# The Qur'ān

With Sūrah Introductions and Appendices

Saheeh International Translation

# The Qur'ān

With Sūrah Introductions and Appendices

Saheeh International Translation

Edited by

A.B. al-Mehri

The Qur'ān Project

www.quranproject.org

# CONTENTS PAGE

Appendices:

## Introduction

The Qur'ān is the word of the Ever-living God; it has been sent down to guide humanity for all times to come. No book can be like it. As you come to the Qur'ān, God speaks to you. To read the Qur'ān is to hear Him, converse with Him and to walk in His ways. It is the encounter of life with the Life-giver. **'God - there is no diety except Him, the Ever-living, the Sustainer of existence. He has sent down upon you the Book with in Truth ... as a guidance for the people ...'** (Qur'ān 3: 2-3).

For those who heard it for the first time from the lips of the Prophet, the Qur'ān was a living reality. They had absolutely no doubt that, through him, God was speaking to them. Their hearts and minds were therefore seized by it. Their eyes overflowed with tears and their bodies shivered. They found each word of it deeply relevant to their concerns and experiences, and integrated it fully into their lives. They were completely transformed by it both as individuals and as a nation - into a totally new, alive and life-giving entity. Those who grazed sheep, herded camels and traded petty merchandise became the leaders of mankind.

### New World

As we come to the Qur'ān, we come to a new world. Each *Ayat* [verse] is a sign of God – informing us of His infinite mercy, power and knowledge. No other venture in our lives can be so momentous and crucial, so blissful and rewarding, as our journey to and through the Qur'ān. It is a journey that will take us through the endless joys and riches of the words that our Creator and Lord has sent to us and all mankind. Here we will find a world of untold treasures of knowledge and wisdom to guide us on the pathways of life, to mould our thoughts and actions. In it we will find deep insights to enrich us and steer us along the right course. From it you will receive a radiant light to illumine the deeper reaches of our soul. Here we will encounter profound emotions, a warmth to melt our hearts and bring tears running down our cheeks.

It is beyond man's power to comprehend, or to describe, the greatness and importance of what the Qur'ān holds for him. It is God's greatest blessing for him. It is the fulfillment of His promise to Adam and his descendants: **'when guidance comes to you from Me, whoever follows My guidance - there will be no fear concerning them, nor will they grieve…'** (2: 38). It is the only weapon to help our frail existence as we struggle against the forces of evil and temptation in this world. It is the only means to overpower our fears and anxieties. It is the only 'light' (*nur*), as we grope in the darkness, with which to find our way to success and salvation. It is the only healing (*shifa'*) for our inner sicknesses, as well as the social ills that may surround us. Its the constant reminder (*dhikr*) of our true nature and destiny, of our station, our duties, our rewards and our perils.

### God - the Greatest

The Qur'ān was brought down by the one who is powerful and trustworthy in the heavens – the angel Gabriel. Its first abode was the pure and sublime heart, the like of which no man has never had - the heart of the Prophet Muhammad, blessings and peace be on him. More than anything, it is the only way to come nearer and closer to our Creator. It tells us of Him, of His attributes, of how He rules over the cosmos and history, of how He relates Himself to us, and how we should relate to Him and to ourselves.

Most important is to remember is that what we read in the Qur'ān is the word of God which He has conveyed to us in a human language, only because of His mercy and care and providence for us. **'The Most-merciful, He has taught the Qur'ān'** (55: 1-2). **'A mercy from your Lord'** (44: 6). The majesty of the Qur'ān, too, is so overpowering that no human being can truly comprehend it. So much so as God says, **'If We had sent down this Qur'ān upon a mountain, you would have seen it humbled and coming apart from fear of God.'** (59: 21). This act of Divine mercy and majesty is enough to awe and overwhelm us, to inspire us to ever-greater heights of gratitude, yearning and endeavour to enter the world of the Qur'ān. Indeed, no treasure is more valuable and precious for us than the Qur'ān, as God says of His generosity, **'O mankind, there has to come to you instruction from your Lord and healing for what is in the breasts and guidance and mercy for the believers.'** (10:57).

The outcome of our entire life depends on how we heed the call given by God. The journey is therefore decisive for our existence, for mankind, for the future of human civilization. A hundred new worlds lie in its verses. Whole centuries are involved in its moments. Know, in that case that it is the Qur'ān, and only the Qur'ān, which can lead us towards success and glory in this-world and in the world-to-come.

We finish by citing a poem;

'My mind ponders and contemplates,
Dwelling on the reality of life,
Yet nothing is as scary as the Realness of the Ever-Living.

His closeness,
His knowledge of my inner self,
The insides tremble and frighten at this reality,

I awake,
Sometimes,
I hear nothing except my heart beating,
Beat after beat it beats,
One thought is flowing in my mind,
All that my mind and body desire at this moment,
Is to stand,
To stand before Him.

This feeling I wouldn't exchange for the world,
To fall prostrate and praise Him, tell Him I love Him and am longing to meet Him.

Life is a journey with many intended ambitions -
Yet mine is simple..............to meet my Lord when I am closest to Him.'

## Editor's Preface

In early 2007, a friend visited me at my home in Birmingham, UK. He was visually emotional and asked if I could give him a translation of the Qur'ān in English. He explained that he had a non-Muslim work colleague who had been enthralled by the Qur'ān and that he, as a Muslim, felt ashamed he had not read it. So I gave him a spare translation I had and began to tell him some basic facts he should know as a seeker of truth –

The Qur'ān is a unique book for a multitude of reasons. To name a few:

- It does not read in chronological order of revelation –
  - i.e. the first verse you read from *Sūrah* 1 is not that first verse revealed
  - nor the last verse from *Sūrah* 114 the very last verse of the Qur'ān.

- The Qur'ān was revealed over 23 years to the Prophet Muhammad –
  - Sometimes a few *Ayats* at a time – (the first revelation began with five ayat, then seven, etc)
  - and at other times, Sūrahs (chapters) were revealed as a whole.

    (An *Ayat* is normally translated as 'a verse' - a more accurate linguistic translation would be 'Sign' [of God])

- The Archangel Gabriel, under instruction from God, informed the Prophet to arrange the various *Ayats* into Sūrahs.

- These Sūrah's (chapters) can be divided into two types –

  - those revealed before the migration of the Muslim community – The Makkan Period
  - and those revealed after the migration – The Madinan period.
  - These *Sūrahs* would often include *Ayats* from both time periods

- The significance of the two periods –

  - in **Makkah** the call to one God was new. The Believers were opposed, beaten and oppressed by the Makkans who were the main proponents of idol-worship in Arabia. The revelations in Makkah were regarding the Oneness of God, Paradise and Hellfire, the Day of Judgment etc. This was a period of many trials and tribulations for the Prophet Muhammad and the Believers.
  - in **Madinah** the Prophet was the leader of the Islāmic state. The revelations here centered on establishing the religion, engaging the enemies of God, social and legal rulings on marriage, divorce, inheritance, punishment, etc.
  - The challenges of both periods were different and the various *Ayats* reflect this.

After explaining the importance of knowing the biography of the Prophet in order to deepen one's understanding of the Qur'ān, I began explaining how amazingly, the Qur'ān has been preserved word for word in written and oral form for over fourteen hundred years – a feat unmatched by any other book, including the Old and New Testament. I then went on to mention the many scientific miracles contained in the Qur'ān and also the prophecies in the Bible about the Prophet Muhammad. All this information I was relaying to my friend was scattered over many books and not contained in a single publication that I could give him. It was at this stage it became evident to me that there was a need to publish a translation of the Qur'ān which would give its reader a complete and informed introduction to the miraculous book. And so, **The Qur'ān Project** was born.

Work then began by first selecting the Saheeh International translation of the Qur'ān as the translation we would use in our print - it is in simple English and corresponds well to the sentence structure of the Arabic. There were two changes that were made to this translation – the word 'Allah' was replaced with 'God' and 'Bismillah ir Rahman nir Raheem' (at the beginning of the Sūrahs) was replaced by 'In the Name of God, the Most Compassionate, the Most Merciful.'

It was then decided to use M. Mawdudi's Sūrah introductions from his commentary of the Qur'ān, 'Towards Understanding the Qur'ān' (available online – www.quranproject.org). These have been edited and abridged to include the most relevant information for a beginner. The following chapters were then selected to also be included:

- Short Biography of the Prophet Muhammad
- Introduction to the Study of the Qur'ān
- The Unique Qur'ānic Generation
- Preservation and Literary Challenge of the Qur'ān
- Scientific Miracles of the Qur'ān;
    - The Qur'ān on the Origin of the Universe
    - The Qur'ān on the 'Big Bang Theory'
    - The Qur'ān on the Expanding Universe
    - The Qur'ān on the Orbital Movement of the Sun and the Moon
    - The Qur'ān on Duality in Creation
    - The Qur'ān on the Origin of Life in Water
    - The Qur'ān on Seas and Rivers
    - Miracle of Iron
    - The Qur'ān on Mountains
    - The Qur'ān on Human Embryonic Development
    - Scientists Acceptance of the Miracles of the Qur'ān
- Miracles Performed
- Old and New Testament Prophecy of Muhammad
- Women in Islām
- How do I become a Muslim?
- Quick Guide to Ablution and Prayer
- Frequently Asked Questions about Islām - Short Answers -

**www.quranproject.org**

The website www.quranproject.org was setup to accompany the publication. Here readers would be able to read it all online, download it, order their free copy, and go through the many additional sections including free online library, audio and video etc.

**Final Note**

Many of those involved have been completely humbled by the opportunity given to them by God to partake in this project. All praise and thanks are for Him and Him alone, the Lord of the Worlds. Often God uses diverse and numerous people for His work and this endeavor has been no different. So many people have offered their time, help and services to this project and are too many to mention here. God knows every single one of them and we ask Him to accept this deed from us and make it as a means of achieving His love, mercy and ultimately Paradise – (ameen).

All that is good and correct in this publication, and anyone who is subsequently guided, this is from God and a mercy from Him. Any mistakes and errors are from ourselves and we ask the forgiveness of God for them.

'O God, Creator of the heavens and the earth – Accept this deed from us and forgive for us for any shortcomings. Enter us and our families into the highest levels of Paradise and protect us from being touched by the Fire even for a moment. Our prayers, sacrifices, lives and death are all for You. Bless us with Your Love, the love of whom You Love and the love of deeds which bring us closer to Your Love. O God, have mercy on us through the Qur'ān and make it for us a Light, Mercy and Guidance - Make the last part of our lives its best, the last deed the best one, and the best day of our lives the Day we meet You.' [ameen]

**A.B. al-Mehri**
Rabi' al-Awwal, 1431 AH
February, 2010
Birmingham, United Kingdom.

## Short Biography of Prophet Muhammad

### The Prophet's Birth

Muhammad, son of Abdullah, son of Abdul Muttalib, of the tribe of Quraysh, was born in Makkah in the year 571 A.D. His father died before he was born, and he was protected first by his grandfather, Abdul Muttalib, and after his grandfather's death, by his uncle Abu Talib.

As a young boy he traveled with his uncle in the merchants' caravan to Syria, and some years later made the same journey in the service of a wealthy widow named Khadijah. So faithfully he conducted her business, and so excellent was the report of his behaviour, which she received from her old servant who had accompanied him, that she soon afterwards married her young agent; and the marriage proved a very happy one, though she was fifteen years older than he was. Throughout the twenty-six years of their life together he remained devoted to her; and after her death, when he took other wives he always mentioned her with the greatest love and reverence. This marriage gave him rank among the notables of Makkah, while his conduct earned for him the title al-Amin, the "trustworthy."

### Physical Description

One of the most comprehensive and detailed descriptions we have of the Prophet Muhammad came from a Bedouin woman who would take care of travelers who passed by her tent. The Prophet once stopped by her with his companions for food and rest. The Prophet asked her if they could buy some meat or dates from her but she could not find anything. The Prophet looked towards a sheep next to the tent. He asked her, "What is wrong with this sheep?" She replied, "The sheep is fatigued and is weaker than the other sheep." The Prophet asked, "Does it milk?" She replied, "I swear by your mother and father, if I saw milk from it then I would milk it." He then called the sheep and moved his hand over its udder; he pronounced the name of God and praised Him. Then he called the woman when the sheep steadied its feet and its udder filled. He asked for a large container and milked it until it was filled. The woman drank until full as did his companions. Then it was milked for a second time until the container was full and they left her and continued on their journey. After a short while, the husband of the Bedouin woman returned from herding goats. He saw the milk and said to his wife, "Where did you get this milk from?" She replied, "I swear by God, a blessed man came to us today" He said, "Describe him to me."

She began; "I saw him to be a man of evident splendor. Fine in figure. His face handsome. Slim in form. His head not too small, elegant and good looking. His eyes large and black [and] his eye lids long. His voice deep. Very intelligent. His brows high and arched [and] his hair in plaits. His neck long and his beard thick. He gave an impression of dignity when silent and of high intelligence when he talked. His words were impressive and his speech decisive, not trivial nor trite. His ideas like pearls moving on their string. He seemed the most splendid and fine looking man from a distance and the very best of all from close by. Medium in height, the eye not finding him too tall nor too short. A tree branch as it were between two others but he was the finest looking of the three. The best proportioned. His companions would surround him, when he spoke they would listen attentively to his speech…"

### The First Revelation

The Makkans claimed descent from Abraham through Ishmail and tradition stated that their temple, the Ka`bah, had been built by Abraham for the worship of the One God. It was still called the House of God, but the chief objects of worship here were a number of idols, which were called "daughters" of God and intercessors.

It was the practice of the Prophet to retire often to a cave in the desert for meditation. His place of retreat was Hira, a cave in a mountain called the Mountain of Light not far from Makkah, and his chosen month was Ramadan, the month of heat. It was there one night towards the end of this quiet month that the first revelation came to him when he was forty years old.

He heard a voice say: "Read!" He said: "I cannot read." The voice again said: "Read!" He said: "I cannot read." A third time the voice, more terrible, commanded: "Read!" He said: "What can I read?" The voice said:

> "Recite in the name of your Lord who created
>
> Created man from a clinging substance.
>
> Recite, and your Lord is the most Generous –
>
> Who taught by the pen –
>
> Taught man that which he knew not."

### The Vision of Cave Hira

He went out of the cave on to the hillside and heard the same awe-inspiring voice say: "O Muhammad! Thou art God's messenger, and I am Gabriel." Then he raised his eyes and saw the angel standing in the sky above the horizon. And again the voice said: "O Muhammad! Thou art God's messenger, and I am Gabriel." Muhammad stood quite still, turning away his face from the brightness of the vision, but wherever he turned his face, there stood the angel confronting him. He remained thus a long while till at length the angel vanished, when he returned in great distress of mind to his wife Khadijah. She did her best to reassure him, saying that his conduct had been such that God would not let a harmful spirit come to him and that it was her hope that he was to become the Prophet of his people. On his return to Makkah she took him to her cousin Waraqa ibn Nawfal, a very old man, "who knew the Scriptures of the Jews and Christians," who declared his belief that the heavenly messenger who came to Moses of old had come to Muhammad, and that he was chosen as the Prophet of his people.

## Message of Islām

Most of the people of Makkah who had acclaimed him as the trustworthy (al-Amīn) and the trustful (as-Sādiq) could not bring themselves to believe in him. Nor could most of the Jews and Christians who had for so long been living in expectation of his arrival. Not that they doubted his truthfulness or integrity but they were not prepared to turn their whole established way of living upside down by submitting to his simple but radical message. He would tell them;

> When I recite the Qur'ān, I find the following clear instruction: God is He who has created you, and the heavens and the earth, He is your only Lord and Master. He is your only Lord and Master. Surrender your being and your lives totally to Him Alone, and worship and serve no one but Him. Let God be the Only God.
>
> The words I speak, He places in my mouth, and I speak on His authority, Obey me and forsake all false claimants to human obedience. Everything in the heavens and on earth belongs to God; no person has a right to be master of another person, to spread oppression and corruption on earth. An eternal life beyond awaits you; where you will meet God face to face, and your life will be judged; for that you must prepare.

This simple message shook the very foundations of Makkan society as well as the seventh-century world. That world, as today, lived under the yoke of many false gods, kings and emperors, priests and monks, feudal lords and rich businessmen, soothsayers and spell-binders who claimed to know what others knew not, and who all lorded over human being.

The Prophet's message challenged them all, exposed them all and threatened them all. His immediate opponents in Makkah could do no better than brand him unconvincingly as a liar, a poet, soothsayer and a man possessed. But how could he who was illiterate, he who had never composed a single verse, who has shown no inclination to lead people, suddenly have words flowing from his lips so full of wisdom and light, morally so uplifting, specifically so enlivening, so beautiful and powerful, that they began to change the hearts and minds and lives of the hearer? His detractors and opponents had no answer. When challenged to produce anything even remotely similar to the words Muhammad claimed he was receiving from God, they could not match God's words.

## Stages of The Call

First privately, then publicly, the Prophet continued to proclaim his message. He himself had an intense, living relationship with God, totally committed to the message and mission entrusted to him. Slowly and gradually, people came forward and embraced Islām. They came from all walks of life – chiefs and slaves, businessmen and artisans, men and women – most of them young. Some simply heard the Qur'ān, and that was enough to transform them. Some saw the Prophet, and were immediately captivated by the light of mercy, generosity and humanity that was visible in his manner and morals, in his words and works and also in his face.

The opposition continued to harden and sharpen. It grew furious and ferocious. Those who joined the Prophet were tortured in innumerable ways; they were mocked, abused, beaten flogged, imprisoned and boycotted. Some were subjected to severe inhuman tortures; made to lie on burning coal fires until the melting body fat extinguished them, or were dragged over burning sand and rocks. Yet such was the strength of their faith that none of them gave it up in the face of such trials and tribulation.

**The Flight to Abyssinia**

However, as the persecutions became unbearable, the Prophet advised those who could, to migrate to Abyssinia. It turned out that there, the Christian king gave the Muslims full protection despite the pleading of the emissaries sent by the Quraysh chiefs. This was the first emigration of Islām.

In the meantime, the Prophet and his Companions continued to nourish their souls and intellect and strengthen their character and resolve for the great task that lay ahead. They met regularly, especially at a house near the Ka'bāh called Dār al-Arqam, to read and study the Qur'ān, to worship and pray and to forge the tied of brotherhood.

**In Makkah**

Years passed and the people of Makkah would not give their allegiance to the Prophet's message nor showed any sign of any easing in their persecution. At the same time, the Prophet lost his closest companion, his wife Khadījah, as well as his uncle Abu Tālib, his chief protector in the tribal world of Makkah. The Prophet now decided to carry his message to the people of the nearby town of Tā'if known for its wealth. In Tā'if, too, the tribal leaders mocked and ridiculed him and rejected his message. They also stirred up their slaves and youth to insult him, mock him and pelt stones at him. Thus he was stoned until he bled and was driven out of Tā'if, and when God placed at his command the Angel of Mountains to crush the Valley of Tā'if if he so wished, he only prayed for them to be guided. Such was the mercy and compassion of the one who is the 'mercy for all the worlds.'

This year is known by historians as the 'Year of Sorrow' due to the grief which the Prophet suffered as a result of all these worldy setbacks. However, as the Qur'ān states that after hardship there is ease, the Prophet was to be blessed with an amazing journey culminating with a meeting with Almighty God himself.

One night the Prophet was awaken and taken, in the company of the Angel Gabriel, first to Jerusalem. There he was met by all the Prophets, who gathered together behind him as he prayed on the Rock at the centre of the site of Masjid Aqsa, the spot where the Dome of the Rock stands today. From the Rock, led by the Archangel, he ascended through the seven heavens and beyond. Thus he saw whatever God made him see, the heavenly worlds which no human eye can see, and which were the focus of this message and mission. It was also during this journey God ordained on the believers the five daily prayers.

## Joy After Sorrow

In quick succession, the Prophet had suffered the terrible loss of Khadījah, his intimate and beloved companion for 25 years, and of Abu Tālib, his guardian and protector against the bloodthirsty Makkan foes, and encountered the worst ever rejection, humiliation and persecution at nearby Tā'if. As the Prophet reached the lowest point in his vocation, God bought him comfort and solace. On the one hand, spiritually, He took him during the Night of Ascension to the Highest of Highs, realities and Divinities, face to face with the Unseen. And on the other, materially, he opened the hearts of the people of Yathrib to the message and mission of Prophet Muhammad.

The message that Makkah and Tā'if rejected, found responsive hearts in Yathrib, a small oasis about four hundred kilometres to the north of Makkah. Now known as Madīnah tunnabī (the city of the Prophet), or Madīnatun Munawwarah (the radiant city), it was destined to be the centre of the Divine light that was to spread to all parts of the world for all time to come.

## The Men of Yathrib

Soon after Prophet Muhammad's return from Tā'if and the Night Journey, at the time of the pilgrimage, six men from Yathrib embraced Islām. They delivered the message of Islām to as many as they could, and at the time of the next pilgrimage in the year 621 CE, 12 people came. They pledged themselves to the Prophet, that they would make no god besides God, that they would neither steal nor commit fornication, nor slay their infants, nor utter slanders, nor disobey him in that which is right. The Prophet said; 'If you fulfil this pledge, then Paradise is yours.' This time the Prophet sent Mus'ab ibn 'Umayr with them to teach them the Qur'ān and Islām and to spread the message of Islām.

More and more people over the course of a year – tribal leaders, men and women – became Muslims. At the time of the next pilgrimage, they decided to send a delegation to the Prophet, make a pledge to him, and invited him and all Muslims in Makkah to Yathrib as a sanctuary and as a base for spearding the Divine message of Islām. In all, 73 men and two women came. They met the Prophet at Aqabah. They pledged to protect the Prophet as they would protect their own women and children, and to fight against all men, red and black, even if their nobles were killed and they suffered the loss of all their possessions. When asked what would be their return if they fulfilled their pledge, the Prophet said; 'Paradise.' Thus the beginning was made, the foundations of the Islāmic society, state and civilization were set.

The road was now open for the persecuted and tortured followers of the Prophet to come to the Land of Islām, that was to be Madinah. Gradually most of the believers found their way to Yathrib. Their Makkan foes could not bear to see the Muslims living in peace. They knew the power of the Prophet's message, they knew the strength of those dedicated believers who cared about nothing for the age-old Arab customs and ties of kinship, and who if they had to, would fight for their faith. The Makkans sensed the danger that the Muslims' presence in Madinah posed for their northern trade caravan routes. They saw no other way to stop all this but to kill the Prophet.

**Plot to Murder the Prophet**

Hence they hatched a conspiracy; one strong and well-connected young man was to be nominated by each clan, and all of them were to pounce upon and kill the Prophet one morning as he came out of his house, so that his blood would be on all the clans' hands. Thus, the Prophets' clan would have to accept blood money in place of revenge. Informed of the plot by the Angel Gabriel, and instructed to leave Makkah for Madinah, the Prophet went to Abu Bakr's house to finalise the travel arrangements. Abu Bakr was overjoyed at having been chosen for the honour and blessing of being the Prophet's companion on this blessed, momentous, sacred and epoch-making journey. He offered his she-camel to the Prophet, but the Prophet insisted on paying its price.

On the fateful night, as darkness fell, the youths selected by the Quraysh leaders to kill the Prophet surrounded his house. They decided to pounce on him when he came out of his house for the dawn prayer. Meanwhile, the Prophet handed over all the money left by the Makkans with him for safe-keeping to Ali. Ali offered to lie in the Prophet's bed. The Prophet slipped out of his house, threw a little dust in their direction, and walked past his enemies, whose eyes were still on the house. He met Abu Bakr at his house, and they both travelled to a nearby cave. When the Quraysh realised that the Prophet had evaded them, they were furious. They looked for him everywhere to no success and then announced a reward of 100 she-camels for anybody who would bring them the Prophet, dead or alive. A tribal chief, Surāqah, sighted the Prophet and followed him, hoping to earn the reward. The Prophet, with bloodthirsty foes in pursuit and an uncertain future ahead of him in Madinah, told Surāqah; A day will soon come when Kisra's golden bracelets will be in Surāqah's hands. Thereafter, Surāqah retreated, and the Prophet proceeded towards Madinah.

**Four stages of the Prophets life in Makkah**

The Makkan period can be summarized in four stages:

1. The first stage began with his appointment as a Messenger and ended with the proclamation of Prophethood three years later. During this period the Message was given secretly to some selected persons only but the common people of Makkah were not aware of it.
2. The second stage lasted for two years after the proclamation of his Prophethood. It began with opposition by individuals: then by and by it took the shape of antagonism, ridicule, derision, accusation, abuse and false propaganda then gangs were formed to persecute those Muslims who were comparatively poor, weak and helpless.
3. The third stage lasted for about six years from the beginning of the persecution to the death of Abu Talib and Khadijah in the tenth year of Prophethood. During this period the persecution of the Muslims became so savage and brutal that many of them were forced to migrate to Abyssinia while social and economic boycott was applied against the remaining Believers.
4. The fourth stage lasted for about three years from the tenth to the thirteenth year of Prophethood. This was a period of hard trials and grievous sufferings for the Prophet and his followers. Life had become unendurable at Makkah and there ap-

peared to be no place of refuge even outside it. So much so that when the Prophet went to Tā'if, it offered no shelter or protection. Besides this, on the occasion of Hajj, he would appeal to each and every Arab clan to accept his invitation to Islām but was met with blank refusal from every quarter. At the same time, the people of Makkah were holding counsels to get rid of him by killing or imprisoning or banishing him from their city. It was at that most critical time that God opened for Islām the hearts of the People of Yathrib where he migrated at their invitation.

### The Hijrah (622 C.E.)

This was al-Hijrah, the emigration – a small distance in space, a mighty leap in history, an event that was to become a threshold in the shaping of the Islāmic Ummah. This is why the Muslims date their calendar from Hijrah (emigration) and not from start of revelation or from the birth of the Prophet.

In Qubah, 10 kilometres outside Madinah, the Prophet made his first stopover. Here he built the first Masjid. Here he also made his first public address; 'Spread peace among yourselves, give away food to the needy, pray while people sleep – and you will enter Paradise, the house of peace.'

Three days later, the Prophet entered Madinah. Men, women, children, the entire populace came out on the streets and jubilantly welcomed him. Never was there a day of grater rejoicing and happiness. 'The Prophet has come! The Prophet has come!' sang the little children.

The first thing the Prophet did after arriving in Madinah was to weld the Muhājirs or Emigrants and the hosts, called the Ansār or Helpers into one brotherhood. Still today this brotherhood remains the hallmark of the Muslims. One person from the Emigrants was made the brother of one from among the Helpers – creating a bond stronger than blood. The Helpers offered to share equally all that they possessed with their new brothers.

### Brotherhood

So, the Muslims were forged into a close-knit community of faith and brotherhood, and the structure of their society was being built. The first structure was also raised. This was the Masjid, the building dedicated to the worship of One God – called Masjid al-Nabi, the Prophet's Masjid. Since then the Masjid has also remained the hallmark of the Muslims' collective and social life, the convenient space for the integration of the religious and political dimension of Islām, a source of identification, a witness to Muslim existence.

At the same time, steps were taken and required institutions built to integrate the entire social life around the centre and pivot of the worship of One God. For this purpose, five daily prayers in congregation were established. Ramadhān, fasting every day from dawn to sunset for an entire month, was also prescribed. Similarly, to establish 'giving' as the way of life, Zakāh, a percentage of one's wealth to be given in the way of God, was made obligatory.

### The Jews and Hypocrites

In the first year of his reign at Yathrib the Prophet made a solemn treaty with the Jewish tribes, which secured to them rights of citizenship and full religious liberty in return for their support of the new state. But their idea of a Prophet was one who would give them dominion, not one who made the Jews who followed him, brothers of every Arab who might happen to believe as they did. When they realised that they could not use the Prophet for their own ends, they tried to shake his faith and his Mission and to seduce his followers, behaviour in which they were encouraged secretly by some professing Muslims who considered they had reason to resent the Prophet's coming, since it robbed them of their local influence. In the Madinan Sūrahs there is frequent mention of these Jews and Hypocrites.

### The First Expeditions

The Prophet's first concern as ruler was to establish public worship and lay down the constitution of the State: but he did not forget that Quraysh had sworn to make an end to his religion, nor that he had received command to fight against them till they ceased from persecution. After twelve months in Yathrib several small expeditions went out, led either by the Prophet himself or other migrants for the purpose of reconnoitering and of dissuading other tribes from siding with Quraysh. One of the other purposes of those expeditions may have been to accustom the Makkan Muslims to engage with enemy forces. For thirteen years they had been strict pacifists, and it is clear, from several passages of the Qur'ān, that many of them disliked the idea of fighting and had to be inured to it.

### The Campaign of Badr

In the second year of the Hijrah (migration) the Makkan merchants' caravan [which had the confiscated possessions of what the Muslims had left in Makkah] was returning from Syria as usual by a road which passed not far from Yathrib. As its leader Abu Sufyan approached the territory of Yathrib he heard of the Prophet's plan to capture the caravan. At once he sent a camel-rider towards Makkah, who arrived in a worn-out state and shouted frantically from the valley to Quraysh to hasten to the rescue unless they wished to lose both wealth and honour. A force of a thousand strong was soon on its way to Yathrib: less, it would seem, with the hope of saving the caravan than with the idea of punishing the raiders, since the Prophet might have taken the caravan before the relief force started from Makkah.

Did the Prophet ever intend to raid the caravan? In Ibn Hisham, in the account of the Tabuk expedition, it is stated that the Prophet on that one occasion did not hide his real objective. The caravan was the pretext in the campaign of Badr; the real objective was the Makkan army.

He had received command to fight his persecutors, and with the promised of victory, he was prepared to venture against any odds, as was well seen at Badr. But the Muslims, ill-equipped for war, would have despaired if they had known from the first instance that they were to face a well-armed force three times their number.

The army of Quraysh had advanced more than half-way to Yathrib before the Prophet set out. All three parties – the army of Quraysh, the Muslim army and the caravan – were heading for the water of Badr. Abu Sufyan, the leader of the caravan, heard from one of his scouts that the Muslims were near the water, and turned back to the coast-plain leaving the Muslims to meet the army of Quraysh by the well of Badr.

Before the battle, the Prophet was prepared, still further to increase the odds against him. He gave leave to all the Ansār (natives of Yathrib) to return to their homes unreproached, since their oath did not include the duty of fighting in the field; but the Ansār were only hurt by the suggestion that they could possibly desert him at a time of danger. The battle went at first against the Muslims, but against the odds with a much weaker army they were victorious.

The victory of Badr gave the Prophet new prestige among the Arab tribes; but thenceforth there was the feud of blood between Quraysh and the Islāmic State in addition to the old religious hatred. Those passages of the Qur'ān which refer to the battle of Badr give warning of much greater struggles yet to come.

In fact in the following year, an army of three thousand came from Makkah to destroy Yathrib. The Prophet's first idea was merely to defend the city, a plan of which Abdullah ibn Ubayy, the leader of "the Hypocrites" ('Muslims by name only'), strongly approved. But the men who had fought at Badr and believed that God would help them against any odds thought it a shame that they should linger behind walls.

**The Battle on Mount Uhud**

The Prophet, approving of their faith and zeal, gave way to them, and set out with an army of one thousand men toward Mt. Uhud, where the enemy were encamped. Abdullah ibn Ubayy was much offended by the change of plan. He thought it unlikely that the Prophet really meant to give battle in conditions so adverse to the Muslims, and was unwilling to take part in a mere demonstration designed to flatter the Muslims. So he withdrew with his men, a fourth or so of the army.

Despite the heavy odds, the battle on Mt. Uhud would have been an even greater victory than that at Badr for the Muslims but for the disobedience of a band of fifty archers whom the Prophet set to guard a pass against the enemy cavalry. Seeing their comrades victorious, these men left their post, fearing to lose their share of the spoils. The cavalry of Quraysh rode through the gap and fell on the exultant Muslims.

The Prophet himself was wounded and the cry arose that he was slain, till someone recognized him and shouted that he was still living; a shout to which the Muslims rallied. Gathering round the Prophet, they retreated, leaving many dead on the hillside.

On the following day the Prophet again ventured forth with what remained of the army, with the intention that the Quraysh might hear that he was in the field and so might perhaps be deterred from attacking the city. The stratagem succeeded, thanks to the behaviour of a friendly Bedouin, who met the Muslims and conversed with them and afterwards met the army of Quraysh. Questioned by Abu Sufyan, he said that Muhammad was in the field, stronger than ever, and thirsting for revenge for yesterday's affair. On that information, Abu Sufyan decided to return to Makkah.

### Massacre of Muslims

The reverse which they had suffered on Mt. Uhud lowered the prestige of the Muslims with the Arab tribes and also with the Jews of Yathrib. Tribes which had inclined toward the Muslims now inclined toward Quraysh. The Prophet's followers were attacked and murdered when they went abroad in little companies. Khubayb, one of his envoys, was captured by a desert tribe and sold to Quraysh, who tortured him to death in Makkah publicly.

### Expulsion of Banu-Nadheer

The Jews, despite their treaty, now hardly concealed their hostility. They even went so far in flattery of Quraysh as to declare the religion of the pagan Arabs superior to Islām. The Prophet was obliged to take punitive action against some of them. The tribe of Banu-Nadheer were besieged in their strong towers, subdued and forced to emigrate. The Hypocrites had sympathized with the Jews and secretly egged them on.

### The War of the Trench

In the fifth year of the Hijrah the idolaters made a great effort to destroy Islām in the War of the Clans or War of the Trench, as it is variously called; when Quraysh with all their clans and the great desert tribe of Ghatafan with all their clans, an army of ten thousand men rode against Al-Madinah (Yathrib). The Prophet (by the advice of Salman the Persian) caused a deep trench to be dug before the city, and himself led the work of digging it.

The army of the clans was stopped by the trench, a novelty in Arab warfare. It seemed impassable for cavalry, which formed their strength. They camped in sight of it and daily showered their arrows on its defenders. While the Muslims were awaiting the assault, news came that Banū Qurays̲h̲ah, a Jewish tribe of Yathrib which had till then been loyal, had gone over to the enemy. The case seemed desperate. But the delay caused by the trench had dampened the zeal of the clans, and one who was secretly a Muslim managed to sow distrust between Quraysh and their Jewish allies, so that both hesitated to act. Then came a bitter wind from the sea, which blew for three days and nights so terribly that not a tent could be kept standing, not a fire lighted, not a pot boiled. The tribesmen were in utter misery. At length, one night the leader of Quraysh decided that the torment could be borne no longer and gave the order to retire. When Ghatafan awoke next morning they found Quraysh had gone and they too took up their baggage and retreated.

### Punishment of Banū Quraythah

On the day of the return from the trench the Prophet ordered war on the treacherous Banū Quraythah, who, conscious of their guilt, had already taken to their towers of refuge. After a siege of nearly a month they had to surrender unconditionally. They only begged that they might be judged by a member of the Arab tribe of which they were adherents. The Prophet granted their request. But the judge, upon whose favor they had counted, condemned their fighting men to death, their women and children to slavery.

Early in the sixth year of the Hijrah the Prophet led a campaign against the Bani al-Mustaliq, a tribe who were preparing to attack the Muslims.

**Al-Hudaybiyah**

In the same year the Prophet had a vision in which he found himself entering the holy place at Makkah unopposed, therefore he determined to attempt the pilgrimage. Attired as pilgrims, and taking with them the customary offerings, a company of fourteen hundred men journeyed to Makkah. As they drew near the holy valley they were met by a friend from the city, who warned the Prophet that Quraysh had put on their leopards-skins (the badge of valour) and had sworn to prevent his entering the sanctuary; their cavalry was on the road before him. On that, the Prophet ordered a detour through mountain gorges and the Muslims were tired out when they came down at last into the valley of Makkah and encamped at a spot called Al-Hudaybiyah; from here he tried to open negotiations with Quraysh, to explain that he came only as a pilgrim.

The first messenger he sent towards the city was maltreated and his camel hamstrung. He returned without delivering his message. Quraysh on their side sent an envoy which was threatening in manner, and very arrogant. Another of their envoys was too familiar and had to be reminded: sternly of the respect due to the Prophet. It was he who, on his return to the city, said: "I have seen Caesar and Chosroes in their pomp, but never have I seen a man honoured as Muhammad is honoured by his comrades."

The Prophet sought some messenger who would impose respect. Uthman was finally chosen because of his kinship with the powerful Umayyad family. While the Muslims were awaiting his return the news came that he had been murdered. It was then that the Prophet, sitting under a tree in Al-Hudaybiyah, took an oath from all his comrades that they would stand or fall together. After a while, however, it became known that Uthman had not been murdered. A troop which came out from the city to molest the Muslims in their camp was captured before they could do any hurt and brought before the Prophet, who forgave them on their promise to renounce hostility.

**Truce of Al-Hudaybiyah**

Then proper envoys came from Quraysh. After some negotiation, the truce of Al-Hudaybiyah was signed. For ten years there were to be no hostilities between the parties. The Prophet was to return to Madinah without visiting the Ka'bāh, but in the following year he might perform the pilgrimage with his comrades, Quraysh promising to evacuate Makkah for three days to allow of his doing so. Deserters from Quraysh to the Muslims during the period of the truce were to be returned; not so deserters from the Muslims to Quraysh. Any tribe or clan who wished to share in, the treaty as allies of the Prophet might do so, and any tribe or clan who wished to share in the treaty as allies of Quraysh might do so.

There was dismay among the Muslims at these terms. They asked one another: "Where is the victory that we were promised?" It was during the return journey from al-Hudaybiyah that the Sūrah entitled "The Conquest" (surah 48) was revealed. This truce proved, in fact, to be the greatest victory that the Muslims had till then achieved. War had been a barrier between them and the idolaters, but now both parties met and talked together, and the religion spread more rapidly. In the two years which elapsed between the signing of the truce and the fall of Makkah the number of reverts was greater than the total number of all previous reverts. The Prophet traveled to Al-Hudaybiyah with 1400 men. Two years later, when the Makkans broke the truce, he marched against them with an army of 10,000.

**The Campaign of Khaybar**

In the seventh year after the Hijrah, the Prophet led a campaign against Khaybar, the stronghold of the Jewish tribes in North Arabia, which had become a hornets' nest of his enemies. The forts of Khaybar were reduced one by one, and the Jews of Khaybar became thenceforth tenants of the Muslims until the expulsion of the Jews from Arabia in the 'Caliphate of Umar.' On the day when the last fort surrendered Ja'far son of Abu Talib, the Prophet's first cousin, arrived with all who remained of the Muslims who had fled to Abyssinia to escape from persecution in the early days.

They had been absent from Arabia for fifteen years. It was at Khaybar that a Jewess prepared for the Prophet poisoned meat, of which he only tasted a morsel without swallowing it, and then warned his comrades that it was poisoned. One Muslim, who had already swallowed a mouthful, died immediately, and the Prophet himself, from the mere taste of it, derived the illness which eventually caused his death. The woman who had cooked the meat was brought before him. When she said that she had done it on account of the humiliation of her people, he forgave her.

**Pilgrimage to Makkah**

In following year the Prophet's vision was fulfilled: he visited the holy place at Makkah unopposed. In accordance with the terms of the truce the idolaters evacuated the city, and from the surrounding heights watched the procedure of the Muslims. At the end of the stipulated three days the chiefs of Quraysh sent a reminder to the Prophet that the time was up. He then withdrew, and the idolaters reoccupied the city.

**Mu'tah Expedition**

In the eighth year of the Hijrah, hearing that the Byzantine emperor was gathering a force in Syria for the destruction of Islām, the Prophet sent three thousand men to Syria under the command of his freed slave Zayd. The campaign was unsuccessful except that it impressed the Syrians with a notion of the reckless valour of the Muslims. The three thousand did not hesitate to join battle with a hundred thousand. When all the three leaders appointed by the Prophet had been killed, the survivors under the command of Khalid ibn al-Walid, who, by his strategy and courage, managed to preserve a remnant and return with them to Madinah.

### Truce Broken by Quraysh

In the same year Quraysh broke the truce by attacking a tribe that was in alliance with the Prophet and massacring them even in the sanctuary at Makkah. Afterwards they were afraid because of what they had done. They sent Abu Sufyan to Madinah to ask for the existing treaty to be renewed and, its term prolonged. They hoped that he would arrive before the tidings of the massacre. But a messenger from the injured tribe had been before him, and his embassy was fruitless.

### Conquest of Makkah

Then the Prophet summoned all the Muslims capable of bearing arms and marched to Makkah. The Quraysh were overawed. Their cavalry put up a show of defence before the town, but were routed without bloodshed; and the Prophet entered his native city on horseback with his head humbled before God as conqueror. The inhabitants expected vengeance for their past misdeeds. The Prophet proclaimed a general amnesty. Only a few known criminals were proscribed, and most of those were in the end forgiven. In their relief and surprise, the whole population of Makkah hastened to swear allegiance. The Prophet caused all the idols which were in the sanctuary to be destroyed, saying: "Truth has come; darkness has vanished away;" and the Muslim call to prayer was heard in Makkah.

### Battle of Hunayn

In the same year there was an angry gathering of pagan tribes eager to regain the Ka'bāh. The Prophet led twelve thousand men against them. At Hunayn, in a deep ravine, his troops were ambushed by the enemy and almost put to flight. It was with difficulty that they were rallied to the Prophet and his bodyguard of faithful comrades who alone stood firm. But the victory, when it came, was complete and the booty enormous, for many of the hostile tribes had brought out with them everything that they possessed.

### Conquest of Tā'if

The tribe of Thaqif was among the enemy at Hunayn. After that victory their city of Tā'if was besieged by the Muslims, and finally reduced. Then the Prophet appointed a governor of Makkah, and himself returned to Madinah to the boundless joy of the Ansār, who had feared lest, now that he had regained his native city, he might forsake them and make Makkah the capital.

### The Tabuk Expedition

In the ninth year of the Hijrah, hearing that an army was again being mustered in Syria, the Prophet called on all the Muslims to support him in a great campaign. The far distance, the hot season, the fact that it was harvest time and the prestige of the enemy caused many to excuse themselves and many more to stay behind without excuse. Those defaulters are denounced in the Qur'ān. But the campaign ended peacefully. The army advanced to Tabuk, on the confines of Syria, and then learnt that the enemy had not yet gathered.

### Declaration of Immunity

Although Makkah had been conquered and its people were now Muslims, the official order of the pilgrimage had not been changed; the pagan Arabs performing it in their manner, and the Muslims in their manner. It was only after the pilgrims' caravan had left Madinah in the ninth year of the Hijrah, when Islām was dominant in North Arabia, that the Declaration of Immunity, as it is called, was revealed (Surah 9). The Prophet sent a copy of it by messenger to Abu Bakr, leader of the pilgrimage, with the instruction that Ali was to read it to the multitudes at Makkah. Its declaration was that after that year, Muslims only were to make the pilgrimage, exception being made for such of the idolaters as had a treaty with the Muslims and had never broken their treaty nor supported anyone against them. Such were to enjoy the privileges of their treaty for the term thereof, but when their treaty expired they would be as other idolaters. That proclamation marks the end of idol-worship in Arabia.

### The Year of Deputations

The ninth year of the Hijrah is called the Year of Deputations, because from all parts of Arabia deputations came to Madinah to swear allegiance to the Prophet and to hear the Qur'ān. The Prophet had become, in fact, the Ruler of Arabia, but his way of life remained as simple as before. He personally controlled every detail of organization, judged every case and was accessible to every suppliant. In the last ten years he destroyed idolatry in Arabia; raised women from the status of a cattle to legal equity with men; effectually stopped the drunkenness and immorality which had till then disgraced the Arabs; made men in love with faith, sincerity and honest dealing; transformed tribes who had been for centuries content with ignorance into a people with the greatest thirst for knowledge; and for the first time in history made universal human brotherhood a fact and principle of common law. And his support and guide in all that work was the Qur'ān.

### The Farewell Pilgrimage

In the tenth year of the Hijrah, the Prophet Muhammad went to Makkah as a pilgrim for the last time – his "pilgrimage of farewell" as it is called – when from Mt. 'Arafat he preached to an enormous throng of pilgrims. He reminded them of all the duties Islām enjoined upon them, and that they would one day have to meet their Lord, who would judge each one of them according to his work. He said:

> "O People, listen well to my words, for I do not know whether, after this year, I shall ever be amongst you again. Therefore listen to what I am saying to you very carefully and take these words to those who could not be present here today.
>
> O People, just as you regard this month, this day, this city as Sacred, so regard the life and property of every Muslim as a sacred trust. Return the goods entrusted to you to their rightful owners. Treat others justly so that no one would be unjust to you. Remember that you will indeed meet your Lord, and that He will indeed reckon your deeds. God has forbidden you to take usury (*riba*), therefore all *riba* obligation shall henceforth be waived. Your capital, however, is yours to keep. You will neither inflict nor suffer inequity....

.... Beware of the devil, for the safety of your religion. He has lost all hope that he will ever be able to lead you astray in big things, so beware of following him in small things.

O People, it is true that you have certain rights over your women, but they also have rights over you. Remember that you have taken them as your wives only under God's trust and with His permission. If they abide by your right then to them belongs the right to be fed and clothed in kindness. Treat your women well and be kind to them, for they are your partners and committed helpers. It is your right that they do not make friends with anyone of whom you do not approve, as well as never to be unchaste...

O People, listen to me in earnest, worship God (The One Creator of the Universe), perform your five daily prayers (*Salah*), fast during the month of Ramadan, and give your financial obligation (zakāh) of your wealth. Perform Hajj if you can afford to.

All mankind are from Adam and Eve - an Arab has no superiority over a non-Arab nor a non-Arab has any superiority over an Arab; also a white has no superiority over a black nor a black has any superiority over white except by piety and good action. Learn that every Muslim is a brother to every Muslim and that the Muslims constitute one brotherhood. Nothing shall be legitimate to a Muslim which belongs to a fellow Muslim unless it was given freely and willingly. Do not, therefore, do injustice to yourselves.

Remember, one day you will appear before God (The Creator) and you will answer for your deeds. So beware, do not stray from the path of righteousness after I am gone.

O People, no prophet or messenger will come after me and no new faith will be born. Reason well, therefore, O People, and understand words which I convey to you. I am leaving you with the Book of God (the Qur'ān) and my Sunnah (practices), if you follow them you will never go astray.

All those who listen to me shall pass on my words to others and those to others again; and may the last ones understand my words better than those who listen to me directly. Be my witness O God, that I have conveyed your message to your people."

### Illness and Death of the Prophet

It was during that last pilgrimage that the Sūrah entitled 'Victory' (surah 110) was revealed, which he received as an announcement of approaching death. Soon after his return to Madinah he fell ill. The tidings of his illness caused dismay throughout Arabia and anguish to the folk of Madinah, Makkah and Tā'if, the hometowns. At early dawn on the last day of his earthly life he came out from his room beside the masjid at Madinah and joined the public prayer, which Abu Bakr had been leading since his illness. And there was great relief among the people, who supposed him well again.

When, later in the day, the rumour grew that he was dead. Umar threatened those who spread the rumour with dire punishment, declaring it a crime to think that the Messenger of God could die. He was storming at the people in that strain when Abu Bakr came into the mosque and overheard him. Abu Bakr went to the chamber of his daughter Aisha, where the Prophet lay. Having ascertained the fact, kissed the dead-man's forehead and went back into the mosque. The people were still listening to Umar, who was saying that the rumour was a wicked lie, that the Prophet who was all in all to them could not be dead. Abu Bakr went up to Umar and tried to stop him by a whispered word. Then, finding he would pay no heed, Abu Bakr called to the people, who, recognizing his voice, left Umar and came crowding round him. He first gave praise to God, and then said: "O people! Lo! As for him who worshipped Muhammad, Muhammad is dead. But as for him who worships God, God is Alive and dies not." He then recited the verse of the Qur'ān:

> **"Muhammad is not but a messenger. [Other] messengers have passed on before him. So if he was to die or be killed, would you turn back on your heels [to unbelief]? And he who turns back on his heels will never harm God at all; but God will reward the grateful."**
>
> Qur'ān 3:144

"And," says the narrator: an eye-witness, "it was as if the people had not known that such a verse had been revealed till Abu Bakr recited it." And another witness tells how Umar used to say: when "I heard Abu Bakr recite that verse my feet were cut from beneath me and I fell to the ground, for I knew that God's messenger was dead, May God bless him!" The final messeneger sent to humanity died at the age of 63 years old in the 10th year of the Hijrah (migration) – 632 A.D.

Such is Prophet Muhammad. According to every standard by which human greatness can be measured he was matchless; no person was ever greater.

Source: A.B. al-Mehri. Edited from following sources –

- M. Pickthall, *Introduction – The Glorious Qur'ān,*
- K. Murrad, *Who is Muhammad?*
- M. Mawdudi, *Tafhim al-Qur'ān*

# The Qur'ān

Saheeh International Translation

**Sūrah 1: al-Fātihah**

**Period of Revelation**

It is one of the very earliest Revelations to the Prophet. As a matter of fact we learn from authentic Hadith (traditions) that it was the first complete Sūrah which was revealed to Prophet Muhammad. Before this only a few verses were revealed which form parts of Sūrah Alaq, Nun, Muzzammil and Muddathir.

**Theme**

This Sūrah is in fact a prayer which God has taught to all those who want to make a study of His Book. It has been placed at the very beginning of the Book to teach this lesson to the reader: if you sincerely want to benefit from the Qur'ān, you should offer this prayer to the Lord of the Universe.

This preface is meant to create a strong desire in the heart of the reader to seek guidance from the Lord of the Universe, who alone can grant it. Thus al-Fātihah indirectly teaches that the best thing for a man is to pray for guidance to the straight path, to study the Qur'ān with the mental attitude of a seeker-after-truth and to recognize the fact that the Lord of the Universe is the source of all knowledge. He should, therefore, begin the study of the Qur'ān with a prayer to him for guidance.

From this theme, it becomes clear that the real relation between al-Fātihah and the Qur'ān is not that of an introduction to a book but that of a prayer and its answer. Al-Fātihah is the prayer from the servant and the Qur'ān is the answer from the the Master to his prayer. The servant prays to God to show him guidance and the Master places the whole of the Qur'ān before him in answer to his prayer, as if to say, "This is the Guidance you begged from Me."

## Sūrah 1: al-Fātihah[1]

1. In the name of God,[2] the Entirely Merciful, the Especially Merciful.[3]

2. [All] praise is [due] to God, Lord[4] of the worlds –

3. The Entirely Merciful, the Especially Merciful,

4. Sovereign of the Day of Recompense.[5]

5. It is You we worship and You we ask for help.

6. Guide us to the straight path –

7. The path of those upon whom You have bestowed favor, not of those who have evoked [Your] anger or of those who are astray.

---

[1] *Al-Fātihah:* The Opening (of the Qur'ān). Note: *Sūrah* titles are not an integral part of the Qur'ān. A distinguishing word in a particular *sūrah* or a word defining its subject matter often became a common means of identification among the Prophet's companions and later scholars. Although some names, such as *al-Fātihah*, were used by the Prophet in reference to a particular *sūrah*, they were not specifically designated by him as titles.

[2] God, Creator and Sustainer of the heavens and the earth and all that is within them, the Eternal and Absolute, to whom alone all worship is due.

[3] *Ar-Rahmān* and a*r-Raheem* are two names of God derived from the word "*rahmāh*" (mercy). In Arabic grammar both are intensive forms of "merciful" (i.e., extremely merciful). A complimentary and comprehensive meaning is intended by using both together.

*Rahmān* is used only to describe God, while *raheem* might be used to describe a person as well. The Prophet was described in the Qur'ān as *raheem. Rahmān* is above the human level (i.e., intensely merciful). Since one usually understands intensity to be something of short duration, God describes Himself also as *raheem* (i.e., continually merciful).

*Rahmān* also carries a wider meaning - merciful to all creation. Justice is a part of this mercy. *Raheem* includes the concept of speciality - especially and specifically merciful to the believers. Forgiveness is a part of this mercy. (See al-Qurtubī's *al-Jāmi'u li Ahkāmil-Qur'ān*, pp.103-107.)

However we will incorporate the translation henceforth, 'In the Name of God, the Most Compassionate, the Most Merciful'

[4] When referring to God, the Arabic term "rabb" (translated as "Lord") includes all of the following meanings: "owner, master, ruler, controller, sustainer, provider, guardian and caretaker."

[5] i.e., repayment and compensation for whatever was earned of good or evil during life on this earth.

## Sūrah 2: al-Baqarah

### Sequence

Though it is a Madani Sūrah, it follows naturally a Makki Sūrah Al-Fātihah, which ended with the prayer: **"Show us the straight way."** It begins with the answer to that prayer, **"This is the Book (that) . . . is guidance."** The greater part of Al-Baqarah was revealed during the first two years of the Prophet's life at Madinah. The smaller part which was revealed at a later period has been included in this Sūrah because its contents are closely related to those dealt with in this Sūrah.

### Historical Background

In order to understand the meaning of this Sūrah, we should know its historical background:

1. At Makkah the Qur'ān generally addressed the polytheist Quraysh who were ignorant of Islām, but at Madinah it was also concerned with the Jews who were acquainted with the creed of the Oneness of God, Prophethood, Revelation, the Hereafter and Angels. They also professed to believe in the law which was revealed by God to their Prophet Moses, and in principle, their way was the same (Islām) that was being taught by Prophet Muhammad. But they had strayed away from it during the centuries of degeneration and had adopted many un-Islāmic creeds, rites and customs of which there was no mention and for which there was no sanction in the Torah. Not only this: they had tampered with the Torah by inserting their own explanations and interpretations into its text. They had distorted even that part of the Word of God which had remained intact in their Scriptures and taken out of it the real spirit of true religion and were now clinging to a lifeless frame of rituals. Consequently their beliefs, their morals and their conduct had gone to the lowest depths of degeneration. The pity is that they were not only satisfied with their condition but loved to cling to it. Besides this, they had no intention or inclination to accept any kind of reform. So they became bitter enemies of those who came to teach them the Right Way and did their worst to defeat every such effort. Though they were originally Muslims, they had swerved from the real Islām and made innovations and alterations in it and had fallen victims to hair splitting and sectarianism. They had forgotten and forsaken God and begun to serve material wealth. So much so that they had even given up their original name "Muslim" and adopted the name "Jew" instead, and made religion the sole monopoly of the children of Israel. This was their religious condition when the Prophet went to Madinah and invited the Jews to the true religion. That is why more than one third of this Sūrah has been addressed to the children of Israel. A critical review of their history, their moral degeneration and their religious perversions has been made. Side by side with this, the high standard of morality and the fundamental principles of the pure religion have been put forward in order to bring out clearly the nature of the degeneration of the community of a prophet when it goes astray and to draw clear lines of demarcation between real piety and formalism, and the essentials and non-essentials of the true religion.

2. At Makkah, Islām was mainly concerned with the propagation of its fundamental principles and the moral training of its followers. But after the migration of the Prophet to Madinah, where Muslims had come to settle from all over Arabia and where a tiny Islāmic State had been set up with the help of the Ansār (local supporters), naturally the Qur'ān had to turn its attention to the social, cultural, economic, political and legal problems as well. This accounts for the difference between the themes of the Sūrahs revealed at Makkah and those at Madinah. Accordingly about half of this Sūrah deals with those principles and regulations which are essential for the integration and solidarity of a community and for the solution of its problems.

After the migration to Madinah, the struggle between Islām and Kufr (disbelief) had also entered a new phase. Before this the Believers, who propagated Islām among their own clans and tribes, had to face its opponents at their own risk. But the conditions had changed at Madinah, where Muslims from all parts of Arabia had come and settled as one community, and had established an independent city state. Here it became a struggle for the survival of the Community itself, for the whole of non-Muslim Arabia was bent upon and united in crushing it totally. Hence the following instructions, upon which depended not only its success but its very survival, were revealed in this Sūrah:

a. The Community should work with the utmost zeal to propagate its ideology and win over to its side the greatest possible number of people.
b. It should so expose its opponents as to leave no room for doubt in the mind of any sensible person that they were adhering to an absolutely wrong position.
c. It should infuse in its members (the majority of whom were homeless and indigent and surrounded on all sides by enemies) that courage and fortitude which is so indispensable to their very existence in the adverse circumstances in which they were struggling and to prepare them to face these boldly.
d. It should also keep them ready and prepared to meet any armed menace, which might come from any side to suppress and crush their ideology, and to oppose it tooth and nail without minding the overwhelming numerical strength and the material resources of its enemies.
e. It should also create in them that courage which is needed for the eradication of evil ways and for the establishment of the Islāmic Way instead. That is why God has revealed in this Sūrah such instructions as may help achieve all the above mentioned objects.

At the time of the revelation of Al-Baqarah, all sorts of hypocrites had begun to appear. God has, therefore, briefly pointed out their characteristics here. Afterwards when their evil characteristics and mischievous deeds became manifest, God sent detailed instructions about them.

**Theme: Guidance**

This Sūrah is an invitation to the Divine Guidance and all the stories, incidents etc., revolve around this central theme. As this Sūrah has particularly been addressed to the Jews, many historical events have been cited from their own traditions to admonish and advise them that their own good lies in accepting the Guidance revealed to the Prophet. They should, therefore, be the first to accept it because it was basically the same that was revealed to Prophet Moses.

## Sūrah 2: al-Baqarah[6]

In the Name of God, the Most Compassionate, the Most Merciful

1. Alif, Lām, Meem.[7]

2. This is the Book about which there is no doubt, a guidance for those conscious of God[8] -

3. Who believe in the unseen, establish prayer,[9] and spend out of what We[10] have provided for them,

4. And who believe in what has been revealed to you, [O Muhammad], and what was revealed before you, and of the Hereafter they are certain [in faith].

5. Those are upon [right] guidance from their Lord, and it is those who are the successful.

6. Indeed, those who disbelieve[11] - it is all the same for them whether you warn them or do not warn them - they will not believe.

7. God has set a seal upon their hearts and upon their hearing, and over their vision is a veil.[12] And for them is a great punishment.

8. And of the people are some who say, "We believe in God and the Last Day," but they are not believers.

9. They [think to] deceive God and those who believe, but they deceive not except themselves and perceive [it] not.

10. In their hearts is disease, so God has increased their disease;[13] and for them is a painful punishment because they [habitually] used to lie.

11. And when it is said to them, "Do not cause corruption on the earth," they say, "We are but reformers."

12. Unquestionably, it is they who are the corrupters, but they perceive [it] not.

13. And when it is said to them, "Believe as the people have believed," they say, "Should we believe as the foolish have believed?" Unquestionably, it is they who are the foolish, but they know [it] not.

14. And when they meet those who believe, they say, "We believe"; but when they are alone with their evil ones, they say, "Indeed, we are with you; we were only mockers."

15. [But] God mocks them and prolongs them in their transgression [while] they wander blindly.

---

[6] *Al-Baqarah*: The Cow. The name is taken from the story in verses 67-73.

[7] These are among the fourteen opening letters which occur in various combinations at the beginning of twenty-nine *sūrahs* in the Qur'ān. Although there has been much speculation as to their meaning, it was not, in fact, revealed by God to anyone and is known only to Him.

[8] Literally, "those who have *taqwā*," i.e., who have piety, righteousness, fear and love of God, and who take great care to avoid His displeasure.

[9] At its proper times and according to its specified conditions.

[10] It is to be noted that the reference of God to Himself as "We" in many Qur'ānic verses is necessarily understood in the Arabic language to denote grandeur and power, as apposed to the more intimate singular form "I" used in specific instances.

[11] Literally, "cover" or "conceal" (faith or truth).

[12] A covering preventing them from discerning guidance. This condition is a direct result of their arrogance and persistence in sin.

[13] The "disease" mentioned here includes doubt, hypocrisy, arrogance and disbelief.

16. Those are the ones who have purchased error [in exchange] for guidance, so their transaction has brought no profit, nor were they guided.

17. Their example is that of one who kindled a fire, but when it illuminated what was around him, God took away their light and left them in darkness [so] they could not see.

18. Deaf, dumb and blind - so they will not return [to the right path].

19. Or [it is] like a rainstorm from the sky within which is darkness, thunder and lightning. They put their fingers in their ears against the thunderclaps in dread of death. But God is encompassing[14] of the disbelievers.

20. The lightning almost snatches away their sight. Every time it lights [the way] for them, they walk therein; but when darkness comes over them, they stand [still]. And if God had willed, He could have taken away their hearing and their sight. Indeed, God is over all things competent.

21. O mankind, worship your Lord, who created you and those before you, that you may become righteous –

22. [He] who made for you the earth a bed [spread out] and the sky a ceiling and sent down from the sky, rain and brought forth thereby fruits as provision for you. So do not attribute to God equals while you know [that there is nothing similar to Him].

23. And if you are in doubt about what We have sent down [i.e., the Qur'ān] upon Our Servant [i.e., Prophet Muhammad], then produce a sūrah the like thereof and call upon your witnesses [i.e., supporters] other than God, if you should be truthful.

24. But if you do not - and you will never be able to - then fear the Fire, whose fuel is men and stones, prepared for the disbelievers.

25. And give good tidings to those who believe and do righteous deeds that they will have gardens [in Paradise] beneath which rivers flow. Whenever they are provided with a provision of fruit therefrom, they will say, "This is what we were provided with before." And it is given to them in likeness. And they will have therein purified spouses, and they will abide therein eternally.

26. Indeed, God is not timid to present an example - that of a mosquito or what is smaller[15] than it. And those who have believed know that it is the truth from their Lord. But as for those who disbelieve, they say, "What did God intend by this as an example?" He misleads many thereby and guides many thereby. And He misleads not except the defiantly disobedient,

27. Who break the covenant of God after contracting it and sever that which God

[14] God states in the Qur'ān that He has certain attributes such as hearing, sight, hands, face, mercy, anger, coming, encompassing, being above the Throne, etc. Yet, He has disassociated Himself from the limitations of human attributes or human imagination. Correct Islāmic belief requires faith in the existence of these attributes as God has described them without applying to them any allegorical meanings or attempting to explain how a certain quality could be (while this is known only to God) and without comparing them to creation or denying that He would have such a quality. His attributes are befitting to Him alone, and "*There is nothing like unto Him.*" (42:11)

[15] Literally, "above it," i.e., greater in smallness.

has ordered to be joined and cause corruption on earth. It is those who are the losers.

28. How can you disbelieve in God when you were lifeless and He brought you to life; then He will cause you to die, then He will bring you [back] to life, and then to Him you will be returned.

29. It is He who created for you all of that which is on the earth. Then He directed Himself[16] to the heaven, [His being above all creation], and made them seven heavens, and He is Knowing of all things.

30. And [mention, O Muhammad], when your Lord said to the angels, "Indeed, I will make upon the earth a successive authority."[17] They said, "Will You place upon it one who causes corruption therein and sheds blood, while we declare Your praise and sanctify You?" He [God] said, "Indeed, I know that which you do not know."

31. And He taught Adam the names - all of them. Then He showed them to the angels and said, "Inform Me of the names of these, if you are truthful."

32. They said, "Exalted are You; we have no knowledge except what You have taught us. Indeed, it is You who is the Knowing, the Wise."

33. He said, "O Adam, inform them of their names." And when he had informed them of their names, He said, "Did I not tell you that I know the unseen [aspects] of the heavens and the earth? And I know what you reveal and what you have concealed."

[16] See footnote to 2:19.

[17] *Khalīfah*: successor, or generations of man, one following another.

34. And [mention] when We said to the angels, "Prostrate before Adam"; so they prostrated, except for Iblees.[18] He refused and was arrogant and became of the disbelievers.

35. And We said, "O Adam, dwell, you and your wife, in Paradise and eat therefrom in [ease and] abundance from wherever you will. But do not approach this tree, lest you be among the wrongdoers."

36. But Satan caused them to slip out of it and removed them from that [condition] in which they had been. And We said, "Go down, [all of you], as enemies to one another, and you will have upon the earth a place of settlement and provision for a time."

37. Then Adam received from his Lord [some] words,[19] and He accepted his repentance. Indeed, it is He who is the Accepting of repentance, the Merciful.

38. We said, "Go down from it, all of you. And when guidance comes to you from Me, whoever follows My guidance - there will be no fear concerning them, nor will they grieve.

39. And those who disbelieve and deny Our signs - those will be companions of the Fire; they will abide therein eternally."

40. O Children of Israel, remember My favor which I have bestowed upon you and fulfill My covenant [upon you] that

[18] The proper name of Satan, who was not an angel but from the *jinn*, as stated in 18:50. Done in obedience to God, this prostration was one of respect, not worship.

[19] God taught Adam words of repentance that would be acceptable to Him.

I will fulfill your covenant [from Me], and be afraid of [only] Me.

41. And believe in what I have sent down confirming that which is [already] with you, and be not the first to disbelieve in it. And do not exchange My signs for a small price, and fear [only] Me.

42. And do not mix the truth with falsehood or conceal the truth while you know [it].

43. And establish prayer and give zakāh[20] and bow with those who bow [in worship and obedience].

44. Do you order righteousness of the people and forget[21] yourselves while you recite the Scripture? Then will you not reason?

45. And seek help through patience and prayer, and indeed, it is difficult except for the humbly submissive [to God]

46. Who are certain that they will meet their Lord and that they will return to Him.

47. O Children of Israel, remember My favor that I have bestowed upon you and that I preferred you over the worlds [i.e., peoples].

48. And fear a Day when no soul will suffice for another soul[22] at all, nor will intercession be accepted from it, nor will compensation be taken from it, nor will they be aided.

[20] An annual expenditure for the benefit of the Islāmic community (see 9:60) required of those Muslims who have excess wealth. Prayer and *zakāh* are among the pillars of Islām.
[21] Make exceptions of.
[22] i.e., fulfil what is due from it.

49. And [recall] when We saved you [i.e., your forefathers] from the people of Pharaoh, who afflicted you with the worst torment, slaughtering your [newborn] sons and keeping your females alive. And in that was a great trial from your Lord.

50. And [recall] when We parted the sea for you and saved you and drowned the people of Pharaoh while you were looking on.

51. And [recall] when We made an appointment with Moses for forty nights. Then you took [for worship] the calf after him [i.e., his departure], while you were wrongdoers.

52. Then We forgave you after that so perhaps you would be grateful.

53. And [recall] when We gave Moses the Scripture and criterion[23] that perhaps you would be guided.

54. And [recall] when Moses said to his people, "O my people, indeed you have wronged yourselves by your taking of the calf [for worship]. So repent to your Creator and kill yourselves [i.e., the guilty among you]. That is best for [all of] you in the sight of your Creator." Then He accepted your repentance; indeed, He is the Accepting of repentance, the Merciful.

55. And [recall] when you said, "O Moses, we will never believe you until we see God outright"; so the thunderbolt took you while you were looking on.

56. Then We revived you after your death that perhaps you would be grateful.

[23] Differentiating between truth and falsehood. "The Scripture and criterion" refers to the Torah.

57. And We shaded you with clouds and sent down to you manna and quails, [saying], "Eat from the good things with which We have provided you." And they wronged Us not - but they were [only] wronging themselves.

58. And [recall] when We said, "Enter this city [i.e., Jerusalem] and eat from it wherever you will in [ease and] abundance, and enter the gate bowing humbly[24] and say, 'Relieve us of our burdens [i.e., sins].' We will [then] forgive your sins for you, and We will increase the doers of good [in goodness and reward]."

59. But those who wronged changed [those words] to a statement other than that which had been said to them, so We sent down upon those who wronged a punishment [i.e., plague] from the sky because they were defiantly disobeying.

60. And [recall] when Moses prayed for water for his people, so We said, "Strike with your staff the stone." And there gushed forth from it twelve springs, and every people [i.e., tribe] knew its watering place. "Eat and drink from the provision of God, and do not commit abuse on the earth, spreading corruption."

61. And [recall] when you said, "O Moses, we can never endure one [kind of] food. So call upon your Lord to bring forth for us from the earth its green herbs and its cucumbers and its garlic and its lentils and its onions." [Moses] said, "Would you exchange what is better for what is less? Go into [any] settlement and indeed, you will have what you have asked." And they were covered with humiliation and poverty and returned with anger from God [upon them]. That was because they [repeatedly] disbelieved in the signs of God and killed the prophets without right. That was because they disobeyed and were [habitually] transgressing.

62. Indeed, those who believed and those who were Jews or Christians or Sabeans [before Prophet Muhammad] - those [among them] who believed in God and the Last Day and did righteousness - will have their reward with their Lord, and no fear will there be concerning them, nor will they grieve.[25]

63. And [recall] when We took your covenant, [O Children of Israel, to abide by the Torah] and We raised over you the mount, [saying], "Take what We have given you with determination and remember what is in it that perhaps you may become righteous."

64. Then you turned away after that. And if not for the favor of God upon you and His mercy, you would have been among the losers.

65. And you had already known about those who transgressed among you concerning the sabbath, and We said to them, "Be apes, despised."

66. And We made it a deterrent punishment for those who were present and those who succeeded [them] and a lesson for those who fear God.

67. And [recall] when Moses said to his people, "Indeed, God commands you to slaughter a cow." They said, "Do you take us in ridicule?" He said, "I

[24] In gratitude to God and admission of sin.

[25] After the coming of Prophet Muhammad no religion other than Islām is acceptable to God, as stated in 3:85.

seek refuge in God from being among the ignorant."

68. They said, "Call upon your Lord to make clear to us what it is." [Moses] said, "[God] says, 'It is a cow which is neither old nor virgin, but median between that,' so do what you are commanded."

69. They said, "Call upon your Lord to show us what is her color." He said, "He says, 'It is a yellow cow, bright in color -pleasing to the observers.' "

70. They said, "Call upon your Lord to make clear to us what it is. Indeed, [all] cows look alike to us. And indeed we, if God wills, will be guided."

71. He said, "He says, 'It is a cow neither trained to plow the earth nor to irrigate the field, one free from fault with no spot upon her.' " They said, "Now you have come with the truth." So they slaughtered her, but they could hardly do it.

72. And [recall] when you slew a man and disputed[26] over it, but God was to bring out that which you were concealing.

73. So We said, "Strike him [i.e., the slain man] with part of it."[27] Thus does God bring the dead to life, and He shows you His signs that you might reason.

74. Then your hearts became hardened after that, being like stones or even harder. For indeed, there are stones from which rivers burst forth, and there are some of them that split open and water comes out, and there are some of them that fall down for fear of God. And God is not unaware of what you do.

[26] i.e., exchanged accusations and denials.

[27] i.e., the cow. Thereupon, God restored life to the man, who informed them of his murderer.

75. Do you covet [the hope, O believers], that they would believe for you while a party of them used to hear the words of God and then distort it [i.e., the Torah] after they had understood it while they were knowing?

76. And when they meet those who believe, they say, "We have believed"; but when they are alone with one another, they say, "Do you talk to them about what God has revealed to you so they can argue with you about it before your Lord?" Then will you not reason?

77. But do they not know that God knows what they conceal and what they declare?

78. And among them are unlettered ones who do not know the Scripture except [indulgement in] wishful thinking, but they are only assuming.

79. So woe[28] to those who write the "scripture" with their own hands, then say, "This is from God," in order to exchange it for a small price. Woe to them for what their hands have written and woe to them for what they earn.

80. And they say, "Never will the Fire touch us, except for [a few] numbered days." Say, "Have you taken a covenant with God? For God will never break His covenant. Or do you say about God that which you do not know?"

81. Yes, [on the contrary], whoever earns evil and his sin has encompassed him - those are the companions of the Fire; they will abide therein eternally.

[28] i.e., death and destruction.

82. But they who believe and do righteous deeds – those are the companions of Paradise; they will abide therein eternally.

83. And [recall] when We took the covenant from the Children of Israel, [enjoining upon them], "Do not worship except God; and to parents do good and to relatives, orphans, and the needy. And speak to people good [words] and establish prayer and give zakāh." Then you turned away, except a few of you, and you were refusing.

84. And [recall] when We took your covenant, [saying], "Do not shed your [i.e., each other's] blood or evict one another from your homes." Then you acknowledged [this] while you were witnessing.

85. Then, you are those [same ones who are] killing one another and evicting a party of your people from their homes, cooperating against them in sin and aggression. And if they come to you as captives, you ransom them, although their eviction was forbidden to you. So do you believe in part of the Scripture and disbelieve in part? Then what is the recompense for those who do that among you except disgrace in worldly life; and on the Day of Resurrection they will be sent back to the severest of punishment. And God is not unaware of what you do.

86. Those are the ones who have bought the life of this world [in exchange] for the Hereafter, so the punishment will not be lightened for them, nor will they be aided.

87. And We did certainly give Moses the scripture [i.e., the Torah] and followed up after him with messengers. And We gave Jesus, the son of Mary, clear proofs and supported him with the Pure Spirit [i.e., the angel Gabriel]. But is it [not] that every time a messenger came to you, [O Children of Israel], with what your souls did not desire, you were arrogant? And a party [of messengers] you denied and another party you killed.

88. And they said, "Our hearts are wrapped."[29] But, [in fact], God has cursed them for their disbelief, so little is it that they believe.

89. And when there came to them a Book [i.e., the Qur'ān] from God confirming that which was with them - although before they used to pray for victory against those who disbelieved - but [then] when there came to them that which they recognized, they disbelieved in it; so the curse of God will be upon the disbelievers.

90. How wretched is that for which they sold themselves - that they would disbelieve in what God has revealed through [their] outrage that God would send down His favor upon whom He wills from among His servants. So they returned having [earned] wrath upon wrath. And for the disbelievers is a humiliating punishment.

91. And when it is said to them, "Believe in what God has revealed," they say, "We believe [only] in what was revealed to us." And they disbelieve in what came after it, while it is the truth confirming that which is with them. Say, "Then why did you kill the prophets of God before, if you are [indeed] believers?"

[29] Covered or sealed against reception of God's word.

92. And Moses had certainly brought you clear proofs. Then you took the calf [in worship] after that, while you were wrongdoers.

93. And [recall] when We took your covenant and raised over you the mount, [saying], "Take what We have given you with determination and listen." They said [instead], "We hear and disobey." And their hearts absorbed [the worship of] the calf because of their disbelief. Say, "How wretched is that which your faith enjoins upon you, if you should be believers."

94. Say, [O Muhammad], "If the home of the Hereafter with God is for you alone and not the [other] people, then wish for death, if you should be truthful."

95. But they will never wish for it, ever, because of what their hands have put forth. And God is Knowing of the wrongdoers.

96. And you will surely find them the most greedy of people for life - [even] more than those who associate others with God. One of them wishes that he could be granted life a thousand years, but it would not remove him in the least from the [coming] punishment that he should be granted life. And God is Seeing of what they do.

97. Say, "Whoever is an enemy to Gabriel - it is [none but] he who has brought it [i.e., the Qur'ān] down upon your heart, [O Muhammad], by permission of God, confirming that which was before it and as guidance and good tidings for the believers."

98. Whoever is an enemy to God and His angels and His messengers and Gabriel and Michael - then indeed, God is an enemy to the disbelievers.

99. And We have certainly revealed to you verses [which are] clear proofs, and no one would deny them except the defiantly disobedient.

100. Is it not [true] that every time they took a covenant a party of them threw it away? But, [in fact], most of them do not believe.

101. And when a messenger from God came to them confirming that which was with them, a party of those who had been given the Scripture threw the Scripture of God [i.e., the Torah] behind their backs as if they did not know [what it contained].

102. And they followed [instead] what the devils had recited during the reign of Solomon. It was not Solomon who disbelieved, but the devils disbelieved, teaching people magic and that which was revealed to the two angels at Babylon, Hārūt and Mārūt. But they [i.e., the two angels] do not teach anyone unless they say, "We are a trial, so do not disbelieve [by practicing magic]."[30] And [yet] they learn from them that by which they cause separation between a man and his wife. But they do not harm anyone through it except by permission of God. And they [i.e., the people] learn what harms them and does not benefit them. But they [i.e., the Children of Israel] certainly knew that whoever purchased it [i.e., magic] would not have in the Hereafter any share. And wretched is that for which they sold themselves, if they only knew.

[30] They warn people against the misuse of what they have learned.

103. And if they had believed and feared God, then the reward from God would have been [far] better, if they only knew.

104. O you who have believed, say not [to God's Messenger], "Rā'inā" but say, "Unthurnā"[31] and listen. And for the disbelievers is a painful punishment.

105. Neither those who disbelieve from the People of the Scripture [i.e., the Jews and Christians] nor the polytheists wish that any good should be sent down to you from your Lord. But God selects for His mercy whom He wills, and God is the possessor of great bounty.

106. We do not abrogate a verse or cause it to be forgotten except that We bring forth [one] better than it or similar to it. Do you not know that God is over all things competent?

107. Do you not know that to God belongs the dominion of the heavens and the earth and [that] you have not besides God any protector or any helper?

108. Or do you intend to ask[32] your Messenger as Moses was asked before? And whoever exchanges faith for disbelief has certainly strayed from the soundness of the way.

109. Many of the People of the Scripture wish they could turn you back to disbelief after you have believed, out of envy from themselves [even] after the truth has become clear to them. So pardon and overlook until God delivers His command. Indeed, God is over all things competent.

110. And establish prayer and give zakāh, and whatever good you put forward for yourselves - you will find it with God. Indeed God, of what you do, is Seeing.

111. And they say, "None will enter Paradise except one who is a Jew or a Christian." That is [merely] their wishful thinking. Say, "Produce your proof, if you should be truthful."

112. Yes, [on the contrary], whoever submits his face [i.e., self] in Islām to God while being a doer of good will have his reward with his Lord. And no fear will there be concerning them, nor will they grieve.

113. The Jews say, "The Christians have nothing [true] to stand on," and the Christians say, "The Jews have nothing to stand on," although they [both] recite the Scripture. Thus do those who know not [i.e., the polytheists] speak the same as their words. But God will judge between them on the Day of Resurrection concerning that over which they used to differ.

114. And who are more unjust than those who prevent the name of God from being mentioned [i.e., praised] in His mosques and strive toward their destruction. It is not for them to enter them except in fear. For them in this world is disgrace, and they will have in the Hereafter a great punishment.

115. And to God belongs the east and the west. So wherever you [might] turn,

---

31 The word "*rā'inā*" in Arabic literally means "consider us," i.e., give us time to hear you and listen to us. The Jews used to use the same word with the meaning of an insult. Therefore, the believers were ordered to avoid this expression and use instead the word "*unthurnā,*" i.e., "wait for us [so that we may understand]."

32 i.e., persistently question or, as in the case of the disbelievers, demand a miracle of the Prophet.

there is the Face[33] of God. Indeed, God is all-Encompassing and Knowing.

116. They say, "God has taken a son." Exalted is He![34] Rather, to Him belongs whatever is in the heavens and the earth. All are devoutly obedient to Him,

117. Originator of the heavens and the earth. When He decrees a matter, He only says to it, "Be," and it is.

118. Those who do not know say, "Why does God not speak to us or there come to us a sign?" Thus spoke those before them like their words. Their hearts resemble each other. We have shown clearly the signs to a people who are certain [in faith].

119. Indeed, We have sent you, [O Muhammad], with the truth as a bringer of good tidings and a warner, and you will not be asked about the companions of Hellfire.

120. And never will the Jews and the Christians approve of you until you follow their religion. Say, "Indeed, the guidance of God is the [only] guidance." If you were to follow their desires after what has come to you of knowledge, you would have against God no protector or helper.

121. Those to whom We have given the Book recite it with its true recital.[35] They [are the ones who] believe in it. And whoever disbelieves in it - it is they who are the losers.

122. O Children of Israel, remember My favor which I have bestowed upon you and that I preferred you over the worlds.

123. And fear a Day when no soul will suffice for another soul[36] at all, and no compensation will be accepted from it, nor will any intercession benefit it, nor will they be aided.

124. And [mention, O Muhammad], when Abraham was tried by his Lord with words [i.e., commands] and he fulfilled them. [God] said, "Indeed, I will make you a leader for the people." [Abraham] said, "And of my descendants?" [God] said, "My covenant does not include the wrongdoers."

125. And [mention] when We made the House [i.e., the Ka'bāh] a place of return for the people and [a place of] security. And take, [O believers], from the standing place of Abraham a place of prayer. And We charged Abraham and Ishmael, [saying], "Purify My House for those who perform tawāf[37] and those who are staying [there] for worship and those who bow and prostrate [in prayer]."

126. And [mention] when Abraham said, "My Lord, make this a secure city and provide its people with fruits - whoever of them believes in God and the Last Day." [God] said. "And whoever disbelieves - I will grant him enjoyment for a little; then I will force him to the punishment of the Fire, and wretched is the destination."

127. And [mention] when Abraham was raising the foundations of the House and [with him] Ishmael, [saying], "Our

[33] See footnote to 2:19.
[34] *Subhānahu* means "far exalted is He above all they falsely attribute to Him."
[35] i.e., applying its teachings to their lives.

[36] See footnote to 2:48.
[37] A form of worship particular to the *Ka'bāh* consisting of going around it in circuits.

Lord, accept [this] from us. Indeed, You are the Hearing, the Knowing.

128. Our Lord, and make us Muslims [in submission] to You and from our descendants a Muslim nation [in submission] to You. And show us our rites [of hajj and 'umrah] and accept our repentance. Indeed, You are the Accepting of repentance, the Merciful.

129. Our Lord, and send among them a messenger from themselves who will recite to them Your verses and teach them the Book and wisdom and purify them. Indeed, You are the Exalted in Might, the Wise."

130. And who would be averse to the religion of Abraham except one who makes a fool of himself. And We had chosen him in this world, and indeed he, in the Hereafter, will be among the righteous.

131. When his Lord said to him, "Submit," he said, "I have submitted [in Islām][38] to the Lord of the worlds."

132. And Abraham instructed his sons [to do the same] and [so did] Jacob, [saying], "O my sons, indeed God has chosen for you this religion, so do not die except while you are Muslims."

133. Or were you witnesses when death approached Jacob, when he said to his sons, "What will you worship after me?" They said, "We will worship your God and the God of your fathers, Abraham and Ishmael and Isaac - one God.[39] And we are Muslims [in submission] to Him."

134. That was a nation which has passed on. It will have [the consequence of] what it earned, and you will have what you have earned. And you will not be asked about what they used to do.

135. They say, "Be Jews or Christians [so] you will be guided." Say, "Rather, [we follow] the religion of Abraham, inclining toward truth, and he was not of the polytheists."[40]

136. Say, [O believers], "We have believed in God and what has been revealed to us and what has been revealed to Abraham and Ishmael and Isaac and Jacob and the Descendants [al-Asbāt][41] and what was given to Moses and Jesus and what was given to the prophets from their Lord. We make no distinction between any of them, and we are Muslims [in submission] to Him."

137. So if they believe in the same as you believe in, then they have been [rightly] guided; but if they turn away, they are only in dissension, and God will be sufficient for you against them. And He is the Hearing, the Knowing.

138. [And say, "Ours is] the religion of God. And who is better than God in [ordaining] religion? And we are worshippers of Him."

139. Say, [O Muhammad], "Do you argue with us about God while He is our Lord and your Lord? For us are our deeds, and for you are your deeds. And

[38] The meaning of the word "Islām" is "submission to the will of God." This is the way of life ordained by God and taught by all of the prophets from Adam to Muhammad. A Muslim is one who submits himself to God.

[39] God alone.

[40] Those who associate others with God in worship.

[41] The twelve tribes of Israel descended from Jacob.

we are sincere [in deed and intention] to Him."

140. Or do you say that Abraham and Ishmael and Isaac and Jacob and the Descendants were Jews or Christians? Say, "Are you more knowing or is God?" And who is more unjust than one who conceals a testimony[42] he has from God? And God is not unaware of what you do.

141. That is a nation which has passed on. It will have [the consequence of] what it earned, and you will have what you have earned. And you will not be asked about what they used to do.

142. The foolish among the people will say, "What has turned them away from their qiblah,[43] which they used to face?"[44] Say, "To God belongs the east and the west. He guides whom He wills to a straight path."

143. And thus We have made you a median [i.e., just] community that you will be witnesses over the people and the Messenger will be a witness over you. And We did not make the qiblah which you used to face except that We might make evident who would follow the Messenger from who would turn back on his heels. And indeed, it is difficult except for those whom God has guided. And never would God have caused you to lose your faith [i.e., your previous prayers]. Indeed God is, to the people, Kind and Merciful.

144. We have certainly seen the turning of your face, [O Muhammad], toward the heaven, and We will surely turn you to a qiblah with which you will be pleased. So turn your face [i.e., yourself] toward al-Masjid al-Harām.[45] And wherever you [believers] are, turn your faces [i.e., yourselves] toward it [in prayer]. Indeed, those who have been given the Scripture [i.e., the Jews and the Christians] well know that it is the truth from their Lord. And God is not unaware of what they do.

145. And if you brought to those who were given the Scripture every sign, they would not follow your qiblah. Nor will you be a follower of their qiblah. Nor would they be followers of one another's qiblah. So if you were to follow their desires after what has come to you of knowledge, indeed, you would then be among the wrongdoers.

146. Those to whom We gave the Scripture know him [i.e., Prophet Muhammad] as they know their own sons. But indeed, a party of them conceal the truth while they know [it].

147. The truth is from your Lord, so never be among the doubters.

148. For each [religious following] is a [prayer] direction toward which it faces. So race to [all that is] good. Wherever you may be, God will bring you forth [for judgement] all together. Indeed, God is over all things competent.

[42] Statements in previous scriptures attesting to the nature of God's religion (Islām) and the coming of Prophet Muhammad.
[43] The direction faced in prayer.
[44] Prior to the command (in verse 144) that the Prophet and his followers turn toward the *Ka'bāh* in Makkah for prayer, they had been facing Jerusalem to the north. The implications of this change are mentioned in succeeding verses.

[45] The Sacred Mosque in Makkah containing the *Ka'bāh.*

149. So from wherever you go out [for prayer, O Muhammad], turn your face toward al-Masjid al-Harām, and indeed, it is the truth from your Lord. And God is not unaware of what you do.

150. And from wherever you go out [for prayer], turn your face toward al-Masjid al-Harām. And wherever you [believers] may be, turn your faces toward it in order that the people will not have any argument against you, except for those of them who commit wrong; so fear them not but fear Me. And [it is] so I may complete My favor upon you and that you may be guided,

151. Just as We have sent among you a messenger from yourselves reciting to you Our verses and purifying you and teaching you the Book and wisdom[46] and teaching you that which you did not know.

152. So remember Me; I will remember you. And be grateful to Me and do not deny Me.

153. O you who have believed, seek help through patience and prayer. Indeed, God is with the patient.

154. And do not say about those who are killed in the way of God, "They are dead." Rather, they are alive, but you perceive [it] not.

155. And We will surely test you with something of fear and hunger and a loss of wealth and lives and fruits, but give good tidings to the patient,

[46] The wisdom taught by the Prophet is his *sunnah*.

156. Who, when disaster strikes them, say, "Indeed we belong to God, and indeed to Him we will return."

157. Those are the ones upon whom are blessings from their Lord and mercy. And it is those who are the [rightly] guided.

158. Indeed, as-Safā and al-Marwah are among the symbols[47] of God. So whoever makes hajj [pilgrimage] to the House or performs 'umrah - there is no blame upon him for walking between them.[48] And whoever volunteers good - then indeed, God is Appreciative and Knowing.

159. Indeed, those who conceal what We sent down of clear proofs and guidance after We made it clear for the people in the Scripture - those are cursed by God and cursed by those who curse,[49]

160. Except for those who repent and correct themselves and make evident [what they concealed]. Those - I will accept their repentance, and I am the Accepting of repentance, the Merciful.

161. Indeed, those who disbelieve and die while they are disbelievers - upon them will be the curse of God and of the angels and the people, all together,

162. Abiding eternally therein. The punishment will not be lightened for them, nor will they be reprieved.

163. And your god is one God. There is no deity [worthy of worship] except Him,

[47] Places designed for the rites of *hajj* and *'umrah*.
[48] Some believers had previously feared that this might be a pagan practice, so God confirms that *sa'i* is among the rites of His religion.
[49] From among the angels and the believers.

the Entirely Merciful, the Especially Merciful.

164. Indeed, in the creation of the heavens and the earth, and the alternation of the night and the day, and the [great] ships which sail through the sea with that which benefits people, and what God has sent down from the heavens of rain, giving life thereby to the earth after its lifelessness and dispersing therein every [kind of] moving creature, and [His] directing of the winds and the clouds controlled between the heaven and earth are signs for a people who use reason.

165. And [yet], among the people are those who take other than God as equals [to Him]. They love them as they [should] love God. But those who believe are stronger in love for God. And if only they who have wronged would consider [that] when they see the punishment, [they will be certain] that all power belongs to God and that God is severe in punishment.

166. [And they should consider that] when those who have been followed disassociate themselves from those who followed [them], and they [all] see the punishment, and cut off from them are the ties [of relationship],

167. Those who followed will say, "If only we had another turn [at worldly life] so we could disassociate ourselves from them as they have disassociated themselves from us." Thus will God show them their deeds as regrets upon them. And they are never to emerge from the Fire.

168. O mankind, eat from whatever is on earth [that is] lawful and good and do not follow the footsteps of Satan. Indeed, he is to you a clear enemy.

169. He only orders you to evil and immorality and to say about God what you do not know.

170. And when it is said to them, "Follow what God has revealed," they say, "Rather, we will follow that which we found our fathers doing." Even though their fathers understood nothing, nor were they guided?

171. The example of those who disbelieve is like that of one who shouts at what hears nothing but calls and cries [i.e., cattle or sheep] - deaf, dumb and blind, so they do not understand.

172. O you who have believed, eat from the good [i.e., lawful] things which We have provided for you and be grateful to God if it is [indeed] Him that you worship.

173. He has only forbidden to you dead animals,[50] blood, the flesh of swine, and that which has been dedicated to other than God. But whoever is forced [by necessity], neither desiring [it] nor transgressing [its limit], there is no sin upon him. Indeed, God is Forgiving and Merciful.

174. Indeed, they who conceal what God has sent down of the Book and exchange it for a small price - those consume not into their bellies except the Fire. And God will not speak to them on the Day of Resurrection, nor will He purify them. And they will have a painful punishment.

---

[50] Those not slaughtered or hunted expressly for food.

175. Those are the ones who have exchanged guidance for error and forgiveness for punishment. How patient they are for [i.e., in pursuit of] the Fire!

176. That is [deserved by them] because God has sent down the Book in truth. And indeed, those who differ over the Book are in extreme dissension.

177. Righteousness is not that you turn your faces toward the east or the west, but [true] righteousness is [in] one who believes in God, the Last Day, the angels, the Book, and the prophets and gives wealth, in spite of love for it, to relatives, orphans, the needy, the traveler, those who ask [for help], and for freeing slaves; [and who] establishes prayer and gives zakāh; [those who] fulfill their promise when they promise; and [those who] are patient in poverty and hardship and during battle. Those are the ones who have been true, and it is those who are the righteous.

178. O you who have believed, prescribed for you is legal retribution for those murdered - the free for the free, the slave for the slave, and the female for the female.[51] But whoever overlooks from his brother [i.e., the killer] anything,[52] then there should be a suitable follow-up and payment to him [i.e., the deceased's heir or legal representative] with good conduct. This is an alleviation from your Lord and a mercy. But whoever transgresses after that[53] will have a painful punishment.

179. And there is for you in legal retribution [saving of] life, O you [people] of understanding, that you may become righteous.

180. Prescribed for you when death approaches [any] one of you if he leaves wealth [is that he should make] a bequest for the parents and near relatives according to what is acceptable - a duty upon the righteous.[54]

181. Then whoever alters it [i.e., the bequest] after he has heard it - the sin is only upon those who have altered it. Indeed, God is Hearing and Knowing.

182. But if one fears from the bequeather [some] error or sin and corrects that which is between them [i.e., the concerned parties], there is no sin upon him. Indeed, God is Forgiving and Merciful.

183. O you who have believed, decreed upon you is fasting as it was decreed upon those before you that you may become righteous -

184. [Fasting for] a limited number of days. So whoever among you is ill or on a journey [during them] - then an equal number of days [are to be made up]. And upon those who are able [to fast, but with hardship] - a ransom [as substitute] of feeding a poor person [each day]. And whoever volunteers good [i.e., excess] - it is better for him. But to fast is best for you, if you only knew.

185. The month of Ramadhān [is that] in which was revealed the Qur'ān, a guidance for the people and clear proofs of guidance and criterion. So whoever

[51] No one else should be executed in place of the killer.

[52] By accepting compensation payment rather than execution.

[53] After acceptance of compensation.

[54] This ruling was abrogated by the revelation in *Sūrah an-Nisā'* stipulating obligatory shares for parents and close relatives. Those who do not inherit by law may be remembered in a bequest. See 4:11-12.

sights [the new moon of] the month,[55] let him fast it; and whoever is ill or on a journey - then an equal number of other days. God intends for you ease and does not intend for you hardship and [wants] for you to complete the period and to glorify God for that [to] which He has guided you; and perhaps you will be grateful.

186. And when My servants ask you, [O Muhammad], concerning Me - indeed I am near. I respond to the invocation of the supplicant when he calls upon Me. So let them respond to Me [by obedience] and believe in Me that they may be [rightly] guided.

187. It has been made permissible for you the night preceding fasting to go to your wives [for sexual relations]. They are clothing for you and you are clothing for them. God knows that you used to deceive yourselves,[56] so He accepted your repentance and forgave you. So now, have relations with them and seek that which God has decreed for you [i.e., offspring]. And eat and drink until the white thread of dawn becomes distinct to you from the black thread [of night]. Then complete the fast until the night [i.e., sunset]. And do not have relations with them as long as you are staying for worship in the mosques. These are the limits [set by] God, so do not approach them. Thus does God make clear His verses [i.e., ordinances] to the people that they may become righteous.

188. And do not consume one another's wealth unjustly or send it [in bribery] to the rulers in order that [they might aid] you [to] consume a portion of the wealth of the people in sin, while you know [it is unlawful].

189. They ask you, [O Muhammad], about the new moons. Say, "They are measurements of time for the people and for hajj [pilgrimage]." And it is not righteousness to enter houses from the back, but righteousness is [in] one who fears God. And enter houses from their doors. And fear God that you may succeed.

190. Fight in the way of God those who fight you but do not transgress. Indeed, God does not like transgressors.

191. And kill them wherever you overtake them and expel them from wherever they have expelled you, and fitnah[57] is worse than killing. And do not fight them at al-Masjid al-Harām until they fight you there. But if they fight you, then kill them. Such is the recompense of the disbelievers.

192. And if they cease, then indeed, God is Forgiving and Merciful.

193. Fight them until there is no [more] fitnah[58] and [until] religion [i.e., worship] is [acknowledged to be] for God. But if they cease, then there is to be no aggression [i.e., assault] except against the oppressors.

194. [Fighting in] the sacred month is for [aggression committed in] the sacred month,[59] and for [all] violations is legal

[55] Also, "whoever is present during the month."

[56] Prior to this revelation, marital relations were unlawful during nights preceding fasting. Some were unable to refrain and secretly disobeyed, but they did not deceive God.

[57] Disbelief and its imposition on others.

[58] Among the meanings of *fitnah* are disbelief, discord, dissension, civil strife, persecution, oppression, injustice, seduction, trial and torment.

[59] The sacred months are Dhul-Qa'dah, Dhul-Hijjah, Muharram and Rajab.

retribution. So whoever has assaulted you, then assault him in the same way that he has assaulted you. And fear God and know that God is with those who fear Him.

195. And spend in the way of God and do not throw [yourselves] with your [own] hands into destruction [by refraining]. And do good; indeed, God loves the doers of good.

196. And complete the hajj and 'umrah for God. But if you are prevented, then [offer] what can be obtained with ease of sacrificial animals. And do not shave your heads until the sacrificial animal has reached its place of slaughter. And whoever among you is ill or has an ailment of the head [making shaving necessary must offer] a ransom of fasting [three days] or charity[60] or sacrifice.[61] And when you are secure,[62] then whoever performs 'umrah [during the hajj months][63] followed by hajj [offers] what can be obtained with ease of sacrificial animals. And whoever cannot find [or afford such an animal] - then a fast of three days during hajj and of seven when you have returned [home]. Those are ten complete [days]. This is for those whose family is not in the area of al-Masjid al-Harām. And fear God and know that God is severe in penalty.

197. Hajj is [during] well-known months,[64] so whoever has made hajj obligatory upon himself therein [by entering the state of ihrām], there is [to be for him]

[60] Feeding six needy persons.

[61] The slaughter of a sheep or goat.

[62] Under normal conditions, i.e., are not prevented.

[63] The months of Shawwal, Dhul-Qa'dạh and Dhul-Hijjah.

[64] See previous footnote.

no sexual relations and no disobedience and no disputing during hajj. And whatever good you do - God knows it. And take provisions, but indeed, the best provision is fear of God. And fear Me, O you of understanding.

198. There is no blame upon you for seeking bounty[65] from your Lord [during hajj]. But when you depart from 'Arafāt, remember God at al-Masha'ar al-Harām.[66] And remember Him, as He has guided you, for indeed, you were before that among those astray.

199. Then depart from the place from where [all] the people depart and ask forgiveness of God. Indeed, God is Forgiving and Merciful.

200. And when you have completed your rites, remember God like your [previous] remembrance of your fathers or with [much] greater remembrance. And among the people is he who says, "Our Lord, give us in this world," and he will have in the Hereafter no share.

201. But among them is he who says, "Our Lord, give us in this world [that which is] good and in the Hereafter [that which is] good and protect us from the punishment of the Fire."

202. Those will have a share of what they have earned, and God is swift in account.

203. And remember God during [specific] numbered days. Then whoever hastens [his departure] in two days - there is no sin upon him; and whoever delays [until the third] - there is no sin upon him - for him who fears God. And fear God

[65] i.e., profit from trade or business.

[66] Which is in Muzdalifah.

and know that unto Him you will be gathered.

204. And of the people is he whose speech pleases you in worldly life, and he calls God to witness as to what is in his heart, yet he is the fiercest of opponents.

205. And when he goes away, he strives throughout the land to cause corruption therein and destroy crops and animals. And God does not like corruption.

206. And when it is said to him, "Fear God," pride in the sin takes hold of him. Sufficient for him is Hellfire, and how wretched is the resting place.

207. And of the people is he who sells himself, seeking means to the approval of God. And God is kind to [His] servants.

208. O you who have believed, enter into Islām completely [and perfectly] and do not follow the footsteps of Satan. Indeed, he is to you a clear enemy.

209. But if you slip [i.e., deviate] after clear proofs have come to you, then know that God is Exalted in Might and Wise.

210. Do they await but that God should come to them in covers of clouds and the angels [as well] and the matter is [then] decided? And to God [all] matters are returned.

211. Ask the Children of Israel how many a sign of evidence We have given them. And whoever exchanges the favor of God [for disbelief] after it has come to him - then indeed, God is severe in penalty.

212. Beautified for those who disbelieve is the life of this world, and they ridicule those who believe. But those who fear God are above them on the Day of Resurrection. And God gives provision to whom He wills without account.

213. Mankind was [of] one religion [before their deviation]; then God sent the prophets as bringers of good tidings and warners and sent down with them the Scripture in truth to judge between the people concerning that in which they differed. And none differed over it [i.e., the Scripture] except those who were given it - after the clear proofs came to them - out of jealous animosity among themselves. And God guided those who believed to the truth concerning that over which they had differed, by His permission. And God guides whom He wills to a straight path.

214. Or do you think that you will enter Paradise while such [trial] has not yet come to you as came to those who passed on before you? They were touched by poverty and hardship and were shaken until [even their] messenger and those who believed with him said, "When is the help of God?" Unquestionably, the help of God is near.

215. They ask you, [O Muhammad], what they should spend. Say, "Whatever you spend of good is [to be] for parents and relatives and orphans and the needy and the traveler. And whatever you do of good - indeed, God is Knowing of it."

216. Fighting has been enjoined upon you while it is hateful to you. But perhaps you hate a thing and it is good for you; and perhaps you love a thing and it is

bad for you. And God knows, while you know not.

217. They ask you about the sacred month[67] - about fighting therein. Say, "Fighting therein is great [sin], but averting [people] from the way of God and disbelief in Him and [preventing access to] al-Masjid al-Harām and the expulsion of its people therefrom are greater [evil] in the sight of God. And fitnah[68] is greater than killing." And they will continue to fight you until they turn you back from your religion if they are able. And whoever of you reverts from his religion [to disbelief] and dies while he is a disbeliever - for those, their deeds have become worthless in this world and the Hereafter, and those are the companions of the Fire; they will abide therein eternally.

218. Indeed, those who have believed and those who have emigrated and fought in the cause of God - those expect the mercy of God. And God is Forgiving and Merciful.

219. They ask you about wine[69] and gambling. Say, "In them is great sin and [yet, some] benefit for people. But their sin is greater than their benefit." And they ask you what they should spend. Say, "The excess [beyond needs]." Thus God makes clear to you the verses [of revelation] that you might give thought

220. To this world and the Hereafter. And they ask you about orphans. Say, "Improvement for them is best. And if you mix your affairs with theirs - they are your brothers. And God knows the corrupter from the amender. And if God had willed, He could have put you in difficulty. Indeed, God is Exalted in Might and Wise."

221. And do not marry polytheistic women until they believe.[70] And a believing slave woman is better than a polytheist, even though she might please you. And do not marry polytheistic men [to your women] until they believe. And a believing slave is better than a polytheist, even though he might please you. Those invite [you] to the Fire, but God invites to Paradise and to forgiveness, by His permission. And He makes clear His verses [i.e., ordinances] to the people that perhaps they may remember.

222. And they ask you about menstruation. Say, "It is harm, so keep away from wives[71] during menstruation. And do not approach them until they are pure. And when they have purified themselves,[72] then come to them from where God has ordained for you. Indeed, God loves those who are constantly repentant and loves those who purify themselves."

223. Your wives are a place of cultivation [i.e., sowing of seed] for you, so come to your place of cultivation however you wish and put forth [righteousness] for yourselves. And fear God and know that you will meet Him. And give good tidings to the believers.

224. And do not make [your oath by] God an excuse against being righteous and fearing God and making peace among people. And God is Hearing and Knowing.

[67] See footnote to 2:194.

[68] See footnote to 2:193.

[69] The word "*khamr*" (wine) includes all intoxicants. The final prohibition is given in 5:90-91.

[70] i.e., worship and obey God alone.

[71] i.e., refrain from sexual intercourse.

[72] By taking a complete bath (*ghusl*).

225. God does not impose blame upon you for what is unintentional in your oaths, but He imposes blame upon you for what your hearts have earned. And God is Forgiving and Forbearing.

226. For those who swear not to have sexual relations with their wives[73] is a waiting time of four months, but if they return [to normal relations] - then indeed, God is Forgiving and Merciful.

227. And if they decide on divorce - then indeed, God is Hearing and Knowing.

228. Divorced women remain in waiting [i.e., do not remarry] for three periods,[74] and it is not lawful for them to conceal what God has created in their wombs if they believe in God and the Last Day. And their husbands have more right to take them back in this [period] if they want reconciliation.[75] And due to them [i.e., the wives] is similar to what is expected of them, according to what is reasonable.[76] But the men [i.e., husbands] have a degree over them [in responsibility and authority]. And God is Exalted in Might and Wise.

229. Divorce is twice. Then [after that], either keep [her] in an acceptable manner or release [her] with good treatment. And it is not lawful for you to take anything of what you have given them unless both fear that they will not be able to keep [within] the limits of God.[77] But if you fear that they will not keep [within] the limits of God, then there is no blame upon either of them concerning that by which she ransoms herself. These are the limits of God, so do not transgress them. And whoever transgresses the limits of God - it is those who are the wrongdoers [i.e., the unjust].

230. And if he has divorced her [for the third time], then she is not lawful to him afterward until [after] she marries a husband other than him.[78] And if he [i.e., the latter husband] divorces her [or dies], there is no blame upon them [i.e., the woman and her former husband] for returning to each other if they think that they can keep [within] the limits of God. These are the limits of God, which He makes clear to a people who know [i.e., understand].

231. And when you divorce women and they have [nearly] fulfilled their term, either retain them according to acceptable terms or release them according to acceptable terms, and do not keep them, intending harm, to transgress [against them]. And whoever does that has certainly wronged himself. And do not take the verses of God in jest. And remember the favor of God upon you and what has been revealed to you of the Book [i.e., the Qur'ān] and wisdom [i.e., the Prophet's sunnah] by which He instructs you. And fear God and know that God is Knowing of all things.

232. And when you divorce women[79] and they have fulfilled their term, do not

[73] Without divorcing them. By such an oath the women is deprived of her right in marriage but is not free to marry another. She may not be kept in such a condition beyond the four-month limit.

[74] Either menstrual periods or periods of purity between menstruation. See also 65:1-7.

[75] The husband may return her to himself during the *'iddah* period of a first and second divorce without a new marriage contract.

[76] The wife has specific rights upon her husband, just as the husband has rights upon her.

[77] i.e., deal fairly with each other.

[78] With the intention of permanence, not merely in order to return to the previous husband.

[79] For the first or second time.

prevent them from remarrying their [former] husbands if they [i.e., all parties] agree among themselves on an acceptable basis. That is instructed to whoever of you believes in God and the Last Day. That is better for you and purer, and God knows and you know not.

233. Mothers may nurse [i.e., breastfeed] their children two complete years for whoever wishes to complete the nursing [period]. Upon the father is their [i.e., the mothers'] provision and their clothing according to what is acceptable. No person is charged with more than his capacity. No mother should be harmed through her child, and no father through his child. And upon the [father's] heir is [a duty] like that [of the father]. And if they both desire weaning through mutual consent from both of them and consultation, there is no blame upon either of them. And if you wish to have your children nursed by a substitute, there is no blame upon you as long as you give payment according to what is acceptable. And fear God and know that God is Seeing of what you do.

234. And those who are taken in death among you and leave wives behind - they, [the wives, shall] wait four months and ten [days]. And when they have fulfilled their term, then there is no blame upon you for what they do with themselves in an acceptable manner.[80] And God is [fully] Acquainted with what you do.

235. There is no blame upon you for that to which you [indirectly] allude concerning a proposal to women or for what you conceal within yourselves. God knows that you will have them in mind. But do not promise them secretly except for saying a proper saying. And do not determine to undertake a marriage contract until the decreed period[81] reaches its end. And know that God knows what is within yourselves, so beware of Him. And know that God is Forgiving and Forbearing.

236. There is no blame upon you if you divorce women you have not touched[82] nor specified for them an obligation.[83] But give them [a gift of] compensation - the wealthy according to his capability and the poor according to his capability - a provision according to what is acceptable, a duty upon the doers of good.

237. And if you divorce them before you have touched them and you have already specified for them an obligation, then [give] half of what you specified - unless they forego the right or the one in whose hand is the marriage contract foregoes it. And to forego it is nearer to righteousness. And do not forget graciousness between you. Indeed God, of whatever you do, is Seeing.

238. Maintain with care the [obligatory] prayers and [in particular] the middle [i.e., 'asr] prayer and stand before God, devoutly obedient.

239. And if you fear [an enemy, then pray] on foot or riding. But when you are secure, then remember God [in prayer], as He has taught you that which you did not [previously] know.

[80] They may remarry if they wish.

[81] The *'iddah* (bereavement period) after the death of a husband.

[82] The marriage has not been consummated.

[83] Require bridal gift (*mahr*).

240. And those who are taken in death among you and leave wives behind - for their wives is a bequest: maintenance for one year without turning [them] out. But if they leave [of their own accord], then there is no blame upon you for what they do with themselves in an acceptable way.[84] And God is Exalted in Might and Wise.

241. And for divorced women is a provision according to what is acceptable - a duty upon the righteous.

242. Thus does God make clear to you His verses [i.e., laws] that you might use reason.

243. Have you not considered those who left their homes in many thousands, fearing death? God said to them, "Die"; then He restored them to life. And God is full of bounty to the people, but most of the people do not show gratitude.

244. And fight in the cause of God and know that God is Hearing and Knowing.

245. Who is it that would loan God a goodly loan so He may multiply it for him many times over? And it is God who withholds and grants abundance, and to Him you will be returned.

246. Have you not considered the assembly of the Children of Israel after [the time of] Moses when they said to a prophet of theirs, "Send to us a king, and we will fight in the way of God?" He said, "Would you perhaps refrain from fighting if fighting was prescribed for you?" They said, "And why should we not fight in the cause of God when we have been driven out from our homes and from our children?" But when fighting was prescribed for them, they turned away, except for a few of them. And God is Knowing of the wrongdoers.

247. And their prophet said to them, "Indeed, God has sent to you Saul as a king." They said, "How can he have kingship over us while we are more worthy of kingship than him and he has not been given any measure of wealth?" He said, "Indeed, God has chosen him over you and has increased him abundantly in knowledge and stature. And God gives His sovereignty to whom He wills. And God is all-Encompassing [in favor] and Knowing."

248. And their prophet said to them, "Indeed, a sign of his kingship is that the chest will come to you in which is assurance[85] from your Lord and a remnant of what the family of Moses and the family of Aaron had left, carried by the angels. Indeed in that is a sign for you, if you are believers."

249. And when Saul went forth with the soldiers, he said, "Indeed, God will be testing you with a river. So whoever drinks from it is not of me, and whoever does not taste it is indeed of me, excepting one who takes [from it] in the hollow of his hand." But they drank from it, except a [very] few of them. Then when he had crossed it along with those who believed with him, they said, "There is no power for us today against Goliath and his soldiers." But those who were certain that they would meet God said, "How many a small company has overcome a large compa-

[84] This directive was abrogated by those later revealed in 2:234 and 4:12.

[85] Signs giving reassurance.

ny by permission of God. And God is with the patient."

250. And when they went forth to [face] Goliath and his soldiers, they said, "Our Lord, pour upon us patience and plant firmly our feet and give us victory over the disbelieving people."

251. So they defeated them by permission of God, and David killed Goliath, and God gave him the kingship and wisdom [i.e., prophethood] and taught him from that which He willed. And if it were not for God checking [some] people by means of others, the earth would have been corrupted, but God is full of bounty to the worlds.

252. These are the verses of God which We recite to you, [O Muhammad], in truth. And indeed, you are from among the messengers.

253. Those messengers - some of them We caused to exceed others. Among them were those to whom God spoke, and He raised some of them in degree. And We gave Jesus, the Son of Mary, clear proofs, and We supported him with the Pure Spirit [i.e., Gabriel]. If God had willed, those [generations] succeeding them would not have fought each other after the clear proofs had come to them. But they differed, and some of them believed and some of them disbelieved. And if God had willed, they would not have fought each other, but God does what He intends.

254. O you who have believed, spend from that which We have provided for you before there comes a Day in which there is no exchange [i.e., ransom] and no friendship and no intercession. And the disbelievers - they are the wrongdoers.

255. God - there is no deity except Him, the Ever-Living, the Sustainer of [all] existence. Neither drowsiness overtakes Him nor sleep. To Him belongs whatever is in the heavens and whatever is on the earth. Who is it that can intercede with Him except by His permission? He knows what is [presently] before them and what will be after them,[86] and they encompass not a thing of His knowledge except for what He wills. His Kursī[87] extends over the heavens and the earth, and their preservation tires Him not. And He is the Most High, the Most Great.

256. There shall be no compulsion in [acceptance of] the religion. The right course has become clear from the wrong. So whoever disbelieves in tāghūt[88] and believes in God has grasped the most trustworthy handhold with no break in it. And God is Hearing and Knowing.

257. God is the ally[89] of those who believe. He brings them out from darknesses into the light. And those who disbelieve - their allies are tāghūt. They take them out of the light into darknesses.[90] Those are the companions of the Fire; they will abide eternally therein.

258. Have you not considered the one who argued with Abraham about his Lord [merely] because God had given him kingship? When Abraham said, "My

[86] God's knowledge encompasses every aspect of His creations in the past, present and future.
[87] Chair or footstool. It is not to be confused with *al-'Arsh* (the Throne), which is infinitely higher and greater than al-Kursī.
[88] False objects of worship, such as idols, heavenly bodies, sprits, human beings, etc.
[89] i.e., patron and supporter.
[90] The light of truth is one, while the darkness of disbelief, doubt and error are many.

Lord is the one who gives life and causes death," he said, "I give life and cause death." Abraham said, "Indeed, God brings up the sun from the east, so bring it up from the west." So the disbeliever was overwhelmed [by astonishment], and God does not guide the wrongdoing people.

259. Or [consider such an example] as the one who passed by a township which had fallen into ruin. He said, "How will God bring this to life after its death?" So God caused him to die for a hundred years; then He revived him. He said, "How long have you remained?" He [the man] said, "I have remained a day or part of a day." He said, "Rather, you have remained one hundred years. Look at your food and your drink; it has not changed with time. And look at your donkey; and We will make you a sign for the people. And look at the bones [of this donkey] - how We raise them and then We cover them with flesh." And when it became clear to him, he said, "I know that God is over all things competent."

260. And [mention] when Abraham said, "My Lord, show me how You give life to the dead." [God] said, "Have you not believed?" He said, "Yes, but [I ask] only that my heart may be satisfied." [God] said, "Take four birds and commit them to yourself.[91] Then [after slaughtering them] put on each hill a portion of them; then call them - they will come [flying] to you in haste. And know that God is Exalted in Might and Wise."

261. The example of those who spend their wealth in the way of God is like a seed [of grain] which grows seven spikes; in each spike is a hundred grains. And God multiplies [His reward] for whom He wills. And God is all-Encompassing and Knowing.

262. Those who spend their wealth in the way of God and then do not follow up what they have spent with reminders [of it] or [other] injury will have their reward with their Lord, and there will be no fear concerning them, nor will they grieve.

263. Kind speech and forgiveness are better than charity followed by injury. And God is Free of need and Forbearing.

264. O you who have believed, do not invalidate your charities with reminders [of it] or injury as does one who spends his wealth [only] to be seen by the people and does not believe in God and the Last Day. His example is like that of a [large] smooth stone upon which is dust and is hit by a downpour that leaves it bare. They are unable [to keep] anything of what they have earned. And God does not guide the disbelieving people.

265. And the example of those who spend their wealth seeking means to the approval of God and assuring [reward for] themselves is like a garden on high ground which is hit by a downpour - so it yields its fruits in double. And [even] if it is not hit by a downpour, then a drizzle [is sufficient]. And God, of what you do, is Seeing.

266. Would one of you like to have a garden of palm trees and grapevines underneath which rivers flow in which he has from every fruit? But he is afflicted with old age and has weak [i.e., immature] offspring, and it is hit by a whirlwind containing fire and is burned.

[91] i.e., train them to come to you on command.

Thus does God make clear to you [His] verses that you might give thought.

267. O you who have believed, spend from the good things which you have earned and from that which We have produced for you from the earth. And do not aim toward the defective therefrom, spending [from that] while you would not take it [yourself] except with closed eyes. And know that God is Free of need and Praiseworthy.

268. Satan threatens you with poverty and orders you to immorality, while God promises you forgiveness from Him and bounty. And God is all-Encompassing and Knowing.

269. He gives wisdom[92] to whom He wills, and whoever has been given wisdom has certainly been given much good. And none will remember except those of understanding.

270. And whatever you spend of expenditures or make of vows - indeed, God knows of it. And for the wrongdoers there are no helpers.

271. If you disclose your charitable expenditures, they are good; but if you conceal them and give them to the poor, it is better for you, and He will remove from you some of your misdeeds [thereby]. And God, with what you do, is [fully] Acquainted.

272. Not upon you, [O Muhammad], is [responsibility for] their guidance, but God guides whom He wills. And whatever good you [believers] spend is for yourselves, and you do not spend except seeking the countenance of God. And whatever you spend of good[93] - it will be fully repaid to you, and you will not be wronged.

273. [Charity is] for the poor who have been restricted for the cause of God, unable to move about in the land. An ignorant [person] would think them self-sufficient because of their restraint, but you will know them by their [characteristic] sign. They do not ask people persistently [or at all]. And whatever you spend of good - indeed, God is Knowing of it.

274. Those who spend their wealth [in God's way] by night and by day, secretly and publicly - they will have their reward with their Lord. And no fear will there be concerning them, nor will they grieve.

275. Those who consume interest[94] cannot stand [on the Day of Resurrection] except as one stands who is being beaten by Satan into insanity. That is because they say, "Trade is [just] like interest." But God has permitted trade and has forbidden interest. So whoever has received an admonition from his Lord and desists may have what is past, and his affair rests with God. But whoever returns [to dealing in interest or usury] - those are the companions of the Fire; they will abide eternally therein.

276. God destroys interest and gives increase for charities. And God does not like every sinning disbeliever.

277. Indeed, those who believe and do righteous deeds and establish prayer and give zakāh will have their reward with

[92] The knowledge and understanding of the religion and of the Qur'ān.

[93] i.e, wealth, property, resources, time, effort, etc.

[94] Included is that given on commercial as well as consumer loans.

their Lord, and there will be no fear concerning them, nor will they grieve.

278. O you who have believed, fear God and give up what remains [due to you] of interest, if you should be believers.

279. And if you do not, then be informed of a war [against you] from God and His Messenger. But if you repent, you may have your principal - [thus] you do no wrong, nor are you wronged.

280. And if someone is in hardship, then [let there be] postponement until [a time of] ease. But if you give [from your right as] charity, then it is better for you, if you only knew.

281. And fear a Day when you will be returned to God. Then every soul will be compensated for what it earned, and they will not be wronged [i.e., treated unjustly].

282. O you who have believed, when you contract a debt for a specified term, write it down. And let a scribe write [it] between you in justice. Let no scribe refuse to write as God has taught him. So let him write and let the one who has the obligation [i.e., the debtor] dictate. And let him fear God, his Lord, and not leave anything out of it. But if the one who has the obligation is of limited understanding or weak or unable to dictate himself, then let his guardian dictate in justice. And bring to witness two witnesses from among your men. And if there are not two men [available], then a man and two women from those whom you accept as witnesses - so that if one of them [i.e., the women] errs, then the other can remind her. And let not the witnesses refuse when they are called upon. And do not be [too] weary to write it, whether it is small or large, for its [specified] term. That is more just in the sight of God and stronger as evidence and more likely to prevent doubt between you, except when it is an immediate transaction which you conduct among yourselves. For [then] there is no blame upon you if you do not write it. And take witnesses when you conclude a contract. Let no scribe be harmed or any witness. For if you do so, indeed, it is [grave] disobedience in you. And fear God. And God teaches you. And God is Knowing of all things.

283. And if you are on a journey and cannot find a scribe, then a security deposit [should be] taken. And if one of you entrusts another, then let him who is entrusted discharge his trust [faithfully] and let him fear God, his Lord. And do not conceal testimony, for whoever conceals it - his heart is indeed sinful, and God is Knowing of what you do.

284. To God belongs whatever is in the heavens and whatever is in the earth. Whether you show what is within yourselves or conceal it, God will bring you to account for it. Then He will forgive whom He wills and punish whom He wills, and God is over all things competent.

285. The Messenger has believed in what was revealed to him from his Lord, and [so have] the believers. All of them have believed in God and His angels and His books and His messengers, [saying], "We make no distinction between any of His messengers." And they say, "We hear and we obey. [We seek] Your forgiveness, our Lord, and to You is the [final] destination."

286. God does not charge a soul except [with that within] its capacity. It will

have [the consequence of] what [good] it has gained, and it will bear [the consequence of] what [evil] it has earned. "Our Lord, do not impose blame upon us if we have forgotten or erred. Our Lord, and lay not upon us a burden like that which You laid upon those before us. Our Lord, and burden us not with that which we have no ability to bear. And pardon us; and forgive us; and have mercy upon us. You are our protector, so give us victory over the disbelieving people."[95]

[95] God concludes this *sūrah* by directing His servants how to supplicate Him, just as He taught them in *sūrah al-Fātihah* how to praise Him and ask for guidance.

## Sūrah 3: Ale-'Imrān

### The Period of Revelation

This Sūrah consists of four discourses: The first discourse (v. 1-32) was probably revealed soon after the Battle of Badr. The second discourse (v. 33-63) was revealed in 9 A.H. on the occasion of the visit of the deputation from the Christians of Najran. The third discourse (v. 64-120) appears to have been revealed immediately after the first one. The fourth discourse (v. 121-200) was revealed after the Battle of Uhud.

### Subject

Though these discourses were revealed at different periods and on different occasions they are so interlinked and so inter-connected in regard to their central theme that they make together one continuous whole. This Sūrah has been especially addressed to two groups; the people of the Book (the Jews and the Christians) and the followers of Muhammad.

The message has been extended to the Jews and the Christians in continuation of the invitation in Sūrah 2: Al-Baqarah in which they have been admonished for their erroneous beliefs and evil morals and advised to accept as a remedy the Truth of the Qur'ān. They have been told here that Muhammad taught the same right way of life that had been preached by their own Prophets; that it alone was the Right Way, the way of God; hence any deviation from it will be wrong even according to their own Scriptures.

The second group, the Muslims who had been declared to be the best Community in Al-Baqarah and appointed torch-bearers of the Truth, were entrusted with the responsibility of reforming the world have been given additional instructions in continuation of those given in the preceding Sūrah. The Muslims have been warned to learn a lesson from the religious and moral degeneration of the former communities and to refrain from treading in their footsteps. Instructions have also been given about the reformative work they had to perform. Besides this they have been taught how to deal with the people of the Book and the hypocrites who were putting different kinds of hindrances in the way of God. Above all they have been warned to guard against those weaknesses which had come to the surface in the Battle Uhud.

### Background

The following is the background of the Sūrah:

1. The Believers had met with all sorts of trials and hardships about which they had been forewarned in Al-Baqarah. Though they had come out victorious in the Battle of Badr they were not out of danger yet. Their victory had aroused the enmity of all those powers in Arabia which were opposed to the Islāmic Movement. Signs of threatening storms had begun to appear on all sides and the Muslims were in a perpetual state of fear and anxiety. It looked as if the whole Arabian world around the tiny state of Madinah - which was no more than a village state at that time - was bent upon blotting out its very existence. This state of war was also adversely affecting its economy which had already been badly disturbed by the influx of the Muslim refugees from Makkah.
2. Then there was the disturbing problem of the Jewish clans who lived in the suburbs of Madinah. They were discarding the treaties of alliance they had made with the Prophet after his migration from Makkah. So much so that on the occasion of the Battle of Badr these people of the Book sympathized with the evil aims of the idolaters in spite of the fact that their fundamental articles of Faith - Oneness of God, Prophethood and Life-after-death - were the same as those of the Muslims. After the Battle of Badr they openly began to incite the Quraysh and other Arab clans to wreak their vengeance on the Muslims. Thus those Jewish clans set aside their centuries-old friendly and neighborly relations with the people of Madinah. At last when their mischievous actions and

breaches of treaties became unbearable the Prophet attacked the Bani-Qaynuqah, the most mischievous of all the other Jewish clans who had conspired with the hypocrites of Madinah and the idolatrous Arab clans to encircle the Believers on all sides. The magnitude of the peril might be judged from the fact that even the life of the Prophet himself was always in danger. Therefore his Companions slept in their armors during that period and kept watch at night to guard against any sudden attack and whenever the Prophet happened to be out of sight even for a short while they would at once set out in search of him.

3. This incitement by the Jews added fuel to the fire which was burning in the hearts of the Quraysh and they began to make preparations to avenge the defeat they had suffered at Badr. A year after this an army of 3000 strong marched out of Makkah to invade Madinah and a battle took place at the foot of Mount Uhud. The Prophet came out of Madinah with one thousand men to meet the enemy. While they were marching to the battlefield three hundred hypocrites deserted the army and returned to Madinah but there still remained a small band of hypocrites among the seven hundred who accompanied the Prophet. They played their part and did their worst to create mischief and chaos in the ranks of the Believers during the Battle. This was the first clear indication of the fact that within the fold of the Muslim Community there was quite a large number of saboteurs who were always ready to conspire with the external enemies to harm their own brethren.
4. Though the devices of the hypocrites had played a great part in the set-back at Uhud the weaknesses of the Muslims themselves contributed no less to it. And it was but natural that the Muslims should show signs of moral weakness for they were a new community which had only recently been formed on a new ideology and had not as yet got a thorough moral training. Naturally in this second hard test of their physical and moral strength some weaknesses came to the surface. That is why a detailed review of the Battle of Uhud was needed to warn the Muslims of their shortcomings and to issue instructions for their reform. It should also be noted that this review of the Battle is quite different from the reviews that are usually made by generals on similar occasions.

**Subject: Guidance**

This Sūrah is the sequel to Al-Baqarah and the invitation therein is continued to the people of the Book. In Al-Baqarah the Jews were pointedly invited to accept the Guidance and in this Sūrah the Christians have particularly been admonished to give up their erroneous beliefs and accept the Guidance of the Qur'ān. At the same time the Muslims have been instructed to nourish the virtues that may enable them to carry out their obligations and spread the Divine Guidance.

## Sūrah 3: Ali-'Imrān[96]

In the Name of God, the Most Compassionate, the Most Merciful

1. Alif, Lām, Meem.[97]

2. God – there is no deity except Him, the Ever-Living, the Sustainer of existence.

3. He has sent down upon you, [O Muhammad], the Book in truth, confirming what was before it. And He revealed the Torah and the Gospel.

4. Before, as guidance for the people. And He revealed the Criterion [i.e., the Qur'ān]. Indeed, those who disbelieve in the verses of God will have a severe punishment, and God is Exalted in Might, the Owner of Retribution.

5. Indeed, from God nothing is hidden in the earth nor in the heaven.

6. It is He who forms you in the wombs however He wills. There is no deity except Him, the Exalted in Might, the Wise.

7. It is He who has sent down to you, [O Muhammad], the Book; in it are verses [that are] precise – they are the foundation of the Book – and others unspecific.[98] As for those in whose hearts is deviation [from truth], they will follow that of it which is unspecific, seeking discord and seeking an interpretation [suitable to them]. And no one knows its [true] interpretation except God. But those firm in knowledge say, "We believe in it. All [of it] is from our Lord." And no one will be reminded except those of understanding,

8. [Who say], "Our Lord, let not our hearts deviate after You have guided us and grant us from Yourself mercy. Indeed, You are the Bestower.

9. Our Lord, surely You will gather the people for a Day about which there is no doubt. Indeed, God does not fail in His promise."

10. Indeed, those who disbelieve – never will their wealth or their children avail them against God at all. And it is they who are fuel for the Fire.

11. [Theirs is] like the custom of the people of Pharaoh and those before them. They denied Our signs, so God seized them for their sins. And God is severe in penalty.

12. Say to those who disbelieve, "You will be overcome and gathered together to Hell, and wretched is the resting place."

13. Already there has been for you a sign in the two armies which met [in combat at Badr] – one fighting in the cause of God and another of disbelievers. They saw them [to be] twice their [own] number by [their] eyesight.[99] But God supports with His victory whom He wills. Indeed in that is a lesson for those of vision.

14. Beautified for people is the love of that which they desire – of women and sons, heaped-up sums of gold and silver, fine branded horses, and cattle and tilled land. That is the enjoyment of

[96] *Ali-'Imrān*: The family of 'Imran.

[97] See footnote to 2:1.

[98] Those which are stated in such a way that they are open to more than one interpretation or whose meaning is known only to God, such as the opening letters on certain *sūrahs*.

[99] The believers saw the disbelievers to be double their own number proceeding the battle of Badr, while, in fact, they were three times their number.

worldly life, but God has with Him the best return [i.e, Paradise].

15. Say, "Shall I inform you of [something] better than that? For those who fear God will be gardens in the presence of their Lord beneath which rivers flow, wherein they abide eternally, and purified spouses and approval from God. And God is Seeing [i.e., aware] of [His] servants –

16. Those who say, "Our Lord, indeed we have believed, so forgive us our sins and protect us from the punishment of the Fire,"

17. The patient, the true, the obedient, those who spend [in the way of God], and those who seek forgiveness before dawn.

18. God witnesses that there is no deity except Him, and [so do] the angels and those of knowledge – [that He is] maintaining [creation] in justice. There is no deity except Him, the Exalted in Might, the Wise.

19. Indeed, the religion in the sight of God is Islām. And those who were given the Scripture did not differ except after knowledge had come to them – out of jealous animosity between themselves. And whoever disbelieves in the verses of God, then indeed, God is swift in [taking] account.

20. So if they argue with you, say, "I have submitted myself to God [in Islām], and [so have] those who follow me." And say to those who were given the Scripture and [to] the unlearned,[100] "Have you submitted yourselves?" And if they submit [in Islām], they are rightly guided; but if they turn away – then upon you is only the [duty of] notification. And God is Seeing of [His] servants.

21. Those who disbelieve in the signs of God and kill the prophets without right and kill those who order justice from among the people – give them tidings of a painful punishment.

22. They are the ones whose deeds have become worthless in this world and the Hereafter, and for them there will be no helpers.

23. Do you not consider, [O Muhammad], those who were given a portion of the Scripture? They are invited to the Scripture of God that it should arbitrate between them;[101] then a party of them turns away, and they are refusing.

24. That is because they say, "Never will the Fire touch us except for [a few] numbered days," and [because] they were deluded in their religion by what they were inventing.

25. So how will it be when We assemble them for a Day about which there is no doubt? And each soul will be compensated [in full for] what it earned, and they will not be wronged.

26. Say, "O God, Owner of Sovereignty, You give sovereignty to whom You will and You take sovereignty away from whom You will. You honour whom You will and You humble whom You will. In Your hand[102] is [all] good. In-

[100] Those who had no scripture (i.e., the pagans).

[101] Referring to the Jews of Madinah who refused to implement the rulings given by God in the Torah or to acknowledge the Prophet, whose coming was mentioned therein.

[102] See footnote to 2:19.

deed, You are over all things competent.

27. You cause the night to enter the day, and You cause the day to enter the night; and You bring the living out of the dead, and You bring the dead out of the living. And You give provision to whom You will without account [i.e., limit or measure]."

28. Let not believers take disbelievers as allies [i.e., supporters or protectors] rather than believers. And whoever [of you] does that has nothing [i.e., no association] with God, except when taking precaution against them in prudence.[103] And God warns you of Himself, and to God is the [final] destination.

29. Say, "Whether you conceal what is in your breasts or reveal it, God knows it. And He knows that which is in the heavens and that which is on the earth. And God is over all things competent.

30. The Day every soul will find what it has done of good present [before it] and what it has done of evil, it will wish that between itself and that [evil] was a great distance. And God warns you of Himself, and God is Kind to [His] servants."

31. Say, [O Muhammad], "If you should love God, then follow me, [so] God will love you and forgive you your sins. And God is Forgiving and Merciful."

32. Say, "Obey God and the Messenger." But if they turn away – then indeed, God does not like the disbelievers.

33. Indeed, God chose Adam and Noah and the family of Abraham and the family of 'Imrān over the worlds –

34. Descendants, some of them from others. And God is Hearing and Knowing.

35. [Mention, O Muhammad], when the wife of 'Imrān said, "My Lord, indeed I have pledged to You what is in my womb, consecrated [for Your service], so accept this from me. Indeed, You are the Hearing, the Knowing."

36. But when she delivered her, she said, "My Lord, I have delivered a female." And God was most knowing of what she delivered, and the male is not like the female. "And I have named her Mary, and I seek refuge for her in You and [for] her descendants from Satan, the expelled [from the mercy of God]."

37. So her Lord accepted her with good acceptance and caused her to grow in a good manner and put her in the care of Zechariah. Every time Zechariah entered upon her in the prayer chamber, he found with her provision. He said, "O Mary, from where is this [coming] to you?" She said, "It is from God. Indeed, God provides for whom He wills without account."

38. At that, Zechariah called upon his Lord, saying, "My Lord, grant me from Yourself a good offspring. Indeed, You are the Hearer of supplication."

39. So the angels called him while he was standing in prayer in the chamber, "Indeed, God gives you good tidings of John, confirming a word[104] from God and [who will be] honourable, abstain-

[103] When fearing harm from an enemy, the believer may pretend as long as his heart and intention are not effected.

[104] Referring to the Prophet Jesus, who was conceived merley by a command from God – the word "Be".

ing [from women], and a prophet from among the righteous."

40. He said, "My Lord, how will I have a boy when I have reached old age and my wife is barren?" He [the angel] said, "Such is God; He does what He wills."

41. He said, "My Lord, make for me a sign." He said, "Your sign is that you will not [be able to] speak to the people for three days except by gesture. And remember your Lord much and exalt [Him with praise] in the evening and the morning."

42. And [mention] when the angels said, "O Mary, indeed God has chosen you and purified you and chosen you above the women of the worlds.

43. O Mary, be devoutly obedient to your Lord and prostrate and bow with those who bow [in prayer]."

44. That is from the news of the unseen which We reveal to you, [O Muhammad]. And you were not with them when they cast their pens[105] as to which of them should be responsible for Mary. Nor were you with them when they disputed.

45. [And mention] when the angels said, "O Mary, indeed God gives you good tidings of a word[106] from Him, whose name will be the Messiah, Jesus, the son of Mary – distinguished in this world and the Hereafter and among those brought near [to God].

46. He will speak to the people in the cradle and in maturity and will be of the righteous."

[105] i.e., threw lots.

[106] See footnote to 3:39.

47. She said, "My Lord, how will I have a child when no man has touched me?" [The angel] said, "Such is God; He creates what He wills. When He decrees a matter, He only says to it, 'Be,' and it is.

48. And He will teach him writing and wisdom[107] and the Torah and the Gospel

49. And [make him] a messenger to the Children of Israel, [who will say], 'Indeed I have come to you with a sign from your Lord in that I design for you from clay [that which is] like the form of a bird, then I breathe into it and it becomes a bird by permission of God. And I cure the blind [from birth] and the leper, and I give life to the dead – by permission of God. And I inform you of what you eat and what you store in your houses. Indeed in that is a sign for you, if you are believers.

50. And [I have come] confirming what was before me of the Torah and to make lawful for you some of what was forbidden to you. And I have come to you with a sign from your Lord, so fear God and obey me.

51. Indeed, God is my Lord and your Lord, so worship Him. That is the straight path.' "

52. But when Jesus felt [persistence in] disbelief from them, he said, "Who are my supporters for [the cause of] God?" The disciples said, "We are supporters for God. We have believed in God and testify that we are Muslims [submitting to Him].

53. Our Lord, we have believed in what You revealed and have followed the

[107] The teachings of the prophets.

messenger [i.e., Jesus], so register us among the witnesses [to truth]."

54. And they [i.e., the disbelievers] planned, but God planned. And God is the best of planners.

55. [Mention] when God said, "O Jesus, indeed I will take you and raise you to Myself and purify [i.e., free] you from those who disbelieve and make those who follow you [in submission to God alone] superior to those who disbelieve until the Day of Resurrection. Then to Me is your return, and I will judge between you concerning that in which you used to differ.

56. And as for those who disbelieved, I will punish them with a severe punishment in this world and the Hereafter, and they will have no helpers."

57. But as for those who believed and did righteous deeds, He will give them in full their rewards, and God does not like the wrongdoers.

58. This is what We recite to you, [O Muhammad], of [Our] verses and the precise [and wise] message [i.e., the Qur'ān].

59. Indeed, the example of Jesus to God[108] is like that of Adam. He created him from dust; then He said to him, "Be," and he was.

60. The truth is from your Lord, so do not be among the doubters.

61. Then whoever argues with you about it after [this] knowledge has come to you – say, "Come, let us call our sons and your sons, our women and your women, ourselves and yourselves, then supplicate earnestly [together] and invoke the curse of God upon the liars [among us]."

62. Indeed, this is the true narration. And there is no deity except God. And indeed, God is the Exalted in Might, the Wise.

63. But if they turn away, then indeed – God is Knowing of the corrupters.

64. Say, "O People of the Scripture, come to a word that is equitable between us and you – that we will not worship except God and not associate anything with Him and not take one another as lords instead of God."[109] But if they turn away, then say, "Bear witness that we are Muslims [submitting to Him]."

65. O People of the Scripture, why do you argue about Abraham while the Torah and the Gospel were not revealed until after him? Then will you not reason?

66. Here you are – those who have argued about that of which you have [some] knowledge, but why do you argue about that of which you have no knowledge? And God knows, while you know not.

67. Abraham was neither a Jew nor a Christian, but he was one inclining toward truth, a Muslim [submitting to God]. And he was not of the polytheists.[110]

68. Indeed, the most worthy of Abraham among the people are those who followed him [in submission to God] and this prophet [i.e., Muhammad] and

[108] i.e., regarding His creation of him.

[109] By obeying another in disobedience to God.

[110] Those who associate others with God.

those who believe [in his message]. And God is the ally of the believers.

69. A faction of the people of the Scripture wish they could mislead you. But they do not mislead except themselves, and they perceive [it] not.

70. O People of the Scripture, why do you disbelieve in the verses of God[111] while you witness [to their truth]?

71. O People of the Scripture, why do you mix [i.e., confuse] the truth with falsehood and conceal the truth while you know [it]?

72. And a faction of the People of the Scripture say [to each other], "Believe in that which was revealed to the believers at the beginning of the day and reject it at its end that perhaps they will return [i.e., abandon their religion],

73. And do not trust except those who follow your religion." Say, "Indeed, the [true] guidance is the guidance of God. [Do you fear] lest someone be given [knowledge] like you were given or that they would [thereby] argue with you before your Lord?" Say, "Indeed, [all] bounty is in the hand[112] of God – He grants it to whom He wills. And God is all-Encompassing and Wise."

74. He selects for His mercy whom He wills. And God is the possessor of great bounty.

75. And among the People of the Scripture is he who, if you entrust him with a great amount [of wealth], he will return it to you. And among them is he who, if you entrust him with a [single] silver coin, he will not return it to you unless you are constantly standing over him [demanding it]. That is because they say, "There is no blame upon us concerning the unlearned."[113] And they speak untruth about God while they know [it].

76. But yes, whoever fulfills his commitment and fears God – then indeed, God loves those who fear Him.

77. Indeed, those who exchange the covenant of God and their [own] oaths for a small price will have no share in the Hereafter, and God will not speak to them or look at them on the Day of Resurrection, nor will He purify them; and they will have a painful punishment.

78. And indeed, there is among them a party who alter the Scripture with their tongues so you may think it is from the Scripture, but it is not from the Scripture. And they say, "This is from God," but it is not from God. And they speak untruth about God while they know.

79. It is not for a human [prophet][114] that God should give him the Scripture[115] and authority and prophethood and then he would say to the people, "Be servants to me rather than God," but [instead, he would say], "Be pious scholars of the Lord because of what you have taught of the Scripture and because of what you have studied."

80. Nor could he order you to take the angels and prophets as lords. Would he

[111] i.e., deliberately reject them.

[112] See footnote to 2:19.

[113] The Jews do not consider it a sin to cheat or lie to a gentile or a pagan.

[114] Or any believer.

[115] Or in the case of the Prophet Muhammad, "the Book" (i.e., the Qur'ān).

order you to disbelief after you had been Muslims?

81. And [recall, O People of the Scripture], when God took the covenant of the prophets, [saying], "Whatever I give you of the Scripture and wisdom and then there comes to you a messenger confirming what is with you, you [must] believe in him and support him." [God] said, "Have you acknowledged and taken upon that My commitment?"[116] They said, "We have acknowledged it." He said, "Then bear witness, and I am with you among the witnesses."

82. And whoever turned away after that – they were the defiantly disobedient.

83. So is it other than the religion of God they desire, while to Him have submitted [all] those within the heavens and earth, willingly or by compulsion, and to Him they will be returned?

84. Say, "We have believed in God and in what was revealed to us and what was revealed to Abraham, Ishmael, Isaac, Jacob, and the Descendants [al-Asbāt], and in what was given to Moses and Jesus and to the prophets from their Lord. We make no distinction between any of them, and we are Muslims [submitting] to Him."

85. And whoever desires other than Islām as religion – never will it be accepted from him, and he, in the Hereafter, will be among the losers.

86. How shall God guide a people who disbelieved after their belief and had witnessed that the Messenger is true and clear signs had come to them? And God does not guide the wrongdoing people.

87. Those – their recompense will be that upon them is the curse of God and the angels and the people, all together,

88. Abiding eternally therein. The punishment will not be lightened for them, nor will they be reprieved,

89. Except for those who repent after that[117] and correct themselves. For indeed, God is Forgiving and Merciful.

90. Indeed, those who disbelieve [i.e., reject the message] after their belief and then increase in disbelief – never will their [claimed] repentance be accepted, and they are the ones astray.

91. Indeed, those who disbelieve and die while they are disbelievers – never would the [whole] capacity of the earth in gold be accepted from one of them if he would [seek to] ransom himself with it. For those there will be a painful punishment, and they will have no helpers.

92. Never will you attain the good [reward][118] until you spend [in the way of God] from that which you love. And whatever you spend – indeed, God is Knowing of it.

93. All food was lawful to the Children of Israel except what Israel [i.e., Jacob] had made unlawful to himself before the Torah was revealed. Say, [O Muhammad], "So bring the Torah and recite it, if you should be truthful."

[116] i.e., Have you accepted this obligation?

[117] After their wrongdoing.

[118] Another meaning is "You will never attain righteousness."

94. And whoever invents about God untruth after that – then those are [truly] the wrongdoers.

95. Say, "God has told the truth. So follow the religion of Abraham, inclining toward truth; and he was not of the polytheists."[119]

96. Indeed, the first House [of worship] established for mankind was that at Bakkah [i.e., Makkah] – blessed and a guidance for the worlds.

97. In it are clear signs [such as] the standing place of Abraham. And whoever enters it [i.e., the Haram] shall be safe. And [due] to God from the people is a pilgrimage to the House – for whoever is able to find thereto a way. But whoever disbelieves [i.e., refuses] – then indeed, God is free from need of the worlds.[120]

98. Say, "O People of the Scripture, why do you disbelieve in the verses of God while God is Witness over what you do?"

99. Say, "O People of the Scripture, why do you avert from the way of God those who believe, seeking to make it [seem] deviant, while you are witnesses [to the truth]? And God is not unaware of what you do."

100. O you who have believed, if you obey a party of those who were given the Scripture, they would turn you back, after your belief, [to being] unbelievers.

101. And how could you disbelieve while to you are being recited the verses of God and among you is His Messenger? And whoever holds firmly to God[121] has [indeed] been guided to a straight path.

102. O you who have believed, fear God as He should be feared and do not die except as Muslims [in submission to Him].

103. And hold firmly to the rope[122] of God all together and do not become divided. And remember the favor of God upon you – when you were enemies and He brought your hearts together and you became, by His favor, brothers. And you were on the edge of a pit of the Fire, and He saved you from it. Thus does God make clear to you His verses that you may be guided.

104. And let there be [arising] from you a nation inviting to [all that is] good, enjoining what is right and forbidding what is wrong,[123] and those will be the successful.

105. And do not be like the ones who became divided and differed after the clear proofs had come to them. And those will have a great punishment

106. On the Day [some] faces will turn white and [some] faces will turn black. As for those whose faces turn black, [to them it will be said], "Did you disbelieve [i.e., reject faith] after your belief? Then taste the punishment for what you used to reject."

107. But as for those whose faces will turn white, [they will be] within the mercy of God. They will abide therein eternally.

---

[119] See footnote to 3:67.

[120] He has no need for His servants' worship; it is they who are in need of Him.

[121] i.e., adhering to His ordinances strictly, then trusting in Him and relying upon Him completely.

[122] Referring either to His covenant or the Qur'ān.

[123] According to the laws of God.

108. These are the verses of God. We recite them to you, [O Muhammad], in truth; and God wants no injustice to the worlds [i.e., His creatures].

109. To God belongs whatever is in the heavens and whatever is on the earth. And to God will [all] matters be returned.

110. You are the best nation produced [as an example] for mankind. You enjoin what is right and forbid what is wrong and believe in God. If only the People of the Scripture had believed, it would have been better for them. Among them are believers, but most of them are defiantly disobedient.

111. They will not harm you except for [some] annoyance. And if they fight you, they will show you their backs [i.e., retreat]; then they will not be aided.

112. They have been put under humiliation [by God] wherever they are overtaken, except for a rope [i.e., covenant] from God and a rope [i.e., treaty] from the people [i.e., the Muslims].[124] And they have drawn upon themselves anger from God and have been put under destitution. That is because they disbelieved in [i.e., rejected] the verses of God and killed the prophets without right. That is because they disobeyed and [habitually] transgressed.

113. They are not [all] the same; among the People of the Scripture is a community[125] standing [in obedience], reciting the verses of God during periods of the night and prostrating [in prayer].

114. They believe in God and the Last Day, and they enjoin what is right and forbid what is wrong and hasten to good deeds. And those are among the righteous.

115. And whatever good they do – never will it be removed from them. And God is Knowing of the righteous.

116. Indeed, those who disbelieve – never will their wealth or their children avail them against God at all, and those are the companions of the Fire; they will abide therein eternally.

117. The example of what they spend in this worldly life is like that of a wind containing frost which strikes the harvest of a people who have wronged themselves [i.e., sinned] and destroys it. And God has not wronged them, but they wrong themselves.

118. O you who have believed, do not take as intimates those other than yourselves, [i.e., believers], for they will not spare you [any] ruin. They wish you would have hardship. Hatred has already appeared from their mouths, and what their breasts conceal is greater. We have certainly made clear to you the signs, if you will use reason.

119. Here you are loving them but they are not loving you, while you believe in the Scripture – all of it.[126] And when they meet you, they say, "We believe." But when they are alone, they bite their fingertips at you in rage. Say, "Die in your

[124] Once they have surrendered, the People of the Scripture retain their rights and honour (in spite of their refusal of Islām) through payment of the *jizyah* tax in place of *zakāh* and military service due from Muslims. They are then under the protection of the Islāmic state.

[125] Of people who accepted Islām.

[126] That of it revealed by God, not what was subsequently altered by men.

rage. Indeed, God is Knowing of that within the breasts."

120. If good touches you, it distresses them; but if harm strikes you, they rejoice at it. And if you are patient and fear God, their plot will not harm you at all. Indeed, God is encompassing of what they do.

121. And [remember] when you, [O Muhammad], left your family in the morning to post the believers at their stations for the battle [of Uhud] – and God is Hearing and Knowing –

122. When two parties among you were about to lose courage, but God was their ally; and upon God the believers should rely.

123. And already had God given you victory at [the battle of] Badr while you were weak [i.e., few in number]. Then fear God; perhaps you will be grateful.

124. [Remember] when you said to the believers, "Is it not sufficient for you that your Lord should reinforce you with three thousand angels sent down?

125. Yes, if you remain patient and conscious of God and they [i.e., the enemy] come upon you [attacking] in rage, your Lord will reinforce you with five thousand angels having marks [of distinction]."

126. And God made it not except as [a sign of] good tidings for you and to reassure your hearts thereby. And victory is not except from God, the Exalted in Might, the Wise –

127. That He might cut down a section of the disbelievers or suppress them so that they turn back disappointed.

128. Not for you, [O Muhammad, but for God], is the decision whether He should [cut them down] or forgive them or punish them, for indeed, they are wrongdoers.

129. And to God belongs whatever is in the heavens and whatever is on the earth. He forgives whom He wills and punishes whom He wills. And God is Forgiving and Merciful.

130. O you who have believed, do not consume usury, doubled and multiplied, but fear God that you may be successful.

131. And fear the Fire, which has been prepared for the disbelievers.

132. And obey God and the Messenger that you may obtain mercy.

133. And hasten to forgiveness from your Lord and a garden [i.e., Paradise] as wide as the heavens and earth, prepared for the righteous

134. Who spend [in the cause of God] during ease and hardship and who restrain anger and who pardon the people – and God loves the doers of good;

135. And those who, when they commit an immorality or wrong themselves [by transgression], remember God and seek forgiveness for their sins – and who can forgive sins except God? – and [who] do not persist in what they have done while they know.

136. Those – their reward is forgiveness from their Lord and gardens beneath which rivers flow [in Paradise], wherein they will abide eternally; and excellent is the reward of the [righteous] workers.

137. Similar situations [as yours] have passed on before you, so proceed throughout the earth and observe how was the end of those who denied.

138. This [Qur'ān] is a clear statement to [all] the people and a guidance and instruction for those conscious of God.

139. So do not weaken and do not grieve, and you will be superior if you are [true] believers.

140. If a wound should touch you – there has already touched the [opposing] people a wound similar to it. And these days [of varying conditions] We alternate among the people so that God may make evident those who believe and [may] take to Himself from among you martyrs – and God does not like the wrongdoers –

141. And that God may purify the believers [through trials] and destroy the disbelievers.

142. Or do you think that you will enter Paradise while God has not yet made evident those of you who fight in His cause and made evident those who are steadfast?

143. And you had certainly wished for death [i.e., martyrdom] before you encountered it, and you have [now] seen it [before you] while you were looking on.

144. Muhammad is not but a messenger. [Other] messengers have passed on before him. So if he was to die or be killed, would you turn back on your heels [to unbelief]? And he who turns back on his heels will never harm God at all; but God will reward the grateful.

145. And it is not [possible] for one to die except by permission of God at a decree determined. And whoever desires the reward of this world – We will give him thereof; and whoever desires the reward of the Hereafter – We will give him thereof. And we will reward the grateful.

146. And how many a prophet [fought and] with him fought many religious scholars. But they never lost assurance due to what afflicted them in the cause of God, nor did they weaken or submit. And God loves the steadfast.

147. And their words were not but that they said, "Our Lord, forgive us our sins and the excess [committed] in our affairs and plant firmly our feet and give us victory over the disbelieving people."

148. So God gave them the reward of this world and the good reward of the Hereafter. And God loves the doers of good.

149. O you who have believed, if you obey those who disbelieve, they will turn you back on your heels, and you will [then] become losers.

150. But God is your protector, and He is the best of helpers.

151. We will cast terror into the hearts of those who disbelieve for what they have associated with God of which He had not sent down [any] authority. And their refuge will be the Fire, and wretched is the residence of the wrongdoers.

152. And God had certainly fulfilled His promise to you when you were killing them [i.e., the enemy] by His permission until [the time] when you lost cou-

rage and fell to disputing about the order [given by the Prophet] and disobeyed after He had shown you that which you love.[127] Among you are some who desire this world, and among you are some who desire the Hereafter. Then he turned you back from them [defeated] that He might test you. And He has already forgiven you, and God is the possessor of bounty for the believers.

153. [Remember] when you [fled and] climbed [the mountain] without looking aside at anyone while the Messenger was calling you from behind. So God repaid you with distress upon distress so you would not grieve for that which had escaped you [of victory and spoils of war] or [for] that which had befallen you [of injury and death]. And God is [fully] Acquainted with what you do.

154. Then after distress, He sent down upon you security [in the form of] drowsiness, overcoming a faction of you, while another faction worried about themselves, thinking of God other than the truth – the thought of ignorance, saying, "Is there anything for us [to have done] in this matter?" Say, "Indeed, the matter belongs completely to God." They conceal within themselves what they will not reveal to you. They say, "If there was anything we could have done in the matter, we [i.e., some of us] would not have been killed right here." Say, "Even if you had been inside your houses, those decreed to be killed would have come out to their death beds." [It was] so that God might test what is in your breasts and purify what is in your hearts. And God is Knowing of that within the breasts.

155. Indeed, those of you who turned back on the day the two armies met [at Uhud] - it was Satan who caused them to slip because of some [blame] they had earned. But God has already forgiven them. Indeed, God is Forgiving and Forbearing.

156. O you who have believed, do not be like those who disbelieved and said about their brothers when they traveled through the land or went out to fight, "If they had been with us, they would not have died or have been killed," so God makes that [misconception] a regret within their hearts. And it is God who gives life and causes death, and God is Seeing of what you do.

157. And if you are killed in the cause of God or die – then forgiveness from God and mercy are better than whatever they accumulate [in this world].

158. And whether you die or are killed, unto God you will be gathered.

159. So by mercy from God, [O Muhammad], you were lenient with them. And if you had been rude [in speech] and harsh in heart, they would have disbanded from about you. So pardon them and ask forgiveness for them and consult them in the matter. And when you have decided, then rely upon God. Indeed, God loves those who rely [upon Him].

160. If God should aid you, no one can overcome you; but if He should forsake you, who is there that can aid you after Him? And upon God let the believers rely.

161. It is not [attributable] to any prophet that he would act unfaithfully [in regard to war booty]. And whoever betrays,

[127] i.e., the spoils of war.

[taking unlawfully], will come with what he took on the Day of Resurrection. Then will every soul be [fully] compensated for what it earned, and they will not be wronged.

162. So is one who pursues the pleasure of God like one who brings upon himself the anger of God and whose refuge is Hell? And wretched is the destination.

163. They are [varying] degrees in the sight of God, and God is Seeing of whatever they do.

164. Certainly did God confer [great] favor upon the believers when He sent among them a Messenger from themselves, reciting to them His verses and purifying them and teaching them the Book [i.e., the Qur'ān] and wisdom,[128] although they had been before in manifest error.

165. Why [is it that] when a [single] disaster struck you [on the day of Uhud], although you had struck [the enemy in the battle of Badr] with one twice as great, you said, "From where is this?" Say, "It is from yourselves [i.e., due to your sin]." Indeed, God is over all things competent.

166. And what struck you on the day the two armies met [at Uhud] was by permission of God that He might make evident the [true] believers

167. And that He might make evident those who are hypocrites. For it was said to them, "Come, fight in the way of God or [at least] defend." They said, "If we had known [there would be] fighting, we would have followed you." They were nearer to disbelief that day than to faith, saying with their mouths what was not in their hearts. And God is most Knowing of what they conceal –

168. Those who said about their brothers while sitting [at home], "If they had obeyed us, they would not have been killed." Say, "Then prevent death from yourselves, if you should be truthful."

169. And never think of those who have been killed in the cause of God as dead. Rather, they are alive with their Lord, receiving provision,

170. Rejoicing in what God has bestowed upon them of His bounty, and they receive good tidings about those [to be martyred] after them who have not yet joined them – that there will be no fear concerning them, nor will they grieve.

171. They receive good tidings of favor from God and bounty and [of the fact] that God does not allow the reward of believers to be lost –

172. Those [believers] who responded to God and the Messenger after injury had struck them. For those who did good among them and feared God is a great reward –

173. Those to whom people [i.e., hypocrites] said, "Indeed, the people have gathered against you, so fear them." But it [merely] increased them in faith, and they said, "Sufficient for us is God, and [He is] the best Disposer of affairs."

174. So they returned with favor from God and bounty, no harm having touched them. And they pursued the pleasure of God, and God is the possessor of great bounty.

---

[128] The Prophet's *sunnah* (examples and sayings)

175. That is only Satan who frightens [you] of his supporters. So fear them not, but fear Me, if you are [indeed] believers.

176. And do not be grieved, [O Muhammad], by those who hasten into disbelief. Indeed, they will never harm God at all. God intends that He should give them no share in the Hereafter, and for them is a great punishment.

177. Indeed, those who purchase disbelief [in exchange] for faith – never will they harm God at all, and for them is a painful punishment.

178. And let not those who disbelieve ever think that [because] We extend their time [of enjoyment] it is better for them. We only extend it for them so that they may increase in sin, and for them is a humiliating punishment.

179. God would not leave the believers in that [state] you are in [presently] until He separates the evil from the good. Nor would God reveal to you the unseen. But [instead], God chooses of His messengers whom He wills, so believe in God and His messengers. And if you believe and fear Him, then for you is a great reward.

180. And let not those who [greedily] withhold what God has given them of His bounty ever think that it is better for them. Rather, it is worse for them. Their necks will be encircled by what they withheld on the Day of Resurrection. And to God belongs the heritage of the heavens and the earth. And God, with what you do, is [fully] Acquainted.

181. God has certainly heard the statement of those [Jews] who said, "Indeed, God is poor, while we are rich." We will record what they said and their killing of the prophets without right and will say, "Taste the punishment of the Burning Fire.

182. That is for what your hands have put forth and because God is not ever unjust to [His] servants."

183. [They are] those who said, "Indeed, God has taken our promise not to believe any messenger until he brings us an offering which fire [from heaven] will consume." Say, "There have already come to you messengers before me with clear proofs and [even] that of which you speak. So why did you kill them, if you should be truthful?"

184. Then if they deny you, [O Muhammad] – so were messengers denied before you, who brought clear proofs and written ordinances and the enlightening Scripture.[129]

185. Every soul will taste death, and you will only be given your [full] compensation on the Day of Resurrection. So he who is drawn away from the Fire and admitted to Paradise has attained [his desire]. And what is the life of this world except the enjoyment of delusion.

186. You will surely be tested in your possessions and in yourselves. And you will surely hear from those who were given the Scripture before you and from those who associate others with God much abuse. But if you are patient and fear God – indeed, that is of the matters [worthy] of determination.

187. And [mention, O Muhammad], when God took a covenant from those who were given the Scripture, [saying], "You

[129] The unaltered, original Torah and Gospel, which were revealed by God.

must make it clear [i.e., explain it] to the people and not conceal it." But they threw it away behind their backs and exchanged it for a small price. And wretched is that which they purchased.

188. And never think that those who rejoice in what they have perpetrated and like to be praised for what they did not do – never think them [to be] in safety from the punishment, and for them is a painful punishment.

189. And to God belongs the dominion of the heavens and the earth, and God is over all things competent.

190. Indeed, in the creation of the heavens and the earth and the alternation of the night and the day are signs for those of understanding -

191. Who remember God while standing or sitting or [lying] on their sides and give thought to the creation of the heavens and the earth, [saying], "Our Lord, You did not create this aimlessly; exalted are You [above such a thing]; then protect us from the punishment of the Fire.

192. Our Lord, indeed whoever You admit to the Fire – You have disgraced him, and for the wrongdoers there are no helpers.

193. Our Lord, indeed we have heard a caller [i.e., Prophet Muhammad] calling to faith, [saying], 'Believe in your Lord,' and we have believed. Our Lord, so forgive us our sins and remove from us our misdeeds and cause us to die with the righteous.

194. Our Lord, and grant us what You promised us through Your messengers and do not disgrace us on the Day of Resurrection. Indeed, You do not fail in [Your] promise."

195. And their Lord responded to them, "Never will I allow to be lost the work of [any] worker among you, whether male or female; you are of one another. So those who emigrated or were evicted from their homes or were harmed in My cause or fought or were killed – I will surely remove from them their misdeeds, and I will surely admit them to gardens beneath which rivers flow as reward from God, and God has with Him the best reward."

196. Be not deceived by the [uninhibited] movement of the disbelievers throughout the land.

197. [It is but] a small enjoyment; then their [final] refuge is Hell, and wretched is the resting place.

198. But those who feared their Lord will have gardens beneath which rivers flow, abiding eternally therein, as accommodation from God. And that which is with God is best for the righteous.

199. And indeed, among the People of the Scripture are those who believe in God and what was revealed to you and what was revealed to them, [being] humbly submissive to God. They do not exchange the verses of God for a small price. Those will have their reward with their Lord. Indeed, God is swift in account.

200. O you who have believed, persevere[130] and endure[131] and remain stationed[132] and fear God that you may be successful.

[130] In your religion and in the face of your enemies.
[131] In patience, outlasting your enemies, and against your own evil inclinations.
[132] Posted at your positions against the enemy or in the mosques, awaiting prayers.

## Sūrah 4: an-Nisā'

### Period of Revelation

This Sūrah comprises several discourses which were revealed on different occasions during the period ranging probably between the end of year 3 A.H. (After Hijrah [migration] from Makkah to Madinah) and the end of 4 A.H. or the beginning of 5 A.H. Although it is difficult to determine the exact dates of their revelations it is possible to assign to them a fairly correct period with the help of the Commandments and the events mentioned therein and the Traditions concerning them. A few instances are given below by way of illustration:

1. We know that the instructions about the division of inheritance of the martyrs and for the safeguard of the rights of the orphans were sent down after the Battle of Uhud in which 70 Muslims were killed. Then naturally the question of the division of the inheritance of the martyrs and the safeguard of the rights of their orphans arose in many families at Madinah. From this we conclude that v. 1 -28 were revealed on that occasion.
2. We learn from the Traditions that the Commandment about Salah (prayer) during war time was given on the occasion of the Zat-ur-Riqa'aan expedition which took place in 4 A.H. From this we conclude that the discourse containing v. 102 was revealed on that occasion
3. The last warning (v. 47) to the Jews was given before the Banu-Nadheer were exiled from Madinah in Rabi'-ulAwwal 4 A.H. From this it may safely be concluded that the discourse containing v. 47 must have been revealed some time before that date.
4. The permission about tayammum(the performance of ablutions with pure dust in case no water be available) was given during the Bani-al-Mustaliq expedition which took place in 5 A.H. Therefore the probable period of the revelation of the discourse containing v. 43 was 5 A.H.

### Topics and Their Background

Let us now consider the social and historical considerations of the period in order to understand the Sūrah. All the discourses in this Sūrah deal with three main problems which confronted the Prophet at the time. First of all he was engaged in bringing about an all round development of the Islāmic Community that had been formed at the time of his migration to Madinah. For this purpose he was introducing new moral cultural social economic and political ways in place of the old ones of the pre-Islāmic period. The second thing that occupied his attention and efforts was the bitter struggle that was going on with the polytheist Arabs, the Jewish clans and the hypocrites who were opposing tooth and nail his mission of reform. Above all he had to propagate Islām in the face of the bitter opposition of these powers of evil with a view to capturing more and more minds and hearts.

Accordingly detailed instructions have been given for the consolidation and strengthening of the Islāmic Community in continuation of those given in Al-Baqarah. Principles for the smooth running of family life have been laid down and ways of settling family disputes have been taught. Rules have been prescribed for marriage and rights of wife and husband have been apportioned fairly and equitably. The status of women in the society has been determined and the declaration of the rights of orphans has been made. Laws and regulations have been laid down for the division of inheritance and instructions have been given to reform economic affairs. The foundation of the penal code has been laid down, drinking has been prohibited and instructions have been given for cleanliness and purity. The Muslims have been taught the kind of relations good men should have with their God and fellow men. Instructions have been given for the maintenance of discipline in the Muslim Community.

The moral and religious condition of the people of the Book has been reviewed to teach lessons to the Muslims and to forewarn them to refrain from following in their footsteps. The conduct of the hypocrites has been criticized and the distinctive features of hypocrisy and true faith have been clearly marked off to enable the Muslims to distinguish between the two. In order to cope with the aftermath of the Battle of Uhud Inspiring discourses were sent down to urge the Muslims to face the enemy bravely for the defeat in the Battle had so emboldened the polytheist Arab clans and the neighboring Jews and the hypocrites at home that they were threatening the Muslims on all sides. At this critical juncture God filled the Muslims with courage and gave them such instructions as were needed during that period of war clouds. In order to counteract the fearful rumors that were being spread by the hypocrites and the Muslims of weak faith they were asked to make a thorough enquiry into them and to inform the responsible people about them. Then they were experiencing some difficulties in offering their salat during the expeditions to some places where no water was available for performing their ablutions etc. In such cases they were allowed to cleanse themselves with pure earth and to shorten the salat or to offer the "Salat of Fear" when they were faced with danger. Instructions were also given for the solution of the puzzling problem of those Muslims who were scattered among the unbelieving Arab clans and were often involved in war. They were asked to migrate to Madinah the abode of Islām.

This Sūrah also deals with the case of Banū Nadir who were showing a hostile and menacing attitude in spite of the peace treaties they had made with the Muslims. They were openly siding with the enemies of Islām and hatching plots against the Prophet and the Muslim Community even at Madinah itself. They were taken to task for their inimical behavior and given a final warning to change their attitude and were at last exiled from Madinah on account of their misconduct.

The problem of the hypocrites, who had become very troublesome at that time, was involving the Believers in difficulties. Therefore they were divided into different categories to enable the Muslims to deal with them appropriately. Clear instructions were also given regarding the attitude they should adopt towards the non-belligerent clans. The most important thing needed at that time was to prepare the Muslims for the bitter struggle with the opponents of Islām. For this purpose greatest importance was attached to their character building, for it was obvious that the small Muslim Community could only come out successful, nay, survive, if the Muslims possessed high moral character. They were, therefore, enjoined to adopt the highest moral qualities and were severely criticized whenever any moral weakness was detected in them.

Though this Sūrah mainly deals with the moral and social reforms, yet due attention has been paid to propagation of Islām. On the one hand, the superiority of the Islāmic morality and culture has been established over that of the Jews, Christians and polytheists; on the other hand, their wrong religious conceptions, their wrong morality and their evil acts have been criticized to prepare the ground for inviting them to the way of the Truth

**Subject: Consolidation of the Islāmic Community**

The main object of this Sūrah is to teach the Muslims the ways that unite a people and make them firm and strong. Introductions for the stability of family, which is the nucleus of community have been given. Then they have been urged to prepare themselves for defense. Side by side with these, they have been taught the importance of the propagation of Islām. Above all, the importance of the highest moral character in the scheme of consolidation of the Community has been impressed.

## Sūrah 4: an-Nisā'[133]

In the Name of God, the Most Compassionate, the Most Merciful

1. O mankind, fear your Lord, who created you from one soul and created from it its mate and dispersed from both of them many men and women. And fear God, through whom[134] you ask one another,[135] and the wombs.[136] Indeed God is ever,[137] over you, an Observer.

2. And give to the orphans their properties and do not substitute the defective [of your own] for the good [of theirs]. And do not consume their properties into your own. Indeed, that is ever a great sin.

3. And if you fear that you will not deal justly with the orphan girls, then marry those that please you of [other] women, two or three or four. But if you fear that you will not be just, then [marry only] one or those your right hands possesses [i.e., slaves]. That is more suitable that you may not incline [to injustice].

4. And give the women [upon marriage] their [bridal] gifts[138] graciously. But if they give up willingly to you anything of it, then take it in satisfaction and ease.[139]

5. And do not give the weak-minded your property,[140] which God has made a means of sustenance for you, but provide for them with it and clothe them and speak to them words of appropriate kindness.

6. And test the orphans [in their abilities] until they reach marriageable age. Then if you perceive in them sound judgement, release their property to them. And do not consume it excessively and quickly, [anticipating] that they will grow up. And whoever, [when acting as guardian], is self-sufficient should refrain [from taking a fee]; and whoever is poor - let him take according to what is acceptable. Then when you release their property to them, bring witnesses upon them. And sufficient is God as Accountant.

7. For men is a share of what the parents and close relatives leave, and for women is a share of what the parents and close relatives leave, be it little or much - an obligatory share.

8. And when [other] relatives and orphans and the needy are present at the [time of] division, then provide for them [something] out of it [i.e., the estate] and speak to them words of appropriate kindness.

9. And let those [executors and guardians] fear [injustice] as if they [themselves] had left weak offspring behind and

---

[133] *An-Nisā'*: The Women.
[134] In whose name.
[135] i.e., request favours and demand rights.
[136] i.e., fear God in regard to relations of kinship.
[137] When used in conjunction with God's attributes, the word "ever" (occurring repeatedly throughout this *sūrah* and elsewhere, such as in *Sūrah al-Ahzāb*) is quite inadequate in imparting the sense of continuation expressed by the word "*kana*" in Arabic, which indicates "always was, is, and always will be."
[138] The obligatory bridal gift (*mahr*).
[139] Knowing that it is lawful.
[140] Although it is their property, God refers to it in the collective sense, reminding us that all wealth is provided by Him for the maintenance of the community as well as of individual members.

feared for them. So let them fear God and speak words of appropriate justice.

10. Indeed, those who devour the property of orphans unjustly are only consuming into their bellies fire. And they will be burned in a Blaze [i.e., Hellfire].

11. God instructs you concerning your children [i.e., their portions of inheritance]: for the male, what is equal to the share of two females. But if there are [only] daughters, two or more, for them is two thirds of one's estate.[141] And if there is only one, for her is half. And for one's parents, to each one of them is a sixth of his estate if he left children. But if he had no children and the parents [alone] inherit from him, then for his mother is one third. And if he had brothers [and/or sisters], for his mother is a sixth,[142] after any bequest he [may have] made or debt.[143] Your parents or your children - you know not which of them are nearest to you in benefit. [These shares are] an obligation [imposed] by God. Indeed, God is ever Knowing and Wise.

12. And for you is half of what your wives leave if they have no child. But if they have a child, for you is one fourth of what they leave, after any bequest they [may have] made or debt. And for them [i.e., the wives] is one fourth if you leave no child. But if you leave a child, then for them is an eighth of what you leave, after any bequest you [may have] made or debt. And if a man or woman leaves neither ascendants nor descendants but has a brother or a sister, then for each one of them is a sixth. But if they are more than two, they share a third,[144] after any bequest which was made or debt, as long as there is no detriment [caused].[145] [This is] an ordinance from God, and God is Knowing and Forbearing.

13. These are the limits [set by] God, and whoever obeys God and His Messenger will be admitted by Him to gardens [in Paradise] under which rivers flow, abiding eternally therein; and that is the great attainment.

14. And whoever disobeys God and His Messenger and transgresses His limits - He will put him into the Fire to abide eternally therein, and he will have a humiliating punishment.

15. Those who commit immorality [i.e., unlawful sexual intercourse] of your women - bring against them four [witnesses] from among you. And if they testify,[146] confine them [i.e., the guilty women] to houses until death takes them or God ordains for them [another] way.[147]

---

141 Literally, "that which he left."

142 Although the siblings themselves do not inherit in this case.

143 Based upon prophetic *hadiths*, scholars have ruled that debt takes precedent over a bequest, that a bequest may not include any who inherit by law, and that the total bequest may not be more than one third of one's estate. After the fulfillment of debts and bequests (if any), the remainder of the estate is to be divided according to the ordinances in this *sūrah*.

144 These shares are divided equally between males and females.

145 This is a condition for any bequest. If it has been violated by the deceased, his bequest is not to be honoured, or it may be adjusted by the executor. See 2:182.

146 The witnesses must swear to actually having seen the act taking place.

147 The "other way" (i.e., penalty) was later revealed in 24:2, cancelling the ruling in this verse.

16. And the two[148] who commit it [i.e., unlawful sexual intercourse] among you – punish [i.e., dishonour] them both. But if they repent and correct themselves, leave them alone. Indeed, God is ever Accepting of repentance and Merciful.

17. The repentance accepted by God is only for those who do wrong in ignorance [or carelessness] and then repent soon after. It is those to whom God will turn in forgiveness, and God is ever Knowing and Wise.

18. But repentance is not [accepted] of those who [continue to] do evil deeds up until, when death comes to one of them, he says, "Indeed, I have repented now," or of those who die while they are disbelievers. For them We have prepared a painful punishment.

19. O you who have believed, it is not lawful for you to inherit women by compulsion.[149] And do not make difficulties for them in order to take [back] part of what you gave them[150] unless they commit a clear immorality [i.e., adultery]. And live with them in kindness. For if you dislike them - perhaps you dislike a thing and God makes therein much good.

20. But if you want to replace one wife with another and you have given one of them a great amount [in gifts], do not take [back] from it anything. Would you take it in injustice and manifest sin?

21. And how could you take it while you have gone in unto each other and they have taken from you a solemn covenant?

22. And do not marry those [women] whom your fathers married, except what has already occurred.[151] Indeed, it was an immorality and hateful [to God] and was evil as a way.

23. Prohibited to you [for marriage] are your mothers, your daughters, your sisters, your father's sisters, your mother's sisters, your brother's daughters, your sister's daughters, your [milk] mothers who nursed you, your sisters through nursing, your wives' mothers, and your step-daughters under your guardianship [born] of your wives unto whom you have gone in. But if you have not gone in unto them, there is no sin upon you. And [also prohibited are] the wives of your sons who are from your [own] loins, and that you take [in marriage] two sisters simultaneously, except for what has already occurred.[152] Indeed, God is ever Forgiving and Merciful.

24. And [also prohibited to you are all] married women except those your right hands possess.[153] [This is] the decree of God upon you. And lawful to you are [all others] beyond these, [provided] that you seek them [in marriage] with [gifts from] your property, desiring chastity, not unlawful sexual intercourse. So for whatever you enjoy [of

[148] Scholars differ over whether "the two" refers to two of the same sex (i.e., homosexuals) or those of opposite sexes. In either case, later rulings outlined in the *sunnah* have replaced this one.

[149] The deceased man's heirs have no rights of marriage or otherwise over his widow.

[150] At the time of marriage as *mahr*.

[151] Before Islām. After the ruling was revealed by God, men were required to release those women unlawful to them (e.g., a stepmother, one of two sisters, or any wives over the limit of four). The same obligation applies to one once he has accepted Islām.

[152] See previous footnote.

[153] i.e., slaves or war captives who had polytheist husbands.

marriage] from them, give them their due compensation[154] as an obligation. And there is no blame upon you for what you mutually agree to beyond the obligation. Indeed, God is ever Knowing and Wise.

25. And whoever among you cannot [find] the means to marry free, believing women, then [he may marry] from those whom your right hands possess of believing slave girls. And God is most knowing about your faith. You [believers] are of one another. So marry them with the permission of their people and give them their due compensation [i.e., mahr] according to what is acceptable. [They should be] chaste, neither [of] those who commit unlawful intercourse randomly nor those who take [secret] lovers. But once they are sheltered in marriage, if they should commit adultery, then for them is half the punishment for free [unmarried] women. This [allowance] is for him among you who fears affliction [i.e., sin], but to be patient is better for you. And God is Forgiving and Merciful.

26. God wants to make clear to you [the lawful from the unlawful] and guide you to the [good] practices of those before you and to accept your repentance. And God is Knowing and Wise.

27. God wants to accept your repentance, but those who follow [their] passions want you to digress [into] a great deviation.

28. And God wants to lighten for you [your difficulties]; and mankind was created weak.

[154] The *mahr*, a specified gift to the bride required of the man upon marriage.

29. O you who have believed, do not consume one another's wealth unjustly[155] but only [in lawful] business by mutual consent. And do not kill yourselves [or one another]. Indeed, God is to you ever Merciful.

30. And whoever does that in aggression and injustice - then We will drive him into a Fire. And that, for God, is [always] easy.

31. If you avoid the major sins which you are forbidden, We will remove from you your lesser sins and admit you to a noble entrance [into Paradise].

32. And do not wish for that by which God has made some of you exceed others. For men is a share of what they have earned, and for women is a share of[156] what they have earned. And ask God of His bounty. Indeed God is ever, of all things, Knowing.

33. And for all, We have made heirs to what is left by parents and relatives. And to those whom your oaths have bound [to you] - give them their share.[157] Indeed God is ever, over all things, a Witness.

34. Men are in charge of women[158] by [right of] what God has given one over the other and what they spend [for maintenance] from their wealth. So righteous women are devoutly obedient, guarding in [the husband's] absence what God would have them

[155] i.e., unlawfully or under false pretence.

[156] This may refer to shares of inheritance, wages and reward in the Hereafter.

[157] By bequest, as only those relatives mentioned in verses 11 and 12 inherit fixed shares.

[158] This applies primarily to the husband-wife relationship.

guard.[159] But those [wives] from whom you fear arrogance - [first] advise them; [then if they persist], forsake them in bed; and [finally], strike them.[160] But if they obey you [once more], seek no means against them. Indeed, God is ever Exalted and Grand.

35. And if you fear dissension between the two, send an arbitrator from his people and an arbitrator from her people. If they both desire reconciliation, God will cause it between them. Indeed, God is ever Knowing and Acquainted [with all things].

36. Worship God and associate nothing with Him, and to parents do good, and to relatives, orphans, the needy, the near neighbor, the neighbor farther away, the companion at your side,[161] the traveler, and those whom your right hands possess. Indeed, God does not like those who are self-deluding and boastful,

37. Who are stingy and enjoin upon [other] people stinginess and conceal what God has given them of His bounty - and We have prepared for the disbelievers a humiliating punishment -

38. And [also] those who spend of their wealth to be seen by the people and believe not in God nor in the Last Day. And he to whom Satan is a companion - then evil is he as a companion.

39. And what [harm would come] upon them if they believed in God and the Last Day and spent out of what God provided for them? And God is ever, about them, Knowing.

40. Indeed, God does not do injustice, [even] as much as an atom's weight; while if there is a good deed, He multiplies it and gives from Himself a great reward.

41. So how [will it be] when We bring from every nation a witness and We bring you, [O Muhammad], against these [people] as a witness?

42. That Day, those who disbelieved and disobeyed the Messenger will wish they could be covered by the earth. And they will not conceal from God a [single] statement.

43. O you who have believed, do not approach prayer while you are intoxicated until you know what you are saying[162] or in a state of janābah,[163] except those passing through [a place of prayer], until you have washed [your whole body]. And if you are ill or on a journey or one of you comes from the place of relieving himself or you have contacted women [i.e., had sexual intercourse] and find no water, then seek clean earth and wipe over your faces and your hands [with it]. Indeed, God is ever Pardoning and Forgiving.

44. Have you not seen those who were given a portion of the Scripture, purchasing error [in exchange for it] and wishing you would lose the way?

[159] i.e., their husbands' property and their own chastity.

[160] As a last resort. It is unlawful to strike the face or to cause bodily injury.

[161] i.e., those whose acquaintance you have made. Also interpreted as the wife.

[162] The use of intoxicants was later prohibited completely. See 5:90-91.

[163] Literally, "distance." The state of one under obligation to perform *ghusl* (a complete bath) due to having had sexual intercourse or ejaculation.

45. And God is most knowing of your enemies; and sufficient is God as an ally, and sufficient is God as a helper.

46. Among the Jews are those who distort words from their [proper] places [i.e., usages] and say, "We hear and disobey" and "Hear but be not heard" and "Rā'inā,"[164] twisting their tongues and defaming the religion. And if they had said [instead], "We hear and obey" and "Wait for us [to understand]," it would have been better for them and more suitable. But God has cursed them for their disbelief, so they believe not, except for a few.[165]

47. O you who were given the Scripture, believe in what We have sent down [to Muhammad], confirming that which is with you, before We obliterate faces and turn them toward their backs or curse them as We cursed the sabbath-breakers.[166] And ever is the matter [i.e., decree] of God accomplished.

48. Indeed, God does not forgive association with Him, but He forgives what is less than that for whom He wills. And he who associates others with God has certainly fabricated a tremendous sin.

49. Have you not seen those who claim themselves to be pure? Rather, God purifies whom He wills, and injustice is not done to them, [even] as much as a thread [inside a date seed].

50. Look how they invent about God untruth, and sufficient is that as a manifest sin.

51. Have you not seen those who were given a portion of the Scripture, who believe in jibt [superstition] and tāghūt [false objects of worship] and say about the disbelievers, "These are better guided than the believers as to the way"?

52. Those are the ones whom God has cursed; and he whom God curses - never will you find for him a helper.

53. Or have they a share of dominion? Then [if that were so], they would not give the people [even as much as] the speck on a date seed.

54. Or do they envy people for what God has given them of His bounty? But We had already given the family of Abraham the Scripture and wisdom[167] and conferred upon them a great kingdom.

55. And some among them believed in it,[168] and some among them were averse to it. And sufficient is Hell as a blaze.

56. Indeed, those who disbelieve in Our verses - We will drive them into a fire. Every time their skins are roasted through We will replace them with other skins so they may taste the punishment. Indeed, God is ever Exalted in Might and Wise.

57. But those who believe and do righteous deeds - We will admit them to gardens beneath which rivers flow, wherein they abide forever. For them therein are purified spouses, and We will admit them to deepening shade.

58. Indeed, God commands you to render trusts to whom they are due and when you judge between people to judge with justice. Excellent is that which God in-

[164] See footnote to 2:104.
[165] Or "except with little belief."
[166] See 7:163-166.

[167] Prophetic teachings.
[168] In what was given to them. Also interpreted as "in him," i.e., Muhammad.

structs you. Indeed, God is ever Hearing and Seeing.

59. O you who have believed, obey God and obey the Messenger and those in authority among you. And if you disagree over anything, refer it to God and the Messenger, if you should believe in God and the Last Day. That is the best [way] and best in result.

60. Have you not seen those who claim to have believed in what was revealed to you, [O Muhammad], and what was revealed before you? They wish to refer legislation to tāghūt,[169] while they were commanded to reject it; and Satan wishes to lead them far astray.

61. And when it is said to them, "Come to what God has revealed and to the Messenger," you see the hypocrites turning away from you in aversion.

62. So how [will it be] when disaster strikes them because of what their hands have put forth and then they come to you swearing by God, "We intended nothing but good conduct and accommodation."

63. Those are the ones of whom God knows what is in their hearts, so turn away from them[170] but admonish them and speak to them a far-reaching [i.e., effective] word.

64. And We did not send any messenger except to be obeyed by permission of God. And if, when they wronged themselves, they had come to you, [O Muhammad], and asked forgiveness of God and the Messenger had asked forgiveness for them, they would have found God Accepting of repentance and Merciful.

65. But no, by your Lord, they will not [truly] believe until they make you, [O Muhammad], judge concerning that over which they dispute among themselves and then find within themselves no discomfort from what you have judged and submit in [full, willing] submission.

66. And if We had decreed upon them, "Kill yourselves" or "Leave your homes," they would not have done it, except for a few of them. But if they had done what they were instructed, it would have been better for them and a firmer position [for them in faith].

67. And then We would have given them from Us a great reward.

68. And We would have guided them to a straight path.

69. And whoever obeys God and the Messenger - those will be with the ones upon whom God has bestowed favor of the prophets, the steadfast affirmers of truth, the martyrs and the righteous. And excellent are those as companions.

70. That is the bounty from God, and sufficient is God as Knower.

71. O you who have believed, take your precaution and [either] go forth in companies or go forth all together.

72. And indeed, there is among you he who lingers behind; and if disaster strikes you, he says, "God has favored me in that I was not present with them."

73. But if bounty comes to you from God, he will surely say, as if [i.e., showing that] there had never been between you

[169] False objects of worship or those transgressors who usurp the divine right of government.
[170] i.e., use not violence against them.

and him any affection, "Oh, I wish I had been with them so I could have attained a great attainment."[171]

74. So let those fight in the cause of God who sell the life of this world for the Hereafter. And he who fights in the cause of God and is killed or achieves victory - We will bestow upon him a great reward.

75. And what is [the matter] with you that you fight not in the cause of God and [for] the oppressed among men, women, and children who say, "Our Lord, take us out of this city of oppressive people and appoint for us from Yourself a protector and appoint for us from Yourself a helper?"

76. Those who believe fight in the cause of God, and those who disbelieve fight in the cause of tāghūt.[172] So fight against the allies of Satan. Indeed, the plot of Satan has ever been weak.

77. Have you not seen those who were told, "Restrain your hands [from fighting][173] and establish prayer and give zakāh?" But then when fighting was ordained for them, at once a party of them feared men as they fear God or with [even] greater fear. They said, "Our Lord, why have You decreed upon us fighting? If only You had postponed [it for] us for a short time." Say, "The enjoyment of this world is little, and the Hereafter is better for he who fears God. And injustice will not be done to you, [even] as much as a thread [inside a date seed]."

[171] The spoils of war. Although having pretended to befriend the believers in support of God's religion, the hypocrite will not be willing to fight except for material gain.

[172] See footnote to 4:60.

[173] Before permission was given by God.

78. Wherever you may be, death will overtake you, even if you should be within towers of lofty construction. But if good comes to them, they say, "This is from God"; and if evil befalls them, they say,[174] "This is from you." Say, "All [things] are from God." So what is [the matter] with those people that they can hardly understand any statement?

79. What comes to you of good is from God, but what comes to you of evil, [O man], is from yourself.[175] And We have sent you, [O Muhammad], to the people as a messenger, and sufficient is God as Witness.

80. He who obeys the Messenger has obeyed God; but those who turn away - We have not sent you over them as a guardian.

81. And they say, "[We pledge] obedience." But when they leave you, a group of them spend the night determining to do other than what you say. But God records what they plan by night. So leave them alone and rely upon God. And sufficient is God as Disposer of affairs.

82. Then do they not reflect upon the Qur'ān?[176] If it had been from [any] other than God, they would have found within it much contradiction.

83. And when there comes to them something [i.e., information] about [public] security or fear, they spread it around. But if they had referred it back to the Messenger or to those of authority among them, then the ones who [can] draw correct conclusions from it would have known about it. And if not for the

[174] Addressing the Prophet.

[175] As a result of your mistakes or sins.

[176] i.e., its meaning and its objective.

favor of God upon you and His mercy, you would have followed Satan, except for a few.

84. So fight, [O Muhammad], in the cause of God; you are not held responsible except for yourself. And encourage the believers [to join you] that perhaps God will restrain the [military] might of those who disbelieve. And God is greater in might and stronger in [exemplary] punishment.[177]

85. Whoever intercedes for a good cause will have a share [i.e., reward] therefrom; and whoever intercedes for an evil cause will have a portion [i.e., burden] therefrom. And ever is God, over all things, a Keeper.[178]

86. And when you are greeted with a greeting, greet [in return] with one better than it or [at least] return it [in a like manner]. Indeed God is ever, over all things, an Accountant.

87. God - there is no deity except Him. He will surely assemble you for [account on] the Day of Resurrection, about which there is no doubt. And who is more truthful than God in statement.

88. What is [the matter] with you [that you are] two groups concerning the hypocrites,[179] while God has made them fall back [into error and disbelief] for what they earned.[180] Do you wish to guide those whom God has sent astray? And he whom God sends astray - never will you find for him a way [of guidance].[181]

89. They wish you would disbelieve as they disbelieved so you would be alike. So do not take from among them allies until they emigrate for the cause of God. But if they turn away [i.e., refuse], then seize them and kill them wherever you find them and take not from among them any ally or helper,

90. Except for those who take refuge with a people between yourselves and whom is a treaty or those who come to you, their hearts strained at [the prospect of] fighting you or fighting their own people. And if God had willed, He could have given them power over you, and they would have fought you. So if they remove themselves from you and do not fight you and offer you peace, then God has not made for you a cause [for fighting] against them.

91. You will find others who wish to obtain security from you and [to] obtain security from their people. Every time they are returned to [the influence of] disbelief, they fall back into it. So if they do not withdraw from you or offer you peace or restrain their hands, then seize them and kill them wherever you overtake them. And those - We have made for you against them a clear authorization.

92. And never is it for a believer to kill a believer except by mistake. And whoever kills a believer by mistake - then the freeing of a believing slave and a compensation payment [diyah] presented to his [i.e., the deceased's] family [is required], unless they give [up their

[177] God is able to defeat them in such a way as to deter others from attempting anything similar.
[178] Providing, protecting, witnessing, keeping precise records and capable of recompense.
[179] i.e., divided between two viewpoints – whether or not they should be fought and killed.
[180] As the result of their disobedience and disloyalty.
[181] God leaves or sends astray those who choose to reject His guidance.

right as] charity. But if he [i.e., the deceased] was from a people at war with you and he was a believer - then [only] the freeing of a believing slave; and if he was from a people with whom you have a treaty - then a compensation payment presented to his family and the freeing of a believing slave. And whoever does not find [one or cannot afford to buy one] - then [instead], a fast for two months consecutively,[182] [seeking] acceptance of repentance from God.[183] And God is ever Knowing and Wise.

93. But whoever kills a believer intentionally - his recompense is Hell, wherein he will abide eternally, and God has become angry with him and has cursed him and has prepared for him a great punishment.

94. O you who have believed, when you go forth [to fight] in the cause of God, investigate; and do not say to one who gives you [a greeting of] peace, "You are not a believer,"[184] aspiring for the goods of worldly life; for with God are many acquisitions. You [yourselves] were like that before; then God conferred His favor [i.e., guidance] upon you, so investigate. Indeed God is ever, with what you do, Acquainted.

95. Not equal are those believers remaining [at home] - other than the disabled - and the mujāhideen, [who strive and fight] in the cause of God with their wealth and their lives. God has preferred the mujāhideen through their wealth and their lives over those who remain [behind], by degrees. And to all [i.e., both] God has promised the best [reward]. But God has preferred the mujāhideen over those who remain [behind] with a great reward -

96. Degrees [of high position] from Him and forgiveness and mercy. And God is ever Forgiving and Merciful.

97. Indeed, those whom the angels take [in death] while wronging themselves[185] - [the angels] will say, "In what [condition] were you?" They will say, "We were oppressed in the land." They [the angels] will say, "Was not the earth of God spacious [enough] for you to emigrate therein?" For those, their refuge is Hell - and evil it is as a destination.

98. Except for the oppressed among men, women, and children who cannot devise a plan nor are they directed to a way[186] -

99. For those it is expected that God will pardon them, and God is ever Pardoning and Forgiving.

100. And whoever emigrates for the cause of God will find on the earth many [alternative] locations and abundance. And whoever leaves his home as an emigrant to God and His Messenger and then death overtakes him - his reward has already become incumbent upon God. And God is ever Forgiving and Merciful.

[182] Uninterrupted except when there is an Islāmically valid reasons, as in Ramadhān.
[183] An accidental death usually results from some degree of negligence or error for which the believer feels the need to repent.
[184] Do not assume that he pretends Islām merely in order to save himself, for he may be sincere in faith.

[185] By preferring to remain among the disbelievers, although they have the means to emigrate, in an environment where a Muslim is unable to practice his religion freely.
[186] They are prevented by circumstances beyond their control.

101. And when you travel throughout the land, there is no blame upon you for shortening the prayer,[187] [especially] if you fear that those who disbelieve may disrupt [or attack] you.[188] Indeed, the disbelievers are ever to you a clear enemy.

102. And when you [i.e., the commander of an army] are among them and lead them in prayer,[189] let a group of them stand [in prayer] with you and let them carry their arms. And when they have prostrated, let them be [in position] behind you and have the other group come forward which has not [yet] prayed and let them pray with you, taking precaution and carrying their arms. Those who disbelieve wish that you would neglect your weapons and your baggage so they could come down upon you in one [single] attack. But there is no blame upon you, if you are troubled by rain or are ill, for putting down your arms, but take precaution. Indeed, God has prepared for the disbelievers a humiliating punishment.

103. And when you have completed the prayer, remember God standing, sitting, or [lying] on your sides. But when you become secure, re-establish [regular] prayer. Indeed, prayer has been decreed upon the believers a decree of specified times.

104. And do not weaken in pursuit of the enemy. If you should be suffering - so are they suffering as you are suffering, but you expect from God that which they expect not. And God is ever Knowing and Wise.

105. Indeed, We have revealed to you, [O Muhammad], the Book in truth so you may judge between the people by that which God has shown you. And do not be for the deceitful an advocate.

106. And seek forgiveness of God. Indeed, God is ever Forgiving and Merciful.

107. And do not argue on behalf of those who deceive themselves. Indeed, God loves not one who is a habitually sinful deceiver.

108. They conceal [their evil intentions and deeds] from the people, but they cannot conceal [them] from God, and He is with them [in His knowledge] when they spend the night in such as He does not accept of speech. And ever is God, of what they do, encompassing.

109. Here you are - those who argue on their behalf in [this] worldly life - but who will argue with God for them on the Day of Resurrection, or who will [then] be their representative?

110. And whoever does a wrong or wrongs himself but then seeks forgiveness of God will find God Forgiving and Merciful.

111. And whoever earns [i.e., commits] a sin only earns it against himself. And God is ever Knowing and Wise.

112. But whoever earns an offense or a sin and then blames it on an innocent [person] has taken upon himself a slander and manifest sin.

113. And if it was not for the favor of God upon you, [O Muhammad], and His

[187] The four *rak'ah* prayers are shortened to two *rak'ahs.*
[188] The example of the Prophet and his companies illustrates that fear is not a condition for this allowance, merely travel.
[189] At time of fear on the battleground.

mercy, a group of them would have determined to mislead you. But they do not mislead except themselves, and they will not harm you at all. And God has revealed to you the Book and wisdom and has taught you that which you did not know. And ever has the favor of God upon you been great.

114. No good is there in much of their private conversation, except for those who enjoin charity or that which is right or conciliation between people. And whoever does that seeking means to the approval of God - then We are going to give him a great reward.

115. And whoever opposes the Messenger after guidance has become clear to him and follows other than the way of the believers - We will give him what he has taken[190] and drive him into Hell, and evil it is as a destination.

116. Indeed, God does not forgive association with Him, but He forgives what is less than that for whom He wills. And he who associates others with God has certainly gone far astray.

117. They call upon instead of Him none but female [deities], and they [actually] call upon none but a rebellious Satan,

118. Whom God has cursed. For he had said, "I will surely take from among Your servants a specific portion.

119. And I will mislead them, and I will arouse in them [sinful] desires, and I will command them so they will slit the ears of cattle, and I will command them so they will change the creation of God." And whoever takes Satan as an ally instead of God has certainly sustained a clear loss.

120. He [i.e., Satan] promises them and arouses desire in them. But Satan does not promise them except delusion.

121. The refuge of those will be Hell, and they will not find from it an escape.

122. But the ones who believe and do righteous deeds - We will admit them to gardens beneath which rivers flow, wherein they will abide forever. [It is] the promise of God, [which is] truth, and who is more truthful than God in statement.

123. It [i.e., Paradise] is not [obtained] by your wishful thinking nor by that of the People of the Scripture. Whoever does a wrong will be recompensed for it, and he will not find besides God a protector or a helper.

124. And whoever does righteous deeds, whether male or female, while being a believer - those will enter Paradise and will not be wronged, [even as much as] the speck on a date seed.

125. And who is better in religion than one who submits himself to God while being a doer of good and follows the religion of Abraham, inclining toward truth? And God took Abraham as an intimate friend.

126. And to God belongs whatever is in the heavens and whatever is on the earth. And ever is God, of all things, encompassing.

127. And they request from you, [O Muhammad], a [legal] ruling concerning women. Say, "God gives you a ruling about them and [about] what has been

[190] i.e., make him responsible for his choice.

recited to you in the Book concerning the orphan girls to whom you do not give what is decreed for them[191] - and [yet] you desire to marry them - and concerning the oppressed among children and that you maintain for orphans [their rights] in justice." And whatever you do of good - indeed, God is ever Knowing of it.

128. And if a woman fears from her husband contempt or evasion, there is no sin upon them if they make terms of settlement between them - and settlement is best. And present in [human] souls is stinginess.[192] But if you do good and fear God - then indeed God is ever, with what you do, Acquainted.

129. And you will never be able to be equal [in feeling] between wives, even if you should strive [to do so]. So do not incline completely [toward one] and leave another hanging.[193] And if you amend [your affairs] and fear God - then indeed, God is ever Forgiving and Merciful.

130. But if they separate [by divorce], God will enrich each [of them] from His abundance. And ever is God Encompassing and Wise.

131. And to God belongs whatever is in the heavens and whatever is on the earth. And We have instructed those who were given the Scripture before you and yourselves to fear God. But if you disbelieve - then to God belongs whatever is in the heavens and whatever is on the earth. And ever is God Free of need and Praiseworthy.

[191] i.e., their rights, in general and their *mahr*, specifically.

[192] i.e., holding on to self-interests.

[193] Neither divorced nor enjoying the rights of marriage.

132. And to God belongs whatever is in the heavens and whatever is on the earth. And sufficient is God as Disposer of affairs.

133. If He wills, He can do away with you, O people, and bring others [in your place]. And ever is God competent to do that.

134. Whoever desires the reward of this world - then with God is the reward of this world and the Hereafter. And ever is God Hearing and Seeing.

135. O you who have believed, be persistently standing firm in justice, witnesses for God, even if it be against yourselves or parents and relatives. Whether one is rich or poor, God is more worthy of both.[194] So follow not [personal] inclination, lest you not be just. And if you distort [your testimony] or refuse [to give it], then indeed God is ever, with what you do, Acquainted.

136. O you who have believed, believe[195] in God and His Messenger and the Book that He sent down upon His Messenger and the Scripture which He sent down before. And whoever disbelieves in God, His angels, His books, His messengers, and the Last Day has certainly gone far astray.

137. Indeed, those who have believed then disbelieved, then believed, then disbelieved, and then increased in disbelief - never will God forgive them, nor will He guide them to a way.

138. Give tidings to the hypocrites that there is for them a painful punishment -

[194] i.e., more knowledgeable of their best interests. Therefore, adhere to what He has enjoyed upon you and testify honestly.

[195] i.e., renew, confirm and adhere to your belief.

139. Those who take disbelievers as allies instead of the believers. Do they seek with them honour [through power]? But indeed, honour belongs to God entirely.[196]

140. And it has already come down to you in the Book [i.e., the Qur'ān] that when you hear the verses of God [recited], they are denied [by them] and ridiculed; so do not sit with them until they enter into another conversation. Indeed, you would then be like them.[197] Indeed, God will gather the hypocrites and disbelievers in Hell all together -

141. Those who wait [and watch] you. Then if you gain a victory from God, they say, "Were we not with you?" But if the disbelievers have a success, they say [to them], "Did we not gain the advantage over you, but we protected you from the believers?" God will judge between [all of] you on the Day of Resurrection, and never will God give the disbelievers over the believers a way [to overcome them].[198]

142. Indeed, the hypocrites [think to] deceive God, but He is deceiving them. And when they stand for prayer, they stand lazily, showing [themselves to] the people and not remembering God except a little,

143. Wavering between them, [belonging] neither to these [i.e., the believers] nor to those [i.e., the disbelievers]. And whoever God leaves astray - never will you find for him a way.

[196] Being the source of all power and honour, God grants them to whom He wills.
[197] In this world, by participation in their blasphemy, and in the next, where you will share their punishment.
[198] In the Hereafter, but possibly in this world as well.

144. O you who have believed, do not take the disbelievers as allies instead of the believers. Do you wish to give God against yourselves a clear case?

145. Indeed, the hypocrites will be in the lowest depths of the Fire - and never will you find for them a helper -

146. Except for those who repent, correct themselves, hold fast to God, and are sincere in their religion for God, for those will be with the believers. And God is going to give the believers a great reward.

147. What would God do with [i.e., gain from] with your punishment if you are grateful and believe? And ever is God Appreciative and Knowing.

148. God does not like the public mention of evil except by one who has been wronged. And ever is God Hearing and Knowing.

149. If [instead] you show [some] good or conceal it or pardon an offense - indeed, God is ever Pardoning and Competent.[199]

150. Indeed, those who disbelieve in God and His messengers and wish to discriminate between God and His messengers and say, "We believe in some and disbelieve in others," and wish to adopt a way in between –

151. Those are the disbelievers, truly. And We have prepared for the disbelievers a humiliating punishment.

152. But they who believe in God and His messengers and do not discriminate be-

[199] God is always able to exact retribution, although He pardons out of His grace.

tween any of them - to those He is going to give their rewards. And ever is God Forgiving and Merciful.

153. The People of the Scripture ask you to bring down to them a book from the heaven. But they had asked of Moses [even] greater than that and said, "Show us God outright," so the thunderbolt struck them for their wrongdoing. Then they took the calf [for worship] after clear evidences had come to them, and We pardoned that. And We gave Moses a clear authority.

154. And We raised over them the mount for [refusal of] their covenant; and We said to them, "Enter the gate bowing humbly"; and We said to them, "Do not transgress on the sabbath"; and We took from them a solemn covenant.

155. And [We cursed them][200] for their breaking of the covenant and their disbelief in the signs of God and their killing of the prophets without right and their saying, "Our hearts are wrapped." [i.e., sealed against reception]. Rather, God has sealed them because of their disbelief, so they believe not, except for a few.[201]

156. And [We cursed them] for their disbelief and their saying against Mary a great slander,[202]

157. And [for] their saying, "Indeed, we have killed the Messiah, Jesus, the son of Mary, the messenger of God." And they did not kill him, nor did they crucify him; but [another] was made to resemble him to them. And indeed, those who differ over it are in doubt about it. They have no knowledge of it except the following of assumption. And they did not kill him, for certain.[203]

158. Rather, God raised him to Himself. And ever is God Exalted in Might and Wise.

159. And there is none from the People of the Scripture but that he will surely believe in him [i.e., Jesus] before his death.[204] And on the Day of Resurrection he will be against them a witness.

160. For wrongdoing on the part of the Jews, We made unlawful for them [certain] good foods which had been lawful to them, and for their averting from the way of God many [people],

161. And [for] their taking of usury while they had been forbidden from it, and their consuming of the people's wealth unjustly. And we have prepared for the disbelievers among them a painful punishment.

162. But those firm in knowledge among them and the believers believe in what has been revealed to you, [O Muhammad], and what was revealed before you. And the establishers of prayer [especially] and the givers of zakāh and the believers in God and the Last Day - those We will give a great reward.

163. Indeed, We have revealed to you, [O Muhammad], as We revealed to Noah and the prophets after him. And we re-

---

200 Another interpretation is "And [We made certain good foods unlawful to them]," based upon verse 160.

201 Or "except with little belief."

202 When they accused her of fornication.

203 Another meaning is "And they did not kill him, being certain [of his identity]," i.e., they killed another assuming it was Jesus.

204 One interpretation is that "his death" refers to that of Jesus after his return to earth. Or it can mean "the death of every individual from among the People of the Scripture."

vealed to Abraham, Ishmael, Isaac, Jacob, the Descendants,[205] Jesus, Job, Jonah, Aaron, and Solomon, and to David We gave the book [of Psalms].

164. And [We sent] messengers about whom We have related [their stories] to you before and messengers about whom We have not related to you. And God spoke to Moses with [direct] speech.

165. [We sent] messengers as bringers of good tidings and warners so that mankind will have no argument against God after the messengers. And ever is God Exalted in Might and Wise.

166. But God bears witness to that which He has revealed to you. He has sent it down with His knowledge, and the angels bear witness [as well]. And sufficient is God as Witness.

167. Indeed, those who disbelieve and avert [people] from the way of God have certainly gone far astray.

168. Indeed, those who disbelieve and commit wrong [or injustice] - never will God forgive them, nor will He guide them to a path,

169. Except the path of Hell; they will abide therein forever. And that, for God, is [always] easy.

170. O mankind, the Messenger has come to you with the truth from your Lord, so believe; it is better for you. But if you disbelieve - then indeed, to God belongs whatever is in the heavens and earth. And ever is God Knowing and Wise.

[205] *Al-Asbāt.* See footnote to 2:136.

171. O People of the Scripture, do not commit excess in your religion[206] or say about God except the truth. The Messiah, Jesus, the son of Mary, was but a messenger of God and His word which He directed to Mary and a soul [created at a command] from Him. So believe in God and His messengers. And do not say, "Three"; desist - it is better for you. Indeed, God is but one God. Exalted is He above having a son. To Him belongs whatever is in the heavens and whatever is on the earth. And sufficient is God as Disposer of affairs.

172. Never would the Messiah disdain to be a servant of God, nor would the angels near [to Him]. And whoever disdains His worship and is arrogant - He will gather them to Himself all together.

173. And as for those who believed and did righteous deeds, He will give them in full their rewards and grant them extra from His bounty. But as for those who disdained and were arrogant, He will punish them with a painful punishment, and they will not find for themselves besides God any protector or helper.

174. O mankind, there has come to you a conclusive proof from your Lord, and We have sent down to you a clear light.[207]

175. So those who believe in God and hold fast to Him - He will admit them to mercy from Himself and bounty and guide them to Himself on a straight path.

176. They request from you a [legal] ruling. Say, "God gives you a ruling concerning one having neither descendants nor

[206] Such as attributing divine qualities to certain creations of God or revering them excessively.
[207] Showing the truth (i.e., the Qur'ān).

ascendants [as heirs]." If a man dies, leaving no child but [only] a sister, she will have half of what he left. And he inherits from her if she [dies and] has no child. But if there are two sisters [or more], they will have two thirds of what he left. If there are both brothers and sisters, the male will have the share of two females. God makes clear to you [His law], lest you go astray. And God is Knowing of all things.

## Sūrah 5: al-Māidah

### Period of Revelation

The theme of this Sūrah indicates and traditions support it, that it was revealed after the treaty of Hudaibiyah at the end of 6 A.H. or in the beginning of 7 A.H. That is why it deals with those problems that arose from this treaty.

The Prophet with 1400 Muslims went to Makkah in 6 A.H. to perform Umrah, but the Quraysh spurred by their enmity prevented him from its performance though it was utterly against all the ancient religious traditions of Arabia. After a good deal of hard and harsh negotiations a treaty was concluded at Hudaibiyah according to which it was agreed that he could perform Umrah the following year. That was a very appropriate occasion for teaching the Muslims the right way of performing a pilgrimage to Makkah with the true Islāmic dignity and enjoining that they should not prevent the disbelievers from performing pilgrimage to Makkah as a retaliation for their misbehaviour. This was not difficult at all as many disbelievers had to pass through Muslim territory on their way to Makkah. This is why the introductory verses deal with the things connected with pilgrimage to Makkah and the same theme has been resumed in v. 101-104. The other topics of this Surah also appear to belong to the same period.

### Occasion of Revelation

This Sūrah was revealed to suit the requirements of the changed conditions which were now different from those prevailing at the time of the revelation of ale-Imrān and an-Nisa. Then the shock of the set-back at Uhud had made the very surroundings of Madinah dangerous for the Muslims. Now Islām had become an invulnerable power and the Islāmic State had extended to Najd on the east, to the Red Sea on the west, to Syria on the north, and to Makkah on the south. This set-back which the Muslims had suffered at Uhud had not broken their determination. It had rather spurred them to action. As a result of their continuous struggle and unparalleled sacrifices the power of the surrounding clans within a radius of 200 miles or so had been broken. The Jewish menace which was always threatening Madinah had been totally removed and the Jews in the other parts of Hijaz had become tributaries of the State of Madinah. The last effort of the Quraysh to suppress Islām had been thwarted in the Battle of the Ditch. After this it had become quite obvious to the Arabs that no power could suppress the Islāmic movement. Now Islām was not merely a creed which ruled over the minds and hearts of the people but had also become a State which dominated over every aspect of the life of the people who lived within its boundaries. This had enabled the Muslims to live their lives without let or hindrance in accordance with their beliefs.

Another development had also taken place during this period. The Muslim civilization had developed in accordance with the principles of Islām and the Islāmic viewpoint. This civilization was quite distinct from all other civilizations in all its details, and distinguished the Muslims clearly from the non-Muslims in their moral, social and cultural behaviour. Mosques had been built in all territories, prayer had been established and an Imām (leader) for every habitation and clan had been appointed. The Islāmic civil and criminal laws had been formulated in detail and were being enforced through the Islāmic courts. New and reformed ways of trade and commerce had taken the place of the old ones. The Islāmic laws of marriage and divorce, of the segregation of the sexes, of the punishment for adultery and calumny and the like had cast the social life of the Muslims in a special mould. Their social behaviour, their conversation, their dress, their very mode of living, their culture etc., had taken a definite shape of its own. As a result of all these changes, the non-Muslims could not expect that the Muslims would ever return to their former fold. Before the treaty of Hudaibiyah, the Muslims were so engaged in their struggle with the non-Muslim Quraysh that they got no time to propagate their message. This hindrance was removed by what was apparently a defeat but in reality a victory at Hudaibiyah. This gave the Muslims not only peace in their own territory but also respite to spread their message in the surrounding territories. Accordingly the Prophet addressed letters to the rulers of Persia, Egypt and the Roman Empire and the chiefs of Arabia, inviting them to Islām. At the same time the missionaries of Islām spread among the clans and tribes and invited them to accept the Divine Way of God. These were the circumstances at the time when al-Maidah was revealed.

**Topics**

It deals with the following three main topics:

1. Commandments and instructions about the religious, cultural and political life of the Muslims. In this connection a code of ceremonial rules concerning the journey for Hajj has been prescribed; the observance of strict respect for the emblems of God has been enjoined; and any kind of obstruction or interference with the pilgrims to the Ka'bāh has been prohibited. Definite rules and regulations have been laid down for what is lawful and unlawful in the matter of food and self-imposed foolish restrictions of the pre-Islāmic age have been abolished. Permission has been given to take food with the people of the Book and to marry their women. Rules and regulations for the performance of Wudu (ablutions) and bath and purification and tayammum (ablutions with dust) have been prescribed. Punishment for rebellion, disturbance of peace and theft have been specified. Drinking and gambling have absolutely been made unlawful. Expiation for the breaking of oath has been laid down and a few more things have been added to the law of evidence.
2. Admonition to the Muslims. Now that the Muslims had become a ruling body it was feared that power might corrupt them. At this period of great trial God had admonished them over and over again to stick to justice and to guard against the wrong behaviour of their predecessors the people of the Book. They have been enjoined to remain steadfast to the Covenant of obedience to God and His Messenger and to observe strictly their commands and prohibitions in order to save themselves from the evil consequences which befell the Jews and the Christians who had violated them. They have been instructed to observe the dictates of the Qur'ān in the conduct of all their affairs and warned against the attitude of hypocrisy.
3. Admonition to the Jews and the Christians. As the power of the Jews had been totally weakened and almost all their habitations in north Arabia had come under the rule of the Muslims they have been warned again about their wrong attitude and invited to follow the Right Way. At the same time a detailed invitation has also been extended to the Christians. The errors of their creeds have been clearly pointed out and they have been admonished to accept the guidance of the Prophet. Incidentally it may be noted that no direct invitation has been made to the Majoos (fire-worshippers) and idolaters living in the adjoining countries because there was no need for a separate address for them as their condition had already been covered by the addresses to the polytheist Arabs.

**Subject: Consolidation of the Islāmic Community.**

In continuation of the instructions about the consolidation of the Islāmic Community given in the previous Sūrah the Muslims have been directed to observe and fulfill all their obligations: further regulations have been prescribed to train the Muslims for that purpose. They have also been particularly warned as rulers to guard against the corruption of power and directed to observe the Covenant of the Qur'ān. They have also been exhorted to learn lessons from the failings of their predecessors the Jews and the Christians who in their turn have been admonished to give up their wrong attitudes towards the Right Way and accept the guidance taught by Prophet Muhammad.

## Sūrah 5: al-Mā'idah[208]

In the Name of God, the Most Compassionate, the Most Merciful

1. O you who have believed, fulfill [all] contracts.[209] Lawful for you are the animals of grazing livestock except for that which is recited to you [in this Qur'ān] - hunting not being permitted while you are in the state of ihrām.[210] Indeed, God ordains what He intends.

2. O you who have believed, do not violate the rites of God or [the sanctity of] the sacred month or [neglect the marking of] the sacrificial animals and garlanding [them] or [violate the safety of] those coming to the Sacred House seeking bounty from their Lord and [His] approval. But when you come out of ihrām, then [you may] hunt. And do not let the hatred of a people for having obstructed you from al-Masjid al-Harām lead you to transgress. And cooperate in righteousness and piety, but do not cooperate in sin and aggression. And fear God; indeed, God is severe in penalty.

3. Prohibited to you are dead animals,[211] blood, the flesh of swine, and that which has been dedicated to other than God, and [those animals] killed by strangling or by a violent blow or by a head-long fall or by the goring of horns, and those from which a wild animal has eaten, except what you [are able to] slaughter [before its death], and those which are sacrificed on stone altars,[212] and [prohibited is] that you seek decision through divining arrows. That is grave disobedience. This day those who disbelieve have despaired of [defeating] your religion; so fear them not, but fear Me. This day I have perfected for you your religion and completed My favor upon you and have approved for you Islām as religion. But whoever is forced by severe hunger with no inclination to sin - then indeed, God is Forgiving and Merciful.

4. They ask you, [O Muhammad], what has been made lawful for them. Say, "Lawful for you are [all] good foods and [game caught by] what you have trained of hunting animals[213] which you train as God has taught you. So eat of what they catch for you, and mention the name of God upon it, and fear God." Indeed, God is swift in account.

5. This day [all] good foods have been made lawful, and the food of those who were given the Scripture is lawful for you and your food is lawful for them. And [lawful in marriage are] chaste women from among the believers and chaste women from among those who were given the Scripture before you, when you have given them their due compensation,[214] desiring chastity, not unlawful sexual intercourse or taking [secret] lovers. And whoever denies the faith - his work has become worthless, and he, in the Hereafter, will be among the losers.

6. O you who have believed, when you rise to [perform] prayer, wash your faces and your forearms to the elbows and

---

[208] *Al-Mā'idah*: The Table, referring to the table spread with food requested by the disciples of Jesus in verse 112.

[209] Which includes promises, covenants, oaths, etc.

[210] The state or ritual consecration for *hajj* or *'umrah*.

[211] See footnote to 2:173.

[212] In the name of anything other that God.

[213] Such as dogs, falcons, etc.

[214] The specified bridal gift (*mahr*).

wipe over your heads and wash your feet to the ankles. And if you are in a state of janābah,[215] then purify yourselves. But if you are ill or on a journey or one of you comes from the place of relieving himself or you have contacted women[216] and do not find water, then seek clean earth and wipe over your faces and hands with it. God does not intend to make difficulty for you, but He intends to purify you and complete His favor upon you that you may be grateful.

7. And remember the favor of God upon you and His covenant with which He bound you when you said, "We hear and we obey"; and fear God. Indeed, God is Knowing of that within the breasts.

8. O you who have believed, be persistently standing firm for God, witnesses in justice, and do not let the hatred of a people prevent you from being just. Be just; that is nearer to righteousness. And fear God; indeed, God is Acquainted with what you do.

9. God has promised those who believe and do righteous deeds [that] for them there is forgiveness and great reward.

10. But those who disbelieve and deny Our signs - those are the companions of Hellfire.

11. O you who have believed, remember the favor of God upon you when a people determined to extend their hands [in aggression] against you, but He withheld their hands from you; and fear God. And upon God let the believers rely.

[215] See footnote to 4:43.

[216] i.e., had sexual intercourse.

12. And God had already taken a covenant from the Children of Israel, and We delegated from among them twelve leaders. And God said, "I am with you. If you establish prayer and give zakāh and believe in My messengers and support them and loan God a goodly loan,[217] I will surely remove from you your misdeeds and admit you to gardens beneath which rivers flow. But whoever of you disbelieves after that has certainly strayed from the soundness of the way."

13. So for their breaking of the covenant We cursed them and made their hearts hard. They distort words from their [proper] places [i.e., usages] and have forgotten a portion of that of which they were reminded.[218] And you will still observe deceit among them, except a few of them. But pardon them and overlook [their misdeeds]. Indeed, God loves the doers of good.

14. And from those who say, "We are Christians" We took their covenant; but they forgot a portion of that of which they were reminded.[219] So We caused among them[220] animosity and hatred until the Day of Resurrection. And God is going to inform them about what they used to do.

15. O People of the Scripture, there has come to you Our Messenger making clear to you much of what you used to conceal of the Scripture and overlook-

[217] By spending in the cause of God, seeking His reward.

[218] In the Torah concerning the coming of Prophet Muhammad.

[219] In the Gospel concerning the coming of Prophet Muhammad.

[220] i.e., among their various denominations or sects.

ing much.[221] There has come to you from God a light and a clear Book [i.e., the Qur'ān]

16. By which God guides those who pursue His pleasure to the ways of peace[222] and brings them out from darknesses into the light, by His permission, and guides them to a straight path.

17. They have certainly disbelieved who say that God is Christ, the son of Mary. Say, "Then who could prevent God at all if He had intended to destroy Christ, the son of Mary, or his mother or everyone on the earth?" And to God belongs the dominion of the heavens and the earth and whatever is between them. He creates what He wills, and God is over all things competent.

18. But the Jews and the Christians say, "We are the children of God and His beloved." Say, "Then why does He punish you for your sins?" Rather, you are human beings from among those He has created. He forgives whom He wills, and He punishes whom He wills. And to God belongs the dominion of the heavens and the earth and whatever is between them, and to Him is the [final] destination.

19. O People of the Scripture, there has come to you Our Messenger to make clear to you [the religion] after a period [of suspension] of messengers, lest you say, "There came not to us any bringer of good tidings or a warner." But there has come to you a bringer of good tidings and a warner. And God is over all things competent.

[221] Of your sin in that regard.

[222] i.e., security, well-being, integrity and escape from Hellfire. Literally, "freedom from all evil."

20. And [mention, O Muhammad], when Moses said to his people, "O my people, remember the favor of God upon you when He appointed among you prophets and made you possessors[223] and gave you that which He had not given anyone among the worlds.

21. O my people, enter the Holy Land [i.e., Palestine] which God has assigned to you and do not turn back [from fighting in God's cause] and [thus] become losers."

22. They said, "O Moses, indeed within it is a people of tyrannical strength, and indeed, we will never enter it until they leave it; but if they leave it, then we will enter."

23. Said two men from those who feared [to disobey] upon whom God had bestowed favor, "Enter upon them through the gate, for when you have entered it, you will be predominant.[224] And upon God rely, if you should be believers."

24. They said, "O Moses, indeed we will not enter it, ever, as long as they are within it; so go, you and your Lord, and fight. Indeed, we are remaining right here."

25. [Moses] said, "My Lord, indeed I do not possess [i.e., control] except myself and my brother, so part us[225] from the defiantly disobedient people."

26. [God] said, "Then indeed, it is forbidden to them for forty years [in which]

[223] Of all that you need – specifically, homes, wives, and servants. Or "sovereigns," i.e., those of independent authority.

[224] i.e., If you obey the command of God trusting in Him, He will fulfil His promise to you.

[225] Or "distinguish us" or "judge between us."

they will wander throughout the land. So do not grieve over the defiantly disobedient people."

27. And recite to them the story of Adam's two sons, in truth, when they both offered a sacrifice [to God], and it was accepted from one of them but was not accepted from the other. Said [the latter], "I will surely kill you." Said [the former], "Indeed, God only accepts from the righteous [who fear Him].

28. If you should raise your hand against me to kill me - I shall not raise my hand against you to kill you. Indeed, I fear God, Lord of the worlds.

29. Indeed, I want you to obtain [thereby] my sin and your sin so you will be among the companions of the Fire. And that is the recompense of wrongdoers."

30. And his soul permitted to him[226] the murder of his brother, so he killed him and became among the losers.

31. Then God sent a crow searching [i.e., scratching] in the ground to show him how to hide the disgrace[227] of his brother. He said, "O woe to me! Have I failed to be like this crow and hide the disgrace [i.e., body] of my brother?" And he became of the regretful.

32. Because of that, We decreed upon the Children of Israel that whoever kills a soul unless for a soul[228] or for corruption [done] in the land[229] - it is as if he had slain mankind entirely. And whoever saves one[230] - it is as if he had saved mankind entirely. And our messengers had certainly come to them with clear proofs. Then indeed many of them, [even] after that, throughout the land, were transgressors.[231]

33. Indeed, the penalty[232] for those who wage war[233] against God and His Messenger and strive upon earth [to cause] corruption is none but that they be killed or crucified or that their hands and feet be cut off from opposite sides or that they be exiled from the land. That is for them a disgrace in this world; and for them in the Hereafter is a great punishment,

34. Except for those who return [repenting] before you overcome [i.e., apprehend] them. And know that God is Forgiving and Merciful.

35. O you who have believed, fear God and seek the means [of nearness] to Him and strive in His cause that you may succeed.

36. Indeed, those who disbelieve - if they should have all that is in the earth and the like of it with it by which to ransom themselves from the punishment of the Day of Resurrection, it will not be accepted from them, and for them is a painful punishment.

37. They will wish to get out of the Fire, but never are they to emerge therefrom, and for them is an enduring punishment.

[226] i.e., the killer allowed himself.
[227] Referring to the dead body, evidence of his shameful deed.
[228] i.e., in legal retribution for murder.
[229] i.e., that requiring the death penalty.
[230] Or refrains from killing.
[231] Heedless of God's limits, negligent of their responsibilities.
[232] Legal retribution.
[233] i.e., commit acts of violence and terrorism against individuals or treason and aggression against the Islāmic state.

38. [As for] the thief, the male and the female, amputate their hands in recompense for what they earned [i.e., committed] as a deterrent [punishment] from God. And God is Exalted in Might and Wise.

39. But whoever repents after his wrongdoing and reforms, indeed, God will turn to him in forgiveness. Indeed, God is Forgiving and Merciful.

40. Do you not know that to God belongs the dominion of the heavens and the earth? He punishes whom He wills and forgives whom He wills, and God is over all things competent.

41. O Messenger, let them not grieve you who hasten into disbelief of those who say, "We believe" with their mouths, but their hearts believe not, and from among the Jews. [They are] avid listeners to falsehood, listening to another people who have not come to you.[234] They distort words beyond their [proper] places [i.e., usages], saying "If you are given this,[235] take it; but if you are not given it, then beware." But he for whom God intends fitnah[236] - never will you possess [power to do] for him a thing against God. Those are the ones for whom God does not intend to purify their hearts. For them in this world is disgrace, and for them in the Hereafter is a great punishment.

42. [They are] avid listeners to falsehood, devourers of [what is] unlawful. So if they come to you, [O Muhammad], judge between them or turn away from them. And if you turn away from them - never will they harm you at all. And if you judge, judge between them with justice. Indeed, God loves those who act justly.

43. But how is it that they come to you for judgement while they have the Torah, in which is the judgement of God? Then they turn away, [even] after that; but those are not [in fact] believers.

44. Indeed, We sent down the Torah, in which was guidance and light. The prophets who submitted [to God] judged by it for the Jews, as did the rabbis and scholars by that with which they were entrusted of the Scripture of God, and they were witnesses thereto. So do not fear the people but fear Me, and do not exchange My verses for a small price [i.e., worldly gain]. And whoever does not judge by what God has revealed - then it is those who are the disbelievers.

45. And We ordained for them therein a life for a life, an eye for an eye, a nose for a nose, an ear for an ear, a tooth for a tooth, and for wounds is legal retribution. But whoever gives [up his right as] charity, it is an expiation for him. And whoever does not judge by what God has revealed - then it is those who are the wrongdoers [i.e., the unjust].

46. And We sent, following in their footsteps,[237] Jesus, the son of Mary, confirming that which came before him in the Torah; and We gave him the Gospel, in which was guidance and light and confirming that which preceded it of the Torah as guidance and instruction for the righteous.

[234] They had not attended the Prophet's gatherings or heard his words.

[235] The legal ruling desired by them.

[236] The meaning here is misbelieve, misconception, or self-delusion as result of one's own refusal of truth.

[237] i.e., following the tradition of the prophets of the Children of Israel.

47. And let the People of the Gospel judge by what God has revealed therein. And whoever does not judge by what God has revealed - then it is those who are the defiantly disobedient.

48. And We have revealed to you, [O Muhammad], the Book [i.e., the Qur'ān] in truth, confirming that which preceded it of the Scripture and as a criterion over it. So judge between them by what God has revealed and do not follow their inclinations away from what has come to you of the truth. To each of you We prescribed a law and a method.[238] Had God willed, He would have made you one nation [united in religion], but [He intended] to test you in what He has given you; so race to [all that is] good.[239] To God is your return all together, and He will [then] inform you concerning that over which you used to differ.

49. And judge, [O Muhammad], between them by what God has revealed and do not follow their inclinations and beware of them, lest they tempt you away from some of what God has revealed to you. And if they turn away - then know that God only intends to afflict them with some of their [own] sins. And indeed, many among the people are defiantly disobedient.

50. Then is it the judgement of [the time of] ignorance they desire? But who is better than God in judgement for a people who are certain [in faith].

51. O you who have believed, do not take the Jews and the Christians as allies. They are [in fact] allies of one another. And whoever is an ally to them among you - then indeed, he is [one] of them. Indeed, God guides not the wrongdoing people.

52. So you see those in whose hearts is disease [i.e., hypocrisy] hastening into [association with] them, saying, "We are afraid a misfortune may strike us." But perhaps God will bring conquest or a decision from Him, and they will become, over what they have been concealing within themselves, regretful.

53. And those who believe will say,[240] "Are these the ones who swore by God their strongest oaths that indeed they were with you?" Their deeds have become worthless, and they have become losers.

54. O you who have believed, whoever of you should revert from his religion - God will bring forth [in place of them] a people He will love and who will love Him [who are] humble toward the believers, powerful against the disbelievers; they strive in the cause of God and do not fear the blame of a critic. That is the favor of God; He bestows it upon whom He wills. And God is all-Encompassing and Knowing.

55. Your ally is none but God and [therefore] His Messenger and those who have believed - those who establish prayer and give zakāh, and they bow [in worship].

56. And whoever is an ally of God and His Messenger and those who have believed - indeed, the party of God - they will be the predominant.

---

[238] Prior to his revelation, which supersedes all previous scriptures.

[239] i.e., obedience to God according to what He enjoined in the Qur'ān and through the *sunnah* of His Prophet.

[240] About the hypocrites after their exposure.

57. O you who have believed, take not those who have taken your religion in ridicule and amusement among the ones who were given the Scripture before you nor the disbelievers as allies. And fear God, if you should [truly] be believers.

58. And when you call to prayer, they take it in ridicule and amusement. That is because they are a people who do not use reason.

59. Say, "O People of the Scripture, do you resent us except [for the fact] that we have believed in God and what was revealed to us and what was revealed before and because most of you are defiantly disobedient?"

60. Say, "Shall I inform you of [what is] worse than that[241] as penalty from God? [It is that of] those whom God has cursed and with whom He became angry and made of them apes and pigs and slaves of tāghūt.[242] Those are worse in position and further astray from the sound way."

61. And when they come to you, they say, "We believe." But they have entered with disbelief [in their hearts], and they have certainly left with it. And God is most knowing of what they were concealing.

62. And you see many of them hastening into sin and aggression and the devouring of [what is] unlawful. How wretched is what they have been doing.

63. Why do the rabbis and religious scholars not forbid them from saying what is sinful and devouring what is unlawful? How wretched is what they have been practicing.

64. And the Jews say, "The hand of God is chained."[243] Chained are their hands, and cursed are they for what they say. Rather, both His hands are extended; He spends however He wills. And that which has been revealed to you from your Lord will surely increase many of them in transgression and disbelief. And We have cast among them animosity and hatred until the Day of Resurrection. Every time they kindled the fire of war [against you], God extinguished it. And they strive throughout the land [causing] corruption, and God does not like corrupters.

65. And if only the People of the Scripture had believed and feared God, We would have removed from them their misdeeds and admitted them to Gardens of Pleasure.

66. And if only they upheld [the law of] the Torah, the Gospel, and what has been revealed to them from their Lord [i.e., the Qur'ān], they would have consumed [provision] from above them and from beneath their feet.[244] Among them are a moderate [i.e., acceptable] community, but many of them - evil is that which they do.

67. O Messenger, announce that which has been revealed to you from your Lord, and if you do not, then you have not conveyed His message. And God will protect you from the people. Indeed, God does not guide the disbelieving people.

---

241 Referring to the punishment of the people of the Scripture (in their censure on the Muslims) claimed was deserved by them.

242 See footnote to 2:256.

243 Implying inability to give or stinginess.

244 i.e., in great abundance.

68. Say, "O People of the Scripture, you are [standing] on nothing until you uphold [the law of] the Torah, the Gospel, and what has been revealed to you from your Lord [i.e., the Qur'ān]." And that which has been revealed to you from your Lord will surely increase many of them in transgression and disbelief. So do not grieve over the disbelieving people.

69. Indeed, those who have believed [in Prophet Muhammad] and those [before him] who were Jews or Sabeans or Christians - those [among them] who believed in God and the Last Day and did righteousness - no fear will there be concerning them, nor will they grieve.[245]

70. We had already taken the covenant of the Children of Israel and had sent to them messengers. Whenever there came to them a messenger with what their souls did not desire, a party [of messengers] they denied, and another party they killed.

71. And they thought there would be no [resulting] punishment, so they became blind and deaf. Then God turned to them in forgiveness; then [again] many of them became blind and deaf. And God is Seeing of what they do.

72. They have certainly disbelieved who say, "God is the Messiah, the son of Mary" while the Messiah has said, "O Children of Israel, worship God, my Lord and your Lord." Indeed, he who associates others with God - God has forbidden him Paradise, and his refuge is the Fire. And there are not for the wrongdoers any helpers.

[245] See footnote to 2:62.

73. They have certainly disbelieved who say, "God is the third of three."[246] And there is no god except one God. And if they do not desist from what they are saying, there will surely afflict the disbelievers among them a painful punishment.

74. So will they not repent to God and seek His forgiveness? And God is Forgiving and Merciful.

75. The Messiah, son of Mary, was not but a messenger; [other] messengers have passed on before him. And his mother was a supporter of truth. They both used to eat food.[247] Look how We make clear to them the signs; then look how they are deluded.

76. Say, "Do you worship besides God that which holds for you no [power of] harm or benefit while it is God who is the Hearing, the Knowing?"

77. Say, "O People of the Scripture, do not exceed limits in your religion beyond the truth and do not follow the inclinations of a people who had gone astray before and misled many and have strayed from the soundness of the way."

78. Cursed were those who disbelieved among the Children of Israel by the tongue of David and of Jesus, the son of Mary. That was because they disobeyed and [habitually] transgressed.

79. They used not to prevent one another from wrongdoing that they did. How wretched was that which they were doing.

[246] i.e., one part of three, referring to the Christians concept of trinity.

[247] They were in need of sustenance, proving that they were creations of God, not divine beings.

80. You see many of them becoming allies of those who disbelieved [i.e., the polytheists]. How wretched is that which they have put forth for themselves in that God has become angry with them, and in the punishment they will abide eternally.

81. And if they had believed in God and the Prophet and in what was revealed to him, they would not have taken them as allies; but many of them are defiantly disobedient.

82. You will surely find the most intense of the people in animosity toward the believers [to be] the Jews and those who associate others with God; and you will find the nearest of them in affection to the believers those who say, "We are Christians." That is because among them are priests and monks and because they are not arrogant.

83. And when they hear what has been revealed to the Messenger, you see their eyes overflowing with tears because of what they have recognized of the truth. They say, "Our Lord, we have believed, so register us among the witnesses.

84. And why should we not believe in God and what has come to us of the truth? And we aspire that our Lord will admit us [to Paradise] with the righteous people."

85. So God rewarded them for what they said[248] with gardens [in Paradise] beneath which rivers flow, wherein they abide eternally. And that is the reward of doers of good.

[248] i.e., their admission and acceptance of the truth and commitment to God's religion (Islām).

86. But those who disbelieved and denied Our signs - they are the companions of Hellfire.

87. O you who have believed, do not prohibit the good things which God has made lawful to you and do not transgress. Indeed, God does not like transgressors.

88. And eat of what God has provided for you [which is] lawful and good. And fear God, in whom you are believers.

89. God will not impose blame upon you for what is meaningless[249] in your oaths, but He will impose blame upon you for [breaking] what you intended of oaths. So its expiation[250] is the feeding of ten needy people from the average of that which you feed your [own] families or clothing them or the freeing of a slave. But whoever cannot find [or afford it] - then a fast of three days [is required]. That is the expiation for oaths when you have sworn. But guard your oaths.[251] Thus does God make clear to you His verses [i.e., revealed law] that you may be grateful.

90. O you who have believed, indeed, intoxicants, gambling, [sacrificing on] stone alters [to other than God], and divining arrows are but defilement from the work of Satan, so avoid[252] it that you may be successful.

[249] i.e., what is sworn to only out of habit of speech or what one utters carelessly without true intent.

[250] i.e., that for a deliberate oath.

[251] i.e., do not take oaths indiscriminately or swear to do that which is sinful, requiring expiation.

[252] The prohibition understood from the word "avoid" is stronger than if God had merely said, "Abstain." The former requires distancing oneself from anything remotely related to these practices.

91. Satan only wants to cause between you animosity and hatred through intoxicants and gambling and to avert you from the remembrance of God and from prayer. So will you not desist?

92. And obey God and obey the Messenger and beware. And if you turn away - then know that upon Our Messenger is only [the responsibility for] clear notification.

93. There is not upon those who believe and do righteousness [any] blame concerning what they have eaten [in the past] if they [now] fear God and believe and do righteous deeds, and then fear God and believe, and then fear God and do good; and God loves the doers of good.

94. O you who have believed, God will surely test you through something of the game that your hands and spears [can] reach, that God may make evident those who fear Him unseen. And whoever transgresses after that - for him is a painful punishment.

95. O you who have believed, do not kill game while you are in the state of ihrām.[253] And whoever of you kills it intentionally - the penalty is an equivalent from sacrificial animals to what he killed, as judged by two just men among you as an offering [to God] delivered to the Ka'bāh, or an expiation: the feeding of needy people or the equivalent of that in fasting, that he may taste the consequence of his matter [i.e., deed]. God has pardoned what is past; but whoever returns [to violation], then God will take retribution from him. And God is Exalted in Might and Owner of Retribution.

96. Lawful to you is game from the sea and its food as provision for you and the travelers,[254] but forbidden to you is game from the land as long as you are in the state of ihrām. And fear God to whom you will be gathered.

97. God has made the Ka'bāh, the Sacred House, standing[255] for the people and [has sanctified] the sacred months and the sacrificial animals and the garlands [by which they are identified]. That is so you may know that God knows what is in the heavens and what is in the earth and that God is Knowing of all things.

98. Know that God is severe in penalty and that God is Forgiving and Merciful.

99. Not upon the Messenger is [responsibility] except [for] notification. And God knows whatever you reveal and whatever you conceal.

100. Say, "Not equal are the evil and the good, although the abundance of evil might impress you." So fear God, O you of understanding, that you may be successful.

101. O you who have believed, do not ask about things which, if they are shown to you, will distress you. But if you ask about them while the Qur'ān is being revealed, they will be shown to you. God has pardoned it [i.e., that which is past]; and God is Forgiving and Forbearing.

[253] See footnote to 5:1.

[254] Fishing and eating whatever is caught from the sea is permitted even during *ihrām*.

[255] Conspicuously as a symbol of God's religion.

102. A people asked such [questions] before you; then they became thereby disbelievers.[256]

103. God has not appointed [such innovations as] bahīrah or sā'ibah or wasīlah or hām.[257] But those who disbelieve invent falsehood about God, and most of them do not reason.

104. And when it is said to them, "Come to what God has revealed and to the Messenger," they say, "Sufficient for us is that upon which we found our fathers." Even though their fathers knew nothing, nor were they guided?

105. O you who have believed, upon you is [responsibility for] yourselves. Those who have gone astray will not harm you when you have been guided. To God is your return all together; then He will inform you of what you used to do.

106. O you who have believed, testimony [should be taken] among you when death approaches one of you at the time of bequest - [that of] two just men from among you or two others from outside if you are traveling through the land and the disaster of death should strike you. Detain them after the prayer and let them both swear by God if you doubt [their testimony, saying], "We will not exchange it [i.e., our oath] for a price [i.e., worldly gain], even if he should be a near relative, and we will not withhold the testimony of [i.e., ordained by] God. Indeed, we would then be of the sinful."

107. But if it is found that those two were guilty of sin [i.e., perjury], let two others stand in their place [who are] foremost [in claim] from those who have a lawful right. And let them swear by God, "Our testimony is truer than their testimony, and we have not transgressed. Indeed, we would then be of the wrongdoers."

108. That is more likely that they will give testimony according to its [true] objective, or [at least] they would fear that [other] oaths might be taken after their oaths. And fear God and listen [i.e., obey Him]; and God does not guide the defiantly disobedient people.

109. [Be warned of] the Day when God will assemble the messengers and say, "What was the response you received?" They will say, "We have no knowledge. Indeed, it is You who is Knower of the unseen" -

110. [The Day] when God will say, "O Jesus, Son of Mary, remember My favor upon you and upon your mother when I supported you with the Pure Spirit [i.e., the angel Gabriel] and you spoke to the people in the cradle and in maturity; and [remember] when I taught you writing and wisdom and the Torah and the Gospel; and when you designed from clay [what was] like the form of a bird with My permission, then you breathed into it, and it became a bird with My permission; and you healed the blind [from birth] and the leper with My permission; and when you brought forth the dead with My permission; and when I restrained the Children of Israel from [killing] you when you came to them with clear proofs and those who disbelieved among them said, "This is not but obvious magic."

---

[256] By their unwillingness to carry out what was commanded to them.

[257] Categories of particular camels which were dedicated to the idols and set free to pasture, liberated from the service of man.

111. And [remember] when I inspired to the disciples, "Believe in Me and in My messenger [i.e., Jesus]." They said, "We have believed, so bear witness that indeed we are Muslims [in submission to God]."

112. [And remember] when the disciples said, "O Jesus, Son of Mary, can your Lord[258] send down to us a table [spread with food] from the heaven? [Jesus] said, "Fear God, if you should be believers."

113. They said, "We wish to eat from it and let our hearts be reassured and know that you have been truthful to us and be among its witnesses."

114. Said Jesus, the son of Mary, "O God, our Lord, send down to us a table [spread with food] from the heaven to be for us a festival for the first of us and the last of us and a sign from You. And provide for us, and You are the best of providers."

115. God said, "Indeed, I will send it down to you, but whoever disbelieves afterwards from among you - then indeed will I punish him with a punishment by which I have not punished anyone among the worlds."

116. And [beware the Day] when God will say, "O Jesus, Son of Mary, did you say to the people, 'Take me and my mother as deities besides God?'" He will say, "Exalted are You! It was not for me to say that to which I have no right. If I had said it, You would have known it. You know what is within myself, and I do not know what is within Yourself. Indeed, it is You who is Knower of the unseen.

117. I said not to them except what You commanded me - to worship God, my Lord and your Lord. And I was a witness over them as long as I was among them; but when You took me up, You were the Observer over them, and You are, over all things, Witness.

118. If You should punish them - indeed they are Your servants; but if You forgive them - indeed it is You who is the Exalted in Might, the Wise."

119. God will say, "This is the Day when the truthful will benefit from their truthfulness." For them are gardens [in Paradise] beneath which rivers flow, wherein they will abide forever, God being pleased with them, and they with Him. That is the great attainment.

120. To God belongs the dominion of the heavens and the earth and whatever is within them. And He is over all things competent.

[258] i.e., will God consent to. (His ability is undoubted)

## Sūrah 6: al-An'ām

### Period of Revelation

According to a tradition of Ibn Abbas the whole of the Sūrah was revealed at one sitting at Makkah. Asma bint Yazid says, '*During the revelation of this Sūrah the Holy Prophet was riding on a she-camel and I was holding her nose-string. The she-camel began to feel the weight so heavily that it seemed as if her bones would break under it.*' We also learn from other hadith that it was revealed during the last year before the Hijrah (migration) and that the Prophet dictated the whole of the Sūrah the same night that it was revealed.

### Occasion of Revelation

After determining the period of its revelation it is easier to visualize the background of the Sūrah. Twelve years had passed since the Prophet had been inviting the people to Islām. The antagonism and persecution by the Quraysh had become most savage and brutal and the majority of the Muslims had to leave their homes and migrate to Abyssinia. Above all the two great supporters of the Prophet, Abu Talib and his wife Khadijah were no more to help and give strength to him. Thus he was deprived of all the worldly support. But in spite of this he carried on his mission in the teeth of opposition. As a result of this on the one hand all the good people of Makkah and the surrounding clans gradually began to accept Islām; on the other hand the community as a whole was bent upon obduracy and rejection. Therefore if anyone showed any inclination towards Islām he was subjected to taunts and derision, physical violence and social boycott. It was in these dark circumstances that a ray of hope gleamed from Yathrib where Islām began to spread freely by the efforts of some influential people of Aws and Khazraj who had embraced Islām at Makkah. This was a humble beginning in the march of Islām towards success and none could foresee at that time the great potentialities that lay hidden in it. To a casual observer it appeared at that time as if Islām was merely a weak movement it had no material backing except the meager support of the Prophet's own family and of the few poor adherents of the Movement. Obviously the latter could not give much help because they themselves had been cast out by their own people who had become their enemies and were persecuting them.

### Topics

These were the conditions when this discourse was revealed. The main topics dealt with in this discourse may be divided under seven headings:

1. Refutation of Shirk (polytheism) and invitation to the creed of Tawhid (Oneness of God).
2. Enunciation of the doctrine of the "Life-after-Death" and refutation of the wrong notion that there was nothing beyond this worldly life.
3. Refutation of the prevalent superstitions.
4. Enunciation of the fundamental moral principles for the building up of the Islāmic Society.
5. Answers to the objections raised against the person of the Prophet and his mission.
6. Comfort and encouragement to the Prophet and his followers who were at that time in a state of anxiety and despondency because of the apparent failure of the mission.
7. Admonition warning and threats to the disbelievers and opponents to give up their apathy and haughtiness. It must however be noted that the above topics have not been dealt with one by one under separate headings but the discourse goes on as a continuous whole and these topics come under discussion over and over again in new and different ways.

### The Background of Makki Sūrahs

As this is the first long Makki Sūrah in the order of the compilation of the Qur'ān it will be useful to explain the historical background of Makki Sūrahs in general so that the reader may easily understand the Makki Sūrahs and our references to its different stages in connection with our commentary on them. First of all it should be noted that comparatively very little material is available in regard to the background of the revelation of Makki Sūrahs whereas the period of the revelation of all the Madani Sūrahs is known or can be determined with a little effort. There are authentic hadith even in regard to the occasions of the revelation of the majority of the verses. On the other hand we do not have such detailed information regarding the Makki Sūrahs. There are only a few Sūrahs and verses which have authentic hadith concerning the time and occasion of their revelation. This is because the history of the Makki period had not been compiled in such detail as that of the Madani period. Therefore we have to depend on the internal evidence of these Sūrahs for determining the period of their revelation: for example the topics they discuss their subject matter their style and the direct or indirect references to the events and the occasions of their revelation. Thus it is obvious that with the help of such evidence as this we cannot say with precision that such and such Sūrah or verse was revealed on such and such an occasion. The most we can do is to compare the internal evidence of a Sūrah with the events of the life of the Prophet at Makkah and then come to a more or less correct conclusion as to what particular stage a certain Sūrah belongs. If we keep the above things in view the history of the mission of the Prophet at Makkah can be divided into four stages.

1. The first stage began with his appointment as a Messenger and ended with the proclamation of Prophethood three years later. During this period the Message was given secretly to some selected persons only but the common people of Makkah were not aware of it.
2. The second stage lasted for two years after the proclamation of his Prophethood. It began with opposition by individuals: then by and by it took the shape of antagonism ridicule derision accusation abuse and false propaganda then gangs were formed to persecute those Muslims who were comparatively poor weak' and helpless.
3. The third stage lasted for about six years from the beginning of the persecution to the death of Abu Talib and Khadijah in the tenth year of Prophethood. During this period the persecution of the Muslims became so savage and brutal that many of them were forced to migrate to Abyssinia while social and economic boycott was applied against the remaining Believers.
4. The fourth stage lasted for about three years from the tenth to the thirteenth year of Prophethood. This was a period of hard trials and grievous sufferings for the Prophet and his followers. Life had become unendurable at Makkah and there appeared to be no place of refuge even outside it. So much so that when the Prophet went to Tā'if, it offered no shelter or protection. Besides this, on the occasion of Hajj, he would appeal to each and every Arab clan to accept his invitation to Islām but met with blank refusal from every quarter. At the same time, the people of Makkah were holding counsels to get rid of him by killing or imprisoning or banishing him from their city. It was at that most critical time that God opened for Islām the hearts of the People of Yathrib where he migrated at their invitation.

In the succeeding Makki Sūrahs, we will determine on the basis of the distinctive features of each stage, and point out in the introduction, the particular stage in which a certain Makki Sūrah was revealed.

**Subject: Islāmic Creed**

This Sūrah mainly discusses the different aspects of the major articles of the Islāmic Creed: Tawhid Life-after-death, Prophethood and their practical application to human life. Side by side with this it refutes the erroneous beliefs of the opponents and answers their objections, warns and admonishes them and comforts the Prophet and his followers who were then suffering from persecution. Of course these themes have not been dealt with under separate heads but have been blended in an excellent manner.

## Sūrah 6: al-An'ām[259]

In the Name of God, the Most Compassionate, the Most Merciful

1. [All] praise is [due] to God, who created the heavens and the earth and made the darkness and the light. Then those who disbelieve equate [others] with their Lord.

2. It is He who created you from clay and then decreed a term[260] and a specified time [known] to Him;[261] then [still] you are in dispute.

3. And He is God, [the only deity] in the heavens and the earth. He knows your secret and what you make public, and He knows that which you earn.

4. And no sign comes to them from the signs of their Lord except that they turn away therefrom.

5. For they had denied the truth when it came to them, but there is going to reach them the news of what they used to ridicule.[262]

6. Have they not seen how many generations We destroyed before them which We had established upon the earth as We have not established you? And We sent [rain from] the sky upon them in showers and made rivers flow beneath them; then We destroyed them for their sins and brought forth after them a generation of others.

7. And even if We had sent down to you, [O Muhammad], a written scripture on a page and they touched it with their hands, the disbelievers would say, "This is not but obvious magic."

8. And they say, "Why was there not sent down to him an angel?"[263] But if We had sent down an angel, the matter would have been decided;[264] then they would not be reprieved.

9. And if We had made him [i.e., the messenger] an angel, We would have made him [appear as] a man, and We would have covered them with that in which they cover themselves [i.e., confusion and doubt].

10. And already were messengers ridiculed before you, but those who mocked them were enveloped by that which they used to ridicule.

11. Say, "Travel through the land; then observe how was the end of the deniers."

12. Say, "To whom belongs whatever is in the heavens and earth?" Say, "To God." He has decreed upon Himself mercy. He will surely assemble you for the Day of Resurrection, about which there is no doubt. Those who will lose themselves [that Day] do not believe.

13. And to Him belongs that which reposes by night and by day, and He is the Hearing, the Knowing.

14. Say, "Is it other than God I should take as a protector, Creator of the heavens and earth, while it is He who feeds and

---

[259] *Al-An'ām*: The Grazing Livestock, specifically: camels, cattle, sheep and goats, as mentioned in verses 143-144 of this *sūrah*.
[260] An appointed time for death.
[261] For resurrection.
[262] They will experience the reality of what they had denied and the consequence of their denial.

[263] In support of his prophethood.
[264] They would have been destroyed immediately with no chance for repentance.

is not fed?" Say, [O Muhammad], "Indeed, I have been commanded to be the first [among you] who submit [to God] and [was commanded], 'Do not ever be of the polytheists.' "

15. Say, "Indeed I fear, if I should disobey my Lord, the punishment of a tremendous Day."

16. He from whom it is averted that Day - [God] has granted him mercy. And that is the clear attainment.

17. And if God should touch you with adversity, there is no remover of it except Him. And if He touches you with good - then He is over all things competent.

18. And He is the subjugator over His servants. And He is the Wise, the Acquainted [with all].

19. Say, "What thing is greatest in testimony?" Say, "God is witness between me and you. And this Qur'ān was revealed to me that I may warn you thereby and whomever it reaches.[265] Do you [truly] testify that with God there are other deities?" Say, "I will not testify [with you]." Say, "Indeed, He is but one God, and indeed, I am free of what you associate [with Him]."

20. Those to whom We have given the Scripture recognize it[266] as they recognize their [own] sons. Those who will lose themselves [in the Hereafter] do not believe.

21. And who is more unjust than one who invents about God a lie or denies His verses? Indeed, the wrongdoers will not succeed.

22. And [mention, O Muhammad], the Day We will gather them all together; then We will say to those who associated others with God, "Where are your 'partners' that you used to claim [with Him]?"

23. Then there will be no [excuse upon] examination except they will say, "By God, our Lord, we were not those who associated."

24. See how they will lie about themselves. And lost from them will be what they used to invent.

25. And among them are those who listen to you,[267] but We have placed over their hearts coverings, lest they understand it, and in their ears deafness. And if they should see every sign, they will not believe in it. Even when they come to you arguing with you, those who disbelieve say, "This is not but legends of the former peoples."

26. And they prevent [others] from him and are [themselves] remote from him. And they do not destroy except themselves, but they perceive [it] not.

27. If you could but see when they are made to stand before the Fire and will say, "Oh, would that we could be returned [to life on earth] and not deny the signs of our Lord and be among the believers."

28. But what they concealed before has [now] appeared to them. And even if they were returned, they would return

[265] At every time and place until the Day of Judgement.

[266] The Qur'ān. Also interpreted as "him," meaning Muhammad.

[267] When you recite the Qur'ān.

to that which they were forbidden; and indeed, they are liars.

29. And they say, "There is none but our worldly life, and we will not be resurrected."

30. If you could but see when they will be made to stand before their Lord. He will say, "Is this not the truth?" They will say, "Yes, by our Lord." He will [then] say, "So taste the punishment because you used to disbelieve."

31. Those will have lost who deny the meeting with God, until when the Hour [of resurrection] comes upon them unexpectedly, they will say, "Oh, [how great is] our regret over what we neglected concerning it [i.e., the Hour]," while they bear their burdens [i.e., sins] on their backs. Unquestionably, evil is that which they bear.

32. And the worldly life is not but amusement and diversion; but the home of the Hereafter is best for those who fear God, so will you not reason?

33. We know that you, [O Muhammad], are saddened by what they say. And indeed, they do not call you untruthful, but it is the verses of God that the wrongdoers reject.

34. And certainly were messengers denied before you, but they were patient over [the effects of] denial, and they were harmed until Our victory came to them. And none can alter the words [i.e., decrees] of God. And there has certainly come to you some information about the [previous] messengers.

35. And if their evasion is difficult for you, then if you are able to seek a tunnel into the earth or a stairway into the sky to bring them a sign, [then do so]. But if God had willed, He would have united them upon guidance. So never be of the ignorant.

36. Only those who hear will respond. But the dead[268] - God will resurrect them; then to Him they will be returned.

37. And they say, "Why has a sign not been sent down to him from his Lord?" Say, "Indeed, God is Able to send down a sign, but most of them do not know."

38. And there is no creature on [or within] the earth or bird that flies with its wings except [that they are] communities like you. We have not neglected in the Register[269] a thing. Then unto their Lord they will be gathered.

39. But those who deny Our verses are deaf and dumb within darknesses. Whomever God wills - He leaves astray; and whomever He wills - He puts him on a straight path.

40. Say, "Have you considered:[270] if there came to you the punishment of God or there came to you the Hour - is it other than God you would invoke, if you should be truthful?"

41. No, it is Him [alone] you would invoke, and He would remove that for which you invoked Him if He willed, and you would forget what you associate [with Him].

42. And We have already sent [messengers] to nations before you, [O Muhammad]; then We seized them with poverty and

[268] i.e., the dead of heart, meaning the disbelievers.

[269] The preserved Slate (*al-Lawh al-Mahfūth*), in which all things are recorded.

[270] The meaning is understood to be "Tell me…"

hardship that perhaps they might humble themselves [to Us].

43. Then why, when Our punishment came to them, did they not humble themselves? But their hearts became hardened, and Satan made attractive to them that which they were doing.

44. So when they forgot that by which they had been reminded,[271] We opened to them the doors of every [good] thing until, when they rejoiced in that which they were given, We seized them suddenly, and they were [then] in despair.

45. So the people that committed wrong were eliminated. And praise to God, Lord of the worlds.

46. Say, "Have you considered:[272] if God should take away your hearing and your sight and set a seal upon your hearts, which deity other than God could bring them [back] to you?" Look how We diversify[273] the verses; then they [still] turn away.

47. Say, "Have you considered: if the punishment of God should come to you unexpectedly or manifestly,[274] will any be destroyed but the wrongdoing people?"

48. And We send not the messengers except as bringers of good tidings and warners. So whoever believes and reforms - there will be no fear concerning them, nor will they grieve.

[271] i.e., their trial by poverty and hardship or the warnings of their prophets.
[272] See footnote to verse 40.
[273] Repeat in various ways for emphasis and clarification.
[274] i.e., before your eyes.

49. But those who deny Our verses - the punishment will touch[275] them for their defiant disobedience.

50. Say, [O Muhammad], "I do not tell you that I have the depositories [containing the provision] of God or that I know the unseen, nor do I tell you that I am an angel. I only follow what is revealed to me." Say, "Is the blind equivalent to the seeing? Then will you not give thought?"

51. And warn by it [i.e., the Qur'ān] those who fear that they will be gathered before their Lord - for them besides Him will be no protector and no intercessor - that they might become righteous.

52. And do not send away those who call upon their Lord morning and afternoon, seeking His countenance. Not upon you is anything of their account and not upon them is anything of your account.[276] So were you to send them away, you would [then] be of the wrongdoers.

53. And thus We have tried some of them through others that they [i.e., the disbelievers] might say, "Is it these whom God has favored among us?" Is not God most knowing of those who are grateful?[277]

54. And when those come to you who believe in Our verses, say, "Peace be upon

[275] i.e., reach and afflict.
[276] No one is held accountable for the deeds or intentions of another. That is left to God's judgement.
[277] Those referred to in verses 52-54 are the poor Muslims who were sincere believers and students of the Prophet. The influential leaders of Quraysh had disdained to sit with them, saying to Prophet Muhammad, "Perhaps if you evicted them, we would follow you."

you. Your Lord has decreed upon Himself mercy: that any of you who does wrong out of ignorance and then repents after that and corrects himself - indeed, He is Forgiving and Merciful."

55. And thus do We detail the verses, and [thus] the way of the criminals will become evident.

56. Say, "Indeed, I have been forbidden to worship those you invoke besides God." Say, "I will not follow your desires, for I would then have gone astray, and I would not be of the [rightly] guided."

57. Say, "Indeed, I am on clear evidence from my Lord, and you have denied it. I do not have that for which you are impatient.[278] The decision is only for God. He relates the truth, and He is the best of deciders."

58. Say, "If I had that for which you are impatient, the matter would have been decided between me and you, but God is most knowing of the wrongdoers."

59. And with Him are the keys of the unseen; none knows them except Him. And He knows what is on the land and in the sea. Not a leaf falls but that He knows it. And no grain is there within the darknesses of the earth and no moist or dry [thing] but that it is [written] in a clear record.

60. And it is He who takes your souls by night[279] and knows what you have committed by day. Then He revives you therein [i.e., by day] that a specified term[280] may be fulfilled. Then to Him will be your return; then He will inform you about what you used to do.

61. And He is the subjugator over His servants, and He sends over you guardian-angels until, when death comes to one of you, Our messengers [i.e., angles of death] take him, and they do not fail [in their duties].

62. Then they [i.e., His servants] are returned to God, their true Lord. Unquestionably, His is the judgement, and He is the swiftest of accountants.

63. Say, "Who rescues you from the darknesses of the land and sea [when] you call upon Him imploring [aloud] and privately, 'If He should save us from this [crisis], we will surely be among the thankful.' "

64. Say, "It is God who saves you from it and from every distress; then you [still] associate others with Him."

65. Say, "He is the [one] Able to send upon you affliction from above you or from beneath your feet or to confuse you [so you become] sects[281] and make you taste the violence of one another." Look how We diversify the signs that they might understand.

66. But your people have denied it while it is the truth. Say, "I am not over you a manager [i.e., authority]."

67. For every news [i.e., happening] is a finality;[282] and you are going to know.

---

[278] The disbelievers would challenge the Prophet, telling him to bring on God's punishment if he should be truthful in his warning.

[279] i.e., when you sleep.

[280] One's decreed life span.

[281] Following your own inclinations rather that the truth, biased and hostile toward each other.

[282] Other shades of meaning include "a permanence," "a realization" and "a time of stability."

68. And when you see those who engage in [offensive] discourse[283] concerning Our verses, then turn away from them until they enter into another conversion. And if Satan should cause you to forget, then do not remain after the reminder with the wrongdoing people.

69. And those who fear God are not held accountable for them [i.e., the disbelievers] at all, but [only for] a reminder - that perhaps they will fear Him.

70. And leave those who take their religion as amusement and diversion and whom the worldly life has deluded. But remind with it [i.e., the Qur'ān], lest a soul be given up to destruction for what it earned; it will have other than God no protector and no intercessor. And if it should offer every compensation, it would not be taken from it [i.e., that soul]. Those are the ones who are given to destruction for what they have earned. For them will be a drink of scalding water and a painful punishment because they used to disbelieve.

71. Say, "Shall we invoke instead of God that which neither benefits us nor harms us and be turned back on our heels after God has guided us? [We would then be] like one whom the devils enticed [to wander] upon the earth confused, [while] he has companions inviting him to guidance, [calling], 'Come to us.' "[284] Say, "Indeed, the guidance of God is the [only] guidance; and we have been commanded to submit to the Lord of the worlds

283 i.e., denials or mockery.

284 The example given is of one who has lost his way and is further confused by the evil ones who tempt him to follow various directions, all leading to destruction. Although his sincere friends call him back to the right path, he ignores them.

72. And to establish prayer and fear Him." And it is He to whom you will be gathered.

73. And it is He who created the heavens and earth in truth. And the day [i.e., whenever] He says, "Be," and it is, His word is the truth.[285] And His is the dominion [on] the Day the Horn is blown. [He is] Knower of the unseen[286] and the witnessed;[287] and He is the Wise, the Acquainted.

74. And [mention, O Muhammad], when Abraham said to his father Āzar, "Do you take idols as deities? Indeed, I see you and your people to be in manifest error."

75. And thus did We show Abraham the realm of the heavens and the earth that he would be among the certain [in faith].

76. So when the night covered him [with darkness], he saw a star. He said, "This is my lord."[288] But when it set, he said, "I like not those that set [i.e., disappear]."

77. And when he saw the moon rising, he said, "This is my lord." But when it set,

285 When interpreted as the "Day" (of resurrection), the sentence would read: "And the Day He says, 'Be,' and it is, His word will be the truth."

286 That which is absent, invisible, or beyond the perception of the senses or of the mind and therefore is unknown to man, except for what God chooses to reveal.

287 What is the present, visible and known to man. The knowledge of God includes the reality of all things and all occurrences, no matter how they might appear to human beings.

288 In verses 76-79, beginning from the People's own assertions, Abraham presents a picture of his dissatisfaction as the only logical conclusion one could reach, in order to show them the futility of their false objects of worship.

he said, "Unless my Lord guides me, I will surely be among the people gone astray."

78. And when he saw the sun rising, he said, "This is my lord; this is greater." But when it set, he said, "O my people, indeed I am free from what you associate with God.

79. Indeed, I have turned my face [i.e., self] toward He who created the heavens and the earth, inclining toward truth, and I am not of those who associate others with God."

80. And his people argued with him. He said, "Do you argue with me concerning God while He has guided me? And I fear not what you associate with Him [and will not be harmed] unless my Lord should will something. My Lord encompasses all things in knowledge; then will you not remember?

81. And how should I fear what you associate while you do not fear that you have associated with God that for which He has not sent down to you any authority? So which of the two parties has more right to security, if you should know?"

82. They who believe and do not mix their belief with injustice[289] - those will have security, and they are [rightly] guided.

83. And that was Our [conclusive] argument which We gave Abraham against his people. We raise by degrees whom We will. Indeed, your Lord is Wise and Knowing.

84. And We gave to him [i.e., Abraham] Isaac and Jacob - all [of them] We guided. And Noah, We guided before; and among his descendants, David and Solomon and Job and Joseph and Moses and Aaron. Thus do We reward the doers of good.

85. And Zechariah and John and Jesus and Elias - and all were of the righteous.

86. And Ishmael and Elisha and Jonah and Lot - and all [of them] We preferred over the worlds.

87. And [some] among their fathers and their descendants and their brothers - and We chose them and We guided them to a straight path.

88. That is the guidance of God by which He guides whomever He wills of His servants. But if they had associated others with God, then worthless for them would be whatever they were doing.

89. Those are the ones to whom We gave the Scripture and authority and prophethood. But if they [i.e., the disbelievers] deny it, then We have entrusted it to a people who are not therein disbelievers.

90. Those are the ones whom God has guided, so from their guidance take an example. Say, "I ask of you for it [i.e., this message] no payment. It is not but a reminder for the worlds."

91. And they did not appraise God with true appraisal[290] when they said, "God did not reveal to a human being anything." Say, "Who revealed the Scripture that Moses brought as light and

[289] Specifically, the association of others in divinity with God.

[290] i.e., they did not appreciate the extent of His ability and wisdom.

guidance to the people? You [Jews] make it into pages, disclosing [some of] it and concealing much. And you[291] were taught that which you knew not - neither you nor your fathers." Say, "God [revealed it]." Then leave them in their [empty] discourse, amusing themselves.

92. And this is a Book which We have sent down, blessed and confirming what was before it, that you may warn the Mother of Cities [i.e., Makkah] and those around it.[292] Those who believe in the Hereafter believe in it, and they are maintaining their prayers.

93. And who is more unjust than one who invents a lie about God or says, "It has been inspired to me," while nothing has been inspired to him, and one who says, "I will reveal [something] like what God revealed." And if you could but see when the wrongdoers are in the overwhelming pangs of death while the angels extend their hands,[293] [saying], "Discharge your souls! Today you will be awarded the punishment of [extreme] humiliation for what you used to say against God other than the truth and [that] you were, toward His verses, being arrogant."

94. [It will be said to them], "And you have certainly come to Us alone [i.e., individually] as We created you the first time, and you have left whatever We bestowed upon you behind you. And We do not see with you your 'intercessors' which you claimed that they were among you associates [of God]. It has [all] been severed between you,[294] and lost from you is what you used to claim."

95. Indeed, God is the cleaver of grain and date seeds.[295] He brings the living out of the dead and brings the dead out of the living. That is God; so how are you deluded?

96. [He is] the cleaver of daybreak and has made the night for rest and the sun and moon for calculation.[296] That is the determination of the Exalted in Might, the Knowing.

97. And it is He who placed for you the stars that you may be guided by them through the darknesses of the land and sea. We have detailed the signs for a people who know.

98. And it is He who produced you from one soul and [gave you] a place of dwelling and of storage.[297] We have detailed the signs for a people who understand.

99. And it is He who sends down rain from the sky, and We produce thereby the growth of all things. We produce from it greenery from which We produce grains arranged in layers. And from the palm trees - of its emerging fruit are clusters hanging low. And [We produce] gardens of grapevines and olives and pomegranates, similar yet varied. Look at [each of] its fruit when it yields and [at] its ripening. Indeed in that are signs for a people who believe.

---

[291] The Jews, or it may refer to the believers, who are taught by the Qur'ān.

[292] i.e., all other peoples.

[293] Striking them, as they are unwilling to give up their souls for judgement.

[294] Between yourselves and the claimed associates and intercessors.

[295] He (God) causes them to split and sprout.

[296] Or "according to calculation," referring to their precise movement.

[297] In the earth. See 77:25-26.

100. But they have attributed to God partners - the jinn, while He has created them - and have fabricated for Him sons and daughters. Exalted is He and high above what they describe.

101. [He is] Originator of the heavens and the earth. How could He have a son when He does not have a companion [i.e., wife] and He created all things? And He is, of all things, Knowing.

102. That is God, your Lord; there is no deity except Him, the Creator of all things, so worship Him. And He is Disposer of all things.

103. Vision perceives Him not,[298] but He perceives [all] vision; and He is the Subtle, the Acquainted.

104. There has come to you enlightenment from your Lord. So whoever will see does so for [the benefit of] his soul, and whoever is blind [does harm] against it. And [say], "I am not a guardian over you." [299]

105. And thus do We diversify the verses so they [i.e., the disbelievers] will say, "You have studied,"[300] and so We may make it [i.e., the Qur'ān] clear for a people who know.

106. Follow, [O Muhammad], what has been revealed to you from your Lord - there is no deity except Him - and turn away from those who associate others with God.

107. But if God had willed, they would not have associated. And We have not appointed you over them as a guardian, nor are you a manager over them.[301]

108. And do not insult those they invoke other than God, lest they insult God in enmity without knowledge. Thus We have made pleasing to every community their deeds. Then to their Lord is their return, and He will inform them about what they used to do.

109. And they swear by God their strongest oaths that if a sign came to them, they would surely believe in it. Say, "The signs are only with [i.e., from] God." And what will make you perceive that even if it [i.e., a sign] came, they would not believe.

110. And We will turn away their hearts and their eyes just as they refused to believe in it [i.e., the revelation] the first time. And We will leave them in their transgression, wandering blindly.

111. And even if We had sent down to them the angels [with the message] and the dead spoke to them [of it] and We gathered together every [created] thing in front of them, they would not believe unless God should will. But most of them, [of that], are ignorant.

112. And thus We have made for every prophet an enemy - devils from mankind and jinn, inspiring to one another decorative speech in delusion. But if your Lord had willed, they would not have done it, so leave them and that which they invent.

298 In the life of this world. The people of Paradise will be able to see God in the Hereafter. See 75:22-23.

299 The Prophet is directed to disassociate himself from all erroneous belief and practice.

300 Accusing the Prophet of having learned from the Jews and Christians.

301 The Prophet's duty did not go beyond delivery of the message.

113. And [it is] so the hearts of those who disbelieve in the Hereafter will incline toward it [i.e., deceptive speech] and that they will be satisfied with it and that they will commit that which they are committing.

114. [Say], "Then is it other than God I should seek as judge while it is He who has revealed to you the Book [i.e., the Qur'ān] explained in detail?" And those to whom We [previously] gave the Scripture know that it is sent down from your Lord in truth, so never be among the doubters.

115. And the word of your Lord has been fulfilled in truth and in justice. None can alter His words, and He is the Hearing, the Knowing.

116. And if you obey most of those upon the earth, they will mislead you from the way of God. They follow not except assumption, and they are not but falsifying.[302]

117. Indeed, your Lord is most knowing of who strays from His way, and He is most knowing of the [rightly] guided.

118. So eat of that [meat] upon which the name of God has been mentioned,[303] if you are believers in His verses [i.e., revealed law].

119. And why should you not eat of that upon which the name of God has been mentioned while He has explained in detail to you what He has forbidden you, excepting that to which you are compelled.[304] And indeed do many lead [others] astray through their [own] inclinations without knowledge. Indeed, your Lord - He is most knowing of the transgressors.

120. And leave [i.e., desist from] what is apparent of sin and what is concealed thereof. Indeed, those who earn [blame for] sin will be recompensed for that which they used to commit.

121. And do not eat of that upon which the name of God has not been mentioned, for indeed, it is grave disobedience. And indeed do the devils inspire their allies [among men] to dispute with you. And if you were to obey them, indeed, you would be associators [of others with Him].[305]

122. And is one who was dead and We gave him life and made for him light by which to walk among the people like one who is in darkness, never to emerge therefrom? Thus it has been made pleasing to the disbelievers that which they were doing.

123. And thus We have placed within every city the greatest of its criminals to conspire therein. But they conspire not except against themselves, and they perceive [it] not.

124. And when a sign comes to them, they say, "Never will we believe until we are given like that which was given to the messengers of God." God is most knowing of where [i.e., with whom] He places His message. There will afflict those who committed crimes debasement before God and severe punishment for what they used to conspire.

[302] Out if ignorance, conjecture and supposition.
[303] At the time of slaughter.
[304] In cases of dire necessity, what is normally prohibited becomes permissible, but only to the extent of the need.

[305] i.e., by your obedience to them - obedience being the bases of worship.

125. So whoever God wants to guide - He expands his breast to [contain] Islām; and whoever He wants to misguide[306] - He makes his breast tight and constricted as though he were climbing into the sky. Thus does God place defilement upon those who do not believe.

126. And this is the path of your Lord, [leading] straight. We have detailed the verses for a people who remember.

127. For them will be the Home of Peace [i.e., Paradise] with their Lord. And He will be their protecting friend because of what they used to do.

128. And [mention, O Muhammad], the Day when He will gather them together [and say], "O company of jinn, you have [misled] many of mankind." And their allies among mankind will say, "Our Lord, some of us made use of others, and we have [now] reached our term which You appointed for us." He will say, "The Fire is your residence, wherein you will abide eternally, except for what God wills. Indeed, your Lord is Wise and Knowing."

129. And thus will We make some of the wrongdoers allies of others for what they used to earn.[307]

130. "O company of jinn and mankind,[308] did there not come to you messengers from among you, relating to you My verses and warning you of the meeting of this Day of yours?" They will say, "We bear witness against ourselves"; and the worldly life had deluded them, and they will bear witness against themselves that they were disbelievers.

131. That is because your Lord would not destroy the cities for wrongdoing[309] while their people were unaware.

132. And for all are degrees [i.e., positions resulting] from what they have done. And your Lord is not unaware of what they do.

133. And your Lord is the Free of need, the possessor of mercy. If He wills, He can do away with you and give succession after you to whomever He wills, just as He produced you from the descendants of another people.

134. Indeed, what you are promised is coming, and you will not cause failure [to God].[310]

135. Say, "O my people, work according to your position; [for] indeed, I am working. And you are going to know who will have succession in the home.[311] Indeed, the wrongdoers will not succeed."

136. And they [i.e., the polytheists] assign to God from that which He created of crops and livestock a share and say, "This is for God," by their claim, "and this is for our 'partners' [associated with Him]." But what is for their "partners" does not reach God, while what is for God - this reaches their "partners." Evil is that which they rule.

---

[306] As a result of the person's arrogance and persistence in sin.

[307] Another interpretation pertaining to this world is "And thus do We make some of the wrongdoers allies of others for what they have been earning."

[308] They will be reproached thus at the Judgement.

[309] Or "unjustly."

[310] i.e., You will neither escape nor prevent its occurrence.

[311] i.e., in the land or in the Hereafter.

137. And likewise, to many of the polytheists their partners[312] have made [to seem] pleasing the killing of their children in order to bring about their destruction and to cover them with confusion in their religion. And if God had willed, they would not have done so. So leave them and that which they invent.

138. And they say, "These animals[313] and crops are forbidden; no one may eat from them except whom we will," by their claim. And there are those [camels] whose backs are forbidden [by them][314] and those upon which the name of God is not mentioned[315] - [all of this] an invention of untruth about Him.[316] He will punish them for what they were inventing.

139. And they say, "What is in the bellies of these animals[317] is exclusively for our males and forbidden to our females. But if it is [born] dead, then all of them have shares therein." He will punish them for their description.[318] Indeed, He is Wise and Knowing.

140. Those will have lost who killed their children in foolishness without knowledge and prohibited what God had provided for them, inventing untruth about God. They have gone astray and were not [rightly] guided.

[312] Their evil associates.
[313] The four categories of grazing livestock called "*an'ām*" collectively.
[314] See 5:103.
[315] At the time of slaughter. Rather, they are dedicated to others among their "deities."
[316] i.e., false assertions that such practices are part of God's religion.
[317] i.e., their milk and offspring.
[318] Of what is lawful and unlawful according to their whims.

141. And He it is who causes gardens to grow, [both] trellised and untrellised, and palm trees and crops of different [kinds of] food and olives and pomegranates, similar and dissimilar. Eat of [each of] its fruit when it yields and give its due [zakāh] on the day of its harvest. And be not excessive.[319] Indeed, He does not like those who commit excess.

142. And of the grazing livestock are carriers [of burdens] and those [too] small. Eat of what God has provided for you and do not follow the footsteps of Satan.[320] Indeed, he is to you a clear enemy.

143. [They are] eight mates - of the sheep, two and of the goats, two. Say, "Is it the two males He has forbidden or the two females or that which the wombs of the two females contain? Inform me with knowledge, if you should be truthful."

144. And of the camels, two and of the cattle, two. Say, "Is it the two males He has forbidden or the two females or that which the wombs of the two females contain? Or were you witnesses when God charged you with this? Then who is more unjust than one who invents a lie about God to mislead the people by [something] other than knowledge? Indeed, God does not guide the wrongdoing people."

145. Say, "I do not find within that which was revealed to me [anything] forbidden to one who would eat it unless it be a dead animal or blood spilled out or the flesh of swine - for indeed, it is impure - or it be [that slaughtered in] disobedience, dedicated to other than God.[321]

[319] In eating, as well as in all things generally.
[320] As the disbelievers have done in making their own rulings about what is permissible and what is prohibited.
[321] Refer to 2:173 and 5:3.

But whoever is forced [by necessity], neither desiring [it] nor transgressing [its limit], then indeed, your Lord is Forgiving and Merciful."

146. And to those who are Jews We prohibited every animal of uncloven hoof; and of the cattle and the sheep We prohibited to them their fat, except what adheres to their backs or the entrails or what is joined with bone. [By] that We repaid them for their injustice. And indeed, We are truthful.

147. So if they deny you, [O Muhammad], say, "Your Lord is the possessor of vast mercy; but His punishment cannot be repelled from the people who are criminals."

148. Those who associated with God will say, "If God had willed, we would not have associated [anything] and neither would our fathers, nor would we have prohibited anything." Likewise did those before deny until they tasted Our punishment. Say, "Do you have any knowledge that you can produce for us? You follow not except assumption, and you are not but falsifying."

149. Say, "With God is the far-reaching [i.e., conclusive] argument. If He had willed, He would have guided you all."

150. Say, [O Muhammad], "Bring forward your witnesses who will testify that God has prohibited this." And if they testify, do not testify with them. And do not follow the desires of those who deny Our verses and those who do not believe in the Hereafter, while they equate [others] with their Lord.

151. Say, "Come, I will recite what your Lord has prohibited to you. [He commands] that you not associate anything with Him, and to parents, good treatment, and do not kill your children out of poverty; We will provide for you and them. And do not approach immoralities - what is apparent of them and what is concealed. And do not kill the soul which God has forbidden [to be killed] except by [legal] right. This has He instructed you that you may use reason."

152. And do not approach the orphan's property except in a way that is best [i.e., intending improvement] until he reaches maturity. And give full measure and weight in justice. We do not charge any soul except [with that within] its capacity. And when you speak [i.e., testify], be just, even if [it concerns] a near relative. And the covenant of God fulfill. This has He instructed you that you may remember.

153. And, [moreover], this is My path, which is straight, so follow it; and do not follow [other] ways, for you will be separated from His way. This has He instructed you that you may become righteous.

154. Then[322] We gave Moses the Scripture, making complete [Our favor] upon the one who did good [i.e., Moses] and as a detailed explanation of all things and as guidance and mercy that perhaps in [the matter of] the meeting with their Lord they would believe.

155. And this [Qur'ān] is a Book We have revealed [which is] blessed, so follow it and fear God that you may receive mercy.

156. [We revealed it] lest you say, "The Scripture was only sent down to two

[322] Meaning "additionally" or "moreover," not denoting time sequence.

groups before us, but we were of their study unaware,"

157. Or lest you say, "If only the Scripture had been revealed to us, we would have been better guided than they." So there has [now] come to you a clear evidence from your Lord and a guidance and mercy. Then who is more unjust than one who denies the verses of God and turns away from them? We will recompense those who turn away from Our verses with the worst of punishment for their having turned away.

158. Do they [then] wait for anything except that the angels should come to them or your Lord should come or that there come some of the signs[323] of your Lord? The Day that some of the signs of your Lord will come no soul will benefit from its faith as long as it had not believed before or had earned through its faith some good. Say, "Wait. Indeed, we [also] are waiting."

159. Indeed, those who have divided their religion and become sects - you, [O Muhammad], are not [associated] with them in anything. Their affair is only [left] to God; then He will inform them about what they used to do.

160. Whoever comes [on the Day of Judgement] with a good deed will have ten times the like thereof [to his credit], and whoever comes with an evil deed will not be recompensed except the like thereof; and they will not be wronged.[324]

161. Say, "Indeed, my Lord has guided me to a straight path - a correct religion - the way of Abraham, inclining toward truth. And he was not among those who associated others with God."

162. Say, "Indeed, my prayer, my rites of sacrifice, my living and my dying are for God, Lord of the worlds.

163. No partner has He. And this I have been commanded, and I am the first [among you] of the Muslims."[325]

164. Say, "Is it other than God I should desire as a lord while He is the Lord of all things? And every soul earns not [blame] except against itself, and no bearer of burdens will bear the burden of another. Then to your Lord is your return, and He will inform you concerning that over which you used to differ."

165. And it is He who has made you successors upon the earth and has raised some of you above others in degrees [of rank] that He may try you through what He has given you. Indeed, your Lord is swift in penalty; but indeed, He is Forgiving and Merciful.

[323] Those denoting the approach of the Last Hour.

[324] i.e., treated unjustly.

[325] i.e., those who submit to the will of God.

## Sūrah 7: al-A'rāf

### Period of Revelation

A study of its contents clearly shows that the period of its revelation is about the same as that of al-An'ām, i.e. the last year of the Prophet's life at Makkah, but it cannot be asserted with certainty which of these two were sent down earlier. Anyhow the manner of its admonition clearly indicates that it belongs to the same period.

### Subject: Invitation to the Divine Message

The principal subject of this Sūrah is "invitation to the Divine Message sent down to Muhammad" which is implied in a warning. This is because the Messenger had spent a long time in admonishing the people of Makkah without any tangible effect on them. Nay, they had turned a deaf ear to his message and become so obdurate and antagonistic that in accordance with the Divine Design, the Messenger was going to be commanded to leave them and turn to other people. That is why they are being admonished to accept the Message but at the same time they are being warned in strong terms of the consequences that followed the wrong attitude of the former people towards their Messengers. Now that the Prophet was going to migrate from Makkah the concluding portion of the address has been directed towards the people of the Book with whom he was going to come into contact. This meant that the time of migration was coming near and the "invitation" was going to be extended to mankind in general and was not to be confined to his own people in particular as before. During the course of the address to the Jews the consequences of their hypocritical conduct towards Prophethood have also been pointed out clearly for they professed to believe in Prophet Moses but in practice opposed his teachings, disobeyed him and worshipped falsehood and consequently were afflicted with humiliation and disgrace.

At the end of the Sūrah some instructions have been given to the Prophet and his followers for carrying out the work of the propagation of Islām with wisdom. The most important of these is that they should show patience and exercise restraint in answer to the provocations of their opponents. Above all they have been advised that under stress of the excitement of feeling they should not take any wrong step that might harm their cause.

## Sūrah 7: al-A'rāf[326]

In the Name of God, the Most Compassionate, the Most Merciful

1. Alif, Lām, Meem, Sād.[327]

2. [This is] a Book revealed to you, [O Muhammad] - so let there not be in your breast distress therefrom - that you may warn thereby and as a reminder to the believers.

3. Follow, [O mankind], what has been revealed to you from your Lord and do not follow other than Him any allies. Little do you remember.

4. And how many cities have We destroyed, and Our punishment came to them at night or while they were sleeping at noon.

5. And their declaration when Our punishment came to them was only that they said, "Indeed, we were wrongdoers!"

6. Then We will surely question those to whom [a message] was sent, and We will surely question the messengers.

7. Then We will surely relate [their deeds] to them with knowledge, and We were not [at all] absent.

8. And the weighing [of deeds] that Day will be the truth. So those whose scales are heavy - it is they who will be the successful.

9. And those whose scales are light - they are the ones who will lose themselves for what injustice they were doing toward Our verses.

10. And We have certainly established you upon the earth and made for you therein ways of livelihood. Little are you grateful.

11. And We have certainly created you, [O mankind], and given you [human] form. Then We said to the angels, "Prostrate to Adam"; so they prostrated, except for Iblees.[328] He was not of those who prostrated.

12. [God] said, "What prevented you from prostrating when I commanded you?" [Satan] said, "I am better than him. You created me from fire and created him from clay [i.e., earth]."

13. [God] said, "Descend from it [i.e., Paradise], for it is not for you to be arrogant therein. So get out; indeed, you are of the debased."

14. [Satan] said, "Reprieve me until the Day they are resurrected."

15. [God] said, "Indeed, you are of those reprieved."

16. [Satan] said, "Because You have put me in error, I will surely sit in wait for them [i.e., mankind] on Your straight path.

17. Then I will come to them from before them and from behind them and on their right and on their left, and You will not find most of them grateful [to You]."

18. [God] said, "Get out of it [i.e., Paradise], reproached and expelled. Whoev-

326 *Al-A'rāf*: The Elevations, referring to the partition between Paradise and Hell.

327 See footnote to 2:1.

328 Satan. See footnote to 2:34.

er follows you among them - I will surely fill Hell with you, all together."

19. And "O Adam, dwell, you and your wife, in Paradise and eat from wherever you will but do not approach this tree, lest you be among the wrongdoers."

20. But Satan whispered to them to make apparent to them that which was concealed from them of their private parts. He said, "Your Lord did not forbid you this tree except that you become angels or become of the immortal."

21. And he swore [by God] to them, "Indeed, I am to you from among the sincere advisors."

22. So he made them fall, through deception. And when they tasted of the tree, their private parts became apparent to them, and they began to fasten together over themselves from the leaves of Paradise. And their Lord called to them, "Did I not forbid you from that tree and tell you that Satan is to you a clear enemy?"

23. They said, "Our Lord, we have wronged ourselves, and if You do not forgive us and have mercy upon us, we will surely be among the losers."

24. [God] said, "Descend, being to one another enemies. And for you on the earth is a place of settlement and enjoyment [i.e., provision] for a time."

25. He said, "Therein you will live, and therein you will die, and from it you will be brought forth."

26. O children of Adam, We have bestowed upon you clothing to conceal your private parts and as adornment. But the clothing of righteousness - that is best. That is from the signs of God that perhaps they will remember.

27. O children of Adam, let not Satan tempt you as he removed your parents from Paradise, stripping them of their clothing[329] to show them their private parts. Indeed, he sees you, he and his tribe, from where you do not see them. Indeed, We have made the devils allies to those who do not believe.

28. And when they commit an immorality, they say, "We found our fathers doing it, and God has ordered us to do it." Say, "Indeed, God does not order immorality. Do you say about God that which you do not know?"

29. Say, [O Muhammad], "My Lord has ordered justice and that you maintain yourselves [in worship of Him] at every place [or time] of prostration, and invoke Him, sincere to Him in religion." Just as He originated you, you will return [to life] -

30. A group [of you] He guided, and a group deserved [to be in] error. Indeed, they [i.e., the latter] had taken the devils as allies instead of God while they thought that they were guided.

31. O children of Adam, take your adornment [i.e., wear your clothing] at every masjid,[330] and eat and drink, but be not excessive. Indeed, He likes not those who commit excess.

32. Say, "Who has forbidden the adornment of [i.e., from] God which He has produced for His servants and the good [lawful] things of provision?" Say,

[329] The garments of Paradise.

[330] Literally, "place of prostration," meaning any place that a Muslim prays upon the earth. The term may also refer specifically to a mosque.

"They are for those who believe during the worldly life [but] exclusively for them on the Day of Resurrection." Thus do We detail the verses for a people who know.

33. Say, "My Lord has only forbidden immoralities - what is apparent of them and what is concealed - and sin,[331] and oppression without right, and that you associate with God that for which He has not sent down authority, and that you say about God that which you do not know."

34. And for every nation is a [specified] term. So when their time has come, they will not remain behind an hour, nor will they precede [it].

35. O children of Adam, if there come to you messengers from among you relating to you My verses [i.e., scriptures and laws], then whoever fears God and reforms - there will be no fear concerning them, nor will they grieve.

36. But the ones who deny Our verses and are arrogant toward them - those are the companions of the Fire; they will abide therein eternally.

37. And who is more unjust than one who invents about God a lie or denies His verses? Those will attain their portion of the decree[332] until, when Our messengers [i.e., angels] come to them to take them in death, they will say, "Where are those you used to invoke besides God?" They will say, "They have departed from us," and will bear witness against themselves that they were disbelievers.

38. [God] will say, "Enter among nations which had passed on before you of jinn and mankind into the Fire." Every time a nation enters, it will curse its sister[333] until, when they have all overtaken one another therein, the last of them[334] will say about the first of them,[335] "Our Lord, these had misled us, so give them a double punishment of the Fire." He will say, "For each is double, but you do not know."

39. And the first of them will say to the last of them, "Then you had not any favor over us, so taste the punishment for what you used to earn."

40. Indeed, those who deny Our verses and are arrogant toward them - the gates of Heaven will not be opened for them, nor will they enter Paradise until a camel enters into the eye of a needle [i.e., never]. And thus do We recompense the criminals.

41. They will have from Hell a bed and over them coverings [of fire]. And thus do We recompense the wrongdoers.

42. But those who believed and did righteous deeds - We charge no soul except [within] its capacity. Those are the companions of Paradise; they will abide therein eternally.

43. And We will have removed whatever is within their breasts of resentment,[336] [while] flowing beneath them are rivers. And they will say, "Praise to God, who has guided us to this; and we would never have been guided if God had not guided us. Certainly the messengers of

331 Any unlawful deed.
332 What is decreed for them.

333 The nation proceeding it.
334 The followers of evil leaders.
335 Their leaders.
336 i.e., ill will or sense of injury for what was inflicted upon them during worldly life.

our Lord had come with the truth." And they will be called, "This is Paradise, which you have been made to inherit for what you used to do."

44. And the companions of Paradise will call out to the companions of the Fire, "We have already found what our Lord promised us to be true. Have you found what your Lord promised to be true?" They will say, "Yes." Then an announcer will announce among them, "The curse of God shall be upon the wrongdoers

45. Who averted [people] from the way of God and sought to make it [seem] deviant while they were, concerning the Hereafter, disbelievers."

46. And between them will be a partition [i.e., wall], and on [its] elevations are men[337] who recognize all[338] by their mark. And they call out to the companions of Paradise, "Peace be upon you." They have not [yet] entered it, but they long intensely.

47. And when their eyes are turned toward the companions of the Fire, they say, "Our Lord, do not place us with the wrongdoing people."

48. And the companions of the Elevations will call to men [within Hell] whom they recognize by their mark, saying, "Of no avail to you was your gathering[339] and [the fact] that you were arrogant."

49. [God will say], "Are these[340] the ones whom you [inhabitants of Hell] swore that God would never offer them mercy? Enter Paradise, [O People of the Elevations]. No fear will there be concerning you, nor will you grieve."

50. And the companions of the Fire will call to the companions of Paradise, "Pour upon us some water or from whatever God has provided you." They will say, "Indeed, God has forbidden them both to the disbelievers

51. Who took their religion as distraction and amusement and whom the worldly life deluded." So today We will forget them just as they forgot the meeting of this Day of theirs and for having rejected Our verses.

52. And We had certainly brought them a Book which We detailed by knowledge - as guidance and mercy to a people who believe.

53. Do they await except its result?[341] The Day its result comes those who had ignored it before will say, "The messengers of our Lord had come with the truth, so are there [now] any intercessors to intercede for us or could we be sent back to do other than what we used to do?" They will have lost themselves, and lost from them is what they used to invent.

54. Indeed, your Lord is God, who created the heavens and earth in six days and then established Himself above the Throne.[342] He covers the night with the

[337] Those whose scales are balanced between good and evil deeds.
[338] Both the inhabitants of Paradise and those of Hell.
[339] i.e., great numbers or gathering of wealth.
[340] The humble believers who are now in Paradise. Another interpretation regards them as the people on the elevated partition.
[341] The fulfilment of what is promised in the Qur'ān.
[342] See footnote to 2:19.

day, [another night] chasing it rapidly; and [He created] the sun, the moon, and the stars, subjected by His command. Unquestionably, His is the creation and the command; blessed is God, Lord of the worlds.

55. Call upon your Lord in humility and privately; indeed, He does not like transgressors.[343]

56. And cause not corruption upon the earth after its reformation. And invoke Him in fear and aspiration. Indeed, the mercy of God is near to the doers of good.

57. And it is He who sends the winds as good tidings before His mercy [i.e., rainfall] until, when they have carried heavy rainclouds, We drive them to a dead land and We send down rain therein and bring forth thereby [some] of all the fruits. Thus will We bring forth the dead; perhaps you may be reminded.

58. And the good land - its vegetation emerges by permission of its Lord; but that which is bad - nothing emerges except sparsely, with difficulty. Thus do We diversify the signs for a people who are grateful.

59. We had certainly sent Noah to his people, and he said, "O my people, worship God; you have no deity other than Him. Indeed, I fear for you the punishment of a tremendous Day."

60. Said the eminent among his people, "Indeed, we see you in clear error."

61. [Noah] said, "O my people, there is not error in me, but I am a messenger from the Lord of the worlds.

62. I convey to you the messages of my Lord and advise you; and I know from God what you do not know.

63. Then do you wonder that there has come to you a reminder from your Lord through a man from among you, that he may warn you and that you may fear God so you might receive mercy?"

64. But they denied him, so We saved him and those who were with him in the ship. And We drowned those who denied Our signs. Indeed, they were a blind people.[344]

65. And to the 'Aad [We sent] their brother Hūd. He said, "O my people, worship God; you have no deity other than Him. Then will you not fear Him?"

66. Said the eminent ones who disbelieved among his people, "Indeed, we see you in foolishness, and indeed, we think you are of the liars."

67. [Hūd] said, "O my people, there is not foolishness in me, but I am a messenger from the Lord of the worlds.

68. I convey to you the messages of my Lord, and I am to you a trustworthy adviser.

69. Then do you wonder that there has come to you a reminder from your Lord through a man from among you, that he may warn you? And remember when He made you successors after the people of Noah and increased you in

343 In supplication or otherwise.

344 For a more detailed account, see 11:25-48.

stature extensively. So remember the favors of God that you might succeed."

70. They said, "Have you come to us that we should worship God alone and leave what our fathers have worshipped? Then bring us what you promise us,[345] if you should be of the truthful."

71. [Hūd] said, "Already have defilement and anger fallen upon you from your Lord. Do you dispute with me concerning [mere] names you have named them,[346] you and your fathers, for which God has not sent down any authority? Then wait; indeed, I am with you among those who wait."

72. So We saved him and those with him by mercy from Us. And We eliminated those who denied Our signs, and they were not [at all] believers.

73. And to the Thamūd [We sent] their brother Sālih. He said, "O my people, worship God; you have no deity other than Him. There has come to you clear evidence from your Lord. This is the she-camel of God [sent] to you as a sign. So leave her to eat within God's land and do not touch her with harm, lest there seize you a painful punishment.

74. And remember when He made you successors after the 'Aad and settled you in the land, [and] you take for yourselves palaces from its plains and carve from the mountains, homes. Then remember the favors of God and do not commit abuse on the earth, spreading corruption."

75. Said the eminent ones who were arrogant among his people to those who were oppressed - to those who believed among them, "Do you [actually] know that Sālih is sent from his Lord?" They said, "Indeed we, in that with which he was sent, are believers."

76. Said those who were arrogant, "Indeed we, in that which you have believed, are disbelievers."

77. So they hamstrung the she-camel and were insolent toward the command of their Lord and said, "O Sālih, bring us what you promise us, if you should be of the messengers."

78. So the earthquake seized them, and they became within their home [corpses] fallen prone.

79. And he [i.e., Sālih] turned away from them and said, "O my people, I had certainly conveyed to you the message of my Lord and advised you, but you do not like advisors."

80. And [We had sent] Lot when he said to his people, "Do you commit such immorality as no one has preceded you with from among the worlds? [i.e., peoples]?

81. Indeed, you approach men with desire, instead of women. Rather, you are a transgressing people."

82. But the answer of his people was only that they said, "Evict them from your city! Indeed, they are men who keep themselves pure."

83. So We saved him and his family, except for his wife; she was of those who remained [with the evildoers].

[345] i.e., God's punishment.

[346] The false objects of worship which you have called "gods."

84. And We rained upon them a rain [of stones]. Then see how was the end of the criminals.

85. And to [the people of] Madyan [We sent] their brother Shu'ayb. He said, "O my people, worship God; you have no deity other than Him. There has come to you clear evidence from your Lord. So fulfill the measure and weight and do not deprive people of their due and cause not corruption upon the earth after its reformation. That is better for you, if you should be believers.

86. And do not sit on every path, threatening and averting from the way of God those who believe in Him, seeking to make it [seem] deviant. And remember when you were few and He increased you. And see how was the end of the corrupters.

87. And if there should be a group among you who has believed in that with which I have been sent and a group that has not believed, then be patient until God judges between us. And He is the best of judges."

88. Said the eminent ones who were arrogant among his people, "We will surely evict you, O Shu'ayb, and those who have believed with you from our city, or you must return to our religion." He said, "Even if we were unwilling?

89. We would have invented against God a lie if we returned to your religion after God had saved us from it. And it is not for us to return to it except that God, our Lord, should will. Our Lord has encompassed all things in knowledge. Upon God we have relied. Our Lord, decide between us and our people in truth, and You are the best of those who give decision."

90. Said the eminent ones who disbelieved among his people, "If you should follow Shu'ayb, indeed, you would then be losers."

91. So the earthquake seized them, and they became within their home [corpses] fallen prone.

92. Those who denied Shu'ayb - it was as though they had never resided there. Those who denied Shu'ayb - it was they who were the losers.

93. And he [i.e., Shu'ayb] turned away from them and said, "O my people, I had certainly conveyed to you the messages of my Lord and advised you, so how could I grieve for a disbelieving people?"

94. And We sent to no city a prophet [who was denied] except that We seized its people with poverty and hardship that they might humble themselves [to God].

95. Then We exchanged in place of the bad [condition], good, until they increased [and prospered] and said, "Our fathers [also] were touched with hardship and ease."[347] So We seized them suddenly while they did not perceive.[348]

96. And if only the people of the cities had believed and feared God, We would have opened [i.e., bestowed] upon them blessings from the heaven and the earth; but they denied [the messengers], so We seized them for what they were earning.[349]

---

[347] Instead of being grateful to God for His blessings, they merely attributed them to the changing fortunes of time.
[348] That they had been tried and tested.
[349] Of blame for their sin.

97. Then did the people of the cities feel secure from Our punishment coming to them at night while they were asleep?

98. Or did the people of the cities feel secure from Our punishment coming to them in the morning while they were at play?[350]

99. Then, did they feel secure from the plan of God? But no one feels secure from the plan of God except the losing people.

100. Has it not become clear to those who inherited the earth after its [previous] people that if We willed, We could afflict them for their sins? But We seal over their hearts so they do not hear.[351]

101. Those cities - We relate to you, [O Muhammad], some of their news. And certainly did their messengers come to them with clear proofs, but they were not to believe in that which they had denied before.[352] Thus does God seal over the hearts of the disbelievers.

102. And We did not find for most of them any covenant;[353] but indeed, We found most of them defiantly disobedient.

103. Then We sent after them Moses with Our signs to Pharaoh and his establishment, but they were unjust toward them.[354] So see how was the end of the corrupters.

[350] i.e., occupied with such activities that have no benefit.
[351] They do not benefit from what they hear.
[352] i.e., they persistently denied every warning given to them.
[353] i.e., they were found to be unfaithful and negligent of God's covenant.
[354] i.e., they rejected and opposed the signs.

104. And Moses said, "O Pharaoh, I am a messenger from the Lord of the worlds

105. [Who is] obligated not to say about God except the truth. I have come to you with clear evidence from your Lord, so send with me the Children of Israel."[355]

106. [Pharaoh] said, "If you have come with a sign, then bring it forth, if you should be of the truthful."

107. So he [i.e., Moses] threw his staff, and suddenly it was a serpent, manifest.[356]

108. And he drew out his hand; thereupon it was white [with radiance] for the observers.

109. Said the eminent among the people of Pharaoh, "Indeed, this is a learned magician

110. Who wants to expel you from your land [through magic], so what do you instruct?"

111. They said,[357] "Postpone [the matter of] him and his brother and send among the cities gatherers

112. Who will bring you every learned magician."

113. And the magicians came to Pharaoh. They said, "Indeed for us is a reward if we are the predominant."

114. He said, "Yes, and, [moreover], you will be among those made near [to me]."

[355] i.e., free them from oppression and allow them to emigrate.
[356] i.e., genuine and not imagined, as a miracle from God.
[357] After mutual consultation and agreement.

115. They said, "O Moses, either you throw [your staff], or we will be the ones to throw [first]."

116. He said, "Throw," and when they threw, they bewitched the eyes of the people and struck terror into them, and they presented a great [feat of] magic.[358]

117. And We inspired to Moses, "Throw your staff," and at once it devoured what they were falsifying.

118 So the truth was established, and abolished was what they were doing.

119. And they [i.e., Pharaoh and his people] were overcome right there and became debased.

120. And the magicians fell down in prostration [to God].

121. They said, "We have believed in the Lord of the worlds,

122. The Lord of Moses and Aaron."

123. Said Pharaoh, "You believed in him[359] before I gave you permission. Indeed, this is a conspiracy which you conspired in the city to expel therefrom its people. But you are going to know.

124. I will surely cut off your hands and your feet on opposite sides; then I will surely crucify you all."

125. They said, "Indeed, to our Lord we will return.

126. And you do not resent us except because we believed in the signs of our Lord when they came to us. Our Lord, pour upon us patience[360] and let us die as Muslims [in submission to You]."

127. And the eminent among the people of Pharaoh said, "Will you leave Moses and his people to cause corruption in the land and abandon you and your gods?" [Pharaoh] said, "We will kill their sons and keep their women alive; and indeed, we are subjugators over them."

128. Said Moses to his people, "Seek help through God and be patient. Indeed, the earth belongs to God. He causes to inherit it whom He wills of His servants. And the [best] outcome is for the righteous."

129. They said, "We have been harmed before you came to us and after you have come to us." He said, "Perhaps your Lord will destroy your enemy and grant you succession in the land and see how you will do."

130. And We certainly seized[361] the people of Pharaoh with years of famine and a deficiency in fruits that perhaps they would be reminded.

131. But when good [i.e., provision] came to them, they said, "This is ours [by right]." And if a bad [condition] struck them, they saw an evil omen in Moses and those with him. Unquestionably, their fortune is with God, but most of them do not know.

132. And they said, "No matter what sign you bring us with which to bewitch us, we will not be believers in you."

358 Their staffs and ropes appeared as withering snakes.

359 i.e., in Moses, avoiding the mention of God.

360 To endure the torture to which we will be subjected.

361 Imposed on them by way of trial and warning.

133. So We sent upon them the flood and locusts and lice and frogs and blood as distinct signs, but they were arrogant and were a criminal people.

134. And when the punishment descended upon them, they said, "O Moses, invoke for us your Lord by what He has promised you. If you [can] remove the punishment from us, we will surely believe you, and we will send with you the Children of Israel."

135. But when We removed the punishment from them until a term which they were to reach,[362] then at once they broke their word.

136. So We took retribution from them, and We drowned them in the sea because they denied Our signs and were heedless of them.

137. And We caused the people who had been oppressed to inherit the eastern regions of the land and the western ones, which We had blessed. And the good word [i.e., decree] of your Lord was fulfilled for the Children of Israel because of what they had patiently endured. And We destroyed [all] that Pharaoh and his people were producing and what they had been building.

138. And We took the Children of Israel across the sea; then they came upon a people intent in devotion to [some] idols of theirs. They [the Children of Israel] said, "O Moses, make for us a god just as they have gods." He said, "Indeed, you are a people behaving ignorantly.

139. Indeed, those [worshippers] - destroyed is that in which they are [engaged], and worthless is whatever they were doing."

140. He said, "Is it other than God I should desire for you as a god[363] while He has preferred you over the worlds?"

141. And [recall, O Children of Israel], when We saved you from the people of Pharaoh, [who were] afflicting you with the worst torment - killing your sons and keeping your women alive. And in that was a great trial from your Lord.

142. And We made an appointment with Moses for thirty nights and perfected them by [the addition of] ten; so the term of his Lord was completed as forty nights. And Moses said to his brother Aaron, "Take my place among my people, do right [by them],[364] and do not follow the way of the corrupters."

143. And when Moses arrived at Our appointed time and his Lord spoke to him, he said, "My Lord, show me [Yourself] that I may look at You." [God] said, "You will not see Me,[365] but look at the mountain; if it should remain in place, then you will see Me." But when his Lord appeared to the mountain, He rendered it level,[366] and Moses fell unconscious. And when he awoke, he said, "Exalted are You! I have repented to You, and I am the first of the believers."

144. [God] said, "O Moses, I have chosen you over the people with My messages and My words [to you]. So take what I have given you and be among the grateful."

---

362 i.e., a specified term which would end with their reversion to disobedience and disbelief.

363 An object of worship.

364 i.e., keep their affairs in order.

365 During the life of this world.

366 It crumbled to dust.

145. And We wrote for him on the tablets [something] of all things - instruction and explanation for all things, [saying], "Take them with determination and order your people to take the best of it. I will show you the home of the defiantly disobedient."[367]

146. I will turn away from My signs those who are arrogant upon the earth without right; and if they should see every sign, they will not believe in it. And if they see the way of consciousness,[368] they will not adopt it as a way; but if they see the way of error, they will adopt it as a way. That is because they have denied Our signs and they were heedless of them.

147. Those who denied Our signs and the meeting of the Hereafter - their deeds have become worthless. Are they recompensed except for what they used to do?

148. And the people of Moses made, after [his departure], from their ornaments a calf - an image having a lowing sound. Did they not see that it could neither speak to them nor guide them to a way? They took it [for worship], and they were wrongdoers.

149. And when regret overcame them[369] and they saw that they had gone astray, they said, "If our Lord does not have mercy upon us and forgive us, we will surely be among the losers."

150. And when Moses returned to his people, angry and grieved, he said, "How wretched is that by which you have replaced me after [my departure]. Were you impatient over the matter of your Lord?" And he threw down the tablets and seized his brother by [the hair of] his head, pulling him toward him. [Aaron] said, "O son of my mother, indeed the people oppressed me and were about to kill me, so let not the enemies rejoice over me[370] and do not place me among the wrongdoing people."

151. [Moses] said, "My Lord, forgive me and my brother and admit us into Your mercy, for You are the most merciful of the merciful."

152. Indeed, those who took the calf [for worship] will obtain anger from their Lord and humiliation in the life of this world, and thus do We recompense the inventors [of falsehood].

153. But those who committed misdeeds and then repented after them and believed - indeed your Lord, thereafter, is Forgiving and Merciful.

154. And when the anger subsided in Moses, he took up the tablets; and in their inscription was guidance and mercy for those who are fearful of their Lord.

155. And Moses chose from his people seventy men for Our appointment.[371] And when the earthquake seized them,[372] he said, "My Lord, if You had willed, You could have destroyed them before and me [as well]. Would You

[367] This is a severe warning from God against rebellion.
[368] i.e., reason and integrity.
[369] Literally, "When their hands had been descended upon," i.e., bitten by them out of severe regret.
[370] i.e., over your humiliation of me.
[371] Whereupon they were to apologize to God for having worshipped the calf.
[372] Upon reaching the appointed place, they said to Moses, "We will not believe until we see God outright." So the mountain convulsed, killing them.

destroy us for what the foolish among us have done? This is not but Your trial by which You send astray whom You will and guide whom You will. You are our Protector, so forgive us and have mercy upon us; and You are the best of forgivers.

156. And decree for us in this world [that which is] good and [also] in the Hereafter; indeed, we have turned back to You." [God] said, "My punishment - I afflict with it whom I will, but My mercy encompasses all things." So I will decree it [especially] for those who fear Me and give zakāh and those who believe in Our verses -

157. Those who follow the Messenger, the unlettered prophet, whom they find written [i.e., mentioned] in what they have of the Torah and the Gospel, who enjoins upon them what is right and forbids them what is wrong and makes lawful for them the good things and prohibits for them the evil and relieves them of their burden[373] and the shackles which were upon them.[374] So they who have believed in him, honoured him, supported him and followed the light which was sent down with him - it is those who will be the successful.

158. Say, [O Muhammad], "O mankind, indeed I am the Messenger of God to you all, [from Him] to whom belongs the dominion of the heavens and the earth. There is no deity except Him; He gives life and causes death." So believe in God and His Messenger, the unlettered prophet, who believes in God and His words, and follow him that you may be guided.

159. And among the people of Moses is a community[375] which guides by truth and by it establishes justice.

160. And We divided them into twelve descendant tribes[376] [as distinct] nations. And We inspired to Moses when his people implored him for water, "Strike with your staff the stone," and there gushed forth from it twelve springs. Every people [i.e., tribe] knew its watering place. And We shaded them with clouds and sent down upon them manna and quails, [saying], "Eat from the good things with which We have provided you." And they wronged Us not, but they were [only] wronging themselves.

161. And [mention, O Muhammad], when it was said to them, "Dwell in this city [i.e., Jerusalem] and eat from it wherever you will and say, 'Relieve us of our burdens [i.e., sins],' and enter the gate bowing humbly; We will [then] forgive you your sins. We will increase the doers of good [in goodness and reward]."

162. But those who wronged among them changed [the words] to a statement other than that which had been said to them. So We sent upon them a punishment from the sky for the wrong that they were doing.

163. And ask them about the town that was by the sea - when they transgressed in [the matter of] the sabbath - when their fish came to them openly on their sab-

373 Difficulties in religious practice.

374 i.e., extreme measure previously required for repentance, and retribution, without recourse to compensation.

375 Those of them who accepted and followed the final prophet, Muhammad.

376 From the twelve sons of Jacob.

bath day, and the day they had no sabbath they did not come to them. Thus did We give them trial because they were defiantly disobedient.

164. And when a community among them said, "Why do you advise [or warn] a people whom God is [about] to destroy or to punish with a severe punishment?" they [the advisors] said, "To be absolved before your Lord and perhaps they may fear Him."

165. And when they [i.e., those advised] forgot that by which they had been reminded, We saved those who had forbidden evil and seized those who wronged, with a wretched punishment, because they were defiantly disobeying.

166. So when they were insolent about that which they had been forbidden, We said to them, "Be apes, despised."

167. And [mention] when your Lord declared that He would surely [continue to] send upon them until the Day of Resurrection those who would afflict them with the worst torment. Indeed, your Lord is swift in penalty; but indeed, He is Forgiving and Merciful.

168. And We divided them throughout the earth into nations. Of them some were righteous, and of them some were otherwise. And We tested them with good [times] and bad that perhaps they would return [to obedience].

169. And there followed them successors who inherited the Scripture [while] taking the commodities[377] of this lower life and saying, "It will be forgiven for us." And if an offer like it[378] comes to them, they will [again] take it. Was not the covenant of the Scripture [i.e., the Torah] taken from them that they would not say about God except the truth, and they studied what was in it? And the home of the Hereafter is better for those who fear God, so will you not use reason?

170. But those who hold fast to the Book [i.e., the Qur'ān] and establish prayer - indeed, We will not allow to be lost the reward of the reformers.

171. And [mention] when We raised the mountain above them as if it was a dark cloud and they were certain that it would fall upon them,[379] [and God said], "Take what We have given you with determination and remember what is in it that you might fear God."

172. And [mention] when your Lord took from the children of Adam - from their loins - their descendants and made them testify of themselves, [saying to them], "Am I not your Lord?" They said, "Yes, we have testified." [This] - lest you should say on the day of Resurrection, "Indeed, we were of this unaware."

173. Or [lest] you say, "It was only that our fathers associated [others in worship] with God before, and we were but descendants after them. Then would You destroy us for what the falsifiers have done?"

174. And thus do We [explain in] detail the verses, and perhaps they will return.[380]

[377] i.e., unlawful gains and pleasures.
[378] i.e., a similar temptation.

[379] For their rebellion and disobedience.
[380] To the way of God, from their diversions and deviations.

175. And recite to them, [O Muhammad], the news of him[381] to whom We gave [knowledge of] Our signs, but he detached himself from them; so Satan pursued him, and he became of the deviators.[382]

176. And if We had willed, We could have elevated him thereby,[383] but he adhered [instead] to the earth[384] and followed his own desire. So his example is like that of the dog: if you chase him, he pants, or if you leave him, he [still] pants. That is the example of the people who denied Our signs.[385] So relate the stories that perhaps they will give thought.

177. How evil an example [is that of] the people who denied Our signs and used to wrong themselves.

178. Whoever God guides - he is the [rightly] guided; and whoever He sends astray[386] - it is those who are the losers.

179. And We have certainly created for Hell many of the jinn and mankind. They have hearts with which they do not understand, they have eyes with which they do not see, and they have ears with which they do not hear. Those are like livestock; rather, they are more astray.[387] It is they who are the heedless.

180. And to God belong the best names, so invoke Him by them. And leave [the company of] those who practice deviation concerning His names.[388] They will be recompensed for what they have been doing.

181. And among those We created is a community[389] which guides by truth and thereby establishes justice.

182. But those who deny Our signs - We will progressively lead them [to destruction][390] from where they do not know.

183. And I will give them time. Indeed, my plan is firm.

184. Then do they not give thought? There is in their companion [i.e., Muhammad] no madness. He is not but a clear warner.

185. Do they not look into the realm of the heavens and the earth and everything that God has created and [think] that perhaps their appointed time has come near? So in what statement [i.e., message] hereafter will they believe?

186. Whoever God sends astray - there is no guide for him. And He leaves them in their transgression, wandering blindly.

187. They ask you, [O Muhammad], about the Hour: when is its arrival?[391] Say,

[381] A man from the Children of Israel at the time of Moses.

[382] Those who deliberately persist in error to the point of destruction.

[383] i.e., through the revelations, signs or evidences of which he had been given knowledge.

[384] i.e., its worldly pleasures.

[385] Whether or not they have been exposed to God's signs or warnings, it is all the same: they will not believe.

[386] As a result of persistence in evil and rejection of truth.

[387] The reference is to their inability (i.e., refusal) to think and reason, while blindly following (as they are accustomed).

[388] i.e., use them improperly or deny them.

[389] The followers of Prophet Muhammad.

[390] God will test them with one favour after another in spite of their disobedience, which only increases them in arrogance and sin.

"Its knowledge is only with my Lord. None will reveal its time except Him. It lays heavily[392] upon the heavens and the earth. It will not come upon you except unexpectedly." They ask you as if you are familiar with it. Say, "Its knowledge is only with God, but most of the people do not know."

188. Say, "I hold not for myself [the power of] benefit or harm, except what God has willed. And if I knew the unseen, I could have acquired much wealth, and no harm would have touched me. I am not except a warner and a bringer of good tidings to a people who believe."

189. It is He who created you from one soul and created from it its mate that he[393] might dwell in security with her. And when he [i.e., man] covers her,[394] she carries a light burden [i.e., a pregnancy] and continues therein. And when it becomes heavy, they both invoke God, their Lord, "If You should give us a good[395] [child], we will surely be among the grateful."

190. But when He gives them a good [child], they[396] ascribe partners to Him concerning that which He has given them. Exalted is God above what they associate with Him.

191. Do they associate with Him those who create nothing and they are [themselves] created?

192. And they [i.e., the false deities] are unable to [give] them help, nor can they help themselves.

193. And if you [believers] invite them to guidance, they will not follow you. It is all the same for you whether you invite them or you are silent.

194. Indeed, those you [polytheists] call upon besides God are servants [i.e., creations] like you. So call upon them and let them respond to you, if you should be truthful.

195. Do they have feet by which they walk? Or do they have hands by which they strike? Or do they have eyes by which they see? Or do they have ears by which they hear? Say, [O Muhammad], "Call your 'partners' and then conspire against me and give me no respite.

196. Indeed, my protector is God, who has sent down the Book; and He is an ally to the righteous.

197. And those you call upon besides Him are unable to help you, nor can they help themselves."

198. And if you invite them to guidance, they do not hear; and you see them looking at you while they do not see.

199. Take what is given freely,[397] enjoin what is good, and turn away from the ignorant.

200. And if an evil suggestion comes to you from Satan, then seek refuge in God. Indeed, He is Hearing and Knowing.

391 Literally, "resting" or "establishment."

392 i.e., it is a source of concern, worry or fear.

393 i.e., man or every descendent of Adam.

394 An allusion to sexual intercourse.

395 Physically sound or righteous.

396 The ungrateful man and woman or the polytheistic man and woman.

397 From the disposition of men or from their wealth. In other words, be easy in dealing with them and avoid causing them difficulty.

201. Indeed, those who fear God - when an impulse touches them from Satan, they remember [Him] and at once they have insight.

202. But their brothers[398] - they [i.e., the devils] increase them in error; then they do not stop short.

203. And when you, [O Muhammad], do not bring them a sign [i.e., miracle], they say, "Why have you not contrived it?" Say, "I only follow what is revealed to me from my Lord. This [Qur'ān] is enlightenment from your Lord and guidance and mercy for a people who believe."

204. So when the Qur'ān is recited, then listen to it and pay attention that you may receive mercy.

205. And remember your Lord within yourself in humility and in fear without being apparent in speech - in the mornings and the evenings. And do not be among the heedless.

206. Indeed, those who are near your Lord [i.e., the angels] are not prevented by arrogance from His worship, and they exalt Him, and to Him they prostrate.

[398] Those among mankind who listen to the devils and obey their orders.

## Sūrah 8: al-Anfāl

### The Period of Revelation

It was revealed in 2 A.H. after the Battle of Badr, the first battle between Islām and Kufr (disbelief). As it contains a detailed and comprehensive review of the Battle it appears that most probably it was revealed all at once at the same time. But it is also possible that some of the verses concerning the problems arising as a result of this Battle might have been revealed later and incorporated at the proper places to make it a continuous whole.

### Historical Background

Before reviewing the Sūrah it is worthwhile to consider the events that led to the Battle of Badr. During the first decade or so of the Prophethood at Makkah the Message had proved its firmness and stability. This was the result of two things. First the Messenger who possessed the highest qualities of character was performing his Mission with wisdom foresight and magnanimity. He had shown by his conduct that he had made up his mind to carry the movement to a successful end and therefore was ready to face all sorts of dangers and obstacles in the way. Secondly the Message was so charming that it attracted the minds and hearts of the people irresistibly towards itself. So much so that all obstacles of ignorance superstition and petty prejudices failed to check its advance. That is why the Arab upholders of the ways of 'ignorance' who looked down upon it in its initial stages had begun to reckon it as a serious menace during the last period of the stay of the Prophet at Makkah and were bent on crushing it with all the force at their command. But in spite of the above-mentioned strength the movement still lacked certain things to lead it to victory.

First, it had not yet been fully proved that it had gathered round it a sufficient number of such followers who not only believed in its truth but also had such an intense devotion to its principles that they were ready to expend all their energies and all that they possessed in the struggle for its success and establishment. So much so that they were ready to sacrifice their lives in the fight against the whole world itself even though they should be their own nearest relative. It is true that the followers of Islām had endured the severest persecutions at the hands of the Quraysh of Makkah and had given a good proof of the firmness of their faith and their strong relation with Islām yet further trials were required to show that Islām had succeeded in acquiring such a band of followers which considered nothing dearer than its ideal and was ready to sacrifice life for it.

Secondly though the voice of Islām had reached every part of the country its effects were yet scattered and its acquired strength was spread here and there: it had not yet gathered sufficient force essential for a decisive conflict with the old established order of 'ignorance'.

Thirdly Islām had yet no home of its own and had not established itself firmly anywhere in the land where it could consolidate its power and make it a base for further action. For the Muslims were scattered all over the country and were living among the unbelievers as aliens whom their bloodthirsty enemies wanted to uproot from their own homes.

Fourthly, the Muslims had not yet had an opportunity to demonstrate practically the blessings of the system of life based on Islām. There was neither any Islāmic culture, nor any social, economic or political system; nor were there any established principles of war and peace for their guidance. Therefore the Muslims had no opportunity for demonstrating those moral principles on which they intended to build their entire system of life; nor had it been proved on the touchstone of trial that the Muslims as a community were sincere in the proclamation of the Message. God created opportunities for making up these deficiencies. During the last four years of the Prophet's stay at Makkah, the voice of Islām had been proving effective at Yathrib (Madinah) and the people for various reasons had been accepting the message more readily than other clans of

Arabia. So much so that in the twelfth year of Prophethood on the occasion of Hajj a deputation of 75 people met the Prophet in the darkness of night. These people not only accepted Islām, but also offered to give him and his followers a home. As this was a most epoch making opportunity provided by God, the Prophet took advantage of it. The significance of this offer was quite clear to the people of Yathrib, and they fully realized that this was not an invitation to a mere fugitive, but to the Messenger of God so that he should become their leader and ruler. Likewise they knew that they were not inviting the Muslim refugees to give them shelter from persecution but to assemble them from all over the country for their integration with themselves to form an organized community. Thus the offer of the people of Yathrib was to make Yathrib the "City of Islām." Accordingly the Prophet accepted their invitation and made it the first "City of Islām" in Arabia. And the people of Yathrib were fully aware of the implications of this offer. It was indeed a declaration of war against the whole of Arabia, and an invitation to their own social and economic boycott as well. And when the Ansār from Yathrib declared their allegiance to the Prophet at Aqabah, they knew fully well its consequences. During the course of the formal declaration of allegiance, Asad bin Zurarah, the youngest of all the delegates from Yathrib, stood up and said, "*O people of Yathrib! Just listen to me and consider the matter carefully in all its aspects. Though we have come to him, regarding him only as a Messenger of God, we should know that we shall be inviting the enmity of the whole of Arabia. For when we take him away to Yathrib, we shall be attacked and our children may be put to the sword. Therefore if you have the courage in your hearts to face it, then and then only, you should declare your allegiance to him and God will give you its reward. But if you love your lives more than him and his Message, then leave this matter and frankly excuse yourselves, for at this time God may accept your excuses.*"

Abbas bin Ubadah bin Naalah, another member of the delegation, reiterated the same thing, saying, *Do you understand the implication of the declaration of your allegiance to this person?*" (Voices, "*Yes, we know it.*") "*You are challenging the whole world to war by your declaration of allegiance to him. There is every likelihood of a serious menace to your lives and properties. Therefore consider it well. If you have any idea lurking in your minds that you will then hand him over to his enemies, it is much better to leave him alone now, because that conduct shall bring shame and disgrace to you in this world and the next. On the other hand, if you have sincerely resolved that you will endure all kinds of consequences that will follow as a result of this invitation, then it would be the best thing to take the oath of allegiance to him because, by God, this will surely bring good to you in this world as well as in the next world.*" At this all the members of the delegation cried with one voice, "*We are ready and prepared to risk all our wealth and our noble kith and kin for his sake.*" It was then that the famous oath of allegiance, which is known as the "Second Oath of Allegiance at Aqabah" was taken.

On the other side, the people of Makkah also understood fully well the implications of this matter from their own point of view. They realized that Muhammad, who they knew well, had a great personality and possessed extraordinary abilities, was going to gain a strong footing, by this allegiance. For this would help integrate his followers, whose constancy, determination, and unwavering faithfulness to the Messenger had been tried, into a disciplined community under his wise leadership and guidance. And they knew that this would spell death for their old ways of life. They also realized the strategic importance of Madinah to their trade, which was their chief means of livelihood. Its geographical position was such that the Muslims could strike with advantage at the caravans traveling on the trade route between Yemen and Syria, and thus strike at the root of their economy and that of other pagan clans very effectively. The value of the trade done by the people of Makkah alone on this route, not to count that of tā'if and other places, amounted to about two hundred thousand dinars annually. As the Quraysh were fully aware of the implications of the oath of allegiance at Aqabah, they were greatly agitated when they got wind of it the same night. At first they tried to win over the people of Madinah to their side. But when they saw that the Muslims were migrating to Madinah in small groups, they realized that the Prophet was also going to emigrate soon from there. Then they decided to adopt an extreme measure to prevent this danger. A few days before his migration, the Quraysh held a council to consider the matter. After a good deal of argument; they decided that one person should be taken from each of the families of Quraysh other than that of Banu Hashim to put an end to the life of the Prophet. This was to make it difficult for the family of the Prophet to fight alone with all the other families of the Quraysh and thus to force them to accept blood-money for his murder instead of taking revenge from them, but by the grace of God their plot against the life of the Prophet failed because of his admirable foresight and full trust in God, and he reached Madinah safe and sound. When they could not prevent his emigration, it occurred to them to exploit Abdullah bin Ubay who had begun to cherish a grievance against the Prophet since his arrival at Madinah. He was an influential chief of Madinah and the people had agreed to make him their king. But when the majority of Aws and Khazraj clan became Muslims and acknowledged the Prophet as their leader, guide and ruler, all his hopes of becoming a king came to an end. Therefore the Quraysh wrote to him, "*As you have given shelter to our enemy, we tell you plainly that you should either fight with him yourself or exile him from your city otherwise we swear by God that we will invade your city, kill your males and make your females our slave girls.*" This letter added fuel to the flames of his jealousy and he was inclined to do some mischief, but the Prophet took timely precautions and defeated his evil designs. The Quraysh got another opportunity to hold out a threat. When Sa'ad bin Mu'adh, another chief of Madinah, went to Makkah to perform Umrah, Abu Jahl interrupted him at the very door of the Ka'bāh, saying, "*Do you think we will let you perform Umrah in peace when you give shelter and help to renegades from us? Had you not been a guest of Ummayyah bin Khalf, you would not have gone alive from here.*" Sa'ad replied, "*By God, if you prevent me from this, I will retaliate in a worse manner and block your route near Madinah.*" This incident virtually led to a declaration from the people of Makkah that they would prevent the Muslims from a pilgrimage to the Ka'bāh, and from the people of Madinah that as a retaliation they would block their trade route to Syria against the opponents of Islām. As a matter of fact there was no other alternative for the Muslims than to keep a strong hold on this route so as to force the Quraysh, and the other clans, whose interests were vitally bound with this route, to reconsider their hostile and antagonistic attitude towards them. That is why the Prophet attached the greatest importance to this problem. As soon as he was free from making the preliminary arrangements for organizing the newly formed Muslim Community and settling peace terms with the neighboring Jewish tribes, he adopted two measures in this connection.

First, he entered into negotiations with those clans who lived between the Red Sea and this route so as to make alliances with them or at east to persuade them to make treaties of neutrality with the Muslims. He was successful in this, and he entered into a treaty of non-alignment with Juhainah, which was a very important clan of the hilly tract near the sea coast. Then, at the end of the first year of Hijrah, he made a treaty of defensive alliance with Bani Damrah. In 2 A.H. Bani Mudlij also joined the alliance, as they were the neighbours and allies of Bani Damrah. Then it so happened that quite a large number of these people were reverted to Islām as a result of the missionary work done by the Muslims.

Secondly, he successively sent small bands of his men on this route to serve as a warning to the Quraysh, and himself accompanied some of them. In the first year of Hijrah, four expeditions were sent there, that is, the expedition under Hamza, the expedition under Ubaidah bin Harith, the expedition under Sa'ad bin Abi Waqqas and the Al-Abwa expedition under the Prophet himself. In the first month of the second year two more incursions were made on the same route. These are known as Buwat Expedition and Zawal Ushairah Expedition. Two things about all these expeditions are noteworthy. First, no blood was shed and no caravans were plundered in any of these expeditions. This proves that the real object of these expeditions was to show to the Quraysh which way the wind was blowing. Secondly, not a single man from the people of Madinah was sent by the Prophet on any of these incursions. All the bands consisted purely of the immigrants from Makkah so that the conflict should remain between the people of the Quraysh themselves and should not further spread by the involvement of other clans. On the other side, the Quraysh of Makkah tried to involve others also in the conflict. When they sent bands towards Madinah, they did not hesitate to plunder the people. For instance, an expedition under the leadership of Kurz bin Jabir al-Fihrl plundered the cattle of the people of Madinah from the very vicinity of the city to show what their real intentions were.

This was the state of affairs when, in Sha'aban, 2 A.H. (February or March, 623 A.D.) a big trade caravan of the Quraysh, carrying goods worth about £50,000, with only a guard of thirty to forty men, on its way back from Syria to Makkah, reached the territory from where it could be easily attacked from Madinah. As the caravan was carrying trade goods worth thousands of pounds, and was scantily guarded, naturally Abu Sufyan, who was in charge of it, from his past experience feared an attack from the Muslims. Accordingly, as soon as he entered the dangerous territory, he despatched a camel rider to Makkah with a frantic appeal for help. When the rider reached Makkah, he, following an old custom of Arabia, tore open the ears of his camel, cut open his nose and overturned the saddle. He began to cry aloud at the top of his voice, "*O people of Quraysh despatch help to protect your caravan from Syria under the charge of Abu Sufyan, for Muhammad with his followers is in pursuit of it; otherwise I don't think you will ever get your goods. Run, run for help.*" This caused great excitement and anger in the whole of Makkah and all the big chiefs of the Quraysh got ready for war. An army, consisting of 600 armoured soldiers and cavalry of 100 riders with great pomp and show marched out for a fight. They intended not only to rescue the caravan but also to put to an end, once for all, the new menace from the Muslims who had consolidated themselves at Madinah. They wanted to crush that rising power and overawe the clans surrounding the route so as to make it absolutely secure for future trade. Now the Prophet, who always kept himself well informed of the state of affairs, felt that the decisive hour has come and that was the right time when he must take a bold step; otherwise the Islāmic Movement would become lifeless for ever and no chance would be left for it to rise again. For if the Quraysh invaded Madinah, the odds would be against the Muslims. The condition of the Muslim Community was still very shaky because the Muhajirin (immigrants) had not been able to stabilize their economy during the short period (less than two years) of their stay at Madinah; their helpers, the Ansār had not yet been tried; and the neighbouring Jewish clans were antagonistic. Then there was a strong group of hypocrites and polytheists in Madinah itself; above all, the surrounding clans lived in awe of the Quraysh and had all their religious sympathies with them. The Prophet, therefore, felt that the consequences of this possible invasion would not be favorable to the Muslims. The second possibility was that they would not invade Madinah but try only to escort their caravan safely and securely by a mere show of force. In that case, too, if the Muslims remained inactive, it would affect their reputation adversely. Obviously, this weak stand in the conflict would embolden the other Arabs also and make the position of the Muslims very insecure in the country and the surrounding clans would, at the instance of the Quraysh, start hostilities against them. And the Jews, the hypocrites and the polytheists of Madinah would openly rise against them and not only endanger their security of life, property and honour but make it difficult for them even to live there. The Muslims would not be able to inspire the enemy with awe so as to keep safe from them their life, property and honour. A careful study of the situation led the Prophet to make up his mind to take a decisive step and go into the battle with whatever little strength he could muster, for thus and thus only could he show whether the Muslim Community had the right to survive or was doomed to perish.

When he arrived at this momentous decision, he called the Muhajirin and the Ansār together and placed the whole position before them, without any reservation. He said, "*God has promised that you will confront one of the two, the trade caravan coming from the north or the army of the Quraysh marching from the south. Now tell me which of the two you want to attack!*" A large majority of the people replied that they wanted to attack the caravan. But the Prophet who had something else before him, repeated the same question. At this Miqdad bin 'Amr, a Muhajir, stood up and said, "*O Messenger of God! Please march to the side to which your Lord commands you; we will accompany you wherever you go. We will not say like the Israelites, 'Go and let you and your Lord fight we will wait'. In contrast to them we say, 'Let you and your Lord fight; we will fight by your side to our last breath'.*" Even then he did not announce any decision but waited for a reply from the Ansār who had not yet taken any part in any battle of Islām. As this was the first opportunity for them to prove that they were ready to fulfill their promise of fighting for the cause of Islām, he repeated the question without directly addressing them. At this, Sa'ad bin Mu'adh, an Ansār, stood up and said, "*...it appears that you are putting the question to us.*" When the Prophet said, "*Yes,*" the Ansār replied, "*We have believed in you and confirmed that what you have brought is the Truth, and have made a solemn pledge with you that we will listen to you and obey you. Therefore, O Messenger of God, do whatever you intend to do. We swear by God Who has sent you with the Truth that we are ready to accompany you to the sea shore and if you enter it, we will plunge into it. We assure you that not a single one of us will remain behind or forsake you, for we will not hesitate at all to go to fight, even if you should lead us to the battlefield tomorrow. We will remain steadfast in the battle and sacrifice our lives in the fight. We do hope that by the grace of God our behavior will gladden your heart. So, trusting in God's blessing, take us to the battlefield.*" After these speeches it was decided that they should march towards the army of the Quraysh and not towards the trade caravan. But it should be noted that the decision was of an ordinary nature. For the number of people, who came forward to go to the battlefield, was only a little more than three hundred (86 Muhajirs, 62 from Aws and 170 from Khazraj). Then the little army was ill-armed and hardly equipped for battle. Only a couple of them had horses to ride and the others had to take their turn in threes and fours on the back of a camel, out of the 70 they had in all. Above all, they had not got enough weapons for the battle; only 60 of them had armor. It is, therefore, no wonder that with the exception of those who were prepared to sacrifice their lives for the cause of Islām, the majority of those who had joined the expedition, were so filled with fear that they felt as if they were knowingly going into the jaws of death. Then there were people who always looked at things from a selfish point of view. Though they had embraced Islām, they did not realize that their faith would demand the sacrifice of their lives and properties from them; they were of the opinion that it was a mad expedition prompted by irrational enthusiasm for religion. But the Prophet and the true Believers had realized the urgency of that critical hour which required the risk of life: therefore they marched straight to the south-west, wherefrom the army of the Quraysh was coming. This is a clear proof of the fact that from the very beginning they had gone out to fight with the army and not to plunder the caravan. For if they had aimed at plundering the caravan they would have taken the north-westerly direction and not the south-westerly one.

The two parties met in combat at Badr on the 17th of Ramadan. When the two armies confronted each other and the Prophet noticed that the Quraysh army outnumbered the Muslims by three to one and was much better equipped, he raised his hands up in supplication and made this earnest prayer with great humility: "*O God! Here are the Quraysh proud of their war material: they have come to prove that Thy Messenger is false. O God! now send that succor that Thou hast promised to give me. O God! If this little army of Thy servants is destroyed, then there will be left none in the land to worship Thee.*" In this combat the emigrants from Makkah were put to the hardest test for they had to fight against their own near and dear relatives and put to the sword their fathers, their sons, their paternal and maternal uncles and their brothers. It is obvious that only such people could have come out successful in this hardest of tests as had accepted the Truth sincerely and cut off all relations with falsehood. And in another way the test to which the Ansār were put was not less hard. So far they had only alienated the powerful Quraysh and their allies by giving shelter to the Muslims against their wishes but now, for the first time, they were going to give fight to them and to sow the seeds of a long and bitter war with them. This was indeed a very hard test for it meant that a small town with a population of a few thousand inhabitants was going to wage a war with the whole of Arabia. It is obvious that only such people could take this bold step who believed in the Truth of Islām so firmly that they were ready to sacrifice every personal interest for its sake. So God accepted the self-sacrifices of the Muhajirin and the Ansār because of their true faith, and rewarded them with His succor. The proud, well-armed Quraysh were routed by these ill-equipped devotees of Islām. Seventy men of their army were killed and seventy captured as prisoners and their arms and equipment came into the hands of the Muslims as spoils of war. All their big chiefs, who were their best soldiers and who had led the opposition to Islām, were killed in this Battle. No wonder that this decisive victory made Islām a power to be reckoned with.

**Topics of Discussion**

The moral lesson of the conflict between the Truth and falsehood has been enunciated and the qualities which lead to success in a conflict have been explained. The Sūrah gives instructions in regard to the spoils of war. The Muslims have been told not to regard these as their right but as a bounty from God. Therefore they should accept with gratitude the share that is granted to them out of it and willingly accede to the share which God sets apart for His cause and for the help of the needy. Then it also gives normal instructions concerning the laws of peace and war for these were urgently needed to be explained at the stage which the Islāmic Movement had entered. It enjoined that the Muslims should refrain from ways of "ignorance" in peace and war and thus should establish their moral superiority in the world. It also meant to demonstrate to the world in actual practical life the morality which it had been preaching to the world from the very beginning of Islām and had been enjoining that practical life should be based on the same. It also states some articles of the Islāmic Constitution which help differentiate the status of the Muslims living within the limits of Dar-ul-Islām (the Abode of Islām) from that of the Muslims living beyond its limits.

## Sūrah 8: al-Anfāl[399]

In the Name of God, the Most Compassionate, the Most Merciful

1. They ask you, [O Muhammad], about the bounties [of war]. Say, "The [decision concerning] bounties is for God and the Messenger." So fear God and amend that which is between you and obey God and His Messenger, if you should be believers.

2. The believers are only those who, when God is mentioned, their hearts become fearful, and when His verses are recited to them, it increases them in faith; and upon their Lord they rely -

3. The ones who establish prayer, and from what We have provided them, they spend.

4. Those are the believers, truly. For them are degrees [of high position] with their Lord and forgiveness and noble provision.

5. [It[400] is] just as when your Lord brought you out of your home [for the battle of Badr] in truth, while indeed, a party among the believers were unwilling,

6. Arguing with you concerning the truth after it had become clear, as if they were being driven toward death while they were looking on.

7. [Remember, O believers], when God promised you one of the two groups[401] - that it would be yours - and you wished that the unarmed one would be yours. But God intended to establish the truth by His words and to eliminate the disbelievers

8. That He should establish the truth and abolish falsehood, even if the criminals disliked it.

9. [Remember] when you asked help of your Lord, and He answered you, "Indeed, I will reinforce you with a thousand from the angels, following one another."

10. And God made it not but good tidings and so that your hearts would be assured thereby. And victory is not but from God. Indeed, God is Exalted in Might and Wise.

11. [Remember] when He overwhelmed you with drowsiness [giving] security from Him and sent down upon you from the sky, rain by which to purify you and remove from you the evil [suggestions] of Satan and to make steadfast your hearts and plant firmly thereby your feet.

12. [Remember] when your Lord inspired to the angels, "I am with you, so strengthen those who have believed. I will cast terror into the hearts of those who disbelieved, so strike [them] upon the necks and strike from them every fingertip."[402]

13. That is because they opposed God and His Messenger. And whoever opposes God and His Messenger - indeed, God is severe in penalty.

---

[399] *Al-Anfāl:* The Bounties, meaning those things acquired in addition to victory, i.e., the spoils of war.

[400] Referring to a dispute which occurred among the Muslims over distribution of war booty.

[401] i.e., either the caravan of Quraysh or their army.

[402] By which they grasp and manipulate their weapons. Also interpreted as "all extremities," i.e., their hands and feet.

14. "That [is yours], so taste it." And indeed for the disbelievers is the punishment of the Fire.

15. O you who have believed, when you meet those who disbelieve advancing [for battle], do not turn to them your backs [in flight].

16. And whoever turns his back to them on such a day, unless swerving [as a strategy] for war or joining [another] company, has certainly returned with anger [upon him] from God, and his refuge is Hell - and wretched is the destination.

17. And you did not kill them, but it was God who killed them.[403] And you threw not, [O Muhammad], when you threw, but it was God who threw[404] that He might test the believers with a good test.[405] Indeed, God is Hearing and Knowing.

18. That [is so], and [also] that God will weaken the plot of the disbelievers.

19. If you [disbelievers] seek the decision [i.e., victory] - the decision [i.e., defeat] has come to you. And if you desist [from hostilities], it is best for you; but if you return [to war], We will return, and never will you be availed by your [large] company at all, even if it should increase; and [that is] because God is with the believers.

403 i.e., Your strength was insufficient to overcome them, but God supported you and gave you victory.

404 When the Prophet threw a handful of dust into the faces of the disbelievers, God caused it to fill the eyes and nose of every soldier, preventing their advance.

405 So that they would appreciate God's favour to them.

20. O you who have believed, obey God and His Messenger and do not turn from him while you hear [his order].

21. And do not be like those who say, "We have heard," while they do not hear.

22. Indeed, the worst of living creatures in the sight of God are the deaf and dumb who do not use reason [i.e., the disbelievers].

23. Had God known any good in them, He would have made them hear. And if He had made them hear, they would [still] have turned away, while they were refusing.

24. O you who have believed, respond to God and to the Messenger when he calls you to that which gives you life. And know that God intervenes between a man and his heart and that to Him you will be gathered.

25. And fear a trial[406] which will not strike those who have wronged among you exclusively, and know that God is severe in penalty.

26. And remember when you were few and oppressed in the land, fearing that people might abduct you, but He sheltered you, supported you with His victory, and provided you with good things - that you might be grateful.

27. O you who have believed, do not betray God and the Messenger or betray your trusts while you know [the consequence].

406 i.e., an affliction or punishment during life upon this earth. When corruption spreads among a people, its consequences will affect everyone.

28. And know that your properties and your children are but a trial and that God has with Him a great reward.

29. O you who have believed, if you fear God, He will grant you a criterion[407] and will remove from you your misdeeds and forgive you. And God is the possessor of great bounty.

30. And [remember, O Muhammad], when those who disbelieved plotted against you to restrain you or kill you or evict you [from Makkah]. But they plan, and God plans. And God is the best of planners.

31. And when Our verses are recited to them, they say, "We have heard. If we willed, we could say [something] like this. This is not but legends of the former peoples."

32. And [remember] when they said, "O God, if this should be the truth from You, then rain down upon us stones from the sky or bring us a painful punishment."

33. But God would not punish them while you, [O Muhammad], are among them, and God would not punish them while they seek forgiveness.

34. But why should God not punish them while they obstruct [people] from al-Masjid al-Harām and they were not [fit to be] its guardians? Its [true] guardians are not but the righteous, but most of them do not know.

35. And their prayer at the House [i.e., the Ka'bāh] was not except whistling and handclapping. So taste the punishment for what you disbelieved [i.e., practiced of deviations].

36. Indeed, those who disbelieve spend their wealth to avert [people] from the way of God. So they will spend it; then it will be for them a [source of] regret; then they will be overcome. And those who have disbelieved - unto Hell they will be gathered.

37. [This is] so that God may distinguish the wicked from the good and place the wicked some of them upon others and heap them all together and put them into Hell. It is those who are the losers.

38. Say to those who have disbelieved [that] if they cease, what has previously occurred will be forgiven for them. But if they return [to hostility] - then the precedent of the former [rebellious] peoples has already taken place.[408]

39. And fight them until there is no fitnah[409] and [until] the religion [i.e., worship], all of it, is for God.[410] And if they cease - then indeed, God is Seeing of what they do.

40. But if they turn away - then know that God is your protector. Excellent is the protector, and Excellent is the helper.

41. And know that anything you obtain of war booty - then indeed, for God is one fifth of it and for the Messenger[411] and for [his] near relatives[412] and the or-

[407] By which to judge between truth and falsehood. Also interpreted as a "way out" of difficulties.

[408] This is a warning that punishment is always the result of rebellion against God and His messengers.

[409] Persecution. See footnote to 2:193.

[410] i.e., until polytheism is no longer dominant.

[411] To be sent in God's cause.

[412] The tribes of Banū Hāshim and Banū Muttalib, who were not eligible for *zakāh*.

phans, the needy, and the [stranded] traveler,[413] if you have believed in God and in that which We sent down to Our Servant[414] on the day of criterion [i.e., decisive encounter] - the day when the two armies met [at Badr]. And God, over all things, is competent.

42. [Remember] when you were on the near side of the valley, and they were on the farther side, and the caravan was lower [in position] than you. If you had made an appointment [to meet], you would have missed the appointment. But [it was] so that God might accomplish a matter already destined - that those who perished [through disbelief] would perish upon evidence and those who lived [in faith] would live upon evidence; and indeed, God is Hearing and Knowing.

43. [Remember, O Muhammad], when God showed them to you in your dream as few; and if He had shown them to you as many, you [believers] would have lost courage and would have disputed in the matter [of whether to fight], but God saved [you from that]. Indeed, He is Knowing of that within the breasts.

44. And [remember] when He showed them to you, when you met, as few in your eyes, and He made you [appear] as few in their eyes so that God might accomplish a matter already destined. And to God are [all] matters returned.

45. O you who have believed, when you encounter a company [from the enemy forces], stand firm and remember God much that you may be successful.

[413] The remaining four fifths are divided among the soldiers.
[414] Prophet Muhammad.

46. And obey God and His Messenger, and do not dispute and [thus] lose courage and [then] your strength would depart; and be patient. Indeed, God is with the patient.

47. And do not be like those who came forth from their homes insolently and to be seen by people and avert [them] from the way of God. And God is encompassing[415] of what they do.

48. And [remember] when Satan made their deeds pleasing to them and said, "No one can overcome you today from among the people, and indeed, I am your protector." But when the two armies sighted each other, he turned on his heels and said, "Indeed, I am disassociated from you. Indeed, I see what you do not see; indeed I fear God. And God is severe in penalty."

49. [Remember] when the hypocrites and those in whose hearts was disease [i.e., arrogance and disbelief] said, "Their religion has deluded those [Muslims]." But whoever relies upon God - then indeed, God is Exalted in Might and Wise.

50. And if you could but see when the angels take the souls of those who disbelieved...[416] They are striking their faces and their backs and [saying], "Taste the punishment of the Burning Fire.

51. That is for what your hands have put forth [of evil] and because God is not ever unjust to His servants."

[415] In knowledge. See footnote to 2:19.
[416] This sentence is left incomplete for additional effect. Its conclusion is left to the imagination of the reader or listener and estimated as "... you would see a dreadful sight."

52. [Theirs is] like the custom of the people of Pharaoh and of those before them. They disbelieved in the signs of God, so God seized them for their sins. Indeed, God is Powerful and severe in penalty.

53. That is because God would not change a favor which He had bestowed upon a people until they change what is within themselves. And indeed, God is Hearing and Knowing.

54. [Theirs is] like the custom of the people of Pharaoh and of those before them. They denied the signs of their Lord, so We destroyed them for their sins, and We drowned the people of Pharaoh. And all [of them] were wrongdoers.

55. Indeed, the worst of living creatures in the sight of God are those who have disbelieved, and they will not [ever] believe -

56. The ones with whom you made a treaty but then they break their pledge every time, and they do not fear God.

57. So if you, [O Muhammad], gain dominance over them in war, disperse by [means of] them those behind them that perhaps they will be reminded.[417]

58. If you [have reason to] fear from a people betrayal, throw [their treaty] back to them, [putting you] on equal terms.[418] Indeed, God does not like traitors.

[417] i.e., kill them and make an example of them to discourage those who follow them.

[418] When you see signs of treachery from those with whom you have made a treaty, announce to them its dissolution so they will know exactly where they stand.

59. And let not those who disbelieve think they will escape. Indeed, they will not cause failure [to God].

60. And prepare against them whatever you are able of power and of steeds of war[419] by which you may terrify the enemy of God and your enemy and others besides them whom you do not know [but] whom God knows. And whatever you spend in the cause of God will be fully repaid to you, and you will not be wronged.

61. And if they incline to peace, then incline to it [also] and rely upon God. Indeed, it is He who is the Hearing, the Knowing.

62. But if they intend to deceive you - then sufficient for you is God. It is He who supported you with His help and with the believers

63. And brought together their hearts. If you had spent all that is in the earth, you could not have brought their hearts together; but God brought them together. Indeed, He is Exalted in Might and Wise.

64. O Prophet, sufficient for you is God and for whoever follows you of the believers.

65. O Prophet, urge the believers to battle. If there are among you twenty [who are] steadfast, they will overcome two hundred. And if there are among you one hundred [who are] steadfast, they will overcome a thousand of those who have disbelieved because they are a people who do not understand.

[419] Or equipment which serves the same purpose.

66. Now, God has lightened [the hardship] for you, and He knows that among you is weakness. So if there are from you one hundred [who are] steadfast, they will overcome two hundred. And if there are among you a thousand, they will overcome two thousand by permission of God. And God is with the steadfast.

67. It is not for a prophet to have captives [of war] until he inflicts a massacre [upon God's enemies] in the land. You [i.e., some Muslims] desire the commodities of this world,[420] but God desires [for you] the Hereafter. And God is Exalted in Might and Wise.

68. If not for a decree from God that preceded,[421] you would have been touched for what you took by a great punishment.

69. So consume what you have taken of war booty [as being] lawful and good, and fear God. Indeed, God is Forgiving and Merciful.

70. O Prophet, say to whoever is in your hands of the captives, "If God knows [any] good in your hearts, He will give you [something] better than what was taken from you, and He will forgive you; and God is Forgiving and Merciful."

71. But if they intend to betray you - then they have already betrayed God before, and He empowered [you] over them. And God is Knowing and Wise.

72. Indeed, those who have believed and emigrated and fought with their wealth and lives in the cause of God and those who gave shelter and aided - they are allies of one another. But those who believed and did not emigrate - for you there is no guardianship of them until they emigrate. And if they seek help of you for the religion, then you must help, except against a people between yourselves and whom is a treaty. And God is Seeing of what you do.

73. And those who disbelieved are allies of one another. If you do not do so [i.e., ally yourselves with other believers], there will be fitnah [i.e., disbelief and oppression] on earth and great corruption.

74. But those who have believed and emigrated and fought in the cause of God and those who gave shelter and aided - it is they who are the believers, truly. For them is forgiveness and noble provision.

75. And those who believed after [the initial emigration] and emigrated and fought with you - they are of you. But those of [blood] relationship are more entitled [to inheritance] in the decree of God.[422] Indeed, God is Knowing of all things.

[420] i.e., material benefit, such as the ransom paid for prisoners.

[421] Three interpretations of the "decree" are given: that by which the companions of Badr were forgiven, that by which indeliberate errors in judgement by believers are not punished, and that which made lawful the spoils of war.

[422] This applies to Muslim relatives only. Others may be given by bequest. See 4:11.

## Sūrah 9: at-Tawbah

This is the only Sūrah of the Qur'ān to which 'In the Name of God, Most Gracious Most Merciful' is not prefixed. Though the commentators have given different reasons for this, the correct one that which has been given by Imām Razi: namely this is because the Prophet himself did not dictate it at the beginning of the Sūrah. Therefore the Companions did not prefix it and their successors followed them. This is a further proof of the fact that utmost care has been taken to keep the Qur'ān intact so that it should remain in its complete and original form.

### Discourses and Periods of Revelation

This Sūrah comprises three discourses. The first discourse (v. 1-37) was revealed in Dhul-Qa'adah 9 A.H. or thereabout. As the importance of the subject of the discourse required its declaration on the occasion of Hajj the Prophet dispatched Ali to follow Abu Bakr who had already left for Makkah as leader of the Pilgrims to the Ka'bāh. He instructed Ali to deliver the discourse before the representatives of the different clans of Arabia so as to inform them of the new policy towards the polytheists.

The second discourse (v. 38-72) was sent down in Rajab 9 A.H. or a little before this when the Prophet was engaged in making preparations for the Campaign of Tabūk. In this discourse the Believers were urged to take active part in Jihād.

The third discourse (v. 73-129) was revealed on his return from the Campaign of Tabūk. There are some pieces in this discourse that were sent down on different occasions during the same period and were afterwards consolidated by the Prophet into the Sūrah in accordance with inspiration from God. But this caused no interruption in its continuity because they dealt with the same subject and formed part of the same series of events. This discourse warns the hypocrites of their evil deeds and rebukes those Believers who had stayed behind in the Campaign of Tabūk. Then after taking them to task God pardons those true Believers who had not taken part in the Jihād in the Way of God for one reason or the other.

### Historical Background

The series of events that have been discussed in this Sūrah took place after the Peace Treaty of Hudaibiyah. By that time one-third of Arabia had come under the sway of Islām which had established itself as a powerful well organized and civilized Islāmic State. There were two important events that followed - the first was the Conquest of Arabia. The Prophet was able to send missions among different clans for the propagation of Islām. The result was that during the short period of two years it became such a great power that it made the old order of ignorance feel helpless before it. So much so that the zealous elements from among the Quraysh were so exasperated that they broke the Treaty in order to encounter Islām in a decisive combat. But the Prophet took prompt action after the breach so as not to allow them any opportunity to gather enough force for this. He made a sudden invasion on Makkah in the month of Ramadan in 8 A.H. and conquered it. Though this conquest broke the backbone of the order of ignorance it made still another attack on Islām in the battlefield of Hunain which proved to be its death-knell. The clans of Hawazin, Thaqif, Naur Jushm and others gathered their entire forces in the battlefield in order to crush the reformative Revolution but they utterly failed in their evil designs. The defeat of 'ignorance' at Hunain paved the way for making the whole of Arabia the 'Abode of Islām' (Dar-ul-Islām). The result was that hardly a year had passed after the Battle of Hunain when the major portion of Arabia came within the fold of Islām and only a few upholders of the old order remained scattered over some corners of the country.

The second event that contributed towards making Islām a formidable power was the Campaign of Tabūk which was necessitated by the provocative activities of the Christians living within or near the boundaries of the Roman Empire to the north of Arabia. Accordingly the Prophet with an army of thirty thousand marched boldly towards the Roman Empire but the Romans evaded the encounter. The result was that the power of the Prophet and Islām increased manifold and deputations from all corners of Arabia began to wait upon him on his return from Tabūk in order to offer their allegiance to Islām and obedience to him. The Qur'ān has described this triumph in Sūrah an-Nasr (s. 110): **"When the victory of God has come and the conquest, And you see the people entering into the religion of God in multitudes..."**

**Campaign to Tabūk**

The Campaign to Tabūk was the result of conflict with the Roman Empire that had started even before the conquest of Makkah. One of the missions sent after the Treaty of Hudaibiyah to different parts of Arabia visited the clans which lived in the northern areas adjacent to Syria. The majority of these people were Christians who were under the influence of the Roman Empire. Contrary to all the principles of the commonly accepted international law they killed fifteen members of the delegation near a place known as Zat-u-Talah. Only Ka'ab bin Umair Ghifari, the head of the delegation, succeeded in escaping and reporting the sad incident. Besides this Shurahbil bin Amr, the Christian governor of Busra who was directly under the Roman Caesar had also put to death Haritli bin Umair the ambassador of the Prophet who had been sent to him on a similar mission.

These events convinced the Prophet that a strong action should be taken in order to make the territory adjacent to the Roman Empire safe and secure for the Muslims. Accordingly in the month of Jamadi-ul-Ula 8 A.H. he sent an army of three thousand towards the Syrian border. When this army reached near Ma'an the Muslims learnt that Shurahbil was marching with an army of one hundred thousand to fight-with them and that the Caesar who himself was at Hims had sent another army consisting of one hundred thousand soldiers under his brother Theodore. But in spite of such fearful news the brave small band of the Muslims marched on fearlessly and encountered the big army of Shurahbil at M'utah. And the result of the encounter in which the Muslirns were fighting against fearful odds (the ratio of the two armies was 1:33) as very favorable for the enemy utterly failed to defeat them. This proved very helpful for the propagation of Islām. As a result those Arabs who were living in a state of semi-independence in Syria and near Syria and the clans of Najd near Iraq who were under the influence of the Persian Empire turned towards Islām and embraced it in thousands. For example the people of Bani Sulaim (whose chief was Abbas bin Mirdas Sulaimi) Ashja'a Ghatafan Zubyan Fazarah etc. came into the fold of Islām at the same time. Above all Farvah bin 'Amral Juzami who was the commander of the Arab armies of the Roman Empire embraced Islām during that time and underwent the trial of his Faith in a way that filled the whole territory with wonder. When the Caesar came to know that Farvah had embraced Islām he ordered that he should be arrested and brought to his court. Then the Caesar said to him, 'You will have to choose one of the two things. Either give up your Islām and win your liberty and your former rank or remain a Muslim and face death.' He calmly chose Islām and sacrificed his life in the way of the Truth.

No wonder that such events as these made the Caesar realize the nature of the danger that was threatening his Empire from Arabia. Accordingly in 9 A.H. he began to make military preparations to avenge the insult he had suffered at M'utah. The Ghassanid and other Arab chiefs also began to muster armies under him. When the Prophet who always kept himself well-informed even of the minutest things that could affect the Islāmic Movement favorably or adversely came to know of these preparations he at once understood their meaning. Therefore without the least hesitation he decided to fight against the great power of the Caesar. He knew that the show of the slightest weakness would result in the utter failure of the Movement which was facing three great dangers at that time. First the dying power of 'ignorance' that had almost been crushed in the battlefield of Hunain might revive again. Secondly the Hypocrites of Madinah who were always on the look-out for such an opportunity might make full use of this to do the greatest possible harm to it. For they had already made preparations for this and had through a monk called Abu Amir, sent secret messages of their evil designs to the Christian king of Ghassan and the Caesar himself. Besides this, they had also built a mosque near Madinah for holding secret meetings for this purpose. The third danger was of an attack by the Caesar himself, who had already defeated Persia, the other great power of that period, and filled with awe the adjacent territories. It is obvious that if all these three elements had been given an opportunity of taking a concerted action against the Muslims, Islām would have lost the fight it had almost won. That is why in this case the Prophet made an open declaration for making preparations for the Campaign against the Roman Empire, which was one of the two greatest empires of the world of that period. The declaration was made though all the apparent circumstances were against such a decision: for there was famine in the country and the long awaited crops were about to ripen: the burning heat of the scorching summer season of Arabia was at its height and there was not enough money for preparations in general, and for equipment and conveyance in particular. But in spite of these handicaps, when the Messenger of God realized the urgency of the occasion, he took this step which was to decide whether the Mission of the Truth was going to survive or perish. The very fact that he made an open declaration for making preparations for such a campaign to Syria against the Roman Empire showed how important it was, for this was contrary to his previous practice. Usually he took every precaution not to reveal beforehand the direction to which he was going nor the name of the enemy whom he was going to attack; nay, he did not move out of Madinah even in the direction of the campaign.

All the parties in Arabia fully realized the grave consequences of this critical decision. The remnants of the lovers of the old order of 'ignorance' were anxiously waiting for the result of the Campaign, for they had pinned all their hopes on the defeat of Islām by the Romans. The 'hypocrites' also considered it to be their last chance of crushing the power of Islām by internal rebellion, if the Muslims suffered a defeat in Syria. They had, therefore, made full use of the Mosque built by them for hatching plots and had employed all their devices to render the Campaign a failure. On the other side, the true Believers also realized fully that the fate of the Movement for which they had been exerting their utmost for the last 22 years was now hanging in the balance. If they showed courage on that critical occasion, the doors of the whole outer world would be thrown open for the Movement to spread. But if they showed weakness or cowardice, then all the work they had done in Arabia would end in smoke. That is why these lovers of Islām began to make enthusiastic preparations for the Campaign. Everyone of them tried to surpass the other in making contributions for the provision of equipment for it. Uthman and Abdur Rahman bin awf presented large sums of money for this purpose. Umar contributed half of the earnings of his life and Abu Bakr the entire earnings of his life. The indigent Companions did not lag behind and presented whatever they could earn by the sweat of their labor and the women parted with their ornaments. Thousands of volunteers, who were filled with the desire of sacrificing their lives for Islām, came to the Prophet and requested that arrangements for weapons and conveyance be made for them so that they should join the expedition. Those who could not be provided with these shed tears of sorrow; the scene was so pathetic that it made the Prophet sad because of his inability to arm them. In short, the occasion became the touchstone for discriminating a true believer from a hypocrite. For, to lag behind in the Campaign meant that the very relationship of a person to Islām was doubtful. Accordingly, whenever a person lagged behind during the journey to Tabūk, the Prophet, on being informed, would spontaneously say, *"Leave him alone. If there be any good in him, God will again join him with you, and if there be no good in him, then thank God that He relieved you of his evil company."*

In short, the Prophet marched out towards Syria in Rajab A.H. 9, with thirty thousand fighters for the cause of Islām. The conditions in which the expedition was undertaken may be judged from the fact that the number of camels with them was so small that many of them were obliged to walk on foot and to wait for their turns for several had to ride at a time on each camel. To add to this, there was the burning heat of the desert and the acute shortage of water. But they were richly rewarded for their firm resolve and sincere adherence to the cause and for their perseverance in the face of those great difficulties and obstacles.

When they arrived at Tabūk, they learnt that the Caesar and his allies had withdrawn their troops from the frontier and there was no enemy to fight with. Thus they won a moral victory that increased their prestige manifold and, that too, without shedding a drop of blood. As a result of this, the boundaries of the Islāmic State were extended right up to the Roman Empire, and the majority of the Arab clans, who were being used by the Caesar against Arabia, became the allies of the Muslims against the Romans. Above all, this moral victory of Tabūk afforded a golden opportunity to the Muslims to strengthen their hold on Arabia before entering into a long conflict with the Romans. For it broke the back of those who had still been expecting that the old order of 'ignorance' might revive in the near future, whether they were the open upholders of shirk or the hypocrites who were hiding their shirk under the garb of Islām. The majority of such people were compelled by the force of circumstances to enter into the fold of Islām and, at least, make it possible for their descendants to become true Muslims. After this a mere impotent minority of the upholders of the old order was left in the field, but it could not stand in the way of the Islāmic Revolution for the perfection of which God had sent His Messenger.

**Problems of the Period**

If we keep in view the preceding background we can easily find out the problems that were confronting the Community at that time. They were: (1)to make the whole of Arabia a perfect Dar-ul-Islām (2)to extend the influence of Islām to the adjoining countries (3)to crush the mischiefs of the hypocrites and (4)to prepare the Muslims for Jihād against the non-Muslim world. A clear declaration was made that all the treaties with the polytheists were abolished and the Muslims would be released from the treaty obligations with them after a respite of four months(v. 1-3). This declaration was necessary for uprooting completely the system of life based on Shirk (polytheism) and to make Arabia exclusively the center of Islām so that it should not in any way interfere with the spirit of Islām nor become an internal danger for it.

A decree was issued that the guardianship of the Ka'bāh, which held central position in all the affairs of Arabia should be wrested from the polytheists and placed permanently in the hands of the Believers (v. 12-18) and that all the customs and practices of the shirk of the era of 'ignorance' should be forcibly abolished: that the polytheists should not be allowed even to come near the "House" (v. 28). This was to eradicate every trace of Shirk from the "House" that was dedicated exclusively to the worship of God. In order to enable the Muslims to extend the influence of Islām outside Arabia they were enjoined to crush with sword the non-Muslim powers and to force them to accept the sovereignty of the Islāmic State. As the great Roman and Persian Empires were the biggest hindrances in the way a conflict with them was inevitable. The object of Jihād was not to coerce them to accept Islām; they were free to accept or not to accept it, but to prevent them from thrusting forcibly their deviations upon others and the coming generations. The Muslims were enjoined to tolerate their misguidance only to the extent that they might have the freedom to remain misguided if they chose to be so provided that they paid Jizyah(v. 29) as a sign of their subjugation to the Islāmic State. The third important problem was to crush the mischiefs of the hypocrites who had hitherto been tolerated in spite of their flagrant crimes. Now that there was practically no pressure upon them from outside the Muslims were enjoined to treat them openly as disbelievers (v. 73). Accordingly the Prophet set on fire the house of Swailim where the hypocrites used to gather for consultations in order to dissuade the people from joining the expedition to Tabūk. Likewise on his return from Tabūk he ordered to pull down and burn the 'Mosque' that had been built to serve as a cover for the hypocrites for hatching plots against the true Believers.

In order to prepare the Muslims for Jihād against the whole non-Muslim world it was necessary to cure them even of that slight weakness of faith from which they were still suffering. For there could be no greater internal danger to the Islāmic Community than the weakness of faith especially where it was going to engage itself single-handed in a conflict with the whole non-Muslim world. That is why those people who had lagged behind in the Campaign to Tabūk or had shown the least negligence were severely taken to task and were considered as hypocrites if they had no plausible excuse for not fulfilling that obligation. Moreover, a clear declaration was made that in future the sole criterion of a Muslim's faith shall be the exertions he makes for the uplift of the Word of God and the role he plays in the conflict between Islām and Kufr (disbelief). Therefore, if anyone will show any hesitation in sacrificing his life, money, time and energies, his faith shall not be regarded as genuine (v. 81-96). If the above-mentioned important points are kept in view during the study of this Sūrah, it will facilitate the understanding of its contents.

## Sūrah 9: at-Tawbah[423]

1. [This is a declaration of] disassociation, from God and His Messenger, to those with whom you had made a treaty among the polytheists.[424]

2. So travel freely, [O disbelievers], throughout the land [during] four months but know that you cannot cause failure to God and that God will disgrace the disbelievers.

3. And [it is] an announcement from God and His Messenger to the people on the day of the greater pilgrimage[425] that God is disassociated from the disbelievers, and [so is] His Messenger. So if you repent, that is best for you; but if you turn away - then know that you will not cause failure to God.[426] And give tidings to those who disbelieve of a painful punishment.

4. Excepted are those with whom you made a treaty among the polytheists and then they have not been deficient toward you in anything or supported anyone against you; so complete for them their treaty until their term [has ended]. Indeed, God loves the righteous [who fear Him].

5. And when the sacred months[427] have passed, then kill the polytheists wherever you find them and capture them and besiege them and sit in wait for them at every place of ambush. But if they should repent, establish prayer, and give zakāh, let them [go] on their way. Indeed, God is Forgiving and Merciful.

6. And if any one of the polytheists seeks your protection, then grant him protection so that he may hear the words of God [i.e., the Qur'ān]. Then deliver him to his place of safety. That is because they are a people who do not know.

7. How can there be for the polytheists a treaty in the sight of God and with His Messenger, except for those with whom you made a treaty at al-Masjid al-Harām? So as long as they are upright toward you,[428] be upright toward them. Indeed, God loves the righteous [who fear Him].

8. How [can there be a treaty] while, if they gain dominance over you, they do not observe concerning you any pact of kinship or covenant of protection? They satisfy you with their mouths, but their hearts refuse [compliance], and most of them are defiantly disobedient.

9. They have exchanged the signs of God for a small price and averted [people] from His way. Indeed, it was evil that they were doing.

10. They do not observe toward a believer any pact of kinship or covenant of protection. And it is they who are the transgressors.

11. But if they repent, establish prayer, and give zakāh, then they are your brothers in religion; and We detail the verses for a people who know.

---

423 *At-Tawbah*: Repentance. This *sūrah* is also known as *Bara'ah,* meaning disassociation, freedom, release or immunity. The words *In the Name of God, the Most Compassionate, the Most Merciful* were not revealed at the beginning of this *sūrah.*

424 But who had violated it.

425 *Hajj*. *'Umrah* is the lesser pilgrimage.

426 i.e., you cannot escape His punishment.

427 The four months mentioned in verse 2, i.e., Muharram, Rajab, Dhul-Qa'dah and Dhul-Hijjah.

428 i.e., maintain the terms of the treaty.

12. And if they break their oaths after their treaty and defame your religion, then fight the leaders of disbelief, for indeed, there are no oaths [sacred] to them; [fight them that] they might cease.

13. Would you not fight a people who broke their oaths and determined to expel the Messenger, and they had begun [the attack upon] you the first time? Do you fear them? But God has more right that you should fear Him, if you are [truly] believers.

14. Fight them; God will punish them by your hands and will disgrace them and give you victory over them and satisfy the breasts [i.e., desires] of a believing people

15. And remove the fury in their [i.e., the believers'] hearts. And God turns in forgiveness to whom He wills; and God is Knowing and Wise.

16. Do you think that you will be left [as you are] while God has not yet made evident those among you who strive [for His cause] and do not take other than God, His Messenger and the believers as intimates? And God is Acquainted with what you do.

17. It is not for the polytheists to maintain the mosques of God [while] witnessing against themselves with disbelief. [For] those, their deeds have become worthless, and in the Fire they will abide eternally.

18. The mosques of God are only to be maintained by those who believe in God and the Last Day and establish prayer and give zakāh and do not fear except God, for it is expected that those will be of the [rightly] guided.

19. Have you made the providing of water for the pilgrim and the maintenance of al-Masjid al-Harām equal to [the deeds of] one who believes in God and the Last Day and strives in the cause of God? They are not equal in the sight of God. And God does not guide the wrongdoing people.

20. The ones who have believed, emigrated and striven in the cause of God with their wealth and their lives are greater in rank in the sight of God. And it is those who are the attainers [of success].

21. Their Lord gives them good tidings of mercy from Him and approval and of gardens for them wherein is enduring pleasure.

22. [They will be] abiding therein forever. Indeed, God has with Him a great reward.

23. O you who have believed, do not take your fathers or your brothers as allies if they have preferred disbelief over belief. And whoever does so among you - then it is those who are the wrongdoers.

24. Say, [O Muhammad], "If your fathers, your sons, your brothers, your wives, your relatives, wealth which you have obtained, commerce wherein you fear decline, and dwellings with which you are pleased are more beloved to you than God and His Messenger and jihād [i.e., striving] in His cause, then wait until God executes His command. And God does not guide the defiantly disobedient people."

25. God has already given you victory in many regions and [even] on the day of Hunayn, when your great number pleased you, but it did not avail you at

all, and the earth was confining for you with [i.e., in spite of] its vastness; then you turned back, fleeing.

26. Then God sent down His tranquillity upon His Messenger and upon the believers and sent down soldiers [i.e., angels] whom you did not see and punished those who disbelieved. And that is the recompense of the disbelievers.

27. Then God will accept repentance after that for whom He wills; and God is Forgiving and Merciful.

28. O you who have believed, indeed the polytheists are unclean, so let them not approach al-Masjid al-Harām after this, their [final] year. And if you fear privation, God will enrich you from His bounty if He wills. Indeed, God is Knowing and Wise.

29. Fight those who do not believe in God or in the Last Day and who do not consider unlawful what God and His Messenger have made unlawful and who do not adopt the religion of truth [i.e., Islām] from those who were given the Scripture - [fight] until they give the jizyah[429] willingly while they are humbled.

30. The Jews say, "Ezra is the son of God"; and the Christians say, "The Messiah is the son of God." That is their statement from their mouths; they imitate the saying of those who disbelieved before [them]. May God destroy them; how are they deluded?

31. They have taken their scholars and monks as lords besides God,[430] and [also] the Messiah, the son of Mary.[431] And they were not commanded except to worship one God; there is no deity except Him. Exalted is He above whatever they associate with Him.

32. They want to extinguish the light of God with their mouths, but God refuses except to perfect His light, although the disbelievers dislike it.

33. It is He who has sent His Messenger with guidance and the religion of truth to manifest it over all religion, although they who associate others with God dislike it.

34. O you who have believed, indeed many of the scholars and the monks devour the wealth of people unjustly[432] and avert [them] from the way of God. And those who hoard gold and silver and spend it not in the way of God - give them tidings of a painful punishment.

35. The Day when it[433] will be heated in the fire of Hell and seared therewith will be their foreheads, their flanks, and their backs, [it will be said], "This is what you hoarded for yourselves, so taste what you used to hoard."

36. Indeed, the number of months with God is twelve [lunar] months in the register of God [from] the day He created the heavens and the earth; of these, four are sacred.[434] That is the

[429] A tax required of non-Muslims exempting them from military service and entitling them to the protection of the Islāmic state. Concurrently, *zakāh* is not taken from them, being an obligation only upon Muslims.

[430] By their obedience to them rather than to what God ordained.

[431] By their worship of him in conjunction with God.

[432] i.e., through false pretence.

[433] The gold and silver which was hoarded, i.e., whose *zakāh* was not paid.

[434] See footnote to 9:5.

correct religion [i.e., way], so do not wrong yourselves during them.[435] And fight against the disbelievers collectively as they fight against you collectively. And know that God is with the righteous [who fear Him].

37. Indeed, the postponing [of restriction within sacred months] is an increase in disbelief by which those who have disbelieved are led [further] astray. They make it[436] lawful one year and unlawful another year to correspond to the number made unlawful by God[437] and [thus] make lawful what God has made unlawful. Made pleasing to them is the evil of their deeds; and God does not guide the disbelieving people.

38. O you who have believed, what is [the matter] with you that, when you are told to go forth in the cause of God, you adhere heavily to the earth?[438] Are you satisfied with the life of this world rather than the Hereafter? But what is the enjoyment of worldly life compared to the Hereafter except a [very] little.

39. If you do not go forth, He will punish you with a painful punishment and will replace you with another people, and you will not harm Him at all. And God is over all things competent.

40. If you do not aid him [i.e., the Prophet] - God has already aided him when those who disbelieved had driven him out [of Makkah] as one of two,[439] when they were in the cave and he [i.e., Muhammad] said to his companion, "Do not grieve; indeed God is with us." And God sent down his tranquillity upon him and supported him with soldiers [i.e., angels] you did not see and made the word[440] of those who disbelieved the lowest,[441] while the word of God[442] - that is the highest. And God is Exalted in Might and Wise.

41. Go forth, whether light or heavy,[443] and strive with your wealth and your lives in the cause of God. That is better for you, if you only knew.

42. Had it been a near [i.e., easy] gain and a moderate trip, they [i.e., the hypocrites] would have followed you, but distant to them was the journey. And they will swear by God,[444] "If we were able, we would have gone forth with you," destroying themselves [through false oaths], and God knows that indeed they are liars.

43. May God pardon you, [O Muhammad]; why did you give them permission [to remain behind]? [You should not have] until it was evident to you who were truthful and you knew [who were] the liars.

44. Those who believe in God and the Last Day would not ask permission of you to be excused from striving [i.e., fighting] with their wealth and their lives.

---

[435] i.e., do not violate the sacred months or commit aggression therein.

[436] Fighting during a sacred month.

[437] If they found it advantageous to violate a sacred month, they would do so, designating another month in its place in which to observe the restrictions concerning fighting.

[438] i.e., inclining toward the comforts of worldly life.

[439] The second was his companion, Abu Bakr.

[440] i.e., their claims and slogans.

[441] i.e., degraded and dishonoured.

[442] "*La ilaha ill-Allāh*" ("There is no deity worthy of worship except God").

[443] i.e., young or old, riding or walking, in ease or in hardship – in all circumstances and conditions.

[444] When you return from the Tabūk expedition.

And God is Knowing of those who fear Him.

45. Only those would ask permission of you who do not believe in God and the Last Day and whose hearts have doubted, and they, in their doubt, are hesitating.

46. And if they had intended to go forth, they would have prepared for it [some] preparation. But God disliked their being sent, so He kept them back, and they were told, "Remain [behind] with those who remain."[445]

47. Had they gone forth with you, they would not have increased you except in confusion, and they would have been active among you, seeking [to cause] you fitnah [i.e., chaos and dissension]. And among you are avid listeners to them. And God is Knowing of the wrongdoers.

48. They had already desired dissension before and had upset matters for you[446] until the truth came and the ordinance [i.e., victory] of God appeared, while they were averse.

49. And among them is he who says, "Permit me [to remain at home] and do not put me to trial." Unquestionably, into trial they have fallen.[447] And indeed, Hell will encompass the disbelievers.

50. If good befalls you, it distresses them; but if disaster strikes you, they say, "We took our matter [in hand] before,"[448] and turn away while they are rejoicing.

51. Say, "Never will we be struck except by what God has decreed for us; He is our protector." And upon God let the believers rely.

52. Say, "Do you await for us except one of the two best things [i.e., martyrdom or victory] while we await for you that God will afflict you with punishment from Himself or at our hands? So wait; indeed we, along with you, are waiting."

53. Say, "Spend willingly or unwillingly; never will it be accepted from you. Indeed, you have been a defiantly disobedient people."

54. And what prevents their expenditures from being accepted from them but that they have disbelieved in God and in His Messenger and that they come not to prayer except while they are lazy and that they do not spend except while they are unwilling.

55. So let not their wealth or their children impress you. God only intends to punish them through them in worldly life and that their souls should depart [at death] while they are disbelievers.

56. And they swear by God that they are from among you while they are not from among you; but they are a people who are afraid.

57. If they could find a refuge or some caves or any place to enter [and hide], they would turn to it while they run heedlessly.

---

[445] i.e., the women and children.

[446] Or "turned matters related to you over [in their minds, considering how to cause you failure]."

[447] By avoiding their obligation, they fell into destruction.

[448] The hypocrites claim to have protected themselves by remaining behind.

58. And among them are some who criticize you concerning the [distribution of] charities. If they are given from them, they approve; but if they are not given from them, at once they become angry.

59. If only they had been satisfied with what God and His Messenger gave them and said, "Sufficient for us is God; God will give us of His bounty, and [so will] His Messenger; indeed, we are desirous toward God,"[449] [it would have been better for them].

60. Zakāh expenditures are only for the poor and for the needy and for those employed to collect [zakāh] and for bringing hearts together [for Islām] and for freeing captives [or slaves] and for those in debt and for the cause of God and for the [stranded] traveler - an obligation [imposed] by God. And God is Knowing and Wise.

61. And among them are those who abuse the Prophet and say, "He is an ear."[450] Say, "[It is] an ear of goodness for you that believes in God and believes the believers and [is] a mercy to those who believe among you." And those who abuse the Messenger of God - for them is a painful punishment.

62. They swear by God to you [Muslims] to satisfy you. But God and His Messenger are more worthy for them to satisfy, if they should be believers.

63. Do they not know that whoever opposes God and His Messenger - that for him is the fire of Hell, wherein he will abide eternally? That is the great disgrace.

64. The hypocrites are apprehensive lest a sūrah be revealed about them, informing them of[451] what is in their hearts. Say, "Mock [as you wish]; indeed, God will expose that which you fear."

65. And if you ask them, they will surely say, "We were only conversing and playing." Say, "Is it God and His verses and His Messenger that you were mocking?"

66. Make no excuse; you have disbelieved [i.e., rejected faith] after your belief. If We pardon one faction of you - We will punish another faction because they were criminals.

67. The hypocrite men and hypocrite women are of one another. They enjoin what is wrong and forbid what is right and close their hands.[452] They have forgotten God, so He has forgotten them [accordingly]. Indeed, the hypocrites - it is they who are the defiantly disobedient.

68. God has promised the hypocrite men and hypocrite women and the disbelievers the fire of Hell, wherein they will abide eternally. It is sufficient for them. And God has cursed them, and for them is an enduring punishment.

69. [You disbelievers are] like those before you; they were stronger than you in power and more abundant in wealth and children. They enjoyed their portion [of worldly enjoyment], and you have enjoyed your portion as those before you enjoyed their portion, and you have engaged [in vanities] like that in which they engaged. [It is] those whose deeds have become worthless in this

[449] Meaning "We desire God and His grace and acceptance," or "We desire whatever God wills to give us of His bounty."
[450] i.e., one who believes everything he hears.

[451] i.e., exposing the truth about.
[452] i.e., refuse to spend in the way of God.

world and in the Hereafter, and it is they who are the losers.

70. Has there not reached them the news of those before them - the people of Noah and [the tribes of] 'Aad and Thamūd and the people of Abraham and the companions [i.e., dwellers] of Madyan and the towns overturned?[453] Their messengers came to them with clear proofs. And God would never have wronged them, but they were wronging themselves.

71. The believing men and believing women are allies of one another. They enjoin what is right and forbid what is wrong and establish prayer and give zakāh and obey God and His Messenger. Those - God will have mercy upon them. Indeed, God is Exalted in Might and Wise.

72. God has promised the believing men and believing women gardens beneath which rivers flow, wherein they abide eternally, and pleasant dwellings in gardens of perpetual residence; but approval from God is greater. It is that which is the great attainment.

73. O Prophet, fight against the disbelievers and the hypocrites and be harsh upon them. And their refuge is Hell, and wretched is the destination.

74. They swear by God that they did not say [anything against the Prophet] while they had said the word of disbelief and disbelieved after their [pretense of] Islām and planned that which they were not to attain.[454] And they were not resentful except [for the fact] that God and His Messenger had enriched them of His bounty.[455] So if they repent, it is better for them; but if they turn away, God will punish them with a painful punishment in this world and the Hereafter. And there will not be for them on earth any protector or helper.

75. And among them are those who made a covenant with God, [saying], "If He should give us from His bounty, we will surely spend in charity, and we will surely be among the righteous."

76. But when He gave them from His bounty, they were stingy with it and turned away while they refused.

77. So He penalized them with hypocrisy in their hearts until the Day they will meet Him - because they failed God in what they promised Him and because they [habitually] used to lie.

78. Did they not know that God knows their secrets and their private conversations and that God is the Knower of the unseen?

79. Those who criticize the contributors among the believers concerning [their] charities and [criticize] the ones who find nothing [to spend] except their effort, so they ridicule them - God will ridicule them, and they will have a painful punishment.

80. Ask forgiveness for them, [O Muhammad], or do not ask forgiveness for them. If you should ask forgiveness for them seventy times - never will God forgive them. That is because they disbelieved in God and His Messenger,

[453] i.e., those to which Lot was sent and which earned for themselves God's punishment. See 11:82-83.

[454] i.e., the murder of Prophet Muhammad.

[455] i.e., for no reason. On the contrary, they should have been grateful.

and God does not guide the defiantly disobedient people.

81. Those who remained behind rejoiced in their staying [at home] after [the departure of] the Messenger of God and disliked to strive with their wealth and their lives in the cause of God and said, "Do not go forth in the heat." Say, "The fire of Hell is more intensive in heat" - if they would but understand.

82. So let them laugh a little and [then] weep much as recompense for what they used to earn.

83. If God should return you to a faction of them [after the expedition] and then they ask your permission to go out [to battle], say, "You will not go out with me, ever, and you will never fight with me an enemy. Indeed, you were satisfied with sitting [at home] the first time, so sit [now] with those who stay behind."

84. And do not pray [the funeral prayer, O Muhammad], over any of them who has died - ever - or stand at his grave. Indeed, they disbelieved in God and His Messenger and died while they were defiantly disobedient.

85. And let not their wealth and their children impress you. God only intends to punish them through them in this world and that their souls should depart [at death] while they are disbelievers.

86. And when a sūrah was revealed [enjoining them] to believe in God and to fight with His Messenger, those of wealth among them asked your permission [to stay back] and said, "Leave us to be with them who sit [at home]."

87. They were satisfied to be with those who stay behind, and their hearts were sealed over, so they do not understand.

88. But the Messenger and those who believed with him fought with their wealth and their lives. Those will have [all that is] good, and it is those who are the successful.

89. God has prepared for them gardens beneath which rivers flow, wherein they will abide eternally. That is the great attainment.

90. And those with excuses among the bedouins came to be permitted [to remain], and they who had lied[456] to God and His Messenger sat [at home]. There will strike those who disbelieved among them a painful punishment.

91. There is not upon the weak or upon the ill or upon those who do not find anything to spend any discomfort [i.e., guilt] when they are sincere to God and His Messenger. There is not upon the doers of good any cause [for blame]. And God is Forgiving and Merciful.

92. Nor [is there blame] upon those who, when they came to you that you might give them mounts, you said, "I can find nothing for you to ride upon." They turned back while their eyes overflowed with tears out of grief that they could not find something to spend [for the cause of God].

93. The cause [for blame] is only upon those who ask permission of you while they are rich. They are satisfied to be with those who stay behind, and God has sealed over their hearts, so they do not know.

[456] i.e., claimed faith.

94. They will make excuses to you when you have returned to them. Say, "Make no excuse - never will we believe you. God has already informed us of your news [i.e., affair]. And God will observe your deeds, and [so will] His Messenger; then you will be taken back to the Knower of the unseen and the witnessed,[457] and He will inform you of what you used to do."

95. They will swear by God to you when you return to them that you would leave them alone. So leave them alone; indeed they are evil; and their refuge is Hell as recompense for what they had been earning.

96. They swear to you so that you might be satisfied with them. But if you should be satisfied with them - indeed, God is not satisfied with a defiantly disobedient people.

97. The bedouins are stronger in disbelief and hypocrisy and more likely not to know the limits of what [laws] God has revealed to His Messenger. And God is Knowing and Wise.

98. And among the bedouins are some who consider what they spend as a loss[458] and await for you turns of misfortune. Upon them will be a misfortune of evil. And God is Hearing and Knowing.

99. But among the bedouins are some who believe in God and the Last Day and consider what they spend as means of nearness to God and of [obtaining] invocations of the Messenger. Unquestionably, it is a means of nearness for them. God will admit them to His mercy. Indeed, God is Forgiving and Merciful.

100. And the first forerunners [in the faith] among the Muhājireen[459] and the Ansār[460] and those who followed them with good conduct - God is pleased with them and they are pleased with Him, and He has prepared for them gardens beneath which rivers flow, wherein they will abide forever. That is the great attainment.

101. And among those around you of the bedouins are hypocrites, and [also] from the people of Madīnah. They have become accustomed to hypocrisy. You, [O Muhammad], do not know them, [but] We know them. We will punish them twice [in this world]; then they will be returned to a great punishment.

102. And [there are] others who have acknowledged their sins. They had mixed [i.e., polluted] a righteous deed with another that was bad.[461] Perhaps God will turn to them in forgiveness. Indeed, God is Forgiving and Merciful.

103. Take, [O, Muhammad], from their wealth a charity by which you purify them and cause them increase, and invoke [God's blessings] upon them. Indeed, your invocations are reassurance for them. And God is Hearing and Knowing.

104. Do they not know that it is God who accepts repentance from His servants

[457] See footnote to 6:73.

[458] i.e., a fine or penalty.

[459] Those who emigrated from Makkah and settled in Madinah for the cause of Islām.

[460] The inhabitants of Madinah who had accepted Islām and assisted the Prophet and other emigrants upon their arrival there.

[461] This refers to their having previously taken part in *jihād* but having abstained on the occasion of Tabūk.

and receives charities and that it is God who is the Accepting of repentance, the Merciful?

105. And say, "Do [as you will], for God will see your deeds, and [so will] His Messenger and the believers. And you will be returned to the Knower of the unseen and the witnessed, and He will inform you of what you used to do."

106. And [there are] others deferred until the command of God - whether He will punish them or whether He will forgive them. And God is Knowing and Wise.

107. And [there are] those [hypocrites] who took for themselves a mosque for causing harm and disbelief and division among the believers and as a station for whoever had warred against God and His Messenger before. And they will surely swear, "We intended only the best." And God testifies that indeed they are liars.

108. Do not stand [for prayer] within it - ever. A mosque founded on righteousness from the first day[462] is more worthy for you to stand in. Within it are men who love to purify themselves; and God loves those who purify themselves.

109. Then is one who laid the foundation of his building on righteousness [with fear] from God and [seeking] His approval better or one who laid the foundation of his building on the edge of a bank about to collapse, so it collapsed with him into the fire of Hell? And God does not guide the wrongdoing people.

110. Their building which they built will not cease to be a [cause of] skepticism in their hearts until their hearts are cut [i.e., stopped]. And God is Knowing and Wise.

111. Indeed, God has purchased from the believers their lives and their properties [in exchange] for that they will have Paradise. They fight in the cause of God, so they kill and are killed. [It is] a true promise [binding] upon Him in the Torah and the Gospel and the Qur'ān. And who is truer to his covenant than God? So rejoice in your transaction which you have contracted. And it is that which is the great attainment.

112. [Such believers are] the repentant, the worshippers, the praisers [of God], the travelers [for His cause], those who bow and prostrate [in prayer], those who enjoin what is right and forbid what is wrong, and those who observe the limits [set by] God. And give good tidings to the believers.

113. It is not for the Prophet and those who have believed to ask forgiveness for the polytheists, even if they were relatives, after it has become clear to them that they are companions of Hellfire.

114. And the request of forgiveness of Abraham for his father was only because of a promise he had made to him. But when it became apparent to him [i.e., Abraham] that he [i.e., the father] was an enemy to God, he disassociated himself from him. Indeed was Abraham compassionate and patient.

115. And God would not let a people stray after He has guided them until He makes clear to them what they should avoid. Indeed, God is Knowing of all things.

[462] This description is of the Qubā' mosque.

116. Indeed, to God belongs the dominion of the heavens and the earth; He gives life and causes death. And you have not besides God any protector or any helper.

117. God has already forgiven the Prophet and the Muhājireen and the Ansār who followed him in the hour of difficulty after the hearts of a party of them had almost inclined [to doubt], and then He forgave them. Indeed, He was to them Kind and Merciful.

118. And [He also forgave] the three who were left behind [and regretted their error] to the point that the earth closed in on them in spite of its vastness[463] and their souls confined [i.e., anguished] them and they were certain that there is no refuge from God except in Him. Then He turned to them so they could repent. Indeed, God is the Accepting of repentance, the Merciful.

119. O you who have believed, fear God and be with those who are true.

120. It was not [proper] for the people of Madīnah and those surrounding them of the bedouins that they remain behind after [the departure of] the Messenger of God or that they prefer themselves over his self.[464] That is because they are not afflicted by thirst or fatigue or hunger in the cause of God, nor do they tread on any ground that enrages the disbelievers, nor do they inflict upon an enemy any infliction but that it is registered for them as a righteous deed. Indeed, God does not allow to be lost the reward of the doers of good.

121. Nor do they spend an expenditure, small or large, or cross a valley but that it is registered for them that God may reward them for the best of what they were doing.

122. And it is not for the believers to go forth [to battle] all at once. For there should separate from every division of them a group [remaining] to obtain understanding in the religion and warn [i.e., advise] their people when they return to them that they might be cautious.

123. O you who have believed, fight those adjacent to you of the disbelievers and let them find in you harshness. And know that God is with the righteous.

124. And whenever a sūrah is revealed, there are among them [i.e., the hypocrites] those who say, "Which of you has this increased faith?" As for those who believed, it has increased them in faith, while they are rejoicing.

125. But as for those in whose hearts is disease, it has [only] increased them in evil [in addition] to their evil.[465] And they will have died while they are disbelievers.

126. Do they not see that they are tried every year once or twice but then they do not repent nor do they remember?

127. And whenever a sūrah is revealed, they look at each other, [saying], "Does anyone see you?" and then they dismiss themselves. God has dismissed their

[463] Thus it seemed to them in their extreme distress.

[464] In times of hardship. Rather, they should have been willing to endure with the Prophet whatever was necessary for Islām.

[465] Literally, "filth," i.e., disbelief and hypocrisy.

hearts because they are a people who do not understand.

128. There has certainly come to you a Messenger from among yourselves. Grievous to him is what you suffer; [he is] concerned over you [i.e., your guidance] and to the believers is kind and merciful.

129. But if they turn away, [O Muhammad], say, "Sufficient for me is God; there is no deity except Him. On Him I have relied, and He is the Lord of the Great Throne."

# Sūrah 10: Yūnus

## Period of Revelation

We learn from hadith the Sūrah was revealed in Makkah. But there are some people who are of the opinion that some of its verses were revealed at Madinah. This is however a superficial view. The continuity of the theme clearly shows that this does not comprise isolated verses or discourses that were revealed at different times and on different occasions. On the contrary it is from the beginning to the end a closely connected discourse which must have been revealed at one sitting. Besides this the nature of its theme is itself a clear proof that the Sūrah belongs to the Makkan period.

## Time of Revelation

We have no hadith in regard to the time of its revelation but its subject matter gives clear indication that it must have been revealed during the last stage of the Prophet's residence at Makkah. For the mode of the discourse suggests that at the time of its revelation the antagonism of the opponents of the Message had become so intense that they could not tolerate even the presence of the Prophet and his followers among themselves and that things had come to such a pass as to leave no hope that they would ever understand and accept the Message of the Prophet. This indicates that the last stage of the Prophet's life among the people had come and the final warning like the one in this Sūrah had to be given. These characteristics of the discourse are clear proof that it was revealed during the last stage of the Movement at Makkah. Another thing that determines more specifically the order of the Sūrahs of the last stage at Makkah is the mention (or absence) of some open or covert hint about Hijrah (Emigration) from Makkah. As this Sūrah does not contain any hint whatsoever about this it is a proof that it preceded those Sūrahs which contain it. Now that we have specified the time of its revelation there is no need of repeating its historical background because that has already been stated in Sūrahs 6 and 7.

## Subject

This discourse deals with the invitation to the Message admonition and warning. In the very introductory verses the invitation has been extended like this: "The people consider it a strange thing that this Message is being conveyed by a human being and charge him with sorcery whereas there is nothing strange in it nor has it any connection with sorcery or sooth saying. It simply informs you of two realities. First God Who has created the universe and manages it is in fact your Master and Lord and He alone is entitled to your worship. The second reality is that after the life in this world there will be another life in the Next World where you shall have to render full account of the life of this world and be rewarded or punished according to whether you adopted the righteous attitude as required by Him after acknowleding Him as your Masters or acted against His will. Both of these realities which the Messenger is presenting before you are "realities" in themselves whether you acknowledge them as such or not. He is inviting you to accept these and regulate your lives in accordance with them; if you accept these you will have a very blessed end; otherwise join shall meet with evil consequences."

## Sūrah 10: Yūnus[466]

In the Name of God, the Most Compassionate, the Most Merciful

1. Alif, Lām, Rā.[467] These are the verses of the wise[468] Book.

2. Have the people been amazed that We revealed [revelation] to a man from among them, [saying], "Warn mankind and give good tidings to those who believe that they will have a [firm] precedence of honor[469] with their Lord"? [But] the disbelievers say, "Indeed, this is an obvious magician."

3. Indeed, your Lord is God, who created the heavens and the earth in six days and then established Himself above the Throne,[470] arranging the matter [of His creation]. There is no intercessor except after His permission. That is God, your Lord, so worship Him. Then will you not remember?

4. To Him is your return all together. [It is] the promise of God [which is] truth. Indeed, He begins the [process of] creation and then repeats it that He may reward those who have believed and done righteous deeds, in justice. But those who disbelieved will have a drink of scalding water and a painful punishment for what they used to deny.

5. It is He who made the sun a shining light and the moon a derived light and determined for it phases - that you may know the number of years and account [of time]. God has not created this except in truth. He details the signs for a people who know.

6. Indeed, in the alternation of the night and the day and [in] what God has created in the heavens and the earth are signs for a people who fear God.

7. Indeed, those who do not expect the meeting with Us and are satisfied with the life of this world and feel secure therein and those who are heedless of Our signs -

8. For those their refuge will be the Fire because of what they used to earn.

9. Indeed, those who have believed and done righteous deeds - their Lord will guide them because of their faith. Beneath them rivers will flow in the Gardens of Pleasure.

10. Their call therein will be, "Exalted are You, O God," and their greeting therein will be, "Peace." And the last of their call will be, "Praise to God, Lord of the worlds!"

11. And if God was to hasten for the people the evil [they invoke][471] as He hastens for them the good, their term would have been ended for them.[472] But We leave the ones who do not expect the meeting with Us, in their transgression, wandering blindly.

12. And when affliction touches man, he calls upon Us, whether lying on his side or sitting or standing; but when We remove from him his affliction, he continues [in disobedience] as if he had

466 *Yūnus*: (The Prophet) Jonah.
467 See footnote to 2:1.
468 The adjective "wise" expresses the qualities of will, purpose, discrimination and precision.
469 i.e., a sure position due to their righteous deeds.
470 See footnote to 2:19.

471 In anger or in heedlessness.
472 i.e., God would have destroyed them on account of that.

never called upon Us to [remove] an affliction that touched him. Thus is made pleasing to the transgressors that which they have been doing.

13. And We had already destroyed generations before you when they wronged, and their messengers had come to them with clear proofs, but they were not to believe. Thus do We recompense the criminal people.

14. Then We made you successors in the land after them so that We may observe how you will do.

15. And when Our verses are recited to them as clear evidences, those who do not expect the meeting with Us say, "Bring us a Qur'ān other than this or change it." Say, [O Muhammad], "It is not for me to change it on my own accord. I only follow what is revealed to me. Indeed I fear, if I should disobey my Lord, the punishment of a tremendous Day."

16. Say, "If God had willed, I would not have recited it to you, nor would He have made it known to you, for I had remained among you a lifetime before it.[473] Then will you not reason?

17. So who is more unjust than he who invents a lie about God or denies His signs? Indeed, the criminals will not succeed.

18. And they worship other than God that which neither harms them nor benefits them, and they say, "These are our intercessors with God." Say, "Do you inform God of something He does not know in the heavens or on the earth?" Exalted is He and high above what they associate with Him.

19. And mankind was not but one community [united in religion], but [then] they differed. And if not for a word[474] that preceded from your Lord, it would have been judged between them [immediately] concerning that over which they differ.

20. And they say, "Why is a sign not sent down to him from his Lord?" So say, "The unseen is only for God [to administer], so wait; indeed, I am with you among those who wait."

21. And when We give the people a taste of mercy after adversity has touched them, at once they conspire against Our verses. Say, "God is swifter in strategy." Indeed, Our messengers [i.e., angels] record that which you conspire.

22. It is He who enables you to travel on land and sea until, when you are in ships and they sail with them[475] by a good wind and they rejoice therein, there comes a storm wind and the waves come upon them from everywhere and they assume that they are surrounded [i.e., doomed], supplicating God, sincere to Him in religion, "If You should save us from this, we will surely be among the thankful."

23. But when He saves them, at once they commit injustice[476] upon the earth without right. O mankind, your injus-

[473] The Prophet lived among his people forty years before receiving any revelation.

[474] God's decree to allow time on earth for His creation or not to punish anyone before evidence has come to him.

[475] The change in pronoun from the second to third person shows that the following description applies specifically to the disbelievers.

[476] By oppression and disobedience or by invoking others besides God.

tice is only against yourselves, [being merely] the enjoyment of worldly life. Then to Us is your return, and We will inform you of what you used to do.

24. The example of [this] worldly life is but like rain which We have sent down from the sky that the plants of the earth absorb - [those] from which men and livestock eat - until, when the earth has taken on its adornment and is beautified and its people suppose that they have capability over it, there comes to it Our command by night or by day, and We make it as a harvest,[477] as if it had not flourished yesterday. Thus do We explain in detail the signs for a people who give thought.

25. And God invites to the Home of Peace [i.e., Paradise] and guides whom He wills to a straight path.

26. For them who have done good is the best [reward] - and extra.[478] No darkness will cover their faces, nor humiliation. Those are companions of Paradise; they will abide therein eternally.

27. But they who have earned [blame for] evil doings - the recompense of an evil deed is its equivalent, and humiliation will cover them. They will have from God no protector. It will be as if their faces are covered with pieces of the night - so dark [are they]. Those are the companions of the Fire; they will abide therein eternally.

28. And [mention, O Muhammad], the Day We will gather them all together - then We will say to those who associated others with God, "[Remain in] your place, you and your 'partners'."[479] Then We will separate them,[480] and their "partners" will say, "You did not used to worship us,[481]

29. And sufficient is God as a witness between us and you that we were of your worship unaware."

30. There, [on that Day], every soul will be put to trial for what it did previously, and they will be returned to God, their master, the Truth, and lost from them is whatever they used to invent.

31. Say, "Who provides for you from the heaven and the earth? Or who controls hearing and sight and who brings the living out of the dead and brings the dead out of the living and who arranges [every] matter?" They will say, "God," so say, "Then will you not fear Him?"

32. For that is God, your Lord, the Truth. And what can be beyond truth except error? So how are you averted?

33. Thus the word [i.e., decree] of your Lord has come into effect upon those who defiantly disobeyed - that they will not believe.

34. Say, "Are there of your 'partners' any who begins creation and then repeats it?" Say, "God begins creation and then repeats it, so how are you deluded?"

35. Say, "Are there of your 'partners' any who guides to the truth?" Say, "God

[477] Its vegetation having been cut down or uprooted, i.e., utterly destroyed.

[478] In addition to the pleasures of Paradise, they will be able to see God, as reported in an authentic *hadith* narrated by Muslim.

[479] Those they had associated with God.

[480] From the believers.

[481] The inanimate objects, such as idols, will not have been aware of their worship of them. But those beings who consented to be worshipped will lie and deny it on the Day of Judgement.

guides to the truth. So is He who guides to the truth more worthy to be followed or he who guides not unless he is guided? Then what is [wrong] with you - how do you judge?"

36. And most of them follow not except assumption. Indeed, assumption avails not against the truth at all. Indeed, God is Knowing of what they do.

37. And it was not [possible] for this Qur'ān to be produced by other than God, but [it is] a confirmation of what was before it and a detailed explanation of the [former] Scripture, about which there is no doubt,[482] from the Lord of the worlds.

38. Or do they say [about the Prophet], "He invented it?" Say, "Then bring forth a sūrah like it and call upon [for assistance] whomever you can besides God, if you should be truthful."

39. Rather, they have denied that which they encompass not in knowledge and whose interpretation has not yet come to them. Thus did those before them deny. Then observe how was the end of the wrongdoers.

40. And of them are those who believe in it, and of them are those who do not believe in it. And your Lord is most knowing of the corrupters.

41. And if they deny you, [O Muhammad], then say, "For me are my deeds, and for you are your deeds. You are disassociated from what I do, and I am disassociated from what you do."

42. And among them are those who listen to you. But can you cause the deaf to hear [i.e., benefit from this hearing], although they will not use reason?

43. And among them are those who look at you. But can you guide the blind although they will not [attempt to] see?

44. Indeed, God does not wrong the people at all, but it is the people who are wronging themselves.

45. And on the Day when He will gather them, [it will be] as if they had not remained [in the world] but an hour of the day, [and] they will know each other. Those will have lost who denied the meeting with God and were not guided.

46. And whether We show you some of what We promise them, [O Muhammad], or We take you in death, to Us is their return; then, [either way], God is a witness concerning what they are doing.

47. And for every nation is a messenger. So when their messenger comes,[483] it will be judged between them in justice, and they will not be wronged.

48. And they say, "When is [the fulfillment of] this promise, if you should be truthful?"

49. Say, "I possess not for myself any harm or benefit except what God should will. For every nation is a [specified] term. When their time has come, then they will not remain behind an hour, nor will they precede [it]."

[482] This phrase refers back to the Qur'ān

[483] To witness on the Day of Judgement. Another meaning is "Once a messenger has come [to them in this world]..."

50. Say, "Have you considered: if His punishment should come to you by night or by day - for which [aspect] of it would the criminals be impatient?"[484]

51. Then is it that when it has [actually] occurred you will believe in it? Now?[485] And you were [once] for it impatient.[486]

52. Then it will be said to those who had wronged, "Taste the punishment of eternity; are you being recompensed except for what you used to earn?"

53. And they ask information of you, [O Muhammad], "Is it true?" Say, "Yes, by my Lord. Indeed, it is truth; and you will not cause failure [to God]."

54. And if each soul that wronged had everything on earth, it would offer it in ransom. And they will confide regret when they see the punishment; and they will be judged in justice, and they will not be wronged.

55. Unquestionably, to God belongs whatever is in the heavens and the earth. Unquestionably, the promise of God is truth, but most of them do not know.

56. He gives life and causes death, and to Him you will be returned.

57. O mankind, there has to come to you instruction from your Lord and healing for what is in the breasts and guidance and mercy for the believers.

58. Say, "In the bounty of God and in His mercy - in that let them rejoice; it is better than what they accumulate."

59. Say, "Have you seen what God has sent down to you of provision of which you have made [some] lawful and [some] unlawful?" Say, "Has God permitted you [to do so], or do you invent [something] about God?"

60. And what will be the supposition of those who invent falsehood about God on the Day of Resurrection?[487] Indeed, God is full of bounty to the people, but most of them are not grateful.

61. And, [O Muhammad], you are not [engaged] in any matter or recite any of the Qur'ān and you [people] do not do any deed except that We are witness over you when you are involved in it. And not absent from your Lord is any [part] of an atom's weight[488] within the earth or within the heaven or [anything] smaller than that or greater but that it is in a clear register.

62. Unquestionably, [for] the allies of God there will be no fear concerning them, nor will they grieve -

63. Those who believed and were fearing God.

64. For them are good tidings in the worldly life and in the Hereafter. No change is there in the words [i.e., decrees] of God. That is what is the great attainment.

65. And let not their speech grieve you. Indeed, honour [due to power] belongs

---

484 "Impatience" refers to the disbelievers' ridicule of the Prophet by telling him to produce God's punishment as proof of his truthfulness.
485 i.e., when it is too late to benefit from belief.
486 Challenging those who warned of it to bring it on immediately.

487 i.e., what do they think He will do with them.
488 Or "the weight of a small ant."

to God entirely. He is the Hearing, the Knowing.

66. Unquestionably, to God belongs whoever is in the heavens and whoever is on the earth. And those who invoke other than God do not [actually] follow [His] "partners." They follow not except assumption, and they are not but falsifying.

67. It is He who made for you the night to rest therein and the day, giving sight.[489] Indeed in that are signs for a people who listen.

68. They[490] have said, "God has taken a son." Exalted is He; He is the [one] Free of need. To Him belongs whatever is in the heavens and whatever is in the earth. You have no authority for this [claim]. Do you say about God that which you do not know?

69. Say, "Indeed, those who invent falsehood about God will not succeed."

70. [For them is brief] enjoyment in this world; then to Us is their return; then We will make them taste the severe punishment because they used to disbelieve.

71. And recite to them the news of Noah, when he said to his people, "O my people, if my residence and my reminding of the signs of God has become burdensome upon you - then I have relied upon God. So resolve upon your plan and [call upon] your associates. Then let not your plan be obscure to you.[491] Then carry it out upon me and do not give me respite.

72. And if you turn away [from my advice] - then no payment have I asked of you. My reward is only from God, and I have been commanded to be of the Muslims [i.e., those who submit to God]."

73. And they denied him, so We saved him and those with him in the ship and made them successors, and We drowned those who denied Our signs. Then see how was the end of those who were warned.

74. Then We sent after him messengers to their peoples, and they came to them with clear proofs. But they were not to believe in that which they had denied before.[492] Thus We seal over the hearts of the transgressors.

75. Then We sent after them Moses and Aaron to Pharaoh and his establishment with Our signs, but they behaved arrogantly and were a criminal people.

76. So when there came to them the truth from Us, they said, "Indeed, this is obvious magic."

77. Moses said, "Do you say [thus] about the truth when it has come to you? Is this magic? But magicians will not succeed."

78. They said, "Have you come to us to turn us away from that upon which we found our fathers and so that you two

[489] i.e., making things visible.
[490] The Christians and others.

[491] i.e., Do not let it be a source of doubt or anxiety to you but let it be clear, open and defined.
[492] i.e., the succeeding generations were persistent in disbelief.

may have grandeur in the land? And we are not believers in you."

79. And Pharaoh said, "Bring to me every learned magician."

80. So when the magicians came, Moses said to them, "Throw down whatever you will throw."

81. And when they had thrown, Moses said, "What you have brought is [only] magic. Indeed, God will expose its worthlessness. Indeed, God does not amend the work of corrupters.

82. And God will establish the truth by His words, even if the criminals dislike it."

83. But no one believed Moses, except [some] offspring [i.e., youths] among his people, for fear of Pharaoh and his establishment that they would persecute them. And indeed, Pharaoh was haughty within the land, and indeed, he was of the transgressors.

84. And Moses said, "O my people, if you have believed in God, then rely upon Him, if you should be Muslims [i.e., submitting to him]."

85. So they said, "Upon God do we rely. Our Lord, make us not [objects of] trial for the wrongdoing people.

86. And save us by Your mercy from the disbelieving people."

87. And We inspired to Moses and his brother, "Settle your people in Egypt in houses and make your houses [facing the] qiblah[493] and establish prayer and give good tidings to the believers."

88. And Moses said, "Our Lord, indeed You have given Pharaoh and his establishment splendor and wealth in the worldly life, our Lord, that they may lead [men] astray from Your way. Our Lord, obliterate their wealth and harden their hearts so that they will not believe until they see the painful punishment."

89. [God] said, "Your supplication has been answered."[494] So remain on a right course and follow not the way of those who do not know."

90. And We took the Children of Israel across the sea, and Pharaoh and his soldiers pursued them in tyranny and enmity until, when drowning overtook him, he said, "I believe that there is no deity except that in whom the Children of Israel believe, and I am of the Muslims."

91. Now? And you had disobeyed [Him] before and were of the corrupters?

92. So today We will save you in body[495] that you may be to those who succeed you a sign. And indeed, many among the people, of Our signs, are heedless.

93. And We had certainty settled the Children of Israel in an agreeable settlement and provided them with good things. And they did not differ until [after] knowledge had come to them. Indeed, your Lord will judge between them on the Day of Resurrection concerning that over which they used to differ.

94. So if you are in doubt, [O Muhammad], about that which We have revealed to

[493] In order that they might pray therein unseen by their enemy.

[494] Literally, "the supplication of both of you," i.e., that of Moses and of Aaron, who joined by saying, "*Ameen*" ("O God, respond").

[495] i.e., his dead body will be preserved and not destroyed.

you, then ask those who have been reading the Scripture before you. The truth has certainly come to you from your Lord, so never be among the doubters.

95. And never be of those who deny the signs of God and [thus] be among the losers.[496]

96. Indeed, those upon whom the word [i.e., decree] of your Lord has come into effect will not believe,

97. Even if every sign should come to them, until they see the painful punishment.

98. Then has there not been a [single] city that believed so its faith benefited it except the people of Jonah? When they believed, We removed from them the punishment of disgrace in worldly life and gave them enjoyment [i.e., provision] for a time.

99. And had your Lord willed, those on earth would have believed - all of them entirely. Then, [O Muhammad], would you compel the people in order that they become believers?

100. And it is not for a soul [i.e., anyone] to believe except by permission of God, and He will place defilement[497] upon those who will not use reason.

101. Say, "Observe what is in the heavens and earth." But of no avail will be signs or warners to a people who do not believe.

102. So do they wait except for like [what occurred in] the days of those who passed on before them? Say, "Then wait; indeed, I am with you among those who wait."

103. Then We will save Our messengers and those who have believed. Thus, it is an obligation upon Us that We save the believers.[498]

104. Say, [O Muhammad], "O people, if you are in doubt as to my religion - then I do not worship those which you worship besides God; but I worship God, who causes your death. And I have been commanded to be of the believers

105. And [commanded], 'Direct your face [i.e., self] toward the religion, inclining to truth, and never be of those who associate others with God;

106. And do not invoke besides God that which neither benefits you nor harms you, for if you did, then indeed you would be of the wrongdoers.' "[499]

107. And if God should touch you with adversity, there is no remover of it except Him; and if He intends for you good, then there is no repeller of His bounty. He causes it to reach whom He wills of His servants. And He is the Forgiving, the Merciful.

108. Say, "O mankind, the truth has come to you from your Lord, so whoever is guided is only guided for [the benefit of] his soul, and whoever goes astray

[496] Among the interpretations of the last two verses is that they were meant to stir the Prophet to declare and confirm his certainty, which he did. Another is that although the words are addressed to the Prophet, they are directed to all people.

[497] Among its meanings are filth, wrath, punishment, disbelief, confusion and error.

[498] From God's punishment.

[499] See footnote to 10:95.

only goes astray [in violation] against it.
And I am not over you a manager."

109. And follow what is revealed to you, [O
Muhammad], and be patient until God
will judge. And He is the best of judges.

## Sūrah 11: Hūd

### Period of Revelation

If we consider its theme deeply we come to the conclusion that it was revealed during the same period as Sūrah Yūnus and most probably followed it immediately.

### Subject

The Sūrah deals with the same subject as Sūrah Yūnus that is invitation to the Message admonition and warning with this difference that the warning is sterner. This is also supported by a hadith: Some time after its revelation Abu Bakr noted to the Prophet that he had been noticing that he was growing older and older. The Prophet replied, *'Sūrah Hūd and the like Sūrahs have made me old.'* This shows that it was a very hard time for the Prophet and these stern warnings added greatly to his anxieties that were caused by the persecution from the Quraysh who were doing their worst to crush down the Message of Islām. For it was obvious to the Prophet that the last limit of the respite given by God was approaching nearer and nearer and he was afraid lest the term of the respite should expire and his people be seized by the torment. The invitation is this: Obey the Messenger of God; discard Shirk (polytheism) and worship God and God alone: establish the entire system of your life on the belief that you shall be called to account in the Hereafter.

The admonition is this: Remember that those people who put their faith in the outward appearance of this worldly life and rejected the Message of the Prophets met with dire consequences. Therefore you should consider it seriously whether you should follow the same way that history has proved to be the path to ruin.

The warning is this: You should not be deluded by the delay in the coming of the punishment: it is because of the respite that God has granted you by His grace so that you might mend your ways: if you do not make use of this opportunity you shall be inflicted with an inevitable punishment that will destroy you all except the Believers.

Instead of addressing the people directly, the Qur'ān has used the stories of the people of Noah, Hud, Sālih, Lot, Shu'aib and Moses to achieve the above mentioned objects. What is most prominent in their stories is that when God passes His judgement on the people He does not spare anyone whatsoever even if he be the nearest relative of the Prophet of the time. Only that one is rescued who had believed in the Prophet and none else not even his own son or wife. More than that: the Faith demands from each and every Believer that he should totally forget his relationships when that judgement comes and remember only the relationship of the Faith. For it is against the spirit of Islām to show any regard whatsoever for the relationships of blood and race. And the Muslims demonstrated these teachings practically in the Battle of Badr four years after the revelation of this Sūrah.

## Sūrah 11: Hūd[500]

In the Name of God, the Most Compassionate, the Most Merciful

1. Alif, Lām, Rā.[501] [This is] a Book whose verses are perfected and then presented in detail from [one who is] Wise and Acquainted

2. [Through a messenger, saying], "Do not worship except God. Indeed, I am to you from Him a warner and a bringer of good tidings,"

3. And [saying], "Seek forgiveness of your Lord and repent to Him, [and] He will let you enjoy a good provision for a specified term and give every doer of favor his favor [i.e., reward]. But if you turn away, then indeed, I fear for you the punishment of a great Day.

4. To God is your return, and He is over all things competent."

5. Unquestionably, they [i.e., the disbelievers] turn away their breasts to hide themselves from Him. Unquestionably, [even] when they cover themselves in their clothing, He [i.e., God] knows what they conceal and what they declare. Indeed, He is Knowing of that within the breasts.

6. And there is no creature on earth but that upon God is its provision, and He knows its place of dwelling and place of storage.[502] All is in a clear register.

7. And it is He who created the heavens and the earth in six days - and His Throne had been upon water - that He might test you as to which of you is best in deed. But if you say, "Indeed, you are resurrected after death," those who disbelieve will surely say, "This is not but obvious magic."

8. And if We hold back from them the punishment for a limited time, they will surely say,[503] "What detains it?" Unquestionably, on the Day it comes to them, it will not be averted from them, and they will be enveloped by what they used to ridicule.

9. And if We give man a taste of mercy from Us and then We withdraw it from him, indeed, he is despairing and ungrateful.

10. But if We give him a taste of favor after hardship has touched him, he will surely say, "Bad times have left me." Indeed, he is exultant and boastful -

11. Except for those who are patient and do righteous deeds; those will have forgiveness and great reward.

12. Then would you possibly leave [out] some of what is revealed to you,[504] or is your breast constrained by it because they say, "Why has there not been sent down to him a treasure or come with him an angel?" But you are only a warner. And God is Disposer of all things.

13. Or do they say, "He invented it"? Say, "Then bring ten sūrahs like it that have been invented and call upon [for assistance] whomever you can besides God, if you should be truthful."

[500] *Hūd:* (The prophet) Hūd.
[501] See footnote to 2:1.
[502] Before birth and after death.
[503] In ridicule and disbelief.
[504] Knowing of the Prophet's difficulties, God urges him to patience, certain that he would not fail to convey the message in its entirety.

14. And if they do not respond to you - then know that it [i.e., the Qur'ān] was revealed with the knowledge of God[505] and that there is no deity except Him. Then,[506] would you [not] be Muslims?

15. Whoever desires the life of this world and its adornments - We fully repay them for their deeds therein,[507] and they therein will not be deprived.

16. Those are the ones for whom there is not in the Hereafter but the Fire. And lost is what they did therein,[508] and worthless is what they used to do.

17. So is one who [stands] upon a clear evidence from his Lord [like the aforementioned]? And a witness[509] from Him follows it,[510] and before it was the Scripture of Moses to lead and as mercy. Those [believers in the former revelations] believe in it [i.e., the Qur'ān]. But whoever disbelieves in it from the [various] factions - the Fire is his promised destination. So be not in doubt about it. Indeed, it is the truth from your Lord, but most of the people do not believe.

18. And who is more unjust than he who invents a lie about God? Those will be presented before their Lord, and the witnesses will say, "These are the ones who lied against their Lord." Unquestionably, the curse of God is upon the wrongdoers

[505] i.e., that knowledge which no one possesses except Him.
[506] After having been convinced by such evidence.
[507] i.e., during worldly life.
[508] i.e., during worldly life.
[509] Referring to Prophet Muhammad or to the angel Gabriel.
[510] Testifying to its truth. Additionally, it can mean "recites it," i.e., the Qur'ān.

19. Who averted [people] from the way of God and sought to make it [seem] deviant while they, concerning the Hereafter, were disbelievers.

20. Those were not causing failure [to God] on earth, nor did they have besides God any protectors. For them the punishment will be multiplied. They were not able to hear, nor did they see.[511]

21. Those are the ones who will have lost themselves, and lost from them is what they used to invent.

22. Assuredly, it is they in the Hereafter who will be the greatest losers.

23. Indeed, they who have believed and done righteous deeds and humbled themselves to their Lord - those are the companions of Paradise; they will abide eternally therein.

24. The example of the two parties is like the blind and deaf, and the seeing and hearing. Are they equal in comparison? Then, will you not remember?

25. And We had certainly sent Noah to his people, [saying], "Indeed, I am to you a clear warner

26. That you not worship except God. Indeed, I fear for you the punishment of a painful day."

27. So the eminent among those who disbelieved from his people said, "We do not see you but as a man like ourselves, and we do not see you followed except by those who are the lowest of us [and]

[511] They refused to listen to the truth or to perceive it.

at first suggestion.[512] And we do not see in you over us any merit; rather, we think you are liars."

28. He said, "O my people, have you considered: if I should be upon clear evidence from my Lord while He has given me mercy from Himself but it has been made unapparent to you, should we force it upon you while you are averse to it?

29. And O my people, I ask not of you for it any wealth. My reward is not but from God. And I am not one to drive away those who have believed. Indeed, they will meet their Lord, but I see that you are a people behaving ignorantly.

30. And O my people, who would protect me from God if I drove them away? Then will you not be reminded?

31. And I do not tell you that I have the depositories [containing the provision] of God or that I know the unseen, nor do I tell you that I am an angel, nor do I say of those upon whom your eyes look down that God will never grant them any good. God is most knowing of what is within their souls. Indeed, I would then be among the wrongdoers [i.e., the unjust]."

32. They said, "O Noah, you have disputed [i.e., opposed] us and been frequent in dispute of us. So bring us what you threaten us, if you should be of the truthful."

33. He said, "God will only bring it to you if He wills, and you will not cause [Him] failure.

[512] i.e., without any thought or hesitation.

34. And my advice will not benefit you - although I wished to advise you - If God should intend to put you in error. He is your Lord, and to Him you will be returned."

35. Or do they say [about Prophet Muhammad], "He invented it"? Say, "If I have invented it, then upon me is [the consequence of] my crime; but I am innocent of what [crimes] you commit."

36. And it was revealed to Noah that, "No one will believe from your people except those who have already believed, so do not be distressed by what they have been doing.

37. And construct the ship under Our observation and Our inspiration and do not address Me concerning those who have wronged; indeed, they are [to be] drowned."

38. And he constructed the ship, and whenever an assembly of the eminent of his people passed by him, they ridiculed him. He said, "If you ridicule us, then we will ridicule you just as you ridicule.

39. And you are going to know who will get a punishment that will disgrace him [on earth] and upon whom will descend an enduring punishment [in the Hereafter]."

40. [So it was], until when Our command came and the oven overflowed,[513] We said, "Load upon it [i.e., the ship] of each [creature] two mates and your family, except those about whom the word [i.e., decree] has preceded, and

[513] As a sign to Noah of the imminence of the flood. The *tannūr* is a large, rounded oven. The word can also mean the earth's lowlands.

[include] whoever has believed." But none had believed with him, except a few.

41. And [Noah] said, "Embark therein; in the name of God is its course and its anchorage. Indeed, my Lord is Forgiving and Merciful."

42. And it sailed with them through waves like mountains, and Noah called to his son who was apart [from them], "O my son, come aboard with us and be not with the disbelievers."

43. [But] he said, "I will take refuge on a mountain to protect me from the water." [Noah] said, "There is no protector today from the decree of God, except for whom He gives mercy." And the waves came between them, and he was among the drowned.

44. And it was said, "O earth, swallow your water, and O sky, withhold [your rain]." And the water subsided, and the matter was accomplished, and it [i.e., the ship] came to rest on the [mountain of] Jūdiyy. And it was said, "Away with the wrongdoing people."

45. And Noah called to his Lord and said, "My Lord, indeed my son is of my family; and indeed, Your promise is true; and You are the most just of judges!"

46. He said, "O Noah, indeed he is not of your family; indeed, he is [one whose] work was other than righteous, so ask Me not for that about which you have no knowledge. Indeed, I advise you, lest you be among the ignorant."

47. [Noah] said, "My Lord, I seek refuge in You from asking that of which I have no knowledge. And unless You forgive me and have mercy upon me, I will be among the losers."

48. It was said, "O Noah, disembark in security from Us and blessings upon you and upon nations [descending] from those with you. But other nations [of them] We will grant enjoyment; then there will touch them from Us a painful punishment."

49. That is from the news of the unseen which We reveal to you, [O Muhammad]. You knew it not, neither you nor your people, before this. So be patient; indeed, the [best] outcome is for the righteous.

50. And to 'Aad [We sent] their brother Hūd. He said, "O my people, worship God; you have no deity other than Him. You are not but inventors [of falsehood].

51. O my people, I do not ask you for it [i.e., my advice] any reward. My reward is only from the one who created me. Then will you not reason?

52. And O my people, ask forgiveness of your Lord and then repent to Him. He will send [rain from] the sky upon you in showers and increase you in strength [added] to your strength. And do not turn away, [being] criminals."

53. They said, "O Hūd, you have not brought us clear evidence, and we are not ones to leave our gods on your say-so. Nor are we believers in you.

54. We only say that some of our gods have possessed you with evil [i.e., insanity]." He said, "Indeed, I call God to witness, and witness [yourselves] that I am free from whatever you associate with God

55. Other than Him. So plot against me all together; then do not give me respite.

56. Indeed, I have relied upon God, my Lord and your Lord. There is no creature but that He holds its forelock [i.e., controls it]. Indeed, my Lord is on a path [that is] straight."

57. But if they turn away, [say], "I have already conveyed that with which I was sent to you. My Lord will give succession to a people other than you, and you will not harm Him at all. Indeed my Lord is, over all things, Guardian."

58. And when Our command came, We saved Hūd and those who believed with him, by mercy from Us; and We saved them from a harsh punishment.

59. And that was 'Aad, who rejected the signs of their Lord and disobeyed His messengers and followed the order of every obstinate tyrant.

60. And they were [therefore] followed in this world with a curse and [as well] on the Day of Resurrection. Unquestionably, 'Aad denied their Lord; then away with 'Aad, the people of Hūd.

61. And to Thamūd [We sent] their brother Sālih. He said, "O my people, worship God; you have no deity other than Him. He has produced you from the earth and settled you in it, so ask forgiveness of Him and then repent to Him. Indeed, my Lord is near and responsive."

62. They said, "O Sālih, you were among us a man of promise before this. Do you forbid us to worship what our fathers worshipped? And indeed we are, about that to which you invite us, in disquieting doubt."

63. He said, "O my people, have you considered: if I should be upon clear evidence from my Lord and He has given me mercy from Himself, who would protect me from God if I disobeyed Him? So you would not increase me except in loss.

64. And O my people, this is the she-camel of God - [she is] to you a sign. So let her feed upon God's earth and do not touch her with harm, or you will be taken by an impending punishment."

65. But they hamstrung her, so he said, "Enjoy yourselves in your homes for three days. That is a promise not to be denied [i.e., unfailing]."

66. So when Our command came, We saved Sālih and those who believed with him, by mercy from Us, and [saved them] from the disgrace of that day.[514] Indeed, it is your Lord who is the Powerful, the Exalted in Might.

67. And the shriek[515] seized those who had wronged, and they became within their homes [corpses] fallen prone

68. As if they had never prospered therein. Unquestionably, Thamūd denied their Lord; then, away with Thamūd.

69. And certainly did Our messengers [i.e., angels] come to Abraham with good tidings; they said, "Peace." He said, "Peace," and did not delay in bringing [them] a roasted calf.

70. But when he saw their hands not reaching for it, he distrusted them and felt

[514] The day of Thamūd's destruction.

[515] A piercing cry or blast from the sky.

from them apprehension.[516] They said, "Fear not. We have been sent to the people of Lot."

71. And his wife was standing, and she smiled.[517] Then We gave her good tidings of Isaac and after Isaac, Jacob.

72. She said, "Woe to me![518] Shall I give birth while I am an old woman and this, my husband, is an old man? Indeed, this is an amazing thing!"

73. They said, "Are you amazed at the decree of God? May the mercy of God and His blessings be upon you, people of the house. Indeed, He is Praiseworthy and Honourable."

74. And when the fright had left Abraham and the good tidings had reached him, he began to argue [i.e., plead] with Us[519] concerning the people of Lot.

75. Indeed, Abraham was forbearing, grieving[520] and [frequently] returning [to God].

76. [The angels said], "O Abraham, give up this [plea]. Indeed, the command of your Lord has come, and indeed, there will reach them a punishment that cannot be repelled."

77. And when Our messengers, [the angels], came to Lot, he was anguished for them and felt for them great discomfort[521] and said, "This is a trying day."

78. And his people came hastening to him, and before [this] they had been doing evil deeds.[522] He said, "O my people, these are my daughters;[523] they are purer for you. So fear God and do not disgrace me concerning my guests. Is there not among you a man of reason?"

79. They said, "You have already known that we have not concerning your daughters [i.e., women] any claim [i.e., desire], and indeed, you know what we want."

80. He said, "If only I had against you some power or could take refuge in a strong support."

81. They [the angels] said, "O Lot, indeed we are messengers of your Lord; [therefore], they will never reach you. So set out with your family during a portion of the night[524] and let not any among you look back - except your wife; indeed, she will be struck by that which strikes them. Indeed, their appointment is [for] the morning. Is not the morning near?"

82. So when Our command came, We made the highest part [of the city] its lowest and rained upon them stones of layered hard clay, [which were]

83. Marked from your Lord. And it [i.e., God's punishment] is not from the wrongdoers [very] far.

---

516 Traditionally, if a guest refused to eat, it meant that he harboured ill will toward the host or intended him harm.

517 In pleasure at the news of the forthcoming punishment of the evil people who denied Prophet Lot.

518 An expression of surprise and amazement.

519 i.e., with Our angels.

520 i.e., sighting or moaning during supplication out of grief for people and fear of God.

521 Prophet Lot feared for the safety and honour of his guests.

522 Referring to their practice of sodomy and homosexual rape of males.

523 i.e., the woman of his community who were available for marriage.

524 i.e., sometime before dawn.

84. And to Madyan [We sent] their brother Shu'ayb. He said, "O my people, worship God; you have no deity other than Him. And do not decrease from the measure and the scale. Indeed, I see you in prosperity, but indeed, I fear for you the punishment of an all-encompassing Day.

85. And O my people, give full measure and weight in justice and do not deprive the people of their due and do not commit abuse on the earth, spreading corruption.

86. What remains [lawful] from God is best for you, if you would be believers. But I am not a guardian over you."

87. They said, "O Shu'ayb, does your prayer [i.e., religion] command you that we should leave what our fathers worship or not do with our wealth what we please? Indeed, you are the forbearing, the discerning!"[525]

88. He said, "O my people, have you considered: if I am upon clear evidence from my Lord and He has provided me with a good provision from Him...?[526] And I do not intend to differ from you in that which I have forbidden you; I only intend reform as much as I am able. And my success is not but through God. Upon Him I have relied, and to Him I return.[527]

89. And O my people, let not [your] dissension from me cause you to be struck by that similar to what struck the people of Noah or the people of Hūd or the people of Sālih. And the people of Lot are not from you far away.

90. And ask forgiveness of your Lord and then repent to Him. Indeed, my Lord is Merciful and Affectionate."

91. They said, "O Shu'ayb, we do not understand much of what you say, and indeed, we consider you among us as weak. And if not for your family, we would have stoned you [to death]; and you are not to us one respected."

92. He said, "O my people, is my family more respected for power by you than God? But you put Him behind your backs [in neglect]. Indeed, my Lord is encompassing of what you do.

93. And O my people, work according to your position; indeed, I am working. You are going to know to whom will come a punishment that will disgrace him and who is a liar. So watch; indeed, I am with you a watcher, [awaiting the outcome]."

94. And when Our command came, We saved Shu'ayb and those who believed with him, by mercy from Us. And the shriek seized those who had wronged, and they became within their homes [corpses] fallen prone

95. As if they had never prospered therein. Then, away with Madyan as Thamūd was taken away.

96. And We did certainly send Moses with Our signs and a clear authority

97. To Pharaoh and his establishment, but they followed the command of Pharaoh, and the command of Pharaoh was not [at all] discerning.

[525] This is a sarcastic description implying the opposite.
[526] The conclusion of the sentence is estimated as "...would it not be my duty to warn you against corruption and disobedience?"
[527] i.e., I turn to God frequently in supplication and repentance.

98. He will precede his people on the Day of Resurrection and lead them into the Fire; and wretched is the place to which they are led.

99. And they were followed in this [world] with a curse and on the Day of Resurrection. And wretched is the gift[528] which is given.

100. That is from the news of the cities, which We relate to you; of them, some are [still] standing and some are [as] a harvest [mowed down].[529]

101. And We did not wrong them, but they wronged themselves. And they were not availed at all by their gods which they invoked other than God when there came the command of your Lord. And they did not increase them in other than ruin.

102. And thus is the seizure of your Lord when He seizes the cities while they are committing wrong. Indeed, His seizure is painful and severe.

103. Indeed in that is a sign for those who fear the punishment of the Hereafter. That is a Day for which the people will be collected, and that is a Day [which will be] witnessed.

104. And We do not delay it except for a limited term.

105. The Day it comes no soul will speak except by His permission. And among them will be the wretched and the prosperous.

106. As for those who were [destined to be] wretched, they will be in the Fire. For them therein is [violent] exhaling and inhaling.[530]

107. [They will be] abiding therein as long as the heavens and the earth endure, except what your Lord should will. Indeed, your Lord is an effecter of what He intends.

108. And as for those who were [destined to be] prosperous, they will be in Paradise, abiding therein as long as the heavens and the earth endure, except what your Lord should will - a bestowal uninterrupted.

109. So do not be in doubt, [O Muhammad], as to what these [polytheists] are worshipping. They worship not except as their fathers worshipped before. And indeed, We will give them their share undiminished.

110. And We had certainly given Moses the Scripture, but it came under disagreement. And if not for a word[531] that preceded from your Lord, it would have been judged between them. And indeed they are, concerning it [i.e., the Qur'ān], in disquieting doubt.

111. And indeed, each [of the believers and disbelievers] - your Lord will fully compensate them for their deeds. Indeed, He is Acquainted with what they do.

112. So remain on a right course as you have been commanded, [you] and those who have turned back with you [to God],

528 i.e., the curse which follows them in both worlds.

529 Their structures have been completely destroyed.

530 i.e., their sighs and sobs, resembling the bray of a donkey.

531 See footnote to 10:19.

and do not transgress. Indeed, He is Seeing of what you do.

113. And do not incline toward those who do wrong, lest you be touched by the Fire, and you would not have other than God any protectors; then you would not be helped.

114. And establish prayer at the two ends of the day and at the approach of the night. Indeed, good deeds do away with misdeeds. That is a reminder for those who remember.

115. And be patient, for indeed, God does not allow to be lost the reward of those who do good.

116. So why were there not[532] among the generations before you those of enduring discrimination forbidding corruption on earth - except a few of those We saved from among them? But those who wronged pursued what luxury they were given therein, and they were criminals.

117. And your Lord would not have destroyed the cities unjustly while their people were reformers.

118. And if your Lord had willed, He could have made mankind one community; but they will not cease to differ,

119. Except whom your Lord has given mercy, and for that He created them. But the word of your Lord is to be fulfilled that, "I will surely fill Hell with jinn and men all together."

120. And each [story] We relate to you from the news of the messengers is that by which We make firm your heart. And there has come to you, in this, the truth and an instruction and a reminder for the believers.

121. And say to those who do not believe, "Work according to your position; indeed, we are working.

122. And wait, indeed, we are waiting."

123. And to God belong the unseen [aspects] of the heavens and the earth and to Him will be returned the matter, all of it, so worship Him and rely upon Him. And your Lord is not unaware of that which you do.

[532] Meaning "if only there had been..."

## Sūrah 12: Yūsuf

### When and Why Revealed?

The subject matter of this Sūrah indicates that it was revealed during the last stage of the Prophet's residence at Makkah when the Quraysh were considering the question of killing or exiling or imprisoning him. At that time some of the disbelievers put this question to test him: "Why did the Israelites go to Egypt?" This question was asked because they knew that their story was not known to the Arabs for there was no mention of it whatever in their traditions and the Prophet had never even referred to it before. Therefore they expected that he would not be able to give any satisfactory answer to this question or would first evade it and afterwards try to enquire about it from some Jew and thus he would be totally exposed. But contrary to their expectations the tables were turned on them for God revealed the whole story of Prophet Joseph then and there and the Prophet recited it on the spot. This put the Quraysh in a very awkward position because it not only foiled their scheme but also administered a warning to them by appropriately applying it to their case as if to say 'As you are behaving towards this Prophet exactly in the same way the brothers of Prophet Joseph behaved towards him; so you shall meet with the same end.'

The fact is that by applying this story to the conflict the Qur'ān had made a bold and clear prophecy which was fulfilled literally by the events that happened in the succeeding ten years. Hardly two years had passed after its revelation when the Quraysh conspired to kill the Prophet like the brothers of Prophet Joseph and he had to emigrate from Makkah to Madinah where he gained the same kind of power as Prophet Joseph had gained in Egypt. Again in the end the Quraysh had to humble themselves before him just like the brothers of Prophet Joseph when they humbly requested 'Show mercy to us for God rewards richly those who show mercy' (v. 88) and Prophet Joseph generously forgave them (though he had complete power to wreak vengeance on them) saying today no penalty shall be inflicted on you. May God forgive you: He is the greatest of all those who forgive (v. 92). The same story of mercy was repeated when after the conquest of Makkah the crest fallen Quraysh stood meekly before the Prophet who had full power to wreak his vengeance on them for each and every cruelty committed by them. But instead he merely asked them 'What treatment do you expect from me now?' They replied 'You are a generous brother and the son of a generous brother. At this he very generously forgave them saying I will give the same answer to your request that Joseph gave to his brothers: '. . . today no penalty shall be inflicted on you: you are forgiven.'

### Topics of Discussion

Moreover the Qur'ān does not relate this story as a mere narrative but uses it as usual for the propagation of the Message in the following ways:

Throughout the narrative the Qur'ān has made it clear that the Faith of Prophets Abraham, Isaac, Jacob and Joseph (God's peace be upon them all) was the same as that of Prophet Muhammad and they invited the people to the same Message to which Muhammad was inviting them.

Then it places the characters of Prophet Jacob and Prophet Joseph side by side with the characters of the brothers of Joseph, the members of the trade caravan the court dignitary; Al Aziz of Egypt and his wife the "ladies" of Egypt and the rulers of Egypt and poses a silent question to the reader as if to say 'Contrast the former characters moulded by Islām on the bedrock of the worship of God and accountability in the Hereafter with the latter moulded by kufr and ignorance' on the worship of the world and disregard of God and the Hereafter and decide for yourselves which of these two patterns you would choose."

The Qur'ān has used this story to bring forth another truth: whatever God wills He fulfils it anyhow and man can never defeat His plan with his counterplans nor prevent it from happening nor change it in any way whatever. Nay, it often so happens that man adopts some measure to fulfil his own design and believes that he has done that very thing which would fulfil his design but in the end he finds to his dismay that he had done something which was against his own and conducive to the Divine purpose. When the brothers of Prophet Joseph cast him into the well they believed that they had once for all got rid of the obstacle in their way but in fact they had paved the way for the Divine purpose of making him the ruler of Egypt before whom they would have to humble themselves in the end. Likewise the wife of Aziz had sent Prophet Joseph to the prison floating over the thought that she had wreaked her vengeance on him but in fact she had provided for him the opportunity for becoming the ruler of Egypt and for putting herself to the shame of confessing her own sin publicly.

And these are not the solitary instances which prove the truth that even if the whole world united to bring about the down fall of the one whom God willed to raise high it could not succeed. Nay, the very "sure and effective" measures that were adopted by the brothers to degrade Joseph were used by God for the success of Joseph and for the humiliation and disgrace of his brothers. On the other hand if God willed the fall of one no measure whatsoever effective could raise him high: nay, it helped to bring about his fall and the disgrace of those who adopted them.

Moreover the story contains other lessons for those who intend to follow the way of God. The first lesson it teaches is that one should remain within the limits prescribed by the Divine Law in one's aims and objects and measures for success and failure are entirely in the hands of God. Therefore if one adopts pure aims and lawful measures but fails at least one will escape humiliation and disgrace. On the other hand the one who adopts an impure aim and unlawful measures to achieve it shall not only inevitably meet with ignominy and disgrace in the Hereafter but also runs the risk of ignominy and disgrace in this world.

The second lesson it teaches is that those who exert for the cause of truth and righteousness and put their trust in God and entrust all their affairs to Him, get consolation and comfort from Him. For this helps them face their opponents with confidence and courage and they do not lose heart when they encounter the apparently terrifying measures of the powerful enemies. They will persevere in their task without fear and leave the results to God.

But the greatest lesson this story teaches is that if the Believer possesses true Islāmic character and is endowed with wisdom, he can conquer a whole country with the strength of his character alone. The marvelous example of Prophet Joseph teaches us that a man of high and pure character comes out successful even under the most adverse circumstances. When Prophet Joseph went to Egypt, he was only a teenager of seventeen years, a foreigner, all alone and without any provisions; nay, he had been sold there as a slave. And the horrible condition of the slaves during that period is known to every student of history. Then he was charged with a heinous moral crime and sent to prison for an indefinite term. But throughout this period of affliction, he evinced the highest moral qualities which raised him to the highest rank in the country.

**Final Note**

Though the story of Prophet Joseph as given in the Qur'ān differs very much in its details from that given in the Bible and the Talmud, the three generally agree in the key events.

## Sūrah 12: Yūsuf[533]

In the Name of God, the Most Compassionate, the Most Merciful

1. Alif, Lām, Rā.[534] These are the verses of the clear Book.

2. Indeed, We have sent it down as an Arabic Qur'ān[535] that you might understand.

3. We relate to you, [O Muhammad], the best of stories in what We have revealed to you of this Qur'ān although you were, before it, among the unaware.

4. [Of these stories mention] when Joseph said to his father,[536] "O my father, indeed I have seen [in a dream] eleven stars and the sun and the moon; I saw them prostrating to me."

5. He said, "O my son, do not relate your vision to your brothers or they will contrive against you a plan. Indeed Satan, to man, is a manifest enemy.

6. And thus will your Lord choose you and teach you the interpretation of narratives [i.e., events of dreams] and complete His favor upon you and upon the family of Jacob, as He completed it upon your fathers before, Abraham and Isaac. Indeed, your Lord is Knowing and Wise."

7. Certainly were there in Joseph and his brothers signs for those who ask, [such as]

8. When they said, "Joseph and his brother[537] are more beloved to our father than we, while we are a clan. Indeed, our father is in clear error.

9. Kill Joseph or cast him out to [another] land; the countenance [i.e., attention] of your father will [then] be only for you, and you will be after that a righteous people."[538]

10. Said a speaker among them, "Do not kill Joseph but throw him into the bottom of the well; some travelers will pick him up - if you would do [something]."

11. They said, "O our father, why do you not entrust us with Joseph while indeed, we are to him sincere counselors?

12. Send him with us tomorrow that he may eat well and play. And indeed, we will be his guardians."

13. [Jacob] said, "Indeed, it saddens me that you should take him, and I fear that a wolf would eat him while you are of him unaware."

14. They said, "If a wolf should eat him while we are a [strong] clan, indeed, we would then be losers."

15. So when they took him [out] and agreed to put him into the bottom of the well...[539] But We inspired to him, "You will surely inform them [someday] about this affair of theirs while they do not perceive [your identity]."

16. And they came to their father at night, weeping.

[533] *Yūsuf*: (The Prophet) Joseph.
[534] See footnote to 2:1.
[535] i.e., revealed in the Arabic language.
[536] The Prophet Jacob.

[537] Benjamin, who was born of the same mother as Joseph.
[538] i.e., You can repent thereafter.
[539] The conclusion of this sentence is estimated to be "...they tormented him."

17. They said, "O our father, indeed we went racing each other and left Joseph with our possessions, and a wolf ate him. But you would not believe us, even if we were truthful."

18. And they brought upon his shirt false blood.[540] [Jacob] said, "Rather, your souls have enticed you to something, so patience is most fitting. And God is the one sought for help against that which you describe."

19. And there came a company of travelers; then they sent their water drawer, and he let down his bucket. He said, "Good news! Here is a boy." And they concealed him, [taking him] as merchandise;[541] and God was knowing of what they did.

20. And they sold him for a reduced price - a few dirhams - and they were, concerning him, of those content with little.

21. And the one from Egypt[542] who bought him said to his wife, "Make his residence comfortable. Perhaps he will benefit us, or we will adopt him as a son." And thus, We established Joseph in the land that We might teach him the interpretation of events [i.e., dreams]. And God is predominant over His affair, but most of the people do not know.

22. And when he [i.e., Joseph] reached maturity, We gave him judgment and knowledge. And thus We reward the doers of good.

[540] They had stained Joseph's shirt with the blood of a lamb but had forgotten to tear it, thereby arousing their father's suspicion.

[541] To be sold as a slave.

[542] The minister in charge of supplies, whose title was al-'Azeez.

23. And she, in whose house he was, sought to seduce him. She closed the doors and said, "Come, you." He said, "[I seek] the refuge of God. Indeed, he[543] is my master, who has made good my residence. Indeed, wrongdoers will not succeed."

24. And she certainly determined [to seduce] him, and he would have inclined to her had he not seen the proof [i.e., sign] of his Lord. And thus [it was] that We should avert from him evil and immorality. Indeed, he was of Our chosen servants.

25. And they both raced to the door, and she tore his shirt from the back, and they found her husband at the door. She said, "What is the recompense of one who intended evil for your wife but that he be imprisoned or a painful punishment?"

26. [Joseph] said, "It was she who sought to seduce me." And a witness from her family testified, "If his shirt is torn from the front, then she has told the truth, and he is of the liars.

27. But if his shirt is torn from the back, then she has lied, and he is of the truthful."

28. So when he [i.e., her husband] saw his shirt torn from the back, he said, "Indeed, it is of your [i.e., women's] plan. Indeed, your plan is great [i.e., vehement].

29. Joseph, ignore this.[544] And, [my wife], ask forgiveness for your sin. Indeed, you were of the sinful."

[543] Her husband, al-'Azeez.

[544] i.e., conceal it and act as if it had not taken place.

30. And women in the city said, "The wife of al-'Azeez is seeking to seduce her slave boy; he has impassioned her with love. Indeed, we see her [to be] in clear error."

31. So when she heard of their scheming, she sent for them and prepared for them a banquet and gave each one of them a knife and said [to Joseph], "Come out before them." And when they saw him, they greatly admired him and cut their hands[545] and said, "Perfect is God![546] This is not a man; this is none but a noble angel."

32. She said, "That is the one about whom you blamed me. And I certainly sought to seduce him, but he firmly refused; and if he will not do what I order him, he will surely be imprisoned and will be of those debased."

33. He said, "My Lord, prison is more to my liking than that to which they invite me. And if You do not avert from me their plan, I might incline toward them and [thus] be of the ignorant."

34. So his Lord responded to him and averted from him their plan. Indeed, He is the Hearing, the Knowing.

35. Then it appeared to them after they had seen the signs[547] that he [i.e., al-'Azeez] should surely imprison him for a time.[548]

36. And there entered the prison with him two young men. One of them said, "Indeed, I have seen myself [in a dream] pressing wine." The other said, "Indeed, I have seen myself carrying upon my head [some] bread, from which the birds were eating. Inform us of its interpretation; indeed, we see you to be of those who do good."

37. He said, "You will not receive food that is provided to you except that I will inform you of its interpretation before it comes to you. That is from what my Lord has taught me. Indeed, I have left the religion of a people who do not believe in God, and they, in the Hereafter, are disbelievers.

38. And I have followed the religion of my fathers, Abraham, Isaac and Jacob. And it was not for us to associate anything with God. That is from the favor of God upon us and upon the people, but most of the people are not grateful.

39. O [my] two companions of prison, are separate lords better or God, the One, the Prevailing?

40. You worship not besides Him except [mere] names you have named them,[549] you and your fathers, for which God has sent down no authority. Legislation is not but for God. He has commanded that you worship not except Him. That is the correct religion, but most of the people do not know.

41. O two companions of prison, as for one of you, he will give drink to his master of wine; but as for the other, he will be crucified, and the birds will eat from his head. The matter has been decreed about which you both inquire."

42. And he said to the one whom he knew would go free, "Mention me before your master." But Satan made him for-

[545] So distracted were they at the sight of him.
[546] In His ability to create such beauty.
[547] Proofs of his innocence.
[548] Until the scandal be forgotten.

[549] The false objects of worship which you have called "gods".

get the mention [to] his master, and he [i.e., Joseph] remained in prison several years.

43. And [subsequently] the king said, "Indeed, I have seen [in a dream] seven fat cows being eaten by seven [that were] lean, and seven green spikes [of grain] and others [that were] dry. O eminent ones, explain to me my vision, if you should interpret visions."

44. They said, "[It is but] a mixture of false dreams, and we are not learned in the interpretation of dreams."

45. But the one who was freed and remembered after a time said, "I will inform you of its interpretation, so send me forth."

46. [He said], "Joseph, O man of truth, explain to us about seven fat cows eaten by seven [that were] lean, and seven green spikes [of grain] and others [that were] dry - that I may return to the people [i.e., the king and his court]; perhaps they will know [about you]."

47. [Joseph] said, "You will plant for seven years consecutively; and what you harvest leave in its spikes, except a little from which you will eat.

48. Then will come after that seven difficult [years] which will consume what you advanced [i.e., saved] for them, except a little from which you will store.

49. Then will come after that a year in which the people will be given rain and in which they will press [olives and grapes]."

50. And the king said, "Bring him to me." But when the messenger came to him, [Joseph] said, "Return to your master and ask him what is the case of the women who cut their hands. Indeed, my Lord is Knowing of their plan."

51. Said [the king to the women], "What was your condition when you sought to seduce Joseph?" They said, "Perfect is God![550] We know about him no evil." The wife of al-'Azeez said, "Now the truth has become evident. It was I who sought to seduce him, and indeed, he is of the truthful.

52. That is so he [i.e., al-'Azeez] will know that I did not betray him in [his] absence and that God does not guide the plan of betrayers.

53. And I do not acquit myself. Indeed, the soul is a persistent enjoiner of evil, except those upon which my Lord has mercy. Indeed, my Lord is Forgiving and Merciful."[551]

54. And the king said, "Bring him to me; I will appoint him exclusively for myself." And when he spoke to him, he said, "Indeed, you are today established [in position] and trusted."

55. [Joseph] said, "Appoint me over the storehouses of the land. Indeed, I will be a knowing guardian."

56. And thus We established Joseph in the land to settle therein wherever he willed. We touch with Our mercy whom We will, and We do not allow to be lost the reward of those who do good.

---

[550] In His ability to create such purity of character.

[551] Although Ibn Katheer attributes the words of verses 52-53 to the wife of al-'Azeez, others have concluded that they were spoken by Joseph, thereby justifying his request for an inquiry and acknowledging God's mercy to him.

57. And the reward of the Hereafter is better for those who believed and were fearing God.

58. And the brothers of Joseph came [seeking food], and they entered upon him; and he recognized them, but he was to them unknown.[552]

59. And when he had furnished them with their supplies, he said, "Bring me a brother of yours from your father.[553] Do not you see that I give full measure and that I am the best of accommodators?

60. But if you do not bring him to me, no measure will there be [hereafter] for you from me, nor will you approach me."

61. They said, "We will attempt to dissuade his father from [keeping] him, and indeed, we will do [it]."

62. And [Joseph] said to his servants, "Put their merchandise[554] into their saddlebags so they might recognize it when they have gone back to their people that perhaps they will [again] return."

63. So when they returned to their father, they said, "O our father, [further] measure has been denied to us, so send with us our brother [that] we will be given measure. And indeed, we will be his guardians."

64. He said, "Should I entrust you with him except [under coercion] as I entrusted you with his brother before? But God is the best guardian, and He is the most merciful of the merciful."

65. And when they opened their baggage, they found their merchandise returned to them. They said, "O our father, what [more] could we desire? This is our merchandise returned to us. And we will obtain supplies [i.e., food] for our family and protect our brother and obtain an increase of a camel's load; that is an easy measurement."[555]

66. [Jacob] said, "Never will I send him with you until you give me a promise [i.e., oath] by God that you will bring him [back] to me, unless you should be surrounded [i.e., overcome by enemies]." And when they had given their promise, he said, "God, over what we say, is Witness."

67. And he said, "O my sons, do not enter from one gate but enter from different gates; and I cannot avail you against [the decree of] God at all. The decision is only for God; upon Him I have relied, and upon Him let those who would rely [indeed] rely."

68. And when they entered from where their father had ordered them, it did not avail them against God at all except [it was] a need [i.e., concern] within the soul of Jacob, which he satisfied. And indeed, he was a possessor of knowledge because of what We had taught him, but most of the people do not know.

69. And when they entered upon Joseph, he took his brother to himself; he said, "Indeed, I am your brother, so do not despair over what they used to do [to me]."

---

[552] Due to the change in his appearance over the years.
[553] i.e., Benjamin, who had been kept at home by his father Jacob.
[554] The goods which they had brought to trade for food supplies.
[555] For them. Or one obtained by us with ease.

70. So when he had furnished them with their supplies, he put the [gold measuring] bowl into the bag of his brother. Then an announcer called out, "O caravan, indeed you are thieves."

71. They said while approaching them, "What is it you are missing?"

72. They said, "We are missing the measure of the king. And for he who produces it is [the reward of] a camel's load, and I am responsible for it."

73. They said, "By God, you have certainly known that we did not come to cause corruption in the land, and we have not been thieves."

74. They [the accusers] said, "Then what would be its recompense[556] if you should be liars?"

75. [The brothers] said, "Its recompense is that he in whose bag it is found - he [himself] will be its recompense.[557] Thus do we recompense the wrongdoers."

76. So he began [the search] with their bags before the bag of his brother; then he extracted it from the bag of his brother. Thus did We plan for Joseph. He could not have taken his brother within the religion [i.e., law] of the king except that God willed. We raise in degrees whom We will, but over every possessor of knowledge is one [more] knowing.[558]

77. They said, "If he steals - a brother of his has stolen before." But Joseph kept it within himself and did not reveal it to them.[559] He said, "You are worse in position, and God is most knowing of what you describe."

78. They said, "O 'Azeez,[560] indeed he has a father [who is] an old man, so take one of us in place of him. Indeed, we see you as a doer of good."

79. He said, "[I seek] the refuge of God [to prevent] that we take except him with whom we found our possession. Indeed, we would then be unjust."

80. So when they had despaired of him, they secluded themselves in private consultation. The eldest of them said, "Do you not know that your father has taken upon you an oath by God and [that] before you failed in [your duty to] Joseph? So I will never leave [this] land until my father permits me or God decides for me,[561] and He is the best of judges.

81. Return to your father and say, 'O our father, indeed your son has stolen, and we did not testify except to what we knew. And we were not witnesses of the unseen.[562]

82. And ask the city in which we were and the caravan in which we came - and indeed, we are truthful,' "

83. [Jacob] said, "Rather, your souls have enticed you to something, so patience is

[556] The punishment for theft.
[557] According to their law, a convicted thief was made a slave of the one from whom he had stolen.
[558] Ending with the ultimate knowledge of God.
[559] He did not answer that he himself had been stolen by them from his father.
[560] Addressing Joseph, who now held the title of "al-'Azeez."
[561] i.e., in my favour by bringing about the release of Benjamin.
[562] i.e., We could not have known when we gave you the oath that he would steal and be apprehended.

most fitting. Perhaps God will bring them to me all together. Indeed, it is He who is the Knowing, the Wise."

84. And he turned away from them and said, "Oh, my sorrow over Joseph," and his eyes became white[563] from grief, for he was [of that] a suppressor.[564]

85. They said, "By God, you will not cease remembering Joseph until you become fatally ill or become of those who perish."

86. He said, "I only complain of my suffering and my grief to God, and I know from God that which you do not know.

87. O my sons, go and find out about Joseph and his brother and despair not of relief from God. Indeed, no one despairs of relief from God except the disbelieving people."

88. So when they entered upon him [i.e., Joseph], they said, "O 'Azeez, adversity has touched us and our family, and we have come with goods poor in quality, but give us full measure and be charitable to us. Indeed, God rewards the charitable."

89. He said, "Do you know what you did with Joseph and his brother when you were ignorant?"

90. They said, "Are you indeed Joseph?" He said, "I am Joseph, and this is my brother. God has certainly favored us. Indeed, he who fears God and is patient, then indeed, God does not allow to be lost the reward of those who do good."

91. They said, "By God, certainly has God preferred you over us, and indeed, we have been sinners."

92. He said, "No blame will there be upon you today. God will forgive you; and He is the most merciful of the merciful.

93. Take this, my shirt, and cast it over the face of my father; he will become seeing. And bring me your family, all together."

94. And when the caravan departed [from Egypt], their father said,[565] "Indeed, I find the smell of Joseph [and would say that he was alive] if you did not think me weakened in mind."

95. They said, "By God, indeed you are in your [same] old error."

96. And when the bearer of good tidings[566] arrived, he cast it over his face, and he returned [once again] seeing. He said, "Did I not tell you that I know from God that which you do not know?"

97. They said, "O our father, ask for us forgiveness of our sins; indeed, we have been sinners."

98. He said, "I will ask forgiveness for you from my Lord. Indeed, it is He who is the Forgiving, the Merciful."

99. And when they entered upon Joseph, he took his parents to himself [i.e., embraced them] and said, "Enter Egypt, God willing, safe [and secure]."

---

[563] i.e., he lost his sight.

[564] He did not express the extent of his grief or his anger at what he suspected his sons had done but was patient, depending only upon God for help.

[565] To those present with him, either some of his sons or other relatives.

[566] He who carried Joseph's shirt from among the brothers.

100. And he raised his parents upon the throne, and they bowed to him in prostration.[567] And he said, "O my father, this is the explanation of my vision of before. My Lord has made it reality. And He was certainly good to me when He took me out of prison and brought you [here] from bedouin life after Satan had induced [estrangement] between me and my brothers. Indeed, my Lord is Subtle in what He wills. Indeed, it is He who is the Knowing, the Wise.

101. My Lord, You have given me [something] of sovereignty and taught me of the interpretation of dreams. Creator of the heavens and earth, You are my protector in this world and in the Hereafter. Cause me to die a Muslim and join me with the righteous."

102. That is from the news of the unseen which We reveal, [O Muhammad], to you. And you were not with them when they put together their plan while they conspired.

103. And most of the people, although you strive [for it], are not believers.

104. And you do not ask of them for it any payment. It is not except a reminder to the worlds.

105. And how many a sign within the heavens and earth do they pass over while they, therefrom, are turning away.

106. And most of them believe not in God except while they associate others with Him.

107. Then do they feel secure that there will not come to them an overwhelming [aspect] of the punishment of God or that the Hour will not come upon them suddenly while they do not perceive?

108. Say, "This is my way; I invite to God with insight, I and those who follow me. And exalted is God; and I am not of those who associate others with Him."

109. And We sent not before you [as messengers] except men to whom We revealed from among the people of cities. So have they[568] not traveled through the earth and observed how was the end of those before them? And the home of the Hereafter is best for those who fear God; then will you not reason?

110. [They continued] until, when the messengers despaired and were certain that they had been denied, there came to them Our victory, and whoever We willed was saved. And Our punishment cannot be repelled from the people who are criminals.

111. There was certainly in their stories a lesson for those of understanding. Never was it [i.e., the Qur'ān] a narration invented, but a confirmation of what was before it and a detailed explanation of all things and guidance and mercy for a people who believe.

567 That of greeting and respect, which was lawful until the time of Prophet Muhammad. Prostration to any person or object other that God was then prohibited conclusively.

568 Those who deny Prophet Muhammad.

## Sūrah 13: ar-Ra'd

### Period of Revelation

The internal evidence (v. 27-31 and v. 34-48) shows that this Sūrah was revealed in the last stage of the Mission of the Prophet at Makkah and during the same period in which Sūrah's Yūnus, Hūd, and al-A'rāf were sent down.

On the one hand his opponents had been scheming different devices to defeat him and his Mission and on the other his followers had been expressing a desire that by showing a miracle the disbelievers might be brought to the Right Way. In answer God impressed on the Believers that it is not His way to revert people by this method and that they should not lose heart if He is giving the enemies of the Truth a rope long enough to hang themselves. Otherwise He is able to show such signs as may bring the dead out of their graves and make them speak (v. 31). But even then these obdurate people will invent an excuse to explain this away. All this decisive evidence clearly proves that this Sūrah was revealed during the last stage of the Prophet's Mission at Makkah.

### Central Theme

The first verse enunciates the main theme of this Sūrah that is The Message of Muhammad is the very Truth but it is the fault of the people that they are rejecting it. This is the pivot on which the whole Sūrah turns. This is why it has been shown over and over again in different ways that the basic components of the Message, Tawhid, Resurrection and Prophethood are a reality: therefore they should believe sincerely in these for their own moral and spiritual good. They have been warned that they shall incur their own ruin if they reject them for kufr by itself is sheer folly and ignorance. Moreover the aim of the Sūrah is not merely to satisfy the minds but also to appeal to the hearts to accept the Faith. Therefore it does not merely put forward logical arguments in support of the truth of the Message and against the people's wrong notions. But at appropriate intervals it makes frequent use of sympathetic and earnest appeals to win over their hearts by warning them of the consequences of Kufr (disbelief) and by holding out the happy rewards of Faith so that the foolish people should give up their stubbornness.

Besides this, the objections of the opponents have been answered without any mention of them and those doubts which are proving a hindrance in the way of the Message or were being created by the opponents have been removed. At the same time the Believers; who had been passing through a long and hard ordeal and were feeling tired and waiting anxiously for God's succour, have been comforted and filled with hope and courage.

## Sūrah 13: ar-Ra'd[569]

In the Name of God, the Most Compassionate, the Most Merciful

1. Alif, Lām, Meem, Rā.[570] These are the verses of the Book; and what has been revealed to you from your Lord is the truth, but most of the people do not believe.

2. It is God who erected the heavens without pillars that you [can] see; then He established Himself above the Throne and made subject[571] the sun and the moon, each running [its course] for a specified term. He arranges [each] matter; He details the signs that you may, of the meeting with your Lord, be certain.

3. And it is He who spread the earth and placed therein firmly set mountains and rivers; and from all of the fruits He made therein two mates; He causes the night to cover the day. Indeed in that are signs for a people who give thought.

4. And within the land are neighboring plots and gardens of grapevines and crops and palm trees, [growing] several from a root or otherwise,[572] watered with one water; but We make some of them exceed others in [quality of] fruit. Indeed in that are signs for a people who reason.

5. And if you are astonished,[573] [O Muhammad] - then astonishing is their saying, "When we are dust, will we indeed be [brought] into a new creation?" Those are the ones who have disbelieved in their Lord, and those will have shackles[574] upon their necks, and those are the companions of the Fire; they will abide therein eternally.

6. They impatiently urge you to bring about evil before good,[575] while there has already occurred before them similar punishments [to what they demand]. And indeed, your Lord is full of forgiveness for the people despite their wrongdoing, and indeed, your Lord is severe in penalty.

7. And those who disbelieved say, "Why has a sign not been sent down to him from his Lord?" You are only a warner, and for every people is a guide.

8. God knows what every female carries[576] and what the wombs lose [prematurely] or exceed.[577] And everything with Him is by due measure.

9. [He is] Knower of the unseen and the witnessed, the Grand, the Exalted.

10. It is the same [to Him] concerning you whether one conceals [his] speech or one publicizes it and whether one is hidden by night or conspicuous [among others] by day.

11. For him [i.e., each one] are successive [angels][578] before and behind him who

---

569 *Ar-Ra'd*: Thunder.

570 See footnote to 2:1

571 For the benefit of mankind

572 i.e., only one from a root.

573 At those who deny resurrection.

574 Iron collars to which their hands are chained.

575 They said, challenging the Prophet in ridicule, "Bring on the punishment, if you are truthful," rather than asking for mercy and forgiveness from God.

576 With absolute knowledge inclusive of every aspect of the fetus' existence.

577 Beyond their normal period of pregnancy and/or the number of fetuses therein.

578 Replacing each other by turn.

protect him by the decree of God.[579] Indeed, God will not change the condition of a people until they change what is in themselves. And when God intends for a people ill,[580] there is no repelling it. And there is not for them besides Him any patron.

12. It is He who shows you lightening, [causing] fear and aspiration, and generates the heavy clouds.

13. And the thunder exalts [God] with praise of Him - and the angels [as well] from fear of Him - and He sends thunderbolts and strikes therewith whom He wills while they dispute about God; and He is severe in assault.

14. To Him [alone] is the supplication of truth. And those they call upon besides Him do not respond to them with a thing, except as one who stretches his hands toward water [from afar, calling it] to reach his mouth, but it will not reach it [thus].[581] And the supplication of the disbelievers is not but in error [i.e., futility].

15. And to God prostrates whoever is within the heavens and the earth, willingly or by compulsion, and their shadows [as well] in the mornings and the afternoons.

16. Say, "Who is Lord of the heavens and earth?" Say, "God." Say, "Have you then taken besides Him allies not possessing [even] for themselves any benefit or any harm?" Say, "Is the blind equivalent to the seeing? Or is darkness equivalent to light? Or have they attributed to God partners who created like His creation so that the creation [of each] seemed similar to them?"[582] Say, "God is the Creator of all things, and He is the One, the Prevailing."

17. He sends down from the sky, rain, and valleys flow according to their capacity, and the torrent carries a rising foam. And from that [ore] which they heat in the fire, desiring adornments and utensils, is a foam like it. Thus God presents [the example of] truth and falsehood. As for the foam, it vanishes, [being] cast off; but as for that which benefits the people, it remains on the earth. Thus does God present examples.

18. For those who have responded to their Lord is the best [reward], but those who did not respond to Him - if they had all that is in the earth entirely and the like of it with it, they would [attempt to] ransom themselves thereby. Those will have the worst account, and their refuge is Hell, and wretched is the resting place.

19. Then is he who knows that what has been revealed to you from your Lord is the truth like one who is blind? They will only be reminded who are people of understanding -

20. Those who fulfill the covenant of God and do not break the contract,

21. And those who join that which God has ordered to be joined[583] and fear

[579] The phrase may also be rendered "...who guard him from [everything except] the decree of God."
[580] i.e., punishment or destruction because of their sins.
[581] The analogy indicates that false deities will never respond to them at all.
[582] The obvious conclusion is that the claimed partners, having no ability to create, cannot be compared to God in any way.
[583] i.e., they uphold the ties of relationship.

their Lord and are afraid of the evil of [their] account,

22. And those who are patient, seeking the countenance of their Lord, and establish prayer and spend from what We have provided for them secretly and publicly and prevent evil with good - those will have the good consequence of [this] home[584] -

23. Gardens of perpetual residence; they will enter them with whoever were righteous among their fathers, their spouses and their descendants. And the angels will enter upon them from every gate, [saying],

24. "Peace [i.e., security] be upon you for what you patiently endured. And excellent is the final home."

25. But those who break the covenant of God after contracting it and sever that which God has ordered to be joined and spread corruption on earth - for them is the curse, and they will have the worst home.[585]

26. God extends provision for whom He wills and restricts [it]. And they rejoice in the worldly life, while the worldly life is not, compared to the Hereafter, except [brief] enjoyment.

27. And those who disbelieved say, "Why has a sign not been sent down to him from his Lord?" Say, [O Muhammad], "Indeed, God leaves astray whom He wills and guides to Himself whoever turns back [to Him] -

28. Those who have believed and whose hearts are assured by the remembrance of God. Unquestionably, by the remembrance of God hearts are assured."

29. Those who have believed and done righteous deeds - a good state is theirs and a good return.

30. Thus have We sent you to a community before which [other] communities have passed on so you might recite to them that which We revealed to you, while they disbelieve in the Most Merciful. Say, "He is my Lord; there is no deity except Him. Upon Him I rely, and to Him is my return."

31. And if there was any qur'ān [i.e., recitation] by which the mountains would be removed or the earth would be broken apart or the dead would be made to speak,[586] [it would be this Qur'ān], but to God belongs the affair entirely. Then have those who believed not accepted that had God willed, He would have guided the people, all of them? And those who disbelieve do not cease to be struck, for what they have done, by calamity - or it will descend near their home - until there comes the promise of God. Indeed, God does not fail in [His] promise.

32. And already were [other] messengers ridiculed before you, and I extended the time of those who disbelieved; then I seized them, and how [terrible] was My penalty.

33. Then is He who is a maintainer of every soul, [knowing] what it has earned, [like any other]? But to God they have attributed partners. Say, "Name them. Or do you inform Him

[584] i.e., the world and its trails, its good consequences being Paradise.

[585] i.e., Hell. Another meaning is (in contrast to verse 22), "...and they will have the bad consequence of [this] home," also referring to Hell.

[586] As suggested by the disbelievers.

of that[587] which He knows not upon the earth or of what is apparent [i.e., alleged] of speech?"[588] Rather, their [own] plan has been made attractive to those who disbelieve, and they have been averted from the way. And whomever God leaves astray - there will be for him no guide.

34. For them will be punishment in the life of [this] world, and the punishment of the Hereafter is more severe. And they will not have from God any protector.

35. The example [i.e., description] of Paradise, which the righteous have been promised, is [that] beneath it rivers flow. Its fruit is lasting, and its shade. That is the consequence for the righteous, and the consequence for the disbelievers is the Fire.

36. And [the believers among] those to whom We have given the [previous] Scripture rejoice at what has been revealed to you, [O Muhammad], but among the [opposing] factions are those who deny part of it [i.e., the Qur'ān]. Say, "I have only been commanded to worship God and not associate [anything] with Him. To Him I invite, and to Him is my return."

37. And thus We have revealed it as an Arabic legislation.[589] And if you should follow their inclinations after what has come to you of knowledge, you would not have against God any ally or any protector.

38. And We have already sent messengers before you and assigned to them wives and descendants. And it was not for a messenger to come with a sign except by permission of God. For every term is a decree.

39. God eliminates what He wills or confirms, and with Him is the Mother of the Book.[590]

40. And whether We show you part of what We promise them or take you in death, upon you is only the [duty of] notification, and upon Us is the account.

41. Have they not seen that We set upon the land, reducing it from its borders?[591] And God decides; there is no adjuster of His decision. And He is swift in account.

42. And those before them had plotted, but to God belongs the plan entirely. He knows what every soul earns, and the disbelievers will know for whom is the final home.

43. And those who have disbelieved say, "You are not a messenger." Say, [O Muhammad], "Sufficient is God as Witness between me and you, and [the witness of] whoever has knowledge of the Scripture."[592]

587 i.e., other "deities."

588 i.e., your attributing of divinity to other than God.

589 i.e., revealed in the Arabic language.

590 The Preserved Slate (*al-Lawh al-Mahfūth*), in which is inscribed the original of every scripture revealed by God.

591 Referring to the spread of Islām through God's Prophet and the diminishing of those areas controlled by the polytheist.

592 i.e., those who recognize the truth through their knowledge of previous scriptures.

## Sūrah 14: Ibrāheem

### Period of Revelation

It appears from the tone of the Sūrah that it belongs to that group of the Sūrahs which were revealed during the last stage of the Makkan period. For instance v.13 (**"And those who disbelieved said to their messengers, "We will surely drive you out of our land, or you must return to our religion." So their Lord inspired to them, "We will surely destroy the wrongdoers."**) clearly indicates that the persecution of the Muslims was at its worst at the time of the revelation of this Sūrah and the people of Makkah were bent on expelling the Believers from there like the disbelievers of the former Prophets.

### Central Theme and Purpose

This Sūrah is an admonition and a warning to the disbelievers who were rejecting the Message of the Prophet and devising cunning schemes to defeat his Mission. But warning, censure and reproach dominate admonition. This is because a good deal of admonition had already been made in the preceding Sūrahs but in spite of this their obduracy, enmity, antagonism, mischief, persecution etc. had rather increased.

## Sūrah 14: Ibrāheem[593]

In the Name of God, the Most Compassionate, the Most Merciful

1. Alif, Lām, Rā.[594] [This is] a Book which We have revealed to you, [O Muhammad], that you might bring mankind out of darknesses into the light by permission of their Lord - to the path of the Exalted in Might, the Praiseworthy -

2. God, to whom belongs whatever is in the heavens and whatever is on the earth. And woe [i.e., destruction] to the disbelievers from a severe punishment -

3. The ones who prefer the worldly life over the Hereafter and avert [people] from the way of God, seeking to make it [seem] deviant. Those are in extreme error.

4. And We did not send any messenger except [speaking] in the language of his people to state clearly for them, and God sends astray [thereby] whom He wills[595] and guides whom He wills. And He is the Exalted in Might, the Wise.

5. And We certainly sent Moses with Our signs, [saying], "Bring out your people from darknesses into the light and remind them of the days[596] of God." Indeed in that are signs for everyone patient and grateful.

6. And [recall, O Children of Israel], when Moses said to His people, "Remember the favor of God upon you when He saved you from the people of Pharaoh, who were afflicting you with the worst torment and were slaughtering your [newborn] sons and keeping your females alive. And in that was a great trial from your Lord.

7. And [remember] when your Lord proclaimed, 'If you are grateful, I will surely increase you [in favor]; but if you deny, indeed, My punishment is severe.'"

8. And Moses said, "If you should disbelieve, you and whoever is on the earth entirely - indeed, God is Free of need and Praiseworthy."

9. Has there not reached you the news of those before you - the people of Noah and 'Aad and Thamūd and those after them? No one knows them [i.e., their number] but God. Their messengers brought them clear proofs, but they returned their hands to their mouths[597] and said, "Indeed, we disbelieve in that with which you have been sent, and indeed we are, about that to which you invite us, in disquieting doubt."

10. Their messengers said, "Can there be doubt about God, Creator of the heavens and earth? He invites you that He may forgive you of your sins, and He delays you [i.e., your death] for a specified term." They said, You are not but men like us who wish to avert us from what our fathers were worshipping. So bring us a clear authority [i.e., evidence]."

11. Their messengers said to them, "We are only men like you, but God confers favor upon whom He wills of His ser-

[593] *Ibrāheem*: (The Prophet) Abraham.
[594] See footnote to 2:1.
[595] i.e., those who refuse His guidance.
[596] Days of blessings bestowed upon the Children of Israel. Also interpreted as days of punishment and destruction of the former nations.

[597] Several explanations have been given as to the meaning. Based upon the conclusion of the verse, Ibn Katheer preferred that this was a gesture of denial and rejection.

vants. It has never been for us to bring you evidence except by permission of God. And upon God let the believers rely.

12. And why should we not rely upon God while He has guided us to our [good] ways. And we will surely be patient against whatever harm you should cause us. And upon God let those who would rely [indeed] rely."

13. And those who disbelieved said to their messengers, "We will surely drive you out of our land, or you must return to our religion." So their Lord inspired to them, "We will surely destroy the wrongdoers.

14. And We will surely cause you to dwell in the land after them. That is for he who fears My position[598] and fears My threat."

15. And they requested decision [i.e., victory from God], and disappointed, [therefore], was every obstinate tyrant.

16. Before him[599] is Hell, and he will be given a drink of purulent water.[600]

17. He will gulp it but will hardly [be able to] swallow it. And death will come to him from everywhere, but he is not to die. And before him is a massive punishment.

18. The example of those who disbelieve in their Lord is [that] their deeds are like ashes which the wind blows forcefully on a stormy day; they are unable [to keep] from what they earned a [single] thing. That is what is extreme error.

19. Have you not seen [i.e., considered] that God created the heavens and the earth in truth? If He wills, He can do away with you and produce a new creation.

20. And that is not difficult for God.

21. And they will come out [for judgement] before God all together, and the weak will say to those who were arrogant, "Indeed, we were your followers, so can you avail us anything against the punishment of God?" They will say, "If God had guided us, we would have guided you. It is all the same for us whether we show intolerance or are patient: there is for us no place of escape."

22. And Satan will say when the matter has been concluded, "Indeed, God had promised you the promise of truth. And I promised you, but I betrayed you. But I had no authority over you except that I invited you, and you responded to me. So do not blame me; but blame yourselves. I cannot be called to your aid, nor can you be called to my aid. Indeed, I deny your association of me [with God] before.[601] Indeed, for the wrongdoers is a painful punishment."

23. And those who believed and did righteous deeds will be admitted to gardens beneath which rivers flow, abiding eternally therein by permission of their Lord; and their greeting therein will be, "Peace!"

598 An alternative meaning is "the standing [for account] before Me."

599 Literally, "after him [in time]," meaning ahead of him.

600 That which oozes from the skins of Hell's inhabitants.

601 By your obedience to me instead of Him during life on earth.

24. Have you not considered how God presents an example, [making] a good word like a good tree, whose root is firmly fixed and its branches [high] in the sky?

25. It produces its fruit all the time, by permission of its Lord. And God presents examples for the people that perhaps they will be reminded.

26. And the example of a bad word is like a bad tree, uprooted from the surface of the earth, not having any stability.

27. God keeps firm those who believe, with the firm word,[602] in worldly life and in the Hereafter.[603] And God sends astray the wrongdoers. And God does what He wills.

28. Have you not considered those who exchanged the favor of God for disbelief[604] and settled their people [in] the home of ruin?

29. [It is] Hell, which they will [enter to] burn, and wretched is the settlement.

30. And they have attributed to God equals to mislead [people] from His way. Say, "Enjoy yourselves, for indeed, your destination is the Fire."

31. [O Muhammad], tell My servants who have believed to establish prayer and spend from what We have provided them, secretly and publicly, before a Day comes in which there will be no exchange [i.e., ransom], nor any friendships.

32. It is God who created the heavens and the earth and sent down rain from the sky and produced thereby some fruits as provision for you and subjected for you[605] the ships to sail through the sea by His command and subjected for you the rivers.

33. And He subjected for you the sun and the moon, continuous [in orbit], and subjected for you the night and the day.

34. And He gave you from all you asked of Him.[606] And if you should count the favor [i.e., blessings] of God, you could not enumerate them. Indeed, mankind is [generally] most unjust and ungrateful.[607]

35. And [mention, O Muhammad], when Abraham said, "My Lord, make this city [i.e., Makkah] secure and keep me and my sons away from worshipping idols.

36. My Lord, indeed they have led astray many among the people. So whoever follows me - then he is of me;[608] and whoever disobeys me - indeed, You are [yet] Forgiving and Merciful.

37. Our Lord, I have settled some of my descendants in an uncultivated valley near Your sacred House, our Lord, that they may establish prayer. So make hearts among the people incline toward them and provide for them from the fruits that they might be grateful.

---

[602] The testimony that there is no deity except God and that Muhammad is the messenger of God.

[603] When questioned in their graves by the angels after death.

[604] They met God's blessing with denial instead of gratitude.

[605] i.e., made serviceable to you.

[606] Something of what you asked and all of what you continually require, according to His wisdom.

[607] i.e., disbelieving and denying of God's favour.

[608] i.e., of my religion.

38. Our Lord, indeed You know what we conceal and what we declare, and nothing is hidden from God on the earth or in the heaven.

39. Praise to God, who has granted to me in old age Ishmael and Isaac. Indeed, my Lord is the Hearer of supplication.

40. My Lord, make me an establisher of prayer, and [many] from my descendants. Our Lord, and accept my supplication.

41. Our Lord, forgive me and my parents and the believers the Day the account is established."

42. And never think that God is unaware of what the wrongdoers do. He only delays them [i.e., their account] for a Day when eyes will stare [in horror].

43. Racing ahead, their heads raised up, their glance does not come back to them,[609] and their hearts are void.

44. And, [O Muhammad], warn the people of a Day when the punishment will come to them and those who did wrong will say, "Our Lord, delay us for a short term; we will answer Your call and follow the messengers." [But it will be said], "Had you not sworn, before, that for you there would be no cessation?[610]

45. And you lived among the dwellings of those who wronged themselves, and it had become clear to you how We dealt with them. And We presented for you [many] examples."

46. And they had planned their plan, but with God is [recorded] their plan, even if their plan had been [sufficient] to do away with the mountains.[611]

47. So never think that God will fail in His promise to His messengers. Indeed, God is Exalted in Might and Owner of Retribution.

48. [It will be] on the Day the earth will be replaced by another earth, and the heavens [as well], and they [i.e., all creatures] will come out before God, the One, the Prevailing,

49. And you will see the criminals that Day bound together in shackles,

50. Their garments of liquid pitch and their faces covered by the Fire

51. So that God will recompense every soul for what it earned. Indeed, God is swift in account.

52. This [Qur'ān] is notification for the people that they may be warned thereby and that they may know that He is but one God and that those of understanding will be reminded.

[609] This is their state at the time of resurrection from the graves. Their heads are upraised in fixed stares of terror, unable even to glance back.

[610] Of the blessings which God had bestowed upon you during life on earth.

[611] An alternative meaning is "...and their plan was not [sufficient] to do away with the mountains," i.e., it had no effect against God's will.

## Sūrah 15: al-Hijr

### Period of Revelation

It is clear from its topics and style that the period of its revelation is similar to that of Sūrah Ibrāhim as two things are quite prominent in its background. Firstly, it appears from the repeated warnings in this Sūrah that despite the fact that the Prophet had been propagating the Message for many years his people in general had not shown any inclination towards its acceptance nay they had become more and more obdurate and stubborn in their antagonism enmity and ridicule with the passage of time. Secondly by that time the Prophet had begun to feel a little tired of making strenuous efforts to eradicate disbelief and opposition of his people. That is why God has consoled and comforted him over and over again by way of encouragement.

### Topics and the Central Theme

Though the main topics of the Sūrah are :

a. warning to those who rejected his Message, opposed it tooth and nail and ridiculed him.
b. comfort and encouragement to the Prophet

It does not mean that this Sūrah does not contain admonition and instructions. As a matter of fact the Qur'ān never confines itself to mere warning; rebuke and censure but resorts to precept in every suitable place. Accordingly this Sūrah contains brief arguments for Tawhid (Monothesim) on the one hand and admonition in the story of Adam and Satan on the other.

## Sūrah 15: al-Hijr[612]

In the Name of God, the Most Compassionate, the Most Merciful

1. Alif, Lām, Rā.[613] These are the verses of the Book and a clear Qur'ān [i.e., recitation].

2. Perhaps those who disbelieve will wish[614] that they had been Muslims.

3. Let them eat and enjoy themselves and be diverted by [false] hope, for they are going to know.

4. And We did not destroy any city but that for it was a known decree.

5. No nation will precede its term, nor will they remain thereafter.

6. And they say, "O you upon whom the message has been sent down, indeed you are mad.[615]

7. Why do you not bring us the angels, if you should be among the truthful?"

8. We do not send down the angels except with truth;[616] and they [i.e., the disbelievers] would not then be reprieved.

9. Indeed, it is We who sent down the message [i.e., the Qur'ān], and indeed, We will be its guardian.

[612] *Al-Hijr*: The valley of stone. It was inhabited by the tribe of Thamūd (mentioned in verses 80-84), who caved palaces and dwellings out of the rock.
[613] See footnote to 2:1.
[614] On the Day of Judgement or at the time of death.
[615] Literally, "possessed by *jinn*."
[616] i.e., with a message or, as the conclusion of the verse suggests, to carry out a promised punishment.

10. And We had certainly sent [messengers] before you, [O Muhammad], among the sects of the former peoples.

11. And no messenger would come to them except that they ridiculed him.

12. Thus do We insert it [i.e., denial] into the hearts of the criminals.

13. They will not believe in it, while there has already occurred the precedent of the former peoples.

14. And [even] if We opened to them a gate from the heaven and they continued therein to ascend,

15. They would say, "Our eyes have only been dazzled. Rather, we are a people affected by magic."

16. And We have placed within the heaven great stars and have beautified it for the observers.

17. And We have protected it from every devil expelled [from the mercy of God]

18. Except one who steals a hearing and is pursued by a clear burning flame.

19. And the earth - We have spread it and cast therein firmly set mountains and caused to grow therein [something] of every well-balanced thing.

20. And We have made for you therein means of living and [for] those for whom you are not providers.[617]

21. And there is not a thing but that with Us are its depositories, and We do not

[617] God has put at your service other men and animals for which He provides. An additional meaning is that God provides means for your living and for all other creatures as well.

send it down except according to a known [i.e., specified] measure.

22. And We have sent the fertilizing winds[618] and sent down water from the sky and given you drink from it. And you are not its retainers.

23. And indeed, it is We who give life and cause death, and We are the Inheritor.[619]

24. And We have already known the preceding [generations] among you, and We have already known the later [ones to come].

25. And indeed, your Lord will gather them; indeed, He is Wise and Knowing.

26. And We did certainly create man out of clay from an altered black mud.

27. And the jinn We created before from scorching fire.

28. And [mention, O Muhammad], when your Lord said to the angels, "I will create a human being out of clay from an altered black mud.

29. And when I have proportioned him and breathed into him of My [created] soul,[620] then fall down to him in prostration."

30. So the angels prostrated - all of them entirely,

31. Except Iblees;[621] he refused to be with those who prostrated.

32. [God] said, "O Iblees, what is [the matter] with you that you are not with those who prostrate?"

33. He said, "Never would I prostrate to a human whom You created out of clay from an altered black mud."

34. [God] said, "Then get out of it,[622] for indeed, you are expelled.

35. And indeed, upon you is the curse until the Day of Recompense."

36. He said, "My Lord, then reprieve me until the Day they are resurrected."

37. [God] said, "So indeed, you are of those reprieved

38. Until the Day of the time well-known."

39. [Iblees] said, "My Lord, because You have put me in error, I will surely make [disobedience] attractive to them [i.e., mankind] on earth, and I will mislead them all

40. Except, among them, Your chosen servants."

41. [God] said, "This is a path [of return] to Me [that is] straight.

42. Indeed, My servants - no authority will you have over them, except those who follow you of the deviators.

43. And indeed, Hell is the promised place for them all.

[618] Causing precipitation in rainclouds or carrying pollen. Another meaning is "pregnant winds," i.e., those carrying rainclouds.

[619] God remains after all creation has passed away.

[620] The element of life and soul which God created for that body, not His own sprit or part of Himself (as some mistakenly believe).

[621] Who was of the *jinn*. See 18:50.

[622] Your position in the heavens.

44. It has seven gates; for every gate is of them [i.e., Satan's followers] a portion designated."

45. Indeed, the righteous will be within gardens and springs,

46. [Having been told], "Enter it in peace, safe [and secure]."

47. And We will remove whatever is in their breasts of resentment,[623] [so they will be] brothers, on thrones facing each other.

48. No fatigue will touch them therein, nor from it will they [ever] be removed.

49. [O Muhammad], inform My servants that it is I who am the Forgiving, the Merciful,

50. And that it is My punishment which is the painful punishment.

51. And inform them about the guests of Abraham,

52. When they entered upon him and said, "Peace." [Abraham] said, "Indeed, we are fearful [i.e., apprehensive] of you."

53. [The angels] said, "Fear not. Indeed, we give you good tidings of a learned boy."

54. He said, "Have you given me good tidings although old age has come upon me? Then of what [wonder] do you inform?"

55. They said, "We have given you good tidings in truth, so do not be of the despairing."

[623] See footnote to 7:43.

56. He said, "And who despairs of the mercy of his Lord except for those astray?"

57. [Abraham] said, "Then what is your business [here], O messengers?"

58. They said, "Indeed, we have been sent to a people of criminals,

59. Except the family of Lot; indeed, we will save them all

60. Except his wife." We [i.e., God] decreed that she is of those who remain behind.[624]

61. And when the messengers came to the family of Lot,

62. He said, "Indeed, you are people unknown."

63. They said, "But we have come to you with that about which they were disputing,

64. And we have come to you with truth, and indeed, we are truthful.

65. So set out with your family during a portion of the night and follow behind them and let not anyone among you look back and continue on to where you are commanded."

66. And We conveyed to him [the decree] of that matter: that those [sinners] would be eliminated by early morning.

67. And the people of the city came rejoicing.[625]

68. [Lot] said, "Indeed, these are my guests, so do not shame me.

[624] For having collaborated with the evildoers.

[625] At the news of Lot's visitors.

69. And fear God and do not disgrace me."

70. They said, "Have we not forbidden you from [protecting] people?"

71. [Lot] said, "These are my daughters[626] - if you would be doers [of lawful marriage]."

72. By your life, [O Muhammad], indeed they were, in their intoxication, wandering blindly.

73. So the shriek[627] seized them at sunrise.

74. And We made the highest part [of the city] its lowest and rained upon them stones of hard clay.

75. Indeed in that are signs for those who discern.

76. And indeed, they [i.e., those cities] are [situated] on an established road.

77. Indeed in that is a sign for the believers.

78. And the companions of the thicket [i.e., the people of Madyan] were [also] wrongdoers,

79. So We took retribution from them, and indeed, both [cities] are on a clear highway.

80. And certainly did the companions of al-Hijr[628] [i.e., the Thamūd] deny the messengers.

81. And We gave them Our signs, but from them they were turning away.

82. And they used to carve from the mountains, houses, feeling secure.

83. But the shriek seized them at early morning,

84. So nothing availed them [from] what they used to earn.

85. And We have not created the heavens and earth and that between them except in truth. And indeed, the Hour is coming; so forgive with gracious forgiveness.

86. Indeed, your Lord - He is the Knowing Creator.

87. And We have certainly given you, [O Muhammad], seven of the often repeated [verses][629] and the great Qur'ān.

88. Do not extend your eyes toward that by which We have given enjoyment to [certain] categories of them [i.e., the disbelievers], and do not grieve over them. And lower your wing [i.e., show kindness] to the believers

89. And say, "Indeed, I am the clear warner" -

90. Just as We had revealed [scriptures] to the separators[630]

91. Who have made the Qur'ān into portions.[631]

92. So by your Lord, We will surely question them all

93. About what they used to do.

[626] i.e., the women of his community who were lawful for marriage.

[627] See footnote to 11:67.

[628] The valley of stone.

[629] Referring to *Sūrah al-Fātihah.*

[630] Specifically, the Jews and Christians, who separated from the teachings of their prophets.

[631] Accepting part and rejecting part according to their own inclinations.

94. Then declare what you are commanded[632] and turn away from the polytheists.[633]

95. Indeed, We are sufficient for you against the mockers

96. Who make [equal] with God another deity. But they are going to know.

97. And We already know that your breast is constrained by what they say.

98. So exalt [God] with praise of your Lord and be of those who prostrate [to Him].

99. And worship your Lord until there comes to you the certainty [i.e., death].

---

632 The implication is "Thereby you will distinguish or separate the disbelievers from the believers."

633 Any who persist in association of others with God.

## Sūrah 16: an-Nahl

### Period of Revelation

The following internal evidence shows that this Sūrah was revealed during the last Makkan stage of Prophet-hood:

1. V. 41 clearly shows that persecution had forced some Muslims to emigrate to Abassinyah before the revelation of this Sūrah.
2. It is evident from v. 106 that at that time the persecution of the Muslims was at its height. Therefore a problem had arisen in regard to the utterance of a blasphemous word without actual disbelief under unbearable conditions. The problem was that if one did so how should he be treated.
3. V. 112-114 clearly refer to the end of a seven year famine that had struck Makkah some years after the appointment of the Prophet as God's Messenger.

### Central Theme

All the topics of the Sūrah revolve around different aspects of the Message i.e., refutation of Shirk (polytheism) proof of Tawhid and warning of the consequences of the rejection of and opposition and antagonism to the Message.

### Topics of Discussion

The very first verse gives direct and strict warning to those who were rejecting the Message outright as if to say God's decision has already been made concerning your rejection of the Message. Why are you then clamouring for hastening it? Why don't you make use of the respite that is being given to you! And this was exactly what the disbelievers of Makkah needed at the time of the revelation of this Sūrah. For they challenged the Prophet over and over again: "Why don't you bring that scourge with which you have been threatening us! For we have not only rejected your Message but have been openly opposing it for a long time." Such a challenge had become a by-word with them which they frequently repeated as a clear proof that Muhammad was not a true Prophet.

Immediately after this warning they have been admonished to give up shirk (polytheism)for this false creed was the main obstacle in the way of the Message. Then the following topics come over and over again one after the other:

1. Very convincing proofs of Tawhid and refutation of Shirk have been based on the plain signs in the universe and in man's own self.
2. The objections of the disbelievers have been answered, their arguments refuted, their doubts removed and their false pretexts exposed.
3. Warnings have been given of the consequences of persistence in false ways and antagonism to the Message.
4. The moral changes which the Message of the Prophet aims to bring practically in human life have been presented briefly in an appealing manner. The polytheists have been told that belief in God which they also professed demanded that it should not be confined merely to lip service but this creed should take a definite shape in moral and practical life.

The Prophet and his companions have been comforted and told about the attitude they should adopt in the face of antagonism and persecution by the disbelievers.

## Sūrah 16: an-Nahl[634]

In the Name of God, the Most Compassionate, the Most Merciful

1. The command of God is coming,[635] so be not impatient for it. Exalted is He and high above what they associate with Him.

2. He sends down the angels, with the inspiration [i.e., revelation] of His command, upon whom He wills of His servants, [telling them], "Warn that there is no deity except Me; so fear Me."

3. He created the heavens and earth in truth. High is He above what they associate with Him.

4. He created man from a sperm-drop; then at once[636] he is a clear adversary.

5. And the grazing livestock He has created for you; in them is warmth[637] and [numerous] benefits, and from them you eat.

6. And for you in them is [the enjoyment of] beauty when you bring them in [for the evening] and when you send them out [to pasture].

7. And they carry your loads to a land you could not have reached except with difficulty to yourselves. Indeed, your Lord is Kind and Merciful.

8. And [He created] the horses, mules and donkeys for you to ride and [as] adornment. And He creates that which you do not know.

9. And upon God[638] is the direction of the [right] way, and among them [i.e., the various paths] are those deviating. And if He willed, He could have guided you all.

10. It is He who sends down rain from the sky; from it is drink and from it is foliage in which you pasture [animals].

11. He causes to grow for you thereby the crops, olives, palm trees, grapevines, and from all the fruits. Indeed in that is a sign for a people who give thought.

12. And He has subjected for you the night and day and the sun and moon, and the stars are subjected by His command. Indeed in that are signs for a people who reason.

13. And [He has subjected] whatever He multiplied for you on the earth of varying colors. Indeed in that is a sign for a people who remember.

14. And it is He who subjected the sea for you to eat from it tender meat and to extract from it ornaments which you wear. And you see the ships plowing through it, and [He subjected it] that you may seek of His bounty; and perhaps you will be grateful.

15. And He has cast into the earth firmly set mountains, lest it shift with you, and [made] rivers and roads, that you may be guided,

---

[634] *An-Nahl*: The Bee.
[635] Literally, "has come," indicating the certainty and nearness of the Last Hour.
[636] As soon as he becomes strong and independent.
[637] i.e., in clothing, tents, furnishings, etc.
[638] God has taken it upon Himself to guide man to the right path. The meaning has also been interpreted as "To God..."

16. And landmarks. And by the stars they are [also] guided. [639]

17. Then is He who creates like one who does not create? So will you not be reminded?

18. And if you should count the favors of God, you could not enumerate them. Indeed, God is Forgiving and Merciful.

19. And God knows what you conceal and what you declare.

20. And those they invoke other than God create nothing, and they [themselves] are created.

21. They are, [in fact], dead,[640] not alive, and they do not perceive when they will be resurrected.

22. Your god is one God. But those who do not believe in the Hereafter - their hearts are disapproving, and they are arrogant.

23. Assuredly, God knows what they conceal and what they declare. Indeed, He does not like the arrogant.

24. And when it is said to them, "What has your Lord sent down?" they say, "Legends of the former peoples,"

25. That they may bear their own burdens [i.e., sins] in full on the Day of Resurrection and some of the burdens of those whom they misguide without [i.e., by lack of] knowledge. Unquestionably, evil is that which they bear.

26. Those before them had already plotted, but God came at [i.e., uprooted] their building from the foundations, so the roof fell upon them from above them,[641] and the punishment came to them from where they did not perceive.

27. Then on the Day of Resurrection He will disgrace them and say, "Where are My 'partners' for whom you used to oppose [the believers]?" Those who were given knowledge will say, "Indeed disgrace, this Day, and evil are upon the disbelievers" -

28. The ones whom the angels take in death [while] wronging themselves,[642] and [who] then offer submission, [saying], "We were not doing any evil." But, yes! Indeed, God is Knowing of what you used to do.

29. So enter the gates of Hell to abide eternally therein, and how wretched is the residence of the arrogant.

30. And it will be said to those who feared God, "What did your Lord send down?" They will say, "[That which is] good." For those who do good in this world is good; and the home of the Hereafter is better. And how excellent is the home of the righteous -

31. Gardens of perpetual residence, which they will enter, beneath which rivers flow. They will have therein whatever they wish. Thus does God reward the righteous -

32. The ones whom the angels take in death, [being] good and pure; [the angels] will say, "Peace be upon you. Enter Paradise for what you used to do."

---

[639] Through the desert or the sea at night.
[640] i.e., inanimate or without understanding.
[641] i.e., God caused their plan to fail and exposed their plot.
[642] i.e., having made punishment due to them for their numerous sins and crimes.

33. Do they [i.e., the disbelievers] await [anything] except that the angels should come to them or there comes the command of your Lord? Thus did those do before them. And God wronged them not, but they had been wronging themselves.

34. So they were struck by the evil consequences of what they did and were enveloped by what they used to ridicule.

35. And those who associate others with God say, "If God had willed, we would not have worshipped anything other than Him, neither we nor our fathers, nor would we have forbidden anything through other than Him." Thus did those do before them. So is there upon the messengers except [the duty of] clear notification?

36. And We certainly sent into every nation a messenger, [saying], "Worship God and avoid tāghūt."[643] And among them were those whom God guided, and among them were those upon whom error was [deservedly] decreed. So proceed [i.e., travel] through the earth and observe how was the end of the deniers.

37. [Even] if you should strive for their guidance, [O Muhammad], indeed, God does not guide those He sends astray,[644] and they will have no helpers.

38. And they swear by God their strongest oaths [that] God will not resurrect one who dies. But yes - [it is] a true promise [binding] upon Him, but most of the people do not know.

39. [It is] so He will make clear to them [the truth of] that wherein they differ and so those who have disbelieved may know that they were liars.

40. Indeed, Our word to a thing when We intend it is but that We say to it, "Be," and it is.

41. And those who emigrated for [the cause of] God after they had been wronged - We will surely settle them in this world in a good place; but the reward of the Hereafter is greater, if only they could know.

42. [They are] those who endured patiently and upon their Lord relied.

43. And We sent not before you except men to whom We revealed [Our message]. So ask the people of the message [i.e., former scriptures] if you do not know.

44. [We sent them] with clear proofs and written ordinances. And We revealed to you the message [i.e., the Qur'ān] that you may make clear to the people what was sent down to them and that they might give thought.

45. Then, do those who have planned evil deeds feel secure that God will not cause the earth to swallow them or that the punishment will not come upon them from where they do not perceive?

46. Or that He would not seize them during their [usual] activity, and they could not cause failure [i.e., escape from Him]?

[643] False objects of worship.
[644] As a result of their choice to reject guidance.

47. Or that He would not seize them gradually [in a state of dread]?[645] But indeed, your Lord is Kind and Merciful.[646]

48. Have they not considered what things God has created? Their shadows incline to the right and to the left, prostrating to God, while they [i.e., those creations] are humble.

49. And to God prostrates whatever is in the heavens and whatever is on the earth of creatures, and the angels [as well], and they are not arrogant.

50. They fear their Lord above them, and they do what they are commanded.

51. And God has said, "Do not take for yourselves two[647] deities. He [i.e., God] is but one God, so fear only Me."

52. And to Him belongs whatever is in the heavens and the earth, and to Him is [due] worship constantly. Then is it other than God that you fear?

53. And whatever you have of favor - it is from God. Then when adversity touches you, to Him you cry for help.

54. Then when He removes the adversity from you, at once a party of you associates others with their Lord

55. So they will deny what We have given them. Then enjoy yourselves, for you are going to know.

56. And they assign to what they do not know[648] [i.e., false deities] a portion of that which We have provided them. By God, you will surely be questioned about what you used to invent.

57. And they attribute to God daughters[649] - exalted is He - and for them is what they desire [i.e., sons].

58. And when one of them is informed of [the birth of] a female, his face becomes dark, and he suppresses grief.

59. He hides himself from the people because of the ill of which he has been informed. Should he keep it in humiliation or bury it in the ground? Unquestionably, evil is what they decide.

60. For those who do not believe in the Hereafter is the description [i.e., an attribute] of evil;[650] and for God is the highest attribute. And He is Exalted in Might, the Wise.

61. And if God were to impose blame on the people for their wrongdoing, He would not have left upon it [i.e., the earth] any creature, but He defers them for a specified term. And when their term has come, they will not remain behind an hour, nor will they precede [it].

62. And they attribute to God that which they dislike [i.e., daughters], and their tongues assert the lie that they will have the best [from Him]. Assuredly, they will have the Fire, and they will be [therein] neglected.[651]

[645] i.e., being aware of what is about to strike them after having seen those near them succumb.
[646] Postponing deserved punishment and giving opportunities for repentance.
[647] Meaning more than one.

[648] i.e., that of which they have no knowledge; rather, they have mere assumption based upon tradition or the claims of misguided men.
[649] By claiming that the angels are His daughters.
[650] Such as that described in the previous two verses.
[651] Another meaning is "...and they will be made to precede [all others thereto]."

63. By God, We did certainly send [messengers] to nations before you, but Satan made their deeds attractive to them. And he is their [i.e., the disbelievers] ally today [as well], and they will have a painful punishment.

64. And We have not revealed to you the Book, [O Muhammad], except for you to make clear to them that wherein they have differed and as guidance and mercy for a people who believe.

65. And God has sent down rain from the sky and given life thereby to the earth after its lifelessness. Indeed in that is a sign for a people who listen.

66. And indeed, for you in grazing livestock is a lesson. We give you drink from what is in their bellies - between excretion and blood - pure milk, palatable to drinkers.

67. And from the fruits of the palm trees and grapevines you take intoxicant and good provision.[652] Indeed in that is a sign for a people who reason.

68. And your Lord inspired to the bee, "Take for yourself among the mountains, houses [i.e., hives], and among the trees and [in] that which they construct.

69. Then eat from all the fruits[653] and follow the ways of your Lord laid down [for you]." There emerges from their bellies a drink, varying in colors, in which there is healing for people. Indeed in that is a sign for a people who give thought.

70. And God created you; then He will take you in death. And among you is he who is reversed to the most decrepit [old] age so that he will not know, after [having had] knowledge, a thing. Indeed, God is Knowing and Competent.

71. And God has favored some of you over others in provision. But those who were favored [i.e., given more] would not hand over their provision to those whom their right hands possess [i.e., slaves] so they would be equal to them therein.[654] Then is it the favor of God they reject?

72. And God has made for you from yourselves mates and has made for you from your mates sons and grandchildren and has provided for you from the good things. Then in falsehood do they believe and in the favor of God they disbelieve?

73. And they worship besides God that which does not possess for them [the power of] provision from the heavens and the earth at all, and [in fact], they are unable.

74. So do not assert similarities to God.[655] Indeed, God knows and you do not know.

75. God presents an example: a slave [who is] owned and unable to do a thing and he to whom We have provided from Us good provision, so he spends from it secretly and publicly. Can they be equal? Praise to God! But most of them do not know.

---

[652] This verse was revealed before the prohibition of intoxicants. It alludes to the fact that there are both evil and good possibilities in certain things.
[653] i.e., delicious substances found by the bee.

[654] The argument presented in this verse is: if they cannot consider their own possessions equal to themselves, then how can they consider God's creations as being equal to Him?
[655] As there is nothing comparable to Him.

76. And God presents an example of two men, one of them dumb and unable to do a thing, while he is a burden to his guardian. Wherever he directs him, he brings no good. Is he equal to one who commands justice, while he is on a straight path?

77. And to God belongs the unseen [aspects] of the heavens and the earth. And the command for the Hour is not but as a glance of the eye or even nearer. Indeed, God is over all things competent.

78. And God has extracted you from the wombs of your mothers not knowing a thing, and He made for you hearing and vision and hearts [i.e., intellect] that perhaps you would be grateful.

79. Do they not see the birds controlled in the atmosphere of the sky? None holds them up except God. Indeed in that are signs for a people who believe.

80. And God has made for you from your homes a place of rest and made for you from the hides of the animals tents which you find light on your day of travel and your day of encampment; and from their wool, fur and hair is furnishing and enjoyment [i.e., provision] for a time.

81. And God has made for you, from that which He has created, shadows [i.e., shade] and has made for you from the mountains, shelters and has made for you garments which protect you from the heat and garments [i.e., coats of mail] which protect you from your [enemy in] battle. Thus does He complete His favor upon you that you might submit [to Him].

82. But if they turn away, [O Muhammad] - then only upon you is [responsibility for] clear notification.

83. They recognize the favor of God; then they deny it. And most of them are disbelievers.

84. And [mention] the Day when We will resurrect from every nation a witness [i.e., their prophet]. Then it will not be permitted to the disbelievers [to apologize or make excuses], nor will they be asked to appease [God].

85. And when those who wronged see the punishment, it will not be lightened for them, nor will they be reprieved.

86. And when those who associated others with God see their "partners," they will say, "Our Lord, these are our partners [to You] whom we used to invoke besides You." But they will throw at them the statement, "Indeed, you are liars."

87. And they will impart to God that Day [their] submission, and lost from them is what they used to invent.

88. Those who disbelieved and averted [others] from the way of God - We will increase them in punishment over [their] punishment for what corruption they were causing.

89. And [mention] the Day when We will resurrect among every nation a witness over them from themselves [i.e., their prophet]. And We will bring you, [O Muhammad], as a witness over these [i.e., your nation]. And We have sent down to you the Book as clarification

for all things and as guidance and mercy and good tidings for the Muslims.[656]

90. Indeed, God orders justice and good conduct and giving to relatives and forbids immorality and bad conduct and oppression. He admonishes you that perhaps you will be reminded.

91. And fulfill the covenant of God when you have taken it, [O believers], and do not break oaths after their confirmation while you have made God, over you, a security [i.e., witness]. Indeed, God knows what you do.

92. And do not be like she who untwisted her spun thread after it was strong [by] taking your oaths as [means of] deceit between you because one community is more plentiful [in number or wealth] than another community.[657] God only tries you thereby. And He will surely make clear to you on the Day of Resurrection that over which you used to differ.

93. And if God had willed, He could have made you [of] one religion, but He causes to stray whom He wills and guides whom He wills.[658] And you will surely be questioned about what you used to do.

94. And do not take your oaths as [means of] deceit between you, lest a foot slip after it was [once] firm, and you would taste evil [in this world] for what [people] you diverted from the way of God,[659] and you would have [in the Hereafter] a great punishment.

95. And do not exchange the covenant of God for a small price. Indeed, what is with God is best for you, if only you could know.

96. Whatever you have will end, but what God has is lasting. And We will surely give those who were patient their reward according to the best of what they used to do.

97. Whoever does righteousness, whether male or female, while he is a believer - We will surely cause him to live a good life, and We will surely give them their reward [in the Hereafter] according to the best of what they used to do.

98. So when you recite the Qur'ān, [first] seek refuge in God from Satan, the expelled [from His mercy].

99. Indeed, there is for him no authority over those who have believed and rely upon their Lord.

100. His authority is only over those who take him as an ally and those who through him associate others with God.

101. And when We substitute a verse in place of a verse - and God is most knowing of what He sends down - they say, "You, [O Muhammad], are but an inventor [of lies]." But most of them do not know.

102. Say, [O Muhammad], "The Pure Spirit [i.e., Gabriel] has brought it down from your Lord in truth to make firm those

656 Those who have submitted themselves to God.
657 i.e., do not swear falsely or break a treaty or contract merely for a worldly advantage.
658 According to His knowledge of each soul's preference.

659 Referring to those who would be dissuaded from Islām as a result of a Muslim's deceit and treachery.

who believe and as guidance and good tidings to the Muslims."

103. And We certainly know that they say, "It is only a human being who teaches him [i.e., the Prophet]." The tongue of the one they refer to is foreign,[660] and this [recitation i.e., Qur'ān] is [in] a clear Arabic language.

104. Indeed, those who do not believe in the verses of God - God will not guide them, and for them is a painful punishment.

105. They only invent falsehood who do not believe in the verses of God, and it is those who are the liars.

106. Whoever disbelieves in [i.e., denies] God after his belief...[661] except for one who is forced [to renounce his religion] while his heart is secure in faith. But those who [willingly] open their breasts to disbelief, upon them is wrath from God, and for them is a great punishment;

107. That is because they preferred the worldly life over the Hereafter and that God does not guide the disbelieving people.

108. Those are the ones over whose hearts and hearing and vision God has sealed, and it is those who are the heedless.

109. Assuredly, it is they, in the Hereafter, who will be the losers.

110. Then, indeed your Lord, to those who emigrated after they had been compelled [to renounce their religion] and thereafter fought [for the cause of God] and were patient - indeed, your Lord, after that, is Forgiving and Merciful

111. On the Day when every soul will come disputing [i.e., pleading] for itself, and every soul will be fully compensated for what it did, and they will not be wronged [i.e., treated unjustly].

112. And God presents an example: a city [i.e., Makkah] which was safe and secure, its provision coming to it in abundance from every location, but it denied the favors of God. So God made it taste the envelopment of hunger and fear for what they had been doing.

113. And there had certainly come to them a Messenger from among themselves, but they denied him; so punishment overtook them while they were wrongdoers.

114. Then eat of what God has provided for you [which is] lawful and good. And be grateful for the favor of God, if it is [indeed] Him that you worship.

115. He has only forbidden to you dead animals,[662] blood, the flesh of swine, and that which has been dedicated to other than God. But whoever is forced [by necessity], neither desiring [it] nor transgressing [its limit] - then indeed, God is Forgiving and Merciful.

116. And do not say about what your tongues assert of untruth, "This is lawful and this is unlawful," to invent falsehood about God. Indeed, those who

[660] Having seen the Prophet speaking with a foreign man on occasion, the Quraysh accused him of repeating the man's words.

[661] Based upon the conclusion of this verse, the omitted phrase concerning the apostate is understood to be "...has earned the wrath of God..."

[662] Those not slaughtered or hunted expressly for food.

invent falsehood about God will not succeed.

117. [It is but] a brief enjoyment, and they will have a painful punishment.

118. And to those who are Jews We have prohibited that which We related to you before.[663] And We did not wrong them [thereby], but they were wronging themselves.

119. Then, indeed your Lord, to those who have done wrong out of ignorance and then repent after that and correct themselves - indeed, your Lord, thereafter, is Forgiving and Merciful.

120. Indeed, Abraham was a [comprehensive] leader,[664] devoutly obedient to God, inclining toward truth, and he was not of those who associate others with God.

121. [He was] grateful for His favors. He [i.e., God] chose him and guided him to a straight path.

122. And We gave him good in this world, and indeed, in the Hereafter he will be among the righteous.

123. Then We revealed to you, [O Muhammad], to follow the religion of Abraham, inclining toward truth; and he was not of those who associate with God.

124. The sabbath was only appointed for those who differed over it. And indeed, your Lord will judge between them on the Day of Resurrection concerning that over which they used to differ.

125. Invite to the way of your Lord with wisdom and good instruction, and argue with them in a way that is best. Indeed, your Lord is most knowing of who has strayed from His way, and He is most knowing of who is [rightly] guided.

126. And if you punish [an enemy, O believers], punish with an equivalent of that with which you were harmed.[665] But if you are patient - it is better for those who are patient.

127. And be patient, [O Muhammad], and your patience is not but through God. And do not grieve over them and do not be in distress over what they conspire.

128. Indeed, God is with those who fear Him and those who are doers of good.

[663] See 6:146.

[664] i.e., embodying all the excellent qualities which make one an example to be followed.

[665] Not exceeding it.

## Sūrah 17: al-Isrā'

### Period of Revelation

The very first verse indicates that this Sūrah was revealed on the occasion of Miraj (Ascension). According to the hadith and books on the life of the Prophet this event happened one year before Hijrah. Thus this Sūrah is one of those which were revealed in the last stage of Prophethood at Makkah.

### Background

The Prophet had been propagating Tawhid (Oneness of God) for the previous twelve years and his opponents had been doing all they could to make his Mission a failure but in spite of all their opposition Islām had spread to every corner of Arabia and there was hardly any clan which had not been influenced by his invitation. In Makkah itself the true Believers had formed themselves into a small community and were ready and willing to face every danger to make Islām a success. Besides them a very large number of the people of Aws and Khazraj (two influential clans of Madinah) had accepted Islām. Thus the time had come for the Prophet to emigrate from Makkah to Madinah and there gather together the scattered Muslims and establish a state based on the principles of Islām.

### Theme and Topics

This Sūrah is a wonderful combination of warning, admonition and instruction which have been blended together in a balanced proportion. The disbelievers of Makkah had been admonished to take a lesson from the miserable end of the Israelites and other communities and mend their ways within the period of respite given by God, which was about to expire. They should therefore accept the invitation that was being extended by Muhammad and the Qur'ān; otherwise they shall be annihilated and replaced by other people. Incidentally the Israelites with whom Islām was going to come in direct contact with in the near future at Madinah have also been warned that they should learn a lesson from the chastisements that have already been inflicted on them. They were warned to take advantage of the Prophethood of Muhammad because that is the last opportunity which is being given to them. If even now you behave as you have been behaving you shall meet with a painful torment.

As regards the education of mankind it has been stressed that human success or failure gain or loss depends upon the right understanding of Tawhid, life-after-death and Prophethood. Accordingly, convincing arguments have been put forward to prove that the Qur'ān is the Book of God and its teachings are true and genuine. The doubts of the disbelievers about these basic realities have been removed and on suitable occasions they have been admonished and rebuked in regard to their ways of ignorance.

In this connection those fundamental principles of morality and civilization on which the Islāmic System of life is meant to be established have been put forward. Thus this was a sort of the Manifesto of the intended Islāmic state which had been proclaimed a year before its actual establishment. It has been explicitly stated that that was the sketch of the system on which Prophet Muhammad intended to build human life, first in his own country and then in the outside world. Besides these the Prophet has been instructed to stick firmly to his stance without minding the opposition and difficulties which he was encountering and should never think of making a compromise with unbelief. Moreover, Salat (prayer) was prescribed in order to reform and purify their souls as if to say, this is the thing which will produce in you those high qualities of character which are essential for everyone who intends to struggle in the righteous way. Incidentally we learn from hadith that Mi'raj was the first occasion on which the five daily Prayers were prescribed to be offered at fixed times.

## Sūrah 17: al-Isrā'[666]

In the Name of God, the Most Compassionate, the Most Merciful

1. Exalted[667] is He who took His Servant [i.e., Prophet Muhammad] by night from al-Masjid al-Harām to al-Masjid al-Aqsā,[668] whose surroundings We have blessed, to show him of Our signs. Indeed, He is the Hearing, the Seeing.

2. And We gave Moses the Scripture and made it a guidance for the Children of Israel that you not take other than Me as Disposer of affairs,[669]

3. O descendants of those We carried [in the ship] with Noah. Indeed, he was a grateful servant.

4. And We conveyed[670] to the Children of Israel in the Scripture that, "You will surely cause corruption on the earth twice, and you will surely reach [a degree of] great haughtiness."

5. So when the [time of] promise came for the first of them,[671] We sent against you servants of Ours - those of great military might, and they probed [even] into the homes,[672] and it was a promise fulfilled.

6. Then We gave back to you a return victory over them. And We reinforced you with wealth and sons and made you more numerous in manpower

7. [And said], "If you do good, you do good for yourselves; and if you do evil, [you do it] to them [i.e., yourselves]." Then when the final [i.e., second] promise came, [We sent your enemies] to sadden your faces and to enter the masjid [i.e., the temple in Jerusalem], as they entered it the first time, and to destroy what they had taken over with [total] destruction.

8. [Then God said], "It is expected, [if you repent], that your Lord will have mercy upon you. But if you return [to sin], We will return [to punishment]. And We have made Hell, for the disbelievers, a prison-bed."

9. Indeed, this Qur'ān guides to that which is most suitable and gives good tidings to the believers who do righteous deeds that they will have a great reward.

10. And that those who do not believe in the Hereafter - We have prepared for them a painful punishment.

11. And man supplicates for evil [when angry] as he supplicates for good, and man is ever hasty.[673]

12. And We have made the night and day two signs, and We erased the sign of the night and made the sign of the day visible[674] that you may seek bounty from your Lord and may know the number of years and the account [of

---

666 *Al-Isrā'*: The Night Journey. The *Sūrah* is also known as *Bani Isrā'eel* (The Children of Israel).

667 Above any imperfection or failure to do as He wills.

668 In Jerusalem.

669 i.e., trust in God, knowing that He is responsible for every occurrence.

670 Foretold out of divine knowledge of what they would do.

671 i.e., the promised punishment for the first of their two transgressions.

672 Violating their sanctity, to kill and plunder.

673 i.e., impatient, emotional, and acting without forethought.

674 Or "giving sight."

time]. And everything We have set out in detail.

13. And [for] every person We have imposed his fate upon his neck,[675] and We will produce for him on the Day of Resurrection a record which he will encounter spread open.

14. [It will be said], "Read your record. Sufficient is yourself against you this Day as accountant."

15. Whoever is guided is only guided for [the benefit of] his soul. And whoever errs only errs against it. And no bearer of burdens will bear the burden of another. And never would We punish until We sent a messenger.

16. And when We intend to destroy a city, We command its affluent[676] but they defiantly disobey therein; so the word [i.e., deserved decree] comes into effect upon it, and We destroy it with [complete] destruction.

17. And how many have We destroyed from the generations after Noah. And sufficient is your Lord, concerning the sins of His servants, as Acquainted and Seeing.

18. Whoever should desire the immediate[677] - We hasten for him from it what We will to whom We intend. Then We have made for him Hell, which he will [enter to] burn, censured and banished.

19. But whoever desires the Hereafter and exerts the effort due to it while he is a believer - it is those whose effort is ever appreciated [by God].

20. To each [category] We extend - to these and to those - from the gift of your Lord. And never has the gift of your Lord been restricted.

21. Look how We have favored [in provision] some of them over others. But the Hereafter is greater in degrees [of difference] and greater in distinction.

22. Do not make [as equal] with God another deity and [thereby] become censured and forsaken.

23. And your Lord has decreed that you not worship except Him, and to parents, good treatment. Whether one or both of them reach old age [while] with you, say not to them [so much as], "uff,"[678] and do not repel them but speak to them a noble word.

24. And lower to them the wing of humility out of mercy and say, "My Lord, have mercy upon them as they brought me up [when I was] small."

25. Your Lord is most knowing of what is within yourselves. If you should be righteous [in intention] - then indeed He is ever, to the often returning [to Him], Forgiving.[679]

26. And give the relative his right, and [also] the poor and the traveler, and do not spend wastefully.[680]

[675] i.e., after having instructed him, We have made him responsible for his own destiny.
[676] To obey God.
[677] i.e., worldly gratifications.

[678] An expression of disapproval or irritation.
[679] For those who intend righteousness, hastening to repent from sins and errors committed through human weakness, God promises forgiveness.
[680] i.e., on that which is unlawful or in disobedience to God.

27. Indeed, the wasteful are brothers of the devils, and ever has Satan been to his Lord ungrateful.

28. And if you [must] turn away from them [i.e., the needy] awaiting mercy from your Lord which you expect,[681] then speak to them a gentle word.

29. And do not make your hand [as] chained to your neck[682] or extend it completely[683] and [thereby] become blamed and insolvent.

30. Indeed, your Lord extends provision for whom He wills and restricts [it]. Indeed He is ever, concerning His servants, Acquainted and Seeing.

31. And do not kill your children for fear of poverty. We provide for them and for you. Indeed, their killing is ever a great sin.

32. And do not approach unlawful sexual intercourse.[684] Indeed, it is ever an immorality and is evil as a way.

33. And do not kill the soul [i.e., person] which God has forbidden, except by right.[685] And whoever is killed unjustly - We have given his heir authority,[686] but let him not exceed limits in [the matter of] taking life. Indeed, he has been supported [by the law].

34. And do not approach the property of an orphan, except in the way that is best,[687] until he reaches maturity. And fulfill [every] commitment. Indeed, the commitment is ever [that about which one will be] questioned.

35. And give full measure when you measure, and weigh with an even [i.e., honest] balance. That is the best [way] and best in result.

36. And do not pursue[688] that of which you have no knowledge. Indeed, the hearing, the sight and the heart - about all those [one] will be questioned.

37. And do not walk upon the earth exultantly. Indeed, you will never tear the earth [apart], and you will never reach the mountains in height.[689]

38. All that [i.e., the aforementioned] - its evil is ever, in the sight of your Lord, detested.

39. That is from what your Lord has revealed to you, [O Muhammad], of wisdom. And, [O mankind], do not make [as equal] with God another deity, lest you be thrown into Hell, blamed and banished.

40. Then, has your Lord chosen you for [having] sons and taken [i.e., adopted] from among the angels daughters? Indeed, you say a grave saying.

41. And We have certainly diversified [the contents] in this Qur'ān that they [i.e., mankind] may be reminded, but it does not increase them [i.e., the disbelievers] except in aversion.

---

[681] i.e., if you have not the means to give them at present.

[682] i.e., refusing to spend.

[683] i.e., being extravagant.

[684] i.e., avoid all situations that might possibly lead to it.

[685] i.e., through legal justice or during *jihād.*

[686] Grounds for legal action.

[687] i.e., to improve or increase it.

[688] i.e., do not assume and do not say.

[689] Man, for all his arrogance, is yet a weak and small creature.

42. Say, [O Muhammad], "If there had been with Him [other] gods, as they say, then they [each] would have sought to the Owner of the Throne a way."[690]

43. Exalted is He and high above what they say by great sublimity.

44. The seven heavens and the earth and whatever is in them exalt Him. And there is not a thing except that it exalts [God] by His praise, but you do not understand their [way of] exalting. Indeed, He is ever Forbearing and Forgiving.

45. And when you recite the Qur'ān, We put between you and those who do not believe in the Hereafter a concealed partition.[691]

46. And We have placed over their hearts coverings, lest they understand it, and in their ears deafness. And when you mention your Lord alone in the Qur'ān, they turn back in aversion.

47. We are most knowing of how they listen to it when they listen to you and [of] when they are in private conversation, when the wrongdoers say, "You follow not but a man affected by magic."

48. Look how they strike for you comparisons;[692] but they have strayed, so they cannot [find] a way.

49. And they say, "When we are bones and crumbled particles, will we [truly] be resurrected as a new creation?"

50. Say, "Be you stones or iron[693]

51. Or [any] creation of that which is great[694] within your breasts." And they will say, "Who will restore us?" Say, "He who brought you forth the first time." Then they will nod their heads toward you[695] and say, "When is that?" Say, "Perhaps it will be soon -

52. On the Day He will call you and you will respond with praise of Him and think that you had not remained [in the world] except for a little."

53. And tell My servants to say that which is best. Indeed, Satan induces [dissension] among them. Indeed Satan is ever, to mankind, a clear enemy.

54. Your Lord is most knowing of you. If He wills, He will have mercy upon you; or if He wills, He will punish you. And We have not sent you, [O Muhammad], over them as a manager.

55. And your Lord is most knowing of whoever is in the heavens and the earth. And We have made some of the prophets exceed others [in various ways], and to David We gave the book [of Psalms].

56. Say, "Invoke those you have claimed [as gods] besides Him, for they do not possess the [ability for] removal of adversity from you or [for its] transfer [to someone else]."

57. Those whom they invoke[696] seek means of access to their Lord, [striving as to] which of them would be nearest, and

---

690 To please Him, recognizing His superiority. Another interpretation is "...they would seek a way" to depose Him and take over His Throne.

691 Preventing guidance from reaching them.

692 Describing the Prophet as a poet, a madman or one under the influence of sorcery.

693 i.e., even if you should be stones or iron.

694 Such as the heavens and earth.

695 In disbelief and ridicule.

696 Among the righteous of God's creation, such as angels, prophets, deceased scholars, etc.

they hope for His mercy and fear His punishment. Indeed, the punishment of your Lord is ever feared.

58. And there is no city but that We will destroy it[697] before the Day of Resurrection or punish it with a severe punishment. That has ever been in the Register[698] inscribed.

59. And nothing has prevented Us from sending signs [i.e., miracles] except that the former peoples denied them. And We gave Thamūd the she-camel as a visible sign, but they wronged her. And We send not the signs except as a warning.

60. And [remember, O Muhammad], when We told you, "Indeed, your Lord has encompassed the people."[699] And We did not make the sight which We showed you[700] except as a trial for the people, as was the accursed tree [mentioned] in the Qur'ān. And We threaten [i.e., warn] them, but it increases them not except in great transgression.

61. And [mention] when We said to the angles, "Prostrate to Adam," and they prostrated, except for Iblees.[701] He said, "Should I prostrate to one You created from clay?"

62. [Iblees] said, "Do You see this one whom You have honoured above me? If You delay me [i.e., my death] until the Day of Resurrection, I will surely destroy[702] his descendants, except for a few."

63. [God] said, "Go, for whoever of them follows you, indeed Hell will be the recompense of [all of] you - an ample recompense.

64. And incite [to senselessness] whoever you can among them with your voice and assault them with your horses and foot soldiers and become a partner in their wealth and their children and promise them." But Satan does not promise them except delusion.

65. Indeed, over My [believing] servants there is for you no authority. And sufficient is your Lord as Disposer of affairs.

66. It is your Lord who drives the ship for you through the sea that you may seek of His bounty. Indeed, He is ever, to you, Merciful.

67. And when adversity touches you at sea, lost are [all] those you invoke except for Him. But when He delivers you to the land, you turn away [from Him]. And ever is man ungrateful.

68. Then do you feel secure that [instead] He will not cause a part of the land to swallow you or send against you a storm of stones? Then you would not find for yourselves an advocate.

69. Or do you feel secure that He will not send you back into it [i.e., the sea] another time and send upon you a hurricane of wind and drown you for what you denied?[703] Then you would not

[697] Because of the sins of its inhabitants.
[698] The Preserved Slate (*al-Lawh al-Mahfūth*), which is with God.
[699] In His knowledge and power, meaning that God would protect him from their harm.
[700] During the *mi'rāj* (ascension) into the heavens.
[701] See footnote to 2:34.
[702] By tempting them and leading them astray.
[703] Or "for your disbelief."

find for yourselves against Us an avenger.[704]

70. And We have certainly honoured the children of Adam and carried them on the land and sea and provided for them of the good things and preferred them over much of what We have created, with [definite] preference.

71. [Mention, O Muhammad], the Day We will call forth every people with their record [of deeds].[705] Then whoever is given his record in his right hand - those will read their records, and injustice will not be done to them, [even] as much as a thread [inside the date seed].

72. And whoever is blind[706] in this [life] will be blind in the Hereafter and more astray in way.

73. And indeed, they were about to tempt you away from that which We revealed to you in order to [make] you invent about Us something else; and then they would have taken you as a friend.

74. And if We had not strengthened you, you would have almost inclined to them a little.

75. Then [if you had], We would have made you taste double [punishment in] life and double [after] death. Then you would not find for yourself against Us a helper.

76. And indeed, they were about to provoke [i.e., drive] you from the land [i.e., Makkah] to evict you therefrom. And then [when they do], they will not remain [there] after you, except for a little.[707]

77. [That is Our] established way for those We had sent before you of Our messengers; and you will not find in Our way any alteration.

78. Establish prayer at the decline of the sun [from its meridian] until the darkness of the night[708] and [also] the Qur'ān [i.e., recitation] of dawn.[709] Indeed, the recitation of dawn is ever witnessed.

79. And from [part of] the night, pray[710] with it [i.e., recitation of the Qur'ān] as additional [worship] for you; it is expected that[711] your Lord will resurrect you to a praised station.[712]

80. And say, "My Lord, cause me to enter a sound entrance[713] and to exit a sound exit[714] and grant me from Yourself a supporting authority."

81. And say, "Truth has come, and falsehood has departed. Indeed is falsehood, [by nature], ever bound to depart."

82. And We send down of the Qur'ān that which is healing and mercy for the be-

[704] Or "someone to demand restitution."
[705] Other meanings are "with their leader" or "with that which they had followed."
[706] i.e., refusing to see the truth.

[707] Only ten years after the Prophet's emigration, Makkah was completely cleared of his enemies.
[708] i.e., the period which includes the *thuhr*, *asr*, *maghrib*, and *'ishā* prayers.
[709] i.e., the *fajr* prayer, in which the recitation of the Qur'ān is prolonged.
[710] Literally, "arise from sleep for prayer."
[711] This is a promise from God to the Prophet Muhammad.
[712] The position of intercession by permission of God and the highest degree in Paradise.
[713] Into Madinah at the time of emigration, or into the grave.
[714] From Makkah, or from the grave at the time of resurrection.

lievers, but it does not increase the wrongdoers except in loss.

83. And when We bestow favor upon man [i.e., the disbeliever], he turns away and distances himself; and when evil touches him, he is ever despairing.

84. Say, "Each works according to his manner, but your Lord is most knowing of who is best guided in way."

85. And they ask you, [O Muhammad], about the soul. Say, "The soul is of the affair [i.e., concern] of my Lord. And you [i.e., mankind] have not been given of knowledge except a little."

86. And if We willed, We could surely do away with that which We revealed to you. Then you would not find for yourself concerning it an advocate against Us.

87. Except [We have left it with you] as a mercy from your Lord. Indeed, His favor upon you has ever been great.

88. Say, "If mankind and the jinn gathered in order to produce the like of this Qur'ān, they could not produce the like of it, even if they were to each other assistants."

89. And We have certainly diversified for the people in this Qur'ān from every [kind of] example, but most of the people refused [anything] except disbelief.

90. And they say, "We will not believe you until you break open for us from the ground a spring

91. Or [until] you have a garden of palm tress and grapes and make rivers gush forth within them in force [and abundance]

92. Or you make the heaven fall upon us in fragments as you have claimed or you bring God and the angels before [us]

93. Or you have a house of ormnament [i.e., gold] or you ascend into the sky. And [even then], we will not believe in your ascension until you bring down to us a book we may read." Say, "Exalted is my Lord! Was I ever but a human messenger?"

94. And what prevented the people from believing when guidance came to them except that they said, "Has God sent a human messenger?"

95. Say, "If there were upon the earth angels walking securely,[715] We would have sent down to them from the heaven an angel [as a] messenger."

96. Say, "Sufficient is God as Witness between me and you. Indeed he is ever, concerning His servants, Acquainted and Seeing."

97. And whoever God guides - he is the [rightly] guided; and whoever He sends astray[716] - you will never find for them protectors besides Him, and We will gather them on the Day of Resurrection [fallen] on their faces - blind, dumb and deaf. Their refuge is Hell; every time it subsides We increase them in blazing fire.

98. That is their recompense because they disbelieved in Our verses and said, "When we are bones and crumbled

[715] i.e., who were settled and established there, as is man.

[716] As a result of his own preference.

particles, will we [truly] be resurrected [in] a new creation?"

99. Do they not see that God, who created the heavens and earth, is [the one] Able to create the likes of them? And He has appointed for them a term, about which there is no doubt. But the wrongdoers refuse [anything] except disbelief.

100. Say [to them], "If you possessed the depositories of the mercy of my Lord, then you would withhold out of fear of spending." And ever has man been stingy.

101. And We had certainly given Moses nine evident signs, so ask the Children of Israel [about] when he came to them and Pharaoh said to him, "Indeed I think, O Moses, that you are affected by magic."

102. [Moses] said, "You have already known that none has sent down these [signs] except the Lord of the heavens and the earth as evidence, and indeed I think,[717] O Pharaoh, that you are destroyed."

103. So he intended to drive them from the land, but We drowned him and those with him all together.

104. And We said after him [i.e., Pharaoh] to the Children of Israel, "Dwell in the land, and when there comes the promise [i.e., appointment] of the Hereafter, We will bring you forth in [one] gathering."

105. And with the truth We have sent it [i.e., the Qur'ān] down, and with the truth it has descended. And We have not sent you, [O Muhammad], except as a bringer of good tidings and a warner.

106. And [it is] a Qur'ān which We have separated [by intervals] that you might recite it to the people over a prolonged period. And We have sent it down progressively.

107. Say, "Believe in it or do not believe. Indeed, those who were given knowledge before it[718] - when it is recited to them, they fall upon their faces in prostration,

108. And they say, "Exalted is our Lord! Indeed, the promise of our Lord has been fulfilled."

109. And they fall upon their faces weeping, and it [i.e., the Qur'ān] increases them in humble submission.

110. Say, "Call upon God or call upon the Most Merciful. [al-Rahmān]. Whichever [name] you call - to Him belong the best names." And do not recite [too] loudly in your prayer or [too] quietly but seek between that an [intermediate] way.

111. And say, "Praise to God, who has not taken a son and has had no partner in [His] dominion and has no [need of a] protector out of weakness; and glorify Him with [great] glorification."

---

[717] i.e., I am certain.

[718] i.e., the righteous among the People of the Scriptures who recognize the truth contained in the Qur'ān.

## Sūrah 18: al-Kahf

### Period of Revelation

This is the first of those Sūrahs which were sent down in the third stage of Prophethood at Makkah. We have already divided the life of the Prophet at Makkah into four stages in the introduction to Sūrah 6. According to that division the third stage lasted from the fifth to the tenth year of Prophethood. What distinguishes this stage from the second and the fourth stages is this: during the second stage the Quraysh mainly resorted to ridiculing, scoffing, threatening, tempting, raising objections and making false propaganda against the Prophet and his followers in order to suppress the Islāmic Movement. But during the third stage they employed the weapons of persecution, man handling and economic pressure for the same purpose. So much so that a large number of the Muslims had to emigrate from Arabia to Abassinyah and those who remained behind were besieged in Shi'ib Abi Talib along with the Prophet and his family. To add to their misery a complete social and economic boycott was applied against them. The only redeeming feature was that there were two personalities, Abu Talib and Khadijah whose personal influence had been conducive to the support of two great families of the Quraysh. However when in the tenth year of Prophethood these two persons died the fourth stage began with such severe persecutions as forced the Prophet and all his Companions to emigrate from Makkah.

It appears from the theme of the Sūrah that it was revealed at the beginning of the third stage when in spite of persecutions and opposition the migration to Abassinyah had not yet taken place. That is why the story of "Ashab-e-Kahf" (the Sleepers of the Cave) has been related to comfort and encourage the persecuted Muslims and to show them how the righteous people have been saving their Faith in the past.

### Subject and Topics

This Sūrah was sent down in answer to the three questions which the polytheists of Makkah in consultation with the people of the Book had put to the Prophet in order to test him. These were:

1. Who were "the Sleepers of the Cave?"
2. What is the real story of Khidr? and
3. What do you know about Dhul-Qarnain?

As these three questions and the stories involved concerned the history of the Christians and the Jews and were unknown in Hijaz (Arabian Peninsula) a choice of these was made to test whether the Prophet possessed any source of the knowledge of the hidden and unseen things. God however not only gave a complete answer to their questions but also employed the three stories to the disadvantage of the opponents of Islām in the conflict that was going on at that time in Makkah between Islām and unbelief.

The questioners were told that "the Sleepers of the Cave" believed in the same doctrine of Tawhid (Oneness of God) which was being put forward in the Qur'ān and that their condition was similar to the condition of the persecuted Muslims of Makkah. On the other hand the persecutors of the Sleepers of the Cave had behaved in the same way towards them as the disbelievers of the Quraysh were behaving towards the Muslims. The story of the Sleepers of the Cave has also been used to warn the chiefs of Makkah who were persecuting the small newly formed Muslim Community. At the same time the Prophet has been instructed that under no circumstances should he make a compromise with their persecutors nor should he consider them to be more important than his poor followers. On the other hand those chiefs have been admonished that they should not be puffed up with the transitory life of pleasure they were then enjoying but should seek after those excellences which are permanent and eternal.

## Sūrah 18: al-Kahf[719]

In the Name of God, the Most Compassionate, the Most Merciful

1. [All] praise is [due] to God, who has sent down upon His Servant [Muhammad] the Book and has not made therein any deviance.[720]

2. [He has made it] straight, to warn of severe punishment from Him and to give good tidings to the believers who do righteous deeds that they will have a good reward [i.e., Paradise]

3. In which they will remain forever

4. And to warn those who say, "God has taken a son."

5. They have no knowledge of it,[721] nor had their fathers. Grave is the word that comes out of their mouths; they speak not except a lie.

6. Then perhaps you would kill yourself through grief over them, [O Muhammad], if they do not believe in this message, [and] out of sorrow.

7. Indeed, We have made that which is on the earth adornment for it that We may test them [as to] which of them is best in deed.

8. And indeed, We will make that which is upon it [into] a barren ground.

9. Or have you thought that the companions of the cave and the inscription were, among Our signs, a wonder?[722]

10. [Mention] when the youths retreated to the cave and said, "Our Lord, grant us from Yourself mercy and prepare for us from our affair right guidance."

11. So We cast [a cover of sleep] over their ears within the cave for a number of years.

12. Then We awakened them that We might show which of the two factions was most precise in calculating what [extent] they had remained in time.

13. It is We who relate to you, [O Muhammad], their story in truth. Indeed, they were youths who believed in their Lord, and We increased them in guidance.

14. And We bound [i.e., made firm] their hearts when they stood up and said, "Our Lord is the Lord of the heavens and the earth. Never will we invoke besides Him any deity. We would have certainly spoken, then, an excessive transgression.

15. These, our people, have taken besides Him deities. Why do they not bring for [worship of] them a clear authority? And who is more unjust than one who invents about God a lie?"

16. [The youths said to one another], "And when you have withdrawn from them and that which they worship other than God, retreat to the cave. Your Lord will spread out for you of His mercy and

[719] *Al-Kahf*: The Cave.
[720] From the truth or the straight path.
[721] i.e., they could not have had knowledge of something which is not true.

[722] Rather, it is only one of the many wonders of God.

will prepare for you from your affair facility."

17. And [had you been present], you would see the sun when it rose, inclining away from their cave on the right, and when it set, passing away from them on the left, while they were [laying] within an open space thereof. That was from the signs of God. He whom God guides is the [rightly] guided, but he whom He leaves astray - never will you find for him a protecting guide.

18. And you would think them awake, while they were asleep. And We turned them to the right and to the left, while their dog stretched his forelegs at the entrance. If you had looked at them, you would have turned from them in flight and been filled by them with terror.

19. And similarly,[723] We awakened them that they might question one another. Said a speaker from among them, "How long have you remained [here]?" They said, "We have remained a day or part of a day." They said, "Your Lord is most knowing of how long you remained. So send one of you with this silver coin of yours to the city and let him look to which is the best of food and bring you provision from it and let him be cautious. And let no one be aware of you.

20. Indeed, if they come to know of you, they will stone you or return you to their religion. And never would you succeed, then - ever."

21. And similarly, We caused them to be found that they [who found them] would know that the promise of God is truth and that of the Hour there is no doubt. [That was] when they[724] disputed among themselves about their affair and [then] said, "Construct over them a structure. Their Lord is most knowing about them." Said those who prevailed in the matter, "We will surely take [for ourselves] over them a masjid."[725]

22. They [i.e., people] will say there were three, the fourth of them being their dog; and they will say there were five, the sixth of them being their dog - guessing at the unseen; and they will say there were seven, and the eighth of them was their dog. Say, [O Muhammad], "My Lord is most knowing of their number. None knows them except a few. So do not argue about them except with an obvious argument[726] and do not inquire about them among [the speculators] from anyone."

23. And never say of anything, "Indeed, I will do that tomorrow,"

24. Except [when adding], "If God wills." And remember your Lord when you forget [it] and say, "Perhaps my Lord will guide me to what is nearer than this to right conduct."

25. And they remained in their cave for three hundred years and exceeded by nine.[727]

26. Say, "God is most knowing of how long they remained. He has [knowledge of] the unseen [aspects] of the heavens and the earth. How Seeing is He and how Hearing! They have not besides

[723] By the will of God.

[724] The people of the city.

[725] i.e., we will make this site a place of worship.

[726] i.e., one from the Qur'ān, which is the only sure argument.

[727] According to the lunar calendar.

Him any protector, and He shares not His legislation with anyone."

27. And recite, [O Muhammad], what has been revealed to you of the Book of your Lord. There is no changer of His words, and never will you find in other than Him a refuge.

28. And keep yourself patient [by being] with those who call upon their Lord in the morning and the evening, seeking His countenance. And let not your eyes pass beyond them, desiring adornments of the worldly life, and do not obey one whose heart We have made heedless of Our remembrance and who follows his desire and whose affair is ever [in] neglect.[728]

29. And say, "The truth is from your Lord, so whoever wills - let him believe; and whoever wills - let him disbelieve." Indeed, We have prepared for the wrongdoers a fire whose walls will surround them. And if they call for relief, they will be relieved with water like murky oil, which scalds [their] faces. Wretched is the drink, and evil is the resting place.

30. Indeed, those who have believed and done righteous deeds - indeed, We will not allow to be lost the reward of any who did well in deeds.

31. Those will have gardens of perpetual residence; beneath them rivers will flow. They will be adorned therein with bracelets of gold and will wear green garments of fine silk and brocade, reclining therein on adorned couches. Excellent is the reward, and good is the resting place.

32. And present to them an example of two men: We granted to one of them two gardens of grapevines, and We bordered them with palm trees and placed between them [fields of] crops.

33. Each of the two gardens produced its fruit and did not fall short thereof in anything. And We caused to gush forth within them a river.

34. And he had fruit, so he said to his companion while he was conversing with him, "I am greater than you in wealth and mightier in [numbers of] men."

35. And he entered his garden while he was unjust to himself.[729] He said, "I do not think that this will perish - ever.

36. And I do not think the Hour will occur. And even if I should be brought back to my Lord, I will surely find better than this as a return."

37. His companion said to him while he was conversing with him, "Have you disbelieved in He who created you from dust and then from a sperm-drop and then proportioned you [as] a man?

38. But as for me, He is God, my Lord, and I do not associate with my Lord anyone.

39. And why did you, when you entered your garden, not say, 'What God willed [has occurred]; there is no power except in God'? Although you see me less than you in wealth and children,

40. It may be that my Lord will give me [something] better than your garden and will send upon it a calamity from

[728] Or "in excess," exceeding the limits of God.

[729] i.e., proud and ungrateful to God.

the sky, and it will become a smooth, dusty ground,

41. Or its water will become sunken [into the earth], so you would never be able to seek it."

42. And his fruits were encompassed [by ruin], so he began to turn his hands about [in dismay] over what he had spent on it, while it had collapsed upon its trellises, and said, "Oh, I wish I had not associated with my Lord anyone."[730]

43. And there was for him no company to aid him other than God, nor could he defend himself.

44. There[731] the authority is [completely] for God, the Truth. He is best in reward and best in outcome.

45. And present to them the example of the life of this world, [its being] like rain which We send down from the sky, and the vegetation of the earth mingles with it[732] and [then] it becomes dry remnants, scattered by the winds. And God is ever, over all things, Perfect in Ability.

46. Wealth and children are [but] adornment of the worldly life. But the enduring good deeds are better to your Lord[733] for reward and better for [one's] hope.

47. And [warn of] the Day when We will remove the mountains and you will see the earth prominent,[734] and We will gather them and not leave behind from them anyone.

48. And they will be presented before your Lord in rows, [and He will say], "You have certainly come to Us just as We created you the first time. But you claimed that We would never make for you an appointment."

49. And the record [of deeds] will be placed [open], and you will see the criminals fearful of that within it, and they will say, "Oh, woe to us! What is this book that leaves nothing small or great except that it has enumerated it?" And they will find what they did present [before them]. And your Lord does injustice to no one.

50. And [mention] when We said to the angels, "Prostrate to Adam," and they prostrated, except for Iblees. He was of the jinn and departed from [i.e., disobeyed] the command of his Lord. Then will you take him and his descendants as allies other than Me while they are enemies to you? Wretched it is for the wrongdoers as an exchange.

51. I did not make them witness to the creation of the heavens and the earth or to the creation of themselves, and I would not have taken the misguiders as assistants.

52. And [warn of] the Day when He will say, "Call 'My partners' whom you claimed," and they will invoke them, but they will not respond to them. And We will put between them [a valley of] destruction.

---

730 He attributed his property to himself rather that to God and disbelieved in the account of the Hereafter.
731 i.e., at such a time or on the Day of Judgement.
732 Absorbs it, growing lush and thick.
733 i.e., in His sight or evaluation.
734 i.e., bare and exposed.

53. And the criminals will see the Fire and will be certain that they are to fall therein. And they will not find from it a way elsewhere.

54. And We have certainly diversified in this Qur'ān for the people from every [kind of] example; but man has ever been, most of anything, [prone to] dispute.

55. And nothing has prevented the people from believing when guidance came to them and from asking forgiveness of their Lord except that there [must] befall them the [accustomed] precedent of the former peoples[735] or that the punishment should come [directly] before them.

56. And We send not the messengers except as bringers of good tidings and warners. And those who disbelieve dispute by [using] falsehood to [attempt to] invalidate thereby the truth and have taken My verses, and that of which they are warned, in ridicule.

57. And who is more unjust than one who is reminded of the verses of his Lord but turns away from them and forgets what his hands have put forth? Indeed, We have placed over their hearts coverings, lest they understand it, and in their ears deafness. And if you invite them to guidance - they will never be guided, then - ever.

58. And your Lord is the Forgiving, full of mercy. If He were to impose blame upon them for what they earned, He would have hastened for them the punishment. Rather, for them is an appointment from which they will never find an escape.

59. And those cities - We destroyed them when they wronged, and We made for their destruction an appointed time.

60. And [mention] when Moses said to his boy [i.e., servant], "I will not cease [traveling] until I reach the junction of the two seas or continue for a long period."

61. But when they reached the junction between them, they forgot their fish, and it took its course into the sea, slipping away.

62. So when they had passed beyond it, [Moses] said to his boy, "Bring us our morning meal. We have certainly suffered in this, our journey, [much] fatigue."

63. He said, "Did you see when we retired to the rock? Indeed, I forgot [there] the fish. And none made me forget it except Satan - that I should mention it. And it took its course into the sea amazingly."

64. [Moses] said, "That is what we were seeking." So they returned, following their footprints.

65. And they found a servant from among Our servants [i.e., al-Khidhr] to whom We had given mercy from Us and had taught him from Us a [certain] knowledge.

66. Moses said to him, "May I follow you on [the condition] that you teach me from what you have been taught of sound judgement?"

[735] Who denied the truth brought by God's messengers.

67. He said, "Indeed, with me you will never be able to have patience.

68. And how can you have patience for what you do not encompass in knowledge?"

69. [Moses] said, "You will find me, if God wills, patient, and I will not disobey you in [any] order."

70. He said, "Then if you follow me, do not ask me about anything until I make to you about it mention [i.e., explanation]."

71. So they set out, until when they had embarked on the ship, he [i.e., al-Khidhr] tore it open. [Moses] said, "Have you torn it open to drown its people? You have certainly done a grave thing."

72. [Al-Khidhr] said, "Did I not say that with me you would never be able to have patience?"

73. [Moses] said, "Do not blame me for what I forgot and do not cover me in my matter with difficulty."

74. So they set out, until when they met a boy, he [i.e., al-Khidhr] killed him. [Moses] said, "Have you killed a pure soul for other than [having killed] a soul? You have certainly done a deplorable thing."

75. [Al-Khidhr] said, "Did I not tell you that with me you would never be able to have patience?"

76. [Moses] said, "If I should ask you about anything after this, then do not keep me as a companion. You have obtained from me an excuse."

77. So they set out, until when they came to the people of a town, they asked its people for food, but they refused to offer them hospitality. And they found therein a wall about to collapse, so he [i.e., al-Khidhr] restored it. [Moses] said, "If you wished, you could have taken for it a payment."

78. [Al-Khidhr] said, "This is parting between me and you. I will inform you of the interpretation of that about which you could not have patience.

79. As for the ship, it belonged to poor people working at sea. So I intended to cause defect in it as there was after them a king who seized every [good] ship by force.

80. And as for the boy, his parents were believers, and we feared that he would overburden them by transgression and disbelief.

81. So we intended that their Lord should substitute for them one better than him in purity and nearer to mercy.

82. And as for the wall, it belonged to two orphan boys in the city, and there was beneath it a treasure for them, and their father had been righteous. So your Lord intended that they reach maturity and extract their treasure, as a mercy from your Lord. And I did it not of my own accord. That is the interpretation of that about which you could not have patience."

83. And they ask you, [O Muhammad], about Dhul-Qarnayn. Say, "I will recite to you about him a report."

84. Indeed, We established him upon the earth, and We gave him to everything a way [i.e., means].

85. So he followed a way

86. Until, when he reached the setting of the sun [i.e., the west], he found it [as if] setting in a spring of dark mud,[736] and he found near it a people. We [i.e., God] said, "O Dhul-Qarnayn, either you punish [them] or else adopt among them [a way of] goodness."

87. He said, "As for one who wrongs,[737] we will punish him. Then he will be returned to his Lord, and He will punish him with a terrible punishment [i.e., Hellfire].

88. But as for one who believes and does righteousness, he will have a reward of the best [i.e., Paradise], and we [i.e., Dhul-Qarnayn] will speak to him from our command with ease."

89. Then he followed a way

90. Until, when he came to the rising of the sun [i.e., the east], he found it rising on a people for whom We had not made against it any shield.

91. Thus.[738] And We had encompassed [all] that he had in knowledge.

92. Then he followed a way

93. Until, when he reached [a pass] between two mountains, he found beside them a people who could hardly understand [his] speech.

94. They said, "O Dhul-Qarnayn, indeed Gog and Magog[739] are [great] corrupters in the land. So may we assign for you an expenditure that you might make between us and them a barrier?"

95. He said, "That in which my Lord has established me is better [than what you offer], but assist me with strength [i.e., manpower]; I will make between you and them a dam.

96. Bring me sheets of iron" - until, when he had leveled [them] between the two mountain walls, he said, "Blow [with bellows]," until when he had made it [like] fire, he said, "Bring me, that I may pour over it molten copper."

97. So they [i.e., Gog and Magog] were unable to pass over it, nor were they able [to effect] in it any penetration.

98. [Dhul-Qarnayn] said, "This is a mercy from my Lord; but when the promise of my Lord[740] comes [i.e., approaches], He will make it level, and ever is the promise of my Lord true."

99. And We will leave them that day[741] surging over each other, and [then] the Horn will be blown, and We will assemble them in [one] assembly.

100. And We will present Hell that Day to the disbelievers, on display -

101. Those whose eyes had been within a cover [removed] from My remembrance,[742] and they were not able to hear.[743]

102. Then do those who disbelieve think that they can take My servants instead of Me as allies? Indeed, We have pre-

[736] Another meaning is "a hot spring."
[737] Persists in disbelief and rebellion.
[738] Such was the affair of Dhul-Qurnayn.
[739] Savage tribes who had ravaged large parts of central Asia, committing every kind of atrocity.
[740] i.e., the Hour of Resurrection.
[741] The day the dam is destroyed.
[742] i.e., God's signs or the Qur'ān.
[743] They refused to listen to the Qur'ān or to understand it.

pared Hell for the disbelievers as a lodging.

103. Say, [O Muhammad], "Shall we [believers] inform you of the greatest losers as to [their] deeds?

104. [They are] those whose effort is lost in worldly life, while they think that they are doing well in work."

105. Those are the ones who disbelieve in the verses of their Lord and in [their] meeting Him, so their deeds have become worthless; and We will not assign to them on the Day of Resurrection any weight [i.e., importance].

106. That is their recompense - Hell - for what they denied and [because] they took My signs and My messengers in ridicule.

107. Indeed, those who have believed and done righteous deeds - they will have the Gardens of Paradise[744] as a lodging,

108. Wherein they abide eternally. They will not desire from it any transfer.

109. Say, "If the sea were ink for [writing] the words[745] of my Lord, the sea would be exhausted before the words of my Lord were exhausted, even if We brought the like of it as a supplement."

110. Say, "I am only a man like you, to whom has been revealed that your god is one God. So whoever would hope for the meeting with his Lord - let him do righteous work and not associate in the worship of his Lord anyone."

---

[744] i.e., the highest part of Paradise, *al-Firdaus.*
[745] The words of God's unlimited knowledge or words describing His attributes and His grandeur or praise of Him.

## Sūrah 19: Maryam

### Period of Revelation

It was revealed before the Migration to Abassinyah. We learn from authentic hadith that Ja'afar recited v. 1-40 of this Sūrah in the court of Negus when he called the migrants to his court.

### Historical Background

We have already briefly referred to the conditions of that period in the introduction to Sūrah al-Kahf. Here we shall give rather fuller details of the same conditions which will be helpful in grasping the meaning of this Sūrah and the other Sūrahs of the period. When the chiefs of the Quraysh felt that they had failed to suppress the Islāmic movement by ridicule and sarcasm, by holding out promises and threats and by making false accusations they resorted to persecution, beating and economic pressure. They would catch hold of the new Muslims of their clans and persecute them, starve them and would even inflict physical torture on them in order to coerce them to give up Islām. The most pitiful victims of their persecution were the poor people and the slaves and the proteges of the Quraysh. They were beaten black and blue, were imprisoned and kept thirsty and hungry and were dragged on the burning sands of Makkah.

When the conditions became unbearable the Prophet in the month of Rajab of the fifth year of Prophethood gave advice to his Companions to this effect: *"You may well migrate to Abassinyah for there is a king who does not allow any kind of injustice to anyone and there is good in his land. You should remain there till the time that God provides a remedy for your affliction."*

Accordingly at first, eleven men and four women left for Abassinyah. The Quraysh pursued them up to the coast but fortunately they got a timely boat for Abassinyah at the sea-port of Shu'aibah and they escaped attest. Then after a few months other people migrated to Abassinyah and their number rose to eighty-three men and eleven women of the Quraysh and seven non-Quraysh. After this only forty persons were left with the Prophet at Makkah.

There was a great hue and cry in Makkah after this Migration for every family of the Quraysh was adversely affected by this. There was hardly a family of the Quraysh which did not lose a son, a son-in-law, a daughter, a brother or a sister. For instance there were among the Migrants the near relatives of Abu Jahl, Abu Sufyan and other chiefs of the Quraysh who were notorious for their persecution of the Muslims. After the migration, the Quraysh held consultations, and decided to send Abdullah bin Abi Rabiy'ah, half brother of Abu Jahl, and Amr bin As to Abassinyah with precious gifts so as to persuade Negus to send the migrants back to Makkah. Umm Salmah (a wife of the Prophet), who was among the migrants, has related this part of the story in detail. She says,

"When these two clever statesmen of the Quraysh reached Abassinyah, they distributed the gifts among the courtiers of the King and persuaded them to recommend strongly to him to send the migrants back. Then they saw Negus himself and, presenting rich gifts to him, said, *'Some headstrong brats of our city have come to your land and our chiefs have sent us to you with the request that you may kindly send them back. These brats have forsaken our faith and have not embraced your faith either, but have invented a new faith'.* As soon as they had finished their speech, all the courtiers recommended their case, saying, *'We should send such people back to their city for their people know them better. It is not proper for us to keep them here'.* At this the King was annoyed and said, *'I am not going to give them back without proper inquiry. As these people have put their trust in my country rather than in any other country and have come here to take shelter, I will not betray them. At first I will send for them and investigate into the allegations these people have made against them. Then I will make my final decision'.* Accordingly, the King sent for the Companions of the Prophet and asked them to come to his court.

When the migrants received the message of the King, they assembled and held consultations as to what they should say to the King. At last they came to this unanimous decision: *"We will present before the King the teachings of the Holy Prophet without adding anything to or withholding anything from them and leave it to him whether he lets us remain here or turns us out of his country'.* When they came to the court, the King put this problem abruptly before them: *'I understand that you have given up the faith of your own people and have neither embraced my faith nor any other existing faith. I would like to know what your new faith is.'* At this, Jafar bin Abi Talib, on behalf of the migrants, made an extempore speech to this effect: *'O King! We were sunk deep in ignorance and had become very corrupt; then Muhammad (God's peace be upon him) came to us as a Messenger of God, and did his best to reform us. But the Quraysh began to persecute his followers, so we have come to your country in the hope that here we will be free from persecution'.* After his speech, the King said, *'Please recite a piece of the Revelation which has been sent down by God to your Prophet'.* In response, Jafar recited that portion of Sūrah Maryam which relates the story of Prophet's John the Baptist and Jesus (God's peace be upon them). The King listened to it and wept, so much so that his beard became wet with tears. When Jafar finished the recital, he said: *'Most surely this Revelation and the Message of Jesus have come from the same source. By God I will not give you up into the hands of these people'.*

Next day Amr bin As went to Negus and said, *'Please send for them again and ask them concerning the creed they hold about Jesus, the son of Mary, for they say a horrible thing about him'.* The King again sent for the migrants, who had already learnt about the scheme of Amr. They again sat together and held consultations in regard to the answer they should give to the King, if he asked about the belief they held about Prophet Jesus. Though this was a very critical situation and all of them were uneasy about it, they decided that they would say the same thing that God and His Messenger had taught them. Accordingly, when they went to the court, the King put them the question that had been suggested by Amr bin As. So Jafar bin Abi Talib stood up and answered without the least hesitation: *'He was a Servant of God and His Messenger. He was a Spirit and a Word of God which had been sent to virgin Mary.' At this the King picked up a straw from the ground and said, 'By God, Jesus was not worth this straw more than what you have said about him.'* After this the King returned the gifts sent by the Quraysh, saying, *'I do not take any bribe'.* Then he said to the migrants, *'You are allowed to stay here in perfect peace'."*

**Theme and Subject**

Keeping in view this historical background it becomes quite obvious that this Sūrah was sent down to serve the migrants as a provision for their journey to Abassinyah, as if to say though you are leaving your country as persecuted emigrants to a Christian country you should not in the least hide anything from the teachings you have received. Therefore you should plainly say to the Christians that Prophet Jesus was not the son of God.

After relating the story of Prophet's John and Jesus in v. 1-40 the story of Prophet Abraham has been related (v. 41-50) also for the benefit of the Migrants for he also had been forced like them to leave his country by the persecution of his father, his family and his country men. On the one hand this meant to console the Emigrants that they were following the footsteps of Prophet Abraham and would attain the same good end as that Prophet did. On the other hand it meant to warn the disbeliever of Makkah that they should note it well that they were in the position of the cruel people who had persecuted their forefather and leader Abraham while the Muslim Emigrants were in the position of Prophet Abraham himself.

Then the mention of the other Prophets has been made in v. 51-65 with a view to impress that Prophet Muhammad had brought the same way of Life that had been brought by the former Prophets but their followers had become corrupt and adopted wrong ways.

In the concluding passage (v. 66-98) a strong criticism has been made of the evil ways of the disbelievers of Makkah while the Believers have been given the good news that they would come out successful and become the beloved of the people in spite of the worst efforts of the enemies of the Truth.

## Sūrah 19: Maryam[746]

In the Name of God, the Most Compassionate, the Most Merciful

1. Kāf, Hā, Yā, 'Ayn, Ṣād.[747]

2. [This is] a mention of the mercy of your Lord to His servant Zechariah

3. When he called to his Lord a private call [i.e., supplication].

4. He said, "My Lord, indeed my bones have weakened, and my head has filled[748] with white, and never have I been in my supplication to You, my Lord, unhappy [i.e., disappointed].

5. And indeed, I fear the successors[749] after me, and my wife has been barren, so give me from Yourself an heir

6. Who will inherit me[750] and inherit from the family of Jacob. And make him, my Lord, pleasing [to You]."

7. [He was told],[751] "O Zechariah, indeed We give you good tidings of a boy whose name will be John. We have not assigned to any before [this] name."

8. He said, "My Lord, how will I have a boy when my wife has been barren and I have reached extreme old age?"

[746] *Maryam*: Mary (the mother of Prophet Jesus).
[747] See footnote to 2:1.
[748] Literally, "ignited." The spread of white hair throughout the head is likened to that of fire in the bush.
[749] Those relatives from the father's side who would inherit religious authority.
[750] Inherit from me religious knowledge and prophethood.
[751] By God through the angels.

9. [An angel] said, "Thus [it will be]; your Lord says, 'It is easy for Me, for I created you before, while you were nothing.' "

10. [Zechariah] said, "My Lord, make for me a sign." He said, "Your sign is that you will not speak to the people for three nights, [being] sound."[752]

11. So he came out to his people from the prayer chamber and signaled to them to exalt [God] in the morning and afternoon.

12. [God said], "O John, take the Scripture [i.e., adhere to it] with determination." And We gave him judgement [while yet] a boy

13. And affection from Us and purity, and he was fearing of God

14. And dutiful to his parents, and he was not a disobedient tyrant.

15. And peace be upon him the day he was born and the day he dies and the day he is raised alive.

16. And mention, [O Muhammad], in the Book [the story of] Mary, when she withdrew from her family to a place toward the east.

17. And she took, in seclusion from them, a screen. Then We sent to her Our Angel [i.e., Gabriel], and he represented himself to her as a well-proportioned man.

18. She said, "Indeed, I seek refuge in the Most Merciful from you, [so leave me], if you should be fearing of God."

[752] i.e., without illness or defect.

19. He said, "I am only the messenger of your Lord to give you [news of] a pure boy [i.e., son]."

20. She said, "How can I have a boy while no man has touched me and I have not been unchaste?"

21. He said, "Thus [it will be]; your Lord says, 'It is easy for Me, and We will make him a sign to the people and a mercy from Us. And it is a matter [already] decreed.' "

22. So she conceived him, and she withdrew with him to a remote place.

23. And the pains of childbirth drove her to the trunk of a palm tree. She said, "Oh, I wish I had died before this and was in oblivion, forgotten."

24. But he[753] called her from below her, "Do not grieve; your Lord has provided beneath you a stream.

25. And shake toward you the trunk of the palm tree; it will drop upon you ripe, fresh dates.

26. So eat and drink and be contented. And if you see from among humanity anyone, say, 'Indeed, I have vowed to the Most Merciful abstention, so I will not speak today to [any] man.' "

27. Then she brought him to her people, carrying him. They said, "O Mary, you have certainly done a thing unprecedented.

[753] There is a difference of opinion among scholars as to whether "he" refers to the baby or to the angel.

28. O sister of Aaron, your father was not a man of evil, nor was your mother unchaste."

29. So she pointed to him. They said, "How can we speak to one who is in the cradle a child?"

30. [Jesus] said, "Indeed, I am the servant of God. He has given me the Scripture and made me a prophet.

31. And He has made me blessed wherever I am and has enjoined upon me prayer and zakāh as long as I remain alive

32. And [made me] dutiful to my mother, and He has not made me a wretched tyrant.

33. And peace is on me the day I was born and the day I will die and the day I am raised alive."

34. That is Jesus, the son of Mary - the word of truth about which they are in dispute.

35. It is not [befitting] for God to take a son; exalted is He![754] When He decrees an affair, He only says to it, "Be," and it is.

36. [Jesus said], "And indeed, God is my Lord and your Lord, so worship Him. That is a straight path."

37. Then the factions differed [concerning Jesus] from among them, so woe to those who disbelieved - from the scene of a tremendous Day.

38. How [clearly] they will hear and see the Day they come to Us, but the wrongdoers today are in clear error.

[754] i.e., far removed is He from any such need.

39. And warn them, [O Muhammad], of the Day of Regret, when the matter will be concluded;[755] and [yet], they are in [a state of] heedlessness, and they do not believe.

40. Indeed, it is We who will inherit the earth and whoever is on it, and to Us they will be returned.

41. And mention in the Book [the story of] Abraham. Indeed, he was a man of truth and a prophet.

42. [Mention] when he said to his father, "O my father, why do you worship that which does not hear and does not see and will not benefit you at all?

43. O my father, indeed there has come to me of knowledge that which has not come to you, so follow me; I will guide you to an even path.

44. O my father, do not worship [i.e., obey] Satan. Indeed Satan has ever been, to the Most Merciful, disobedient.

45. O my father, indeed I fear that there will touch you a punishment from the Most Merciful so you would be to Satan a companion [in Hellfire]."

46. [His father] said, "Have you no desire for my gods, O Abraham? If you do not desist, I will surely stone you, so avoid me a prolonged time."

47. [Abraham] said, "Peace [i.e., safety] will be upon you.[756] I will ask forgiveness for you of my Lord. Indeed, He is ever gracious to me.

48. And I will leave you and those you invoke other than God and will invoke my Lord. I expect that I will not be in invocation to my Lord unhappy [i.e., disappointed]."

49. So when he had left them and those they worshipped other than God, We gave him Isaac and Jacob, and each [of them] We made a prophet.

50. And We gave them of Our mercy, and We made for them a mention [i.e., reputation] of high honour.

51. And mention in the Book, Moses. Indeed, he was chosen, and he was a messenger and a prophet.[757]

52. And We called him from the side of the mount[758] at [his] right and brought him near, confiding [to him].

53. And We gave him out of Our mercy his brother Aaron as a prophet.

54. And mention in the Book, Ishmael. Indeed, he was true to his promise, and he was a messenger and a prophet.

55. And he used to enjoin on his people prayer and zakāh and was to his Lord pleasing [i.e., accepted by Him].

56. And mention in the Book, Idrees. Indeed, he was a man of truth and a prophet.

57. And We raised him to a high station.

58. Those were the ones upon whom God bestowed favor from among the

[755] i.e., "judged" or "accomplished."
[756] Meaning "You are secure" or "I will not harm you."

[757] A messenger (*rasūl*) is one who was charged by God to reform society. A prophet (*nabī*) is one who received revelation from God, the latter being more numerous than the former.
[758] Mount Sinai.

prophets of the descendants of Adam and of those We carried [in the ship] with Noah, and of the descendants of Abraham and Israel [i.e., Jacob], and of those whom We guided and chose. When the verses of the Most Merciful were recited to them, they fell in prostration and weeping.

59. But there came after them successors [i.e., later generations] who neglected prayer and pursued desires; so they are going to meet evil [759] -

60. Except those who repent, believe and do righteousness; for those will enter Paradise and will not be wronged at all.

61. [Therein are] gardens of perpetual residence which the Most Merciful has promised His servants in the unseen. Indeed, His promise has ever been coming.[760]

62. They will not hear therein any ill speech - only [greetings of] peace - and they will have their provision therein, morning and afternoon.

63. That is Paradise, which We give as inheritance to those of Our servants who were fearing of God.

64. [Gabriel said],[761] "And we [angels] descend not except by the order of your Lord. To Him belongs that before us and that behind us and what is in between. And never is your Lord forgetful -

65. Lord of the heavens and the earth and whatever is between them - so worship Him and have patience for His worship. Do you know of any similarity to Him?"

66. And man [i.e., the disbeliever] says, "When I have died, am I going to be brought forth alive?"

67. Does man not remember that We created him before, while he was nothing?

68. So by your Lord, We will surely gather them and the devils; then We will bring them to be present around Hell upon their knees.[762]

69. Then We will surely extract from every sect those of them who were worst against the Most Merciful in insolence.

70. Then, surely it is We who are most knowing of those most worthy of burning therein.

71. And there is none of you except he will come to it.[763] This is upon your Lord an inevitability decreed.

72. Then We will save those who feared God and leave the wrongdoers within it, on their knees.

73. And when Our verses are recited to them as clear evidences, those who disbelieve say to those who believe, "Which of [our] two parties is best in position and best in association?"[764]

74. And how many a generation have We destroyed before them who were better

[759] Described as a valley in Hell or may be rendered "the consequence of error."
[760] Literally, "that to which all will come."
[761] In answer to the Prophet's wish that Gabriel would visit him more often.
[762] i.e., fallen on their knees from terror or dragged there unwillingly on their knees.
[763] i.e., be exposed to it. However, the people of Paradise will not be harmed thereby.
[764] In regard to worldly interests.

in possessions and [outward] appearance?

75. Say, "Whoever is in error - let the Most Merciful extend for him an extension [in wealth and time] until, when they see that which they were promised - either punishment [in this world] or the Hour [of resurrection] - they will come to know who is worst in position and weaker in soldiers."

76. And God increases those who were guided, in guidance, and the enduring good deeds are better to your Lord[765] for reward and better for recourse.

77. Then, have you seen he who disbelieved in Our verses and said, "I will surely be given wealth and children [in the next life]?"

78. Has he looked into the unseen, or has he taken from the Most Merciful a promise?

79. No! We will record what he says and extend [i.e., increase] for him from the punishment extensively.

80. And We will inherit him [in] what he mentions,[766] and he will come to Us alone.

81. And they have taken besides God [false] deities that they would be for them [a source of] honour.

82. No! They [i.e., those "gods"] will deny their worship of them and will be against them opponents [on the Day of Judgement].

[765] i.e., in the sight or evaluation of God.

[766] Instead of giving him wealth and children in the Hereafter, God will take from him those he had in worldly life at time of his death.

83. Do you not see that We have sent the devils upon the disbelievers, inciting them [to evil] with [constant] incitement?

84. So be not impatient over them. We only count out [i.e., allow] to them a [limited] number.[767]

85. On the Day We will gather the righteous to the Most Merciful as a delegation

86. And will drive the criminals to Hell in thirst

87. None will have [power of] intercession except he who had taken from the Most Merciful a covenant.[768]

88. And they say, "The Most Merciful has taken [for Himself] a son."

89. You have done an atrocious thing.

90. The heavens almost rupture therefrom and the earth splits open and the mountains collapse in devastation

91. That they attribute to the Most Merciful a son.

92. And it is not appropriate for the Most Merciful that He should take a son.

93. There is no one in the heavens and earth but that he comes to the Most Merciful as a servant.

94. He has enumerated them and counted them a [full] counting.

95. And all of them are coming to Him on the Day of Resurrection alone.

[767] Of breaths, of days, or of evil deeds.

[768] Not to worship other than Him.

96. Indeed, those who have believed and done righteous deeds - the Most Merciful will appoint for them affection.[769]

97. So, [O Muhammad], We have only made it [i.e., the Qur'ān] easy in your tongue [i.e., the Arabic language] that you may give good tidings thereby to the righteous and warn thereby a hostile people.

98. And how many have We destroyed before them of generations? Do you perceive of them anyone or hear from them a sound?

[769] From Himself and from among each other.

## Sūrah 20: Tā Hā

### Period of Revelation

The period of its revelation is the same as of Surah Maryam. It is just possible that it was sent down during the Migration to Abassinyah or just after it. Anyhow it is certain that this Sūrah was revealed before Umar embraced Islām.

According to a well known and authentic hadith when Umar set out to kill the Prophet he met a certain person who said *'Before you do anything else you should know that your own sister and brother-in-law have embraced Islām'* Hearing this he directly went to the house of his sister. There he found his sister Fātimah and his brother-in-law Said bin Zayd learning the contents of a scroll from Khabbab bin Art. When Fātimah saw him coming she hid the scroll at once but Umar had heard the recital so he began to interrogate them about it. Then he began to thrash his brother-in-law and wounded his sister who tried to protect him. At last both of them confessed *'We have become Muslims; you may do whatever you like.'* As Umar was moved to see blood running down from her head he said, *'Show me the thing you were reading.'* The sister asked him to promise on oath that he would not tear it and added *'You cannot touch it unless you have a bath.'* Accordingly , Umar took his bath and when he began to read the scroll which contained this Sūrah he spontaneously spoke out, *'What an excellent thing!'* At this Khabbab who had hidden himself at the sound of his footsteps came out of his hiding and said, *'By God I have high expectations that God will get great service from you to propagate the Message of His Prophet for just yesterday I heard the Holy Prophet praying to God 'My Lord make Abul Hakam bin Hisham (Abu Jahl) or Umar bin Khattab a supporter of Islām.' So O Umar turn to God turn to God.'* These words proved to be so persuasive that he at once accompanied Khabbab and went to the Prophet to embrace Islām. This happened a short time after the Migration to Abassinyah.

### Theme and Topics of Discussion

This Sūrah begins with the enunciation of the object of the Revelation of the Qur'ān to this effect: "O Muhammad this Qur'ān has not been sent down to you to put you unnecessarily to some great affliction. It does not demand from you to perform the impossible task of imbuing the hearts of the obdurate disbelievers with Faith. It is merely an admonition meant to guide on to the Right Path those who fear God and want to save themselves from His punishment. This Qur'ān is the Word of the Master of the earth and the heavens and God-head belongs to Him alone:These two facts are eternal whether one believes them or not."

After this introduction the Surah abruptly moves on to relate the story of Prophet Moses without any apparent relevancy and without even hinting at its applicability to the events of the period. However if we read between the lines we realize that the discourse is addressed very relevantly to the people of Makkah. But before we explain the hidden meaning of the discourse we must keep in view the fact that the Arabs in general acknowledged Moses as a Prophet of God. This was so because they had "been influenced by the large number of the Jews around them and by" the neighbouring Christian kingdoms. Now let us state those things which are hidden between the lines of the story:

1. God does not appoint a Prophet by the beat of drums or by celebrating the occasion in a regular and formal ceremony as if to say We are appointing such and such a person as Our Prophet from today. On the contrary He bestows Prophethood in a confidential manner just as He did in the case of Prophet Moses. Therefore you should not consider it strange if Muhammad has been appointed as a Prophet all of a sudden and without any public proclamation.
2. The fundamental principles presented by Prophet Muhammad, Tawhid (oneness of God) and the Hereafter are just the same as were taught to Prophet Moses at the time of his appointment.
3. Prophet Muhammad has been made the standard bearer of the Message of the Truth among the people of the Quraysh all by himself without material provisions just as Prophet Moses was entrusted with the Mission to go to a tyrant king like Pharaoh and ask him to give up his attitude of

rebellion. These are the mysterious ways of God. He catches hold of a way farer of Midian on his way to Egypt and says Go and fight with the greatest tyrant of the time. He did not provide him with armies and provisions for this Mission. The only thing He did was to appoint his brother as his assistant at his request.

4. You O People of Makkah should note it well that Pharaoh employed the same devices against Prophet Moses as you are employing against Prophet Muhammad; frivolous objections accusations and cruel persecutions. You should know that God's Prophet came out victorious over Pharaoh who possessed large armies and war equipments. Incidentally the Muslims have been consoled and comforted though not in so many words that they should not be afraid of fighting with the Quraysh against fearful odds for the mission which is supported by God comes out victorious in the end. At the same time the Muslims have been exhorted to follow the excellent example of the magicians of Egypt who remained steadfast in their Faith though Pharaoh threatened them with horrible vengeance.
5. An incident from the story of the Israelites has been cited to show in what ridiculous manner the idolisation of false gods and goddesses starts and that the Prophets of God do not tolerate even the slightest tinge of this preposterous practice. Likewise Prophet Muhammad is following the former Prophets in opposing shirk and idol worship today.

Thus the story of Moses has been used to throw light on all those matters which were connected with the conflict between the Prophet and the Quraysh. Then at the end of the story the Quraysh have been briefly admonished as if to say The Qur'ān has been sent down in your tongue for your own good. If you listen to it and follow its admonition, you will be doing so for your own good but if you reject it, you will yourselves meet with an evil end."

After this the story of Prophet Adam has been related, as if to tell the Quraysh, "The way you are following is the way of Satan, whereas the right way for a man is to follow his father Adam. He was beguiled by Satan, but when he realized his error, he plainly confessed it and repented and again turned back to the service of God and won His favor. On the other hand, if a person follows Satan and sticks to his error obdurately in spite of admonition, he does harm to himself alone like Satan."

In the end, the Prophet and the Muslims have been advised not to be impatient in regard to the punishment to the disbelievers, as if to say, "God has His Own scheme concerning them. He does not seize them at once but gives them sufficient respite. Therefore you should not grow impatient but bear the persecutions with fortitude and go on conveying the Message."

In this connection, great emphasis has been laid on salat so that it may create in the believers the virtues of patience, forbearance, contentment, resignation to the will of God and self analysis for these are greatly needed in the service of the Message of the Truth.

## Sūrah 20: Tā Hā[770]

In the Name of God, the Most Compassionate, the Most Merciful

1. Tā, Hā.[771]

2. We have not sent down to you the Qur'ān that you be distressed

3. But only as a reminder for those who fear [God] -

4. A revelation from He who created the earth and highest heavens,

5. The Most Merciful [who is] above the Throne established.[772]

6. To Him belongs what is in the heavens and what is on the earth and what is between them and what is under the soil.

7. And if you speak aloud - then indeed, He knows the secret and what is [even] more hidden.

8. God - there is no deity except Him. To Him belong the best names.

9. And has the story of Moses reached you? -

10. When he saw a fire and said to his family, "Stay here; indeed, I have perceived a fire; perhaps I can bring you a torch or find at the fire some guidance."

11. And when he came to it, he was called, "O Moses,

12. Indeed, I am your Lord, so remove your sandals. Indeed, you are in the sacred valley of Tuwā.

13. And I have chosen you, so listen to what is revealed [to you].

14. Indeed, I am God. There is no deity except Me, so worship Me and establish prayer for My remembrance.

15. Indeed, the Hour is coming - I almost conceal it[773] - so that every soul may be recompensed according to that for which it strives.

16. So do not let one avert you from it[774] who does not believe in it and follows his desire, for you [then] would perish.

17. And what is that in your right hand, O Moses?"

18. He said, "It is my staff; I lean upon it, and I bring down leaves for my sheep and I have therein other uses."

19. [God] said, "Throw it down, O Moses."

20. So he threw it down, and thereupon it was a snake, moving swiftly.

21. [God] said, "Seize it and fear not; We will return it to its former condition.

22. And draw in your hand to your side; it will come out white without disease - another sign,

23. That We may show you [some] of Our greater signs.

[770] *Tā Hā*: (the letters) *tā and hā.*
[771] See footnote to 2:1.
[772] i.e., having ascendancy over all creation. See footnote to 2:19.
[773] Meaning that God keeps knowledge of the Hour hidden from everyone except Himself.
[774] From preparation for the Hour or for the Hereafter.

24. Go to Pharaoh. Indeed, he has transgressed [i.e., tyrannized]."

25. [Moses] said, "My Lord, expand [i.e., relax] for me my breast [with assurance]

26. And ease for me my task

27. And untie the knot from my tongue

28. That they may understand my speech.

29. And appoint for me a minister [i.e., assistant] from my family -

30. Aaron, my brother.

31. Increase through him my strength

32. And let him share my task

33. That we may exalt You much

34. And remember You much.

35. Indeed, You are of us ever Seeing."

36. [God] said, "You have been granted your request, O Moses.

37. And We had already conferred favor upon you another time,

38. When We inspired to your mother what We inspired,

39. [Saying], 'Cast him into the chest and cast it into the river, and the river will throw it onto the bank; there will take him an enemy to Me and an enemy to him.' And I bestowed upon you love from Me[775] that you would be brought up under My eye [i.e., observation and care].

[775] God put love of Moses into the hearts of the people.

40. [And We favored you] when your sister went and said, 'Shall I direct you to someone who will be responsible for him?' So We restored you to your mother that she might be content and not grieve. And you killed someone,[776] but We saved you from retaliation and tried you with a [severe] trial. And you remained [some] years among the people of Madyan. Then you came [here] at the decreed time, O Moses.

41. And I produced you for Myself.[777]

42. Go, you and your brother, with My signs and do not slacken in My remembrance.

43. Go, both of you, to Pharaoh. Indeed, he has transgressed.

44. And speak to him with gentle speech that perhaps he may be reminded or fear [God]."

45. They said, "Our Lord, indeed we are afraid that he will hasten [punishment] against us or that he will transgress."

46. [God] said, "Fear not. Indeed, I am with you both; I hear and I see.

47. So go to him and say, 'Indeed, we are messengers of your Lord, so send with us the Children of Israel and do not torment them. We have come to you with a sign from your Lord. And peace[778] will be upon he who follows the guidance.

[776] The Copt who died after being struck by Moses.

[777] God had already selected Moses and made him strong in body and character according to the requirements of his mission.

[778] i.e., safety and security from God's Punishment.

48. Indeed, it has been revealed to us that the punishment will be upon whoever denies and turns away.' "

49. [Pharaoh] said, "So who is the Lord of you two, O Moses?"

50. He said, "Our Lord is He who gave each thing its form and then guided [it]."

51. [Pharaoh] said, "Then what is the case of the former generations?"

52. [Moses] said, "The knowledge thereof is with my Lord in a record. My Lord neither errs nor forgets."

53. [It is He] who has made for you the earth as a bed [spread out] and inserted therein for you roadways and sent down from the sky, rain and produced thereby categories of various plants.

54. Eat [therefrom] and pasture your livestock. Indeed, in that are signs for those of intelligence.

55. From it [i.e., the earth] We created you, and into it We will return you, and from it We will extract you another time.

56. And We certainly showed him [i.e., Pharaoh] Our signs - all of them - but he denied and refused.

57. He said, "Have you come to us to drive us out of our land with your magic, O Moses?

58. Then we will surely bring you magic like it, so make between us and you an appointment, which we will not fail to keep and neither will you, in a place assigned."[779]

59. [Moses] said, "Your appointment is on the day of the festival when the people assemble at mid-morning."[780]

60. So Pharaoh went away, put together his plan, and then came [to Moses].

61. Moses said to them [i.e., the magicians summoned by Pharaoh], "Woe to you! Do not invent a lie against God or He will exterminate you with a punishment; and he has failed who invents [such falsehood]."

62. So they disputed over their affair among themselves and concealed their private conversation.

63. They said, "Indeed, these are two magicians who want to drive you out of your land with their magic and do away with your most exemplary way [i.e., religion or tradition].

64. So resolve upon your plan and then come [forward] in line. And he has succeeded today who overcomes."

65. They said, "O Moses, either you throw or we will be the first to throw."

66. He said, "Rather, you throw." And suddenly their ropes and staffs seemed to him from their magic that they were moving [like snakes].

67. And he sensed within himself apprehension, did Moses.

---

[779] Literally, "marked", as to be known. Another meaning is "a place midway [between us]" or "a level place."

[780] So that the signs of God would be seen clearly.

68. We [i.e., God] said, "Fear not. Indeed, it is you who are superior.

69. And throw what is in your right hand; it will swallow up what they have crafted. What they have crafted is but the trick of a magician, and the magician will not succeed wherever he is."

70. So the magicians fell down in prostration.[781] They said, "We have believed in the Lord of Aaron and Moses."

71. [Pharaoh] said, "You believed him [i.e., Moses] before I gave you permission. Indeed, he is your leader who has taught you magic. So I will surely cut off your hands and your feet on opposite sides, and I will crucify you on the trunks of palm trees, and you will surely know which of us is more severe in [giving] punishment and more enduring."

72. They said, "Never will we prefer you over what has come to us of clear proofs and [over] He who created us.[782] So decree whatever you are to decree. You can only decree for this worldly life.

73. Indeed, we have believed in our Lord that He may forgive us our sins and what you compelled us [to do] of magic. And God is better and more enduring." [783]

74. Indeed, whoever comes to his Lord as a criminal - indeed, for him is Hell; he will neither die therein nor live.

75. But whoever comes to Him as a believer having done righteous deeds - for those will be the highest degrees [in position]:

76. Gardens of perpetual residence beneath which rivers flow, wherein they abide eternally. And that is the reward of one who purifies himself.[784]

77. And We had inspired to Moses, "Travel by night with My servants and strike for them a dry path through the sea; you will not fear being overtaken [by Pharaoh] nor be afraid [of drowning]."

78. So Pharaoh pursued them with his soldiers, and there covered them from the sea that which covered them,[785]

79. And Pharaoh led his people astray and did not guide [them].

80. O Children of Israel, We delivered you from your enemy, and We made an appointment with you[786] at the right side of the mount, and We sent down to you manna and quails,

81. [Saying], "Eat from the good things with which We have provided you and do not transgress [or oppress others] therein, lest My anger should descend upon you. And he upon whom My anger descends has certainly fallen [i.e., perished]."

82. But indeed, I am the Perpetual Forgiver of whoever repents and believes and does righteousness and then continues in guidance.

---

[781] After they had seen the miracles which God had given Moses and that they were realities and not merely impressions of magic.

[782] This phrase has also been interpreted as an oath, i.e., "...by Him who created us."

[783] In reward and in punishment.

[784] From all uncleanliness, the greatest of which is worship and obedience to other than God.

[785] i.e., not only the water but that which only God knows – terror, pain, regret, etc.

[786] i.e., with your prophet, to receive the scripture for you.

83. [God] said, "And what made you hasten from your people, O Moses?"

84. He said, "They are close upon my tracks, and I hastened to You, my Lord, that You be pleased."

85. [God] said, "But indeed, We have tried your people after you [departed], and the Sāmirī[787] has led them astray."

86. So Moses returned to his people, angry and grieved.[788] He said, "O my people, did your Lord not make you a good promise?[789] Then, was the time [of its fulfillment] too long for you, or did you wish that wrath from your Lord descend upon you, so you broke your promise [of obedience] to me?"

87. They said, "We did not break our promise to you by our will, but we were made to carry burdens from the ornaments of the people [of Pharaoh], so we threw them [into the fire], and thus did the Sāmirī throw."

88. And he extracted for them [the statue of] a calf which had a lowing sound, and they said, "This is your god and the god of Moses, but he forgot."

89. Did they not see that it could not return to them any speech [i.e., response] and that it did not possess for them any harm or benefit?

90. And Aaron had already told them before [the return of Moses], "O my people, you are only being tested by it, and indeed, your Lord is the Most Merciful, so follow me and obey my order."

91. They said, "We will never cease being devoted to it [i.e., the calf] until Moses returns to us."

92. [Moses] said, "O Aaron, what prevented you, when you saw them going astray,

93. From following me? Then have you disobeyed my order?"

94. [Aaron] said, "O son of my mother, do not seize [me] by my beard or by my head. Indeed, I feared that you would say, 'You caused division among the Children of Israel, and you did not observe [or await] my word.' "

95. [Moses] said, "And what is your case, O Sāmirī?"

96. He said, "I saw what they did not see, so I took a handful [of dust] from the track of the messenger[790] and threw it,[791] and thus did my soul entice me."

97. [Moses] said, "Then go. And indeed, it is [decreed] for you in [this] life to say, 'No contact.'[792] And indeed, you have an appointment [in the Hereafter] you will not fail to keep. And look at your 'god' to which you remained devoted. We will surely burn it and blow it [i.e., its ashes] into the sea with a blast.

98. Your god is only God, except for whom there is no deity. He has encompassed all things in knowledge."

787 Translated as "the Samaritan" (from Samaria), a hypocrite among them who led the Children of Israel into idol-worship.
788 The meaning may also be "angry and enraged."
789 That He would send down the Torah, containing guidance for you.
790 i.e., a hoof-print in the sand left by the angel Gabriel's horse.
791 Into the fire upon the melted ornaments in order to form the calf.
792 i.e., Do not touch me. As chastisement, he was to be completely shunned by all people.

99. Thus, [O Muhammad], We relate to you from the news of what has preceded. And We have certainly given you from Us a message [i.e., the Qur'ān.]

100. Whoever turns away from it - then indeed, he will bear on the Day of Resurrection a burden [i.e., great sin],

101. [Abiding] eternally therein,[793] and evil it is for them on the Day of Resurrection as a load -

102. The Day the Horn will be blown. And We will gather the criminals, that Day, blue-eyed.[794]

103. They will murmur among themselves, "You remained not but ten [days in the world]."

104. We are most knowing of what they say when the best of them in manner [i.e., wisdom or speech] will say, "You remained not but one day."

105. And they ask you about the mountains, so say, "My Lord will blow them away with a blast.[795]

106. And He will leave it [i.e., the earth] a level plain;

107. You will not see therein a depression or an elevation."

108. That Day, they [i.e., everyone] will follow [the call of] the Caller[796] [with] no deviation therefrom, and [all] voices will be stilled before the Most Merciful, so you will not hear except a whisper [of footsteps].

[793] i.e., in the state of sin.
[794] From terror, or blinded completely.
[795] Once they have been reduced to dust.
[796] To the gathering for judgement.

109. That Day, no intercession will benefit except [that of] one to whom the Most Merciful has given permission and has accepted his word.

110. He [i.e., God] knows what is [presently] before them and what will be after them,[797] but they do not encompass it [i.e., what He knows] in knowledge.

111. And [all] faces will be humbled before the Ever-Living, the Sustainer of existence. And he will have failed who carries injustice.[798]

112. But he who does of righteous deeds while he is a believer - he will neither fear injustice nor deprivation.

113. And thus We have sent it down as an Arabic Qur'ān[799] and have diversified therein the warnings that perhaps they will avoid [sin] or it would cause them remembrance.

114. So high [above all] is God, the Sovereign, the Truth. And, [O Muhammad], do not hasten with [recitation of] the Qur'ān before its revelation is completed to you, and say, "My Lord, increase me in knowledge."

115. And We had already taken a promise from Adam before, but he forgot; and We found not in him determination.[800]

116. And [mention] when We said to the angels, "Prostrate to Adam," and they prostrated, except Iblees;[801] he refused.

[797] See footnote to 2:255.
[798] i.e., sin or wrongdoing towards God or any of His creation.
[799] i.e., revealed in the Arabic language.
[800] To resist temptation.
[801] See footnote to 2:34.

117. So We said, "O Adam, indeed this is an enemy to you and to your wife. Then let him not remove you from Paradise so you would suffer.

118. Indeed, it is [promised] for you not to be hungry therein or be unclothed.

119. And indeed, you will not be thirsty therein or be hot from the sun."

120. Then Satan whispered to him; he said, "O Adam, shall I direct you to the tree of eternity and possession that will not deteriorate?"

121. And they [i.e., Adam and his wife] ate of it, and their private parts became apparent to them, and they began to fasten over themselves from the leaves of Paradise. And Adam disobeyed his Lord and erred.

122. Then his Lord chose him and turned to him in forgiveness and guided [him].

123. [God] said, "Descend from it [i.e., Paradise] - all, [your descendants] being enemies to one another. And if there should come to you guidance from Me - then whoever follows My guidance will neither go astray [in the world] nor suffer [in the Hereafter].

124. And whoever turns away from My remembrance - indeed, he will have a depressed [i.e., difficult] life, and We will gather [i.e., raise] him on the Day of Resurrection blind."

125. He will say, "My Lord, why have you raised me blind while I was [once] seeing?"

126. [God] will say, "Thus did Our signs come to you, and you forgot [i.e., disregarded] them; and thus will you this Day be forgotten."

127. And thus do We recompense he who transgressed and did not believe in the signs of his Lord. And the punishment of the Hereafter is more severe and more enduring.[802]

128. Then, has it not become clear to them how many generations We destroyed before them as they walk among their dwellings? Indeed in that are signs for those of intelligence.

129. And if not for a word[803] that preceded from your Lord, it [i.e., punishment] would have been an obligation [due immediately],[804] and [if not for] a specified term [decreed].

130. So be patient over what they say and exalt [God] with praise of your Lord before the rising of the sun and before its setting; and during periods of the night [exalt Him] and at the ends of the day, that you may be satisfied.

131. And do not extend your eyes toward that by which We have given enjoyment to [some] categories of them, [its being but] the splendor of worldly life by which We test them. And the provision of your Lord is better and more enduring.

132. And enjoin prayer upon your family [and people] and be steadfast therein. We ask you not for provision; We provide for you, and the [best] outcome is for [those of] righteousness.

---

[802] Than that of this world.

[803] See footnote to 10:19.

[804] God would have punished the disbelievers in this world as He did with previous peoples.

133. And they say, "Why does he not bring us a sign from his Lord?" Has there not come to them evidence of what was in the former scriptures?[805]

134. And if We had destroyed them with a punishment before him,[806] they would have said, "Our Lord, why did You not send to us a messenger so we could have followed Your verses [i.e., teachings] before we were humiliated and disgraced?"

135. Say, "Each [of us] is waiting;[807] so wait. For you will know who are the companions of the sound path and who is guided."

---

[805] Is not the Qur'ān an adequate proof of Muhammad's prophethood and sufficient as a lasting miracle?

[806] Prophet Muhammad. Also interpreted as "before it," i.e., the Qur'ān.

[807] For the outcome of this matter.

# Sūrah 21: al-Anbiyā'

## Period of Revelation

Both the subject matter and the style of the Sūrah indicate that it was sent down in the third stage of the life of the Prophet at Makkah (see introduction to Sūrah 6).

## Subject and Topics

This Sūrah discusses the conflict between the Prophet and the chiefs of Makkah which was rampant at the time of its Revelation and answers those objections and doubts which were being put forward concerning his Prophethood and the doctrines of Tawhid and the Hereafter. The chiefs of Makkah have also been rebuked for their machinations against the Prophet and warned of the evil consequences of their wicked activities. They have been admonished to give up their indifference and heedlessness that they were showing about the Message. At the end of the Sūrah they have been told that the person whom they considered to be a "distress and affliction" had in reality come to them as a blessing.

## Main Themes

In v. 1-47 the following themes have been discussed in particular :

1. The objection of the disbelievers that a human being could not be a Messenger and therefore they could not accept Muhammad as a Prophet has been refuted.
2. They have been taken to task for raising multifarious and contradictory objections against the Prophet and the Qur'ān.
3. Their wrong conception of life has been proved to be false because it was responsible for their indifferent and heedless attitude towards the Message of the Prophet. They believed that life was merely a sport and pastime and had no purpose behind or before it and there was no accountability or reward or punishment.
4. The main cause of the conflict between the disbelievers and the Prophet was their insistence on the doctrine of Shirk (polytheism) and antagonism to the Doctrine of Tawhid (Oneness of God). So the doctrine of Shirk has been refuted and the doctrine of Tawhid reinforced by weighty and impressive though brief arguments.
5. Arguments and admonitions have been used to remove another misunderstanding of theirs. They presumed that Muhammad was a false prophet and his warnings of a scourge from God were empty threats just because no scourge was visiting them in spite of their persistent rejection of the Prophet. In v. 48-91 instances have been cited from the important events of the life stories of the Prophets to show that all the Prophets who were sent by God were human beings and had all the characteristics of a man except those which were exclusive to Prophethood. They had no share in Godhead and they had to implore God to fulfil each and every necessity of theirs.
6. All the Prophets had to pass through distress and affliction; their opponents did their worst to thwart their mission but in spite of it they came out successful by the extraordinary succour from God.
7. All the Prophets had one and the same 'way of life' the same as was being presented by Muhammad and that was the only Right Way of Life and all other ways invented and introduced by mischievous people were utterly wrong.

In v. 92-106 it has been declared that only those who follow the Right Way will come out successful in the final judgment of God and those who discard it shall meet with the worst consequences. In v. 107-112 the people have been told that it is a great favour of God that He has sent His Messenger to inform them beforehand of this Reality and that those who consider his coming to be an affliction instead of a blessing are foolish people.

## Sūrah 21: al-Anbiyā'[808]

In the Name of God, the Most Compassionate, the Most Merciful

1. [The time of] their account has approached for the people, while they are in heedlessness turning away.

2. No mention [i.e., revelation] comes to them anew from their Lord except that they listen to it while they are at play

3. With their hearts distracted. And those who do wrong conceal their private conversation, [saying], "Is this [Prophet] except a human being like you? So would you approach magic while you are aware [of it]?"

4. He [the Prophet] said, "My Lord knows whatever is said throughout the heaven and earth, and He is the Hearing, the Knowing."

5. But they say, "[The revelation is but] a mixture of false dreams; rather, he has invented it; rather, he is a poet. So let him bring us a sign just as the previous [messengers] were sent [with miracles]."

6. Not a [single] city which We destroyed believed before them,[809] so will they believe?

7. And We sent not before you, [O Muhammad], except men to whom We revealed [the message], so ask the people of the message [i.e., former scriptures] if you do not know.

[808] *Al-Anbiyā':* The Prophets.
[809] Even though they had witnessed signs and miracles.

8. And We did not make them [i.e., the prophets] forms not eating food,[810] nor were they immortal [on earth].

9. Then[811] We fulfilled for them the promise, and We saved them and whom We willed and destroyed the transgressors.

10. We have certainly sent down to you a Book [i.e., the Qur'ān] in which is your mention.[812] Then will you not reason?

11. And how many a city which was unjust[813] have We shattered and produced after it another people.

12. And when they [i.e., its inhabitants] perceived Our punishment, at once they fled from it.

13. [Some angels said], "Do not flee but return to where you were given luxury and to your homes - perhaps you will be questioned."[814]

14. They said, "O woe to us! Indeed, we were wrongdoers."

15. And that declaration of theirs did not cease until We made them [as] a harvest [mowed down], extinguished [like a fire].

16. And We did not create the heaven and earth and that between them in play.

[810] Like the angels. Rather, they were human beings with human attributes.
[811] Once they had conveyed the message.
[812] This implies the honour of having been mentioned or addressed. Another meaning is "your reminder."
[813] i.e., its inhabitants persisting in wrongdoing.
[814] About what happened to you. This is said to them in sarcasm and ridicule.

17. Had We intended to take a diversion,[815] We could have taken it from [what is] with Us - if [indeed] We were to do so.

18. Rather, We dash the truth upon falsehood, and it destroys it,[816] and thereupon it departs. And for you is destruction from that which you describe.[817]

19. To Him belongs whoever is in the heavens and the earth. And those near Him [i.e., the angels] are not prevented by arrogance from His worship, nor do they tire.

20. They exalt [Him] night and day [and] do not slacken.

21. Or have they [i.e., men] taken for themselves gods from the earth who resurrect [the dead]?

22. Had there been within them [i.e., the heavens and earth] gods besides God, they both would have been ruined. So exalted is God, Lord of the Throne, above what they describe.

23. He is not questioned about what He does, but they will be questioned.

24. Or have they taken gods besides Him? Say, [O Muhammad], "Produce your proof. This [Qur'ān] is the message for those with me and the message of those before me."[818] But most of them do not know the truth, so they are turning away.

25. And We sent not before you any messenger except that We revealed to him that, "There is no deity except Me, so worship Me."

26. And they say, "The Most Merciful has taken a son." Exalted is He! Rather, they[819] are [but] honoured servants.

27. They cannot precede Him in word, and they act by His command.

28. He knows what is [presently] before them and what will be after them,[820] and they cannot intercede except on behalf of one whom He approves. And they, from fear of Him, are apprehensive.

29. And whoever of them should say, "Indeed, I am a god besides Him"— that one We would recompense with Hell. Thus do We recompense the wrongdoers.

30. Have those who disbelieved not considered that the heavens and the earth were a joined entity, and We separated them and made from water every living thing? Then will they not believe?

31. And We placed within the earth firmly set mountains, lest it should shift with them, and We made therein [mountain] passes [as] roads that they might be guided.

32. And We made the sky a protected ceiling, but they, from its signs,[821] are turning away.

33. And it is He who created the night and the day and the sun and the moon; all

[815] Such as a wife or a child.

[816] Literally, "strikes its brain," disabling or killing it.

[817] Of untruth concerning God, particularly here the claim that He has a son or other "partner" in divinity.

[818] All previous prophets called for the worship of God alone.

[819] Those they claim to be "children" of God, such as the angels, Ezra, Jesus etc.

[820] See footnote to 2:255.

[821] The signs present in the heavens.

[heavenly bodies] in an orbit are swimming.

34. And We did not grant to any man before you eternity [on earth]; so if you die - would they be eternal?

35. Every soul will taste death. And We test you with evil and with good as trial; and to Us you will be returned.

36. And when those who disbelieve see you, [O Muhammad], they take you not except in ridicule, [saying], "Is this the one who mentions [i.e., insults] your gods?" And they are, at the mention of the Most Merciful, disbelievers.

37. Man was created of haste [i.e., impatience]. I will show you My signs [i.e., vengeance], so do not impatiently urge Me.

38. And they say, "When is this promise, if you should be truthful?"

39. If those who disbelieved but knew the time when they will not avert the Fire from their faces or from their backs and they will not be aided...[822]

40. Rather, it will come to them unexpectedly and bewilder them, and they will not be able to repel it, nor will they be reprieved.

41. And already were messengers ridiculed before you, but those who mocked them were enveloped by what they used to ridicule.

42. Say, "Who can protect you at night or by day from the Most Merciful?" But they are, from the remembrance of their Lord, turning away.

43. Or do they have gods to defend them other than Us? They are unable [even] to help themselves, nor can they be protected from Us.

44. But, [on the contrary], We have provided good things for these [disbelievers] and their fathers until life was prolonged for them. Then do they not see that We set upon the land, reducing it from its borders?[823] So it is they who will overcome?

45. Say, "I only warn you by revelation." But the deaf do not hear the call when they are warned.

46. And if [as much as] a whiff of the punishment of your Lord should touch them, they would surely say, "O woe to us! Indeed, we have been wrongdoers."

47. And We place the scales of justice for the Day of Resurrection, so no soul will be treated unjustly at all. And if there is [even] the weight of a mustard seed,[824] We will bring it forth. And sufficient are We as accountant.

48. And We had already given Moses and Aaron the criterion and a light and a reminder[825] for the righteous

49. Who fear their Lord unseen,[826] while they are of the Hour apprehensive.

---

822 The completion of the sentence is understood to be "....they would not be asking in disbelief and ridicule to be shown the punishment."

823 See footnote to 13:41.

824 i.e., anything as small or insignificant as a mustard seed.

825 These are three qualities of the Torah.

826 Which can mean "Him being unseen" by them or "though they are unseen" by others.

50. And this [Qur'ān] is a blessed message which We have sent down. Then are you with it unacquainted?[827]

51. And We had certainly given Abraham his sound judgement before,[828] and We were of him well-Knowing

52. When he said to his father and his people, "What are these statues to which you are devoted?"

53. They said, "We found our fathers worshippers of them."

54. He said, "You were certainly, you and your fathers, in manifest error."

55. They said, "Have you come to us with truth, or are you of those who jest?"

56. He said, "[No], rather, your Lord is the Lord of the heavens and the earth who created them, and I, to that, am of those who testify.

57. And [I swear] by God, I will surely plan against your idols after you have turned and gone away."

58. So he made them into fragments, except a large one among them, that they might return to it [and question].

59. They said, "Who has done this to our gods? Indeed, he is of the wrongdoers."

60. They said, "We heard a young man mention them who is called Abraham."

61. They said, "Then bring him before the eyes of the people that they may testify."[829]

[827] i.e., pretending ignorance, disapproving or refusing to acknowledge it?

[828] i.e., before Moses. God had guided him from early youth.

62. They said, "Have you done this to our gods, O Abraham?"

63. He said, "Rather, this - the largest of them - did it, so ask them, if they should [be able to] speak."

64. So they returned to [blaming] themselves and said [to each other], "Indeed, you are the wrongdoers."

65. Then they reversed themselves,[830] [saying], "You have already known that these do not speak!"

66. He said, "Then do you worship instead of God that which does not benefit you at all or harm you?

67. Uff[831] to you and to what you worship instead of God. Then will you not use reason?"

68. They said, "Burn him and support your gods — if you are to act."

69. We [i.e., God] said, "O fire, be coolness and safety upon Abraham."

70. And they intended for him a plan [i.e., harm], but We made them the greatest losers.

71. And We delivered him and Lot to the land which We had blessed for the worlds [i.e., peoples].

72. And We gave him Isaac and Jacob in addition, and all [of them] We made righteous.

[829] To what they heard him say. It may also mean "....that they may witness [what will be done to him as punishment]."

[830] After first admitting to their error, they were seized by pride and obstinacy.

[831] An exclamation of anger and displeasure.

73. And We made them leaders guiding by Our command. And We inspired to them the doing of good deeds, establishment of prayer, and giving of zakāh; and they were worshippers of Us.

74. And to Lot We gave judgement and knowledge, and We saved him from the city that was committing wicked deeds. Indeed, they were a people of evil, defiantly disobedient.

75. And We admitted him into Our mercy. Indeed, he was of the righteous.

76. And [mention] Noah, when he called [to God][832] before [that time], so We responded to him and saved him and his family from the great affliction [i.e., the flood].

77. And We aided [i.e., saved] him from the people who denied Our signs. Indeed, they were a people of evil, so We drowned them, all together.

78. And [mention] David and Solomon, when they judged concerning the field - when the sheep of a people overran it [at night],[833] and We were witness to their judgement.

79. And We gave understanding of it [i.e., the case] to Solomon, and to each [of them] We gave judgement and knowledge. And We subjected the mountains to exalt [Us], along with David and [also] the birds. And We were doing [that].[834]

80. And We taught him the fashioning of coats of armor to protect you from your [enemy in] battle. So will you then be grateful?

81. And to Solomon [We subjected] the wind, blowing forcefully, proceeding by his command toward the land which We had blessed. And We are ever, of all things, Knowing.

82. And of the devils [i.e., jinn] were those who dived for him and did work other than that. And We were of them a guardian.[835]

83. And [mention] Job, when he called to his Lord, "Indeed, adversity has touched me, and you are the Most Merciful of the merciful."

84. So We responded to him and removed what afflicted him of adversity. And We gave him [back] his family and the like thereof with them as mercy from Us and a reminder for the worshippers [of God].

85. And [mention] Ishmael and Idrees and Dhul-Kifl; all were of the patient.

86. And We admitted them into Our mercy. Indeed, they were of the righteous.

87. And [mention] the man of the fish [i.e., Jonah], when he went off in anger[836] and thought that We would not decree [anything] upon him.[837] And he called out within the darknesses,[838] "There is no deity except You; exalted are You.

[832] i.e., supplicated against his people who had persisted in denial and animosity. See 17:26-28.
[833] Eating and destroying the crops.
[834] Meaning that God has always been capable of accomplishing whatever He wills.
[835] Preventing any disobedience or deviation by them from Solomon's instructions and protecting him from being harmed by them.
[836] At the disbelief of his people.
[837] Or "would not restrict him" in the belly of the fish.
[838] That of the night, of the sea, and of the fish's interior.

Indeed, I have been of the wrong-doers."

88. So We responded to him and saved him from the distress. And thus do We save the believers.

89. And [mention] Zechariah, when he called to his Lord, "My Lord, do not leave me alone [with no heir], while You are the best of inheritors."

90. So We responded to him, and We gave to him John, and amended for him his wife. Indeed, they used to hasten to good deeds and supplicate Us in hope and fear, and they were to Us humbly submissive.

91. And [mention] the one who guarded her chastity [i.e., Mary], so We blew into her [garment] through Our angel [i.e., Gabriel], and We made her and her son a sign for the worlds.

92. Indeed this, your religion, is one religion,[839] and I am your Lord, so worship Me.

93. And [yet] they divided their affair [i.e., that of their relegion] among themselves,[840] [but] all to Us will return.

94. So whoever does righteous deeds while he is a believer — no denial will there be for his effort,[841] and indeed We [i.e., Our angels], of it, are recorders.

95. And there is prohibition upon [the people of] a city which We have destroyed that they will [ever] return[842]

96. Until when [the dam of] Gog and Magog has been opened and they, from every elevation, descend

97. And [when] the true promise [i.e., the resurrection] has approached; then suddenly the eyes of those who disbelieved will be staring [in horror, while they say], "O woe to us; we had been unmindful of this; rather, we were wrongdoers."

98. Indeed, you [disbelievers] and what you worship other than God are the firewood of Hell. You will be coming to [enter] it.

99. Had these [false deities] been [actual] gods, they would not have come to it, but all are eternal therein.

100. For them therein is heavy sighing, and they therein will not hear.

101. Indeed, those for whom the best [reward] has preceded from Us — they are from it far removed.

102. They will not hear its sound, while they are, in that which their souls desire, abiding eternally.

103. They will not be grieved by the greatest terror,[843] and the angels will meet them, [saying], "This is your Day which you have been promised" -

104. The Day when We will fold the heaven like the folding of a [written] sheet for

[839] i.e., a collective way of life or course of conduct followed by a community.
[840] Becoming sects and denominations.
[841] Such a person will not be deprived of his due reward.
[842] They cannot return to this world, nor can they repent to God.
[843] The events of the Last Hour or of the Resurrection.

the records. As We began the first creation, We will repeat it. [That is] a promise binding upon Us. Indeed, We will do it.[844]

105. And We have already written in the book [of Psalms][845] after the [previous] mention[846] that the land [of Paradise] is inherited by My righteous servants.

106. Indeed, in this [Qur'ān] is notification for a worshipping people.

107. And We have not sent you, [O Muhammad], except as a mercy to the worlds.

108. Say, "It is only revealed to me that your god is but one God; so will you be Muslims [in submission to Him]?"

109. But if they turn away, then say, "I have announced to [all of] you equally.[847] And I know not whether near or far is that which you are promised.

110. Indeed, He knows what is declared of speech, and He knows what you conceal.

111. And I know not; perhaps it[848] is a trial for you and enjoyment for a time."

112. [The Prophet] has said, "My Lord, judge [between us] in truth. And our Lord is the Most Merciful, the one whose help is sought against that which you describe."[849]

[844] More literally, "Indeed, We are ever doers" of what We will.
[845] *Az-Zabūr* can also mean "scriptures" in general.
[846] i.e., the Torah. The "mention" may also refer to the original inscription with God, i.e., the Preserved Slate (*al-Lawh al Mahfūth*).
[847] The Prophet made this message known to all people, not concealing any of it from anyone or preferring any group over another.
[848] The postponement of punishment.
[849] i.e., their lies and disbelief.

## Sūrah 22: al-Hajj

### Period of Revelation

As this Sūrah contains the characteristics of both the Makki and the Madani Sūrahs the commentators have differed as to its period of revelation but in the light of its style and themes we are of the opinion that a part of it (v. 1-24) was sent down in the last stage of the Makki life of the Prophet a little before migration and the rest (v. 25-78) during the first stage of his Madani life. That is why this Sūrah combines the characteristics of both the Makki and the Madani Sūrahs.

According to Ibn Abbas, Mujahid, Qatadah and other great commentators, v. 39 is the first verse that grants the Muslims permission to wage war. Collections of hadith and books on the life of the Prophet confirm that after this permission actual preparations for war were started and the first expedition was sent to the coast of the Red Sea in Safar 2 A.H. which is known as the Expedition of Waddan or Al-Abwa.

### Subject Matter and Theme

This Sūrah is addressed to:

1. The polytheists of Makkah
2. the wavering Muslims and
3. the True Believers.

The polytheists have been warned in a forceful manner to this effect: "You have obdurately and impudently persisted in your ideas of ignorance and trusted in your deities instead of God though they possess no power at all and you have repudiated the Divine Messenger. Now you will meet the same end as has been the doom of those like you before. You have only harmed yourselves by rejecting Our Prophet and by persecuting the best element of your own community; now your false deities shall not be able to save you from the wrath of God." At the same time they have been admonished time and again for their creed of Shirk (polytheism) and sound arguments have been given in favour of Tawhid and the Hereafter. The wavering Muslims who had embraced Islām but were not prepared to endure any hardship in its way have been admonished to this effect: "What is this faith of yours? On the one hand you are ready to believe in God and become His servants provided you are given peace and prosperity but on the other if you meet with afflictions and hardships in His Way you discard your God and cease to remain His servant. You should bear in mind that this wavering attitude of yours cannot avert those misfortunes and losses which God has ordained for you."

As regards the true Believers they have been addressed in two ways:

1. in a general way so as to include the common people of Arabia also and
2. in an exclusive way.

The Believers have been told that the polytheists of Makkah had no right to debar them from visiting the Holy Mosque. They had no right to prevent anyone from performing Hajj because the Holy Mosque was not their private property. This objection was not only justified but it also acted as an effective political weapon against the Quraysh. For it posed this question to the other clans of Arabia: Were the Quraysh mere attendants of the Holy Mosque or its owners? It implied that if they succeeded in debarring the Muslims from Hajj without any protest from others, they would feel encouraged in future to debar from Hajj and Umrah the people of any other clan, who happened to have strained relations with the Quraysh. In order to emphasize this point, the history of the construction of the Holy Mosque has been cited to show that it was built by Prophet Abraham by the Command of God and he had invited all the peoples to perform Hajj there. That is why those coming from outside had enjoyed equal rights by the local people from the very beginning. It has also been made clear that that House had not been built for the rituals of shirk but for the worship of One God. Thus it was sheer tyranny that the worship of God was being forbidden there while the worship of idols enjoyed full licence

In order to counteract the tyranny of the Quraysh, the Muslims were allowed to fight with them. They were also given instructions to adopt the right and just attitude as and when they acquired power to rule in the land. Moreover, the Believers have been officially given the name of "Muslims" saying, "You are the real heirs to Abraham and you have been chosen to become witnesses of the Truth before mankind. Therefore you should establish salat and pay the zakāt dues in order to become the best models of righteous life and perform Jihād for propagating the Word of God (v. 41,77, 78.) It will be worth while to keep in view the introductions to Sūrahs 2 (al-Baqarah) and 8 (al Anfāl).

## Sūrah 22: al-Hajj[850]

In the Name of God, the Most Compassionate, the Most Merciful

1. O mankind, fear your Lord. Indeed, the convulsion of the [final] Hour is a terrible thing.

2. On the Day you see it every nursing mother will be distracted from that [child] she was nursing, and every pregnant woman will abort her pregnancy, and you will see the people [appearing] intoxicated while they are not intoxicated; but the punishment of God is severe.

3. And of the people is he who disputes about God without knowledge and follows every rebellious devil.

4. It has been decreed for him [i.e., every devil] that whoever turns to him – he will misguide him and will lead him to the punishment of the Blaze.

5. O People, if you should be in doubt about the Resurrection, then [consider that] indeed, We created you from dust, then from a sperm-drop, then from a clinging clot, and then from a lump of flesh, formed and unformed[851] – that We may show you.[852] And We settle in the wombs whom We will for a specified term, then We bring you out as a child, and then [We develop you] that you may reach your [time of] maturity. And among you is he who is taken in [early] death, and among you is he who is returned to the most decrepit [old] age so that he knows, after [once having] knowledge, nothing. And you see the earth barren, but when We send down upon it rain, it quivers and swells and grows [something] of every beautiful kind.

6. That is because God is the Truth and because He gives life to the dead and because He is over all things competent

7. And [that they may know] that the Hour is coming – no doubt about it – and that God will resurrect those in the graves.

8. And of the people is he who disputes about God without knowledge or guidance or an enlightening book [from Him],

9. Twisting his neck [in arrogance] to mislead [people] from the way of God. For him in the world is disgrace, and We will make him taste on the Day of Resurrection the punishment of the Burning Fire [while it is said],

10. "That is for what your hands have put forth and because God is not ever unjust to [His] servants."

11. And of the people is he who worships God on an edge.[853] If he is touched by good, he is reassured by it; but if he is struck by trial, he turns on his face [to the other direction]. He has lost [this] world and the Hereafter. That is what is the manifest loss.

12. He invokes instead of God that which neither harms him nor benefits him. That is what is the extreme error.

[850] *Al-Hajj*: The pilgrimage.
[851] That which is incomplete. This may include what is aborted at that stage.
[852] Our power and creative ability.
[853] At the edge of his religion, so to speak, i.e., with uncertainty, hypocrisy or heedlessness.

13. He invokes one whose harm is closer than his benefit – how wretched the protector and how wretched the associate.

14. Indeed, God will admit those who believe and do righteous deeds to gardens beneath which rivers flow. Indeed, God does what He intends.

15. Whoever should think that God will not support him [i.e., Prophet Muhammad] in this world and the Hereafter – let him extend a rope to the ceiling, then cut off [his breath],[854] and let him see: will his effort remove that which enrages [him]?

16. And thus have We sent it [i.e., the Qur'ān] down as verses of clear evidence and because God guides whom He intends.

17. Indeed, those who have believed and those who were Jews and the Sabeans and the Christians and the Magians and those who associated with God – God will judge between them on the Day of Resurrection. Indeed God is, over all things, Witness.

18. Do you not see [i.e., know] that to God prostrates whoever is in the heavens and whoever is on the earth and the sun, the moon, the stars, the mountains, the trees, the moving creatures and many of the people? But upon many the punishment has been justified.[855] And he whom God humiliates – for him there is no bestower of honour. Indeed, God does what He wills.

[854] i.e., strangle himself.
[855] And therefore decreed.

19. These[856] are two adversaries who have disputed over their Lord. But those who disbelieved will have cut out for them garments of fire. Poured upon their heads will be scalding water

20. By which is melted that within their bellies and [their] skins.

21. And for [striking] them are maces of iron.

22. Every time they want to get out of it [i.e., Hellfire] from anguish, they will be returned to it, and [it will be said], "Taste the punishment of the Burning Fire!"

23. Indeed, God will admit those who believe and do righteous deeds to gardens beneath which rivers flow. They will be adorned therein with bracelets of gold and pearl, and their garments therein will be silk.

24. And they had been guided [in worldly life] to good speech, and they were guided to the path of the Praiseworthy.

25. Indeed, those who have disbelieved and avert [people] from the way of God and [from] al-Masjid al-Harām, which We made for the people – equal are the resident therein and one from outside - and [also] whoever intends [a deed] therein[857] of deviation [in religion] or wrongdoing – We will make him taste of a painful punishment.

26. And [mention, O Muhammad], when We designated for Abraham the site of

[856] i.e., the believers and the disbelievers.
[857] Whether inside its boundaries or intending from afar to do evil therein. The Haram is unique in that the mere intention of sin therein (whether or not it is actually carried out) is sufficient to bring punishment from God.

the House, [saying], "Do not associate anything with Me and purify My House for those who perform tawāf[858] and those who stand [in prayer] and those who bow and prostrate.

27. And proclaim to the people the hajj [pilgrimage]; they will come to you on foot and on every lean camel; they will come from every distant pass –

28. That they may witness [i.e., attend] benefits for themselves and mention the name of God on known [i.e., specific] days over what He has provided for them of [sacrificial] animals.[859] So eat of them and feed the miserable and poor.

29. Then let them end their untidiness and fulfill their vows and perform tawāf around the ancient House."

30. That [has been commanded], and whoever honours the sacred ordinances of God – it is best for him in the sight of his Lord. And permitted to you are the grazing livestock, except what is recited to you.[860] So avoid the uncleanliness of idols and avoid false statement,

31. Inclining [only] to God, not associating [anything] with Him. And he who associates with God – it is as though he had fallen from the sky and was snatched by the birds or the wind carried him down into a remote place.

32. That [is so]. And whoever honours the symbols [i.e., rites] of God – indeed, it is from the piety of hearts.

33. For you therein [i.e., the animals marked for sacrifice] are benefits for a specified term;[861] then their place of sacrifice is at the ancient House.[862]

34. And for all religion We have appointed a rite [of sacrifice][863] that they may mention the name of God over what He has provided for them of [sacrificial] animals. For your god is one God, so to Him submit. And, [O Muhammad], give good tidings to the humble [before their Lord]

35. Who, when God is mentioned, their hearts are fearful, and [to] the patient over what has afflicted them, and the establishers of prayer and those who spend from what We have provided them.

36. And the camels and cattle We have appointed for you as among the symbols [i.e., rites] of God; for you therein is good. So mention the name of God upon them when lined up [for sacrifice]; and when they are [lifeless] on their sides, then eat from them and feed the needy [who does not seek aid] and the beggar. Thus have We subjected them to you that you may be grateful.

37. Their meat will not reach God, nor will their blood, but what reaches Him is piety from you. Thus have We subjected them to you that you may glorify God for that [to] which He has guided you; and give good tidings to the doers of good.

---

858 See footnote to 2:125.

859 *Al-An'ām*: camels, cattle, sheep and goats.

860 See 5:3.

861 i.e., they may be milked or ridden (in the case of camels) before the time of slaughter.

862 i.e., within the boundaries of the Haram, which includes Minā.

863 i.e., the right to sacrifice has always been a part of God's revealed religion.

38. Indeed, God defends those who have believed. Indeed, God does not like everyone treacherous and ungrateful.

39. Permission [to fight] has been given to those who are being fought,[864] because they were wronged. And indeed, God is competent to give them victory.

40. [They are] those who have been evicted from their homes without right – only because they say, "Our Lord is God." And were it not that God checks the people, some by means of others, there would have been demolished monasteries, churches, synagogues, and mosques in which the name of God is much mentioned [i.e., praised]. And God will surely support those who support Him [i.e., His cause]. Indeed, God is Powerful and Exalted in Might.

41. [And they are] those who, if We give them authority in the land, establish prayer and give zakāh and enjoin what is right and forbid what is wrong. And to God belongs the outcome of [all] matters.

42. And if they deny you, [O Muhammad] - so, before them, did the people of Noah and 'Aad and Thamūd deny [their prophets],

43. And the people of Abraham and the people of Lot

44. And the inhabitants of Madyan. And Moses was denied, so I prolonged enjoyment for the disbelievers; then I seized them, and how [terrible] was My reproach.

45. And how many a city did We destroy while it was committing wrong – so it is [now] fallen into ruin[865] – and [how many] an abandoned well and [how many] a lofty palace.[866]

46. So have they not traveled through the earth and have hearts by which to reason and ears by which to hear? For indeed, it is not eyes that are blinded, but blinded are the hearts which are within the breasts.

47. And they urge you to hasten the punishment. But God will never fail in His promise. And indeed, a day with your Lord is like a thousand years of those which you count.

48. And for how many a city did I prolong enjoyment while it was committing wrong. Then I seized it, and to Me is the [final] destination.

49. Say, "O people, I am only to you a clear warner."

50. And those who have believed and done righteous deeds – for them is forgiveness and noble provision.

51. But the ones who strove against Our verses, [seeking] to cause failure[867] – those are the companions of Hellfire.

52. And We did not send before you any messenger or prophet except that when he spoke [or recited], Satan threw into it [some misunderstanding]. But God abolishes that which Satan throws in;

864 Referring here to the Prophet's companions.

865 Literally, "fallen in upon its roofs," i.e., after the roofs of its buildings had caved in, the walls collapsed over them.

866 i.e., How many wells have been left inoperative, and how many palaces have been emptied of their occupants in the past.

867 i.e., trying to undermine their credibility and thereby defeat the Prophet.

then God makes precise His verses.[868] And God is Knowing and Wise.

53. [That is] so He may make what Satan throws in [i.e., asserts] a trial for those within whose hearts is disease[869] and those hard of heart. And indeed, the wrongdoers are in extreme dissension.

54. And so those who were given knowledge may know that it is the truth from your Lord and [therefore] believe in it, and their hearts humbly submit to it. And indeed is God the Guide of those who have believed to a straight path.

55. But those who disbelieve will not cease to be in doubt of it until the Hour comes upon them unexpectedly or there comes to them the punishment of a barren Day.[870]

56. [All] sovereignty that Day is for God;[871] He will judge between them. So they who believed and did righteous deeds will be in the Gardens of Pleasure.

57. And they who disbelieved and denied Our signs – for those there will be a humiliating punishment.

58. And those who emigrated for the cause of God and then were killed or died – God will surely provide for them a good provision. And indeed, it is God who is the best of providers.

59. He will surely cause them to enter an entrance with which they will be pleased, and indeed, God is Knowing and Forbearing.

60. That [is so]. And whoever responds [to injustice] with the equivalent of that with which he was harmed and then is tyrannized – God will surely aid him. Indeed, God is Pardoning and Forgiving.[872]

61. That[873] is because God causes the night to enter the day and causes the day to enter the night and because God is Hearing and Seeing.

62. That is because God is the Truth, and that which they call upon other than Him is falsehood, and because God is the Most High, the Grand.

63. Do you not see that God has sent down rain from the sky and the earth becomes green? Indeed, God is Subtle and Acquainted.[874]

64. To Him belongs what is in the heavens and what is on the earth. And indeed, God is the Free of need, the Praiseworthy.

65. Do you not see that God has subjected to you whatever is on the earth and the ships which run through the sea by His command? And He restrains the sky from falling upon the earth, unless by His permission. Indeed God, to the people, is Kind and Merciful.

---

868 Clarifying those issues which were misunderstood to remove any doubt.
869 See footnote to 2:10.
870 One which will not be followed by night and therefore will not give birth to a new day, referring to the Day of Resurrection.
871 None will compete with Him for authority at that time.
872 In spite of His ability to take vengeance. The statement contains a suggestion that the believers pardon as well.
873 i.e., God's capability to give assistance or victory to the oppressed.
874 With His creation and with the needs of His creatures.

66. And He is the one who gave you life; then He causes you to die and then will [again] give you life. Indeed, mankind is ungrateful.

67. For every religion We have appointed rites which they perform. So, [O Muhammad], let them [i.e., the disbelievers] not contend with you over the matter but invite them to your Lord. Indeed, you are upon straight guidance.

68. And if they dispute with you, then say, "God is most knowing of what you do.

69. God will judge between you on the Day of Resurrection concerning that over which you used to differ."

70. Do you not know that God knows what is in the heaven and earth? Indeed, that is in a Record.[875] Indeed that, for God, is easy.

71. And they worship besides God that for which He has not sent down authority and that of which they have no knowledge. And there will not be for the wrongdoers any helper.

72. And when Our verses are recited to them as clear evidences, you recognize in the faces of those who disbelieve disapproval. They are almost on the verge of assaulting those who recite to them Our verses. Say, "Then shall I inform you of [what is] worse than that?[876] [It is] the Fire which God has promised those who disbelieve, and wretched is the destination."

73. O people, an example is presented, so listen to it. Indeed, those you invoke besides God will never create [as much as] a fly, even if they gathered together for it [i.e., that purpose]. And if the fly should steal from them a [tiny] thing, they could not recover it from him. Weak are the pursuer and pursued.[877]

74. They have not appraised God with true appraisal.[878] Indeed, God is Powerful and Exalted in Might.

75. God chooses from the angels messengers and from the people. Indeed, God is Hearing and Seeing.

76. He knows what is [presently] before them and what will be after them.[879] And to God will be returned [all] matters.

77. O you who have believed, bow and prostrate and worship your Lord and do good – that you may succeed.

78. And strive for God with the striving due to Him. He has chosen you and has not placed upon you in the religion any difficulty. [It is] the religion of your father, Abraham. He [i.e., God] named you "Muslims" before [in former scriptures] and in this [revelation] that the Messenger may be a witness over you and you may be witnesses over the people. So establish prayer and give zakāh and hold fast to God. He is your protector; and excellent is the protector, and excellent is the helper.

875 The Preserved Slate (*al-Lawh al-Mahfūth*), which is with God.

876 i.e., worse than the rage you feel against those who recite God's verses or worse than your threats against them.

877 A comparison is made here to the worshipper of a false deity and that which he worships.

878 They have not assessed Him with the assessment due to Him, meaning that they did not take into account His perfect attributes.

879 See footnote to 2:255.

## Sūrah 23: al-Mu'minūn

### Period of Revelation

Both its style and theme indicate that it was revealed during the middle stage of Prophethood at Makkah. Reading between the lines one feels that a bitter conflict had begun between the Prophet and the disbelievers of Makkah though the persecution by them had not yet become tyrannical. It appears that the Sūrah was sent down during the climax of the "Famine" in Makkah (v. 75-76) which according to authentic traditions occurred during the middle stage of Prophethood. Moreover, according to a tradition related by 'Urwah bin Zubair, Hadarat Umar who had embraced Islām by that time said, '*This Sūrah was revealed in my presence and I myself observed the state of the Holy Prophet during its revelation. When the revelation ended the Holy Prophet remarked 'On this occasion ten such verses have been sent down to me that the one who measures up to them will most surely go to Paradise'.* Then he recited the initial verses of the Sūrah. (Ahmad and Tirmidhi)

### Theme Topics

The central theme of the Sūrah is to invite the people to accept and follow the Message of the Prophet and the whole Sūrah revolves round this theme.

## Sūrah 23: al-Mu'minūn[880]

In the Name of God, the Most Compassionate, the Most Merciful

1. Certainly will the believers have succeeded:

2. They who are during their prayer humbly submissive

3. And they who turn away from ill speech

4. And they who are observant of zakāh

5. And they who guard their private parts

6. Except from their wives or those their right hands possess,[881] for indeed, they will not be blamed –

7. But whoever seeks beyond that, then those are the transgressors –

8. And they who are to their trusts and their promises attentive

9. And they who carefully maintain their prayers –

10. Those are the inheritors

11. Who will inherit al-Firdaus.[882] They will abide therein eternally.

12. And certainly did We create man from an extract of clay.

13. Then We placed him as a sperm-drop[883] in a firm lodging [i.e., the womb].

14. Then We made the sperm-drop into a clinging clot, and We made the clot into a lump [of flesh], and We made [from] the lump, bones, and We covered the bones with flesh; then We developed him into another creation. So blessed is God, the best of creators.[884]

15. Then indeed, after that you are to die.

16. Then indeed you, on the Day of Resurrection, will be resurrected.

17. And We have created above you seven layered heavens, and never have We been of [Our] creation unaware.

18. And We have sent down rain from the sky in a measured amount and settled it in the earth. And indeed, We are Able to take it away.

19. And We brought forth for you thereby gardens of palm trees and grapevines in which for you are abundant fruits and from which you eat.

20. And [We brought forth] a tree issuing from Mount Sinai which produces oil and food [i.e., olives] for those who eat.

21. And indeed, for you in livestock is a lesson. We give you drink from that which is in their bellies, and for you in them are numerous benefits, and from them you eat.

22. And upon them and on ships you are carried.

23. And We had certainly sent Noah to his people, and he said, "O my people, worship God; you have no deity other than Him; then will you not fear Him?"

880 *Al- Mu'minūn*: The Believers.
881 Female slaves or captives under their ownership.
882 The highest part of Paradise.
883 Or "as a zygote."
884 i.e., the most skilful and only true Creator.

24. But the eminent among those who disbelieved from his people said, "This is not but a man like yourselves who wishes to take precedence over you; and if God had willed [to send a messenger], He would have sent down angels. We have not heard of this among our forefathers.

25. He is not but a man possessed with madness, so wait concerning him for a time."

26. [Noah] said, "My Lord, support me because they have denied me."

27. So We inspired to him, "Construct the ship under Our observation, and Our inspiration, and when Our command comes and the oven overflows,[885] put into it [i.e., the ship] from each [creature] two mates and your family, except those for whom the decree [of destruction] has proceeded. And do not address Me concerning those who have wronged; indeed, they are to be drowned.

28. And when you have boarded the ship, you and those with you, then say, 'Praise to God who has saved us form the wrongdoing people.'

29. And say, 'My Lord, let me land at a blessed landing place, and You are the best to accommodate [us].' "

30. Indeed in that are signs, and indeed, We are ever testing [Our servants].

31. Then We produced after them a generation of others.

[885] See footnote to 11:40.

32. And We sent among them a messenger[886] from themselves, [saying], "Worship God; you have no deity other than Him; then will you not fear Him?"

33. And the eminent among his people who disbelieved and denied the meeting of the Hereafter while We had given them luxury in the worldly life said, "This is not but a man like yourselves. He eats of that from which you eat and drinks of what you drink.

34. And if you should obey a man like yourselves, indeed, you would then be losers.

35. Does he promise you that when you have died and become dust and bones that you will be brought forth [once more]?

36. How far, how far, is that which you are promised.[887]

37. It [i.e., life] is not but our worldly life – we die and live, but we will not be resurrected.

38. He is not but a man who has invented a lie about God, and we will not believe him."

39. He said, "My Lord, support me because they have denied me."

40. [God] said, "After a little, they will surely become regretful."

41. So the shriek[888] seized them in truth,[889] and We made them as [plant] stubble.

[886] Prophet Hūd, who was sent to the tribe of 'Aad.
[887] i.e., how distant and improbable it is.
[888] See footnote to 11:67.
[889] i.e., by right or in justice.

Then away with the wrongdoing people.

42. Then We produced after them other generations.

43. No nation will precede its time [of termination], nor will they remain [thereafter].

44. Then We sent Our messengers in succession. Every time there came to a nation its messenger, they denied him, so We made them follow one another [to destruction], and We made them narrations.[890] So away with a people who do not believe.

45. Then We sent Moses and his brother Aaron with Our signs and a clear authority

46. To Pharaoh and his establishment, but they were arrogant and were a haughty people.

47. They said, "Should we believe two men like ourselves while their people are for us in servitude?"

48. So they denied them and were of those destroyed.

49. And We certainly gave Moses the Scripture that perhaps they[891] would be guided.

50. And We made the son of Mary and his mother a sign and sheltered them within a high ground having level [areas] and flowing water.

51. [God said], "O messengers, eat from the good foods and work righteousness. Indeed I, of what you do, am Knowing.

52. And indeed this, your religion, is one religion,[892] and I am your Lord, so fear Me."

53. But they [i.e., the people] divided their religion among them into portions [i.e., sects] – each faction, in what it has,[893] rejoicing.

54. So leave them in their confusion for a time.

55. Do they think that what We extend to them of wealth and children

56. Is [because] We hasten for them good things? Rather, they do not perceive.[894]

57. Indeed, they who are apprehensive from fear of their Lord

58. And they who believe in the signs of their Lord

59. And they who do not associate anything with their Lord

60. And they who give what they give while their hearts are fearful[895] because they will be returning to their Lord –

61. It is those who hasten to good deeds, and they outstrip [others] therein.

62. And We charge no soul except [with that within] its capacity, and with Us is a record which speaks with truth; and they will not be wronged.

---

[890] i.e., history or lessons for mankind.

[891] The Children of Israel.

[892] See footnote to 21:92.

[893] Of beliefs, opinions, customs, etc.

[894] That the good things given to them in this world are but a trial for them.

[895] Lest their deeds not be acceptable.

63. But their hearts are covered with confusion over this, and they have [evil] deeds besides that [i.e., disbelief] which they are doing,

64. Until when We seize their affluent ones with punishment,[896] at once they are crying [to God] for help.

65. Do not cry out today. Indeed, by Us you will not be helped.

66. My verses had already been recited to you, but you were turning back on your heels

67. In arrogance regarding it,[897] conversing by night, speaking evil.

68. Then have they not reflected over the word [i.e., the Qur'ān], or has there come to them that which had not come to their forefathers?

69. Or did they not know their Messenger, so they are toward him disacknowledging?

70. Or do they say, "In him is madness?" Rather, he brought them the truth, but most of them, to the truth, are averse.

71. But if the Truth [i.e., God] had followed their inclinations, the heavens and the earth and whoever is in them would have been ruined. Rather, We have brought them their message,[898] but they, from their message, are turning away.

[896] In worldly life, before the punishment of the Hereafter. Although general, the description includes specifically the punishment of the Quraysh by famine.
[897] The revelation. Or "him," i.e., the Prophet.
[898] Or "reminder."

72. Or do you, [O Muhammad], ask them for payment? But the reward of your Lord is best, and He is the best of providers.

73. And indeed, you invite them to a straight path.

74. But indeed, those who do not believe in the Hereafter are deviating from the path.

75. And even if We gave them mercy and removed what was upon them of affliction, they would persist in their transgression, wandering blindly.

76. And We had gripped them with suffering [as a warning], but they did not yield to their Lord, nor did they humbly supplicate, [and will continue thus]

77. Until when We have opened before them a door of severe punishment, immediately they will be therein in despair.

78. And it is He who produced for you hearing and vision and hearts [i.e., intellect]; little are you grateful.

79. And it is He who has multiplied you throughout the earth, and to Him you will be gathered.

80. And it is He who gives life and causes death, and His is the alternation of the night and the day. Then will you not reason?

81. Rather,[899] they say like what the former peoples said.

[899] Instead of understanding or reasoning.

82. They said, "When we have died and become dust and bones, are we indeed to be resurrected?

83. We have been promised this, we and our forefathers, before; this is not but legends of the former peoples."

84. Say, [O Muhammad], "To whom belongs the earth and whoever is in it, if you should know?"

85. They will say, "To God." Say, "Then will you not remember?"

86. Say, "Who is Lord of the seven heavens and Lord of the Great Throne?"

87. They will say, "[They belong] to God." Say, "Then will you not fear Him?"

88. Say, "In whose hand is the realm of all things – and He protects while none can protect against Him – if you should know?"

89. They will say, "[All belongs] to God." Say, "Then how are you deluded?"

90. Rather, We have brought them the truth, and indeed they are liars.

91. God has not taken any son, nor has there ever been with Him any deity. [If there had been], then each deity would have taken what it created, and some of them would have sought to overcome others. Exalted is God above what they describe [concerning Him].

92. [He is] Knower of the unseen and the witnessed, so high is He above what they associate [with Him].

93. Say, [O Muhammad], "My Lord, if You should show me that which they are promised,

94. My Lord, then do not place me among the wrongdoing people."

95. And indeed, We are able to show you what We have promised them.

96. Repel, by [means of] what is best, [their] evil. We are most knowing of what they describe.

97. And say, "My Lord, I seek refuge in You from the incitements of the devils,

98. And I seek refuge in You, my Lord, lest they be present with me."

99. [For such is the state of the disbelievers], until, when death comes to one of them, he says, "My Lord, send me back

100. That I might do righteousness in that which I left behind."[900] No! It is only a word he is saying; and behind them is a barrier until the Day they are resurrected.

101. So when the Horn is blown, no relationship will there be among them that Day, nor will they ask about one another.

102. And those whose scales are heavy [with good deeds] – it is they who are the successful.

103. But those whose scales are light – those are the ones who have lost their souls, [being] in Hell, abiding eternally.

104. The Fire will sear their faces, and they therein will have taut smiles.[901]

[900] Or "in that which I neglected."

[901] Their lips having been contracted by scorching until the teeth are exposed.

105. [It will be said]. "Were not My verses recited to you and you used to deny them?"

106. They will say, "Our Lord, our wretchedness overcame us, and we were a people astray.

107. Our Lord, remove us from it, and if we were to return [to evil], we would indeed be wrongdoers."

108. He will say, "Remain despised therein and do not speak to Me.

109. Indeed, there was a party of My servants who said, 'Our Lord, we have believed, so forgive us and have mercy upon us, and You are the best of the merciful.'

110. But you took them in mockery to the point that they made you forget My remembrance, and you used to laugh at them.

111. Indeed, I have rewarded them this Day for their patient endurance – that they are the attainers [of success]."

112. [God] will say, "How long did you remain on earth in number of years?"

113. They will say, "We remained a day or part of a day; ask those who enumerate."

114. He will say, "You stayed not but a little – if only you had known.

115. Then did you think that We created you uselessly and that to Us you would not be returned?"

116. So exalted is God, the Sovereign, the Truth; there is no deity except Him, Lord of the Noble Throne.

117. And whoever invokes besides God another deity for which he has no proof – then his account is only with his Lord. Indeed, the disbelievers will not succeed.

118. And, [O Muhammad], say, "My Lord, forgive and have mercy, and You are the best of the merciful."

## Sūrah 24: an-Nūr

### Period of Revelation

The consensus of opinion is that it was sent down after the Campaign against Bani al-Mustaliq and this is confirmed by v. 11-20 that deal with the incident of the "Slander" which occurred during that Campaign. But there is a difference of opinion as to whether this Campaign took place in 5 A.H. before the Battle of the Trench or in 6 A.H. after it.

### Historical Background

Now let us review the circumstances existing at the time of the revelation of this Sūrah. It should be kept in mind that the incident of the "Slander" which was the occasion of its revelation was closely connected with the conflict between Islām and the disbelievers.

After the victory at Badr the Islāmic movement began to gain strength day by day; so much so that by the time of the Battle of the Trench it had become so strong that the united forces of the enemy numbering about ten thousand failed to crush it and had to raise the siege of Madinah after one month. It meant this and both the parties understood it well that the war of aggression which the Disbelievers had been waging for several years had come to an end. The Prophet himself declared: *"After this year the Quraysh will not be able to attack you; now you will take the offensive."*

When the disbelievers realized that they could not defeat Islām on the battlefield they chose the moral front to carry on the conflict. It cannot be said with certainty whether this change of tactics was the outcome of deliberate consultations or it was the inevitable result of the humiliating retreat in the Battle of the Trench for which all the available forces of the enemy had been concentrated: They knew it well that the rise of Islām was not due to the numerical strength of the Muslims, nor to their superior arms and ammunition and not to their greater material resources; nay the Muslims were fighting against fearful odds on all these fronts. They owed their success to their moral superiority. Their enemies realized that the pure and noble qualities of the Prophet and his followers were capturing the hearts of the people and were also binding them together into a highly disciplined community. As a result of this they were defeating the polytheists and the Jews both on the peace and on the war front because the latter lacked discipline and character.

Under the above mentioned circumstances the wicked designs of the disbelievers led them to start a campaign of vilification against the Prophet and the Muslims in order to destroy the bulwark of morale that was helping them to defeat their enemies. Therefore the strategy was to attain the assistance of the hypocrites to spread slanders against the Prophet and his followers so that the polytheists and the Jews could exploit these to sow the seeds of discord among the Muslims and undermine their discipline.

The first opportunity for the use of the new strategy was afforded in Dhul-Qa'dah 5 A.H. when the Prophet married Zainab (daughter of Jahsh) who was the divorced wife of his adopted son Zayd bin Harithah. The Prophet had arranged this marriage in order to put an end to the custom of ignorance which gave the same status to the adopted son that was the right only of the son from one's own loins. The hypocrites however considered it a golden opportunity to vilify the Prophet from inside the community and the Jews and the polytheists exploited it from outside to ruin his high reputation by this malicious slander. For this purpose fantastic stories were concocted and spread to this effect: *"One day Muhammad happened to see the wife of his adopted son and fell in love with her; he manouvered her divorce and married her."* Though this was an absurd fiction it was spread with such skill, cunning and artfulness that it succeeded in its purpose; so much so that some Muslim traditionalists and commentators also have cited some parts of it in their writings and the orientalists have exploited these fully to vilify the Prophet. As a matter of fact Zainab was never a stranger to the Prophet that he should see her by chance and fall in love with her at first sight. For she was his first cousin being the daughter of his real paternal aunt Umaimah daughter of Abdul Muttalib. He had known her from her childhood to her youth. A year before this incident, he himself had persuaded her against her will to marry Zayd in order to demonstrate practically that the Quraysh and the liberated slaves were equal as human being. As she never reconciled herself to her marriage, they could not pull on together for long, which inevitably led to her divorce. The above mentioned facts were well known to all, yet the slanderers succeeded in their false propaganda with the result that even today there are people who exploit these things to defame Islām

The second slander was made on the honour of Ā'isha, a wife of the Prophet, in connection with an incident which occurred while he was returning from the Campaign against Bani al-Mustaliq. As this attack was even severer than the first one and was the main background of this Sūrah, we shall deal with it in greater detail.

Let us say a few words about Abdullah bin Ubayy, who played the part of a villain in this attack. He belonged to the clan of Khazraj and was one of the most important chiefs of Madinah. The people had even intended to make him their king a little before the Prophet's migration there, but the scheme had to be dropped because of the changed circumstances. Though he had embraced Islām, he remained at heart a hypocrite and his hypocrisy was so manifest that he was called the "Chief of the Hypocrites." He never lost any opportunity to slander Islām in order to take his revenge.

Now the main theme. When in Sha'aban 6 A.H. the Prophet learned that the people of Bani al-Mustaliq were making preparations for a war against the Muslims and were trying to muster other clans also for this purpose, he fore-stalled and took the enemy by surprise. After capturing the people of the clan and their belongings, the Prophet made a halt near Muraisi, a spring in their territory. One day a dispute concerning taking water from the spring started between a servant of Umar and an ally of the clan of Khazraj, and developed into a quarrel between the Muhajirs (immigrants) and the Ansār (Muslims of Madina), but was soon settled. This, however, did not suit the strategy of Abdullah bin Ubayy, who also had joined the expedition with a large number of hypocrites. So he began to incite the Ansār, saying, *"You yourselves brought these people of the Quraysh from Makkah and made them partners in your wealth and property. And now they have become your rivals and want domination over you. If even now you withdraw your support from them, they shall be forced to leave your city."* Then he swore and declared, *"As soon as we reach back Madinah, the respectable people will turn out the degraded people from the city."*

When the Prophet came to know of this, he ordered the people to set off immediately and march back to Madinah. The forced march continued up to noon the next day without a halt on the way so that the people became exhausted and had no time for idle talk.

Though this wise judgment and quick action by the Prophet averted the undesirable consequences of the mischief, Abdullah bin Ubayy got another opportunity for doing a far more serious and greater mischief, i.e. by engineering a "Slander" against Ā'isha, for that was a mischief which might well have involved the young Muslim Community in a civil war, if the Prophet and his sincere and devoted followers had not shown wisdom, forbearance and marvelous discipline in dealing with it. In order to understand the events that led to the incident of the "Slander," we cite the story in Ā'isha's own words. She says *"Whenever the Holy Prophet went out on a journey, he decided by lots as to which of his wives should accompany him. Accordingly, it was decided that I should accompany him during the expedition to Bani al-Mustaliq. On the return journey, the Holy Prophet halted for the night at a place which was the last stage on the way back to Madinah . It was still night, when they began to make preparations for the march. So I went outside the camp to ease myself. When I returned and came near my halting place, I noticed that my necklace had fallen down somewhere. I went back in search for it but in the meantime the caravan moved off and I was left behind all alone. The four carriers of the litter had placed it on my camel without noticing that it was empty. This happened because of my light weight due to lack of food in those days. I wrapped myself in my sheet and lay down in the hope that when it would be found that I had been left behind, a search party would come back to pick me up. In the meantime I fell asleep. In the morning, when Safwan bin Mu'attal Sulami passed that way, he saw me and recognized me for he had seen me several times before the Commandment about purdah had been sent down. No sooner did he see me than he stopped his camel and cried out spontaneously : "How sad! The wife of the Holy Prophet has been left here!" At this I woke up all of a sudden and covered my face with my sheet. Without uttering another word, he made his camel kneel by me and stood aside, while I climbed on to the camel back. He led the camel by the nose-string and we overtook the caravan at about noon, when it had just halted and nobody had yet noticed that I had been left behind. I learnt afterwards that this incident had been used to slander me and Abdullah bin Ubayy was foremost among the slanderers."* (According to other traditions, when Ā'isha reached the camp on the camel, led by Safwan, and it was known that she had been left behind, Abdullah bin Ubayy cried out, *'By God, she could not have remained chaste. Look, there comes the wife of your Prophet openly on the camel led by the person with whom she passed the night.'*)

*"When I reached Madinah, I fell ill and stayed in bed for more than a month. Though I was quite unaware of it, the news of the "Slander" was spreading like a scandal in the city, and had also reached the Holy Prophet. Anyhow, I noticed that he did not seem as concerned about my illness as he used to be. He would come but without addressing me directly, would inquire from others how I was and leave the house. Therefore it troubled my mind that something had gone wrong somewhere. So I took leave of him and went to my mother's house for better nursing. While I was there, one night I went out of the city to ease myself in the company of Mistah's mother, who was a first cousin of my mother. As she was walking along she stumbled over something and cried out spontaneously, 'May Mistah perish!' To this I retorted, 'What a good mother you are that you curse your own son, the son who took part in the Battle of Badr.' She replied, 'My dear daughter, are you not aware of his scandal mongering?' Then she told me everything about the campaign of the 'Slander'. Hearing this horrible story, my blood curdled, and I immediately returned home, and passed the rest of the night in crying over it.*

*"During my absence the Holy Prophet took counsel with Ali and Usamah bin Zayd about this matter. Usamah said good words about me to this effect: 'O Messenger of God, we have found nothing but good in your wife. All that is being spread about her is a lie and calumny.' As regards Ali, he said, 'O Messenger of God, there is no dearth of women; you may, if you like, marry another wife. If, however, you would like to investigate into the matter, you may send for her maid servant and inquire into it through her.' Accordingly, the maid servant was sent for and questioned. She replied, 'I declare on an oath by God, Who has sent you with the Truth, that I have never seen any evil thing in her, except that she falls asleep when I tell her to look after the kneaded dough in my absence and a goat comes and eats it.' On that same day the Holy Prophet addressed the people from the pulpit, saying: 'O Muslims, who from among you will defend my honour against the attacker of the person who has transgressed all bounds in doing harm to me by slandering my wife. By God, I have made a thorough inquiry and found nothing wrong with her nor with the man, whose name has been linked with the "Slander".' At this Usaid bin Hudair (or Sa'd bin Mauz) according to other traditions) stood up and said, 'O Messenger of God, if that person belongs to our clan, we will kill him by ourselves, but if he belongs to the Khazraj clan, we will kill him if you order us to do so.' Hearing this Sa'd bin 'Ubadah, chief of the Khazraj clan, stood up and said, 'You lie you can never kill him. You are saying this just because the person belongs to our clan of Khazraj. Had he belonged to your clan, you would never have said so.' Usaid retorted, 'You are a hypocrite: that is why you are defending a hypocrite.' At this, there was a general turmoil in the mosque, which would have developed into a riot, even though the Holy Prophet was present there the whole time. But he cooled down their anger and came down from the pulpit."*

Let us point out the enormity of the mischief that was engineered by Abdullah bin Ubayy:

1. It implied an attack on the honour of the Prophet and Abu Bakr Siddiq.
2. He meant to undermine the high moral superiority which was the greatest asset of the Islāmic Movement.
3. He intended to ignite civil war between the Muhajirs and the Ansār, and between Aus and Khazraj, the two clans of the Ansār.

**Themes and Topics**

This Sūrah and v. 28-73 of Sūrah al-Ahzāb (of which this is the sequel) were sent down to strengthen the moral front, which at that time was the main target of the attack, v. 28-73 of al-Ahzāb were sent down concerning the Prophet's marriage with Zainab, and on the occasion of the second attack (the "Slander" about Ā'isha), Sūrah An-Nūr was sent down to repair the cracks that had appeared in the unity of the Muslim Community. If we keep this in view during the study of the two Sūrahs, we shall understand the wisdom that underlies the Commandments about the Veil. God sent the following instructions to strengthen and safeguard the moral front, and to counteract the storm of propaganda that was raised on the occasion of the marriage of Zainab:

1. The wives of the Prophet were enjoined to remain within their private quarters, to avoid display of adornments and to be cautious in their talk with other persons (v. 32, 33).
2. The other Muslims were forbidden to enter the private rooms of the Prophet and instructed to ask whatever they wanted from behind the curtain (v. 53).
3. A line of demarcation was drawn between the mahram and the non-mahram relatives. Only the former were allowed to enter the private rooms of those wives of the Prophet with whom they were so closely related as to prohibit marriage with them (v. 55).
4. The Muslims were told that the wives of the Prophet were prohibited for them just like their own real mothers; therefore every Muslim should regard them with the purest of intentions (v. 53, 54).
5. The Muslims were warned that they would invite the curse and scourge of God if they offended the Prophet. Likewise it was a heinous sin to attack the honour of or slander any Muslim man or woman (v. 57, -8).
6. All the Muslim women were enjoined to cover their faces with their sheets if and when they had to go out of their houses (v. 59).

On the occasion of the second attack, this Sūrah was sent down to keep pure and strengthen the moral fibre of the Muslim society, which had been shaken by the enormity of the slander. We give below a summary of the Commandments and instructions in their chronological order so that one may understand how the Qur'ān makes use of the psychological occasion to reform the Community by the adoption of legal, moral and social measures.

1. Fornication which had already been declared to be a social crime (4:15,16) was now made a criminal offence and was to be punished with a hundred lashes.
2. It was enjoined to boycott the adulterous men and women and the Muslims were forbidden to have any marriage relations with them.
3. The one, who accused the other of adultery but failed to produce four witnesses, was to be punished with eighty lashes.
4. The Law of Lian was prescribed to decide the charge of adultery against his own wife by a husband.
5. The Muslims were enjoined to learn a lesson from the incident of the "Slander" about Ā'isha, as if to say, "You should be very cautious in regard to charges of adultery against the people of good reputation, and should not spread these; nay, you should refute and suppress them immediately." In this connection, a general principle was enunciated that the proper spouse for a pure man is a pure woman, for he cannot pull on with a wicked woman for long, and the same is the case with a pure woman, as if to say, "When you knew that the Prophet was a pure man, nay, the purest of all human beings, how could you believe that he had experienced happiness with a wicked woman and exalted her as the most beloved of his wives? For it was obvious that an adulterous woman could not have been able to deceive, with her affected behavior, a pure man like the Prophet. You ought also to have considered the fact that the accuser was a mean person while the accused was a pure woman. This should have been enough to convince you that the accusation was not worth your consideration; nay, it was not even conceivable.
6. Those who spread news and evil rumors and propagate wickedness in the Muslim Community, deserve punishment and not encouragement.
7. A general principle was laid down that relations in the Muslim Community should be based on good faith and not on suspicion: everyone should be treated as innocent unless he is proved to be guilty and vice versa.
8. The people were forbidden to enter the houses of others unceremoniously and were instructed to take permission for this.

9. Both men and women were instructed to lower their gaze and forbidden to cast glances or make eyes at each other.
10. Women were enjoined to cover their heads and breasts even inside their houses.
11. Women were forbidden to appear with make-up before other men except their servants or such relatives with whom their marriage is prohibited.
12. They were enjoined to hide their make-ups when they went out of their houses, and even forbidden to put on jingling ornaments, while they moved out of their houses.
13. Marriage was encouraged and enjoined even for slaves and slave girls, for unmarried people help spread indecency.
14. The institution of slavery was discouraged and the owners and other people were enjoined to give financial help to the slaves to earn their freedom under the law of Mukatabāt.
15. Prostitution by slave girls was forbidden in the first instance, for prostitution in Arabia was confined to this class alone. This in fact implied the legal prohibition of prostitution.
16. Sanctity of privacy in home life was enjoined even for servants and under age children including one's own. They were enjoined not to enter the private rooms of any man or woman without permission; especially in the morning, at noon and at night.
17. Old women were given the concession that they could set aside their head covers within their houses but should refrain from display of adornments. Even they were told that it was better for them to keep themselves covered with head wrappers.
18. The blind, lame, crippled and sick persons were allowed to take any article of food from the houses of other people without permission, for it was not to be treated like theft and cheating, which are cognizable offenses.
19. On the other hand, the Muslims were encouraged to develop mutual relationships by taking their meals together, and the nearest relatives and intimate friends were allowed to take their meals in each other's house without any formal invitation. This was to produce mutual affection and sincere relationships between them to counteract any future mischief. Side by side with these instructions, clear signs of the Believers and the hypocrites were stated to enable every Muslim to discriminate between the two. At the same time the Community was bound together by adopting disciplinary measures in order to make it stronger and firmer than it was at the time so as to discourage the enemies from creating mischief in it.

Above all, the most conspicuous thing about this discourse is that it is free from the bitterness which inevitably follows such shameful and absurd attacks. Instead of showing any wrath at this provocation, the discourse prescribes some laws and regulations and enjoins reformative commandments and issues wise instructions that were required at the time for the education and training of the Community. Incidentally, this teaches us how to deal with such provocative mischiefs coolly, wisely and generously. At the same time, it is a clear proof that this is not the word of Prophet Muhammad but of a Being Who is observing all human conditions and affairs from the highest level, and guiding mankind without any personal prejudices, feelings and leanings. Had this been the word of the Prophet; there would have been at least some tinge of natural bitterness in spite of his great generosity and forbearance, for it is but human that a noble man naturally becomes enraged when his own honour is attacked in this mean manner.

## Sūrah 24: an-Nūr[902]

In the Name of God, the Most Compassionate, the Most Merciful

1. [This is] a sūrah which We have sent down and made [that within it] obligatory and revealed therein verses of clear evidence that you might remember.

2. The [unmarried] woman or [unmarried] man found guilty of sexual intercourse[903] - lash each one of them with a hundred lashes,[904] and do not be taken by pity for them in the religion [i.e., Law] of God,[905] if you should believe in God and the Last Day. And let a group of the believers witness their punishment.

3. The fornicator does not marry except a [female] fornicator or polytheist, and none marries her except a fornicator[906] or a polytheist, and that [i.e., marriage to such persons] has been made unlawful to the believers.

4. And those who accuse chaste women and then do not produce four witnesses - lash them with eighty lashes and do not accept from them testimony ever after. And those are the defiantly disobedient,

5. Except for those who repent thereafter and reform, for indeed, God is Forgiving and Merciful.

6. And those who accuse their wives [of adultery] and have no witnesses except themselves - then the witness of one of them[907] [shall be] four testimonies [swearing] by God that indeed, he is of the truthful.

7. And the fifth [oath will be] that the curse of God be upon him if he should be among the liars.

8. But it will prevent punishment from her if she gives four testimonies [swearing] by God that indeed, he is of the liars.

9. And the fifth [oath will be] that the wrath of God be upon her if he was of the truthful.

10. And if not for the favor of God upon you and His mercy…[908] and because God is Accepting of repentance and Wise.

11. Indeed, those who came with falsehood[909] are a group among you. Do not think it bad for you; rather it is good for you. For every person among them is what [punishment] he has earned from the sin, and he who took upon himself the greater portion thereof [910] - for him is a great punishment [i.e., Hellfire].

---

902 *An-Nūr*: Light.

903 Either by voluntary confession by the offender or the testimony of four male witnesses to having actually seen the act take place. Otherwise, there can be no conviction.

904 The ruling in this verse is applicable to unmarried fornicators. Execution by stoning is confirmed in the *sunnah* for convicted adulterers.

905 i.e., Do not let sympathy for a guilty person move you to alter anything ordained by God, for His law is protection for society as a whole.

906 Included in this ruling is the adulterer as well. Such persons cannot be married to believers unless they have repented and reformed.

907 The husbands have been betrayed.

908 The phrase omitted is estimated to be "…you would surely have been punished, destroyed or scandalized," or "…you would have suffered many difficult situations."

909 Referring to the incident when the Prophet's wife 'Ā'isha was falsely accused by the hypocrites.

910 i.e., 'Abdullah bin 'Ubayy, leader of the hypocrites.

12. Why, when you heard it, did not the believing men and believing women think good of themselves [i.e., one another] and say, "This is an obvious falsehood"?

13. Why did they [who slandered] not produce for it four witnesses? And when they do not produce the witnesses, then it is they, in the sight of God, who are the liars.

14. And if it had not been for the favor of God upon you and His mercy in this world and the Hereafter, you would have been touched for that [lie] in which you were involved by a great punishment

15. When you received it with your tongues[911] and said with your mouths that of which you had no knowledge and thought it was insignificant while it was, in the sight of God, tremendous.

16. And why, when you heard it, did you not say, "It is not for us to speak of this. Exalted are You, [O God]; this is a great slander"?

17. God warns you against returning to the likes of this [conduct], ever, if you should be believers.

18. And God makes clear to you the verses [i.e., His rulings], and God is Knowing and Wise.

19. Indeed, those who like that immorality[912] should be spread [or publicized] among those who have believed will have a painful punishment in this world and the Hereafter. And God knows[913] and you do not know.

20. And if it had not been for the favor of God upon you and His mercy...[914]and because God is Kind and Merciful.

21. O you who have believed, do not follow the footsteps of Satan. And whoever follows the footsteps of Satan - indeed, he enjoins immorality and wrongdoing. And if not for the favor of God upon you and His mercy, not one of you would have been pure, ever, but God purifies whom He wills, and God is Hearing and Knowing.

22. And let not those of virtue among you and wealth swear not to give [aid] to their relatives and the needy and the emigrants for the cause of God, and let them pardon and overlook. Would you not like that God should forgive you? And God is Forgiving and Merciful.

23. Indeed, those who [falsely] accuse chaste, unaware and believing women are cursed in this world and the Hereafter; and they will have a great punishment

24. On a Day when their tongues, their hands and their feet will bear witness against them as to what they used to do.

25. That Day, God will pay them in full their true [i.e., deserved] recompense, and they will know that it is God who is the manifest Truth [i.e., perfect in justice].

26. Evil words are for evil men, and evil men are [subjected] to evil words. And

[911] Rather than your ears, i.e., not thinking about what you had heard but hastening to repeat it carelessly.
[912] Specifically, unlawful sexual relations.
[913] The hidden aspects of all things: what is beneficial and what is harmful.
[914] See footnote to verse 10.

good words are for good men, and good men are [an object] of good words.[915] Those [good people] are declared innocent of what they [i.e., slanderers] say. For them is forgiveness and noble provision.

27. O you who have believed, do not enter houses other than your own houses until you ascertain welcome and greet[916] their inhabitants. That is best for you; perhaps you will be reminded [i.e., advised].

28. And if you do not find anyone therein, do not enter them until permission has been given you. And if it is said to you, "Go back,"[917] then go back; it is purer for you. And God is Knowing of what you do.

29. There is no blame upon you for entering houses not inhabited in which there is convenience[918] for you. And God knows what you reveal and what you conceal.

30. Tell the believing men to reduce [some] of their vision[919] and guard their private parts.[920] That is purer for them. Indeed, God is Acquainted with what they do.

31. And tell the believing women to reduce [some] of their vision[921] and guard their private parts and not expose their adornment[922] except that which [necessarily] appears thereof[923] and to wrap [a portion of] their headcovers over their chests and not expose their adornment [i.e., beauty] except to their husbands, their fathers, their husbands' fathers, their sons, their husbands' sons, their brothers, their brothers' sons, their sisters' sons, their women, that which their right hands possess [i.e., slaves], or those male attendants having no physical desire,[924] or children who are not yet aware of the private aspects of women. And let them not stamp their feet to make known what they conceal of their adornment. And turn to God in repentance, all of you, O believers, that you might succeed.

32. And marry the unmarried among you and the righteous among your male slaves and female slaves. If they should be poor, God will enrich them from His bounty, and God is all-Encompassing and Knowing.

33. But let them who find not [the means for] marriage abstain [from sexual relations] until God enriches them from His bounty. And those who seek a contract [for eventual emancipation] from among whom your right hands pos-

[915] Another accepted interpretation is "Evil women are for evil men, and evil men are for evil women. And good women are for good men, and good men are for good women."

[916] By the words "*As-salāmu 'alaykum*" ("Peace be upon you").

[917] Or a similar expression showing that the occupants are not prepared to receive visitors (which should be respected).

[918] Some benefit such as rest, shelter, commodities, one's personal belongings, etc.

[919] Looking only at what is lawful and averting their eyes from what is unlawful.

[920] From being seen and from unlawful acts.

[921] Looking only at what is lawful and averting their eyes from what is unlawful.

[922] Both natural beauty, such as hair or body shape, and that with which a woman beautifies herself of clothing, jewelry, etc.

[923] i.e., the outer garments or whatever might appear out of necessity, such as a part of the face or the hands.

[924] Referring to an abnormal condition in which a man is devoid of sexual feeling.

sess[925] - then make a contract with them if you know there is within them goodness and give them from the wealth of God which He has given you. And do not compel your slave girls to prostitution, if they desire chastity, to seek [thereby] the temporary interests of worldly life. And if someone should compel them, then indeed, God is [to them], after their compulsion, Forgiving and Merciful.

34. And We have certainly sent down to you distinct verses[926] and examples from those who passed on before you and an admonition for those who fear God.

35. God is the Light[927] of the heavens and the earth. The example of His light[928] is like a niche within which is a lamp,[929] the lamp is within glass, the glass as if it were a pearly [white] star lit from [the oil of] a blessed olive tree, neither of the east nor of the west, whose oil would almost glow even if untouched by fire. Light upon light. God guides to His light whom He wills. And God presents examples for the people, and God is Knowing of all things.

36. [Such niches are] in houses [i.e., mosques] which God has ordered to be raised and that His name be mentioned [i.e., praised] therein; exalting Him within them in the morning and the evenings[930]

37. [Are] men whom neither commerce nor sale distracts from the remembrance of God and performance of prayer and giving of zakāh. They fear a Day in which the hearts and eyes will [fearfully] turn about -

38. That God may reward them [according to] the best of what they did and increase them from His bounty. And God gives provision to whom He wills without account [i.e., limit].

39. But those who disbelieved - their deeds are like a mirage in a lowland which a thirsty one thinks is water until, when he comes to it, he finds it is nothing but finds God before Him, and He will pay him in full his due; and God is swift in account.

40. Or [they are] like darknesses within an unfathomable sea which is covered by waves, upon which are waves, over which are clouds - darknesses, some of them upon others. When one puts out his hand [therein], he can hardly see it. And he to whom God has not granted light - for him there is no light.

41. Do you not see that God is exalted by whomever is within the heavens and the earth and [by] the birds with wings spread [in flight]? Each [of them] has known his [means of] prayer and exalting [Him], and God is Knowing of what they do.

42. And to God belongs the dominion of the heavens and the earth, and to God is the destination.

925 i.e., those slaves who desire to purchase their freedom from their owners for a price agreed upon by both.
926 i.e., rulings and ordinances, in particular those in this *Sūrah*.
927 i.e., the source and bestower of light and enlightenment.
928 His guidance in the heart of a believing servant.
929 Literally, "a burning wick," which is the essence of a lamp.

930 The term used here can refer to either afternoon or evening.

43. Do you not see that God drives clouds? Then He brings them together, then He makes them into a mass, and you see the rain emerge from within it. And He sends down from the sky, mountains [of clouds] within which is hail, and He strikes with it whom He wills and averts it from whom He wills. The flash of its lightening almost takes away the eyesight.

44. God alternates the night and the day. Indeed in that is a lesson for those who have vision.

45. God has created every [living] creature from water. And of them are those that move on their bellies, and of them are those that walk on two legs, and of them are those that walk on four. God creates what He wills. Indeed, God is over all things competent.

46. We have certainly sent down distinct verses. And God guides whom He wills to a straight path.

47. But they [i.e., the hypocrites] say, "We have believed in God and in the Messenger, and we obey"; then a party of them turns away after that. And those are not believers.

48. And when they are called to [the words of] God and His Messenger to judge between them, at once a party of them turns aside [in refusal].

49. But if the right is theirs, they come to him in prompt obedience.

50. Is there disease in their hearts? Or have they doubted? Or do they fear that God will be unjust to them, or His Messenger? Rather, it is they who are the wrongdoers [i.e., the unjust].

51. The only statement of the [true] believers when they are called to God and His Messenger to judge between them is that they say, "We hear and we obey." And those are the successful.

52. And whoever obeys God and His Messenger and fears God and is conscious of Him - it is those who are the attainers.

53. And they swear by God their strongest oaths that if you ordered them, they would go forth [in God's cause]. Say, "Do not swear. [Such] obedience is known.[931] Indeed, God is Acquainted with that which you do."

54. Say, "Obey God and obey the Messenger; but if you turn away - then upon him is only that [duty] with which he has been charged, and upon you is that with which you have been charged. And if you obey him, you will be [rightly] guided. And there is not upon the Messenger except the [responsibility for] clear notification."

55. God has promised those who have believed among you and done righteous deeds that He will surely grant them succession [to authority] upon the earth just as He granted it to those before them and that He will surely establish for them [therein] their religion which He has preferred for them and that He will surely substitute for them, after their fear, security, [for] they worship Me, not associating anything with Me. But whoever disbelieves[932] after that - then those are the defiantly disobedient.

[931] i.e., the hypocrites' pretense of obedience is known to be a lie.

[932] i.e., denies the favour of God or does not live by His ordinance.

56. And establish prayer and give zakāh and obey the Messenger - that you may receive mercy.

57. Never think that the disbelievers are causing failure [to God] upon the earth. Their refuge will be the Fire - and how wretched the destination.

58. O you who have believed, let those whom your right hands possess and those who have not [yet] reached puberty among you ask permission of you [before entering] at three times: before the dawn prayer and when you put aside your clothing [for rest] at noon and after the night prayer. [These are] three times of privacy[933] for you. There is no blame upon you nor upon them beyond these [periods], for they continually circulate among you - some of you, among others. Thus does God make clear to you the verses [i.e., His ordinances]; and God is Knowing and Wise.

59. And when the children among you reach puberty, let them ask permission [at all times] as those before them have done. Thus does God make clear to you His verses; and God is Knowing and Wise.

60. And women of post-menstrual age who have no desire for marriage - there is no blame upon them for putting aside their outer garments [but] not displaying adornment. But to modestly refrain [from that] is better for them. And God is Hearing and Knowing.

61. There is not upon the blind [any] constraint nor upon the lame [any] constraint nor upon the ill [any] constraint nor upon yourselves if you eat from your [own] houses or the houses of your fathers or the houses of your mothers or the houses of your brothers or the houses of your sisters or the houses of your fathers' brothers or the houses of your fathers' sisters or the houses of your mothers' brothers or the houses of your mothers' sisters or [from houses] whose keys you possess or [from the house] of your friend. There is no blame upon you whether you eat together or separately. But when you enter houses, give greetings of peace[934] upon each other - a greeting from God, blessed and good. Thus does God make clear to you the verses [of ordinance] that you may understand.

62. The believers are only those who believe in God and His Messenger and, when they are [meeting] with him for a matter of common interest, do not depart until they have asked his permission. Indeed, those who ask your permission, [O Muhammad] - those are the ones who believe in God and His Messenger. So when they ask your permission for something of their affairs, then give permission to whom you will among them and ask forgiveness for them of God. Indeed, God is Forgiving and Merciful.

63. Do not make [your] calling of the Messenger among yourselves as the call of one of you to another. Already God knows those of you who slip away, concealed by others. So let those beware who dissent from his [i.e., the Prophet's] order,[935] lest fitnah[936] strike them or a painful punishment.

[933] Literally, "exposure" or "being uncovered."

[934] Saying, "*As-salāmu 'alaykum*" ("Peace be upon you").

[935] Meaning also his way or his *sunnah*.

[936] Trials, affliction, dissension, strife, etc.

64. Unquestionably, to God belongs whatever is in the heavens and earth. Already He knows that upon which you [stand][937] and [knows] the Day[938] when they will be returned to Him and He will inform them of what they have done. And God is Knowing of all things.

[937] i.e., your position – the basis for your actions (whether sincere faith or hypocrisy) and the condition of your souls.
[938] The meaning can also be rendered "…and [let them beware of] the Day…"

# Sūrah 25: al- Furqān

## Period of Revelation

It appears from its style and subject matter that like Sūrah al-Mu'minūn it was also revealed during the third stage of Prophethood at Makkah. Ibn Jarir and Imām Razi have cited a tradition of Dahhak bin Muzahim that this Sūrah was revealed eight years before Sūrah 4: an-Nisa.

## Subject Matter and Topics

The Sūrah deals with the doubts and objections that were being raised against the Qur'ān, the Prophethood of Muhammad and his teachings by the disbelievers of Makkah. Appropriate answers to each and every objection have been given and the people have been warned of the consequences of rejecting the Truth. At the end of the Sūrah a clear picture of the moral superiority of the Believers has been depicted as in the beginning of Sūrah al-Mu'minūn as if to say 'Here is the criterion for distinguishing the genuine from the counterfeit. This is the noble character of those people who have believed in and followed the teachings of the Prophet and this is the kind of people that he is trying to train. You may yourselves compare and contrast this type of people with those Arabs who have not as yet accepted the Message and who are upholding "ignorance" and exerting their utmost to defeat the Truth. Now you may judge for yourselves as to which you would like to choose." Though this question was not posed in so many words it was placed before every one in Arabia in a tangible shape. It may be noted that during the next few years the practical answer given to this question by the whole nation with the exception of a small minority was that they chose Islām.

## Sūrah 25: al- Furqān[939]

In the Name of God, the Most Compassionate, the Most Merciful

1. Blessed is He who sent down the Criterion upon His Servant that he may be to the worlds a warner -

2. He to whom belongs the dominion of the heavens and the earth and who has not taken a son and has not had a partner in dominion and has created each thing and determined it with [precise] determination.

3. But they have taken besides Him gods which create nothing, while they are created, and possess not for themselves any harm or benefit and possess not [power to cause] death or life or resurrection.

4. And those who disbelieve say, "This [Qur'ān] is not except a falsehood he invented, and another people assisted him in it." But they have committed an injustice and a lie.

5. And they say, "Legends of the former peoples which he has written down, and they are dictated to him morning and afternoon."

6. Say, [O Muhammad], "It has been revealed by He who knows [every] secret within the heavens and the earth. Indeed, He is ever Forgiving and Merciful."

7. And they say, "What is this messenger that eats food and walks in the markets? Why was there not sent down to him an angel so he would be with him a warner?

8. Or [why is not] a treasure presented to him [from heaven], or does he [not] have a garden from which he eats?" And the wrongdoers say, "You follow not but a man affected by magic."

9. Look how they strike for you comparisons;[940] but they have strayed, so they cannot [find] a way.

10. Blessed is He who, if He willed, could have made for you [something] better than that - gardens beneath which rivers flow - and could make for you palaces.

11. But they have denied the Hour, and We have prepared for those who deny the Hour a Blaze.

12. When it [i.e., the Hellfire] sees them from a distant place, they will hear its fury and roaring.

13. And when they are thrown into a narrow place therein bound in chains, they will cry out thereupon for destruction.

14. [They will be told], "Do not cry this Day for one destruction but cry for much destruction."

15. Say, "Is that better or the Garden of Eternity which is promised to the righteous? It will be for them a reward and destination.

16. For them therein is whatever they wish, [while] abiding eternally. It is ever upon

939 *Al-Furqān*: The Criterion, which is another name for the Qur'ān and means "that which distinguishes truth from falsehood and right from wrong."

940 From their own imaginations in order to deny and discredit you.

your Lord a promise [worthy to be] requested.[941]

17. And [mention] the Day He will gather them and that which they worship besides God and will say, "Did you mislead these, My servants, or did they [themselves] stray from the way?"

18. They will say, "Exalted are You! It was not for us to take besides You any allies [i.e., protectors]. But You provided comforts for them and their fathers until they forgot the message and became a people ruined."

19. So they will deny you, [disbelievers], in what you say,[942] and you cannot avert [punishment] or [find] help. And whoever commits injustice[943] among you - We will make him taste a great punishment.

20. And We did not send before you, [O Muhammad], any of the messengers except that they ate food and walked in the markets. And We have made some of you [people] as trial for others - will you have patience? And ever is your Lord, Seeing.

21. And those who do not expect the meeting with Us say, "Why were not angels sent down to us, or [why] do we [not] see our Lord?" They have certainly become arrogant within themselves[944] and [become] insolent with great insolence.

22. The day they see the angels[945] - no good tidings will there be that day for the criminals, and [the angels] will say, "Prevented and inaccessible."[946]

23. And We will approach [i.e., regard][947] what they have done of deeds and make them as dust dispersed.

24. The companions of Paradise, that Day, are [in] a better settlement and better resting place.

25. And [mention] the Day when the heaven will split open with [emerging] clouds,[948] and the angels will be sent down in successive descent.

26. True sovereignty, that Day, is for the Most Merciful. And it will be upon the disbelievers a difficult Day.

27. And the Day the wrongdoer will bite on his hands [in regret] he will say, "Oh, I wish I had taken with the Messenger a way.[949]

28. Oh, woe to me! I wish I had not taken that one[950] as a friend.

29. He led me away from the remembrance[951] after it had come to me. And ever is Satan, to man, a deserter."[952]

30. And the Messenger has said, "O my Lord, indeed my people have taken this Qur'ān as [a thing] abandoned."[953]

---

[941] Or "...a promise requested [for them by the angels]."
[942] At the time of Judgement the false objects of worship will betray their worshippers and deny them.
[943] Specifically, association of others with God.
[944] Additional meaning are "among themselves" and "over [the matter of] themselves."
[945] i.e., at the time of death.
[946] Referring to any good tidings.
[947] On the Day of Judgement.
[948] Within which are the angels.
[949] i.e., followed the Prophet on a path of guidance.
[950] The person who misguided him.
[951] i.e., the Qur'ān or the remembrance of God.
[952] Forsaking him once he has led him into evil.

31. And thus have We made for every prophet an enemy from among the criminals. But sufficient is your Lord as a guide and a helper.

32. And those who disbelieve say, "Why was the Qur'ān not revealed to him all at once?" Thus [it is] that We may strengthen thereby your heart. And We have spaced it distinctly.[954]

33. And they do not come to you with an example [i.e., argument] except that We bring you the truth and the best explanation.

34. The ones who are gathered on their faces to Hell - those are the worst in position and farthest astray in [their] way.

35. And We had certainly given Moses the Scripture and appointed with him his brother Aaron as an assistant.

36. And We said, "Go both of you to the people who have denied Our signs." Then We destroyed them with [complete] destruction.

37. And the people of Noah - when they denied the messengers,[955] We drowned them, and We made them for mankind a sign. And We have prepared for the wrongdoers a painful punishment.

38. And [We destroyed] 'Aad and Thamūd and the companions of the well[956] and many generations between them.

39. And for each We presented examples [as warnings], and each We destroyed with [total] destruction.

40. And they have already come upon the town which was showered with a rain of evil [i.e., stones]. So have they not seen it? But they are not expecting resurrection.[957]

41. And when they see you, [O Muhammad], they take you not except in ridicule, [saying], "Is this the one whom God has sent as a messenger?

42. He almost would have misled us from our gods had we not been steadfast in [worship of] them." But they are going to know, when they see the punishment, who is farthest astray in [his] way.

43. Have you seen the one who takes as his god his own desire? Then would you be responsible for him?

44. Or do you think that most of them hear or reason? They are not except like livestock.[958] Rather, they are [even] more astray in [their] way.

45. Have you not considered your Lord - how He extends the shadow, and if He willed, He could have made it statio-

[953] i.e., avoiding it, not listening to or understanding it, not living by it, or preferring something else to it.
[954] Also, "recited it with distinct recitation."
[955] Their denial of Noah was as if they had denied all those who brought the same message from God.
[956] Said to be a people who denied Prophet Shu'ayb or possibly those mentioned in *Sūrah Yā Seen*, 36:13-29.
[957] So they do not benefit from lessons of the past.
[958] i.e., cattle or sheep, that follow without question wherever they are led.

nary? Then We made the sun for it an indication.[959]

46. Then We hold it in hand for a brief grasp.[960]

47. And it is He who has made the night for you as clothing[961] and sleep [a means for] rest and has made the day a resurrection.[962]

48. And it is He who sends the winds as good tidings before His mercy [i.e., rainfall], and We send down from the sky pure water

49. That We may bring to life thereby a dead land and give it as drink to those We created of numerous livestock and men.

50. And We have certainly distributed it among them that they might be reminded,[963] but most of the people refuse except disbelief.

51. And if We had willed, We could have sent into every city a warner.[964]

52. So do not obey the disbelievers, and strive against them with it [i.e., the Qur'ān] a great striving.

53. And it is He who has released [simultaneously] the two seas [i.e., bodies of water], one fresh and sweet and one salty and bitter, and He placed between them a barrier and prohibiting partition.

54. And it is He who has created from water [i.e., semen] a human being and made him [a relative by] lineage and marriage. And ever is your Lord competent [concerning creation].

55. But they worship rather than God that which does not benefit them or harm them, and the disbeliever is ever, against his Lord, an assistant [to Satan].

56. And We have not sent you, [O Muhammad], except as a bringer of good tidings and a warner.

57. Say, "I do not ask of you for it any payment - only that whoever wills might take to his Lord a way."

58. And rely upon the Ever-Living who does not die, and exalt [God] with His praise. And sufficient is He to be, with the sins of His servants, Acquainted -

59. He who created the heavens and the earth and what is between them in six days and then established Himself above the Throne[965] - the Most Merciful, so ask about Him one well informed [i.e., the Prophet].

60. And when it is said to them, "Prostrate to the Most Merciful," they say, "And what is the Most Merciful? Should we prostrate to that which you order us?" And it increases them in aversion.

61. Blessed is He who has placed in the sky great stars and placed therein a [burning] lamp and luminous moon.

---

[959] i.e., showing the existence of a shadow or making it apparent by contrast.
[960] i.e., when the sun is overhead at noon.
[961] Covering and concealing you in its darkness.
[962] For renewal of life and activity.
[963] Of God's ability to bring the dead to life.
[964] However, God willed that Prophet Muhammad be sent as the final messenger for all peoples of the earth until the Day of Resurrection.

[965] See footnote to 2:19.

62. And it is He who has made the night and the day in succession for whoever desires to remember or desires gratitude.

63. And the servants of the Most Merciful are those who walk upon the earth easily,[966] and when the ignorant address them [harshly], they say [words of] peace,[967]

64. And those who spend [part of] the night to their Lord prostrating and standing [in prayer]

65. And those who say, "Our Lord, avert from us the punishment of Hell. Indeed, its punishment is ever adhering;

66. Indeed, it is evil as a settlement and residence."

67. And [they are] those who, when they spend, do so not excessively or sparingly but are ever, between that, [justly] moderate

68. And those who do not invoke with God another deity or kill the soul which God has forbidden [to be killed], except by right, and do not commit unlawful sexual intercourse. And whoever should do that will meet a penalty.

69. Multiplied for him is the punishment on the Day of Resurrection, and he will abide therein humiliated -

70. Except for those who repent, believe and do righteous work. For them God will replace their evil deeds with good. And ever is God Forgiving and Merciful.

[966] i.e., gently, with dignity but without arrogance.
[967] Or "safety," i.e., words free from fault or evil.

71. And he who repents and does righteousness does indeed turn to God with [accepted] repentance.

72. And [they are] those who do not testify to falsehood, and when they pass near ill speech, they pass by with dignity.

73. And those who, when reminded of the verses of their Lord, do not fall upon them deaf and blind.

74. And those who say, "Our Lord, grant us from among our wives and offspring comfort to our eyes[968] and make us a leader [i.e., example] for the righteous."

75. Those will be awarded the Chamber[969] for what they patiently endured, and they will be received therein with greetings and [words of] peace,

76. Abiding eternally therein. Good is the settlement and residence.

77. Say, "What would my Lord care for you if not for your supplication?"[970] For you [disbelievers] have denied, so it [i.e., your denial] is going to be adherent.[971]

[968] i.e., a source of happiness due to their righteousness.
[969] The most elevated portion of Paradise.
[970] i.e., faith and worship. An alternative meaning is "What would my Lord do with you…"
[971] It will remain with them, causing punishment to be required and imperative upon them.

## Sūrah 26: ash- Shu'arā'

### Period of Revelation

The subject matter and the style show, and the hadith confirm that it was revealed during the middle Makkan period. According to Ibn Abbas, Sūrah Tā Hā was revealed first, then Sūrah al-Wāqi'ah and then Sūrah ash-Shu'arā'.

### Subject Matter and Topics

The background of the Sūrah is that the disbelievers of Makkah were persistently refusing on one pretext or the other to accept the message of Islām given by the Prophet. Sometimes they would say that he did not show them any sign to convince them of his Prophethood; sometimes they would brand him as a poet or a sorcerer and mock his message; and sometimes they would ridicule his Mission saying that his followers were either a few foolish youth or the poor people and slaves. They argued that if his Mission had really some value for the people the nobles and the elders would have accepted it first. Meanwhile on the one hand the Prophet was becoming wearied by his efforts to show them rationally the errors of their creeds and prove the truth of the Doctrines of Tawhid (Oneness of God) and the Hereafter, the disbelievers on the other were never tired of adopting one kind of obduracy after the other. This state of affairs was causing great anguish and grief to the Prophet. Such were the conditions when this Sūrah was revealed. It begins with words of consolation to the Prophet implying, why do you fret for their sake? If these people have not believed in you it is not because they have not seen any Sign but because they are stubborn. They will not listen to reason and they want to see a Sign which makes them bow their heads in humility. When this Sign is shown in due course of time they will themselves realize that what was being presented to them was the Truth.

After this introduction till verse 191 one and the same theme has been presented continuously and it is said: "The whole earth abounds in such Signs as can guide a seeker after truth to Reality but the stubborn and misguided people have never believed even after seeing the Signs whether these were the Signs of the natural phenomena or the miracles of the Prophets. These wretched people have stubbornly adhered to their erroneous creeds till the Divine scourge actually overtook them." It is to illustrate this, that the history of seven of the ancient tribes has been told who persisted in disbelief just like the disbelievers of Makkah. In this connection the following points have been stressed:

1. The Signs are of two kinds:
    a. Those which are scattered all over the earth and by seeing which an intelligent person can judge for himself whether what the Prophet is presenting is the Truth or not and
    b. Those which were seen by Pharaoh and his people, Noah's people, the people of 'Aad and the Thamūd, Lot's people and the people of Aiykah. Now it is for the disbelievers to decide which kind of the Signs they are eager to see.
2. The mentality of thc disbeliever has been the same throughout the ages; their arguments, their objections, their excuses and ploys for not believing have been similar and ultimately the fates that they met have also been the same. Likewise the Prophets in every age presented the same teachings, their personal character, their reasoning and arguments against their opponents were the same and they were all similarly blessed with mercy by God Almighty. Both these patterns of behaviour and conduct are found in history and the disbelievers could themselves see as to which respective patterns they and the Prophet belonged.
3. God is All Mighty, All Powerful and All Merciful at the same time. History contains instances of His Wrath as well as of His Mercy. Now therefore it is for the people to decide whether they would like to deserve God's Merey or His Wrath.
4. Lastly the discussion has been summed up saying "O disbelievers if at all you want to see the Signs why should you insist on seeing those horrible Signs that visited the doomed communities of the past? Why don't you see the Qur'ān which is being presented in your own language? Why don't you

see Muhammad and his Companions? Can the revelations of the Qur'ān be the work of a satan or a Jinn? Does the recipient of the Qur'ān appear to be a sorcerer? Are Muhammad and his Companions no different from a poet and his admirers? Why don't you give up disbelief and search your hearts for their judgment? When in the heart of your hearts you yourselves believe that the Revelations of the Qur'ān have nothing in common with sorcery and poetry, then you should know that you are being cruel and unjust, and will certainly meet the doom meant for the cruel and unjust."

## Sūrah 26: ash- Shu'arā'[972]

In the Name of God, the Most Compassionate, the Most Merciful

1. Tā, Seen, Meem.[973]

2. These are the verses of the clear Book.

3. Perhaps, [O Muhammad], you would kill yourself with grief that they will not be believers.

4. If We willed, We could send down to them from the sky a sign for which their necks would remain humbled.[974]

5. And no mention [i.e., revelation] comes to them anew from the Most Merciful except that they turn away from it.

6. For they have already denied, but there will come to them the news of that which they used to ridicule.

7. Did they not look at the earth - how much We have produced therein from every noble kind?

8. Indeed in that is a sign, but most of them were not to be believers.

9 And indeed, your Lord - He is the Exalted in Might, the Merciful.

10. And [mention] when your Lord called Moses, [saying], "Go to the wrong-doing people -

11. The people of Pharaoh. Will they not fear God?"

12. He said, "My Lord, indeed I fear that they will deny me

13. And that my breast will tighten and my tongue will not be fluent, so send for Aaron.

14. And they have upon me a [claim due to] sin, so I fear that they will kill me."

15. [God] said, "No. Go both of you with Our signs; indeed, We are with you, listening.

16. Go to Pharaoh and say, 'We are the messengers[975] of the Lord of the worlds,

17. [Commanded to say], 'Send with us the Children of Israel." ' "

18. [Pharaoh] said, "Did we not raise you among us as a child, and you remained among us for years of your life?

19. And [then] you did your deed which you did,[976] and you were of the ungrateful."

20. [Moses] said, "I did it, then, while I was of those astray [i.e., ignorant].

21. So I fled from you when I feared you. Then my Lord granted me judgement [i.e., wisdom and prophethood] and appointed me [as one] of the messengers.

22. And is this a favor of which you remind me - that you have enslaved the Children of Israel?"

---

972 *Ash- Shu'arā'*: The Poets.

973 See footnote to 2:1.

974 i.e., they would be compelled to believe.

975 The singular form in Arabic indicates that both were sent with a single message.

976 i.e., striking the Copt, who died as a result.

23. Said Pharaoh, "And what is the Lord of the worlds?"

24. [Moses] said, "The Lord of the heavens and earth and that between them, if you should be convinced."

25. [Pharaoh] said to those around him, "Do you not hear?"

26. [Moses] said, "Your Lord and the Lord of your first forefathers."

27. [Pharaoh] said,[977] "Indeed, your 'messenger' who has been sent to you is mad."

28. [Moses] said, "Lord of the east and the west and that between them, if you were to reason."

29. [Pharaoh] said, "If you take a God other than me, I will surely place you among those imprisoned."

30. [Moses] said, "Even if I brought you something [i.e., proof] manifest?"

31. [Pharaoh] said, "Then bring it, if you should be of the truthful."

32. So [Moses] threw his staff, and suddenly it was a serpent manifest.[978]

33. And he drew out his hand; thereupon it was white for the observers.

34. [Pharaoh] said to the eminent ones around him, "Indeed, this is a learned magician.

35. He wants to drive you out of your land by his magic, so what do you advise?"

36. They said, "Postpone [the matter of] him and his brother and send among the cities gatherers

37. Who will bring you every learned, skilled magician."

38. So the magicians were assembled for the appointment of a well-known day.[979]

39. And it was said to the people, "Will you congregate

40. That we might follow the magicians if they are the predominant?"

41. And when the magicians arrived, they said to Pharaoh, "Is there indeed for us a reward if we are the predominant?"

42. He said, "Yes, and indeed, you will then be of those near [to me]."

43. Moses said to them, "Throw whatever you will throw."

44. So they threw their ropes and their staffs and said, "By the might of Pharaoh, indeed it is we who are predominant."

45. Then Moses threw his staff, and at once it devoured what they falsified.

46. So the magicians fell down in prostration [to God].

47. They said, "We have believed in the Lord of the worlds,

48. The Lord of Moses and Aaron."

---

[977] Angrily addressing those present.
[978] i.e., clearly genuine.

[979] i.e., the morning of the day of festival. See 20:58-59.

49. [Pharaoh] said, "You believed him [i.e., Moses] before I gave you permission. Indeed, he is your leader who has taught you magic, but you are going to know. I will surely cut off your hands and your feet on opposite sides, and I will surely crucify you all."

50. They said, "No harm. Indeed, to our Lord we will return.

51. Indeed, we aspire that our Lord will forgive us our sins because we were the first of the believers."

52. And We inspired to Moses, "Travel by night with My servants; indeed, you will be pursued."

53. Then Pharaoh sent among the cities gatherers[980]

54. [And said], "Indeed, those are but a small band,

55. And indeed, they are enraging us,

56. And indeed, we are a cautious society..."

57. So We removed them from gardens and springs

58. And treasures and honourable station[981] -

59. Thus. And We caused to inherit it the Children of Israel.

60. So they pursued them at sunrise.

61. And when the two companies saw one another, the companions of Moses said, "Indeed, we are to be overtaken!"

62. [Moses] said, "No! Indeed, with me is my Lord; He will guide me."

63. Then We inspired to Moses, "Strike with your staff the sea," and it parted, and each portion was like a great towering mountain.

64. And We advanced thereto the others [i.e., the pursuers].

65. And We saved Moses and those with him, all together.

66. Then We drowned the others.

67. Indeed in that is a sign, but most of them were not to be believers.

68. And indeed, your Lord - He is the Exalted in Might, the Merciful.

69. And recite to them the news of Abraham,

70. When he said to his father and his people, "What do you worship?"

71. They said, "We worship idols and remain to them devoted."

72. He said, "Do they hear you when you supplicate?

73. Or do they benefit you, or do they harm?"

74. They said, "But we found our fathers doing thus."

75. He said, "Then do you see what you have been worshipping,

[980] Recruiters of an army to prevent the emigration of the Children of Israel.
[981] God caused them to abandon their wealth and property in pursuit of the Israelites.

76. You and your ancient forefathers?

77. Indeed, they are enemies to me, except the Lord of the worlds,[982]

78. Who created me, and He [it is who] guides me.

79. And it is He who feeds me and gives me drink.

80. And when I am ill, it is He who cures me

81. And who will cause me to die and then bring me to life

82. And who I aspire that He will forgive me my sin on the Day of Recompense."

83. [And he said], "My Lord, grant me authority and join me with the righteous.

84. And grant me a mention [i.e., reputation] of honour among later generations.

85. And place me among the inheritors of the Garden of Pleasure.

86. And forgive my father. Indeed, he has been of those astray.

87. And do not disgrace me on the Day they are [all] resurrected -

88. The Day when there will not benefit [anyone] wealth or children

89. But only one who comes to God with a sound heart."

90. And Paradise will be brought near [that Day] to the righteous.

91. And Hellfire will be brought forth for the deviators,

92. And it will be said to them, "Where are those you used to worship

93. Other than God? Can they help you or help themselves?"

94. So they will be overturned into it [i.e., Hellfire], they and the deviators

95. And the soldiers of Iblees, all together.

96. They will say while they dispute therein,

97. "By God, we were indeed in manifest error

98. When we equated you with the Lord of the worlds.

99. And no one misguided us except the criminals.

100. So now we have no intercessors

101. And not a devoted friend.

102. Then if we only had a return [to the world] and could be of the believers..."[983]

103. Indeed in that is a sign, but most of them were not to be believers.

104. And indeed, your Lord - He is the Exalted in Might, the Merciful.

105. The people of Noah denied the messengers[984]

---

[982] The people worshipped idols in addition to God.

[983] The conclusion of this verse is estimated as "...we would do this or that."

106. When their brother Noah said to them, "Will you not fear God?

107. Indeed, I am to you a trustworthy messenger.

108. So fear God and obey me.

109. And I do not ask you for it any payment. My payment is only from the Lord of the worlds.

110. So fear God and obey me."

111. They said, "Should we believe you while you are followed by the lowest [class of people]?"

112. He said, "And what is my knowledge of what they used to do?

113. Their account is only upon my Lord, if you [could] perceive.

114. And I am not one to drive away the believers.

115. I am only a clear warner."

116. They said, "If you do not desist, O Noah, you will surely be of those who are stoned."

117. He said, "My Lord, indeed my people have denied me.

118. Then judge between me and them with decisive judgement and save me and those with me of the believers."

119. So We saved him and those with him in the laden ship.

120. Then We drowned thereafter the remaining ones.

121. Indeed in that is a sign, but most of them were not to be believers.

122. And indeed, your Lord - He is the Exalted in Might, the Merciful.

123. 'Aad denied the messengers

124. When their brother Hūd said to them, "Will you not fear God?

125. Indeed, I am to you a trustworthy messenger.

126. So fear God and obey me.

127. And I do not ask you for it any payment. My payment is only from the Lord of the worlds.

128. Do you construct on every elevation a sign,[985] amusing yourselves,

129. And take for yourselves constructions [i.e., places and fortresses] that you might abide eternally?

130. And when you strike, you strike as tyrants.

131. So fear God and obey me.

132. And fear He who provided you with that which you know,

133. Provided you with grazing livestock and children

134. And gardens and springs.

135. Indeed, I fear for you the punishment of a terrible day."

---

[984] See footnote to 25:37.

[985] i.e., a symbol or indication of their wealth and power. They used to build lofty structures along the road to be seen by all those who passed by.

136. They said, "It is all the same to us whether you advise or are not of the advisors.

137. This is not but the custom of the former peoples,

138. And we are not to be punished."

139. And they denied him, so We destroyed them. Indeed in that is a sign, but most of them were not to be believers.

140. And indeed, your Lord - He is the Exalted in Might, the Merciful.

141. Thamūd denied the messengers

142. When their brother Sālih said to them, "Will you not fear God?

143. Indeed, I am to you a trustworthy messenger.

144. So fear God and obey me.

145. And I do not ask you for it any payment. My payment is only from the Lord of the worlds.

146. Will you be left in what is here, secure [from death],

147. Within gardens and springs

148. And fields of crops and palm trees with softened fruit?

149. And you carve out of the mountains, homes, with skill.

150. So fear God and obey me.

151. And do not obey the order of the transgressors,

152. Who cause corruption in the land and do not amend."

153. They said, "You are only of those affected by magic.

154. You are but a man like ourselves, so bring a sign, if you should be of the truthful."

155. He said, "This is a she-camel.[986] For her is a [time of] drink, and for you is a [time of] drink, [each] on a known day.

156. And do not touch her with harm, lest you be seized by the punishment of a terrible day."

157. But they hamstrung her and so became regretful.

158. And the punishment seized them. Indeed in that is a sign, but most of them were not to be believers.

159. And indeed, your Lord - He is the Exalted in Might, the Merciful.

160. The people of Lot denied the messengers

161. When their brother Lot said to them, "Will you not fear God?

162. Indeed, I am to you a trustworthy messenger.

163. So fear God and obey me.

164. And I do not ask you for it any payment. My payment is only from the Lord of the worlds.

165. Do you approach males among the worlds[987]

[986] Miraculously sent to them as a sign by God.

166. And leave what your Lord has created for you as mates? But you are a people transgressing."

167. They said, "If you do not desist, O Lot, you will surely be of those evicted."

168. He said, "Indeed, I am, toward your deed, of those who detest [it].

169. My Lord, save me and my family from [the consequence of] what they do."

170. So We saved him and his family, all,

171. Except an old woman[988] among those who remained behind.

172. Then We destroyed the others.

173. And We rained upon them a rain [of stones], and evil was the rain of those who were warned.

174. Indeed in that is a sign, but most of them were not to be believers.

175. And indeed, your Lord - He is the Exalted in Might, the Merciful.

176. The companions of the thicket [i.e., the people of Madyan] denied the messengers

177. When Shu'ayb said to them, "Will you not fear God?

178. Indeed, I am to you a trustworthy messenger.

179. So fear God and obey me.

[987] i.e., Are there, out of all God's creatures, any besides you who commit this unnatural act?

[988] Lot's wife, who had collaborated with the evildoers.

180. And I do not ask you for it any payment. My payment is only from the Lord of the worlds.

181. Give full measure and do not be of those who cause loss.

182. And weigh with an even [i.e., honest] balance.

183. And do not deprive people of their due and do not commit abuse on earth, spreading corruption.

184. And fear He who created you and the former creation."[989]

185. They said, "You are only of those affected by magic.

186. You are but a man like ourselves, and indeed, we think you are among the liars.

187. So cause to fall upon us fragments of the sky, if you should be of the truthful."

188. He said, "My Lord is most knowing of what you do."

189. And they denied him, so the punishment of the day of the black cloud seized them. Indeed, it was the punishment of a terrible day.

190. Indeed in that is a sign, but most of them were not to be believers.

191. And indeed, your Lord - He is the Exalted in Might, the Merciful.

192. And indeed, it [i.e., the Qur'ān] is the revelation of the Lord of the worlds.

[989] i.e., previous generations.

193. The Trustworthy Spirit [i.e., Gabriel] has brought it down

194. Upon your heart, [O Muhammad] - that you may be of the warners -

195. In a clear Arabic language.

196. And indeed, it is [mentioned] in the scriptures of former peoples.

197. And has it not been a sign to them that it is recognized by the scholars of the Children of Israel?

198. And even if We had revealed it to one among the foreigners[990]

199. And he had recited it to them [perfectly],[991] they would [still] not have been believers in it.

200. Thus have We inserted it [i.e., disbelief] into the hearts of the criminals.

201. They will not believe in it until they see the painful punishment.

202. And it will come to them suddenly while they perceive [it] not.

203. And they will say, "May we be reprieved?"

204. So for Our punishment are they impatient?

205. Then have you considered if We gave them enjoyment for years

206. And then there came to them that which they were promised?

207. They would not be availed by the enjoyment with which they were provided.

208. And We did not destroy any city except that it had warners

209. As a reminder; and never have We been unjust.

210. And the devils have not brought it [i.e., the revelation] down.[992]

211. It is not allowable for them, nor would they be able.

212. Indeed they, from [its] hearing, are removed.[993]

213. So do not invoke with God another deity and [thus] be among the punished.

214. And warn, [O Muhammad], your closest kindred.

215. And lower your wing [i.e., show kindness] to those who follow you of the believers.

216. And if they disobey you, then say, "Indeed, I am disassociated from what you are doing."

217. And rely upon the Exalted in Might, the Merciful,

218. Who sees you when you arise[994]

219. And your movement among those who prostrate.[995]

[990] i.e., the non-Arabs or those who are not fluent in the Arabic language.
[991] As a miracle from God.

[992] As was asserted by the disbelievers. Rather, it was brought by Gabriel, the Trustworthy Spirit.
[993] As mentioned in 72:9.
[994] From your bed at night for prayer while you are alone.

220. Indeed, He is the Hearing, the Knowing.

221. Shall I inform you upon whom the devils descend?

222. They descend upon every sinful liar.

223. They pass on what is heard,[996] and most of them are liars.

224. And the poets - [only] the deviators follow them;

225. Do you not see that in every valley they roam[997]

226. And that they say what they do not do?
-

227. Except those [poets] who believe and do righteous deeds and remember God often and defend [the Muslims][998] after they were wronged. And those who have wronged are going to know to what [kind of] return they will be returned.

---

[995] i.e., among those who pray with you in congregation.
[996] This was before they were prevented, as described in 72:8-9.
[997] Speaking lies indiscriminately and praising and disparaging others according to whim.
[998] By replying through poetry to the attacks of hostile poets.

## Sūrah 27: an-Naml

### Period of Revelation

The subject matter and the style bear full resemblance with the Sūrahs of the middle Makkan period and this is supported by various hadith as well.

### Theme and Topics

The Sūrah consists of two discourses, the first from the beginning of the Sūrah to the end of verse 58 and the second from verse 59 to the end of the Sūrah. The theme of the first discourse is that only those people can benefit from the guidance of the Qur'ān and become worthy of the good promises made in it who accept the realities which this Book presents as the basic realities of the universe and then follow up their belief with obedience and submission in their practical lives aswell. But the greatest hindrance for man to follow this way is the denial of the Hereafter. For it makes him irresponsible, selfish and given to worldly life which in turn makes it impossible for him to submit himself before God and to accept the moral restrictions on his lusts and desires. After this introduction three types of character have been presented.

1. The first type is characterised by Pharoah, the chiefs of Thamūd and the rebels of the people of Lot who were all heedless of the accountability of the Hereafter and had consequently become the slaves of the world. These people did not believe even after seeing the miracles. Rather they turned against those who invited them to goodness and piety. They persisted in their evil ways which are held in abhorrence by every sensible person. They did not heed the admonition even until a moment before they were overtaken by the scourge of God.
2. The second type of character is of the Prophet Solomon who had been blessed by God with wealth, kingdom and grandeur to an extent undreamt of by the chiefs of the disbelievers of Makkah. But since he regarded himself as answerable before God and had the feeling that whatever he had was only due to God's bounty, he had adopted the attitude of obediance before Him and there was no tinge of vanity in his character.
3. The third type is of the queen of Sheba who ruled over a most wealthy and well known people in the history of Arabia. She possessed all those means of life which could cause a person to become vain and conceited. Her wealth and possessions far exceeded the wealth and possessions of the Quraysh. Then she professed Shirk (polytheism) which was not only an ancestral way of life with her but she had to follow it in order to maintain her position as a ruler. Therefore it was much more difficult for her to give up shirk and adopt the way of Tawhid (Oneness of God) than it could be for a common polytheist. But when the Truth became evident to her nothing could stop her from accepting it. Her deviation was in fact due to her being born and brought up in a polytheistic environment and not because of her being a slave to her lusts and desires. Her conscience was not devoid of the sense of accountability before God.

In the second discourse at the outset attention has been drawn to some of the most glaring and visible realities of the universe and the disbelievers of Makkah have been asked one question after the other to the effect: "Do these realities testify to the creed of Shirk (polytheism) which you are following or to the truth of Tawhid (Oneness of God) to which the Qur'ān invites you?" In conclusion, the real invitation of the Qur'ān, that is, the invitation to serve One God alone, has been presented in a concise but forceful manner, and the people warned that accepting it would be to their own advantage and rejecting it to their own disadvantage. For if they deferred their faith until they saw those Signs of God after the appearance of which they would be left with no choice but to believe and submit, they should bear in mind the fact that that would be the time of judgment and believing then would be of no avail.

## Sūrah 27: an-Naml[999]

In the Name of God, the Most Compassionate, the Most Merciful

1. Tā, Seen.[1000] These are the verses of the Qur'ān [i.e., recitation] and a clear Book

2. As guidance and good tidings for the believers

3. Who establish prayer and give zakāh, and of the Hereafter they are certain [in faith].

4. Indeed, for those who do not believe in the Hereafter, We have made pleasing to them their deeds, so they wander blindly.

5. Those are the ones for whom there will be the worst of punishment, and in the Hereafter they are the greatest losers.

6. And indeed, [O Muhammad], you receive the Qur'ān from one Wise and Knowing.

7 [Mention] when Moses said to his family, "Indeed, I have perceived a fire. I will bring you from there information or will bring you a burning torch that you may warm yourselves."

8. But when he came to it, he was called, "Blessed is whoever is at the fire and whoever is around it. And exalted is God, Lord of the worlds.

9. O Moses, indeed it is I - God, the Exalted in Might, the Wise."

10. And [he was told], "Throw down your staff." But when he saw it writhing as if it were a snake, he turned in flight and did not return.[1001] [God said], "O Moses, fear not. Indeed, in My presence the messengers do not fear.

11. Otherwise, he who wrongs, then substitutes good after evil - indeed, I am Forgiving and Merciful.

12. And put your hand into the opening of your garment [at the breast]; it will come out white without disease. [These are] among the nine signs [you will take] to Pharaoh and his people. Indeed, they have been a people defiantly disobedient."

13. But when there came to them Our visible signs, they said, "This is obvious magic."

14. And they rejected them, while their [inner] selves were convinced thereof, out of injustice and haughtiness. So see how was the end of the corrupters.

15. And We had certainly given to David and Solomon knowledge, and they said, "Praise [is due] to God, who has favored us over many of His believing servants."

16. And Solomon inherited David. He said, "O people, we have been taught the language of birds, and we have been given from all things. Indeed, this is evident bounty."

17. And gathered for Solomon were his soldiers of the jinn and men and birds, and they were [marching] in rows

18. Until, when they came upon the valley of the ants, an ant said, "O ants, enter your dwellings that you not be crushed

999 *An-Naml*: The Ants.
1000 See footnote to 2:1.

1001 Or "did not look back."

by Solomon and his soldiers while they perceive not."

19. So [Solomon] smiled, amused at her speech, and said, "My Lord, enable me[1002] to be grateful for Your favor which You have bestowed upon me and upon my parents and to do righteousness of which You approve. And admit me by Your mercy into [the ranks of] Your righteous servants."[1003]

20. And he took attendance of the birds and said, "Why do I not see the hoopoe - or is he among the absent?

21. I will surely punish him with a severe punishment or slaughter him unless he brings me clear authorization."

22. But he [i.e., the hoopoe] stayed not long and said, "I have encompassed [in knowledge] that which you have not encompassed, and I have come to you from Sheba with certain news.

23. Indeed, I found [there] a woman ruling them, and she has been given of all things, and she has a great throne.

24. I found her and her people prostrating to the sun instead of God, and Satan has made their deeds pleasing to them and averted them from [His] way, so they are not guided,

25. [And] so they do not prostrate to God, who brings forth what is hidden within the heavens and the earth and knows what you conceal and what you declare -

[1002] More literally, "gather within me the utmost strength and ability."
[1003] Or "with Your righteous servants [into paradise]."

26. God - there is no deity except Him, Lord of the Great Throne."

27. [Solomon] said, "We will see whether you were truthful or were of the liars.

28. Take this letter of mine and deliver it to them. Then leave them and see what [answer] they will return."

29. She said, "O eminent ones, indeed, to me has been delivered a noble letter.

30. Indeed, it is from Solomon, and indeed, it is [i.e., reads]: 'In the name of God, the Entirely Merciful, the Especially Merciful,

31. Be not haughty with me but come to me in submission [as Muslims].' "

32. She said, "O eminent ones, advise me in my affair. I would not decide a matter until you witness [for] me."[1004]

33. They said, "We are men of strength and of great military might, but the command is yours, so see what you will command."

34. She said, "Indeed kings - when they enter a city, they ruin it and render the honoured of its people humbled. And thus do they do.

35. But indeed, I will send to them a gift and see with what [reply] the messengers will return."

36. So when they came to Solomon, he said, "Do you provide me with wealth? But what God has given me is better than what He has given you. Rather, it is you who rejoice in your gift.

[1004] i.e., are present with me or testify in my favor.

37. Return to them, for we will surely come to them with soldiers that they will be powerless to encounter, and we will surely expel them therefrom in humiliation, and they will be debased."

38. [Solomon] said, "O assembly [of jinn], which of you will bring me her throne before they come to me in submission?"

39. A powerful one from among the jinn said, "I will bring it to you before you rise from your place, and indeed, I am for this [task] strong and trustworthy."

40. Said one who had knowledge from the Scripture, "I will bring it to you before your glance returns to you." And when [Solomon] saw it placed before him, he said, "This is from the favor of my Lord to test me whether I will be grateful or ungrateful. And whoever is grateful - his gratitude is only for [the benefit of] himself. And whoever is ungrateful - then indeed, my Lord is Free of need and Generous."

41. He said, "Disguise for her her throne; we will see whether she will be guided [to truth] or will be of those who is not guided."

42. So when she arrived, it was said [to her], "Is your throne like this?" She said, "[It is] as though it was it." [Solomon said], "And we were given knowledge before her, and we have been Muslims [in submission to God].

43. And that which she was worshipping other than God had averted her [from submission to Him]. Indeed, she was from a disbelieving people."

44. She was told, "Enter the palace." But when she saw it, she thought it was a body of water[1005] and uncovered her shins [to wade through]. He said, "Indeed, it is a palace [whose floor is] made smooth with glass." She said, "My Lord, indeed I have wronged myself, and I submit with Solomon to God, Lord of the worlds."

45. And We had certainly sent to Thamūd their brother Sālih, [saying], "Worship God," and at once they were two parties conflicting.

46. He said, "O my people, why are you impatient for evil before [i.e., instead of] good?[1006] Why do you not seek forgiveness of God that you may receive mercy?"

47. They said, "We consider you a bad omen, you and those with you." He said, "Your omen [i.e., fate] is with God. Rather, you are a people being tested."[1007]

48. And there were in the city nine family heads causing corruption in the land and not amending [its affairs].

49. They said, "Take a mutual oath by God that we will kill him by night, he and his family. Then we will say to his executor,[1008] 'We did not witness the destruction of his family, and indeed, we are truthful.' "

50. And they planned a plan, and We planned a plan, while they perceived not.

---

1005 The floor was transparent, and beneath it was flowing water.

1006 By challenging Sālih to bring on the promised punishment rather than asking for mercy from God.

1007 Or "being tempted [by Satan]."

1008 i.e., the one responsible for executing his will and avenging his blood.

51. Then look how was the outcome of their plan - that We destroyed them and their people, all.

52. So those are their houses, desolate because of the wrong they had done. Indeed in that is a sign for people who know.

53. And We saved those who believed and used to fear God.

54. And [mention] Lot, when he said to his people, "Do you commit immorality[1009] while you are seeing?[1010]

55. Do you indeed approach men with desire instead of women? Rather, you are a people behaving ignorantly."

56. But the answer of his people was not except that they said, "Expel the family of Lot from your city. Indeed, they are people who keep themselves pure."

57. So We saved him and his family, except for his wife; We destined her to be of those who remained behind.

58. And We rained upon them a rain [of stones], and evil was the rain of those who were warned.

59. Say, [O Muhammad], "Praise be to God, and peace upon His servants whom He has chosen. Is God better or what they associate with Him?"

60. [More precisely], is He [not best] who created the heavens and the earth and sent down for you rain from the sky, causing to grow thereby gardens of joyful beauty which you could not [otherwise] have grown the trees thereof? Is there a deity with God?[1011] [No], but they are a people who ascribe equals [to Him].

61. Is He [not best] who made the earth a stable ground and placed within it rivers and made for it firmly set mountains and placed between the two seas a barrier? Is there a deity with God? [No], but most of them do not know.

62. Is He [not best] who responds to the desperate one when he calls upon Him and removes evil and makes you inheritors of the earth?[1012] Is there a deity with God? Little do you remember.

63. Is He [not best] who guides you through the darknesses of the land and sea and who sends the winds as good tidings before His mercy? Is there a deity with God? High is God above whatever they associate with Him.

64. Is He [not best] who begins creation and then repeats it and who provides for you from the heaven and earth? Is there a deity with God? Say, "Produce your proof, if you should be truthful."

65. Say, "None in the heavens and earth knows the unseen except God, and they do not perceive when they will be resurrected."

66. Rather, their knowledge is arrested concerning the Hereafter. Rather, they are in doubt about it. Rather, they are, concerning it, blind.

---

1009 Homosexual acts.

1010 i.e., openly. Another meaning is "...while you are aware [that it is wrong]."

1011 Three meanings are implied: "Is there another god who did all of this with God?" or "Is there any deity to be worshipped along with God?" or "Is there a deity to be compared with God?"

1012 Generation after generation.

67. And those who disbelieve say, "When we have become dust as well as our forefathers, will we indeed be brought out [of the graves]?

68. We have been promised this, we and our forefathers, before. This is not but legends of the former peoples."

69. Say, [O Muhammad], "Proceed [i.e., travel] through the land and observe how was the end of the criminals."

70. And grieve not over them or be in distress from what they conspire.

71. And they say, "When is [the fulfillment of] this promise, if you should be truthful?"

72. Say, "Perhaps it is close behind you [i.e., very near] - some of that for which you are impatient.

73. And indeed, your Lord is full of bounty for the people, but most of them do not show gratitude."

74. And indeed, your Lord knows what their breasts conceal and what they declare.

75. And there is nothing concealed[1013] within the heaven and the earth except that it is in a clear Register.[1014]

76. Indeed, this Qur'ān relates to the Children of Israel most of that over which they disagree.

77. And indeed, it is guidance and mercy for the believers.

78. Indeed, your Lord will judge between them by His [wise] judgement. And He is the Exalted in Might, the Knowing.

79. So rely upon God; indeed, you are upon the clear truth.

80. Indeed, you will not make the dead hear, nor will you make the deaf hear the call when they have turned their backs retreating.

81. And you cannot guide the blind away from their error. You will only make hear those who believe in Our verses so they are Muslims [i.e., submitting to God].

82. And when the word [i.e., decree] befalls them,[1015] We will bring forth for them a creature from the earth speaking to them, [saying] that the people were, of Our verses, not certain [in faith].

83. And [warn of] the Day when We will gather from every nation a company of those who deny Our signs, and they will be [driven] in rows

84. Until, when they arrive [at the place of Judgement], He will say, "Did you deny My signs while you encompassed them not in knowledge, or what [was it that] you were doing?"

85. And the decree will befall them[1016] for the wrong they did, and they will not [be able to] speak.

86. Do they not see that We made the night that they may rest therein and the day giving sight? Indeed in that are signs for a people who believe.

---

1013 Literally, "absent [from the senses]."
1014 The Preserved Slate (*al-Lawh al-Mahfūṯẖ*), which is with God.

1015 At the approach of the Hour.
1016 God's decree will come into effect upon them, and His promise will be fulfilled.

87. And [warn of] the Day the Horn will be blown, and whoever is in the heavens and whoever is on the earth will be terrified except whom God wills. And all will come to Him humbled.

88. And you see the mountains, thinking them rigid, while they will pass as the passing of clouds. [It is] the work of God, who perfected all things. Indeed, He is Acquainted with that which you do.

89. Whoever comes [at Judgement] with a good deed will have better than it, and they, from the terror of that Day, will be safe.

90. And whoever comes with an evil deed[1017] - their faces will be overturned into the Fire, [and it will be said], "Are you recompensed except for what you used to do?"

91. [Say, O Muhammad], "I have only been commanded to worship the Lord of this city,[1018] who made it sacred and to whom [belongs] all things. And I am commanded to be of the Muslims [i.e., those who submit to God]

92. And to recite the Qur'ān." And whoever is guided is only guided for [the benefit of] himself; and whoever strays - say, "I am only [one] of the warners."

93. And say, "[All] praise is [due] to God. He will show you His signs, and you will recognize them. And your Lord is not unaware of what you do."

---

[1017] Without having repented. It may refer generally to any sin or more specifically to association of another with God.
[1018] Or region, meaning Makkah and its surroundings.

## Sūrah 28: al-Qasas

### Period of Revelation

According to Ibn Abbas the Sūrahs ash-Shu'arā', an-Naml and al-Qasas were sent down one after the other. The language, the style and the theme also show that the period of the revelation of these three Sūrahs is nearly the same. Another reason for their close resemblance is that the different parts of the story of Prophet Moses is mentioned in these Sūrahs together to make up a complete story.

### Theme and Topics

The main theme is to remove the doubts and objections that were being raised against the Prophethood of the Prophet Muhammad and to invalidate the excuses which were being offered for not believing in him. For this purpose first the story of the Prophet Moses has been related which by analogy with the period of revelation impresses the following points in the listener's mind automatically:

1. First God provides the means and motives of whatever He wills to do in imperceptible ways. Thus God so arranged things that the child through whom Pharaoh had to be removed from power was bred and brought up in his own house and he could not know whom he was fostering. Who can then fight God and frustrate Him by his machinations.
2. Secondly Prophethood is not granted to a person amid festivities by issuing a proclamation from the earth and heavens. You wonder how Muhammad has been blessed with Prophethood unexpectedly all of a sudden but Moses whom you yourselves acknowledge as a Prophet (v.48) had also become a Prophet unexpectedly while on a journey and nobody had known what event had occurred in the desolation at the foot of Mt. Sinai. Even Moses himself did not know a moment before what he was going to be blessed with. He in fact had gone to bring a piece of the fire but had returned with the gift of Prophethood
3. Thirdly the person from whom God wants to take some service comes out without any army and armour and without an apparent helper or force at his back yet he puts to rout much stronger and better equipped opponents. The contrast that existed between the strengths of Moses and Pharaoh was much more prominent and glaring than that which existed between Muhammad and the Quraysh; yet the world knows who had come out victorious in the end and who had been routed.
4. Fourthly you refer to Moses again and again and say, 'Why has Muhammad not been given the same which was given to Moses?' i. e. miracles of the staff and the shining hand etc. as if to suggest that you would readily believe only if you were shown the kind of the miracles that were shown by Moses to Pharaoh. But do you know what sort of response was made by those who were shown those miracles? They had not believed even after seeing the miracles and had only said, 'This is magic' for they were involved in stubbornness and hostility to the Truth. The same malady afflicts you today. Will you believe only when you are shown the same kind of miracles? Then do you know what fate the disbelievers had met even after seeing the miracles? They were annihilated by God. Do you now wish to meet the same doom by asking for the miracles in your obstinacy?

These were the things which were automatically impressed in the mind of every listener who heard this story in the pagan environment of Makkah for a similar conflict was going on at that time between the Prophet and disbelievers of Makkah as had already taken place between the Prophet Moses and Pharaoh before. This was the background against which the story of the Prophet Moses was narrated so that a perfect analogy was established automatically in every detail between the conditions prevailing then in Makkah and those existing in the time of the Prophet Moses. Then from verse 43 onward the discourse turns to the real theme.

In the first place the narration of a two thousand year old historical event by the Prophet with such accuracy and detail is presented as a proof of his Prophethood although he was un-lettered and the people of his city and clan knew full well that he had no access to any source of such information as they could point out.

Then his appointment as a Prophet is put forward as God's mercy to them, for they were heedless and God had made this arrangement for their guidance. Then their oft-repeated objection, "Why has not this Prophet brought the miracles which Moses had brought?" has been answered. It is said to them, "How can you be justified in demanding miracles from this Prophet when you did not believe in Moses either, who, as you yourselves acknowledge, had brought miracles from God? You can still see the truth only if you do not serve your lusts and whims. But if you remained afflicted with this malady, you would never see it even though you were shown any kind of miracles."

Then the disbelievers of Makkah have been warned and put to shame for an event that occurred in those very days. Some Christians had come to Makkah and embraced Islām when they heard the Qur'ān from the Prophet. Instead of learning any lesson from this the Makkans were so upset at this that their leader, Abu Jahl, disgraced those people publicly. In conclusion, the excuse that the disbelievers put forward for not believing in the Prophet has been dealt with. What they feared was this: "If we give up the polytheistic creed of the Arabs and accept the doctrine of Tawhid instead, this will put an end to our supremacy in the religious, political and economic fields, which, in turn, will destroy our position of the most influential tribe of Arabia and we shall be left with no refuge anywhere in the land." As this was the real motive of the chiefs of the Quraysh for their antagonism towards the Truth, and their doubts and objections were only the pretenses, which they invented to deceive the common people, God has dealt with these fully till the end of the Sūrah, considered each aspect of these in a wise manner and offered the remedy for their basic ailment due to which those people judged the Truth and falsehood only from the viewpoint of their worldly interests.

## Sūrah 28: al-Qasas[1019]

In the Name of God, the Most Compassionate, the Most Merciful

1. Tā, Seen, Meem.[1020]

2. These are the verses of the clear Book.

3. We recite to you from the news of Moses and Pharaoh in truth for a people who believe.

4. Indeed, Pharaoh exalted himself in the land and made its people into factions, oppressing a sector among them, slaughtering their [newborn] sons and keeping their females alive. Indeed, he was of the corrupters.

5. And We wanted to confer favor upon those who were oppressed in the land and make them leaders and make them inheritors

6. And establish them in the land and show Pharaoh and [his minister] Hāmān and their soldiers through them[1021] that which they had feared.

7. And We inspired to the mother of Moses, "Suckle him; but when you fear for him, cast him into the river and do not fear and do not grieve. Indeed, We will return him to you and will make him [one] of the messengers."

8. And the family of Pharaoh picked him up [out of the river] so that he would become to them an enemy and a [cause of] grief. Indeed, Pharaoh and Hāmān and their soldiers were deliberate sinners.

9. And the wife of Pharaoh said, "[He will be] a comfort of the eye [i.e., pleasure] for me and for you. Do not kill him; perhaps he may benefit us, or we may adopt him as a son." And they perceived not.[1022]

10. And the heart of Moses' mother became empty [of all else]. She was about to disclose [the matter concerning] him had We not bound fast her heart that she would be of the believers.

11. And she said to his sister, "Follow him"; so she watched him from a distance while they perceived not.

12. And We had prevented from him [all] wet nurses before,[1023] so she said, "Shall I direct you to a household that will be responsible for him for you while they are to him [for his upbringing] sincere?"

13. So We restored him to his mother that she might be content and not grieve and that she would know that the promise of God is true. But most of them [i.e., the people] do not know.

14. And when he attained his full strength and was [mentally] mature, We bestowed upon him judgement and knowledge. And thus do We reward the doers of good.

15. And he entered the city at a time of inattention by its people[1024] and found therein two men fighting: one from his faction and one from among his ene-

---

1019 *Al-Qasas*: The Narrative (or Story).

1020 See footnote to 2:1.

1021 By means of those whom they had oppressed and enslaved.

1022 What would be the result of that.

1023 Prior to that, Moses had refused to nurse from any other woman.

1024 i.e., during the noon period of rest.

my. And the one from his faction called for help to him against the one from his enemy, so Moses struck him and [unintentionally] killed him. [Moses] said, "This is from the work of Satan. Indeed, he is a manifest, misleading enemy."

16. He said, "My Lord, indeed I have wronged myself, so forgive me," and He forgave him. Indeed, He is the Forgiving, the Merciful.

17. He said, "My Lord, for the favor You bestowed upon me, I will never be an assistant to the criminals."

18. And he became inside the city fearful and anticipating [exposure], when suddenly the one who sought his help the previous day cried out to him [once again]. Moses said to him, "Indeed, you are an evident, [persistent] deviator."

19. And when he wanted to strike the one who was an enemy to both of them, he[1025] said, "O Moses, do you intend to kill me as you killed someone yesterday? You only want to be a tyrant in the land and do not want to be of the amenders."

20. And a man came from the farthest end of the city, running. He said, "O Moses, indeed the eminent ones are conferring over you [intending] to kill you, so leave [the city]; indeed, I am to you of the sincere advisors."

21. So he left it, fearful and anticipating [apprehension]. He said, "My Lord, save me from the wrongdoing people."

22. And when he directed himself toward Madyan, he said, "Perhaps my Lord will guide me to the sound way."

23. And when he came to the water [i.e., well] of Madyan, he found there a crowd of people watering [their flocks], and he found aside from them two women driving back [their flocks]. He said, "What is your circumstance?" They said, "We do not water until the shepherds dispatch [their flocks]; and our father is an old man."

24. So he watered [their flocks] for them; then he went back to the shade and said, "My Lord, indeed I am, for whatever good You would send down to me, in need."

25. Then one of the two women came to him walking with shyness. She said, "Indeed, my father invites you that he may reward you for having watered for us." So when he came to him[1026] and related to him the story, he said, "Fear not. You have escaped from the wrongdoing people."

26. One of the women said, "O my father, hire him. Indeed, the best one you can hire is the strong and the trustworthy."

27. He said, "Indeed, I wish to wed you one of these, my two daughters, on [the condition] that you serve me for eight years; but if you complete ten, it will be [as a favor] from you. And I do not wish to put you in difficulty. You will

[1025] i.e., the Israelite, thinking that Moses meant to strike him. Some commentators have attributed the words to the Copt; however, the Israelite was the only one who knew of the previous occurrence.

[1026] Prophet Shu'ayb, the father of the two women.

find me, if God wills, from among the righteous."

28. [Moses] said, "That is [established] between me and you. Whichever of the two terms I complete - there is no injustice to me, and God, over what we say, is Witness."

29. And when Moses had completed the term and was traveling with his family, he perceived from the direction of the mount a fire. He said to his family, "Stay here; indeed, I have perceived a fire. Perhaps I will bring you from there [some] information or burning wood from the fire that you may warm yourselves."

30. But when he came to it, he was called from the right side of the valley in a blessed spot - from the tree,[1027] "O Moses, indeed I am God, Lord of the worlds."

31. And [he was told], "Throw down your staff." But when he saw it writhing as if it was a snake, he turned in flight and did not return.[1028] [God said], "O Moses, approach and fear not. Indeed, you are of the secure.

32. Insert your hand into the opening of your garment; it will come out white, without disease. And draw in your arm close to you [as prevention] from fear, for those are two proofs from your Lord to Pharaoh and his establishment. Indeed, they have been a people defiantly disobedient."

33. He said, "My Lord, indeed, I killed from among them someone, and I fear they will kill me.

[1027] Which was within the fire.
[1028] Or "did not look back."

34. And my brother Aaron is more fluent than me in tongue, so send him with me as support, verifying me. Indeed, I fear that they will deny me."

35. [God] said, "We will strengthen your arm through your brother and grant you both supremacy so they will not reach you. [It will be] through Our signs; you and those who follow you will be the predominant."

36. But when Moses came to them with Our signs as clear evidences, they said, "This is not except invented magic, and we have not heard of this [religion] among our forefathers."

37. And Moses said, "My Lord is more knowing [than we or you] of who has come with guidance from Him and to whom will be succession in the home.[1029] Indeed, wrongdoers do not succeed."

38. And Pharaoh said, "O eminent ones, I have not known you to have a god other than me. Then ignite for me, O Hāmān, [a fire] upon the clay[1030] and make for me a tower that I may look at the God of Moses. And indeed, I do think he is among the liars."

39. And he was arrogant, he and his soldiers, in the land, without right, and they thought that they would not be returned to Us.

40. So We took him and his soldiers and threw them into the sea.[1031] So see how was the end of the wrongdoers.

[1029] i.e., in this world or in the Hereafter.
[1030] From which bricks are made.
[1031] God caused them to leave all their wordly wealth behind and enter the sea in pursuit of the Children of Israel. See 26:52-66.

41. And We made them leaders[1032] inviting to the Fire, and on the Day of Resurrection they will not be helped.

42. And We caused to overtake them in this world a curse, and on the Day of Resurrection they will be of the despised.[1033]

43. And We gave Moses the Scripture, after We had destroyed the former generations, as enlightenment for the people and guidance and mercy that they might be reminded.

44. And you, [O Muhammad], were not on the western side [of the mount] when We revealed to Moses the command, and you were not among the witnesses [to that].

45. But We produced [many] generations [after Moses], and prolonged was their duration.[1034] And you were not a resident among the people of Madyan, reciting to them Our verses, but We were senders [of this message].[1035]

46. And you were not at the side of the mount when We called [Moses] but [were sent] as a mercy from your Lord to warn a people to whom no warner had come before you that they might be reminded.

47. And if not that a disaster should strike them for what their hands put forth [of sins] and they would say, "Our Lord, why did You not send us a messenger so we could have followed Your verses and been among the believers?"...[1036]

48. But when the truth came to them from Us, they said, "Why was he not given like that which was given to Moses?" Did they not disbelieve in that which was given to Moses before? They said, "[They are but] two works of magic supporting each other,[1037] and indeed we are, in both, disbelievers."

49. Say, "Then bring a scripture from God which is more guiding than either of them that I may follow it, if you should be truthful."

50. But if they do not respond to you - then know that they only follow their [own] desires. And who is more astray than one who follows his desire without guidance from God? Indeed, God does not guide the wrongdoing people.

51. And We have [repeatedly] conveyed to them the word [i.e., the Qur'ān] that they might be reminded.

52. Those to whom We gave the Scripture before it - they[1038] are believers in it.

53. And when it is recited to them, they say, "We have believed in it; indeed, it is the truth from our Lord. Indeed we were, [even] before it, Muslims [i.e., submitting to God]."

---

[1032] i.e., examples or precedents, followed by subsequent tyrants.
[1033] Literally, "those made hideous," who will be far removed from all good and mercy.
[1034] So they forgot and neglected the ordinances of God
[1035] The Prophet had no way of obtaining this information except through God's revelation.
[1036] The conclusion of the sentence is understood to be "...We would not have sent messengers," meaning that God sent messengers and sent Muhammad with the final scripture to mankind so that no one could claim that punishment was imposed unjustly without warning.
[1037] The reference is by the disbelievers of Quraysh to the Qu'rān and the Torah.
[1038] i.e., the sincere believers among them.

54. Those will be given their reward twice for what they patiently endured and [because] they avert evil through good, and from what We have provided them they spend.

55. And when they hear ill speech, they turn away from it and say, "For us are our deeds, and for you are your deeds. Peace will be upon you;[1039] we seek not the ignorant."

56. Indeed, [O Muhammad], you do not guide whom you like, but God guides whom He wills. And He is most knowing of the [rightly] guided.

57. And they [i.e., the Quraysh] say, "If we were to follow the guidance with you, we would be swept[1040] from our land." Have We not established for them a safe sanctuary to which are brought the fruits of all things as provision from Us? But most of them do not know.

58. And how many a city have We destroyed that was insolent in its [way of] living, and those are their dwellings which have not been inhabited after them except briefly.[1041] And it is We who were the inheritors.

59. And never would your Lord have destroyed the cities until He had sent to their mother [i.e., principal city] a messenger reciting to them Our verses. And We would not destroy the cities except while their people were wrongdoers.

60. And whatever thing you [people] have been given - it is [only for] the enjoyment of worldly life and its adornment. And what is with God is better and more lasting; so will you not use reason?

61. Then is he whom We have promised a good promise which he will meet [i.e., obtain] like he for whom We provided enjoyment of worldly life [but] then he is, on the Day of Resurrection, among those presented [for punishment in Hell]?

62. And [warn of] the Day He will call them and say, "Where are My 'partners' which you used to claim?"

63. Those upon whom the word[1042] will have come into effect will say, "Our Lord, these are the ones we led to error. We led them to error just as we were in error. We declare our disassociation [from them] to You. They did not used to worship [i.e., obey] us."[1043]

64. And it will be said, "Invoke your 'partners,' " and they will invoke them; but they will not respond to them, and they will see the punishment. If only they had followed guidance!

65. And [mention] the Day He will call them and say, "What did you answer the messengers?"

66. But the information[1044] will be unapparent to them that Day, so they will not [be able to] ask one another.

[1039] This is not the Islāmic greeting of "Peace be upon you." Rather, it means "You are secure from being treated in a like manner by us."
[1040] By the other Arab tribes.
[1041] By travellers seeking temporary shelter. The reference is to the ruins which were visible to the Quraysh during their journeys.

[1042] The decree for their punishment.
[1043] i.e., We did not compel them, and they did not obey us; instead, they obeyed their own desires and inclinations.
[1044] By which they might invent lies or excuses.

67. But as for one who had repented, believed, and done righteousness, it is expected [i.e., promised by God] that he will be among the successful.

68. And your Lord creates what He wills and chooses; not for them was the choice. Exalted is God and high above what they associate with Him.

69. And your Lord knows what their breasts conceal and what they declare.

70. And He is God; there is no deity except Him. To Him is [due all] praise in the first [life] and the Hereafter. And His is the [final] decision, and to Him you will be returned.

71. Say, "Have you considered:[1045] if God should make for you the night continuous until the Day of Resurrection, what deity other than God could bring you light? Then will you not hear?"

72. Say, "Have you considered: if God should make for you the day continuous until the Day of Resurrection, what deity other than God could bring you a night in which you may rest? Then will you not see?"

73. And out of His mercy He made for you the night and the day that you may rest therein and [by day] seek from His bounty and [that] perhaps you will be grateful.

74. And [warn of] the Day He will call them and say, "Where are my 'partners' which you used to claim?"

75. And We will extract from every nation a witness and say, "Produce your proof," and they will know that the truth belongs to God, and lost from them is that which they used to invent.

76. Indeed, Qārūn was from the people of Moses, but he tyrannized them. And We gave him of treasures whose keys would burden a band of strong men; thereupon his people said to him, "Do not exult. Indeed, God does not like the exultant.

77. But seek, through that which God has given you, the home of the Hereafter; and [yet], do not forget your share of the world. And do good as God has done good to you. And desire not corruption in the land. Indeed, God does not like corrupters."

78. He said, "I was only given it because of knowledge I have." Did he not know that God had destroyed before him of generations those who were greater than him in power and greater in accumulation [of wealth]? But the criminals, about their sins, will not be asked.[1046]

79. So he came out before his people in his adornment. Those who desired the worldly life said, "Oh, would that we had like what was given to Qārūn. Indeed, he is one of great fortune."

80. But those who had been given knowledge said, "Woe to you! The reward of God is better for he who believes and does righteousness. And none are granted it except the patient."

81. And We caused the earth to swallow him and his home. And there was for him no company to aid him other than

[1045] Meaning "Inform me if you really know."

[1046] There will be no need to enumerate their sins separately, as their quantity is obvious and more than sufficient to warrant punishment in Hell.

God, nor was he of those who [could] defend themselves.

82. And those who had wished for his position the previous day began to say, "Oh, how God extends provision to whom He wills of His servants and restricts it! If not that God had conferred favor on us, He would have caused it to swallow us. Oh, how the disbelievers do not succeed!"

83. That home of the Hereafter We assign to those who do not desire exaltedness upon the earth or corruption. And the [best] outcome is for the righteous.

84. Whoever comes [on the Day of Judgement] with a good deed will have better than it; and whoever comes with an evil deed - then those who did evil deeds will not be recompensed except [as much as] what they used to do.

85. Indeed, [O Muhammad], He who imposed upon you the Qur'ān will take you back to a place of return.[1047] Say, "My Lord is most knowing of who brings guidance and who is in clear error."

86. And you were not expecting that the Book would be conveyed to you, but [it is] a mercy from your Lord. So do not be an assistant to the disbelievers.[1048]

87. And never let them avert you from the verses of God after they have been revealed to you. And invite [people] to your Lord. And never be of those who associate others with God.

88. And do not invoke with God another deity. There is no deity except Him. Everything will be destroyed except His Face.[1049] His is the judgement, and to Him you will be returned.

[1047] Meaning to Makkah (in this life) or to Paradise (in the Hereafter).
[1048] In their religion by making any concessions to their beliefs.

[1049] i.e., except Himself.

## Sūrah 29: al-'Ankabūt

### Period of Revelation

Verses 56 to 60 clearly show that this Sūrah was sent down a little before the migration to Abassinyah and this is supported by the internal evidence of the subject matter as well. Some commentators have opined that since it mentions the hypocrites and hypocrisy appeared in Madinah the first ten verses of this Sūrah were revealed at Madinah and the rest of it at Makkah; whereas the people whose hypocrisy has been mentioned here are those who had adopted a hypocritical way of life because they were afraid of the oppression and extreme physical torture to which the Muslims were being subjected by the disbelievers. Evidently this kind of hypocrisy could be there only at Makkah and not at Madinah. Similarly some other commentators seeing that in this Sūrah the Muslims have been exhorted to migrate have regarded it as the last Sūrah to be revealed at Makkah whereas the Muslims had migrated to Abassinyah even before their migration to Madinah. These opinions are not based on any tradition but on the internal evidence of the subject matter. The internal evidence when considered against the subject matter of the Sūrah as a whole points to the conditions prevailing in the time of the migration to Abassinyah and not to the last stage at Makkah.

### Theme and Subject Matter

A perusal of the Sūrah shows that the period of its revelation was the period of extreme persecution of the Muslims at Makkah. The disbelievers were opposing and fighting Islām tooth and nail and the new reverts were being subjected to the severest oppression. Such were the conditions when God sent down this Sūrah to strengthen and encourage the sincere Muslims as well as to put to shame those who were showing weakness of the faith. Besides, the disbelievers of Makkah have been threatened and warned not to invite for themselves the fate that the antagonists of the Truth have been experiencing in every age.

In this connection the questions that some young men were facing in those days have also been answered. For instance their parents were urging them to abandon Muhammad and return to their ancestral religion for they argued: "The Qur'ān in which you have put your faith regards the rights of the parents as the uppermost; therefore listen to what we say; otherwise you will be working against the dictates of your own Faith." This has been answered in verse 8. Similarly the people of some clans said to the new reverts to Islām, 'Leave the question of punishments etc. to us. Listen to us and abandon this man. If God seizes you in the Hereafter we will come forward and say 'Lord these people are innocent: we had forced them to give up the Faith; therefore seize us.' This has been dealt with in v. 12-13.

The stories mentioned in this Sūrah also impress the same point mostly as if to say, 'Look at the Prophets of the past: they were made to suffer great hardships and were treated cruelly for long periods. Then at last they were helped by God. Therefore take heart: God's succour will certainly come. But a period of trial and tribulation has to be undergone. Besides teaching this lesson to the Muslims the disbelievers also have been warned as if to say, if you are not being immediately seized by God you should not form the wrong impression that you will never be seized. The signs of the doomed nations of the past are before you. Just see how they met their doom and how God succoured the Prophets.

Then the Muslims have been instructed to the effect: "If you feel that the persecution has become unbearable for you, you should give up your homes instead of giving up your Faith: God's earth is vast: seek a new place where you can worship God with the full peace of mind." Besides all this the disbelievers also have been urged to understand Islām. The realities of Tawhid (Oneness of God) and the Hereafter have been impressed with rational arguments, Shirk (polytheism) has been refuted and drawing their attention towards the signs in the universe they have been told that all these Signs confirm the teachings that the Prophet is presenting before them.

## Sūrah 29: al-'Ankabūt[1050]

In the Name of God, the Most Compassionate, the Most Merciful

1. Alif, Lām, Meem[1051]

2. Do the people think that they will be left to say, "We believe" and they will not be tried?

3. But We have certainly tried those before them, and God will surely make evident those who are truthful, and He will surely make evident the liars.

4. Or do those who do evil deeds think they can outrun [i.e., escape] Us? Evil is what they judge.

5. Whoever should hope for the meeting with God - indeed, the term [decreed] by God is coming. And He is the Hearing, the Knowing.

6. And whoever strives only strives for [the benefit of] himself. Indeed, God is free from need of the worlds.

7. And those who believe and do righteous deeds - We will surely remove from them their misdeeds and will surely reward them according to the best of what they used to do.

8. And We have enjoined upon man goodness to parents. But if they endeavor to make you associate with Me that of which you have no knowledge,[1052] do not obey them. To Me is your return, and I will inform you about what you used to do.

9. And those who believe and do righteous deeds - We will surely admit them among the righteous [into Paradise].

10. And of the people are some who say, "We believe in God," but when one [of them] is harmed for [the cause of] God, they consider the trial [i.e., harm] of the people as [if it were] the punishment of God. But if victory comes from your Lord, they say, "Indeed, We were with you." Is not God most knowing of what is within the breasts of all worlds [i.e., all creatures]?

11. And God will surely make evident those who believe, and He will surely make evident the hypocrites.

12. And those who disbelieve say to those who believe, "Follow our way, and we will carry your sins."[1053] But they will not carry anything of their sins. Indeed, they are liars.

13. But they will surely carry their [own] burdens and [other] burdens along with their burdens,[1054] and they will surely be questioned on the Day of Resurrection about what they used to invent.

14. And We certainly sent Noah to his people, and he remained among them a thousand years minus fifty years, and the flood seized them while they were wrongdoers.

15. But We saved him and the companions of the ship, and We made it[1055] a sign for the worlds.

---

[1050] *Al-'Ankabūt:* The Spider.
[1051] See footnote to 2:1.
[1052] i.e., no knowledge of its divinity. There can be no knowledge about something which is nonexistent or untrue.
[1053] The phrase may also read: "and let us carry your sins," i.e., the responsibility for your sins.
[1054] Besides their own sins, they will carry those of the people they misled, although it will not lessen the burden of the latter.
[1055] i.e., the ship, the event or the story.

16. And [We sent] Abraham, when he said to his people, "Worship God and fear Him. That is best for you, if you should know.

17. You only worship, besides God, idols, and you produce a falsehood. Indeed, those you worship besides God do not possess for you [the power of] provision. So seek from God provision and worship Him and be grateful to Him. To Him you will be returned."

18. And if you [people] deny [the message] - already nations before you have denied. And there is not upon the Messenger except [the duty of] clear notification.[1056]

19. Have they not considered how God begins creation and then repeats it? Indeed that, for God, is easy.

20. Say, [O Muhammad], "Travel through the land and observe how He began creation. Then God will produce the final creation [i.e., final development]. Indeed God, over all things, is competent."

21. He punishes whom He wills and has mercy upon whom He wills, and to Him you will be returned.

22. And you will not cause failure [to God] upon the earth or in the heaven. And you have not other than God any protector or any helper.

23. And the ones who disbelieve in the signs of God and the meeting with Him - those have despaired of My mercy, and they will have a painful punishment.

24. And the answer of his [i.e., Abraham's] people was not but that they said, "Kill him or burn him," but God saved him from the fire. Indeed in that are signs for a people who believe.

25. And [Abraham] said, "You have only taken, other than God, idols as [a bond of] affection among you in worldly life. Then on the Day of Resurrection you will deny one another and curse one another, and your refuge will be the Fire, and you will not have any helpers."

26. And Lot believed him. [Abraham] said, "Indeed, I will emigrate to [the service of] my Lord. Indeed, He is the Exalted in Might, the Wise."

27. And We gave to Him Isaac and Jacob and placed in his descendants prophethood and scripture. And We gave him his reward in this world, and indeed, he is in the Hereafter among the righteous.

28. And [mention] Lot, when he said to his people, "Indeed, you commit such immorality as no one has preceded you with from among the worlds.

29. Indeed, you approach men and obstruct the road[1057] and commit in your meetings [every] evil." And the answer of his people was not but they said, "Bring us the punishment of God, if you should be of the truthful."

30. He said, "My Lord, support me against the corrupting people."

[1056] Commentators have differed over this verse – whether it is a continuation of the words of Prophet Abraham or words of comfort given by God to Prophet Muhammad, which according to context seems more likely.

[1057] i.e., commit highway robbery and acts of aggression against travellers.

31. And when Our messengers [i.e., angels] came to Abraham with the good tidings,[1058] they said, "Indeed, we will destroy the people of that [i.e., Lot's] city. Indeed, its people have been wrongdoers."

32. [Abraham] said, "Indeed, within it is Lot." They said, "We are more knowing of who is within it. We will surely save him and his family, except his wife. She is to be of those who remain behind."

33. And when Our messengers [i.e., angels] came to Lot, he was distressed for them and felt for them great discomfort.[1059] They said, "Fear not, nor grieve. Indeed, we will save you and your family, except your wife; she is to be of those who remain behind.

34. Indeed, we will bring down on the people of this city punishment from the sky because they have been defiantly disobedient."

35. And We have certainly left of it a sign as clear evidence for a people who use reason.

36. And to Madyan [We sent] their brother Shu'ayb, and he said, "O my people, worship God and expect the Last Day and do not commit abuse on the earth, spreading corruption."

37. But they denied him, so the earthquake seized them, and they became within their home [corpses] fallen prone.

38. And [We destroyed] 'Aad and Thamūd, and it has become clear to you from their [ruined] dwellings. And Satan had made pleasing to them their deeds and averted them from the path, and they were endowed with perception.

39. And [We destroyed] Qārūn and Pharaoh and Hāmān. And Moses had already come to them with clear evidences, and they were arrogant in the land, but they were not outrunners [of Our punishment].

40. So each We seized for his sin; and among them were those upon whom We sent a storm of stones, and among them were those who were seized by the blast [from the sky], and among them were those whom We caused the earth to swallow, and among them were those whom We drowned. And God would not have wronged them, but it was they who were wronging themselves.

41. The example of those who take allies other than God is like that of the spider who takes [i.e., constructs] a home. And indeed, the weakest of homes is the home of the spider, if they only knew.

42. Indeed, God knows whatever thing they call upon other than Him. And He is the Exalted in Might, the Wise.

43. And these examples We present to the people, but none will understand them except those of knowledge.

44. God created the heavens and the earth in truth. Indeed in that is a sign for the believers.

45. Recite, [O Muhammad], what has been revealed to you of the Book and establish prayer. Indeed, prayer prohibits immorality and wrongdoing, and the

[1058] Of the birth of Isaac and his descendent, Jacob.

[1059] See footnote to 11:77.

remembrance of God is greater. And God knows that which you do.

46. And do not argue with the People of the Scripture except in a way that is best, except for those who commit injustice among them, and say, "We believe in that which has been revealed to us and revealed to you. And our God and your God is one; and we are Muslims [in submission] to Him."

47. And thus We have sent down to you the Book [i.e., the Qur'ān]. And those to whom We [previously] gave the Scripture believe in it. And among these [people of Makkah] are those who believe in it. And none reject Our verses except the disbelievers.

48. And you did not recite before it any scripture, nor did you inscribe one with your right hand. Then [i.e., otherwise] the falsifiers would have had [cause for] doubt.

49. Rather, it [i.e., the Qur'ān] is distinct verses [preserved] within the breasts of those who have been given knowledge. And none reject Our verses except the wrongdoers.

50. But they say, "Why are not signs sent down to him from his Lord?" Say, "The signs are only with God, and I am only a clear warner."

51. And is it not sufficient for them that We revealed to you the Book [i.e., the Qur'ān] which is recited to them? Indeed in that is a mercy and reminder for a people who believe.

52. Say, "Sufficient is God between me and you as Witness. He knows what is in the heavens and earth. And they who have believed in falsehood and disbelieved in God - it is those who are the losers."

53. And they urge you to hasten the punishment. And if not for [the decree of] a specified term, punishment would have reached them. But it will surely come to them suddenly while they perceive not.

54. They urge you to hasten the punishment. And indeed, Hell will be encompassing of the disbelievers

55. On the Day the punishment will cover them from above them and from below their feet and it is said, "Taste [the result of] what you used to do."

56. O My servants who have believed, indeed My earth is spacious, so worship only Me.

57. Every soul will taste death. Then to Us will you be returned.

58. And those who have believed and done righteous deeds - We will surely assign to them of Paradise [elevated] chambers beneath which rivers flow, wherein they abide eternally. Excellent is the reward of the [righteous] workers

59. Who have been patient and upon their Lord rely.

60. And how many a creature carries not its [own] provision. God provides for it and for you. And He is the Hearing, the Knowing.

61. If you asked them, "Who created the heavens and earth and subjected the sun and the moon?" they would surely say, "God." Then how are they deluded?

62. God extends provision for whom He wills of His servants and restricts for him. Indeed God is, of all things, Knowing.

63. And if you asked them, "Who sends down rain from the sky and gives life thereby to the earth after its lifelessness?" they would surely say "God." Say, "Praise to God"; but most of them do not reason.

64. And this worldly life is not but diversion and amusement. And indeed, the home of the Hereafter - that is the [eternal] life, if only they knew.

65. And when they board a ship, they supplicate God, sincere to Him in religion [i.e., faith and hope]. But when He delivers them to the land, at once they associate others with Him

66. So that they will deny what We have granted them, and they will enjoy themselves. But they are going to know.[1060]

67. Have they not seen that We made [Makkah] a safe sanctuary, while people are being taken away[1061] all around them? Then in falsehood do they believe, and in the favor of God they disbelieve?

68. And who is more unjust than one who invents a lie about God or denies the truth when it has come to him? Is there not in Hell a [sufficient] residence for the disbelievers?

69. And those who strive for Us - We will surely guide them to Our ways.[1062] And indeed, God is with the doers of good.

1060 Grammatically, the verse may also be read as a threat, i.e., "So let them deny what We have granted them and let them enjoy themselves, for they are going to know."

1061 i.e., killed and taken captive.

1062 The various ways and means to attain the acceptance and pleasure of God.

## Sūrah 30: ar-Rūm

### Period of Revelation

The period of the revelation of this Sūrah is determined absolutely by the historical event that has been mentioned at the outset. It says: **"The Romans have been defeated in the neighbouring land."** In those days the Byzantine occupied territories adjacent to Arabia were Jordan, Syria and Palestine and in these territories the Romans were completely overpowered by the Persians in 615 A. D. Therefore it can be said with absolute certainty that this Sūrah was sent down in the same year and this was the year in which the migration to Abassinyah took place.

### Historical Background

The prediction made in the initial verses of this Sūrah is one of the most outstanding evidences of the Qur'ān's being the Word of God and the Prophet Muhammad's being a true Messenger of God. Let us have a look at the historical background relevant to the verses.

Eight years before the Prophet's advent as a Prophet the Byzantine Emperor Maurice was overthrown by Phocus who captured the throne and became king. Phocus first got the Emperor's five sons executed in front of him and then got the Emperor also killed and hung their heads in a thoroughfare in Constantinople. A few days after this he had the empress and her three danghters also put to death. The event provided Khusrau Parvez the Sassanid king of Persia; a good moral excuse to attack Byzantium. For Emperor Maurice had been his benefactor; with his help he had got the throne of Persia. Therefore he declared that he would avenge his Godfather's and his children's murder upon Phocus the usurper. So he started war against Byzantium in 603 A. D. and within a few years of putting the Phocus armies to rout in succession he reached Edessa (modern Urfa) in Asia Minor on the one hand and Aleppo and Antioch in Syria on the other. When the Byzantine ministers saw that Phocus could not save the country they sought the African governor's help who sent his son Heraclius to Constantinople with a strong fleet. Phocus was immediately deposed and Heraclius made emperor. He treated Phocus as he had treated Maurice. This happened in 610 A.D. the year the Prophet was appointed to Prophethood.

The moral excuse for which Khusrau Parvez had started the war was no more valid after the deposition and death of Phocus. Had the object of his war really been to avenge the murder of his ally on Phocus for his cruelty he would have come to terms with the new Emperor after the death of Phocus. But he continued the war and gave it the colour of a crusade between Zoroastrianism and Christianity. The sympathies of the Christian sects (i. e. Nestorians and Jacobians etc.) which had been excommunicated by the Roman ecclesiastical authority and tyrannized for years also went with the Magian (Zoroastrian) invaders and the Jews also joined hands with them; so much so that the number of the Jews who enlisted in Khusrau's army rose up to 26, 000.

Heraclius could not stop this storm. The very first news that he received from the East after ascending the throne was that of the Persian occupation of Antioch. After this Damascus fell in 613 A. D. Then in 614 A.D. the Persians occupying Jerusalem played havoc with the Christian world. Ninety thousand Christians were massacred and the Holy Sepulchre was desecrated. The Original Cross on which according to the Christian belief Jesus had died was seized and carried to Mada'in. The chief priest Zacharia was taken prisoner and all the important churches of the city were destroyed. How puffed up was Khusrau Parvez at this victory can be judged from the letter that he wrote to Heraclius from Jerusalem. He wrote: "From Khusrau the greatest of all gods, the master of the whole world: To Heraclius his most wretched and most stupid servant: 'You say that you have trust in your Lord. why didn't then your Lord save Jerusalem from me?'"

Within a year after this victory the Persian armies over-ran Jordan, Palestine and the whole of the Sinai Peninsula and reached the frontiers of Egypt. In those very days another conflict of a far greater historical consequence was going on in Makkah. The believers in One God under the leadership of the Prophet Muhammad were fighting for their existence against the followers of Shirk (polytheism) under the command of the chiefs of the Quraysh and the conflict had reached such a stage that in 615 A. D. a substantial number of the Muslims had to leave their homes and take refuge with the Christian kingdom of Abassinyah which was an ally of the Byzantine Empire. In those days the Sassanid victories against Byzantium were the talk of the town, and the pagans of Makkah were delighted and were taunting the Muslims to the effect: "Look the fire worshipers of Persia are winning victories and the Christian believers in Revelation and Prophethood are being routed everywhere. Likewise, we, the idol worshipers of Arabia, will exterminate you and your religion."

These were the conditions when this Sūrah of the Qur'ān was sent down, and in it a prediction was made, saying: **"The Byzantines have been defeated. In the nearest land. But they, after their defeat, will overcome. Within three to nine years. To God belongs the command before and after. And that day the believers will rejoice. In the victory of God. He gives victory to whom He wills, and He is the Exalted in Might, the Merciful."** It contained not one but two predictions: First, the Romans shall be Victorious; and second, the Muslims also shall win a victory at the same time. Apparently, there was not a remote chance of the fulfillment of the either prediction in the next few years. On the one hand, there were a handful of the Muslims, who were being beaten and tortured in Makkah, and even till eight years after this prediction there appeared no chance of their victory and domination. On the other, the Romans were losing more and more ground every next day. By 619 A.D. the whole of Egypt had passed into Sassanid hands and the Magian armies had reached as far as Tripoli. In Asia Minor they beat and pushed back the Romans to Bosporus, and in 617 A.D. they captured Chalcedon (modern, Kadikoy) just opposite Constantinople. The Emperor sent an envoy to Khusrau, praying that he was ready to have peace on any terms, but he replied, "I shall not give protection to the emperor until he is brought in chains before me and gives up obedience to his crucified God and adopts submission to the fire God." At last, the Emperor became so depressed by defeat that he decided to leave Constantinople and shift to Carthage (modern, Tunis). The conditions were such that no one could even imagine that the Byzantine Empire would ever gain an upper hand over Persia. Not to speak of gaining domination, no one could hope that the Empire, under the circumstances, would even survive.

When these verses of the Qur'ān were sent down, the disbelievers of Makkah made great fun of them, and Ubayy bin Khalaf bet Abu Bakr ten camels if the Romans became victorious within three years. When the Prophet came to know of the bet, he said, *"The Qur'ān has used the words* ***bid-i-sinin****, and the word bid in Arabic applies to a number up to ten. Therefore, make the bet for ten years and increase the number of camels to a hundred."* So, Abu Bakr spoke to Ubayy again and bet a hundred camels for ten years.

In 622 A.D. as the Prophet migrated to Madinah, the Emperor Heraclius set off quietly for Trabzon from Constantinople via the Black Sea and started preparations to attack Persia from the rear. For this he asked the Church for money, and Pope Sergius lent him the Church collections on interest, in a bid to save Christianity from Zoroastrianism. Heraclius started his counter attack in 623 A.D. from Armenia. Next year, in 624 A.D., he entered Azerbaijan and destroyed Clorumia, the birthplace of Zoroaster, and ravaged the principal fire temple of Persia. Great are the powers of God, this was the very year when the Muslims achieved a decisive victory at Badr for the first time against the polytheists. Thus both the predictions made in Sūrah Rum were fulfilled simultaneously within the stipulated period of ten years.

The Byzantine forces continued to press the Persians hard and in the decisive battle at Nineveh (627 A.D.) they dealt them the hardest blow. They captured the royal residence of Dastagerd, and then pressing forward reached right opposite to Ctesiphon, capital of Persia in those days. In 628 A. D. in an internal revolt, Khusrau Parvez was imprisoned and 18 of his sons were executed in front of him and a few days later he himself died in the prison. This was the year when the peace treaty of Hudaibiya was concluded, which the Qur'ān has termed as "the supreme victory," and in this very year Khusrau's son, Qubad II, gave up all the occupied Roman territories and made peace with Byzantium.

After this no one could have any doubt about the truth of the prophecy of the Qur'ān, with the result that most of the Arab polytheists accepted Islām. The heirs of Ubayy bin Khalaf lost their bet and had to give a hundred camels to Abu Bakr Siddiq. He took them before the Prophet, who ordered that they be given away in charity, because the bet had been made at a time when gambling had not yet been forbidden by the Shariah; now it was forbidden. Therefore, the bet was allowed to be accepted from the belligerent disbelievers, but instruction given that it should be given away in charity and should not be brought in personal use.

**Theme and Subject Matter**

The discourse begins with the theme that the Romans have been overcome and the people the world over think that the empire is about to collapse, but the fact is that within a few years the tables will be turned and the vanquished will again become victorious.

This introductory theme contains the great truth that man is accustomed to seeing only what is apparent and superficial. That which is behind the apparent and superficial he does not know. When in the petty matters of life, this habit to see only the apparent and superficial can lead man to misunderstandings and miscalculations, and when he is liable to make wrong estimates only due to lack of knowledge about "what will happen tomorrow," how stupendous will be his error if he risks his whole life-activity by placing reliance only upon what is visible and apparent with respect to his worldly life as a whole. Then, from the question of the conflict between Byzantium and Persia the direction of the discourse turns to the theme of the Hereafter, and as far as verse 27, man has been made to understand in different ways that the Hereafter is possible as well as rational and necessary; then for the sake of keeping the system of his life also stable and balanced it is absolutely necessary that he should plan and order his present life on the faith in the Hereafter; otherwise he will commit the same error as has always been the result of placing one's reliance only upon the apparent and the visible.

In this connection, the Signs of the universe which have been presented as evidence to prove the doctrine of the Hereafter are precisely the same which support the doctrine of Tawhid (Oneness of God). Therefore from verse 28 onward, the discourse turns to the affirmation of Tawhid and the refutation of Shirk (polytheism), and it is stressed that the natural way of life for man is none else but to serve One God exclusively. Shirk is opposed to the nature of the universe as to the nature of man. Therefore, whenever man has adopted this deviation, chaos has resulted. Again here, an allusion has been made to the great chaos that had gripped the world on account of the war between the two major powers of the time, and it has been indicated that this chaos too, is the result of shirk, and all the nations who were ever involved in mischief and chaos in the history of mankind were also polytheists.

In conclusion, a parable has been presented to make the people understand that just as dead earth comes to life, all of a sudden, by a shower of rain sent by God and swells with vegetation and plant life, so is the case with the dead humanity. When God sends a shower of His mercy in the form of Revelation and Prophethood, it also gives a new life to mankind and causes it to grow and develop and flourish. Therefore: "If you take full advantage of this opportunity, the barren land of Arabia will bloom by God's mercy and the whole advantage will be your. But if you do not take advantage of it, you will harm only your selves. Then no regret will avail and no opportunity will be provided to make amends."

## Sūrah 30: ar-Rūm[1063]

In the Name of God, the Most Compassionate, the Most Merciful

1. Alif, Lām, Meem.[1064]

2. The Byzantines have been defeated[1065]

3. In the nearest land. But they, after their defeat, will overcome

4. Within three to nine years. To God belongs the command [i.e., decree] before and after. And that day the believers will rejoice

5. In the victory of God.[1066] He gives victory to whom He wills, and He is the Exalted in Might, the Merciful.

6. [It is] the promise of God. God does not fail in His promise, but most of the people do not know.

7. They know what is apparent of the worldly life, but they, of the Hereafter, are unaware.

8. Do they not contemplate within themselves?[1067] God has not created the heavens and the earth and what is between them except in truth and for a specified term. And indeed, many of the people, in [the matter of] the meeting with their Lord, are disbelievers.

9. Have they not traveled through the earth and observed how was the end of those before them? They were greater than them in power, and they plowed [or excavated] the earth and built it up more than they [i.e., the Makkans] have built it up, and their messengers came to them with clear evidences. And God would not ever have wronged them, but they were wronging themselves.

10. Then the end of those who did evil was the worst [consequence] because they denied the signs of God and used to ridicule them.

11. God begins creation; then He will repeat it; then to Him you will be returned.

12. And the Day the Hour appears the criminals will be in despair.

13. And there will not be for them among their [alleged] partners any intercessors, and they will [then] be disbelievers in their partners.

14. And the Day the Hour appears - that Day they will become separated.

15. And as for those who had believed and done righteous deeds, they will be in a garden [of Paradise], delighted.

16. But as for those who disbelieved and denied Our verses and the meeting of the Hereafter, those will be brought into the punishment [to remain].

17. So exalted is God when you reach the evening and when you reach the morning.

18. And to Him is [due all] praise throughout the heavens and the earth. And [ex-

---

1063 *Ar-Rūm*: The Byzantines (of the Eastern Roman Empire) or Romaeans.
1064 See footnote to 2:1.
1065 By the Persians.
1066 i.e., the victory given by God to a people of the scripture (Christians) over the Magians of Persia.
1067 An additional meaning is "Do they not contemplate concerning themselves."

alted is He] at night and when you are at noon.

19. He brings the living out of the dead and brings the dead out of the living and brings to life the earth after its lifelessness. And thus will you be brought out.[1068]

20. And of His signs is that He created you from dust; then, suddenly you were human beings dispersing [throughout the earth].

21. And of His signs is that He created for you from yourselves mates that you may find tranquillity in them; and He placed between you affection and mercy. Indeed in that are signs for a people who give thought.

22. And of His signs is the creation of the heavens and the earth and the diversity of your languages and your colors. Indeed in that are signs for those of knowledge.

23. And of His signs is your sleep by night and day and your seeking of His bounty. Indeed in that are signs for a people who listen.

24. And of His signs is [that] He shows you the lightening [causing] fear and aspiration, and He sends down rain from the sky by which He brings to life the earth after its lifelessness. Indeed in that are signs for a people who use reason.

25. And of His signs is that the heaven and earth stand [i.e., remain] by His command. Then when He calls you with a [single] call from the earth, immediately you will come forth.

[1068] Of the graves or out of the earth at the time of resurrection.

26. And to Him belongs whoever is in the heavens and earth. All are to Him devoutly obedient.

27. And it is He who begins creation; then He repeats it, and that is [even] easier for Him. To Him belongs the highest description [i.e., attribute] in the heavens and earth. And He is the Exalted in Might, the Wise.

28. He presents to you an example from yourselves. Do you have among those whom your right hands possess [i.e., slaves] any partners in what We have provided for you so that you are equal therein [and] would fear them as your fear of one another [within a partnership]?[1069] Thus do We detail the verses for a people who use reason.

29. But those who wrong follow their [own] desires without knowledge. Then who can guide one whom God has sent astray? And for them there are no helpers.

30. So direct your face [i.e., self] toward the religion, inclining to truth. [Adhere to] the fitrah[1070] of God upon which He has created [all] people. No change should there be in the creation of God.[1071] That is the correct religion, but most of the people do not know.

31. [Adhere to it], turning in repentance to Him, and fear Him and establish prayer and do not be of those who associate others with God

[1069] See footnote to 16:71.

[1070] The natural inborn inclination of man to worship his Creator prior to the corruption of his nature by external influences. Thus, Islāmic monotheism is described as the religion of *fitrah* – that of the inherent nature of mankind.

[1071] i.e., let people remain true to their *fitrah* within the religion of Islām.

32. [Or] of those who have divided their religion and become sects, every faction rejoicing in what it has.[1072]

33. And when adversity touches the people, they call upon their Lord, turning in repentance to Him. Then when He lets them taste mercy from Him, at once a party of them associate others with their Lord,

34. So that they will deny what We have granted them.[1073] Then enjoy yourselves, for you are going to know.

35. Or have We sent down to them an authority [i.e., a proof or scripture], and it speaks of what they were associating with Him?

36. And when We let the people taste mercy, they rejoice therein, but if evil afflicts them for what their hands have put forth, immediately they despair.

37. Do they not see that God extends provision for whom He wills and restricts [it]? Indeed, in that are signs for a people who believe.

38. So give the relative his right, as well as the needy and the traveler. That is best for those who desire the countenance of God, and it is they who will be the successful.

39. And whatever you give for interest [i.e., advantage] to increase within the wealth of people[1074] will not increase with God. But what you give in zakāh,[1075] desiring the countenance of God - those are the multipliers.[1076]

40. God is the one who created you, then provided for you, then will cause you to die, and then will give you life. Are there any of your "partners" who does anything of that? Exalted is He and high above what they associate with Him.

41. Corruption has appeared throughout the land and sea by [reason of] what the hands of people have earned so He [i.e., God] may let them taste part of [the consequence of] what they have done that perhaps they will return [to righteousness].

42. Say, [O Muhammad], "Travel through the land and observe how was the end of those before. Most of them were associators [of others with God].

43. So direct your face [i.e., self] toward the correct religion before a Day comes from God of which there is no repelling. That Day, they will be divided.[1077]

44. Whoever disbelieves - upon him is [the consequence of] his disbelief. And whoever does righteousness - they are for themselves preparing,

45. That He may reward those who have believed and done righteous deeds out of His bounty. Indeed, He does not like the disbelievers.

---

1072 Of beliefs, opinions, customs, etc.

1073 Or "So let them deny what We have granted them."

1074 The phrase includes several connotations, among them: a) that which is given as usury or interest, b) that which is given on the condition that it be repaid with interest, and c) a gift given with the intention of obtaining from the recipient greater benefit or a larger gift.

1075 The meaning of *sadaqah* (voluntary charity) is included here.

1076 Of their blessings on earth and their rewards in the Hereafter.

1077 Into those destined for Paradise and those destined for Hell.

46. And of His signs is that He sends the winds as bringers of good tidings and to let you taste His mercy [i.e., rain] and so the ships may sail at His command and so you may seek of His bounty, and perhaps you will be grateful.

47. And We have already sent messengers before you to their peoples, and they came to them with clear evidences; then We took retribution from those who committed crimes, and incumbent upon Us was support[1078] of the believers.

48. It is God who sends the winds, and they stir the clouds and spread them in the sky however He wills, and He makes them fragments so you see the rain emerge from within them. And when He causes it to fall upon whom He wills of His servants, immediately they rejoice

49. Although they were, before it was sent down upon them - before that, in despair.

50. So observe the effects of the mercy of God - how He gives life to the earth after its lifelessness. Indeed, that [same one] will give life to the dead, and He is over all things competent.

51. But if We should send a [bad] wind and they saw [their crops] turned yellow, they would remain thereafter disbelievers.[1079]

52. So indeed, you will not make the dead hear, nor will you make the deaf hear the call when they turn their backs, retreating.

[1078] i.e., aid or the bestowal of victory.

[1079] Denying and ungrateful for the previous favours of God.

53. And you cannot guide the blind away from their error. You will only make hear those who believe in Our verses so they are Muslims [in submission to God].

54. God is the one who created you from weakness, then made after weakness strength, then made after strength weakness and white hair. He creates what He wills, and He is the Knowing, the Competent.

55. And the Day the Hour appears the criminals will swear they had remained but an hour. Thus they were deluded.

56. But those who were given knowledge and faith will say, "You remained the extent of God's decree until the Day of Resurrection, and this is the Day of Resurrection, but you did not used to know."[1080]

57. So that Day, their excuse will not benefit those who wronged, nor will they be asked to appease [God].

58. And We have certainly presented to the people in this Qur'ān from every [kind of] example. But, [O Muhammad], if you should bring them a sign, the disbelievers will surely say, "You [believers] are but falsifiers."

59. Thus does God seal the hearts of those who do not know.[1081]

60. So be patient. Indeed, the promise of God is truth. And let them not disquiet you who are not certain [in faith].

[1080] i.e., acknowledge the truth.

[1081] i.e., those who do not wish to know the truth and refuse it.

## Sūrah 31: Luqmān

### Period of Revelation

A perusal of the subject matter shows that it was sent down in the period when persecution to suppress and thwart the invitation to Islām had begun and every sort of machination had started being employed for the purpose. This is borne out by v.14 in which the young reverts to Islām have been told that although the rights of the parents are the uppermost after God they should not listen to them if they prevented them from accepting Islām or compelled them to revert to the creed of Shirk (polytheism). The same thing has been said in Sūrah al-Ankabut which indicates that both these Sūrahs were sent down in the same period. A study of the style and subject matter of the two Sūrahs on the whole however shows that Sūrah Luqman was sent down earlier for one does not see any sign of the antagonism in its background, though contrary to this while studying Sūrah Al-Ankabut one can clearly feel that the Muslims were being severely persecuted during the period of its revelation.

### Theme and Subject Matter

In this Sūrah the people have been made to understand the meaninglessness and absurdity of Shirk (polytheism) and the truth and reasonableness of Tawhid (Oneness of God). They have been invited to give up blind imitation of their forefathers, consider with a cool mind the teachings which the Prophet Muhammad is presenting from the Lord of the worlds and see with open eyes the manifest Signs found in the universe around them and in their own selves which bear evidence to its truth.

In this connection it has also been pointed out that this is not a new teaching which might have been presented in the world or in the land of Arabia for the first time and with which the people might be unfamiliar. The learned and wise people of the past ages said and taught the same thing which Muhammad is teaching today. It is as if to say, 'O people: In your own country there has lived a wise man named Luqmān whose wisdom has been well known among you, whose proverbs and wise sayings are cited in your daily conversation and who is often quoted by your poets and orators. Now you should see for yourselves what creed and what morals he used to teach.'

## Sūrah 31: Luqmān[1082]

In the Name of God, the Most Compassionate, the Most Merciful

1. Alif, Lām, Meem.[1083]

2. These are verses of the wise[1084] Book,

3. As guidance and mercy for the doers of good

4. Who establish prayer and give zakāh, and they, of the Hereafter, are certain [in faith].

5. Those are on [right] guidance from their Lord, and it is those who are the successful.

6. And of the people is he who buys the amusement of speech[1085] to mislead [others] from the way of God without knowledge and who takes it [i.e., His way] in ridicule. Those will have a humiliating punishment.

7. And when our verses are recited to him, he turns away arrogantly as if he had not heard them, as if there was in his ears deafness. So give him tidings of a painful punishment.

8. Indeed, those who believe and do righteous deeds - for them are the Gardens of Pleasure,

9. Wherein they abide eternally; [it is] the promise of God [which is] truth. And He is the Exalted in Might, the Wise.

10. He created the heavens without pillars that you see and has cast into the earth firmly set mountains, lest it should shift with you, and dispersed therein from every creature. And We sent down rain from the sky and made grow therein [plants] of every noble kind.

11. This is the creation of God. So show Me what those other than Him have created. Rather, the wrongdoers are in clear error.

12. And We had certainly given Luqmān wisdom [and said], "Be grateful to God." And whoever is grateful is grateful for [the benefit of] himself. And whoever denies [His favor] - then indeed, God is Free of need and Praiseworthy.

13. And [mention, O Muhammad], when Luqmān said to his son while he was instructing him, "O my son, do not associate [anything] with God. Indeed, association [with Him] is great injustice."

14. And We have enjoined upon man [care] for his parents. His mother carried him, [increasing her] in weakness upon weakness, and his weaning is in two years. Be grateful to Me and to your parents; to Me is the [final] destination.

15. But if they endeavor to make you associate with Me that of which you have

---

[1082] *Luqmān*: Luqmān, the Wise, whose learning and wisdom was known among pre-Islāmic Arabs. He was said to have been an Abyssinian or Nubian slave who lived in the area of Madyan and thus knew Arabic.

[1083] See footnote to 2:1.

[1084] See footnote to 10:1.

[1085] i.e., that which has no benefit. Described by different *sahābah* as *shirk* (association with God), misleading stories, frivolous songs, or music but includes all which distracts or diverts one from the Qur'ān and remembrance of God.

no knowledge,[1086] do not obey them but accompany them in [this] world with appropriate kindness and follow the way of those who turn back to Me [in repentance]. Then to Me will be your return, and I will inform you about what you used to do.

16. [And Luqmān said], "O my son, indeed if it [i.e., wrong] should be the weight of a mustard seed and should be within a rock or [anywhere] in the heavens or in the earth, God will bring it forth. Indeed, God is Subtle and Acquainted.

17. O my son, establish prayer, enjoin what is right, forbid what is wrong, and be patient over what befalls you. Indeed, [all] that is of the matters [requiring] determination.[1087]

18. And do not turn your cheek [in contempt] toward people[1088] and do not walk through the earth exultantly. Indeed, God does not like everyone self-deluded and boastful.

19. And be moderate in your pace and lower your voice; indeed, the most disagreeable of sounds is the voice of donkeys."

20. Do you not see that God has made subject to you whatever is in the heavens and whatever is in the earth and amply bestowed upon you His favors, [both] apparent and unapparent? But of the people is he who disputes about God without knowledge or guidance or an enlightening Book [from Him].

21. And when it is said to them, "Follow what God has revealed," they say, "Rather, we will follow that upon which we found our fathers." Even if Satan was inviting them to the punishment of the Blaze?

22. And whoever submits his face [i.e., self] to God while he is a doer of good - then he has grasped the most trustworthy handhold. And to God will be the outcome of [all] matters.

23. And whoever has disbelieved - let not his disbelief grieve you. To Us is their return, and We will inform them of what they did. Indeed, God is Knowing of that within the breasts.

24. We grant them enjoyment for a little; then We will force them to a massive punishment.

25. And if you asked them, "Who created the heavens and earth?" they would surely say, "God." Say, "[All] praise is [due] to God"; but most of them do not know.

26. To God belongs whatever is in the heavens and earth. Indeed, God is the Free of need, the Praiseworthy.

27. And if whatever trees upon the earth were pens and the sea [was ink], replenished thereafter by seven [more] seas, the words[1089] of God would not be exhausted. Indeed, God is Exalted in Might and Wise.

28. Your creation and your resurrection will not be but as that of a single soul.[1090] Indeed, God is Hearing and Seeing.

---

[1086] See footnote to 29:8.
[1087] For the reason that they are enjoined by God.
[1088] Rather, respect them by directing your face and attention to them.
[1089] See footnote to 18:109.
[1090] The re-creation and resurrection of one or of all is accomplished with equal ease by God.

29. Do you not see [i.e., know] that God causes the night to enter the day and causes the day to enter the night and has subjected the sun and the moon, each running [its course] for a specified term, and that God, with whatever you do, is Acquainted?

30. That is because God is the Truth, and that what they call upon other than Him is falsehood, and because God is the Most High, the Grand.

31. Do you not see that ships sail through the sea by the favor of God that He may show you of His signs? Indeed in that are signs for everyone patient and grateful.

32. And when waves come over them like canopies, they supplicate God, sincere to Him in religion [i.e., faith]. But when He delivers them to the land, there are [some] of them who are moderate [in faith]. And none rejects Our signs except everyone treacherous and ungrateful.

33. O mankind, fear your Lord and fear a Day when no father will avail his son, nor will a son avail his father at all. Indeed, the promise of God is truth, so let not the worldly life delude you and be not deceived about God by the Deceiver [i.e., Satan].

34. Indeed, God [alone] has knowledge of the Hour and sends down the rain and knows what is in the wombs.[1091] And no soul perceives what it will earn tomorrow, and no soul perceives in what land it will die. Indeed, God is Knowing and Acquainted.

[1091] i.e., every aspect of the fetus' present and future existence.

## Sūrah 32: as-Sajdah

### Period of Revelation

From the style of the Sūrah it appears that it was sent down during the middle Makkah period, more particularly in its initial stage for one does not find in its background that severity of the persecution and tyranny which one finds in the Sūrahs sent down in the later stages.

### Themes and Topics

The main theme of the Sūrah is to remove the doubts of the people concerning Tawhid (Oneness of God), the Hereafter, the Prophethood and to invite them to all these three realities. The disbelievers of Makkah when they talked of the Prophet in private said to one another 'This person is forging strange things, sometimes he gives news of what will happen after death. He says: 'When you have become dust you will be called to render your accounts and there will be Hell and Heaven.' Sometimes he says: 'These gods and goddesses and saints are nonentities: One God alone is the Deity.' And sometimes he says: 'The discourses which I recite are not my own but God's Word. All these are strange things which he presents.' The answer to these doubts and misgivings forms the theme and subject matter of this Sūrah.

In this connection the disbelievers have been told: "Most certainly it is God's Word which has been sent down in order to arouse a people who are sunk in heedlessness being deprived of the bounties and blessings of Prophethood. How can you call it a fabrication when its having been sent down from God is manifest and self-evident?" Then they have been asked - Use your common sense and judge for yourselves which of the things presented by the Qur'ān is strange and novel? Look at the administration of the heavens and the earth: consider your own creation and structure. Don't these things testify to the teaching which this Prophet is presenting before you in the Qur'ān? Does the system of the universe point to Tawhid (Oneness of God) or to Shirk (polytheism)?

Then a scene of the Hereafter has been depicted, the fruits of belief and the evil consequences of disbelief have been mentioned and the people exhorted to give up disbelief even before they meet their doom and accept the teaching of the Qur'ān which will be to their own advantage in the Hereafter. Then they have been told: It is God's supreme Mercy that He does not seize man immediately for his errors, to punish him finally and decisively but warns him beforehand by afflicting him with small troubles, hardships, calamities, losses and strokes of misfortune so that he may wake up and take admonition. Then it is said: "This is not the first and novel event of its kind that a Book has been sent down upon a man from God. Before this the Book had been sent upon Moses also which you all know. There is nothing strange in this at which you should marvel. Be assured that this Book has come down from God and note it well that the same will happen now as has already happened in the time of Moses. Leadership now will be bestowed only on those who will accept this Divine Book. Those who reject it shall be doomed to failure. Will you like to meet the same doom yourself? Do not be deluded by the apparent and superficial. Today you see that no one is listening to Muhammad except a few young men, some slaves and poor men and he is being made the target of curses and ugly remarks from every side. From this you have formed the wrong impression that his mission will fail. But this is only a deception of your eyes. Don't you see the phenomenon in your daily life that a land previously lying absolutely barren starts swelling with vegetation and plant life everywhere, just by a single shower of the rain though before this no one could ever imagine that under the layers of its soil there lay hidden such treasures of greenery and herbage?" In conclusion, the Prophet has been addressed to the effect: "These people mock at what you say and ask as to when you will attain this decisive victory. Tell them: when the time comes for the final judgment regarding you and us, believing then will not profit you at all. If you have to believe, believe now. But if you intend to await the final judgment, then await it as you please."

## Sūrah 32: as-Sajdah[1092]

In the Name of God, the Most Compassionate, the Most Merciful

1. Alif, Lām, Meem.[1093]

2. [This is] the revelation of the Book about which there is no doubt from the Lord of the worlds.

3. Or do they say, "He invented it"? Rather, it is the truth from your Lord, [O Muhammad], that you may warn a people to whom no warner has come before you [so] perhaps they will be guided.

4. It is God who created the heavens and the earth and whatever is between them in six days; then He established Himself above the Throne.[1094] You have not besides Him any protector or any intercessor; so will you not be reminded?

5. He arranges [each] matter from the heaven to the earth; then it will ascend to Him in a Day, the extent of which is a thousand years of those which you count.

6. That is the Knower of the unseen and the witnessed, the Exalted in Might, the Merciful,

7. Who perfected everything which He created and began the creation of man from clay.

8. Then He made his posterity out of the extract of a liquid disdained.

[1092] *As-Sajdah*: Prostration.

[1093] See footnote to 2:1.

[1094] See footnote to 2:19.

9. Then He proportioned him and breathed into him from His [created] soul[1095] and made for you hearing and vision and hearts [i.e., intellect]; little are you grateful.

10. And they say, "When we are lost [i.e., disintegrated] within the earth, will we indeed be [recreated] in a new creation?" Rather, they are, in [the matter of] the meeting with their Lord, disbelievers.

11. Say, "The angel of death will take you who has been entrusted with you. Then to your Lord you will be returned."

12. If you could but see when the criminals are hanging their heads before their Lord, [saying], "Our Lord, we have seen and heard, so return us [to the world]; we will work righteousness. Indeed, we are [now] certain."

13. And if We had willed, We could have given every soul its guidance, but the word[1096] from Me will come into effect [that] "I will surely fill Hell with jinn and people all together.

14. So taste [punishment] because you forgot the meeting of this, your Day; indeed, We have [accordingly] forgotten you. And taste the punishment of eternity for what you used to do."

15. Only those believe in Our verses who, when they are reminded by them, fall down in prostration and exalt [God] with praise of their Lord, and they are not arrogant.

16. Their sides part [i.e., they arise] from [their] beds; they supplicate their Lord

[1095] i.e., element of life. See footnote to 15:29.

[1096] Deserved by the evildoers.

in fear and aspiration, and from what We have provided them, they spend.[1097]

17. And no soul knows what has been hidden for them of comfort for eyes [i.e., satisfaction] as reward for what they used to do.

18. Then is one who was a believer like one who was defiantly disobedient? They are not equal.

19. As for those who believed and did righteous deeds, for them will be the Gardens of Refuge as accommodation for what they used to do.

20. But as for those who defiantly disobeyed, their refuge is the Fire. Every time they wish to emerge from it, they will be returned to it while it is said to them, "Taste the punishment of the Fire which you used to deny."

21. And We will surely let them taste the nearer punishment[1098] short of the greater punishment that perhaps they will return [i.e., repent].

22. And who is more unjust than one who is reminded of the verses of his Lord; then he turns away from them? Indeed We, from the criminals, will take retribution.

23. And We certainly gave Moses the Scripture, so do not be in doubt over his meeting.[1099] And We made it [i.e., the Torah] guidance for the Children of Israel.

24. And We made from among them leaders guiding by Our command when they were patient and [when] they were certain of Our signs.

25. Indeed, your Lord will judge between them on the Day of Resurrection concerning that over which they used to differ.

26. Has it not become clear to them how many generations We destroyed before them, [as] they walk among their dwellings? Indeed in that are signs; then do they not hear?

27. Have they not seen that We drive the water [in clouds] to barren land and bring forth thereby crops from which their livestock eat and [they] themselves? Then do they not see?

28. And they say, "When will be this conquest,[1100] if you should be truthful?"

29. Say, [O Muhammad], "On the Day of Conquest the belief of those who had disbelieved will not benefit them, nor will they be reprieved."

30. So turn away from them and wait. Indeed, they are waiting.

[1097] In the cause of God.
[1098] i.e., the disasters and calamities of this world.
[1099] i.e., Muhammad's meeting Moses on the night of *al-Mi'rāj* (ascent).

[1100] Or "decision," i.e., judgement.

## Sūrah 33: al-Ahzāb

### Period of Revelation

The Sūrah discusses three important events which are: the Battle of the Trench (or Al-Ahzāb: the Confederates) which took place in the month of Shawwal 5 A.H.; the raid on Banū Quraythah which was made in Dhil-Qa'dah 5 A.H.; and the Prophet's marriage with Zaynab which also was contracted in Dhil-Qa'dah 5 A.H.. These historical events accurately determine the period of the revelation of this Sūrah.

### Historical Background

The Islāmic army's setback in the Battle of Uhud (3 A.H.) that resulted from the error of the archers appointed by the Prophet so boosted up the morale of the Arab pagans, the Jews and the hypocrites that they started entertaining the hope that they would soon be able to exterminate Islām and the Muslims completely. Their high state of morale can be judged from the events that occurred in the first year after Uhud. Hardly two months had passed then the tribe of Bani Asad of Najd began to make preparations for a raid on Madinah and the Prophet had to despatch an expedition under Abu Salamah to counteract them. In Safar 4 A.H. some people of the tribes of Adal and Qarah asked the Prophet to send some men to instruct them in Islām. Accordingly six of the Companions were allowed to accompany them for the purpose. But when they reached Raji (a place between Rabigh and Jeddah) they summoned Hudhail against them who killed four of the Companions and took the other two (Khubaib bin Adi and Zayd bin ad-Dathinnah) to Makkah and sold them to the enemy. Then in the same month of Safar on the request of a chief of Bani Amir the Prophet sent another deputation of 40 (according to others 70) preachers consisting of the Ansār young men to Najd. But they were also betrayed. The people of Usayyah, Ri'l and Dhakwan tribes of Bani Sulaim surrounded them suddenly at Bir Maunah and slew all of them. Meanwhile, the Jewish tribe of Banu-Nadheer of Madinah getting encouragement continued to commit breaches of the treaties; so much so that in Rabi'ul Awwal 4 A.H. they plotted against the life of the Prophet himself. Then in Jamadi al-Ula 4 A.H. Bani Thalbah and Bani Muharib the two tribes of Banu Ghatafan started making preparations to attack Madinah and the Prophet had to go to punish them. Thus after their setback at Uhud the Muslims went on encountering repercussions continuously for seven to eight months.

However, it was the Prophet's determination and wisdom and his great Companions' spirit of sacrifice that changed these adverse conditions completely within a short span of time. The economic boycott by the Arabs had made life hard for the people of Madinah. All the polytheistic tribes around Madinah were becoming rebellious. Inside Madinah itself the Jews and the hypocrites were bent upon mischief. But the successive steps taken by a handful of the sincere Muslims under the leadership of the Prophet not only restored the image of strength of Islām in Arabia but also increased it manifold.

### Raids Preceding the Battle of the Trench

The first such step was taken immediately after the Battle of Uhud. The very next day when quite a large number of Muslims lay wounded and the martyrdom of the near and dear ones was being mourned in many houses and the Prophet himself was injured and sad at the martyrdom of his uncle Hamza he called out to the devoted servants of Islām to accompany him in pursuit of the pagans so as to deter them from returning and attacking Madinah again. The Prophet's assessment was absolutely correct. He knew that although the Quraysh had retreated without taking any advantage of their almost complete victory, they would certainly regret their folly when they would halt, consider the whole matter coolly on the way and would return to attack Madinah again. Therefore he decided to go in pursuit of them and 630 of of the Muslims at once volunteered to accompany him. When they reached Hamra al-Asad on the way to Makkah and camped there for three days the Prophet came to know through a sympathetic non-Muslim that Abu Sufyan had stayed at ar-Rauha, 36 miles short of Madinah with an army 2,978 strong: they were regretting their error and were in fact planning to return and attack Madinah once again. But when they heard that the Prophet was coming in pursuit of them with an army, they lost heart and gave up their plan. Thus, not only were the Quraysh deterred by this action, but the other enemies living around Madinah also realized that the Muslims were being led by a person who was highly well informed, wise and resolute, and that the Muslims were ever ready to lay down their lives at his command.

Then as soon as the Bani Asad started making preparations for a raid on Madinah, the Prophet's secret agents gave him timely information about their intention. Thus, before they could come in force to attack Madinah, he sent an army 150 strong, under Abu Salamah (the first husband of Umm Salamah) to punish them. They took Bani Asad by surprise, who fled in panic leaving all their possessions behind, which fell into the Muslim hands.

After this came the turn of the Banu-Nadheer. The day they plotted against the life of the Prophet, and the secret was disclosed, the Prophet ordered them to leave Madinah within ten days and warned that anyone who remained behind after that would be put to death. Abdullah bin Ubayy, the chief of the hypocrites of Madinah, encouraged them to defy the order and refuse to leave Madinah. He even promised to help them with 2,000 men, and assured them that the Banu Ghatafan from Najd also would come to their aid. Accordingly, the Banu-Nadheer sent word that they would not leave no matter what the Prophet might do.

As soon as the time limit of ten days come to an end, the Prophet laid siege to their quarters, but none of their supporters had the courage to come to their rescue. At last, they surrendered on condition that every three of them would be allowed to load a camel with whatever they could carry and go away leaving the rest of their possessions behind. Thus, the whole suburbs of the city which were inhabited by the Banu-Nadheer, and their gardens, their fortresses and other properties fell to the Muslims and the people of this treacherous tribe became scattered in Khaiber, Wad-il-Qura and Syria. Then the Prophet turned his attention to the Banu Ghatafan, who were preparing for a war against Madinah. He took 400 of the Muslims and overtook them at Dhat-ar-Riqa. They were so taken by surprise that they fled their houses without a struggle and took refuge in the mountains.

After this in Shaban 4 A.H., the Prophet went forth to Badr to fight Abu Sufyan. At the end of the Battle of Uhud, he had challenged the Prophet and the Muslims, saying, *"We shall again meet you in combat at Badr next year."* In reply the Prophet announced through a Companion: *"All right: we accept your challenge."* Accordingly, at the appointed time he reached Badr with 1,500 of the Muslims. From the other side, Abu Sufyan left Makkah with an army of 2,000 men, but could not have the courage to march beyond Marr-az-Zahran (modern, Wadi Fātimah). The Prophet waited for him at Badr for eight days; the Muslims during these days did profitable business with a trading party. This incident helped more than restore the image of strength of the Muslims that had been tarnished at Uhud. It also made the whole of Arabia realize that the Quraysh alone could no longer resist Muhammad.

This image and position of the Muslims was further strengthened by another event. Dumat al-Jandal (modern, Al-Jauf) was an important place at the border between Arabia and Syria. When the caravans of the Arabs, trading between Iraq in the south and Syria and Egypt in the north, passed that way, they were harassed and looted by the natives. In Rabi al-Awwal, 5 A.H., the Prophet himself went to punish them with an army of 1,000 men. They could not muster up courage to come out and fight him and, therefore, fled the place. This caused the whole of northern Arabia to dread the power of Islām, and the tribes began to realize that the great power emerging from Madinah was formidable and could no longer be resisted by one or a few of the tribes.

### The Battle of the Trench

Such were the conditions when the Battle of the Trench took place. It was in fact a combined raid by many of the Arab tribes who wanted to crush the power of Madinah. It had been instigated by the leaders of the Banu-Nadheer who had settled in Khaiber after their banishment from Madinah. They went round to the

Quraysh, Ghatafan, Hudhail and many other tribes and induced them to gather all their forces together and attack Madinah jointly. Thus in Shawwal 5 A.H. an unprecedentedly large army of the Arab tribes marched against the small city of Madinah. From the north came Jews of Banu-Nadheer and Bani-Qaynuqah who after their banishment from Madinah had settled in Khaiber and Wad-il-Qura. From the east advanced the tribes of Ghatafan, Bani Sulaim, Fazarah, Murrah, Ashja, Sad Asad etc. and from the south the Quraysh along with a large force of their allies. Together they numbered from ten to twelve thousand men.

Had it been a sudden attack it would have been disastrous. But the Prophet was not unaware of this in Madinah. His intelligence men and the sympathisers of the Islāmic movement and the people influenced by it were present in every tribe who kept him informed of the enemy's movements. Even before the enemy could reach his city he got a trench dug out on the north-west of Madinah in six days and took up a defensive position with 3,000 men in the protection of the Trench. To the south of Madinah there were many gardens (even now there are) so that it could not be attacked from that side. To the east there are lava rocks which are impassable for a large army. The same is the case with the south western side. The attack therefore could be made only from the eastern and western sides of the Uhud which the Prophet had secured by digging a trench. The disbelievers were not at all aware that they would have to counter the trench outside Madinah. This kind of a defensive stratagem was unknown to the Arabs. Thus they had to lay a long siege in winter for which they had not come prepared.

After this, only one alternative remained with the disbelievers: to incite the Jewish tribe of Banū Quraythah who inhabited the south eastern part of the city to rebellion. As the Muslims had entered a treaty with them, that in case of an attack on Madinah they would defend the city along with them. The Muslims had made no defensive arrangement there and had even sent their families to take shelter in the forts situated on that side. The invaders perceived this weakness of the Islāmic defenses. They sent Huyayy bin Akhtab the Jewish leader of the Banu-Nadheer to the Banū Quraythah so as to induce them to break the treaty and join the war. In the beginning they refused to oblige and said that they had a treaty with Muhammad who had faithfully abided by it and given them no cause for complaint. But when Ibn Akhtab said to them, look I have summoned the united force of entire Arabia against him: this is a perfect opportunity to get rid of him. If you lose it you will never have another opportunity. The anti Islāmic Jewish mind prevailed over every moral consideration and the Banū Quraythah were persuaded to break the treaty.

The Prophet received news of this. He at once told Sad bin Ubadah, Sad bin Muadh, Abdullah bin Rawahah and Khawwat bin Jubair chiefs of the Ansār to go and find out the truth. He advised them that if they found Banū Quraythah still loyal to the treaty they should return and say so openly before the Muslim army; however if they found that they were bent upon treachery they should only inform him so that the common Muslims would not be disheartened. On reaching there the Companions found the Banū Quraythah fully bent on mischief. They told the Companions openly that there is no agreement and no treaty between us and Muhammad. At this they returned to the Islāmic army and submitted their report to the Prophet, saying, "*'Adal and Qarah.*" That is, "*The Quraidhah are bent upon doing what the Adal and Qarah had done with the preachers of Islām at Raji.*"

This news spread among the Muslims and caused great consternation among them, for they had been encircled and their city had been endangered on the side where there existed no defensive arrangement and where they had also sent their families to take shelter in the forts. This further increased the activities of the hypocrites and they started making psychological attacks to break the morale of the Muslims. One said, "*How strange! We were being foretold that the lands of Caesar and Chosroes would fall to us, but here we are that not one of us can go out even to relieve himself.*" Another one asked for permission to leave his post at the Trench so that he could go and protect his own house which was in danger. Another one started making secret propaganda to the effect: "*Settle your affair with the invaders yourselves and hand over Muhammad to them.*" This was a highly critical hour of trial, which exposed every person who harbored any hypocrisy in his heart. Only the true and sincere Muslims remained firm and steadfast in their resolve and devotion.

The Prophet at that critical moment initiated peace negotiations with the Banu Ghatafan and tried to persuade them to accept one third of the fruit harvest of Madinah and withdraw. But when he asked Sad bin Ubadah and Sad bin Muadh, chief of the Ansār, for their opinion about the conditions of peace, they said, "*O Messenger of God: Is it your personal wish that we should agree on these conditions, or is it God's Command that we have no option but to accept it? Or, are you giving this proposal only in order to save us from the enemy?*" The Prophet replied, "*I am proposing this only to save you: I see that the whole of Arabia has formed a united front against you. I want to divide the enemy.*" At this the two chiefs protested; saying, "*if you want to conclude this pact for our sake, kindly forget it. These tribes could not subdue us under tribute when we were polytheists. Now that we have the honour of believing in God and His Messenger, will they make us sink to this depth of ignominy? The sword now shall be the arbiter till God passes His judgment between them and us.*" With these words they tore up the draft for the treaty which had not yet been signed.

In the meantime Nuaim bin Masud, a member of the Ashja branch of the Ghatafan tribe, became a Muslim and came before the Prophet and submitted: "*No one as yet knows that I have embraced Islām: You can take from me whatever service you please.*" The Prophet replied: "*Go and sow the seeds of discord among the enemy.*" So, first of all, Nuaim went to the Quraidhah with whom he was on friendly terms, and said to them, "*The Quraysh and the Ghatafan can become wearied of the siege and go back, and they will lose nothing, but you have to live here with the Muslims. Just consider what will be your position if the matter turns that way. Therefore, I would advise you not to join the enemy until the outsiders should send some of their prominent men as hostages to you.*" This had the desired effect upon the Banū Quraythah and they decided to demand hostages from the united front of the tribes. Then he went to the chiefs of the Quraysh and the Ghatafan and said to them, "*The Banū Quraythah seem to be slack and irresolute. Maybe they demand some men as hostage from you, and then hand them over to Muhammad to settle their affair with him. Therefore, be very firm and cautious in your dealing with them.*" This made the leaders of the united front suspicious of Banū Quraythah, and they sent them a message, saying, "*We are tired of the long siege; let there be a decisive battle; let us, therefore, make a general assault simultaneously from both the sides.*" The Banū Quraythah sent back the word, saying, "*We cannot afford to join the war unless you hand over some of your prominent men to us as hostages.*" The leaders of the united front became convinced that what Nuaim had said was true. They refused to send hostages. And the Banū Quraythah, on the other side, also felt that Nuaim had given them the correct counsel. Thus, the strategy worked: it divided the enemy against itself.

The siege was prolonged for more than 25 days. It was winter. The supply of food and water and forage was becoming more and more scarce everyday and division in the camp was also a great strain on the state of morale of the besiegers. Then, suddenly one night a severe windstorm accompanied by thunder and lightning hit the camp. It added to the cold and darkness. The wind overthrew the tents and put the enemy in disarray. They could not stand this severe blow of nature. They left the battleground even during the night and returned to their homes. When the Muslims awoke in the morning, there was not a single enemy soldier to be seen on the battlefield. The Prophet, finding the battlefield completely empty, said: "*The Quraysh will never be able to attack you after this: now you will take the offensive.*" This was a correct assessment of the situation. Not only the Quraysh but the united front of all the enemy tribes had made their final assault against Islām and had failed. Now they could no longer dare invade Madinah; now the Muslims were on the offensive.

**Social Reforms**

Though the period of two years between the Battles of Uhud and the Trench was a period of disturbance and turmoil and the Prophet and his Companions could hardly relax in peace and security even for a day the work of reform as a whole and the reconstruction of the Muslim society continued uninterrupted. This was the time when the Islāmic laws pertaining to marriage and divorce were complemented; the law of inheritance was introduced drinking and gambling were prohibited and the new laws and regulations concerning many other aspects of the economic and social life were enforced.

In this connection an important thing that needed to be reformed was the question of the adoption of a son. Whoever was adopted by the Arabs as a son was regarded as one of their own offspring: he got share in inheritance; he was treated like a real son and real brother by the adopted mother and the adopted sister; he could not marry the daughter of his adopted father and his widow after his death. And the same was the case if the adopted son died or divorced a wife. The adopted father regarded the woman as his real daughter-in-law. This custom clashed in every detail with the laws of marriage, divorce and inheritance enjoined by God in Sūrahs al-Baqarah and an-Nisā. It made a person who could get no share in inheritance entitled to it at the expense of those who were really entitled to it. It prohibited marriage between the men and the women who could contract marriage perfectly lawfully. And above all it helped spread the immoralities which the Islāmic Law wanted to eradicate. For a real mother and a real sister and a real daughter cannot be like the adopted mother, the adopted sister and the adopted daughter however one may try to sanctify the adopted relations as a custom. When the artificial relations endued with customary sanctity are allowed to mix freely like the real relations it cannot but produce evil results. That is why the Islāmic law of marriage, divorce, the law of inheritance and the law of the prohibition of adultery required that the concept and custom of regarding the adopted son as the real son should be eradicated completely.

This concept, however could not be rooted out by merely passing a legal order saying the adopted son is not the real son. The centuries old prejudices and superstitions cannot be changed by mere word of mouth. Even if the people had accepted the command that these relations were not the real relations they would still have looked upon marriage between the adopted mother and the adopted son, the adopted brother and the sister, the adopted father and the daughter and the adopted father- in-law and the daughter-in-law loathsome and detestable. Moreover there would still exist some freedom of mixing together freely. Therefore it was inevitable that the custom should be eradicated practically and through the Prophet himself. For no Muslim could ever conceive that a thing done by the Prophet himself and done by him under God's Command could be detestable. Therefore a little before the Battle of the Trench the Prophet was inspired by God that he should marry the divorced wife of his adopted son Zayd bin Harithah and he acted on this Command during the siege of the Banū Quraythah which had immediately followed the Battle of Trench.

**Storm of Propaganda at the Marriage of Zaynab**

As soon as the marriage was contracted, there arose a storm of propaganda against the Prophet. The polytheists, the hypocrites and the Jews, all were burning with jealousy at his triumphs which followed one after the other. The way they had been humbled within two years after Uhud, in the Battle of the Trench, and in the affair of the Quraidhah, had made them sore at heart. They had also lost hope that they could ever subdue him on the battlefield. Therefore, they seized the question of this marriage as a Godsend for themselves and thought they would put an end to his moral superiority, which was the real secret of his power and success. Therefore, stories were concocted that Muhammad, God forbid, had fallen in love with his daughter-in-law, and when the son had come to know of this, he divorced his wife, and the father married his daughter-in-law. The propaganda, however, was absurd on the face of it. Zaynab was the Prophet's first cousin. He had known her from childhood to youth. So, there could be no question of his falling in love with her at first sight. Then he himself had arranged her marriage with Zayd under his personal influence, although her whole family had opposed it. They did not like that a daughter of the noble Quraysh should be given in marriage to a freed slave. Zainab herself was not happy at this arrangement. But everyone had to submit to the Prophet's command. The marriage was solemnized and a precedent was set in Arabia that Islām had raised a freed slave to the status of the Quraysh nobility. If the Prophet had in reality any desire for Zainab, there was no need of marrying her to Zayd; he himself could have married her. But in spite of all this, the shameless opponents invented stories of love, spread them with great exaggeration and publicized them so vehemently that even some Muslims also began to accept them as true.

**Preliminary Commandments of the Veil**

The fact that the tales invented by the enemies also became topics of conversation among the Muslims was a clear sign that the element of sensuality in society had crossed all limits. If this malady had not been there it was not possible that minds would have paid any attention whatever to such absurd and disgusting stories about a righteous and pure person like the Prophet. This was precisely the occasion when the reformative commandments pertaining to the law of Hijab or Purdah were first enforced in the Islāmic society. These reforms were introduced in this Sūrah and complemented a year later in Sūrah an-Nūr when a slander was made on the honour of Ā'isha. (For further details see introduction to Sūrah an-Nūr).

### Domestic Affairs of the Prophet

There were two other problems which needed attention at that time. Though apparently they pertained to the Prophet's domestic life it was necessary to resolve them for the domestic and mental peace of the person who was exerting every effort to promote the cause of God's Religion and was day and night absorbed in this great mission. Therefore God took these two problems also officially in His own hand.

The first problem was that economically the Prophet at that time was in straitened circumstances. During the first four years he had no source of income whatever. In 4 A.H.after the banishment of the Banu-Nadheer a portion of their evacuated lands was reserved for his use by the Command of God but it was not enough for his family requirements. On the other hand the duties of the office of Prophethood were so onerous that they were absorbing all his energies of the mind and body and heart and every moment of his time and he could not make any effort at all for earning his livelihood. In conditions such as these when his wives happened to disturb his mental peace because of economic hardships he would feel doubly strained and taxed. The other problem was that before marrying Zaynab he had four wives already in the houses: Saudah, Ā'isha, Hafsa and Umm Salamah. Zaynab was his fifth wife. At this the opponents raised the objection. The Muslims also started entertaining doubts that as for others it had been forbidden to keep more than four wives at a time but how the Prophet himself had taken a fifth wife also.

### Subject Matter and Topics

These were the questions that were engaging the attention of the Prophet and the Muslims at the time Sūrah Al-Ahzāb was revealed and replies to the same form the subject matter of this Sūrah.

A perusal of the theme and the background shows that the Sūrah is not a single discourse which was sent down in one piece but it consists of several injunctions, commandments and discourses which were sent down one after the other in connection with the important events of the time and then were put together in one Sūrah. Its following parts stand out clearly distinguished from one another:

1. Verses 1-8 seem to have been sent down before the Battle of the Trench. Their perusal keeping the historical background in view shows that at the time of their revelation Zayd had already divorced Zaynab. The Prophet was feeling the necessity that the concepts and customs and superstitions of ignorance concerning the adoption of the son should be eradicated and he was also feeling that the delicate and deep sentiments the people cherished about the adopted relations merely on emotional grounds would not be rooted out until he himelf took the initiative to eradicate the custom practically. But at the same time he was hesitant and considering seriously that if he married the divorced wife of Zayd then the hypocrites, the Jews and the polytheists who were already bent on mischief would get a fresh excuse to start a propaganda campaign against Islām. This was the occasion of the revelation of v. 1-8.
2. In verses 9-27 an appraisal has been made of the Battle of the Trench and the raid against the Banū Quraythah. This is a clear proof that these verses were sent down after these events. The discourse contained in v. 28-35 consists of two parts. In the first part God has given a notice to the wives of the Prophet who were being impatient of the straitened circumstances to the effect: "..**If you should desire the worldly life and its adornment, then come, I will provide for you and give you a gracious release. But if you should desire God and His Messenger and the home of the Hereafter - then indeed, God has prepared for the doers of good among you a great reward.**"

3. In the second part initial steps were taken towards the social reforms whose need was being felt by the minds moulded in the Islāmic pattern themselves. In this regard reform was started from the house of the Prophet himself and his wives were commanded to avoid behaving and conducting themselves in the ways of the pre Islāmic days of ignorance to remain in their houses with dignity and to exercise great caution in their conversation with the other men. This was the beginning of the Commandments of the Veil.
4. Verses 36-48 deal with the Prophet's marriage with Zainab. In this section the opponents' objection about this marriage have been answered; the doubts that were being created in the minds of the Muslims have been removed; the Muslims have been acquainted with the Prophet's position and status; and the Prophet himself has been counselled to exercise patience on the false propaganda of the disbelievers and the hypocrites.
5. In verse 49 a clause of the law of divorce has been laid down. This is a unique verse which was sent down on some occasion probably in connection with the same events.
6. In verses 50-52 a special regulation of marriage has been laid down for the Prophet which points out that he is an exception to the several restrictions that have been imposed on the other Muslims in regard to marital life.
7. In verses 53-55 the second step was taken towards social reform. It consists of the following injunctions: Restriction on the other men to visit the houses of the Prophet's wives; Islāmic etiquette concerning visits and invitations; the law that only the near relatives could visit the wives in their houses; as for the other men, they could speak to or ask them a thing from behind a curtain; the injunction that the Prophet's wives were forbidden for the Muslims like their mothers; and none could marry any of them after him.
8. In verses 56-57 warning was given to stop criticizing the Prophet's marriage and his domestic life, and the believers instructed not to indulge in fault finding like the enemies of Islām, but to invoke the blessings of God for their Prophet; moreover, they were instructed that they should avoid falsely accusing one another even among themselves, not to speak of the person of the Prophet.
9. In verse 59 the third step for social reform was taken. All the Muslim women were commanded that they should come out well covered with the outer garments and covering their faces whenever they came out of their houses for a genuine need.

After this till the end of the Sūrah the hypocrites and other foolish and mean people have been rebuked for the propaganda that they were carrying on at that time against Islām and the Muslims.

## Sūrah 33: al-Ahzāb[1101]

In the Name of God, the Most Compassionate, the Most Merciful

1. O Prophet, fear God and do not obey the disbelievers and the hypocrites. Indeed, God is ever Knowing and Wise.

2. And follow that which is revealed to you from your Lord. Indeed God is ever, with what you do, Acquainted.

3. And rely upon God; and sufficient is God as Disposer of affairs.

4. God has not made for a man two hearts in his interior. And He has not made your wives whom you declare unlawful[1102] your mothers. And He has not made your claimed [i.e., adopted] sons your [true] sons. That is [merely] your saying by your mouths, but God says the truth, and He guides to the [right] way.

5. Call them[1103] by [the names of] their fathers; it is more just in the sight of God. But if you do not know their fathers - then they are [still] your brothers in religion and those entrusted to you. And there is no blame upon you for that in which you have erred but [only for] what your hearts intended. And ever is God Forgiving and Merciful.

6. The Prophet is more worthy of the believers than themselves,[1104] and his wives are [in the position of] their mothers. And those of [blood] relationship are more entitled [to inheritance] in the decree of God than the [other] believers and the emigrants, except that you may do to your close associates a kindness [through bequest]. That was in the Book[1105] inscribed.

7. And [mention, O Muhammad], when We took from the prophets their covenant and from you and from Noah and Abraham and Moses and Jesus, the son of Mary; and We took from them a solemn covenant.

8. That He may question the truthful about their truth.[1106] And He has prepared for the disbelievers a painful punishment.

9. O you who have believed, remember the favor of God upon you when armies came to [attack] you and We sent upon them a wind and armies [of angels] you did not see. And ever is God, of what you do, Seeing.

10. [Remember] when they came at you from above you and from below you, and when eyes shifted [in fear], and hearts reached the throats, and you assumed about God [various] assumptions.

---

1101 *Al-Azḥāb*: The Companies or The Combined Forces, referring to the alliance of disbelieving Arab tribes against the Muslims in Madinah for the battle called *"al-Ahzāb"* or *"al-Khunduq"* (the Trench).

1102 By the expression "You are to me like the back of my mother." Such an oath taken against approaching one's wife was a pre-Islāmic practice declared by God to be a sin requiring expiation as described in 58:3-4.

1103 Those children under your care.

1104 He is more worthy of their obedience and loyalty and is more concerned for them than they are for one another.

1105 The Preserved Slate (*al-Lawh al-Mahfūth*).

1106 i.e., that He may ask the prophets what they conveyed to their people and what response they received. "The truthful" may also refer to those who believed in the message conveyed by the prophets and imparted it to others.

11. There the believers were tested and shaken with a severe shaking.

12. And [remember] when the hypocrites and those in whose hearts is disease said, "God and His Messenger did not promise us except delusion,"

13. And when a faction of them said, "O people of Yathrib,[1107] there is no stability for you [here], so return [home]." And a party of them asked permission of the Prophet, saying, "Indeed, our houses are exposed [i.e., unprotected]," while they were not exposed. They did not intend except to flee.

14. And if they had been entered upon from all its [surrounding] regions and fitnah [i.e., disbelief] had been demanded of them, they would have done it and not hesitated over it except briefly.

15. And they had already promised God before not to turn their backs [i.e., flee]. And ever is the promise to God [that about which one will be] questioned.

16. Say, [O Muhammad], "Never will fleeing benefit you if you should flee from death or killing; and then [if you did], you would not be given enjoyment [of life] except for a little."

17. Say, "Who is it that can protect you from God[1108] if He intends for you an ill or intends for you a mercy?" And they will not find for themselves besides God any protector or any helper.

18. Already God knows the hinderers[1109] among you and those [hypocrites] who say to their brothers, "Come to us,"[1110] and do not go to battle, except for a few,[1111]

19. Indisposed[1112] toward you. And when fear comes, you see them looking at you, their eyes revolving like one being overcome by death. But when fear departs, they lash you with sharp tongues, indisposed toward [any] good. Those have not believed, so God has rendered their deeds worthless, and ever is that, for God, easy.

20. They think the companies have not [yet] withdrawn.[1113] And if the companies should come [again], they would wish they were in the desert among the bedouins, inquiring [from afar] about your news. And if they should be among you, they would not fight except for a little.

21. There has certainly been for you in the Messenger of God an excellent pattern[1114] for anyone whose hope is in God and the Last Day and [who] remembers God often.

22. And when the believers saw the companies, they said, "This is what God and His Messenger had promised us, and God and His Messenger spoke the truth." And it increased them only in faith and acceptance.

---

[1107] The name by which al-Madinah was known before the arrival of the Prophet.
[1108] i.e., prevent the will of God from being carried out.

[1109] Those who dissuade others from supporting the Prophet in battle.
[1110] Rather than joining the Prophet.
[1111] Who went out of ulterior motives.
[1112] Literally, "stingy," i.e., unwilling to offer any help.
[1113] In their excessive fear the cowardly hypocrites could not believe the enemy forces had been defeated.
[1114] An example to be followed.

23. Among the believers are men true to what they promised God. Among them is he who has fulfilled his vow [to the death], and among them is he who awaits [his chance]. And they did not alter [the terms of their commitment] by any alteration -

24. That God may reward the truthful for their truth and punish the hypocrites if He wills or accept their repentance. Indeed, God is ever Forgiving and Merciful.

25. And God repelled those who disbelieved, in their rage, not having obtained any good. And sufficient was God for the believers in battle, and ever is God Powerful and Exalted in Might.

26. And He brought down those who supported them among the People of the Scripture[1115] from their fortresses and cast terror into their hearts [so that] a party [i.e., their men] you killed, and you took captive a party [i.e., the women and children].

27. And He caused you to inherit their land and their homes and their properties and a land which you have not trodden.[1116] And ever is God, over all things, competent.

28. O Prophet, say to your wives, "If you should desire the worldly life and its adornment, then come, I will provide for you and give you a gracious release.

29. But if you should desire God and His Messenger and the home of the Hereafter - then indeed, God has prepared for the doers of good among you a great reward."

30. O wives of the Prophet, whoever of you should commit a clear immorality - for her the punishment would be doubled two fold, and ever is that, for God, easy.

31. And whoever of you devoutly obeys God and His Messenger and does righteousness - We will give her her reward twice; and We have prepared for her a noble provision.

32. O wives of the Prophet, you are not like anyone among women. If you fear God, then do not be soft in speech [to men],[1117] lest he in whose heart is disease should covet, but speak with appropriate speech.

33. And abide in your houses and do not display yourselves as [was] the display of the former times of ignorance. And establish prayer and give zakāh and obey God and His Messenger. God intends only to remove from you the impurity [of sin], O people of the [Prophet's] household, and to purify you with [extensive] purification.

34. And remember what is recited in your houses of the verses of God and wisdom.[1118] Indeed, God is ever Subtle and Acquainted [with all things].

35. Indeed, the Muslim men and Muslim women, the believing men and believing women, the obedient men and obedient women, the truthful men and truthful women, the patient men and

[1115] The Jews of Banū Quraythah, who had violated their treaty with the Muslims.

[1116] i.e., that taken in subsequent conquests.

[1117] The meaning has also been given as "You are not like any among women if you fear God. So do not be soft in speech…"

[1118] The teachings of the Prophet or his *sunnah* (sayings and practices).

patient women, the humble men and humble women, the charitable men and charitable women, the fasting men and fasting women, the men who guard their private parts and the women who do so, and the men who remember God often and the women who do so - for them God has prepared forgiveness and a great reward.

36. It is not for a believing man or a believing woman, when God and His Messenger have decided a matter, that they should [thereafter] have any choice about their affair. And whoever disobeys God and His Messenger has certainly strayed into clear error.

37. And [remember, O Muhammad], when you said to the one on whom God bestowed favor and you bestowed favor,[1119] "Keep your wife and fear God," while you concealed within yourself that which God is to disclose.[1120] And you feared the people,[1121] while God has more right that you fear Him.[1122] So when Zayd had no longer any need for her, We married her to you in order that there not be upon the believers any discomfort [i.e., guilt] concerning the wives of their claimed [i.e., adopted] sons when they no longer have need of them. And ever is the command [i.e., decree] of God accomplished.

38. There is not to be upon the Prophet any discomfort concerning that which God has imposed upon him.[1123] [This is] the established way of God with those [prophets] who have passed on before. And ever is the command of God a destiny decreed.

39. [God praises] those who convey the messages of God[1124] and fear Him and do not fear anyone but God. And sufficient is God as Accountant.

40. Muhammad is not the father of [any] one of your men, but [he is] the Messenger of God and seal [i.e., last] of the prophets. And ever is God, of all things, Knowing.

41. O you who have believed, remember God with much remembrance

42. And exalt Him morning and afternoon.

43. It is He who confers blessing upon you,[1125] and His angels [ask Him to do so] that He may bring you out from darknesses into the light. And ever is He, to the believers, Merciful.

44. Their greeting the Day they meet Him will be, "Peace." And He has prepared for them a noble reward.

45. O Prophet, indeed We have sent you as a witness and a bringer of good tidings and a warner.

---

[1119] Referring to the Prophet's freed slave, Zayd bin Hārithah.

[1120] i.e., God's command to the Prophet to marry Zaynab after Zayd divorced her. This was to demonstrate that a man may marry a woman formally married to his adopted son.

[1121] i.e., feared their saying that the Prophet had married the (former) wife of his son (which is prohibited by God in the case if a true, begotten son).

[1122] By making known His command.

[1123] Or permitted to him.

[1124] i.e., the prophets (peace be upon them all) and after them, the followers of the final prophet, Muhammad, who honestly convey God's message to the people.

[1125] i.e., God cares for you and covers you with His mercy. An additional meaning is that He praises you in the presence of the angels.

46. And one who invites to God, by His permission, and an illuminating lamp.

47. And give good tidings to the believers that they will have from God great bounty.

48. And do not obey the disbelievers and the hypocrites but do not harm them, and rely upon God. And sufficient is God as Disposer of affairs.

49. O you who have believed, when you marry believing women and then divorce them before you have touched them [i.e., consummated the marriage], then there is not for you any waiting period to count concerning them. So provide for them and give them a gracious release.

50. O Prophet, indeed We have made lawful to you your wives to whom you have given their due compensation[1126] and those your right hand possesses from what God has returned to you [of captives] and the daughters of your paternal uncles and the daughters of your paternal aunts and the daughters of your maternal uncles and the daughters of your maternal aunts who emigrated with you and a believing woman if she gives herself to the Prophet [and] if the Prophet wishes to marry her, [this is] only for you, excluding the [other] believers. We certainly know what We have made obligatory upon them concerning their wives and those their right hands possess, [but this is for you] in order that there will be upon you no discomfort [i.e., difficulty]. And ever is God Forgiving and Merciful.

[1126] i.e., bridal gifts (*mahr*).

51. You, [O Muhammad], may put aside whom you will of them[1127] or take to yourself whom you will. And any that you desire of those [wives] from whom you had [temporarily] separated - there is no blame upon you [in returning her]. That is more suitable that they should be content and not grieve and that they should be satisfied with what you have given them - all of them. And God knows what is in your hearts. And ever is God Knowing and Forbearing.

52. Not lawful to you, [O Muhammad], are [any additional] women after [this], nor [is it] for you to exchange them for [other] wives, even if their beauty were to please you, except what your right hand possesses. And ever is God, over all things, an Observer.

53. O you who have believed, do not enter the houses of the Prophet except when you are permitted for a meal, without awaiting its readiness. But when you are invited, then enter; and when you have eaten, disperse without seeking to remain for conversation. Indeed, that [behavior] was troubling the Prophet, and he is shy of [dismissing] you. But God is not shy of the truth. And when you ask [his wives] for something, ask them from behind a partition. That is purer for your hearts and their hearts. And it is not [conceivable or lawful] for you to harm the Messenger of God or to marry his wives after him, ever. Indeed, that would be in the sight of God an enormity.

54. Whether you reveal a thing or conceal it, indeed God is ever, of all things, Knowing.

[1127] Those mentioned in the previous verse as being lawful to the Prophet or his wives to which he was married.

55. There is no blame upon them [i.e., women] concerning their fathers or their sons or their brothers or their brothers' sons or their sisters' sons or their women or those their right hands possess [i.e., slaves].[1128] And fear God. Indeed God is ever, over all things, Witness.

56. Indeed, God confers blessing upon the Prophet, and His angels [ask Him to do so]. O you who have believed, ask [God to confer] blessing upon him and ask [God to grant him] peace.

57. Indeed, those who abuse God and His Messenger - God has cursed them in this world and the Hereafter and prepared for them a humiliating punishment.

58. And those who harm believing men and believing women for [something] other than what they have earned [i.e., deserved] have certainly born upon themselves a slander and manifest sin.

59. O Prophet, tell your wives and your daughters and the women of the believers to bring down over themselves [part] of their outer garments.[1129] That is more suitable that they will be known[1130] and not be abused. And ever is God Forgiving and Merciful.[1131]

[1128] It is permissible for a woman to appear before these people without complete covering and to be alone with them. The brothers of both parents (uncles) are included as "fathers" or "parents," according to *hadith*.

[1129] The *jilbāb*, which is defined as a cloak covering the head and reaching to the ground, thereby covering the woman's entire body.

[1130] As chaste believing women.

[1131] Or "and God was forgiving and Merciful" of what occurred before this injunction or before knowledge of it.

60. If the hypocrites and those in whose hearts is disease[1132] and those who spread rumors in al-Madīnah do not cease, We will surely incite you against them; then they will not remain your neighbors therein except for a little.

61. Accursed wherever they are found, [being] seized and massacred completely.

62. [This is] the established way of God with those who passed on before; and you will not find in the way of God any change.

63. People ask you concerning the Hour. Say, "Knowledge of it is only with God. And what may make you perceive? Perhaps the Hour is near."

64. Indeed, God has cursed the disbelievers and prepared for them a Blaze.

65. Abiding therein forever, they will not find a protector or a helper.

66. The Day their faces will be turned about in the Fire, they will say, "How we wish we had obeyed God and obeyed the Messenger."

67. And they will say, "Our Lord, indeed we obeyed our masters and our dignitaries,[1133] and they led us astray from the [right] way.

68. Our Lord, give them double the punishment and curse them with a great curse."

69. O you who have believed, be not like those who abused Moses; then God

[1132] Referring here to those who commit adultery or fornication.

[1133] Also interpreted to mean "our noble ones and our elders [i.e., distinguished scholars]."

cleared him of what they said. And he, in the sight of God, was distinguished.

70. O you who have believed, fear God and speak words of appropriate justice.

71. He will [then] amend for you your deeds and forgive you your sins. And whoever obeys God and His Messenger has certainly attained a great attainment.

72. Indeed, We offered the Trust[1134] to the heavens and the earth and the mountains, and they declined to bear it and feared it; but man [undertook to] bear it. Indeed, he was unjust and ignorant.[1135]

73. [It[1136] was] so that God may punish the hypocrite men and hypocrite women and the men and women who associate others with Him and that God may accept repentance from the believing men and believing women. And ever is God Forgiving and Merciful.

[1134] The acceptance of obligations and obedience to God.

[1135] Coveting its reward while forgetting the penalty for failure to keep his commitment.

[1136] The reason for which mankind was permitted to carry the Trust.

## Sūrah 34: Saba'

### Period of Revelation

The exact period of its revelation is not known from any reliable hadith. However the style shows that it is either the middle or the early Makkan period. If it is the middle period it was probably its initial stage when the persecution had not yet become tyrannical and the Islāmic movement was being suppressed only by resort to derision and ridicule, rumour mongering, false allegations and casting of evil suggestions in the peoples minds.

### Theme and Subject Matter

The Sūrah deals with those objections of the disbelievers which they were raising against the Prophet's message of Tawhid (oneness of God), the Hereafter and about his Prophethood itself. This was mostly in the form of absurd allegations, taunts and mockery. These objections have been answered sometimes by citing them and sometimes without citing them while the discourse itself shows which objection is being answered at a particular place. The answers mostly take the form of instruction and admonition and argument but at some places the disbelievers have been warned also of the evil consequences of their stubborness. In this connection the stories of the Sabaeans and the Prophets David and Solomon have been related to impress this lesson: "You have both these historical precedents before you. On the one hand there were the Prophets David and Solomon who had been blessed by God with great powers and such grandeur and glory as had been granted to hardly any people before them. In spite of this they were not proud and arrogant but remained grateful servants of their Lord. They were never rebellious. On the other hand there were the people of Saba who when blessed by God became proud and were consequently so thoroughly destroyed and dispersed as to be remembered only in myths and legends. With these precedents in view you may see and judge for yourselves as to which bind of the life is better: that which is built on belief in Tawhid, the Hereafter and the attitude of gratefulness to God or that which is based on disbelief, shirk, denial of the Hereafter and the worship of the world."

## Sūrah 34: Saba'[1137]

In the Name of God, the Most Compassionate, the Most Merciful

1. [All] praise is [due] to God, to whom belongs whatever is in the heavens and whatever is in the earth, and to Him belongs [all] praise in the Hereafter. And He is the Wise, the Acquainted.

2. He knows what penetrates into the earth and what emerges from it and what descends from the heaven and what ascends therein. And He is the Merciful, the Forgiving.

3. But those who disbelieve say, "The Hour will not come to us." Say, "Yes, by my Lord, it will surely come to you. [God is] the Knower of the unseen." Not absent from Him is an atom's weight[1138] within the heavens or within the earth or [what is] smaller than that or greater, except that it is in a clear register -

4. That He may reward those who believe and do righteous deeds. Those will have forgiveness and noble provision.

5. But those who strive against Our verses [seeking] to cause failure[1139] - for them will be a painful punishment of foul nature.

6. And those who have been given knowledge see that what is revealed to you from your Lord is the truth, and it guides to the path of the Exalted in Might, the Praiseworthy.

7. But those who disbelieve say, "Shall we direct you to a man who will inform you [that] when you have disintegrated in complete disintegration, you will [then] be [recreated] in a new creation?

8. Has he invented about God a lie or is there in him madness?" Rather, they who do not believe in the Hereafter will be in the punishment and [are in] extreme error.

9. Then, do they not look at what is before them and what is behind them of the heaven and earth? If We should will, We could cause the earth to swallow them or [could] let fall upon them fragments from the sky. Indeed in that is a sign for every servant turning back [to God].

10. And We certainly gave David from Us bounty. [We said], "O mountains, repeat [Our] praises with him, and the birds [as well]." And We made pliable for him iron,

11. [Commanding him], "Make full coats of mail and calculate [precisely] the links, and work [all of you] righteousness. Indeed I, of what you do, am Seeing."

12. And to Solomon [We subjected] the wind - its morning [journey was that of] a month - and its afternoon [journey was that of] a month, and We made flow for him a spring of [liquid] copper. And among the jinn were those who worked for him by the permission of his Lord. And whoever deviated among them from Our command - We will make him taste of the punishment of the Blaze.

[1137] *Saba'*; (The People of) Saba' or Sabeans.
[1138] Or "the weight of a small ant."
[1139] i.e., to undermine their credibility in order to defeat the Prophet.

13. They made for him what he willed of elevated chambers,[1140] statues,[1141] bowls like reservoirs, and stationary kettles. [We said], "Work, O family of David, in gratitude." And few of My servants are grateful.

14. And when We decreed for him [i.e., Solomon] death, nothing indicated to them [i.e., the jinn] his death except a creature of the earth eating his staff.[1142] But when he fell, it became clear to the jinn that if they had known the unseen, they would not have remained in humiliating punishment.[1143]

15. There was for [the tribe of] Saba' in their dwelling place a sign: two [fields of] gardens on the right and on the left. [They were told], "Eat from the provisions of your Lord and be grateful to Him. A good land [have you], and a forgiving Lord."

16. But they turned away [refusing], so We sent upon them the flood of the dam,[1144] and We replaced their two [fields of] gardens with gardens of bitter fruit, tamarisks and something of sparse lote trees.

17. [By] that We repaid them because they disbelieved. And do We [thus] repay except the ungrateful?

18. And We placed between them and the cities which We had blessed[1145] [many] visible cities. And We determined between them the [distances of] journey,[1146] [saying], "Travel between them by night or day in safety."

19. But [insolently] they said, "Our Lord, lengthen the distance between our journeys," and wronged themselves, so We made them narrations[1147] and dispersed them in total dispersion. Indeed in that are signs for everyone patient and grateful.

20. And Iblees had already confirmed through them[1148] his assumption,[1149] so they followed him, except for a party of believers.

21. And he had over them no authority except [it was decreed] that We might make evident who believes in the Hereafter from who is thereof in doubt. And your Lord, over all things, is Guardian.

22. Say, [O Muhammad], "Invoke those you claim [as deities] besides God." They do not possess an atom's weight [of ability] in the heavens or on the earth, and they do not have therein any partnership [with Him], nor is there for Him from among them any assistant.

23. And intercession does not benefit with Him except for one whom He permits.

---

[1140] Described by commentators as palaces, dwellings, or places of prayer.

[1141] Which were not prohibited until the time of Prophet Muhammad.

[1142] Upon which he was leaning at the time of his death. A termite continued to gnaw into the stick until it collapsed under his weight.

[1143] i.e., hard labor. This verse is evidence that the *jinn* do not possess knowledge of the unseen, which belongs exclusively to God.

[1144] i.e., caused by a break in their dam. Another meaning is "the overwhelming flood."

[1145] In the lands of what is now southern Syria and Palestine.

[1146] i.e., We placed the intermediate settlements at calculated distances for the convenience of travellers.

[1147] Stories related to others as lessons or examples.

[1148] i.e., the people of Saba' or mankind in general.

[1149] That mankind could readily be misled by him.

[And those wait] until, when terror is removed from their hearts,[1150] they will say [to one another], "What has your Lord said?" They will say, "The truth." And He is the Most High, the Grand.

24. Say, "Who provides for you from the heavens and the earth?" Say, "God. And indeed, we or you are either upon guidance or in clear error."

25. Say, "You will not be asked about what we committed, and we will not be asked about what you do."

26. Say, "Our Lord will bring us together; then He will judge between us in truth. And He is the Knowing Judge."

27. Say, "Show me those whom you have attached to Him as partners. No! Rather, He [alone] is God, the Exalted in Might, the Wise."

28. And We have not sent you except comprehensively[1151] to mankind as a bringer of good tidings and a warner. But most of the people do not know.

29. And they say, "When is this promise, if you should be truthful?"

30. Say, "For you is the appointment of a Day [when] you will not remain thereafter an hour, nor will you precede [it]."

31. And those who disbelieve say, "We will never believe in this Qur'ān nor in that before it." But if you could see when the wrongdoers are made to stand before their Lord, refuting each others' words...[1152] Those who were oppressed will say to those who were arrogant, "If not for you, we would have been believers."

32. Those who were arrogant will say to those who were oppressed, "Did we avert you from guidance after it had come to you? Rather, you were criminals."

33. Those who were oppressed will say to those who were arrogant, "Rather, [it was your] conspiracy of night and day when you were ordering us to disbelieve in God and attribute to Him equals." But they will [all] confide regret when they see the punishment; and We will put shackles on the necks of those who disbelieved. Will they be recompensed except for what they used to do?

34. And We did not send into a city any warner except that its affluent said, "Indeed we, in that with which you were sent, are disbelievers."

35. And they[1153] said, "We are more [than the believers] in wealth and children, and we are not to be punished."

36. Say, "Indeed, my Lord extends provision for whom He wills and restricts [it], but most of the people do not know."

37. And it is not your wealth or your children that bring you nearer to Us in position, but it is [by being] one who has believed and done righteousness. For them there will be the double reward

[1150] i.e., the hearts of the angels who will be permitted to intercede.

[1151] Literally, "inclusively, without exception."

[1152] Having been left to the imagination, the conclusion of this sentence is estimated to be "...you would see a dreadful sight."

[1153] The affluent ones in general or the people of Makkah specifically.

for what they did, and they will be in the upper chambers [of Paradise], safe [and secure].

38. And the ones who strive against Our verses to cause [them] failure[1154] - those will be brought into the punishment [to remain].

39. Say, "Indeed, my Lord extends provision for whom He wills of His servants and restricts [it] for him. But whatever thing you spend [in His cause] - He will compensate it; and He is the best of providers."

40. And [mention] the Day when He will gather them all and then say to the angels, "Did these [people] used to worship you?"

41. They will say, "Exalted are You! You, [O God], are our benefactor excluding [i.e., not] them. Rather, they used to worship the jinn; most of them were believers in them."

42. But today [i.e., the Day of Judgement] you do not hold for one another [the power of] benefit or harm, and We will say to those who wronged, "Taste the punishment of the Fire, which you used to deny."

43. And when our verses are recited to them as clear evidences, they say, "This is not but a man who wishes to avert you from that which your fathers were worshipping." And they say, "This is not except a lie invented." And those who disbelieve say of the truth when it has come to them, "This is not but obvious magic."

44. And We had not given them any scriptures which they could study, and We had not sent to them before you, [O Muhammad], any warner.

45. And those before them denied, and they [i.e., the people of Makkah] have not attained a tenth of what We had given them. But they [i.e., the former peoples] denied My messengers, so how [terrible] was My reproach.

46. Say, "I only advise you of one [thing] - that you stand for God, [seeking truth] in pairs and individually, and then give thought." There is not in your companion any madness. He is only a warner to you before a severe punishment.

47. Say, "Whatever payment I might have asked of you - it is yours. My payment is only from God, and He is, over all things, Witness."

48. Say, "Indeed, my Lord projects the truth, Knower of the unseen."

49. Say, "The truth has come, and falsehood can neither begin [anything] nor repeat [it]."[1155]

50. Say, "If I should err, I would only err against myself. But if I am guided, it is by what my Lord reveals to me. Indeed, He is Hearing and near."

51. And if you could see[1156] when they are terrified but there is no escape, and they will be seized from a place nearby.

52. And they will [then] say, "We believe in it!" But how for them will be the tak-

[1154] See footnote to 34:5.

[1155] This expression alludes to complete inability, meaning that falsehood was abolished.

[1156] i.e., have a glimpse of the Hereafter.

ing[1157] [of faith] from a place far away?[1158]

53. And they had already disbelieved in it before and would assault[1159] the unseen from a place far away.[1160]

54. And prevention will be placed between them and what they desire,[1161] as was done with their kind before. Indeed, they were in disquieting doubt [i.e., denial].

1157 Literally, "taking of something within easy reach," in other words, "How can they expect to obtain faith at this point?"
1158 i.e., their former life on earth, wherein they had every opportunity but which is now gone, never to return.
1159 Verbally, by conjecture and denial.
1160 i.e., a position far from truth.
1161 Meaning the attainment of faith and its benefits or entrance into Paradise.

## Sūrah 35: Fātir

### Period of Revelation

The internal evidence of the style shows that the period of the revelation of this Sūrah is probably the middle Makkan period when antagonism had grown quite strong so every sort of mischief was being adopted to frustrate the mission of the Prophet.

### Subject Matter and Theme

The discourse is meant to warn and reprove the people of Makkah and their chiefs for their antagonistic attitude that they had then adopted towards the Prophet's message of Tawhid (Oneness of God) like a well wisher and also to admonish them like a teacher as if to say: "O foolish people the way to which this Prophet is calling you is to your own advantage. Your anger, your tricks, plotting against it and your conspiracies and designs to frustrate it are not directed against him but against your own selves. If you do not listen to him you will be harming your own selves not him. Just consider and ponder over what he says: there is nothing wrong in it. He repudiates shirk. If you look around carefully you will yourself realize that there is no basis for shirk in the world. He presents the doctrine of Tawhid. If you use your common sense you will come to the conclusion that there is no being beside God, the Creator of the Universe which might possess divine attributes, powers and authority. He tells you that you have not been created to be irresponsible in this world but you have to render an account of your deeds before your God and that there is life after the life of this world when everyone will meet the consequences of what he has done here. If you think a little you will see that your doubts and your astonishment about it are absolutely baseless. Don't you see the phenomenon of the creation of day and night. How can then your own recreation be impossible for that God Who created you from an insignificant sperm drop? Doesn't your own intellect testify that the good and the evil cannot be alike? Then think and judge for yourselves as to what is reasonable: should the good and the evil meet with the same fate and end up in the dust or should the good be requited with good and the evil with evil? Now, if you do not admit and acknowledge these rational and reasonable things and do not abandon your false gods and wish to continue living only as irresponsible people in the world the Prophet will not lose anything. It is you yourselves only who will suffer the consequences. The Prophet's only responsibility was to make the truth plain to you which be has done."

In this connection the Prophet has been consoled again and again as if to say: "When you are doing full justice to the preaching of your mission you do not incur any responsibility for those who persist in their error and do not accept and follow the right way." Furthermore he has also been consoled to the effect "You should neither grieve on account of those who do not want to believe nor consume yourself with the thought of how to bring them to the right path. Instead of this you should pay your full attention to those who are inclined to listen to you."

The believers also in this connection have been given the good news so that they may feel strengthened, encouraged and remain steadfast on the path of the truth with full faith in the promises made by God.

## Sūrah 35: Fātir[1162]

In the Name of God, the Most Compassionate, the Most Merciful

1. [All] praise is [due] to God, Creator of the heavens and the earth, [who] made the angels messengers having wings, two or three or four. He increases in creation what He wills. Indeed, God is over all things competent.

2. Whatever God grants to people of mercy - none can withhold it; and whatever He withholds - none can release it thereafter. And He is the Exalted in Might, the Wise.

3. O mankind, remember the favor of God upon you. Is there any creator other than God who provides for you from the heaven and earth? There is no deity except Him, so how are you deluded?

4. And if they deny you, [O Muhammad] - already were messengers denied before you. And to God are returned [all] matters.

5. O mankind, indeed the promise of God is truth, so let not the worldly life delude you and be not deceived about God by the Deceiver [i.e., Satan].

6. Indeed, Satan is an enemy to you; so take him as an enemy. He only invites his party to be among the companions of the Blaze.

7. Those who disbelieve will have a severe punishment, and those who believe and do righteous deeds will have forgiveness and great reward.

8. Then is one to whom the evil of his deed has been made attractive so he considers it good [like one rightly guided]? For indeed, God sends astray whom He wills and guides whom He wills. So do not let yourself perish over them in regret. Indeed, God is Knowing of what they do.

9. And it is God who sends the winds, and they stir the clouds, and We drive them to a dead land and give life thereby to the earth after its lifelessness. Thus is the resurrection.

10. Whoever desires honour [through power] - then to God belongs all honour.[1163] To Him ascends good speech, and righteous work raises it.[1164] But they who plot evil deeds will have a severe punishment, and the plotting of those - it will perish.

11. And God created you from dust, then from a sperm-drop; then He made you mates. And no female conceives nor does she give birth except with His knowledge. And no aged person is granted [additional] life nor is his lifespan lessened but that it is in a register. Indeed, that for God is easy.

12. And not alike are the two seas [i.e., bodies of water]. One is fresh and sweet, palatable for drinking, and one is salty and bitter. And from each you eat tender meat and extract ornaments which you wear, and you see the ships plowing through [them] that you might seek

[1162] *Fātir*: The Creator, Originator (of creation), or He who brings (it) into existence from nothing. Also called *al-Malā'ikah* (The Angels).

[1163] See footnote to 4:139.

[1164] For acceptance by God, meaning that righteous deeds are confirmation and proof of what is uttered by the tongue.

of His bounty; and perhaps you will be grateful.

13. He causes the night to enter the day, and He causes the day to enter the night and has subjected the sun and the moon - each running [its course] for a specified term. That is God, your Lord; to Him belongs sovereignty. And those whom you invoke other than Him do not possess [as much as] the membrane of a date seed.

14. If you invoke them, they do not hear your supplication; and if they heard, they would not respond to you. And on the Day of Resurrection they will deny your association.[1165] And none can inform you like [one] Acquainted [with all matters].

15. O mankind, you are those in need of God, while God is the Free of need, the Praiseworthy.

16. If He wills, He can do away with you and bring forth a new creation.

17. And that is for God not difficult.

18. And no bearer of burdens will bear the burden of another. And if a heavily laden soul calls [another] to [carry some of] its load, nothing of it will be carried, even if he should be a close relative. You can only warn those who fear their Lord unseen and have established prayer. And whoever purifies himself only purifies himself for [the benefit of] his soul. And to God is the [final] destination.

19. Not equal are the blind and the seeing,

20. Nor are the darknesses and the light,

21. Nor are the shade and the heat,[1166]

22. And not equal are the living and the dead. Indeed, God causes to hear whom He wills, but you cannot make hear those in the graves.[1167]

23. You, [O Muhammad], are not but a warner.

24. Indeed, We have sent you with the truth as a bringer of good tidings and a warner. And there was no nation but that there had passed within it a warner.

25. And if they deny you - then already have those before them denied. Their messengers came to them with clear proofs and written ordinances and with the enlightening Scripture.

26. Then I seized the ones who disbelieved, and how [terrible] was My reproach.

27. Do you not see that God sends down rain from the sky, and We produce thereby fruits of varying colors? And in the mountains are tracts, white and red of varying shades and [some] extremely black.

28. And among people and moving creatures and grazing livestock are various colors similarly. Only those fear God, from among His servants, who have knowledge. Indeed, God is Exalted in Might and Forgiving.

29. Indeed, those who recite the Book of God and establish prayer and spend [in

[1165] Of them with God or your worship of them.

[1166] Of the sun or of a scorching wind.

[1167] The four comparisons given by God in verses 19-22 are those of the believer and unbeliever, various kinds of misbelief and (true) belief, Paradise and Hellfire, and those receptive to guidance and those unreceptive.

His cause] out of what We have provided them, secretly and publicly, [can] expect a transaction [i.e., profit] that will never perish -

30. That He may give them in full their rewards and increase for them of His bounty. Indeed, He is Forgiving and Appreciative.

31. And that which We have revealed to you, [O Muhammad], of the Book is the truth, confirming what was before it. Indeed, God, of His servants, is Acquainted and Seeing.

32. Then We caused to inherit the Book those We have chosen of Our servants;[1168] and among them is he who wrongs himself [i.e., sins], and among them is he who is moderate, and among them is he who is foremost in good deeds by permission of God. That [inheritance] is what is the great bounty.

33. [For them are] gardens of perpetual residence which they will enter. They will be adorned therein with bracelets of gold and pearls, and their garments therein will be silk.

34. And they will say, "Praise to God, who has removed from us [all] sorrow. Indeed, our Lord is Forgiving and Appreciative -

35. He who has settled us in the home of duration [i.e., Paradisre] out of His bounty. There touches us not in it any fatigue, and there touches us not in it weariness [of mind]."

36. And for those who disbelieve will be the fire of Hell. [Death] is not decreed for them[1169] so they may die, nor will its torment be lightened for them. Thus do We recompense every ungrateful one.

37. And they will cry out therein, "Our Lord, remove us;[1170] we will do righteousness - other than what we were doing!" But did We not grant you life enough for whoever would remember therein to remember, and the warner had come to you? So taste [the punishment], for there is not for the wrongdoers any helper.

38. Indeed, God is Knower of the unseen [aspects] of the heavens and earth. Indeed, He is Knowing of that within the breasts.

39. It is He who has made you successors upon the earth. And whoever disbelieves - upon him will be [the consequence of] his disbelief. And the disbelief of the disbelievers does not increase them in the sight of their Lord except in hatred; and the disbelief of the disbelievers does not increase them except in loss.

40. Say, "Have you considered[1171] your 'partners' whom you invoke besides God? Show me what they have created from the earth, or have they partnership [with Him] in the heavens? Or have We given them a book so they are [standing] on evidence therefrom? [No], rather, the wrongdoers do not promise each other except delusion."[1172]

1168 The followers of Prophet Muhammad.

1169 Or "They are not killed."

1170 The implication is "Return us to the previous world."

1171 Understood to mean "Tell me about…"

1172 By telling their followers that the so-called deities will intercede for them with God.

41. Indeed, God holds the heavens and the earth, lest they cease. And if they should cease, no one could hold them [in place] after Him. Indeed, He is Forbearing and Forgiving.

42. And they swore by God their strongest oaths that if a warner came to them, they would be more guided than [any] one of the [previous] nations. But when a warner came to them, it did not increase them except in aversion.

43. [Due to] arrogance in the land and plotting of evil; but the evil plot does not encompass except its own people. Then do they await except the way [i.e., fate] of the former peoples? But you will never find in the way [i.e., established method] of God any change, and you will never find in the way of God[1173] any alteration.[1174]

44. Have they not traveled through the land and observed how was the end of those before them? And they were greater than them in power. But God is not to be caused failure [i.e., prevented] by anything in the heavens or on the earth. Indeed, He is ever Knowing and Competent.

45. And if God were to impose blame on the people for what they have earned, He would not leave upon it [i.e., the earth] any creature. But He defers them for a specified term. And when their time comes, then indeed God has ever been, of His servants, Seeing.

---

[1173] i.e., in His punishment of those who deny the prophets.
[1174] Or "transfer" of punishment to others in place of them.

## Sūrah 36: Yā Seen

**Period of Revelation**

A study of the style shows that it was either sent down during the last stage of the middle Makkan period or it is one of those Sūrahs which were sent down during the last stage of the Prophet's stay at Makkah.

**Subject Matter and Theme**

The object of the discourse is to warn the Quraysh of the consequences of not believing in the Prophethood of Muhammad and of resisting and opposing it with tyranny, ridicule and mockery. The aspect of the warning is dominant and conspicuous although along with repeatedly giving the warnings, arguments also have been given for the correct understanding by the people.

Arguments have been given for three things:

(1) For Tawhid (Oneness of God) from the signs of the universe and from common sense; (2) for the Hereafter from the signs of the universe, from common sense and from man's own existence itself; and (3) for the Prophethood of the Prophet Muhammad. This was from the fact that he was facing all kinds of hardships in the preaching of his message without any selfish motive and from this that whatever he was inviting the people to was rational and reasonable, accepting which was in the people's own interest.

On the strength of these arguments themes of reprobation, reproof and warning have been presented repeatedly in a highly forceful manner so that hearts are shaken up and those which have any capacity for accepting the truth left in them should not remain unmoved.

Imām Ahmad has related on the authority of Ma'qil bin Yasar that the Prophet said: *"Sūrah Yā Seen is the heart of the Qur'ān."* This is similar to describing the Sūrah Al-Fātihah as the Umm al Qur'ān (the essence or core of the Qur'ān) because Al-Fātihah contains the sum and substance of the teaching of the whole Qur'ān. The Sūrah Yā Seen has been called the throbbing heart of the Qur'ān because it presents the message of the Qur'ān in a most forceful manner which breaks the inertness and stirs the spirit of man to action. The object is not only to revive and refresh the whole Islāmic creed in the mind of the dying person but also bring before him in particular a complete picture of the Hereafter so that he may know what stages he would have to pass through after crossing the stage of this worldly life.

## Sūrah 36: Yā Seen[1175]

In the Name of God, the Most Compassionate, the Most Merciful

1. Yā, Seen.[1176]

2. By the wise[1177] Qur'ān.

3. Indeed you, [O Muhammad], are from among the messengers,

4. On a straight path.

5. [This is] a revelation of the Exalted in Might, the Merciful,

6. That you may warn a people whose forefathers were not warned, so they are unaware.

7. Already the word [i.e., decree] has come into effect upon most of them, so they do not believe.

8. Indeed, We have put shackles on their necks, and they are to their chins, so they are with heads [kept] aloft.

9. And We have put before them a barrier and behind them a barrier and covered them, so they do not see.

10. And it is all the same for them whether you warn them or do not warn them - they will not believe.

11. You can only warn one who follows the message and fears the Most Merciful unseen. So give him good tidings of forgiveness and noble reward.

12. Indeed, it is We who bring the dead to life and record what they have put forth and what they left behind, and all things We have enumerated in a clear register.

13. And present to them an example: the people of the city, when the messengers came to it -

14. When We sent to them two but they denied them, so We strengthened them with a third, and they said, "Indeed, we are messengers to you."

15. They said, "You are not but human beings like us, and the Most Merciful has not revealed a thing. You are only telling lies."

16. They said, "Our Lord knows that we are messengers to you,

17. And we are not responsible except for clear notification."

18. They said, "Indeed, we consider you a bad omen. If you do not desist, we will surely stone you, and there will surely touch you, from us, a painful punishment."

19. They said, "Your omen [i.e., fate] is with yourselves. Is it[1178] because you were reminded? Rather, you are a transgressing people."

20. And there came from the farthest end of the city a man, running. He said, "O my people, follow the messengers.

21. Follow those who do not ask of you [any] payment, and they are [rightly] guided.

[1175] *Yā Seen*: (the letters) *yā* and *seen*.
[1176] See footnote to 2:1.
[1177] See footnote to 10:1.

[1178] Your threat against us.

22. And why should I not worship He who created me and to whom you will be returned?

23. Should I take other than Him [false] deities [while], if the Most Merciful intends for me some adversity, their intercession will not avail me at all, nor can they save me?

24. Indeed, I would then be in manifest error.

25. Indeed, I have believed in your Lord, so listen to me."

26. It was said, "Enter Paradise."[1179] He said, "I wish my people could know

27. Of how my Lord has forgiven me and placed me among the honoured."

28. And We did not send down upon his people after him any soldiers from the heaven, nor would We have done so.

29. It was not but one shout,[1180] and immediately they were extinguished.

30. How regretful for the servants. There did not come to them any messenger except that they used to ridicule him.

31. Have they not considered how many generations We destroyed before them - that they to them[1181] will not return?

32. And indeed, all of them will yet be brought present before Us.

[1179] An abrupt transfer to the Hereafter conveys the meaning that the man met a violent death at the hands of the disbelievers and so was martyred for the cause of God.
[1180] From Gabriel or a blast from the sky.
[1181] i.e., to those living presently in the world.

33. And a sign for them is the dead earth. We have brought it to life and brought forth from it grain, and from it they eat.

34. And We placed therein gardens of palm trees and grapevines and caused to burst forth therefrom some springs -

35. That they may eat of His fruit.[1182] And their hands have not produced it,[1183] so will they not be grateful?

36. Exalted is He who created all pairs[1184] - from what the earth grows and from themselves and from that which they do not know.

37. And a sign for them is the night. We remove[1185] from it the [light of] day, so they are [left] in darkness.

38. And the sun runs [on course] toward its stopping point. That is the determination of the Exalted in Might, the Knowing.

39. And the moon - We have determined for it phases, until it returns [appearing] like the old date stalk.

40. It is not allowable [i.e., possible] for the sun to reach the moon, nor does the night overtake the day, but each, in an orbit, is swimming.

41. And a sign for them is that We carried their forefathers[1186] in a laden ship.

[1182] i.e., that which God has produced for them.
[1183] An alternative meaning is "And [eat from] what their hands have produced [i.e., planted and harvested]." Both are grammatically correct.
[1184] Or "all species."
[1185] Literally, "strip" or "peel." Sunlight projected onto the earth is removed from it as the earth turns and night approaches.
[1186] Usually meaning "descendents" or "offspring" the word "*dhurriyyah*" is used here to

42. And We created for them from the likes of it that which they ride.

43. And if We should will, We could drown them; then no one responding to a cry would there be for them, nor would they be saved

44. Except as a mercy from Us and provision for a time.

45. But when it is said to them, "Beware of what is before you and what is behind you;[1187] perhaps you will receive mercy..."[1188]

46. And no sign comes to them from the signs of their Lord except that they are from it turning away.

47. And when it is said to them, "Spend from that which God has provided for you," those who disbelieve say to those who believe, "Should we feed one whom, if God had willed, He would have fed? You are not but in clear error."

48. And they say, "When is this promise, if you should be truthful?"

49. They do not await except one blast[1189] which will seize them while they are disputing.

50. And they will not be able [to give] any instruction, nor to their people can they return.

51. And the Horn will be blown;[1190] and at once from the graves to their Lord they will hasten.

52. They will say, "O woe to us! Who has raised us up from our sleeping place?" [The reply will be], "This is what the Most Merciful had promised, and the messengers told the truth."

53. It will not be but one blast, and at once they are all brought present before Us.

54. So today [i.e., the Day of Judgement] no soul will be wronged at all, and you will not be recompensed except for what you used to do.

55. Indeed the companions of Paradise, that Day, will be amused in [joyful] occupation -

56. They and their spouses - in shade, reclining on adorned couches.

57. For them therein is fruit, and for them is whatever they request [or wish]

58. [And] "Peace," a word from a Merciful Lord.

59. [Then He will say], "But stand apart today, you criminals.[1191]

60. Did I not enjoin upon you, O children of Adam, that you not worship Satan - [for] indeed, he is to you a clear enemy -

61. And that you worship [only] Me? This is a straight path.

denote forefathers (their being the offspring of Noah), who were saved from the flood.

1187 Of sins or of life in this world and the Hereafter.

1188 The conclusion of this sentence is understood to be "...they ignored the warning."

1189 Literally, "cry" or "shriek," meaning the first blast of the Horn which will strike dead every living thing on the earth without warning.

1190 For the second time, signalling the Resurrection.

1191 i.e., remove yourself from the ranks of the believers to be distinguished from them.

62. And he had already led astray from among you much of creation, so did you not use reason?

63. This is the Hellfire which you were promised.

64. [Enter to] burn therein today for what you used to deny."[1192]

65. That Day, We will seal over their mouths, and their hands will speak to Us, and their feet will testify about what they used to earn.

66. And if We willed, We could have obliterated their eyes, and they would race to [find] the path, and how could they see?[1193]

67. And if We willed, We could have deformed them, [paralyzing them] in their places so they would not be able to proceed, nor could they return.[1194]

68. And he to whom We grant long life We reverse in creation;[1195] so will they not understand?

69. And We did not give him [i.e., Prophet Muhammad] knowledge of poetry, nor is it befitting for him. It is not but a message and a clear Qur'ān

70. To warn whoever is alive[1196] and justify the word [i.e., decree] against the disbelievers.

71. Do they not see that We have created for them from what Our hands[1197] have made, grazing livestock, and [then] they are their owners?

72. And We have tamed them for them, so some of them they ride, and some of them they eat.

73. And for them therein are [other] benefits and drinks, so will they not be grateful?

74. But they have taken besides God [false] deities that perhaps they would be helped.

75. They are not able to help them, and they [themselves] are for them soldiers in attendance.[1198]

76. So let not their speech grieve you. Indeed, We know what they conceal and what they declare.

77. Does man not consider that We created him from a [mere] sperm drop - then at once[1199] he is a clear adversary?

78. And he presents for Us an example[1200] and forgets his [own] creation. He says, "Who will give life to bones while they are disintegrated?"

79. Say, "He will give them life who produced them the first time; and He is, of all creation, Knowing."

80. [It is] He who made for you from the green tree, fire, and then from it you ignite.

[1192] Or "because you used to disbelieve."
[1193] God could have left man without means of guidance in the life of this world, although in His mercy He did not.
[1194] He (Almighty) could have prevented man from taking any action to benefit himself in this world or the Hereafter, yet He did not.
[1195] In his physical and mental capacity.
[1196] In heart and mind, i.e., the believers.
[1197] See footnote to 2:19.
[1198] Maintaining and protecting their "gods." Another interpretation is that they (i.e., the gods) will be soldiers set against them in Hellfire.
[1199] i.e., as soon as he becomes self-sufficient.
[1200] Attempting to establish the finality of death.

81. Is not He who created the heavens and the earth Able to create the likes of them? Yes, [it is so]; and He is the Knowing Creator.

82. His command is only when He intends a thing that He says to it, "Be," and it is.

83. So exalted is He in whose hand is the realm of all things, and to Him you will be returned.

## Sūrah 37: as-Sāffāt

### Period of Revelation

The subject matter and the style show that this Sūrah probably was sent down in the middle of the Makkan period or perhaps in the last stage of the middle Makkan period. The style clearly indicates that antagonism is raging strong in the background and the Prophet and his Companions are passing through very difficult and discouraging circumstances.

### Subject Matter and Theme

The disbelievers of Makkah have been severely warned for their attitude of mockery and derision with which they were responding to the Prophet's message of Tawhid (Oneness of God), and the Hereafter and for their utter refusal to accept and acknowledge his claim to Prophethood. In the end they have been plainly warned that the Prophet whom they are mocking and ridiculing will overwhelm them in spite of their power and pelf and they will find the army of God encamping in the very courtyards of their houses (v. 171-179). This notice was given at a time when there appeared no chance whatever of the Prophet's success and triumph. The Muslims (who have been called God's army in these verses) were being made the target of severe persecution. Three quarters of their population had already emigrated and hardly 40 to 50 of the Companions were left with the Prophet in Makkah who were experiencing all sorts of the excesses with utter helplessness. Under such circumstances in view of the apparent conditions no one could believe that the Prophet and the handful of his ill equipped Companions would ultimately attain dominance. The people rather thought that the new movement would end and be buried in the ravines of Makkah. But hardly 15 to 16 years had passed when on the conquest of Makkah precisely the same thing happened of which the disbelievers had been forewarned. Along with administering warnings this Sūrah has done full justice also to the theme of inducement and instruction in a balanced way. Brief but impressive arguments have been given about the validity of the doctrines of Tawhid (Oneness of God) and the Hereafter. Criticism has been made of the creed of the polytheist, showing the absurdity of their beliefs; they have been informed of the evil consequences of their deviations which have been contrasted with the splendid results of the faith and righteous acts.

The most instructive of the historical narratives presented in this Sūrah is the important event of the pious life of the Prophet Abraham who became ready to sacrifice his only son as soon as he received an inspiration from God. In this there was a lesson not only for the disbelieving Quraysh who waxed proud of their blood relationship with him but also for the Muslims who had believed in God and His Messenger. By narrating this event they were told what is the essence and the real spirit of Islām and how a true believer should be ready to sacrifice his all for the pleasure and approval of God after he has adopted it as his Faith and Creed. In these verses they were given the good news that they should not be disheartened at the hardships and difficulties they had to encounter in the beginning for in the end they alone would attain dominance and the standard bearers of falsehood who appeared to be dominant at the time would be overwhelmed and vanquished at their hands. A few years later the turn the events took proved that it was not an empty consolation but an inevitable reality of which they had been foretold in order to strengthen their hearts.

## Sūrah 37: as-Sāffāt[1201]

In the Name of God, the Most Compassionate, the Most Merciful

1. By those [angels] lined up in rows

2. And those who drive [the clouds]

3. And those who recite the message,[1202]

4. Indeed, your God is One,

5. Lord of the heavens and the earth and that between them and Lord of the sunrises.[1203]

6. Indeed, We have adorned the nearest heaven with an adornment of stars

7. And as protection against every rebellious devil

8. [So] they may not listen to the exalted assembly [of angels] and are pelted from every side,[1204]

9. Repelled; and for them is a constant punishment,

10. Except one who snatches [some words] by theft, but they are pursued by a burning flame, piercing [in brightness].

11. Then inquire of them, [O Muhammad], "Are they a stronger [or more difficult] creation or those [others] We have created?" Indeed, We created them [i.e., men] from sticky clay.

12. But you wonder, while they mock,

13. And when they are reminded, they remember not.

14. And when they see a sign, they ridicule

15. And say, "This is not but obvious magic.

16. When we have died and become dust and bones, are we indeed to be resurrected?

17. And our forefathers [as well]?"

18. Say, "Yes, and you will be [rendered] contemptible."

19. It will be only one shout, and at once they will be observing.

20. They will say, "O woe to us! This is the Day of Recompense."

21. [They will be told], "This is the Day of Judgement which you used to deny."

22. [The angels will be ordered], "Gather those who committed wrong, their kinds,[1205] and what they used to worship

23. Other than God, and guide them to the path of Hellfire

24. And stop them; indeed, they are to be questioned."

25. [They will be asked], "What is [wrong] with you? Why do you not help each other?"

26. But they, that Day, are in surrender.

---

[1201] *As-Sāffāt*: Those Lined Up.
[1202] To the prophets or among themselves. God swears by these three kinds of angels to the fact mentioned in the following verse.
[1203] i.e., each point or place of sunrise.
[1204] By flaming meteors.

[1205] Those similar to them in evil deeds. Another possible meaning is "their wives."

27. And they will approach one another asking [i.e., blaming] each other.

28. They will say, "Indeed, you used to come at us from the right."[1206]

29. They [i.e., the oppressors] will say, "Rather, you [yourselves] were not believers,

30. And we had over you no authority, but you were a transgressing people.

31. So the word [i.e., decree] of our Lord has come into effect upon us; indeed, we will taste [punishment].

32. And we led you to deviation; indeed, we were deviators."

33. So indeed they, that Day, will be sharing in the punishment.

34. Indeed, that is how We deal with the criminals.

35. Indeed they, when it was said to them, "There is no deity but God," were arrogant

36. And were saying, "Are we to leave our gods for a mad poet?"

37. Rather, he [i.e., the Prophet] has come with the truth and confirmed the [previous] messengers.

38. Indeed, you [disbelievers] will be tasters of the painful punishment,

39. And you will not be recompensed except for what you used to do -

[1206] i.e., from our position of strength, oppressing us. Or from where we would have grasped the truth, preventing us.

40. But not the chosen servants of God.

41. Those will have a provision determined -

42. Fruits;[1207] and they will be honoured

43. In gardens of pleasure

44. On thrones facing one another.

45. There will be circulated among them a cup [of wine] from a flowing spring,

46. White and delicious to the drinkers;

47. No bad effect is there in it, nor from it will they be intoxicated.

48. And with them will be women limiting [their] glances,[1208] with large, [beautiful] eyes,

49. As if they were [delicate] eggs, well-protected.

50. And they will approach one another, inquiring of each other.

51. A speaker among them will say, "Indeed, I had a companion [on earth]

52. Who would say, 'Are you indeed of those who believe

53. That when we have died and become dust and bones, we will indeed be recompensed?' "

54. He will say,[1209] "Would you [care to] look?"

55. And he will look and see him[1210] in the midst of the Hellfire.

[1207] Meaning everything delicious.

[1208] i.e., chaste and modest, looking only at their mates.

[1209] To his companions in Paradise.

56. He will say, "By God, you almost ruined me.

57. If not for the favor of my Lord, I would have been of those brought in [to Hell].

58. Then, are we not to die

59. Except for our first death, and we will not be punished?"

60. Indeed, this is the great attainment.

61. For the like of this let the workers [on earth] work.

62. Is that [i.e., Paradise] a better accommodation or the tree of zaqqūm?

63. Indeed, We have made it a torment for the wrongdoers.

64. Indeed, it is a tree issuing from the bottom of the Hellfire,

65. Its emerging fruit as if it was heads of the devils.

66. And indeed, they will eat from it and fill with it their bellies.

67. Then indeed, they will have after it a mixture of scalding water.

68. Then indeed, their return will be to the Hellfire.

69. Indeed they found their fathers astray.

70. So they hastened [to follow] in their footsteps.

71. And there had already strayed before them most of the former peoples,

72. And We had already sent among them warners.

73. Then look how was the end of those who were warned -

74. But not the chosen servants of God.

75. And Noah had certainly called Us, and [We are] the best of responders.

76. And We saved him and his family from the great affliction.

77. And We made his descendants those remaining [on the earth]

78. And left for him [favorable mention] among later generations:

79. "Peace upon Noah among the worlds."

80. Indeed, We thus reward the doers of good.

81. Indeed, he was of Our believing servants.

82. Then We drowned the others [i.e., disbelievers].

83. And indeed, among his kind was Abraham,

84. When he came to his Lord with a sound heart

85. [And] when he said to his father and his people, "What do you worship?

86. Is it falsehood [as] gods other than God you desire?

[1210] The companion who had tried to dissuade him from belief on earth.

87. Then what is your thought about the Lord of the worlds?"

88. And he cast a look at the stars

89. And said, "Indeed, I am [about to be] ill."

90. So they turned away from him, departing.

91. Then he turned to their gods and said, "Do you not eat?[1211]

92. What is [wrong] with you that you do not speak?"

93. And he turned upon them a blow with [his] right hand.

94. Then they [i.e., the people] came toward him, hastening.

95. He said, "Do you worship that which you [yourselves] carve,

96. While God created you and that which you do?"

97. They said, "Construct for him a structure [i.e., furnace] and throw him into the burning fire."

98. And they intended for him a plan, [i.e., harm] but We made them the most debased.

99. And [then] he said, "Indeed, I will go to [where I am ordered by] my Lord; He will guide me.

100. My Lord, grant me [a child] from among the righteous."

[1211] Consume the offerings placed before them.

101. So We gave him good tidings of a forbearing boy.

102. And when he reached with him [the age of] exertion,[1212] he said, "O my son, indeed I have seen in a dream that I [must] sacrifice you, so see what you think." He said, "O my father, do as you are commanded. You will find me, if God wills, of the steadfast."

103. And when they had both submitted[1213] and he put him down upon his forehead,

104. We called to him, "O Abraham,

105. You have fulfilled the vision." Indeed, We thus reward the doers of good.

106. Indeed, this was the clear trial.

107. And We ransomed him with a great sacrifice,[1214]

108. And We left for him [favorable mention] among later generations:

109. "Peace upon Abraham."

110. Indeed, We thus reward the doers of good.

111. Indeed, he was of Our believing servants.

112. And We gave him good tidings of Isaac, a prophet from among the righteous.[1215]

[1212] i.e., the ability to work and be of assistance.
[1213] To the command of God.
[1214] God sent a huge ram to be sacrificed in place of Ishmael.
[1215] This verifies that the firstborn son who was to be sacrificed was Ishmael and not Isaac, as claimed by the Jews and Christians.

113. And We blessed him and Isaac. But among their descendants is the doer of good and the clearly unjust to himself [i.e., sinner].

114. And We did certainly confer favor upon Moses and Aaron.

115. And We saved them and their people from the great affliction,

116. And We supported them so it was they who overcame.

117. And We gave them the explicit Scripture [i.e., the Torah],

118. And We guided them on the straight path.

119. And We left for them [favorable mention] among later generations:

120. "Peace upon Moses and Aaron."

121. Indeed, We thus reward the doers of good.

122. Indeed, they were of Our believing servants.

123. And indeed, Elias was from among the messengers,

124. When he said to his people, "Will you not fear God?

125. Do you call upon Ba'l[1216] and leave the best of creators -

126. God, your Lord and the Lord of your first forefathers?"

127. And they denied him, so indeed, they will be brought [for punishment],

128. Except the chosen servants of God.

129. And We left for him [favorable mention] among later generations:

130. "Peace upon Elias."[1217]

131. Indeed, We thus reward the doers of good.

132. Indeed, he was of Our believing servants.

133. And indeed, Lot was among the messengers.

134. [So mention] when We saved him and his family, all,

135. Except an old woman [i.e., his wife] among those who remained [with the evildoers].

136. Then We destroyed the others.

137. And indeed, you pass by them in the morning

138. And at night. Then will you not use reason?

139. And indeed, Jonah was among the messengers.

140. [Mention] when he ran away to the laden ship.

141. And he drew lots[1218] and was among the losers.

---

[1216] The name of a great idol worshipped by the people and said to mean "lord."

[1217] *Ilyāseen* is said by some commentators to be a plural form, meaning "Elias and those who followed him."

[1218] To determine who would be cast overboard in order to save the other passengers. Having

142. Then the fish swallowed him, while he was blameworthy.[1219]

143. And had he not been of those who exalt God,

144. He would have remained inside its belly until the Day they are resurrected.[1220]

145. But We threw him onto the open shore while he was ill.

146. And We caused to grow over him a gourd vine.[1221]

147. And We sent him[1222] to [his people of] a hundred thousand or more.

148. And they believed, so We gave them enjoyment [of life] for a time.

149. So inquire of them, [O Muhammad], "Does your Lord have daughters while they have sons?[1223]

150. Or did We create the angels as females while they were witnesses?"

151. Unquestionably, it is out of their [invented] falsehood that they say,

152. "God has begotten," and indeed, they are liars.

153. Has He chosen daughters over sons?

154. What is [wrong] with you? How do you make judgement?

155. Then will you not be reminded?

156. Or do you have a clear authority?

157. Then produce your scripture, if you should be truthful.

158. And they have made [i.e., claimed] between Him and the jinn a lineage, but the jinn have already known that they [who made such claims] will be brought [to punishment].

159. Exalted is God above what they describe,

160. Except the chosen servants of God [who do not share in that sin].

161. So indeed, you [disbelievers] and whatever you worship,

162. You cannot tempt [anyone] away from Him

163. Except he who is to [enter and] burn in the Hellfire.[1224]

164. [The angels say],[1225] "There is not among us any except that he has a known position.[1226]

165. And indeed, we are those who line up [for prayer].

166. And indeed, we are those who exalt God."

been overloaded, the ship was on the verge of sinking.

[1219] For having given up hope on his people prematurely and having left them without permission from God.

[1220] Meaning that the belly of the fish would have become his grave.

[1221] Which is known to give cooling shade and to be a repellent of flies.

[1222] i.e., returned him thereafter.

[1223] The people of Makkah claimed that the angels were daughters of God, yet they preferred sons for themselves.

[1224] Due to his disbelief and evil deeds.

[1225] Refuting what the disbelievers had said about them.

[1226] For worship. Or "an assigned task" to perform.

167. And indeed, they [i.e., the disbelievers] used to say,[1227]

168. "If we had a message from [those of] the former peoples,

169. We would have been the chosen servants of God."

170. But they disbelieved in it,[1228] so they are going to know.

171. And Our word [i.e., decree] has already preceded for Our servants, the messengers,

172. [That] indeed, they would be those given victory

173. And [that] indeed, Our soldiers [i.e., the belivers] will be those who overcome.[1229]

174. So, [O Muhammad], leave them for a time.

175. And see [what will befall] them, for they are going to see.

176. Then for Our punishment are they impatient?

177. But when it descends in their territory, then evil is the morning of those who were warned.

178. And leave them for a time.

179. And see, for they are going to see.

180. Exalted is your Lord, the Lord of might, above what they describe.

181. And peace upon the messengers.

182. And praise to God, Lord of the worlds.

[1227] Before the revelation of the Qur'ān.
[1228] i.e., in their own message, the Qur'ān.
[1229] If not in this world, then definitely in the Hereafter.

# Sūrah 38: Sād

## Period of Revelation

As will be explained below according to some hadith, this Sūrah was sent down in the period when the Prophet had started calling the people openly to Islām in Makkah and this had caused great alarm among the chiefs of the Quraysh. If this be true its period of revelation would be about the 4th year of the Prophethood. According to some other hadith it was sent down after Umar's embracing Islām and this happened as is well known after the migration to Abassinyah. Another chain of the traditions shows that the event which occasioned the revelation of this Sūrah took place during the last illness of Abu Talib. If this be correct the period of its revelation would be the 10th or 11th year of the Prophethood.

## Historical Background

Here is a resume of the hadith related by Imām Ahmad, Nasa'i, Tirmidhi, Ibn Jarir, Ibn Abi Shaibah, Ibn Abi Hatim Muhammad, Ibn Ishaq and others:

When Abu Talib fell ill and the Quraysh chiefs knew that his end was near they held consultations and decided to approach the old chief with the request that he should solve the dispute between them and his nephew. For they feared that if Abu Talib died and then they subjected Muhammad to a harsh treatment after his death the Arabs would taunt them saying, 'they were afraid of the old chief as long as he lived now that he is dead they have started maltreating his nephew.' At least 25 of the Quraysh chiefs including Abu Jahl, Abu Sufyan, Umayyah bin Khalaf, Aa's bin Wa'il Aswad bin al-Muttalib, 'Uqbah bin Abi Mu'ait, Utbah and Shaibah went to Abu Talib. First they put before him their complaints against the Prophet as usual then said, '*We have come to present before you a just request and it is this : let your nephew leave us to our religion and we shall leave him to his. He may worship whomever he may please: we shall not stand in his way in this matter; but he should not condemn our gods and should not try to force us to give them up. Please tell him to make terms with us on this condition.*' Abu Talib called the Prophet and said, '*Dear nephew these people of your tribe have come to me with a request. They want you to agree with them on a just matter so as to put an end to your dispute with them.*' Then he told him about the request of the chiefs of the Quraysh. The Prophet replied, '*Dear uncle: I shall request them to agree upon a thing which if they accept will enable them to conquer the whole of Arabia and subject the non-Arab world to their domination.*' Hearing this the people were first confounded; they did not know how they should turn down such a proposal. Then after they had considered the matter they replied: '*You speak of one word: we are prepared to repeat ten others like it but please tell us what it is.*' The Prophet said: '*La ilaha ill-Allāh.*' (There is none worthy of worship except God) At this they got up all together and left the place saying what God has narrated in the initial part of this Sūrah.

Ibn Sa'd in his Tabaqat has related this event just as cited above but according to him this did not happen during Abu Talibs last illness but at the time when the Prophet had started preaching Islām openly and the news of the conversion of one person or the other was being heard almost daily in Makkah. In those days the Quraysh chiefs had led several deputations to Abu Talib and had asked him to stop Muhammad from preaching his message and it was with one of those deputations that this conversation had taken place.

## Subject Matter and Topics

The Sūrah begins with a review of the aforesaid meeting. Making the dialogue between the Prophet and the disbelievers the basis, God says that the actual reason with those people for their denial is not any defect in the message of Islām but their own arrogance, jealousy and insistence on following the blind. They are not prepared to believe in a man from their own clan as a Prophet of God and follow him. They want to persist in the ideas of ignorance which they have found their ancestors following. And when a person exposes this ignorance and presents the truth before them, they are alarmed and regard it as an oddity, rather as a novel and impossible thing. For them the concept of Tawhid and the Hereafter is not only an unacceptable creed but also a concept which only deserves to be ridiculed and mocked.

Then, God, both in the initial part of the Sūrah and in its last sentences, has precisely warned the disbelievers, as if to say, "The man whom you are ridiculing today and whose guidance you reject will soon overpower you, and the time is not far when in this very city of Makkah, where you are persecuting him, he will overwhelm you completely." Then describing nine of the Prophets, one after the other, with greater details of the story of the Prophets David and Solomon; God has emphasized the point that His Law of Justice is impartial and objective, that only the right attitude of man is acceptable to Him, that He calls to account and punishes every wrongdoer, whoever he be, and that He likes only those people who do not persist in wrongdoing but repent as soon as they are warned of it, and pass their life in the world keeping in mind their accountability in the Hereafter.

After this, the final end that the obedient servants and the disobedient people will meet in the Hereafter, has been depicted, and two things have been especially impressed on the disbelievers:

1. That the leaders and guides whom the ignorant people are following blindly in the world, on the way of deviation, will have reached Hell even before their followers in the Hereafter, and the two groups will be cursing each other there;
2. That the disbelievers will be amazed to see that there is no trace whatever in Hell of the believers whom they used to regard as contemptible in the world and will themselves be involved in its torment.

In conclusion, mention has been made of the story of Adam and Iblis (Satan), which is meant to tell the disbelieving Quraysh that the same arrogance and vanity which was preventing them from bowing before Muhammad had prevented Iblis also from bowing before Adam. Iblis felt jealous of the high rank God had given to Adam and became accursed when he disobeyed His Command. Likewise, "You, O people of Quraysh, are feeling jealous of the high rank God has bestowed on Muhammad and are not prepared to obey him whom God has appointed His messenger. Therefore, you will be doomed ultimately to the same fate as will be met by Satan."

## Sūrah 38: Ṣād[1230]

In the Name of God, the Most Compassionate, the Most Merciful

1. Ṣād.[1231] By the Qur'ān containing reminder...[1232]

2. But those who disbelieve are in pride and dissension.

3. How many a generation have We destroyed before them, and they [then] called out; but it was not a time for escape.

4. And they wonder that there has come to them a warner [i.e., Prophet Muhammad] from among themselves. And the disbelievers say, "This is a magician and a liar.

5. Has he made the gods [only] one God? Indeed, this is a curious thing."

6. And the eminent among them went forth, [saying], "Continue, and be patient over [the defense of] your gods. Indeed, this is a thing intended.[1233]

7. We have not heard of this in the latest religion.[1234] This is not but a fabrication.

8. Has the message been revealed to him out of [all of] us?" Rather, they are in doubt about My message. Rather, they have not yet tasted My punishment.

9. Or do they have the depositories of the mercy of your Lord, the Exalted in Might, the Bestower?

10. Or is theirs the dominion of the heavens and the earth and what is between them? Then let them ascend through [any] ways of access.[1235]

11. [They are but] soldiers [who will be] defeated there among the companies [of disbelievers].

12. The people of Noah denied before them, and [the tribe of] 'Aad and Pharaoh, the owner of stakes,[1236]

13. And [the tribe of] Thamūd and the people of Lot and the companions of the thicket [i.e., people of Madyan]. Those are the companies.[1237]

14. Each of them denied the messengers, so My penalty was justified.

15. And these [disbelievers] await not but one blast [of the Horn]; for it there will be no delay.[1238]

16. And they say, "Our Lord, hasten for us our share [of the punishment] before the Day of Account."

17. Be patient over what they say and remember Our servant, David, the possessor of strength; indeed, he was one who repeatedly turned back [to God].

---

1230 *Ṣād*: (the letter) *ṣād*.
1231 See footnote to 2:1.
1232 The completion of the oath is understood to be that the Qur'ān is inimitable and thus a miracle from God.
1233 Planned by Prophet Muhammad in order to gain influence and prestige for himself.
1234 Referring to Christianity or possibly the pagan religion of the Quraysh.
1235 To oversee the affairs of their dominion.
1236 By which he tortured people.
1237 That were defeated, among whom will be the disbelievers of Quraysh and others.
1238 Or "respite." More literally, "a period between two milkings of a she-camel," which also alludes to the meanings of "return" or "repetition."

18. Indeed, We subjected the mountains [to praise] with him, exalting [God] in the [late] afternoon and [after] sunrise.

19. And the birds were assembled, all with him repeating [praises].

20. And We strengthened his kingdom and gave him wisdom and discernment in speech.

21. And has there come to you the news of the adversaries, when they climbed over the wall of [his] prayer chamber -

22. When they entered upon David and he was alarmed by them? They said, "Fear not. [We are] two adversaries, one of whom has wronged the other, so judge between us with truth and do not exceed [it] and guide us to the sound path.

23. Indeed this, my brother, has ninety-nine ewes, and I have one ewe; so he said, 'Entrust her to me,' and he overpowered me in speech."

24. [David] said, "He has certainly wronged you in demanding your ewe [in addition] to his ewes. And indeed, many associates oppress one another, except for those who believe and do righteous deeds - and few are they." And David became certain that We had tried him, and he asked forgiveness of his Lord[1239] and fell down bowing [in prostration] and turned in repentance [to God].

25. So We forgave him that; and indeed, for him is nearness to Us and a good place of return.

26. [We said], "O David, indeed We have made you a successor upon the earth, so judge between the people in truth and do not follow [your own] desire, as it will lead you astray from the way of God." Indeed, those who go astray from the way of God will have a severe punishment for having forgotten the Day of Account.

27. And We did not create the heaven and the earth and that between them aimlessly. That is the assumption of those who disbelieve, so woe to those who disbelieve from the Fire.

28. Or should We treat those who believe and do righteous deeds like corrupters in the land? Or should We treat those who fear God like the wicked?

29. [This is] a blessed Book which We have revealed to you, [O Muhammad], that they might reflect upon its verses and that those of understanding would be reminded.

30. And to David We gave Solomon. An excellent servant, indeed he was one repeatedly turning back [to God].

31. [Mention] when there were exhibited before him in the afternoon the poised [standing] racehorses.

32. And he said, "Indeed, I gave preference to the love of good [things] over the remembrance of my Lord until it [i.e., the sun] disappeared into the curtain [of darkness]."

[1239] For his errors, such as fear and suspicion of the two men at the outset, any mistake in judgement he might have made, concealed feelings of partiality, etc.

33. [He said], "Return them to me," and set about striking[1240] [their] legs and necks.

34. And We certainly tried Solomon and placed on his throne a body;[1241] then he returned.[1242]

35. He said, "My Lord, forgive me and grant me a kingdom such as will not belong to anyone after me. Indeed, You are the Bestower."

36. So We subjected to him the wind blowing by his command, gently, wherever he directed,

37. And [also] the devils [of jinn] - every builder and diver

38. And others bound together in shackles.

39. [We said], "This is Our gift, so grant or withhold without account."

40. And indeed, for him is nearness to Us and a good place of return.

41. And remember Our servant Job, when he called to his Lord, "Indeed, Satan has touched me with hardship and torment."

42. [So he was told], "Strike [the ground] with your foot; this is a [spring for a] cool bath and drink."

43. And We granted him his family and a like [number] with them as mercy from Us and a reminder for those of understanding.

44. [We said], "And take in your hand a bunch [of grass] and strike with it and do not break your oath."[1243] Indeed, We found him patient, an excellent servant. Indeed, he was one repeatedly turning back [to God].

45. And remember Our servants, Abraham, Isaac and Jacob - those of strength and [religious] vision.

46. Indeed, We chose them for an exclusive quality: remembrance of the home [of the Hereafter].

47. And indeed they are, to Us, among the chosen and outstanding.

48. And remember Ishmael, Elisha and Dhul-Kifl, and all are among the outstanding.

49. This is a reminder. And indeed, for the righteous is a good place of return -

50. Gardens of perpetual residence, whose doors will be opened to them.

51. Reclining within them, they will call therein for abundant fruit and drink.

52. And with them will be women limiting [their] glances[1244] and of equal age.

53. This is what you, [the righteous], are promised for the Day of Account.

54. Indeed, this is Our provision; for it there is no depletion.

---

[1240] With his sword as expiation. Some commentaries have also suggested the meaning of "stroking" with the hand.

[1241] Said to be a devil or a lifeless body (one without capability), but God alone knows.

[1242] To sovereignty and to God in repentance.

[1243] At a point during his illness, Job became very angry with his wife and swore that if he recovered, he would punish her with one hundred lashes. According to God's instruction, the oath was fulfilled by striking her once with one hundred blades of grass.

[1244] To their mates alone.

55. This [is so]. But indeed, for the transgressors is an evil place of return -

56. Hell, which they will [enter to] burn, and wretched is the resting place.

57. This - so let them taste it - is scalding water and [foul] purulence

58. And other [punishments] of its type [in various] kinds.

59. [Its inhabitants will say], "This is a company bursting in with you. No welcome for them. Indeed, they will burn in the Fire."

60. They will say, "Nor you! No welcome for you. You, [our leaders], brought this upon us, and wretched is the settlement."

61. They will say, "Our Lord, whoever brought this upon us - increase for him double punishment in the Fire."

62. And they will say, "Why do we not see men whom we used to count among the worst?[1245]

63. Is it [because] we took them in ridicule, or has [our] vision turned away from them?"

64. Indeed, that is truth [i.e., reality] - the quarreling of the people of the Fire.

65. Say, [O Muhammad], "I am only a warner, and there is not any deity except God, the One, the Prevailing,

66. Lord of the heavens and the earth and whatever is between them, the Exalted in Might, the Perpetual Forgiver."

[1245] They are referring to the believers.

67. Say, "It is great news

68. From which you turn away.

69. I had no knowledge of the exalted assembly [of angels] when they were disputing [the creation of Adam].

70. It has not been revealed to me except that I am a clear warner."

71. [So mention] when your Lord said to the angels, "Indeed, I am going to create a human being from clay.

72. So when I have proportioned him and breathed into him of My [created] soul,[1246] then fall down to him in prostration."

73. So the angels prostrated - all of them entirely.

74. Except Iblees;[1247] he was arrogant and became among the disbelievers.

75. [God] said, "O Iblees, what prevented you from prostrating to that which I created with My hands?[1248] Were you arrogant [then], or were you [already] among the haughty?"

76. He said, "I am better than him. You created me from fire and created him from clay."

77. [God] said, "Then get out of it [i.e., Paradise], for indeed, you are expelled.

78. And indeed, upon you is My curse until the Day of Recompense."

[1246] See footnote to 15:29.
[1247] See footnote to 2:34.
[1248] See footnote to 2:19.

79. He said, "My Lord, then reprieve me until the Day they are resurrected."

80. [God] said, "So indeed, you are of those reprieved

81. Until the Day of the time well-known."

82. [Iblees] said, "By your might, I will surely mislead them all

83. Except, among them, Your chosen servants."

84. [God] said, "The truth [is My oath], and the truth I say -

85. [That] I will surely fill Hell with you and those of them that follow you all together."

86. Say, [O Muhammad], "I do not ask you for it [i.e., the Qur'ān] any payment, and I am not of the pretentious.

87. It is but a reminder to the worlds.

88. And you will surely know [the truth of] its information after a time."

## Sūrah 39: az-Zumar

### Period of Revelation

In verse 10 (wa ardullah-i-wasi atun: and God's earth is spacious) there is abundant evidence that this Sūrah was sent down before the migration to Abassinyah. Some hadith provide the explanation that this verse was sent down in respect of Ja'far bin Abi Talib and his companions when they made up their mind to emigrate to Abassinyah.

### Theme and Subject Matter

The entire Sūrah is a most eloquent and effective address which was given some time before the emigration to Abassinyah, in an environment filled with tyranny and persecution, ill-will and antagonism, at Makkah. It is a sermon whose addressees mainly are the unbelieving Quraysh, although here and there the believers also have been addressed. In it the real aim of the invitation of Muhammad had been enunciated, which is this: Man should adopt God's servitude sincerely, and should not pollute his worship with the service of any other. Presenting this cardinal principle in different ways over and over again, the truth of Tawhid (Oneness of God) and the excellent results of accepting it, and the falsehood of shirk and the evil consequences of following it, have been explained in a most forceful way, and the people exhorted to give up their wrong way of life and return to the mercy of their Lord. In this very connection, the believers have been instructed, as if to say: "If a place has become narrow for the worship and service of God, His earth is vast: you may emigrate to some other place in order to save your faith: God will reward you for your patience." On the other hand, the Prophet has been encouraged, so as to say: "Tell the disbelievers plainly that they may do whatever they like, but their persecutions and tyrannies will never deter you from the way of Islām; that they may go on doing their worst to obstruct your way, but you will continue to perform your mission in spite of the adverse conditions and circumstances."

## Sūrah 39: az-Zumar[1249]

In the Name of God, the Most Compassionate, the Most Merciful

1. The revelation of the Book [i.e., the Qur'ān] is from God, the Exalted in Might, the Wise.

2. Indeed, We have sent down to you the Book, [O Muhammad], in truth. So worship God, [being] sincere to Him in religion.

3. Unquestionably, for God is the pure religion.[1250] And those who take protectors besides Him [say], "We only worship them that they may bring us nearer to God in position." Indeed, God will judge between them concerning that over which they differ. Indeed, God does not guide he who is a liar and [confirmed] disbeliever.

4. If God had intended to take a son, He could have chosen from what He creates whatever He willed. Exalted is He; He is God, the One, the Prevailing.

5. He created the heavens and earth in truth. He wraps the night over the day and wraps the day over the night and has subjected the sun and the moon, each running [its course] for a specified term. Unquestionably, He is the Exalted in Might, the Perpetual Forgiver.

6. He created you from one soul. Then He made from it its mate, and He produced for you from the grazing livestock eight mates.[1251] He creates you in the wombs of your mothers, creation after creation, within three darknesses.[1252] That is God, your Lord; to Him belongs dominion. There is no deity except Him, so how are you averted?

7. If you disbelieve - indeed, God is Free from need of you. And He does not approve for His servants disbelief. And if you are grateful, He approves [i.e., likes] it for you; and no bearer of burdens will bear the burden of another. Then to your Lord is your return, and He will inform you about what you used to do. Indeed, He is Knowing of that within the breasts.

8. And when adversity touches man, he calls upon his Lord, turning to Him [alone]; then when He bestows on him a favor from Himself, he forgets Him whom he called upon before,[1253] and he attributes to God equals to mislead [people] from His way. Say, "Enjoy your disbelief for a little; indeed, you are of the companions of the Fire."

9. Is one who is devoutly obedient during periods of the night, prostrating and standing [in prayer], fearing the Hereafter and hoping for the mercy of his Lord, [like one who does not]? Say, "Are those who know equal to those who do not know?" Only they will remember [who are] people of understanding.

10. Say,[1254] "O My servants who have believed, fear your Lord. For those who do good in this world is good, and the earth of God is spacious. Indeed, the

[1249] *Az-Zumar*: The Groups.
[1250] i.e., acceptable to God is that none be associated with Him in worship and obedience.
[1251] See 6:143-144.
[1252] i.e., the belly, the womb, and the amniotic membrane.
[1253] Or "that for which he called upon Him before."
[1254] The Prophet is instructed to say on behalf of God to His believing servants.

patient will be given their reward without account [i.e., limit]."

11. Say, [O Muhammad], "Indeed, I have been commanded to worship God, [being] sincere to Him in religion.

12. And I have been commanded to be the first [among you] of the Muslims."

13. Say, "Indeed I fear, if I should disobey my Lord, the punishment of a tremendous Day."

14. Say, "God [alone] do I worship, sincere to Him in my religion,

15. So worship what you will besides Him." Say, "Indeed, the losers are the ones who will lose themselves and their families on the Day of Resurrection. Unquestionably, that is the manifest loss."

16. They will have canopies [i.e., layers] of fire above them and below them, canopies. By that God threatens [i.e., warms] His servants. O My servants, then fear Me.

17. But those who have avoided tāghūt,[1255] lest they worship it, and turned back to God - for them are good tidings. So give good tidings to My servants

18. Who listen to speech and follow the best of it. Those are the ones God has guided, and those are people of understanding.

19. Then, is one who has deserved the decree of punishment [to be guided]? Then, can you save one who is in the Fire?

20. But those who have feared their Lord - for them are chambers,[1256] above them chambers built high, beneath which rivers flow. [This is] the promise of God. God does not fail in [His] promise.

21. Do you not see that God sends down rain from the sky and makes it flow as springs [and rivers] in the earth; then He produces thereby crops of varying colors; then they dry and you see them turned yellow; then He makes them [scattered] debris. Indeed in that is a reminder for those of understanding.

22. So is one whose breast God has expanded to [accept] Islām and he is upon [i.e., guided by] a light from his Lord [like one whose heart rejects it]? Then woe to those whose hearts are hardened against the remembrance of God. Those are in manifest error.

23. God has sent down the best statement: a consistent Book wherein is reiteration. The skins shiver therefrom of those who fear their Lord; then their skins and their hearts relax at the remembrance [i.e., mention] of God. That is the guidance of God by which He guides whom He wills. And one whom God leaves astray - for him there is no guide.

24. Then is he who will shield with his face[1257] the worst of the punishment on the Day of Resurrection [like one secure from it]? And it will be said to the wrongdoers, "Taste what you used to earn."

[1255] i.e., Satan or any false object of worship.

[1256] i.e., elevated rooms, dwellings or palaces.

[1257] Rather than his hands, which will be chained to his neck.

25. Those before them denied, and punishment came upon them from where they did not perceive.

26. So God made them taste disgrace in worldly life. But the punishment of the Hereafter is greater, if they only knew.

27. And We have certainly presented for the people in this Qur'ān from every [kind of] example - that they might remember.

28. [It is] an Arabic Qur'ān, without any deviance[1258] that they might become righteous.[1259]

29. God presents an example: a man [i.e., slave] owned by quarreling partners and another belonging exclusively to one man - are they equal in comparison? Praise be to God! But most of them do not know.

30. Indeed, you are to die, and indeed, they are to die.

31. Then indeed you, on the Day of Resurrection, before your Lord, will dispute.

32. So who is more unjust than one who lies about God and denies the truth when it has come to him? Is there not in Hell a residence for the disbelievers?

33. And the one who has brought the truth [i.e., the Prophet] and [they who] believed in it - those are the righteous.

34. They will have whatever they desire with their Lord. That is the reward of the doers of good -

[1258] From the truth.

[1259] Through consciousness of God.

35. That God may remove from them the worst of what they did and reward them their due for the best of what they used to do.

36. Is not God sufficient for His Servant [i.e., Prophet Muhammad]? And [yet], they threaten you with those [they worship] other than Him. And whoever God leaves astray - for him there is no guide.

37. And whoever God guides - for him there is no misleader. Is not God Exalted in Might and Owner of Retribution?

38. And if you asked them, "Who created the heavens and the earth?" they would surely say, "God." Say, "Then have you considered[1260] what you invoke besides God? If God intended me harm, are they removers of His harm; or if He intended me mercy, are they withholders of His mercy?" Say, "Sufficient for me is God; upon Him [alone] rely the [wise] reliers."

39. Say, "O my people, work according to your position, [for] indeed, I am working; and you are going to know

40. To whom will come a torment disgracing him and on whom will descend an enduring punishment."

41. Indeed, We sent down to you the Book for the people in truth. So whoever is guided - it is for [the benefit of] his soul; and whoever goes astray only goes astray to its detriment. And you are not a manager [i.e., authority] over them.

42. God takes the souls at the time of their death, and those that do not die [He

[1260] i.e., "Tell me about..."

takes] during their sleep. Then He keeps those for which He has decreed death and releases the others for a specified term. Indeed in that are signs for a people who give thought.

43. Or have they taken other than God as intercessors? Say, "Even though they do not possess [power over] anything, nor do they reason?"

44. Say, "To God belongs [the right to allow] intercession entirely. To Him belongs the dominion of the heavens and the earth. Then to Him you will be returned."

45. And when God is mentioned alone, the hearts of those who do not believe in the Hereafter shrink with aversion, but when those [worshipped] other than Him are mentioned, immediately they rejoice.

46. Say, "O God, Creator of the heavens and the earth, Knower of the unseen and the witnessed, You will judge between your servants concerning that over which they used to differ."

47. And if those who did wrong had all that is in the earth entirely and the like of it with it, they would [attempt to] ransom themselves thereby from the worst of the punishment on the Day of Resurrection. And there will appear to them from God that which they had not taken into account.[1261]

48. And there will appear to them the evils they had earned, and they will be enveloped by what they used to ridicule.

49. And when adversity touches man, he calls upon Us; then when We bestow on him a favor from Us, he says, "I have only been given it because of [my] knowledge." Rather, it is a trial, but most of them do not know.

50. Those before them had already said it, but they were not availed by what they used to earn.

51. And the evil consequences of what they earned struck them. And those who have wronged of these [people] will be struck [i.e., afflicted] by the evil consequences of what they earned; and they will not cause failure.[1262]

52. Do they not know that God extends provision for whom He wills and restricts [it]? Indeed in that are signs for a people who believe.

53. Say, "O My servants who have transgressed against themselves [by sinning], do not despair of the mercy of God. Indeed, God forgives all sins.[1263] Indeed, it is He who is the Forgiving, the Merciful."

54. And return [in repentance] to your Lord and submit to Him before the punishment comes upon you; then you will not be helped.

55. And follow the best of what was revealed to you from your Lord [i.e., the Qur'ān] before the punishment comes upon you suddenly while you do not perceive,

56. Lest a soul should say,[1264] "Oh [how great is] my regret over what I neglected in regard to God and that I was among the mockers."

1261 Of His anger and punishment.

1262 i.e., prevent God from what He wills or escape from the punishment.

1263 For those who repent and correct themselves.

1264 On the Day of Resurrection.

57. Or [lest] it say, "If only God had guided me, I would have been among the righteous."

58. Or [lest] it say when it sees the punishment, "If only I had another turn[1265] so I could be among the doers of good."

59. But yes, there had come to you My verses, but you denied them and were arrogant, and you were among the disbelievers.

60. And on the Day of Resurrection you will see those who lied about God [with] their faces blackened. Is there not in Hell a residence for the arrogant?

61. And God will save those who feared Him by their attainment;[1266] no evil will touch them, nor will they grieve.

62. God is the Creator of all things, and He is, over all things, Disposer of affairs.

63. To Him belong the keys of the heavens and the earth. And they who disbelieve in the verses of God - it is those who are the losers.

64. Say, [O Muhammad], "Is it other than God that you order me to worship, O ignorant ones?"

65. And it was already revealed to you and to those before you that if you should associate [anything] with God, your work would surely become worthless, and you would surely be among the losers."

[1265] At worldly life.

[1266] i.e., their success in the trials of worldly life and attainment of Paradise.

66. Rather, worship [only] God and be among the grateful.

67. They have not appraised God with true appraisal,[1267] while the earth entirely will be [within] His grip[1268] on the Day of Resurrection, and the heavens will be folded in His right hand.[1269] Exalted is He and high above what they associate with Him.

68. And the Horn will be blown, and whoever is in the heavens and whoever is on the earth will fall dead except whom God wills. Then it will be blown again, and at once they will be standing, looking on.

69. And the earth will shine with the light of its Lord, and the record [of deeds] will be placed, and the prophets and the witnesses will be brought, and it will be judged between them in truth, and they will not be wronged.

70. And every soul will be fully compensated [for] what it did; and He is most knowing[1270] of what they do.

71. And those who disbelieved will be driven to Hell in groups until, when they reach it, its gates are opened and its keepers will say, "Did there not come to you messengers from yourselves, reciting to you the verses of your Lord and warning you of the meeting of this Day of yours?" They will say, "Yes, but the word [i.e., decree] of punishment has come into effect upon the disbelievers."

[1267] i.e., appreciation of His attributes.

[1268] Literally, "no more than a handful of His."

[1269] See footnote to 2:19.

[1270] With no need for any record or witnesses, which are but means to establish proof to the soul itself in addition to its own knowledge of what it has done.

72. [To them] it will be said, "Enter the gates of Hell to abide eternally therein, and wretched is the residence of the arrogant."

73. But those who feared their Lord will be driven to Paradise in groups until, when they reach it while its gates have been opened and its keepers say, "Peace be upon you; you have become pure; so enter it to abide eternally therein," [they will enter].[1271]

74. And they will say, "Praise to God, who has fulfilled for us His promise and made us inherit the earth [so] we may settle in Paradise wherever we will. And excellent is the reward of [righteous] workers."

75. And you will see the angels surrounding the Throne, exalting [God] with praise of their Lord. And it will be judged between them in truth, and it will be said, "[All] praise to God, Lord of the worlds."

[1271] In such honour and joy that is beyond description – thus, the omission of this conclusion in the Arabic text.

## Sūrah 40: Ghāfir

### Period of Revelation

According to Ibn Abbas, this Sūrah was sent down consecutively after Sūrah az-Zumar and its present position in the order of the Sūrahs in the Qur'ān is the same as its chronological order.

### Background of Revelation

There are clear indications in the subject matter of this Sūrah to the conditions in which it was revealed. The disbelievers of Makkah at that time were engaged in two kinds of the activities against the Prophet. First, they were creating every kind of suspicion and misgiving in the minds of the people about the teaching of the Qur'ān and the message of Islām and about the Prophet himself by starting many disputes and discussions, raising irrelevant objections and bringing ever new accusations so that the Prophet and the believers were sick of trying to answer them. Second, they were preparing the ground for putting an end to the Prophet himself. They were devising one plot after the other, and on one occasion had even taken the practical steps to execute a plot. Bukhari has related a hadith on the authority of Abdullah bin Amr bin As saying that one day when the Prophet was offering his Prayer in the precincts of the Ka'bāh, suddenly 'Uqbah bin Abi Mu'ait, rushed forward and putting a piece of cloth round his neck started twisting it so as to strangle him to death. Abu Bakr, who happened to go there in time, pushed him away. Abdullah says that when Abu Bakr was struggling with the cruel man, he was saying words to the effect: "Would you kill a man only because he says: God is my Lord?"

## Sūrah 40: Ghāfir[1272]

In the Name of God, the Most Compassionate, the Most Merciful

1. Hā, Meem.[1273]

2. The revelation of the Book [i.e., the Qur'ān] is from God, the Exalted in Might, the Knowing.

3. The forgiver of sin, acceptor of repentance, severe in punishment, owner of abundance. There is no deity except Him; to Him is the destination.

4. No one disputes concerning the signs of God except those who disbelieve, so be not deceived by their [uninhibited] movement throughout the land.

5. The people of Noah denied before them and the [disbelieving] factions after them, and every nation intended [a plot] for their messenger to seize him, and they disputed by [using] falsehood to [attempt to] invalidate thereby the truth. So I seized them, and how [terrible] was My penalty.

6. And thus has the word [i.e., decree] of your Lord come into effect upon those who disbelieved that they are companions of the Fire.

7. Those [angels] who carry the Throne and those around it exalt [God] with praise of their Lord and believe in Him and ask forgiveness for those who have believed, [saying], "Our Lord, You have encompassed all things in mercy and knowledge, so forgive those who have repented and followed Your way and protect them from the punishment of Hellfire.

8. Our Lord, and admit them to gardens of perpetual residence which You have promised them and whoever was righteous among their fathers, their spouses and their offspring. Indeed, it is You who is the Exalted in Might, the Wise.

9. And protect them from the evil consequences [of their deeds]. And he whom You protect from evil consequences that Day - You will have given him mercy. And that is the great attainment."

10. Indeed, those who disbelieve will be addressed, "The hatred of God for you was [even] greater than your hatred of yourselves [this Day in Hell] when you were invited to faith, but you disbelieved [i.e., refused]."

11. They will say, "Our Lord, You made us lifeless twice and gave us life twice, and we have confessed our sins. So is there to an exit any way?"

12. [They will be told], "That is because, when God was called upon alone, you disbelieved; but if others were associated with Him, you believed. So the judgement is with God, the Most High, the Grand."

13. It is He who shows you His signs and sends down to you from the sky, provision. But none will remember except he who turns back [in repentance].

14. So invoke God, [being] sincere to Him in religion, although the disbelievers dislike it.

15. [He is] the Exalted above [all] degrees, Owner of the Throne; He places the

---

1272 *Ghāfir*: The Forgiver, i.e., God. This *sūrah* is also known as *al-Mu'min* (The Believer).

1273 See footnote to 2:1.

inspiration of His command [i.e., revelation] upon whom He wills of His servants to warn of the Day of Meeting.

16. The Day they come forth nothing concerning them will be concealed from God. To whom belongs [all] sovereignty this Day? To God, the One, the Prevailing.

17. This Day every soul will be recompensed for what it earned. No injustice today! Indeed, God is swift in account.

18. And warn them, [O Muhammad], of the Approaching Day, when hearts are at the throats, filled [with distress]. For the wrongdoers there will be no devoted friend and no intercessor [who is] obeyed.

19. He knows that which deceives the eyes and what the breasts conceal.

20. And God judges with truth, while those they invoke besides Him judge not with anything. Indeed, God - He is the Hearing, the Seeing.

21. Have they not traveled through the land and observed how was the end of those who were before them? They were greater than them in strength and in impression on the land, but God seized them for their sins. And they had not from God any protector.

22. That was because their messengers were coming to them with clear proofs, but they disbelieved, so God seized them. Indeed, He is Powerful and severe in punishment.

23. And We did certainly send Moses with Our signs and a clear authority

24. To Pharaoh, Hāmān and Qārūn, but they said, "[He is] a magician and a liar."

25. And when he brought them the truth from Us, they said, "Kill the sons of those who have believed with him and keep their women alive." But the plan of the disbelievers is not except in error.

26. And Pharaoh said, "Let me kill Moses and let him call upon his Lord. Indeed, I fear that he will change your religion or that he will cause corruption[1274] in the land."

27. But Moses said, "Indeed, I have sought refuge in my Lord and your Lord from every arrogant one who does not believe in the Day of Account."

28. And a believing man from the family of Pharaoh who concealed his faith said, "Do you kill a man [merely] because he says, 'My Lord is God' while he has brought you clear proofs from your Lord? And if he should be lying, then upon him is [the consequence of] his lie; but if he should be truthful, there will strike you some of what he promises you. Indeed, God does not guide one who is a transgressor and a liar.

29. O my people, sovereignty is yours today, [your being] dominant in the land. But who would protect us from the punishment of God if it came to us?" Pharaoh said, "I do not show you except what I see, and I do not guide you except to the way of right conduct."

[1274] i.e., dissension or civil strife.

30. And he who believed said, "O my people, indeed I fear for you [a fate] like the day of the companies[1275] -

31. Like the custom of the people of Noah and of 'Aad and Thamūd and those after them. And God wants no injustice for [His] servants.

32. And O my people, indeed I fear for you the Day of Calling[1276] -

33. The Day you will turn your backs fleeing; there is not for you from God any protector. And whoever God leaves astray - there is not for him any guide.

34. And Joseph had already come to you before with clear proofs, but you remained in doubt of that which he brought to you, until when he died, you said, 'Never will God send a messenger after him.' Thus does God leave astray he who is a transgressor and skeptic."

35. Those who dispute concerning the signs of God without an authority having come to them - great is hatred [of them] in the sight of God and in the sight of those who have believed. Thus does God seal over every heart [belonging to] an arrogant tyrant.

36. And Pharaoh said, "O Hāmān, construct for me a tower that I might reach the ways[1277] -

37. The ways into the heavens - so that I may look at the deity of Moses; but indeed, I think he is a liar." And thus was made attractive to Pharaoh the evil of his deed, and he was averted from the [right] way. And the plan of Pharaoh was not except in ruin.

38. And he who believed said, "O my people, follow me; I will guide you to the way of right conduct.

39. O my people, this worldly life is only [temporary] enjoyment, and indeed, the Hereafter - that is the home of [permanent] settlement.

40. Whoever does an evil deed will not be recompensed except by the like thereof; but whoever does righteousness, whether male or female, while he is a believer - those will enter Paradise, being given provision therein without account.

41. And O my people, how is it that I invite you to salvation while you invite me to the Fire?

42. You invite me to disbelieve in God and associate with Him that of which I have no knowledge, and I invite you to the Exalted in Might, the Perpetual Forgiver.

43. Assuredly, that to which you invite me has no [response to a] supplication in this world or in the Hereafter; and indeed, our return is to God, and indeed, the transgressors will be companions of the Fire.

44. And you will remember what I [now] say to you, and I entrust my affair to God. Indeed, God is Seeing of [His] servants."

45. So God protected him from the evils they plotted, and the people of Pharaoh

[1275] i.e., the days on which God sent His punishment upon those who rejected their prophets in former times.

[1276] i.e., the Day of Judgement, when the criminals will cry out in terror, the people will call to each other (see 7:44-51), and the angels will call out the results of each person's judgement.

[1277] Means of ascent, pathways.

were enveloped by the worst of punishment -

46. The Fire, they are exposed to it morning and evening.[1278] And the Day the Hour appears [it will be said], "Make the people of Pharaoh enter the severest punishment."

47. And [mention] when they will argue within the Fire, and the weak will say to those who had been arrogant, "Indeed, we were [only] your followers, so will you relieve us of a share of the Fire?"

48. Those who had been arrogant will say, "Indeed, all [of us] are in it. Indeed, God has judged between the servants."

49. And those in the Fire will say to the keepers of Hell, "Supplicate your Lord to lighten for us a day from the punishment."

50. They will say, "Did there not come to you your messengers with clear proofs?" They will say, "Yes." They will reply, "Then supplicate [yourselves], but the supplication of the disbelievers is not except in error [i.e., futility]."

51. Indeed, We will support Our messengers and those who believe during the life of this world and on the Day when the witnesses will stand -

52. The Day their excuse will not benefit the wrongdoers, and they will have the curse, and they will have the worst home [i.e., Hell].

53. And We had certainly given Moses guidance, and We caused the Children of Israel to inherit the Scripture

54. As guidance and a reminder for those of understanding.

55. So be patient, [O Muhammad]. Indeed, the promise of God is truth. And ask forgiveness for your sin[1279] and exalt [God] with praise of your Lord in the evening and the morning.

56. Indeed, those who dispute concerning the signs of God without [any] authority having come to them - there is not within their breasts except pride, [the extent of] which they cannot reach. So seek refuge in God. Indeed, it is He who is the Hearing, the Seeing.

57. The creation of the heavens and earth is greater than the creation of mankind, but most of the people do not know.

58. And not equal are the blind and the seeing, nor are those who believe and do righteous deeds and the evildoer. Little do you remember.

59. Indeed, the Hour is coming - no doubt about it - but most of the people do not believe.

60. And your Lord says, "Call upon Me; I will respond to you." Indeed, those who disdain My worship will enter Hell [rendered] contemptible.

61. It is God who made for you the night that you may rest therein and the day giving sight.[1280] Indeed, God is full of

[1278] From the time of their death until the Day of Resurrection, when they will be driven into it.

[1279] What is intended is "fault" or "error" in judgement, since all prophets were protected by God from falling into sin. The implication is that all believers should seek forgiveness for their sins.

[1280] i.e., making things visible.

bounty to the people, but most of the people are not grateful.

62. That is God, your Lord, Creator of all things; there is no deity except Him, so how are you deluded?

63. Thus were those [before you] deluded who were rejecting the signs of God.

64. It is God who made for you the earth a place of settlement and the sky a structure [i.e., ceiling] and formed you and perfected your forms and provided you with good things. That is God, your Lord; then blessed is God, Lord of the worlds.

65. He is the Ever-Living; there is no deity except Him, so call upon Him, [being] sincere to Him in religion. [All] praise is [due] to God, Lord of the worlds.

66. Say, [O Muhammad], "Indeed, I have been forbidden to worship those you call upon besides God once the clear proofs have come to me from my Lord, and I have been commanded to submit to the Lord of the worlds."

67. It is He who created you from dust, then from a sperm-drop, then from a clinging clot; then He brings you out as a child; then [He develops you] that you reach your [time of] maturity, then [further] that you become elders. And among you is he who is taken in death before [that], so that you reach a specified term;[1281] and perhaps you will use reason.

68. He it is who gives life and causes death; and when He decrees a matter, He but says to it, "Be," and it is.

69. Do you not consider those who dispute concerning the signs of God - how are they averted?

70. Those who deny the Book [i.e., the Qur'ān] and that with which We sent Our messengers - they are going to know,

71. When the shackles are around their necks and the chains; they will be dragged

72. In boiling water; then in the Fire they will be filled [with flame].

73. Then it will be said to them, "Where is that which you used to associate [with Him in worship]

74. Other than God?" They will say, "They have departed from us; rather, we did not used to invoke previously anything." Thus does God put astray the disbelievers.

75. [The angels will say], "That was because you used to exult upon the earth without right and you used to behave insolently.

76. Enter the gates of Hell to abide eternally therein, and wretched is the residence of the arrogant."

77. So be patient, [O Muhammad]; indeed, the promise of God is truth. And whether We show you some of what We have promised them or We take you in death, it is to Us they will be returned.

78. And We have already sent messengers before you. Among them are those [whose stories] We have related to you, and among them are those [whose stories] We have not related to you. And it

[1281] The time decreed for your death.

was not for any messenger to bring a sign [or verse] except by permission of God. So when the command of God comes, it will be concluded [i.e., judged] in truth, and the falsifiers will thereupon lose [all].

79. It is God who made for you the grazing animals upon which you ride, and some of them you eat.

80. And for you therein are [other] benefits and that you may realize upon them a need which is in your breasts;[1282] and upon them and upon ships you are carried.

81. And He shows you His signs. So which of the signs of God do you deny?

82. Have they not traveled through the land and observed how was the end of those before them? They were more numerous than themselves and greater in strength and in impression on the land, but they were not availed by what they used to earn.

83. And when their messengers came to them with clear proofs, they [merely] rejoiced in what they had of knowledge, but they were enveloped by what they used to ridicule.

84. And when they saw Our punishment, they said, "We believe in God alone and disbelieve in that which we used to associate with Him."

85. But never did their faith benefit them once they saw Our punishment. [It is] the established way of God which has preceded among His servants. And the disbelievers thereupon lost [all].

---

[1282] i.e., that you may use the animals to carry your loads to distant places, according to need.

## Sūrah 41: Fussilat

### Period of Revelation

According to authentic hadith, it was sent down after the affirmation of the Faith by Hamza, the uncle of the Prophet and before the affirmation of the Faith by Umar. Muhammad bin Ishaq, the earliest biographer of the Prophet, has related on the authority of Muhammad bin Ka'b al-Qurzi, the famous follower of the Companions, that one day some of the Quraysh chiefs were sitting in their assembly in the Masjid al-Haram, while in another corner of the Mosque there was the Prophet sitting by himself. This was the time when Hamza had already embraced Islām and the people of the Quraysh were feeling upset at the growing numbers of the Muslims. On this occasion, Utbah bin Rabi'ah (the father-in-law of Abu Sufyan) said to the Quraysh chiefs: *"Gentlemen, if you like I would go and speak to Muhammad and put before him some proposals; maybe that he accepts one of them, to which we may also agree, and so he stops opposing us."* They all agreed to this, and Utbah went and sat by the Prophet. When the Prophet turned to him, he said: *"Nephew, you know the high status that you enjoy in the community by virtue of your ancestry and family relations, but you have put your people to great trouble: you have created divisions among them and you consider them to be fools: you talk ill of their religion and gods, and say things as though all our forefathers were pagans. Now listen to me and I shall make some suggestions. Consider them well: maybe that you accept one of them."* The Prophet said: *"Abul Walid, say what you want to say and I shall listen to you."* He said, *"Nephew, if by what you are doing, you want wealth, we will give you enough of it so that you will be the richest man among us; if you want to became an important man, we will make you our chief and will never decide a matter without you; if you want to be a king, we will accept you as our king; and if you are visited by a Jinn, whom you cannot get rid of by your own power, we will arrange the best physicians and have you treated at our own expense."* 'Utbah went on speaking in this strain and the Prophet went on listening to him quietly. Then he said, *"Have you said, O Abul Walid, what you had to say?"* He replied that he had. The Prophet said: *"Well, now listen to me."* Then pronouncing Bismillah ir Rahman-ir-Rahim he began to recite this very Sūrah, and Utbah kept on listening to it, putting his hands behind his back and leaning on them as he listened. Coming to the verse of prostration (v. 37) the Prophet prostrated himself; then raising his head, said, *"This was my reply, O Abul Walid, now you may act as you please."* Then Utbah arose and walked back towards the chiefs, the people saw him from afar, and said: *"By God! Utbah's face is changed. He does not look the same man that he was when he went from here."* Then, when he came back and sat down, the people asked, *"What have you heard?"* He replied, *"By God! I have heard something the like of which I had never heard before. By God, it's neither poetry, nor sorcery, nor magic. O chiefs of the Quraysh, listen to what I say and leave this man to himself. I think what he recites is going to have its effect. If the other Arabs overcome him, you will be saved from raising your hand against your brother, and the others will deal with him. But if he overcame Arabia, his sovereignty would be your sovereignty and his honour your honour."* Hearing this the chiefs spoke out: *"You too, O father of Walid, have been bewitched by his tongue."* Utbah replied, *"I have given you my opinion; now you may act as you please."* (Ibn Hisham, vol. I, pp. 313-314).

### Theme and Subject Matter

In the discourse that God sent down in response to what Utbah said, no attention whatever was paid to the absurd proposals that he had made to the Prophet. For what he had said was, in fact, an attack on the Prophet's intention and his intellect. His assumption was that as there was no possibility of his being a Prophet and the Qur'ān being God's Revelation, inevitably the motive of his invitation must either be the desire to obtain wealth and political power, or, God forbid, he had lost his reason. In the first case, he wanted to make a bargain with the Prophet; in the second, he was insulting him when he said that the Quraysh chiefs would have him cured of his madness at their own expense. Obviously, when the opponents come down to such absurd things, no gentleman would like to answer them, but would ignore them and say what he himself had to say.

Therefore, ignoring what Utbah said, this Sūrah makes antagonism its subject of discussion, which the unbelieving Quraysh were showing stubbornly and wickedly in order to defeat the message of the Qur'ān. They would say to the Prophet, "You may try however hard you try: we would not listen to you. We have put coverings on our hearts and we have closed our ears. There is a wall between you and us, which would never let us meet together."

They had given a clear notice to the Prophet to the effect: "You may continue your mission of inviting the people to yourself, but we would go on opposing you as hard as we can to frustrate your mission."

For this object they had devised the following plan: Whenever the Prophet or a follower of his would try to recite the Qur'ān before the people, they would at once raise such a hue and cry that no one could hear anything. They were desperately trying to misconstrue the verses of the Qur'ān and spread every kind of misunderstanding among the people. They misconstrued everything and found fault even with the straightforward things. They would isolate words and sentences from their right context, from here and there, and would add their own words in order to put new meanings on them so as to mislead the people about the Qur'ān and the Messenger who presented it.

They would raise strange objections a specimen of which has been presented in this Sūrah. They said, "If an Arab presents a discourse in Arabic, what could be the miracle in it? Arabic is his mother tongue. Anyone could compose anything that he pleased in his mother tongue and then make the claim that he had received it from God. It would be a miracle if the person would suddenly arise and make an eloquent speech in a foreign tongue which he did not know. Then only could one say that the discourse was not of his own composition but a revelation from God."

Here is a resume of what has been said in answer to this deaf and blind opposition:

1. The Qur'ān is most certainly the Word of God, which He has sent down in Arabic. The ignorant people do not find any light of knowledge in the truths that have been presented in it plainly and clearly, but the people of understanding are seeing this light as well as benefiting by it. It is surely God's mercy that He has sent down this Word for the guidance of man. If a person regarded it as an affliction, it would be his own misfortune. Good news is for those who benefit by it and warning for those who turn away from it.
2. If you have put coverings on your hearts and have made yourselves deaf, it is none of the Prophet's job to make the one hear who does not want to hear, and the one who does not want to understand, understand forcibly. He is a man like you; he can make only those to hear and understand, who are inclined to hear and understand.
3. Whether you close down your eyes and ears and put coverings on your hearts, the fact, however, is that your God is only One God, and you are not the servant of any one else. Your stubbornness cannot change this reality in any way. If you accept this truth and correct your behavior accordingly you will do good only to yourselves, and if you reject it, you will only be preparing your own doom.
4. Do you have any understanding as to whom you disbelieve and with whom you associate others in divinity? It is with regard to that God Who has created this limitless universe, Who is the Creator of the earth and heavens, from Whose blessings you are benefiting on the earth, and on Whose provisions you are being fed and sustained. You set up His mean creatures as His associates and then you are made to understand the truth you turn away in stubbornness.
5. If you still do not believe, then be aware that a sudden torment is about to visit you, the like of which had visited the 'Aad and the Thamūd, and this torment also will not be the final punishment of your crimes, but there is in addition the accountability and the fire of Hell in the Hereafter.
6. Wretched is the man who gets as company such satans from among men and Jinn, who show him nothing but green and pleasant, who make his follies seem fair to him, who neither let him think aright himself nor let him hear right from others. But on the Day of Reckoning when their doom overtakes them, each one of them will say that if he happened to get hold of those who had misled and deceived him in the world, he would trample them under his foot.

7. This Qur'ān is an unchangeable Book. You can not defeat it by your machinations and falsehoods. Whether falsehood comes from the front or makes a secret and indirect attack from behind, it cannot succeed in refuting it.
8. Today when this Qur'ān is being presented in your own language so that you may understand it, you say that it should have been sent down in some foreign tongue. But had We sent it in a foreign tongue for your guidance, you would yourselves have called it a joke, as if to say, "What a strange thing! The Arabs are being given guidance in a non-Arabic language, which nobody understands." This means that you, in fact, have no desire to obtain guidance. You are only inventing ever new excuses for not affirming the faith.
9. Have you ever considered that if it became established that the Qur'ān was really from God, then what fate you would meet by denying it and opposing it so vehemently as you do?
10. Today you do not believe but soon you will see with your own eyes that the message of this Qur'ān had pervaded the whole world and you have yourselves been overwhelmed by it. Then you will come to know that what you were being told was the very truth.

Besides giving these answers to the opponents, attention has been paid to the problems which the believers and the Prophet himself were facing in that environment of active resistance. Not to speak of preaching the message to others, the believers were even finding it difficult to follow the way of the Faith. Any one about whom it became known that he had become a Muslim, life would become an agony. As against the dreadful combination of the enemy and its all pervading power, they were feeling utterly helpless and powerless. In this state, in the first place, they were consoled and encouraged, as if to say: "You are not, in fact, helpless and powerless, for any person who believes in God as his Lord and adheres to this belief and way of life resolutely, God's angels descend on him and help and support him at every stage, from the life of this world till the Hereafter." Then they were encouraged with the consolation: "The best man is he who does good, invites others to God and proclaims firmly that he is a Muslim."

The question the Prophet had at that time was as to how he should carve out a way of preaching his message when he had to face such heavy odds on every side. The solution he was given to this question was: "Although apparently the obstacles seem to be insurmountable, the weapon of good morals and character can smash and melt them away. Use this weapon patiently, and whenever Satan provokes you and incites you to use some other device, seek refuge in God."

## Sūrah 41: Fussilat[1283]

In the Name of God, the Most Compassionate, the Most Merciful

1. Hā, Meem.[1284]

2. [This is] a revelation from the Entirely Merciful, the Especially Merciful –

3. A Book whose verses have been detailed, an Arabic Qur'ān[1285] for a people who know,

4. As a giver of good tidings and a warner; but most of them turn away, so they do not hear.

5. And they say, "Our hearts are within coverings [i.e., screened] from that to which you invite us, and in our ears is deafness, and between us and you is a partition, so work;[1286] indeed, we are working."

6. Say, [O Muhammad], "I am only a man like you to whom it has been revealed that your god is but one God; so take a straight course to Him and seek His forgiveness." And woe to those who associate others with God –

7. Those who do not give zakāh, and in the Hereafter they are disbelievers.

8. Indeed, those who believe and do righteous deeds – for them is a reward uninterrupted.

9. Say, "Do you indeed disbelieve in He who created the earth in two days and attribute to Him equals? That is the Lord of the worlds."

10. And He placed on it [i.e., the earth] firmly set mountains over its surface, and He blessed it and determined therein its [creatures'] sustenance in four days without distinction[1287] – for [the information of] those who ask.

11. Then He directed Himself[1288] to the heaven while it was smoke and said to it and to the earth, "Come [into being],[1289] willingly or by compulsion." They said, "We have come willingly."

12. And He completed them as seven heavens within two days and inspired [i.e., made known] in each heaven its command. And We adorned the nearest heaven with lamps [i.e., stars, for beauty] and as protection.[1290] That is the determination of the Exalted in Might, the Knowing.

13. But if they turn away, then say, "I have warned you of a thunderbolt like the thunderbolt [that struck] 'Aad and Thamūd.

14. [That occurred] when the messengers had come to them before them and after them, [saying], "Worship not except God." They said, "If our Lord had willed,[1291] He would have sent down the angels, so indeed we, in that with which you have been sent, are disbelievers."

15. As for 'Aad, they were arrogant upon the earth without right and said, "Who

---

[1283] *Fussilat*: They (i.e., God's verses) Have Been Detailed or Presented in Detail. The *sūrah* is also referred to as *Hā Meem as-Sajdah*.
[1284] See footnote to 2:1.
[1285] i.e., revealed in the Arabic language.
[1286] For your own religion or work against us.
[1287] Also "four equal days" or "four days of completion."
[1288] See footnote to 2:19.
[1289] Literally, "become" or "do [as commanded]."
[1290] From the devils who attempt to steal information from the angels.
[1291] To send messengers.

is greater than us in strength?" Did they not consider that God who created them was greater than them in strength? But they were rejecting Our signs.

16. So We sent upon them a screaming wind during days of misfortune to make them taste the punishment of disgrace in the worldly life; but the punishment of the Hereafter is more disgracing, and they will not be helped.

17. And as for Thamūd, We guided them, but they preferred blindness over guidance, so the thunderbolt of humiliating punishment seized them for what they used to earn.

18. And We saved those who believed and used to fear God.

19. And [mention, O Muhammad], the Day when the enemies of God will be gathered to the Fire while they are [driven], assembled in rows,

20. Until, when they reach it, their hearing and their eyes and their skins will testify against them of what they used to do.

21. And they will say to their skins, "Why have you testified against us?" They will say, "We were made to speak by God, who has made everything speak; and He created you the first time, and to Him you are returned.

22. And you were not covering [i.e., protecting] yourselves,[1292] lest your hearing testify against you or your sight or your skins, but you assumed that God does not know much of what you do.

[1292] With righteousness or by fearing God.

23. And that was your assumption which you assumed about your Lord. It has brought you to ruin, and you have become among the losers."

24. So [even] if they are patient, the Fire is a residence for them; and if they ask to appease [God], they will not be of those who are allowed to appease.

25. And We appointed for them companions[1293] who made attractive to them what was before them and what was behind them [of sin], and the word [i.e., decree] has come into effect upon them among nations which had passed on before them of jinn and men. Indeed, they [all] were losers.

26. And those who disbelieve say, "Do not listen to this Qur'ān and speak noisily[1294] during [the recitation of] it that perhaps you will overcome."

27. But We will surely cause those who disbelieve to taste a severe punishment, and We will surely recompense them for the worst of what they had been doing.

28. That is the recompense of the enemies of God – the Fire. For them therein is the home of eternity as recompense for what they, of Our verses, were rejecting.

29. And those who disbelieved will [then] say, "Our Lord, show us those who misled us of the jinn and men [so] we

[1293] In this world amoung the evil *jinn* and men.
[1294] Other meanings include "speak improperly" and/or "make a clamor." The purpose of this was to prevent the hearing or understanding of the Qur'ān.

may put them under our feet[1295] that they will be among the lowest."

30. Indeed, those who have said, "Our Lord is God" and then remained on a right course – the angels will descend upon them, [saying], "Do not fear and do not grieve but receive good tidings of Paradise, which you were promised.

31. We [angels] were your allies in worldly life and [are so] in the Hereafter. And you will have therein whatever your souls desire, and you will have therein whatever you request [or wish]

32. As accommodation from a [Lord who is] Forgiving and Merciful."

33. And who is better in speech than one who invites to God and does righteousness and says, "Indeed, I am of the Muslims."

34. And not equal are the good deed and the bad. Repel [evil] by that [deed] which is better; and thereupon, the one whom between you and him is enmity [will become] as though he was a devoted friend.

35. But none is granted it except those who are patient, and none is granted it except one having a great portion [of good].

36. And if there comes to you from Satan an evil suggestion, then seek refuge in God. Indeed, He is the Hearing, the Knowing.

37. And of His signs are the night and day and the sun and moon. Do not prostrate to the sun or to the moon, but prostate to God, who created them, if it should be Him that you worship.[1296]

38. But if they are arrogant – then those who are near your Lord [i.e., the angels] exalt Him by night and by day, and they do not become weary.

39. And of His signs is that you see the earth stilled, but when We send down upon it rain, it quivers and grows. Indeed, He who has given it life is the Giver of Life to the dead. Indeed, He is over all things competent.

40. Indeed, those who inject deviation into Our verses[1297] are not concealed from Us. So, is he who is cast into the Fire better or he who comes secure on the Day of Resurrection? Do whatever you will; indeed, He is Seeing of what you do.

41. Indeed, those who disbelieve in the message [i.e., the Qur'ān][1298] after it has come to them...[1299] And indeed, it is a mighty[1300] Book.

42. Falsehood cannot approach it from before it or from behind it; [it is] a revelation from a [Lord who is] Wise and Praiseworthy.

43. Nothing is said to you, [O Muhammad], except what was already said to the messengers before you. Indeed, your Lord is a possessor of forgiveness and a possessor of painful penalty.

[1295] In the lowest depths of Hell. Or "that we may step on them" in revenge.

[1296] i.e., Do not worship God through His creations but worship Him directly and exclusively.

[1297] Through deviant recitations or interpretations.

[1298] i.e., reject it or prefer deviant interpretation.

[1299] The conclusion is understood to be "...will have earned an indescribable punishment."

[1300] Inimitable, resistant to attack, protected by God.

44. And if We had made it a foreign [i.e., non-Arabic] Qur'ān, they would have said, "Why are its verses not explained in detail [in our language]? Is it a foreign [recitation] and an Arab [messenger]?" Say, "It is, for those who believe, a guidance and cure." And those who do not believe – in their ears is deafness, and it is upon them blindness. Those are being called from a distant place.[1301]

45. And We had already given Moses the Scripture, but it came under disagreement.[1302] And if not for a word [i.e., decree][1303] that preceded from your Lord, it would have been concluded between them. And indeed they are, concerning it [i.e., the Qur'ān], in disquieting doubt.

46. Whoever does righteousness – it is for his [own] soul; and whoever does evil [does so] against it. And your Lord is not ever unjust to [His] servants.

47. To Him [alone] is attributed knowledge of the Hour. And fruits emerge not from their coverings nor does a female conceive or give birth except with His knowledge. And the Day He will call to them, "Where are My 'partners'?" they will say, "We announce to You that there is [no longer] among us any witness [to that]."

48. And lost from them will be those they were invoking before, and they will be certain that they have no place of escape.

49. Man is not weary of supplication for good [things], but if evil touches him, he is hopeless and despairing.

50. And if We let him taste mercy from Us after an adversity which has touched him, he will surely say, "This is [due] to me,[1304] and I do not think the Hour will occur; and [even] if I should be returned to my Lord, indeed, for me there will be with Him the best." But We will surely inform those who disbelieved about what they did, and We will surely make them taste a massive punishment.

51. And when We bestow favor upon man, he turns away and distances himself; but when evil touches him, then he is full of extensive supplication.

52. Say, "Have you considered: if it [i.e., the Qur'ān] is from God and you disbelieved in it, who would be more astray than one who is in extreme dissension?"

53. We will show them Our signs in the horizons and within themselves until it becomes clear to them that it is the truth.[1305] But is it not sufficient concerning your Lord that He is, over all things, a Witness?

54. Unquestionably, they are in doubt about the meeting with their Lord. Unquestionably He is, of all things, encompassing.

1301 For all practical purposes, since they neither hear nor understand.

1302 An alternative meaning is "he was opposed over it."

1303 See footnote to 10:19.

1304 Because of my effort, knowledge, excellence, etc.

1305 Or "that He is the Truth."

## Sūrah 42: ash-Shūrā

### Period of Revelation

Although it could not be known from any authentic traditions, yet one feels after a study of its subject matter that this Sūrah might have been sent down consecutively after Fussilat, for it seems to be, in a way, a supplement to it. This will become clear to every person who first studies Sūrah Fussilat carefully and then goes through this Sūrah. He will see that in that Sūrah the Quraysh chiefs had been taken to tack for their deaf and blind opposition so that anyone in Makkah and in its out-skirts, who had any sense of morality and nobility left in him, should know how unreasonably the chiefs of the people were opposing Muhammad (upon whom be God's peace), and as against them, how serious he was in everything he said, how rational was his standpoint and how noble his character and conduct. Immediately after that warning this Sūrah was sent down, which did full justice to teaching and instruction, and made the truth of the Prophet's message plain in such an impressive way that anyone who had any element of the love of the truth in him and who had not been blinded by the errors of ignorance, could not help being influenced by it.

### Theme and Subject Matter

The discourse begins in a way as if to say: "Why are you expressing surprise and amazement at what Our Prophet is presenting before you? What he says is not new or strange, nor anything novel, which might have been presented for the first time in history: that Revelation should come down to a man from God and he should be given instructions for the guidance of mankind. God has been sending similar Revelations with similar instructions to the former Prophets before this. It is not surprising that the Owner of the Universe should be acknowledged as Deity and Ruler, but what is strange is that one should accept another as divine and deity in spite of being His subject and slave. You are being angry with him who is presenting Tawhid (Oneness of God) before you, where as the shirk that you are practicing with regard to the Master of the Universe is such a grave crime as may cause the heavens to break asunder. The angels are amazed at this boldness of yours and fear that the wrath of God might descend on you any moment."

After this the people have been told that a person's being appointed to Prophethood and his presenting himself as a Prophet does not mean that he has been made master of the people's destinies and he has come to the world with that very claim. God has kept the destinies in His own hand. The Prophet has come only to arouse the heedless and guide the strayed ones to the Right Path. To call to account those who do not listen to him and to punish or not to punish them is God's own responsibility, and not part of the Prophet's work. Therefore, they should take it out of their head that the Prophet has come with a claim similar to those that are made by their so called religious guides and saints to the effect that he who would not listen to them, or would behave insolently towards them, would be burnt to death: In this very connection, the people have also been told that the Prophet has not come to condemn them but he is their well wisher; he is warning them that the way they are following will only lead to their own destruction.

Then, an answer has been given to the question: Why didn't God make all human beings righteous by birth, and why did He allow the difference of viewpoint owing to which the people start following each and every way of thought and action? The answer given is this: Owing to this very fact has it become possible for man to attain to the special mercy of God, which is not meant for other dumb creatures, but is only meant for those endowed with power and authority, who should take God as Patron and Guardian not instinctively but consciously by willing choice. God supports the man who adopts this way and guides and helps him to do good and right and admits him into His special mercy. On the contrary, the man who misuses his option and makes his patron those who are not, in fact, the guardians, and cannot be, are deprived of divine mercy. In this connection, it has also been made clear that only God is the Patron of man and of all other creatures. Others are neither the patron nor have the power to do full justice to patronage. Man's success depends only on this that he should make no mistake in choosing a patron for himself by the use of his free choice, and should take only Him his Guide Who, in reality, is the real Patron.

After this, it has been explained what the Faith (Din) being presented by the Prophet Muhammad really is : Its primary basis that as God Almighty is the Creator, Master and real Patron of the Universe and Man, He alone is Man's Ruler, He alone has the right to give Man Faith (Din) and Law (system of belief and practice) and judge the disputes of man and tell what is Truth and what is falsehood. No other being has any right whatever to be man's lawgiver. In other words, like the natural sovereignty, the sovereignty with regard to lawmaking also is vested only in God. No man or creature, apart from God, can be the bearer of this sovereignty. And if a person does not recognize and accept this Divine rule of God, it is merely futile for him to recognize the natural sovereignty of God.

On this very basis has God ordained a Din (True Religion) for Man from the very beginning. It was one and the same Religion that was vouchsafed in every age to all the Prophets. No Prophet ever founded any separate religion of his own. The same one Religion has been enjoined by God for all Mankind since the beginning of creation, and all the Prophets have been following it and inviting others to follow it.

This Religion and Creed was not sent so that man may rest content only with believing in it, but it was sent with the purpose and intention that it alone should be introduced, established and enforced in the world, and no man made religion be made to prevail in God's earth apart from His Religion. The Prophets had not been appointed only to preach this Religion but to establish it particularly in the world.

This same was the original Religion of mankind, but after the death of the Prophets, selfish people created new creeds by creating schisms for vested interests due to self-conceit, vanity and ostentation. All the different religions and creeds found in the world today have resulted from corruption of the original Divine Truth.

Now, the Prophet Muhammad has been sent so that he may present before the people the same and original Religion in place of the various practices and artificial creeds and man made religions, and may try to establish the same. On this, if instead of being grateful, you feel angry and come out to fight him, it is your folly; the Prophet will not abandon his mission only because of your foolishness. He has been enjoined to adhere to his faith at all costs and to carry out the mission to which he has been appointed. Therefore, the people should not cherish any false hope that in order to please them he would cater to the same whims and superstitions of ignorance which has corrupted God's Religion before.

You do not understand how great an impudence it is against God to adopt a man made religion and law instead of the Religion and Law enjoined by God. You think it is an ordinary thing and there is nothing wrong with it. But in the sight of God it is the worst kind of shirk and a grave crime whose punishment will be imposed on all those who enforced their own religion on God's earth and those who adopted and followed their religion.

Thus, after presenting a clear and visible concept of Religion it is said: "The best possible method that could be employed for your instruction and for bringing you to the Right Path has already been employed. On the one hand, God has sent down His Book, which is teaching you the truth in a most impressive way in your own language; and on the other, the lives of the Prophet Muhammad and his Companions are present before you by which you can see for yourselves what kind of men are prepared by the guidance given in this Book. Even then if you do not accept this guidance, nothing else in the world can bring you to the Right Path. The only alternative, therefore, is that you should be allowed to persist in the same error in which you have remained involved in for centuries, and made to meet with the same doom which has been destined by God for such wrongdoers."

While stating these truths, brief arguments have been given, here and there, for Tawhid (Oneness of God) and the Hereafter, the world worshipers have been warned of the evil consequences and their punishment in the life hereafter, and the disbelievers have been criticized for the moral weaknesses, which were the real cause of their deviation from the truth. The Sūrah has been concluded with two important themes.

First, that the Prophet was wholly unaware of this concept of the "Book" or the True Faith during the first forty years of his life and then his sudden appearance before the people with those two things, is a manifest proof of his being a Prophet.

Secondly, his presenting his own teaching as the teaching of God does not mean that he claims to have spoken to God, face to face, but God has conveyed to him this Guidance, as in the case of all other Prophets, in three ways: He speaks to His Prophets either through Revelation, or from behind a veil, or He sends an angel with the message. This thing was clarified so that the opponents did not have an opportunity of accusing the Prophet of claiming to have spoken to God, face to face, and the lovers of the truth should know by what methods God gave instruction to the man whom He had appointed to the mission of Prophethood.

## Sūrah 42: ash-Shūrā[1306]

In the Name of God, the Most Compassionate, the Most Merciful

1. Hā, Meem.

2. 'Ayn, Seen, Qāf.[1307]

3. Thus has He revealed to you, [O Muhammad], and to those before you - God, the Exalted in Might, the Wise.

4. To Him belongs whatever is in the heavens and whatever is in the earth, and He is the Most High, the Most Great.

5. The heavens almost break from above them,[1308] and the angels exalt [God] with praise of their Lord and ask forgiveness for those on earth. Unquestionably, it is God who is the Forgiving, the Merciful.

6. And those who take as allies other than Him - God is [yet] Guardian over them; and you, [O Muhammad], are not over them a manager.

7. And thus We have revealed to you an Arabic Qur'ān that you may warn the Mother of Cities [i.e., Makkah] and those around it[1309] and warn of the Day of Assembly, about which there is no doubt. A party will be in Paradise and a party in the Blaze.

8. And if God willed, He could have made them [of] one religion, but He admits whom He wills[1310] into His mercy. And the wrongdoers have not any protector or helper.

9. Or have they taken protectors [or allies] besides him? But God - He is the Protector, and He gives life to the dead, and He is over all things competent.

10. And in anything over which you disagree - its ruling is [to be referred] to God. [Say], "That is God, my Lord; upon Him I have relied, and to Him I turn back."[1311]

11. [He is] Creator of the heavens and the earth. He has made for you from yourselves, mates, and among the cattle, mates; He multiplies you thereby. There is nothing like unto Him,[1312] and He is the Hearing, the Seeing.

12. To Him belong the keys of the heavens and the earth. He extends provision for whom He wills and restricts [it]. Indeed He is, of all things, Knowing.

13. He has ordained for you of religion what He enjoined upon Noah and that which We have revealed to you, [O Muhammad], and what We enjoined upon Abraham and Moses and Jesus - to establish the religion and not be divided therein. Difficult for those who associate others with God is that to which you invite them. God chooses for Himself whom He wills and guides to Himself whoever turns back [to Him].

14. And they did not become divided until after knowledge had come to them - out of jealous animosity between them-

[1306] *Ash-Shūrā*: Consultation.
[1307] See footnote to 2:1.
[1308] i.e., from the grandeur of God above them.
[1309] i.e., all other peoples.
[1310] i.e., those who desire His guidance and His acceptance of them.

[1311] In remembrance and repentance.
[1312] There is no similarity whatsoever between the Creator and His creation in essence, in attributes or in deed.

selves. And if not for a word[1313] that preceded from your Lord [postponing the penalty] until a specified time, it would have been concluded between them. And indeed, those who were granted inheritance of the Scripture after them are, concerning it, in disquieting doubt.

15. So to that [religion of God] invite, [O Muhammad],[1314] and remain on a right course as you are commanded and do not follow their inclinations but say, "I have believed in what God has revealed of scripture [i.e., the Qur'ān], and I have been commanded to do justice among you. God is our Lord and your Lord. For us are our deeds, and for you your deeds.[1315] There is no [need for] argument between us and you.[1316] God will bring us together, and to Him is the [final] destination."

16. And those who argue concerning God after He has been responded to[1317] - their argument is invalid with their Lord, and upon them is [His] wrath, and for them is a severe punishment.

17. It is God who has sent down the Book in truth and [also] the balance [i.e., justice]. And what will make you perceive? Perhaps the Hour is near.

18. Those who do not believe in it are impatient for it,[1318] but those who believe are fearful of it and know that it is the truth. Unquestionably, those who dispute concerning the Hour are in extreme error.

19. God is Subtle [i.e., gentle] with His servants; He gives provisions to whom He wills. And He is the Powerful, the Exalted in Might.

20. Whoever desires the harvest of the Hereafter - We increase for him in his harvest [i.e., reward]. And whoever desires the harvest [i.e., benefits] of this world - We give him thereof, but there is not for him in the Hereafter any share.

21. Or have they partners [i.e., other deities] who have ordained for them a religion to which God has not consented? But if not for the decisive word,[1319] it would have been concluded between them. And indeed, the wrongdoers will have a painful punishment.

22. You will see the wrongdoers fearful of what they have earned, and it will [certainly] befall them. And those who have believed and done righteous deeds will be in lush regions of the gardens [in Paradise] having whatever they will in the presence of their Lord. That is what is the great bounty.

23. It is that of which God gives good tidings to His servants who believe and do righteous deeds. Say, [O Muhammad], "I do not ask you for it [i.e., this message] any payment [but] only good will through [i.e., due to] kinship." And

[1313] Decree. See footnote to 10:19.
[1314] Another meaning understood from the Arabic is "So because of that [division and separation into sects], invite [them back to God]..."
[1315] i.e., the consequences thereof.
[1316] Since the truth has been made clear and since those who refuse it do so only out of stubbornness or worldly interests.
[1317] i.e., after people have accepted the truth from God, in an attempt to turn the believers away from His religion of Islām.

[1318] They had challenged the Prophet to bring it on immediately.
[1319] Decree. See footnote to 10:19.

whoever commits a good deed - We will increase for him good therein. Indeed, God is Forgiving and Appreciative.

24. Or do they say, "He has invented about God a lie"? But if God willed, He could seal over your heart.[1320] And God eliminates falsehood and establishes the truth by His words. Indeed, He is Knowing of that within the breasts.

25. And it is He who accepts repentance from his servants and pardons misdeeds, and He knows what you do.

26. And He answers [the supplication of] those who have believed and done righteous deeds and increases [for] them from His bounty. But the disbelievers will have a severe punishment.

27. And if God had extended [excessively] provision for His servants, they would have committed tyranny throughout the earth. But He sends [it] down in an amount which He wills. Indeed He is, of His servants, Acquainted and Seeing.

28. And it is He who sends down the rain after they had despaired and spreads His mercy. And He is the Protector, the Praiseworthy.

29. And of his signs is the creation of the heavens and earth and what He has dispersed throughout them of creatures. And He, for gathering them when He wills, is competent.

30. And whatever strikes you of disaster - it is for what your hands have earned; but He pardons much.

[1320] i.e., He could make you forget the Qur'ān and deprive you of it.

31. And you will not cause failure [to God][1321] upon the earth. And you have not besides God any protector or helper.

32. And of His signs are the ships in the sea, like mountains.

33. If He willed, He could still the wind, and they would remain motionless on its surface. Indeed in that are signs for everyone patient and grateful.

34. Or He could destroy them[1322] for what they earned; but He pardons much.

35. And [that is so] those who dispute concerning Our signs may know that for them there is no place of escape.

36. So whatever thing you have been given - it is but [for] enjoyment of the worldly life. But what is with God is better and more lasting for those who have believed and upon their Lord rely

37. And those who avoid the major sins and immoralities, and when they are angry, they forgive,

38. And those who have responded to their lord and established prayer and whose affair is [determined by] consultation among themselves, and from what We have provided them, they spend,

39. And those who, when tyranny strikes them, they defend themselves.[1323]

40. And the retribution for an evil act is an evil one like it, but whoever pardons

[1321] i.e., escape from Him.

[1322] Meaning that God could sink the ships by means of violent winds.

[1323] Or avenge themselves in a just manner, restoring their rights and not allowing aggressors to take advantage of them out of weakness.

and makes reconciliation - his reward is [due] from God. Indeed, He does not like wrongdoers.

41. And whoever avenges himself after having been wronged - those have not upon them any cause [for blame].

42. The cause is only against the ones who wrong the people and tyrannize upon the earth without right. Those will have a painful punishment.

43. And whoever is patient and forgives - indeed, that is of the matters [requiring] determination.[1324]

44. And he whom God sends astray - for him there is no protector beyond Him. And you will see the wrongdoers, when they see the punishment, saying, "Is there for return [to the former world] any way?"

45. And you will see them being exposed to it [i.e., the Fire], humbled from humiliation, looking from [behind] a covert glance. And those who had believed will say, "Indeed, the [true] losers are the ones who lost themselves and their families on the Day of Resurrection. Unquestionably, the wrongdoers are in an enduring punishment."

46. And there will not be for them any allies to aid them other than God. And whoever God sends astray - for him there is no way.

47. Respond to your Lord before a Day comes from God of which there is no repelling. No refuge will you have that day, nor for you will there be any denial.[1325]

48. But if they turn away - then We have not sent you, [O Muhammad], over them as a guardian; upon you is only [the duty of] notification. And indeed, when We let man taste mercy from Us, he rejoices in it; but if evil afflicts him for what his hands have put forth, then indeed, man is ungrateful.

49. To God belongs the dominion of the heavens and the earth; He creates what he wills. He gives to whom He wills female [children], and He gives to whom He wills males.

50. Or He makes them [both] males and females, and He renders whom He wills barren. Indeed, He is Knowing and Competent.

51. And it is not for any human being that God should speak to him except by revelation or from behind a partition or that He sends a messenger [i.e., angel] to reveal, by His permission, what He wills. Indeed, He is Most High and Wise.

52. And thus We have revealed to you an inspiration of Our command [i.e., the Qur'ān]. You did not know what is the Book or [what is] faith, but We have made it a light by which We guide whom We will of Our servants. And indeed, [O Muhammad], you guide to a straight path -

[1324] On the part of those seeking the reward of God.

[1325] Of your sins or "disapproval" of your punishment.

53. The path of God, to whom belongs whatever is in the heavens and whatever is on the earth. Unquestionably, to God do [all] matters evolve [i.e., return].

## Sūrah 43: az-Zukhruf

### Period of Revelation

It could not be known from any authentic tradition, but a study of its subject matter shows that this Sūrah also was sent down in the same period in which the Sūrah's al-Mumin, as-Sajdah and ash-Shura, were sent down. It appears that the revelation of this series of the Sūrahs began when the disbelievers of Makkah were planning to put an end to the Prophet's life. Day and night they were holding consultations in their assemblies as how to eliminate him, and even an attack on his life also had been made as has been clearly referred to in v. 79-80.

### Theme and Topics

In this Sūrah a forceful and severe criticism has been made of the Quraysh and the common Arabs creeds and superstitions of ignorance in which they persisted, and their stubbornness has been exposed in a firm and effective way, so that every member of the society, who was reasonable in some degree, should be made to consider the evils in which the community was involved and its tyrannical treatment of the person who was trying to redeem it.

The discourse starts in a way as if to say: "You, by means of your mischiefs, want that the revelation of this Book should be stopped, but God has never withheld the appointment of His Prophets and the revelation of His Books because of the mischief of the people, but has destroyed the wicked people, who obstructed the way of His guidance. The same He will do again. A little further in v. 41-43 and 79-80 the same thing has been reiterated. Though the people who were plotting against his life are meant, the Prophet has been addressed to the effect: "whether you remain alive or not, We will certainly punish the wicked," and the people themselves have been plainly warned to the effect: "If you have decided to take an action against Our Prophet, We too will take a decisive action."

Then, it has been told what is the reality of the religion that the people are following so devotedly and what are the arguments on whose strength they are resisting Muhammad.

They themselves admit that the Creator of the earth and heavens and of themselves and their deities is only God. They also know and admit that the blessings they are benefiting from, have been bestowed by God; yet they insist on making others associates of God in His Sovereingty. They regard the servants as the children of God, and that too daughters, whom they regard as disgraceful for themselves.

They believe that the angels are Goddesses; they have carved their images as females; they adorn them with female dresses and ornaments, and call them daughters of God: they worship them and invoke them for the fulfillment of their needs. How did they know that the angels were female?

When they are rebuked for these superstitions, they present the pretense of destiny and say: "Had God disapproved of these our practices, we could not have worshipped these images, whereas the means of finding out whether God had approved of something or not, are His Books and not those things which are happening in the world according to His Will. For under His Will not only idol worship but crimes like theft and adultery, robbery, murder, etc. also are being committed. Can this argument be used to justify as right and proper this commission of every crime and evil in the world?

When it is asked: Have you any other authority, apart from this wrong argument, for this polytheism of yours? They reply, "The same has been the practice since the time of our forefathers." In other words, this in their opinion is a strong enough argument for a creed's being right and true, whereas the Prophet Abrahim, descent from whom is the only basis of their pride and distinction, had rejected the religion of his elders and left his home, and he had discarded every such blind imitation of his forefathers, which did not have the support of any rational argument. Then, if these people had to follow their elders only, for this also they selected their most ignorant elders and abandoned their most illustrious elders like the Prophets Abraham and Ishmael.

When they are asked: "Has ever a Prophet or a Book sent down by God also given this teaching that others beside God too are worthy of worship? They present this practice of the Christians as an argument that they took Jesus son of Mary as son of God and worshipped him; whereas the question was not whether the community of a Prophet had committed shirk or not, but whether a Prophet had himself taught Shirk (polytheism). Jesus son of Mary had never said that he was son of God and that the people should worship him. His own was the same teaching which every other Prophet had given: "My Lord as well as your Lord is God: so worship Him alone."

They were disinclined to believe in the Prophethood of the Prophet because he was neither a rich man nor a person of high worldly position and rank. They said "Had God willed to appoint a prophet among us, He would have appointed one of the great men of our two cities (Makkah and Tā'if). On that very basis, Pharaoh also had looked down upon the Prophet Moses and said: "If God, the King of the heavens, had to send a messenger to me, the king of the earth, He would have sent him with bracelets of gold and a company of angels in attendance. Wherefrom has this mendicant appeared? I am superior to him, for the kingdom of Egypt belongs to me, and the canals of the River Nile are flowing under my control. What is the status of this man as against me? He has neither wealth nor authority."

Thus, after criticizing each practice of ignorance of the disbelievers and rejecting it with rational arguments, it has been pointed out: "Neither has God any offspring, nor are there separate gods of the earth and heavens, nor is there any intercessor who may be able to protect from His punishment those who adopt deviation knowingly. God is far above this that He should have children. He alone is the God of the whole Universe: all others are His servants and not associates in His attributes and powers, and only such men can intercede with Him, who are themselves followers of the Truth and they also can intercede only for those who may have adopted obedience of the Truth in the world."

## Sūrah 43: az-Zukhruf[1326]

In the Name of God, the Most Compassionate, the Most Merciful

1. Hā, Meem.[1327]

2. By the clear Book,

3. Indeed, We have made it an Arabic Qur'ān that you might understand.

4. And indeed it is, in the Mother of the Book[1328] with Us, exalted and full of wisdom.[1329]

5. Then should We turn the message away, disregarding you, because you are a transgressing people?

6. And how many a prophet We sent among the former peoples,

7. But there would not come to them a prophet except that they used to ridicule him.

8. And We destroyed greater than them[1330] in [striking] power, and the example of the former peoples has preceded.

9. And if you should ask them, "Who has created the heavens and the earth?" they would surely say, "They were created by the Exalted in Might, the Knowing,"

10. [The one] who has made for you the earth a bed and made for you upon it roads that you might be guided

11. And who sends down rain from the sky in measured amounts, and We revive thereby a dead land - thus will you be brought forth -

12. And who created the species, all of them, and has made for you of ships and animals those which you mount

13. That you may settle yourselves upon their backs and then remember the favor of your Lord when you have settled upon them and say, "Exalted is He who has subjected this to us, and we could not have [otherwise] subdued it.[1331]

14. And indeed we, to our Lord, will [surely] return."

15. But they have attributed to Him from His servants a portion.[1332] Indeed, man is clearly ungrateful.

16. Or has He taken, out of what He has created, daughters and chosen you for [having] sons?

17. And when one of them is given good tidings of that which he attributes to the Most Merciful in comparison [i.e., a daughter], his face becomes dark, and he suppresses grief.

18. So is one brought up in ornaments while being during conflict unevident[1333] [attributed to God]?

---

1326 *Az-Zukhruf*: Ornament, originally meaning gold but including other types of decoration.
1327 See footnote to 2:1.
1328 i.e., the Preserved Slate (*al-Lawh al-Mahfūth*).
1329 Also, "precise" or "specific."
1330 The disbelievers of the Quraysh, who denied Prophet Muhammad.

1331 Literally, "made it a companion" or "made it compatible."
1332 By claiming that He has a son or daughters, as it is said that a child is part of his parent. This concept is totally incompatible with God's unity and exclusiveness.

19. And they have made the angels, who are servants of the Most Merciful, females. Did they witness their creation? Their testimony will be recorded, and they will be questioned.

20. And they said, "If the Most Merciful had willed, we would not have worshipped them." They have of that no knowledge. They are not but falsifying.

21. Or have We given them a book before it [i.e., the Qur'ān] to which they are adhering?

22. Rather, they say, "Indeed, we found our fathers upon a religion, and we are in their footsteps [rightly] guided."

23. And similarly, We did not send before you any warner into a city except that its affluent said, "Indeed, we found our fathers upon a religion, and we are, in their footsteps, following."

24. [Each warner] said, "Even if I brought you better guidance than that [religion] upon which you found your fathers?" They said, "Indeed we, in that with which you were sent, are disbelievers."

25. So we took retribution from them; then see how was the end of the deniers.

26. And [mention, O Muhammad], when Abraham said to his father and his people, "Indeed, I am disassociated from that which you worship

27. Except for He who created me; and indeed, He will guide me."

[1333] Not "obvious" or "distinct" in an argument. Or not "seen," i.e., absent from battles. The reference is to a daughter.

28. And he made it[1334] a word remaining among his descendants that they might return [to it].

29. However, I gave enjoyment to these [people of Makkah] and their fathers[1335] until there came to them the truth and a clear Messenger.[1336]

30. But when the truth came to them, they said, "This is magic, and indeed we are, concerning it, disbelievers."

31. And they said, "Why was this Qur'ān not sent down upon a great man from [one of] the two cities?"[1337]

32. Do they distribute the mercy of your Lord? It is We who have apportioned among them their livelihood in the life of this world and have raised some of them above others in degrees [of rank] that they may make use of one another for service. But the mercy of your Lord is better than whatever they accumulate.

33. And if it were not that the people would become one community [of disbelievers],[1338] We would have made for those who disbelieve in the Most Merciful - for their houses - ceilings and stairways of silver upon which to mount

34. And for their houses - doors and couches [of silver] upon which to recline

[1334] i.e., his testimony that none is worthy of worship except God.
[1335] The descendants of Abraham.
[1336] i.e., one who is obvious with a clear message, meaning Muhammad.
[1337] Referring to Makkah and at-Tā'if.
[1338] Who assumed that God's generosity to them was a sign of His approval or who would hasten to disbelief in order to obtain wealth.

35. And gold ornament. But all that is not but the enjoyment of worldly life. And the Hereafter with your Lord is for the righteous.

36. And whoever is blinded from remembrance of the Most Merciful - We appoint for him a devil, and he is to him a companion.

37. And indeed, they [i.e., the devils] avert them from the way [of guidance] while they think that they are [rightly] guided

38. Until, when he comes to Us [at Judgement], he says [to his companion], "Oh, I wish there was between me and you the distance between the east and west - how wretched a companion."

39. And never will it benefit you that Day, when you have wronged, that you are [all] sharing in the punishment.

40. Then will you make the deaf hear, [O Muhammad], or guide the blind or he who is in clear error?

41. And whether [or not] We take you away [in death], indeed, We will take retribution upon them.

42. Or whether [or not] We show you that which We have promised them, indeed, We are Perfect in Ability.

43. So adhere to that which is revealed to you. Indeed, you are on a straight path.

44. And indeed, it is a remembrance[1339] for you and your people, and you [all] are going to be questioned.

45. And ask those We sent before you of Our messengers; have We made besides the Most Merciful deities to be worshipped?

46. And certainly did We send Moses with Our signs to Pharaoh and his establishment, and he said, "Indeed, I am the messenger of the Lord of the worlds."

47. But when he brought them Our signs, at once they laughed at them.

48. And We showed them not a sign except that it was greater than its sister, and We seized them with affliction that perhaps they might return [to faith].

49. And they said [to Moses], "O magician, invoke for us your Lord by what He has promised you. Indeed, we will be guided."

50. But when We removed from them the affliction, at once they broke their word.

51. And Pharaoh called out among his people; he said, "O my people, does not the kingdom of Egypt belong to me, and these rivers flowing beneath me; then do you not see?

52. Or am I [not] better than this one [i.e., Moses] who is insignificant and hardly makes himself clear?[1340]

53. Then why have there not been placed upon him bracelets of gold or come with him the angels in conjunction?"

54. So he bluffed his people, and they obeyed him. Indeed, they were [them-

[1339] i.e., an honour. Or "a reminder."

[1340] That was true previous to his appointment as a prophet, at which time God corrected his speech impediment.

selves] a people defiantly disobedient [of God].

55. And when they angered Us, We took retribution from them and drowned them all.

56. And We made them a precedent and an example for the later peoples.

57. And when the son of Mary was presented as an example,[1341] immediately your people laughed aloud.

58. And they said, "Are your gods better, or is he?"[1342] They did not present it [i.e., the comparison] except for [mere] argument. But, [in fact], they are a people prone to dispute.

59. He [i.e., Jesus] was not but a servant upon whom We bestowed favor, and We made him an example for the Children of Israel.

60. And if We willed, We could have made [instead] of you angels succeeding [one another][1343] on the earth.

61. And indeed, he [i.e., Jesus] will be [a sign for] knowledge of the Hour, so be not in doubt of it, and follow Me.[1344] This is a straight path.

62. And never let Satan avert you. Indeed, he is to you a clear enemy.

63. And when Jesus brought clear proofs, he said, "I have come to you with wisdom [i.e., prophethood] and to make clear to you some of that over which you differ, so fear God and obey me.

64. Indeed, God is my Lord and your Lord, so worship Him. This is a straight path."

65. But the denominations from among them differed [and separated], so woe to those who have wronged from the punishment of a painful Day.

66. Are they waiting except for the Hour to come upon them suddenly while they perceive not?

67. Close friends, that Day, will be enemies to each other, except for the righteous

68. [To whom God will say], "O My servants, no fear will there be concerning you this Day, nor will you grieve,

69. [You] who believed in Our verses and were Muslims.

70. Enter Paradise, you and your kinds,[1345] delighted."

71. Circulated among them will be plates and vessels of gold. And therein is whatever the souls desire and [what] delights the eyes, and you will abide therein eternally.

72. And that is Paradise which you are made to inherit for what you used to do.

73. For you therein is much fruit[1346] from which you will eat.

[1341] Of a creation of God which is being worshipped along with Him.
[1342] Implying that they must all be the same.
[1343] Or "succeeding [you]."
[1344] i.e., follow the guidance and instruction of God.

[1345] i.e., those like you. Another meaning may be "your spouses," i.e., the righteous among them.
[1346] Meaning everything delicious.

74. Indeed, the criminals will be in the punishment of Hell, abiding eternally.

75. It will not be allowed to subside for them, and they, therein, are in despair.

76. And We did not wrong them, but it was they who were the wrongdoers.

77. And they will call, "O Mālik,[1347] let your Lord put an end to us!" He will say, "Indeed, you will remain."

78. We had certainly brought you the truth, but most of you, to the truth, were averse.

79. Or have they devised [some] affair?[1348] But indeed, We are devising [a plan].

80. Or do they think that We hear not their secrets and their private conversations? Yes, [We do], and Our messengers [i.e., angels] are with them recording.

81. Say, [O Muhammad], "If the Most Merciful had a son, then I would be the first of [his] worshippers."[1349]

82. Exalted is the Lord of the heavens and the earth, Lord of the Throne, above what they describe.

83. So leave them to converse vainly and amuse themselves until they meet their Day which they are promised.

84. And it is He [i.e., God] who is [the only] deity in the heaven, and on the earth [the only] deity. And He is the Wise, the Knowing.

[1347] Addressing the keeper of Hell.
[1348] Conspiracy against the Prophet. The reference here is to the disbelievers of Makkah.
[1349] Only supposing it were so, which it is not.

85. And blessed is He to whom belongs the dominion of the heavens and the earth and whatever is between them and with whom is knowledge of the Hour and to whom you will be returned.

86. And those they invoke besides Him do not possess [power of] intercession; but only those who testify to the truth [can benefit], and they know.[1350]

87. And if you asked them[1351] who created them, they would surely say, "God." So how are they deluded?

88. And [God acknowledges] his saying,[1352] "O my Lord, indeed these are a people who do not believe."

89. So turn aside from them and say, "Peace."[1353] But they are going to know.

[1350] That intercession is granted exclusively by permission of God to those He wills.
[1351] Those who associate others with God.
[1352] i.e., the complaint of Prophet Muhammad about his people.
[1353] Meaning safety or security, i.e., "I will not harm you." This was before permission was granted for armed struggle.

## Sūrah 44: ad-Dukhān

### Period of Revelation

Its period of revelation also could not be determined from any authentic tradition, but the internal evidence of the subject matter shows that this Sūrah too was sent down in the same period in which Sūrah az-Zukhruf and a few other earlier Sūrahs had been revealed. However, this Sūrah was sent down somewhat later. Its historical background is this: When the disbelievers of Makkah became more and more antagonistic in their attitude and conduct, the Prophet prayed: O God, help me with a famine like the famine of Joseph. He thought that when the people would be afflicted with a calamity, they would remember God, their hearts would soften and they would accept the admonition. God granted his prayer, and the whole land was overtaken by such a terrible famine that the people were sorely distressed. At last, some of the Quraysh chiefs among whom Abdullah bin Masud has particularly mentioned the name of Abu Sufyan came to the Prophet and requested him to pray to God to deliver his people from the calamity. On this occasion God sent down this Sūrah.

### Subject Matter and Topics

The introduction to the address revealed on this occasion for the admonition and warning of the people of Makkah contained some important points, which are as follows:

1. "You, O People of Makkah, are wrong in thinking that the Qur'ān is being composed by Muhammad . This Book by itself bears the clear testimony that it is not the composition of a man but of God, Lord of the worlds."
2. "You are making a wrong estimate of the worth of this Book. You think it is a calamity that has descended on you, whereas the Hour when God, out of sheer mercy, decided to send His Messenger and His Book to you was highly blessed."
3. "You are foolishly involved in the misunderstanding that you will fight this Messenger and this Book and will win, whereas the fact is that the Messenger has been raised and the Book sent down in that particular Hour when God decides the destinies, and God's decisions are not so weak that they may be changed to a person's liking, nor are they based on ignorance and folly that there may be the likelihood of a mistake or error or weakness in them. They are rather the firm and unalterable decisions of the Ruler of the Universe, Who is All Hearing, All Knowing and All Wise. Therefore, they cannot be treated lightly.
4. "You yourselves acknowledge that God alone is the Master and Lord of the earth and heavens and of everything in the Universe and also admit that life and death are only in His power, yet you insist on making others your deities, for which the only argument you offer is that that had been the practice since the time of your forefathers, whereas if a person has the conviction that God alone is the Master, Sustainer and Giver of life and death, he can never entertain the doubt that there can be other gods also beside Him, who can be worthy of worship. If your forefathers had committed this folly, there is no reason why you also should continue committing it blindly. As a matter of fact, their Lord too was only One God, Who is your Lord, and they also should have worshipped only Him, Whom you should worship."
5. "The only demand of God's Providence and Mercifulness is not this that He should feed you, but also this that He should arrange guidance for you. For this very guidance He has sent His Messenger and His Book."

After this introduction, the question of the famine that was raging in Makkah has been discussed. As already mentioned, this famine had occurred on the Prophet's prayer, and he had prayed for it so that when the calamity befell it would break the stubbornness of the disbelievers and then they would listen to the rebuke. It looked as if this expectation was being fulfilled to some extent, for some of the most stubborn enemies of the Truth, on account of the severity of the famine, had cried out: "O Lord, avert this torment from us and we will believe." At this, on the one hand, the Prophet has been foretold: "These people will not learn any lesson from such calamities. When they have turned away from the Messenger, whose life, character, works and speech clearly show that he is God's true Messenger, how will a mere famine help remove their disbelief?" On the other, the unbelievers have been addressed, so as to say : "You lie when you say that you will believe as soon as the torment is removed from you. We shall just remove it to see how sincere you are in your promise. There is a graver disaster about to fall upon you. You need a much more crushing blow: minor misfortunes cannot set you right."

In this very connection, a reference has been made a little below to Pharaoh and his people, implying that those people also had met with precisely the same trial as the chiefs of the disbelieving Quraysh are now afflicted. To them also a similar noble and honourable Messenger had come; they also had seen those express pointers and signs which clearly showed that he had been appointed by God; they also had gone on witnessing one sign after the other but they did not give up their stubbornness, till at last they made up their mind to put an end to the Messenger's life, and they met their doom, which has since become an object lesson for the people for ever.

After this the theme of the Hereafter has been taken up, which the disbelievers of Makkah vehemently denied. They said: "We have never seen anyone rising back to life after death. Raise our forefathers back to life if you are true in your claim about the life hereafter." In response to this, two arguments for the Hereafter have been presented briefly:

1. That the denial of this creed has always proved destructive for the morals
2. That the universe is not a plaything of a thoughtless deity, but it is a wise system and no work of wisdom is ever vain or useless.

Then the disbelievers' demand to bring their forefathers back to life has been answered, thus: "This cannot be done every day to meet the demand of the individuals, but God has appointed a time when He will resurrect all mankind simultaneously and will subject them to accountability in His Court. If one has to protect oneself there, one should think about it here. For no one will be able to save himself there by his own power, nor by the power of any one else."

In connection with this Court of God, mention has been made of the fate of those who will be declared as culprits and of the rewards of those who will be declared as successful. The discourse has been concluded with this warning: "This Qur'ān has been revealed in simple language in your own tongue so that you may understand it; yet if you do not understand it and insist on seeing your evil end, you may wait; Our Prophet too is waiting. Whatever is to happen, will happen at its own appointed time."

## Sūrah 44: ad-Dukhān[1354]

In the Name of God, the Most Compassionate, the Most Merciful

1. Hā, Meem.[1355]

2. By the clear Book,

3. Indeed, We sent it down during a blessed night.[1356] Indeed, We were to warn [mankind].

4. Therein [i.e., on that night] is made distinct[1357] every precise matter -

5. [Every] matter [proceeding] from Us. Indeed, We were to send [a messenger]

6. As mercy from your Lord. Indeed, He is the Hearing, the Knowing,

7. Lord of the heavens and the earth and that between them, if you would be certain.

8. There is no deity except Him; He gives life and causes death. [He is] your Lord and the Lord of your first forefathers.

9. But they are in doubt, amusing themselves.

10. Then watch for the Day when the sky will bring a visible smoke.

11. Covering the people; this is a painful torment.

12. [They will say], "Our Lord, remove from us the torment; indeed, we are believers."

13. How will there be for them a reminder [at that time]? And there had come to them a clear Messenger.

14. Then they turned away from him and said, "[He was] taught [and is] a madman."

15. Indeed, We will remove the torment for a little. Indeed, you [disbelievers] will return [to disbelief].

16. The Day We will strike with the greatest assault, indeed, We will take retribution.

17. And We had already tried before them the people of Pharaoh, and there came to them a noble messenger [i.e., Moses],

18. [Saying], "Render to me the servants of God.[1358] Indeed, I am to you a trustworthy messenger,"

19. And [saying], "Be not haughty with God. Indeed, I have come to you with clear authority.

20. And indeed, I have sought refuge in my Lord and your Lord, lest you stone me.[1359]

21. But if you do not believe me, then leave me alone."

22. And [finally] he called to his Lord that these were a criminal people.

---

[1354] *Ad-Dukhān*: Smoke.

[1355] See footnote to 2:1.

[1356] The Night of Decree (*Qadr*). See *sūrah* 97.

[1357] Or "is separated" or "apportioned," from what is inscribed in the Preserved Slate. The angels record and descend with whatever God has decreed for the coming year.

[1358] i.e., the Children of Israel.

[1359] To death. Or "lest you assault me [with your tongues or harm me otherwise]."

23. [God said], "Then set out with My servants by night. Indeed, you are to be pursued.

24. And leave the sea in stillness.[1360] Indeed, they are an army to be drowned."

25. How much they left behind of gardens and springs

26. And crops and noble sites

27. And comfort wherein they were amused.

28. Thus. And We caused to inherit it another people.

29. And the heaven and earth wept not for them, nor were they reprieved.

30. And We certainly saved the Children of Israel from the humiliating torment -

31. From Pharaoh. Indeed, he was a haughty one among the transgressors.

32. And We certainly chose them by knowledge over [all] the worlds.

33. And We gave them of signs that in which there was a clear trial.

34. Indeed, these [disbelievers] are saying,

35. "There is not but our first death, and we will not be resurrected.

36. Then bring [back] our forefathers, if you should be truthful."

37. Are they better or the people of Tubba'[1361] and those before them? We destroyed them, [for] indeed, they were criminals.

38. And We did not create the heavens and earth and that between them in play.

39. We did not create them except in truth, but most of them do not know.

40. Indeed, the Day of Judgement is the appointed time for them all -

41. The Day when no relation[1362] will avail a relation at all, nor will they be helped -

42. Except those [believers] on whom God has mercy. Indeed, He is the Exalted in Might, the Merciful.

43. Indeed, the tree of zaqqūm

44. Is food for the sinful.

45. Like murky oil, it boils within bellies

46. Like the boiling of scalding water.

47. [It will be commanded], "Seize him and drag him into the midst of the Hellfire,

48. Then pour over his head from the torment of scalding water."

49. [It will be said], "Taste! Indeed, you are the honoured, the noble![1363]

50. Indeed, this is what you used to dispute."

51. Indeed, the righteous will be in a secure place:

[1360] After it has parted, in order that soldiers of Pharoah would follow the Children of Israel and be drowned.

[1361] The tribe of Saba'.

[1362] i.e., patron, protector or close associate.

[1363] As he had claimed upon the earth. He is taunted with these words in Hell as a reminder and additional torment.

52. Within gardens and springs,

53. Wearing [garments of] fine silk and brocade, facing each other.

54. Thus. And We will marry them to fair women with large, [beautiful] eyes.

55. They will call therein for every [kind of] fruit - safe and secure.

56. They will not taste death therein except the first death, and He will have protected them from the punishment of Hellfire

57. As bounty from your Lord. That is what is the great attainment.

58. And indeed, We have eased it [i.e., the Qur'ān] in your tongue that they might be reminded.

59. So watch, [O Muhammad]; indeed, they are watching [for your end].

## Sūrah 45: al-Jāthiyah

### Period of Revelation

The period of the revelation of this Sūrah also has not been mentioned in any authentic hadith, but its subject matter clearly shows that it was revealed consecutively after Sūrah ad-Dukhān. The close resemblance between the contents of the two Sūrahs makes them look like the twin Sūrahs.

### Subject Matter and Topics

It answers the doubts and objections of the disbelievers of Makkah about Tawhid (Oneness of God) and the Hereafter and warns them for their attitude that they had adopted against the message of the Qur'ān.

The discourse begins with the arguments for Tawhid (Oneness of God). In this connection, reference has been made to the countless Signs that are found in the world, from man's own body to the earth and heavens, and it is pointed out that everywhere around him man finds things which testify to Tawhid which he refuses to acknowledge. If man sees carefully the variety of animals, the day and night, the rainfall and the vegetation thereby, the winds and his own creation, and ponders over them intelligently, without prejudice, he will find these Signs sufficiently convincing of the truth that this universe is not Godless, nor under the control of many gods, but it has been created by One God, and He alone is its Controller and Ruler. However, the case of the person who is determined not to acknowledge and wants to remain involved in doubts and suspicions is different. He cannot be blessed with the faith and conviction from anywhere in the world.

A little below, in the beginning of the second section, it has been reiterated that the things man is exploiting in the world, and the countless forces and agencies that are serving his interests in the universe, did not come into being just accidentally, nor have they been provided by the gods and goddesses, but it is One God alone, Who has supplied and subjected these to him from Himself. If only a person uses his mind properly and rightly, his own intellect will proclaim that God alone is man's real Benefactor and He alone deserves that man should pay obeisance to Him.

After this, the disbelievers of Makkah have been taken to task and reproved for their stubbornness, arrogance, mockery and insistence on disbelief with which they were resisting the invitation of the Qur'ān; they have been warned that this Qur'ān has brought the same blessing which had been granted to the children of Israel before, by virtue of which they became distinguished above all the people of the world. Then, when they failed to recognize the true worth of this blessing and disputed their religion and lost it, this blessing now has been sent to them. This is such a code of guidance which shows the clear highway of Religion to man. The people who would turn it down by their own folly, would only prepare for their own doom, and only such people would become worthy of God's succor and mercy who would adopt obedience to it and lead a life of piety and righteousness.

In this connection, the followers of the Prophet have been instructed that they should forbear and pardon the absurd and foolish behavior towards them of the people fearless of God, for if they showed patience God Himself would deal with their opponents and would reward them for their fortitude.

Then, there is a criticism of the erroneous ideas that the disbelievers hold about the Hereafter. They said that life was only this worldly life and there was no life hereafter. Man dies in the course of time just as a watch stops functioning suddenly. The body is not survived by any soul, which might be seized and then breathed again into the human body some time in the future. In this regard, they challenged the Prophet, saying: "If you lay a claim to this, then raise our dead forefathers back to life." In answer to this, God has given the following arguments:

1. "You do not say this on the basis of any knowledge but are uttering this grave thing on the basis of conjecture. Do you really have the knowledge that there is no other life after death, and the souls are not seized but are annihilated?"
2. "Your claim rests mainly on this: that you have not seen any dead person rising back to life and returning to the world. Is this basis strong enough for a person to make a claim that the dead people will never rise to life? When you do not experience and observe a thing, does it mean that you have the knowledge that it does not exist at all?
3. It is utterly against reason and justice that the good and the bad, the obedient and the disobedient, the oppressor and the oppressed, should be made equal ultimately. Neither a good act should bear a good result nor an evil act an evil result; neither the grievances of the oppressed be redressed nor the oppressor be punished, but everyone should meet with the same fate ultimately. Whoever has formed this view about the universe of God, has formed a patently wrong view. The unjust and wicked people adopt this view because they do not want to face the evil results of their deeds, but this world of God is not a lawless kingdom; it is rather a system based on the Truth, in which there can be no question of the injustice of regarding the good and the bad as equal.
4. That the creed of the denial of the Hereafter is highly destructive of morals. This is adopted only by such people as are the slaves of their lusts, and for the reason that they should have full freedom to serve their lusts. Then, when they have adopted this creed, it goes on making them more and more perverse till at last their moral sense becomes dead and all avenues of guidance are closed against them.

After giving these arguments God says most emphatically: "Just as you did not become living of your own accord, but became living by Our power, so you do not die of your own accord, but die when We send death on you. And a time is certainly coming when you will all be gathered together. If you do not believe in this because of your ignorance and folly today, you may not; when the time arrives, you will see for yourself that you are present before your God and your whole book of conduct is ready accurately, which bears evidence against each of your misdeeds. Then you will come to know how dearly has your denial of the Hereafter and your mockery of it cost you."

## Sūrah 45: al-Jāthiyah[1364]

In the Name of God, the Most Compassionate, the Most Merciful

1. Hā, Meem.[1365]

2. The revelation of the Book is from God, the Exalted in Might, the Wise.

3. Indeed, within the heavens and earth are signs for the believers.

4. And in the creation of yourselves and what He disperses of moving creatures are signs for people who are certain [in faith].

5. And [in] the alternation of night and day and [in] what God sends down from the sky of provision [i.e., rain] and gives life thereby to the earth after its lifelessness and [in His] directing of the winds are signs for a people who reason.

6. These are the verses of God which We recite to you in truth. Then in what statement after God and His verses will they believe?

7. Woe to every sinful liar

8. Who hears the verses of God recited to him, then persists arrogantly as if he had not heard them. So give him tidings of a painful punishment.

9. And when he knows anything of Our verses, he takes them in ridicule. Those will have a humiliating punishment.

10. Before them[1366] is Hell, and what they had earned will not avail them at all nor what they had taken besides God as allies. And they will have a great punishment.

11. This [Qur'ān] is guidance. And those who have disbelieved in the verses of their Lord will have a painful punishment of foul nature.

12. It is God who subjected to you the sea so that ships may sail upon it by His command and that you may seek of His bounty; and perhaps you will be grateful.

13. And He has subjected to you whatever is in the heavens and whatever is on the earth - all from Him. Indeed in that are signs for a people who give thought.

14. Say, [O Muhammad], to those who have believed that they [should] forgive those who expect not the days of God [i.e., of His retribution] so that He may recompense a people[1367] for what they used to earn.

15. Whoever does a good deed - it is for himself; and whoever does evil - it is against it [i.e., the self or soul]. Then to your Lord you will be returned.

16. And We did certainly give the Children of Israel the Scripture and judgement[1368] and prophethood, and We provided them with good things and preferred them over the worlds.

[1364] *Al-Jāthiyah*: Kneeling (in dread of the Judgement).
[1365] See footnote to 2:1.

[1366] See footnote to 14:16.
[1367] In the Hereafter, where those who forgive will be rewarded and those who earned evil will be punished. This was at the outset of *da'wah* (invitation to God) before permission for *jihād*.
[1368] Understanding of the law.

17. And We gave them clear proofs of the matter [of religion]. And they did not differ except after knowledge had come to them - out of jealous animosity between themselves. Indeed, your Lord will judge between them on the Day of Resurrection concerning that over which they used to differ.

18. Then We put you, [O Muhammad], on an ordained way concerning the matter [of religion]; so follow it and do not follow the inclinations of those who do not know.

19. Indeed, they will never avail you against God at all. And indeed, the wrongdoers are allies of one another; but God is the protector of the righteous.

20. This [Qur'ān] is enlightenment for mankind and guidance and mercy for a people who are certain [in faith].

21. Or do those who commit evils think We will make them like those who have believed and done righteous deeds - [make them] equal in their life and their death?[1369] Evil is that which they judge [i.e., assume].

22. And God created the heavens and earth in truth and so that every soul may be recompensed for what it has earned, and they will not be wronged.

23. Have you seen he who has taken as his god his [own] desire, and God has sent him astray due to knowledge[1370] and has set a seal upon his hearing and his heart and put over his vision a veil? So who will guide him after God? Then will you not be reminded?

24. And they say, "There is not but our worldly life; we die and live,[1371] and nothing destroys us except time." And they have of that no knowledge; they are only assuming.

25. And when Our verses are recited to them as clear evidences, their argument is only that they say, "Bring [back] our forefathers, if you should be truthful."

26. Say, "God causes you to live, then causes you to die; then He will assemble you for the Day of Resurrection, about which there is no doubt, but most of the people do not know."

27. And to God belongs the dominion of the heavens and the earth. And the Day the Hour appears - that Day the falsifiers will lose.

28. And you will see every nation kneeling [from fear]. Every nation will be called to its record [and told], "Today you will be recompensed for what you used to do.

29. This, Our record, speaks about you in truth. Indeed, We were having transcribed[1372] whatever you used to do."

30. So as for those who believed and did righteous deeds, their Lord will admit them into His mercy. That is what is the clear attainment.

31. But as for those who disbelieved, [it will be said], "Were not Our verses re-

1369 Another meaning is "...[the evildoers being] equal in their life and their death," i.e., unresponsive to guidance.

1370 This can refer to God's knowledge of that person and of his preference for his own inclinations or to that person's knowledge of the truth while he refuses it.

1371 i.e., some people die and others live, replacing them.

1372 By recording angels.

cited to you, but you were arrogant and became a people of criminals?

32. And when it was said, 'Indeed, the promise of God is truth and the Hour [is coming] - no doubt about it,' you said, 'We know not what is the Hour. We assume only assumption, and we are not convinced.' "

33. And the evil consequences of what they did will appear to them, and they will be enveloped by what they used to ridicule.

34. And it will be said, "Today We will forget you as you forgot the meeting of this Day of yours, and your refuge is the Fire, and for you there are no helpers.

35. That is because you took the verses of God in ridicule, and worldly life deluded you." So that Day they will not be removed from it, nor will they be asked to appease [God].

36. Then, to God belongs [all] praise - Lord of the heavens and Lord of the earth, Lord of the worlds.

37. And to Him belongs [all] grandeur within the heavens and the earth, and He is the Exalted in Might, the Wise.

## Sūrah 46: al-Ahqāf

### Period of Revelation

It is determined by an historical event that has been mentioned in v. 29-32. This incident of the visit of the Jinn and their going back after listening to the Qur'ān had occurred, according to agreed hadith and biographical literature, at the time when the Prophet had halted at Makkah during his return journey from Tā'if to Makkah. And according to all authentic hadith he had gone to Tā'if three years before the Hijrah; therefore it is determined that this Sūrah was sent down towards the end of the 10th year or in the early part of the 11th year of the Prophethood.

### Historical Background

The 10th year of the Prophethood was a year of extreme persecution and distress in the Prophet's life. The Quraysh and the other tribes had continued their boycott of the Banu Hashim and the Muslims for three years and the Prophet, the people of his family and Companions lay besieged in Shi'b Abi Talib. The Quraysh had blocked up this locality from every side so that no supplies of any kind could reach the besieged people. Only during the Hajj season they were allowed to come out and buy some articles of necessity. But even at that time whenever Abu Lahab noticed any of them approaching the market place or a trading caravan he would call out to the merchants exhorting them to announce forbidding rates of their articles for them, and would pledge that he himself would buy those articles so that they did not suffer any loss. This boycott which continued uninterrupted for three years had broken the back of the Muslims and the Banu Hashim; so much so that at times they were even forced to eat grass and the leaves of trees.

At last, when the siege was lifted this year, Abu Talib, the Prophet's uncle, who had been shielding him for ten long years, died, and hardly a month later his wife, Khadijah, who had been a source of peace and consolation for him ever since the beginning of the call, also passed away. Because of these tragic incidents, which closely followed each other, the Prophet used to refer to this year as the year of sorrow and grief.

After the death of Khadijah and Abu Talib the disbelievers of Makkah became even bolder against the Prophet. They started treating him even more harshly. So much so that it became difficult for him to step out of his house. Of these days Ibn Hisham has related the incident that a Quraysh scoundrel one day threw dust at him openly in the street.

At last, the Prophet left for Tā'if with the intention that he should invite the Bani Thaqif to Islām, for even if they did not accept Islām, they might at least be persuaded to allow him to work for his mission peacefully. He did not have the facility of any conveyance at that time, and traveled all the way to Tā'if on foot. According to some hadith, he had gone there alone, but according to others, he was accompanied by Zayd bin Harithah. He stayed at Tā'if for a few days, and approached each of the chiefs and nobles of the Bani Thaqif and talked to him about his mission. But not only they refused to listen to him, but plainly gave him the notice that he should leave their city, for they feared that his preaching might "spoil" their younger generation. Thus, he was compelled to leave Tā'if. When he was leaving the city, the chiefs of Thaqif set their slaves and scoundrels behind him, who went on crying at him, abusing him and pelting him with stones for a long way from either side of the road till he became broken down with wounds and his shoes were filled with blood. Wearied and exhausted he took shelter in the shade of the wall of a garden outside Tā'if, and prayed:

*"O God, to Thee I complain of my weakness, little resource, and lowliness before men. O Most Merciful, Thou art the Lord of the weak, and Thou art my Lord. To whom wilt Thou confide me? To one afar who will misuse me? Or to an enemy to whom Thou hast given power over me? If Thou art not angry with me I care not. Thy favor is more wide for me. I take refuge in the light of Thy countenance by which the darkness is illumined, and the things of this world and the next are rightly ordered, lest Thy anger descend upon me or Thy wrath light upon me. It is for Thee to be satisfied until Thou art well pleased. There is no power and no might save in Thee."*

Grieved and heartbroken when he returned and reached near Qarn al-Manazil, he felt as though the sky was overcast by clouds. He looked up and saw Gabriel in front of him, who called out: "*God has heard the way your people have responded. He has, therefore, sent this angel in charge of the mountains. You may command him as you please.*" Then the angel of the mountains greeted him and submitted: "*If you like I would overturn the mountains from either side upon these people.*" The Prophet replied: "*No, but I expect that God will create from their seed those who will worship none but God, the One.*" (Bukhari)

After this he went to stay for a few days at Makkah, perplexed as to how he would face the people of Makkah, who, he thought, would be still further emboldened against him after hearing what had happened at Tā'if. It was here that one night when he was reciting the Qur'ān in the Prayer, a group of the Jinn happened to pass by and listened to the Qur'ān, believed in it, and returned to their people to preach Islām. Thus, God gave His Prophet the good news that if the men were running away from his invitation, there were many of the Jinn, who had become its believers, and they were spreading his message among their own kind.

**Subject Matter and Topics**

Such were the conditions when this Sūrah was sent down. Anyone who keeps this background in view, on the one hand, and studies this Sūrah, on the other, will have no doubt left in his mind that this is not at all the composition of Muhammad , but "a Revelation from the All Mighty, All Wise God." For nowhere in this Sūrah, from the beginning to the end, does one find even a tinge of the human feelings and reactions, which are naturally produced in a man who is passing through such hard conditions. Had it been the word of Muhammad whom the occurrence of personal griefs one after the other and the countless and the recent bitter experience at Tā'if had caused extreme anguish and distress, it would have reflected in some degree the state of the mind of the man who was the subject of these afflictions and griefs. Consider the prayer that we have cited above: it contains his own language, its every word is saturated with the feelings that he had at the time. But this Sūrah which was sent down precisely in the same period and was recited even by him under the same conditions, is absolutely free from every sign or trace of the time.

The subject matter of the Sūrah is to warn the disbelievers of the errors in which they were involved, and also persisted arrogantly, and were condemning the man who was trying to redeem them. They regarded the world as a useless and purposeless place where they were not answerable to anyone. They thought that invitation to Tawhid (Oneness of God) was false and stuck to the belief that their own deities were actually the associates of God. They were not inclined to believe that the Qur'ān was the Word of the Lord of the worlds. They had a strange erroneous concept of apostleship on the basis of which they were proposing strange criteria of judging the Prophet's claim to it. In their estimation one great proof of Islām's not being based on the truth was that their elders and important chiefs of the tribes and so called leaders of their nation were not accepting it and only a few young men, and some poor folks and some slaves had affirmed faith in it. They thought that Resurrection and life after death and the rewards and punishments of the Hereafter were fabrications whose occurrence was absolutely out of the question.

In this Sūrah each of these misconceptions has been refuted in a brief but rational way, and the disbelievers have been warned that if they would reject the invitation of the Qur'ān and the Prophethood of the Prophet Muhammad by prejudice and stubbornness instead of trying to understand its truth rationally, they would only be preparing for their own doom.

## Sūrah 46: al-Ahqāf[1373]

In the Name of God, the Most Compassionate, the Most Merciful

1. Hā, Meem.[1374]

2. The revelation of the Book is from God, the Exalted in Might, the Wise.

3. We did not create the heavens and earth and what is between them except in truth and [for] a specified term. But those who disbelieve, from that of which they are warned, are turning away.

4. Say, [O Muhammad], "Have you considered that which you invoke besides God? Show me what they have created of the earth; or did they have partnership in [creation of] the heavens? Bring me a scripture [revealed] before this or a [remaining] trace of knowledge, if you should be truthful."

5. And who is more astray than he who invokes besides God those who will not respond to him until the Day of Resurrection [i.e., never], and they, of their invocation, are unaware.

6. And when the people are gathered [that Day], they [who were invoked] will be enemies to them, and they will be deniers of their worship.

7. And when Our verses are recited to them as clear evidences, those who disbelieve say of the truth when it has come to them, "This is obvious magic."

8. Or do they say, "He has invented it"? Say, "If I have invented it, you will not possess for me [the power of protection] from God at all. He is most knowing of that in which you are involved.[1375] Sufficient is He as Witness between me and you, and He is the Forgiving the Merciful."

9. Say, "I am not something original among the messengers,[1376] nor do I know what will be done with me or with you. I only follow that which is revealed to me, and I am not but a clear warner."

10. Say, "Have you considered: if it [i.e., the Qur'ān] was from God, and you disbelieved in it while a witness from the Children of Israel has testified to something similar[1377] and believed while you were arrogant...?"[1378] Indeed, God does not guide the wrongdoing people.

11. And those who disbelieve say of those who believe, "If it had [truly] been good, they would not have preceded us to it." And when they are not guided by it, they will say, "This is an ancient falsehood."

12. And before it was the scripture of Moses to lead and as a mercy. And this is a confirming Book in an Arabic tongue to warn those who have wronged and as good tidings to the doers of good.

---

[1373] *Al-Ahqāf*: The Curving Sand Tracts, a characteristic of the region once inhabited by the tribe of 'Aad.

[1374] See footnote to 2:1.

[1375] Of false implications and suggestions.

[1376] i.e., I am neither the first messenger to be sent, nor do I bring something different from the other messengers.

[1377] Based upon information from the Torah.

[1378] The conclusion is estimated to be "...would you not then be the most unjust of people?" or "...in what condition would you then be?"

13. Indeed, those who have said, "Our Lord is God," and then remained on a right course - there will be no fear concerning them, nor will they grieve.

14. Those are the companions of Paradise, abiding eternally therein as reward for what they used to do.

15. And We have enjoined upon man, to his parents, good treatment. His mother carried him with hardship and gave birth to him with hardship, and his gestation and weaning [period] is thirty months. [He grows] until, when he reaches maturity and reaches [the age of] forty years, he says, "My Lord, enable me[1379] to be grateful for Your favor which You have bestowed upon me and upon my parents and to work righteousness of which You will approve and make righteous for me my offspring. Indeed, I have repented to You, and indeed, I am of the Muslims."

16. Those are the ones from whom We will accept the best of what they did and overlook their misdeeds, [their being] among the companions of Paradise. [That is] the promise of truth which they had been promised.

17. But one who says to his parents, "Uff[1380] to you; do you promise me that I will be brought forth [from the earth] when generations before me have already passed on [into oblivion]?" while they call to God for help [and to their son], "Woe to you! Believe! Indeed, the promise of God is truth." But he says, "This is not but legends of the former peoples" -

18. Those are the ones upon whom the word [i.e., decree] has come into effect, [who will be] among nations which had passed on before them of jinn and men. Indeed, they [all] were losers.

19. And for all there are degrees [of reward and punishment] for what they have done, and [it is] so that He may fully compensate them for their deeds, and they will not be wronged.

20. And the Day those who disbelieved are exposed to the Fire [it will be said], "You exhausted your pleasures during your worldly life and enjoyed them, so this Day you will be awarded the punishment of [extreme] humiliation because you were arrogant upon the earth without right and because you were defiantly disobedient."

21. And mention, [O Muhammad], the brother of 'Aad,[1381] when he warned his people in [the region of] al-Ahqāf - and warners had already passed on before him and after him - [saying], "Do not worship except God. Indeed, I fear for you the punishment of a terrible day."[1382]

22. They said, "Have you come to delude us away from our gods? Then bring us what you promise us, if you should be of the truthful."

23. He said, "Knowledge [of its time] is only with God, and I convey to you that with which I was sent; but I see you [to be] a people behaving ignorantly."

[1379] Literally, "gather within me the utmost strength and ability."
[1380] An expression of distaste and irritation.

[1381] i.e., the prophet Hūd.
[1382] Upon the earth. It could also refer to "a tremendous Day," i.e., that of resurrection.

24. And when they saw it as a cloud approaching their valleys, they said, "This is a cloud bringing us rain!" Rather, it is that for which you were impatient:[1383] a wind, within it a painful punishment,

25. Destroying everything by command of its Lord. And they became so that nothing was seen [of them] except their dwellings. Thus do We recompense the criminal people.

26. And We had certainly established them in such as We have not established you, and We made for them hearing and vision and hearts [i.e., intellect]. But their hearing and vision and hearts availed them not from anything [of the punishment] when they were [continually] rejecting the signs of God; and they were enveloped by what they used to ridicule.

27. And We have already destroyed what surrounds you of [those] cities, and We have diversified the signs [or verses] that perhaps they might return [from disbelief].

28. Then why did those they took besides God as deities by which to approach [Him][1384] not aid them? But they had strayed [i.e., departed] from them. And that was their falsehood and what they were inventing.

29. And [mention, O Muhammad], when We directed to you a few of the jinn, listening to the Qur'ān. And when they attended it, they said, "Listen quietly." And when it was concluded, they went back to their people as warners.

30. They said, "O our people, indeed we have heard a [recited] Book revealed after Moses confirming what was before it which guides to the truth and to a straight path.

31. O our people, respond to the Caller [i.e., Messenger] of God[1385] and believe in him; He [i.e., God] will forgive for you your sins and protect you from a painful punishment.

32. But he who does not respond to the Caller of God will not cause failure [to Him] upon earth, and he will not have besides Him any protectors. Those are in manifest error."

33. Do they not see that God, who created the heavens and earth and did not fail in their creation, is able to give life to the dead? Yes. Indeed, He is over all things competent.

34. And the Day those who disbelieved are exposed to the Fire [it will be said], "Is this not the truth?" They will say, "Yes, by our Lord." He will say, "Then taste the punishment because you used to disbelieve."[1386]

35. So be patient, [O Muhammad], as were those of determination among the messengers and do not be impatient for them.[1387] It will be - on the Day they see that which they are promised - as though they had not remained [in the world] except an hour of a day. [This is] notification. And will [any] be destroyed except the defiantly disobedient people?

[1383] When you challenged your prophet. See verse 22 of this *sūrah*.
[1384] According to their claim.
[1385] Prophet Muhammad.
[1386] Or "for what you used to deny."
[1387] i.e., for God's punishment of the disbelievers.

# Sūrah 47: Muhammad

## Period of Revelation

The contents of this Sūrah testify that it was sent down after the Hijrah at Madinah at the time when the fighting had been enjoined, though active fighting had not yet been undertaken.

## Historical Background

The conditions at the time when this Sūrah was sent down were such that the Muslims were being made the target of persecution and tyranny in Makkah in particular and in Arabia in general, and life had become miserable for them. Although the Muslims had emigrated to the haven of Madinah from every side, the disbelieving Quraysh were not prepared to leave them alone and let them live in peace even there. Thus, the small settlement of Madinah was hemmed in by the enemy, who was bent upon exterminating it completely. The only alternative left with the Muslims were that either they should surrender to the forces of ignorance, giving up their mission of preaching the true Faith, or even following it in their private lives, or should rise to wage a war at the cost of their lives to settle finally and for ever whether Islām would stay in Arabia or the creed of ignorance. On this occasion God showed the Muslims the same way of resolution and will, which is the only way for the true believers. He first permitted them to fight in Sūrah al-Hajj: 39 and then enjoined fighting in Sūrah al-Baqarah: 190. But at that time everyone knew fully well what it meant to wage a war in those conditions. There were only a handful of Muslims in Madinah, who could not muster even a thousand soldiers; yet they were being urged to take up the sword and clash against the pagan forces of the whole of Arabia. Then the kind of the weapons needed to equip its soldiers for war could hardly be afforded by the town in which hundreds of emigrants were still homeless and unsettled even by resort to starving its members at a time when it had been boycotted economically by the Arabs on all sides.

## Theme and Subject Matter

Such were the conditions when this Sūrah was revealed. Its theme is to prepare the believers for war and to give them preliminary instructions in this regard. That is why it has also been entitled al-Qital. It deals with the following topics:

At the outset it is said that of the two groups confronting each other at this time, one has refused to accept the Truth and has become an obstruction for others on the way of God, while the other group has accepted the Truth which had been sent down by God to His servant, Muhammad. Now, God's final decision is that He has rendered fruitless and vain all the works of the former group and set right the condition and affairs of the latter group.

After this, the Muslims have been given the initial war instructions and they have been reassured of God's help and guidance: they have been given hope for the best rewards on offering sacrifices in the cause of God and they have been assured that their struggle in the cause of the Truth will not go to waste, but they will be abundantly rewarded both in this world and in the Hereafter.

Furthermore, about the disbelievers it has been said that they are deprived of God's support and guidance: none of their designs will succeed in their conflict with the believers, and they will meet a most evil fate both in this world and in the Hereafter. They thought they had achieved a great success by driving the Prophet of God out of Makkah, but in fact by this they had hastened their own doom.

After this, the discourse turns to the hypocrites, who were posing to be sincere Muslims before the command to fight was sent down, but were confounded when this command actually came down, and began to conspire with the disbelievers in order to save themselves from the hazards of war. They have been plainly warned to the effect that no act and deed is acceptable to God of those who adopt hypocrisy with regard to

Him and His Prophet. There, the basic issue against which all those who profess the Faith are being tried is whether one is on the side of the Truth or Falsehood, whether one's sympathies are with Islām and the Muslims or with disbelief and the disbelievers, whether one keeps one's own self and interests dearer or the Truth which one professes to believe in and follow. One who fails in this test is not at all a believer; his Prayer and his Fasting and his discharging of the Zakāh deserve no reward from God.

Then the Muslims have been exhorted not to lose heart for being small in numbers and ill equipped as against the great strength of the disbelievers: they should not show weakness by offering peace to them, which might still further embolden them against Islām and the Muslims, but they should come out with trust in God and clash with the mighty forces of disbelief. God is with the Muslims: they alone shall triumph; and the might of disbelief will be humbled and vanquished.

In conclusion, the Muslims have been invited to spend their wealth in the cause of God. Although at that time they were economically very weak, the problem that they confronted was the very survival of Islām and the Muslims. The importance and delicacy of the problem demanded that the Muslims should not only risk their lives for safeguarding themselves and their Faith from the dominance of disbelief and for exalting God's Religion but should also expend their economic resources as far as possible in the preparations for war. Therefore, they were clearly warned to the effect: Anyone who adopted a niggardly attitude at the time, would not, in fact, harm God at all, but would result in his own destruction, for God does not stand in need of help from men. If one group of men shirked offering sacrifices in the cause of His Religion, God would remove them and bring another group in its place.

## Sūrah 47: Muhammad[1388]

In the Name of God, the Most Compassionate, the Most Merciful

1. Those who disbelieve and avert [people] from the way of God - He will waste their deeds.[1389]

2. And those who believe and do righteous deeds and believe in what has been sent down upon Muhammad - and it is the truth from their Lord - He will remove from them their misdeeds and amend their condition.

3. That is because those who disbelieve follow falsehood, and those who believe follow the truth from their Lord. Thus does God present to the people their comparisons.[1390]

4. So when you meet those who disbelieve [in battle], strike [their] necks until, when you have inflicted slaughter upon them, then secure their bonds,[1391] and either [confer] favor[1392] afterwards or ransom [them] until the war lays down its burdens.[1393] That [is the command]. And if God had willed, He could have taken vengeance upon them [Himself], but [He ordered armed struggle] to test some of you by means of others. And those who are killed in the cause of God - never will He waste their deeds.

5. He will guide them and amend their condition

6. And admit them to Paradise, which He has made known to them.

7. O you who have believed, if you support God, He will support you and plant firmly your feet.

8. But those who disbelieve - for them is misery, and He will waste their deeds.

9. That is because they disliked what God revealed, so He rendered worthless their deeds.

10. Have they not traveled through the land and seen how was the end of those before them? God destroyed [everything] over them,[1394] and for the disbelievers is something comparable.

11. That is because God is the protector of those who have believed and because the disbelievers have no protector.

12. Indeed, God will admit those who have believed and done righteous deeds to gardens beneath which rivers flow, but those who disbelieve enjoy themselves and eat as grazing livestock eat, and the Fire will be a residence for them.

13. And how many a city was stronger than your city [i.e., Makkah] which drove you out? We destroyed them; and there was no helper for them.

14. So is he who is on clear evidence from his Lord like him to whom the evil of his work has been made attractive and they follow their [own] desires?

---

1388 *Muhammad*: (The Prophet) Muhammad.
1389 i.e., cause them to be lost or make them worthless, earning no reward.
1390 So that they may know the results of their choice.
1391 i.e., take those remaining as captives.
1392 i.e., release them without ransom.
1393 i.e., its armour, machinery, etc., meaning "until the war is over."

1394 i.e., destroyed them and all they owned.

15. Is the description of Paradise, which the righteous are promised, wherein are rivers of water unaltered,[1395] rivers of milk the taste of which never changes, rivers of wine delicious to those who drink, and rivers of purified honey, in which they will have from all [kinds of] fruits and forgiveness from their Lord, like [that of] those who abide eternally in the Fire and are given to drink scalding water that will sever their intestines?

16. And among them, [O Muhammad], are those who listen to you, until when they depart from you, they say to those who were given knowledge,[1396] "What has he said just now?" Those are the ones of whom God has sealed over their hearts and who have followed their [own] desires.

17. And those who are guided - He increases them in guidance and gives them their righteousness.[1397]

18. Then do they await except that the Hour should come upon them unexpectedly? But already there have come [some of] its indications. Then how [i.e., what good] to them, when it has come, will be their remembrance?

19. So know, [O Muhammad], that there is no deity except God and ask forgiveness for your sin[1398] and for the believing men and believing women. And God knows of your movement and your resting place.

20. Those who believe say, "Why has a sūrah[1399] not been sent down?" But when a precise sūrah is revealed and fighting is mentioned therein, you see those in whose hearts is disease [i.e., hypocrisy] looking at you with a look of one overcome by death. And more appropriate for them[1400] [would have been]

21. Obedience and good words. And when the matter [of fighting] was determined, if they had been true to God, it would have been better for them.

22. So would you perhaps, if you turned away,[1401] cause corruption on earth and sever your [ties of] relationship?

23. Those [who do so] are the ones that God has cursed, so He deafened them and blinded their vision.

24. Then do they not reflect upon the Qur'ān, or are there locks upon [their] hearts?

25. Indeed, those who reverted back [to disbelief] after guidance had become clear to them - Satan enticed them and prolonged hope for them.

26. That is because they said to those who disliked what God sent down,[1402] "We will obey you in part of the matter." And God knows what they conceal.

[1395] In taste or smell, neither stagnant nor polluted.

[1396] From among the Prophet's companions.

[1397] *Tāqwa*, meaning piety, consciousness and fear of God, and care to avoid His displeasure.

[1398] See footnote to 40:55.

[1399] i.e., one in which permission is given the believers to fight their enemies.

[1400] The words "*awlā lahum*" can also be interpreted as "woe to them!" In that case, the following verse would begin, "[Better for them would have been] obedience and good words."

[1401] From Islām or from *jihād* (struggling in the cause of God).

[1402] i.e., the Jews of Madinah.

27. Then how [will it be] when the angels take them in death, striking their faces and their backs?

28. That is because they followed what angered God and disliked [what earns] His pleasure, so He rendered worthless their deeds.

29. Or do those in whose hearts is disease think that God would never expose their [feelings of] hatred?

30. And if We willed, We could show them to you, and you would know them by their mark; but you will surely know them by the tone of [their] speech. And God knows your deeds.

31. And We will surely test you until We make evident those who strive among you [for the cause of God] and the patient, and We will test your affairs.

32. Indeed, those who disbelieved and averted [people] from the path of God and opposed the Messenger after guidance had become clear to them - never will they harm God at all, and He will render worthless their deeds.

33. O you who have believed, obey God and obey the Messenger and do not invalidate your deeds.

34. Indeed, those who disbelieved and averted [people] from the path of God and then died while they were disbelievers - never will God forgive them.

35. So do not weaken and call for peace while you are superior; and God is with you and will never deprive you of [the reward of] your deeds.

36. [This] worldly life is only amusement and diversion. And if you believe and fear God, He will give you your rewards and not ask you for your properties.

37. If He should ask you for them and press you, you would withhold, and He would expose your hatred [i.e., unwillingness].

38. Here you are - those invited to spend in the cause of God - but among you are those who withhold [out of greed]. And whoever withholds only withholds [benefit] from himself; and God is the Free of need, while you are the needy. And if you turn away [i.e., refuse], He will replace you with another people; then they will not be the likes of you.

## Sūrah 48: al-Fath

### Period of Revelation

Hadith concur that it was sent down in Dhul Qa'dah, 6 A.H., at a time when the Prophet was on his return journey to Madinah after concluding the Truce of Hudaibiyah with the disbelievers of Makkah.

### Historical Background

The events in connection with which this Sūrah was sent down began life like this: One day the Prophet saw in a dream that he had gone to Makkah with his Companions and had performed the Umrah (smaller pilgrimage) there. Obviously, the Prophet's dream could not be a mere dream and fiction for it is a kind of Divine inspiration as God Himself has confirmed in verse 27 below and said that He Himself had shown that dream to His Messenger. Therefore, it was not merely a dream but a Divine inspiration which the Prophet had to obey and follow.

Apparently, there was no possible way of acting on this inspiration. The disbelieving Quraysh had debarred the Muslims from proceeding to the Ka'bāh for the past six years and no Muslim had been allowed during that period to approach the Ka'bāh for the purpose of performing Hajj and Umrah. Therefore, it could not be expected that they would allow the Prophet to enter Makkah along with a party of his Companions. If they had proceeded to Makkah in the pilgrim garments with the intention of performing umrah, along with their arms, this would have provoked the enemy to war, and if they had proceeded unarmed, this would have meant endangering his own as well as his Companions' lives. Under conditions such as these nobody could see and suggest how the Divine inspiration could be acted upon.

But the Prophet's position was different. It demanded that he should carry out whatever Command his Lord gave fearlessly and without any apprehension and doubt. Therefore, the Prophet informed his Companions of his dream and began to make preparations for the journey. Among the tribes living in the suburbs also he had the public announcement made that he was proceeding for umrah and the people could join him. Those who could only see the apparent conditions thought that he and his Companions were going into the very jaws of death and none of them therefore was inclined to accompany him in the expedition. But those who had true faith in God and His Messenger were least bothered about the consequences. For them this information was enough that it was a Divine inspiration and God's Prophet had made up his mind to carry it into effect. After this nothing could hinder them from accompanying the Messenger of God. Thus, 1,400 of the Companions became ready to follow him on this highly dangerous journey.

This blessed caravan set off from Madinah in the beginning of Dhul Qa'dah, 6 A.H. At Dhul Hulaifah they entered the pilgrims robe with the intention of Umrah, took 70 camels with collars round their necks indicating that they were sacrificial animals; kept only a sword each in sheaths, which the pilgrims to the Ka'bāh were allowed to carry according to the recognized custom of Arabia, but no other weapon. Thus, the caravan set out for the Ka'bāh, the House of God, at Makkah, chanting the prescribed slogan of '*Labbaik, Allahuma labbaik.*' (I respond to you O God I respond to you)

The nature of the relations between Makkah and Madinah in those days was known too well to every Arab. Just the previous year, in Shawwal 5 A.H., the Quraysh mustering the united strength of the Arab tribes had invaded Madinah and the well known Battle of the Trench had taken place. Therefore, when the Prophet along with such a large caravan set off for the home of his blood-thirsty enemy, the whole of Arabia looked up with amazement, and the people also noticed that the caravan was not going with the intention to fight but was proceeding to the House of God in a forbidden month in the pilgrims garb carrying sacrificial animals and was absolutely unarmed.

The Quraysh were confounded at this bold step taken by the Prophet. Dhul Qa'dah was one of those forbidden months which had been held as sacred for pilgrimage in Arabia for centuries. Nobody had a right to interfere with a caravan which might be coming for Hajj or Umrah in the pilgrims garb in this month; so much so that even an enemy tribe could not hinder it from passing through its territory according to the recognized law of the land. The Quraysh therefore were caught in a dilemma, for if they attacked this caravan from Madinah and stopped it from entering Makkah, this would arouse a clamor of protest in the whole country, and all the Arab tribes would have the misgiving that the Quraysh had monopolized the Ka'bāh as exclusively their own, and every tribe would be involved in the mistrust that now it depended on the will of the Quraysh to allow or not to allow anyone to perform Hajj or Umrah in the future and that they would stop any tribe with which they were angry from visiting the Ka'bāh just as they had stopped the Madinese pilgrims. This they thought would be a grave mistake, which would cause the entire Arabia to revolt against them. But, on the other hand, if they allowed Muhammad and his large caravan to enter their city safely, they would lose their image of power in Arabia and the people would say that they were afraid of Muhammad. At last, after a great deal of confusion, perplexity and hesitation they were overcome by their false sense of honour and for the sake of their prestige they took the decision that they would at no cost allow the caravan to enter the city of Makkah.

The Prophet had despatched a man of the Bani Ka'b as a secret agent so that he may keep him fully informed of the intentions and movements of the Quraysh. When the Prophet reached Usfan, he brought the news that the Quraysh had reached Dhi Tuwa with full preparations and they had sent Khalid bin Walid with two hundred cavalry men in advance towards Kura'al-Ghamim to intercept him. The Quraysh wanted somehow to provoke the Prophet's Companions into fighting so that they may tell the Arabs that those people had actually come to fight and had put on the pilgrims garments for Umrah only to deceive others.

Immediately on receipt of this information the Prophet changed his route and following a very rugged, rocky track reached Hudaibiyah, which was situated right on the boundary of the sacred Makkan territory. Here, he was visited by Budail bin Warqa the chief of the Bani Khuza'ah, along with some men of his tribe. They asked what he had come for. The Prophet replied that he and his Companions had come only for pilgrimage to the House of God and for going round it in worship and not for war. The men of Khuza'ah went and told this to the Quraysh chiefs and counseled them not to interfere with the pilgrims. But the Quraysh were obstinate. They sent Hulays bin Alqamah, the chief of the Ahabish, to the Prophet to persuade him to go back. Their object was that when Muhammad would not listen to Hulays, he would come back disappointed and then the entire power of the Ahabish would be on their side. But when Hulays went and saw that the whole caravan had put on the pilgrims garments, had brought sacrificial camels with festive collars round their necks, and had come for doing reverence to the House of God and not to fight, he returned to Makkah without having any dialogue with the Prophet and told the Quraysh chiefs plainly that those people had no other object but to pay a visit to the Ka'bāh; if they debarred them from it, the Ahabish would not join them in that, because they had not become their allies to support them even if they violated the sacred customs and traditions.

Then the Quraysh sent Urwah bin Mas'ud Thaqafi; he had lengthy negotiations with the Prophet in an effort to persuade him to give up his intention to enter Makkah. But the Prophet gave him also the same reply that he had given to the chief of the Khuza'ah, that they had not come to fight but to do honour to the House of God and carry out a religious duty. Urwah went back and said to the Quraysh: *"I have been to the courts of the Caesar and Khosroes, and the Negus also, but by God, never have I seen any people so devoted to a king as are the Companions of Muhammad to him. If Muhammad makes his ablutions they would not let the water thereof fall on the ground but would rub it on their bodies and clothes. Now you may decide as to what you should do."*

In the meantime when the messages were coming and the negotiations were going on, the Quraysh tried again and again to quietly launch sudden attacks on the Muslim camp in order to provoke the Companions and somehow incite them to war, but every time they did so the Companions' forbearance and patience and the Prophet's wisdom and sagacity frustrated their designs. On one occasion forty or fifty of their men came at night and attacked the Muslim camp with stones and arrows. The Companions arrested all of them and took them before the Prophet, but he let them go. On another occasion 80 men came from the direction of Tan'im right at the time of the Fajr Prayer and made a sudden attack. They were also caught, but the Prophet forgave them, too. Thus, the Quraysh went on meeting failure after failure in every one of their designs.

At last, the Prophet sent Uthman as his own messenger to Makkah with the message that they had not come to fight but only for pilgrimage and had brought their sacrificial camels along, and they would go back after performing the rite of pilgrimage and offering the sacrifice. But the Quraysh did not agree and withheld Uthman in the city. In the meantime a rumor spread that Uthman had been killed; and when he did not return in time the Muslims took the rumor to be true. Now they could show no more forbearance. Entry into Makkah was different for there was no intention to use force. But when the ambassador was put to death, the Muslims had no alternative but to prepare for war. Therefore, the Prophet summoned all his Companions together and took a solemn pledge from them that they would fight to death. In view of the critical occasion it was not an ordinary undertaking. The Muslims numbered only 1,400 and had come without any weapons, were encamping at the boundary of Makkah, 250 miles away from their own city, and the enemy could attack them in full strength, and could surround them with its allies from the adjoining tribes as well. In spite of this, none from the caravan except one man failed to give his pledge to fight to death, and there could be no greater proof of their dedication and sincerity than that in the cause of God. This pledge is well known in the history of Islām as the pledge of Ridwan.

Later it was known that the news about Uthman was false. Not only did he return but under Suhail bin 'Amr from the Quraysh also arrived a deputation to negotiate peace with the Prophet. Now, the Quraysh no more insisted that they would disallow the Prophet and his Companions to enter Makkah. However, in order to save their face they only insisted that he went back that year but could come the following year to perform the umrah. After lengthy negotiations peace was concluded on the following terms:

1. War would remain suspended for ten years, and no party would indulge in any hostility, open or secret, against the other.
2. If any one during that period from among the Quraysh went over to Muhammad, without his guardian's permission, he would return him to them, but if a Companion of Muhammad came oven to the Quraysh, they would not return him to him.
3. Every Arab tribe would have the option to join either side as its ally and enter the treaty.
4. Muhammad and his men would go back that year and could come the following year for Umrah and stay in Makkah for three days, provided that they brought only one sheathed sword each, and no other weapon of war. In those three days the Makkans would vacate the city for them (so that there was no chance of a clash), but they would not be allowed to take along any Makkan on return. When the conditions of the treaty were being settled, the whole of the Muslim army was feeling greatly upset. No one understood the expedience because of which the Prophet was accepting the conditions. No one was farsighted enough to foresee the great benefit that was to result from this treaty. The disbelieving Quraysh looked at it as their victory, and the Muslims were upset as to why they should be humiliated to accepting those mean conditions. Even a statesman of the caliber of Umar says that he had never given way to doubt since the time he had embraced Islām but on this occasion he also could not avoid it. Impatient he went to Abu Bakr and said "*Is he (the Prophet) not God's Messenger, and are we not Muslims, and are they not polytheists? Then, why should we agree to what is humiliating to our Faith?*" He replied "*O Umar, he is surely God's Messenger, and God will never make him the loser.*" Unsatisfied he went to the Prophet himself and put the same questions to him, and he also gave him the same replies as Abu Bakr had given. Afterwards Umar continued to offer voluntary prayers and give alms so that God may pardon his insolence that he had shown on that occasion.

Two things in the treaty were highly disturbing for the Muslims first, the second condition, about which they said that it was an expressly unfair condition, for if they had to return a fugitive from Makkah, why should not the Quraysh return a fugitive from Madinah? To this the Prophet replied: "*What use would be he to us, who fled from us to them? May God keep him away from us! And if we return the one who flees to us from them, God will create some other way out for him."* The other thing that was rankling in their minds was the fourth condition. The Muslims thought that agreeing to it meant that they were going back unsuccessful and this was humiliating. Furthermore, the question that was causing them to feel upset was that they had accepted the condition of going back without performing the pilgrimage to the Ka'bāh, whereas the Prophet had seen in the vision that they were performing tawaf at Makkah. To this the Prophet replied that in his vision the year had not been specified. According to the treaty conditions, therefore, they would perform the Tawaf (encircling of the Ka'bāh) the following year if it pleased God.

Right at the time when the document was being written, Suhail bin 'Amr's own son, Abu Jandal, who had become a Muslim and been imprisoned by the pagans of Makkah somehow escaped to the Prophet's camp. He had fetters on his feet and signs of violence on his body. He implored the Prophet that he help secure his release from imprisonment. The scene only increased the Companions' dejection, and they were moved beyond control. But Suhail bin 'Amr said the conditions of the agreement had been concluded between them although the writing was not yet complete; therefore, the boy should be returned to them. The Prophet admitted his argument and Abu Jandal was returned to his oppressors.

When the document was finished, the Prophet spoke to the Companions and told them to slaughter their sacrificial animals at that very place, shave their heads and put off the pilgrim garments, but no one moved from his place. The Prophet repeated the order thrice but the Companions were so overcome by depression and dejection that they did not comply. During his entire period of apostleship on no occasion had it ever happened that he should command his Companions to do a thing and they should not hasten to comply with it. This caused him a great shock, and he repaired to his tent and expressed his grief before his wife, Umm Salamah. She said, *"You may quietly go and slaughter your own camel and call the barber and have your head shaved. After that the people would automatically do what you did and would understand that whatever decision had been taken would not be changed."* Precisely the same thing happened. The people slaughtered their animals, shaved their heads or cut their hair short and put off the pilgrim garb, but their hearts were still afflicted with grief.

Later, when this caravan was returning to Madinah, feeling depressed and dejected at the truce of Hudaibiyah, this Sūrah came down at Dajnan (or according to some others, at Kura' al-Ghamim), which told the Muslims that the treaty that they were regarding as their defeat, was indeed a great victory. After it had come down, the Prophet summoned the Muslims together and said: *"Today such a thing has been sent down to me, which is more valuable to me than the world and what it contains."* Then be recited this Sūrah, especially to Umar, for he was the one who was feeling most dejected.

Although the believers were satisfied when they heard this Divine Revelation, not much longer afterwards the advantages of this treaty began to appear one after the other until every one became fully convinced that this peace treaty indeed was a great victory:

1. In it for the first time the existence of the Islāmic State in Arabia was duly recognized. Before this in the eyes of the Arabs the position of the Prophet Muhammad and his Companions was no more than of mere rebels against the Quraysh and other Arab tribes, and they regarded them as the outlaws. Now the Quraysh themselves by concluding this agreement with the Prophet recognized his sovereignty over the territories of the Islāmic State and opened the way for the Arab tribes to enter treaties of alliance with either of the political powers they liked.
2. By admitting the right of pilgrimage to the House of God for the Muslims, the Quraysh also admitted that Islām was not an anti-religious creed, as they had so far been thinking, but it was one of the admitted religions of Arabia, and like the other Arabs, its followers also had the right to perform the rites of Hajj and Umrah. This diminished the hatred in the Arabs hearts that had been caused by the propaganda made by the Quraysh against Islām.
3. The signing of a no-war pact for ten years provided full peace to the Muslims, and spreading to every nook and corner of Arabia they preached Islām with such spirit and speed that within two

years after Hudaibiyah the number of the people who embraced Islām far exceeded those who had embraced it during the past 19 years or so. It was all due to this treaty that two years later when in consequence of the Quraysh's violating the treaty the Prophet invaded Makkah, he was accompanied by an army 10,000 strong, whereas on the occasion of Hudaibiyah only 1,400 men had joined him in the march.

4. After the suspension of hostilities by the Quraysh the Prophet had the opportunity to establish and strengthen Islāmic rule in the territories under him and to turn the Islāmic society into a full fledged civilization and way of life by the enforcement of Islāmic law.
5. Another gain that accrued from the truce with the Quraysh was that being assured of peace from the south the Muslims overpowered all the opponent forces in the north and central Arabia easily. Just three months after Hudaibiyah, Khaiber, the major stronghold of the Jews, was conquered and after it the Jewish settlements of Fadak, Wad-il Qura, Taima and Tabūk also fell to Islām one after the other. Then all other tribes of central Arabia, which were bound in alliance with the Jews and Quraysh, came under the sway of Islām. Thus, within two years after Hudaibiyah the balance of power in Arabia was so changed that the strength of the Quraysh and pagan gave way and the domination of Islām became certain.

These were the blessings that the Muslims gained from the peace treaty which they were looking upon as their defeat and the Quraysh as their victory. However, what had troubled the Muslims most in this treaty, was the condition about the fugitives from Makkah and Madinah, that the former would be returned and the latter would not be returned. But not much long after- wards this condition also proved to be disadvantageous for the Quraysh, and experience revealed what far reaching consequences of it had the Prophet foreseen and then accepted it. A few days after the treaty a Muslim of Makkah, Abu Basir, escaped from the Quraysh and reached Madinah. The Quraysh demanded him back and the Prophet returned him to their men who had been sent from Makkah to arrest him. But while on the way to Makkah he again fled and went and sat on the road by the Red Sea shore, which the trade caravans of the Quraysh took to Syria. After that every Muslim who succeeded in escaping from the Quraysh would go and join Abu Basir instead of going to Madinah, until 70 men gathered there. They would attack any Quraysh caravan that passed the way and cut it into pieces at last, the Quraysh themselves begged the Prophet to call those men to Madinah, and the condition relating to the return of the fugitives of itself became null and void. The Sūrah should be read with this historical background in view in order to fully understand it.

## Sūrah 48: al-Fath[1403]

In the Name of God, the Most Compassionate, the Most Merciful

1. Indeed, We have given you, [O Muhammad], a clear conquest[1404]

2. That God may forgive for you what preceded of your sin [i.e., errors] and what will follow and complete His favor upon you and guide you to a straight path

3. And [that] God may aid you with a mighty victory.

4. It is He who sent down tranquillity into the hearts of the believers that they would increase in faith along with their [present] faith. And to God belong the soldiers of the heavens and the earth, and ever is God Knowing and Wise.

5. [And] that He may admit the believing men and the believing women to gardens beneath which rivers flow to abide therein eternally and remove from them their misdeeds - and ever is that, in the sight of God, a great attainment -

6. And [that] He may punish the hypocrite men and hypocrite women, and the polytheist men and polytheist women - those who assume about God an assumption of evil nature. Upon them is a misfortune of evil nature; and God has become angry with them and has cursed them and prepared for them Hell, and evil it is as a destination.

7. And to God belong the soldiers of the heavens and the earth. And ever is God Exalted in Might and Wise.

8. Indeed, We have sent you as a witness and a bringer of good tidings and a warner

9. That you [people] may believe in God and His Messenger and honour him and respect him [i.e., the Prophet] and exalt Him [i.e., God] morning and afternoon.

10. Indeed, those who pledge allegiance to you, [O Muhammad] - they are actually pledging allegiance to God. The hand[1405] of God is over their hands.[1406] So he who breaks his word only breaks it to the detriment of himself. And he who fulfills that which he has promised God - He will give him a great reward.

11. Those who remained behind of the bedouins will say to you, "Our properties and our families occupied us, so ask forgiveness for us." They say with their tongues what is not within their hearts. Say, "Then who could prevent God at all if He intended for you harm or intended for you benefit? Rather, ever is God, with what you do, Acquainted.

12. But you thought that the Messenger and the believers would never return to their families, ever, and that was made pleasing in your hearts. And you assumed an assumption of evil and became a people ruined."

[1403] *Al-Fath*: The Conquest.

[1404] Ibn Mas'ud said, "You [people] consider the conquest to be that of Makkah, but we consider it to be the Treaty of al-Hudaybiyyah." Al Bukhāri reported a similar quotation from al-Barā' bin 'Āzib. Although initially regarded by the companions as a setback, the treaty, in effect, served to promote the spread of Islām, which led to the conquest of Makkah two years later.

[1405] See footnote to 2:19.

[1406] Meaning that He (Almighty) accepted their pledge.

13. And whoever has not believed in God and His Messenger - then indeed, We have prepared for the disbelievers a Blaze.

14. And to God belongs the dominion of the heavens and the earth. He forgives whom He wills and punishes whom He wills. And ever is God Forgiving and Merciful.

15. Those who remained behind will say when you set out toward the war booty to take it, "Let us follow you." They wish to change the words of God. Say, "Never will you follow us. Thus did God say before." So they will say, "Rather, you envy us." But [in fact] they were not understanding except a little.[1407]

16. Say to those who remained behind of the bedouins, "You will be called to [face] a people of great military might; you may fight them, or they will submit.[1408] So if you obey, God will give you a good reward; but if you turn away as you turned away before, He will punish you with a painful punishment."

17. There is not upon the blind any guilt or upon the lame any guilt or upon the ill any guilt [for remaining behind]. And whoever obeys God and His Messenger - He will admit him to gardens beneath which rivers flow; but whoever turns away - He will punish him with a painful punishment.

18. Certainly was God pleased with the believers when they pledged allegiance to you, [O Muhammad], under the tree, and He knew what was in their hearts, so He sent down tranquillity upon them and rewarded them with an imminent conquest[1409]

19. And much war booty which they will take. And ever is God Exalted in Might and Wise.

20. God has promised you much booty that you will take [in the future] and has hastened for you this [victory] and withheld the hands of people from you - that it may be a sign for the believers and [that] He may guide you to a straight path.

21. And [He promises] other [victories] that you were [so far] unable to [realize] which God has already encompassed.[1410] And ever is God, over all things, competent.

22. And if those [Makkans] who disbelieve had fought you, they would have turned their backs [in flight]. Then they would not find a protector or a helper.

23. [This is] the established way of God which has occurred before. And never will you find in the way of God any change.

24. And it is He who withheld their hands from you and your hands from them within [the area of] Makkah after He caused you to overcome them. And ever is God of what you do, Seeing.

25. They are the ones who disbelieved and obstructed you from al-Masjid al-Harām while the offering[1411] was pre-

[1407] i.e., they only understood the material aspects of life.

[1408] To God in Islām.

[1409] That of Khaybar, which preceded the conquest of Makkah.

[1410] i.e., prepared for you or decreed.

[1411] i.e., seventy camels intended for sacrifice and feeding of the poor.

vented from reaching its place of sacrifice. And if not for believing men and believing women whom you did not know - that you might trample [i.e., kill] them and there would befall you because of them dishonour without [your] knowledge - [you would have been permitted to enter Makkah]. [This was so] that God might admit to His mercy whom He willed. If they had been apart [from them], We would have punished those who disbelieved among them with painful punishment

26. When those who disbelieved had put into their hearts chauvinism - the chauvinism of the time of ignorance. But God sent down His tranquillity upon His Messenger and upon the believers and imposed upon them the word of righteousness, and they were more deserving of it and worthy of it. And ever is God, of all things, Knowing.

27. Certainly has God showed to His Messenger the vision [i.e., dream] in truth. You will surely enter al-Masjid al-Harām, if God wills, in safety, with your heads shaved and [hair] shortened,[1412] not fearing [anyone]. He knew what you did not know and has arranged before that a conquest near [at hand].

28. It is He who sent His Messenger with guidance and the religion of truth to manifest it over all religion. And sufficient is God as Witness.

29. Muhammad is the Messenger of God; and those with him are forceful against the disbelievers, merciful among themselves. You see them bowing and prostrating [in prayer], seeking bounty from God and [His] pleasure. Their mark [i.e., sign] is on their faces [i.e., foreheads] from the trace of prostration. That is their description in the Torah. And their description in the Gospel is as a plant which produces its offshoots and strengthens them so they grow firm and stand upon their stalks, delighting the sowers - so that He [i.e., God] may enrage by them[1413] the disbelievers. God has promised those who believe and do righteous deeds among them forgiveness and a great reward.

[1412] i.e., having completed the rites of *'umrah*.

[1413] The given examples depict the Prophet and his companions.

## Sūrah 49: al-Hujurāt

### Period of Revelation

Ahadith show that this Sūrah is a collection of the commandments and instructions sent down on different occasions. Moreover, the hadith also show that most of these commandments were sent down during the final stage of the Prophet's life at Madinah. For instance, about verse 4, the commentators state that it was sent down concerning the Bani Tamim whose deputation had arrived in Madinah and started calling out to the Prophet from outside the apartments (hujurat) of his wives, and according to all biographical books on the Prophet's life this deputation had visited Madinah in 9 A.H. Likewise, about verse 6 a large number of the hadith confirm that it was sent down concerning Walid bin Uqbah whom the Prophet had sent to collect the Zakāh from the Bani al-Mustaliq, and it is well known that Walid bin Uqabah had become a Muslim on the conquest of Makkah.

### Subject Matter and Topics

The subject matter of this Sūrah is to teach the Muslims the manners worthy of true believers. In the first five verses they have been taught the manners they should observe with regard to God and His Messenger.

Then, they have been given the instruction that it is not right to believe in every news blindly and to act according to it, without due thought. If information is received about a person, a group or a community, it should be seen carefully whether the means of the information is reliable or not. If the means is not reliable, it should be tested and examined to see whether the news is authentic or not before taking any action on it.

Then, it has been told what attitude should the other Muslims adopt in case two groups of the Muslims fall to mutual fighting. Then the Muslims have been exhorted to safeguard against the evils that corrupt collective life and spoil mutual relationships. Mocking and taunting each other, calling others by nicknames, creating suspicions, prying into other people's affairs and backbiting are the evils which are not only sins in themselves but they also corrupt society. God has mentioned all these evils separately and forbidden them as unlawful.

After this, the national and racial distinctions that cause universal corruption in the world have been condemned. Nations and tribes and families pride of ancestry and their looking down upon others as inferior to themselves and their pulling down others only for the sake of establishing their own superiority is an important factor that has filled the world with injustices and tyranny. God in a brief verse has cut at the root of this evil by stating that all men are descendants of the same one pair and their division into tribes and communities is only for the sake of recognition, not for boasting and pride, and there is no lawful basis of one man's superiority over the other except on the basis of moral excellence.

In conclusion, the people have been told that the real thing is not the verbal Profession of the Faith but to believe in God and His messenger truly, to obey them in practical life and to exert sincerely with one's self and wealth in the cause of God. True believers are only those who adopt this attitude. As for those who profess Islām merely orally without affirmation by the heart and then adopt an attitude as if they had done someone a favor by accepting Islām, may be counted among the Muslims in the world, may even be treated as Muslims in society, but they cannot be counted as believers in the sight of God.

## Sūrah 49: al-Hujurāt[1414]

In the Name of God, the Most Compassionate, the Most Merciful

1. O you who have believed, do not put [yourselves] before God and His Messenger[1415] but fear God. Indeed, God is Hearing and Knowing.

2. O you who have believed, do not raise your voices above the voice of the Prophet or be loud to him in speech like the loudness of some of you to others, lest your deeds become worthless while you perceive not.

3. Indeed, those who lower their voices before the Messenger of God - they are the ones whose hearts God has tested for righteousness. For them is forgiveness and great reward.

4. Indeed, those who call you, [O Muhammad], from behind the chambers - most of them do not use reason.

5. And if they had been patient until you [could] come out to them, it would have been better for them. But God is Forgiving and Merciful.

6. O you who have believed, if there comes to you a disobedient one with information, investigate, lest you harm a people out of ignorance and become, over what you have done, regretful.

7. And know that among you is the Messenger of God. If he were to obey you in much of the matter, you would be in difficulty, but God has endeared to you the faith and has made it pleasing in your hearts and has made hateful to you disbelief, defiance and disobedience. Those are the [rightly] guided.

8. [It is] as bounty from God and favor. And God is Knowing and Wise.

9. And if two factions among the believers should fight, then make settlement between the two. But if one of them oppresses the other, then fight against the one that oppresses until it returns to the ordinance of God. And if it returns, then make settlement between them in justice and act justly. Indeed, God loves those who act justly.

10. The believers are but brothers, so make settlement between your brothers. And fear God that you may receive mercy.

11. O you who have believed, let not a people ridicule [another] people; perhaps they may be better than them; nor let women ridicule [other] women; perhaps they may be better than them. And do not insult one another and do not call each other by [offensive] nicknames. Wretched is the name [i.e., mention] of disobedience after [one's] faith. And whoever does not repent - then it is those who are the wrongdoers.

12. O you who have believed, avoid much [negative] assumption. Indeed, some assumption is sin. And do not spy or backbite each other. Would one of you like to eat the flesh of his brother when dead? You would detest it. And fear God; indeed, God is Accepting of repentance and Merciful.

13. O mankind, indeed We have created you from male and female and made you peoples and tribes that you may

---

1414 *Al-Hujurāt*: The Chambers, referring to the rooms in which the wives of the Prophet lived.

1415 Rather, wait for instruction and follow the way of the Prophet.

know one another. Indeed, the most noble of you in the sight of God is the most righteous[1416] of you. Indeed, God is Knowing and Acquainted.

14. The bedouins say, "We have believed." Say, "You have not [yet] believed; but say [instead], 'We have submitted,' for faith has not yet entered your hearts. And if you obey God and His Messenger, He will not deprive you from your deeds[1417] of anything. Indeed, God is Forgiving and Merciful."

15. The believers are only the ones who have believed in God and His Messenger and then doubt not but strive with their properties and their lives in the cause of God. It is those who are the truthful.

16. Say, "Would you acquaint God with your religion while God knows whatever is in the heavens and whatever is on the earth, and God is Knowing of all things?"

17. They consider it a favor to you that they have accepted Islām. Say, "Do not consider your Islām a favor to me. Rather, God has conferred favor upon you that He has guided you to the faith, if you should be truthful."

18. Indeed, God knows the unseen [aspects] of the heavens and the earth. And God is Seeing of what you do.

[1416] Literally, "he who has the most *taqwā*," i.e., consciousness and fear of God, piety and righteousness.
[1417] i.e., the reward thereof.

# Sūrah 50: Qāf

## Period of Revelation

There is no authentic hadith to show as to when exactly this Sūrah was sent down. A study of the subject matter, however, reveals that its period of revelation is the second stage of the Prophet's life at Makkah, which lasted from the third year of the Prophethood till the fifth year.

## Theme and Topics

Authentic traditions show that the Prophet used to recite this Sūrah generally in the Prayer on the Eid days. A woman named Umm Hisham bin Harithah, who was a neighbor of the Prophet, says that she was able to commit Sūrah Qaf to memory only because she often heard it from the Prophet in the Friday sermons. According to some other traditions he often recited it in the Fajr (dawn) Prayer. This makes it abundantly clear that this was an important Sūrah in the sight of the Prophet. That is why he made sure that its contents reached as many people as possible over and over again.

The reason for this importance can be easily understood by a careful study of the Sūrah. The theme of the entire Sūrah is the Hereafter. When the Prophet started preaching his message in Makkah what surprised the people most was the news that people would be resurrected after death, and they would have to render an account of their deeds. They said that "that was impossible"; human mind could not believe that, that would happen. After all, how could it be possible that when the body had disintegrated into dust the scattered particles would be reassembled after hundreds of thousands of years to make up the same body once again and raised up as a living body. God in response sent down this discourse. In it, on the one hand, arguments have been given for the possibility and occurrence of the Hereafter in a brief way, in short sentences, and, on the other, the people have been warned, as if to say: "Whether you express wonder and surprise, or you regard it as something remote from reason, or deny it altogether, in any case it cannot change the truth. The absolute, unalterable truth is that God knows the whereabouts of each and every particle of your body that has scattered away in the earth, and knows where and in what state it is. God's one signal is enough to make all the scattered particles gather together again and to make you rise up once again as you had been made in the first instance. Likewise, this idea that you have been created and left free to yourselves in the world and that you have not been made answerable to anyone, is no more than a misunderstanding. The fact is that not only is God Himself directly aware of each act and word of yours, even of the ideas that pass in your mind, but His angels also are attached to each one of you, who are preserving the record of whatever you do and utter. When the time comes, you will come out of your graves at one call just as young shoots of vegetable sprout up from the earth on the first shower of the rain. Then this heedlessness which obstructs your vision will be removed and you will see with your own eyes all that you are denying today. At that time you will realize that you had not been created to be irresponsible in this world but accountable to all your deeds. The meting out of the rewards and punishments, the Hell and Heaven, which you regard as impossible and imaginary things, will at that time become visible realities for you. In consequence of your enmity and opposition to the Truth you will be cast into the same Hell which you regard as remote from reason today and the ones who fear the Merciful God and return to the path of righteousness, will be admitted to the same Paradise at whose mention you now express wonder and surprise.

## Sūrah 50: Qāf[1418]

In the Name of God, the Most Compassionate, the Most Merciful

1. Qāf.[1419] By the honoured Qur'ān...[1420]

2. But they wonder that there has come to them a warner from among themselves, and the disbelievers say, "This is an amazing thing.

3. When we have died and have become dust, [we will return to life]? That is a distant [i.e., unlikely] return."

4. We know what the earth diminishes [i.e., consumes] of them, and with Us is a retaining record.

5. But they denied the truth when it came to them, so they are in a confused condition.

6. Have they not looked at the heaven above them - how We structured it and adorned it and [how] it has no rifts?

7. And the earth - We spread it out and cast therein firmly set mountains and made grow therein [something] of every beautiful kind,

8. Giving insight and a reminder for every servant who turns [to God].

9. And We have sent down blessed rain from the sky and made grow thereby gardens and grain from the harvest

10. And lofty palm trees having fruit arranged in layers –

[1418] *Qāf*: (the letter) *qāf*.
[1419] See footnote to 2:1.
[1420] See footnote to 38:1.

11. As provision for the servants, and We have given life thereby to a dead land. Thus is the emergence [i.e., resurrection].

12. The people of Noah denied before them,[1421] and the companions of the well[1422] and Thamūd

13. And 'Aad and Pharaoh and the brothers [i.e., people] of Lot

14. And the companions of the thicket and the people of Tubba'. All denied the messengers, so My threat was justly fulfilled.

15. Did We fail in the first creation? But they are in confusion over a new creation.

16. And We have already created man and know what his soul whispers to him, and We are closer[1423] to him than [his] jugular vein

17. When the two receivers [i.e., recording angels] receive,[1424] seated on the right and on the left.

18. He [i.e., man] does not utter any word except that with him is an observer prepared [to record].

19. And the intoxication of death will bring the truth; that is what you were trying to avoid.

20. And the Horn will be blown. That is the Day of [carrying out] the threat.

[1421] i.e., before the disbelievers of Makkah.
[1422] See footnote to 25:38.
[1423] In absolute knowledge of everything about him. "We" has also been interpreted to mean the angels who are mentioned in the following verse.
[1424] And record each word and deed.

21. And every soul will come, with it a driver and a witness.[1425]

22. [It will be said], "You were certainly in unmindfulness of this, and We have removed from you your cover,[1426] so your sight, this Day, is sharp."

23. And his companion, [the angel], will say, "This [record] is what is with me, prepared."

24. [God will say], "Throw into Hell every obstinate disbeliever,

25. Preventer of good, aggressor, and doubter,

26. Who made [as equal] with God another deity; then throw him into the severe punishment."

27. His [devil] companion will say, "Our Lord, I did not make him transgress, but he [himself] was in extreme error."

28. [God] will say, "Do not dispute before Me, while I had already presented to you the threat [i.e., warning].

29. The word [i.e., decree] will not be changed with Me, and never will I be unjust to the servants."

30. On the Day We will say to Hell, "Have you been filled?" and it will say, "Are there some more,"

31. And Paradise will be brought near to the righteous, not far,

[1425] i.e., one angel driving the soul to the Judgement and one to testify as to its deeds.

[1426] Of heedlessness, or that which had sealed your hearing, your vision and your heart from guidance.

32. [It will be said], "This is what you were promised - for every returner [to God] and keeper [of His covenant]

33. Who feared the Most Merciful unseen and came with a heart returning [in repentance].

34. Enter it in peace. This is the Day of Eternity."

35. They will have whatever they wish therein, and with Us is more.

36. And how many a generation before them did We destroy who were greater than them in [striking] power and had explored throughout the lands. Is there any place of escape?

37. Indeed in that is a reminder for whoever has a heart or who listens while he is present [in mind].

38. And We did certainly create the heavens and earth and what is between them in six days, and there touched Us no weariness.

39. So be patient, [O Muhammad], over what they say and exalt [God] with praise of your Lord before the rising of the sun and before its setting,

40. And [in part] of the night exalt Him and after prostration [i.e., prayer].

41. And listen on the Day when the Caller[1427] will call out from a place that is near -

42. The Day they will hear the blast [of the Horn] in truth. That is the Day of Emergence [from the graves].

[1427] An angel who will call out God's command for the Resurrection.

43. Indeed, it is We who give life and cause death, and to Us is the destination

44. On the Day the earth breaks away from them [and they emerge] rapidly; that is a gathering easy for Us.

45. We are most knowing of what they say, and you are not over them a tyrant.[1428] But remind by the Qur'ān whoever fears My threat.

[1428] Forcing people to belief or submission.

## Sūrah 51: adh-Dhāriyāt

### Period of Revelation

The subject matter and the style clearly show that it was sent down in the period when persecution had not yet started. Although the Prophet's invitation was being resisted and opposed with denial and ridicule and false accusations stubbornly. Therefore, this Sūrah also seems to have been revealed in the same period in which the Sūrah Qaf was revealed.

### Subject Matter and Topics

The Sūrah mostly deals with the Hereafter, and in the end it presents the invitation to Tawhid. In addition, the people have also been warned that refusal to accept the message of the Prophets and persistence in the concepts and creeds of ignorance have proved to be disastrous for those nations themselves which have adopted this attitude and way of life in the past.

About the Hereafter what this Sūrah presents in short but brief sentences is this: The people's different and conflicting beliefs about the end of human life are themselves an express proof that none of these beliefs and creeds is based on knowledge. Everyone by himself has formed an ideology on the basis of conjecture and made the same his creed. Someone thought that there would be no life-after-death; someone believed in the life-after-death, but in the form of the transmigration of souls; someone believed in the life hereafter and the meting out of the rewards and punishments but invented different sorts of props and supports to escape retribution. About a question of such vital and fundamental importance a wrong view of which renders man's whole life-work wrong and waste and ruins his future for ever, it would be a disastrous folly to build an ideology only on the basis of speculation and conjecture, without knowledge. It would mean that man should remain involved in a grave misunderstanding, pass his whole life in the heedlessness of error, and after death should suddenly meet with a situation for which he had made no preparation at all. There is only one way of forming the right opinion about such a question, and it is this: Man should seriously ponder over the knowledge about the Hereafter that the Prophet of God is conveying to him from Him, and should study carefully the system of the earth and heavens and his own existence. One should see whether the evidence of that knowledge's being sound and correct is afforded by everything around him or not. In this regard, the arrangement of the wind and rain, the structure of the earth and the creatures found on it, man's own self, the creation of the heavens and of everything in the world in the form of pairs have been presented as evidence of the Hereafter, and instances have been cited from human history to show that the temper of the empire of the Universe requires that the law of retribution must operate here.

In this very connection, it has also been stated that whenever the Prophets of God have been opposed and resisted, they have not been opposed and resisted on the basis of any rational ground but on the basis of the same obduracy and stubbornness and false pride that is being shown against the Prophet Muhammad, and there is no other motive for it than rebellion and arrogance. Then the Prophet has been instructed not to bother about the rebels but to go on performing his mission of invitation and admonition, for it is useful and beneficial for the believers although it may not be so for the other people. As for the wicked people who still persist in their rebellion, they should know that their predecessors who followed the same way of life, have already received their shares of the punishment, and these people's share of the punishment has been made ready for them.

## Sūrah 51: adh-Dhāriyāt[1429]

In the Name of God, the Most Compassionate, the Most Merciful

1. By those [winds] scattering [dust] dispersing [it]

2. And those [clouds] carrying a load [of water]

3. And those [ships] sailing with ease

4. And those [angels] apportioning [each] matter,

5. Indeed, what you are promised is true.

6. And indeed, the recompense is to occur.

7. By the heaven containing pathways,[1430]

8. Indeed, you are in differing speech.[1431]

9. Deluded away from it [i.e., the Qur'ān] is he who is deluded.

10. Destroyed are the falsifiers[1432]

11. Who are within a flood [of confusion] and heedless.

12. They ask, "When is the Day of Recompense?"

13. [It is] the Day they will be tormented over the Fire

14. [And will be told], "Taste your torment. This is that for which you were impatient."

15. Indeed, the righteous will be among gardens and springs,

16. Accepting what their Lord has given them. Indeed, they were before that doers of good.

17. They used to sleep but little of the night,[1433]

18. And in the hours before dawn they would ask forgiveness,

19. And from their properties was [given] the right of the [needy] petitioner and the deprived.

20. And on the earth are signs for the certain [in faith]

21. And in yourselves. Then will you not see?

22. And in the heaven is your provision and whatever you are promised.

23. Then by the Lord of the heaven and earth, indeed, it is truth - just as [sure as] it is that you are speaking.

24. Has there reached you the story of the honoured guests of Abraham?[1434] -

25. When they entered upon him and said, "[We greet you with] peace." He answered, "[And upon you] peace; [you are] a people unknown."

26. Then he went to his family and came with a fat [roasted] calf

27. And placed it near them; he said, "Will you not eat?"

---

[1429] *Adh-Dhāriyāt*: The Scattering Winds.

[1430] Explained as tracks, layers or orbits.

[1431] About Prophet Muhammad and the Qur'ān.

[1432] Or "May they be destroyed" or "cursed."

[1433] i.e., spending a portion of the night in prayer and supplication.

[1434] Who were angels given honoured positions by God.

28. And he felt from them apprehension.[1435] They said, "Fear not," and gave him good tidings of a learned boy.

29. And his wife approached with a cry [of alarm] and struck her face and said, "[I am] a barren old woman!"

30. They said, "Thus has said your Lord; indeed, He is the Wise, the Knowing."

31. [Abraham] said, "Then what is your business [here], O messengers?"

32. They said, "Indeed, we have been sent to a people of criminals[1436]

33. To send down upon them stones of clay,

34. Marked in the presence of your Lord for the transgressors."

35. So We brought out whoever was in them [i.e., the cities] of the believers.

36. And We found not within them other than a [single] house of Muslims.[1437]

37. And We left therein a sign for those who fear the painful punishment.

38. And in Moses [was a sign], when We sent him to Pharaoh with clear authority.

39. But he turned away with his supporters and said, "A magician or a madman."

40. So We took him and his soldiers and cast them into the sea, and he was blameworthy.

[1435] See footnote to 11:70.
[1436] i.e., those who defied Lot.
[1437] i.e., Lot and his family, excepting his wife.

41. And in 'Aad [was a sign], when We sent against them the barren wind.[1438]

42. It left nothing of what it came upon but that it made it like disintegrated ruins.

43. And in Thamūd, when it was said to them, "Enjoy yourselves for a time."

44. But they were insolent toward the command of their Lord, so the thunderbolt seized them while they were looking on.

45. And they were unable to arise, nor could they defend themselves.

46. And [We destroyed] the people of Noah before; indeed, they were a people defiantly disobedient.

47. And the heaven We constructed with strength, and indeed, We are [its] expander.

48. And the earth We have spread out, and excellent is the preparer.

49. And of all things We created two mates [i.e., counterparts]; perhaps you will remember.

50. So flee to God.[1439] Indeed, I am to you from Him a clear warner.

51. And do not make [as equal] with God another deity. Indeed, I am to you from Him a clear warner.

52. Similarly, there came not to those before them any messenger except that they said, "A magician or a madman."

[1438] Barren of any benefit, i.e., evil.
[1439] i.e., turn to God and take refuge in Him from disbelief and sin, thereby escaping His punishment.

53. Did they suggest it to them?[1440] Rather, they [themselves] are a transgressing people.

54. So leave them, [O Muhammad], for you are not to be blamed.

55. And remind, for indeed, the reminder benefits the believers.

56. And I did not create the jinn and mankind except to worship Me.

57. I do not want from them any provision, nor do I want them to feed Me.

58. Indeed, it is God who is the [continual] Provider, the firm possessor of strength.

59. And indeed, for those who have wronged is a portion [of punishment] like the portion of their companions [i.e., predecessors], so let them not impatiently urge Me.

60. And woe to those who have disbelieved from their Day which they are promised.

[1440] i.e., Did the former disbelievers pass on these words to the Makkans so that they repeat the same expressions?

## Sūrah 52: at-Tūr

### Period of Revelation

From the internal evidence of the subject matter it appears that this Sūrah too was revealed in the same stage of the Prophet's life at Makkah in which the Sūrah adh-Dhariyat was revealed. While going through it one can clearly feel that during the period of its revelation the Prophet was being showered with objections and accusations but there is no evidence yet to show that severe persecution of the Muslims had started.

### Subject Matter and Topics

The subject matter of its first section (v. 1-28) is the Hereafter. As arguments for its possibility, necessity and occurrence had already been given in Sūrah adh-Dhariyat, these have not been repeated here. However, swearing an oath by some realities and signs which testify to the Hereafter, it has been stated most emphatically that it will surely come to pass, and none has the power to prevent its occurrence. Then, it has been stated as to what will be the fate of those who deny it when it actually occurs, and how will those who believe in it and adopt the way of piety and righteousness accordingly, be blessed by God.

Then, in the second section (v. 29-49) the Quraysh chiefs' attitude towards the message of the Prophet has been criticized. They called him a sorcerer, a madman, or a poet, and would thus mislead the common people against him so that they should not pay any serious attention to the message he preached. They looked upon him as a calamity that had suddenly descended on them and would openly wish that he met with a disaster so that they were rid of him. They accused him of fabricating the Qur'ān by himself and of presenting it in the name of God, and this was, God forbid, a fraud that he was practicing. They would often taunt him, saying that God could not have appointed an ordinary man like him to the office of Prophethood. They expressed great disgust at his invitation and message and would avoid him as if he was asking them for a reward for it. They would sit and take counsels together to devise schemes in order to put an end to his mission. And while they did all this they never realized what creeds of ignorance they were involved in and how selflessly and sincerely was Muhammad exerting himself to deliver them from their error. While criticizing them for this attitude and conduct, God has put to them certain questions, one after the other, each of which is either an answer to some objection of theirs, or a criticism of some error. Then, it has been said that it would absolutely be of no avail to show them a miracle in order to convince them of his Prophethood, for they were such stubborn people as would misinterpret anything they were shown only to avoid affirming the faith.

In the beginning of this section as well as in its end, the Prophet has been given the instruction that he should persistently continue giving his invitation and preaching his message in spite of the accusations and objections of his opponents and enemies, and should endure their resistance patiently till God's judgment comes to pass. Besides, he has been consoled, as if to say "Your Lord has not left you alone to face your enemies, after raising you as a Prophet, but He is constantly watching over you. Therefore, endure every hardship patiently till the Hour of His judgment comes, and seek through praising and glorifying your Lord the power that is required for exerting in the cause of God under such conditions."

## Sūrah 52: at-Tūr[1441]

In the Name of God, the Most Compassionate, the Most Merciful

1. By the mount

2. And [by] a Book inscribed[1442]

3. In parchment spread open

4. And [by] the frequented House[1443]

5. And [by] the ceiling [i.e., heaven] raised high

6. And [by] the sea filled [with fire],[1444]

7. Indeed, the punishment of your Lord will occur.

8. Of it there is no preventer.

9. On the Day the heaven will sway with circular motion

10. And the mountains will pass on, departing[1445] -

11. Then woe, that Day, to the deniers,

12. Who are in [empty] discourse amusing themselves.

13. The Day they are thrust toward the fire of Hell with a [violent] thrust, [its angels will say],

14. "This is the Fire which you used to deny.

15. Then is this magic, or do you not see?

16. [Enter to] burn therein; then be patient or impatient - it is all the same for you. You are only being recompensed [for] what you used to do."

17. Indeed, the righteous will be in gardens and pleasure,

18. Enjoying what their Lord has given them, and their Lord protected them from the punishment of Hellfire.

19. [They will be told], "Eat and drink in satisfaction for what you used to do."

20. They will be reclining on thrones lined up, and We will marry them to fair women with large, [beautiful] eyes.

21. And those who believed and whose descendants followed them in faith - We will join with them their descendants, and We will not deprive them of anything of their deeds.[1446] Every person, for what he earned, is retained.[1447]

22. And We will provide them with fruit and meat from whatever they desire.

23. They will exchange with one another a cup [of wine] wherein [results] no ill speech or commission of sin.

24. There will circulate among them [servant] boys [especially] for them, as if they were pearls well-protected.

---

[1441] *At-Tūr:* The Mount, where God spoke to Moses.
[1442] Interpreted as the Preserved Slate or possibly the Qur'ān.
[1443] The house of worship for the angels in the seventh heaven, comparable to the *Ka'bāh* on earth.
[1444] On the Day of Resurrection. Or "the sea which has overflowed."
[1445] Becoming dust and moving as clouds.

[1446] i.e., the reward thereof.
[1447] i.e., subject or held responsible. Literally, "a hostage."

25. And they will approach one another, inquiring of each other.

26. They will say, "Indeed, we were previously among our people fearful [of displeasing God].

27. So God conferred favor upon us and protected us from the punishment of the Scorching Fire.

28. Indeed, we used to supplicate Him before. Indeed, it is He who is the Beneficent, the Merciful."

29. So remind, [O Muhammad], for you are not, by the favor of your Lord, a soothsayer or a madman.

30. Or do they say [of you], "A poet for whom we await a misfortune of time"?[1448]

31. Say, "Wait, for indeed I am, with you, among the waiters."

32. Or do their minds[1449] command them to [say] this, or are they a transgressing people?

33. Or do they say, "He has made it up"? Rather, they do not believe.

34. Then let them produce a statement like it, if they should be truthful.

35. Or were they created by nothing, or were they the creators [of themselves]?

36. Or did they create the heavens and the earth? Rather, they are not certain.

37. Or have they the depositories [containing the provision] of your Lord? Or are they the controllers [of them]?

38. Or have they a stairway [into the heaven] upon which they listen? Then let their listener produce a clear authority [i.e., proof].

39. Or has He daughters while you have sons?

40. Or do you, [O Muhammad], ask of them a payment, so they are by debt burdened down?

41. Or have they [knowledge of] the unseen, so they write [it] down?

42. Or do they intend a plan? But those who disbelieve - they are the object of a plan.

43. Or have they a deity other than God? Exalted is God above whatever they associate with Him.

44. And if they were to see a fragment from the sky falling,[1450] they would say, "[It is merely] clouds heaped up."

45. So leave them until they meet their Day in which they will be struck insensible -

46. The Day their plan will not avail them at all, nor will they be helped.

47. And indeed, for those who have wronged is a punishment[1451] before that, but most of them do not know.

[1448] i.e., some accident or inevitable death.

[1449] In this expression is also a subtle allusion to the leaders of the Quraysh, who considered themselves to be great minds.

[1450] Marking the onset of God's punishment, as they had requested.

[1451] If not in this world, in the grave.

48. And be patient, [O Muhammad], for the decision of your Lord, for indeed, you are in Our eyes [i.e., sight]. And exalt [God] with praise of your Lord when you arise

49. And in a part of the night exalt Him and after [the setting of] the stars.

## Sūrah 53: an-Najm

### Period of Revelation

According to a hadith related by Bukhari and Muslim on the authority of Abdullah bin Mas'ud, the first Sūrah in which a verse requiring the performance of a sajdah (prostration) was sent down, is Sūrah an-Najm. The parts of this Hadith which have been reported by Aswad bin Yazid, Abu Ishaq and Zubair bin Mu'awiyah from Ibn Mas'ud, indicate that this is the first Sūrah of the Qur'ān, which the Prophet had publicly recited before an assembly of the Quraysh (and according to Ibn Marduyah, in the Ka'bāh) in which both the believers and the disbelievers were present. At the end, when he recited the verse requiring the performance of a sajdah and fell down in prostration, the whole assembly also fall down in prostration with him. Even those chiefs of the polytheists who were in the forefront of the opposition to the Prophet could not resist falling down in prostration. Ibn Mas'ud says that he saw only one man, Umayyah bin Khalaf, from among the disbelievers, who did not fall down in prostration but took a little dust and rubbing it on his forehead said that that was enough for him. Later, as Ibn Mas'ud relates, he saw this man being killed in the state of disbelief.

Another eye witness of this incident is Muttalib bin Abi Wada'ah, who had not yet become a Muslim. Nasai and Musnad Ahmad contain his own words to the effect: *"When the Prophet recited the Sūrah An-Najm and performed the sajdah and the whole assembly fell down in prostration along with him, I did not perform the sajdah. Now to compensate for the same whenever I recite this Sūrah I make sure never to abandon its performance."*

Ibn Sad says that before this, in the Rajab of the 5th year of Prophethood, a small group of the Companions had emigrated to Abyssinia. Then, when in the Ramadan of the same year this incident took place the news spread that the Prophet had recited Sūrah an-Najm publicly in the assembly of the Quraysh and the whole assembly, including the believers as well as the disbelievers, had fallen down in prostration with him. When the emigrants to Abyssinia heard this news they formed the impression that the disbelievers of Makkah had become Muslims. Thereupon, some of them returned to Makkah in the Shawwal of the 5th year of Prophethood, only to learn that the news was wrong and the conflict between Islām and disbelief was raging as furiously as before. Consequently, the second emigration to Abyssinia took place, in which many more people left Makkah. Thus, it becomes almost certain that this Sūrah was revealed in the Ramadan of the 5th year of Prophethood.

### Historical Background

The details of the period of revelation as given above, point to the conditions in which this Sūrah was revealed. During the first five years of his appointment as a Prophet, the Prophet had been extending invitation to God's Religion by presenting the Divine Revelations before the people only in private and restricted meetings and assemblies. During this whole period he could never have a chance to recite the Qur'ān before a common gathering openly, mainly because of the strong opposition and resistance from the disbelievers. They were well aware of how magnetic and captivating the Prophet's personality was and in addition were impressed by the Revelations of the Qur'ān and his way of preaching. Therefore, they tried their best to avoid hearing it themselves and to stop others also from hearing it and to suppress his invitation by false propaganda by spreading every kind of suspicion against him. For this object, on the one hand, they were telling the people that Muhammad had gone astray and was now bent upon misleading others as well; on the other hand, they would raise an uproar whenever he tried to present the Qur'ān before the people so that no one could know what it was for which he was being branded as a misled and misguided person.

Such were the conditions when the Prophet suddenly stood up one day to make a speech in the sacred precincts of the Ka'bāh, where a large number of the Quraysh had gathered together. God at that time made him deliver this discourse, which we have now in the form of the Sūrah An-Najm with us. Such was the intensity of the impression that when the Prophet started reciting it, the opponents were so completely overwhelmed that they could not think of raising any disorder, and when at the conclusion he fell down in prostration, they too fell down in prostration along with him. Later they felt great remorse at the weakness they had involuntarily shown. The people also started taunting them to the effect that whereas they had been forbidding others to listen to the Qur'ān, that day not only had they themselves listened to it, with complete absorption but had even fallen down in prostration along with Muhammad. At last, they had to invent a story in order to get rid of the people's taunt and ridicule. They said, *"After he had recited afara'ait-ul Lata wal Uzza wa Manat ath-thalitha-al ukhra, we heard from Muhammad the words: tilk al-gharaniqa- tal-'ula, wa anna shafa'at-u-hunna latarja: 'They are exalted Goddesses: indeed, their intercession may be expected.' From this we understood that Muhammad had returned to our faith."* As a matter of fact, only a mad person could think that in the context of this Sūrah the sentences they claimed to have heard could have any place and relevance.

**Subject Matter and Topics**

The theme of the discourse is to warn the disbelievers of Makkah about the error of the attitude that they had adopted towards the Qur'ān and the Prophet Muhammad.

The discourse starts in a way as if to say: "Muhammad is neither deluded nor gone astray, as you are telling others in your propaganda against him, nor has he fabricated this teaching of Islām and its message, as you seem to think he has. In fact, whatever he is presenting is nothing but Revelation which is sent down to him. The verities that he presents before you, are not the product of his own assumtions and speculation but realities of which he himself is an eye witness. He has himself seen the Angel through whom this knowledge is conveyed to him. He has been directly made to observe the great Signs of his Lord: whatever he says is not what he has himself thought out but what he has seen with his own eyes. Therefore, your disputing and wrangling with him is just like the disputing and wrangling of a blind man with a man of sight over a thing which the blind man cannot see but he can see."

After this, three things have been presented in their successive order: First, the listeners have been made to understand that: "The religion that you are following is based on mere conjecture and invented ideas. You have set up a few goddesses like Lat and Manat and Uzza as your deities, whereas they have no share whatever in divinity. You regard the angels as the daughters of God, whereas you regard a daughter as disgraceful for your own selves. You think that these deities of yours can influence God in your favor, whereas the fact is that all the angels together, who are stationed closest to God, cannot influence Him even in their own favor. None of such beliefs that you have adopted, is based on knowledge and reason, but are wishes and desires for the sake of which you have taken some whims as realities. This is a grave error. The right and true religion is that which is in conformity to the reality, and the reality is never subject to the people's wishes and desires so that whatever they may regard as a reality and truth should become the reality and truth. Speculation and conjecture cannot help to determine as to what is according to the truth and what is not; it is knowledge. When that knowledge is presented before you, you turn away from it, and brand the one who tells you the truth as misguided. The actual cause of your being involved in this error is that you are heedless of the Hereafter. Only this world is your goal. Therefore, you have neither any desire for the knowledge of reality, nor do you bother to see whether the beliefs you hold are according to the truth or not.

Secondly, the people have been told that: God is the Master and Sovereign of the entire Universe. The righteous is he who follows His way, and the misguided he who has turned away from His way. The error of the misguided and the righteousness of the righteous are not hidden from Him. He knows whatever everyone is doing: He will requite the evil with evil and the good with good. The final judgment will not depend on what you consider yourself to be, and on tall claims you make of your purity and chastity but on whether you are pious or impious, righteous or unrighteous, in the sight of God. If you refrain from major sins, He in His mercy will overlook your minor errors."

Thirdly, a few basic principles of the true Religion which had been presented hundreds of years before the revelation of the Qur'ān in the Books of the Prophets Abraham and Moses have been reiterated so that the people did not remain involved in the misunderstanding that the Prophet Muhammad had brought some new and novel religion, but they should know that these are the fundamental truths which the former Prophets of God have always been presenting in their respective ages. Besides, the same Books have been quoted to confirm the historical facts that the destruction of the 'Aad and the Thamūd and of the people of the Prophets Noah and Lot was not the result of accidental calamities, but God has destroyed them in consequence of the same wickedness and rebellion from which the disbelievers of Makkah were not inclined to refrain and desist in any case.

After presenting these themes and discourses the Sūrah has been concluded, thus: "The Hour of Judgment has approached near at hand, which no one can avert. Before the occurrence of that Hour you are being warned through Muhammad and the Qur'ān in the like manner as the former people had been warned before. Now, is it this warning that you find novel and strange? Which you mock and ridicule? Which you turn away from and cause disorder so that no one else also is able to hear what it is? Don't you feel like weeping at your folly and ignorance? Abandon this attitude and behaviour, bow down to God and serve Him alone!"

This was that impressive conclusion hearing which even the most hardened deniers of the Truth were completely overwhelmed, and when after reciting these verses of Divine Word the Messenger of God fell down in prostration, they too could not help falling down in prostration along with him.

## Sūrah 53: an-Najm[1452]

In the Name of God, the Most Compassionate, the Most Merciful

1. By the star when it descends,

2. Your companion [i.e., Muhammad] has not strayed, nor has he erred,

3. Nor does he speak from [his own] inclination.

4. It is not but a revelation revealed,

5. Taught to him by one intense in strength [i.e., Gabriel] -

6. One of soundness.[1453] And he rose to [his] true form[1454]

7. While he was in the higher [part of the] horizon.[1455]

8. Then he approached and descended

9. And was at a distance of two bow lengths or nearer.

10. And he revealed to His Servant[1456] what he revealed [i.e., coveyed].

11. The heart[1457] did not lie [about] what it saw.

12. So will you dispute with him over what he saw?

13. And he certainly saw him in another descent[1458]

14. At the Lote Tree of the Utmost Boundary -

15. Near it is the Garden of Refuge [i.e., Paradise] -

16. When there covered the Lote Tree that which covered [it].[1459]

17. The sight [of the Prophet] did not swerve, nor did it transgress [its limit].

18. He certainly saw of the greatest signs of his Lord.

19. So have you considered al-Lāt and al-'Uzzā?

20. And Manāt, the third - the other one?[1460]

21. Is the male for you and for Him the female?

22. That, then, is an unjust division.[1461]

23. They are not but [mere] names you have named them - you and your forefathers - for which God has sent down no authority. They follow not except assumption and what [their] souls desire, and there has already come to them from their Lord guidance.

[1452] *An-Najm*: The Star.

[1453] *i.e.*, strength of body and of mind.

[1454] Gabriel appeared to Muhammad at the outset of his prophethood in the angelic form in which God originally created him.

[1455] i.e., in the sky, above the eastern horizon.

[1456] i.e., to the Servant of God, Prophet Muhammad.

[1457] i.e., mind or perception (of the Prophet)

[1458] i.e., on another occasion. During his ascent into the heavens (*al-Mi'rāj*), the Prophet also saw Gabriel in his true form.

[1459] Then and there he saw Gabriel in angelic form.

[1460] The three names given in this and the previous verse are those of well-known "goddesses" which were worshipped by the pagan Arabs before the spread of Islām.

[1461] According to their own standards.

24. Or is there for man whatever he wishes?

25. Rather, to God belongs the Hereafter and the first [life].

26. And how many angels there are in the heavens whose intercession will not avail at all except [only] after God has permitted [it] to whom He wills and approves.

27. Indeed, those who do not believe in the Hereafter name the angels female names,

28. And they have thereof no knowledge. They follow not except assumption, and indeed, assumption avails not against the truth at all.

29. So turn away from whoever turns his back on Our message and desires not except the worldly life.

30. That is their sum of knowledge. Indeed, your Lord is most knowing of who strays from His way, and He is most knowing of who is guided.

31. And to God belongs whatever is in the heavens and whatever is in the earth - that He may recompense those who do evil with [the penalty of] what they have done and recompense those who do good with the best [reward] -

32. Those who avoid the major sins and immoralities, only [committing] slight ones. Indeed, your Lord is vast in forgiveness. He was most knowing of you when He produced you from the earth and when you were fetuses in the wombs of your mothers. So do not claim yourselves to be pure; He is most knowing of who fears Him.

33. Have you seen the one who turned away

34. And gave a little and [then] refrained?

35. Does he have knowledge of the unseen, so he sees?[1462]

36. Or has he not been informed of what was in the scriptures of Moses

37. And [of] Abraham, who fulfilled [his obligations] -

38. That no bearer of burdens will bear the burden of another

39. And that there is not for man except that [good] for which he strives

40. And that his effort is going to be seen -

41. Then he will be recompensed for it with the fullest recompense

42. And that to your Lord is the finality

43. And that it is He who makes [one] laugh and weep

44. And that it is He who causes death and gives life

45. And that He creates the two mates - the male and female -

46. From a sperm-drop when it is emitted

47. And that [incumbent] upon Him is the other [i.e., next] creation

48. And that it is He who enriches and suffices

1462 Knows that his provision will be exhausted if he spends on the poor, while God has promised otherwise.

49. And that it is He who is the Lord of Sirius[1463]

50. And that He destroyed the first [people of] 'Aad

51. And Thamūd - and He did not spare [them] -

52. And the people of Noah before. Indeed, it was they who were [even] more unjust and oppressing.

53. And the overturned towns[1464] He hurled down

54. And covered them by that which He covered.[1465]

55. Then which of the favors of your Lord do you doubt?

56. This [Prophet] is a warner from [i.e., like] the former warners.

57. The Approaching Day has approached.

58. Of it, [from those] besides God, there is no remover.

59. Then at this statement do you wonder?

60. And you laugh and do not weep

61. While you are proudly sporting?[1466]

62. So prostrate to God and worship [Him].

---

[1463] A star worshipped by some of the pagan Arabs.
[1464] Whose inhabitants defied Prophet Lot.
[1465] i.e., a rain of stones.
[1466] Additional meanings are "singing [with expanded chest]," "heedless," or "lost in vain amusements."

## Sūrah 54: al-Qamar

### Period of Revelation

The incident of the shaqq-al-Qamar (splitting of the moon) that has been mentioned in this Sūrah, determines its period of revelation precisely. The traditionists and commentators are agreed that this incident took place at Mina in Makkah about five years before the Prophet's Hijra (migration) to Madinah.

### Theme and Subject Matter

In this Sūrah the disbelievers of Makkah have been warned for their stubbornness which they had adopted against the invitation of the Prophet. The amazing and wonderful phenomenon of the splitting of the Moon was a manifest sign of the truth that the Resurrection, of which the Prophet was giving them the news, could take place and that it had approached near at hand. The great sphere of the Moon had split into two distinct parts in front of their very eyes. The two parts had separated and receded so much apart from each other that to the on-lookers one part had appeared on one side of the mountain and the other on the other side of it. Then, in an instant the two had rejoined. This was a manifest proof of the truth that the system of the Universe was neither eternal nor immortal, it could be disrupted. Huge stars and planets could split asunder, disintegrate, collide with each other, and everything that had been depicted in the Qur'ān in connection with the description of the details of Resurrection, could happen. Not only this: it was also a portent that the disintegration of the system of the Universe had begun and the time was near when Resurrection would take place. The Prophet invited the people's attention to this event only with this object in view and asked them to mark it and be a witness to it. But the disbelievers described it as a magical illusion and persisted in their denial. For this stubbornness they have been reproached in this Sūrah.

At the outset it has been said: "These people neither believe in the admonition, nor learn a lesson from history, nor affirm faith after witnessing manifest signs with their eyes. Now they would believe only when Resurrection has taken place and they would be rushing out of their graves towards the Summoner on that Day." Then, the stories of the people of Noah and of 'Aad and Thamūd and of the peoples of Lot and the Pharaoh have been related briefly and they have been reminded of the terrible punishments that these nations suffered when they belied and disregarded the warnings given by the Prophets of God. After the narration of each story the refrain that has been provided is: "This Qur'ān is an easy means of admonition, which if a nation takes to heart and thereby takes the Right Way, the torment that descended on the former nations could be avoided. But it would indeed be a folly if instead of heeding the admonition through this easy means, one persisted in heedlessness and disbelieved until one was overtaken by the torment itself."

Likewise, after citing admonitory precedents from the history of the former nations, the disbelievers at Makkah have been addressed and warned to this effect: "If you too adopt the same attitude and conduct for which the other nations have already been punished, why will you not be punished for it? Are you in any way a superior people that you should be treated differently from others? Or, have you received a deed of amnesty that you will not be punished for the crime for which others have been punished? And if you feel elated at your great numbers, you will soon see that these very numbers of yours are put to rout (on the battlefield) and on the Day of Resurrection you will be dealt with even more severely." In the end, the disbelievers have been told that God does not need to make lengthy preparations to bring about Resurrection. No sooner does He give a simple command for it than it will take place immediately. Like everything else the Universe and mankind also have a destiny. According to this destiny everything happens at its own appointed time. It cannot be so that whenever somebody gives a challenge, Resurrection is brought about in order to convince him. If you adopt rebellion because you do not see it coming, you will only be adding to your own distress and misfortune. For your record which is being prepared by Divine agents, has not left any misdeed of yours, great or small, unrecorded.

## Sūrah 54: al-Qamar[1467]

In the Name of God, the Most Compassionate, the Most Merciful

1. The Hour has come near, and the moon has split [in two].[1468]

2. And if they see a sign [i.e., miracle], they turn away and say, "Passing magic."[1469]

3. And they denied and followed their inclinations. But for every matter is a [time of] settlement.

4. And there has already come to them of information that in which there is deterrence -

5. Extensive wisdom - but warning does not avail [them].

6. So leave them, [O Muhammad]. The Day the Caller[1470] calls to something forbidding,

7. Their eyes humbled, they will emerge from the graves as if they were locusts spreading,

8. Racing ahead toward the Caller. The disbelievers will say, "This is a difficult Day."

9. The people of Noah denied before them, and they denied Our servant and said, "A madman," and he was repelled.

10. So he invoked his Lord, "Indeed, I am overpowered, so help."

11. Then We opened the gates of the heaven with rain pouring down

12. And caused the earth to burst with springs, and the waters met for a matter already predestined.

13. And We carried him on a [construction of] planks and nails,

14. Sailing under Our observation as reward for he who had been denied.

15. And We left it as a sign, so is there any who will remember?

16. And how [severe] were My punishment and warning.[1471]

17. And We have certainly made the Qur'ān easy for remembrance, so is there any who will remember?

18. 'Aad denied; and how [severe] were My punishment and warning.

19. Indeed, We sent upon them a screaming wind on a day of continuous misfortune,

20. Extracting the people[1472] as if they were trunks of palm trees uprooted.

21. And how [severe] were My punishment and warning.

22. And We have certainly made the Qur'ān easy for remembrance, so is there any who will remember?

---

1467 *Al-Qamar*: The Moon.

1468 This was a sign given by God to Prophet Muhammad when the Quraysh challenged him to show them a miracle.

1469 Or "continuing magic."

1470 Said to be an angel announcing the account and judgement.

1471 To those after them, who were expected to derive a lesson from previous occurrences.

1472 From their hiding places.

23. Thamūd denied the warning

24. And said, "Is it one human being[1473] among us that we should follow? Indeed, we would then be in error and madness.

25. Has the message been sent down upon him from among us? Rather, he is an insolent liar."

26. They will know tomorrow who is the insolent liar.

27. Indeed, We are sending the she-camel as trial for them, so watch them and be patient.[1474]

28. And inform them that the water is shared between them ,[1475] each [day of] drink attended [by turn].

29. But they called their companion,[1476] and he dared[1477] and hamstrung [her].

30. And how [severe] were My punishment and warning.

31. Indeed, We sent upon them one shriek [i.e., blast from the sky], and they became like the dry twig fragments of an [animal] pen.

32. And We have certainly made the Qur'ān easy for remembrance, so is there any who will remember?

33. The people of Lot denied the warning.

34. Indeed, We sent upon them a storm of stones, except the family of Lot - We saved them before dawn

35. As favor from Us. Thus do We reward he who is grateful.

36. And he had already warned them of Our assault, but they disputed the warning.

37. And they had demanded from him his guests, but We obliterated their eyes, [saying], "Taste My punishment and warning."

38. And there came upon them by morning an abiding punishment.

39. So taste My punishment and warning.

40. And We have certainly made the Qur'ān easy for remembrance, so is there any who will remember?

41. And there certainly came to the people of Pharaoh warning.

42. They denied Our signs, all of them, so We seized them with a seizure of one Exalted in Might and Perfect in Ability.

43. Are your disbelievers better than those [former ones], or have you immunity in the scriptures?

44. Or do they say, "We are an assembly supporting [each other]"?

45. [Their] assembly will be defeated, and they will turn their backs [in retreat].[1478]

---

1473 i.e., the Prophet Salih.

1474 This and the following verse are an address to Salih.

1475 i.e., between the tribe of Thamūd and the she-camel – a day for each to drink.

1476 i.e., the worst and most despicable among them.

1477 Or "he took," referring to his sword or to the she-camel.

1478 This foretold event took place on the day of Badr.

46. But the Hour is their appointment [for due punishment], and the Hour is more disastrous and more bitter.

47. Indeed, the criminals are in error and madness.[1479]

48. The Day they are dragged into the Fire on their faces [it will be said], "Taste the touch of Saqar."[1480]

49. Indeed, all things We created with predestination.

50. And Our command is but one, like a glance of the eye.

51. And We have already destroyed your kinds,[1481] so is there any who will remember?

52. And everything they did is in written records.

53. And every small and great [thing] is inscribed.

54. Indeed, the righteous will be among gardens and rivers,

55. In a seat of honour near a Sovereign, Perfect in Ability.

---

[1479] Or "in blazing fires."

[1480] One of the proper names of Hell.

[1481] i.e., those similar to you in attitude and behaviour when they rejected God's messengers.

## Sūrah 55: ar-Rahman

### Period of Revelation

The commentators generally hold the view that this is a Makki Sūrah, though according to some traditions which have been cited on the authority of Abdullah bin Abbas, Ikrimah and Qatadah, it was revealed in Madinah.

### Theme and Subject Matter

This is the only Sūrah of the Qur'ān in which besides men, the Jinn - who are the other creation of the earth endowed with freedom of will and action - have been directly addressed. Both men and Jinn have been made to realize the wonders of God's power, His countless blessings, their own helplessness and accountability before Him, and have been warned of the evil consequences of His disobedience and made aware of the best results of His obedience. At several other places in the Qur'ān there are clear pointers to show that like the men the Jinn too are a creation who have been endowed with freedom of will and action and are accountable, who have been granted the freedom of belief and unbelief, of obedience and disobedience, and among them too there are the believers and the unbelievers, the obedient and the rebellious, as among human beings. And among them too there exist such groups as have believed in the Prophets sent by God and in the Divine Books. This Sūrah clearly points out that the message of the Prophet and the Qur'ān is meant both for men and for Jinn and that his Prophethood is not restricted to human beings alone.

Although in the beginning of the Sūrah the address is directed only to human beings, for to them only belongs the vicegerency of the earth, among them only have the Messengers of God been raised, and in their tongues only have the Divine Books been revealed, yet from verse 13 onwards both the men and the Jinn have been addressed and one and the same invitation has been extended to both.

## Sūrah 55: ar-Rahmān[1482]

In the Name of God, the Most Compassionate, the Most Merciful

1. The Most Merciful

2. Taught the Qur'ān,

3. Created man,

4. [And] taught him eloquence.

5. The sun and the moon [move] by precise calculation,

6. And the stars and trees prostrate.[1483]

7. And the heaven He raised and imposed the balance

8. That you not transgress within the balance.

9. And establish weight in justice and do not make deficient the balance.

10. And the earth He laid [out] for the creatures.

11. Therein is fruit and palm trees having sheaths [of dates]

12. And grain having husks and scented plants.

13. So which of the favors of your Lord would you[1484] deny?

14. He created man from clay like [that of] pottery.

15. And He created the jinn from a smokeless flame of fire.

16. So which of the favors of your Lord would you deny?

17. [He is] Lord of the two sunrises and Lord of the two sunsets.[1485]

18. So which of the favors of your Lord would you deny?

19. He released the two seas,[1486] meeting [side by side];

20. Between them is a barrier [so] neither of them transgresses.

21. So which of the favors of your Lord would you deny?

22. From both of them emerge pearl and coral.

23. So which of the favors of your Lord would you deny?

24. And to Him belong the ships [with sails] elevated in the sea like mountains.

25. So which of the favors of your Lord would you deny?

26. Everyone upon it [i.e., the earth] will perish,

27. And there will remain the Face[1487] of your Lord, Owner of Majesty and Honour.

28. So which of the favors of your Lord would you deny?

---

[1482] *Ar-Rahmān*: The Most Merciful, or more literally, "The Entirely Merciful." See footnote to 1:1.
[1483] They submit obediently to the laws of God. See 22:18.
[1484] Literally, "you two," addressing the species of mankind and *jinn*.
[1485] i.e., the points of sunrise in the east and sunset in the west in both summer and winter.
[1486] The two bodies of water: fresh and salt.
[1487] See footnote to 2:19.

29. Whoever is within the heavens and earth asks Him; every day He is in [i.e., bringing about] a matter.[1488]

30. So which of the favors of your Lord would you deny?

31. We will attend to you, O prominent beings.[1489]

32. So which of the favors of your Lord would you deny?

33. O company of jinn and mankind, if you are able to pass beyond the regions of the heavens and the earth, then pass. You will not pass except by authority [from God].

34. So which of the favors of your Lord would you deny?

35. There will be sent upon you a flame of fire and smoke,[1490] and you will not defend yourselves.

36. So which of the favors of your Lord would you deny?

37. And when the heaven is split open and becomes rose-colored like oil[1491] -

38. So which of the favors of your Lord would you deny? -

39. Then on that Day none will be asked about his sin among men or jinn.[1492]

40. So which of the favors of your Lord would you deny?

41. The criminals will be known by their marks, and they will be seized by the forelocks and the feet.

42. So which of the favors of your Lord would you deny?

43. This is Hell, which the criminals deny.

44. They will go around between it and scalding water, heated [to the utmost degree].

45. So which of the favors of your Lord would you deny?

46. But for he who has feared the position of his Lord[1493] are two gardens -

47. So which of the favors of your Lord would you deny? -

48. Having [spreading] branches.

49. So which of the favors of your Lord would you deny?

50. In both of them are two springs, flowing.

51. So which of the favors of your Lord would you deny?

52. In both of them are of every fruit, two kinds.

53. So which of the favors of your Lord would you deny?

54. [They are] reclining on beds whose linings are of silk brocade, and the fruit of the two gardens is hanging low.

---

1488 For each of His creatures.

1489 Specifically two: mankind and *jinn*.

1490 Another possible meaning is liquefied brass or copper.

1491 Or "like a tanned skin."

1492 Once they have been condemned to the Fire.

1493 An alternative meaning is "the standing [for account] before his Lord."

55. So which of the favors of your Lord would you deny?

56. In them are women limiting [their] glances,[1494] untouched[1495] before them by man or jinnī -

57. So which of the favors of your Lord would you deny? -

58. As if they were rubies and coral.[1496]

59. So which of the favors of your Lord would you deny?

60. Is the reward for good [anything] but good?

61. So which of the favors of your Lord would you deny?

62. And below them both [in excellence] are two [other] gardens -

63. So which of the favors of your Lord would you deny? -

64. Dark green [in color].

65. So which of the favors of your Lord would you deny?

66. In both of them are two springs, spouting.

67. So which of the favors of your Lord would you deny?

68. In both of them are fruit and palm trees and pomegranates.

69. So which of the favors of your Lord would you deny?

70. In them are good and beautiful women -

71. So which of the favors of your Lord would you deny? -

72. Fair ones reserved in pavilions -

73. So which of the favors of your Lord would you deny? -

74. Untouched before them by man or jinnī -

75. So which of the favors of your Lord would you deny? -

76. Reclining on green cushions and beautiful fine carpets.

77. So which of the favors of your Lord would you deny?

78. Blessed is the name of your Lord, Owner of Majesty and Honour.

[1494] To their own mates, i.e., being chaste and modest.

[1495] Literally, they have not been caused to bleed by loss of virginity.

[1496] In purity, colour and beauty.

## Sūrah 56: al-Wāqi'ah

### Period of Revelation

According to the chronological order that Abdullah bin Abbas has given of the Sūrahs, first Sūrah Tā Hā was sent down, then al-Wāqi'ah and then ash-Shuara.

### Theme and Subject Matter

Its theme is the Hereafter, Tawhid (Oneness of God) and refutation of the Makkan disbelievers suspicions about the Qur'ān. What they regarded as utterly incredible was that Resurrection would ever take place, then the entire system of the earth and heavens would be upset, and when all the dead would be resurrected and called to account, after which the righteous would be admitted to Paradise and the wicked cast into Hell. They regarded all this as imaginary, which could not possibly happen in actual fact. In answer to this, it was said: "When the inevitable event will take place, there will be none to believe its happening, nor will anyone have the Power to avert it, nor prove it to be an unreal happening. At that time all nations will be divided into three classes:

1. The foremost in rank and position;
2. The common righteous people;
3. Those who denied the Hereafter and persisted in disbelief and polytheism and major sins till the last.

How these three classes of the people will be rewarded and punished has been described in detail in v. 7-56.

Then, in v. 57-74 arguments have been given, one after the other, to prove the truth of the two basic doctrines of Islām, which the disbelievers were refusing to accept; the doctrines of Tawhid (oneness of God) and the Hereafter. In these arguments, apart from everything else that exists in the earth and heavens, man's attention has been drawn to his own body and to the food that he eats and to the water that he drinks and to the fire on which he cooks his food, and he has been invited to ponder the question: What right do you have to behave independently of, or serve any other than, the God Whose creative power has brought you into being, and Whose provisions sustain you? And how can you entertain the idea that after having once brought you into existence He has become so helpless and powerless that He cannot recreate you once again even if he wills to?

Then, in v. 75-82 their suspicions in respect of the Qur'ān have been refuted and they have been made to realize how fortunate they are that instead of deriving any benefit from the great blessing that the Qur'ān is, they are treating it with scarce attention and have set only this share of theirs in it that they deny it. If one seriously considers this matchless argument that has been presented in two brief sentences about the truth of the Qur'ān, one will find in it the same kind of firm and stable system as exists among the stars and planets of the Universe - and the same is the proof of the fact that its Author is the same Being Who has created the Universe. Then the disbelievers have been told that this Book is inscribed in that Writ of Destiny which is beyond the reach of the creatures, as if to say "You think it is brought down by the devils to Muhammad, whereas none but the pure angels has any access to the means by which it reaches Muhammad from the well guarded Tablet."

In conclusion, man has been warned, as if to say: "You may brag and boast as you like and may shut your eyes to the truths in your arrogance of independence, but death is enough to open your eyes. At death you become helpless: you cannot save your own parents; you cannot save your children; you cannot save your religious guided and beloved leaders. They all die in front of your very eyes while you look on helplessly. If there is no supreme power ruling over you, and this assumption is correct that you are all in all in the world, and there is no God, then why don't you restore to the dying person his soul? Just as you are helpless in this, so it is also beyond your power to stop God from calling the people to account and mete out rewards and punishments to them. You may or may not believe it, but every dying person will surely see his own end after death. If he belongs to those nearest to God, he will see the good end meant for them if he be from among the righteous, he will see the end prepared for the righteous; and if he be from among the deniers of the truth, he will see the end destined for the criminals.

## Sūrah 56: al-Wāqi'ah[1497]

In the Name of God, the Most Compassionate, the Most Merciful

1. When the Occurrence occurs,

2. There is, at its occurrence, no denial.

3. It will bring down [some] and raise up [others].[1498]

4. When the earth is shaken with convulsion

5. And the mountains are broken down, crumbling

6. And become dust dispersing.

7. And you become [of] three kinds:

8. Then the companions of the right - what are the companions of the right?[1499]

9. And the companions of the left - what are companions of the left?[1500]

10. And the forerunners, the forerunners[1501] -

11. Those are the ones brought near [to God]

12. In the Gardens of Pleasure,

13. A [large] company of the former peoples

14. And a few of the later peoples,

15. On thrones woven [with ornament],

16. Reclining on them, facing each other.

17. There will circulate among them young boys made eternal

18. With vessels, pitchers and a cup [of wine] from a flowing spring -

19. No headache will they have therefrom, nor will they be intoxicated -

20. And fruit of what they select

21. And the meat of fowl, from whatever they desire.

22. And [for them are] fair women with large, [beautiful] eyes,

23. The likenesses of pearls well-protected,

24. As reward for what they used to do.

25. They will not hear therein ill speech or commission of sin -

26. Only a saying: "Peace, peace."

27. The companions of the right - what are the companions of the right?

28. [They will be] among lote trees with thorns removed

29. And [banana] trees layered [with fruit]

30. And shade extended

31. And water poured out

---

1497 *Al-Wāqi'ah*: The Occurrence, literally, "That which befalls," meaning the Resurrection.
1498 According to their deeds rather than wealth and social position, as is the case in this world.
1499 i.e., those given their records in their right hand and who are destined for Paradise.
1500 i.e., those given their records in their left hand and who are destined for Hell.
1501 The words can also be understood as a complete sentence, i.e., "The forerunners [in good deeds] are the forerunners [in entering Paradise]."

32. And fruit, abundant [and varied],

33. Neither limited [to season] nor forbidden,

34. And [upon] beds raised high.

35. Indeed, We have produced them [i.e., the women of Paradise] in a [new] creation

36. And made them virgins,

37. Devoted [to their husbands] and of equal age,

38. For the companions of the right [who are]

39. A company of the former peoples

40. And a company of the later peoples.

41. And the companions of the left - what are the companions of the left?

42. [They will be] in scorching fire and scalding water

43. And a shade of black smoke,

44. Neither cool nor beneficial.

45. Indeed they were, before that, indulging in affluence,

46. And they used to persist in the great violation,[1502]

47. And they used to say, "When we die and become dust and bones, are we indeed to be resurrected?

48. And our forefathers [as well]?"

[1502] i.e., *shirk* (association with God) or disbelief.

49. Say, [O Muhammad], "Indeed, the former and the later peoples

50. Are to be gathered together for the appointment of a known Day."

51. Then indeed you, O those astray [who are] deniers,

52. Will be eating from trees of zaqqūm

53. And filling with it your bellies

54. And drinking on top of it from scalding water

55. And will drink as the drinking of thirsty camels.

56. That is their accommodation on the Day of Recompense.

57. We have created you, so why do you not believe?

58. Have you seen that which you emit?[1503]

59. Is it you who creates it, or are We the Creator?

60. We have decreed death among you, and We are not to be outdone

61. In that We will change your likenesses and produce you in that [form] which you do not know.[1504]

62. And you have already known the first creation, so will you not remember?

[1503] i.e., semen, which contains the potential for human life.

[1504] An alternative meaning has also been given: "...in that We will replace the likes of you [with others upon the earth] and create you [in the Hereafter] in that which you do not know."

63. And have you seen that [seed] which you sow?

64. Is it you who makes it grow, or are We the grower?

65. If We willed, We could make it [dry] debris, and you would remain in wonder,[1505]

66. [Saying], "Indeed, we are [now] in debt;

67. Rather, we have been deprived."

68. And have you seen the water that you drink?

69. Is it you who brought it down from the clouds, or is it We who bring it down?

70. If We willed, We could make it bitter, so why are you not grateful?

71. And have you seen the fire that you ignite?

72. Is it you who produced its tree, or are We the producer?

73. We have made it a reminder[1506] and provision for the travelers,[1507]

74. So exalt the name of your Lord, the Most Great.

75. Then I swear by the setting of the stars,[1508]

[1505] At what had happened or remain in a state of shock. Another meaning is "in regret."
[1506] Of the great fire of Hell.
[1507] In the form of flints or other means by which to ignite fire. Travellers are mentioned because of the special convenience to them, although it is a provision for all people in general.
[1508] God confirms absolutely by oath.

76. And indeed, it is an oath - if you could know - [most] great.

77. Indeed, it is a noble Qur'ān

78. In a Register well-protected;[1509]

79. None touch it except the purified [i.e., the angels].

80. [It is] a revelation from the Lord of the worlds.

81. Then is it to this statement that you are indifferent

82. And make [the thanks for] your provision that you deny [the Provider]?

83. Then why, when it [i.e., the soul at death] reaches the throat

84. And you are at that time looking on -

85. And We [i.e., Our angels] are nearer to him than you, but you do not see -

86. Then why do you not, if you are not to be recompensed,

87. Bring it back,[1510] if you should be truthful?

88. And if he [i.e., the deceased] was of those brought near [to God],

89. Then [for him is] rest and bounty and a garden of pleasure.

90. And if he was of the companions of the right,

[1509] The Preserved Slate (*al-Lawh al-Mahfūth*), which is with God.
[1510] i.e., return the soul to the body, meaning that just as you cannot prevent death when it is decreed, you will not escape the recompense when it is decreed.

91. Then [the angels will say], "Peace for you; [you are] from the companions of the right."

92. But if he was of the deniers [who were] astray,

93. Then [for him is] accommodation of scalding water

94. And burning in Hellfire.

95. Indeed, this is the true certainty,

96. So exalt the name of your Lord, the Most Great.

## Sūrah 57: al-Hadeed

### Period of Revelation

This is unanimously a Madani Sūrah, and a study of its subject matter shows that it was probably sent down some time during the interval between the Battle of Uhud and the Truce of Hudaibiyah. This was the time when the tiny Islāmic State of Madinah had been hemmed in by the disbelievers and the handful of the ill equipped Muslims were entrenched against the combined power of entire Arabia. In this state Islām not only stood in need of the sacrifice of Life from its followers, but it also needed monetary help and assistance. In this Sūrah a forceful appeal has been made for the same. This view is further strengthened by verse 10 in which God has addressed the believers to the effect: "Those of you who would spend and fight after the victory can never be equal to those who have spent and fought before the victory." And the same is supported by the traditions that Ibn Marduyah has related on the authority of Anas. In respect of the verse 'Alam ya'n-i lilladhina aamanu an takhsha'a qulubu-hum li-dhikrillah-i,' he says that 17 years after the commencement of the revelation of the Qur'ān this verse was sent down to arouse the believers to action. Reckoned thus the period of the revelation of this Sūrah falls between the 4th and the 5th year after the Hijra (migration).

### Theme and Subject Matter

The theme of this Sūrah is to exhort the Muslims to spend in the cause of God. At the most critical juncture of the history of Islām when it was engaged in a life and death struggle against Arab paganism, this Sūrah was revealed to persuade the Muslim's to make monetary sacrifices in particular, and to make them realize that Islām did not merely consist in verbal affirmation and some outward practices but its essence and spirit is sincerity towards God and His Religion. The faith of the one who was devoid of this spirit and who regarded his own self and wealth as dearer to himself than God and His Religion, was hollow and therefore of little worth in the sight of God. For this object, first the attributes of God Almighty have been mentioned so that the listeners may fully realize as to Who is addressing them. Then, the following themes have been expressed in sequence:

1. The inevitable demand of the Faith is that one should not avoid spending one's wealth for the sake of God. This would not only be contrary to the Faith but also wrong realistically. For the wealth indeed belongs to God, on which man has been given proprietary rights only as His vicegerent. Yesterday this wealth was in other people's possession; today it is with one particular man, and tomorrow it will pass into someone else's hand. Ultimately, it will go back to God, Who is the inheritor of everything in the universe. The only amount of wealth that will be of any use to a man, is that amount which he spends in the cause of God during the period it is in his possession.
2. Although making sacrifices for the sake of God is commendable in any case, the true worth of these sacrifices is determined by the nature of the occasion. There is an occasion when the power of paganism is overwhelming and there is a danger that it might subdue and overcome Islām completely; there is another occasion when Islām is in a stronger position in its struggle against un-Islām and the believers are attaining victories. Both these states are not equal as regards their respective importance. Therefore, the sacrifices that are made in these different states would also not be equal. Those who sacrifice their lives and expend their wealth to further promote the cause of Islām when it is already strong cannot attain to the rank of those who struggled with their lives and their wealth to promote and uphold the cause of Islām when it was weak.
3. Whatever is spent for the cause of the Truth is a loan on God, and God will not only return it increasing it manifold but will also give from Himself the best reward for it.
4. In the Hereafter the Light shall be bestowed only on those believers who would have spent their wealth in the cause of God. As for the hypocrites who watched and served only their own interests in the world, and who least bothered whether the Truth or falsehood prevailed will be segregated

from the believers in the Hereafter although they might have lived in close association with them in the world. They will be deprived of the Light, and they will be counted among the disbelievers.

5. The Muslims should not behave like those followers of the earlier Books, whose lives have been spent in the worship of the world and whose hearts have become hardened due to negligence with the passage of time. He cannot be a believer whose heart does not melt at the remembrance of God and does not bow to the Truth sent down by Him.
6. The sincere upholders of the Truth and the true witnesses of the Faith in the sight of God are only those believers who spend their wealth in His way sincerely, without any desire of show.
7. The life of this world is only a short lived spring and a means of pride and show. Its sports and pastimes, its adornments and decorations, its pride of place, its wealth and possessions, for which the people try to oppose with one another, are transient. Its likeness is of the crop which flourishes and blooms, then turns pale and then finally is reduced to chaff. The everlasting life is the life hereafter when results of great consequence will be announced. Therefore, if one has to complete with another for something, one should strive for Paradise.
8. Whatever good man meets with and whatever hardship he suffers in the world, are preordained by God. A true believer is he who does not lose heart in affliction and is not puffed up with pride in good times. It is the character of a hypocrite and disbeliever that he is puffed up with pride when God favors him with His blessings, behaved boastfully and shows stinginess when called upon to spend in the cause of the same God Who blessed him, and also counsels others to be stingy like himself.
9. God sent His Messengers with clear signs and the Book and the Law of Justice so that the people may adhere to justice; besides, He sent down iron also so that power may be used to establish the Truth and vanquish falsehood. Thus, God likes to see as to who from among the people would rise to support and succor His true Religion even at the risk of their lives. These opportunities God has created for man's own advantage and development; otherwise God does not stand in need of others for His works.
10. Prophets came from God in the past, and by their preaching some people adopted the Right Path, but most of them persisted in wickedness. Then the Prophet Jesus came, whose teachings brought about many moral improvements in the lives of the people, but his community invented monasticism. Now God has sent the Prophet Muhammad. Those who affirm faith in him and pass their life fearing God's accountability, will be given by God a double share of His mercy and He will bless them with the Light by which they will see and walk the straight path among the crooked paths met with at every step in the life of this world. Although the followers of the earlier revelation regard themselves as the monopolists of God's bounties, the fact remains that God Himself controls His bounties He may bless with these whomever He pleases.

## Sūrah 57: al-Hadeed[1511]

In the Name of God, the Most Compassionate, the Most Merciful

1. Whatever is in the heavens and earth exalts God,[1512] and He is the Exalted in Might, the Wise.

2. His is the dominion of the heavens and earth. He gives life and causes death, and He is over all things competent.

3. He is the First and the Last, the Ascendant[1513] and the Intimate,[1514] and He is, of all things, Knowing.

4. It is He who created the heavens and earth in six days and then established Himself above the Throne.[1515] He knows what penetrates into the earth and what emerges from it and what descends from the heaven and what ascends therein; and He is with you[1516] wherever you are. And God, of what you do, is Seeing.

5. His is the dominion of the heavens and earth. And to God are returned [all] matters.

6. He causes the night to enter the day and causes the day to enter the night, and He is Knowing of that within the breasts.

[1511] *Al-Hadeed*: Iron.
[1512] By praising Him and declaring Him far above and beyond any failure or imperfection.
[1513] Nothing being above Him. Another meaning is "the Apparent," i.e., evident through His creation and revelation.
[1514] Nothing being nearer than Him by way of His knowledge. Another meaning is "the Unapparent," i.e., concealed from man's physical senses.
[1515] See footnote to 2:19.
[1516] In knowledge – observing and witnessing.

7. Believe in God and His Messenger and spend out of that in which He has made you successors. For those who have believed among you and spent,[1517] there will be a great reward.

8. And why do you not believe in God while the Messenger invites you to believe in your Lord and He has taken your covenant, if you should [truly] be believers?

9. It is He who sends down upon His Servant [Muhammad] verses of clear evidence that He may bring you out from darknesses into the light. And indeed, God is to you Kind and Merciful.

10. And why do you not spend in the cause of God while to God belongs the heritage of the heavens and the earth? Not equal among you are those who spent before the conquest [of Makkah] and fought [and those who did so after it]. Those are greater in degree than they who spent afterwards and fought. But to all God has promised the best [reward]. And God, with what you do, is Acquainted.

11. Who is it that would loan God a goodly loan so He will multiply it for him and he will have a noble reward?

12. On the Day you see the believing men and believing women, their light proceeding before them and on their right, [it will be said], "Your good tidings today are [of] gardens beneath which rivers flow, wherein you will abide eternally." That is what is the great attainment.

13. On the [same] Day the hypocrite men and hypocrite women will say to those who believed, "Wait for us that we may

[1517] In ways pleasing to God.

acquire some of your light." It will be said, "Go back behind you[1518] and seek light." And a wall will be placed between them with a door, its interior containing mercy, but on the outside of it is torment.

14. They [i.e., the hypocrites] will call to them [i.e., the believers], "Were we not with you?" They will say, "Yes, but you afflicted yourselves[1519] and awaited [misfortune for us] and doubted, and wishful thinking deluded you until there came the command of God. And the Deceiver [i.e., Satan] deceived you concerning God.

15. So today no ransom will be taken from you or from those who disbelieved. Your refuge is the Fire. It is most worthy of you, and wretched is the destination.

16. Has the time not come for those who have believed that their hearts should become humbly submissive at the remembrance of God and what has come down of the truth? And let them not be like those who were given the Scripture before, and a long period passed over them, so their hearts hardened; and many of them are defiantly disobedient.

17. Know that God gives life to the earth after its lifelessness. We have made clear to you the signs; perhaps you will understand.[1520]

18. Indeed, the men who practice charity and the women who practice charity and [they who] have loaned God a goodly loan - it will be multiplied for them, and they will have a noble reward.

19. And those who have believed in God and His messengers - those are [in the ranks of] the supporters of truth and the martyrs, with their Lord. For them is their reward and their light.[1521] But those who have disbelieved and denied Our verses - those are the companions of Hellfire.

20. Know that the life of this world is but amusement and diversion and adornment and boasting to one another and competition in increase of wealth and children - like the example of a rain whose [resulting] plant growth pleases the tillers; then it dries and you see it turned yellow; then it becomes [scattered] debris. And in the Hereafter is severe punishment and forgiveness from God and approval. And what is the worldly life except the enjoyment of delusion.

21. Race [i.e., compete] toward forgiveness from your Lord and a Garden whose width is like the width of the heavens and earth, prepared for those who believed in God and His messengers. That is the bounty of God which He gives to whom He wills, and God is the possessor of great bounty.

22. No disaster strikes upon the earth or among yourselves except that it is in a register[1522] before We bring it into being - indeed that, for God, is easy -

[1518] To where light was acquired, i.e., in the worldly life.

[1519] By hypocrisy or by falling into temptations.

[1520] That similarly, God can soften a heart after its hardness and guide one who had previously been astray.

[1521] Another accepted meaning is "And those who have believed in God and His messengers – they are the supporters of truth. And the martyrs, with their Lord, will have their reward and their light."

[1522] i.e., the Preserved Slate (*al-Lawh al-Mahfūth*).

23. In order that you not despair over what has eluded you and not exult [in pride] over what He has given you. And God does not like everyone self-deluded and boastful -

24. [Those] who are stingy and enjoin upon people stinginess. And whoever turns away[1523] - then indeed, God is the Free of need, the Praiseworthy.

25. We have already sent Our messengers with clear evidences and sent down with them the Scripture and the balance that the people may maintain [their affairs] in justice. And We sent down [i.e., created] iron, wherein is great military might and benefits for the people, and so that God may make evident those who support Him and His messengers unseen. Indeed, God is Powerful and Exalted in Might.

26. And We have already sent Noah and Abraham and placed in their descendants prophethood and scripture; and among them is he who is guided, but many of them are defiantly disobedient.

27. Then We sent following their footsteps [i.e., traditions] Our messengers and followed [them] with Jesus, the son of Mary, and gave him the Gospel. And We placed in the hearts of those who followed him compassion and mercy and monasticism, which they innovated; We did not prescribe it for them except [that they did so] seeking the approval of God. But they did not observe it with due observance. So We gave the ones who believed among them their reward, but many of them are defiantly disobedient.

28. O you who have believed, fear God and believe in His Messenger; He will [then] give you a double portion of His mercy and make for you a light by which you will walk and forgive you; and God is Forgiving and Merciful.

29. [This is] so that the People of the Scripture may know that they are not able [to obtain] anything from the bounty of God[1524] and that [all] bounty is in the hand[1525] of God; He gives it to whom He wills. And God is the possessor of great bounty.

[1523] Refusing to spend for God's cause or refusing obedience to Him.

[1524] As long as they refuse to believe in the message of God which was conveyed through Muhammad.

[1525] See footnote to 2:19.

## Sūrah 58: al-Mujādilah

### Period of Revelation

There is no hadith to tell as to when this incident of pleading and arguing took place, but there is a hint in the subject matter of the Sūrah on the basis of which it can be said with certainty that it happened some time after the battle of the Trench (Shawwal, 5 A.H.). In Sūrah al-Ahzab, God while negating that an adopted son could be one's real son, had just said this and no more; "And God has not made those of your wives whom you divorce by zihar your mothers." But in that Sūrah there was nothing to the effect that to divorce a wife by zihar was a sin or a crime, nor anything about the legal injunction concerning it. Contrary to it, in this Sūrah the whole law relating to zihar has been laid down, which shows that these detailed injunctions were sent down some time after the brief reference to it in Sūrah al-Ahzab.

### Subject Matter and Topics

In this Sūrah instructions have been given to the Muslims about the different problems that confronted them at that time. From the beginning of the Sūrah to verse 6 legal injunctions about zihar have been given, along with which the Muslims have been strictly warned that it is contrary to their profession of the Faith. That they should still persist in the practices of ignorance after they have accepted Islām, that they should break the bounds set by God, or refuse to abide by them, or that they should make their own rules and regulations contradictory to them. For this there is not only the punishment of disgrace and humiliation in the world but in the Hereafter too there will be strict accountability for it.

In v. 7-10 the hypocrites have been taken to task for their secret whisperings and consultations by which they conspired and intrigued against the Prophet, and because of their hidden malice and grudge greeted him, like the Jews, in a manner as to wish him ill instead of well. In this connection, the Muslims have been consoled, as if to say: "These whisperings of the hypocrites can do no harm to you; therefore, you should go on doing your duty with full trust in God." Besides, they have also been taught this moral lesson: "The true believers, when they talk secretly together, do not talk of sin and transgression and disobedience to the Messenger if they have to talk secretly together they should talk of goodness and piety."

In v. 11-13 the Muslims have been taught certain manners of social behavior and given instructions to eradicate certain social evils which were prevalent among the people then as they are today. If some people are sitting in an assembly, and more people arrive, they do not show even the courtesy as to squeeze in so as to make room for others, with the result that the new-comers have to keep standing, or to sit in the door-way, or to go back, or seeing that there is enough room yet start jumping over the people's heads to find room for themselves. This often used to be experienced in the Prophet's assemblies. Therefore, God gave the instruction, as if to say: "Do not behave selfishly and narrow mindedly in your assemblies but do accommodate the new-comers also with an open heart."

Likewise, another vice found among the people is that when they go on a visit to somebody (an important person, in particular), they prolong their sitting and do not mind at all that encroaching upon his time unduly would cause him hardship. Then, if he tells them to leave, they mind it; if he himself rises up from their assembly, they complain of his lack of manners; if he tells them indirectly that he has some other business also to attend to, for which he needs time, they turn a deaf ear to his request. The Prophet himself also had to experience such misconduct of the people, who in their earnestness to benefit by his teaching did not at all see that they were wasting his precious time so badly needed for other important works. At last, God in order to eradicate this bad manner, enjoined that when the people are asked to rise up from an assembly, they should rise up and disperse.

Another vice prevalent among the people was that each person wished to have secret counsel individually with the Prophet without any real need, or would like that he should approach him during an assembly and whisper something to him. This was not only embarrassing for the Prophet but also annoying for the people who sat in the assembly. That is why God imposed the restriction that anyone who wanted to consult him in private, should first give away something in charity. The object was that the people should be warned of this bad manner and made to give it up. Thus, the restriction was kept in force for a short while, and when the people had corrected their behavior, it was withdrawn.

From verse 14 to the end of the Sūrah members of the Muslim society, which was a mixture of the sincere Muslims and the hypocrites and the waverers, have been told plainly as to what is the criterion of sincerity in Islām. One kind of Muslims are those who are friends with the enemies of Islām: they do not hesitate for the sake of their interests to be treacherous to the religion which they profess to believe in; they spread all sorts of doubts and suspicions against Islām and prevent the people from adopting the Way of God. But since they are part of the Muslim community their false profession of Faith serves them as a cover and shield. The second kind of Muslims are those who, in the matter of God's Religion, do not care even for their own father, brother, children, and family, to say nothing of others. They do not cherish any feeling of love for the person who is an enemy of God and His Messenger and His Religion. God in these verses has explicitly stated that the people of the first kind, in fact, belong to Satan's party however hard they may try to convince others of their Islām by swearing oaths. And the honour of belonging to God's party is possessed only by the Muslims of the second kind. They alone are the true Muslims: they alone will attain to true success, and with them alone is God well pleased.

## Sūrah 58: al-Mujādilah[1526]

In the Name of God, the Most Compassionate, the Most Merciful

1. Certainly has God heard the speech of the one who argues [i.e., pleads] with you, [O Muhammad], concerning her husband and directs her complaint to God. And God hears your dialogue; indeed, God is Hearing and Seeing.

2. Those who pronounce thihār[1527] among you [to separate] from their wives - they are not [consequently] their mothers. Their mothers are none but those who gave birth to them. And indeed, they are saying an objectionable statement and a falsehood. But indeed, God is Pardoning and Forgiving.

3. And those who pronounce thihār from their wives and then [wish to] go back on what they said - then [there must be] the freeing of a slave before they touch one another. That is what you are admonished thereby; and God is Acquainted with what you do.

4. And he who does not find [a slave] - then a fast for two months consecutively[1528] before they touch one another; and he who is unable - then the feeding of sixty poor persons. That is for you to believe [completely] in God and His Messenger; and those are the limits [set by] God. And for the disbelievers is a painful punishment.

5. Indeed, those who oppose God and His Messenger are abased as those before them were abased. And We have certainly sent down verses of clear evidence. And for the disbelievers is a humiliating punishment.

6. On the Day when God will resurrect them all and inform them of what they did. God had enumerated it, while they forgot it; and God is, over all things, Witness.

7. Have you not considered that God knows what is in the heavens and what is on the earth? There is in no private conversation three but that He is the fourth of them,[1529] nor are there five but that He is the sixth of them - and no less than that and no more except that He is with them [in knowledge] wherever they are. Then He will inform them of what they did, on the Day of Resurrection. Indeed God is, of all things, Knowing.

8. Have you not considered those who were forbidden from private conversation [i.e., ridicule and conspiracy], then they return to that which they were forbidden and converse among themselves about sin and aggression and disobedience to the Messenger? And when they come to you, they greet you with that [word] by which God does not greet you[1530] and say among themselves, "Why does God not punish us for what we say?" Sufficient for them is Hell, which they will [enter to] burn, and wretched is the destination.

---

[1526] *Al-Mujādilah*: The Arguing (or Pleading) Woman.

[1527] The saying by a husband to his wife, "You are to me like the back of my mother," meaning unlawful to approach. This was a type of divorce practiced by the Arabs before the prophethood of Muhammad.

[1528] See footnote to 4:92.

[1529] Through His knowledge of them and their secrets.

[1530] This is in reference to the Jews who would greet the Muslims with the words "Death be upon you," rather than "Peace."

9. O you who have believed, when you converse privately, do not converse about sin and aggression and disobedience to the Messenger but converse about righteousness and piety. And fear God, to whom you will be gathered.

10. Private conversation is only from Satan that he may grieve those who have believed,[1531] but he will not harm them at all except by permission of God. And upon God let the believers rely.

11. O you who have believed, when you are told, "Space yourselves" in assemblies, then make space; God will make space for you.[1532] And when you are told, "Arise,"[1533] then arise; God will raise those who have believed among you and those who were given knowledge, by degrees. And God is Acquainted with what you do.

12. O you who have believed, when you [wish to] privately consult the Messenger, present before your consultation a charity. That is better for you and purer. But if you find not [the means] - then indeed, God is Forgiving and Merciful.

13. Have you feared to present before your consultation charities? Then when you do not and God has forgiven you, then [at least] establish prayer and give zakāh and obey God and His Messenger. And God is Acquainted with what you do.

14. Have you not considered those who make allies of a people with whom God has become angry? They are neither of you nor of them, and they swear to untruth while they know [they are lying].

15. God has prepared for them a severe punishment. Indeed, it was evil that they were doing.

16. They took their [false] oaths as a cover, so they averted [people] from the way of God, and for them is a humiliating punishment.

17. Never will their wealth or their children avail them against God at all. Those are the companions of the Fire; they will abide therein eternally

18. On the Day God will resurrect them all, and they will swear to Him as they swear to you and think that they are [standing] on something.[1534] Unquestionably, it is they who are the liars.

19. Satan has overcome them and made them forget the remembrance of God. Those are the party of Satan. Unquestionably, the party of Satan - they will be the losers.

20. Indeed, the ones who oppose God and His Messenger - those will be among the most humbled.

21. God has written [i.e., decreed], "I will surely overcome, I and My messen-

[1531] The reference may be to the sinful type of conversation, as mentioned in the previous verses, or to the practice of two persons speaking in confidence in the presence of a third, which might lead him to assume that he is the subject of their conversation. Such behaviour was prohibited by the Prophet in narrations of al-Bukhāri and Muslim.

[1532] In His mercy, in Paradise, or in everything good.

[1533] To prayer, to battle, or to good deeds.

[1534] They assume that their lies will be believed and they will escape detection as they did in worldly life.

gers." Indeed, God is Powerful and Exalted in Might.

22. You will not find a people who believe in God and the Last Day having affection for those who oppose God and His Messenger, even if they were their fathers or their sons or their brothers or their kindred. Those - He has decreed within their hearts faith and supported them with spirit[1535] from Him. And We will admit them to gardens beneath which rivers flow, wherein they abide eternally. God is pleased with them, and they are pleased with Him - those are the party of God. Unquestionably, the party of God - they are the successful.

[1535] i.e., "that which gives life," explained as the guidance of the Qur'ān or victory over their opponents.

## Sūrah 59: al-Hashr

### Period of Revelation

Bukhari and Muslim contain a hadith from Sa'id bin Jubair to the effect "When I asked Abdullah bin Abbas about Sūrah Al-Hashr, he replied that it was sent down concerning the battle against the Banu-Nadheer just as Sūrah Al-Anfal was sent down concerning the Battle of Badr. "As for the question as to when this battle took place, Imām Zuhri has stated on the authority of Urwah bin Zubair that it took place six months after the Battle of Badr. However, Ibn Sa'd, Ibn Hisham and Baladhuri regard it as an event of Rabi' al-Awwal, 4 A.H.

### Historical Background

In order to understand the subject matter of this Sūrah well, it is necessary to have a look at the history of Madinah and the Jews of Hijaz, for without it one cannot know precisely the real causes of the Prophet's dealing with their different tribes the way he did.

No authentic history of the Arabian Jews exists in the world. They have not left any writing of their own in the form of a book or a tablet which might throw light on their past, nor have the Jewish historians and writers of the non-Arab world made any mention of them, the reason being that after their settlement in the Arabian peninsula they had detached themselves from the main body of the nation, and the Jews of the world did not count them as among themselves. For they had given up Hebrew culture and language, even the names, and adopted Arabism instead. In the tablets that have been unearthed in the archaeological research in the Hijaz no trace of the Jews is found before the first century of the Christian era, except for a few Jewish names. Therefore, the history of the Arabian Jews is based mostly on the verbal traditions prevalent among the Arabs most of which are bad, and have been spread by the Jews themselves.

The Jews of the Hijaz claimed that they had come to settle in Arabia during the last stage of the life of the Prophet Moses. They said that the Prophet Moses had despatched an army to expel the Amalekites from the land of Yathrib (previous name of Madinah) and had commanded it not to spare even a single soul of that tribe. The Israelite army carried out the Prophet's command, but spared the life of a handsome prince of the Amalekite king and returned with him to Palestine. By that time the Prophet Moses had passed away. His successors took great exception to what the army had done, for by sparing the life of an Amalekite it had clearly disobeyed the Prophet and violated the Mosaic law. Consequently, they excluded the army from their community, and it had to return to Yathrib and settle there for ever. (Kitab al-Aghani, vol. xix, p. 94). Thus the Jews claimed that they had been living in Yathrib since about 1200 B.C. But, this had in fact no historical basis and probably the Jews had invented this story in order to overawe the Arabs into believing that they were of noble lineage and the original inhabitants of the land.

The second Jewish immigration, according to the Jews, took place in 587 B.C. when Nebuchadnezzer, the king of Babylon, destroyed Jerusalem and dispersed the Jews throughout the world. The Arab Jews said that several of their tribes at that time had come to settle in Wadi al-Qura, Taima, and Yathrib. (Al-Baladhuri, Futuh al-Buldan). But this too has no historical basis. By this also they might have wanted to prove that they were the original settlers of the area.

As a matter of fact, what is established is that when in 70 A.D. The Romans massacred the Jews in Palestine, and then in 132 A.D. expelled them from that land, many of the Jewish tribes fled to find an asylum in the Hijaz, a territory that was contiguous to Palestine in the south. There, they settled wherever they found water springs and greenery, and then by intrigue and through money lending businesses gradually occupied the fertile lands. Ailah, Maqna, Tabūk, Taima, Wadi al Qura, Fadak and Khaiber came under their control in that very period, and Banl Quraidhah, Banu-Nadheer, Bani Bahdal, and Bani-Qaynuqah also came in the same period and occupied Yathrib.

Among the tribes that settled in Yathrib the Banu-Nadheer and the Banū Quraythah were more prominent for they belonged to the Cohen or priest class. They were looked upon as of noble descent and enjoyed religious leadership among their co-religionists. When they came to settle in Madinah (Yathrib) there were some other tribes living there before, whom they subdued and became practically the owners of this green and fertile land. About three centuries later, in 450 or 451 A.D., the great flood of Yemen occurred which has been mentioned in v. 16-17 of Sūrah Saba. As a result of this different tribes of the people of Saba were compelled to leave Yemen and disperse in different parts of Arabia. Thus, the Bani Ghassan went to settle in Syria, Bani Lakhm in Hirah (Iraq), Bani Khuza'ah between Jeddah and Makkah and the Aws and the Khazraj went to settle in Yathrib. As Yathrib was under Jewish domination, they at first did not allow the Aws and the Khazraj to gain a footing and the two Arab tribes had to settle on lands that had not yet been brought under cultivation, where they could hardly produce just enough to enable them to survive. At last, one of their chiefs went to Syria to ask for the assistance of their Ghassanide brothers; he brought an army from there and broke the power of the Jews. Thus, the Aws and the Khazraj were able to gain complete dominance over Yathrib, with the result that two of the major Jewish tribes, Banu-Nadheer and Banū Quraythah were forced to take quarters outside the city. Since the third tribe, Bani-Qaynuqah, was not on friendly terms with the other two tribes, it stayed inside the city as usual, but had to seek protection of the Khazraj tribe. As a counter measure to this Banu-Nadheer and Banū Quraythah took protection of the Aws tribe so that they could live in peace in the suburbs of Yathrib.

Before the Prophet's arrival at Madinah until his emigration the following were the main features of the Jews' position in Hijaz in general and in Madinah (Yathrib) in particular:

1. In the matter of language, dress, civilization and way of life they had completely adopted Arabism, even their names had become Arabian. Of the 12 Jewish tribes that had settled in Hijaz, none except the Bani Zaura retained its Hebrew name. Except for a few scattered scholars none knew Hebrew. In fact, there is nothing in the poetry of the Jewish poets of the pre-Islāmic days to distinguish it from the poetry of the Arab poets in language, ideas and themes. They even intermarried with the Arabs. In fact, nothing distinguished them from the common Arabs except religion. Notwithstanding this, they had not lost their identity among the Arabs and had kept their Jewish prejudice alive most ardently and jealously. They had adopted superficial Arabism because they could not survive in Arabia without it.
2. Because of this Arabism the western orientalists have been misled into thinking that perhaps they were not really Israelites but Arabs who had embraced Judaism, or that at least majority of them consisted of the Arab Jews. But there is no historical proof to show that the Jews ever engaged in any proselytizing activities in Hijaz, or their rabbis invited the Arabs to embrace Judaism like the Christian priests and missionaries. On the contrary, we see that they prided themselves upon their Israelite descent and racial prejudices. They called the Arabs the Gentiles, which did not mean illiterate or uneducated but savage and uncivilized people. They believed that the Gentiles did not possess any human rights; these were only reserved for the Israelites, and therefore, it was lawful and right for the Israelites to defraud them of their properties by every fair and foul means. Apart from the Arab chiefs, they did not consider the common Arabs fit enough to have equal status with them even if they entered Judaism. No historical proof is available, nor is there any evidence in the Arabian traditions, that some Arab tribe or prominent clan might have accepted Judaism. However, mention has been made of some individuals, who had become Jews. The Jews, however, were more interested in their trade and business than in the preaching of their religion. That is why Judaism did not spread as a religion and creed in Hijaz but remained only as a mark of pride and distinction of a few Israelite tribes. The Jewish rabbis, however, had a flourishing business in granting amulets and charms, fortune telling and sorcery, because of which they were held in great awe by the Arabs for their "knowledge" and practical wisdom.
3. Economically they were much stronger than the Arabs. Since they had emigrated from more civilized and culturally advanced countries of Palestine and Syria, they knew many such arts as were unknown to the Arabs; they also enjoyed trade relations with the outside world. Hence, they had

captured the business of importing grain in Yathrib and the upper Hijaz and exporting dried dates to other countries. Poultry farming and fishing also were mostly under their controls. They were good at cloth weaving too. They had also set up wine shops here and there, where they sold wine which they imported from Syria. The Bani-Qaynuqah generally practiced crafts such as that of the goldsmith, blacksmith and vessel makers. In all these occupations, trade and business these Jews earned excessive profits, but their chief occupation was trading in money lending in which they had ensnared the Arabs of the surrounding areas. More particularly the chiefs and elders of the Arab tribes who were given to a life of pomp, bragging and boasting on the strength of borrowed money were deeply indebted to them. They lent money on high rates of interest and then would charge compound interest, which one could hardly clear off once one was involved in it. Thus, they had rendered the Arabs economically hollow, but it had naturally induced a deep rooted hatred among the common Arabs against the Jews.

4. The demand of their trade and economic interests was that they should neither estrange one Arab tribe by befriending another, nor take part in their mutual wars. But, on the other hand, it was also in their interests, that they should not allow the Arabs to be united and should keep them fighting and entrenched against each other, for they knew that whenever the Arab tribes united, they would not allow them to remain in possession of their large properties, gardens and fertile lands, which they had come to own through their profiteering and money lending business. Furthermore, each of their tribes also had to enter into alliance with one or another powerful Arab tribe for the sake of its own protection so that no other powerful tribe should overawe it by its might. Because of this they had not only to take part in the mutual wars of the Arabs but they often had to go to war in support of the Arab tribe to which their tribe was tied in alliance against another Jewish tribe which was allied to the enemy tribe. In Yathrib the Banū Quraythah and the Banu-Nadheer were the allies of the Aws while the Bani-Qaynuqah of the Khazraj. A little before the Prophet's emigration, these Jewish tribes had confronted each other in support of their respective allies in the bloody war that took place between the Aws and the Khazraj at Buath.

Such were the conditions when Islām came to Madinah, and ultimately an Islāmic State came into existence after the Prophet's arrival there. One of the first things that he accomplished soon after establishing this state was unification of the Aws and the Khazraj and the Emigrants into a brotherhood. The second was that he concluded a treaty between the Muslims and the Jews on definite conditions, in which it was pledged that neither party would encroach on the rights of the other, and both would unite in a joint defense against the external enemies. Some important clauses of this treaty are as follows, which clearly show what the Jews and the Muslims had pledged to adhere to in their mutual relationship:

"The Jews must bear their expenses and the Muslims their expenses. Each must help the other against anyone who attacks the people of this document. They must seek mutual advice and consultation, and loyalty is a protection against treachery. They shall sincerely wish one another well. Their relations will be governed by piety and recognition of the rights of others, and not by sin and wrongdoing. The wronged must be helped. The Jews must pay with the believers so long as the war lasts. Yathrib shall be a sanctuary for the people of this document. If any dispute or controversy likely to cause trouble should arise, it must be referred to God and to Muhammad the Apostle of God; Quraysh and their helpers shall not be given protection. The contracting parties are bound to help one another against any attack on Yathrib; Every one shall be responsible for the defense of the portion to which he belongs." (Ibn Hisham, vol. ii, pp. 147 to 150).

This was on absolute and definitive covenant to the conditions of which the Jews themselves had agreed. But not very long after this they began to show hostility towards the Prophet of God and Islām and the Muslims, and their hostility and perverseness went on increasing day by day. Its main causes were three:

First, they envisaged the Prophet merely as a chief of his people, who should be content to have concluded a political agreement with them and should only concern himself with the worldly interests of his group. But they found that he was extending an invitation to belief in God and the Apostleship and the Book (which also included belief in their own Prophets and scriptures), and was urging the people to give up disobedience of God and adopt obedience to the Divine Commands and abide by the moral laws of their own prophets. This they could not put up with. They feared that if this universal ideological movement gained momentum it would destroy their rigid religiosity and wipe out their racial nationhood.

Second, when they saw that the Aws and the Khazraj and the Emigrants were uniting into a brotherhood and the people from the Arab tribes of the surrounding areas, who entered Islām, were also joining this Islāmic Brotherhood of Madinah and forming a religious community, they feared that the selfish policy that they had been following of sowing discord between the Arab tribes for the promotion of their own well being and interests for centuries, would not work in the new system, but they would face a united front of the Arabs against which their scheming and machinations would not succeed.

Third, the work that the Messenger of God was carrying out of reforming the society and civilization included putting an end to all unlawful methods in business and mutual dealings. More than that; he had declared taking and giving of interest also as impure and unlawful earning. This caused them the fear that if his rule became established in Arabia, he would declare interest legally forbidden, and in this they saw their own economic disaster and death.

For these reasons they made resistance and opposition to the Prophet their national ideal. They would never hesitate to employ any trick and machination, any device and cunning, to harm him. They spread every kind of falsehood so as to cause distrust against him in the people's minds. They created every kind of doubt, suspicion and misgiving in the hearts of the new reverts so as to turn them back from Islām. They would make false profession of Islām and then would turn apostate so that it may engender more and more misunderstandings among the people against Islām and the Prophet. They would conspire with the hypocrites to create mischief and would cooperate with every group and tribe hostile to Islām. They would create rifts between the Muslims and would do whatever they could to stir them up to mutual feuds and fighting. The people of the Aws and the Khazraj tribes were their special target, with whom they had been allied for centuries. Making mention of the war of Buath before them they would remind them of their previous enmities so that they might again resort to the sword against each other and shatter their bond of fraternity into which Islām had bound them. They would resort to every kind of deceit and fraud in order to harm the Muslims economically. Whenever one of those with whom they had business dealings, would accept Islām, they would do whatever they could to cause him financial loss. If he owed them something they would worry and harass him by making repeated demands, and if they owed him something, they would withhold the payment and would publicly say that at the time the bargain was made he professed a different religion, and since he had changed his religion, they were no longer under any obligation towards him. Several instances of this nature have been cited in the explanation of verse 75 of Sūrah ali-Imrān given in the commentaries by Tabari, Nisaburi, Tabrisi and in Ruh al Ma'ani.

They had adopted this hostile attitude against the covenant even before the Battle of Badr. But when the Prophet and the Muslims won a decisive victory over the Quraysh at Badr, they were filled with grief and anguish, malice and anger. They were in fact anticipating that in that war the powerful Quraysh would deal a death blow to the Muslims. That is why even before the news of the Islāmic victory reached Madinah they had begun to spread the rumor that the Prophet had fallen a martyr and the Muslims had been routed, and the Quraysh army under Abu Jahl was advancing on Madinah. But when the battle was decided against their hopes and wishes, they burst with anger and grief. Ka'b bin Ashraf, the chief of the Banu-Nadheer, cried out: *"By God, if Muhammad has actually killed these nobles of Arabia, the earth's belly would be better for us than its back."* Then he went to Makkah and incited the people to vengeance by writing and reciting provocative elegies for the Quraysh chiefs killed at Badr. Then he returned to Madinah and composed lyrical verses of an insulting nature about the Muslim women. At last, enraged with his mischief, the Prophet sent Muhammad bin Maslamah Ansāri in Rabi al-Awwal, 3 A.H., and had him slain.

The first Jewish tribe which, after the Battle of Badr, openly and collectively broke their covenant were the Bani-Qaynuqah. They lived in a locality inside the city of Madinah. As they practiced the crafts of the goldsmith, blacksmith and vessel makers, the people of Madinah had to visit their shops fairly frequently. They were proud of their bravery and valor. Being blacksmiths by profession even their children were well armed, and they could instantly muster 700 fighting men from among themselves. They were also arrogantly aware that they enjoyed relations of confederacy with the Khazraj and Abdullah bin Ubbay, the chief of the Khazraj, who was their chief supporter. At the victory of Badr, they became so provoked than they began to trouble and harass the Muslims and their women in particular, who visited their shops. By and by things came to such a pass that one day a Muslim woman was stripped naked publicly in their bazaar. This led to a brawl in which a Muslim and a Jew were killed. Thereupon the Prophet himself visited their locality, got them together and counseled them on decent conduct. But the reply that they gave was; *"O Muhammad, you perhaps think we are like the Quraysh; they did not know fighting; therefore, you overpowered them. But when you come in contact with us, you will see how men fight."* This was in clear words a declaration of war. Consequently, the Prophet laid siege to their quarters towards the end of Shawwal (and according to some others, of Dhul Qa'dah) 2 A.H. The siege had hardly lasted for a fortnight when they surrendered and all their fighting men were tied and taken prisoners. Now Abdullah bin Ubayy came up in support of them and insisted that they should be pardoned. The Prophet conceded his request and decided that the Bani-Qaynuqah would be exiled from Madinah leaving their properties, armor and tools of trade behind.(Ibn Sa'd, Ibn Hisham, Tarikh Tabari).

For some time after these punitive measures (i.e. the banishment of the Qainuqa and killing of Ka'b bin Ashraf) the Jews remained so terror stricken that they did not dare commit any further mischief. But later when in Shawwal, 3 A.H., the Quraysh in order to avenge themselves for the defeat at Badr, marched against Madinah with great preparations, and the Jews saw that only a thousand men had marched out with the Prophet as against three thousand men of the Quraysh, and even they were deserted by 300 hypocrites who returned to Madinah, they committed the first and open breach of the treaty by refusing to join the Prophet in the defense of the city although they were bound to it. Then, when in the Battle of Uhud the Muslims suffered reverses, they were further emboldened. So much so that the Banu-Nadheer made a secret plan to kill the Prophet, though the plan failed before it could be executed. According to the details, after the incident of Bi'r Maunah (Safar, 4 A.H.) Amr bin Umayyah Damri slew by mistake two men of the Bani Amir in retaliation, who actually belonged to a tribe which was allied to the Muslims, but Amr had mistaken them for the men of the enemy. Because of this mistake their blood money became obligatory on the Muslims. Since the Banu-Nadheer were also a party in the alliance with the Bani Amir, the Prophet went to their clan along with some of his Companions to ask for their help in paying the blood money. Outwardly they agreed to contribute, as he wished, but secretly they plotted that a person should go up to the top of the house by whose wall the Prophet was sitting and drop a rock on him to kill him. But before they could execute their plan, God informed him in time and be immediately got up and returned to Madinah.

Now there was no question of showing them any further concession. The Prophet at once sent to them the ultimatum that the treachery they had meditated against him had come to his knowledge; therefore, they were to leave Madinah within ten days; if anyone of them was found staying behind in their quarters, he would be put to the sword. Meanwhile Abduliah bin Ubayy sent them the message that he would help them with two thousand men and that the Banū Quraythah and Banu Ghatafan also would come to their aid; therefore, they should stand firm and should not go. On this false assurance they responded to the Prophet's ultimatum saying that they would not leave Madinah and he could do whatever was in his power. Consequently, in Rabi' al-Awwal, 4 A.H., the Prophet laid siege to them, and after a few days of the siege (which according to some traditions were 6 and according to others 15 days) they agreed to leave Madinah on the condition that they could retain all their property which they could carry on thee camels, except the armour. Thus, Madinah was rid of this second mischievous tribe of Jews. Only two of the Banu-Nadheer became Muslims and stayed behind. Others went to Syria and Khaiber.

**Theme and Subject Matter**

The theme of the Sūrah as stated above, is an appraisal of the battle against the Banu-Nadheer. In this, on the whole, four things have been discussed.

1. In the first four verses the world has been admonished to take heed of the fate that had just befallen the Banu-Nadheer. A major tribe which was as strong in numbers as the Muslims, whose people boasted of far more wealth and possession who were by no means ill-equipped militarily and whose forts were well fortified could not stand siege even for a few days, and expressed their readiness to accept banishment from their centuries-old, well established settlement even though not a single man from among them was slain. God says that this happened not because of any power possessed by the Muslims but because the Jews had tried to resist and fight God and His Messenger, and those who dare to resist the power of God, always meet with the same fate.
2. In verse 5, the rule of the law of war that has been enunciated is: the destruction caused in the enemy territory for military purposes does not come under "spreading mischief in the earth."
3. In v. 6-10 it has been stated how the lands and properties which come under the control of the Islāmic State as a result of war or peace terms, are to be managed. As it was the first ever occasion that the Muslims took control of a conquered territory, the law concerning it was laid down for their guidance.
4. In v. 11-17 the attitude that the hypocrites had adopted on the occasion of the battle against the Banu-Nadheer has been reviewed and the causes underlying it have been pointed out.
5. The whole of the last section (v. 18-24) is an admonition for all those people who had professed to have affirmed the faith and joined the Muslim community, but were devoid of the true spirit of the faith. In it they have been told what is the real demand of the Faith, what is the real difference between piety and wickedness, what is the place and importance of the Qur'ān which they professed to believe in, and what are the attributes of God in Whom they claimed to have believed.

## Sūrah 59: al-Hashr[1536]

In the Name of God, the Most Compassionate, the Most Merciful

1. Whatever is in the heavens and whatever is on the earth exalts God,[1537] and He is the Exalted in Might, the Wise.

2. It is He who expelled the ones who disbelieved among the People of the Scripture[1538] from their homes at the first gathering.[1539] You did not think they would leave, and they thought that their fortresses would protect them from God; but [the decree of] God came upon them from where they had not expected, and He cast terror into their hearts [so] they destroyed their houses by their [own] hands and the hands of the believers. So take warning, O people of vision.

3. And if not that God had decreed for them evacuation, He would have punished them in [this] world, and for them in the Hereafter is the punishment of the Fire.

4. That is because they opposed God and His Messenger. And whoever opposes God - then indeed, God is severe in penalty.

5. Whatever you have cut down of [their] palm trees or left standing on their trunks - it was by permission of God and so He would disgrace the defiantly disobedient.

6. And what God restored [of property] to His Messenger from them - you did not spur for it [in an expedition] any horses or camels,[1540] but God gives His messengers power over whom He wills, and God is over all things competent.

7. And what God restored to His Messenger from the people of the towns - it is for God and for the Messenger and for [his] near relatives[1541] and orphans and the [stranded] traveler[1542] - so that it will not be a perpetual distribution among the rich from among you. And whatever the Messenger has given you - take; and what he has forbidden you - refrain from. And fear God; indeed, God is severe in penalty.

8. For the poor emigrants who were expelled from their homes and their properties, seeking bounty from God and [His] approval and supporting God and His Messenger, [there is also a share]. Those are the truthful.

9. And [also for] those who were settled in the home [i.e., al-Madīnah] and [adopted] the faith before them.[1543] They love those who emigrated to them and find not any want in their breasts of what they [i.e., the emigrants] were given but give [them] preference over themselves, even though they are

[1536] *Al-Hashr*: The Gathering.
[1537] See footnote to 57:1.
[1538] Referring to the Jews of Banu-Na<u>dh</u>eer, who broke their pact with the Messenger of God.
[1539] This was the first time they had ever been gathered and expelled.

[1540] Meaning that they went through no hardship (i.e., war) to obtain it.
[1541] Those of Banā Hāshim and Banū Muttalib, whom he (Muhammad) had prohibited from accepting *zakāh*.
[1542] This ruling concerning properties abandoned by an enemy without a war effort differs from that in *Sūrah al-Anfāl*, verse 41, which refers to spoils of war in which four-fifths is distributed among those who fought in God's cause.
[1543] Before the settlement of the emigrants (Muhājireen) among the Ansār, for whom a share is delegated as well.

in privation. And whoever is protected from the stinginess of his soul - it is those who will be the successful.

10. And [there is a share for] those who came after them, saying, "Our Lord, forgive us and our brothers who preceded us in faith and put not in our hearts [any] resentment toward those who have believed. Our Lord, indeed You are Kind and Merciful."

11. Have you not considered those who practice hypocrisy, saying to their brothers [i.e., associates] who have disbelieved among the People of the Scripture, "If you are expelled, we will surely leave with you, and we will not obey, in regard to you, anyone - ever; and if you are fought, we will surely aid you." But God testifies that they are liars.

12. If they are expelled, they will not leave with them, and if they are fought, they will not aid them. And [even] if they should aid them, they will surely turn their backs; then [thereafter] they will not be aided.

13. You [believers] are more fearful within their breasts than God. That is because they are a people who do not understand.

14. They will not fight you all except within fortified cities or from behind walls. Their violence [i.e., enmity] among themselves is severe. You think they are together, but their hearts are diverse. That is because they are a people who do not reason.

15. [Theirs is] like the example of those shortly before them: they tasted the bad consequence of their affair, and they will have a painful punishment.

16. [The hypocrites are] like the example of Satan when he says to man, "Disbelieve." But when he disbelieves, he says, "Indeed, I am disassociated from you. Indeed, I fear God, Lord of the worlds."

17. So the outcome for both of them is that they will be in the Fire, abiding eternally therein. And that is the recompense of the wrongdoers.

18. O you who have believed, fear God. And let every soul look to what it has put forth for tomorrow - and fear God. Indeed, God is Acquainted with what you do.

19. And be not like those who forgot God, so He made them forget themselves. Those are the defiantly disobedient.

20. Not equal are the companions of the Fire and the companions of Paradise. The companions of Paradise - they are the attainers [of success].

21. If We had sent down this Qur'ān upon a mountain, you would have seen it humbled and coming apart from fear of God. And these examples We present to the people that perhaps they will give thought.

22. He is God, other than whom there is no deity, Knower of the unseen and the witnessed.[1544] He is the Entirely Merciful, the Especially Merciful.

23. He is God, other than whom there is no deity, the Sovereign, the Pure, the Perfection,[1545] the Bestower of Faith,[1546] the Overseer, the Exalted in

[1544] See footnotes to 6:73.

[1545] Literally, "Free" from any imperfection or "the Security."

[1546] Or "of Safety."

Might, the Compeller, the Superior. Exalted is God above whatever they associate with Him.

24. He is God, the Creator, the Inventor, the Fashioner; to Him belong the best names.[1547] Whatever is in the heavens and earth is exalting Him. And He is the Exalted in Might, the Wise.

[1547] As for the names and attributes of God, their translation is surely an impossibility, for even in Arabic they cannot represent more than an approximation limited by human understanding. To any description by God of Himself in human terminology, the mind is required to apply the concept of absoluteness and perfection befitting Him.

## Sūrah 60: al-Mumtahinah

### Period of Revelation

The Sūrah deals with two incidents, the time of the occurrence of which is well known historically. The first relates to Hatib bin Abz Balta'a, who, a little before the conquest of Makkah, had sent a secret letter to the Quraysh chiefs informing them of the Prophet's intention to attack them. The second relates to the Muslim women, who had started emigrating from Makkah to Madinah, after the conclusion of the Truce of Hudaibiyah, and the problem arose whether they also were to be returned to the disbelievers, like the Muslim men, according to the conditions of the Truce. The mention of these two things absolutely determines that this Sūrah came down during the interval between the Truce of Hudaibiyah and the Conquest of Makkah. Besides, there is a third thing also that has been mentioned at the end of the Sūrah to the effect: What should the Prophet make the women to pledge when they come to take the oath of allegiance before him as believers? About this part also the guess is that this too was sent down some time before the conquest of Makkah, for after this conquest a large number of the Quraysh women, like their men, were going to enter Islām simultaneously and had to be administered the oath of allegiance collectively.

### Theme and Topics

This Sūrah has three parts;

The first part consists of v. 1-9, and the concluding verse 13 also relates to it. In this strong exception has been taken to the act of Hatib bin Abi Balta'a in that he had tried to inform the enemy of a very important war secret of the Prophet only for the sake of safe guarding his family. This would have caused great bloodshed at the conquest of Makkah had it not been made ineffective in time. It would have cost the Muslims many precious lives; many of the Quraysh would have been killed, who were to render great services to Islām afterward; the gains which were to accrue from conquering Makkah peacefully would have been lost, and all these serious losses would have resulted only because one of the Muslims had wanted to safeguard his family from the dangers of war. Administering a severe warning at this blunder God has taught the believers the lesson that no believer should, under any circumstances and for any motive, have relations of love and friendship with the disbelievers, who are actively hostile to Islām, and a believer should refrain from everything which might be helpful to them in the conflict between Islām and disbelief. However, there is no harm in dealing kindly and justly with those disbelievers, who may not be practically engaged in hostile activities against Islām and persecution of the Muslims.

The second part consists of v. 10-11. In this a social problem has been settled, which was agitating the minds at that time. There were many Muslim women in Makkah, whose husbands were pagans, but they were emigrating and reaching Madinah somehow. Likewise, there were many Muslim men in Madinah, whose wives were pagans and had been left behind in Makkah. The question arose whether the marriage bond between them continued to be valid or not. God settled this problem for ever, saying that the pagan husband is not lawful for the Muslim women, nor the pagan wife lawful for the Muslim husband. This decision leads to very important legal consequences, which we shall explain in our notes below.

The third section consists of verse 12, in which the Prophet has been instructed to ask the women who accept Islām to pledge that they would refrain from the major evils that were prevalent among the womenfolk of the pre-Islāmic Arab society, and to promise that they would henceforth follow the ways of goodness which the Messenger of God may enjoin.

## Sūrah 60: al-Mumtahinah[1548]

In the Name of God, the Most Compassionate, the Most Merciful

1. O you who have believed, do not take My enemies and your enemies as allies,[1549] extending to them affection while they have disbelieved in what came to you of the truth, having driven out the Prophet and yourselves [only] because you believe in God, your Lord. If you have come out for jihād [i.e., fighting or striving] in My cause and seeking means to My approval, [take them not as friends]. You confide to them affection [i.e., instruction], but I am most knowing of what you have concealed and what you have declared. And whoever does it among you has certainly strayed from the soundness of the way.

2. If they gain dominance over you, they would be [i.e., behave] to you as enemies and extend against you their hands and their tongues with evil, and they wish you would disbelieve.

3. Never will your relatives or your children benefit you; the Day of Resurrection He will judge between you. And God, of what you do, is Seeing.

4. There has already been for you an excellent pattern[1550] in Abraham and those with him, when they said to their people, "Indeed, we are disassociated from you and from whatever you worship other than God. We have denied you, and there has appeared between us and you animosity and hatred forever until you believe in God alone," - except for the saying of Abraham to his father, "I will surely ask forgiveness for you, but I have not [power to do] for you anything against God. Our Lord, upon You we have relied, and to You we have returned, and to You is the destination.

5. Our Lord, make us not [objects of] torment for the disbelievers and forgive us, our Lord. Indeed, it is You who is the Exalted in Might, the Wise."

6. There has certainly been for you in them an excellent pattern for anyone whose hope is in God and the Last Day. And whoever turns away - then indeed, God is the Free of need, the Praiseworthy.

7. Perhaps God will put, between you and those to whom you have been enemies among them, affection. And God is competent,[1551] and God is Forgiving and Merciful.

8. God does not forbid you from those who do not fight you because of religion and do not expel you from your homes - from being righteous toward them and acting justly toward them. Indeed, God loves those who act justly.

9. God only forbids you from those who fight you because of religion and expel you from your homes and aid in your expulsion - [forbids] that you make allies[1552] of them. And whoever makes allies of them, then it is those who are the wrongdoers.

---

[1548] *Al-Mumtahinah*: That (Sūrah) Which Examines. Also called "*al-Mumtahanah*," meaning "The Woman Examined."

[1549] i.e., close associates and friends.

[1550] An example to be followed.

[1551] To accomplish this or whatever He should will.

[1552] See footnote to verse 1 of this *sūrah*.

10. O you who have believed, when the believing women come to you as emigrants, examine [i.e., test] them. God is most knowing as to their faith. And if you know them to be believers, then do not return them to the disbelievers; they are not lawful [wives] for them, nor are they lawful [husbands] for them. But give them [i.e., the disbelievers] what they have spent.[1553] And there is no blame upon you if you marry them when you have given them their due compensation [i.e., mahr]. And hold not to marriage bonds with disbelieving women, but ask for what you have spent and let them [i.e., the disbelievers] ask for what they have spent.[1554] That is the judgement of God; He judges between you. And God is Knowing and Wise.

11. And if you have lost any of your wives to the disbelievers and you subsequently obtain [something],[1555] then give those whose wives have gone the equivalent of what they had spent. And fear God, in whom you are believers.

12. O Prophet, when the believing women come to you pledging to you that they will not associate anything with God, nor will they steal, nor will they commit unlawful sexual intercourse, nor will they kill their children, nor will they bring forth a slander they have invented between their arms and legs,[1556] nor will they disobey you in what is right - then accept their pledge and ask forgiveness for them of God. Indeed, God is Forgiving and Merciful.

13. O you who have believed, do not make allies of a people with whom God has become angry. They have despaired of [reward in] the Hereafter just as the disbelievers have despaired of [meeting] the companions [i.e., inhabitants] of the graves.

[1553] For marriage, i.e., compensate their loss.
[1554] When a disbelieving wife chose to join the disbelievers, a Muslim husband could demand in return the equivalent of her *mahr*. Likewise, the disbelievers had a similar right when a believing woman joined the Muslims. This and the following verses were revealed subsequent to the Treaty of al-Hudaybiyyah.
[1555] From the side of the disbelievers, i.e., war booty or a believing woman seeking refuge with the Muslims.

[1556] This is an allusion to pregnancy and childbirth, i.e., to falsely attribute a child (whether adopted or born of adultery) to a woman's husband.

## Sūrah 61: as-Saff

### Period of Revelation

It could not be known from any reliable hadith, but a study of its subject-matter shows that this Sūrah probably was sent down in the period closely following the Battle of Uhud, for by reading between the lines perceives a clear description of the conditions that prevailed in that period.

### Theme and Subject Matter

Its theme is to exhort the Muslims to adopt sincerity in Faith and to struggle with their lives in the cause of God. It is addressed to the Muslims with weak faith as well as those who had entered Islām with a false profession of the Faith and also those who were sincere in their profession. Some verses are addressed to the first two groups, some only to the hypocrites, and some only to the sincere Muslims. The style itself shows where one particular group has been addressed and where the other.

At the outset the believers have been warned to the effect; "God indeed hates those people who say one thing and do another, and He indeed loves those who fight in the cause of the Truth, standing like a solid structure, against the enemies of God."

In v. 5-7 the people of the Prophet's community have been warned that their attitude towards their Messenger and their Religion should not be like the attitude that the Israelites had adopted towards the Prophets Moses and Jesus. In spite of acknowledging the Prophet Moses as a Messenger of God they continued to malign him as long as he lived, and in spite of witnessing clear signs from the Prophet Jesus they denied him without any hesitation. Consequently, the Israelites became perverse, incapable of benefiting from divine guidance. This is certainly not an enviable state which another nation should imitate.

Then, in v. 8-9 a proclamation has been made with the challenge: "The Jews and the Christians, and the hypocrites, who are conspiring with them, may try however hard they may to extinguish this Light of God, it will shine forth and spread in the world in all its fullness, and the Religion brought by the true Messenger of God shall prevail over every other religion however hateful it may be to the pagans and polytheists."

In v. 10-13, the believers have been told that the way to success both here and in the Hereafter is only one: that they should believe in God and His Messenger sincerely and should exert their utmost in God's Way with their selves and their wealth. As a reward for this they will earn immunity from God's punishment, forgiveness of their sins and the eternal Paradise in the Hereafter, and will be blessed with God's good pleasure, assistance and victory in the world.

In conclusion, the believers have been exhorted to the effect that just as the disciples of the Prophet Jesus had helped him in the cause of God, so should they also become "helpers of God," so that they too are blessed with the same kind of good pleasure and approval of God as had been the believers before them against the disbelievers.

## Sūrah 61: as-Saff[1557]

In the Name of God, the Most Compassionate, the Most Merciful

1. Whatever is in the heavens and whatever is on the earth exalts God,[1558] and He is the Exalted in Might, the Wise.

2. O you who have believed, why do you say what you do not do?

3. Great is hatred in the sight of God that you say what you do not do.

4. Indeed, God loves those who fight in His cause in a row as though they are a [single] structure joined firmly.

5. And [mention, O Muhammad], when Moses said to his people, "O my people, why do you harm me while you certainly know that I am the messenger of God to you?" And when they deviated, God caused their hearts to deviate. And God does not guide the defiantly disobedient people.

6. And [mention] when Jesus, the son of Mary, said, "O children of Israel, indeed I am the messenger of God to you confirming what came before me of the Torah and bringing good tidings of a messenger to come after me, whose name is Ahmad."[1559] But when he came to them with clear evidences, they said, "This is obvious magic."[1560]

7. And who is more unjust than one who invents about God untruth while he is being invited to Islām. And God does not guide the wrongdoing people.

8. They want to extinguish the light of God with their mouths, but God will perfect His light, although the disbelievers dislike it.

9. It is He who sent His Messenger with guidance and the religion of truth to manifest it over all religion, although those who associate others with God dislike it.

10. O you who have believed, shall I guide you to a transaction that will save you from a painful punishment?

11. [It is that] you believe in God and His Messenger and strive in the cause of God with your wealth and your lives. That is best for you, if you should know.

12. He will forgive for you your sins and admit you to gardens beneath which rivers flow and pleasant dwellings in gardens of perpetual residence. That is the great attainment.

13. And [you will obtain] another [favor] that you love - victory from God and an imminent conquest; and give good tidings to the believers.

14. O you who have believed, be supporters of God, as when Jesus, the son of Mary, said to the disciples, "Who are my supporters for God?" The disciples said, "We are supporters of God." And a faction of the Children of Israel believed and a faction disbelieved. So We supported those who believed against their enemy, and they became dominant.

[1557] *As-Saff*: The Row.
[1558] See footnote to 57:1.
[1559] Another name of Prophet Muhammad.
[1560] i.e., fraud or deception.

## Sūrah 62: al-Jumu'ah

### Period of Revelation

The period of the revelation of the first section (v. 1-8) is 7 A.H., and probably it was sent down on the occasion of the conquest of Khaiber or soon after it. Bukhari, Muslim, Tirmidhi, Nasa'i and Ibn Jarir have related on the authority of Abu Hurairah that he and other Companions were sitting in the Prophet's assembly when these verses were revealed. About Abu Hurairah it is confirmed historically that he entered Islām after the truce of Hudaibiyah and before the conquest of Khaiber, and Khaiber was conquered, according to Ibn Hisham, in the month of Muharram, and according to Ibn Sa'd, in Jamadi al-Awwal, 7 A.H. Thus presumably God might have sent down these verses, addressing the Jews, when their last stronghold had fallen to the Muslims, or these might have been revealed when, seeing the fate of Khaiber, all the Jewish settlements of northern Hijaz had surrendered to the Islāmic government.

The second section (v. 9-11) was sent down shortly after the emigration, for the Prophet had established the Friday congregational Prayer on the 5th day after his arrival at Madinah. The incident that has been referred to in the last verse of this section must have occurred at a time when the people had not yet received full training in the etiquette of religious congregations.

### Theme and Subject Matter

As we have explained above, the two sections of this Sūrah were sent down in two different periods. That is why their themes as well as their audiences are different. Although there is a kind of harmony between them on account of which they have been put together in one Sūrah, yet we should understand their themes separately before we consider the question of their harmony.

The first section was sent down at a time when all Jewish efforts to obstruct the message of Islām during the past six years had failed. First, in Madinah as many as three of their powerful tribes had done whatever they could to frustrate the mission of the Prophet, with the result that one of the tribes was completely exterminated and the other two were exiled. Then by deception and conspiracy they brought many of the Arab tribes together to advance on Madinah, but in the Battle of the Trench they were all repulsed. After this, Khaiber had become their stronghold, where a large number of the Jews expelled from Madinah also had taken refuge. At the time these verses were revealed, that too was taken without any extraordinary effort, and the Jews at their own request agreed to live there as tenants of the Muslims. After this final defeat the Jewish power in Arabia came to an end. Then, Wad-il-Qura, Fadak Taima', Tabūk, all surrendered one after the other, so much so that all Arabian Jews became subdued to the same Islām which they were not prepared to tolerate before. This was the occasion when God Almighty once again addressed them in this Sūrah, and probably this was the last and final address that was directed to them in the Qur'ān. In this they have been reminded of three things:

1. "You refused to believe in this Messenger only because he was born among a people whom you contemptuously call the "gentiles." You were under the false delusion that the Messenger must necessarily belong to your own community. You seemed to have been convinced that anyone who claimed to be a prophet from outside your community, must be an impostor for this office had been reserved for your race, and a messenger could never be raised among the "gentiles." But among the same gentiles God has raised a Messenger who is reciting His Book in front of your very eyes, is purifying souls, and showing the Right Way to the people whose misdeeds are well known to you. This is God's bounty, which He may bestow on anyone He may please. You have no monopoly over it so that He may bestow it over whomever you may please and may withhold it from whomever you may desire it to be withheld."
2. "You had been made bearers of the Torah, but you did not understand your responsibility for it nor discharged it as you should have. You are like the donkey which is loaded with books, and which

does not know what burden it is bearing. Rather you are worse than the donkey, for the donkey is devoid of sense, but you are intelligent. You not only evade your responsibility of being bearers of God's book, but you do not even hesitate to deny God's revelations deliberately. Yet, you are under the delusion that you are God's favourites and the blessing of apostleship has been reserved for you alone. More than that, you seem to entertain the notion that whether you fulfill the demands of God's message or not, God in any case is bound not to make any other than you the bearer of His message."

3. "If you really were God's favourites and you were sure of having a place of honour and high rank reserved with Him, you would not have feared death so much as to prefer a life of disgrace to death. It is only because of this fear of death that you have suffered humiliation after humiliation during the past few years. This condition is by itself a proof that you are fully conscious of your misdeeds, and your conscience is aware that if you die with these misdeeds, you will meet with a greater disgrace before God in the Hereafter than in this world."

This is the subject matter of the first section. The second section that was sent down many years later, was appended to this Sūrah because in it God has bestowed Friday on the Muslims as against the Sabbath of the Jews, and God wanted to warn the Muslims not to treat their Friday as the Jews had treated their Sabbath. This section was sent down on an occasion when a trade caravan arrived in Madinah right at the time of the Friday congregational service and hearing its clamor and drum the audience, except for 12 men, left the Prophet's Mosque and rushed out to the caravan, although the Prophet at that time was delivering the Sermon. Thereupon it was enjoined that after the call is sounded for the Friday Prayer all trade and business and other occupations become forbidden. The believers should then suspend every kind of transaction and hasten to the remembrance of God. However, when the Prayer is over, they have the right to disperse in the land to resume their normal occupations. This section could be made an independent Sūrah in view of the commandments that it contains about the congregational service on Friday, and could also be included in some other Sūrah, but instead, it has been included here particularly in the verses in which the Jews have been warned of the causes of their evil end. Its wisdom in our opinion is the same as we have explained above.

## Sūrah 62: al-Jumu'ah[1561]

In the Name of God, the Most Compassionate, the Most Merciful

1. Whatever is in the heavens and whatever is on the earth is exalting God,[1562] the Sovereign, the Pure, the Exalted in Might, the Wise.

2. It is He who has sent among the unlettered a Messenger from themselves reciting to them His verses and purifying them and teaching them the Book [i.e., the Qur'ān] and wisdom [i.e., the sunnah] - although they were before in clear error -

3. And [to] others of them who have not yet joined them. And He is the Exalted in Might, the Wise.

4. That is the bounty of God, which He gives to whom He wills, and God is the possessor of great bounty.

5. The example of those who were entrusted with the Torah and then did not take it on[1563] is like that of a donkey who carries volumes [of books].[1564] Wretched is the example of the people who deny the signs of God. And God does not guide the wrongdoing people.

6. Say, "O you who are Jews, if you claim that you are allies of God, excluding the [other] people, then wish for death, if you should be truthful."

7. But they will not wish for it, ever, because of what their hands have put forth. And God is Knowing of the wrongdoers.

8. Say, "Indeed, the death from which you flee - indeed, it will meet you. Then you will be returned to the Knower of the unseen and the witnessed, and He will inform you about what you used to do."

9. O you who have believed, when [the adhān] is called for the prayer on the day of Jumu'ah [Friday], then proceed to the remembrance of God and leave trade. That is better for you, if you only knew.

10. And when the prayer has been concluded, disperse within the land and seek from the bounty of God, and remember God often that you may succeed.

11. But [on one accasion] when they saw a transaction or a diversion, [O Muhammad], they rushed to it and left you standing. Say, "What is with God is better than diversion and than a transaction, and God is the best of providers."

---

[1561] *Al-Jumu'ah*: Friday.
[1562] See footnote to 57:1.
[1563] i.e., neglected their responsibility towards it by not putting its teachings into practice.
[1564] But does not benefit from their contents.

## Sūrah 63: al-Munāfiqūn

### Period of Revelation

As we shall explain below this Sūrah was sent down either during the Prophet's return journey from his campaign against Bani al-Mustaliq, or immediately after his arrival back at Madinah. And we have established by argument and research in the introduction to Sūrah an-Nur that the campaign against Bani al-Mustaliq had taken place in Sha'aban 6 A.H. Thus, the date of the revelation of this Sūrah is determined precisely.

### Historical Background

Before we mention the particular incident about which this Sūrah was sent down, it is necessary to have a look at the history of the hypocrites of Madinah, for the incident that occurred on this occasion was not a chance happening but had a whole series of events behind it, which ultimately led up to it. Before the Prophet's emigration to Madinah the tribes of the Aws and the Khazraj, fed up with their mutual rivalries and civil wars, had almost agreed on the leadership of one man and were making preparations to crown him their king. This was Abdullah bin Ubayy bin Salul, the chief of the Khazraj. Muhammad bin Ishaq has stated that among the people of Khazraj his authority was never contested and never had the Aws and the Khazraj rallied to one man before this.

Such were the conditions when the voice of Islām reached Madinah and the influential people of both the tribes started becoming Muslims. When before the Emigration, invitation was being extended to the Prophet to come to Madinah, Abbas bin Ubadah bin Nadlah Ansāri wanted to defer this invitation for the reason that Abdullah bin Ubayy also might join in the declaration of allegiance and invitation to the Prophet, so that Madinah might become the center of Islām by common consent. But the delegation that arrived in Makkah to declare their allegiance did not give any importance to the proposal of Abbas bin Ubadah, and all its members, who included 75 men from both the tribes, became ready to invite the Prophet in the face of every danger (Ibn Hisham, vol. II, p. 89).

Then, when the Prophet arrived in Madinah, Islām had so deeply penetrated every house of the Ansār that Abdullah bin Ubayy became helpless and did not see any other way to save his leadership than to become a Muslim himself. So, he entered Islām along with many of his followers from among the chiefs and leaders of both the tribes although their hearts were burning with rage from within. Ibn Ubayy in particular was filled with grief, for the Prophet had deprived him of his kingship. For several years his hypocritical faith and grief of being deprived of his kingdom manifested itself in different ways. On the one hand, when on Fridays the Prophet took his seat to deliver the Sermon, Abdullah bin Ubayy would stand up and say "*O people, the Messenger of God is present among you, by whom God has honoured you; therefore, you should support him and listen to what he says and obey him.*" On the other, his hypocrisy was being exposed day by day and the true Muslims were realizing that he and his followers bore great malice against Islām, the Prophet and the Muslims.

Once when the Prophet was passing on the way Abdullah bin Ubayy spoke to him in harsh words. When the Prophet complained of it to Sa'd bin Ubadah; he said: *"O Messenger of God, don't be hard on him, for when God sent you to us we were making a diadem to crown him, and, by God, he thinks that you have robbed him of his kingdom."* After the Battle of Badr when the Prophet invaded the Jewish tribe of Bani-Qaynuqah on their breaking the agreement and unprovoked revolt, this man stood up in support of them, and holding the Prophet by his armor, said: *"These 700 fighters have been helping and protecting me against every enemy; would you cut them down in one morning? By God, I will not leave you until you pardon my clients."*

On the occasion of the Battle of Uhud this man committed open treachery and withdrew from the battlefield with 300 of his companions. One should note that at this critical moment when he so acted, the Quraysh had marched upon Madinah with 3,000 troops and the Prophet had marched out with only 1,000 men to resist them. Of these 1,000 this hypocrite broke away with 300 men and the Prophet was left with only 700 men to meet 3,000 troops of the enemy in the field.

After this incident the common Muslims of Madinah came to realize fully that he was certainly a hypocrite and those Companions also were found who were his associates in hypocrisy. That is why when on the very first Friday, after the Battle of Uhud, this man stood up as usual to make a speech before the Prophet's Sermon, the people pulled at his garment, saying *"Sit down you are not worthy to say such things."* That was the first occasion in Madinah when this man was publicly disgraced. Thereupon he was so filled with rage that he left the mosque jumping over the heads of the people. At the door of the Mosque some of the Ansār said to him, *"What are you doing? Go back and ask the Holy Prophet to pray for your forgiveness."* He retorted *"I do not want him to pray for my forgiveness."*

Then in 4 A.H. the Battle of Banu-Nadheer took place. On this occasion he and his companions supported the enemies of Islām even more openly. On the one side, the Prophet and his devoted Companions were preparing for war against their enemy, the Jews, and on the other, these hypocrites were secretly sending messages to the Jews to the effect: *"Stand firm we are with you: if you are attacked, we will help you, and if you are driven out, we too will go out with you."* The secret of this intrigue was exposed by God Himself, as has been explained in Sūrah al-Hashr: 11-17 above.

But in spite of being so exposed the reason why the Prophet was still treating him kindly was that he had a large band of the hypocrites behind him. Many of the chiefs of both the Aws and the Khazraj were his supporters. At least a third of the population of Madinah consisted of his companions, as became manifest on the occasion of the Battle of Uhud. Under such conditions it was not prudent to wage a war with these internal enemies combined with the external enemies. On this very account, in spite of being fully aware of their hypocrisy the Prophet continued to deal with them according to their apparent profession of faith for a long time. On the other hand, these people too neither possessed the power nor the courage to fight the believers openly as disbelievers, or to join hands with an invader and face them in the battlefield. Apparently they were a strong hand but inwardly they had the weakness which God has vividly portrayed in Sūrah al-Hashr: 12-14. Therefore; they thought their wellbeing lay only in posing as Muslims. They came to the mosque, offered the prayers, gave away the Zakāh, and would make tall oral claims to the faith, which the true Muslims never felt the need to do. They would offer a thousand justifications for each of their hypocritical acts by which they would try to deceive their compatriots, the Ansār, into believing that they were with them. By these designs they were not only saving themselves from the disadvantages which could naturally accrue if they separated themselves from the Ansār brotherhood, but also taking advantage of the opportunities to make mischief which were available to them as members of the Muslim brotherhood.

These were the causes which enabled Abdullah bin Ubayy and like minded hypocrites to get an opportunity to accompany the Prophet in his campaign against the Bani al-Mustaliq, and they simultaneously engineered two great mischiefs which could shatter the Muslim unity to pieces. However, by virtue of the wonderful training in discipline that the Muslims had received through the pure teaching of the Qur'ān and the companionship of the Prophet both mischiefs were stopped in time, and the hypocrites themselves were disgraced instead. One of these was the mischief that has been mentioned in Sūrah An-Nur above, and the other which has been mentioned in this Sūrah.

This incident has been related by Bukhari, Muslim, Ahmad, Nasai, Tirmidhi, Baihaqi, Tabari, Ibn Marduyah, Abdur Razzaq, Ibn Jarir Tabari, Ibn Sa'd and Muhammad bin Ishaq through many reliable channels. In some hadith the expedition in which it took place has not been named, and in others it has been connected with the Battle of Tabūk. But the authorities on the battles fought by the Prophet and history are agreed that this incident took place on the occasion of the campaign against the Bani al-Mustaliq. The following seems to be the real story when all the traditions are read together.

When after crushing down the power of Bani al-Mustaliq the Islāmic army had made a halt in the settlement at the well of al Muraisi. Suddenly a dispute arose between two men on taking water from the well; one of them was Jehjah bin Masud Ghifari, a servant of Umar appointed to lead his horse. The other was Sinan bin Wabar al-Juhani, whose tribe was an ally of a clan of the Khazraj. Harsh words between them led to fighting and Jehjah kicked Sinan, which the Ansār, on account of their ancient Yemenite tradition, took as a great insult and disgrace. At this Sinan called out the men of Ansār and Jehjah called the Emigrants for help. Hearing about the quarrel Ibn Ubayy started inciting and calling the men of the Aws and the Khazraj to come out and help their ally. From the other side some Emigrants also came out. The dispute might have led to a fight between the Ansār and the Muhajirin themselves at the very place where they had just fought an enemy tribe jointly and crushing it had halted in its own territory. But hearing the noise the Prophet emerged and said: "*What is this call of paganism? What have you to do with such a call? Leave it: it is a dirty thing.*" Thereupon the leading men of the two sides met and settled the dispute; Sinan pardoned Jehjah and peace was restored.

After this every person whose heart was disaffected came to Abdullah hin Ubayy and they all said to him, "*Until now we had our hopes attached to you and you were protecting us, but now it seems you have become a helper of these paupers against us.*" Ibn Ubayy was already enraged. These words made him burst out, thus: *"This is what you have done to yourselves. You have given these people shelter in your country, and have divided your property among them. So much so that they have now become our rivals. Nothing so fits us and the paupers of Quraysh (or the Companions of Muhammad) as the ancient saying 'Feed your dog to fatten it and it will devour you.' If you hold back your property from them, they would go elsewhere. By God, when we return to Madinah, the honourable ones will drive out from it the mean ones."*

Zayd bin Arqam, a young boy, also happened to be present in the assembly at that time. He heard this and mentioned it before his uncle, and his uncle who was one of the Ansār chiefs went to the Prophet and told him the whole story. The Prophet called Zayd and asked him what had happened and he repeated every word of what he had heard. The Prophet said, *"Zayd, you are perhaps displeased with Ibn Ubayy; you might have been mistaken in hearing; you might have imagined Ibn Ubayy said this."* But Zayd was sure and firm. He said, *"No, I swear by God I have heard him say this and that.*" Thereupon the Prophet called Ibn Ubayy, and he came and swore that he had not said any such thing. The people of the Ansār also said *"...a boy says this: he might have been mistaken in what he heard. Ibn Ubayy is a venerable old man and our chief. Do not believe what a boy says against him.*" The elderly people of the tribe reproved Zayd also, who became depressed and held his peace. But the Prophet knew Zayd as well as Abdullah bin Ubayy. Therefore, he fully understood what had actually happened.

When Umar came to know of this, he came to the Prophet and said: *"Please allow me to put this hypocrite to the sword. Or, if you do not think it is fit to give me the permission you may tell Muadh bin Jabal, or Abbad bin Bishr, or Sad bin Mu'adh, or Muhammad bin Maslamah from among the Ansār, to go and kill him."* But the Prophet said: "*No, the people will say Muhammad kills his own Companions.*" After this he ordered the people to set off immediately, although it was at a time when the Prophet was not accustomed to travel. The forced march continued for 30 hours at a stretch so that the people became exhausted. Then he halted, and as soon as they touched the ground they fell asleep. This he did to distract their minds from what had happened at the well of al-Muraisi. On the way, Usaid bin Hudair, an Ansār chief, met the Prophet, and said: *"O Messenger of God, today you ordered the people to set off at a time which was disagreeable for traveling, a thing you have never done before."* The Prophet replied: *"Have you. not heard of what your friend said?"* When he asked who he meant, the Prophet replied: *"Abdullah bin Ubayy."* He asked what he had said. The Prophet answered: *"He has asserted that when he returns to Madinah the honourable ones will drive out from it the mean ones."* He answered: *"By God, O Messenger of God, you are the honourable one and he is the mean one; you will drive him out whenever you want to."*

By and by the news spread among the Ansār soldiers and it enraged them against Ibn Ubayy. The people advised him to go to the Prophet and request for his forgiveness, but he retorted : *"You asked me to believe in him, and I believed in him; you asked me to pay the Zakāh on my property, and I paid the Zakāh too; now the only thing left is that I should bow down to Muhammad."* This further enraged the believing Ansār and everyone started reproaching and cursing him roughly. When the caravan was about to enter Madinah, Abullah, the son of Abdullah bin Ubayy, stood before his father with a drawn out sword, and said: *"You had said that when you reached Madi-*

*nah, the honourable ones would drive out the mean ones. Now, you will know who is honourable, you or God and His Messenger. By God, you cannot enter Madinah until the Messenger of God permits you to enter."* At this Ibn Uhayy cried out: *"O people of Khazraj, look, my own son is preventing me from entering Madinah."* The people conveyed this news to the Prophet, and he said: *"Tell Abdullah to let his father come home."* Abdullah said, *"If this is the Holy Prophet's order, then you may enter."* Thereupon the Prophet said to Umar: *"Now what do you think, Umar? Had you killed him on the day when you asked my permission to kill him, many people woujd have trembled with rage. Today if I order them to kill him, they will kill him immediately."* Umar replied, *"By God, I realize there was greater wisdom behind what the Apostle of God said than what I said."* These were the circumstances under which this Sūrah was sent down most probably after the Prophet's return to Madinah.

## Sūrah 63: al-Munāfiqūn[1565]

In the Name of God, the Most Compassionate, the Most Merciful

1. When the hypocrites come to you, [O Muhammad], they say, "We testify that you are the Messenger of God." And God knows that you are His Messenger, and God testifies that the hypocrites are liars.

2. They have taken their oaths as a cover, so they averted [people] from the way of God. Indeed, it was evil that they were doing.

3. That is because they believed, and then they disbelieved; so their hearts were sealed over, and they do not understand.

4. And when you see them, their forms please you, and if they speak, you listen to their speech. [They are] as if they were pieces of wood propped up[1566] - they think that every shout is against them. They are the enemy, so beware of them. May God destroy them; how are they deluded?

5. And when it is said to them, "Come, the Messenger of God will ask forgiveness for you," they turn their heads aside and you see them evading while they are arrogant.

6. It is all the same for them whether you ask forgiveness for them or do not ask forgiveness for them; never will God forgive them. Indeed, God does not guide the defiantly disobedient people.

7. They are the ones who say, "Do not spend on those who are with the Messenger of God until they disband." And to God belongs the depositories of the heavens and the earth, but the hypocrites do not understand.

8. They say, "If we return to al-Madīnah, the more honoured [for power] will surely expel therefrom the more humble." And to God belongs [all] honour, and to His Messenger, and to the believers, but the hypocrites do not know.

9. O you who have believed, let not your wealth and your children divert you from remembrance of God. And whoever does that - then those are the losers.

10. And spend [in the way of God] from what We have provided you before death approaches one of you and he says, "My Lord, if only You would delay me for a brief term so I would give charity and be among the righteous."

11. But never will God delay a soul when its time has come. And God is Acquainted with what you do.

---

1565 *Al-Munāfiqūn*: The Hypocrites.

1566 i.e., bodies with empty minds and empty hearts.

## Sūrah 64: at-Taghābun

### Period of Revelation

Muqatil and Kalbi say that it was partly revealed at Makkah and partly at Madinah. Abdullah bin Abbas and Ata bin Yasar say that v. 1-13 were revealed at Makkah and v. 14-18 at Madinah. But the majority of commentators regard the whole of the Sūrah as a Madinan Revelation. Although there is no internal evidence to help determine its exact period of revelation, yet a study of its subject matter shows that it might probably have been sent down at an early stage at Madinah. That is why it partly resembles the Makkah Sūrahs and partly the Madinan Sūrahs.

### Theme and Subject Matter

The theme of this Sūrah is invitation to the Faith and obedience (to God) and the teaching of good morals. The sequence followed is that the first four verses are addressed to all men; verses 5-10 to those men who do not believe in the invitation of the Qur'ān; and verses 11-18 to those who accept and believe in this invitation. In the verses addressed to all men, they have been made aware in a few brief sentences of the four fundamental truths:

First, that the universe in which they live is not Godless, but its Creator, Master and Ruler is an All Powerful God, and everything in it testifies to His being most Perfect and absolutely faultless.

Second, that the universe is not without purpose and wisdom, but its Creator has created it with truth; no one should be under the delusion that it is a mock show, which began without a purpose and will come to an end without a purpose.

Third, that the excellent form that God has created you with and the choice that He has given you to choose between belief and unbelief is not a useless and meaningless activity so that it may be of no consequence whether you choose belief or unbelief. In fact, God is watching as to how you exercise your choice.

Fourth, that you have not been created irresponsible and unanswerable. You have to return ultimately to your Creator, and have to meet the Being who is aware of everything in the universe, from Whom nothing is hidden, to Whom even the innermost thoughts of the minds are known.

After stating these four fundamental truths about the Universe and Man, the address turns to the people who adopted the way of unbelief, and their attention is drawn to a phenomenon which has persisted throughout human history, namely that nation after nation has arisen and ultimately gone to its doom. Man by his intellect and reason has been explaining this phenomenon in a thousand ways, but God tells the real truth and declares that the fundamental causes of the destruction of the nations were only two.

First, that they refused to believe in the Messengers whom He sent for their guidance, with the result that God too left them to themselves, and they invented their own philosophies of life and went on groping their way from one error to another.

Second, that they also rejected the doctrine of Hereafter, and thought this worldly life to be an end in itself, and that there was no life hereafter when they would have to render an account of their deeds before God. This corrupted their whole attitude towards life, and their impure morals and character so polluted the world that eventually the scourge of God itself had to descend and eliminate them from the scene.

After stating these two instructive truths of human history, the deniers of the message of Truth have been admonished to wake up and believe in God, His Messenger and the Light of Guidance that God has sent in the form of the Qur'ān if they want to avoid the fate met by the former peoples. Besides, they have been warned that the Day shall eventually come when all the former and the latter generations will be collected at one place and the fraud and embezzlement committed by each will be exposed before all mankind. Then the fate of each man will be decided finally on the basis as to who had adopted the path of the Faith and righteousness and who had followed the way of disbelief and denial of the Truth. The first group shall deserve eternal Paradise and the second shall be doomed to everlasting Hell. Then, addressing those who adopt the way of the Faith, a few important instructions have been given:

First, that whatever affliction befalls a person in the world, it befalls him by God's leave. Whoever in this state of affliction remains steadfast to the Faith, God blesses his heart with guidance; otherwise although the affliction of the one who in confusion or bewilderment turns away from the path of the Faith, cannot be averted except by God's leave, yet he becomes involved in another, the greatest affliction of all, namely that his heart is deprived of the guidance of God.

Secondly, that the believer is not required to affirm the faith with the tongue only, but after the affirmation of the Faith he should practically obey God and His Messenger. If he turns away from obedience he would himself be responsible for his loss, for the Messenger of God has become absolved from the responsibility after having delivered the message of Truth.

Thirdly, that the believer should place his trust in God alone and not in his own power or some other power of the world.

Fourthly, that the worldly goods and children are a great trial and temptation for the believer, for it is their love which generally distracts man from the path of faith and obedience. Therefore, the believers have to beware some of their children, and wives lest they become robbers for them on the Way of God directly or indirectly; and they should spend their wealth for the sake of God so that their self remains safe against the temptations of Satan.

Fifthly, that every man is responsible only to the extent of his power and ability. God does not demand that man should exert himself beyond his power and ability. However, the believer should try his best to live in fear of God as far as possible, and should see that he does not transgress the bounds set by God in his speech, conduct and dealings through his own negligence.

## Sūrah 64: at-Taghābun[1567]

In the Name of God, the Most Compassionate, the Most Merciful

1. Whatever is in the heavens and whatever is on the earth is exalting God.[1568] To Him belongs dominion, and to Him belongs [all] praise, and He is over all things competent.

2. It is He who created you, and among you is the disbeliever, and among you is the believer. And God, of what you do, is Seeing.

3. He created the heavens and earth in truth and formed you and perfected your forms; and to Him is the [final] destination.

4. He knows what is within the heavens and earth and knows what you conceal and what you declare. And God is Knowing of that within the breasts.

5. Has there not come to you the news of those who disbelieved before? So they tasted the bad consequence of their affair, and they will have a painful punishment.

6. That is because their messengers used to come to them with clear evidences, but they said, "Shall human beings guide us?" and disbelieved and turned away. And God dispensed [with them]; and God is Free of need and Praiseworthy.

7. Those who disbelieve have claimed that they will never be resurrected. Say, "Yes, by my Lord, you will surely be resurrected; then you will surely be informed of what you did. And that, for God, is easy."

8. So believe in God and His Messenger and the light [i.e., the Qur'ān] which We have sent down. And God is Acquainted with what you do.

9. The Day He will assemble you for the Day of Assembly - that is the Day of Deprivation.[1569] And whoever believes in God and does righteousness - He will remove from him his misdeeds and admit him to gardens beneath which rivers flow, wherein they will abide forever. That is the great attainment.

10. But the ones who disbelieved and denied Our verses - those are the companions of the Fire, abiding eternally therein; and wretched is the destination.

11. No disaster strikes except by permission of God. And whoever believes in God - He will guide his heart. And God is Knowing of all things.

12. And obey God and obey the Messenger; but if you turn away - then upon Our Messenger is only [the duty of] clear notification.

13. God - there is no deity except Him. And upon God let the believers rely.

14. O you who have believed, indeed, among your wives and your children are enemies to you, so beware of them. But if you pardon and overlook and forgive - then indeed, God is Forgiving and Merciful.

---

1567 *At-Taghābun*: Deprivation, another name for the Day of Judgement. See footnote 1569.

1568 See footnote to 57:1.

1569 "*At-Taghābun*" suggests having been outdone by others in the acquisition of something valued. That Day, the disbelievers will suffer the loss of Paradise to the believers.

15. Your wealth and your children are but a trial, and God has with Him a great reward.

16. So fear God as much as you are able and listen and obey and spend [in the way of God]; it is better for your selves. And whoever is protected from the stinginess of his soul - it is those who will be the successful.

17. If you loan God a goodly loan, He will multiply it for you and forgive you. And God is Most Appreciative and Forbearing,

18. Knower of the unseen and the witnessed, the Exalted in Might, the Wise.

## Sūrah 65: at-Talāq

### Period of Revelation

Abdullah bin Masud has pointed out, and the internal evidence of the "When you marry the believing...." subject matter of the Sūrah confirms the same, that it must have been sent down after those verses of Sūrah al-Baqarah in which commandments concerning divorce were given for the first time. Although it is difficult to determine precisely what is its exact date of revelation, yet the traditions in any case indicate that when the people started making errors in understanding the commandments of Sūrah Al-Baqarah, and practically also they began to commit mistakes, God sent down these instructions for their correction.

### Theme and Subject Matter

In order to understand the commandments of this Sūrah, it would be useful to refresh one's memory about the instructions which have been given in the Qur'ān concerning divorce and the waiting period (Iddat) above.

> **"Divorce is twice. Then [after that], either keep [her] in an acceptable manner or release [her] with good treatment."**
>
> Sūrah al-Baqarah 2:229
>
> **"Divorced women remain in waiting [i.e., do not marry] for three periods, and it is not lawful for them to conceal what God has created in their wombs if they believe in God and the Last Day. And their husbands have more right to take them back in this [period] if they want reconciliation."**
>
> Sūrah al-Baqarah 2:228
>
> **"And if he has divorced her [for the third time], then she is not lawful to him afterward until [after] she marries a husband..."**
>
> Sūrah al-Baqarah 2:230
>
> **"O You who have believed, when you marry believing women and then divorce them before you have touched them [i.e., consummated the marriage], then there is not for you any waiting period to count concerning them. So provide for them and give them a gracious release."**
>
> Sūrah al-Ahzāb 33:49
>
> **"And those who are taken in death among you and leave wives behind - they, [the wives, shall] wait four months and ten [days]."**
>
> Sūrah al-Baqarah 2:234

The rules prescribed in these verses were as follows:

1. A man can pronounce at the most three divorces on his wife.
2. In case the husband has pronounced one or two divorces he is entitled to keep the woman back as his wife within the waiting period and if after the expiry of the waiting period the two desire to remarry, they can re-marry; there is no condition of legalization (tahlil). But if the husband has pronounced three divorces, he forfeits his right to keep her as his wife within the waiting period, and they cannot re-marry unless the woman remarries another husband and he subsequently divorces her of his own free will.
3. The waiting period of the woman, who menstruates and marriage with whom has been consummated, is that she should pass three monthly courses. The waiting period in case of one or two divorces is that the woman is still the legal wife of the husband and he can keep her back as his wife

within the waiting period. But if the husband has pronounced three divorces, this waiting period cannot be taken advantage of for the purpose of reconciliation, but it is only meant to restrain the woman from re-marrying another person before it comes to an end.

4. There is no waiting period for the woman, marriage with whom has not been consummated, and who is divorced even before she is touched. She can re-marry, if she likes, immediately after the divorce.
5. The waiting period of the woman whose husband dies, is four months and ten days.

Here, one should understand well that Sūrah at-Talaq was not sent down to annul any of these rules or amend it, but it was sent down for two purposes: first, that the man who has been given the right to pronounce divorce should be taught such judicious methods of using this right as do not lead to separation, as far as possible however, if separation does take place, it should only be in case all possibilities of mutual reconciliation have been exhausted. For in the Divine Law provision for divorce has been made only as an unavoidable necessity; otherwise God does not approve that the marriage relationship that has been established between a man and a woman should ever break. The Prophet has said "*God has not made lawful anything more hateful in His sight than divorce.*" And: "*Of all the things permitted by the Law, the most hateful in the sight of God is the divorce.*" (Abu Dawud)

The second object was to complement this section of the family law of Islām by supplying answers to the questions that had remained after the revelation of the commandments in Sūrah al-Baqarah. So, answers have been supplied to the following questions: What would be the waiting period of the women, marriage with whom has been consummated and who no longer menstruate, or those who have not yet menstruated, in case they are divorced? What would be the waiting period of the woman, who is pregnant, or the woman whose husband dies, if she is divorced? And what arrangements would be made for the maintenance and lodging of the different categories of divorced women, and for the fosterage of the child whose parents have separated on account of a divorce?

## Sūrah 65: at-Talāq[1570]

In the Name of God, the Most Compassionate, the Most Merciful

1. O Prophet, when you [Muslims] divorce women, divorce them for [the commencement of] their waiting period[1571] and keep count of the waiting period, and fear God, your Lord. Do not turn them out of their [husbands'] houses, nor should they [themselves] leave [during that period] unless they are committing a clear immorality. And those are the limits [set by] God. And whoever transgresses the limits of God has certainly wronged himself. You know not; perhaps God will bring about after that a [different] matter.[1572]

2. And when they have [nearly] fulfilled their term, either retain them according to acceptable terms or part with them according to acceptable terms. And bring to witness two just men from among you and establish the testimony for [the acceptance of] God. That is instructed to whoever should believe in God and the Last day. And whoever fears God - He will make for him a way out[1573]

3. And will provide for him from where he does not expect. And whoever relies upon God - then He is sufficient for him. Indeed, God will accomplish His purpose. God has already set for everything a [decreed] extent.

4. And those who no longer expect menstruation among your women - if you doubt, then their period is three months, and [also for] those who have not menstruated. And for those who are pregnant, their term is until they give birth.[1574] And whoever fears God - He will make for him of his matter ease.

5. That is the command of God, which He has sent down to you; and whoever fears God - He will remove for him his misdeeds and make great for him his reward.

6. Lodge them[1575] [in a section] of where you dwell out of your means and do not harm them in order to oppress them.[1576] And if they should be pregnant, then spend on them until they give birth. And if they breastfeed for you, then give them their payment and confer among yourselves in the acceptable way; but if you are in discord, then there may breastfeed for him [i.e., the father] another woman.[1577]

7. Let a man of wealth spend from his wealth, and he whose provision is restricted - let him spend from what God has given him. God does not charge a soul except [according to] what He has given it. God will bring about, after hardship, ease [i.e., relief].

8. And how many a city was insolent toward the command of its Lord and His messengers, so We took it to severe ac-

[1570] *At-Talāq*: Divorce.
[1571] See rulings in 2:228-233. A wife should not be divorced except after the completion of her menstrual period but before sexual intercourse has occurred, or else during a confirmed pregnancy. The pronouncement of divorce begins her waiting period (*'iddah*).
[1572] Such as regret or renewed desire for the wife.
[1573] i.e., relief from distress.

[1574] The ruling concerning pregnancy applies also in the case of the husband's death.
[1575] During their waiting period (referring to wives whose divorce has been pronounced).
[1576] So that they would be forced to leave or ransom themselves.
[1577] See 2:233.

count and punished it with a terrible punishment.

9. And it tasted the bad consequence of its affair [i.e., rebellion], and the outcome of its affair was loss.

10. God has prepared for them a severe punishment; so fear God, O you of understanding who have believed. God has sent down to you a message [i.e., the Qur'ān]. [1578]

11. [He sent] a Messenger [i.e., Muhammad] reciting to you the distinct verses of God that He may bring out those who believe and do righteous deeds from darknesses into the light. And whoever believes in God and does righteousness - He will admit him into gardens beneath which rivers flow to abide therein forever. God will have perfected for him a provision.

12. It is God who has created seven heavens and of the earth, the like of them.[1579] [His] command descends among them so you may know that God is over all things competent and that God has encompassed all things in knowledge.

[1578] Some scholars have interpreted "*dhikr*" here as "a reminder," meaning the Messenger, since he is mentioned in the following verse.
[1579] i.e., a similar number: seven.

## Sūrah 66: at-Tahreem

### Period of Revelation

In connection with the incident of Tahreem (prohibition) referred to in this Sūrah, the traditions mention two wives of the Prophet. There are differing narrations about the cause of revelation, but it seems the most authentic narrations allude to the incident surrounding the Prophet prohibiting of honey for himself.

### Theme and Topics

This is a very important Sūrah in which light has been thrown on some questions of grave significance with reference to some incidents concerning the wives of the Prophet. First, that the powers to prescribe the bounds of the lawful and the unlawful, the permissible and the forbidden, are entirely and absolutely in the hand of God and nothing has been delegated even to the Prophet of God himself, not to speak of any other man. The Prophet as such can declare something lawful or unlawful only if he receives an inspiration from God to do so whether that inspiration is embodied in the Qur'ān, or imparted to him secretly. However, even the Prophet is not authorized to declare anything made permissible by God unlawful by himself, much less to say of another man.

Second, that in any society the position of a Prophet is very delicate. A minor incident experienced by an ordinary man in his life may not be of any consequence, but it assumes the status of law when experienced by a Prophet. That is why the lives of the Prophets have been kept under close supervision by God so that none of their acts, not even a most trivial one, may deviate from Divine Will. Whenever such an act has emanated from a Prophet, it was rectified and rectified immediately so that the Islāmic law and its principles should reach the people in their absolute purity not only through the Divine Book but also through the excellent example of the Prophet, and they should include nothing which may be in disagreement with Divine Will.

Thirdly, and this automatically follows from the above mentioned point, that when the Prophet was checked on a minor thing, which was not only corrected but also recorded, it gives us complete satisfaction that whatever actions and commands and instructions we now find in the pure life of the Prophet concerning which there is nothing on record in the nature of criticism or correction from God, they are wholly based on truth, are in complete conformity with Divine Will and we can draw guidance from them with full confidence and peace of mind.

The fourth thing that we learn from this discourse is that about the Messenger himself, whose reverence and respect God Himself has enjoined as a necessary part of the Faith of His servants, it has been stated in this Sūrah that once during his sacred life he made a thing declared lawful by God unlawful for himself only to please his wives; then God has severely reproved for their errors those very wives of the Prophet, whom He Himself has declared as mothers of the faithful and worthy of the highest esteem and honour by them. Then, this criticism of the Prophet and the administration of the warning to the wives also has not been made secretly but included in the Book, which the entire Ummah (nation of Muslims) has to read and recite forever. Obviously, neither the intention of making mention of it in the Book of God was, nor it could be, that God wanted to degrade His Messenger and the mothers of the faithful in the eyes of the believers; and this also is obvious that no Muslim has lost respect for them, in his heart after reading this Sūrah of the Qur'ān. Now, there cannot be any other reason of mentioning this thing in the Qur'ān than that God wants to acquaint the believers with the correct manner of reverence for their great personalities. The Prophet is a Prophet, not God, that he may commit no error. Respect of the Prophet has not been enjoined because he is infallible, but because he is a perfect representative of Divine Will, and God has not permitted any of his errors to pass by unnoticed. This gives us the satisfaction that the noble pattern of life left by the Prophet wholly and fully represents the will of God. Likewise, the Companions of the wives of the Prophet, were human, not angels or supermen. They could commit mistakes. Whatever ranks they achieved became possible only because the guidance given by God and the training imparted by God's Messenger had molded them into the finest models. Whatever esteem and reverence they deserve is on this very basis and not on the presumption that they were infallible. For this reason, whenever in the sacred lifetime of the Prophet, the Companions or wives happened to commit an error due to human weakness, they were checked. Some of their errors were corrected by the Prophet, as has been mentioned at many places in the Hadith; some other errors were mentioned in the Qur'ān and God Himself corrected them so that the Muslims might not form any exaggerated notion of the respect and reverence of their elders and great men, which might raise them from humanity to the position of gods and goddesses. If one studies the Qur'ān carefully, one will see instances of this one after the other.

The fifth thing that has been explicitly mentioned in this Sūrah is that God's Religion is absolutely fair and just. It has for every person just that of which he becomes worthy on the basis of his faith and works. No relationship or connection even with the most righteous person can be beneficial for him in any way and no relationship or connection with the most evil and wicked person can be harmful for him in any way. In this connection three kinds of women have been cited as examples before the wives in particular. One example is of the wives of the Prophets Noah and Lot, who, if they had believed and cooperated with their illustrious husbands, would have occupied the same rank and position in the Muslim community which is enjoyed by the wives of the Prophet Muhammad. But since they were disbelievers, their being the wives of the Prophets did not help them and they fell into Hell. The second example is of the wife of Pharaoh, who in spite of being the wife of a staunch enemy of God believed and chose a path of action separate from that followed by the Pharaoh's people, and her being the wife of a staunch disbeliever did not cause her any harm, and God made her worthy of Paradise. The third example is of Maryam (Mary) who attained to the high rank because she submitted to the severe test to which God had decided to put her. Apart from Mary no other chaste and righteous girl in the world ever has been put to such a hard test that in spite of being unmarried, she might have been made pregnant miraculously by God's command and informed what service her Lord willed to take from her. When Mary accepted this decision, and agreed to bear, like a true believer, everything that she inevitably had to bear in order to fulfill God's will, then did God exalt her to the noble rank of Sayyidatu an-nisa' fil-Jannah: "Leader of the women in Paradise" (Musnad Ahmad).

Besides, another truth that we learn from this Sūrah is that the Prophet did not receive from God only that knowledge which is included and recorded in the Qur'ān, but he was given information about other things also by revelation, which has not been recorded in the Qur'ān. Its clear proof is verse 3 of this Sūrah. In it we are told that the Prophet confided a secret to one of his wives, and she told it to another. God informed the Prophet of this secret. Then, when the Prophet warned his particular wife on the mistake of disclosure and she said: "Who told you this?" He replied: "I was informed by the Knowing, the Acquainted."

## Sūrah 66: at-Tahreem[1580]

In the Name of God, the Most Compassionate, the Most Merciful

1. O Prophet, why do you prohibit [yourself from] what God has made lawful for you, seeking the approval of your wives? And God is Forgiving and Merciful.

2. God has already ordained for you [Muslims] the dissolution of your oaths.[1581] And God is your protector, and He is the Knowing, the Wise.

3. And [remember] when the Prophet confided to one of his wives a statement; and when she informed [another] of it and God showed it to him, he made known part of it and ignored a part. And when he informed her about it, she said, "Who told you this?" He said, "I was informed by the Knowing, the Acquainted."

4. If you two [wives] repent to God, [it is best], for your hearts have deviated. But if you cooperate against him - then indeed God is his protector, and Gabriel and the righteous of the believers and the angels, moreover, are [his] assistants.

5. Perhaps his Lord, if he divorced you [all], would substitute for him wives better than you - submitting [to God], believing, devoutly obedient, repentant, worshipping, and traveling[1582] - [ones] previously married and virgins.

[1580] *At-Tahreem*: Prohibition.
[1581] By means of a *kaffārah* (expiation). This is required when one is unable to fulfill an oath or when one has taken an oath which would not be pleasing to God. See 5:89.
[1582] Emigrating for the cause of God.

6. O you who have believed, protect yourselves and your families from a Fire whose fuel is people and stones, over which are [appointed] angels, harsh and severe; they do not disobey God in what He commands them but do what they are commanded.

7. O you who have disbelieved, make no excuses that Day. You will only be recompensed for what you used to do.

8. O you who have believed, repent to God with sincere repentance. Perhaps[1583] your Lord will remove from you your misdeeds and admit you into gardens beneath which rivers flow [on] the Day when God will not disgrace the Prophet and those who believed with him. Their light will proceed before them and on their right; they will say, "Our Lord, perfect for us our light and forgive us. Indeed, You are over all things competent."

9. O Prophet, strive against the disbelievers and the hypocrites and be harsh upon them. And their refuge is Hell, and wretched is the destination.

10. God presents an example of those who disbelieved: the wife of Noah and the wife of Lot. They were under two of Our righteous servants but betrayed them,[1584] so they [i.e., those prophets] did not avail them from God at all, and it was said, "Enter the Fire with those who enter."

11. And God presents an example of those who believed: the wife of Pharaoh, when she said, "My Lord, build for me near You a house in Paradise and save

[1583] i.e., it is expected or promised.
[1584] In the matter of religion.

me from Pharaoh and his deeds and save me from the wrongdoing people."

12. And [the example of] Mary, the daughter of 'Imrān, who guarded her chastity, so We blew into [her garment] through Our angel [i.e., Gabriel], and she believed in the words of her Lord and His scriptures and was of the devoutly obedient.

## Sūrah 67: al-Mulk

### Period of Revelation

It could not be known from any authentic hadith when this Sūrah was revealed, but the subject matter and the style indicate that it is one of the earliest Sūrahs to be revealed at Makkah.

### Theme and Subject Matter

In this Sūrah, on the one hand, the teachings of Islām have been introduced briefly, and on the other, the people living in heedlessness have been aroused from their slumber in a most effective way. A characteristic of the earliest Sūrahs of the Makkan period is that they present the entire teachings of Islām and the object of the Prophet's mission, not in detail, but briefly, so that they are assimilated by the people easily. Moreover, they are particularly directed to make the people shun heedlessness, to make them think, and to arouse their dormant conscience.

In the first five verses man has been made to realize that the universe in which he lives is a most well organized and fortified Kingdom in which he cannot detect any fault, any weakness or flaw, how ever hard he may try to probe. This Kingdom has been brought from nothing into existence by God Almighty Himself and all the powers of controlling, administering and ruling it are also entirely in God's hand and His power is infinite. Besides, man has also been told that in this wise system he has not been created without a purpose, but he has been sent here for a test and in this test he can succeed only by his righteous deeds and conduct.

In v. 6-11, dreadful consequences of disbelief which will appear in the Hereafter have been mentioned, and the people are told that God, by sending His Prophets, has warned them of these consequences in this very world, as if to say "Now, if you do not believe in what the Prophets say and correct your attitude and behavior accordingly, in the Hereafter you will yourself have to admit that you really deserved the punishment that was being meted out to you."

In v. 12-14, the truth that has been impressed on the minds is that the Creator cannot be unaware of His creation, as if to say: "He is aware of each open and hidden secret of yours, even of the innermost ideas of your hearts. Hence, the right basis of morality is that man should avoid evil, fearing the accountability of the unseen God, whether in the world there is a power to take him to task for this or not, and whether in the world there is a possibility of being harmed by such a power or not. Those who adopt such a conduct in the world alone will deserve forgiveness and a rich reward in the Hereafter."

In v. 15-23, making allusions, one after the other to those common truths of daily occurrence, which man does not regard as worthy of much attention, he has been invited to consider them seriously. It has been said: "Look: the earth on which you move about with full satisfaction and peace of mind, and from which you obtain your sustenance has been subdued for you by God; otherwise this earth might at any time start shaking suddenly so as to cause your destruction, or a typhoon might occur, which may annihilate you completely. Look at the birds that fly above you; it is only God Who is sustaining them in the air. Look at your own means and resources: if God wills to inflict you with a scourge, none can save you from it; and if God wills to close the doors of sustenance on you, none can open them for you. These things are there to make you aware of the truth, but you see them like animals, which are unable to draw conclusions from observations, and you do not use your sight, hearing and minds which God has bestowed on you as men; that is why you do not see the right way."

In v. 24-27, it has been said: "You have ultimately to appear before your God in any case. It is not for the Prophet to tell you the exact time and date of the event. His only duty is to warn you beforehand of its inevitable occurrence. Today you do not listen to him and demand that he should cause the event to occur and appear prematurely before you; but when it does occur, and you see it with your own eyes, you will then be astounded. Then, it will be said to you: "This is the very thing you were calling to be hastened."

In v. 28-29 replies have been given to what the disbelievers of Makkah said against the Prophet and his Companions. They cursed the Prophet and prayed for his and the believers destruction. To this it has been said: "Whether those who call you to the right way are destroyed, or shown mercy by God, how will their fate change your destiny? You should look after yourselves and consider who would save you if you were overtaken by the scourge of God? You regard those who believe in God and put their trust in Him as the misguided. A time will come when it will become evident as to who was misguided in actual truth."

In conclusion, the people have been asked this question and left to ponder over it: "If the water which has come out from the earth at some place in the desert or hill of Arabia and upon which depends your whole life activity, should sink and vanish underground, who beside God can restore to you this life-giving water?"

## Sūrah 67: al-Mulk[1585]

In the Name of God, the Most Compassionate, the Most Merciful

1. Blessed is He in whose hand is dominion, and He is over all things competent -

2. [He] who created death and life to test you [as to] which of you is best in deed - and He is the Exalted in Might, the Forgiving -

3. [And] who created seven heavens in layers.[1586] You do not see in the creation of the Most Merciful any inconsistency. So return [your] vision [to the sky]; do you see any breaks?

4. Then return [your] vision twice again.[1587] [Your] vision will return to you humbled while it is fatigued.

5. And We have certainly beautified the nearest heaven with lamps [i.e., stars] and have made [from] them what is thrown at the devils[1588] and have prepared for them the punishment of the Blaze.

6. And for those who disbelieved in their Lord is the punishment of Hell, and wretched is the destination.

7. When they are thrown into it, they hear from it a [dreadful] inhaling while it boils up.

8. It almost bursts with rage. Every time a company is thrown into it, its keepers ask them, "Did there not come to you a warner?"

9. They will say, "Yes, a warner had come to us, but we denied and said, 'God has not sent down anything. You are not but in great error.' "

10. And they will say, "If only we had been listening or reasoning, we would not be among the companions of the Blaze."

11. And they will admit their sin, so [it is] alienation[1589] for the companions of the Blaze.

12. Indeed, those who fear their Lord unseen will have forgiveness and great reward.

13. And conceal your speech or publicize it; indeed, He is Knowing of that within the breasts.

14. Does He who created not know,[1590] while He is the Subtle, the Acquainted?

15. It is He who made the earth tame[1591] for you - so walk among its slopes and eat of His provision - and to Him is the resurrection.

16. Do you feel secure that He who [holds authority] in the heaven would not cause the earth to swallow you and suddenly it would sway?[1592]

17. Or do you feel secure that He who [holds authority] in the heaven would not send against you a storm of stones? Then you would know how [severe] was My warning.

---

[1585] *Al-Mulk*: Dominion.

[1586] i.e., one covering or fitting over the other.

[1587] i.e., repeatedly.

[1588] Therby driving them from the heavens and preventing them from eavesdropping. See 72:8-9.

[1589] From all good and from God's mercy.

[1590] Another accepted meaning is "Does He not know those whom He created…?"

[1591] i.e., stable and subservient.

[1592] In a circular motion, as in an earthquake.

18. And already had those before them denied, and how [terrible] was My reproach.

19. Do they not see the birds above them with wings outspread and [sometimes] folded in? None holds them [aloft] except the Most Merciful. Indeed He is, of all things, Seeing.

20. Or who is it that could be an army for you to aid you other than the Most Merciful? The disbelievers are not but in delusion.

21. Or who is it that could provide for you if He withheld His provision? But they have persisted in insolence and aversion.

22. Then is one who walks fallen on his face better guided or one who walks erect on a straight path?

23. Say, "It is He who has produced you and made for you hearing and vision and hearts [i.e., intellect]; little are you grateful."

24. Say, "It is He who has multiplied you throughout the earth, and to Him you will be gathered."

25. And they say, "When is this promise, if you should be truthful?"

26. Say, "The knowledge is only with God, and I am only a clear warner."

27. But when they see it[1593] approaching, the faces of those who disbelieve will be distressed, and it will be said, "This is that for which you used to call."[1594]

[1593] The punishment of which they were warned.
[1594] When they challenged their prophets, saying, "Bring on the punishment, if you are truthful."

28. Say, [O Muhammad], "Have you considered:[1595] whether God should cause my death and those with me or have mercy upon us, who can protect the disbelievers from a painful punishment?"

29. Say, "He is the Most Merciful; we have believed in Him, and upon Him we have relied. And you will [come to] know who it is that is in clear error."

30. Say, "Have you considered: if your water was to become sunken [into the earth], then who could bring you flowing water?"

[1595] i.e., inform me.

## Sūrah 68: al-Qalam

### Period of Revelation

This too is one of the earliest Sūrahs to be revealed at Makkah, but its subject matter shows that it was sent down at the time when opposition to the Prophet had grown very harsh and tyrannical.

### Theme and Subject Matter

It consists of three themes: Replies to the opponents objections, administration of warning and admonition to them, and exhortation to the Prophet to patience and constancy.

At the outset, the Prophet has been addressed, to the effect: "The disbelievers call you a madman whereas the Book that you are presenting and the sublime conduct that you practice, are by themselves sufficient to refute their false accusations. Soon they will see as to who was mad and who was sane; therefore, do not at all yield to the commotion of opposition being kicked up against you, for all this is actually meant to intimidate you and make you resort to a compromise with them."

Then, in order to enlighten the common people the character of a prominent man from among the opponents, whom the people of Makkah fully well recognized, has been presented, without naming him: At that time, the Prophet's pure and sublime conduct was before them, and every discerning eye could also see what sort of character and morals were possessed by the chiefs of Makkah, who were leading the opposition against him. Then, in v. 17-33, the parable of the owners of a garden has been presented, who after having been blessed by God turned ungrateful to Him, and did not heed the admonition of the best man among them when it was given them. Consequently, they were deprived of the blessing and they realized this, when all they had lay devastated. With this parable the people of Makkah have been warned to the effect: "With the appointment of the Prophet to Prophethood, you, O people of Makkah, too, have been put to a test similar to the one to which the owners of the garden had been put. If you do not listen to him, you too will be afflicted with a punishment in the world, and the punishment of the Hereafter is far greater."

Then, in v. 34-47 continuously, the disbelievers have been admonished, in which the address sometimes turns to them directly and sometimes they are warned through the Prophet. A summary of what has been said in this regard, is this: Well being in the Hereafter inevitably belongs to those who spend their lives in the world in full consciousness of God. It is utterly against reason that the obedient servants should meet in the Hereafter the same fate as the guilty. There is absolutely no basis of the disbelievers misunderstanding that God will treat them in the manner they choose for themselves, whereas they have no guarantee for this. Those who are being called upon to bow before God in the world and they refuse to do so, would be unable to prostrate themselves on the Day of Resurrection even if they wanted to do so, and thus would stand disgraced and condemned. Having denied the Qur'ān they cannot escape Divine punishment. The rein they are being given, has deluded them. They think that since they are not being punished in spite of their denial, they must be on the right path, whereas they are following the path of ruin. They have no reasonable ground for opposing the Messenger, for he is a preacher without any vested interest: he is not asking any reward of them for himself, and they cannot either make the claim that they know with certainty that he is not a true Messenger, nor that what he says is false.

In conclusion, the Prophet has been exhorted to the effect: "Bear with patience the hardships that you may have to face in the way of preaching the Faith till God's judgment arrives, and avoid the impatience which caused suffering and affliction to the Prophet Jonah."

## Sūrah 68: al-Qalam[1596]

In the Name of God, the Most Compassionate, the Most Merciful

1. Nūn.[1597] By the pen and what they inscribe,

2. You are not, [O Muhammad], by the favor of your Lord, a madman.

3. And indeed, for you is a reward uninterrupted.

4. And indeed, you are of a great moral character.

5. So you will see and they will see

6. Which of you is the afflicted [by a devil].

7. Indeed, your Lord is most knowing of who has gone astray from His way, and He is most knowing of the [rightly] guided.

8. Then do not obey the deniers.

9. They wish that you would soften [in your position], so they would soften [toward you].

10. And do not obey every worthless habitual swearer

11. [And] scorner, going about with malicious gossip -

12. A preventer of good, transgressing and sinful,

13. Cruel, moreover, and an illegitimate pretender.[1598]

14. Because he is a possessor of wealth and children,

15. When Our verses are recited to him, he says, "Legends of the former peoples."

16. We will brand him upon the snout.[1599]

17. Indeed, We have tried them as We tried the companions of the garden, when they swore to cut its fruit in the [early] morning

18. Without making exception.[1600]

19. So there came upon it [i.e., the garden] an affliction from your Lord while they were asleep.

20. And it became as though reaped.

21. And they called one another at morning,

22. [Saying], "Go early to your crop if you would cut the fruit."

23. So they set out, while lowering their voices,

24. [Saying], "There will surely not enter it today upon you [any] poor person."

25. And they went early in determination, [assuming themselves] able.[1601]

---

1596 *Al-Qalam*: The Pen.

1597 See footnote to 2:1.

1598 i.e., claiming a particular lineage falsely. The description given in these verses is of al-Waleed bin al-Mugheerah (see also 74:11-25) or possibly, as asserted by Ibn Katheer, al-Akhnas bin Shurayq.

1599 Literally, "trunk," meaning the nose of an elephant or pig.

1600 i.e., without conceding that nothing can be accomplished unless God wills, saying, "...if God wills ("in-shā'-Allāh"). See 18:23-24.

1601 To carry out their plan, confident of their ability.

26. But when they saw it, they said, "Indeed, we are lost;

27. Rather, we have been deprived."

28. The most moderate of them said, "Did I not say to you, 'Why do you not exalt [God]?' "[1602]

29. They said, "Exalted is our Lord! Indeed, we were wrongdoers."

30. Then they approached one another, blaming each other.

31. They said, "O woe to us; indeed we were transgressors.

32. Perhaps our Lord will substitute for us [one] better than it. Indeed, we are toward our Lord desirous."[1603]

33. Such is the punishment [of this world]. And the punishment of the Hereafter is greater, if they only knew.

34. Indeed, for the righteous with their Lord are the Gardens of Pleasure.

35. Then will We treat the Muslims like the criminals?

36. What is [the matter] with you? How do you judge?

37. Or do you have a scripture in which you learn

38. That indeed for you is whatever you choose?

39. Or do you have oaths [binding] upon Us, extending until the Day of Resurrection, that indeed for you is whatever you judge?

40. Ask them which of them, for that [claim], is responsible.

41. Or do they have partners?[1604] Then let them bring their partners, if they should be truthful.

42. The Day the shin will be uncovered[1605] and they are invited to prostration but they [i.e., the disbelievers] will not be able,

43. Their eyes humbled, humiliation will cover them. And they used to be invited to prostration while they were sound.[1606]

44. So leave Me, [O Muhammad], with [the matter of] whoever denies this statement [i.e., the Qur'ān]. We will progressively lead them [to punishment] from where they do not know.[1607]

45. And I will give them time. Indeed, My plan is firm.

46. Or do you ask of them a payment, so they are by debt burdened down?

47. Or have they [knowledge of] the unseen, so they write [it] down?

---

[1602] i.e., remember or mention Him by saying, "...if God wills." An additional meaning is "praise" or "thank" Him for His bounty.
[1603] Of His mercy, forgiveness and bounty.

[1604] i.e., those to whom they attribute divinity other than God or partners from among themselves.
[1605] i.e., when everyone will find before him great difficulty. In accordance with authentic *hadiths*, "the shin" might also refer to that of God, before which every believer will prostrate on the Day of Judgement. See footnote to 2:19.
[1606] During worldly life.
[1607] God will increase His favours to them in this world by way of trial, whereby they will sink deeper into sin and thus into destruction.

48. Then be patient for the decision of your Lord, [O Muhammad], and be not like the companion of the fish [i.e., Jonah] when he called out while he was distressed.

49. If not that a favor [i.e., mercy] from his Lord overtook him, he would have been thrown onto the naked shore while he was censured.[1608]

50. And his Lord chose him and made him of the righteous.

51. And indeed, those who disbelieve would almost make you slip with their eyes [i.e., looks] when they hear the message, and they say, "Indeed, he is mad."

52. But it is not except a reminder to the worlds.

---

[1608] But instead, God accepted his repentance and provided means for his recovery. See 37:139-148.

## Sūrah 69: al-Hāqqah

### Period of Revelation

This too is one of the earliest Sūrahs to be revealed at Makkah. Its subject matter shows that it was sent down at the time when opposition to the Prophet had started but had not yet become tyrannical. Musnad Ahmad contains a hadith from Umar, saying: *"Before embracing Islām one day I came out of my house with a view to causing trouble to the Holy Prophet, but he had entered the Masjid al-Haram before me. When I arrived I found that he was reciting Sūrah Al-Haaqqah in the Prayer. I stood behind him and listened. As he recited the Qur'ān I wondered at its literary charm and beauty. Then suddenly an idea came to my mind that he must be a poet as the Quraysh alleged. Just at that moment he recited the words: "This is the Word of an honourable Messenger: it is not the word of a poet." I said to myself: Then, he must be a soothsayer, if not a poet. Thereupon he recited the words: "Nor is it the word of a soothsayer: little it is that you reflect. It is a Revelation from the Lord and Sustainer of the worlds. On hearing this Islām entered deep into my heart."* This hadith of Umar shows that this Sūrah had been sent down long before his acceptance of Islām, for even after this event he did not believe for a long time, and he continued to be influenced in favor of Islām by different incidents from time to time, till at last in the house of his own sister he came by the experience that made him surrender and submit to the Faith completely.

### Theme and Subject Matter

The first section (v. 1-37) is about the Hereafter and the second (v. 38-52) about the Qur'ān's being a revelation from God and the Prophet's being a true Messenger of God. The first section opens with the assertion that the coming of the Resurrection and the occurrence of the Hereafter is a truth which has to take place inevitably. Then in v. 4-12, it has been stated that the communities that denied the Hereafter in the past became worthy of God's scourge ultimately. In v. 13-17 the occurrence of Resurrection has been depicted. In v. 18-37 the real object for which God has destined a second life for mankind after the present worldly life has been enunciated. In it we are told that on that Day all men shall appear in the Court of their Lord, where no secret of theirs shall remain hidden; each man's record will be placed in his hand. Those who had spent lives in the world with the realization that one day they would have to render an account of their deeds before their Lord, and who had worked righteously in the world and provided beforehand for their well being in the Hereafter, will rejoice when they see that they have been acquitted and blessed with the eternal bliss of Paradise. On the contrary, those who neither recognized the rights of God, nor discharged the rights of men, will have no one to save them from the punishment of God, and they will be cast into Hell.

In the second section (v. 38-52) the disbelievers of Makkah have been addressed and told: "You think this Qur'ān is the word of a poet or soothsayer, whereas it is a Revelation sent down by God, which is being presented by the noble Messengers. The Messenger by himself had no power to increase or decrease a word in it. If he forges something of his own composition into it, We will cut off his neck-vein (or heart-vein). For this is the Truth absolute and pure: and those who give it a lie, will have ultimately to regret and repent."

## Sūrah 69: al-Hāqqah[1609]

In the Name of God, the Most Compassionate, the Most Merciful

1. The Inevitable Reality -

2. What is the Inevitable Reality?

3. And what can make you know what is the Inevitable Reality?

4. Thamūd and 'Aad denied the Striking Calamity [i.e., the Resurrection].

5. So as for Thamūd, they were destroyed by the overpowering [blast].

6. And as for 'Aad, they were destroyed by a screaming,[1610] violent wind

7. Which He [i.e., God] imposed upon them for seven nights and eight days in succession, so you would see the people therein fallen as if they were hollow trunks of palm trees.

8. Then do you see of them any remains?

9. And there came Pharaoh and those before him and the overturned cities[1611] with sin.

10. And they disobeyed the messenger of their Lord, so He seized them with a seizure exceeding [in severity].

11. Indeed, when the water overflowed, We carried you [i.e., your ancestors] in the sailing ship[1612]

12. That We might make it for you a reminder and [that] a conscious ear would be conscious of it.

13. Then when the Horn is blown with one blast

14. And the earth and the mountains are lifted and leveled with one blow [i.e., stroke] -

15. Then on that Day, the Occurrence [i.e., Resurrection] will occur,

16. And the heaven will split [open], for that Day it is infirm.[1613]

17. And the angels are at its edges. And there will bear the Throne of your Lord above them, that Day, eight [of them].

18. That Day, you will be exhibited [for judgement]; not hidden among you is anything concealed.[1614]

19. So as for he who is given his record in his right hand, he will say, "Here, read my record!

20. Indeed, I was certain that I would be meeting my account."

21. So he will be in a pleasant life -

22. In an elevated garden,

23. Its [fruit] to be picked hanging near.

24. [They will be told], "Eat and drink in satisfaction for what you put forth[1615] in the days past."

---

1609 *Al-Hāqqah*: The Inevitable Reality or That Which Manifests Realities – another name for the Resurrection.

1610 Or "cold."

1611 Those to which Lot was sent (see 11:82-83) or generally, all cities which were destroyed due to their denial of a messenger from God.

1612 Which was constructed by Noah.

1613 i.e., weak, enfeebled and unstable.

1614 i.e., any person or any secret you might attempt to conceal.

1615 Literally, "advanced" in anticipation of reward in the Hereafter.

25. But as for he who is given his record in his left hand, he will say, "Oh, I wish I had not been given my record

26. And had not known what is my account.

27. I wish it [i.e., my death] had been the decisive one.[1616]

28. My wealth has not availed me.

29. Gone from me is my authority."

30. [God will say], "Seize him and shackle him.

31. Then into Hellfire drive him.

32. Then into a chain whose length is seventy cubits insert him."

33. Indeed, he did not used to believe in God, the Most Great,

34. Nor did he encourage the feeding of the poor.

35. So there is not for him here this Day any devoted friend

36. Nor any food except from the discharge of wounds;

37. None will eat it except the sinners.

38. So I swear by what you see

39. And what you do not see

40. [That] indeed, it [i.e., the Qur'ān] is the word of a noble Messenger.

41. And it is not the word of a poet; little do you believe.

42. Nor the word of a soothsayer; little do you remember.

43. [It is] a revelation from the Lord of the worlds.

44. And if he [i.e., Muhammad] had made up about Us some [false] sayings,

45. We would have seized him by the right hand;[1617]

46. Then We would have cut from him the aorta.[1618]

47. And there is no one of you who could prevent [Us] from him.

48. And indeed, it [i.e., the Qur'ān] is a reminder for the righteous.

49. And indeed, We know that among you are deniers.

50. And indeed, it will be [a cause of] regret upon the disbelievers.

51. And indeed, it is the truth of certainty.

52. So exalt the name of your Lord, the Most Great.

[1616] i.e., ending life rather than being the gateway to eternal life.

[1617] Another interpretation is "by [Our] right hand," i.e., God would have exacted revenge with might and power.

[1618] Causing immediate death.

## Sūrah 70: al-Ma'ārij

**Period of Revelation**

The subject matter bears evidence that this Sūrah too was sent down in conditions closely resembling those under which Sūrah al-Hāqqah was sent down.

**Theme and Subject Matter**

It admonishes and gives warning to the disbelievers who made fun of the news about Resurrection and the Hereafter, and Hell and Heaven, and challenged the Prophet to cause Resurrection with which he threatened them to take place if what he said was true and they had become worthy of the punishment in Hell by denying it. The whole Sūrah is meant to answer this denial.

The Sūrah opens with words to the effect: "A demander has demanded a torment, the torment which must befall the deniers; and when it takes place, there will be none to prevent it, but it will take place at its own appointed time. God has His own way of doing things, but He is not unjust. Therefore, have patience, O Prophet, at what they say. They think it is far off, but We see it as near at hand."

Then it is said: "Resurrection, which they desire to be hastened out of jest and fun, is terrible, and when it comes, it will cause great distress to the culprits. At that time they will even be prepared to give away their wives and children and their nearest kinsfolk in ransom to escape the punishment, but they will not be able to escape it.

Then the people have been warned to the effect; "On that Day the destinies of men will be decided strictly on the basis of their belief and their conduct. Those who turn away from the Truth in the world and amass wealth and withhold it from the needy, will be doomed to Hell; and those who fear the punishment of God here, believe in the Hereafter, keep up the Prayer, discharge the rights of the needy out of their wealth, strictly avoid immoral and wicked deeds, practice honesty in all their dealings, fulfill their pledges and trust and bear true witness, will have a place of honour in Paradise."

In conclusion, the disbelievers of Makkah who rushed in upon the Prophet from every side as soon as they saw him, in order to make fun of him, have been warned to the effect: "If you do not believe, God will replace you by other people who will be better than you," and the Prophet has been consoled, so as to say: "Do not take to heart their mockery and jesting; leave them to indulge in their idle talk and foolish conduct if they are bent upon experiencing the disgrace and humiliation of the Resurrection; they will themselves see their evil end."

## Sūrah 70: al-Ma'ārij[1619]

In the Name of God, the Most Compassionate, the Most Merciful

1. A supplicant asked for a punishment bound to happen[1620]

2. To the disbelievers; of it there is no preventer.

3. [It is] from God, owner of the ways of ascent.

4. The angels and the Spirit [i.e., Gabriel] will ascend to Him during a Day the extent of which is fifty thousand years.

5. So be patient with gracious patience.

6. Indeed, they see it [as] distant,

7. But We see it [as] near.

8. On the Day the sky will be like murky oil,[1621]

9. And the mountains will be like wool,[1622]

10. And no friend will ask [anything of] a friend,

11. They will be shown each other. The criminal will wish that he could be ransomed from the punishment of that Day by his children

12. And his wife and his brother

13. And his nearest kindred who shelter him

14. And whoever is on earth entirely [so] then it could save him.

15. No![1623] Indeed, it is the Flame [of Hell],

16. A remover of exteriors.[1624]

17. It invites he who turned his back [on truth] and went away [from obedience]

18. And collected [wealth] and hoarded.

19. Indeed, mankind was created anxious:

20. When evil touches him, impatient,

21. And when good touches him, withholding [of it],

22. Except the observers of prayer -

23. Those who are constant in their prayer

24. And those within whose wealth is a known right[1625]

25. For the petitioner and the deprived -

26. And those who believe in the Day of Recompense

27. And those who are fearful of the punishment of their Lord -

28. Indeed, the punishment of their Lord is not that from which one is safe -

[1619] *Al-Ma'ārij*: Ways of Ascent, i.e., those of the angels into the heavens.

[1620] In the Hereafter. Disbelievers had challenged the Prophet by invoking God to bring on His punishment. See 8:32.

[1621] Or "molten metal."

[1622] i.e., in the process of disintegration.

[1623] An emphatic refusal meaning "It is not to be."

[1624] This refers to the skin of the head or of the body or to the body extremities – which will be burned away.

[1625] i.e., a specified share, meaning the obligatory *zakāh*.

29. And those who guard their private parts

30. Except from their wives or those their right hands possess,[1626] for indeed, they are not to be blamed -

31. But whoever seeks beyond that, then they are the transgressors -

32. And those who are to their trusts and promises attentive

33. And those who are in their testimonies upright

34. And those who [carefully] maintain their prayer:

35. They will be in gardens,[1627] honoured.

36. So what is [the matter] with those who disbelieve, hastening [from] before you, [O Muhammad],

37. [To sit] on [your] right and [your] left in separate groups?[1628]

38. Does every person among them aspire to enter a garden of pleasure?

39. No! Indeed, We have created them from that which they know.[1629]

40. So I swear by the Lord of [all] risings and settings[1630] that indeed We are able

41. To replace them with better than them; and We are not to be outdone.

42. So leave them to converse vainly and amuse themselves until they meet their Day which they are promised -

43. The Day they will emerge from the graves rapidly as if they were, toward an erected idol, hastening.[1631]

44. Their eyes humbled, humiliation will cover them. That is the Day which they had been promised.

---

[1626] i.e., female slaves.

[1627] In Paradise.

[1628] They sat at a distance in order to oppose and mock the Prophet, claiming that they would enter Paradise before the believers.

[1629] i.e., a liquid disdained. So how can they expect to enter Paradise except by the will of their Creator?

[1630] i.e., God who determines the point at which the sun, moon and stars rise and set according to season and every position of observation.

[1631] i.e., just as they used to race, whenever an idol was newly appointed, to be the first of its worshippers.

## Sūrah 71: Nūh

### Period of Revelation

This also is one of the earliest Sūrahs to be revealed at Makkah, but the internal evidence of its subject matter shows that it was sent down in the period when opposition to the Prophet's message of Islām by the disbelievers of Makkah had grown very strong and active.

### Theme and Subject

In this Sūrah the story of the Prophet Noah has not been related only for the sake of storytelling, but its object is to warn the disbelievers of Makkah, so as to say: "You, O people of Makkah, are adopting towards Muhammad the same attitude as the people of the Prophet Noah had adopted towards him; if you do not change this attitude, you too would meet with the same end." This had not been said in so many words anywhere in the Sūrah, but in the background of the conditions under which this story was narrated to the people of Makkah, this subject itself became obvious.

Verse 2-4 briefly explain how he began his mission and what he preached. Then after suffering hardships and troubles in the way of preaching his mission for ages the report that he made to his Lord has been given in v. 5-20. In it he states how he had been trying to bring his people to the right path and how his people had stubbornly opposed him.

After this, the Prophet Noah's final submission has been recorded in v. 21-24, in which he prays to his Lord, saying: "These people have rejected my invitation: they are blindly following their chiefs, who have devised a tremendous plot of deceit and cunning. Time now has come when these people should be deprived of every grace to accept guidance." This was not an expression of impatience by the Prophet Noah, but when after having preached his message under extremely trying circumstances for centuries be became utterly disappointed with his people, he formed the opinion that no chance whatever was left of their coming to the right path. His opinion fully conformed to God's own decision. Thus, in the next verse (25), it has been said: "The torment of God descended on those people because of their misdeeds."

In the concluding verse, the Prophet Noah's supplication that he made to his Lord, right at the time the torment descended, has been recorded. He prays for his own and for all the believers' forgiveness, and makes a submission to God to the effect: "Do not leave any of the disbelievers alive on the earth, for they have become utterly devoid of every good: they will not beget any but disbelieving and wicked descendent."

While studying this Sūrah one should keep in view the details of the Prophet Noah's story which have been given in the Qur'ān. For this see the following al-A'raf: 59-64 Yunus: 71,73, Hud: 25-49, al-Mu'minun: 23-31, ash- Shua'ra: 105-122, al-Ankabut: 14,15, as-Saffat: 75-82, al-Qamar: 9-16.

## Sūrah 71: Nūh[1632]

In the Name of God, the Most Compassionate, the Most Merciful

1. Indeed, We sent Noah to his people, [saying], "Warn your people before there comes to them a painful punishment."

2. He said, "O my people, indeed I am to you a clear warner,

3. [Saying], 'Worship God, fear Him and obey me.

4. He [i.e., God] will forgive you of your sins and delay you for a specified term. Indeed, the time [set by] God, when it comes, will not be delayed, if you only knew.' "

5. He said, "My Lord, indeed I invited my people [to truth] night and day.

6. But my invitation increased them not except in flight [i.e., aversion].

7. And indeed, every time I invited them that You may forgive them, they put their fingers in their ears, covered themselves with their garments,[1633] persisted, and were arrogant with [great] arrogance.

8. Then I invited them publicly.

9. Then I announced to them and [also] confided to them secretly

10. And said, 'Ask forgiveness of your Lord. Indeed, He is ever a Perpetual Forgiver.

11. He will send [rain from] the sky upon you in [continuing] showers

12. And give you increase in wealth and children and provide for you gardens and provide for you rivers.

13. What is [the matter] with you that you do not attribute to God [due] grandeur

14. While He has created you in stages?[1634]

15. Do you not consider how God has created seven heavens in layers[1635]

16. And made the moon therein a [reflected] light and made the sun a burning lamp?

17. And God has caused you to grow from the earth a [progressive] growth.

18. Then He will return you into it and extract you [another] extraction.

19. And God has made for you the earth an expanse

20. That you may follow therein roads of passage.' "

21. Noah said, "My Lord, indeed they have disobeyed me and followed him whose wealth and children will not increase him except in loss.

22. And they conspired an immense conspiracy.

23. And said, 'Never leave your gods and never leave Wadd or Suwā' or Yaghūth and Ya'ūq and Nasr.'[1636]

---

[1632] *Nūh*: (The Prophet) Noah.
[1633] Refusing to look or listen.

[1634] i.e., in various progressive states and conditions. See 22:5 and 23:12-14.
[1635] See footnote to 67:3.
[1636] These were the names of specific idols named after pious men of earlier generations.

24. And already they have misled many. And, [my Lord], do not increase the wrongdoers except in error."

25. Because of their sins they were drowned and put into the Fire, and they found not for themselves besides God [any] helpers.

26. And Noah said, "My Lord, do not leave upon the earth from among the disbelievers an inhabitant.

27. Indeed, if You leave them, they will mislead Your servants and not beget except [every] wicked one and [confirmed] disbeliever.

28. My Lord, forgive me and my parents and whoever enters my house a believer and the believing men and believing women. And do not increase the wrongdoers except in destruction."

## Sūrah 72: al-Jinn

### Period o Revelation

According to a hadith related in Bukhari and Muslim, on the authority of Abdullah bin Abbas, once the Prophet was going to Visit the Fair of Ukaz with some of his Companions. On the way be led the Fajr Prayer at Nakhlah. At that time a company of the Jinn happened to pass that way. When they heard the Qur'ān being recited, they stopped and listened to it attentively. This very event has been described in this Sūrah.

Most of the commentators, on the basis of this hadith, believe that this relates to the Prophet's well known journey to Tā'if, which had taken place three years before the Hijrah in the 10th year of the Prophethood. But this is not correct for several reasons. The Jinn's hearing the Qur'ān during the journey to Tā'if has been related in al-Ahqaf 29-32. A cursory reading of those verses shows that the Jinn who had believed after hearing the Qur'ān on that occasion were already believers in the Prophet Moses and the previous scriptures. On the contrary, v. 2-7 of this Sūrah clearly show that the Jinn who heard the Qur'ān on this occasion were polytheists and deniers of the Hereafter and Prophethood. Then, it is confirmed historically that in his journey to Tā'if none accompanied the Prophet except Zayd bin Harithah. On the contrary, concerning this journey Ibn Abbas says that the Prophet was accompanied by some of his Companions. Furthermore, the hadith also agree that in that journey the Jinn heard the Qur'ān when the Prophet had stopped at Nakhlah on his return journey from Tā'if to Makkah, and in this journey, according to the hadith of Ibn Abbas, the event of the Jinn's hearing the Qur'ān occurred when the Prophet was going to Ukaz from Makkah. Therefore, in view of these reasons what seems to be correct is that in Sūrah al-Ahqaf and Sūrah al-Jinn, one and the same event has not been narrated, but these were two separate events, which took place during two separate journeys.

As far as Sūrah al-Ahqaf is concerned, it is agreed that the event mentioned in it occurred on the return journey from Tā'if in the 10th year of Prophethood. As for the question, when this second event took place, its answer is not given by the tradition of Ibn Abbas, nor any other historical tradition shows as to when the Prophet had gone to the Fair of Ukaz along with some of his Companions. However, a little consideration of v 8-10 of this Sūrah shows that this could only be an event of the earliest stage of Prophethood. In these verses it has been stated that before the appointment of the Prophet to Divine Mission the Jinn used to have one or another opportunity to eavesdrop in the heavens in order to hear news of the unseen, but after it they suddenly found that angels had been set as guards and meteorites were being shot on every side so that they could find no place of safety from where they could hear the secret news. Thereupon they had set about searching for the unusual thing that had occurred on the earth, or was going to occur, because of which the security measures had been tightened up. Probably since then many companies of the Jinn must have been moving about in search of the unusual occurrence and one of them after having heard the Qur'ān from the Prophet must have formed the opinion that that was the very thing for the sake of which all the gates of the heavens had been shut against the Jinn.

### Reality of Jinn

Before one starts the study of this Sūrah one must clearly know what is the reality of the Jinn so as to avoid any possible mental confusion. Many people of the modern times are involved in the misunderstanding that the Jinn are not real, but only a figment of the ancient superstition and myths. They have not formed this opinion on the basis that they have known all the realities and truths about the universe and have thus discovered that the Jinn do not exist. They cannot claim to possess any such knowledge either. But they have assumed without reason and proof that nothing exists in the universe except what they can see, whereas the sphere of human perceptions as against the vastness of this great universe is not even comparable to a drop of water as against the ocean. Here, the person who thinks that what he does not perceive, does not exist, and what exists must necessarily be perceived, in fact, provides a proof of the narrowness of his own mind. With this mode of thought, not to speak of the Jinn, man cannot even accept and acknowledge any reality, which he cannot directly experience and observe, and he cannot even admit the existence of God, to say nothing of admitting any other unseen reality.

Those of the Muslims who have been influenced by modernism, but cannot deny the Qur'ān either, have given strange interpretations of the clear statements of the Qur'ān about the Jinn, Iblis and Satan. They say that this does not refer to any hidden creation, which may have its own independent existence, but it sometimes implies man's own animal forces, which have been called Satan, and sometimes it implies savage and wild mountain tribes, and sometimes the people who used to listen to the Qur'ān secretly. But the statements of the Qur'ān in this regard are so clear and explicit that these interpretations bear no relevance to them whatever.

The Qur'ān frequently mentions the Jinn and the men in a manner as to indicate that they are two separate creations. For this, see al-A'raf: 38, Hud: 119, Ha-Mim As-Sajdah: 25,29, Ahqaf: 18, Adh-Dhariyat: 56, and the entire Sūrah ar-Rahman, which bears such clear evidence as to leave no room to regard the Jinn as a human species.

In Sūrah al-A'raf: 12, al-Hijr: 26-27 and ar-Rahman: 14-19, it has been expressly stated that man was created out of clay and Jinn out of fire. In Sūrah al-Hijr: 27, it has been said that the Jinn had been created before man. The same thing is testified by the story of Adam and Iblis, which has been told at seven different places in the Qur'ān, and at every place it confirms that Iblis was already there at the creation of man. Moreover, in Sūrah al-Kahf: 50, it has been stated that Iblis belonged to the Jinn. In Sūrah al-A'raf: 27, it has been stated in clear words that the Jinn see the human beings but the human beings do not see them. In Sūrah al-Hijr: 16-18, Sūrah as-Saffat: 6-10 and Sūrah al-Mulk: 5, it has been said that although the Jinn can ascend to the heavens, they cannot exceed a certain limit; if they try to ascend beyond that limit and try to hear what goes on in the heavens, they are not allowed to do so, and if they try to eavesdrop they are driven away by meteorites. By this the belief of the polytheistic Arabs that the Jinn possess the knowledge of the unseen, or have access to Divine secrets, has been refuted. The same error has also been refuted in Saba: 14, al-Baqarah: 30-34 and al-Kahf: 50 show that God has entrusted man with the vicegerency of the earth and the men are superior to the Jinn. Although the Jinn also have been given certain extraordinary powers and abilities an example of which is found in an-Naml 39, yet the animals likewise have been given some powers greater than man, but these are no argument that the animals are superior to man.

The Qur'ān also explains that the Jinn, like men, are a creation possessed of power and authority, and they, just like them, can choose between obedience and disobedience, faith and disbelief. This is confirmed by the story of Satan and the event of the Jinn affirming the faith as found in Sūrahs al-Ahqaf and al-Jinn.

At scores of places in the Qur'ān, it has also been stated that Iblis at the very creation of Adam had resolved to misguide mankind, and since then the Satanic Jinn have been persistently trying to mislead man, but they do not have the power to overwhelm him and make him do something forcibly. However, they inspire him with evil suggestions, beguile him and make evil seem good to him. For this, see an-Nisa 117-120, al-A'raf: 11-17, Ibrahim 22, al-Hijr 30-42, an-Nahl 98-100, al-Isra 61-65. The Qur'ān also tells us that in the pre-Islāmic ignorance the polytheistic Arabs regarded the Jinn as associates of God, worshipped them and thought they were descended from God. For this, see al-An'am: 100, Saba: 40-41, as-Saffat: 158.

From these details, it becomes abundantly clear that the Jinn have their own objective existence and are a concealed creation of an entirely different species from man. Because of their mysterious qualities, ignorant people have formed exaggerated notions and concepts about them and their powers, and have even worshipped them, but the Qur'ān has explained the whole truth about them, which shows what they are and what they are not.

**Theme and Topics**

In this Sūrah in v. 1-15, it has been told what was the impact of the Qur'ān on the company of the Jinn when they heard it and what they said to their fellow Jinn when they returned to them. God, in this connection, has not cited their whole conversation but only those particular things which were worthy of mention. That is why the style is not that of a continuous speech but sentences have been cited so as to indicate that they said this and this. If one studies these sentences spoken by the Jinn carefully, one can easily understand the real object of the narration of this event of their affirming the faith and or mentioning this conversation of theirs with their people in the Qur'ān.

After this, in v. 16-18, the people have been admonished to the effect: "If you refrain from polytheism and follow the way of righteousness firmly, you will be blessed; otherwise if you turn away from the admonition sent down by God, you will meet with a severe punishment." Then, in v. 19-23, the disbelievers of Makkah have been reproached, as if to say: When the Messenger of God calls you towards God, you surround and mob him from every side, whereas the only duty of the Messenger is to convey the messages of God. He does not claim to have any power to bring any gain or cause any harm to the people." Then, in v. 24-25 the disbelievers have been warned to the effect: "Today you are trying to overpower and suppress the Messenger seeing that he is helpless and friendless, but a time will come when you will know who in actual fact is helpless and friendless. Whether that time is yet far off, or near at hand, the Messenger has no knowledge thereof, but it will come to pass in any case." In conclusion, the people have been told: The Knower of the unseen is God alone. The Messenger receives only that knowledge which God is pleased to give him. This knowledge pertains to matters connected with the performance of the duties of Prophethood and it is delivered to him in such security which does not admit of any external interference whatever.

## Sūrah 72: al-Jinn[1637]

In the Name of God, the Most Compassionate, the Most Merciful

1. Say, [O Muhammad], "It has been revealed to me that a group of the jinn listened and said, 'Indeed, we have heard an amazing Qur'ān [i.e., recitation].

2. It guides to the right course, and we have believed in it. And we will never associate with our Lord anyone.

3. And [it teaches] that exalted is the nobleness of our Lord; He has not taken a wife or a son

4. And that our foolish one [i.e., Iblees][1638] has been saying about God an excessive transgression.

5. And we had thought that mankind and the jinn would never speak about God a lie.

6. And there were men from mankind who sought refuge in men from the jinn, so they [only] increased them in burden [i.e., sin].

7. And they had thought, as you thought, that God would never send anyone [as a messenger].

8. And we have sought [to reach] the heaven but found it filled with powerful guards and burning flames.

9. And we used to sit therein in positions for hearing,[1639] but whoever listens now will find a burning flame lying in wait for him.

10. And we do not know [therefore] whether evil is intended for those on earth or whether their Lord intends for them a right course.

11. And among us are the righteous, and among us are [others] not so; we were [of] divided ways.[1640]

12. And we have become certain that we will never cause failure to God upon earth, nor can we escape Him by flight.

13. And when we heard the guidance [i.e., the Qur'ān], we believed in it. And whoever believes in his Lord will not fear deprivation or burden.[1641]

14. And among us are Muslims [in submission to God], and among us are the unjust.[1642] And whoever has become Muslim - those have sought out the right course.

15. But as for the unjust, they will be, for Hell, firewood.'

16. And [God revealed] that if they had remained straight on the way, We would have given them abundant rain [i.e., provision]

17. So We might test them therein. And whoever turns away from the remem-

---

1637 *Al-Jinn:* The Jinn, a species of beings created by God from fire.

1638 A plural form may also be understood, i.e., "the foolish ones among us."

1639 Before the prophethood of Muhammad the *jinn* used to collect information by eavesdropping on the angels and then pass it on to fortunetellers and soothsayers.

1640 In opinion, belief and religious practice.

1641 In regard to his account in the Hereafter. Nothing of his good will be diminished, nor will the evil of another be placed upon him.

1642 i.e., those who deviate from truth and act tyrannically.

brance of his Lord[1643] He will put into arduous punishment.

18. And [He revealed] that the masjids[1644] are for God, so do not invoke with God anyone.

19. And that when the Servant [i.e., Prophet] of God stood up supplicating Him, they almost became about him a compacted mass."[1645]

20. Say, [O Muhammad], "I only invoke my Lord and do not associate with Him anyone."

21. Say, "Indeed, I do not possess for you [the power of] harm or right direction."

22. Say, "Indeed, there will never protect me from God anyone [if I should disobey], nor will I find in other than Him a refuge.

23. But [I have for you] only notification from God, and His messages." And whoever disobeys God and His Messenger - then indeed, for him is the fire of Hell; they will abide therein forever.

24. [The disbelievers continue] until, when they see that which they are promised, then they will know who is weaker in helpers and less in number.

25. Say, "I do not know if what you are promised is near or if my Lord will grant for it a [long] period."

26. [He is] Knower of the unseen, and He does not disclose His [knowledge of the] unseen to anyone

27. Except whom He has approved of messengers, and indeed, He sends before him [i.e., each messenger] and behind him observers[1646]

28. That he [i.e., Muhammad] may know[1647] that they have conveyed the messages of their Lord; and He has encompassed whatever is with them and has enumerated all things in number.

[1643] i.e., refuses obedience to Him.

[1644] The term "*masjid*" here includes every place of worship or the earth in general.

[1645] Crowding on top of each other in the manner of locusts in order to hear him. "They" may refer to the *jinn* or to the disbelievers among the Arabs.

[1646] Guardian angels to protect the messenger and the message.

[1647] This phrase may also read: "So He [i.e., God] may make evident."

## Sūrah 73: al-Muzzammil

### Period of Revelation

The two sections of this Sūrah were revealed in two separate periods. The first section (v. 1-19) is unanimously a Makki Revelation, and this is supported both by its subject matter and by the hadith. As for the question, in which specific period of the life at Makkah it was revealed, it is not answered by the tradition, but the internal evidence of the subject matter of this section helps to determine the period of its revelation.

First, in it the Prophet has been instructed to the effect: "Arise during the night and worship God so that you may develop the capability to shoulder the heavy burden of Prophethood and to discharge its responsibilities." This shows that this Command must have been given in the earliest period of the Prophethood when training was being imparted to the Prophet by God for this office.

Secondly, a Command has been given in it that the Qur'ān be recited in the Tahajjud Prayer for half the night, or thereabouts. This Command by itself points out that by that time at least so much of the Qur'ān had been revealed as could be recited for that long.

Thirdly, in this section the Prophet has been exhorted to have patience at the excesses being committed by his opponents, and the disbelievers of Makkah have been threatened with the torment. This shows that this section was revealed at a time when the Prophet had openly started preaching Islām and the opposition to him at Makkah had grown active and strong.

About the second section (v. 20) although many of the commentators have expressed the opinion that this too was sent down at Makkah, yet some other commentators regard it as a Madani Revelation, and this same opinion is confirmed by the subject matter of this section. For it mentions fighting in the way of God, and obviously, there could be no question of it at Makkah; it also contains the Command to pay the obligatory Zakāh, and it is fully confirmed that the Zakāh at a specific rate and with an exemption limit (nisab) was enjoined at Madinah.

### Theme and Subject Matter

In the first seven verses the Prophet has been commanded to the effect: "Prepare yourself to shoulder the responsibilities of the great Mission that has been entrusted to you; its practical form is that you should rise during the hours of night and stand up in Prayer for half the night, or for a little more or less of it."

In v. 8-14, he has been exhorted to the effect: "Devote yourself exclusively to that God Who is the Owner of the whole universe, entrust all your affairs to Him with full satisfaction of the heart. Bear with patience whatever your opponents may utter against you. Do not be intimate with them. Leave their affair to God: He Himself will deal with them."

Then, in v. 15-19, those of the people of Makkah, who were opposing the Prophet have been warned, so as to say: "We have sent a Messenger to you just as We sent a Messenger to the Pharaoh. Just consider what fate the Pharaoh met when he did not accept the invitation of the Messenger of God. Supposing that you are not punished by a torment in this world, how will you save yourselves from the punishment for disbelief on the Day of Resurrection."

This is the subject matter of the first section. The second section, according to a hadith from Sa'id bin Jubair, was sent down ten years later, and in it the initial Command given in connection with the Tahajjud Prayer, in the beginning of the first section, was curtailed. The new Command enjoined, "Offer as much of the Tahajjud Prayer as you easily can, but what the Muslims should particularly mind and attend to is the five times obligatory Prayer a day, they should establish it regularly and punctually; they should discharge their Zakāh dues accurately; and they should spend their wealth with sincere intentions for the sake of God. In conclusion, the Muslims have been exhorted, saying: "Whatever good works you do in the world, will not go waste, but they are like the provision which a traveler sends up in advance to his permanent place of residence. Whatever good you send up from the world, you will find it with God, and the provision thus sent up is much better than what you will have to leave behind in the world, and with God you will also get a much better and richer reward than what you have actually sent up before."

## Sūrah 73: al-Muzzammil[1648]

In the Name of God, the Most Compassionate, the Most Merciful

1. O you who wraps himself [in clothing],[1649]

2. Arise [to pray] the night, except for a little -

3. Half of it - or subtract from it a little

4. Or add to it, and recite the Qur'ān with measured recitation.

5. Indeed, We will cast upon you a heavy word.[1650]

6. Indeed, the hours of the night are more effective for concurrence [of heart and tongue][1651] and more suitable for words.[1652]

7. Indeed, for you by day is prolonged occupation.

8. And remember the name of your Lord and devote yourself to Him with [complete] devotion.

9. [He is] the Lord of the East and the West; there is no deity except Him, so take Him as Disposer of [your] affairs.[1653]

10. And be patient over what they say and avoid them with gracious avoidance.

11. And leave Me with [the matter of] the deniers, those of ease [in life], and allow them respite a little.

12. Indeed, with Us [for them] are shackles and burning fire

13. And food that chokes and a painful punishment -

14. On the Day the earth and the mountains will convulse and the mountains will become a heap of sand pouring down.

15. Indeed, We have sent to you a Messenger as a witness upon you just as We sent to Pharaoh a messenger.

16. But Pharaoh disobeyed the messenger, so We seized him with a ruinous seizure.

17. Then how can you fear, if you disbelieve, a Day that will make the children white-haired?[1654]

18. The heaven will break apart therefrom;[1655] ever is His promise fulfilled.

19. Indeed, this is a reminder, so whoever wills may take to his Lord a way.

20. Indeed, your Lord knows, [O Muhammad], that you stand [in prayer] almost two thirds of the night or half of it or a third of it, and [so do] a group of those

[1648] *Al-Muzzammil*: The One Who Wraps Himself (in clothing).
[1649] God addresses the Prophet, who was asleep, wrapped in his garments.
[1650] i.e., the revelation, which when descending on the Prophet bore down upon him with a great weight. Another meaning is "important ordinances."
[1651] Another accepted interpretation of the same words is "Indeed, arising at night is more difficult...," meaning that it will only be done by sincere believers and not others.
[1652] i.e., for recitation of the Qur'ān and for hearing and understanding it.
[1653] i.e., trust in God and rely upon Him.
[1654] Another meaning is "How can you avoid [punishment]" on such a Day?
[1655] From the terror of that Day.

with you. And God determines [the extent of] the night and the day. He has known that you [Muslims] will not be able to do it[1656] and has turned to you in forgiveness, so recite what is easy [for you] of the Qur'ān. He has known that there will be among you those who are ill and others traveling throughout the land seeking [something] of the bounty of God and others fighting for the cause of God. So recite what is easy from it and establish prayer and give zakāh and loan God a goodly loan.[1657] And whatever good you put forward for yourselves - you will find it with God. It is better and greater in reward. And seek forgiveness of God. Indeed, God is Forgiving and Merciful.

[1656] God has known that if they were to continue in such long periods of worship each night, the people would be caused much hardship.
[1657] In the form of charities and contributions to His cause.

## Sūrah 74: al-Muddathir

### Period of Revelation

The first seven verses of this Sūrah belong to the earliest period at Makkah. Even according to some hadith which have been related in Bukhari, Muslim, Tirmidhi, Musnad Ahmad, etc., on the authority of Jabir bin Abdullah, these are the very earliest verses of the Qur'ān to be revealed to the Prophet. But the Muslim Ummah almost unanimously agreed that the earliest revelation to the Prophet consisted of the first five verses of Sūrah al-Alaq (96) However, what is established by authentic hadith that after this first Revelation, no Revelation came down to the Prophet for quite some time. Then, when it was resumed, it started with the verses of Sūrah al-Muddathir - Imām Zuhri has given the following details of it:

"Revelation to the Prophet remained suspended for quite some time, and it was such a period of deep grief and distress for him that he started going early to the tops of the mountains to throw himself down from them. But whenever he stood on the edge of a peak, the Angel Gabriel would appear and tell him that he was God's Prophet. This would console him and restore to him full peace of mind." (Ibn Jarir). After this Imām Zuhri relates the following tradition on the authority of Jabir bin Abdullah; "The Messenger of God describing the period of falrat al-wahi (break in revelation) said: One day when I was passing on the way, I suddenly heard a call from heaven. I raised my head and saw that the same Angel who had visited me in the Cave of Hira was sitting on a throne between heaven and earth. This struck terror in my heart, and reaching home quickly, I said: 'Cover me up, cover me up'. So the people of the house covered me up with a quilt (or blanket). At that time God sent down the Revelation: Ya ayyuhal-Muddathiru... From then on revelation became intense and continuous." (Bukhari, Muslim Musnad Ahmad, Ibn Jarir).

The rest of the Sūrah (v. 8-56) was revealed when the first Hajj season came after public preaching of Islām had begun in Makkah.

### Theme and Subject Matter

As has been explained above, the earliest Revelation to the Prophet consisted of the first five verses of Sūrah Al-Alaq:

**Recite in the name of your Lord who created. Created man from a clinging substance. Recite, and your Lord is the most Generous. Who taught by the pen. Taught man that which he knew not.**

This was the first experience of Revelation by the Prophet. In this message it was not told what great mission he had been entrusted with and what duties he had to perform in future. He was only initiated into it and then left alone for a time so that the great strain this experience had caused should pass away and he should mentally become prepared to receive the Revelation and perform the prophetic mission in the future. After this intermission when Revelation was resumed, the first seven verses of this Sūrah were revealed: In these he was for the first time commanded to arise and warn the people of the consequences of the way of life they were following and to proclaim the greatness of God in the world where others were being magnified without any right. Along with that he was given this instruction: The demand of the Unique mission that you have to perform, now is that your life should be pure in every respect and you should carry out the duty of reforming your people sincerely irrespective of any worldly gain. Then, in the last sentence, he was exhorted to endure with patience, for the sake of his Lord, all the hardships and troubles that he might have to face while performing his mission.

In the implementation of this Divine Command when the Messenger of God began to preach Islām and recite the Qur'ānic Sūrahs revealed successively, the people of Makkah felt alarmed, and it provoked a great storm of opposition and hostility. A few months passed in this state until the Hajj season approached. The people of Makkah feared that if Muhammad started visiting the caravans of the pilgrims coming from all over Arabia at their halting places and reciting the spellbinding and unique Revelations of the Qur'ān in their assemblies on the occasion of Hajj, his message would reach every part of Arabia and influence countless people. Therefore, the Quraysh chiefs held a conference and settled that they would start a propaganda campaign against the Prophet among the pilgrims as soon as they arrived. After they had agreed on this, Walid bin al-Mughirah said to the assembled people: *'If you said contradictory things about Muhammad , we all would lose our trust among the people. Therefore, let us agree upon one opinion, which we should all say without dispute.* Some people said that they would call Muhammad a soothsayer. Walid said: *'No, by God, he is not a soothsayer. We have seen the soothsayers: what they murmur and what they utter has no remote resemblance with the Qur'ān.'* Some other people said: *'Then we say he is possessed.'* Walid said: *He is not a possessed one: we have seen bad and insane people; the way one talks disjointedly and behaves foolishly in that state is known to all: who would believe that what Muhammad presented was the incoherent speech of a madman?* The people said: *'Then we say he is a poet.'* Walid said: *'No, he is not a poet, for we know poetry in all its forms, and what he presents conforms to no form of it.'* The people said: *'Then he is a sorcerer.'* Walid said: *'He is no sorcerer either: we have seen sorcerers and we also know what methods they adopt for their sorcery. This also does not apply to Muhammad.'* Then he said: *'Whichever of these things you said about Muhammad, it would be known to be a false accusation. By God, his speech is sweet, his root is deep and his branches are fruitful.'* At this Abu Jahl, urging on Walid, said: *'Your people will never be pleased with you unless you say something about Muhammad.'* He said: *'Let me think over it awhile.'* Then, after prolonged thought and consideration, he said: *'The nearest thing to the truth is that you tell the Arabs that he is a sorcerer, who has brought a message by which he separates a man from his father; and from his brother, and from his wife and children, and from his family.'* They all agreed on what Walid had proposed. Then, according to a scheme the men of Quraysh spread among the pilgrims in the Hajj season and they warned everyone they met of the sorcery of Muhammad and of his stirring up divisions in the families by it. But the result was that by their this plan the Quraysh chiefs themselves made the name of the Messenger known throughout Arabia. That Walid had made this proposal on the insistence of Abu Jahl has been related by Ibn Jarir in his Tafsir on the authority of Ikrimah.

In conclusion, it has been explicitly stated: God does not stand in need of anybody's faith that He may fulfill his conditions. The Qur'ān is an admonition that has been presented before the people openly; now whoever wills may accept it. God has a right that the people should fear His disobedience and He alone has the power to forgive the one who adopts piety and an attitude of God consciousness even though one may have committed many acts of disobedience in the past.

## Sūrah 74: al-Muddathir[1658]

In the Name of God, the Most Compassionate, the Most Merciful

1. O you who covers himself [with a garment],[1659]
2. Arise and warn
3. And your Lord glorify
4. And your clothing purify
5. And uncleanliness[1660] avoid
6. And do not confer favor to acquire more[1661]
7. But for your Lord be patient.
8. And when the trumpet is blown,
9. That Day will be a difficult day
10. For the disbelievers - not easy.
11. Leave Me with the one I created alone[1662]
12. And to whom I granted extensive wealth
13. And children present [with him]
14. And spread [everything] before him, easing [his life].
15. Then he desires that I should add more.
16. No! Indeed, he has been toward Our verses obstinate.
17. I will cover him with arduous torment.
18. Indeed, he thought and deliberated.[1663]
19. So may he be destroyed [for] how he deliberated.
20. Then may he be destroyed [for] how he deliberated.
21. Then he considered [again];
22. Then he frowned and scowled;
23. Then he turned back and was arrogant
24. And said, "This is not but magic imitated [from others].
25. This is not but the word of a human being."
26. I will drive him into Saqar.[1664]
27. And what can make you know what is Saqar?
28. It lets nothing remain and leaves nothing [unburned],
29. Altering [i.e., blackening] the skins.
30. Over it are nineteen [angels].

[1658] *Al-Muddathir*: The One Who Covers Himself (with a garment).
[1659] Referring to the Prophet.
[1660] Specifically, idols or generally, bad conduct and morals.
[1661] An alternative meaning is "Do not consider any favour you have conferred to be great."
[1662] i.e., without wealth or children. The reference is to al-Waleed bin al-Mugheerah, who after inclining toward the Qur'ān, denied it publicly in order to win the approval of the Quraysh.

[1663] About what he would say concerning the Qur'ān and how he might discredit the Prophet.
[1664] One of the proper names of Hell.

31. And We have not made the keepers of the Fire except angels. And We have not made their number except as a trial for those who disbelieve - that those who were given the Scripture will be convinced and those who have believed will increase in faith and those who were given the Scripture and the believers will not doubt and that those in whose hearts is disease [i.e., hypocrisy] and the disbelievers will say, "What does God intend by this as an example?" Thus does God leave astray whom He wills and guides whom He wills. And none knows the soldiers of your Lord except Him. And it [i.e., mention of the Fire] is not but a reminder to humanity.

32. No! By the moon

33. And [by] the night when it departs

34. And [by] the morning when it brightens,

35. Indeed, it [i.e., the Fire] is of the greatest [afflictions]

36. As a warning to humanity -

37. To whoever wills among you to proceed[1665] or stay behind.

38. Every soul, for what it has earned, will be retained[1666]

39. Except the companions of the right,[1667]

40. [Who will be] in gardens, questioning each other

41. About the criminals,

42. [And asking them], "What put you into Saqar?"

43. They will say, "We were not of those who prayed,

44. Nor did we used to feed the poor.

45. And we used to enter into vain discourse with those who engaged [in it],

46. And we used to deny the Day of Recompense

47. Until there came to us the certainty [i.e., death]."

48. So there will not benefit them the intercession of [any] intercessors.

49. Then what is [the matter] with them that they are, from the reminder, turning away

50. As if they were alarmed donkeys

51. Fleeing from a lion?

52. Rather, every person among them desires that he[1668] would be given scriptures spread about.[1669]

53. No! But they do not fear the Hereafter.

54. No! Indeed, it [i.e., the Qur'ān] is a reminder

55. Then whoever wills will remember it.

---

[1665] To righteousness by acceptance of the warning.

[1666] i.e., subject or held responsible.

[1667] i.e., the righteous who receive their records in their right hands.

[1668] Instead of Prophet Muhammad

[1669] i.e., made public. Much of their refusal of his message was due to envy and jealousy of the Prophet.

56. And they will not remember except that God wills. He is worthy of fear and adequate for [granting] forgiveness.

## Sūrah 75: al-Qiyāmah

### Period of Revelation

Although there is no tradition to indicate its period of revelation, yet there is in the subject matter of this Sūrah an internal evidence, which shows that it is one of the earliest Sūrahs to be sent down at Makkah. After verse 15 the discourse is suddenly interrupted and the Prophet told: "Do not move your tongue to remember this Revelation hastily. It is Our responsibility to have it remembered and read. Therefore, when We are reciting it, listen to its recital carefully. Again, it is Our responsibility to explain its meaning." Then, from verse 20 onward the same theme which was interrupted at verse 15, is resumed. This parenthetical passage, according to both the context and the traditions, has been interposed here for the reason that when the Angel Gabriel was reciting this Sūrah to the Prophet, the Prophet, lest he should forget its words later, was repeating them at the same moment. This in fact happened at the time when the coming down and receipt of Revelation was yet a new experience for him and he was not yet fully used to receiving it calmly. There are two other instances also of this in the Qur'ān. First, in Sūrah Ta-Ha the Prophet has been told: "And see that you do not hasten to recite the Qur'ān before its revelation is completed to you." (v. 114). Then, in Sūrah al-A'la, it has been said: "We shall enable you to recite:, then you shall never forget." (v. 6). Later, when the Prophet became fully used to receiving the Revelation well, there remained no need to give him any such instruction. That is why except for these three, there is no other instance of this in the Qur'ān.

### Theme and Subject Matter

Most of the Sūrahs, from here till the end of the Qur'ān, in view of their content and style, seem to have been sent down in the period when after the first seven verses of Sūrah al-Muddathir, revelation of the Qur'ān began like a shower of rain: Thus, in the successively revealed Sūrahs Islām and its fundamental concepts and moral teachings were presented so forcefully and effectively in concise, brief sentences and the people of Makkah warned so vehemently on their errors and deviations that the Quraysh chiefs were utterly confounded. Therefore, before the next Hajj season came they held the conference for devising schemes to defeat the Prophet as has been mentioned in the introduction to Sūrah al-Muddathir previously.

In this Sūrah, addressing the deniers of the Hereafter, replies have been given to each of their doubts and objections, strong arguments have been given to prove the possibility, occurrence and necessity of the Resurrection and Hereafter, and also it has been pointed out clearly that the actual reason of the people's denying the Hereafter is not that they regard it as impossible rationally but because their selfish motives do not allow them to affirm it. At the same time, the people have been warned, as if to say: "The event, the occurrence of which you deny, will inevitably come: all your deeds will be brought and placed before you. As a matter of fact, even before any of you sees his record, he will be knowing fully well what he has done in the world, for no man is unaware of himself, no matter what excuses and pretenses he may offer to deceive the world and deceive himself in respect of his misdeeds."

## Sūrah 75: al-Qiyāmah[1670]

In the Name of God, the Most Compassionate, the Most Merciful

1. I swear by the Day of Resurrection

2. And I swear by the reproaching soul[1671] [to the certainty of resurrection].

3. Does man think that We will not assemble his bones?

4. Yes. [We are] Able [even] to proportion his fingertips.

5. But man desires to continue in sin.[1672]

6. He asks, "When is the Day of Resurrection?"

7. So when vision is dazzled

8. And the moon darkens

9. And the sun and the moon are joined,

10. Man will say on that Day, "Where is the [place of] escape?"

11. No! There is no refuge.

12. To your Lord, that Day, is the [place of] permanence.

13. Man will be informed that Day of what he sent ahead[1673] and kept back.[1674]

14. Rather, man, against himself, will be a witness,[1675]

15. Even if he presents his excuses.

16. Move not your tongue with it, [O Muhammad], to hasten with it [i.e., recitation of the Qur'ān].

17. Indeed, upon Us is its collection [in your heart] and [to make possible] its recitation.

18. So when We have recited it [through Gabriel], then follow its recitation.

19. Then upon Us is its clarification [to you].

20. No! But you [i.e., mankind] love the immediate

21. And leave [i.e., neglect] the Hereafter.

22. [Some] faces, that Day, will be radiant,

23. Looking at their Lord.[1676]

24. And [some] faces, that Day, will be contorted,

25. Expecting that there will be done to them [something] backbreaking.

26. No! When it [i.e., the soul] has reached the collar bones[1677]

27. And it is said, "Who will cure [him]?"

28. And he [i.e., the dying one] is certain that it is the [time of] separation

---

[1670] *Al-Qiyāmah*: The resurrection.

[1671] i.e., that of the believer, which blames him when he falls into sin or error.

[1672] Literally, "to sin ahead of him." This refers to the disbeliever, who denies the Day of Account.

[1673] i.e., his deeds, which await him in the Hereafter.

[1674] i.e., that which he did not do or which he delayed.

[1675] As described in 36:65 and 41:20-23.

[1676] The people of Paradise will actually see their Creator in the Hereafter.

[1677] At the time it is about to leave the body when one is on the verge of death.

29. And the leg is wound about the leg,[1678]

30. To your Lord, that Day, will be the procession.[1679]

31. And he [i.e., the disbeliever] had not believed, nor had he prayed.

32. But [instead], he denied and turned away.

33. And then he went to his people, swaggering [in pride].

34. Woe to you, and woe!

35. Then woe to you, and woe!

36. Does man think that he will be left neglected?[1680]

37. Had he not been a sperm from semen emitted?

38. Then he was a clinging clot, and [God] created [his form] and proportioned [him]

39. And made of him two mates, the male and the female.

40. Is not that [Creator] Able to give life to the dead?

---

[1678] From the difficulties the person faces at death or his sudden awareness of the realities of both this world and the Hereafter. It may also refer to his shrouding after death.

[1679] Literally, "driving" or herding" or "the place to which one is driven."

[1680] i.e., to no end, without responsibility, or without being returned to the Creator for judgement.

## Sūrah 76: al-Insān

### Period of Revelation

Most of the commentators, including Allama Zamakhshari, Imām Razi, Qadi, Baidawi, Allama Nizam ad-Din Nisaburi, Ibn Kathir and many others, regard it as a Makki Sūrah, and, according to Allama Alusi, the same is the opinion of the majority of scholars. However, some commentators hold the view that the Sūrah was revealed at Madinah, and some others say that it was revealed at Makkah but v. 8-10 of it were sent down at Madinah.

As far as the subject matter and the style of the Sūrah are concerned, these are very different from those of the Madani Sūrahs. A little study of it rather shown that it is not only a Makki Sūrah but it was revealed during the earliest period at Makkah, which began just after the revelation of the first seven verses of Sūrah Al-Muddathir.

### Theme and Subject Matter

The theme of this Sūrah is to inform man of his true position in the world and to tell him that if he understood his true position rightly and adopted the attitude of gratefulness, he would meet with such and such good end, and if he adopted the way of disbelief, he would meet with such and such evil ends. In the longer Sūrahs of the Qur'ān this same theme has been presented at length, but a special characteristic of the style of the earliest Sūrahs revealed at Makkah is that the subjects dealt with at length in the later period, "have been presented in a brief but highly effective way in this period in such concise, elegant sentences as may automatically be preserved in the memory of the hearers."

In this Sūrah, first of all man has been reminded that there was a time when he was nothing; then a humble beginning of him was made with a mixed drop of sperm and ovum of which even his mother was not aware; even she did not know that he had been conceived nor anyone else seeing the microscopic cell could say that it was a man, who in future would become the best of creation on the earth. After this, man has been warned, so as to say: "Beginning your creation in this way We have developed and shaped you into what you are today in order to test and try you in the world. That is why, unlike other creatures, you were made intelligent and sensible and were shown both the way of gratitude and the way of ingratitude clearly so that you may show, in the interval that you have been granted here for work, whether you have emerged as a grateful servant from the test or an unbelieving, ungrateful wretch!"

Then, just in one sentence, it has been stated decisively what will be the fate to be met with in the Hereafter by those who emerged as unbelievers from this test.

After this, in v. 5-22 continuously, the blessings with which those who do full justice to servitude in the world, will be favored, have been mentioned in full detail. In these verses, not only have their best rewards been mentioned but they have also been told briefly what are the acts on the basis of which they would become worthy of those rewards. Another special characteristic of the earliest Sūrahs revealed at Makkah is that besides introducing in them briefly the fundamental beliefs and concepts of Islām, here and there, those moral qualities and virtuous acts have been mentioned, which are praiseworthy according to Islām, and also those evils of deed and morality of which Islām strives to cleanse human life. And these two things have not been mentioned with a view to show what good or evil result is entailed by them in the transitory life of the world, but they have been mentioned only to point out what enduring results they will produce in the eternal and everlasting life of the Hereafter, irrespective of whether an evil quality may prove useful or a good quality may prove harmful in the world.

This is the subject matter of the first section (v. 1-22). In the second section, addressing the Prophet , three things have been stated: first, that "it is in fact We Ourself Who are revealing this Qur'ān gradually to you, and this is intended to inform the disbelievers, not you, that the Qur'ān is not being fabricated by Muhammad but it is "We Who are revealing it, and it is Our Own wisdom which requires that We should reveal it piece by piece and not all at once." Second, the Prophet has been told: "No matter how long it may take for the decree of your Lord to be enforced and no matter what afflictions may befall you in the meantime, in any case you should continue to perform your mission of Apostleship patiently, and not to yield to the pressure tactics of any of these wicked and unbelieving people." The third thing he has been told is: "Remember God day and night, perform the Prayer and spend your nights in the worship of God, for it is these things which sustain and strengthen those who call to God in the face of iniquity and disbelief."

Then in one single sentence, the actual cause of the disbelievers' wrong attitude has been stated: they have forgotten the Hereafter and are enamored of the world. In the second sentence, they have been warned to the effect: "You have not come into being by yourself: We have created you. You have not made these broad chests, and strong, sturdy hands and feet for yourselves, it is We Who made these for you; and it so lies in Our power to treat you as We please. We can distort your figures, We can destroy you and replace you by some other nation. We can cause you to die and can recreate you in whatever form we like."

In conclusion, it has been said: This is an Admonition: whoever wills may accept it and take a path to his Lord. But man's own will and desire is not everything in the world. No one's will and desire can be fulfilled unless God (also) so wills. And God's willing is not haphazard: whatever He wills, He wills it on the basis of His knowledge and wisdom. He admits into His mercy whomever He regards as worthy of His mercy on the basis of His knowledge and wisdom, and He has prepared a painful torment for those whom He finds unjust and wicked.

## Sūrah 76: al-Insān[1681]

In the Name of God, the Most Compassionate, the Most Merciful

1. Has there [not] come upon man a period of time when he was not a thing [even] mentioned?

2. Indeed, We created man from a sperm-drop mixture[1682] that We may try him; and We made him hearing and seeing.

3. Indeed, We guided him to the way, be he grateful or be he ungrateful.

4. Indeed, We have prepared for the disbelievers chains and shackles and a blaze.

5. Indeed, the righteous will drink from a cup [of wine] whose mixture is of Kāfūr,[1683]

6. A spring of which the [righteous] servants of God will drink; they will make it gush forth in force [and abundance].

7. They [are those who] fulfill [their] vows and fear a Day whose evil will be widespread.

8. And they give food in spite of love for it[1684] to the needy, the orphan, and the captive,

9. [Saying], "We feed you only for the countenance [i.e., approval] of God. We wish not from you reward or gratitude.

10. Indeed, We fear from our Lord a Day austere and distressful."

11. So God will protect them from the evil of that Day and give them radiance and happiness

12. And will reward them for what they patiently endured [with] a garden [in Paradise] and silk [garments].

13. [They will be] reclining therein on adorned couches. They will not see therein any [burning] sun or [freezing] cold.

14. And near above them are its shades, and its [fruit] to be picked will be lowered in compliance.

15. And there will be circulated among them vessels of silver and cups having been [created] clear [as glass],

16. Clear glasses [made] from silver of which they have determined the measure.

17. And they will be given to drink a cup [of wine] whose mixture is of ginger

18. [From] a fountain within it [i.e., Paradise] named Salsabeel.

19. There will circulate among them young boys made eternal. When you see them, you would think them [as beautiful as] scattered pearls.

20. And when you look there [in Paradise], you will see pleasure and great dominion.

21. Upon them [i.e., the inhabitants] will be green garments of fine silk and brocade. And they will be adorned with

---

1681 *Al-Insān*: Man. Also entitled *Sūrah ad-Dahr* (Time).

1682 i.e., a combination of the male and female substance, within the womb.

1683 A sweet-smelling spring in Paradise.

1684 The meaning here may also be "out of love for Him," i.e., God.

bracelets of silver, and their Lord will give them a purifying drink.

22. [And it will be said], "Indeed, this is for you a reward, and your effort has been appreciated."

23. Indeed, it is We who have sent down to you, [O Muhammad], the Qur'ān progressively.

24. So be patient for the decision of your Lord and do not obey from among them a sinner or ungrateful [disbeliever].

25. And mention the name of your Lord [in prayer] morning and evening

26. And during the night prostrate to Him and exalt [i.e., praise] Him a long [part of the] night.

27. Indeed, these [disbelievers] love the immediate and leave behind them[1685] a grave Day.

28. We have created them and strengthened their forms, and when We will, We can change their likenesses with [complete] alteration.

29. Indeed, this is a reminder, so he who wills may take to his Lord a way.

30. And you do not will except that God wills. Indeed, God is ever Knowing and Wise.

31. He admits whom He wills into His mercy; but the wrongdoers - He has prepared for them a painful punishment.

---

[1685] i.e., neglect. The meaning may also be "leave ahead of them."

## Sūrah 77: al-Mursalāt

### Period of Revelation

Its subject matter bears full evidence that it was revealed in the earliest period at Makkah. If this Sūrah is read together with the two Sūrahs preceding it, namely al-Qiyamah and ad-Dahr [al-Insan], and the two Sūrahs following it, namely an-Naba and an-Naziat, it becomes obvious that all these Sūrahs are the Revelations of the same period, and they deal with one and the same theme, which has been impressed on the people of Makkah in different ways.

### Theme and Subject Matter

Its theme is to affirm the Resurrection and Hereafter and to warn the people of the consequences which will ultimately follow the denial and the affirmation of these truths.

In the first seven verses, the system of winds has been presented as an evidence of the truth that the Resurrection which is being foretold by the Qur'ān and the Prophet Muhammad must come to pass. The reasoning is that the power of All-Mighty God Who established this wonderful system on the earth, cannot be helpless in bringing about the Resurrection, and the express wisdom which underlies this system bears full evidence that the Hereafter must appear, for no act of an All-Wise Creator can be vain and purposeless, and if there was no Hereafter, it would mean that the whole of one's life was useless and absurd.

The people of Makkah repeatedly asked, "Bring about the Resurrection with which you threaten us; only then shall we believe in it." In v. 8-15, their demand has been answered, saying: "Resurrection is no sport or fun so that whenever a jester should ask for it, it should be brought forth immediately. It is indeed the Day of Judgment to settle the account of all mankind and of all its individuals. For it God has fixed a specific time it will take place, and when it takes place with all its dreads and horrors, it will confound those who are demanding it for fun today. Then their cases will be decided only on the evidence of those Messengers whom these deniers of the truth are repudiating with impunity. Then they will themselves realize how they are responsible for their dooms."

In v. 16-28 arguments have been given continuously for the occurrence and necessity of the Resurrection and Hereafter. In these it has been stated that man's own history, his own birth, and the structure of the earth on which he lives, bear the testimony that the coming of Resurrection and the establishment of the Hereafter are possible as well as the demand of God Almighty's wisdom. History tells us that the nations which denied the Hereafter ultimately became corrupted and met with destruction. This means that the Hereafter is a truth which if denied and contradicted by a nation by its conduct and attitude, will cause it to meet the same doom, which is met by a blind man who rushes headlong into an approaching train. And it also means that in the kingdom of the universe only physical laws are not at work but a moral law also is working in it, under which in this very world the process of retribution is operating. But since in the present life of the world retribution is not taking place in its complete and perfect form, the moral law of the universe necessarily demands that there should come a time when it should take its full course and all those good works and evil deeds, which could not be rewarded here, or which escaped their due punishment should be fully rewarded and punished. For this it is inevitable that there should be a second life after death. If man only considers how he takes his birth in the world, his intellect, provided it is sound intellect, he cannot deny that for the God Who began his creation from an insignificant sperm drop and developed him into a perfect man, it is certainly possible to create the same man once again. After death the particles of man's body do not disappear but continue to exist on the same earth on which he lived his whole life. It is from the resources and treasures of this very earth that he is made and nourished and then into the same treasures of the earth he is deposited. The God who caused him to emerge from the treasures of the earth, in the first instance, can also cause him to re-emerge from the same treasures after he has been restored to them at death. If one only considers the powers of God, one cannot deny that He can do this; and if one considers the wisdom of God, one also cannot deny that it is certainly the very demand of His wisdom to call man to account for the right and wrong use of the powers that He has granted him on the earth; it would rather be against wisdom to let him off without rendering an account.

Then, in v. 28-40, the fate of the deniers of the Hereafter has been depicted, and in v. 41-45 of those who affirming faith in it in their worldly life, endeavored to improve their Hereafter, and abstained from the evils of disbelief and thought, morality and deed, conduct and character which might be helpful in man's worldly life, but are certainly ruinous for his life hereafter.

In the end, the deniers of the Hereafter and those who turn away from God-worship, have been warned as if to say: "Enjoy your short-lived worldly pleasure as you may, but your end will ultimately be disastrous." The discourse concludes with the assertion that the one who fails to obtain guidance from a Book like the Qur'ān, can have no other source in the world to afford him Guidance.

## Sūrah 77: al-Mursalāt[1686]

In the Name of God, the Most Compassionate, the Most Merciful

1. By those [winds] sent forth in gusts

2. And the winds that blow violently

3. And [by] the winds that spread [clouds]

4. And those [angels] who bring criterion[1687]

5. And those [angels] who deliver a message

6. As justification or warning,

7. Indeed, what you are promised is to occur.

8. So when the stars are obliterated

9. And when the heaven is opened

10. And when the mountains are blown away

11. And when the messengers' time has come...[1688]

12. For what Day was it postponed?[1689]

13. For the Day of Judgement.

14. And what can make you know what is the Day of Judgement?

15. Woe,[1690] that Day, to the deniers.

16. Did We not destroy the former peoples?

17. Then We will follow them with the later ones.

18. Thus do We deal with the criminals.

19. Woe, that Day, to the deniers.

20. Did We not create you from a liquid disdained?

21. And We placed it in a firm lodging [i.e., the womb]

22. For a known extent.

23. And We determined [it], and excellent [are We] to determine.

24. Woe, that Day, to the deniers.

25. Have We not made the earth a container

26. Of the living and the dead?

27. And We placed therein lofty, firmly set mountains and have given you to drink sweet water.

28. Woe, that Day, to the deniers.

29. [They will be told], "Proceed to that which you used to deny.

30. Proceed to a shadow [of smoke] having three columns

31. [But having] no cool shade and availing not against the flame."

---

1686 *Al-Mursalāt*: Those sent forth.
1687 To God's human messengers.
1688 i.e., when they are gathered to witness concerning their nations. The sentence's conclusion is understood to be "...the promised judgement will then take place."
1689 "It" may refer to either the aforementioned occurrences collectively or to the testimony of the messengers.

1690 i.e., death and destruction.

32. Indeed, it throws sparks [as huge] as a fortress,

33. As if they were yellowish [black] camels.

34. Woe, that Day, to the deniers.

35. This is a Day they will not speak,

36. Nor will it be permitted for them to make an excuse.

37. Woe, that Day, to the deniers.

38. This is the Day of Judgement; We will have assembled you and the former peoples.

39. So if you have a plan, then plan against Me.

40. Woe, that Day, to the deniers.

41. Indeed, the righteous will be among shades and springs

42. And fruits from whatever they desire,

43. [Being told], "Eat and drink in satisfaction for what you used to do."

44. Indeed, We thus reward the doers of good.

45. Woe, that Day, to the deniers.

46. [O disbelievers], eat and enjoy yourselves a little; indeed, you are criminals.

47. Woe, that Day, to the deniers.

48. And when it is said to them, "Bow [in prayer]," they do not bow.

49. Woe, that Day, to the deniers.

50. Then in what statement after it [i.e., the Qur'ān] will they believe?

## Sūrah 78: an-Naba'

### Period of Revelation

As we have explained in the introduction to Sūrah al-Mursalat, the themes of all the Sūrahs, from al-Qiyamah to an-Naziat, closely resemble one another, and all these seem to have been revealed in the earliest period at Makkah.

### Theme and Subject Matter

Its theme also is the same as of Sūrah Al-Mursalat, i.e. to affirm the Resurrection and Hereafter, and to warn the people of the consequences of acknowledging or disacknowledging it.

When the Prophet first started to preach Islām in Makkah, his message consisted of three elements:

1. That none be held as an associate with God in Godhead;
2. That God had appointed him as His Messenger;
3. That this world will come to an end one day and then another world will be established when all the former and the latter generations will be resurrected with the same bodies in which they lived and worked in the world; then they will be called to account for their beliefs and deeds and those who emerge as believing and righteous in this accountability will go to Paradise and those who are proved to be disbelieving and wicked will live in Hell for ever.

Of these, although the first thing was highly unpleasant for the people of Makkah, yet in any case they were not disbelievers in the existence of God. They believed in His Being the Supreme Sustainer, Creator and Providence and also admitted that all those beings whom they regarded as their deities, were themselves God's creatures. Therefore, in this regard the only thing they disputed was whether they had any share in the attributes and powers of Divinity and in the Divine Being itself or not.

As for the second thing, the people of Makkah were not prepared to accept it. However, what they could not possibly deny was that during the 40 years life that the Prophet had lived among them before his claim to Prophethood, they had never found him a lying deceitful person or the one who would adopt unlawful methods for selfish ends. They themselves admitted that he was a man possessed of wisdom, righteousness and moral superiority. Therefore, in spite of charging him with a thousand false accusations, to say nothing of making others believe, they were finding it difficult even for themselves to believe that although he was an honest and upright man in every other affair and dealing of life, yet, God forbid, a liar only in his claim to be a Prophet.

Thus, the first two things were not in fact so perplexing for the people of Makkah as the third thing. When this was presented before them, they mocked it most of all, expressed unusual wonder at it, and regarding it as remote from reason and impossible, started talking against it as incredible, even inconceivable, in their assemblies. But in order to bring them to the way of Islām it was absolutely essential that the doctrine of the Hereafter should be instilled into their minds, for without belief in this doctrine, it was not at all possible that they could adopt a serious attitude with regard to the truth and falsehood, could change their standard of values in respect of good and evil, and giving up worship of the world, could be inclined to follow the way that Islām urged them to follow. That is why in the earliest Sūrahs revealed at Makkah the doctrine of the Hereafter has been impressed and stressed more than anything else. However, the arguments for it have been given in such a way that the doctrine of the Oneness of God (Tawhid) also is impressed on the minds automatically. This also contains brief arguments, here and there, to confirm the truth of the Holy Messenger of God and the Qur'ān.

After understanding well why the theme of the Hereafter has been so frequently repeated in the Sūrahs of this period, let us now have a look at the subject matter of this Sūrah. In it first of all, allusion has been made to the common talk and the doubts that were being expressed in every street of Makkah and in every assembly of the people of Makkah on hearing the news about Resurrection. Then, the deniers have been asked: "Don't you see this earth which We have spread as a carpet for you? Don't you see the high mountains which we have so firmly placed in the earth? Don't you consider your own selves how We have created you as pairs of men and women? Don't you consider your sleep by which We make you seek a few hours rest after every few hours labor and toil so as to keep you fit for work in the world? Don't you see the alternation of the night and day which We are so regularly perpetuating precisely according to your needs and requirements? Don't you see the strongly fortified system of the heavens above you? Don't you see the sun by means of which you are receiving your light and heat? Don't you see the rains which fall from the clouds and help produce corn and vegetables and luxuriant gardens? Do these things only tell you that the power of the Almighty Being Who has created them, will be unable to bring about Resurrection and establish the Next World? Then, from the supreme wisdom which is clearly working in this world around you, do you only understand this that although each part of it and each function of it is purposive, yet life is meaningless? Nothing could be more absurd and meaningless that after appointing man to the office of foreman and granting him vast powers of appropriation, in this workhouse, when he leaves the world after fulfilling his role, he should be let off without any accountability. He should neither be rewarded and granted pension on satisfactory work, nor subjected to any accountability and punishment on unsatisfactory performance of duty.

After giving these arguments it has been emphatically stated that the Day of Judgment shall certainly come to pass on its appointed time. No sooner is the Trumpet sounded than whatever is being foretold shall appear before the eyes, and whether you believe in it today, or not, at that time you will come out in your multitudes from wherever you would be lying dead and buried to render your account. Your denial cannot in any way avert this inevitable event.

Then, in v. 21-30; it has been stated that every single misdeed of those who do not expect any accountability to take place and have thus belied Our Revelations, lies reckoned and recorded with Us, and Hell is ever lying an ambush to punish them and punish them fully for all their doings. Then, in v. 31-36, the best rewards of those who lived as responsible people in the world and have provided for their Hereafter beforehand have been mentioned. They have been reassured that they will not only be rewarded richly for their services but in addition they will also be given sufficient gifts.

In conclusion, the Divine Court in the Hereafter has been depicted, making it plain that there will be no question of somebody's being adamant in the matter of getting his followers and associates forgiven, none will speak without leave, and leave will be granted on the condition that intercession be made only for the one to whom leave of intercession will have been given, and the intercessor will say only what is right. Moreover, leave for intercession will be given only for those who had acknowledged the Truth in the world but were sinners; rebels of God and rejecters of the Truth will deserve no intercession at all.

The discourse has been concluded with this warning: The Day the coming of which is being foretold, shall certainly come to pass. Do not think it is yet far off, it is close at hand. Now, whoever wills, let him believe in it and take the way towards his Lord. But he who disbelieves, in spite of the warning, "will have all his deeds placed before him: and he will exclaim regretfully: "Oh, would that I were not born in the world!" At that time, his regrets will be about the same world of which he is so enamored today!

## Sūrah 78: an-Naba'[1691]

In the Name of God, the Most Compassionate, the Most Merciful

1. About what are they asking one another?

2. About the great news[1692] -

3. That over which they are in disagreement.

4. No! They are going to know.

5. Then, no! They are going to know.

6. Have We not made the earth a resting place?

7. And the mountains as stakes?[1693]

8. And We created you in pairs

9. And made your sleep [a means for] rest

10. And made the night as clothing[1694]

11. And made the day for livelihood

12. And constructed above you seven strong [heavens]

13. And made [therein] a burning lamp

14. And sent down, from the rain clouds, pouring water

15. That We may bring forth thereby grain and vegetation

16. And gardens of entwined growth.

17. Indeed, the Day of Judgement is an appointed time -

18. The Day the Horn is blown and you will come forth in multitudes

19. And the heaven is opened and will become gateways

20. And the mountains are removed and will be [but] a mirage.

21. Indeed, Hell has been lying in wait

22. For the transgressors, a place of return,

23. In which they will remain for ages [unending].

24. They will not taste therein [any] coolness or drink

25. Except scalding water and [foul] purulence -

26. An appropriate recompense.[1695]

27. Indeed, they were not expecting an account

28. And denied Our verses with [emphatic] denial.

29. But all things We have enumerated in writing.

30. "So taste [the penalty], and never will We increase you except in torment."[1696]

31. Indeed, for the righteous is attainment[1697] -

---

[1691] *An-Naba'*: The News (or Happening).

[1692] i.e., the Resurrection.

[1693] To stabilize the land and balance the earth.

[1694] Covering and concealing you in its darkness.

[1695] In proportion to and comparable with their crimes.

[1696] This announcement will be made to the companions of Hell.

[1697] Of security, success and reward, including escape and safety from Hell.

32. Gardens and grapevines

33. And full-breasted [companions] of equal age

34. And a full cup.[1698]

35. No ill speech will they hear therein or any falsehood -

36. [As] reward from your Lord, [a generous] gift [made due by] account,[1699]

37. [From] the Lord of the heavens and the earth and whatever is between them, the Most Merciful. They possess not from Him [authority for] speech.[1700]

38. The Day that the Spirit [i.e., Gabriel] and the angels will stand in rows, they will not speak except for one whom the Most Merciful permits, and he will say what is correct.

39. That is the True [i.e., certain] Day; so he who wills may take to his Lord a [way of] return.[1701]

40. Indeed, We have warned you of a near punishment on the Day when a man will observe what his hands have put forth[1702] and the disbeliever will say, "Oh, I wish that I were dust!"

---

[1698] Of wine which is delicious and does not intoxicate.
[1699] i.e., as a result of both their own righteous deeds and the limitless generosity of God. Another meaning is a "gift calculated [to be adequate]."
[1700] None of God's creatures can plead with Him on the Day of Judgement except by His permission.
[1701] i.e., a direct route through correct beliefs and righteous deeds.
[1702] i.e., the deeds he did in this world, which await him in the Hereafter.

## Sūrah 79: an-Nāzi'āt

### Period of Revelation

According to Abdullah bin Abbas, this Sūrah was sent down after Sūrah an-Naba. Its subject matter also testifies that it belongs to the earliest period at Makkah.

### Theme and Subject Matter

Its theme is affirmation of Resurrection and the life hereafter; it also warns of the consequences of belying the Messenger of God.

The Sūrah opens with oaths sworn by the angels who take the soul at deaths and those who hasten to carry out God's Commands, and those who conduct the affairs of the universe according to Divine Will, to assure that the Resurrection will certainly come to pass and the second life after death will certainly take place. For the angels who are employed to pluck out the soul today can also be employed to restore the soul tomorrow, and the angels who promptly execute God's Commands and conduct the affairs of the universe today can also upset the order of the universe tomorrow by orders of the same God and can also bring about a new order.

After this the people have been told, so as to say: "This work which you regard as absolutely impossible, is not any difficult for God, for which He may have to make lengthy preparations. Just a single jolt will upset this system of the world and a second jolt will be enough to cause you to appear as living beings in the new world. At that time the same people who deny it, would be trembling with fear and seeing with awe struck eyes all that they thought was impossible.

Then, relating the story of the Prophet Moses and Pharaoh briefly, the people have been warned to the effect: "You know full well what fate the Pharaoh met in consequence of belying the Messenger and rejecting the guidance brought by him and endeavoring to defeat his mission by trickery and deceit. If you do not learn any lesson from it and do not change your ways and attitude accordingly, you also will have to meet the same fate.

Then, in v. 27-13, arguments have been given for the Hereafter and life after death. In this regard, the deniers have been asked the question: "Is your resurrection a more difficult task or the creation of the huge Universe which spreads around you to infinite distances with myriads of its stars and planets? Your recreation cannot be difficult for the God for Whom this was an easy task. Thus, after presenting, in a single sentence, a decisive argument for the possibility of the Hereafter, attention has been drawn to the earth and its provisions that have been arranged in it for the sustenance of man and animal and of which everything testifies that it has been created with great wisdom for fulfilling some special purpose. Pointing to this the question has been left for the intellect of man to ponder for itself and form the opinion whether calling man to account after having delegated authority and responsibilities to a creature like him in this wise system would be more in keeping with the demands of wisdom, or that he should die after committing all sorts of misdeeds in the world and should perish and mix in the dust for ever and should never be called to account as to how he employed the authority and fulfilled the responsibilities entrusted to him. Instead of discussing this question, in v. 34-41, it has been said: "When the Hereafter is established, men's eternal future will be determined on the criterion as to which of them rebelled against his God transgressing the bounds of service and made the material benefits and pleasures his objective of life and which of them feared standing before his Lord and refrained from fulfilling the unlawful desires of the self." This by itself provides the right answer to the above question to every such person who considers it honestly, free from stubbornness. For the only rational, logical and moral demand of giving authority and entrusting responsibilities to man in the world is that he should be called to account on this very basis ultimately and rewarded or punished accordingly.

In conclusion, the question of the disbelievers of Makkah as to when Resurrection will take place, has been answered. They asked the Prophet this question over and over again. In reply it has been said that the knowledge of the time of its occurrence rests with God alone. The Messenger is there only to give the warning that it will certainly come. Now whoever wishes may mend his ways, fearing its coming, and whoever wishes may behave and conduct himself as he likes, fearless of its coming. When the appointed time comes, those very people who loved the life of this world and regarded its pleasures as the only object of life, would feel that they had stayed in the world only for an hour or so. Then they will realize how utterly they had ruined their future for ever for the sake of the short lived pleasures of the world.

## Sūrah 79: an-Nāzi'āt[1703]

In the Name of God, the Most Compassionate, the Most Merciful

1. By those [angels] who extract with violence[1704]

2. And [by] those who remove with ease[1705]

3. And [by] those who glide [as if] swimming[1706]

4. And those who race each other in a race[1707]

5. And those who arrange [each] matter,[1708]

6. On the Day the blast [of the Horn] will convulse [creation],

7. There will follow it the subsequent [one].

8. Hearts,[1709] that Day, will tremble,

9. Their eyes[1710] humbled.

10. They are [presently] saying, "Will we indeed be returned to [our] former state [of life]?

11. Even if we should be decayed bones?"[1711]

12. They say, "That, then, would be a losing return."[1712]

13. Indeed, it will be but one shout,

14. And suddenly they will be [alert] upon the earth's surface.

15. Has there reached you the story of Moses? -

16. When his Lord called to him in the sacred valley of Tuwā,

17. "Go to Pharaoh. Indeed, he has transgressed.

18. And say to him, 'Would you [be willing to] purify yourself

19. And let me guide you to your Lord so you would fear [Him]?' "

20. And he showed him the greatest sign,[1713]

21. But he [i.e., Pharaoh] denied and disobeyed.

22. Then he turned his back, striving [i.e., plotting].[1714]

23. And he gathered [his people] and called out

---

1703 An-Nāzi'āt: The Extractors.
1704 i.e., those who tear out the souls of those destined for Hell.
1705 i.e., those angels who ease out the souls of those destined for Paradise.
1706 Speeding to execute God's commands.
1707 Racing to deliver the souls of the believers to Paradise.
1708 According to God's decree.
1709 Those of the disbelievers who denied the Resurrection.
1710 Those of the disbelievers.

1711 The disbelievers say this in ridicule of the warning.
1712 i.e., "If that were so, we would not be able to escape punishment."
1713 i.e., the miracle of his staff becoming a great snake.
1714 An alternative meaning is "running [from the snake]."

24. And said, "I am your most exalted lord."

25. So God seized him in exemplary punishment for the last and the first [transgression].[1715]

26. Indeed in that is a lesson [i.e., warning] for whoever would fear [God].

27. Are you a more difficult creation or is the heaven? He [i.e., God] constructed it.

28. He raised its ceiling and proportioned it.

29. And He darkened its night and extracted its brightness.[1716]

30. And after that He spread the earth.

31. He extracted from it its water and its pasture,

32. And the mountains He set firmly

33. As enjoyment [i.e., provision] for you and your grazing livestock.

34. But when there comes the greatest Overwhelming Calamity[1717] -

35. The Day when man will remember that for which he strove,

36. And Hellfire will be exposed for [all] those who see -

37. So as for he who transgressed

38. And preferred the life of the world,

39. Then indeed, Hellfire will be [his] refuge.

40. But as for he who feared the position of his Lord[1718] and prevented the soul from [unlawful] inclination,

41. Then indeed, Paradise will be [his] refuge.

42. They ask you, [O Muhammad], about the Hour: when is its arrival?[1719]

43. In what [position] are you that you should mention it?[1720]

44. To your Lord is its finality.[1721]

45. You are only a warner for those who fear it.

46. It will be, on the Day they see it,[1722] as though they had not remained [in the world] except for an afternoon or a morning thereof.

[1715] i.e., for Pharaoh's setting himself up as a deity and for his previous oppression of the people and denial of Moses.

[1716] i.e., created the day from within the surrounding darkness.

[1717] i.e., the Day of Resurrection.

[1718] See footnote to 55:46.

[1719] Literally, "resting" or establishment."

[1720] Meaning that Muhammad had no knowledge of it, so how could he inform them?

[1721] i.e., its destination and termination. And to Him belongs ultimate knowledge of it.

[1722] i.e., the Hour, the Resurrection.

## Sūrah 80: 'Abasa

### Period of Revelation

The commentators and traditionists are unanimous about the occasion of the revelation of this Sūrah. According to them, once some big chiefs of Makkah were sitting in the Prophet's assembly and he was earnestly engaged in trying to persuade them to accept Islām. At that very point, a blind man, named Ibn Umm Maktum, approached him to seek explanation of some point concerning Islām. The Prophet disliked his interruption and ignored him. Thereupon God sent down this Sūrah. From this historical incident the period of the revelation of this Sūrah can be precisely determined.

In the first place, it is confirmed that Ibn Umm Maktum was one of the earliest reverts to Islām. Ibn Hajar and Ibn Kathir have stated that he was one of those who had accepted Islām at a very early stage at Makkah.

Secondly, some of the hadith which relate this incident show that he had already accepted Islām and some others show that be was inclined to accept it and had approached the Prophet in search of the truth. Ā'isha states that coming to the Prophet he had said: *"O Messenger of God, guide me to the straight path."* (Tirmidhi, Hakim, Ibn Hibban, Ibn Jarir, Abu Ya'la. According to Abdullah bin Abbas, he had asked the meaning of a verse of the Qur'ān and said to the Prophet: *"O Messenger of God, teach me the knowledge that God has taught you."* Ibn Jarir, Ibn Abu Hatim). These statements show that he had acknowledged the Prophet as a Messenger of God and the Qur'ān as a Book of God.

Thirdly, the names of the people who were sitting in the Prophet's assembly at that time, have been given in different hadith. In this list we find the names of `Utbah, Shaibah, Abu Jahl, Umayyah bin Khalaf, Ubayy bin Khalaf, who were the bitterest enemies of Islām. This shows that the incident took place in the period when these chiefs were still on meeting terms with the Prophet and their antagonism to Islām had not yet grown so strong as to have stopped their paying visits to him and having dialogues with him off and on. All these arguments indicate that this is one of the very earliest Sūrahs to be revealed at Makkah.

### Theme and Subject Matter

In view of the apparent style with which the discourse opens, one feels that in this Sūrah God has expressed His displeasure against the Prophet for his treating the blind man with indifference and attending to the big chiefs exclusively. But when the whole Sūrah is considered objectively, one finds that the displeasure, in fact, has been expressed against the disbelieving Quraysh, who because of their arrogant attitude and indifference to the truth, were rejecting with contempt the message of truth being conveyed by the Prophet. Then, besides teaching him the correct method of preaching, the error of the method that he was adopting at the start of his mission has also been pointed out. His treating the blind man with neglect and disregard and devoting all his attention to the Quraysh chiefs was not for the reason that he regarded the rich as noble and a poor blind man as contemptible, and, God forbid, there was some rudeness in his manner for which God reproved him. But, as a matter of fact, when a caller to Truth embarks on his mission of conveying his message to the people, he naturally wants the most influential people of society to accept his message so that his task becomes easy, for even if his invitation spreads among the poor and weak people, it cannot make much difference. Almost the same attitude had the Prophet also adopted in the beginning, his motive being only sincerity and a desire to promote his mission and not any idea of respect for the big people and hatred for the small people. But God made him realize that that was not the correct method of extending invitation to Islām, but from his mission's point of view, every man, who was a seeker after truth, was important, even if he was weak, or poor, and every man, who was heedless to the truth, was unimportant, even if he occupied a high position in society. Therefore, he should openly proclaim and convey the teachings of Islām to all and sundry, but the people who were really worthy of his attention, were those who were inclined to accept the Truth, and his sublime and noble message was too high to be presented before those haughty people who in their arrogance and vanity thought that they did not stand in need of him but rather he stood in need of them.

This is the theme of v. 1-16. From verse 17 onward the rebuke directly turns to the disbelievers, who were repudiating the invitation of the Messenger of God. In this, first they have been reproved for their attitude which they had adopted against their Creator, Providence and Sustainer. In the end, they have been warned of the dreadful fate that they would meet in consequence of their conduct on the Day of Resurrection.

## Sūrah 80: 'Abasa[1723]

In the Name of God, the Most Compassionate, the Most Merciful

1. He [i.e., the Prophet] frowned and turned away

2. Because there came to him the blind man,[1724] [interrupting].

3. But what would make you perceive, [O Muhammad], that perhaps he might be purified[1725]

4. Or be reminded and the remembrance would benefit him?

5. As for he who thinks himself without need,[1726]

6. To him you give attention.

7. And not upon you [is any blame] if he will not be purified.[1727]

8. But as for he who came to you striving [for knowledge]

9. While he fears [God],

10. From him you are distracted.

11. No! Indeed, they [i.e., these verses] are a reminder;

12. So whoever wills may remember it.[1728]

13. [It is recorded] in honoured sheets,

14. Exalted and purified,

15. [Carried] by the hands of messenger-angels,

16. Noble and dutiful.

17. Destroyed [i.e., cursed] is man;[1729] how disbelieving is he.

18. From what thing [i.e., substance] did He create him?

19. From a sperm-drop He created him and destined for him;[1730]

20. Then He eased the way for him;[1731]

21. Then He causes his death and provides a grave for him.[1732]

22. Then when He wills, He will resurrect him.

23. No! He [i.e., man] has not yet accomplished what He commanded him.

24. Then let mankind look at his food -

25. How We poured down water in torrents,

26. Then We broke open the earth, splitting [it with sprouts],

27. And caused to grow within it grain

28. And grapes and herbage

---

1723 *'Abasa*: He frowned.
1724 'Abdullah, the son of Umm Maktūm.
1725 As a result of what he learns from you.
1726 i.e., without need of faith or need of God. Here it is in reference to a certain influential member of the Quraysh whom the Prophet had hoped to bring to Islām.
1727 The Prophet was responsible only for conveying the message, not for ultimate guidance.
1728 The revelation. Or "Him," i.e., God.
1729 i.e., those who deny God's message.
1730 His proportions, provisions, life span, etc.
1731 Into this world (i.e., his birth). It may also refer to life itself, which has been made easier by God's guidance.
1732 To conceal his decaying body.

29. And olive and palm trees

30. And gardens of dense shrubbery

31. And fruit and grass -

32. [As] enjoyment [i.e., provision] for you and your grazing livestock.

33. But when there comes the Deafening Blast[1733]

34. On the Day a man will flee from his brother

35. And his mother and his father

36. And his wife and his children,

37. For every man, that Day, will be a matter adequate for him.[1734]

38. [Some] faces, that Day, will be bright -

39. Laughing, rejoicing at good news.

40. And [other] faces, that Day, will have upon them dust.

41. Blackness will cover them.

42. Those are the disbelievers, the wicked ones.

---

[1733] The piercing blast of the Horn which signals resurrection. *As-Sākhkhah* is also a name for the Day of Resurrection.

[1734] i.e., to occupy him. He will be concerned only with himself, thus forgetting all others.

## Sūrah 81: at-Takweer

### Period of Revelation

The subject matter and the style clearly show that it is one of the earliest Sūrahs to be revealed at Makkah.

### Theme and Subject Matter

It has two themes: the Hereafter and the institution of Apostleship.

In the first six verses the first stage of the Resurrection has been mentioned when the sun will lose its light, the stars will scatter, the mountains will be uprooted and will disperse, the people will become heedless of their dearest possessions, the beasts of the jungle will be stupefied and will gather together, and the seas will boil up. Then in the next seven verses the second stage has been described when the souls will be reunited with the bodies, the records will be laid open, the people will be called to account for their crimes, the heavens will be unveiled, and Hell and Heaven will be brought into full view. After depicting the Hereafter thus, man has been left to ponder his own self and deeds, saying: "Then each man shall himself know what he has brought with him."

After this the theme of Apostleship has been taken up. In this the people of Makkah have been addressed, as if to say "Whatever Muhammad is presenting before you, is not the bragging of a madman, nor an evil suggestion inspired by Satan, but the word of a noble, exalted and trustworthy messenger sent by God, whom Muhammad has seen with his own eyes in the bright horizon of the clear sky in broad day light. Where then are you going having turned away from this teaching?"

## Sūrah 81: at-Takweer[1735]

In the Name of God, the Most Compassionate, the Most Merciful

1. When the sun is wrapped up [in darkness]

2. And when the stars fall, dispersing,

3. And when the mountains are removed

4. And when full-term she-camels[1736] are neglected

5. And when the wild beasts are gathered

6. And when the seas are filled with flame[1737]

7. And when the souls are paired[1738]

8. And when the girl [who was] buried alive is asked

9. For what sin she was killed

10. And when the pages[1739] are spread [i.e., made public]

11. And when the sky is stripped away

12. And when Hellfire is set ablaze

13. And when Paradise is brought near,

14. A soul will [then] know what it has brought [with it].[1740]

15. So I swear by the retreating stars -

16. Those that run [their courses] and disappear [i.e., set] -

17. And by the night as it closes in[1741]

18. And by the dawn when it breathes [i.e., stirs]

19. [That] indeed, it [i.e., the Qur'ān] is a word [conveyed by] a noble messenger [i.e., Gabriel]

20. [Who is] possessed of power and with the Owner of the Throne, secure [in position],

21. Obeyed there [in the heavens] and trustworthy.

22. And your companion [i.e., Prophet Muhammad] is not [at all] mad.[1742]

23. And he has already seen him [i.e., Gabriel] in the clear horizon.[1743]

24. And he [i.e., Muhammad] is not a withholder of [knowledge of] the unseen.[1744]

25. And it [i.e., the Qur'ān] is not the word of a devil, expelled [from the heavens].

26. So where are you going?[1745]

---

1735 *At-Takweer*: The Wrapping.

1736 Those ten months pregnant and nearing delivery. This verse alludes to distraction from the most valued of possessions.

1737 Or "when the seas have overflowed [into each other]."

1738 With another like soul. It can also mean "joined" (with their groups or sects).

1739 On which are recorded the deeds of all people.

1740 i.e., all of one's deeds from worldly life, which have accompanied the soul to the Hereafter.

1741 An alternative meaning is "as it departs."

1742 Literally, "possessed by *jinn*."

1743 i.e., the eastern horizon, where the sun rises. See footnote to 53:6.

1744 Prophet Muhammad did not withhold that knowledge of the unseen which God had revealed to him in the Qur'ān.

27. It is not except a reminder to the worlds

28. For whoever wills among you to take a right course.

29. And you do not will except that God wills - Lord of the worlds.

[1745] In your denial of the Qur'ān and in your accusations against the Prophet. The meaning is essentially "Surely, you have strayed far from God's path."

## Sūrah 82: al-Infitār

### Period of Revelation

This Sūrah and the Sūrah at-Takwir closely resemble each other in their subject matter. This shows that both were sent down in about the same period.

### Theme and Subject Matter

Its theme is the Hereafter. According to a hadith related in Musnad Ahmad, Tirmidhi, Ibn al-Mundhir, Tabarani, Hakim and Ibn Marduyah, on the authority of Abdullah bin Umar, the Messenger said: *"The one who wants that he should see the Resurrection Day as one would see it with one's eyes, should read Sūrah At-Takwir, Sūrah Al-Infitār and Sūrah Al-Ishiqaq."*

In this Sūrah first the Resurrection Day has been described and it is said that when it occurs, every person will see whatever he has done in the world. After this, man has been asked to ponder the question: "O man, what has deluded you into thinking that the God, Who brought you into being and by Whose favor and bounty you possess the finest body, limbs and features among all creatures, is only bountiful and not just? His being bountiful and generous does not mean that you should become fearless of His justice." Then, man has been warned, so as to say: "Do not remain involved in any misunderstanding. Your complete record is being prepared. There are trustworthy writers who are writing down whatever you do." In conclusion, it has been forcefully stated that the Day of Resurrection will surely take place when the righteous shall enjoy every kind of bliss in Paradise and the wicked shall be punished in Hell. On that day no one shall avail anyone anything. All powers of judgment shall be with God.

## Sūrah 82: al-Infitār[1746]

In the Name of God, the Most Compassionate, the Most Merciful

1. When the sky breaks apart

2. And when the stars fall, scattering,

3. And when the seas are erupted

4. And when the [contents of] graves are scattered [i.e., exposed],

5. A soul will [then] know what it has put forth and kept back.

6. O mankind, what has deceived you concerning your Lord, the Generous,

7. Who created you, proportioned you, and balanced you?

8. In whatever form He willed has He assembled you.

9. No! But you deny the Recompense.

10. And indeed, [appointed] over you are keepers,[1747]

11. Noble and recording;

12. They know whatever you do.

13. Indeed, the righteous will be in pleasure,

14. And indeed, the wicked will be in Hellfire.

15. They will [enter to] burn therein on the Day of Recompense,

16. And never therefrom will they be absent.

17. And what can make you know what is the Day of Recompense?

18. Then, what can make you know what is the Day of Recompense?

19. It is the Day when a soul will not possess for another soul [power to do] a thing; and the command, that Day, is [entirely] with God.

---

1746 *Al-Infitār*: The Breaking Apart.

1747 Angels who preserve the deeds of men in records.

## Sūrah 83: al-Mutaffifeen

### Period of Revelation

The style of the Sūrah and its subject matter clearly show that it was revealed in the earliest stage at Makkah, when Sūrah after Sūrah was being revealed to impress the doctrine of the Hereafter on the people's minds. This Sūrah was revealed when they had started ridiculing the Muslims and disgracing them publicly in the streets and in their assemblies, but persecution and manhandling of the Muslims had not yet started.

### Theme and Subject Matter

The theme of this Sūrah too is the Hereafter. In the first six verses the people have been taken to task for the prevalent evil practice in their commercial dealings. When they had to receive their due from others, they demanded that it be given in full, but when they had to measure or weigh for others, they would give less than what was due. Taking this one evil as an example out of countless evils prevalent in society, it has been said that it is an inevitable result of the heedlessness of the Hereafter. Unless the people realized that one day they would have to appear before God and account for each single act they performed in the world, it was not possible that they would adopt piety and righteousness in their daily affairs. Even if a person might practice honesty in some of his less important dealings in view of "honesty is the best policy," he would never practice honesty on occasions when dishonesty would seem to be "the best policy." Man can develop true and enduring honesty only when he fears God and sincerely believes in the Hereafter, for then he would regard honesty not merely as "a policy" but as "a duty" and obligation, and his being constant in it, or otherwise, would not be dependent on its being useful or useless in the world.

Thus, after making explicit the relation between morality and the doctrine of the Hereafter in an effective and impressive way, in v. 7-17, it has been said: The deeds of the wicked are already being recorded in the black list of the culprits, and in the Hereafter they will meet with utter ruin. Then in v. 18-28, the best end of the virtuous has been described and it has been laid that their deeds are being recorded in the list of the exalted people, on which are appointed the angels nearest to God.

In conclusion, the believers have been consoled, and the disbelievers warned, as if to say: "The people who are disgracing and humiliating the believers today, are culprits who, on the Resurrection Day, will meet with a most evil end in consequence of their conduct, and these very believers will feel comforted when they see their fate."

## Sūrah 83: al-Mutaffifeen[1748]

In the Name of God, the Most Compassionate, the Most Merciful

1. Woe to those who give less [than due],[1749]

2. Who, when they take a measure from people, take in full.

3. But if they give by measure or by weight to them, they cause loss.

4. Do they not think that they will be resurrected

5. For a tremendous Day -

6. The Day when mankind will stand before the Lord of the worlds?

7. No! Indeed, the record of the wicked is in sijjeen.

8. And what can make you know what is sijjeen?

9. It is [their destination[1750] recorded in] a register inscribed.

10. Woe, that Day, to the deniers,

11. Who deny the Day of Recompense.

12. And none deny it except every sinful transgressor.

13. When Our verses are recited to him, he says, "Legends of the former peoples."

[1748] *Al-Mutaffifeen*: Those Who Give Less.

[1749] i.e., those who cheat people by giving them less than what they paid for when weighing or measuring – an amount so little as to hardly be noticed.

[1750] The lowest depths of Hell.

14. No! Rather, the stain has covered their hearts of that which they were earning.[1751]

15. No! Indeed, from their Lord, that Day, they will be partitioned.[1752]

16. Then indeed, they will [enter and] burn in Hellfire.

17. Then it will be said [to them], "This is what you used to deny."

18. No! Indeed, the record of the righteous is in 'illiyyūn.

19. And what can make you know what is 'illiyyūn?

20. It is [their destination[1753] recorded in] a register inscribed

21. Which is witnessed by those brought near [to God].

22. Indeed, the righteous will be in pleasure

23. On adorned couches, observing.

24. You will recognize in their faces the radiance of pleasure.

25. They will be given to drink [pure] wine[1754] [which was] sealed.

26. The last of it[1755] is musk. So for this let the competitors compete.

27. And its mixture is of Tasneem,[1756]

[1751] i.e., their sins.

[1752] i.e., they will not be able to see Him.

[1753] The highest elevations of Paradise.

[1754] Which is delicious and does not intoxicate.

[1755] i.e., its lingering odor.

[1756] The highest spring in Paradise and the most favored drink of its inhabitants.

28. A spring from which those near [to God] drink.

29. Indeed, those who committed crimes used to laugh at those who believed.

30. And when they passed by them, they would exchange derisive glances.

31. And when they returned to their people, they would return jesting.

32. And when they saw them, they would say, "Indeed, those are truly lost."

33. But they had not been sent as guardians over them.

34. So Today[1757] those who believed are laughing at the disbelievers,

35. On adorned couches, observing.

36. Have the disbelievers [not] been rewarded [this Day] for what they used to do?

[1757] On the Day of Judgement.

# Sūrah 84: al-Inshiqāq

## Period of Revelation

This too is one of the earliest Sūrahs to be revealed at Makkah. The internal evidence of its subject matter indicates that persecution of the Muslims had not yet started; however, the message of the Qur'ān was being openly repudiated at Makkah and the people were refusing to acknowledge that Resurrection would ever take place when they would have to appear before their God to render an account of their deeds.

## Theme and Subject Matter

Its theme is the Resurrection and Hereafter. In the first five verses not only have the state of Resurrection been described vividly but an argument of its being true and certain also have been given. It has been stated that the heavens on that Day will split asunder, the earth will be spread out plain and smooth, and it will throw out whatever lies inside it of the dead bodies of men and evidences of their deeds so as to become completely empty from within. The argument given for it is that such will be the Command of their Lord for the heavens and the earth; since both are His creation and cannot dare disobey His Command. For them the only right and proper course is that they should obey the Command of their Lord.

Then, in v. 6-19 it has been said that whether man is conscious of this fact or not, he in any case is moving willy nilly to the destination when he will appear and stand before his Lord. At that time all human beings will divide into two parts: first those whose records will be given in their right hands: they will be forgiven without any severe reckoning; second those whose records will be given them behind their back. They will wish that they should die somehow, but they will not die; instead they will be cast into Hell. They will meet with this fate because in the world they remained lost in the misunderstanding that they would never have to appear before God to render an account of their deeds, whereas their Lord was watching whatever they were doing, and there was no reason why they should escape the accountability for their deeds. Their moving gradually from the life of the world to the meting out of rewards and punishments in the Hereafter was as certain as the appearance of twilight after sunset, the coming of the night after the day, the returning of men and animals to their respective abodes at night, and the growing of the crescent into full moon.

In conclusion, the disbelievers who repudiate the Qur'ān instead of bowing down to God when they hear it, have been forewarned of a grievous punishment and the good news of limitless rewards has been given to the believers and the righteous.

## Sūrah 84: al-Inshiqāq[1758]

In the Name of God, the Most Compassionate, the Most Merciful

1. When the sky has split [open]

2. And has listened [i.e., responded][1759] to its Lord and was obligated [to do so]

3. And when the earth has been extended[1760]

4. And has cast out that within it[1761] and relinquished [it]

5. And has listened [i.e., responded] to its Lord and was obligated [to do so] -

6. O mankind, indeed you are laboring toward your Lord with [great] exertion[1762] and will meet it.[1763]

7. Then as for he who is given his record in his right hand,

8. He will be judged with an easy account

9. And return to his people in happiness.

10. But as for he who is given his record behind his back,

11. He will cry out for destruction

12. And [enter to] burn in a Blaze.

13. Indeed, he had [once] been among his people in happiness;

14. Indeed, he had thought he would never return [to God].

15. But yes! Indeed, his Lord was ever, of him, Seeing.

16. So I swear by the twilight glow

17. And [by] the night and what it envelops

18. And [by] the moon when it becomes full

19. [That] you will surely embark upon [i.e., experience] state after state.[1764]

20. So what is [the matter] with them [that] they do not believe,

21. And when the Qur'ān is recited to them, they do not prostrate [to God]?

22. But those who have disbelieved deny,

23. And God is most knowing of what they keep within themselves.

24. So give them tidings of a painful punishment,

25. Except for those who believe and do righteous deeds. For them is a reward uninterrupted.

[1758] *Al-Inshiqāq*: The Splitting.
[1759] It will have heard God's command and will have inclined immediately to compliance and willing obedience.
[1760] i.e., stretched flat and spread out.
[1761] Of the dead and all else buried therein.
[1762] i.e., striving throughout your life until you meet your Lord, hastening toward death.
[1763] i.e., you will find all that you intended and accomplished awaiting you in the Hereafter. Another meaning is "And will meet Him [i.e., your Lord]" and be recompensed in full by Him.

[1764] i.e., various stages, both in this life and the Hereafter.

## Sūrah 85: al-Burūj

### Period of Revelation

The subject matter itself indicates that this Sūrah was sent down at Makkah in the period when persecution of the Muslims was at its climax and the disbelievers of Makkah were trying their utmost by tyranny and coercion to turn away the new reverts from Islām.

### Theme and Subject Matter

Its theme is to warn the disbelievers of the evil consequences of the persecution and tyranny that they were perpetrating on the reverts to Islām, and to console the believers, so as to say: "If you remain firm and steadfast against tyranny and coercion, you will be rewarded richly for it, and God will certainly avenge Himself on your persecutors on your behalf."

In this connection, first of all the story of the people of the ditch (ashāb al-ukhdud) had been related, who had burnt the believers to death by casting them into pits full of fire. By means of this story the believers and the disbelievers have been taught a few lessons. First, that just as the people of the ditch became worthy of God's curse and punishment, so are the chiefs of Makkah also becoming worthy of it. Second, that just as the believers at that time had willingly accepted to sacrifice their lives by being burnt to death in the pits of fire instead of turning away from the faith, so also the believers now should endure every persecution but should never give up the faith. Third, that God, acknowledging Whom displeases the disbelievers and is urged on by the believers, is Dominant and Master of the Kingdom of the earth and heavens; He is self-praiseworthy and is watching what the two groups are striving for. Therefore, it is certain that the disbelievers will not only be punished in Hell for their disbelief but, more than that, they too will suffer punishment by fire as a fit recompense for their tyranny and cruelties. Likewise, this also is certain that those, who believe and follow up their belief with good deeds, should go to Paradise and this indeed is the supreme success. Then the disbelievers have been warned, so as to say: "God's grip is very severe. If you are proud of the strength of your hosts, you should know that the hosts of Pharaoh and Thamūd were even stronger and more numerous. Therefore, you should learn a lesson from the fate they met. God's power has so encompassed you that you cannot escape His encirclement, and the Qur'ān that you are bent upon belying, is unchangeable: it is inscribed in the Preserved Tablet, which cannot be corrupted in any way."

## Sūrah 85: al-Burūj[1765]

In the Name of God, the Most Compassionate, the Most Merciful

1. By the sky containing great stars

2. And [by] the promised Day

3. And [by] the witness and what is witnessed,

4. Destroyed [i.e., cursed] were the companions of the trench[1766]

5. [Containing] the fire full of fuel,

6. When they were sitting near it

7. And they, to what they were doing against the believers, were witnesses.[1767]

8. And they resented them not except because they believed in God, the Exalted in Might, the Praiseworthy,

9. To whom belongs the dominion of the heavens and the earth. And God, over all things, is Witness.

10. Indeed, those who have tortured[1768] the believing men and believing women and then have not repented will have the punishment of Hell, and they will have the punishment of the Burning Fire.

11. Indeed, those who have believed and done righteous deeds will have gardens beneath which rivers flow. That is the great attainment.

12. Indeed, the assult [i.e., vengeance] of your Lord is severe.

13. Indeed, it is He who originates [creation] and repeats.

14. And He is the Forgiving, the Affectionate,

15. Honourable Owner of the Throne,

16. Effecter of what He intends.

17. Has there reached you the story of the soldiers -

18. [Those of] Pharaoh and Thamūd?

19. But they who disbelieve are in [persistent] denial,

20. While God encompasses them from behind.[1769]

21. But this is an honoured Qur'ān

22. [Inscribed] in a Preserved Slate.

---

[1765] *Al-Burūj*: The Great Stars. Also explained as "the planets" or their "high positions in the heaven."

[1766] Or "May they be destroyed" or "cursed." The "companions of the trench" (or ditch) were agents of a tyrannical king who refused to allow his people to believe in God. Their evil deed in obedience to their ruler earned for them the curse of God.

[1767] After casting the believers into a trench filled with fire, they sat at its edge, watching them burn to death. This event occurred before the time of Prophet Muhammad.

[1768] Or, in this instance, the literal meaning of "burned" is also appropriate.

[1769] See footnote to 2:19.

# Sūrah 86: at-Tāriq

**Period of Revelation**

The style of its subject matter resembles that of the earliest Sūrahs revealed at Makkah, but this Sūrah was sent down at a stage when the disbelievers of Makkah were employing all sorts of devices and plans to defeat and frustrate the message of the Qur'ān and Muhammad.

**Theme and Subject Matter**

It discuses two themes: first, that man has to appear before God after death; second, that the Qur'ān is a decisive Word which no plan or device of the disbelievers can defeat or frustrate.

First of all, the stars of the heavens have been cited as an evidence that there is nothing in the universe which may continue to exist and survive without a guardian over it. Then man has been asked to consider his own self as to how he has been brought into existence from a mere sperm drop and shaped into a living human being. Then it has been said that the God, Who has so brought him into existence, has certainly the power to create him once again, and this resurrection will be for the purpose to subject to scrutiny all the secrets of man which remained hidden in the world. At that time, man will neither be able to escape the consequences of his deeds by his own power, nor will anyone else come to his rescue.

In conclusion, it has been pointed out that just as the falling of rain from the sky and the sprouting of plants and crops from the earth is no child's play but a serious task, so also the truths expressed in the Qur'ān are no jest but a firm and unchangeable reality. The disbelievers are involved in the misunderstanding that their plans and devices will defeat the invitation of the Qur'ān, but they do not know that God too is devising a plan which will bring to nought all their scheming and planning. Then in one sentence the discourse has been summed up, with a word of consolation to the Prophet and a tacit warning to the disbelievers, saying: "Have patience for a while: let the disbelievers do their worst. Before long they will themselves realize whether they have been able to defeat the Qur'ān by their scheming or the Qur'ān has dominated them in the very place where they are exerting their utmost to defeat it."

## Sūrah 86: at-Tāriq[1770]

In the Name of God, the Most Compassionate, the Most Merciful

1. By the sky and the night comer -

2. And what can make you know what is the night comer?

3. It is the piercing star[1771] -

4. There is no soul but that it has over it a protector.

5. So let man observe from what he was created.

6. He was created from a fluid, ejected,

7. Emerging from between the backbone and the ribs.

8. Indeed, He [i.e., God], to return him [to life], is Able.

9. The Day when secrets will be put on trial,[1772]

10. Then he [i.e., man] will have no power or any helper.

11. By the sky which returns [rain]

12. And [by] the earth which cracks open,[1773]

13. Indeed, it [i.e., the Qur'ān] is a decisive statement,

14. And it is not amusement.

15. Indeed, they are planning a plan,

16. But I am planning a plan.

17. So allow time for the disbelievers. Leave them awhile.[1774]

[1770] *At-Tāriq*: That Which Comes at Night.
[1771] Whose light pierces through the darkness.
[1772] i.e., exposed, examined and judged.
[1773] With the growth of plants.

[1774] i.e., Do not be in haste for revenge, for you will see what will become of them.

## Sūrah 87: al-A'lā

### Period of Revelation

The subject matter shows that this too is one of the earliest Sūrahs to be revealed, and the words: "We shall enable you to recite, then you shall never forget" of verse 6 also indicate that it was sent down in the period when the Messenger was not yet fully accustomed to receive Revelation and at the time Revelation came down he feared lest he should forget its words. If this verse is read along with verse 114 of Sūrah Tā Hā and verses 16-19 of al-Qiyāmah and the three verses are also considered with regard to their styles and contexts, the sequence of events seems to be that first in this Sūrah the Prophet was reassured to the effect: "Do not at all worry: We shall enable you to recite this Word, then you shall not forget it." Then after a lapse of time, on another occasion, when the Sūrah Al-Qiyāmah was being revealed, the Prophet involuntarily began to rehearse the words of the Revelation. Thereupon it was said: "O Prophet do not move your tongue to remember this Revelation hastily. It is for Us to have it remembered and read. Therefore when We are reciting it, listen to its recital carefully. Again, it is for Us to explain its meaning." Last of all, on the occasion of the revelation of Sūrah Tā Hā, the Prophet on account of human weakness, again became afraid lest his memory should fail to preserve some portion of the 113 verses which were continuously revealed at that time, and therefore, he began to memorize them. Thereupon, it was said: "And see that you do not hasten to recite the Qur'ān before its revelation is completed to you." After this, it never so happened that he felt any such danger, for apart from these three places, there is no other place in the Qur'ān where there might be a reference to this matter.

### Theme and Subject Matter

This short Sūrah contains three themes.Tawhid, instructions to the Prophet and the Hereafter.

In the first verse, the doctrine of Tawhid (Oneness of God) has been compressed into a single sentence, saying that God's name should be glorified and exalted, i.e. He should not be remembered by any name which might reflect a deficiency, fault, weakness, or an aspect of likeness, with created beings, for the root of all false creeds in the world are wrong concepts about God, which assumed the form of an erroneous name for His glorious and exalted Being. Therefore, for the correction of the creed, the primary thing is that God Almighty should be remembered only by the beautiful names which suit and befit Him.

In the next three verses, it has been said: "Your Lord, glorification of Whose name is being enjoined, is He Who created everything in the Universe, proportioned it, set it a destiny, taught it to perform the function for which it is created, and you witness this manifestation of His power day and night that He creates vegetation on the earth as well as reduces it to mere rubbish. No other being has the power to bring about spring nor the power to prevent autumn."

Then, in the following two verses, the Prophet is being consoled, as if to say: "Do not worry as to how you will remember word for word the Qur'ān that is being revealed to you. It is for Us to preserve it in your memory, and its preservation is not in any way the result of any excellence in you but the result of Our bounty and favor, otherwise if We so will, We can cause you to forget it."

Then, the Prophet has been told: "You have not been made responsible to bring everyone on to the right path; your only duty is to convey the truth, and the simplest way of conveying the truth is that admonition be given to him who is inclined to listen to the admonition and accept it, and the one who is not inclined to it, should not be pursued. The one who fears the evil consequences of deviation and falsehood, will listen to the truth and accept it, and the wretched one who avoids listening to and accepting it, will himself see his evil end."

The discourse has been summed up, saying: "Success is only for those who adopt purity of belief, morals and deed, and remember the name of their Lord and perform the Prayer. But, on the contrary, the people are wholly lost in seeking the ease, benefits and pleasures of the world, whereas they should actually endeavor for their well being in the Hereafter, for the world is transitory and the Hereafter everlasting and the blessings of the Hereafter are far better than the blessings of the world. This truth has not been expressed only in the Qur'ān but in the books of the Prophets Abraham and Moses too, it had been brought to the notice of man.

## Sūrah 87: al-A'lā[1775]

In the Name of God, the Most Compassionate, the Most Merciful

1. Exalt the name of your Lord, the Most High,

2. Who created and proportioned

3. And who destined and [then] guided

4. And who brings out the pasture

5. And [then] makes it black stubble.

6. We will make you recite, [O Muhammad], and you will not forget,

7. Except what God should will. Indeed, He knows what is declared and what is hidden.

8. And We will ease you toward ease.[1776]

9. So remind, if the reminder should benefit;[1777]

10. He who fears [God] will be reminded.

11. But the wretched one will avoid it -

12. [He] who will [enter and] burn in the greatest Fire,

13. Neither dying therein nor living.

14. He has certainly succeeded who purifies himself

15. And mentions the name of his Lord and prays.

16. But you prefer the worldly life,

17. While the Hereafter is better and more enduring.

18. Indeed, this is in the former scriptures,

19. The scriptures of Abraham and Moses.

[1775] *Al-A'lā*: The Most High.
[1776] To the path of God's religion, which is easy and natural, or toward Paradise, by giving opportunities for righteous deeds.
[1777] i.e., wherever it will be heard and understood.

## Sūrah 88: al-Ghāshiyah

**Period of Revelation**

The whole subject matter of the Sūrah indicates that this too is one of the earliest Sūrahs to be revealed; but this was the period when the Prophet had started preaching his message publicly, and the people of Makkah were hearing it and ignoring it carelessly and thoughtlessly.

**Theme and Subject Matter**

To understand the subject matter well one should keep in view the fact that in the initial stage the preaching of the Prophet mostly centered around two points which he wanted to instill in the people's minds: Tawhid and the Hereafter: and the people of Makkah were repudiating both. Let us now consider the subject matter and the style of this Sūrah.

At the outset, in order to arouse the people from their heedlessness, they have been plainly asked: "Do you have any knowledge of the time when an overwhelming calamity will descend?" Immediately after this details of the impending calamity are given as to how the people will be divided into two separate groups and will meet separate ends. One group of the people will go to Hell and they will suffer punishment; the second group will go to the sublime Paradise and will be provided with blessings.

After thus arousing the people the theme suddenly changes and the question is asked: Do not these people, who frown and scorn the teaching of Tawhid and the news of the Hereafter being given by the Qur'ān, observe the common things which they experience daily in their lives? Do they never consider how the camels, on whom their whole life activity in the Arabian desert depends, came into being, endowed precisely with the same characteristics as were required for the beast needed in their desert life? When they go on their journeys, they see the sky, the mountains, or the earth. Let them ponder over these three phenomena and consider as to how the sky was stretched above them, how the mountains were erected and how the earth was spread beneath them? Has all this come about without the skill and craftsmanship of an All-Powerful, All Wise Designer? If they acknowledge that a Creator has created all this with great wisdom and power and that no one else is an associate with Him in their creation, why then do they refuse to accept Him alone as their Lord and Sustainer? And if they acknowledge that God had the power to create all this, then on what rational ground do they hesitate to acknowledge that God also has the power to bring about Resurrection, to recreate man, and to make Hell and Heaven?

After making the truth plain by this concise and rational argument, the address turns from the disbelievers to the Prophet and he is told: "If these people do not acknowledge the truth, they may not; you have not been empowered to act with authority over them, so that you should coerce them into believing: your only task is to exhort, so exhort them. Ultimately they have to return to Us; then We shall call them to full account and shall inflict a heavy punishment on those who do not believe."

## Sūrah 88: al-Ghāshiyah[1778]

In the Name of God, the Most Compassionate, the Most Merciful

1. Has there reached you the report of the Overwhelming [event]?

2. [Some] faces, that Day, will be humbled,

3. Working [hard] and exhausted.[1779]

4. They will [enter to] burn in an intensely hot Fire.

5. They will be given drink from a boiling spring.

6. For them there will be no food except from a poisonous, thorny plant

7. Which neither nourishes nor avails against hunger.

8. [Other] faces, that Day, will show pleasure.

9. With their effort [they are] satisfied

10. In an elevated garden,

11. Wherein they will hear no unsuitable speech.[1780]

12. Within it is a flowing spring.

13. Within it are couches raised high

14. And cups put in place

15. And cushions lined up

16. And carpets spread around.

17. Then do they not look at the camels - how they are created?

18. And at the sky - how it is raised?

19. And at the mountains - how they are erected?

20. And at the earth - how it is spread out?

21. So remind, [O Muhammad]; you are only a reminder.

22. You are not over them a controller.

23. However, he who turns away and disbelieves -

24. Then God will punish him with the greatest punishment.

25. Indeed, to Us is their return.

26. Then indeed, upon Us is their account.

---

[1778] *Al-Ghāshiyah*: The Overwhelming, one of the names of the Resurrection.

[1779] Another accepted meaning is "They were working hard and exhausted," i.e., doing deeds during worldly life which did not benefit them since they were not accompanied by faith or done for the acceptance of God.

[1780] i.e., any insult, falsehood, immorality, idle or vain talk, etc.

## Sūrah 89: al-Fajr

### Period of Revelation

Its contents show that it was revealed at the stage when persecution of the new reverts to Islām had begun in Makkah. On that very basis the people of Makkah have been warned of the evil end of the tribes of 'Aad and Thamūd and of Pharaoh.

### Theme and Subject Matter

Its theme is to affirm the meting out of rewards and punishments in the Hereafter, which the people of Makkah were not prepared to acknowledge. Let us consider the reasoning in the order in which it has been presented. First of all, swearing oaths by the dawn, the ten nights, the even and the odd, and the departing night, the listeners have been asked: "Are these things not enough to testify to the truth of that which you are refusing to acknowledge?" From the explanation that we have given of these four things in the corresponding notes, it will become clear that these things are a symbol of the regularity that exists in the night and day, and swearing oaths by these the question has been asked in the sense: Even after witnessing this wise system established by God, do you still need any other evidence to show that it is not beyond the power of that God Who has brought about this system to establish the Hereafter, and that it is the very requirement of His wisdom that He should call man to account for his deeds?

Then, reasoning from man's own history, the evil end of the 'Aad and the Thamūd and Pharaoh has been cited as an example to show that when they transgressed all limits and multiplied corruption in the earth, God laid upon them the scourge of His chastisement. This is a proof of the fact that the system of the universe is not being run by deaf and blind forces, nor is the world a lawless kingdom of a corrupt ruler, but a Wise Ruler is ruling over it. The demand of Whose wisdom and justice is continuously visible in the world itself in man's own history that He should call to account, and reward and punish accordingly, the being whom He has blessed with reason and moral sense and given the right of appropriation in the world. After this, an appraisal has been made of the general moral state of human society of which Arab paganism was a conspicuous example; two aspects of it in particular, have been criticized: first, the materialistic attitude of the people on account of which overlooking the moral good and evil, they regarded only the achievement of worldly wealth, rank and position, or the absence of it, as the criterion of honor or disgrace, and had forgotten that neither riches was a reward nor poverty a punishment, but that God is trying man in both conditions to see what attitude he adopts when blessed with wealth and how he behaves when afflicted by poverty. Second, the people's attitude under which the orphan child in their society was left destitute on the death of the father. Nobody asked after the poor; whoever could, usurped the whole heritage left by the deceased parent, and drove away the weak heirs fraudulently. The people were so afflicted with an insatiable greed for wealth that they were never satisfied however much they might hoard and amass. This criticism is meant to make them realize as to why the people with such an attitude and conduct in the life of the world should not be called to account for their misdeeds.

The discourse has been concluded with the assertion that accountability shall certainly be held and it will be held on the Day when the Divine Court will be established. At that time the deniers of the judgment will understand that which they are not understanding now in spite of instruction and admonition, but understanding then will be of no avail. The denier will regret and say, "Would that I had provided for this Day before while I lived in the world." But his regrets will not save him from God's punishment. However, as for the people who would have accepted the Truth, which the heavenly books and the Prophets of God were presenting, with full satisfaction of the heart in the world, God will be pleased with them and they will be well pleased with the rewards bestowed by God. They will be called upon to join the righteous and enter Paradise.

## Sūrah 89: al-Fajr[1781]

In the Name of God, the Most Compassionate, the Most Merciful

1. By the dawn

2. And [by] ten nights[1782]

3. And [by] the even [number] and the odd

4. And [by] the night when it passes,

5. Is there [not] in [all] that an oath [sufficient] for one of perception?[1783]

6. Have you not considered how your Lord dealt with 'Aad -

7. [With] Iram[1784] - who had lofty pillars,[1785]

8. The likes of whom had never been created in the land?

9. And [with] Thamūd, who carved out the rocks in the valley?

10. And [with] Pharaoh, owner of the stakes?[1786] -

11. [All of] whom oppressed within the lands

12. And increased therein the corruption.

13. So your Lord poured upon them a scourge of punishment.

14. Indeed, your Lord is in observation.

15. And as for man, when his Lord tries him and [thus] is generous to him and favors him, he says, "My Lord has honoured me."[1787]

16. But when He tries him and restricts his provision, he says, "My Lord has humiliated me."

17. No![1788] But you do not honour the orphan

18. And you do not encourage one another to feed the poor.

19. And you consume inheritance, devouring [it] altogether,[1789]

20. And you love wealth with immense love.

21. No! When the earth has been leveled - pounded and crushed -

22. And your Lord has come[1790] and the angels, rank upon rank,

23. And brought [within view], that Day, is Hell - that Day, man will remember, but how [i.e., what good] to him will be the remembrance?

24. He will say, "Oh, I wish I had sent ahead [some good] for my life."[1791]

---

[1781] *Al-Fajr*: The Dawn.
[1782] Usually interpreted as the first ten nights of the month of Dhul-Hijjah.
[1783] Based upon the following verses, what has been sworn to by God is that He will certainly punish the disbelievers.
[1784] Another name for the first people of 'Aad, to whom Prophet Hūd was sent.
[1785] Supporting their tents or buildings.
[1786] By which he tortured people.

[1787] He is proud rather than grateful, attributing the favour to his own merit.
[1788] It is not like you imagine. Rather, God tries people through prosperity and hardship and rewards both gratitude and patience with honour in the Hereafter.
[1789] Not caring whether it is lawful or unlawful.
[1790] To pass judgement. See footnote to 2:19.

25. So on that Day, none will punish [as severely] as His punishment,

26. And none will bind [as severely] as His binding [of the evildoers].

27. [To the righteous it will be said], "O reassured soul,

28. Return to your Lord, well-pleased and pleasing [to Him],

29. And enter among My [righteous] servants

30. And enter My Paradise."

[1791] The everlasting life of the Hereafter.

## Sūrah 90: al-Balad

### Period of Revelation

Its subject matter and style resemble those of the earliest Sūrahs revealed at Makkah, but it contains a pointer which indicates that it was sent down in the period when the disbelievers of Makkah had resolved to oppose the Prophet, and made it lawful for themselves to commit tyranny and excess against him.

### Theme and Subject Matter

In this Sūrah a vast subject has been compressed into a few brief sentences, and it is a miracle of the Qur'ān that a complete ideology of life which could hardly be explained in a thick volume has been abridged most effectively in brief sentences of this short Sūrah. Its theme is to explain the true position of man in the world and of the world in relation to man and to tell that God has shown to man both the highways of good and evil, has also provided for him the means to judge and see and follow them, and now it rests upon man's own effort and judgment whether he chooses the path of virtue and reaches felicity or adopts the path of vice and meets with doom.

First, the city of Makkah and the hardships being faced therein by the Prophet and the state of the children of Adam have been cited as a witness to the truth that this world is not a place of rest and ease for man, where he might have been born to enjoy life, but here he has been created into toil and struggle. If this theme is read with verse 39 of Sūrah an-Najm (Laisa lil insani illa ma saa: there is nothing for man but what he has striven for), it becomes plain that in this world the future of man depends on his toil and struggle, effort and striving.

After this, man's misunderstanding that he is all in all in this world and that there is no superior power to watch what he does and to call him to account, has been refuted.

Then, taking one of the many moral concepts of ignorance held by man, as an example, it has been pointed out what wrong criteria of merit and greatness he has proposed for himself in the world. The person who for ostentation and display squanders heaps of wealth, not only himself prides upon his extravagances but the people also admire him for it enthusiastically, whereas the Being Who is watching over his deeds, sees by what methods he obtained the wealth and in what ways and with what motives and intention he spent it.

Then God says: We have given man the means of knowledge and the faculties of thinking and understanding and opened up before him both the highways of virtue and vice: one way leads down to moral depravity, and it is an easy way pleasing for the self; the other way leads up to moral heights, which is steep like an uphill road, for scaling which man has to exercise self-restraint. It is man's weakness that he prefers slipping down into the abyss to scaling the cliff.

Then, God has explained what the steep road is by following which man can ascend to the heights. It is that he should give up spending for ostentation, display and pride and should spend his wealth to help the orphans and the needy, should believe in God and His Religion and joining the company of believers, should participate in the construction of a society which should fulfill the demands of virtue and righteousness patiently and should be compassionate to the people. The end of those who follow this way is that they would become worthy of God's mercies. On the contrary, the end of those who follow the wrong way, is the fire of Hell from which there is no escape.

## Sūrah 90: al-Balad[1792]

In the Name of God, the Most Compassionate, the Most Merciful

1. I swear by this city, [i.e., Makkah] -

2. And you, [O Muhammad], are free of restriction in this city -

3. And [by] the father[1793] and that which was born [of him],

4. We have certainly created man into hardship.

5. Does he think that never will anyone overcome him?

6. He says, "I have spent wealth in abundance."

7. Does he think that no one has seen him?

8. Have We not made for him two eyes?

9. And a tongue and two lips?

10. And have shown him the two ways?[1794]

11. But he has not broken through the difficult pass.[1795]

12. And what can make you know what is [breaking through] the difficult pass?

13. It is the freeing of a slave

14. Or feeding on a day of severe hunger

15. An orphan of near relationship

16. Or a needy person in misery

17. And then being among those who believed and advised one another to patience and advised one another to compassion.

18. Those are the companions of the right.[1796]

19. But they who disbelieved in Our signs - those are the companions of the left.[1797]

20. Over them will be fire closed in.[1798]

[1792] *Al-Balad*: The City.
[1793] Said to be Adam.
[1794] Of good and evil.
[1795] i.e., the steep incline or obstacle. In other words, he has not spent in the cause of God but only boasts of spending in front of others.

[1796] Or "the companions of good fortune," i.e., those who receive their records in their right hands and proceed to Paradise.
[1797] Or "the companions of ill fortune," i.e., those who receive their records in their left hands and proceed to Hell.
[1798] The cover over Hell will be sealed and locked, containing its fire and its inhabitants.

## Sūrah 91: ash-Shams

### Period of Revelation

The subject matter and the style show that this Sūrah too was revealed in the earliest period at Makkah at a stage when opposition to the Prophet had grown very strong and intense.

### Theme and Subject Matter

Its theme is to distinguish the good from the evil and to warn the people, who were refusing to understand this distinction and insisting on following the evil way, of the evil end.

In view of the subject matter this Sūrah consists of two parts. The first part consists of v. 1-10, and the second of v. 11-15. The first part deals with three things:

1. That just as the sun and the moon, the day and the night, the earth and the sky, are different from each other and contradictory in their effects and results, so are the good and the evil different from each other and contradictory in their effects and results; they are neither alike in their outward appearance nor can they be alike in their results.
2. That God after giving the human self powers of the body, sense and mind has not left it uninformed in the world, but has instilled into his unconscious by means of a natural inspiration the distinction between good and evil, right and wrong, and the sense of the good to be good and of the evil to be evil.
3. That the future of man depends on how by using the powers of discrimination, will and judgment that God has endowed him with, he develops the good and suppresses the evil tendencies of the self. If he develops the good inclination and frees his self of the evil inclinations, he will attain to eternal success, and if, on the contrary, he suppresses the good and promotes the evil, he will meet with disappointment and failure.

In the second part, citing the historical precedent of the people of Thamūd, the significance of Apostleship has been brought out. A Messenger is raised in the world, because the inspirational knowledge of good and evil that God has placed in human nature is by itself not enough for the guidance of man, but on account of his failure to understand it fully man has been proposing wrong criteria and theories of good and evil and thus going astray. That is why God sent down clear and definite Revelation to the Prophets (peace be upon them) to augment man's natural inspiration so that they may expound to the people as to what is good and what is evil. Likewise, the Prophet Sālih was sent to the people of Thamūd, but the people overwhelmed by the evil of their self, had become so rebellious that they rejected him. And when he presented before them the miracle of the she camel, as demanded by themselves, the most wretched one of them, in spite of his warning, hamstrung it, in accordance with the will and desire of the people. Consequently, the entire tribe was overtaken by a disaster.

While narrating this story of the Thamūd nowhere in the Sūrah has it been said - O people of Quraysh, if you rejected your Prophet, Muhammad, as the Thamūd had rejected theirs, you too would meet with the same fate as they met. The conditions at that time in Makkah were similar to those that had been created by the wicked among the people of Thamūd against the Prophet Sālih. Therefore, the narration of this story in those conditions was by itself enough to suggest to the people of Makkah how precisely this historical precedent applied to them.

## Sūrah 91: ash-Shams[1799]

In the Name of God, the Most Compassionate, the Most Merciful

1. By the sun and its brightness

2. And [by] the moon when it follows it

3. And [by] the day when it displays it[1800]

4. And [by] the night when it covers [i.e., conceals] it

5. And [by] the sky and He who constructed it

6. And [by] the earth and He who spread it

7. And [by] the soul and He who proportioned it[1801]

8. And inspired it [with discernment of] its wickedness and its righteousness,

9. He has succeeded who purifies it,

10. And he has failed who instills it [with corruption].

11. Thamūd denied [their prophet] by reason of their transgression,

12. When the most wretched of them was sent forth.[1802]

13. And the messenger of God [i.e., Sālih] said to them, "[Do not harm] the she-camel of God or [prevent her from] her drink."

14. But they denied him and hamstrung[1803] her. So their Lord brought down upon them destruction for their sin and made it equal [upon all of them].

15. And He does not fear the consequence thereof.[1804]

---

[1799] *Ash-Shams*: The Sun.

[1800] The earth. Also interpreted as the sun. The same applies to the following verse.

[1801] i.e., balanced and refined it, creating in it sound tendencies and consciousness.

[1802] To hamstring the she-camel which had been sent by God as a sign to them.

[1803] And then killed.

[1804] God is not asked about what He does, but His servants will be asked. See 21:23.

# Sūrah 92: al-Layl

## Period of Revelation

Its subject matter so closely resembles that of Sūrah ash-Shams that each Sūrah seems to be an explanation of the other. It is one and the same thing which has been explained in Sūrah ash-Shams in one way and in this Sūrah in another. This indicates that both these Sūrahs were sent down in about the same period.

## Theme and Subject Matter

Its theme is to distinguish between the two different ways of life and to explain the contrast between their ultimate ends and results. In view of the subject matter this Sūrah consists of two parts, the first part consisting of v. 1-11 and the second of v. 12-21.

In the first part, at the outset it has been pointed out that the strivings and doings that the individuals, nations and groups of mankind are engaged in in the world, are, in respect of their moral nature, as divergent as the day is from the night, and the male from the female. After this, according to the general style of the brief Sūrahs of the Qur'ān, three moral characteristics of one kind and three moral characteristics of the other kind have been presented as an illustration from among a vast collection of the strivings and activities of man, from which every man can judge which style of life is represented by one kind of the characteristics and which style of life by the other kind. Both these styles have been described in such brief, elegant, and pithy sentences that they move the heart and go down into memory as soon as one hears them. Characteristics of the first kind are that one should spend one's wealth, adopt God-consciousness and piety, and acknowledge the good as good. The second kind of the characteristics are that one should be miserly, should least care for God's pleasure and His displeasure, and should repudiate what is good and right. Then it has been stated that these two modes of action which are clearly divergent, cannot be equal and alike in respect of their results. But, just as they are divergent in their nature, so they are divergent in their results. The person (or group of persons) who adopts the first mode of action, God will make easy for him the correct way of life, so much so that doing good will become easy for him and doing evil difficult. On the contrary, he who adopts the second mode of life, God will make easy for him the difficult and hard way of life, so much so that doing evil will become easy for him and doing good difficult. This passage has been concluded with a most effective and touching sentence, saying: "This worldly wealth for the sake of which man is even prepared to risk his life: will not go down with him into the grave; therefore, what will it avail him after death?"

In the second part also three truths have been stated equally briefly. First, that God has not left man uninformed in the examination hall of the world, but He has taken on Himself the responsibility to tell him which one is the straight and right way out of the different ways of life. Here, there was no need to point out that by sending His Messenger and His Book. He has fulfilled His responsibility, for both the Messenger and the Book were present to afford the guidance. Second, that the Master of both the world and the Hereafter is God alone. If you seek the world, it is He Who will give it, and if you seek the Hereafter, again it is He Who will give it. Now, it is for you to decide what you should seek from Him. The third truth that has been stated is that the wretched one who rejects the good, which is being presented through the Messenger and the Book, and turns away from it, will have a blazing fire ready for him. As for the God fearing person who spends his wealth in a good cause, without any selfish motive, only for the sake of winning his Lord's good pleasure, his Lord will be pleased with him and will bless him with so much that he will be well pleased with Him.

## Sūrah 92: al-Layl[1805]

In the Name of God, the Most Compassionate, the Most Merciful

1. By the night when it covers[1806]

2. And [by] the day when it appears

3. And [by] He who created the male and female,

4. Indeed, your efforts are diverse.

5. As for he who gives and fears God

6. And believes in the best [reward],

7. We will ease him toward ease.

8. But as for he who withholds and considers himself free of need

9. And denies the best [reward],

10. We will ease him toward difficulty.

11. And what will his wealth avail him when he falls?[1807]

12. Indeed, [incumbent] upon Us is guidance.

13. And indeed, to Us belongs the Hereafter and the first [life].

14. So I have warned you of a Fire which is blazing.

15. None will [enter to] burn therein except the most wretched one

16. Who had denied and turned away.

17. But the righteous one will avoid it -

18. [He] who gives [from] his wealth to purify himself

19. And not [giving] for anyone who has [done him] a favor to be rewarded[1808]

20. But only seeking the countenance of his Lord, Most High.

21. And he is going to be satisfied.

[1805] *Al-Layl*: The Night.
[1806] With darkness.
[1807] i.e., when he dies or is destroyed. It can also mean when he falls into the Hellfire.

[1808] i.e., without intending reciprocation for some benefit to himself.

## Sūrah 93: adh-Dhuhā

### Period of Revelation

Its subject matter clearly indicates that it belongs to the earliest period at Makkah. Hadith also show that the revelations were suspended for a time, which caused the Prophet to be deeply distressed and grieved. On this account he felt very anxious that perhaps he had committed some error because of which his Lord had become angry with him and had forsaken him. Thereupon he was given the consolation that revelation had not been stopped because of some displeasure but this was necessitated by the same expediency as underlies the peace and stillness of the night after the bright day, as if to say: "If you had continuously been exposed to the intensely bright light of Revelation (Wahi) your nerves could not have endured it. Therefore, an interval was given in order to afford you peace and tranquillity." This state was experienced by the Prophet in the initial stage of the Prophethood when he was not yet accustomed to hear the intensity of Revelation. On this basis, observance of a pause in between was necessary. This we have already explained in the introduction to Sūrah al-Muddathir.

### Theme and Subject Matter

Its theme is to console the Prophet and its object to remove his anxiety and distress, which he had been caused by the suspension of Revelation. First of all, swearing an oath by the bright morning and the stillness of night, he has been reassured, so as to say: "Your Lord has not at all forsaken you, nor is he displeased with you." Then, he has been given the good news that the hardships that he was experiencing in the initial stage of his mission, would not last long, for every later period of life for him would be better than the former period, and before long God would bless him so abundantly that he would be well pleased. This is one of the express prophecies of the Qur'ān, which proved literally true, afterwards, whereas when this prophecy was made there seemed not to be the remotest chance that the helpless and powerless man who had come out to wage a war against the ignorance and paganism of the entire nation, would ever achieve such wonderful success.

Then, addressing His Prophet God says: "O My dear Prophet, what has caused you the anxiety and distress that your Lord has forsaken you, and that We are displeased with you? Whereas the fact is that We have been good to you with kindness after kindness ever since the day of your birth. You were born an orphan, We made the best arrangement for your upbringing and care: you were unaware of the Way, We showed you the Way; you were indigent, We made you rich. All this shows that you have been favored by Us from the very beginning and Our grace and bounty has been constantly focused on you." Here, one should also keep in view v. 37-42 of Sūrah Tā Hā, where God, while sending the Prophet Moses to confront a tyrant like Pharaoh, encouraged and consoled him, saying: "We have been looking after you with kindness ever since your birth; therefore, you should be satisfied that you will not be left alone in this dreadful mission. Our bounty will constantly be with you."

In conclusion, God has instructed His Prophet telling him how he should treat the creatures of God to repay for the favors He has done him and how he should render thanks for the blessings He has bestowed on him.

## Sūrah 93: adh-Dhuhā[1809]

In the Name of God, the Most Compassionate,
the Most Merciful

1. By the morning brightness

2. And [by] the night when it covers with darkness,[1810]

3. Your Lord has not taken leave of you, [O Muhammad], nor has He detested [you].

4. And the Hereafter is better for you than the first [life].

5. And your Lord is going to give you, and you will be satisfied.

6. Did He not find you an orphan and give [you] refuge?

7. And He found you lost and guided [you],

8. And He found you poor and made [you] self-sufficient.

9. So as for the orphan, do not oppress [him].

10. And as for the petitioner,[1811] do not repel [him].

11. But as for the favor of your Lord, report [it].

[1809] *Adh-Dhuhā*: The Morning Brightness, i.e., the brightness or heat of the sun.
[1810] And becomes still.
[1811] Anyone who seeks aid or knowledge.

## Sūrah 94: ash-Sharh

### Period of Revelation

Its subject matter so closely resembles that of Sūrah adh-Dhuhā that both these Sūrah seem to have been revealed in about the same period under similar conditions. According to Abdullah bin Abbas, it was sent down in Makkah just after Sūrah adh-Dhuhā.

### Theme and Subject Matter

The aim and object of this Sūrah too is to console and encourage the Messenger. Before his call he never had to encounter the conditions which he suddenly had to encounter after it when he embarked on his mission of inviting the people to Islām. This was by itself a great revolution in his own life of which he had no idea in his life before Prophethood. No sooner had he started preaching the message of Islām than the same society which had esteemed him with unique honour, turned hostile to him. The same relatives and friends, the same clansmen and neighbors, who used to treat him with the highest respect, began to shower him with abuse and invective. No one in Makkah was prepared to listen to him; he began to be ridiculed and mocked in the street and on the road; and at every step he had to face new difficulties. Although gradually he became accustomed to the hardships, even much severer ones, yet the initial stage was very discouraging for him. That is why first Sūrah adh-Dhuhā was sent down to console him, and then this Sūrah.

In it, at the outset, God says: "We have favored you, O Prophet, with three great blessings; therefore you have no cause to be disheartened. The first is the blessing of Sharh Sadr (opening up of the breast), the second of removing from you the heavy burden that was weighing down your back before the call, and the third of exalting your renown the like of which has never been granted to any man before. Further below in the notes we have explained what is implied by each of these blessings and how great and unique these blessings indeed are!

After this, the Lord and Sustainer of the universe has reassured His Servant and Messenger that the period of hardships which he is passing through, is not very long, but following close behind it there is also a period of ease. This same thing has been described in Sūrah adh-Dhuhā, saying: "Every later period is better for you than the former period, and soon your Lord will give you so much that you will be well pleased."

In conclusion, the Prophet has been instructed, so as to say, "You can develop the power to bear and resist the hardships of the initial stage only by one means, and it is this: `When you are free from your occupations, you should devote yourself to the labour and toil of worship, and turn all your attention exclusively to your Lord'." This same instruction has been given to him in much greater detail in Sūrah Al-Muzzammil 1-9.

## Sūrah 94: ash-Sharh[1812]

In the Name of God, the Most Compassionate, the Most Merciful

1. Did We not expand for you, [O Muhammad], your breast?[1813]

2. And We removed from you your burden[1814]

3. Which had weighed upon your back

4. And raised high for you your repute.

5. For indeed, with hardship [will be] ease [i.e., relief].

6. Indeed, with hardship [will be] ease.

7. So when you have finished [your duties], then stand up [for worship].

8. And to your Lord direct [your] longing.

---

1812 *Ash-Sharh* or *al-Inshirāh*: Expansion.

1813 i.e., enlighten, assure and gladden your heart with guidance.

1814 By forgiving any errors which you may have committed previously or might commit consequently. "Burden" can also refer to the anxiety experienced by the Prophet at the beginning of his mission.

## Sūrah 95: at-Teen

### Period of Revelation

According to Qatadah, this Sūrah is Madani. Two different views have been reported from Ibn Abbas: first that it is a Makki Sūrah, and second that it is Madani. But the majority of scholars regard it as a Makki revelation, a manifest symbol of which is the use of the words ha-dhal-balad-il-amin (this city of peace) for Makkah.

### Theme and Subject Matter

Its theme is the rewards and punishments of the Hereafter. For this purpose first swearing an oath by the habitats of some illustrious Prophets, it has been stated that God has created man in the most excellent of molds. Although at other places in the Qur'ān, this truth has been expressed in different ways, for example, at some places it has been said: **"God appointed man His vicegerent on the earth and commanded the angels to bow down to him** "(al-Baqarah: 30,34, al-An'ām: 165, al-A'rāf: 11, al-Hijr 28,29, an-Naml: 62) at others that: **"Man has become bearer of the Divine trust, which the earth and the heavens and the mountains did not have the power to bear"** (al-Ahzāb 72); and at still others that: **"And We have certainly honoured the children of Adam and carried them on the land and sea and provided for them of the good things and preferred them over much of what We have created, with [definite] preference."** (al-Isrā': 70), yet here the statement made an oath in particular by the habitats of the Prophets that man has been created in the finest of molds, signifies that mankind has been blessed with such an excellent mould and nature that it gave birth to men capable of attaining to the highest position of Prophethood, a higher position than which has not been attained by any other creature of God.

Then, it has been stated that there are two kinds of men; those who in spite of having been created in the finest of mould, become inclined to evil and their moral degeneration causes them to be reduced to the lowest of the low, and those who by adopting the way of faith and righteousness remain secure from the degeneration and consistent with the noble position, which is the necessary demand of their having been created in the best of molds. The existence among mankind of both these kinds of men is such a factual thing which no one can deny, for it is being observed and experienced in society everywhere at all times.

In conclusion, this factual reality has been used as an argument to prove that when among the people there are these two separate and quite distinct kinds, how can one deny the judgment and retribution for deeds? If the morally degraded are not punished and the morally pure and exalted are not rewarded and both end in the dust alike, it would mean that there is no justice in the Kingdom of God; whereas human nature and common sense demand that a judge should do justice. How then can one conceive that God, Who is the most just of all judges, would not do justice?

## Sūrah 95: at-Teen[1815]

In the Name of God, the Most Compassionate, the Most Merciful

1. By the fig and the olive[1816]

2. And [by] Mount Sinai

3. And [by] this secure city [i.e., Makkah],

4. We have certainly created man in the best of stature;[1817]

5. Then We return him to the lowest of the low,[1818]

6. Except for those who believe and do righteous deeds, for they will have a reward uninterrupted.

7. So what yet causes you to deny the Recompense?[1819]

8. Is not God the most just of judges?

---

1815 *At-Teen*: The Fig.
1816 Referring to the places known for their production, i.e., Damascus and Jerusalem, respectively. It could also refer to the fig and olive trees or to the fruits themselves.
1817 i.e., upright, symmetrical, and balanced in form and nature.
1818 This can refer to the depths of Hell, to decrepit old age or to immorality.
1819 More literally, "What makes you lie concerning it?"

## Sūrah 96: al-'Alaq

### Period of Revelation

This Sūrah has two parts: the first part consists of v. 1-5, and the second of v. 6-19. About the first part, a great majority of the Islāmic scholars are in agreement that it forms the very first Revelation to be sent down to the Prophet. In this regard, the Hadith from Ā'isha, which Imām Ahmad, Bukhari, Muslim, and other traditionists have related with several chains of authorities, is one of the most authentic hadith on the subject. In it Ā'isha has narrated the full story of the beginning of revelation as she herself heard it from the Messenger of God. Besides, Ibn Abbas, Abu Musa al-Ashari and a group of the Companions also are reported to have stated that these were the very first verses of the Qur'ān to be revealed to the Prophet. The second part was sent down afterwards when the Prophet began to perform the prescribed Prayer in the precincts of the Ka'bāh and Abu Jahl tried to prevent him from this with threats.

### Beginning of Revelation

The traditionists have related on the strength of their respective authorities the story of the beginning of revelation from Iman Az-Zuhri, who had it from Urwah bin Zubair, who had it from Ā'isha, his aunt. She states that revelations to the Prophet began in the form of true (according to other hadith, good) visions. Whichever vision he saw it seemed as though he saw it in broad daylight. Afterwards solitude became dear to him and he would go to the Cave of Hira to engage in worship there for several days and nights (Ā'isha has used the word tahannuth, which Imām Zuhri has explained as ta'abbud: devotional exercises. This was some kind of worship which he performed, for until then he had not been taught the method of performing the Prayer by God). He would take provisions with him and stay there for several days, then would return to Khadijah who would again provide for him for a few more days. One day when he was in the Cave of Hira, Revelation came down to him unexpectedly and the Angel said, to him: *"Read."* After this Ā'isha reports the words of the Prophet himself, to the effect, "*I said: I cannot read! Thereupon the Angel took me and pressed me until I could bear it no more. Then he left me and said: Read. I said: I cannot read! He pressed me a second time until I could bear it no more. Then he left me and said: Read. I again said: I cannot read! He pressed me for the third time until I could bear it no more. Then he left me and said: Iqra bismi Rabbi kal- ladhi khalaqa: (Read in the name of your Lord Who created) till he reached ma lam ya lam (what he did not know).*" Ā'isha says: *"Then the Holy Messenger returned home to Khadijah trembling with fear, and said to her: `Cover me, cover me', and he was covered. When terror left him, he said: `O Khadijah, what has happened to me?' Then he narrated to her whatever had happened, and said: `I fear for my life'. She said; `No never! Be of good cheer. By God, never will God debase you: you treat the kindred well, you speak the truth, (one tradition adds: you restore what is entrusted to you), you bear the burden of the helpless, you help the poor, you entertain the guests, and you cooperate in good works.' Then she took him to Waraqah bin Naufal, who was her cousin. He had become a Christian in pre-Islāmic days, wrote the Gospel in Arabic and Hebrew, and had become very old and blind. Khadijah said: `Brother, listen to the son of your brother.' Waraqah said to the Holy Prophet: `What have you seen, nephew?' The Holy Prophet described what he had seen. Waraqah said; `This is the same Namus (the Angel of Revelation) which God had sent down to Moses. Would that I were a young man during your Prophethood! Would that I were alive when your tribe would expel you!' The Holy Prophet said: `Will they expel me?' Waraqah said; `Yes, never has it so happened that a person brought what you have brought and was not treated as an enemy. If I live till then I would help you with all the power at my command.' But not very long after this Waraqah died."*

This narrative is explicit that even until a moment before the coming of the Angel to the Messenger of God he was intimately aware of his life, his affairs and dealings. When he also heard of his experience, he did not regard it as an evil suggestion, but immediately said that it was the Namus who had descended on Moses. This meant that even according to him the Prophet was such a sublime person that there was nothing surprising in his being elevated to the office of Prophethood.

**Occasion of Revelation of v. 6-19**

This second part of the Sūrah was revealed when the Messenger of God began to perform the Prayer in the Islāmic way in the Ka'bāh and Abu Jahl threatened and tried to prevent him from this. It so happened that after his appointment to Prophethood even before he could start preaching Islām openly, he began to perform the Prayer in the precincts of the Ka'bāh in the way God taught him; and from this the Quraysh felt for the first time that he had adopted a new religion. The other people were watching it with curiosity, but Abu Jahl in his arrogance and pride threatened the Prophet and forbade him to worship in that way in the Ka'bāh. In this connection, quite a number of the hadith have been related from Abdullah ibn Abbas and Abu Huraira, which mention the foolish behavior of Abu Jahl.

Abu Hurairah says that Abu Jahl asked the people of Quraysh: *"Does Muhammad set his face on the ground before you?"* When they replied in the affirmative, he said: *"By Lat and Uzza, if I ever catch him in that act of worship, I would set my foot on his neck and rub his face in the dust."* Then it so happened that he saw the Messenger in that posture and came forward to set his foot on his neck, but suddenly turned back as if in a fright and being asked what was the matter, he said there was a ditch of fire and a terrible spirit between himself and Muhammad and some wings. On hearing this the Prophet remarked: *"Had he come near me, the angels would have smitten and torn him to pieces."* (Ahmad, Muslim, Nasai, Ibn Jarir, Ibn AbI Hatim, Ibn al-Mundhir, lbn Marduyah, Abu Nu'aim Isfahani, Baihaqi).

According to lbn Abbas, Abu Jahl said: "If I caught Muhammad performing his Prayer by the Ka'bāh, I would trample his neck down." When the Prophet heard of it, he said: "If he acted so, the angels would seize him there and then." (Bukhari and Tirmidhi)

According to another hadith from Ibn Abbas, the Prophet was performing his Prayer at the Maqam Ibrahim. Abu Jahl passed that way and said: *"O Muhammad, did I not forbid you this,"* and then he started to threaten him. In reply the Prophet rebuked him severely. There upon he said: *"O Muhammad, on what strength do you rebuke me? By God, my followers in this valley far exceed yours in number."* (Ahmad, Tirmidhi, Nasai, Ibn Jarir, lbn Abi Shaibah, Ibn al-Mundhir, Tabarani, Ibn Marduyah).

Because of these very incidents the portion of this Sūrah beginning with **'Kalla inn al-insana la yat gha'** (v. 6) was sent down. Naturally the place of this part should be the same as assigned to it in this Sūrah of the Qur'ān, for after the coming down of the first Revelation the Prophet had given expression to Islām first of all by the act of Prayer, and his conflict with the pagans.

## Sūrah 96: al-'Alaq[1820]

In the Name of God, the Most Compassionate, the Most Merciful

1. Recite in the name of your Lord who created -

2. Created man from a clinging substance.

3. Recite, and your Lord is the most Generous -

4. Who taught by the pen -

5. Taught man that which he knew not.

6. No! [But] indeed, man transgresses

7. Because he sees himself self-sufficient.

8. Indeed, to your Lord is the return.

9. Have you seen the one who forbids

10. A servant when he prays?

11. Have you seen if he is upon guidance

12. Or enjoins righteousness?

13. Have you seen if he denies and turns away -

14. Does he not know that God sees?

15. No! If he does not desist, We will surely drag him by the forelock[1821] -

16. A lying, sinning forelock.

17. Then let him call his associates;

18. We will call the angels of Hell.[1822]

19. No! Do not obey him. But prostrate and draw near [to God].

[1820] *Al-'Alaq*: The Clinging (or Suspended) Substance. The *sūrah* has also been called *Iqra'*, meaning "recite" or "read."

[1821] It may also mean "slap him" or "blacken his face at the forelock."

[1822] Those who push the wicked into the Fire.

## Sūrah 97: al-Qadr

### Period of Revelation

Whether it is a Makki or a Madani revelation is disputed. Abu Hayyan in Al-Bahr al-Muhti has made the claim that the majority of scholars regard it as a Madani Sūrah. Ibn Mardayah has cited Ibn Abbas, Ibn Zubair and Ā'isha as saying that this Sūrah was revealed at Makkah. A study of the contents also shows that it should have been revealed at Makkah as we shall explain below.

### Theme and Subject Matter

Its theme is to acquaint man with the value, worth and importance of the Qur'ān. Its being placed just after Sūrah al-'Alaq in the arrangement of the Qur'ān by itself explains that the Holy Book, the revelation of which began with the first five verses of Sūrah al-'Alaq was sent down in a destiny making night. It is a glorious Book and its revelation for mankind is full of blessings.

At the outset, God says: **"We have sent the Qur'ān down."** That is, it is not a composition of Muhammad himself, but We Ourself have revealed it.

Then, it is said that "We sent it down in the Night of Destiny." Night of Destiny has two meanings and both are implied here. First, that it is the night during which destinies are decided; or, in other words, it is not an ordinary night like the other nights, but a night in which destinies are made or marred. The revelation of this Book in this night is not merely the revelation of a book but an event which will change the destiny of not only the Quraysh, or of Arabia, but of, the entire world. The same thing has been said in Sūrah ad-Dukhān (please see Introduction to that Sūrah). The other meaning is that this is a night of unique honour, dignity and glory; so much so that it is better than a thousand months. Thus, the disbelievers of Makkah have been warned, as if to say: "You on account of your ignorance regard this Book, which Muhammad has presented, as a calamity for yourselves and complain that a disaster has befallen you, whereas the night in which it was decreed to be sent down was such a blessed night that a task was accomplished in it for the well being of mankind, which had never been accomplished even during a thousand months of history. This also has been said in verse 3 of Ad-Dukhān in another way, which we have explained in the introduction to that Sūrah.

In conclusion, it has been stated that in this night the angels and Gabriel descend with every decree (which in verse 4 of Sūrah ad-Dukhān has been described as arm-hakim: wise decree) by the leave of their Lord, and it is all peace from evening till morning; that is, there is no interference of evil in it, for all decrees of God are intended to promote good and not evil. So much so that even if a decision to destroy a nation is taken, it is taken for the sake of ultimate good, not evil.

## Sūrah 97: al-Qadr[1823]

In the Name of God, the Most Compassionate,
the Most Merciful

1. Indeed, We sent it [i.e., the Qur'ān] down during the Night of Decree.

2. And what can make you know what is the Night of Decree?

3. The Night of Decree is better than a thousand months.

4. The angels and the Spirit [i.e., Gabriel] descend therein by permission of their Lord for every matter.[1824]

5. Peace it is[1825] until the emergence of dawn.

---

[1823] *Al-Qadr*: Decree or Destiny. Other meanings are "precise measurement [i.e., amount or extent]," "value," "gravity" or "greatness."
[1824] They bring down the decree for everything destined to occur in the coming year.
[1825] Upon the believers.

## Sūrah 98: al-Bayyinah

### Period of Revelation

Where it was revealed, at Makkah or Madinah, is also disputed. Ibn Zubair and Ata bin Yasar hold the view that it is Madani. Ibn Abbas and Qatadah are reported to have held two views, first that it is Makki, second that it is Madani. Ā'isha regards it as a Makki Sūrah. As for its contents, there is nothing in it to indicate whether it was revealed at Makkah or at Madinah.

### Theme and Subject Matter

Having been placed after Sūrah al-'Alaq and al-Qadr in the arrangement of the Qur'ān is very meaningful. Sūrah Al-'Alaq contains the very first revelation, while Sūrah Al-Qadr shows as to when it was revealed, and in this Sūrah it has been explained why it was necessary to send a Messenger along with this Holy Book.

First of all the need of sending a Messenger has been explained, saying: The people of the world, be they from among the followers of the earlier scriptures or from among the idolaters, could not possibly be freed from their state of unbelief, until a Messenger was sent whose appearance by itself should be a clear proof of his apostleship, and he should present the Book of God before the people in its original, pristine form, which should be free from every mixture of falsehood corrupting the earlier Divine Books; and which should comprise sound teachings.

Then, about the errors of the followers of the earlier Books it has been said that the cause of their straying into different creeds was not that God had not provided any guidance to them, but they strayed only after a clear statement of the Right Creed had come to them. From this it automatically follows that they themselves were responsible for their error and deviation. Now, if even after the coming of the clear statement through this Messenger, they continued to stray, their responsibility would further increase.

In this very connection, it has been stated that the Prophets who came from God and the Books sent down by Him, did not enjoin anything but that the way of sincere and true service to God be adopted, apart from all other ways, no one else's worship, service or obedience be mixed with His, the salat be established and the Zakāh be paid. From this also it automatically follows that the followers of the earlier scriptures, straying from this true religion, have added unrelated things to it, which are false, and God's Messenger has come to invite them back to the same original faith.

In conclusion, it has been pointed out clearly that the followers of the earlier Books and the idolaters who would refuse to acknowledge this Messenger are the worst of creatures: their punishment is an everlasting Hell; and the people who would believe and act righteously, and would spend life in the world in awe of God, are the best of creatures: their reward is eternal Paradise wherein they will live forever. God became well pleased with them and they became well pleased with God.

## Sūrah 98: al-Bayyinah[1826]

In the Name of God, the Most Compassionate, the Most Merciful

1. Those who disbelieved among the People of the Scripture and the polytheists were not to be parted [from misbelief][1827] until there came to them clear evidence -

2. A Messenger from God, reciting purified[1828] scriptures

3. Within which are correct writings [i.e., rulings and laws].

4. Nor did those who were given the Scripture become divided[1829] until after there had come to them clear evidence.

5. And they were not commanded except to worship God, [being] sincere to Him in religion, inclining to truth, and to establish prayer and to give zakāh. And that is the correct religion.

6. Indeed, they who disbelieved among the People of the Scripture and the polytheists will be in the fire of Hell, abiding eternally therein. Those are the worst of creatures.

7. Indeed, they who have believed and done righteous deeds - those are the best of creatures.

8. Their reward with God will be gardens of perpetual residence beneath which rivers flow, wherein they will abide forever, God being pleased with them and they with Him. That is for whoever has feared his Lord.

---

[1826] *Al-Bayyinah*: Clear Evidence.
[1827] i.e., from their erroneous beliefs and superstitions.
[1828] i.e., containing no falsehood.
[1829] Into sects and denominations.

## Sūrah 99: az-Zalzalah

### Period of Revelation

Whether or not it was revealed at Makkah or Madina, is disputed. Ibn Masud, Ata, Jabir, and Mujahid say that it is a Makki Sūrah and a statement of Ibn Abbas also supports this view. On the contrary, Qatadah and Muqatil say that it is Madini and another statement of Ibn Abbas also has been cited in support of this view.

### Theme end Subject Matter

Its theme is the second life after death and presentation in it before man of the full record of the deeds done by him in the world. In the first three sentences it has been told briefly how the second life after death will take place and how confounding it will be for man. In the next two sentences it has been said that this very earth on which man has lived and performed all kinds of deeds thoughtlessly, and about which he never could fancy that this lifeless thing would at some time in the future bear witness to his deeds, will speak out on that Day by God's command and will state in respect of each individual person what act he had committed at a particular time and place. Then, it has been said that men on that Day, rising from their graves, will come out in their varied groups from all corners of the earth, to be shown their deeds and works, and their presentation of the deeds will be so complete and detailed that not an atom's weight of any good or evil act will be left unnoticed or hidden from his eyes.

## Sūrah 99: az-Zalzalah[1830]

In the Name of God, the Most Compassionate, the Most Merciful

1. When the earth is shaken with its [final] earthquake

2. And the earth discharges its burdens[1831]

3. And man says,[1832] "What is [wrong] with it?" -

4. That Day, it will report its news

5. Because your Lord has inspired [i.e., commanded] it.

6. That Day, the people will depart[1833] separated [into categories] to be shown [the result of] their deeds.

7. So whoever does an atom's weight[1834] of good will see it,

8. And whoever does an atom's weight of evil will see it.

---

[1830] *Az-Zalzalah*: The Earthquake.
[1831] See verse 84:4.
[1832] In terror and amazement.
[1833] From the place of Judgement to their final abode. Another interpretation is "emerge separately" (from the graves).
[1834] Or "the weight of a small ant."

## Sūrah 100: al-'Aadiyāt

### Period of Revelation

Whether it is a Makki or a Madani Sūrah is disputed. Abdullāh bin Masud, Jabir, Hasan Basri, Ikrimah, and Ata say that it is Makki. Anas bin Malik, and Qatadah say that it is Madani; and from Ibn Abbas two views have been reported, first that it is a Makki Sūrah, and second that it is Madani. But the subject matter of the Sūrah and its style clearly indicate that it is not only Makki but was revealed in the earliest stage of Makkah.

### Theme and Subject Matter

Its object is to make the people realize how evil man becomes when he denies the Hereafter, or becomes heedless of it, and also to warn them that in the Hereafter not only their visible and apparent deeds but even the secrets hidden in their hearts too will be subjected to scrutiny.

For this purpose the general chaos and confusion prevailing in Arabia, with which the whole country was in turmoil, has been presented as an argument. Bloodshed, loot and plunder raged on every side. Tribes were subjecting tribes to raids, and no one could have peaceful sleep at night from fear that some enemy tribe might raid his settlement early in the morning. Every Arab was fully conscious of this state of affairs and realized that it was wrong. Although the plundered bemoaned his miserable, helpless state and the plunderer rejoiced, yet when the plunderer himself was plundered, he too realized how wretched was the condition in which the whole nation was involved. Referring to this very state of affairs, it has been said: Unaware of the second life after death and his accountability before God in it, man has become ungrateful to his Lord and Sustainer. He is using the powers and abilities given by God for perpetrating tyranny and pillage; blinded by the love of worldly wealth he tries to obtain it by every means, however impure and filthy, and his own state itself testifies that by abusing the powers bestowed by his Lord he is being ungrateful to Him. He would never have behaved so, had he known the time when the dead will be raised from the graves, and when the intentions and motives with which he had done all sorts of deeds in the world, will be exposed and brought out before everyone to see. At that time the Lord and Sustainer of men shall be well informed of what one had done and what punishment or reward one deserved.

## Sūrah 100: al-'Aadiyāt[1835]

In the Name of God, the Most Compassionate, the Most Merciful

1. By the racers, panting,[1836]

2. And the producers of sparks [when] striking[1837]

3. And the chargers at dawn,[1838]

4. Stirring up thereby [clouds of] dust,

5. Arriving thereby in the center[1839] collectively,

6. Indeed mankind, to his Lord, is ungrateful.

7. And indeed, he is to that a witness.[1840]

8. And indeed he is, in love of wealth, intense.

9. But does he not know that when the contents of the graves are scattered

10. And that within the breasts is obtained,[1841]

11. Indeed, their Lord with them, that Day, is [fully] Acquainted.

---

1835 *Al-'Aadayāt*: The Racers.

1836 i.e., the horses of those fighting for God's cause as they race to attack the enemy.

1837 Their hoofs while galloping over rocky terrain.

1838 While the enemy is unaware.

1839 i.e., penetrating into the enemy ranks during a surprise attack.

1840 Through his speech and his actions.

1841 i.e., when all secrets are made known.

## Sūrah 101: al-Qāri'ah

**Period of Revelation**

There is no dispute about its being a Makki Sūrah. Its contents show that this too is one of the earliest Sūrahs to be revealed at Makkah.

**Theme and Subject Matter**

Its theme is Resurrection and the Hereafter. At the outset, the people have been aroused and alarmed, saying: "The Great Disaster! What is the Great Disaster? And what can make you know what the Great Disaster is?" Thus, after preparing the listeners for the news of the dreadful calamity, Resurrection has been depicted before them in two sentences, saying that on that Day people will be running about in confusion and bewilderment just like so many scattered moths around a light, and the mountains uprooted, will their cohesion and will fly about like carded wool. Then, it has been said that when God's Court is established in the Hereafter, the people are called upon to account for their deeds. The people whose good deeds are found to be heavier than their evil deeds, will be blessed with bliss and happiness, and the people whose good deeds are found to be lighter than their evil deeds, will be cast into the deep pit full of burning fire.

## Sūrah 101: al-Qāri'ah[1842]

In the Name of God, the Most Compassionate, the Most Merciful

1. The Striking Calamity -
2. What is the Striking Calamity?
3. And what can make you know what is the Striking Calamity?
4. It is the Day when people will be like moths, dispersed,[1843]
5. And the mountains will be like wool, fluffed up.[1844]
6. Then as for one whose scales are heavy [with good deeds],
7. He will be in a pleasant life.
8. But as for one whose scales are light,
9. His refuge[1845] will be an abyss.[1846]
10. And what can make you know what that is?
11. It is a Fire, intensely hot.

---

[1842] *Al-Qāri'ah*: That Which Strikes or The Sudden Calamity, another name for the Resurrection.
[1843] The people will be as such after having been expelled from their graves.
[1844] i.e., beginning to disintegrate.
[1845] Literally, "mother" (a man's original refuge), which will envelop him as in an embrace.
[1846] i.e., the pit of Hellfire.

## Sūrah 102: at-Takāthur

**Period of Revelation**

Abu Hayyan and Shawkani say that this Sūrah, according to all commentators, is Makki, and this same is the well known view according to Iman Suyuti.

**Theme and Subject Matter**

In it the people have been warned of the evil consequences of world worship because of which they spend their lives in acquiring more and more of worldly wealth, material benefits and pleasures, and position and power, till death, and in vying with one another and bragging and boasting about their acquisitions. This one pursuit has so occupied them that they are left with no time or opportunity for pursuing the higher things in life. After warning the people of its evil end they have been told as if to say: "These blessings which you are amassing and enjoying thoughtlessly, are not mere blessings but are also a means of your trial. For each one of these blessings and comforts you will surely be called to account in the Hereafter."

## Sūrah 102: at-Takāthur[1847]

In the Name of God, the Most Compassionate, the Most Merciful

1. Competition in [worldly] increase diverts you
2. Until you visit the graveyards.[1848]
3. No! You are going to know.
4. Then, no! You are going to know.
5. No! If you only knew with knowledge of certainty...[1849]
6. You will surely see the Hellfire.
7. Then you will surely see it with the eye of certainty.[1850]
8. Then you will surely be asked that Day about pleasure.[1851]

---

1847 *At-Takāthur*: Competition in Increase.

1848 i.e., remain in them temporarily, meaning until the Day of Resurrection.

1849 The conclusion of this verse is estimated to be "...you would not have been distracted from preparing for the Hereafter."

1850 i.e., with actual eyesight.

1851 i.e., the comforts of worldly life and whether you were grateful to God for His blessings.

## Sūrah 103: al-'Asr

### Period of Revelation

Although Mujahid, Qatadah and Muqatil regard it as a Madani Sūrah, yet a great majority of the commentators opine that it is Makki; its subject matter also testifies that it must have been sent down in the earliest stage at Makkah, when the message of Islām was being presented in brief but highly impressive sentences so that the listeners who heard them once could not forget them even if they wanted to, for they were automatically committed to memory.

### Theme and Subject Matter

This Sūrah is a matchless specimen of comprehensiveness and brevity. A whole world of meaning has been compressed into its few brief words, which is too vast in content to be fully expressed even in a book. In it, in a clear and plain way it has been stated what is the way to true success for man and what is the way to ruin and destruction for him. Imām Shafi'i has very rightly said that if the people only considered this Sūrah well, it alone would suffice them for their guidance. How important this Sūrah was in the sight of the Companions can be judged from the tradition cited from Abdullah bin Hisn ad-Darimi Abu Madinah, according to which whenever any two of them met they would not part company until they had recited Sūrah Al-'Asr to each other. (Tabarani)

## Sūrah 103: al-'Asr[1852]

In the Name of God, the Most Compassionate,
the Most Merciful

1. By time,[1853]

2. Indeed, mankind is in loss,

3. Except for those who have believed and done righteous deeds and advised each other to truth and advised each other to patience.

1852 *Al-'Asr*: Time.
1853 An oath in which God swears by time throughout the ages.

## Sūrah 104: al-Humazah

**Period of Revelation**

All commentators are in agreement that it is a Makki Sūrah; a study of its subject matter and style shows that this too is one of the earliest Sūrahs to be revealed at Makkah.

**Theme and Subject Matter**

In it some of the evils prevalent among the materialistic hoarders of wealth in the pre-Islāmic days have been condemned. Every Arab knew that they actually existed in their society; they regarded them as evils and nobody thought they were good. After calling attention to this kind of ugly character, the ultimate end in the Hereafter of the people having this kind of character has been stated. Both these things (i.e. the character and his fate in the Hereafter) have been depicted in a way which makes the listener automatically reach the conclusion that such a man properly deserves to meet such an end. And since in the world, people of such character do not suffer any punishment, but seem to be thriving instead, the occurrence of the Hereafter becomes absolutely inevitable.

If this Sūrah is read in the sequence of the Sūrahs beginning with az-Zalzalah, one can fully well understand how the fundamental beliefs of Islām and its teachings were impressed on the peoples minds in the earliest stage in Makkah. In Sūrah az-Zalzalah, it was said that in the Hereafter man's full record will be placed before him and not an atom's weight of good or evil done by him in the world will have been left unrecorded. In Sūrah al-'Aadiyat, attention was drawn to the plunder and loot, blood-shed and vandalism, prevailing in Arabia before Islām; then making the people realize that the way the powers given by God were being abused was indeed an expression of sheer ingratitude to Him; they were told that the matter would not end up in the world, but in the second life after death - not only their deeds but their intentions and motives too would be examined, and their Lord fully well knows which of them deserves what reward or punishment. In Sūrah al-Qāri'ah after depicting Resurrection the people were warned that in the Hereafter a man's good or evil end will be dependent on whether the scale of his good deeds was heavier, or the scale of his evil deeds was heavier: In Sūrah at-Takāthur the people were taken to task for the materialistic mentality because of which they remained occupied in seeking increase in worldly benefits, pleasures, comforts and position, and in vying with one another for abundance of everything until death overtook them. Then, warning them of the evil consequences of their heedlessness, they were told that the world was not an open table of food for them to pick and choose whatever they pleased, but for every single blessing that they were enjoying in the world, they would have to render an account to their Lord and Sustainer as to how they obtained it and how they used it. In Sūrah al-Asr it was declared that each member, each group and each community of mankind, even the entire world of humanity, was in manifest loss, if its members were devoid of Faith and righteous deeds and of the practice of exhorting others to truth and patience. Immediately after this comes Sūrah al-Humazah in which after presenting a specimen of leadership of the pre-Islāmic age of ignorance, the people have been asked the question: "What should such a character deserve if not loss and perdition?"

## Sūrah 104: al-Humazah[1854]

In the Name of God, the Most Compassionate, the Most Merciful

1. Woe to every scorner and mocker

2. Who collects wealth and [continuously] counts it.[1855]

3. He thinks that his wealth will make him immortal.

4. No! He will surely be thrown into the Crusher.[1856]

5. And what can make you know what is the Crusher?

6. It is the fire of God, [eternally] fueled,

7. Which mounts directed at the hearts.[1857]

8. Indeed, it [i.e., Hellfire] will be closed down upon them

9. In extended columns.[1858]

---

1854 *Al-Humazah*: The Scorner.
1855 Rather than spending in the way of God.
1856 i.e., Hellfire, which crushes and destroys all that enters it.
1857 Covering them and penetrating them.
1858 Interpreted to be either columns of fire or columns of iron to which are chained the inmates of Hell.

## Sūrah 105: al-Fīl

### Historical Background

In retaliation for the persecution of the followers of the Prophet Jesus in Najran by the Jewish ruler Dhu-Nuwas of Yemen, the Christian kingdom of Abyssinia invaded Yemen and put an end to the Himyarite rule there, and in 525 A.D. this whole land passed under Abyssinian control. This happened, in fact, through collaboration between the Byzantine empire of Constantinople and the Abyssinian kingdom, for the Abyssinians at that time had no naval fleet. The fleet was provided by Byzantium and Abyssinia sent 70,000 of its troops by it across the Red Sea to Yemen. At the outset one should understand that all this did not happen under the religious zeal but there were economic and political factors also working behind it, and probably these were the real motive, and retaliation for the Christian blood was just an excuse. Since the time the Byzantine empire had occupied Egypt and Syria, it had been trying to gain control over the trade going on between East Africa, India, Indonesia, etc., and the Byzantine dominions: from the Arabs, who had been controlling it for centuries, so as to earn maximum profits by eliminating the intermediary Arab merchants. For this purpose, in 24 or 25 B.C., Caesar Augustus sent a large army under the Roman general, Aelius Gallus, which landed on the western coast of Arabia, in order to intercept and occupy the sea route between southern Arabia and Syria. But the campaign failed to achieve its objective on account of the extreme geographical conditions of Arabia. After this, the Byzantines brought their fleet into the Red Sea and put an end to the Arab trade which they carried out by sea, with the result that they were left only with the land route. To capture this very land route they conspired with the Abyssinian Christians and aiding them with their fleet helped them to occupy Yemen.

The Arab historians statements about the Abyssinian army that invaded Yemen are different. Hafiz Ibn Kathir says that it was led by two commanders, Aryat and Abrahah, and according to Muhammad bin Ishaq, its commander was Aryat, and Abrahah was included in it. They both agree that Aryat and Abrahah fell out, Aryat was killed in the encounter, and Abrahah took possession of the country; then somehow he persuaded the Abyssinian king to appoint him his viceroy over Yemen. On the contrary, the Greek and Syriac historians state that when after the conquest of Yemen, the Abyssinians started putting to death the Yemenite chiefs, who had put up resistance, one of the chiefs, named As-Sumayfi Ashwa (whom the Greek historians call Esymphaeus) yielded to the Abyssinians and promising to pay tribute obtained the Abyssinian king's warrant to be governor over Yemen. But the Abyssinian army revolted against him and made Abrahah governor in his place. This man was the slave of a Greek merchant of the Abyssinian seaport of Adolis, who by clever diplomacy had come to wield great influence in the Abyssinian army occupying Yemen. The troops sent by the Negus to punish him either warned him or were defeated by him. Subsequently, after the death of the king, his successor was reconciled to accept him as his vicegerent of Yemen. (The Greek historians write him as Abrames and the Syriac historians as Abraham. Abrahah perhaps is an Abyssinian variant of Abraham, for its Arabic version is Ibrahim).

This man through passage of time became an independent ruler of Yemen. He acknowledged the sovereignty of the Negus only in name and described himself as his deputy. The influence he wielded can be judged from the fact that after the restoration of the dam of Marib in 543 A.D. he celebrated the event by holding a grand feast, which was attended by the ambassadors of the Byzantine emperor, king of Persia, king of Hirah, and king of Ghassan. Its full details are given in the inscription that Abrahah installed on the dam. This inscription is extant and Glaser has published it.

After stabilizing his rule in Yemen Abrahah turned his attention to the objective which from the very beginning of this campaign had been before the Byzantine empire and its allies, the Abyssinian Christians, i.e. to spread Christianity in Arabia, on the one hand, and to capture the trade that was carried out through the Arabs between the eastern lands and the Byzantine dominions, on the other. The need for this increased because the Byzantine struggle for power against the Sasanian empire of Persia had blocked all the routes of the Byzantine trade with the East.

To achieve this objective, Abrahah built in Sana, the capital of Yemen, a magnificent cathedral, called by the Arabian historians al-Qalis, al-Qullais, or al-Qulais, this word being an Arabic version of the Greek word Ekklesia, church. According, to Muhammad bin Ishaq, after having completed the building, he wrote to the Negus, saying: "I shall not rest until I have diverted the Arabs pilgrimage to it." Ibn Kathir writes that he openly declared his intention in Yemen and got it publicly announced. He, in fact, wanted to provoke the Arabs into doing something which should provide him with an excuse to attack Makkah and destroy the Ka'bāh. Muhammad bin Ishaq says that an Arab, enraged at this public proclamation somehow went into the cathedral and defiled it. Ibn Kathir says this was done by a Qurayshite and according to Muqatil bin Suleman, some young men of the Quraysh had set fire to the cathedral. Either might have happened, for Abrahah's proclamation was certainly provocative and in the ancient pre-Islāmic age it cannot be impossible that an Arab, or a Qurayshite youth, might have been enraged and might have defiled the cathedral, or set fire to it. Whatever happened, when the report reached Abrahah that the devotees of the Ka'bāh had thus defiled his cathedral, he swore that he would not rest until he had destroyed the Ka'bāh.

So, in 570 or 571 A.D., he took 60,000 troops and 13 elephants (according to another tradition, 9 elephants) and set off for Makkah. On the way, first a Yemeni chief, Dhu Nafr by name, mustering an army of the Arabs, resisted him but was defeated and taken prisoner. Then in the country of Khath'am he was opposed by Nufail bin Habib al-Khath'am, with his tribe, but he too was defeated and taken prisoner, and in order to save his life he accepted to serve him as guide in the Arab country. When he reached near Tā'if, Bani Thaqif felt that they would not be able to resist such a big force and feeling the danger lest he should destroy the temple of their deity Lat, too; their chief, Mas'ud came out to Abrahah with his men, and he told him that their temple was not the temple he had come to destroy. The temple He sought was in Makkah, and they would send with him a man to guide him there. Abrahah accepted the offer, and Bani Thaqif sent Abu Righal as guide with him. When they reached al-Mughammas (or al-Mughammis), a place about 3 miles short of Makkah, Abu Righal died, and the Arabs stoned his grave and the practice survives to this day. They cursed the Bani Thaqif too, for in order to save the temple of Lat they had cooperated with the invaders of the House of God.

According to Muhammad bin Ishaq, from al-Mughammas, Abrahah sent forward his vanguard and they brought him the plunder of the people of Tihamah and Quraysh, which included two hundred camels of Abdul Muttalib, the grandfather of the Messenger of God. Then, he sent an envoy of his to Makkah with the message that he had not come to fight the people of Makkah but only to destroy the House (i.e. the Ka'bāh). If they offered no resistance, there would be no cause for bloodshed. Abrahah also instructed his envoy that if the people of Makkah wanted to negotiate, he should return with their leading chief to him. The leading chief of Makkah at that time was Abdul Muttalib. The envoy went to him and delivered Abrahah's message. Abdul Muttalib replied: *"We have no power to fight Abrahah. This is God's House. If He wills He will save His House."* The envoy asked him to go with him to Abrahah. He agreed and accompanied him to the king. Now Abdul Muttalib was such a dignified and handsome man that when Abrahah saw him he was much impressed; he got off his throne and sat beside him on the carpet. Then he asked him what he wanted. Abdul Muttalib replied that he wanted the king to return his camels which he had taken. Abrahah said: *"I was much impressed when I saw you but your reply has brought you down in my eyes: you only demand your camels but you say nothing about this House which is your sanctuary and the sanctuary of your forefathers."* He replied: *"I am the owner of my camels and am requesting you to return them. As for the House, it has its own Owner: He will defend it."* When Abrahah said that He would not be able to defend it against him, Abdul Muttalib said that that rested between Him and him. With this Abdul Muttalib left Abrahah and he restored to him his camels.

One thing which becomes evident is that the tribes living in and around Makkah did not have the power to fight such a big force and save the Ka'bāh. Therefore, obviously, the Quraysh did not try to put up any resistance. The Quraysh on the occasion of the Battle of the Trench (Ahzāb) had hardly been able to muster strength numbering ten to twelve thousand men in spite of the alliance with the pagan and Jewish tribes; they could not have resisted an army 60,000 strong.

Muhammad bin Ishaq says that after returning from the camp of Abrahah Abdul Muttalib ordered the Quraysh to withdraw from the city and go to the mountains along with their families for fear of a general massacre. Then he went to the Ka'bāh along with some chiefs of the Quraysh and taking hold of the iron ring of the door, prayed to God Almighty to protect His House and its keepers. There were at that time 360 idols in and around the Ka'bāh, but on that critical moment they forgot them and implored only God for help. Their supplications which have been reported in the books of history do not contain any name but of God, the One. Ibn Hisham in his Life of the Prophet has cited some verses of Abdul Muttalib, which are to the following effect:

*"O God, a man protects his house, so protect Your House; Let not their cross and their craft tomorrow overcome Your craft. If You will to leave them and our qiblah to themselves, You may do as You please." Suhail in Raud al-Unuf has cited this verse also in this connection: "Help today Your devotees against the devotees of the cross and its worshipers."*

After making these supplications Abdul Muttalib and his companions also went off to the mountains. Next morning Abrahah prepared to enter Makkah, but his special elephant, Mahmud, which was in the forefront, knelt down. It was beaten with iron bars, goaded, even scarified, but it would not get up. When they made it face south, north, or east, it would immediately start off, but as soon as they directed it towards Makkah, it knelt down. In the meantime swarms of birds appeared carrying stones in their beaks and claws and showered these on the troops. Whoever was hit would start disintegrating. According to Muhammad bin Ishaq and Ikrimah, this was smallpox, which was seen in Arabia for the first time in that year. Ibn Abbas says that whoever was struck by a pebble, would start scratching his body resulting in breaking of the skin and falling off of the flesh. In another tradition Ibn Abbas says that the flesh and blood flowed like water and bones in the body became visible. The same thing happened with Abrahah too. His flesh fell in pieces and there arose bores on his body emitting pus and blood. In confusion they withdrew and fled towards Yemen. Nufail bin Habib, whom they had brought as guide from the country of Khatham, was searched out and asked to guide them back to Yemen, but he refused and said: "Now where can one flee when God pursues?

The split nose (Abrahah) is the conquered; not the conqueror."

As they withdrew they were continually falling by the bay and dying. Ata bin Yasar says that all the troops did not perish at the spot; some perished there and others perished by the wayside as they withdrew. Abrahah died in the country of Khatham.

This event took place at Muhassir by the Muhassab valley, between Muzdalifah and Mina. According to the Sahih of Muslim and Abu Dawud, in the description of the Prophet's farewell pilgrimage that Imām Jafar as-Sadiq has related from his father, Imām Muhammad Baqir, and he from Jabir bin Abdullah, he says that when the Prophet proceeded from Muzdalifah to Mina, he increased his speed in the valley of Muhassir. Imām Nawawi has explained it saying that the incident of the people of the elephant had occurred there; therefore, the pilgrims have been enjoined to pass by quickly, for Muhassir is a tormented place. Imām Malik in Muwatta has related that the Prophet said that the whole of Muzdalifah is a fit place for staying but one should not stay in the valley of Muhassir. In the verses of Nufail bin Habib, which Ibn Ishaq has cited, he describes this event as an eyewitness;

*"Would that you had seen, O Rudaina, but you would not see, What we saw by the valley of Muhassab. I praised God when I saw the birds, and I feared lest the stones should fall upon us. Everyone was asking for Nufail as though I owned the Abyssinians a debt."*

This was such a momentous event that it soon spread throughout Arabia and many poets made it the subject of their laudatory poems. In these poems one thing is quite evident that everyone regarded it as a manifestation of God Almighty's miraculous power, and no one, even by allusion, said that the idols which were worshipped in the Ka'bāh, had anything to do with it. For example, Abdullah ibn Az-Zibara says:

*"The sixty thousand returned not home, Nor did their sick man (Abrahah) survive on return. Ad and Jurham were there before them, and there is God, above the servants, Who sustains it."* Abu Qais bin Aslat says; *"Rise and worship your Lord and anoint the Corners of the House of God between the Mountains of Makkah and Mina. When the help of the Owner of the Throne reached you, His armies repulsed them so that they were lying in dust, pelted with stones."*

Not only this, but according to Umm Hani and Zubair bin al-Awwam, the Prophet said: *"The Quraysh did not worship anyone but God, the Only and One, for ten years"* (and according to others, for seven years).

The Arabs describe the year in which this event took place as Am al-Fil (the year of the elephants), and in the same year the Messenger of God was born. The traditionists and historians almost unanimously state that the event of the people of the elephant had occurred in Muharram and the Prophet was born in Rabi al-Awwal. A majority of them states that he was born 50 days after the event of the elephant.

**Theme and Substance**

If Sūrah al-Fil is studied in the light of the historical details as given above, one can fully well understand why in this Sūrah only God's inflicting His punishment on the people of the elephant has been referred and described so briefly. It was an event of recent occurrence, and everyone in Makkah and Arabia was fully aware of it. The Arabs believed that the Ka'bāh had been protected in this invasion not by any God or Goddess but by God Almighty Himself. Then God alone had been invoked by the Quraysh chiefs for help, and for quite a few years the people of Quraysh having been impressed by this event, had worshipped none but God. Therefore, there was no need to mention the details in Sūrah al-Fil, but only a reference to it was enough so that the people of Quraysh, in particular, and the people of Arabia, in general, should consider well in their hearts the message that the Prophet Muhammad was giving. For the only message that he gave was that they should worship and serve none but God, the Only and One. Then, they should also consider that if they used force to suppress this invitation to the truth, they would only be inviting the wrath of God, Who had so completely routed and destroyed the people of the elephants.

## Sūrah 105: al-Fīl[1859]

In the Name of God, the Most Compassionate,
the Most Merciful

1. Have you not considered, [O Muhammad], how your Lord dealt with the companions of the elephant?[1860]

2. Did He not make their plan into misguidance?[1861]

3. And He sent against them birds in flocks,

4. Striking them with stones of hard clay,

5. And He made them like eaten straw.[1862]

---

1859 *Al-Fīl:* The Elephant.
1860 i.e., the army under the command of Abrahah al-Ashram which was accompanied by a huge elephant and came with the intention of destroying the *Ka'bāh* at Makkah.
1861 Causing them to perish.
1862 i.e., husks which have been chewed by cattle. This event took place in the year of the Prophet's birth.

## Sūrah 106: Quraysh

### Period of Revelation

A great majority of the commentators are agreed that it is Makki, and a manifest evidence of this are the words Rabba hadhal-Bait (Lord of this House) of this Sūrah itself.

### Historical Background

To understand the Sūrah well it is essential that one should keep the historical background relevant to the contents of this Sūrah and of Sūrah Al-Fil in view.

The tribe of Quraysh was scattered throughout Hijaz until the time of Qusayy bin Kilab, the ancestor of the Prophet. First of all, Qusayy gathered it in Makkah and this tribe was able to gain authority over the Ka'bāh. On that very basis Qusayy was called mujammi (unite, assembler) by his people. This man by his sagacity and wisdom founded a city state in Makkah and made excellent arrangements for the welfare of the pilgrims coming from all over Arabia, with the result that the Quraysh were able to gain great influence among the Arabian tribes and lands. After Qusayy the offices of the state of Makkah were divided between his sons, Abdi Manaf and Abd ad-Dar, but of the two Abdi Manaf gained greater fame even during his father's life-time and was held in high esteem throughout Arabia. Abdi Manaf had four sons: Hashim, Abdi Shams, Al-Muttalib, and Naufal. Of these Hashim, father of Abdul Muttalib and grandfather of the Prophet, first conceived the idea to take part in the trade that passed between the eastern countries and Syria and Egypt through Arabia, and also to purchase the necessities of life for the Arabians so that the tribes living by the trade route bought these from them and the merchants living in the interior of the country were attracted to the market of Makkah. This was the time when the Sasanian kingdom of Persia had captured the international trade that was carried out between the northern lands and the eastern countries and Byzantine empire through the Persian Gulf. This had boosted up the trade activity on the trade route leading from southern Arabia to Syria and Egypt along the Red Sea coast. As against the other Arabian caravans, the Quraysh had the advantage that the tribes on the route held them in high esteem on account of their being keepers of the Ka'bāh. They stood indebted to them for the great generosity with which the Quraysh treated them in the Hajj season. That is why the Quraysh felt no fear that their caravans would be robbed or harmed any where on the way. The tribes on the way did not even charge them the heavy transit taxes that they demanded from the other caravans. Hashim taking advantage of this prepared the trade scheme and made his three brothers partners in it. Thus, Hashim obtained trade privileges from the Ghassanide king of Syria, Abdi Shams from the Negus, Al-Muttalib from the Yemeni nobles and Naufal from the governments of Iraq and Iran, and their trade began to flourish. That is how the four brothers became famous as traders and began to be called ashab al-ilaf (generators of love and affection) on account of their friendly relations with the tribes and states of the surrounding lands.

Because of their business relations with Syria, Egypt, Iraq, Persia, Yemen and Abyssinia, the Quraysh came across such opportunities and their direct contact with the culture and civilization of different countries so enhanced the level of their knowledge and wisdom that no tribe in Arabia could match and equal them. As regards wealth and worldly goods they became the most affluent tribe, and Makkah became the most important commercial center of the Arabian peninsula. Another great advantage that accursed from these international relations was that they brought from Iraq tile script which later was used for writing down the Qur'ān. No other Arabian tribe could boast of so many literate people as Quraysh. For these very reasons the Prophet said: *"Quraysh are the leaders of men."* (Musnad Ahmad). And according to a hadith from Ali in Baihaqi, the Prophet said: *"First the leadership of the Arabians was in the hands of the people of Himyar, then God withdrew it from them and gave it to Quraysh."*

The Quraysh were thus prospering and flourishing when the event of Abrahah's invasion of Makkah took place. Had Abrahah at that time succeeded in taking this Holy City and destroying the Ka'bāh, the glory and renown of not only the Quraysh but of the Ka'bāh itself, would have faded away, the belief of the pre-Islāmic Arabia that the House indeed was God's House would have been shattered, and the high esteem in which Quraysh were held for being keepers of the House throughout the country would have been tarnished. Then, after the Abyssinian advance to Makkah, the Byzantium also would have taken the initiative to gain control over the trade route between Syria and Makkah: and the Quraysh would have been reduced to a plight worse than that in which they were involved before Qusayy bin Kilab. But when God showed this manifestation of His power that the swarms of birds destroyed 60,000 Abyssinian troops brought by Abrahah by pelting them with stones, and from Makkah to Yemen they went on falling and dying by the wayside, the faith of the Arabs that the Ka'bāh indeed was God's House increased manifold, and the glory and renown of Quraysh too was enhanced considerably throughout the country. Now the Arabs were convinced that they were under God's special favor; therefore, they visited every part of Arabia fearlessly and passed through every land with their trade caravans unharmed. No one could dare touch them with an evil intention. Not to speak of touching them, even if they had a non-Quraysh under their protection, he too was allowed to pass unharmed.

**Theme and Substance**

As all this was well known in the time of the Prophet's appointment to Prophethood, there was no need to mention them. That is why in the four brief sentences of this Sūrah, Quraysh were simply asked to consider: "When you yourselves acknowledge this House (i.e. the Ka'bāh) to be God's House, and not of the idols, and when you fully well know that it is God alone Who has granted you peace by virtue of this House, made your trade and commerce flourish and saving you from destitution favored you with prosperity, you should then worship and serve Him alone!"

## Sūrah 106: Quraysh[1863]

In the Name of God, the Most Compassionate, the Most Merciful

1. For the accustomed security of the Quraysh[1864] -
2. Their accustomed security [in] the caravan of winter and summer[1865] -
3. Let them worship the Lord of this House,[1866]
4. Who has fed them, [saving them] from hunger and made them safe, [saving them] from fear.

[1863] *Quraysh*: (The tribe of) Quraysh.
[1864] i.e., the honour and reputation God had given them as guardians of the Holy *Ka'bāh*, which allowed them to travel without fear of being harmed.
[1865] i.e., the trading caravans that travelled south in winter and north in summer.
[1866] i.e., the *Ka'bāh*.

## Sūrah 107: al-Mā'ūn

### Period of Revelation

There are narrations from Ibn Abbas, Qatadah and Dahhak as saying that this Sūrah was revealed at Madinah. In our opinion there is an internal piece of evidence in the Sūrah itself which points to its being a Madani Revelation. It holds out a threat of destruction to those praying ones who are unmindful of their Prayers and who pray only to be seen. These kind of hypocrites were found only at Madinah, for it was there that Islām and the Muslims gained such strength that many people were compelled to believe from expedience, had to visit the Mosque, join the congregational Prayer and prayed only to be seen of others, so as to be counted among Muslims. Contrary to this is, at Makkah conditions were altogether different. No one had to pray to be seen. There it was difficult even for the believers to pray in congregation; they prayed secretly and if a person prayed openly he did so only at the risk of his life. These kind of hypocrites found in Makkah did not comprise those who believed and prayed to be seen but those who in their hearts had known and acknowledged the Messenger of God to be on the true path, but were avoiding to accept Islām in order to maintain their position of leadership and authority, or were not prepared to take the risk of being afflicted with the kind of hardships with which they found the believers afflicted in the society around them. This condition of the hypocrites at Makkah has been described in v. 10-11 of Sūrah Al-Ankabūt.

### Theme and Subject Matter

Its theme is to point out what kind of morals a man develops when he refuses to believe in the Hereafter. In v. 2-3 the condition of the disbelievers who openly belie the Hereafter has been described, and in the last four verses the state of those hypocrites who apparently are Muslims but have no idea of the Hereafter, its judgment, and the meting out of rewards and punishments accordingly has been described. On the whole, the object of depicting the attitude and conduct of two kinds of people is to impress the point that man cannot develop a strong, stable and pure character in himself unless he believes in the Hereafter.

## Sūrah 107: al-Mā'ūn[1867]

In the Name of God, the Most Compassionate, the Most Merciful

1. Have you seen the one who denies the Recompense?

2. For that is the one who drives away the orphan

3. And does not encourage the feeding of the poor.

4. So woe to those who pray

5. [But] who are heedless of their prayer[1868] -

6. Those who make show [of their deeds]

7. And withhold [simple] assistance.

---

1867 *Al-Mā'ūn*: Assistance.

1868 i.e., the hypocrites who are unconcerned if they miss prayers when no one sees them.

## Sūrah 108: al-Kawthar

### Period of Revelation

Ibn Marduyah has cited Abdullah bin Abbas, Abdullah bin az-Zubair and Ā'isha as saying that this Sūrah is Makki. Kalbi and Muqatil also regard it as Makki, and the same is the view held by the majority of commentators. But Hasan Basri, Ikrimah, Mujahid and Qatadah regard it as Madani. Imām Suyuti in Al-Itqan has confirmed this same view, and Imām Nawawi in his commentary of the Sahih of Muslim has also preferred the same. The reason for this assumption is the tradition which traditionists of the rank of Imām Ahmad, Muslim, Abu Daud, Nasai, Ibn Abi Shaibah, Ibn al-Mundhir, Ibn Marduyah, Baihaqi and others have related from Anas bin Malik, saying: "The Holy Prophet was among us. In the meantime he dozed; then he raised his head, smiling, according to some traditions, the people asked what for he was smiling, according to others, he himself told them that a Sūrah had just been revealed to him. Then, with Bismillah ir-Rahman ir-Rahim, he recited Sūrah al-Kawthar; then he asked the people whether they knew what al-Kawthar was. When they said that God and his Messenger had the best knowledge, he said; It is a river which my Lord has granted me in Paradise." (The details follow under "Kawthar"). The basis of the reasoning from this tradition for this Sūrah's being Madani is that Anas belonged to Madinah, and his saying that this Sūrah was revealed in his presence is a proof that it was Madani.

But, in the first place, from this same Anas, Imām Ahmad, Bukhari, Muslim, Abu Da'ud, Tirmidhi and Ibn Jarir have related the traditions which say that this river of Paradise (al-Kawthar) had been shown to the Prophet on the occasion of the miraj (ascension) and everyone knows that miraj had taken place at Makkah before the Hijrah. Secondly, when during the miraj the Prophet had not only been informed of this gift of God Almighty but also shown it, there was no reason why Sūrah al-Kawthar should have be revealed at Madinah to give him the good news of it. Thirdly, if in an assembly of the Companions the Holy Prophet himself had given the news of the revelation of Sūrah al-Kawthar which Anas has mentioned in his tradition, and it meant that that Sūrah had been revealed for the first time then, it was not possible that well-informed Companions like Ā'isha, Abdullah bin Abbas and Abdullah bin Zubair should have declared this Sūrah to be a Makki revelation and most of the commentators also should have regarded it as Makki. If the matter is considered carefully, there appears to be a flaw in the tradition from Anas in that it does not say what was the subject under discussion in the assembly in which the Prophet gave the news about Sūrah al-Kawthar. It is possible that at that time the Prophet was explaining something. In the meantime he was informed by revelation that that point was further explained by Sūrah al-Kawthar, and he mentioned the same thing, saying that that Sūrah was revealed to him just then. Such incidents did take place on several occasions, on the basis of which the commentators have opined about certain verses that they were revealed twice. This second revelation, in fact, meant that the verse had been revealed earlier, but on some later occasion the Prophet's attention was invited to it by revelation for the second time. In such traditions, the mention of the revelation of a certain verse is not enough to decide whether it was revealed at Makkah or Madinah, and when precisely it was revealed.

Had this tradition of Anas not been there to cause doubt, the whole content of the Sūrah al-Kawthar by itself bears evidence that it was revealed at Makkah, and in the period when the Prophet was passing through extremely discouraging conditions.

### Historical Background

Before this in Sūrahs Adh-Dhuhā and Alam Nashrah we have seen that when in the earliest phase of Prophethood the Prophet was passing through the most trying conditions when the whole nation had turned hostile, there was resistance and opposition on every side, and the Prophet and a handful of his Companions did not see any remote chance of success. God in order to console and encourage him at that time had sent down several verses. In Sūrah Adh-Dhuhā it was said: "And surely the later period (i.e. every later period) is better for you than the former period, and soon your Lord shall give you so much that you shall be well pleased." In Sūrah Alam Nashrah: "And We exalted your renown for you." That is, "Though the enemies are trying to defame you throughout the country, We, on the contrary, have arranged to exalt your name and fame." And: "The fact is that along with every hardship there is also ease." That is, "You should not be disheartened by the severity of conditions at this time; this period of hardships will soon pass, and the period of success and victory will follow."

Such were the conditions in which God by sending down Sūrah al-Kawthar consoled the Prophet as well as foretold the destruction of his opponents. The disbelieving Quraysh said: "Muhammad cut off from his community and reduced to a powerless and helpless individual. According to Ikrimah when the Prophet was appointed a Prophet, and he began to call the people to Islām, the Quraysh said: "Muhammad is cut off from his people as a tree is cut off from its root, which might fall to the ground any moment." (Ibn Jarir). Muhammad bin Ishaq says: "Whenever the Prophet was mentioned before As bin Wa'il as-Sehmi, the chief of Makkah, he used to say: "Let him alone for he is only a childless man (abtar) with no male offspring. When he dies, there will be no one to remember him." Shamir bin Atiyyah says that Uqbah bin Abi Mu'ait, also used to say similar things about the Prophet (Ibn Jarir). According to Ibn Abbas, once Ka'b bin Ashraf (the Jewish chief of Madinah) came to Makkah and the Quraysh chiefs said to him: "Just see this boy, who is cut off from his people; he thinks he is superior to us, whereas we manage the Hajj, look after the Ka'bāh and water the pilgrims." (Bazzar) Concerning this very incident Ikrimah reports that the Quraysh had used the words as-sunbur al-munbatir min qaumi-hi (a weak, helpless and childless man who is cut off from his people) for the Prophet. (Ibn Jarir) Ibn Sa'd and Ibn Asakir have related that Abdullah bin Abbas said; "The eldest son of the Prophet was Qasim; next to him was Zainab, next to her Abdullah and next to him three daughters, viz. Umm Kulthum, Fātimah and Ruqayyah. Of them first Qasim died and then Abdullah. Thereupon As bin Wail said: "His line has come to an end: now he is abtar (i.e. cut off from root)." Some traditions add that As said "Muhammad is abtar: he has no son to succeed him. When he dies, his memory will perish and you will be rid of him." The tradition from Ibn Abbas, which Abd bin Humaid has related, shows that Abu Jahl also had said similar words on the death of the Prophet's son, Abdullah. Ibn Abi Hatim has related on the authority of Shmir bin Atiyyah that the same kind of meanness was shown by Uqbah bin Abi Mu'ait by rejoicing at this bereavement of the Prophet. Ata says that when the second son of the Prophet died, his own uncle, Abu Lahab (whose house was next to his) hastened to the pagans and gave them the "good news:" Batira Muhammadun al-lail: "Muhammad has become childless this night, or he is cut off from root."

Such were the disturbing conditions under which Sūrah al-Kawthar was sent down. The Quraysh were angry with him because he worshipped and served only God and repudiated their idolatry publicly. For this very reason he was deprived of the rank, esteem and honour that he enjoyed among his people before Prophethood and was now as cut off from his community. The handful of his Companions also were helpless, poor people who were being persecuted and tyrannized. Furthermore, he was bereaved by the death of two sons, one after the other, whereas the near relatives and the people of his clan, brotherhood and neighborhood were rejoicing and uttering such words as were disheartening and disturbing for a noble person who had treated even his enemies most kindly. At this God just in one sentence of this brief Sūrah gave him the good news, better news than which has never been given to any man in the world, besides the decision that it will be his opponents who will be cut off from their root and not he.

## Sūrah 108: al-Kawthar[1869]

In the Name of God, the Most Compassionate, the Most Merciful

1. Indeed, We have granted you, [O Muhammad], al-Kawthar.

2. So pray to your Lord and sacrifice [to Him alone].

3. Indeed, your enemy is the one cut off.[1870]

[1869] Al-Kawthar: Literally, "the most abundant good." Also, a river in Paradise.
[1870] From all good in this world and the Hereafter.

## Sūrah 109: al-Kāfirūn

### Period of Revelation

Abdullah bin Mas'ud, Hasan Basri and Ikrimah, say that this Sūrah, is Makki, while Abdullah bin Zubair says that it is Madani. Two different views have been reported from Abdullah bin Abbas and Qatadah, first that it is Makki, and second that it is Madani. However, according to the majority of commentators, it is a Makki Sūrah, and its subject matter itself points to its being a Makki revelation.

### Historical Background

There was a time in Makkah when although a storm of opposition had arisen in the pagan society of Quraysh against the message of Islām preached by the Prophet , yet the Quraysh chiefs had not yet lost hope that they would reach some sort of a compromise with him. Therefore, from time to time they would visit him with different proposals of compromise so that he accepted one of them and the dispute between them was brought to an end. In this connection, different traditions have been related in the Hadith.

According to Abdullah bin Abbas, the Quraysh proposed to the Prophet; "We shall give you so much of wealth that you will become the richest man of Makkah; we shall give you whichever woman you like in marriage; we are prepared to follow and obey you as our leader, only on the condition that you will not speak ill of our gods. If you do not agree to this, we present another proposal which is to your as well as to our advantage." When the Prophet asked what it was, they said that if he would worship their gods, Lāt and 'Uzza, for a year, they would worship his God for the same space of time. The Prophet said: "Wait awhile; let me see what my Lord commands in this regard." Thereupon the revelation came down: Qul ya-ayyuhal-kafirun...and: Qul afa-ghair Allah...(Az-Zumar: 64): "Say to them: ignorant people do you bid me to worship others than God?" (Ibn Jarir, Ibn Abi Hatim, Tabarani) According to another tradition from Ibn Abbas, the Quraysh said to the Prophet: "O Muhammad, if you kiss our gods, the idols, we shall worship your God." Thereupon, this Sūrah was sent down. (Abd bin Humaid)

Said bin Mina (the freed slave of Abul Bakhtari) has related that Walid bin Mughirah, As bin Wail, Aswad bin al-Muttalib and Umayyah bin Khalaf met the Prophet and said to him: "O Muhammad, let us agree that we would worship your God and you would worship our gods, and we would make you a partner in all our works. If what you have brought was better than what we possess, we would be partners in it with you, and have our share in it, and if what we possess is better than what you have brought, you would be partner in it with us and have your share of it." At this God sent down: Qul ya-ayyuhal-kafirun (Ibn Jarir, Ibn Abi Hatim, Ibn Hisham also has related this incident in the Sirah).

Wahb bin Munabbih has related that the people of Quraysh said to God's Messenger: "If you like we would enter your faith for a year and you would enter our faith for a year."(Abd bin Humaid, Ibn Abi Hatim)

These traditions show that the Quraysh had proposed such things to the Prophet not once, in one sitting, but at different times and on different occasions; and there was need that they should be given a definite, decisive reply so that their hope that he would come to terms with them on the principle of "give and take" was frustrated forever.

### Theme and Subject Matter

If the Sūrah is read with this background in mind, one finds that it was not revealed to preach religious tolerance as some people of today seem to think, but it was revealed in order to exonerate the Muslims from the disbelievers religion, their rites of worship, and their gods, and to express their total disgust and unconcern with them and to tell them that Islām and kufr (unbelief) had nothing in common and there was no possibility of their being combined and mixed into one entity. Although it was addressed in the beginning to the disbelieving Quraysh in response to their proposals of compromise, yet it is not confined to them only, but having made it a part of the Qur'ān, God gave the Muslims the eternal teaching that they should exonerate themselves by word and deed from the creed of kufr wherever and in whatever form it be, and should declare without any reservation that they cannot make any compromise with the disbelievers in the matter of Faith. That is why this Sūrah continued to be recited when the people to whom it was addressed as a rejoinder, had died and been forgotten, and those Muslims also continued to recite it who were disbelievers at the time it was revealed, and the Muslims still recite it centuries after they have passed away, for expression of disgust with and dissociation from kufr and its rites is a perpetual demand of Faith.

As for the esteem in which the Prophet held this Sūrah, it can be judged from the following few hadith:

Abdullah bin Umar (may God be pleased with him) has related that on many occasions he heard the Prophet recite Sūrahs *Qul Ya-ayyuhal-kafirun* and *Qul Huwu-Allahu-ahad* in the two rakahs before the Fajr obligatory Prayer and in the two rakahs after the Maghrib obligatory Prayer. Several traditions on this subject with a little variation in wording have been related by Imām Ahmad, Tirmidhi, Nasai, Ibn Majah, Ibn Hibban, Ibn Marduyah from Ibn Umar.

Khabbab says: "The Prophet said to me: when you lie down in bed to sleep, recite Qul ya-ayyuhal kafirun, and this was the Prophet's own practice also; when he lay down to sleep, he recited this Sūrah." (Bazzar, Tabarani, Ibn Marduyah)

According to Ibn Abbas, the Prophet said to the people: "Should I tell you the word which will protect you from polytheism? It is that you should recite Qul ya-ayyuhal kafirun when you go to bed."(Abu Ya'la, Tabarani)

Anas says that the Prophet said to Mu'adh bin Jabal; "Recite Qul ya-ayyuhal-kafirun at the time you go to bed, for this is immunity from polytheism." (Baihaqi in Ash-Shu'ab)

Both Fardah bin Naufal and Abdur Rahman bin Naufal have stated that their father, Naufal bin Muawiyah al-Ashjai, said to the Prophet: "Teach me something which I may recite at the time I go to bed." The Prophet replied: "Recite Qul ya-ayyuhal kafirun to the end and then sleep, for this is immunity from polytheism." (Musnad Ahmad, Aba Da'ud, Tirmidhi, Nasai, Ibn Abi Shaibah, Hakim, Ibn Marduyah, Baihaqi in Ash-Shuab). A similar request was made by Jabalah bin Harithah, brother of Said bin Harithah, to the Prophet and to him also he gave the same reply. (Musnad Ahmad, Tabarani)

## Sūrah 109: al-Kāfirūn[1871]

In the Name of God, the Most Compassionate, the Most Merciful

1. Say, "O disbelievers,

2. I do not worship what you worship.

3. Nor are you worshippers of what I worship.

4. Nor will I be a worshipper of what you worship.

5. Nor will you be worshippers of what I worship.

6. For you is your religion, and for me is my religion."

---

[1871] *Al-Kāfirūn*: The Disbelievers. The Prophet mentioned that this *sūrah* is disassociation from *shirk* (worship of anything other than God) for him whom recites it. (Narrated by Ahmad, Abū Dāwūd and Tirmidhī – *hasan*.)

## Sūrah 110: an-Nasr

### Period of Revelation

Abdullah bin Abbas states that this is the last Sūrah of the Qur'ān to be revealed, i.e. no complete Sūrah was sent down to the Prophet after it. (Muslim Nasai, Tabarani, Ibn Abi Shaibah, Ibn Marduyah) According to Abdullah bin Umar, this Sūrah was sent down on the occasion of the Farewell Pilgrimage in the middle of the Tashriq Days at Mina, and after it the Prophet rode his she camel and gave his well known Sermon. (Tirmidhi, Bazzar, Baihaqi, Ibn Abi Shaibah, Abd bin Humaid, Abn Yala, Ibn Marduyah) Baihaqi in Kilab al-Hajj has related from the tradition of Sarra bint-Nabhan the Sermon which the Prophet gave on this occasion. She says: "At the Farewell Pilgrimage I heard the Prophet say: O people, do you know what day it is? They said: God and His Messenger have the best knowledge. He said: This is the middle day of the Tashriq Days. Then he said: Do you know what place it is? They said: God and His Messenger have the best knowledge. He said: This is Masharil-Haram. Then he said: I do not know, I might not meet you here again. Beware, your bloods and your honours are forbidden, until you appear before your Lord, and He questions you about your deeds. Listen: let the one who is near convey it to him who is far away. Listen: have I conveyed the message to you? Then, when we returned to Madinah, the Prophet passed away not many days after that."

If both these traditions are read together, it appears that there was an interval of three months and some days between the revelation of Sūrah An-Nasr and the Prophet's death, for historically the same was the interval between the Farewell Pilgrimage and the passing away of the Prophet.

Ibn Abbas says that when this Sūrah was revealed, the Prophet said that he had been informed of his death and his time had approached. (Musnad Ahmad, Ibn Jarir, Ibn al-Mundhir, Ibn Marduyah). In the other traditions related from Abdullah bin Abbas, it has been stated that at the revelation of this Sūrah the Prophet understood that he had been informed of his departure from the world.(Musnad Ahmad, Ibn Jarir, Tabarani, Nasai, Ibn Abi Hatim, Ibn Marduyah)

Mother of the Believers, Umm Habibah, says that when this Sūrah was revealed the Prophet said that he would leave the world that year. Hearing this Fātimah wept. Thereat he said: "From among my family you will be the first to join me." Hearing this she laughed. (Ibn Abi Hatim, Ibn Marduyah) A tradition containing almost the same theme has been related by Baihaqi from Ibn Abbas.

Ibn Abbas says: "Umar used to invite me to sit in his assembly along with some of the important elderly Companions who had fought at Badr. This was not liked by some of them. They complained that they also had sons who were like the boy. Why then was he in particular invited to sit in the assembly? (Imām Bukhari and Ibn Jarir have pointed out that such a thing was said by Abdur Rahman bin Auf). Umar said that the boy enjoyed the position and distinction because of his knowledge. Then one day he invited the Companions of Badr and called me also to sit with them. I understood that he had invited me to the assembly to prove his contention. During the conversation Umar asked the Companions of Badr: "What do you say about Idha jaa nasrullahi wal-fath?" Some said: "In it we have been enjoined to praise God and ask for His forgiveness when His succor comes and we attain victory." Some others said that it implied the conquest of cities and forts. Some kept quiet. Then Umar said: "Ibn Abbas, do you also say the same?" I said no. He asked: "What then is your view?" I submitted that it implied the last hour of God's Messenger; in it he was informed that when God's succor came and victory was attained, it would be a sign that his hour had come; therefore, he, should praise God and ask for His forgiveness. There at Umar said "I know nought but what you have said." In another tradition there is the addition that, Umar said to the Companions: "How can you blame me when you yourselves have seen why I invite this boy to join the assembly?" (Bukhari, Musnad Ahmad, Tirmidhi, Ibn Jarir, Ibn Marduyah, Baghawi, Baihaqi, Ibn al-Mundhir)

**Theme and Subject Matter**

As is shown by the above traditions, God in this Sūrah had informed His Messenger that when Islām attained complete victory in Arabia and the people started entering God's religion in great numbers, it would mean that the mission for which he had been sent to the world, had been fulfilled. Then, he was enjoined to busy himself in praising and glorifying God by Whose bounty he had been able to accomplish such a great task, and should implore Him to forgive whatever failings and frailties he might have shown in the performance of the service. Here, by a little consideration one can easily see the great difference that there is between a Prophet and a common worldly leader. If a worldly leader in his own lifetime is able to bring about a revolution, which has the aim and objective of his struggle, this would be an occasion for exultation for him. But here we witness quite another phenomenon. The Messenger of God in a brief space of 23 years revolutionized an entire nation as regards its beliefs, thoughts, customs, morals, civilization, ways of living, economy, politics and fighting ability, and raising it from ignorance and barbarism enabled it to conquer the world and become leader of nations; yet when he had accomplished this unique task, he was not enjoined to celebrate it but to glorify and praise God and to pray for His forgiveness, and he busied himself humbly the implementation of that command.

Ā'isha says: "The Messenger often used to recite Subhanak-Allahumma wa bi-hamdika astaghfiruka wa atubu ilaika (according to some other traditions, Subhan Allahi wa bi hamdi-hi as-taghfirullaha wa atubu ilaihi) before his death. I asked: O Messenger of God, what are these words that you have started reciting now? He replied: A sign has been appointed for me so that when I see it, I should recite these words, and it is: Idha jaa nasrullahi wal-fathu." (Musnad Ahmad, Muslim, Ibn Jarir, Ibn al-Mundhir, Ibn Marduyah) In some other traditions on the same subject Ā'isha has reported that the Prophet often recited the following words in his ruku and sajdah: Subhanak-Allahumma wa-bi hamdika, Allahumma-aghfirli. This was the interpretation of the Qur'ān (i.e. of Sūrah An-Nasr) that he had made. (Bukhari, Muslim Abu Daud, Nasai, Ibn Majah, Ibn Jarir)

Unm Salamah says that the Prophet during his last days very often recited the following words sitting and standing, going out of the house and coming back to it: Subhan Allahi wa-bi hamdi-hi. I one day asked: "Why do you recite these words so often O Messenger of God?" He replied: "I have been enjoined to do so. Then he recited this Sūrah." (Ibn Jarir)

According to Abdullah bin Masud, when this Sūrah was revealed, the Messenger of God frequently began to recite the words Subhanak-Allahumma wa bi-hamdika, Allahumm-aghfirli, subhanaka Rabbana wa bi-hamdika, Allahumm-aghfirli, innaka anta at-Tawwab al-Ghafur. (Ibn Jarir, Musnad Ahmad, Ibn Abi Hatim)

Ibn Abbas has stated that after the revelation of this Sūrah the Messenger began to labor so intensively and devotedly hard for the Hereafter as he had never done before.

## Sūrah 110: an-Nasr[1872]

In the Name of God, the Most Compassionate,
the Most Merciful

1. When the victory of God has come and the conquest,[1873]

2. And you see the people entering into the religion of God in multitudes,

3. Then exalt [Him] with praise of your Lord and ask forgiveness of Him. Indeed, He is ever Accepting of repentance.

[1872] *An-Nasr:* Victory.
[1873] The conquest of Makkah.

## Sūrah 111: al-Masad

### Period of Revelation

Although the commentators have not disputed its being a Makki Sūrah, yet it is difficult to determine in which phase of the life at Makkah precisely it was revealed. However, in view of Abu Lahab's role and conduct against the Prophet's message of Truth, it can be assumed that it must have been revealed in the period when he had transgressed all limits in his mad hostility to him, and his attitude was becoming a serious obstruction in the progress of Islām. It may well have been revealed in the period when the Quraysh had boycotted the Prophet together with the people of his clan and besieged them in Shi'b Abi Talib, and Abu Lahab was the only person to join with the enemies against his own relatives. The basis of this assumption is that Abu Lahab was the Prophet's uncle, and public condemnation of the uncle by the tongue of the nephew could not be proper until the extreme excesses committed by the uncle had become visible to everyone. If the Sūrah had been revealed before this, in the very beginning, the people would have regarded it as morally discourteous that the nephew should so condemn the uncle.

### Background

This is the only place in the Qur'ān where a person from among the enemies of Islām has been condemned by name, whereas in Makkah as well as in Madinah, after the migration, there were many people who were in no way less inimical to Islām and the Prophet Muhammad than Abu Lahab. The question is, what was the special trait of the character of this person, which became the basis of this condemnation by name? To understand that it is necessary that one should understand the Arabian society of that time and the role that Abu Lahab played in it.

In ancient days since there prevailed chaos and confusion, bloodshed and plunder throughout Arabia, and the condition since centuries was that a person could have no guarantee of the protection of life, honour and property except with the help and support of his clansmen and blood relations, therefore silah rehmi (good treatment of the kindred) was esteemed most highly among the moral values of the Arabian society and breaking off of connections with the kindred was regarded as a great sin. Under the influence of the same Arabian tradition when the Prophet began to preach the message of Islām, the other clans of Quraysh and their chiefs resisted and opposed him tooth and nail, but the Banu Hashim and the Bani al-Muttalib (children of al-Muttalib, brother of Hashim) not only did not oppose him but continued to support him openly, although most of them had not yet believed in his Prophethood. The other clans of Quraysh themselves regarded this support by the blood relations of the Prophet as perfectly in accordance with the moral traditions of Arabia. That is why they never taunted the Banu Hashim and the Bani al-Muttalib in that they had abandoned their ancestral faith by supporting a person who was preaching a new faith. They knew and believed that they could in no case hand over an individual of their clan to his enemies, and their support and aid of a clansman was perfectly natural in the sight of the Quraysh and the people of Arabia.

This moral principle, which the Arabs even in the pre-Islāmic days of ignorance, regarded as worthy of respect and inviolable was broken only by one man in his enmity of Islām, and that was Abu Lahab, son of Abdul Muttalib. He was an uncle of the Prophet, whose father and he were sons of the same father. In Arabia, an uncle represented the father especially when the nephew was fatherless. The uncle was expected to look after the nephew as one of his own children. But this man in his hostility to Islām and love of kufr trampled all the Arab traditions underfoot.

The traditionists have related from Ibn Abbas with several chains of transmitters the tradition that when the Prophet was commanded to present the message of Islām openly, and he was instructed in the Qur'ān to warn first of all his nearest kinsfolk of the punishment of God, he ascended the Mount Safa one morning and called out aloud: Ya sabahah (O, the calamity of the morning!) This alarm in Arabia was raised by the person who noticed early at dawn an enemy tribe advancing against his tribe. When the Messenger made this call, the people inquired as to who had made the call. They were told that it was Muhammad. There at the people of all the clans of Quraysh rushed out. Everyone who could, came; he who could not, sent another one for himself. When the People had assembled, the Messenger calling out each clan by name, viz. O Banu Hashim, O Bani Abdul Muttalib, O Bani Fir, O Bani so and so, said: "If I were to tell you that behind the hill there was an enemy host ready to fall upon you, would you believe me?" The people responded with one voice, saying that they never had so far experienced a lie from him. The Prophet said: "Then I warn you that you are heading for a torment." Thereupon, before anyone else could speak, Abu Lahab, the Prophet's uncle, said: "May you perish! Did you summon us for this?" Another tradition adds that he picked up a stone to throw at the Prophet. (Musnad Ahmad, Bukhari, Muslim, Tirmidhi, Ibn Jarir, and others)

According to Ibn Zayd, one day Abu Lahab asked the Prophet: "If I were to accept your religion, what would I get?" The Prophet replied: "You would get what the other believers would get." He said: "Is there no preference or distinction for me?" The Prophet replied: "What else do you want?" Thereupon he said: "May this religion perish in which I and all other people should be equal and alike!" (Ibn Jarir)

In Makkah Abu Lahab was the next door neighbor of the Prophet. Their houses were separated by a wall. Besides him, Hakam bin As (Father of Marwan), Uqbah bin Abi Muait, Adi bin Hamra and Ibn al-Asda il-Hudhali also were his neighbors. These people did not allow him to have peace even in his own house. Sometimes when he was performing the Prayer, they would place the goat's stomach on him; sometimes when food was being cooked in the courtyard, they would throw filth at the cooking pot. The Prophet would come out and say: "O Bani Abdi Manaf, what kind of neighborliness is it?" Abu Lahab's wife, Umm Jamil (Abu Sufyan's sister), had made it a practice to cast thorns at his door in the night so that when he or his children came out of the house at dawn, they should run thorns in the foot. (Baihaqi, Ibn Abi Hatim, Ibn Jarir, Ibn Asakir, Ibn Hisham)

Before the proclamation of Prophethood, two of the Prophet's daughters were married to two of Abu Lahab's sons, Utbah and Utaibah. After his call when the Prophet began to invite the people to Islām, Abu Lahab said to both his sons: "I would forbid myself seeing and meeting you until you divorced the daughters of Muhammad." So, both of them divorced their wives. Utaibah in particular became so nasty in his spitefulness that one day he came before the Prophet and said: "I repudiate An-najmi idha haw and Alladhi dana fatadalla" and then he spat at him, but his spittle did not fall on him. The Prophet prayed: "O God, subject him to the power of a dog from among Your dogs." Afterwards, Utaibah accompanied his father in his journey to Syria. During the journey the caravan halted at a place which, according to local people, was visited by wild beasts at night. Abu Lahab told his companions, the Quraysh: "Make full arrangements for the protection of my son, for I fear the curse invoked by Muhammad (upon whom be God's peace) on him." Accordingly, the people made their camels sit all around Utaibah and went to sleep. At night a tiger came which crossed the circle of the camels and devoured Utaibah tearing him to pieces. (Ibn Abdul Barr: Al- Istiab; Ibn Hajar: Al-Isabah; Abu Nuaim al-Isfahani: Dalail an-Nubuwwat; As-Suhaili: Raud al-Unuf. Here there is a difference of opinion. Some reporters say that the divorce took place after the Prophet's proclamation of Prophethood and some say that it took place after the revelation of Tabbat yada Abi Lahab. There is also a difference of opinion about whether Abu Lahab's son was Utbah or Utaibah. But this much is confirmed: that after the conquest of Makkah, Utbah embraced Islām and took the oath of allegiance at the Prophet's hand. Therefore, the correct view is that it was Utaibah).

Abu Lahab's wickedness can be judged from the fact that when after the death of the Prophet's son Qasim, his second son, Abdullah, also died, this man instead of condoling with his nephew in his bereavement, hastened to the Quraysh chiefs joyfully to give them the news that Muhammad had become childless that night. This we have already related in the commentary of Sūrah al-Kawthar.

Wherever the Prophet went to preach his message of Islām, this man followed him and forbade the people to listen to him. Rabiah bin Abbad ad-Dill has related: "I was a young boy when I accompanied my father to the face of Dhul-Majaz. There I saw the Messenger who was exhorting the people, saying: 'O people, say:

there is no deity but God, you will attain success.' Following behind him I saw a man, who was telling the people; `This fellow is a liar: he has gone astray from his ancestral faith.' I asked; who is he? The people replied: He is his uncle, Abu Lahab." (Musnad Ahmad, Baihaqi). Another tradition from Rabiah is to the effect; "I saw that the Prophet went to the halting place of each tribe and said: `O children of so and so, I have been appointed God's Messenger to you. I exhort you to worship only God and to associate none with Him. So, affirm faith in me and join me so that I may fulfill the mission for which I have been sent.' Following close behind him there was a man who was saying: `O children of so and so, he is leading you astray from Lat and Uzza and inviting you to the religion of error and innovation which he has brought. Do not at all listen to what he says and do not follow him.' I asked my father: who is he? He replied: he is his uncle, Abu Lahab." (Musnad Ahmad, Tabarani). Tariq bin Abdullah al-Muharibi's tradition is similar. He says: "I saw in the fare of Dhul-Majaz that the Messenger was exhorting the people, saying: `O people, say La ilaha ill-Allah, you will attain success', and behind him there was a man who was casting stones at him, until his heels bled, and he was telling the people: 'Do not listen to him, he is a liar.' I asked the people who he was. They said he was his uncle, Abu Lahab." (Tirmidhi)

In the 7th year of Prophethood, when all the clans of Quraysh boycotted the Banu Hashim and the Bani al-Muttalib socially and economically, and both these clans remaining steadfast to the Prophet's support, were besieged in Shib Abi Talib, Abu Lahab was the only person, who sided with the disbelieving Quraysh against his own clan. This boycott continued for three years, so much so that the Banu Hashim and the Bani al-Muttalib began to starve. This, however, did not move Abu Lahab. When a trade caravan came to Makkah and a besieged person from Shib Abi Talib approached it to buy some article of food, Abu Lahab would shout out to the merchants to demand a forbidding price, telling them that he would make up for any loss that they incurred. Thus, they would demand exorbitant rates and the poor customer had to return empty handed to his starving children. Then Abu Lahab would purchase the same articles from them at the market rates. (Ibn Sa'd, Ibn Hisham).

On account of these very misdeeds this man was condemned in this Sūrah by name, and there was a special need for it. When the Prophet's own uncle followed and opposed him before the Arabs who came for hajj from outside Makkah, or gathered together in the fares held at different places, they regarded it as against the established traditions of Arabia that an uncle should run down his nephew without a reason, should pelt stones at him and bring false accusations against him publicly. They were, therefore, influenced by what Abu Lahab said and were involved in doubt about the Prophet. But when this, Sūrah was revealed, and Abu Lahab, filled with rage, started uttering nonsense, the people realized that what he said in opposition to the Prophet was not at all reliable, for he said all that in his mad hostility to his nephew.

Besides, when his uncle was condemned by name, the people's expectation that the Messenger could treat some relative leniently in the matter of religion was frustrated forever. When the Messenger's own uncle was taken to task publicly the people understood that there was no room for preference or partiality in their faith. A non-relative could become a near and dear one if he believed, and a near relation a non-relative if he disbelieved. Thus, there is no place for the ties of blood in religion.

## Sūrah 111: al-Masad[1874]

In the Name of God, the Most Compassionate,
the Most Merciful

1. May the hands of Abū Lahab be ruined, and ruined is he.[1875]

2. His wealth will not avail him or that which he gained.

3. He will [enter to] burn in a Fire of [blazing] flame

4. And his wife [as well] - the carrier of firewood.[1876]

5. Around her neck is a rope of [twisted] fiber.

[1874] *Al-Masad*: Fiber. This *sūrah* is also known as *al-Lahab* (Flame).
[1875] Abū Lahab (the Prophet's uncle), who was an enemy of Islām.
[1876] She used to put thorns in the Prophet's path and slander him. The word "firewood" was used by the Arabs to allude to slander and backbiting.

## Sūrah 112: al-Ikhlās

### Period of Revelation

Whether it is a Makki or a Madani Sūrah is disputed, and the difference of opinion has been caused by the traditions which have been related concerning the occasion of its revelation. We give them below ad seriatum:

1. Abdullah bin Masud has reported that the Quraysh said to the Prophet: "Tell us of the ancestry of your Lord." Thereupon this Sūrah was sent down. (Tabarani).
2. Abul Aliyah has related on the authority of Ubayy bin Kab that the polytheists said to the Prophet: Tell us of your Lord's ancestry. Thereupon God sent down this Sūrah. (Musnad Ahmad, Ibn Abi Harim, Ibn Jarir, Tirmidhi, Bukhari in At-Tarikh, Ibn al-Mundhir, Hakim, Baihaqi). Tirmidhi has related a tradition on the same theme from Abul Aliyah, which does not contain any reference to Ubayy bin Kab, and has declared it to be more authentic.
3. Jabir bin Abdullah has stated that a bedouin (according to other traditions, some people) said to the Prophet: "Tell us of your Lord's ancestry." Thereupon God sent down this Sūrah. (Abu Yala, Ibn Jarir, Ibn al-Mundhir, Tabarani in Al-Ausat, Baihaqi, Abu Nuaim in Al-Hilyah)
4. Ikrimah has related a tradition form Ibn Abbas, saying that a group of the Jews, including Kab bin Ashraf, Huyayy bin Akhtab and other, came before the Prophet and said: "O Muhammad, tell us of the attributes of your Lord, Who has sent you as a Prophet." Thereupon God sent down this Sūrah. (Ibn Abi Hatim, Ibn Adi, Baihaqi in Al-Asma was-Sifat)

In addition to these, some other traditions also have been cited by Ibn Taimiyyah in his commentary of Sūrah Al-Ikhlās, which are as follows:

These traditions show that different people on different occasions had questioned the Prophet about the essence and nature of the God to Whose service and worship he invited the people, and on every occasion he recited by God's command this very Sūrah in response. First of all, the pagans of Quraysh asked him this question in Makkah, and in reply this Sūrah was sent down. Then, at Madinah, sometimes the Christians, and sometimes the other people of Arabia, asked him questions of this nature, and every time God inspired him to recite this very Sūrah in answer to them. In each of these traditions, it has been said that this Sūrah was revealed on this or that occasion. From this one should not form the impression that all these traditions are mutually contradictory. The fact is that whenever there existed with the Prophet a verse or a Sūrah previously revealed in respect of a particular question or matter, and later the same question was presented before him, God inspired him to recite the same verse or Sūrah to the people as it contained the answer to their question. The reporters of Hadith describe the same thing, saying: When such and such a question or matter was presented before the Prophet, such and such a verse or Sūrah was revealed. This has also been described as repetition of revelation, i.e. the revelation of a verse or Sūrah several times.

Thus, the fact is that this Sūrah is Makki, rather in view of its subject matter a Sūrah revealed in the earliest period at Makkah, when detailed verses of the Qur'ān dealing with the essence and attributes of God Almighty had not yet been revealed, and the people hearing, the Prophet's invitation to God, wanted to know what was his Lord like to whose worship and service he was calling them. Another proof of this Sūrah's being one of the earliest Sūrahs to be revealed is that when in Makkah Umayyah bin Khalaf, the master of Bilal, made him lie down on burning sand and placed a heavy stone on his chest, Bilal used to cry "Ahad, Ahad!" This word was derived from this very Sūrah.

### Theme and Subject Matter

A little consideration of the traditions regarding the occasion of the revelation of this Sūrah shows what were the religious concepts of the world at the time the Prophet began to preach the message of Tawhid. The idolatrous polytheists were worshipping gods made of wood, stone, gold, silver and other substances. These gods had a form, shape and body. The gods and goddesses were descended from each other. No goddess was without a husband and no god without a wife. They stood in need of food and drink and their devotees arranged these for them. A large number of the polytheists believed that God assumed human form and there were some people who descended from Him. Although the Christians claimed to believe in One God, yet their God also had at least a son, and besides the Father and Son, the Holy Ghost also had the honour of being an associate in Godhead: so much so that God had a mother and a mother-in-law too. The Jews also claimed to believe in One God, but their God too was not without physical, material and other human qualities and characteristics. He went for a stroll, appeared in human form, wrestled with a servant of His, and was father of a son, Ezra. Besides these religious communities, the zoroastrianism were fire worshipers, and the Sabeans star worshipers. Under such conditions when the people were invited to believe in God, the One; Who has no associate, it was inevitable that questions arose in the minds as to what kind of a God it was, Who was the one and Only Lord and invitation to believe in Whom was being given at the expense of all other gods and deities. It is a miracle of the Qur'ān that in a few words briefly it answered all the questions and presented such a clear concept of the Being of God as destroyed all polytheistic concepts, without leaving any room for the ascription of any of the human qualities to His Being.

**Merit and Importance**

That is why the Messenger of God held this Sūrah in great esteem, and he made the Muslims realize its importance in different ways so that they recited it frequently and disseminated it among the people. For it states the foremost and fundamental doctrine of Islām (viz. Tawhid) in four such brief sentences as are immediately impressed on human memory and can be read and recited easily. There are a great number of the traditions of Hadith, which show that the Prophet on different occasions and in different ways told the people that this Sūrah is equivalent to one-third of the Qur'ān. Several hadith on this subject have been related in Bukhari, Muslim, Abu Daud; Nasai, Tirmidhi, Ibn Majah, Musnad Ahmad, Tabarani and other books, on the authority of Abu Said Khudri, Abu Hurairah, Abu Ayyub Ansāri, Abu ad-Darda, Muadh bin Jabal, Jabir bin Abdullah, Ubayy bin Kab, Umm Kulthum bint Uqbah bin Abi Muait, Ibn Umar, Ibn Masud, Qatadah bin an-Numan, Anas bin Malik, and Abu Masud (may God be pleased with all of them). The commentators have given many explanations of the Prophet's saying this. But in our opinion it simply means that the religion presented by the Qur'ān is based on three doctrines: Tawhid, Apostleship and the Hereafter. This Sūrah teaches Tawhid, pure and undefiled. Therefore, the Prophet regarded it as equal to one-third of the Qur'ān.

A tradition on the authority of Ā'isha has been related in Bukhari, Muslim and other collections of the hadith, saying that the Prophet sent a man as leader of an expedition. During the journey he concluded his recitation of the Qur'ān in every Prayer with Qul Huwa-Allahu ahad. On their return him companions mentioned this before the Prophet. He said: "Ask him why he did so." When the man was asked, he replied: "In this Sūrah the attributes of the Merciful God have been stated; therefore, I love to recite it again and again." When the Prophet heard this reply, he said to the people: "Inform him that God holds him in great love and esteem."

A similar incident has been related in Bukhari, on the authority of Anas. He says: "A man from among the Ansār led the Prayers in the Quba Mosque. His practice was that in every rakah he first recited this Sūrah and then would join another Sūrah to it. The people objected to it and said to him: 'Don't you think that Sūrah Ikhlas is by itself enough? Why do you join another Sūrah to it? You should either recite only this Sūrah, or should leave it and recite some other Sūrah'. He said: 'I cannot leave it, I would rather give up leadership in the Prayer, if you so desired'. The people did not approve that another man be appointed leader instead of him. At last, the matter was brought before the Prophet. He asked the man, 'What prevents you from conceding what your companions desire? What makes you recite this particular Sūrah in every rakah?' The man replied: 'I have great love for it.' The Prophet remarked: 'Your love for this Sūrah has earned you entry into Paradise'."

## Sūrah 112: al-Ikhlās[1877]

In the Name of God, the Most Compassionate,
the Most Merciful

1. Say, "He is God, [who is] One,[1878]

2. God, the Eternal Refuge.[1879]

3. He neither begets nor is born,

4. Nor is there to Him any equivalent."

[1877] *Al-Ikhlās*: Purification, i.e., the purification of faith – the *sūrah's* theme. In narrations by al-Bukhārī and Ahmad, the Prophet described this *sūrah* as being equivalent to one third of the Qur'ān.
[1878] i.e., single, unique and indivisible.
[1879] i.e., the one sought in times of difficulty and need, the one depended upon by all existence.

## Sūrah 113 and 114: al-Falaq and an-Nās

Although these two Sūrahs of the Qur'ān are separate entities and are written in the Mushaf also under separate names, yet they are so deeply related mutually and their contents so closely resemble each other's that they have been designated by a common name Mu'awwidhatayn (the two Sūrahs in which refuge with God has been sought). Imām Baihaqi in Dala'il an-Nubuwwat has written that these Sūrahs were revealed together, that is why the combined name of both is Mu'awwidhatayn. We are writing the same one Introduction to both, for they discuss and deal with just the same matters and topics. However, they will be explained and commented on separately below.

### Period of Revelation

Hasan Basri, 'Ikrimah, 'Ata and Jabir bin Zayd say that these Sūrahs are Makki. A tradition from 'Abdullah bin 'Abbas also supports the same view. However, according to another tradition from him, it is Madani and the same view is held also by 'Abdullah bin Zubair and Qatadah. One of the traditions which strengthens this second view is the Hadith which Muslim, Tirmidhi, Nasa'i and Imām Ahmad bin Hanbal have related on the authority of 'Uqbah bin 'Amir. He says that the Prophet one day said to him: "Do you know what kind of verses have been revealed to me tonight? - these matchless verses are A'udhu bi-Rabbil-falaq and A'udhu bi-Rabbin-nas (i.e. these two Sūrahs). This Hadith is used as an argument for these Sūrahs to be Madani because 'Uqbah bin 'Amir had become a Muslim in Madinah after the Hijrah (migration). Other traditions which have lent strength to this view are those related by Ibn Sa'd, Baghawi, Imām Baihaqi, Ibn Hajar and others to the effect that these Sūrahs were revealed when the Jews had worked magic on the Prophet in Madinah and he had fallen ill under its effect.

But as we have explained in the Introduction to Sūrah Al-Ikhlās, when it is said about a certain Sūrah or verse that it was revealed on this or that particular occasion, it does not necessarily mean that it was revealed for the first time on that very occasion. Rather it sometimes so happened that a Sūrah or a verse had previously been revealed, then on the occurrence or appearance of a particular incident or situation, the Prophet's attention was drawn to it by God for the second time, or even again and again. In our opinion the same also was the case with the Mu'awwidhatayn. The subject matter of these Sūrahs is explicit that these were sent down at Makkah in the first instance when opposition to the Prophet there had grown very intense. Later, when at Madinah storms of opposition were raised by the hypocrites, Jews and polytheists, the Prophet was instructed to recite these very Sūrahs, as has been mentioned in the above cited tradition from Uqbah bin Amir. After this, when magic was worked on him, and his illness grew intense, Gabriel came and instructed him by God's command to recite these very Sūrahs. Therefore, in our opinion, the view held by the commentators who describe both these Sūrahs as Makki is more reliable. Regarding them as connected exclusively with the incident of magic is difficult, for to this incident related only one verse (v.4), the remaining verses of Sūrah al Falaq and the whole of Sūrah An-Nas have nothing to do with it directly.

### Theme and Subject-Matter

The conditions under which these two Sūrahs were sent down in Makkah were as follows. As soon as the Prophet began to preach the message of Islām, it seemed as though he had provoked all classes of the people around him. As his message spread the opposition of the disbelieving Quraysh also became more and more intense. As long as they had any hope that they would be able to prevent him from preaching his message by throwing some temptation in his way, or striking some bargain with him, their hostility did not become very active. But when the Prophet disappointed them completely that he would not effect any kind of compromise with them in the matter of faith, and in Sūrah Al-Kāfirūn they were plainly told: "I do not worship those who you worship nor are you worshipers of Him Whom I worship. For you is your religion and for me is mine," the hostility touched its extreme limits. More particularly, the families whose members (men or women, boys or girls) had accepted Islām, were burning with rage from within against the Prophet. They were cursing him, holding secret consultations to kill him quietly in the dark of the night so that the Banu

Hashim could not discover the murderer and take revenge; magic and charms were being worked on him so as to cause his death, or make him fall ill, or become mad; satans from among the men and the Jinn spread on every side so as to whisper one or another evil into the hearts of the people against him and the Qur'ān brought by him so that they became suspicious of him and fled him. There were many people who were burning with jealousy against him, for they could not tolerate that a man from another family or clan than their own should flourish and become prominent. For instance, the reason why Abu Jahl was crossing every limit in his hostility to him has been explained by himself: "We and the Bani Abdi Manaf (to which the Prophet belonged) were rivals of each other: they fed others, we too fed others; they provided conveyances to the people, we too did the same; they gave donations, we too gave donations, so much so that when they and we have become equal in honour and nobility, they now proclaim that they have a Prophet who is inspired from the heaven; how can we compete with them in this field? By God, we will never acknowledge him, nor affirm faith in him." (Ibn Hisham, vol. I, pp. 337-338)

Such were the conditions when the Prophet was commanded to tell the people: "I seek refuge with the Lord of the dawn, from the evil of everything that He has created, and from the evil of the darkness of night and from the evil of magicians, men and women, and from the evil of the envious," and to tell them: "I seek refuge with the Lord of mankind, the King of mankind, and the Deity of mankind, from the evil of the whisperer, who returns over and over again, who whispers (evil) into the hearts of men, whether he be from among the Jinn or men." This is similar to what the Prophet Moses had been told to say when Pharaoh had expressed his design before his full court to kill him: "I have taken refuge with my Lord and your Lord against every arrogant person who does not believe in the Day of Reckoning." (al-Mu'min: 27) And: "I have taken refuge with my Lord and your Lord lest you should assail me." (ad-Dukhān: 20)

On both occasions these illustrious Prophets of God were confronted with well-equipped, resourceful and powerful enemies. On both occasions they stood firm on their message of Truth against their strong opponents, whereas they had no material power on the strength of which they could fight them, and on both occasions they utterly disregarded the threats and dangerous plans and hostile devices of the enemy, saying: "We have taken refuge with the Lord of the universe against you." Obviously, such firmness and steadfastness can be shown only by the person who has the conviction that the power of His Lord is the supreme power, that all powers of the world are insignificant against Him, and that no one can harm the one who has taken His refuge. Only such a one can say: "I will not give up preaching the Word of Truth. I care the least for what you may say or do, for I have taken refuge with my Lord and your Lord and Lord of all universe."

### Relation between Sūrah Al-Fātihah and the Mu'awwidhatayn

The last thing which is noteworthy with regard to the Mu'awwidhatayn is the relation between the beginning and the end of the Qur'ān. Although the Qur'ān has not been arranged chronologically, the Prophet arranged in the present order the verses and Sūrahs revealed during 23 years on different occasions to meet different needs and situations not by himself but by the command of God Who revealed them. According to this order, the Qur'ān opens with the Sūrah Al-Fātihah and ends with the Mu'awwidhatayn. Now, let us have a look at the two. In the beginning, after praising and glorifying God, Who is Lord of the worlds, Kind, Merciful and Master of the Judgment Day, the servant submits: "Lord, You alone I worship and to You alone I turn for help, and the most urgent help that I need from You is to be guided to the Straight Way." In answer, he is given by God the whole Qur'ān to show him the Straight Way, which is concluded thus: Man prays to God, Who is Lord of dawn, Lord of men, King of men, Deity of men, saying: "I seek refuge only with You for protection from every evil and mischief of every creature, and in particular, from the evil whisperings of devils, be they from among men or Jinn, for they are the greatest obstacle in following the Straight Way." The relation that the beginning bears with the end, cannot remain hidden from anyone who has understanding and insight.

## Sūrah 113: al-Falaq[1880]

In the Name of God, the Most Compassionate,
the Most Merciful

1. Say, "I seek refuge in the Lord of daybreak

2. From the evil of that which He created

3. And from the evil of darkness when it settles

4. And from the evil of the blowers in knots[1881]

5. And from the evil of an envier when he envies."

---

1880 *Al-Falaq*: Daybreak. This and the following *sūrah* were revealed together and are recited when seeking God's protection from all kinds of evil.
1881 i.e., those who practice magic.

## Sūrah 114: an-Nās[1882]

In the Name of God, the Most Compassionate, the Most Merciful

1. Say, "I seek refuge in the Lord of mankind,

2. The Sovereign of mankind,

3. The God of mankind,

4. From the evil of the retreating whisperer[1883] -

5. Who whispers [evil] into the breasts of mankind -

6. From among the jinn and mankind."[1884]

[1882] *An-Nās*: People or Mankind.
[1883] i.e., a devil who makes evil suggestions to man but disappears when one remembers God.
[1884] Evil prompters may be from men as well as from *jinn*.

# APPENDICES

## Introduction to the Study of the Qur'ān

We are accustomed to reading books which present information, ideas and arguments systematically and coherently. So, when we embark on the study of the Qur'ān, we expect that this book too will revolve around a definite subject, that the subject matter of the book will be clearly defined at the beginning and will then be neatly divided into sections and chapters, after which discussion will proceed in a logical sequence. We likewise expect a separate and systematic arrangement of instruction and guidance for each of the various aspects of human life.

However, as soon as we open the Qur'ān we encounter a hitherto completely unfamiliar genre of literature. We notice that it embodies precepts of belief and conduct, moral directives, legal prescriptions, exhortation and admonition, censure and condemnation of evildoers, warnings to deniers of the Truth, good tidings and words of consolation and good cheer to those who have suffered for the sake of God, arguments and corroborative evidence in support of its basic message, allusions to anecdotes from the past and to signs of God visible in the universe. Moreover, these myriad subjects alternate without any apparent system; quite unlike the books to which we are accustomed, the Qur'ān deals with the same subject over and over again, each time couched in a different phraseology.

The reader also encounters abrupt transitions between one subject matter and another. Audience and speaker constantly change as the message is directed now to one and now to another group of people. There is no trace of familiar division into chapters and sections. Likewise, the treatment of different subjects is unique. If a historical subject is raised, the narrative does not follow the pattern familiar in historical accounts. In discussions of philosophical or metaphysical questions, we miss the familiar expressions and terminology of formal logic and philosophy. Cultural and political matters, or questions pertaining to man's social and economic life, are discussed in a way very different from that usual in works of social sciences. Juristic principles and legal injunctions are elucidated, but quite differently from the manner of conventional works. When we come across an ethical instruction, we find its form differs entirely from anything to be found elsewhere in the literature of ethics.

The reader may find all this so foreign that the notion of what a book should be - that they may become so confused as to feel that the Qur'ān is a piece of disorganized, incoherent and unsystematic writing, comprising nothing but a disjointed conglomeration of comments of varying lengths put together arbitrarily. Hostile critics use this as a basis for their criticism, while those more favorably inclined resort to far-fetched explanations, or else conclude that the Qur'ān consists of unrelated pieces, thus making it amenable to all kinds of interpretations, even interpretations quite opposed to the intent of God Who revealed the Book.

What kind of a book is the Qur'ān? In what manner was it revealed? What underlies its arrangement? What is the subject? What is its true purpose? What is the central theme to which its diverse topics are intrinsically related? What kind of reasoning and style does it adopt in elucidating its central theme? If we could obtain clear, lucid answers to these and other related questions we might avoid some dangerous pitfalls, thus making it easier to reflect upon and to grasp the meaning and purpose of the Qur'ānic verses. If we begin studying the Qur'ān in the expectation of reading a book on religion we shall find it hard, since our notions of religion and of a book are naturally circumscribed by our range of experience. We need, therefore, to be told in advance that this Book is unique in the manner of its composition, in its theme and in its contents and arrangement. We should be forewarned that the concept of a book which we have formed from our previous readings is likely to be a hindrance, rather than a help, towards a deep understanding of the Qur'ān. We should realize that as a first step towards understanding it we must empty our minds of all preconceived notions.

The student of the Qur'ān should grasp, from the outset, the fundamental claims that the Qur'ān make for itself. Whether one ultimately decides to believe in the Qur'ān or not, one must recognize the fundamental statements made by the Qur'ān and the man to whom it was revealed, the Prophet Muhammad, to be the starting point of one's study. These claims are:

1. The Lord of the creation, the Creator and Sovereign of the entire universe, created man on earth (which is merely a part of His boundless realm). He also endowed man with the capacity for cognition, reflection, and understanding, with the ability to distinguish between good and evil, with the freedom of choice and volition, and with the power to exercise his latent potentialities. In short, God bestowed upon man a kind of autonomy and appointed him His vicegerent on earth.

2. Although man enjoys this status, God made it abundantly plain to him that He alone is man's Lord and Sovereign, even as He is the Lord and Sovereign of the whole universe. Man was told that he was not entitled to consider himself independent and that only God was entitled to claim absolute obedience, service and worship. It was also made clear to man that life in this world, for which he had been placed and invested with a certain honour and authority, was in fact a temporary term, and was meant to test him; that after the end of the earthly life man must return to God, who will judge him on the basis of his performance, declaring who has succeeded and who has failed.

The right way for man is to regard God as his only Sovereign and the only object of his worship and adoration, to follow the guidance revealed by God, to act in this world in the consciousness that earthly life is merely a period of trial, and to keep his eyes fixed on the ultimate objective - success in God's final judgment. Every other way is wrong.

It was also explained to man that if he chose to adopt the right way of life - and in this choice he was free - he would enjoy peace and contentment in this world and be assigned on his return to God the abode of eternal bliss and happiness known as Paradise. Should man follow any other way - although he was free to do so - he would experience the evil effects of corruption and disorder in the life of this world and be consigned to eternal grief and torment when he crosses the borders of the present world and arrives in the Hereafter.

3. Having explained all this, the Lord of the universe placed man on earth and communicated to Adam and Eve, the first human beings to live on the earth, the guidance which they and their offspring were required to follow. These first human beings were not born in a state of ignorance and darkness. On the contrary, they began their life in the broad daylight of Divine Guidance. They had intimate knowledge of reality and the Law which they were to follow was communicated to them. Their way of life consisted of obedience to God (i.e. Islām) and they taught their children to live in obedience to Him (i.e. to live as Muslims)

In the course of time, however, men gradually deviated from their true way of life and began to follow various erroneous ways. They allowed true guidance to be lost through heedlessness and negligence and sometimes, even deliberately, distorted it out of evil perversity. They associated with God a number of beings, human and non human, real as well as imaginary, and adored them as deities. They adulterated the God-given knowledge of reality with all kinds of fanciful ideas, superstitions and philosophical concepts, thereby giving birth to innumerable religions. They disregarded or distorted the sound and equitable principle of individual morality and of collective conduct and made their own laws in accordance with their base desires and prejudices. As a result, the world became filled with wrong and injustice.

4. It was insistent with the limited autonomy conferred upon man by God that He should exercise His overwhelming power and compel man to righteousness. It was also inconsistent with the fact that God had granted a term to the human species in which to show their worth that He should afflict men with catastrophic destruction as soon as they showed signs of rebellion. Moreover, God had undertaken from the beginning of creation that true guidance would be made available to man throughout the term granted to him and that his guidance would be available in a manner consistent with man's autonomy. To fulfill this self-assumed responsibility God chose to appoint those human beings whose faith in Him was outstanding and who followed the way pleasing to Him. God chose these people to be His envoys. He had His messages communicated to them, honoured them with an intimate knowledge of reality, provided them with the true laws of life and entrusted them with the task of recalling man to the original path from which he had strayed.

5. These Prophets were sent to different people in different lands and over a period of time covering thousands and thousands of years. They all had the same religion; the one originally revealed to man as the right way for him. All of them followed the same guidance; those principles of morality and collective life prescribed for man at the very outset of his existence. All these Prophets had the same mission - to call man to his true religion and subsequently to organize all who accepted this message into a community which would be bounded by the Law of God, which would strive to establish its observance and would seek to prevent its violation. All the Prophets discharged their missions creditably in their own time. However, there were always many who refused to accept their guidance and consequently those who did accept it and became a "Muslim" (Muslim would be anyone obeying God) community gradually degenerated, causing the Divine Guidance either to be lost, distorted or adulterated.

6. At last the Lord of the Universe sent Muhammad to Arabia and entrusted him with the same mission that He had entrusted to the earlier Prophets. This last Messenger of God addressed the followers of the earlier Prophets as well as the rest of humanity. The mission of each Prophet was to call men to the right way of life, to communicate God's true guidance afresh and to organize into one community all who responded to his mission and accepted the guidance revealed to him. Such a community was to be dedicated to the two-fold task of molding its own life in accordance with God's guidance and striving for the reform of the world. The Qur'ān is the Book which embodies this mission and guidance, as revealed by God to Prophet Muhammad.

If we remember these basic facts about the Qur'ān it becomes easy to grasp its true subject, its central theme and the objective it seeks to achieve. Insofar as it seeks to explain the ultimate causes of man's success or failure the subject of the Book is MAN.

Its central theme is that concepts relating to God, the universe and man which have emanated from man's own limited knowledge run counter to reality. The same applies to concepts which have been either woven by man's intellectual fancies or which have evolved through man's obsession with animal desires. The ways of life which rest on these false foundations are both contrary to reality and ruinous for man. The essence of true knowledge is that which God revealed to man when He appointed him his vicegerent. Hence, the way of life which is in accordance with the reality and conducive to human good is that which we have characterized above as "the right way." The real object for the Book is to call people to this "right way" and to illuminate God's true guidance, which has often been lost either through man's negligence and heedlessness or distorted by his wicked perversity.

If we study the Qur'ān with these facts in mind it is bound to strike us that the Qur'ān does not deviate one iota from its main subject, its central theme and its basic objective. All the various themes occurring in the Qur'ān are related to the central theme; just as beads of different sizes and color may be strung together to form a necklace. The Qur'ān speaks of the structure of the heavens and the earth and of man, refers to the signs of reality in the various phenomena of the universe, relates anecdotes of bygone nations, criticizes the beliefs, morals, and deeds of different peoples, elucidates supernatural truths and discusses many other things besides. All this the Qur'ān does, not in order to provide instruction in physics, history, philosophy or any other particular branch of knowledge, but rather to remove the misconception people have about reality and to make that reality manifest to them.

It emphasizes that the various ways men follow, which are not in conformity with reality, are essentially false, and full of harmful consequences for mankind. It calls on men to shun all such ways and to follow instead the way which both conforms to reality and yields best practical results. This is why the Qur'ān mentions everything only to the extent and in the manner necessary for the purpose it seeks to serve. The Qur'ān confines itself to essentials thereby omitting any irrelevant details. Thus all its contents consistently revolve around this call.

Likewise, it is not possible to fully appreciate either the style of the Qur'ān, the order underlying the arrangement of its verses or the diversity of the subjects treated in it, without fully understanding the manner in which it was revealed.

The Qur'ān, as we have noted earlier, is not a book in the conventional sense of the term. God did not compose and entrust it in one piece to Prophet Muhammad so that he could spread its message and call people to adopt an attitude to life consistent with its teachings. Nor is the Qur'ān one of those books which discusses their subjects and main themes in the conventional manner. Its arrangement differs from that of ordinary books, and its style is correspondingly different. The nature of this Book is that God chose a man in Makkah to serve as His Messenger and asked him to preach His message, starting in his own city and with his own tribe (Quraysh). At this initial stage, instructions were confined to what was necessary at this particular juncture of the mission. Three themes in particular stand out:

1. Directives were given to the Prophet on how he should prepare himself for his great mission and how he should begin working for the fulfillment of his task.

2. A fundamental knowledge of reality was furnished and misconceptions commonly held by people in that regard - misconceptions which gave rise to wrong orientations in life - were removed.

3. People were exhorted to adopt the right attitude towards life. Moreover, the Qur'ān also elucidated those fundamental principles which, if followed, lead to man's success and happiness.

In keeping with the character of the mission at this stage the early revelations generally consisted of short verses, couched in language of uncommon grace and owner, and clothed in a literary style suited to the taste and temperament of the people to whom they were originally addressed, and whose hearts they were meant to penetrate. The rhythm, melody and vitality of these verses drew rapt attention, and such was their stylistic grace and charm that people began to recite them involuntarily.

The local color of these early messages is conspicuous, for while the truths they contained were universal, the arguments and illustration used to elucidate them were drawn from the immediate environment familiar to the first listeners. Allusions were made to their history and traditions and to the visible traces of the past which had crept into the beliefs, and into the moral and social life of Arabia. All this was calculated to enhance the appeal the message held for its immediate audience. This early stage lasted for four or five years, during which period the following reactions to the Prophet's message manifested themselves:

1. A few people responded to the call and agreed to join the Ummah (nation) committed, of its own volition, to submit to the Will of God.

2. Many people reacted with hostility, either from ignorance or egotism, or because of chauvinistic attachment to the way of life of their forefathers.

3. The call of the Prophet did not remain confined to Makkah, it began to meet with favorable response beyond the borders.

In spite of the strong and growing resistance and opposition, the Islāmic movement continued to spread. There was hardly a family left in Makkah one of whose members at least had not embraced Islām.

During the Prophet's long and arduous struggle God continued to inspire him with revelations. These messages instructed the believers in their basic duties, inculcated in them a sense of community and belonging, exhorted them to piety, moral excellence and purity of character, taught them how to preach the true faith, sustained their spirit by promises of success and Paradise in the Hereafter, aroused them to struggle in the cause of God with patience, fortitude and high spirits, and filled their hearts with such zeal and enthusiasm that they were prepared to endure every sacrifice, brave every hardship and face every adversity.

This stage was unfolded in several phases. In each phase, the preaching of the message assumed ever wider proportions, as the struggle for the cause of Islām and opposition to it became increasingly intense and severe, and as the believers encountered people of varying outlooks and beliefs. All these factors had the effect of increasing the variety of the topics treated in the messages revealed during this period. Such, in brief, was the situation forming the background of the Makkan Sūrahs (chapters) of the Qur'ān.

It is now clear to us that the revelation of the Qur'ān began and went hand in hand with the preaching of the message. This message passed through many stages and met with diverse situations from the very beginning and throughout a period of twenty-three years. The different parts of the Qur'ān were revealed step by step according to the various, changing needs and requirements of the Islāmic movement during these stages. It therefore could not possibly possess the kind of coherence and systematic sequence expected of a doctoral dissertation. Moreover, the various fragments of the Qur'ān which were revealed in harmony with the growth of the Islāmic movement were not published in the form of written treatises, but were spread orally. Their style, therefore, bore an oratorical flavor rather than the characteristics of literary composition.

Furthermore, these orations were delivered by one whose task meant he had to appeal simultaneously to the mind, to the heart and to the emotions, and to people of different mental levels and dispositions. He had to revolutionize people's thinking, to arouse in them a storm of noble emotions in support of his cause, to persuade his companions and inspire them with real devotion and with the desire to improve and reform their lives. He had to raise their morale and steel their determination, turn enemies into friends and opponents into admirers, disarm those out to oppose his message and show their position to be morally untenable. In short, he had to do everything necessary to carry his movement through to a successful conclusion. Orations revealed in conformity with requirements of a message and movement will inevitably have a style different from that of a professional lecture.

This explains the repetitions we encounter in the Qur'ān. The interests of a message and a movement demand that during a particular stage emphasis should be placed only on those subjects which are appropriate at that stage, to the exclusion of matters pertaining to later stages. As a result, certain subjects may require continual emphasis for months or even years. On the other hand, constant repetition in the same manner becomes exhausting. Whenever a subject is repeated, it should therefore be expressed in different phraseology, in new forms and with stylistic variations so as to ensure that the ideas and beliefs being put over find their way into the hearts of the people.

At the same time, it was essential that the fundamental beliefs and principles on which the movement was based should always be kept fresh in people's minds; a necessity which dictated that they should be repeated continually through all stages of the movement. If these ideas had lost their hold on the hearts and minds of people, the Islāmic movement could not have moved forward in its true spirit. If we reflect on this, it also becomes clear that the Prophet did not arrange the Qur'ān in the sequence in which it was revealed. As we have noted, the context in which the Qur'ān was revealed in the course of twenty-three years was the mission and movement of the Prophet; the revelations correspond with the various stages of this mission and movement. Now, it is evident that when the Prophet's mission was completed, the chronological sequence of the various parts of the Qur'ān - revealed in accordance with the growth of the prophet's mission - could in no way be suitable to the changed situation. What was now required was a different sequence in tune with the changed context resulting from the completion of the mission.

Initially, the Prophet's message was addressed to people totally ignorant of Islām. Their instruction had to start with the most elementary things. After the mission had reached its successful completion, the Qur'ān acquired a compelling relevance for those who had decided to believe in the prophet. By virtue of that belief they had become a new religious community - the Muslim Ummah. Not only that, they had been made responsible for carrying on the Prophet's mission, which he had bequeathed to them, in a perfected form on both conceptual and practical levels. It was no longer necessary for the Qur'ānic verses to be arranged in chronological sequence. In the changed context, it had become necessary for the bearers of the mission of the Prophet to be informed of their duties and of the true principles and laws governing their lives. They also had to be warned against the deviations and corruptions which had appeared among the followers of earlier Prophets.

It would be foreign to the very nature of the Qur'ān to group together in one place all verses relating to a specific subject; the nature of the Qur'ān requires that the reader should find teachings revealed during the Madinan period interspersed with those of the Makkan period, and vice versa. It requires the scrutiny of early discourses with instructions from the later period of the life of the Prophet. This blending of the teachings from different periods helps to provide an overall view and an integrated perspective of Islām, and acts as a safeguard against lopsidedness. Furthermore, a chronological arrangement of the Qur'ān would have been meaningful to later generations only if it had been supplemented with explanatory notes and these would have had to be treated as inseparable appendices to the Qur'ān. This would have been quite contrary to God's purpose in revealing the Qur'ān; the main purpose of its revelation was that all human beings - children and young people, old men and women, town and country dwellers, laymen and scholars - should be able to refer to the Divine Guidance available to them in composite form and providentially secured against adulteration. This was necessary to enable people of every level of intelligence and understanding to know what God required of them. This purpose would have been defeated had the reader been obliged solemnly to recite historical notes and explanatory comments along with the Book of God.

Those who object to the present arrangement of the Qur'ān appear to be suffering from a misapprehension as to its true purpose. Sometimes, they almost seem to be under the illusion that it was revealed merely for the benefit of students of history and sociology!

The present arrangement of the Qur'ān is not the work of later generations, but was made by the Prophet under God's direction. Whenever a Sūrah was revealed, the Prophet summoned his scribes, to whom he carefully dictated its contents, and instructed them where to place it in relation to the other Sūrahs. The Prophet followed the same order of Sūrahs and verses when reciting during ritual Prayer as on other occasions, and his Companions followed the same practice in memorizing the Qur'ān. It is therefore a historical fact that the collection of the Qur'ān came to an end on the very day that its revelation ceased.

Since Prayers were obligatory for the Muslims from the very outset of the Prophet's mission, and recitation of the Qur'ān was an obligatory part of those prayers, Muslims were committing the Qur'ān to memory while its revelation continued. Thus, as soon as a fragment of the Qur'ān was revealed, it was memorized by some of the Companions. Hence the preservation of the Qur'ān was not solely dependent on its verses being inscribed on palm leaves, pieces of bone, leather and scraps of parchment - the materials used by the Prophet's scribes for writing down Qur'ānic verses. Instead the verses came to be inscribed upon scores, then hundreds, then thousands, then hundreds of thousands of human hearts, soon after they had been revealed, so that no scope was left for any devil to alter so much as one word of them.

When, after the death for the Prophet, the storm of apostasy convulsed Arabia and the companions had to plunge into bloody battles to suppress it, many companions who had memorized the Qur'ān had become martyrs. This led Umar to plead that the Qur'ān ought to be preserved in writing, as well as orally. He therefore impressed the urgency of this upon Abu Bakr (The first Caliph). After slight hesitation, the latter agreed and entrusted that task to Zayd ibn Thabit, who had worked as a scribe of the Prophet.

The Qur'ān that we possess today corresponds exactly to the edition which was prepared on the orders of Abu Bakr and copies of which were officially sent, on the orders of Uthman, to various cities and provinces. Several copies of this original edition of the Qur'ān still exist today [see chapter - Preservation and Literary Challenge of the Qur'ān.]

The Qur'ān is a Book to which innumerable people turn for innumerable purposes. It is difficult to offer advice appropriate to all. The readers to whom this work is addressed are those who are concerned to acquire a serious understanding of the Book, and who seek the guidance it has to offer in relation to the various problems of life. For such people we have a few suggestions to make, and we shall offer some explanations in the hope of facilitating their study of the Qur'ān. Anyone who really wishes to understand the Qur'ān, irrespective of whether or not he believes must divest his mind, as far as possible, of every preconceived notion, bias and prejudice, in order to embark upon his study with an open mind. Anyone who begins to study the Qur'ān with a set of preconceived ideas is likely to read those very ideas into the Book. No book can be profitably studied with this kind of attitude, let alone the Qur'ān which refuses to open its treasure-house to such readers.

For those who want only a superficial acquaintance with the doctrines of the Qur'ān one reading is perhaps sufficient. For those who want to fathom its depths several readings are not even enough. These people need to study the Qur'ān over and over again, taking notes of everything that strikes them as significant. Those who are willing to study the Qur'ān in this manner should do so at least twice to begin with, so as to obtain a broad grasp of the system of beliefs and practical prescriptions that it offers. In this preliminary survey, they should try to gain an overall perspective of the Qur'ān and to grasp the basic ideas which it expounds, and the system of life that it seeks to build on the basis of those ideas. If, during the course of this study, anything agitates the mind of the reader, he should note down the point concerned and patiently persevere with his study. He is likely to find that, as he proceeds, the difficulties are resolved. (When a problem has been solved, it is advisable to note down the solution alongside the problem). Experience suggests that any problems still unsolved after a first reading of the Qur'ān are likely to be resolved by a careful second reading.

Only after acquiring a total perspective of the Qur'ān should a more detailed study be attempted. Again the reader is well advised to keep noting down the various aspects of the Qur'ānic teachings. For instance, he should note the human model that the Qur'ān extols as praiseworthy, and the model it denounces. It might be helpful to make two columns, one headed 'praiseworthy qualities', the other headed 'blameworthy qualities', and then to enter into the respective columns all that is found relevant in the Qur'ān. To take another instance, the reader might proceed to investigate the Qur'ānic point of view on what is conducive to human success and felicity, as against what leads to man's ultimate failure and perdition. In the same way, the reader should take down notes about Qur'ānic teachings on questions of belief and morals, man's rights and obligations, family life and collective behaviour, economic and political life, law and social organization, war and peace, and so on. Then he should use these various teachings to try to develop an image of the Qur'ānic teachings vis-à-vis each particular aspect of human life. This should be followed by an attempt at integrating these images so that he comes to grasp the total scheme of life envisaged by the Qur'ān.

Moreover, anyone wishing to study in depth the Qur'ānic viewpoint on any particular problem of life should, first of all, study all the significant strands of human thought concerning that problem. Ancient and modern works on the subject should be studied. Unresolved problems where human thinking seems to have got stuck should be noted. The Qur'ān should then be studied with these unresolved problems in mind, with a view to finding out what solutions the Qur'ān has to offer. Personal experience again suggests that anyone who studies the Qur'ān in this manner will find his problem solved with the help of verses which he may have read scores of times without it ever crossing his mind that they could have any relevance to the problems at hand.

It should be remembered, nevertheless, that full appreciation of the spirit of the Qur'ān demands practical involvement with the struggle to fulfill its mission. The Qur'ān is neither a book of abstract theories and cold doctrines which the reader can grasp while seated in a cozy armchair, nor is it merely a religious book like other religious books, the secrets of which can be grasped in seminaries and oratories. On the contrary, it is the blueprint and guidebook of a message, of a mission, of a movement. As soon as this Book was revealed, it drove a quiet, kind-hearted man from his isolation and seclusion, and placed him upon the battlefield of life to challenge a world that had gone astray. It inspired him to raise his voice against falsehood, and pitted him in grim struggle against the standard-bearers of unbelief, of disobedience of God, of waywardness and error.

One after the other, it sought out everyone who had a pure and noble soul, mustering them together under the standard of the Messenger. It also infuriated all those who by their nature were bent on mischief and drove them to wage war against the bearers of the Truth. This is the Book which inspired and directed that great movement which began with the preaching of a message by an individual, and continued for no fewer than twenty three years, until the Kingdom of God was truly established on earth. In this long and heart-rending struggle between Truth and Falsehood, this Book unfailingly guided its followers to the eradication of the latter and the consolidation and enthronement of the former. How then could one expect to get to the heart of the Qur'ānic truths merely by reciting its verses, without so much as stepping upon the field of battle between faith and unbelief, between Islām and ignorance? To appreciate the Qur'ān fully one must take it up and launch into the task of calling people to God, making it one's guide at every stage.

Then, and only then, does one meet the various experiences encountered at the time of its revelation. One experiences the initial rejection of the message of Islām by the city of Makkah, the persistent hostility leading to the quest for a haven in the refuge of Abyssinia, and the attempt to win a favorable response from Tā'if which led, instead, to cruel persecution of the bearer for the Qur'ānic message. One experiences also the campaigns of Badr, of Uhud, of Hunayn and of Tabuk. One comes face to face with Abu Jahl and Abu Lahab, with hypocrites and with Jews, with those who instantly respond to this call as well as those who, lacking clarity of perception and moral strength, were drawn into Islām only at a later stage.

This will be an experience different from any so-called "mystic-experience." I designate it the "Qur'ānic mystic experience." One of the characteristics of this 'experience' is that at each stage one almost automatically finds certain Qur'ānic verses to guide one, since they were revealed at a similar stage and therefore contain the guidance appropriate to it. A person engaged in this struggle may not grasp all the linguistic and grammatical subtleties, he may also miss certain finer points in the rhetoric and semantics of the Qur'ān, yet it is impossible for the Qur'ān to fail to reveal its true spirit to him.

It is well known that the Qur'ān claims to be capable of guiding all mankind. Yet the student of the Qur'ān finds that it is generally addressed to the people of Arabia, who lived in the time of its revelation. Although the Qur'ān occasionally addresses itself to all mankind - its contents are, on the whole, vitally related to the taste and temperament, the environment and history, and the customs and usages of Arabia. When one notices this, one begins to question why a Book which seeks to guide all mankind to salvation should assign such importance to certain aspects of a particular people's life, and to things belonging to a particular age and time. Failure to grasp the real cause of this may lead one to believe that the Book was originally designed to reform the Arabs of that particular age alone, and that it is only an altogether novel interpretation. If, while addressing the people of a particular area at a particular period of time, attempting to refute their polytheistic beliefs and adducing arguments in support of its own doctrine of the Oneness of God, the Qur'ān draws upon facts with which those people were familiar, this does not warrant the conclusion that its message is relevant only for that particular people or for that particular period of time.

What ought to be considered is whether or not the Qur'ānic statements in refutation of the polytheistic beliefs of the Arabs of those days apply as well to other forms of polytheism in other parts of the world. Can the arguments advanced by the Qur'ān in that connection be used to rectify the beliefs of other polytheists? Is the Qur'ānic line of argument for establishing the Oneness of God, with minor adaptations, valid and persuasive for every age? If the answers are positive, there is no reason why a universal teaching should be dubbed exclusive to a particular people and age merely because it happened to be addressed originally to that people and at that particular period of time.

Indeed, what marks out a time-bound doctrine from an eternal one, and a particularistic national doctrine from a universal one, is the fact that the former either seeks to exalt a people or claims special privileges for it or else comprises ideas and principles so vitally related to that people's life and traditions as to render it totally inapplicable to the conditions of other people. A universal doctrine, on the other hand, is willing to accord equal rights and status to all, and its principles have an international character in that they are equally applicable to other nations. Likewise, the validity of those doctrines which seek to come to grips merely with the questions of a transient and superficial nature is time-bound. If one studies the Qur'ān with these considerations in mind, can one really conclude that it has only a particularistic national character, and that its validity is therefore time-bound?

Those who embark upon a study of the Qur'ān often proceed with the assumption that this Book is, as it is commonly believed to be, a detailed code of guidance. However, when they actually read it, they fail to find detailed regulations regarding social, political and economic matters. In fact, they notice that the Qur'ān has not laid down detailed regulations even in respect of such oft-repeated subjects as Prayers and Zakāh. The reader finds this somewhat disconcerting and wonders in what sense the Qur'ān can be considered a code of guidance.

The uneasiness some people feel about this arises because they forget that God did not merely reveal a Book, but that he also designated a Prophet. Suppose some laymen were to be provided with the bare outlines of a construction plan on the understanding that they would carry out the construction as they wished. In such a case, it would be reasonable to expect that they should have very elaborate directives as to how the construction should be carried out. Suppose, however, that along with the broad outline of the plan of construction, they were also provided with a competent engineer to supervise the task. In that case, it would be quite unjustifiable to disregard the work of the engineer, on the expectation that detailed directives would form an integral part of the construction plan, and then to complain of imperfection in the plan itself. The Qur'ān, to put it succinctly, is a Book of broad general principles rather than of legal minutiae. The Book's main aim is to expound, clearly and adequately, the intellectual and moral foundations of the Islāmic programme for life. It seeks to consolidate these by appealing to both the person's mind and to his/her heart. Its method of guidance for practical Islāmic life does not consist of laying down minutely detailed laws and regulations. It prefers to outline the basic framework for each aspect of human activity, and to lay down certain guidelines within which man can order his life in keeping with the Will of God. The mission of the Prophet was to give practical shape to the Islāmic vision of the good life, by offering the world a model of an individual character and of a human state and society, as living embodiments of the principles of the Qur'ān.

Source: M. Mawdudi, *Introduction – Towards Understanding the Qur'ān,* (complete tafsir [explanation] of the Qur'ān), available in full online: www.quranproject.org

## The Unique Qur'ānic Generation

The callers to Islām in every country and in every period should give thought to one particular aspect of the history of Islām, and they should ponder over it deeply. This is related to the method of inviting people to Islām and its ways of training.

At one time this Message created a generation - the generation of the Companions of the Prophet, may God be pleased with them - without comparison in the history of Islām, even in the entire history of man. After this, no other generation of this calibre was ever again to be found. It is true that we do find some individuals of this calibre here and there in history, but never again did a great number of such people exist in one region as was the case during the first period of Islām.

This is an obvious and open truth of history, and we ought to ponder over it deeply so that we may reach its secret.

The Qur'ān of this Message is still in our hands, and the Hadith (prophetic traditions) of the Messenger of God, i.e. his guidance in practical affairs, and the history of his sacred life are also in our hands, as they were in the hands of the first Muslim community whose equal history could not produce again. The only difference is the person of the Messenger of God; but is this the secret?

Had the person of the Prophet been absolutely essential for the establishment and fruition of this message, God Almighty would not have made Islām a universal message, ordained it as the religion for the whole of mankind, given it the status of the last Divine Message for humanity, and made it to be a guide for all the inhabitants of this planet in all their affairs until the end of time.

God Almighty has taken the responsibility for preserving the Holy Qur'ān on Himself because He knows that Islām can be established and can benefit mankind even after the time of the Prophet. Hence He called His Prophet back to His mercy after twenty three years of messengership and declared this religion to be valid until the end of time. Therefore the absence of the Messenger of God is not the real cause nor does it explain this phenomenon.

We look, therefore, for some other reasons, and for this purpose we look at that clear spring from which the first generation of Muslims quenched their thirst. Perhaps something has been mixed with that clear spring. We should look at the manner in which they received their training. Perhaps some changes have found their way into it.

The spring from which the Companions of the Prophet drank was the Holy Qur'ān; only the Qur'ān, as the Hadith of the Prophet and his teachings were offspring of this fountainhead. When someone asked the Mother of the Believers, Aisha - may God be pleased with her, about the character of the Prophet, she answered, '*His character was the Qur'ān.*'

The Holy Qur'ān was the only source from which they quenched their thirst, and this was the only mould in which they formed their lives. This was the only guidance for them, not because there was no civilization or culture or science or books or schools. Indeed, there was the Roman culture, its civilization, its books and its laws which even today are considered to be the foundation of European culture. There was the heritage of Greek culture, its logic, its philosophy and its arts, which are still a source of inspiration for Western thought. There was the Persian civilization, its art, its poetry and its legends, and its religion and system of government.

There were many other civilizations, near or far, such as the Indian and Chinese cultures, and so on. The Roman and Persian cultures were established to the north and to the south of the Arabian Peninsula, while the Jews and Christians were settled in the heart of Arabia. Thus we believe that this generation did not place sole reliance on the Book of God for the understanding of their religion because of any ignorance of civilization and culture, but it was all according to a well thought out plan and method. An example of this purpose is found in the displeasure expressed by the Messenger of God when Umar, may God be pleased with him, brought some pages from the Torah. The Messenger of God said, '*By God, if even Moses had been alive among you today, he would have no recourse except to follow me.*'

It is clear from this incident that the Messenger of God deliberately limited the first generation of Muslims, which was undergoing the initial stages of training, to only one source of guidance, and that was the Book of God. His intention was that this group should dedicate itself purely to the Book of God and arrange its lives solely according to its teachings. That is why the Messenger of God was upset when Umar, may God be pleased with him, turned to a source different from the Qur'ān.

In fact, the Messenger of God intended to prepare a generation pure in heart, pure in mind, pure in understanding. Their training was to be based on the method prescribed by God Almighty who saved the Holy Qur'ān, purified from the influence of all other sources.

This generation, then, drank solely from this spring and thus attained a unique distinction in history. In later times it happened that other sources mingled with it. Other sources used by later generations included Greek philosophy and logic, ancient Persian legends and their ideas, Jewish scriptures and traditions, Christian theology, and, in addition to these, fragments of other religions and civilizations. These mingled with the commentaries on the Holy Qur'ān and with scholastic theology, as they were mingled with jurisprudence and its principles. Later generations after this generation obtained their training from this mixed source, and hence the like of this generation never arose again.

Thus we can say without any reservations that the main reason for the difference between the first unique and distinguished group of Muslims and later Muslims is that the purity of the first source of Islāmic guidance was mixed with various other sources, as we have indicated.

There is another basic cause, which has operated in creating this difference. That difference is in the art of learning of this unique generation. They of the first generation did not approach the Qur'ān for the purpose of acquiring culture and information, nor for the purpose of taste or enjoyment. None of them came to the Qur'ān to increase his sum total of knowledge for the sake of knowledge itself or to solve some scientific or legal problem, or to remove some defect in his understanding. Rather, he turned to the Qur'ān to find out what the Almighty Creator had prescribed for him and for the group in which he lived, for his life and for the life of the group. He approached it to act on what he heard immediately, as a soldier on the battlefield reads '*Today's Bulletin*' so that he may know what is to be done. He did not read many verses of the Qur'ān in one session, as he understood that this would lay an unbearable burden of duties and responsibilities on his shoulders. At most he would read ten verses, memorize them, and then act upon them. We know this from a tradition reported by Abdullah ibn Masud.

This understanding, the understanding that instruction is for action, opened the doors to spiritual fulfilment and to knowledge. If they had read the Qur'ān only for the sake of discussion, learning and information, these doors would not have opened. Moreover, action became easy, the weight of responsibilities became light, and the Qur'ān became a part of their personalities, mingling with their lives and characters so that they became living examples of faith; a faith not hidden in intellects or books, but expressing itself in a dynamic movement, which changed conditions and events and the course of life.

Indeed, this Qur'ān does not open its treasures except to him who accepts it with this spirit: the spirit of knowing with the intention of acting upon it. It did not come to be a book of intellectual content, or a book of literature, or to be considered as a book of stories or history, although it has all these facets. It came to become a way of life, a way dedicated to God Almighty. Thus, God Most High imparted it to them in a gradual manner, to be read at intervals:

> **"And (it is) a Qur'ān which We have separated (by intervals) that you might recite it to the people over a long period. And We have sent it down progressively."**

Qur'ān 17:106

The Qur'ān did not come down all at once; rather it came down according to the needs of the Islāmic society in facing new problems, according to the growth of ideas and concepts, according to the progress of general social life and according to new challenges faced by the Muslim community in its practical life. One verse or a few verses would be revealed according to the special circumstances and events, and they would answer questions which arose in the minds of people, would explain the nature of a particular situation, and would prescribe a way of dealing with it. These verses would correct their mistakes, either of understanding or of practice, would bring them closer to God, and would explain to them the wisdom of the various aspects of the universe in the light of God's attributes. Thus they clearly realised that every moment of their lives was under the continuous guidance and direction of the Almighty Creator and that they were traversing the path of life under the wings of God's mercy. Because of this sense of constant relationship with God Almighty, their lives were moulded according to that sacred way of life, which was being instructed by Him.

Thus, instruction to be translated into action was the method of the first group of Muslims. The method of later generations was instruction for academic discussion and enjoyment. And without doubt this is the second major factor, which made later generations different from the first unique generation of Islām.

A third cause is also operative in the history of Muslims; we ought to look at it also.

When a person embraced Islām during the time of the Prophet he would immediately cut himself off from *Jahiliyyahh* (pre-Islāmic ignorance). When he stepped into the circle of Islām, he would start a new life, separating himself completely from his past life under ignorance of the Divine Law. He would look upon the deeds during his life of ignorance with mistrust and fear, with a feeling that these were impure and could not be tolerated in Islām! With this feeling, he would turn toward Islām for new guidance; and if at any time temptations overpowered him, or the old habits attracted him, or if he became lax in carrying out the injunctions of Islām, he would become restless with a sense of guilt and would feel the need to purify himself of what had happened, and would turn to the Qur'ān to mould himself according to its guidance.

Thus, there would be a break between the Muslim's present Islām and his past *Jahiliyyahh*, and this after a well thought out decision, as a result of which all his relationships with *Jahiliyyahh* would be cut off and he would be joined completely to Islām, although there would be some give-and-take with the polytheists in commercial activity and daily business; yet relationships of understanding are one thing and daily business is something else.

This renunciation of the *Jahili* (pre-Islāmic ignorance) environment, its customs and traditions, its ideas and concepts, proceeded from the replacement of polytheism by the concept of the Oneness of God, of the *Jahili* view of life and the world by that of the Islāmic view, and from absorption into the new Islāmic community under a new leadership and dedication of all loyalties and commitments to this new society and new leadership.

This was the parting of the ways and the starting of a new journey, a journey free from the pressures of the values, concepts and traditions of the *Jahili* society. The Muslim encountered nothing burdensome except the torture and oppression; but he had already decided in the depths of his heart that he would face it with equanimity, and hence no pressure from the *Jahili* society would have any effect on his continuing steadfastness.

We are also surrounded by *Jahiliyyahh* today, which is of the same nature as it was during the first period of Islām, perhaps a little deeper. Our whole environment, people's beliefs and ideas, habits and art, rules and laws is *Jahiliyyahh*, even to the extent that what we consider to be Islāmic culture, Islāmic sources, Islāmic philosophy and Islāmic thought are also constructs of *Jahiliyyahh*.

This is why the true Islāmic values never enter our hearts, why our minds are never illuminated by Islāmic concepts, and why no group of people arises among us who are of the calibre of the first generation of Islām.

It is therefore necessary, in the way of the Islāmic movement, that in the early stages of our training and education we should remove ourselves from all the influences of the *Jahiliyyahh* in which we live and from which we derive benefits. We must return to that pure source from which those people derived their guidance, the source that is free from any mixing or pollution. We must return to it to derive from it our concepts of the nature of the universe, the nature of human existence, and the relationship of these two with the Perfect, the Real Being: God Most High. From it we must also derive our concepts of life, our principles of government, politics, economics and all other aspects of life.

We must return to it with a sense of instruction for obedience and action, and not for academic discussion and enjoyment.

We should return to it to find out what kind of person it asks us to be, and then be like that. During this process, we will also discover the artistic beauty in the Qur'ān, the marvelous tales in the

Qur'ān, the scenes of the Day of Judgment in the Qur'ān, the intuitive logic of the Qur'ān, and all other such benefits, which are sought in the Qur'ān by academic and literary people. We will enjoy all these other aspects, but these are not the main object of our study. Our primary purpose is to know what way of life is demanded of us by the Qur'ān, the total view of the universe which the Qur'ān wants us to have, what is the nature of our knowledge of God taught to us by the Qur'ān, the kind of morals and manners which are enjoined by it, and the kind of legal and constitutional system it asks us to establish in the world.

We must also free ourselves from the clutches of *Jahili* society, *Jahili* concepts, *Jahili* traditions and *Jahili* leadership. Our mission is not to compromise with the practices of *Jahili* society, nor can we be loyal to it. *Jahili* society, because of its *Jahili* characteristics, is not worthy to be compromised with. Our aim is first to change ourselves so that we may later change the society.

Our foremost objective is to change the practices of this society. Our aim is to change the *Jahili* system at its very roots, this system which is fundamentally at variance with Islām and which, with the help of force and oppression, is keeping us from living the sort of life which is demanded by our Creator.

Our first step will be to raise ourselves above the *Jahili* society, and all its values and concepts. We will not change our own values and concepts either more or less to make a bargain with this *Jahili* society. Never! Even if we were on different roads, and if we take even one step in its company, we will lose our goal entirely and lose our way as well.

We know that in this we will have difficulties and trials, and we will have to make great sacrifices. But if we are to walk in the footsteps of the first generation of Muslims, through whom God established His system and gave it victory over *Jahiliyyahh*, then God must be the Master of our wills.

It is therefore desirable that we should be aware at all times of the nature of our course of action, of the nature of our position, and the nature of the road which we must traverse to come out of ignorance, as the distinguished and unique generation of the Companions of the Prophet came out of it.

Source: Chapter 1 from *Milestones* by Sayyid Qutb, Maktabah Booksellers and Publishers, available in full online: www.quranproject.org

# Preservation and Literary Challenge of the Qur'ān

## Memorization

'In the ancient times, when writing was scarcely used, memory and oral transmission was exercised and strengthened to a degree now almost unknown.'[1885] relates Michael Zwettler. It was in to this 'oral' society that Prophet Muhammad was born. During its revelation, which spanned twenty three years, not only did the Prophet teach the Qur'ān, he memorized it entirely himself as did many of his Companions amongst them; Abu Bakr, Umar, Uthman, Ali, Ibn Masud, Abu Hurairah, Abdullah bin Abbas, Abdullah bin Amr bin al-As, Aisha, Hafsa, and Umm Salama. The Angel Gabriel would spend every night in the month of Ramadhan with the Prophet, on a yearly basis, to refresh his Qur'ānic memory.

The lives of Muslims revolved solely around the Qur'ān; they would memorize it, teach it, recite portions from it every day for their obligatory Prayers – and many would stand a third of the night in prayer reciting from it. There existed so many memorizers of the Qur'ān, that it was considered strange to find a family without someone amongst them who had not memorized the Qur'ān entirely.

As time progressed, literally thousands of schools were opened devoted specifically to the teaching of the Qur'ān to children for the purpose of memorization. The teachers in these schools would have unbroken *Tazkiya's* [authoritative chains of learning] going back to the Prophet himself through his many Companions – and this system exists even today.

Indeed, we live in a world where there are millions of memorizers of the Qur'ān, scattered in every city and country spanning the whole globe. These memorizers range from ages 6 and up; males, females, Arabs, non-Arabs, blacks, whites, Orientals, rich and poor.

There does not exist a single book, secular or religious, which has as many memorizers of it, as the Qur'ān. In reality, if one considers the 'greatest' writings of the world; Old and New Testament, Aristotle, Plato, Shakespeare, Orwell, Marx, Dickens, Machiavelli, Sun Tzu etc.– one may ask, how many people have memorized them? Seldom do we find a single individual.

Hypothetically, if we were loose all the books of the world, by throwing them into the sea for instance, the only book we could resurrect entirely word-for-word would be the Qur'ān – and, amazingly, it could be done simultaneously in every country of the world within twenty-four hours.

Kenneth Cragg writes, "This phenomenon of Qur'ānic recital means that the text has traversed the centuries in an unbroken living sequence of devotion. It cannot, therefore, be handled as an antiquarian thing, nor as a historical document out of a distant past. The fact of *Hifdh* (Qur'ānic Memorization) has made the Qur'ān a present possession through all the lapse of Muslim time and given it a human currency in every generation never allowing its relegation to a bare authority for reference alone."[1886]

---

1885 Zwettler, Michael –*The Oral Tradition of Classical Arabic Poetry,* p. 14.

1886 Cragg, Kenneth - *The Mind of the Qur'ān*, London: George Allen & Unwin, 1973, p.26.

**Written Text**

The entire Qur'ān was in writing at the time of revelation from the Prophet's dictation by some of his literate companions, the most prominent of them being Zayd ibn Thabit.[1887] Others among his noble scribes were Ubayy ibn Ka'b, Ibn Mas'ud, Mu'awiyah ibn Abu Sufyan, Khalid ibn Waleed and Zubayr ibn Awwam.[1888] The verses were recorded on leather, parchment, scapulae (shoulder bones of animals) and the stalks of date palms.[1889]

The codification of the Qur'ān (i.e. into a 'single book form') was done soon after the Battle of Yamamah (11AH/633CE), after the Prophet's death and during the Caliphate of Abu Bakr. Many companions became martyrs in that battle, and it was feared that unless a written copy of the entire revelation was produced, large parts of the Qur'ān might be lost with the death of those who had memorized it. Therefore, at the suggestion of Umar to collect the Qur'ān in the form of writing, Zayd ibn Thabit was requested by Abu Bakr to head a committee which would gather together the scattered recordings of the Qur'ān and prepare a mushaf - loose sheets which bore the entire revelation on them.[1890] To safeguard the compilation from errors, the committee accepted only material which had been written down in the presence of the Prophet himself, and which could be verified by at least two reliable witnesses who had actually heard the Prophet recite the passage in question[1891]. Once completed and unanimously approved of by the Prophet's Companions, these sheets were kept with the Caliph Abu Bakr (d. 13AH/634CE), then passed on to the Caliph Umar (13-23AH/634-644CE), and then Umar's daughter and the Prophet's widow, Hafsa.[1892]

The third Caliph Uthman (23AH-35AH/644-656CE) requested Hafsa to send him the manuscript of the Qur'ān which was in her safekeeping, and ordered the production of several bounded copies of it (masaahif, *sing.* mushaf). This task was entrusted to the Companions Zayd ibn Thabit, Abdullah ibn Az-Zubair, Sa'eed ibn As-'As, and Abdur-Rahman ibn Harith ibn Hisham.[1893] Upon completion (in 25AH/646CE), Uthman returned the original manuscript to Hafsa and sent the copies to the major Islāmic provinces.

A number of non-Muslim scholars who have studied the issue of the compilation and preservation of the Qur'ān have also stated its authenticity. John Burton, at the end of his substantial work on the Qur'ān's compilation, states that the Qur'ān as we have it today is:

"...the text which has come down to us in the form in which it was organized and approved by the Prophet.... What we have today in our hands is the mushaf of Muhammad."[1894]

Kenneth Cragg describes the transmission of the Qur'ān from the time of revelation to today as occurring in *"an unbroken living sequence of devotion."*[1895] Schwally concurs that:

[1887] Suyuti, Jalal al-Din - *Al-Itqan fee 'Uloom al-Qur'ān*, Beirut: Maktab al-Thiqaafiyya, 1973, Vol.1, p.41 & 99.
[1888] al-'Asqalani, Ibn Hajar - *Al-Isabah fee Taymeez as-Sahabah*, and in Azami, M.M. *Kuttab al-Nabi* – list 48 persons who used to write for the Prophet (saw).
[1889] al-Muhasabi, al-Harith - *Kitab Fahm al-Sunan*, cited in Suyuti, *Al-Itqan fi 'Uloom al-Qur'ān*, Vol.1, p.58.
[1890] Bukhari, Vol.6, hadith no. 201 & 509 and vol.9, hadith no.301.
[1891] al-'Asqalani, Ibn Hajar - *Fath al-Bari*, vol.9, p.10-11.
[1892] Bukhari, vol.6, hadith no.201.
[1893] Bukhari, vol.4, hadith no.709 and vol.6, hadith no.507.
[1894] Burton, John - *The Collection of the Qur'ān*, Cambridge University Press, 1977, p.239-40.

"As far as the various pieces of revelation are concerned, we may be confident that their text has been generally transmitted exactly as it was found in the Prophet's legacy." [1896]

The historical credibility of the Qur'ān is further established by the fact that one of the copies sent out by the Caliph Uthman is still in existence today. It lies in the Museum of the City of Tashkent in Uzbekistan, Central Asia.[1897] According to Memory of the World Program, UNESCO, an arm of the United Nations, *'it is the definitive version, known as the Mushaf of Uthman.'*[1898]

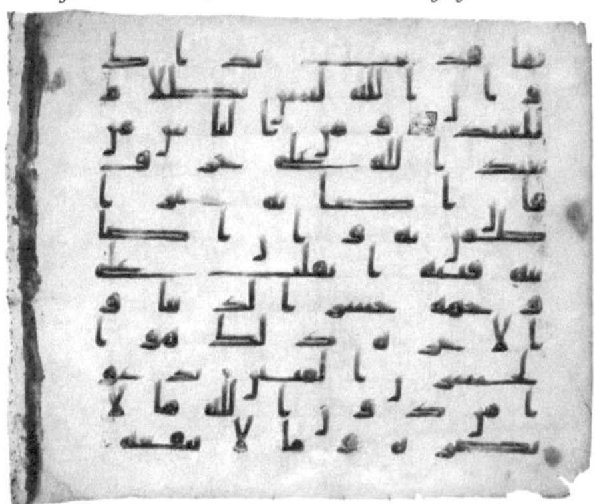

This manuscript, held by the Muslim Board of Uzbekistan, is the earliest existent written version of the Qur'ān. It is the definitive version, known as the Mushaf of Uthman.[1899]

A facsimile of the mushaf in Tashkent is available at the Columbia University Library in the United States of America and the Topkapi Museum, Turkey.

1895 Cragg, Kenneth - *The Mind of the Qur'ān*, London: George Allen & Unwin, 1973, p.26.

1896 Geschichte des Qorans, Schwally - *Leipzig: Dieterich'sche Verlagsbuchhandlung*,1909-38, Vol.2, p.120.

1897 al-Nur, Yusuf Ibrahi - *Ma' al-Masaahif*, Dubai: Dar al-Manar, 1st ed., 1993, p.117; Makhdum, Isma'il - *Tarikh al-Mushaf al-Uthmani fi Tashqand*, Tashkent: Al-Idara al-Diniya, 1971, p.22ff.

1898 http://www.unesco.org - I. Mendelsohn, *"The Columbia University Copy Of The Samarqand Kufic Qur'ān,"* The Moslem World, 1940, p. 357-358. A. Jeffery & I. Mendelsohn, *"The Orthography Of The Samarqand Qur'ān Codex,"* Journal Of The American Oriental Society, 1942, Volume 62, pp. 175-195.

1899 Image courtesy of Memory of the World Register, UNESCO.

A copy of the mushaf sent to Syria (duplicated before a fire in 1310AH/1892CE destroyed the Jaami' Masjid where it was housed) also exists in the Topkapi Museum in Istanbul,[1900] and an early manuscript on gazelle parchment exists in Dar al-Kutub as-Sultaniyyah in Egypt.

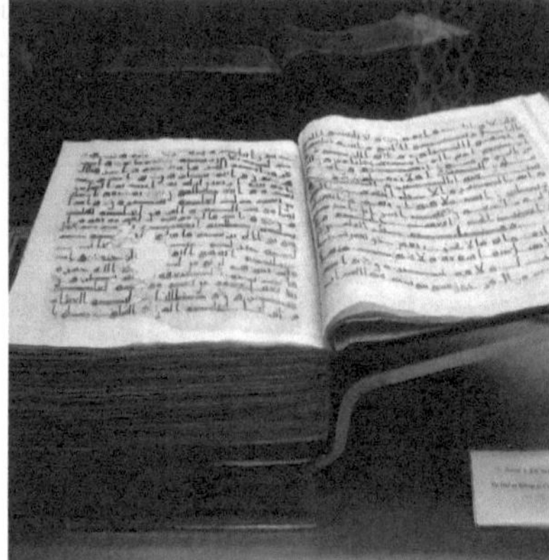

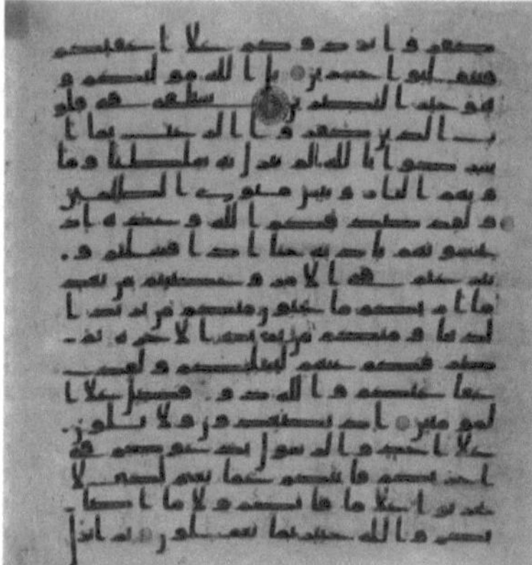

This manuscript held at the Topkapi Museum in Istanbul can be dated back to the late 1st century Hijri.

This Qur'ānic manuscript is housed at the al-Hussein mosque in Cairo and is amongst the oldest of all the manuscripts, and is either Uthmanic or an exact copy from the original.

More ancient manuscripts from all periods of Islāmic history, found in the Library of Congress in Washington, the Chester Beatty Museum in Dublin (Ireland) and the London Museum, have been compared with those in Tashkent, Turkey and Egypt, with results confirming that there have not been any changes in the text from its original time of writing and is proof that the text of the

1900 al-Nur, Yusuf Ibrahim - *Ma' al-Masaahif*, Dubai: Dar al-Manar, 1st ed., 1993, p.113.

Qur'ān we have in circulation today is identical with that of the time of the Prophet and his companions.

The Institute for Koranforschung, for example, in the University of Munich (Germany), collected over 42,000 complete or incomplete ancient copies of the Qur'ān. After around fifty years of research, they reported that there was no variance between the various copies, except the occasional mistakes of the copyist which could easily be ascertained. This Institute was unfortunately destroyed by bombs during WWII.[1901]

Thus, due to the efforts of the early companions, with God's assistance, the Qur'ān as we have it today is recited in the same manner as it was revealed. This makes it the only religious scripture that is still completely retained and understood in its original language. Indeed, as Sir William Muir states, *"There is probably no other book in the world which has remained twelve centuries (now fourteen) with so pure a text."*[1902]

The evidence above confirms God's promise in the Qur'ān:

**"Indeed, it is We who sent down the Qur'ān and indeed, We will be its guardian."**
Qur'ān 15:9

The Qur'ān has been preserved in both oral and written form in a way no other book has, with each form providing a check and balance for the authenticity of the other.[1903]

**Explanation of Qur'ān's Inimitability**

State of the Prophet Muhammad:

- He was an ordinary human being.
- He was illiterate. He could neither read nor write.
- He was more than forty years old when he received the first revelation. Until then he was not known to be an orator, poet, or a man of letters; he was just a merchant. He did not compose a single poem or deliver even one sermon before he was chosen to be a prophet.
- He brought a book attributing it to God, and all Arabs of his time were in agreement it was inimitable.

How do we know it is from God?

William Shakespeare, who was an English poet and playwright, widely regarded as the greatest writer in the English language, is often used as an example of unique literature. The argument posed is that if Shakespeare expressed his poetry and prose in a unique manner - and he is a human being - then surely no matter how unique the Qur'ān is, it must also be from a human being. However there are some problems with the above argument. It does not take into account the nature of the Qur'ān's uniqueness and it doesn't understand the uniqueness of literary geniuses such as

1901 Hamidullah, Mohammed - *Muhammad Rasullullah*, Lahore: Idara-e-Islāmiat, n.d., p.179.
1902 Sir William Muir, *Life of Mohamet*, London, 1894, Vol.1, Introduction.
1903 Source - http://www.islamreligion.com/articles/18/

Shakespeare. Although Shakespeare composed poetry and prose that received an unparalleled aesthetic reception, the literary form he expressed his works in was not unique. In many instances Shakespeare used the common Iambic Pentameter (The Iambic pentameter is a meter in poetry. It refers to a line consisting of five iambic feet. The word "pentameter" simply means that there are five feet in the line.)

However in the case of the Qur'ān, its language is in an entirely unknown and unmatched literary form. The structural features of the Qur'ānic discourse render it unique and not the subjective appreciation of its literary and linguistic makeup.

With this in mind there are two approaches that can show that there are greater reasons to believe that the Qur'ān is from the divine and a miraculous text. The first approach is rational deduction and the second is the philosophy of miracles.

**Rational Deduction**

Rational deduction is the thinking process where logical conclusions are drawn from a universally accepted statement or provable premises. This process is also called rational inference or logical deduction. In the context of the Qur'ān's uniqueness the universally accepted statement supported by eastern and western scholarship is: "The Qur'ān was not successfully imitated by the Arabs at the time of revelation"

From this statement the following logical conclusions can be drawn:

1. The Qur'ān could not have come from an Arab as the Arabs, at the time of revelation, were linguists *par excellence* and they failed to challenge the Qur'ān. They had even admitted that the Qur'ān could have not come from a human being – the accusation being that the Prophet was a magician or was being taught by some Jinn.

2. The Qur'ān could not have come from a Non-Arab as the language in the Qur'ān is Arabic, and the knowledge of the Arabic language is a pre-requisite to successfully challenge the Qur'ān.

3. The Qur'ān could not have come from the Prophet Muhammad due to the following reasons:

    a. The Prophet Muhammad was an Arab himself and all the Arabs failed to challenge the Qur'ān.
    b. The Arab linguists at the time of revelation never accused the Prophet of being the author of the Qur'ān.
    c. The Prophet Muhammad experienced many trials and tribulations during the course of his Prophetic mission. For example his children died, his beloved wife Khadija passed away, he was boycotted, his close companions were tortured and killed, yet the Qur'ān's literary character remains that of the divine voice and character. Nothing in the Qur'ān expresses the turmoil and emotions of the Prophet Muhammad. It is almost a psychological and physiological impossibility to go

through what the Prophet went through and yet none of the emotions are expressed in the literary character of the Qur'ān.

d. The Qur'ān is a known literary masterpiece yet its verses were at many times revealed for specific circumstances and events that occurred. However, without revision or deletion they are literary masterpieces. All literary masterpieces have undergone revision and deletion to ensure literary perfection, however the Qur'ān was revealed instantaneously.

e. All types of human expression can be imitated if the blueprint of that expression exists. For example artwork can be imitated even though some art is thought to be extraordinary or amazingly unique. But in the case of the Qur'ān we have the blueprint - the Qur'ān itself - yet no one has been able to imitate its unique literary form.

4. The Qur'ān could not have come from another being such as a Jinn or Spirit because the basis of their existence is the Qur'ān and revelation itself. Their existence is based upon revelation and not empirical evidence. Therefore if someone claims that the source of the Qur'ān to be another being then they would have to prove its existence and in this case proving revelation. In the case of using the Qur'ān as the revelation to establish Jinns existence then that would mean the whole rational deduction exercise would not be required in the first place, as the Qur'ān would already have been established as a divine text, because to believe in Jinns existence would mean belief in the Qur'ān in the first place.

5. The Qur'ān can only have come from the Divine as it is the only logical explanation as all other explanations have been discarded because they do not explain the uniqueness of the Qur'ān in a comprehensive and coherent manner.

**Philosophy of Miracles**

The word miracle is derived from the Latin word 'miraculum' meaning "something wonderful." A miracle is commonly defined as a violation of a natural law (lex naturalis); however this is an incoherent definition. This incoherence is due our understanding of natural laws, as the Philosopher Bilynskyj observes "...so long as natural laws are conceived of as universal inductive generalisations the notion of violation of a nature law is incoherent." Natural laws are inductive generalizations of patterns we observe in the universe. If the definition of a miracle is a violation of a natural law, in other words a violation of the patterns we observe in the universe, then an obvious conceptual problem occurs. The problem is: why can't we take this perceived violation of the pattern as part of the pattern?

Therefore the more coherent description of a miracle is not a 'violation' but an 'impossibility'. The Philosopher William Lane Craig rejects the definition of a miracle as a "violation of a natural law" and replaces it with the coherent definition of "events which lie outside the productive capacity of nature." What this means is that miracles are acts of impossibilities concerning causal or logical connections.

What makes the Qur'ān a miracle, is that it lies outside the productive capacity of the nature of the Arabic language. The productive capacity of nature, concerning the Arabic language, is that any grammatically sound expression of the Arabic language will always fall within the known Arabic literary forms of Prose and Poetry.

The Qur'ān is a miracle as its literary form cannot be explained via the productive capacity of the Arabic language, because all the possible combinations of Arabic words, letters and grammatical rules have been exhausted and yet the Qur'ān's literary form has not been imitated. The Arabs who were known to have been Arab linguists par excellence failed to successfully challenge the Qur'ān. Forster Fitzgerald Arbuthnot who was a notable British Orientalist and translator states: "…and that though several attempts have been made to produce a work equal to it as far as elegant writing is concerned, none has as yet succeeded."

The implication of this is that there is no link between the Qur'ān and the Arabic language; however this seems impossible because the Qur'ān *is* made up of the Arabic language! On the other hand, all the combinations of Arabic words and letters have been used to try and imitate the Qur'ān. Therefore, it can only be concluded that a supernatural explanation is the only coherent explanation for this impossible Arabic literary form – the Qur'ān. When we look at the productive nature of the Arabic language to find an answer for the unique literary form of the Qur'ān, we find no link between it and the divine text, thus making it an impossibility requiring supernatural explanation. So it logically follows that if the Qur'ān is a literary event that lies outside the productive capacity of the Arabic language, then, by definition, it is a miracle.

The Qur'ān is a literary and linguistic miracle. It has challenged those who doubt its divine authorship, and history has shown that it indeed is a miracle as there can be no natural explanation to comprehensively explain its unmatched unique expression. Professor Bruce Lawrence correctly asserts, "As tangible signs, Qur'ānic verse are expressive of an inexhaustible truth, they signify meaning layered with meaning, light upon light, miracle after miracle." [1904]

**Revelation Related to Contemporary Events**

The fact that specific passages of the Holy Qur'ān were revealed at the same time as the events they describe is not particularly surprising. What is extraordinary to note, however, is the content.

Anybody who reads the Qur'ān for the first time may be struck not only by what the revelation contains, but also by that which is absent. For example, the Prophet Muhammad outlived his first love and first wife, the woman with whom he spent twenty-five years of his youth, Khadijah. She died after two long, painful years during which the Makkan pagans ostracized, persecuted, and starved Prophet Muhammad and his followers. Twenty-five years of love, support, caring, and kindness - gone. His first wife, so beloved that he remained faithful to her throughout their marriage and throughout his youth - gone. The first person to believe in his prophethood, the wife who bore all but one of his eight children - gone. So devoted was she that she exhausted her wealth and sacrificed her tribal relationships in support of him. After which, she was gone.

Musicians croon over their lost loves; artists immortalize their infatuations in marble and on canvas, photographers fill albums with glossy memorials and poets pour their hearts onto paper with the ink of liquid lamentation. Yet despite what a person might expect, nowhere does the Qur'ān

[1904] www.theinimitablequran.com

mention the name Khadijah. Not once. The wives of Pharaoh, Noah, and Lot are alluded to, but Khadijah is not even given passing mention. Compounding the peculiarity is the startling fact that the only woman the Qur'ān mentions by name is Mary, an Israelite and the mother of Jesus. And she is mentioned in glowing terms. As a matter of fact, a whole surah bears her name [surah 19].

Many orientalists claim that the Qur'ān is not revelation but was the product of the Prophet Muhammad's mind. One could question if this could be the product of the mind of a man when he excluded the women who filled his life and memory from the revelation he claimed, in favor of an Israelite woman and the mother of an Israelite prophet, this drives recklessly against the flow of reasonable expectation.

During the Prophet Muhammad's life, he saw every one of his four sons die. All but one of his four daughters pre-deceased him. His favored uncle, Hamzah, was killed in battle and mutilated in a horrific manner. The Prophet Muhammad and his followers were regularly insulted, humiliated, beaten, and on occasion murdered. On one occasion the offal of a slaughtered camel was dumped on the Prophet's back while he was prostrate in prayer. The sheer weight of this offal reportedly pinned him to the ground until his daughter uncovered him. Now, camels smell bad enough while they're living. Try to imagine the smell of their decomposing guts in the tropical sun. Then try to imagine being buried in the tangled mass of their slimy offense, rivulets of rotting camel juice running down exposed arms, cheeks and, oh yes, behind the ears. A refreshing massage-head shower is a couple thousand calendar pages away, with soap not yet registered in the patent office. Such events must have tortured Prophet Muhammad's memory. Yet they are described nowhere in the Qur'ān.

So the Qur'ān is remarkable in that its content does not reflect the mind of the messenger. In fact, in some cases the Qur'ān does the exact opposite, and corrects Prophet Muhammad's errors in judgment. For example, many passages defined issues with which Prophet Muhammad and his companions were immediately concerned, or delivered lessons regarding contemporaneous events. Such passages are legion. However, instead of affirming Prophet Muhammad's judgment, the Qur'ān not only admonishes certain of the believers, but even corrects Prophet Muhammad on occasion. Surah 80 admonishes Prophet Muhammad for having frowned and turned his back on a blind Muslim who, in seeking guidance, interrupted a conversation to which Prophet Muhammad mistakenly assigned priority. The error in judgment was understandable, but it was an error nonetheless. And according to the Holy Qur'ān, it was an error deserving of correction.

On other occasions, revelation admonished Prophet Muhammad for forbidding himself the use of honey [after being deceived into believing it gave his breath a bad odour - 66:1], for directing his adopted son to keep his marriage when divorce was preferable, and for praying for forgiveness of the Hypocrites [Muslims-in-name-only who were denied the mercy of Allah due to their obstinate rebellion]. The admonishment for his error of judgment with regard to his adopted son, Zaid, and his unhappy marriage to Zainab, was of such extreme embarrassment that Prophet Muhammad's wife, A'ishah, later commented to the effect that, "Were Prophet Muhammad to have concealed anything from the revelation, he would have concealed this verse."

In one case Prophet Muhammad was corrected for being vengeful, in another for being lenient. Although such errors of judgment were rare, they highlight his humanity. Equally important, they reveal his sincerity, for Prophet Muhammad's errors required correction by the One Whom

Prophet Muhammad represented, lest they be misperceived as bearing God's approval. However, unlike a false prophet, who would have concealed his shortcomings, Prophet Muhammad conveyed revelation that immortalized his mistakes, and Allah's admonition thereof. So here is a man who claimed every letter of revelation was from God, including the passages that corrected his own errors and instructed him to repent. Weird. If, that is, we imagine the Qur'ān to have been authored by a false prophet. False prophets are either liars or deluded, and both types attempt to build confidence in their followers by portraying themselves as perfect.[1905]

Initially, the Makkan disbelievers said Muhammad is the author of the Qur'ān. God responded to them:

**" Or do they say, "He has made it up?" Rather, they do not believe. Then let them produce a statement like it, if they should be truthful. Or were they created by nothing, or were they the creators [of themselves]?"**

Qur'ān 52:33-35

First, God challenged them to produce ten chapters like the Qur'ān:

**"Or do they say, "He invented it?" Say, "Then bring ten sūrahs like it that have been invented and call upon [for assistance] whomever you can besides God, if you should be truthful. And if they do not respond to you - then know that the Qur'ān was revealed with the knowledge of God and that there is no deity except Him. Then, would you [not] be Muslims?"**

Qur'ān 11:13-14

But, when they were unable to meet the challenge of ten chapters, God reduced it to a single chapter:

**"And if you are in doubt about what We have sent down [i.e., the Qur'ān] upon Our Servant [i.e Prophet Muhammad], then produce a sūrah the like thereof and call upon your witnesses[i.e supporters] other than God, if you should be truthful. But if you do not - and you will never be able to - then fear the Fire, whose fuel is men and stones, prepared for the disbelievers."**

Qur'ān 2:23-24

Finally, God foretold their eternal failure to meet the divine challenge:

**Say, "If mankind and the jinn gathered in order to produce the like of this Qur'ān, they could not produce the like of it, even if they were to each other assistants."**

Qur'ān 17:88

The Prophet said, *"Every Prophet was given 'signs' because of which people believed in him. Indeed, I have been given the Divine Revelation that God has revealed to me. So, I hope to have the most followers of all the prophets on the Day of Resurrection."* [1906]

---

[1905] Edited from, *The First and Final Commandment*, Dr. Laurence B. Brown.

[1906] Bukhari

The physical miracles performed by the prophets were time-specific, valid only for those who witnessed them, whereas the like of the continuing miracle of our Prophet, the Noble Qur'ān, was not granted to any other prophet. Its linguistic superiority, style, clarity of message, strength of argument, quality of rhetoric, and the human inability to match even its shortest chapter till the end of time grant it an exquisite uniqueness. Those who witnessed the revelation and those who came after, all can drink from its fountain of wisdom. That is why the Prophet of Mercy hoped he would have the most followers out of all the prophets, and prophesized that he would at a time when Muslims were few, but then they began to embrace Islām in floods. Thus, this prophecy came true.

## Scientific Miracles of the Qur'ān

The Qur'ān is not a book of Science, Philosophy, Geology, History, etc - It is revelation from God as guidance for Mankind. However, if experts from any of the human sciences were to read it, they would conclude beyond doubt, that the words of the Qur'ān are not from any human being but from God Almighty. The field of Science is no different. The Qur'ān contains countless scientific facts which were unknown to man even a hundred years ago, and considering it was revealed fourteen hundred years ago, clearly/absolutely proves its divine origin.

### The Qur'ān on the Origin of the Universe

The science of modern cosmology, observational and theoretical, clearly indicates that, at one point in time, the whole universe was nothing but a cloud of 'smoke' (i.e. an opaque highly dense and hot gaseous composition).[1907] This is one of the undisputed principles of standard modern cosmology. Scientists now can observe new stars forming out of the remnants of that 'smoke' (see figures 1 and 2).

**Figure 1:** A new star forming out of a cloud of gas and dust (nebula), which is one of the remnants of the 'smoke' that was the origin of the whole universe. (*The Space Atlas, Heather and Henbest, p. 50.*)

**Figure 2:** The Lagoon nebula is a cloud of gas and dust, about 60 light years in diameter. It is excited by the ultraviolet radiation of the hot stars that have recently formed within its bulk. (*Horizons, Exploring the Universe, Seeds, plate 9, from Association of Universities for Research in Astronomy, Inc.)*

The illuminating stars we see at night were, just as was the whole universe, in that 'smoke' material. God has said in the Qur'ān:

**"Then He directed Himself to the heaven while it was smoke..."**

Qur'ān 41:11

Because the earth and the heavens above (the sun, the moon, stars, planets, galaxies, etc.) have been formed from this same 'smoke,' we conclude that the earth and the heavens were one con-

[1907] Weinberg, *The First Three Minutes, a Modern View of the Origin of the Universe*, pp. 94-105.

nected entity. Then out of this homogeneous 'smoke,' they formed and separated from each other. God has said in the Qur'ān:

> **"Have those who disbelieved not considered that the heavens and the earth were a joined entity, and We separated them and made from water every living thing? Then will they not believe?"**
>
> Qur'ān 21:30

We know that our world, the sun and the stars did not come about immediately after the primeval explosion. For the universe was in a gaseous state before the formation of the stars. This gaseous state was initially made of hydrogen and helium. Condensation and compression shaped the planets, the earth, the sun and the stars that were but products of the gaseous state. The discovery of these phenomena has been rendered possible thanks to successive findings as a result of observations and theoretical developments.

The knowledge of all contemporary communities during the time of the Prophet would not suffice for the assertion that the universe had once been in a gaseous state. The Prophet himself did not claim to be the author of the statements in the Qur'ān as it often reminded, declaring that he is simply a messenger of God.

> **"That is from the news of the unseen which We reveal to you, [O Muhammad]. You knew it not, neither you nor your people, before this. So be patient; indeed, the [best] outcome is for the righteous."**
>
> Qur'ān 11: 49

Dr. Alfred Kroner is one of the world's renowned geologists from Johannes Gutenberg University in Germany. He said: "*Thinking where Muhammad came from . . . I think it is almost impossible that he could have known about things like the common origin of the universe, because scientists have only found out within the last few years, with very complicated and advanced technological methods, that this is the case....Somebody who did not know something about nuclear physics fourteen hundred years ago could not, I think, be in a position to find out from his own mind, for instance, that the earth and the heavens had the same origin.*" [1908]

### The Qur'ān on the 'Big Bang Theory'

> **"Have those who disbelieved not considered that the heavens and the earth were a [*ratq*] joined entity, and We [*fataqa*] separated them....Then will they not believe?"**
>
> Qur'ān 21:30

[1908] Stated by Dr. Alfred in *This is the Truth* (videotape). To view this visit www.Islām-guide.com/truth.htm

The word '*ratq*' translated as 'sewn to' means 'mixed in each, blended' in Arabic. It is used to refer to two different substances that make up a whole. The phrase '*fataqa*' is 'unstitched' and implies that something comes into being by tearing apart or destroying the structure of things that are sewn to one another.

In the verse, heaven and earth are at first subject to the status of '*ratq*.' They are separated (*fataqa*) with one coming out of the other. Intriguingly, when we think about the first moments of the 'Big Bang' we see that the entire matter of the universe collected at one single point. In other words, everything including 'the heavens and earth' which were not created yet were in an interwoven and inseparable condition. Then, this point exploded violently, causing its matter to disunite.

The 'Big Bang' theory holds that about 20,000,000,000 years ago the universe began with the explosive expansion of a single, extremely condensed state of matter. The Nobel Prize for science in 1977 was awarded for this discovery, whereas it was stated by the Qur'ān centruries before.

### The Qur'ān on the Expanding Universe

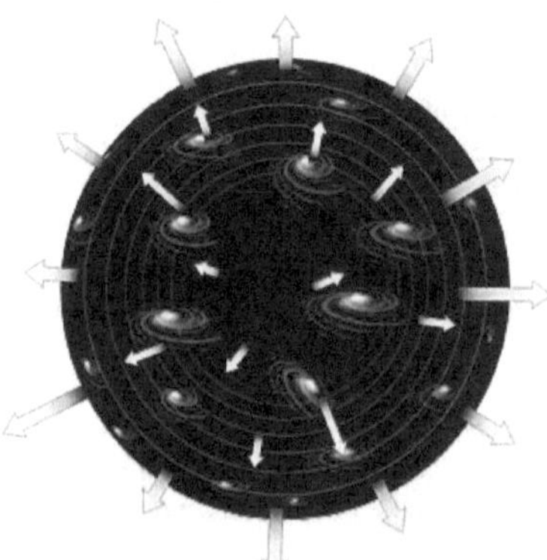

**"And the heaven We constructed with strength, and indeed, We are [its] expander."**

Qur'ān 51: 47

It was only after the development of the radio telescope in 1937 that the expansion of the universe was observed and established. While observing the sky with a telescope, Edwin Hubble, the American astronomer, discovered that the stars and galaxies were constantly moving away from each other. This discovery is regarded as one of the greatest in the history of astronomy. During these observations, Hubble established that the stars emit a light that turns redder according to their distance.

That is because according to the known laws of physics, light heading towards a point of observation turns violet, and light moving away from that point assumes a more reddish hue. During his observations, Hubble noted a tendency towards the colour red in the light emitted by stars. In short, the stars were moving further and further away, all the time. The stars and galaxies were not only moving away from us, but also from each other. A universe where everything constantly moves away from everything else implied a constantly expanding universe.

**The Qur'ān on the Orbital Movement of the Sun and the Moon**

**"And it is He who created the night and the day and the sun and the moon; all [heavenly bodies] in an [*falak*] orbit are [*yasbahoon*] swimming."**

Qur'ān 21: 33

**"It is not allowable [i.e., possible] for the sun to reach the moon, nor does the night overtake the day, but each, in an [*falak*] orbit, is [*yasbahoon*] swimming."**

Qur'ān 36: 40

The Arabic words used in these verses are *falak* and *yasbahoon* which can be translated as 'sphere or orbit' and 'swimming.' This concept of the movement of the sun and the moon and the other planets is in perfect harmony with recent discovery. It is inconceivable that an Arab, living centuries ago in the most primitive part of the world, could have rightly used such a specific term to describe the movements of planets without divine guidance. It should be noted that the discovery of the orbital movement of all celestial bodies was due to the invention of telescopes.

**The Qur'ān on Duality in Creation**

**"Exalted is He who created all pairs - from what the earth grows and from themselves and from that which they do not know."**

Qur'ān 36: 36

This Qur'ānic verse outlines the fact that all creatures, whether living beings or solid matter, are created in pairs. It refers to everything that was created. Amazingly, the outstanding truth and generality of this and similar verses came to be gradually realized, and more so recently, during 14 centuries since the Qur'ān was first revealed in a primitive world.

Millions of animal species discovered, classified and investigated only during the last two centuries, were found to be invariably in "pairs," male and female. Electron microscopy has clarified that all living creatures, however minute, are in pairs. The smallest microbes, viruses, and bacteria have their counterpart antibodies.

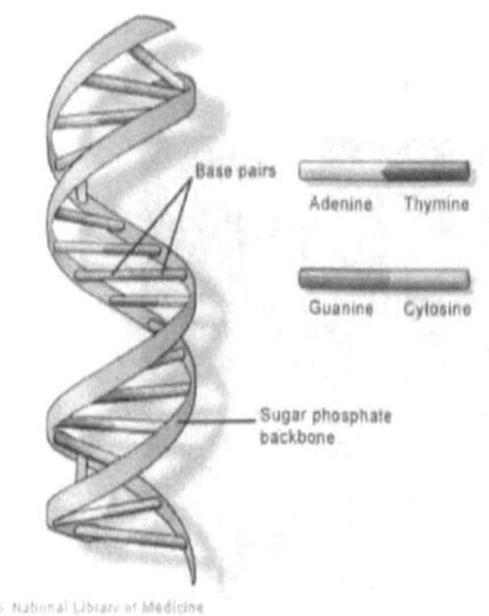


Take for example DNA – it is made up of thousands of different genes, and genes are made up of base pairs. These "base pairs" are made of two paired up nucleotides. In order to form a base pair, we need to pair up specific nucleotides. Each type of nucleotide has a specific shape, so only certain combinations fit.

The sequence, composition, and orientation of these "pairs" of nucleotides control the genetic information carried by the DNA. A chromosome consists of different types of protein bound tightly with a single DNA molecule chain.

The DNA is a large long (up to 1 meter long) amino acid chain. It consists of a "pair" of spiral strands, connected with steps. Each step consists of a "pair" of chemical components, so-called nucleotides.

There are 4 nucleotides. Adenine, Thymine, Guanine and Cytosine represented respectively by the letters A,T,G and C. Due to their shapes only A and T or G and C fit into one another.

Base Pairs [A-T, G-C] (billions of these matching pairs) --->
Genes (thousands of these) --> DNA --> Chromosomes -->
Nucleotides --> Nucleus (the 'brain' of the cell).[1909]

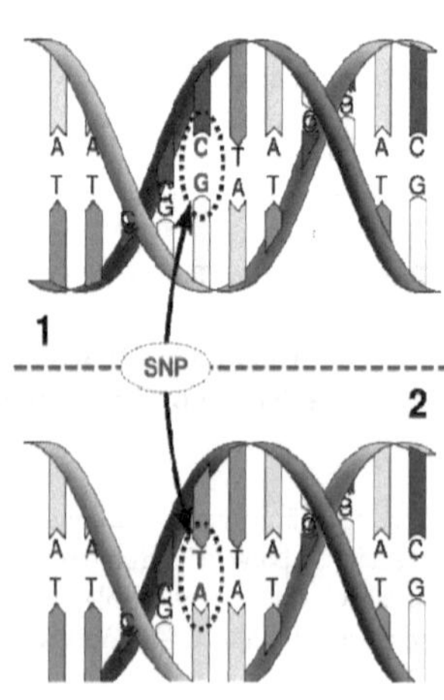


All life systems including plant, animal, and human consist of different types of cells. A cell consists of a nucleus surrounded with cytoplasm which is usually enclosed, within a cell wall. The cell nucleus, carries the chromosomes that control all the cell functions. All cells of a particular organism have exactly the same number of chromosomes; the number varies widely between different species. Proteins are formed from various combinations of amino acids. Specifically, 20 types of amino acid are used in different combinations to form more than a million types of protein, present in a human being. Every type of amino acid can exist in either of a pair of structures (right-handed isomer or left-handed isomer), with opposite polarized light rotation direction. The same applies to the proteins formed thereof.

[1909] International Human Genome Sequencing Consortium (2004). "Finishing the euchromatic sequence of the human genome". Nature 431 (7011): 931–45.

The wide variety of creatures including living species, solid matter, liquids, and gases are marvelous combinations of the same list of building blocks: atoms. These basic units, were long known to consist of a "pair" of a positively charged nucleus surrounded by negative electrons. The nucleus consists of protons that carry the positive charge, together with neutrons. Even the neutral neutrons have their counterpart, the anti-neutrons. Later advances in nuclear physics has demonstrated that each of these particles is, in effect, a complex structure of much smaller nuclear particles. Over 200 of such elementary particles are now known.

At the atomic level, atoms can, literally, ionize i.e. either lose or gain electrons to form positive cations or negative anions. "Pairs" of cations/anions combine to produce the wide variety of chemical (inorganic) compounds. This is one of the conclusions made by British physicist Paul Dirac, winner for Nobel Prize for Physics in 1933. His finding, known as "parity," revealed the duality known as matter and anti-matter.

Another example of duality in creation is plants. Botanists only discovered that there is a gender distinction in plants some 100 years ago. Yet, the fact that plants are created in pairs was revealed in the verses of the Qur'ān 1,400 years ago. It was only after the discovery of microscopes that human beings knew that plants have male organs (stamens) and female organs (ovaries) and that the wind, together with other factors, carries the pollen from one type to the opposite one so that reproduction can take place.

Every animal species of the wide animal kingdom reproduce sexually. Sexual reproduction results from the combination of a female ovum and a male sperm. The formation of this zygote "pair" is the starting point in the reproduction cycle. The sperms, in turn are of "two" kinds, the first carries the hereditary male characteristics, while the other carries the female ones. Flowering plants, of which more than 250,000 have been discovered so far, also reproduce sexually. They have both female (ovaries containing eggs) and male (stamens carrying pollens); either combined in the same flower or in different flowers. In the latter case, fertilization occurs when pollens are transferred by wind or insects to an adjacent flower.

Non-flowering plants, on the other hand, amounting to 150,000 species, reproduce in a double-stage cycle of sexual and asexual reproduction. Yet, the asexual reproduction stage is essentially a process of breaking up the DNA "pair" of strands into two; followed by each of which re-forming its complementary strand. Thus, a new "pair" of identical DNA molecules results in the cell, just before it divides into a "pair" of identical cells. The same applies to the asexual reproduction of bacteria.

Each bacterium consists of a single cell, the smallest biological unit able to function independently. A single bacterium reproduces the same way explained above, i.e. by splitting into a pair of identical cells. As we have seen, cell division occurs through the process of DNA replication, in which the two strands of the DNA molecules are separated; and each strand re-synthesizes a complementary strand to itself. So, "asexual" reproduction of bacteria involves the DNA "pair" of strands splitting and reformation into a new "pair" of cells.

### The Qur'ān on the Origin of Life in Water

> **"Have those who disbelieved not considered that the heavens and the earth were a joined entity, and We separated them and made from water every living thing? Then will they not believe?"**
>
> Qur'ān 21:30

The origin of life is now such a basic scientific fact that it is accepted without hesitation. This could lessen one's appreciation for these verses. Yet it must be borne in mind that the Arabian peninsula is a desert land without a single lake or river, these verses describe something unimaginable to those at the time of Prophet Muhammad.

A point to note - animals in dry regions have been created with mechanisms to protect their metabolisms from water loss and to ensure maximum benefit from water use. If water loss takes place in the body for any reason, and if that loss is not made good, death will result in a few days.

### The Qur'ān on Seas and Rivers

Modern Science has discovered that in the places where two different seas meet, there is a barrier between them. This barrier divides the two seas so that each sea has its own temperature, salinity, and density.[1910] For example, Mediterranean sea water is warm, saline, and less dense, compared to Atlantic ocean water. When Mediterranean sea water enters the Atlantic over the Gibraltar sill, it moves several hundred kilometers into the Atlantic at a depth of about 1000 meters with its own warm, saline, and less dense characteristics. The Mediterranean water stabilizes at this depth[1911] (see figure 1).

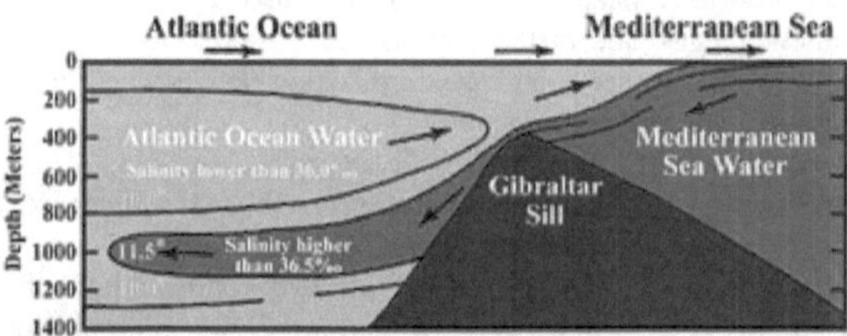


**Figure 1:** The Mediterranean sea water as it enters the Atlantic over the Gibraltar sill with its own warm, saline, and less dense characteristics, because of the barrier that distinguishes between them. Temperatures are in degrees Celsius (C°). (Marine Geology, Kuenen, p. 43, with a slight enhancement.)

Although there are large waves, strong currents, and tides in these seas, they do not mix or transgress this barrier.

The Qur'ān mentioned that there is a barrier between two seas that meet and that they do not transgress. God has said:

---

[1910] Davis, *Principles of Oceanography*, pp. 92-93.
[1911] Ibid 93.

**"He released the two seas, meeting [side by side]; Between them is a barrier [so] neither of them transgresses."**

Qur'ān 55:19-20

But when the Qur'ān speaks about the divider between fresh and salt water, it mentions the existence of "a forbidding partition" with the barrier. God has said in the Qur'ān:

**"And it is He who has released [simultaneously] the two seas, one fresh and sweet and one salty and bitter, and He placed between them a barrier and prohibiting partition."**

Qur'ān 25:53

One may ask, why did the Qur'ān mention the partition when speaking about the divider between fresh and salt water, but did not mention it when speaking about the divider between the two seas?

Modern science has discovered that in estuaries, where fresh (sweet) and salt water meet, the situation is somewhat different from what is found in places where two seas meet. It has been discovered that what distinguishes fresh water from salt water in estuaries is a "pycnocline zone with a marked density discontinuity separating the two layers."[1912] This partition (zone of separation) has a different salinity from the fresh water and from the salt water (see figure 2).

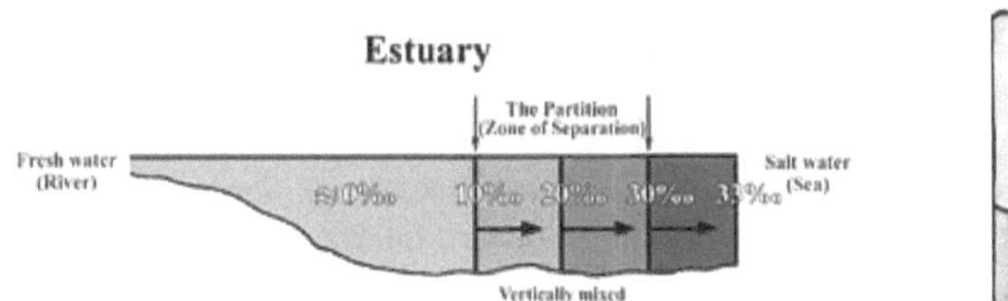


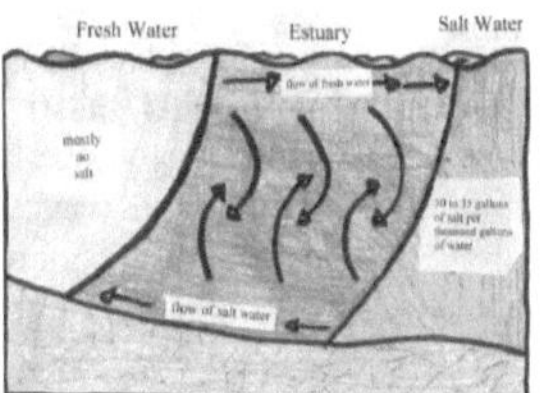


Figure 2: Longitudinal section showing salinity (parts per thousand ‰) in an estuary. We can see here the partition (zone of separation) between the fresh and the salt water.[1913]

This information has been discovered only recently, using advanced equipment to measure temperature, salinity, density, oxygen dissolubility, etc. The human eye cannot see the difference between the two seas that meet, rather the two seas appear to us as one homogeneous sea. Likewise, the human eye cannot see the division of water in estuaries into the three kinds: fresh water, salt water, and the partition (zone of separation).

God has said in the Qur'ān:

**"Or [they are] like darknesses within an unfathomable sea which is covered by waves, upon which are waves, over which are clouds - darknesses, some of them upon others. When one puts out his hand [therein], he can hardly see it...."**

Qur'ān 24:40

[1912] Gross, *Oceanography*, p. 242.
[1913] Thurman, *Introductory Oceanography*, pp. 300-301.

This verse mentions the darkness found in deep seas and oceans, where if a man stretches out his hand, he cannot see it. The darkness in deep seas and oceans is found around a depth of 200 meters and below. At this depth, there is almost no light (see figure 3). Below a depth of 1000 meters there is no light at all.[1914] Human beings are not able to dive more than forty meters without the aid of submarines or special equipment. Human beings cannot survive unaided in the deep dark part of the oceans, such as at a depth of 200 meters.

**Figure 3:** Between 3 and 30 percent of the sunlight is reflected at the sea surface. Then almost all of the seven colors of the light spectrum are absorbed one after another in the first 200 meters, except the blue light. (*Oceans*, Elder and Pernetta, p. 27.)

Scientists have recently discovered this darkness by means of special equipment and submarines that have enabled them to dive into the depths of the oceans.

We can also understand from the following sentences in the previous verse, **"...in a deep sea. It is covered by waves, above which are waves, above which are clouds....,"** that the deep waters of seas and oceans are covered by waves, and above these waves are other waves. It is clear that the second set of waves are the surface waves that we see, because the verse mentions that above the second waves there are clouds. But what about the first waves? Scientists have recently discovered that there are internal waves which "occur on density interfaces between layers of different densities."[1915] (see figure 4).

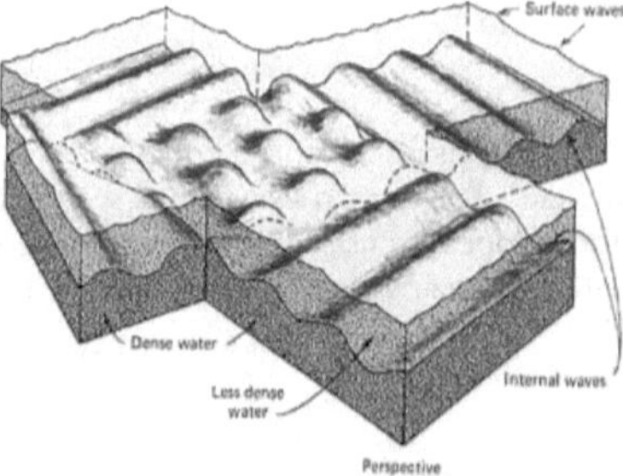


**Figure 4:** Internal waves at interface between two layers of water of different densities. One is dense (the lower one), the other one is less dense (the upper one).

The internal waves cover the deep waters of seas and oceans because the deep waters have a higher density than the waters above them. Internal waves act like surface waves. They can also break,

[1914] *Oceans*, Elder and Pernetta, p. 27.
[1915] Gross, *Oceanography*, p. 205.

just like surface waves. Internal waves cannot be seen by the human eye, but they can be detected by studying temperature or salinity changes at a given location.[1916]

**Miracle of Iron**

Iron is one of the elements highlighted in the Qur'ān. In the chapter known *Al-Hadeed*, meaning Iron, we are informed:

> **"And We sent down iron, wherein is great military might and benefits for the people, and so that God may make evident those who support Him and His messengers unseen. Indeed, God is Powerful and Exalted in Might."**
>
> Qur'ān 57:25

The word "*anzalna*," translated as "sent down" and used for iron in the verse, could be thought of having a metaphorical meaning to explain that iron has been given to benefit people. But, when we take into consideration the literal meaning of the word, which is, being physically sent down from the sky, as this word usage had not been employed in the Qur'ān except literally, like the descending of the rain or revelation, we realize that this verse implies a very significant scientific miracle. Because, modern astronomical findings have disclosed that the iron found in our world has come from giant stars in outer space.[1917]

Not only the iron on earth, but also the iron in the entire Solar System, comes from outer space, since the temperature in the Sun is inadequate for the formation of iron. The sun has a surface temperature of 6,000 degrees Celsius, and a core temperature of approximately 20 million degrees. Iron can only be produced in much larger stars than the Sun, where the temperature reaches a few hundred million degrees. When the amount of iron exceeds a certain level in a star, the star can no longer accommodate it, and it eventually explodes in what is called a "nova" or a "supernova." These explosions make it possible for iron to be given off into space.

One scientific source provides the following information on this subject: *"There is also evidence for older supernova events: Enhanced levels of iron-60 in deep-sea sediments have been interpreted as indications that a supernova explosion occurred within 90 light-years of the sun about 5 million years ago. 60 is a radioactive isotope of iron, formed in supernova explosions, which decays with a half life of 1.5 million years. An enhanced presence of this isotope in a geologic layer indicates the recent nucleosynthesis of elements nearby in space and their subsequent transport to the earth (perhaps as part of dust grains).*"[1918]

All this shows that iron did not form on the Earth, but was carried from Supernovas, and was "sent down," as stated in the verse. It is clear that this fact could not have been known in the 7th century, when the Qur'ān was revealed. Nevertheless, this fact is related in the Qur'ān, the Word of God, Who encompasses all things in His infinite knowledge. The fact that the verse specifically mentions iron is quite astounding, considering that these discoveries were made at the end of the 20th century. In his book Nature's Destiny, the well-known microbiologist Michael Denton emphasizes the importance of iron:

1916 *Oceanography*, Gross, p. 205.

1917 Kazi, Dr. Mazhar U. *130 Evident Miracles in the Qur'ān*, p. 110-111;

1918 Frisch, Priscilla, *The Galactic Environment of the Sun*, American Scientist, January-February 2000.

*"Of all the metals there is none more essential to life than iron. It is the accumulation of iron in the center of a star which triggers a supernova explosion and the subsequent scattering of the vital atoms of life throughout the cosmos. It was the drawing by gravity of iron atoms to the center of the primeval earth that generated the heat which caused the initial chemical differentiation of the earth, the out-gassing of the early atmosphere, and ultimately the formation of the hydrosphere. It is molten iron in the center of the earth which, acting like a gigantic dynamo, generates the earth's magnetic field, which in turn creates the Van Allen radiation belts that shield the earth's surface from destructive high-energy-penetrating cosmic radiation and preserve the crucial ozone layer from cosmic ray destruction…Without the iron atom, there would be no carbon-based life in the cosmos; no supernova, no heating of the primitive earth, no atmosphere or hydrosphere. There would be no protective magnetic field, no Van Allen radiation belts, no ozone layer, no metal to make hemoglobin [in human blood], no metal to tame the reactivity of oxygen, and no oxidative metabolism…The intriguing and intimate relationship between life and iron, between the red color of blood and the dying of some distant star, not only indicates the relevance of metals to biology but also the bio-centricity of the cosmos…"*[1919]

This account clearly indicates the importance of the iron atom. The fact that particular attention is drawn to iron in the Qur'ān also emphasizes the importance of the element.

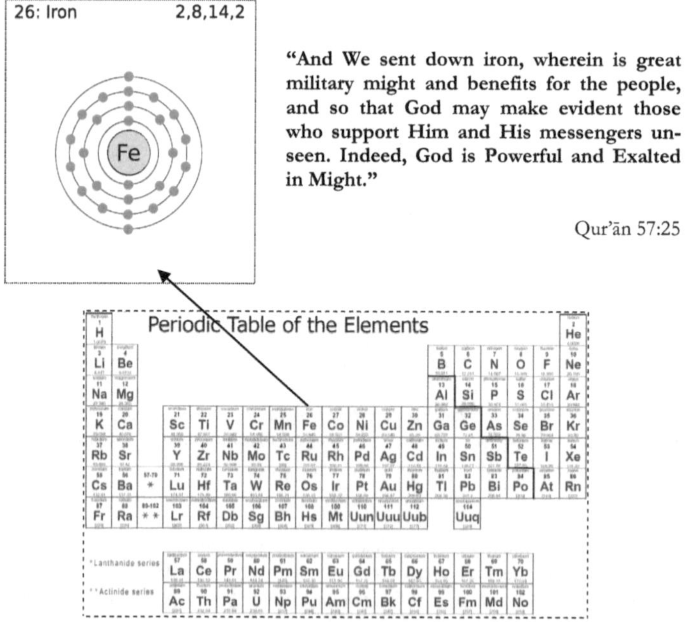


**"And We sent down iron, wherein is great military might and benefits for the people, and so that God may make evident those who support Him and His messengers unseen. Indeed, God is Powerful and Exalted in Might."**

Qur'ān 57:25

Zaghloul El-Naggar, professor of earth science and geology, has an interesting theory. He concludes that the Qur'ānic account of the celestial origin of iron is coupled by another miraculous aspect which is represented by the fact that the number of both the Qur'ānic chapter on iron and

1919 Denton, Michael J., *Nature's Destiny*, p.198.

of the verse that mentions this element in the same chapter precisely correspond to both the atomic weight (55.847 or roughly 56) and the atomic number (26) of iron, respectively.

Indeed the number of Surah al-Hadeed (the Qur'ānic Chapter on Iron) is "57" and the number of the verse is "25," but the Qur'ān in its text separates its introduction (Surat Al-Fātihah or the Opening) from the rest of the Book, and considers the "Basmalah" (In the Name of God, the Most Compassionate, the Most Merciful) as a Qur'ānic verse at the beginning of this Sūrah (Al-Fātihah) and of every other Qur'ānic Sūrah where it is mentioned.

Taking this Qur'ānic direction into consideration, the number of Surah al-Hadeed becomes "56" which is the closest figure to the atomic weight of the most abundant iron isotope (55.847), and the number of the verse becomes "26" which is the **exact atomic number** of iron. The existence of an iron isotope with the atomic weight of 57 also fits very well with the current numbering of the chapter on iron in the Glorious Qur'ān. [God knows better]

## The Qur'ān on Mountains

The book entitled 'Earth' is a basic reference textbook in many universities around the world. One of its two authors is Professor Emeritus Frank Press. He was the Science Advisor to former US President Jimmy Carter, and for 12 years was the President of the National Academy of Sciences, Washington, DC. His book says that mountains have underlying roots.[1920] These roots are deeply embedded in the ground, thus, mountains have a shape like a peg (see figures 1, 2 and 3).

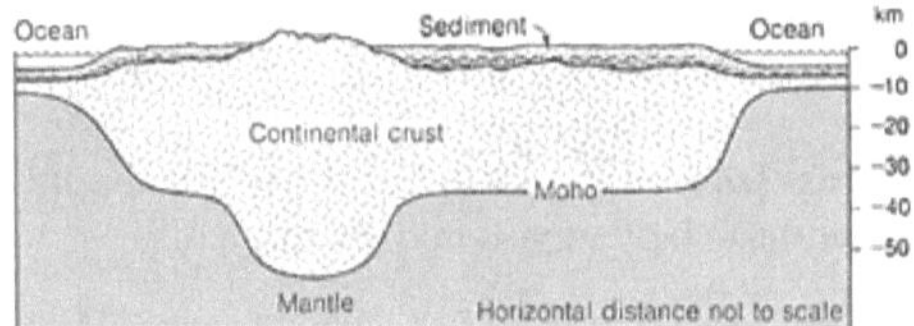


Figure 1: Mountains have deep roots under the surface of the ground.[1921]

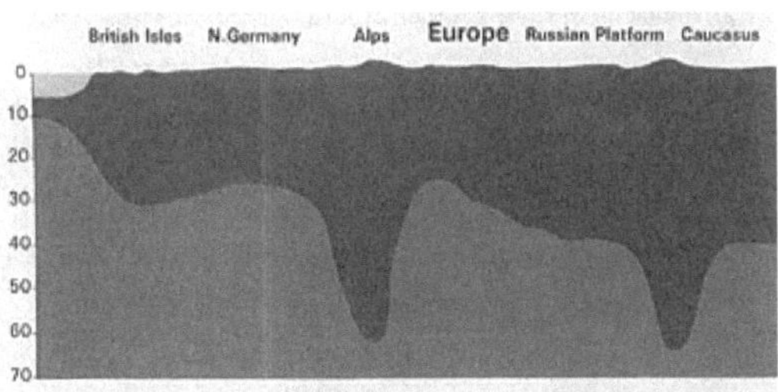


Figure 2: Schematic section. The mountains, like pegs, have deep roots embedded in the ground.[1922]

[1920] Press, E.F., *Earth*, p. 435.

[1921] Ibid, p. 413.

[1922] Cailleux, *Anatomy of the Earth*, p. 220.

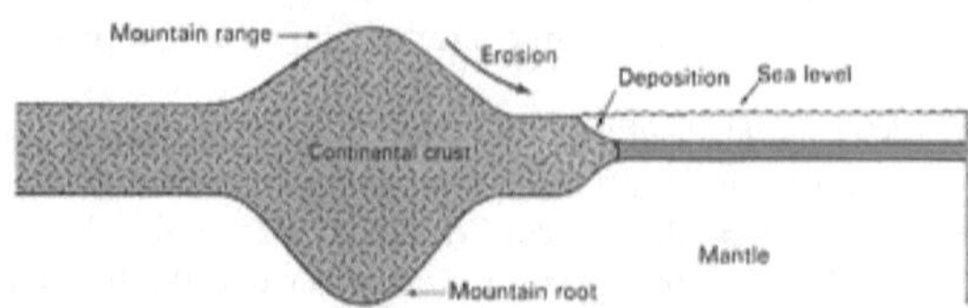


**Figure 3:** Another illustration shows how the mountains are peg-like in shape, due to their deep roots.[1923]

This is how the Qur'ān has described mountains. God has said in the Qur'ān:

**"Have We not made the earth a resting place? And the mountains as stakes (pegs)?"**
Qur'ān 78: 6-7

Modern earth sciences have proven that mountains have deep roots under the surface of the ground (see figure 3) and that these roots can reach several times their elevations above the surface of the ground.[1924] So the most suitable word to describe mountains on the basis of this information is the word 'peg,' since most of a properly set peg is hidden under the surface of the ground. The history of science tells us that the theory of mountains having deep roots was introduced only in the latter half of the nineteenth century.[1925]

Mountains also play an important role in stabilizing the crust of the earth.[1926] They hinder the shaking of the earth. God has said in the Qur'ān:

"**And He has cast [*fi*] into the earth firmly set mountains, lest it shift with you, and [made] rivers and roads, that you may be guided."**
Qur'ān 16: 15

Likewise, the modern theory of plate tectonics holds that mountains work as stabilizers for the earth. This knowledge about the role of mountains as stabilizers for the earth has just begun to be understood in the framework of plate tectonics since the late 1960's.[1927]

Could anyone during the time of the Prophet Muhammad have known of the true shape of mountains? Could anyone imagine that the solid massive mountain which he sees before him actually extends deep into the earth and has a root, as scientists assert? A large number of books of geology, when discussing mountains, only describe that part which is above the surface of the earth. This is because these books were not written by specialists in geology. However, modern geology has confirmed the truth of the Qur'ānic verses.

---

[1923] Tarbuck and Lutgens, Earth Science, p. 158.
[1924] Naggar, El-, *The Geological Concept of Mountains in the Qur'ān*, p. 5.
[1925] Ibid, p.5.
[1926] Ibid p.44 -45.
[1927] Ibid p.5.

### The Qur'ān on Human Embryonic Development

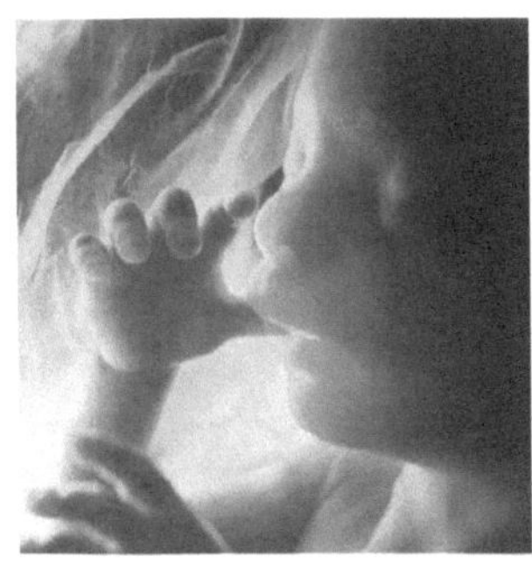

In the Holy Qur'ān, God speaks about the stages of man's embryonic development:

**"And certainly did We create man from an extract of clay. Then We placed him as a sperm-drop [*nutfah*] in a firm lodging [i.e., womb]. Then We made the sperm-drop into a clinging clot [*alaqah*], and We made the clot [*alaqah*] into a lump [of flesh], and We made [from] the lump, bones, and We covered the bones with flesh; then We developed him into another creation. So blessed is God, the best of creators."**

Qur'ān 23:12-14

### Nutfah and Manii

The *Nutfah* literally means 'a [single] drop' of fluid whereas *Manii* means 'semen.'

In the Qur'ān and Hadith, Nutfah is used in three different but interwoven connotations:

1. The Male Nutfah
2. The Female Nutfah
3. Nutfah Amshaj – mixed or mingled Male and Female Nutfah

In the male context, the Nutfah is a **single particle** from the Manii when it is ejaculated – i.e. a single cell [sperm] from amongst the 200-300 million sperm cells. The word Nutfah was mentioned twelve different times in the Qur'ān and the word Manii was mentioned thrice.

### The Male Nutfah

> **"Does man think that he will be left neglected? Had he not been a sperm [nutfah] from semen [manii] emitted? Then he was a clinging clot [alaqah], and [God] created [his form] and proportioned [him]. And made of him two mates, the male and the female. Is not that [Creator] Able to give life to the dead?"**
>
> Qur'ān 75:36-40

> **"And that He creates the two mates - the male and female - From a sperm-drop [nutfah] when it is emitted."**
>
> Qur'ān 53:45-46

In these ayats, there are a lot of facts that require careful consideration. We know the sex of the new born is determined by the male - it is definitively stated that the male and female are fashioned from a sperm-drop from the semen that has been ejaculated. We know that the sex of the new born is determined by the sperm which will fertilize the ovum. If the sperm carrying an X chromosome fertilizes an ovum [which always contains an X chromosome], the offspring will be a girl, while if the fertilizing sperm contains a Y chromosome, the offspring will be a boy.

The Qur'ān has stated this fact 1400 years ago, before anybody knew anything about X and Y chromosomes.

**The Female Nutfah**

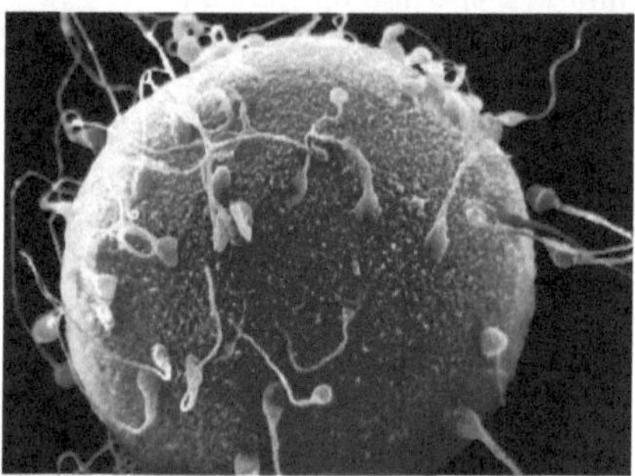

The Female Nutfah [ovum] per se is not mentioned explicitly in the Qur'ān but is inferred in the term Nutfah Amshaj – i.e. mingled from both male and female. However, it is clearly stated in the hadith from the Prophet.

A Jew came to the Prophet and asked, 'O Muhammad. Tell me from what thing man is created.' The Prophet said, 'O Jew. From both Male and Female Nutfah man is created.' [Musnad Ahmad]

This is a very astonishing revelation, as it is only recently that we came to know that both male and female cells [sperm and ovum] join together to form the human zygote – a fact not known before the 19th century.

**The Role of Genes**

> **'From what substance did He create him? From a sperm-drop [*nutfah*] He created him and destined [*qadr*] for him.'**
>
> Qur'ān 80:18-19

In a single Male Nutfah [sperm cell], which measures 60 microns [1 micron = 1/1000 mm], there are 23 Chromosomes – long spiral double strand helix. They contain the genes which determine every type of characteristics the body has like hair colour, skin type, etc.

Hence, it is within this Nutfah that God has determined and destined all the physical characterisitics that an individual has. It is amazing that the description of these realities are so accurately stated by God in the Qur'ān.

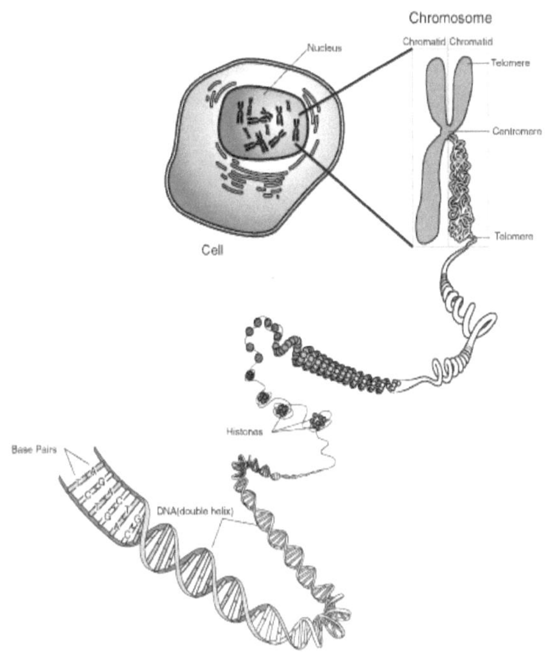


The Prophet said, 'God has ordained an angel that accompanies the different stages of develepment of the Nutfah. The Alaqa, the Mudgha and in every stage he asks God, 'O God, what to do next?' If God determines its full development, the angel asks, 'Is it a boy or a girl? Happy or unhappy, his livelihood and his life span. All is written [determined] while he is in mother's womb.' [Bukhari]

### Alaqah

> **"And certainly did We create man from an extract of clay. Then We placed him as a sperm-drop [nutfah] in a firm lodging [womb]. Then We made the sperm-drop [nutfah] into a clinging clot [alaqah], and We made the clot [alaqah] into a lump [of flesh - mudghah], and We made [from] the lump [mudghah], bones, and We covered the bones with flesh; then We developed him into another creation. So blessed is God, the best of creators."**
>
> Qur'ān 23:12-14

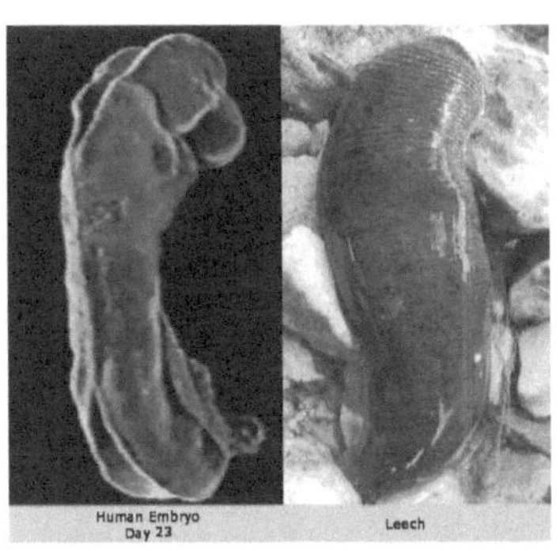


Literally, the Arabic word *alaqah* has three meanings: (1) leech, (2) suspended thing, and (3) blood clot.

In comparing a leech to an embryo in the *alaqah* stage, we find similarity between the two as we can see in figure 1. Also, the embryo at this stage obtains nourishment from the blood of the mother, similar to the leech, which feeds on the blood of others.

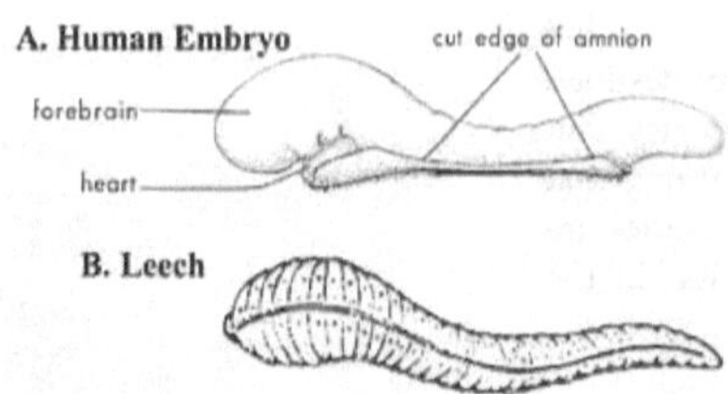


**Figure 1:** Drawings illustrating the similarities in appearance between a leech and a human embryo at the *alaqah* stage.[1928]

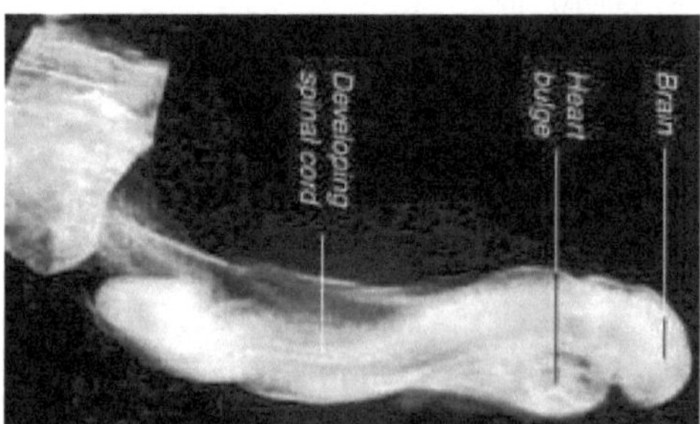


X-ray of *alaqah* on day 23

The second meaning of the word *alaqah* is "suspended thing." This is what we can see above the suspension of the embryo, during the *alaqah* stage, in the womb of the mother.

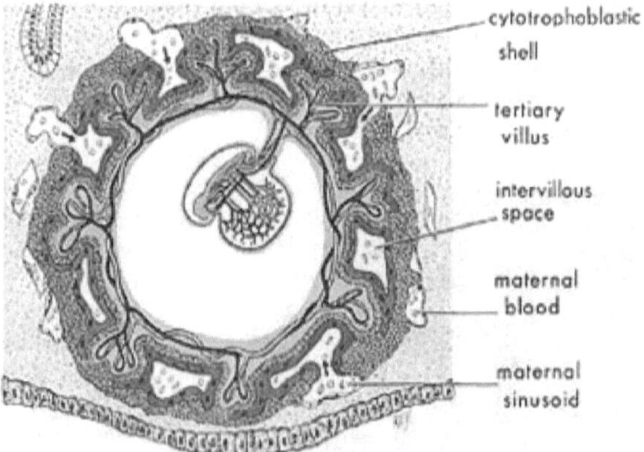


**Figure 2:** We can see in this diagram the suspension of an embryo during the *alaqah* stage in the womb (uterus) of the mother.[1929]

1928 Leech drawing taken from Moore, K., *Human Development as Described in the Qur'ān and Sunnah*, p. 37 and p.73, Hickman, *Integrated Principles of Zoology*.

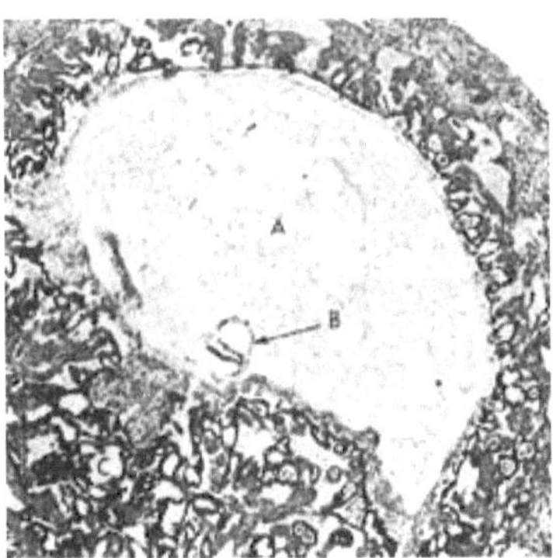


Figure 3: In this photomicrograph, we can see the suspension of an embryo (marked B) during the *alaqah* stage (about 15 days old) in the womb of the mother. The actual size of the embryo is about 0.6 mm.[1930]

The third meaning of the word *alaqah* is "blood clot." We find that the external appearance of the embryo and its sacs during the *alaqah* stage is similar to that of a blood clot. This is due to the presence of relatively large amounts of blood present in the embryo during this stage (see figure 4). Also during this stage, the blood in the embryo does not circulate until the end of the third week. Thus, the embryo at this stage is like a clot of blood.

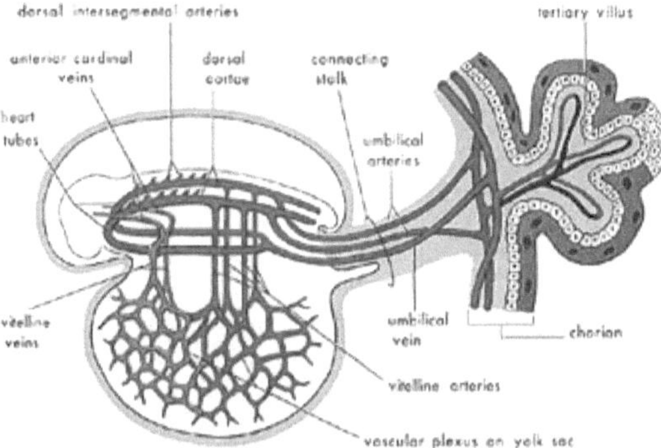


Figure 4: Diagram of the primitive cardiovascular system in an embryo during the *alaqah* stage. The external appearance of the embryo and its sacs is similar to that of a blood clot, due to the presence of relatively large amounts of blood present in the embryo.[1931]

So the three meanings of the word *alaqah* correspond accurately to the descriptions of the embryo at the *alaqah* stage.

---

1929 Moore and Persaud, *The Developing Human*, 5th ed., p. 66.
1930 Moore, *The Developing Human*, Moore, 3rd ed., p. 66, from Histology, Leeson and Leeson.
1931 Moore, *The Developing Human*, Moore, 5th ed., p. 65.

## Mudghah

The next stage mentioned in the verse is the *mudghah* stage. The Arabic word *mudghah* means "chewed substance." If one were to take a piece of gum and chew it in his or her mouth and then compare it with an embryo at the *mudghah* stage, we would conclude that the embryo at the *mudghah* stage acquires the appearance of a chewed substance. This is because of the somites at the back of the embryo that "somewhat resemble teeth-marks in a chewed substance."[1932] (see figures 5 and 6).

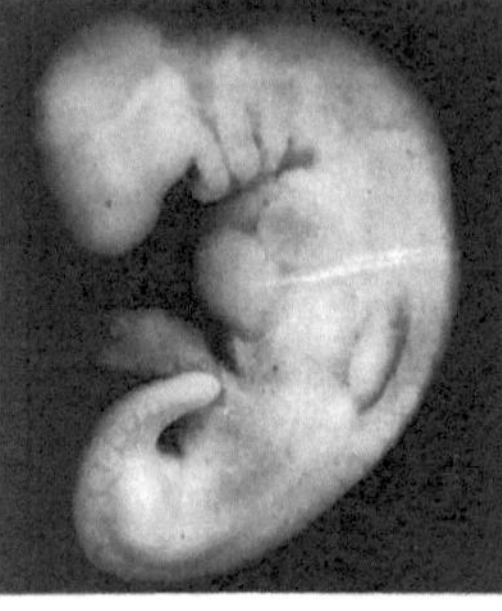

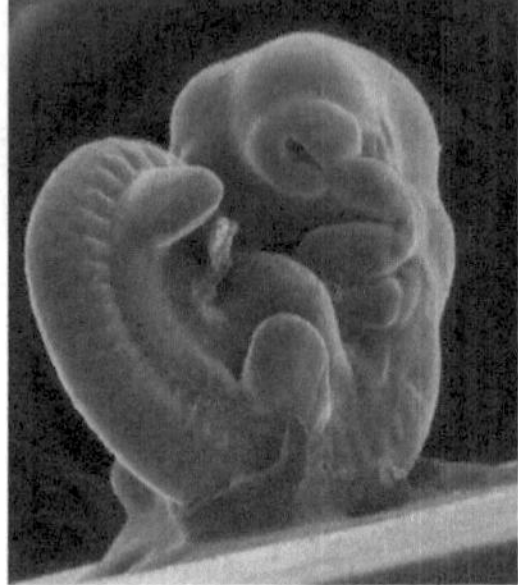

**Figure 5:** Top left photograph of an embryo at the mudghah stage (28 days old). The embryo at this stage acquires the appearance of a chewed substance, because the somites at the back of the embryo somewhat resemble teeth marks in a chewed substance. The actual size of the embryo is 4 mm.[1933]

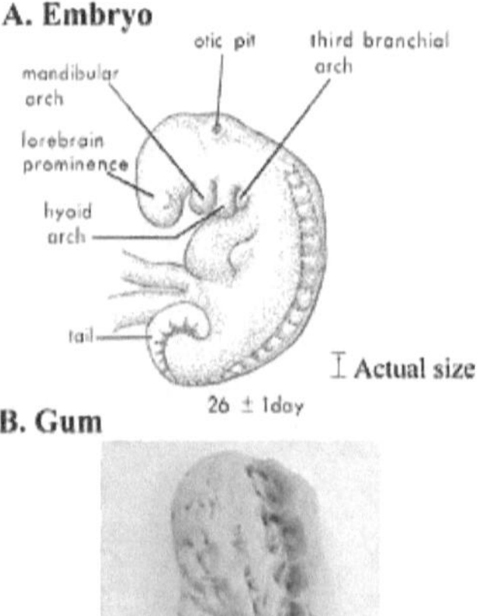


**Figure 6:** When comparing the appearance of an embryo at the mudghah stage with a piece of gum that has been chewed, we find similarity between the two.

**A.** Drawing of an embryo at the mudghah stage. We can see here the somites at the back of the embryo that look like teeth marks. ( Moore and Persaud, *The Developing Human*, 5th ed., p. 79.)

**B.** Photograph of a piece of gum that has been chewed.

---

[1932] Moore and Persaud, *The Developing Human*, 5th ed., p. 8.

[1933] Moore and Persaud, *The Developing Human*, 5th ed., p. 82 – from Professor Hideo Nishimura, Kyoto University, Japan.

How could Prophet Muhammad, may the blessing and mercy of God be upon him, have possibly known all this 1400 years ago, when scientists have only recently discovered this using advanced equipment and powerful microscopes which did not exist at that time? Hamm and Leeuwenhoek were the first scientists to observe human sperm cells (spermatozoa) using an improved microscope in 1677 (more than 1000 years after Prophet Muhammad). They mistakenly thought that the sperm cell contained a miniature preformed human being that grew when it was deposited in the female genital tract.[1934]

Professor Emeritus Keith L. Moore is one of the world's most prominent scientists in the fields of anatomy and embryology and is the author of the book entitled 'The Developing Human', which has been translated into eight languages. This book is a scientific reference work and was chosen by a special committee in the United States as the best book authored by one person. Dr. Keith Moore is Professor Emeritus of Anatomy and Cell Biology at the University of Toronto, Toronto, Canada. There, he was Associate Dean of Basic Sciences at the Faculty of Medicine and for 8 years was the Chairman of the Department of Anatomy. In 1984, he received the most distinguished award presented in the field of anatomy in Canada, the J.C.B. Grant Award from the Canadian Association of Anatomists. He has directed many international associations, such as the Canadian and American Association of Anatomists and the Council of the Union of Biological Sciences.

In 1981, during the Seventh Medical Conference in Dammam, Saudi Arabia, Professor Moore said: *"It has been a great pleasure for me to help clarify statements in the Qur'ān about human development. It is clear to me that these statements must have come to Muhammad from God, because almost all of this knowledge was not discovered until many centuries later. This proves to me that Muhammad must have been a messenger of God."*[1935]

Consequently, Professor Moore was asked the following question: "*Does this mean that you believe that the Qur'ān is the word of God?*" He replied: "*I find no difficulty in accepting this.*"[1936]

During one conference, Professor Moore stated: "*....Because the staging of human embryos is complex, owing to the continuous process of change during development, it is proposed that a new system of classification could be developed using the terms mentioned in the Qur'ān and Sunnah (what Muhammad, may the blessing and mercy of God be upon him, said, did, or approved of). The proposed system is simple, comprehensive, and conforms with present embryological knowledge. The intensive studies of the Qur'ān and hadeeth (reliably transmitted reports by the Prophet Muhammad's companions of what he said, did, or approved of) in the last four years have revealed a system for classifying human embryos that is amazing since it was recorded in the seventh century A.D. Although Aristotle, the founder of the science of embryology, realized that chick embryos developed in stages from his studies of hen's eggs in the fourth century B.C., he did not give any details about these stages. As far as it is known from the history of embryology, little was known about the staging and classification of human embryos until the twentieth century. For this reason, the descriptions of the human embryo in the Qur'ān cannot be based on scientific knowledge in the seventh century. The only reasonable conclusion is: these descriptions were revealed to Muhammad from God. He could not have known such details because he was an illiterate man with absolutely no scientific training.*"[1937]

---

1934 Moore and Persaud, *The Developing Human*, 5th ed., p. 9.

1935 Professor Moore stated this in *This is the Truth* (videotape). To view this and more extracts from him visit www.Islām-guide.com/truth.htm

1936 Ibid

1937 *This is the Truth* - www.Islām-guide.com/truth.htm

**Scientists Acceptance of the Miracles of the Qur'ān**

The following are some comments of scientists on the scientific miracles in the Holy Qur'ān. All of these comments have been taken from the videotape entitled *This is the Truth.*[1938]

**Dr. T. V. N. Persaud** is Professor of Anatomy, Professor of Pediatrics and Child Health, and Professor of Obstetrics, Gynecology, and Reproductive Sciences at the University of Manitoba, Winnipeg, Manitoba, Canada. There, he was the Chairman of the Department of Anatomy for 16 years. He is well-known in his field. He is the author or editor of 22 textbooks and has published over 181 scientific papers. In 1991, he received the most distinguished award presented in the field of anatomy in Canada, the J.C.B. Grant Award from the Canadian Association of Anatomists. When he was asked about the scientific miracles in the Qur'ān which he has researched, he stated the following:

"The way it was explained to me is that Muhammad was a very ordinary man. He could not read, didn't know [how] to write. In fact, he was an illiterate. And we're talking about twelve [actually about fourteen] hundred years ago. You have someone illiterate making profound pronouncements and statements and that are amazingly accurate about scientific nature. And I personally can't see how this could be a mere chance. There are too many accuracies and, like Dr. Moore, I have no difficulty in my mind that this is a divine inspiration or revelation which led him to these statements."

Professor Persaud has included some Qur'ānic verses and sayings of the Prophet Muhammad, may the blessing and mercy of God be upon him, in some of his books. He has also presented these verses and sayings of the Prophet Muhammad at several conferences.

**Dr. Joe Leigh Simpson** is the Chairman of the Department of Obstetrics and Gynecology, Professor of Obstetrics and Gynecology, and Professor of Molecular and Human Genetics at the Baylor College of Medicine, Houston, Texas, USA. Formerly, he was Professor of Ob-Gyn and the Chairman of the Department of Ob-Gyn at the University of Tennessee, Memphis, Tennessee, USA. He was also the President of the American Fertility Society. He has received many awards, including the Association of Professors of Obstetrics and Gynecology Public Recognition Award in 1992. Professor Simpson studied the following two sayings of the Prophet Muhammad:

*"In every one of you, all components of your creation are collected together in your mother's womb by forty days...'* [1939]
*"If forty-two nights have passed over the embryo, God sends an angel to it, who shapes it and creates its hearing, vision, skin, flesh, and bones...."* [1940]

He studied these two sayings of the Prophet Muhammad extensively, noting that the first forty days constitute a clearly distinguishable stage of embryo-genesis. He was particularly impressed by the absolute precision and accuracy of those sayings of the Prophet Muhammad. Then, during one conference, he gave the following opinion:

---

[1938] Video clips available online on www.Islāmreligion.com/articles/219/
[1939] Bukhari, Hadith no. 3208.
[1940] Muslim, Hadith no. 2645.

"So that the two *hadeeths* (the sayings of the Prophet Muhammad) that have been noted provide us with a specific timetable for the main embryological development before forty days. Again, the point has been made, I think, repeatedly by other speakers this morning: these *hadeeths* could not have been obtained on the basis of the scientific knowledge that was available [at] the time of their writing . . . . It follows, I think, that not only is there no conflict between genetics and religion but, in fact, religion can guide science by adding revelation to some of the traditional scientific approaches, that there exist statements in the Qur'ān shown centuries later to be valid, which support knowledge in the Qur'ān having been derived from God."

**Dr. E. Marshall Johnson** is Professor Emeritus of Anatomy and Developmental Biology at Thomas Jefferson University, Philadelphia, Pennsylvania, USA. There, for 22 years he was Professor of Anatomy, the Chairman of the Department of Anatomy, and the Director of the Daniel Baugh Institute. He was also the President of the Teratology Society. He has authored more than 200 publications. In 1981, during the Seventh Medical Conference in Dammam, Saudi Arabia, Professor Johnson said in the presentation of his research paper:

"Summary: The Qur'ān describes not only the development of external form, but emphasizes also the internal stages, the stages inside the embryo, of its creation and development, emphasizing major events recognized by contemporary science."

Also he said: "As a scientist, I can only deal with things which I can specifically see. I can understand embryology and developmental biology. I can understand the words that are translated to me from the Qur'ān. As I gave the example before, if I were to transpose myself into that era, knowing what I knew today and describing things, I could not describe the things which were described. I see no evidence for the fact to refute the concept that this individual, Muhammad, had to be developing this information from some place. So I see nothing here in conflict with the concept that divine intervention was involved in what he was able to write."[1941]

**Dr. William W. Hay** is a well-known marine scientist. He is Professor of Geological Sciences at the University of Colorado, Boulder, Colorado, USA. He was formerly the Dean of the Rosenstiel School of Marine and Atmospheric Science at the University of Miami, Miami, Florida, USA. After a discussion with Professor Hay about the Qur'ān's mention of recently discovered facts on seas, he said:

"I find it very interesting that this sort of information is in the ancient scriptures of the Holy Qur'ān, and I have no way of knowing where they would come from, but I think it is extremely interesting that they are there and that this work is going on to discover it, the meaning of some of the passages." And when he was asked about the source of the Qur'ān, he replied: "Well, I would think it must be the divine being."

**Dr. Gerald C. Goeringer** is Course Director and Associate Professor of Medical Embryology at the Department of Cell Biology, School of Medicine, Georgetown University, Washington, DC, USA. During the Eighth Saudi Medical Conference in Riyadh, Saudi Arabia, Professor Goeringer stated the following in the presentation of his research paper:

[1941] The Prophet Muhammad was illiterate. He could not read nor write, but he dictated the Qur'ān to his Companions and commanded some of them to write it down.

"In a relatively few *aayahs* (Qur'ānic verses) is contained a rather comprehensive description of human development from the time of commingling of the gametes through organogenesis. No such distinct and complete record of human development, such as classification, terminology, and description, existed previously. In most, if not all, instances, this description antedates by many centuries the recording of the various stages of human embryonic and fetal development recorded in the traditional scientific literature."

**Dr. Yoshihide Kozai** is Professor Emeritus at Tokyo University, Hongo, Tokyo, Japan, and was the Director of the National Astronomical Observatory, Mitaka, Tokyo, Japan. He said:

"I am very much impressed by finding true astronomical facts in [the] Qur'ān, and for us the modern astronomers have been studying very small pieces of the universe. We've concentrated our efforts for understanding of [a] very small part. Because by using telescopes, we can see only very few parts [of] the sky without thinking [about the] whole universe. So, by reading [the] Qur'ān and by answering the questions, I think I can find my future way for investigation of the universe."

**Professor Tejatat Tejasen** is the Chairman of the Department of Anatomy at Chiang Mai University, Chiang Mai, Thailand. Previously, he was the Dean of the Faculty of Medicine at the same university. During the Eighth Saudi Medical Conference in Riyadh, Saudi Arabia, Professor Tejasen stood up and said:

"During the last three years, I became interested in the Qur'ān . . . . From my study and what I have learned from this conference, I believe that everything that has been recorded in the Qur'ān fourteen hundred years ago must be the truth, that can be proved by the scientific means. Since the Prophet Muhammad could neither read nor write, Muhammad must be a messenger who relayed this truth, which was revealed to him as an enlightenment by the one who is eligible [as the] creator. This creator must be God. Therefore, I think this is the time to say *La ilaha illa Allah*, there is no diety to worship except God, *Muhammadur rasoolu Allah*, Muhammad is Messenger (Prophet) of Allah (God). Lastly, I must congratulate for the excellent and highly successful arrangement for this conference . . . . I have gained not only from the scientific point of view and religious point of view but also the great chance of meeting many well-known scientists and making many new friends among the participants. The most precious thing of all that I have gained by coming to this place is *La ilaha illa Allah, Muhammadur rasoolu Allah*, and to have become a Muslim."

After all these examples we have seen about the scientific miracles in the Holy Qur'ān and all these scientists' comments on this, let us ask ourselves these questions:

Could it be a coincidence that all this recently discovered scientific information from different fields was mentioned in the Qur'ān, which was revealed fourteen centuries ago? Could this Qur'ān have been authored by Muhammad, may the blessing and mercy of God be upon him, or by any other human being?

The only answer is that the Qur'ān is the word of God, revealed by Him.

## Miracles Performed

Apart from the greatest miracle given to him, the Qur'ān, the Prophet performed many physical miracles witnessed by his contemporaries numbering in hundreds, and in some cases thousands. The miracle reports have reached us by a reliable and strong methods of transmission unmatched in world history – the hadith. It is as if the miracles were performed in front of our eyes. These miracles were witnessed by thousands of believers and skeptics, following which portions of the Qur'ān were revealed mentioning the supernatural events.

The Qur'ān made some miracles eternal by etching them in the conscious of the believers. The ancient detractors would simply remain silent when these verses were recited. Through these events, the believers grew more certain of the truth of Prophet Muhammad and the Qur'ān.

The Prophet Muhammad, through prayer or invoking blessings from God, was seen bringing milk to the udders of dry sheep, transforming camels virtually too weary to walk into the fastest and most energetic of the bunch, transforming a stick of wood into a sword for soldier whose sword had broken [Ukashah ibn Mihsan at the Battle of Badr], and feeding and watering the masses from miniscule quantities. Scores of hungry poor were fed from a bowl of milk which appeared sufficient for only one. An entire army numbering more than a thousand were fed from a measure of flour and pot of meat so small as to be thought sufficient for only ten persons at the 'Battle of the Trench,' after which the flour and the meat seemed undiminished. So much was left over that a gift of food was made to the neighbour of the house in which the meal was prepared. Another army of 1,400, headed for the Battle of Tabuk, was fed from a few handfuls of mixed foodstuffs, over which the Prophet invoked blessings, and the increase was sufficient to fill not only the stomachs of the army, but their depleted saddlebags as well.

Evil spirits [Jinn] were exorcised, the broken leg of Abdullah ibn Ateeq and the war-wounded leg of Salama ibn Aqwa were healed on the spot [each on separate occasions], the bleeding wound of al-Harith ibn Aws cauterized and healed instantly, the poisonous sting of Abu Bakr's foot quieted, and the vision of a blind man restored. On a separate occasion, Qatadah ibn an-Nu'man was wounded, in the Battle of Badr, so severely that his eye prolapsed into his cheek. His companions wanted to cut off the remaining attachments, but the Prophet supplicated over the eye, replaced it, and from that day on Qatadah could not tell which was the injured eye and which was not.

When called to wrestle Rukanah, an unbeaten champion, the Prophet won miraculously. Merely touching Rukanah on the shoulder, he fell down, defeated. In rematch, the miracle was repeated. A third challenge brought the same result.

When asked to call for rain, he did, and rain fell. When requested to feed the people his supplications brought sustenance, from where, the people did not know. When interceding as a healer, wounds and injuries disappeared.

In short, the prayers and supplications of the Prophet brought relief and blessings to the believers. And yet, whether being stoned on Ta'if, starved at Makkah, beaten in front of the Ka'bah, or humiliated a amidst his tribe and loved ones, the Prophet's example appears to have been one of facing personal trials, of which there was an abundance, by relying upon internal patience to calling for divine intervention.[1942]

### Splitting of the Moon: A Miracle

> **"The Hour has come near, and the moon has split [in two]. And if they see a sign [i.e., miracle], they turn away and say, "Passing magic."**
>
> Qur'ān 54:1-2

During the time of the Prophet, the pagans of Makkah had asked Prophet Muhammad for a miracle. In response, the Prophet split the moon, one part remaining over the mountain and the other part disappearing behind it [the mountain]. However, the pagans said, 'Muhammad has enchanted us, but he cannot bewitch the world; so let us wait for people to come from the neighbouring parts of the land and hear what they have to say.'

### Historical Evidence

A skeptic might ask, do we have any independent historical evidence to suggest the moon was ever split? After all, people around the world should have seen this marvelous event and recorded it. The answer to this question is twofold.

First, people around the world could not have seen it as it would have been daytime, late night, or early morning many parts of the world. The following table will give the reader some idea of corresponding world times to 9:00 pm Makkah time:

| Country | Time |
|---|---|
| Makkah | 9:00 pm |
| India | 11:30 pm |
| Perth | 2:00 am |
| Reykjavik | 6:00 pm |
| Washington D.C. | 2:00 pm |
| Rio de Janeiro | 3:00 pm |
| Tokyo | 3:00 am |
| Beijing | 2:00 am |

[1942] Edited from, *The First and Final Commandment*, Dr. Laurence B. Brown.

Also, it is not likely that a large number of people in lands close by would be observing the moon at the exact same time. They had no reason to. Even if some one did, it does not necessarily mean people believed him and kept a written record of it, especially when many civilizations at that time did not preserve their own history in writing.

Second, we actually have an independent, and quite amazing, historical corroboration of the event from an Indian king of that time.

Kerala is a state of India. The state stretches for 360 miles along the Malabar Coast on the southwestern side of the Indian peninsula. King Chakrawati Farmas of Malabar was a Chera king, Cheraman perumal of Kodungallure. He is recorded to have seen the moon split. The incident is documented in a manuscript kept at the India Office Library, London, reference number: Arabic, 2807, 152-173.

A group of Muslim merchant's passing by Malabar on their way to China spoke to the king about how God had supported the Arabian prophet with the miracle of splitting of the moon. The shocked king said he had seen it with his own eyes as well, deputized his son, and left for Arabia to meet the Prophet in person.

The Malabari king met the Prophet, and bore the two testimonies of faith, learned the basics of faith, but passed away on his way back and was buried in the port city of Zafar, Yemen.

It is said that the contingent, led by a Muslim, Malik bin Dinar, continued to Kodungallure, the Chera capital, and built the first, and India's oldest, mosque in the area in 629 CE which exists today. The news of his accepting Islam reached Kerala where people accepted Islam. The people of Lakshadweep and the Moplas [Mapillais] from the Calicut province of Kerala are converts from those days. The king was also considered a 'companion' – a term used for a person who met the Prophet and died as a Muslim – his name registered in the mega-compendiums chronicling the Prophet's companions. Abu Sa'id al-Khudri, a companion of Prophet Muhammad, states: "The Indian king gifted the Prophet with a jar of ginger. The companions ate it piece by piece. I took a bite as well."

A pre-renovation picture of the Cheraman Juma Masjid, India's oldest mosque dating back to 629 CE.

**Moon Split – Visible Today**

Dr. Zaghloul El-Naggar, professor of earth science and geology, recalls, '[firstly] the Indian and Chinese calendars have recorded the incident of the splitting of the moon.... While I was giving a lecture at the Faculty of Medicine at Cardiff University, in Wales, a Muslim asked me a question about the verses....about the splitting of the moon, and whether it is considered as one of the scientific signs which are mentioned in the Qur'ān and whether there is any scientific evidence discovered to explain this incident. My answer was that this incident is considered one of the most tangible miracles, which took place to support the Prophet when he was challenged by the polytheists and disbelievers of Quraish, showing them this miracle to prove that he is a Messenger of God. Anyway, miracles take place as unusual incidents that break all regular laws of nature. Therefore, conventional science is unable to explain how miracles take place, and if they were not mentioned in the Qur'ān and in the Sunnah of the Prophet we would not have been obliged to believe in them...When I finished my speech, a British man from the audience named Dawud Musa Pidcock...asked to add something to my answer.

He said: "It is these verses, at the beginning of Surah al-Qamar that made me embrace Islam in the late seventies." This occurred while he was doing extensive research in comparative religion, and one of the Muslims gave him a copy of translation of the meanings of the Qur'ān. When he opened this copy for the first time, he came across Surat al-Qamar, and he read the verses at the beginning of the surah, and could not believe that the moon had split into two distinct parts and they were rejoined, so he closed the copy of the translation and kept it aside.'

In 1978 Mr. Pidcock was destined by God's Will to watch a program on BBC, where the host was talking with three American space scientists and accusing the USA of over spending and wasting millions of dollars on space projects while millions of people were in a state of poverty here on Earth. The scientist responded, "We were studying the moon surface to examine the extent of similarities with the Earth's surface...we were astonished to find a belt of melted rocks that cuts across the surface and deep into the core of the moon. This information was promptly given to our geologists, where they were shocked by their findings and stated that this phenomenon could never happen unless the moon at one time was split and brought back together and the surface rocky belt is the resulting collision at the moment of this occurrence."

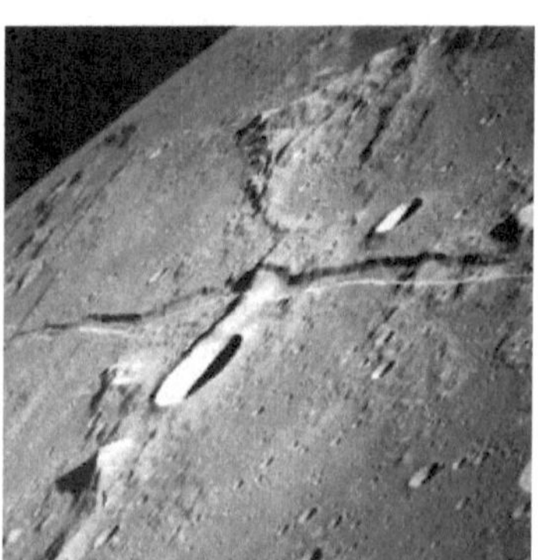

A rocky streak [gap] is clearly shown across the moon surface

Mr. Pidcock went on to say, "When I heard this, I jumped off my chair , and said this is a miracle which took place fourteen hundred years ago to support Muhammad and the Qur'ān narrates it in such a detailed way. After this long period and during the age of science and technology, God employs people (non-Muslims) who spent all this money for nothing but to prove that this miracle had actually happened. Then, I said to myself, this must be the true religion, and I went back to the translation of the meanings of the Qur'ān, reading it eagerly. It was these verses at the opening of Surah al-Qamar that lie behind my...[conversion] to Islam."

# Old and New Testament Prophecies of Muhammad

## Old Testament Prophecies

### God promises the lineage of Abraham to be named through both Ishmael and Isaac

"...through Isaac shall your descendants be named. And I will make a nation of the son of the slave woman [Ishamel] also, because he is your offspring." (Genesis 21:13-14)

### The descendants of Ishmael to be a great nation

Abraham had left Hagar and their newborn, Ishamel in Makkah (or Paran). "..when the water in the skin was gone, she cast the child under one of the bushes. Then she went, and sat down over against him a good way off, about the distance of a bowshot; for she said, "Let me not look upon the death of the child." And as she sat over against him, the child lifted up his voice and wept. And God heard the voice of the lad; and the angel of God called to Hagar from heaven, and said to her, "What troubles you, Hagar? Fear not; for God has heard the voice of the lad where he is. Arise, lift up the lad, and hold him fast with your hand; for I will make **him a great nation.**" (Genesis 21:16-19)

### Ishmael settles in Makkah (refered to as Paran)

"And God was with the lad [Ishmael], and he grew up; he lived in the wilderness, and became an expert with the bow. He lived in the wilderness of Paran;" (Genesis 21:21)

### Reference to Moses, Jesus and Muhammad (in order)

"This is the blessing with which Moses the man of God blessed the children of Israel before his death. He said, "The LORD came from **Sinai**, and dawned from **Se'ir** upon us; he shone forth from Mount **Paran**, he came from the ten thousands of holy ones....." (Deuteronomy 33:1-3)

**Sinai** - is reference to Moses. It is an obvious reference to Mount Sinai where Moses received revelation. **Se'ir** – is reference to Jesus. It is usually associated with the chain of mountains west and south of the Dead Sea extending through Jerusalem, and Bethlehem, the birthplace of Jesus. **Paran** – is reference to the location where Ishmael settled. The Prophet Muhammad was born in Paran (Makkah) and having migrated from Makkah, he returned to conquer the city with 10,000 of his companions.

### Prophet just like Moses

Deuteronomy 18:18 "I (God) will raise them up a Prophet from among their brethren, like unto thee (Moses), and will put my words in his mouth; and he shall speak unto them all that I shall command him."

Many Christians believe this prophecy foretold by Moses to be in regards to Jesus. Indeed Jesus was foretold in the Old Testament, but as will be clear, this prophecy does not fit him, but rather is more deserving of Muhammad, may the blessing and mercy of God be upon him. Moses foretold the following:

1. The Prophet Will Be Like Moses

| **Areas of Comparison** | **Moses** | **Jesus** | **Muhammad** |
|---|---|---|---|
| Birth | normal birth | miraculous, virgin birth | normal birth |
| Mission | prophet only | said to be Son of God | prophet only |
| Parents | father & mother | mother only | father & mother |
| Family Life | married with children | never married | married with children |
| Acceptance by own people | Jews accepted him | Jews rejected him[1943] | Arabs accepted him |
| Political Authority | Moses had it (Num 15:36) | Jesus refused it[1944] | Muhammad had it |
| Victory Over Opponents | Pharaoh drowned | said to be crucified | Makkans defeated |
| Death | natural death | claimed to be crucified | natural death |
| Burial | buried in grave | Empty tomb | buried in grave |
| Divinity | not divine | divine to Christians | not divine |
| Began Mission at age | 40 | 30 | 40 |
| Resurrection on Earth | not resurrected | resurrection claimed | not resurrected |

2. The Awaited Prophet will be from the *Brethren* of the Jews

The verse in discussion is explicit in saying that the prophet will come amongst the Brethren of the Jews. Abraham had two sons: Ishmael and Isaac. The Jews are the descendants of Isaac's son, Jacob. The Arabs are the children of Ishmael. Thus, the Arabs are the brethren of the Jewish nation. The Bible affirms:

'And he (Ishmael) shall dwell in the presence of all his brethren.' (Genesis 16:12)

'And he (Ishmael) died in the presence of all his brethren.' (Genesis 25:18)

The children of Isaac are the brethren of the Ishmaelites. Likewise, Muhammad is from among the brethren of the Israelites, because he was a descendant of Ishmael the son of Abraham.

**3. God will Put His Words in the Mouth of the Awaited Prophet**

The Qur'ān says of Prophet Muhammad:

**"Nor does he speak from [his own] inclination. It is not but a revelation revealed."**

Qur'ān 53:3-4

[1943] "He (Jesus) came unto his own, but his own received him not" (John 1:11)
[1944] John 18:36.

This is quite similar to the verse in Geneses 18:15:

"I will raise them up a Prophet from among their brethren, like unto thee, *and will put my words in his mouth*; and he shall speak unto them all that I shall command him" (Geneses 18:18)

The Prophet Muhammad came with a message to the whole world, and from them, the Jews. All, including the Jews, must accept his prophethood, and this is supported by the following words:

"The Lord thy God will raise up unto thee a Prophet from the midst of thee, of thy brethren, like unto me; unto him ye shall hearken." (Deuteronomy 18:15)

**4. A Warning to Rejecters**

The prophecy continues:

Deuteronomy 18:19 "And it shall come to pass, [that] whosoever will not hearken unto my words which he shall speak in my name, I will require [it] of him." (in some translations: "I will be the Revenger").

Interestingly, Muslims begin every chapter of the Qur'ān in the name of God by saying:

*Bismillah ir-Rahman ir-Raheem* - ""In the Name of God, the Most Gracious Most Merciful."

Abdul-Ahad Dawud, the former Rev. David Benjamin Keldani, BD, a Roman Catholic priest of the Uniate-Chaldean sect. After accepting Islām, he wrote the book, 'Muhammad in the Bible.' He writes about this prophecy:

"If these words do not apply to Muhammad, they still remain unfulfilled. Jesus himself never claimed to be the prophet alluded to. Even his disciples were of the same opinion: they looked to the second coming of Jesus for the fulfillment of the prophecy (Acts 3: 17-24). So far it is undisputed that the first coming of Jesus was not the advent of the Prophet like unto thee and his second advent can hardly fulfill the words. Jesus, as is believed by his Church, will appear as a Judge and not as a law-giver; but the promised one has to come with a "fiery law" in his right hand."

**New Testament Prophecy**

John 14:16 "And I will pray the Father, and he shall give you another Comforter, that he may abide with you for ever."

In this verse, Jesus promises that another "Comforter" will appear, and thus, we must discuss some issues concerning this "Comforter."

The Greek word paravklhtoß, *ho parakletos*, has been translated as 'Comforter.' *Parakletos* more precisely means 'one who pleads another's cause, an intercessor.'[1945] The *ho parakletos* is a person in the Greek language, not an incorporeal entity. In the Greek language, every noun possesses gender; that is, it is masculine, feminine or neutral. In the Gospel of John, Chapters 14, 15 and 16 the *ho parakletos* is actually a person. All pronouns in Greek must agree in gender with the word to which they refer and the pronoun "he" is used when referring to the *parakletos.* The NT uses the word *pneuma*, which means "breath" or "spirit," the Greek equivalent of *ruah*, the Hebrew word for "spirit" used in the Old Testament. *Pneuma* is a grammatically neutral word and is always represented by the pronoun "it."

All present day Bibles are compiled from "ancient manuscripts," the oldest dating back to the fourth century C.E. No two ancient manuscripts are identical.[1946] All Bibles today are produced by combining manuscripts with no single definitive reference. The Bible translators attempt to "choose" the correct version. In other words, since they do not know which "ancient manuscript" is the correct one, they decide for us which "version" for a given verse to accept. Take John 14:26 as an example. John 14:26 is the only verse of the Bible which associates the *Parakletos* with the Holy Spirit. But the "ancient manuscripts" are not in agreement that the "*Parakletos*" is the 'Holy Spirit.' For instance, the famous Codex Syriacus, written around the fifth century C.E., and discovered in 1812 on Mount Sinai, the text of 14:26 reads; "Paraclete, the Spirit"; and not "Paraclete, the *Holy Spirit.*"

Muslim scholars state that what Jesus actually said in Aramaic represents more closely the Greek word *periklytos* which means the 'admired one.' In Arabic the word 'Muhammad' means the 'praiseworthy, admired one.' In other words, *periklytos* is "Muhammad" in Greek. We have two strong reasons in its support. First, due to several documented cases of similar word substitution in the Bible, it is quite possible that both words were contained in the original text but were dropped by a copyist because of the ancient custom of writing words closely packed, with no spaces in between. In such a case the original reading would have been, "and He will give you another comforter (*parakletos*), the admirable one (*periklytos*)." Second, we have the reliable testimony of at least four Muslim authorities from different eras who ascribed 'admired, praised one' as a possible meaning of the Greek or Syriac word to Christians scholars.

The following are some who attest that the Paraclete is indeed an allusion to Prophet Muhammad,

**The First Witness**

Anselm Turmeda (1352/55-1425 CE), a priest and Christian scholar, was a witness to the prophecy. After accepting Islām he wrote the book, *"Tuhfat al-arib fi al-radd 'ala Ahl al-Salib."*

[1945] Vine's Expository Dictionary of New Testament Words.

[1946] "Besides the larger discrepancies, such as these, there is scarcely a verse in which there is not some variation of phrase in some copies [of the ancient manuscripts from which the Bible has been collected]. No one can say that these additions or omissions or alterations are matters of mere indifference." 'Our Bible and the Ancient Manuscripts,' by Dr. Frederic Kenyon, Eyre and Spottiswoode, p. 3.

### The Second Witness

Abdul-Ahad Dawud, the former Rev. David Abdu Benjamin Keldani, BD, a Roman Catholic priest of the Uniate-Chaldean sect.. After accepting Islām, he wrote the book, 'Muhammad in the Bible.' He writes in this book: "There is not the slightest doubt that by "Periqlyte," Prophet Muhammad, i.e. Ahmad, is intended."

### The Third Witness

Commenting on the verse where Jesus predicts the coming of Prophet Muhammad:

**"...a messenger who shall come after me, whose name shall be Ahmad..."**
Qur'ān 61:6

... Asad explains that the word Parakletos:

"...[it] is almost certainly a corruption of Periklytos ('the Much-Praised'), an exact Greek translation of the Aramaic term or name Mawhamana. (It is to be borne in mind that Aramaic was the language used in Palestine at the time of, and for some centuries after Jesus and was thus undoubtedly the language in which the original - now lost - texts of the Gospels were composed.) In view of the phonetic closeness of Periklytos and Parakletos it is easy to understand how the translator - or, more probably, a later scribe - confused these two expressions. It is significant that both the Aramaic Mawhamana and the Greek Periklytos have the same meaning as the two names of the Last Prophet, Muhammad and Ahmad, both of which are derived from the Hebrew verb hamida ('he praised') and the Hebrew noun hamd ('praise')."

### Holy spirit or Prophet -

Why is it important? It is significant because in biblical language a "spirit," simply means "a prophet."

"Beloved, believe not every spirit, but try the spirits whether they are of God: because many false prophets are gone out into the world."[1947]

It is instructive to know that several biblical scholars considered *parakletos* to be an 'independent salvific (having the power to save) figure,' not the Holy Ghost.[1948]

Let us further study whether Jesus' *parakletos*, Comforter, was a 'Holy Ghost' or a person (a prophet) to come after him? When we continue reading beyond chapter 14:16 and chapter 16:7, we find that Jesus predicts the specific details of the arrival and identity of the *parakletos*. Therefore, according to the context of John 14 & 16 we discover the following facts.

[1947] 1 John 4: 1-3

[1948] '...Christian tradition has identified this figure (Paraclete) as the Holy Spirit, but scholars like Spitta, Delafosse, Windisch, Sasse, Bultmann, and Betz have doubted whether this identification is true to the original picture and have suggested that the Paraclete was once an independent salvific figure, later confused with the Holy Spirit." 'the Anchor Bible, Doubleday & Company, Inc, Garden City, N.Y. 1970, Volume 29A, p. 1135.

**1. Jesus said the parakletos is a human being:**

John 16:13 "He will speak."

John 16:7 "…for if I go not away, the Comforter will not come unto you."

It is impossible that the Comforter be the "Holy Ghost" because the Holy Ghost was present long before Jesus and during his ministry.[1949]

John 16:13 Jesus referred to the paraclete as 'he' and not 'it' seven times, no other verse in the Bible contains seven masculine pronouns. Therefore, *paraclete* is a person, not a ghost.

**2. Jesus is called a parakletos:**

"And if any man sin, we have an advocate (parakletos) with the Father, Jesus Christ the righteous." (1 John 2:1)

Here we see that parakletos is a physical and human intercessor.

**3. The Divinity of Jesus a later innovation**

Jesus was not accepted as divine until the Council of Nicea, 325 CE, but everyone, except Jews, agree he was a prophet of God, as indicated by the Bible:

Matthew 21:11 "...This is Jesus the prophet of Nazareth of Galilee."

Luke 24:19 "...Jesus of Nazareth, which was a prophet mighty in deed and word before God and all the people."

**4. Jesus prayed to God for another parakletos:**

John 14:16 "And I will pray the Father, and he shall give you another parakletos."

**5. Jesus describes the function of the other Parakletos:**

John 16:13 "He will guide you into all the truth."

God says in the Qur'ān:

> **"O mankind! The Messenger has now come unto you with the truth from your Lord, so believe; it is better for you…"**
>
> Qur'ān 4:170

[1949] Genesis 1: 2, 1 Samuel 10: 10, 1 Samuel 11: 6, Isaiah 63: 11, Luke 1: 15, Luke 1: 35, Luke 1: 41, Luke 1: 67, Luke 2: 25, Luke 2: 26, Luke 3:22, John 20: 21-22.

**John 16:14 "He will glorify Me."**

The Qur'ān brought by Muhammad glorifies Jesus:

> **"[And mention] when the angels said, "O Mary, indeed God gives you good tidings of a word from Him, whose name will be the Messiah, Jesus, the son of Mary – distinguished in this world and the Hereafter and among those brought near [to God]."**

Qur'ān 3:45

The Prophet Muhammad also glorified Jesus, He said "*Whoever testifies that none deserves worship except God, who has no partner, and that Muhammad is His servant and Messenger, and that Jesus is the servant of God, His Messenger, and His Word which He bestowed in Mary, and a spirit created from Him, and that Paradise is true, and that Hell is true, God will admit him into Paradise, according to his deeds.*"[1950]

John 16:8 "he will convince the world of its sin, and of God's righteousness, and of the coming judgment."

The Qur'ān announces:

> **"They have certainly disbelieved who say, "God is the Messiah, the son of Mary" while the Messiah has said, "O Children of Israel, worship God, my Lord and your Lord." Indeed, he who associates others with God - God has forbidden him Paradise, and his refuge is the Fire. And there are not for the wrongdoers any helpers."**

Qur'ān 5:72

John 16:13 "he shall not speak of himself; but whatsoever he shall hear, [that] shall he speak."

The Qur'ān says of Prophet Muhammad:

> "**Nor does he speak from [his own] inclination. It is not but a revelation revealed."**

Qur'ān 53:3-4

John 14:26 "and bring all things to your remembrance, whatsoever I have said unto you."
The words of the Qur'ān:

> **"...while the Messiah has said, 'O Children of Israel, worship God, my Lord and your Lord.'"**

Qur'ān 5:72

...reminds people of the first and greatest command of Jesus they have forgotten: "The first of all the commandments is, 'Hear, O Israel; the Lord our God is one Lord.'" (Mark 12:29)

---

[1950] Bukhari and Muslim.

John 16:13 "…and He will disclose to you what is to come."

The Qur'ān states:

**"That is from the news of the unseen which We reveal, [O Muhammad], to you…"**

Qur'ān 12:102

Hudhaifa, a companion of Prophet Muhammad, tells us: *"The Prophet once delivered a speech in front of us wherein he left nothing but mentioned everything that would happen till the Hour (of Judgment).*"[1951]

John 14:16 "that he may abide with you for ever."

…meaning his original teachings will remain forever. Muhammad was God's last prophet to humanity. His teachings are perfectly preserved. He lives in the hearts and minds of his adoring followers who worship God in his exact imitation. No man, including Jesus or Muhammad, has an eternal life on earth. *Parakletos* is not an exception either. This cannot be an allusion to the Holy Ghost, for present day creed of the Holy Ghost did not exist until the Council of Chalcedon, in 451 CE, four and half centuries after Jesus.

John 14:17 "he will be the spirit of truth" **…meaning he will a true prophet, see 1 John 4: 1-3.**

John 14:17 "the world neither sees him..."

Many people in the world today do not know Muhammad.

John 14:17 "...nor knows him"

Fewer people recognize the real Muhammad, God's Prophet of Mercy.

John 14:26 "the Advocate (parakletos)"

Prophet Muhammad will be the advocate of humanity at large and of sinful believers on Judgment Day. People will look for those who can intercede on their behalf to God to reduce the distress and suffering on Day of Judgment. Adam, Noah, Abraham, Moses, and Jesus will excuse themselves. Then they will come to the Prophet Muhammad and he will say, "I am the one who is able." So he will intercede for the people in the Great Plain of Gathering, so judgment may be passed. This is the 'Station of Praise' God promises Him in the Qur'ān:

> **"…It may be that your Lord will raise you to Station of Praise (the honour of intercession on the Day of Resurrection)"**

Qur'ān 17:79

The Prophet Muhammad said: *'My intercession will be for those of my nation who committed major sins."* [1952] *and 'I shall be the first intercessor in Paradise."* [1953]

[1951] Bukhari.

[1952] Tirmidhi.

## Gospel of Barnabas

> **"And [mention] when Jesus, the son of Mary, said, "O children of Israel, indeed I am the messenger of God to you confirming what came before me of the Torah and bringing good tidings of a messenger to come after me, whose name is Ahmad [another name of the Prophet Muhmmad]. But when he came to them with clear evidences, they said, "This is obvious magic."**

Qur'ān 61:6

The Gospel of Barnabas is attributed to Barnabas, one of the twelve disciples of Jesus. The complete authenticity of this Gospel has not been established, but it is nevertheless startling, that there are many references explicitly naming the Prophet Muhammad in it. In chapter 163 of the Gospel we read;

"Jesus went into the wilderness beyond Jordan with his disciples, and when the midday prayer was done he sat down near to a palm-tree, and under the shadow of the palm-tree his disciples sat down. Then Jesus said: 'So secret is predestination, O brethren, that I say to you, truly, only to one man shall it be clearly known. He it is whom the nations look for, to whom the secrets of God are so clear that, when he comes into the world, blessed shall they be that shall listen to his words, because God shall overshadow them with his mercy even as this palm-tree overshadows us. Yes, even as this tree protects us from the burning heat of the sun, even so the mercy of God will protect from Satan them that believe in that man.' The disciples answered, "O Master, who shall that man be of whom you speak, who shall come into the world?" Jesus answered with joy of heart: 'He is **Muhammad; Messenger of God**, and when he comes into the world, even as the rain makes the earth to bear fruit when for a long time it has not rained, even so shall he be occasion of good works among men, through the abundant mercy which he shall bring. For he is a white cloud full of the mercy of God, which mercy God shall sprinkle upon the faithful like rain."

A complete translation of the Gospel of Barnabas is available online: www.quranproject.org

### Recommended Reading:

- 'What did Jesus Really Say?' by Misha'al ibn Abdullah
- 'Izhar ul-Haq' [Truth Revealed] by Rahmatullah Kairanvi
- 'The Choice' by Ahmed Deedat
- 'The First and Final Commandment – A Search for Truth in Revelation within Abrahamic Religions' by Dr. Laurence B. Brown
- 'Muhammad in World Scriptures – The Parsi, Hindu and Bhuddist Scriptures' by Abdul Haq Vidyarthi
- 'Muhammad in the Bible' by Prof. Abdul-Ahad Dawud
- 'The Bible's Last Prophet' by Faisal Siddiqui
- 'The Dead Sea Scrolls, The Gospel of Barnabas and the New Testament' by M.A. Yussuff
- 'Al-Jawab as-Sahih' by Ibn Taymiyyah

[1953] Muslim.

# Women in Islām

## Introduction

The issue of gender equity is important, relevant, and current. Debates and writings on the subject are increasing and are diverse in their perspectives. The Islāmic perspective on the issue is the least understood and most misrepresented by non-Muslims and some Muslims as well. This article is intended to provide a brief and authentic exposition of what Islām stands for in this regard.

## Women in Ancient Civilizations

One major objective of this article is to provide a fair evaluation of what Islām contributed toward the restoration of woman's dignity and rights. In order to achieve this objective, it may be useful to review briefly how women were treated in general in previous civilizations and religions, especially those which preceded Islām (before 610 AD). Part of the information provided here, however, describes the status of woman as late as this century, more than 13 centuries after Islām.

Describing the status of the Indian woman, The Encyclopedia Britannica, 1911, states: "In India, subjection was a cardinal principle. Day and night must women be held by their protectors in a state of dependence says Manu. The rule of inheritance was agnatic, that is descent traced through males to the exclusion of females." In Hindu scriptures, the description of a good wife is as follows: "a woman whose mind, speech and body are kept in subjection, acquires high renown in this world, and, in the next, the same abode with her husband." (Mace, Marriage East and West).

In Athens, women were not better off than either the Indian or the Roman women: "Athenian women were always minors, subject to some male - to their father, to their brother, or to some of their male kin." (Allen, E. A., History of Civilization). Her consent in marriage was not generally thought to be necessary and "she was obliged to submit to the wishes of her parents, and receive from them her husband and her lord, even though he were stranger to her." (Previous Source)

A Roman wife was described by a historian as: "a babe, a minor, a ward, a person incapable of doing or acting anything according to her own individual taste, a person continually under the tutelage and guardianship of her husband." (Previous Source). In The Encyclopedia Britannica, 1911, we find a summary of the legal status of women in the Roman civilization: "In Roman Law a woman was even in historic times completely dependent. If married she and her property passed into the power of her husband . . . the wife was the purchased property of her husband, and like a slave acquired only for his benefit. A woman could not exercise any civil or public office . . . could not be a witness, surety, tutor, or curator; she could not adopt or be adopted, or make will or contract."

Among the Scandinavian races women were: "under perpetual tutelage, whether married or unmarried. As late as the Code of Christian V, at the end of the 17th Century, it was enacted that if a woman married without the consent of her tutor he might have, if he wished, (taken) administration and usufruct of her goods during her life." (The Encyclopedia Britannica, 1911).

In Britain, the right of married women to own property was not recognized until the late 19th Century, "By a series of acts starting with the Married Women's Property Act in 1870, amended in 1882 and 1887, married women achieved the right to own property and to enter into contracts on a par with spinsters, widows, and divorcees." (Encyclopedia Britannica, 1968). In France, it was not until 1938 that the French Law was amended so as to recognize the eligibility of women to contract. A married woman, however, was still required to secure her husband's permission before she could dispense with her private property.

In the Mosaic (Jewish) Law, the wife was betrothed. Explaining this concept, the Encyclopedia Biblica, 1902, states: "To betroth a wife to oneself meant simply to acquire possession of her by payment of the purchase money; the betrothed is a girl for whom the purchase money has been paid." From the legal point of view, the consent of the girl was not necessary for the validation of her marriage. "The girl's consent is unnecessary and the need for it is nowhere suggested in the Law." (Previous Source). As to the right of divorce, we read in the Encyclopedia Biblica: "The woman being man's property, his right to divorce her follows as a matter of course." The right to divorce was held only by man, The Encyclopedia Britannica, 1911, states: "In the Mosaic Law divorce was a privilege of the husband only."

The position of the Christian Church until recent centuries seems to have been influenced by both the Mosaic Law and by the streams of thought that were dominant in its contemporary cultures. In their book, Marriage East and West, David and Vera Mace wrote: "Let no one suppose, either, that our Christian heritage is free of such slighting judgments. It would be hard to find anywhere a collection of more degrading references to the female sex than the early Church Fathers provide. Lecky, the famous historian, speaks of 'these fierce incentives which form so conspicuous and so grotesque a portion of the writing of the Fathers . . . woman was represented as the door of hell, as the mother of all human ills. She should be ashamed at the very thought that she is a woman. She should live in continual penance on account of the curses she has brought upon the world. She should be ashamed of her dress, for it is the memorial of her fall. She should be especially ashamed of her beauty, for it is the most potent instrument of the devil.' One of the most scathing of these attacks on woman is that of Tertullian: 'Do you know that you are each an Eve? The sentence of God on this sex of yours lives in this age; the guilt must of necessity live too. You are the devil's gateway; you are the unsealer of that forbidden tree; you are the first deserters of the divine law; you are she who persuades him whom the devil was not valiant enough to attack.' Not only did the church affirm the inferior status of woman, it deprived her of legal rights she had previously enjoyed."

### Foundations of Spiritual and Human Equity in Islām

In the midst of the darkness that engulfed the world, the divine revelation echoed in the wide desert of Arabia in the seventh century with a fresh, noble, and universal message to humanity, described below. According to the Holy Qur'ān, men and women have the same human spiritual nature:

> **"O mankind, fear your Lord, who created you from one soul and created from it its mate and dispersed from both of them many men and women..."**

Qur'ān 4:1, (see also 7:189, 42:11, 16:72, 32:9, and 15:29)

The Qur'ān does not blame woman for the "fall of man," nor does it view pregnancy and childbirth as punishments for "eating from the forbidden tree." On the contrary, the Qur'ān depicts Adam and Eve as equally responsible for their sin in the Garden, never singling out Eve for blame. Both repented, and both were forgiven (see the Qur'ān 2:36-37 and 7:19-27). In fact, in one verse (Qur'ān 20:121) Adam specifically was blamed. The Qur'ān also esteems pregnancy and childbirth as sufficient reasons for the love and respect due to mothers from their children (Qur'ān 31:14 and 46:15).

Men and women have the same religious and moral duties and responsibilities. Each human being shall face the consequences of his or her deeds:

> **"And their Lord responded to them (saying): Never will I allow to be lost the work of (any) worker among you, whether male or female; you are of one another..."**
>
> Qur'ān 3:195 (see also 74:38, 16:97, 4:124, 33:35, and 57:12)

The Qur'ān is quite clear about the issue of the claimed superiority or inferiority of any human, male or female. The sole basis for superiority of any person over another is piety and righteousness not gender, color, or nationality (see the Qur'ān 49:13).

**The Economic Aspect of Women in Islām**

(1) The Right to Possess Personal Property: Islām decreed a right of which woman was deprived both before Islām and after it (even as late as the 20th century), the right of independent ownership. The Islāmic Law recognizes the full property rights of women before and after marriage. They may buy, sell, or lease any or all of their properties at will. For this reason, Muslim women may keep (and in fact they have traditionally kept) their maiden names after marriage, an indication of their independent property rights as legal entities.

(2) Financial Security and Inheritance Laws: Financial security is assured for women. They are entitled to receive marital gifts without limit and to keep present and future properties and income for their own security, even after marriage. No married woman is required to spend any amount at all from her property and income on the household. The woman is entitled also to full financial support during marriage and during the "waiting period" (iddah) in case of divorce or widowhood. Some jurists require, in addition, one year's support for divorce and widowhood (or until they remarry, if remarriage takes place before the year is over). A woman who bears a child in marriage is entitled to child support from the child's father. Generally, a Muslim woman is guaranteed support in all stages of her life, as a daughter, wife, mother, or sister. The financial advantages accorded to women and not to men in marriage and in family have a social counterpart in the provisions that the Qur'ān lays down in the laws of inheritance, which afford the male, in most cases, twice the inheritance of a female. Males inherit more but ultimately they are financially responsible for their female relatives: their wives, daughters, mothers, and sisters. Females inherit less but retain their share for investment and financial security, without any legal obligation to spend any part of it, even for their own sustenance (food, clothing, housing, medication, etc). It should be noted that before Islām, women themselves were sometimes objects of inheritance (see the Qur'ān 4:19). In some western countries, even after the advent of Islām, the whole estate of the deceased was given

to his/her eldest son. The Qur'ān, however, made it clear that both men and women are entitled to a specified share of the estate of their deceased parents or close relatives. God has said:

> **"For men is a share of what the parents and close relatives leave, and for women is a share of what the parents and close relatives leave, be it little or much, an obligatory share."**
>
> Qur'ān 4:7

(3) Employment: With regard to the woman's right to seek employment, it should be stated first that Islām regards her role in society as a mother and a wife as her most sacred and essential one. Neither maids nor baby sitters can possibly take the mother's place as the educator of an upright, complex-free, and carefully-reared child. Such a noble and vital role, which largely shapes the future of nations, cannot be regarded as idleness. However, there is no decree in Islām that forbids women from seeking employment whenever there is a necessity for it, especially in positions which fit her nature best and in which society needs her most. Examples of these professions are nursing, teaching (especially children), medicine, and social and charitable work.

### The Social Aspect of Women in Islām

#### A) As a Daughter:

(1) The Qur'ān ended the cruel practice of female infanticide, which was before Islām. God has said: **"And when the girl (who was) buried alive is asked, for what sin she was killed."** (Qur'ān 81:8-9)

(2) The Qur'ān went further to rebuke the unwelcoming attitude of some parents upon hearing the news of the birth of a baby girl, instead of a baby boy. God has said: **"And when one of them is informed of (the birth of) a female, his face becomes dark, and he suppresses grief. He hides himself from the people because of the ill of which he has been informed. Should he keep it in humiliation or bury it in the ground? Certainly, evil is what they decide."** (Qur'ān 16:58-59)

(3) Parents are duty-bound to support and show kindness and justice to their daughters. The Prophet Muhammad, may God praise him, said: "Whosoever supports two daughters until they mature, he and I will come on the Day of Judgment as this (and he pointed with his fingers held together)."

(4) A crucial aspect in the upbringing of daughters that greatly influences their future is education. Education is not only a right but a responsibility for all males and females. The Prophet Muhammad said: "Seeking knowledge is mandatory for every Muslim." The word "Muslim" here is inclusive of both males and females.

(5) Islām neither requires nor encourages female circumcision. And while it is maybe practiced by some Muslims in certain parts of Africa, it is also practiced by other peoples, including Christians, in those places, a reflection merely of the local customs and practices there.

**B) As a Wife:**

(1) Marriage in Islām is based on mutual peace, love, and compassion, and not just the mere satisfying of human sexual desire. Among the most notable verses in the Qur'ān about marriage is the following:

**"And of His signs is: that He created for you from yourselves mates that you may find tranquility in them; and He placed between you affection and mercy. Indeed in that are signs for a people who give thought."** (Qur'ān 30:21, see also 42:11 and 2:228)

(2) The female has the right to accept or reject marriage proposals. According to the Islāmic Law, women cannot be forced to marry anyone without their consent.

(3) The husband is responsible for the maintenance, protection, and overall leadership of the family, within the framework of consultation (see the Qur'ān 2:233) and kindness (see the Qur'ān 4:19). The mutuality and complementary nature of the role of husband and wife does not mean subservience by either party to the other. The Prophet Muhammad instructed Muslims regarding women: "I commend you to be good to women." And "The best among you are those who are best to their wives." The Qur'ān urges husbands to be kind and considerate to their wives, even if a wife falls out of favor with her husband or disinclination for her arises within him:

**"...And live with them in kindness. For if you dislike them, perhaps you dislike a thing and God makes therein much good."** (Qur'ān 4:19)

It also outlawed the Arabian practice before Islām whereby the stepson of the deceased father was allowed to take possession of his father's widow(s) (inherit them) as if they were part of the estate of the deceased (see the Qur'ān 4:19).

(4) Should marital disputes arise, the Qur'ān encourages couples to resolve them privately in a spirit of fairness and goodness. Indeed, the Qur'ān outlines an enlightened step and wise approach for the husband and wife to resolve persistent conflict in their marital life. In the event that dispute cannot be resolved equitably between husband and wife, the Qur'ān prescribes mediation between the parties through family intervention on behalf of both spouses (see the Qur'ān 4:35).

(5) Divorce is a last resort, permissible but not encouraged, for the Qur'ān esteems the preservation of faith and the individual's right -male and female alike- to felicity. Forms of marriage dissolution include an enactment based upon mutual agreement, the husband's initiative, the wife's initiative (if part of her marital contract), the court's decision on a wife's initiative (for a legitimate reason), and the wife's initiative without a cause, provided that she returns her marital gift to her husband. When the continuation of the marriage relationship is impossible for any reason, men are still taught to seek a gracious end for it. The Qur'ān states about such cases:

**"And when you divorce women and they have fulfilled their term (i.e. waiting period), either keep them in kindness or release them in kindness, and do not keep them, intending harm, to transgress (against them)."** (Qur'ān 2:231, see also 2:229 and 33:49)

(6) Associating polygyny with Islām, as if it was introduced by it or is the norm according to its teachings, is one of the most persistent myths perpetuated in Western literature and media. Polygyny existed in almost all nations and was even sanctioned by Judaism and Christianity until recent centuries. Islām did not outlaw polygyny, as did many peoples and religious communities; rather, it regulated and restricted it. It is not required but simply permitted with conditions (see the Qur'ān 4:3). Spirit of law, including timing of revelation, is to deal with individual and collective contingencies that may arise from time to time (e.g. imbalances between the number of males and females created by wars) and to provide a moral, practical, and humane solution for the problems of widows and orphans.

**C) As a Mother:**

(1) The Qur'ān elevates kindness to parents (especially mothers) to a status second to the worship of God:

**"Your Lord has commanded that you worship none but Him, and that you be kind to your parents. If one of them or both of them reach old age with you, do not say to them a word of disrespect, or scold them, but say a generous word to them. And act humbly to them in mercy, and say, 'My Lord, have mercy on them, since they cared for me when I was small.'"** (Qur'ān 17:23-24, see also 31:14, 46:15, and 29:8)

(2) Naturally, the Prophet Muhammad specified this behavior for his followers, rendering to mothers an unequalled status in human relationships. A man came to the Prophet Muhammad and said, "O Messenger of God! Who among the people is the most worthy of my good companionship?" The Prophet said: "Your mother." The man said, "Then who?" The Prophet said: "Then your mother." The man further asked, "Then who?" The Prophet said: "Then your mother." The man asked again, "Then who?" The Prophet said: "Then your father."

**D) As a Sister in Faith (In General):**

(1) According to the Prophet Muhammad's sayings: "women are but shaqa'iq (twin halves or sisters) of men." This saying is a profound statement that directly relates to the issue of human equality between the genders. If the first meaning of the Arabic word shaqa'iq, "twin halves," is adopted, it means that the male is worth one half (of society), while the female is worth the other half. If the second meaning, "sisters," is adopted, it implies the same.

(2) The Prophet Muhammad taught kindness, care, and respect toward women in general: "I commend you to be good to women." It is significant that such instruction of the Prophet was among his final instructions and reminders in the farewell pilgrimage address given shortly before his passing away.

(3) Modesty and social interaction: The parameters of proper modesty for males and females (dress and behavior) are based on revelatory sources (the Qur'ān and prophetic sayings) and, as such, are regarded by believing men and women as divinely-based guidelines with legitimate aims and divine wisdom behind them. They are not male-imposed or socially imposed restrictions. It is

interesting to know that even the Bible encourages women to cover their head: "If a woman does not cover her head, she should have her hair cut off; and if it is a disgrace for a woman to have her hair cut or shaved off, she should cover her head." (1 Corinthians 11:6).

**The Legal and Political Aspect of Women in Islām**

(1) Equality before the Law: Both genders are entitled to equality before the Law and courts of Law. Justice is genderless (see the Qur'ān 5:38, 24:2, and 5:45). Women do possess an independent legal entity in financial and other matters.

(2) Participation in Social and Political Life: The general rule in social and political life is participation and collaboration of males and females in public affairs (see the Qur'ān 9:71). There is sufficient historical evidence of participation by Muslim women in the choice of rulers, in public issues, in Law making, in administrative positions, in scholarship and teaching, and even in the battlefield. Such involvement in social and political affairs was conducted without the participants' losing sight of the complementary priorities of both genders and without violating Islāmic guidelines of modesty and virtue.

**Conclusion**

The status which non-Muslim women reached during the present era was not achieved due to the kindness of men or due to natural progress. It was rather achieved through a long struggle and sacrifice on woman's part and only when society needed her contribution and work, more especially during the two world wars, and due to the escalation of technological change. While in Islām such compassionate and dignified status was decreed, not because it reflects the environment of the seventh century, nor under the threat or pressure of women and their organizations, but rather because of its intrinsic truthfulness.

If this indicates anything, it would demonstrate the Divine origin of the Qur'ān and the truthfulness of the message of Islām, which, unlike human philosophies and ideologies, was far from proceeding from its human environment; a message which established such humane principles that neither grew obsolete during the course of time, nor can become obsolete in the future. After all, this is the message of the All-Wise and All-Knowing God whose wisdom and knowledge are far beyond the ultimate in human thought and progress.[1954]

---

[1954] M. Malaekah, *Women in Islām,* http://www.islāmreligion.com/articles/2132/

## How do I become a Muslim?

The word "Muslim" means one who submits to the will of God, regardless of their race, nationality or ethnic background. Becoming a Muslim is a simple and easy process that requires no prerequisites. If anyone has a real desire to be a Muslim and has full conviction and strong belief that Islām is the true religion of God, then, all one needs to do is pronounce the "Shahada," the testimony of faith, without further delay, ideally witnessed by fellow Muslims.

The "Shahada" is the first and most important of the five pillars of Islām. With the pronunciation of this testimony, or "Shahada," with sincere belief and conviction, one enters the fold of Islām. Upon entering the fold of Islām purely for the Pleasure of God, all of one's previous sins are forgiven, and one starts a new life of piety and righteousness. The Prophet said to a person who had placed the condition upon the Prophet in accepting Islām that God would forgive his sins: "Do you not know that accepting Islām destroys all sins which come before it?" [1955]

When one accepts Islām, they in essence repent from the ways and beliefs of their previous life. One need not be overburdened by sins committed before their acceptance. The person's record is clean, and it is as if he was just born from his mother's womb. One should try as much as possible to keep his records clean and strive to do as many good deeds as possible.

The Qur'ān and Hadeeth (Prophetic sayings) both stress the importance of following Islām. God states:

> **"Indeed, the religion in the sight of God is Islām."**
>
> Qur'ān 3:19

In another verse of the Holy Qur'ān, God states:

> **"And whoever desires other than Islām as religion – never will it be accepted from him, and he, in the Hereafter, will be among the losers."**
>
> Qur'ān 3:85

The Prophet Muhammad said "Whoever testifies that there in none worthy of being worshipped but God, Who has no partner, and that Muhammad is His slave and Prophet, and that Jesus is the Slave of God, His Prophet, and His word which He bestowed in Mary and a spirit created from Him; and that Paradise (Heaven) is true, and that the Hellfire is true, God will eventually admit him into Paradise, according to his deeds." [1956]

The Prophet of God also said, "Indeed God has forbidden to reside eternally in Hell the person who says: "I testify that none has the right to worship except Allah (God),' seeking thereby the Face of God." [1957]

---

[1955] Saheeh Muslim.
[1956] Bukhari.
[1957] Bukhari.

**The Declaration of the Testimony (Shahada)**

To convert [or more accurately revert] to Islām and become a Muslim, a person needs to pronounce the below testimony with conviction and understanding its meaning - with other Muslims present:

"Ash hadu Anla ilaha Illa Allah...Wa Ash hadu Anna MuHammadan Rasoolu Allah."

**"I testify that there is no true God (deity) but Allah (God), and that Muhammad is the Messenger of Allah (God)."**

When someone pronounces the testimony with conviction, then he/she has become a Muslim.

The **first** part of the testimony consists of the most important truth that God revealed to mankind: that there is nothing divine or worthy of being worshipped except for Almighty God. God states in the Holy Qur'ān:

> **"And We sent not before you any messenger except that We revealed to him that, "There is no deity except Me, so worship Me."**

Qur'ān 21:25

This conveys that all forms of worship, whether it be praying, fasting, invoking, seeking refuge in, and offering an animal as sacrifice, must be directed to God and to God alone. Directing any form of worship to other than God (whether it be an angel, a messenger, Jesus, Muhammad, a saint, an idol, the sun, the moon, a tree) is seen as a contradiction to the fundamental message of Islām, and it is an unforgivable sin unless it is repented from before one dies. All forms of worship must be directed to God only.

Worship means the performance of deeds and sayings that please God, things which He commanded or encouraged to be performed, either by direct textual proof or by analogy. Thus, worship is not restricted to the implementation of the five pillars of Islām, but also includes every aspect of life. Providing food for one's family, and saying something pleasant to cheer a person up are also considered acts of worship, if such is done with the intention of pleasing God. This means that, to be accepted, all acts of worship must be carried out sincerely for the Sake of God alone.

The **second** part of the testimony means that Prophet Muhammad is the servant and chosen messenger of God. This implies that one obeys and follows the commands of the Prophet. One must believe in what he has said, practice his teachings and avoid what he has forbidden. One must therefore worship God only according to his teaching alone, for all the teachings of the Prophet were in fact revelations and inspirations conveyed to him by God.

One must try to mold their lives and character and emulate the Prophet, as he was a living example for humans to follow. God says:

**"And indeed, you are of a great moral character."**

Qur'ān 68:4

**"There has certainly been for you in the Messenger of God an excellent pattern for anyone whose hope is in God and the Last Day and [who] remembers God often.."**

Qur'ān 33:21

He was sent in order to practically implement the Qur'ān, in his saying, deeds, legislation as well as all other facets of life. Aisha, the wife of the Prophet, when asked about the character of the Prophet, replied: "His character was that of the Qur'ān."

To truly adhere to the second part of the Shahada is to follow his example in all walks of life. God says:

**"Say (O Muhammad to mankind): 'If you (really) love God, then follow me.'"**

Qur'ān 3:31

It also means that Muhammad is the Final Prophet and Messenger of God, and that no (true) Prophet can come after him.

**"Muhammad is not the father of [any] one of your men, but [he is] the Messenger of God and last of the prophets. And ever is God, of all things, Knowing."**

Qur'ān 33:40

All who claim to be prophets or receive revelation after Muhammad are imposters, and to acknowledge them would be tantamount to disbelief.

We welcome you to Islām, congratulate you for your decision, and will try to help you in any way we can, God willing. Logon to www.quranproject.org/newmuslim for more information.

## Short Guide to Ablution and Prayer [1958]

Below is a quick and basic guide to prayer which highlight the main pillars of prayer and ablution. For a more detailed and thorough guide to the rules/methods of prayer then logon to www.quranproject.org/prayer

### Wudu – The Ablution

The Wudu is a pre-requisite for the prayer

1. Make intention for the ablution and say, 'Bismillah' (In the name of God)
2. Wash your hands
3. Rinse your mouth and nose
4. Wash the face
5. Wash the right arm including hand upto the elbow, then do the same for the left
6. Wipe the head back and forth once
7. Wash the right foot including its ankle, then do the same for the left

All actions of washing can be done once, twice or thrice except for wiping of the head which is done only once.

### The Five Daily Prayers

For exact timings of each prayer, visit your local masjid and obtain a prayer timetable

| *Name* | *Time of Day* | *Units of Prayer* |
|---|---|---|
| Fajr | Dawn | 2 |
| Dhuhr | Midday | 4 |
| Asr | Late-Afternoon | 4 |
| Maghrib | Sunset | 3 |
| Isha | Night | 4 |

**Note**

Any part of what you find difficult to memorize you can replace with a supplication in your mother tongue like, 'Glory be to Allah, All praise is due to Allah, Allah is the Greatest, and there is no diety worthy of worhip except Allah.' Until you can memorize it in Arabic.

[1958] al-Muntada al-Islāmi, London.

**The first unit of Prayer (rak'ah)**

In a standing position, face the Qiblah (prayer direction)

Note: The Qiblah is approx South East for the UK, but changes according to your location in the world

.....And make the intention in your heart to pray that particular prayer.

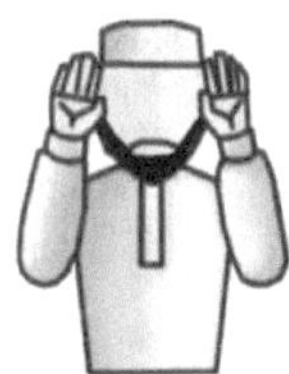

**1.** Raise your hands up to the level of your shoulders/face saying, *'Allah u Akbar'*

**2.**...Then place them on your chest, the right hand on the left.

**3. Whilst standing recite the opening chapter (al-Fātihah) of the Qur'ān:**

Bismillahi Rahmani Raheem
Alhamdu lillahi Rabbil alameen.
Ar-Rahmanir Raheem.
Maliki Yawmid deen.
Iyyaka na'budu wa iyyaka nasta'een.
Ihdinas siratal mustaqeem.
Siratal latheena an'amta alayhim.
Ghayril maghdubi alayhim walad daalleen.'

Then say: *'Ameen'*

'In the name of God, the Most Gracious, Most Merciful.
[All] praise is [due] to God, Lord of the worlds
The Entirely Merciful, the Especially Merciful,
Sovereign of the Day of Recompense
It is You we worship and You we ask for help.
Guide us to the straight path
The path of those upon whom You have bestowed favor,
not of those who have evoked [Your] anger or of those who are astray.'

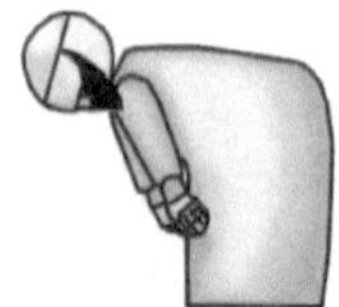

**4.** Say *'Allah u Akbar'* then bow down. Then say *'Subhana rabbiyal Adheem'* three times, while bowing down

**5.**....Return to a standing position saying, *'Sami Allahu liman hamidah, Rabbana wa lakal hamd.'*

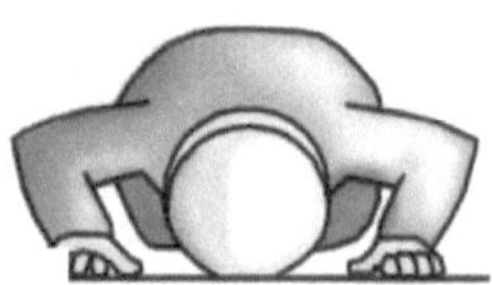

**6.** Say *'Allah u Akbar'* and prostrate yourself with the forehead and the nose touching the ground and say while prostrating *'Subhana Rabbiyal a'la'* three times...

**7.**...Sit up saying 'Allahu Akbar' then say while seated *'Rabbigh firli war hamni.'*

**8.** Prostrate yourself again saying *'Allahu Akbar'* and repeat the same supplication *'Subhana Rabbiyal a'la.'*

**The second unit of Prayer (rak'ah)**

Return to a standing position for the second unit of prayet (rak'ah) saying 'Allahu Akbar.' Start with reading the opening chapter, and continue this unit of prayer as you did in the first.

**At-Tashahhud (The Testimony)**

In the three or four unit prayer, after the second unit, sit down after your prostration and say the following supplication

'At-tahiyyatu lillahi was-salawatu wat -tayyibat. Assalamu alayka ayyahun nabiyyu wa rahmatul-lahi wa barakatahuh. Assalamu alayna wa ala ibadillahis saliheen Ashhadu alla ilaha ilal-ha wa ashadu anna Muhammadan abduhu wa rasuluh.'

'Words of Praise and glorification are for Allah, and Prayers and pure words. Peace and salutations upon you O Prophet and the Mercy of Allah and His Blessings. And peace be upon us and upon all of Allah's righteous servants. I testify that none has the right to be worshipped except Allah, and testify that Muhammad is His Slave and Messenger.'

In the final rak'ah (unit prayer) say the previous (point 10) supplication and add the following supplication:

'Allahumm salli 'ala Muhammad wa 'ala ali Muhammad kama sallayta ala Ibraheem wa 'ala ali Ibraheem innaka hameedun majeed. Allahumma barik 'ala Muhammad wa 'ala Muhammad kama barakta 'ala Ibraheem wa 'ala ali Ibraheem innaka hameedun majeed'

'O Lord, bless Muhammad and his family as You blessed Ibrahim and his family. You are the Most-Praised, The Most Glorious. O Lord, bestow Your grace on Muhammad and his family as You bestowed it on Ibrahim and his family. You are the Most-Praised, the Most- Glorious".

After you say the supplication turn your face right saying

'Assalam alaykum wa rahmatullah'.....

....Then turn left saying the same.

Now your Prayer is complete

## Short Phrases Translated

Moving in Prayer - *'Allah u Akbar'* – God is the Greatest

Bowing - '*Subhana rabbiyal Adheem*' – Glory be to God the most Magnificent

After Bowing while Standing - '*Sami Allahu liman hamidah*' – God hears those who praises Him
- *Rabbana wa lakal hamd.*' Our Lord to You belong all the praise

While Prostrating - '*Subhana Rabbiyal a'la*' – Glory be to God, Most High

In between Prostrations - *'Rabbigh firli war hamni.'* - My Lord forgive me and have mercy on me

Completing the Prayer - *'Assalam alaykum wa rahmatullah'* – May the Peace and Mercy of God be upon you

Frequently Asked Questions about Islām

## - Brief Answers -

**Q: What is Islām?**

A: Islām means submission to the will of God. Islām teaches belief in only one God, the Day of Judgment and individual accountability for actions. One who submits to God is called a Muslim – this being the precondition to enter Paradise.

**Q: Who is Allah?**

A: Allah is simply the Arabic word for God, the same God worshiped by Christians and Jews. It is the God of Abraham and Moses, not a different God. Christian Arabs also refer to God as Allah.

**Q: What is the Qur'ān/Koran?**

A: The Qur'ān is the holy book of Islām. Muslims believe that the Qur'ān was divinely revealed and is the last testament of God. The Qur'ān is preserved in its original Arabic form and is unanimoussly accepted that it has never been altered – preserved both orally and in written form.

**Q: What are the basic teachings of Islām?**

A: There are five Pillars in Islām:

1) *Declaration of the Faith:* To testify there is no diety worthy of worship except God and Muhammad is the Messenger of God
2) *Prayer:* Pray towards Makkah five times each day
3) *Charity:* Donate a portion of your wealth to the poor
4) *Fasting:* Go without food, drink and having relations with your spouses from dawn until sunset during the month of Ramadan
5) *Pilgrimage:* Visit Makkah and perform the Hajj once in a lifetime, if you have the means to do so.

These pillars are built on the Articles of Faith – which can simply be broken down into the following:

1) *God:* There is only one God with no associate or partner. All that happened in the past, is happening now and is going to happen in the future is by the will of God.
2) *The Angels:* Angels are created from light and execute the commands of God without question.
3) *The Books of God:* These include the Torah, the Psalms of David, The Gospel revealed to Jesus and the Qur'ān.
4) *Prophets of God:* There were thousands of prophets who preached God's message. Prophet Muhammad was the last prophet for all humanity and completed the message of God.
5) *Day of Judgment:* On this day all mankind will be raised back to life and judged by God. Those whose good deeds outweigh their bad deeds will be allowed to enter Paradise and those whose bad deeds outweigh their good deeds will be condemned to Hell except whom God has mercy on.

6) *Divine Decree:* God's predestination of all things and events and His Decree. Nothing in the universe can occur without the knowledge of God. Whatever He desires, it occurs and whatever He does not desire, it doesn't occur. There is no power or any movement except by God.
7) *Life after Death:* The eternal life in Paradise where one will be rewarded for living a righteous life on Earth, or the fire of Hell where one will be punished for the evil that one committed.

**Q: Why do Muslims pray five times a day?**

A: Muslims pray five times a day because God prescribed it. For those who do not know the values of prayer may think it is too much. For those who practice the prayer, take solace in it as they are praising, glorifying and talking to the Greatest. Hence at five times during the day no matter what circumstances surround them they focus back to God and the true realities of life. Indeed, some prefer to pray more in order to attain happiness, peace and tranquillity.

**Q: In order to pray you perform the ablution. Why do you do such a ritual? Can't you pray without ablution?**

A: For every activity in life, there are rules and regulations. Sometimes there are pre-requisites to the general requirements too. In Islām there are also some rules and regulations for the systems that God had legislated. In schools, each teacher has his requirements for every course that he/she teaches. Through their knowledge and wisdom they have designed the course and the requirement so that the students will be able to pass the course. The prayer (salat) in Islām has its rules and regulations. It has its spiritual and physical dimensions – spiritually any minor sins that have been accumulated since the previous ablution are cleansed and physically it removes and cleans the body from all types of impurities. Islām also encourages the use of a toothstick to clean our teeth and apply scent – all in preparation for the Believer to presents him/herself before the King of kings, God himself.

**Q: Why do Muslims have to pray towards Ka'aba in Makkah?**

A: The Ka'bāh is the first house built for the worship of God on earth. It was originally built by Adam and then rebuilt by Abraham and his son Ishmael. God has chosen the Ka'bāh as a focal point of unity of pray for all the Believers all over the world.

**Q: What is a Mosque/Masjid?**

A: A Mosque or Masjid is a place of worship for Muslims. Muslims pray in a masjid in the same way that Christians pray in a church.

**Q: I know Muslims fast in Ramadhan. Why do you fast the whole month not eating and drinking anything during the day?**

A: Fasting the whole month of Ramadan is the fourth pillar in Islām. This month is the 9th lunar month of the Islāmic calendar and is the month in which the Qur'ān was revelaed. For the whole month Muslims fast from dawn until sunset. During the Prophet's life, the Angel Gabriel would descend every night of the month and go over the verses that had been revealed up to that point with him. In additional to his spiritual cleansing of the soul, fasting has many religious, social, cultural, economic, and educational benefits to all – including the control of egos, appetites, lusts. Fasting has also been prescribed on other people before Islām too, like the Jews and Christians.

**Q: What is Hajj?**

A: The pilgrimage to Makkah (the Hajj) is an obligation only for those who are physically and financially able to do so. Nevertheless, over two million people go to Makkah each year from every corner of the globe providing a unique opportunity for those of different nations to meet one another. The annual Hajj begins in the twelfth month of the Islāmic year. Pilgrims wear special clothes: simple garments that strip away distinctions of class and culture, so that all stand equal before God. The rites of the Hajj, which are of Abrahamic origin, include going around the Ka'bāh seven times, and going seven times between the hills of Safa and Marwa as did Hagar (Abraham's wife) during her search for water. The pilgrims later stand together on the wide plains of 'Arafat (a large expanse of desert outside Makkah) and join in prayer for God's forgiveness, in what is often thought as a preview of the Day of Judgment. The close of the Hajj is marked by a festival, the Eid al Adha, which is celebrated with prayers and the exchange of gifts in Muslim communities everywhere. This and the Eid al Fitr, a festive day celebrating the end of Ramadan, are the two holidays of the Islāmic calendar.

**Q: Who was the Prophet Muhammad?**

A: Prophet Muhammad was the last and final prophet sent by God. He completed the lineage of prophets which included Adam, Noah, Abraham, Ishmael, Isaac, Moses and Jesus. He was born in Makkah in the year 570 CE, during the period of history Europeans call the Middle Ages. The Prophet Muhammad was the son of Abdullah, a noble from the tribe of the Quraysh. His father died before his birth and his mother, Aminah died shortly afterwards. He was then raised by his uncle, Abu Talib. As he grew up, Muhammad became known for his truthfulness, generosity and sincerity, earning the title of al-Amin, the trustworthy one. He was of a contemplative nature, and had long detested the decadence of his society. It became his habit to retreat from time to time in the Cave of Hira' near the summit of 'Mountain of Light' near Makkah.

**Q: How did Muhammad become a prophet and messenger of God?**

A: At the age of 40, while engaged in a meditative retreat, he received his first revelation from God through the Archangel Gabriel. This revelation, which continued for twenty-three years, is known as the Qur'ān. The Prophet Muhammad began to recite the words he heard from Gabriel and to preach the truth which God had revealed to him. The people of Makkah were steeped in their ways of ignorance and opposed him and his small group of followers in every way. These early Muslims suffered bitter persecution. In the year 622 CE, God gave the Muslim community the command to emigrate. This event, the hijrah or migration, in which they left Makkah for the city of Madinah, some 260 miles to the North, marks the beginning of the Muslim calendar.

Madinah provided the Prophet Muhammad and the Muslims the safe and nurturing haven in which the Muslim community grew and here He established the Islāmic state. After several years, the Prophet and his followers returned as conquerors. He was now supreme ruler of Arabia cleansing the land from idolatry and dedicated the Ka'bāh to the worship of the One God. He died at the age of 63, and within a century of his death, Islām had spread to Spain in the west and as far east as China.

**Q: Is it true that Muslims worship Muhammad?**

A: Not at all! Muslims only worship God alone. For this reason they are not called Muhammadans. For example, Christians worship Christ and are hence called Christians. It is the greatest sin in Islām to worship anybody or anything else alongside God.

**Q: I thought that Muslims believe only in Muhammad as their Prophet. Is this true?**

A: No! Muslims believe in all of the Prophets and Messengers that God sent to mankind from the days of Adam to the days of the Prophet Muhammad. God sent over 124,000 Prophets in the history of mankind. However, God mentioned 25 names in the Qur'ān some of them being: Adam, Enoch, Noah, Abraham, Lot, Ishmael, Isaac, Jacob, Joseph, Job, Moses, Aaron, King David, King Soleman, Jonah, Zachariah, John the Baptist, Jesus and Muhammad. Muslims believe in all of them and do not differentiate in their missions – all of whom were calling to the worship of one God. Any time any Prophet's name is mentioned, Muslims say peace be upon him (pbuh).

**Q: I was surprised to know that Muslims believe in Jesus and Mary?**

A: Muslims are obligated to believe in Jesus and Mary. They deeply respect them and consider them to be amongst the greatest of human beings with Jesus being one of the greatest Messengers of God and His mother the greatest of all women. In the Qur'ān there is one chapter (Sūrah) in the name of Mary herself – Sūrah 19. No other women's name was revealed explicitly in the Qur'ān except that of Mary.

**Q: I am also surprised to know that Muslims believe in Moses. I thought Moses was the Prophet of the Jews only.**

A: Moses was not the Prophet of the Jews. He was the Prophet of God to the children of Israel. He was sent to save them from the persecution of Pharaoh of Egypt. However, Moses was a Muslim. He preached the Message of God and taught them to believe in God, the Creator of the Universe. He instructed them to pray, fast and pay charity as well. Muslims believe in Prophet Moses in as much as they believe in all the other Prophets and Messengers without any discrimination.

**Q: Is it true that Muhammad is the last Prophet and the last Messenger? If yes, how come?! Don't you think that we need more Prophets today?**

A: Yes! Muhammad is the last Prophet and the last Messenger of God to all mankind. His teachings are meant for Christians, Jews, Bhudists, Hindus and others. You may need another Prophet if his teachings were distorted or lost. The originality, totality and authenticity of the Qur'ān are well documented and proved to be intact. The teachings of Islām are meant for all human beings. This was not true to the previous Prophets who came for a particular tribe, nation, or even for a particular era and area. The Qur'ān was revealed as the last testament to mankind.

**Q: Christians believe that we were born sinful and therefore we have to be baptized. What does Islām say about original sin?**

A: In Islām, every person is born free of sin. It would be inhumane and unjust that God would create us with sins. God is so merciful. He created us as pure as crystal ice. It is only after the age of puberty that one will be accounted for his deeds and actions preceded by intention. At that time, we will be rewarded ten times for any good deeds, and we will be charged once for every bad deed. If we ask forgiveness from God, He will forgive us. Because we are born free of sins, we do not need to be baptized. We are already born as Muslims.

**Q: In Christianity, one must believe in Jesus as our personal Savior to enter Paradise. What does Islām say about Salvation?**

A: Salvation in Islām does not depend on someone else to do it for us. We are responsible for our deeds and actions preceded by our good intentions. Therefore, everyone has to work hard with good intention. Our intention as Muslims is to please the Creator. Whoever believes in God; in all the Prophets and Messengers that God sent to mankind; in the Day of Judgment; and do good deeds to all without personal ego or without exploitation; then and only then God assures us eternal Salvation. Through His Mercy, Forgiveness and Blessings, people will be given Salvation.

**Q: Once I was talking to a Muslim saying to him that Christians believe in the Unity of God. He informed me that Muslims do not believe in the Unity of God but in the Oneness of God. I got confused. Would you kindly elaborate for me the difference.**

A: Thank you very much for raising a very fundamental principle in Islām. Muslims believe in the Oneness of God. They do not believe in the concept of Unity of God. The word unity may give a wrong impression about the concept of God. It may mean two gods in one, or three gods in one. Christians believe in three gods in one: God the father, god the son and god the holy spirit. Three in One. This is the concept of Unity of God. Muslims do not subscribe to this concept. God is the only One. He is One-in-One. He begets no one; and no one has begotten Him. He is the Creator of the whole universe. No one shares with Him His Sovereignty.

**Q: During Christmas, I realized that Muslims don't participate in this celebration. Since Muslims believe in Jesus, why then they don't celebrate Christmas?**

A: Muslims believe in the Prophet Jesus. He was one of the five Mighty Messengers of God. However, Muslims don't celebrate the birth of any Prophet. Even those Prophets did not celebrate their own birthdays. Its origins lie in the Pagan feast of the Roman Empire.

**Q: Does Islām consider Christians and Jews as Believers?**

A: Jews and Christians are referred to in the Qur'ān as the 'People of the Book' – meaning their orgins lie in scripture revealed by God. However these scriptures have not remained untouched by human insertions and have been distorted. When each prophet was sent, the people of that era were obliged to follow him and would be defined as people of the truth or simply 'Muslims' – so when Moses came – people were obliged to follow him and these Jews were Believers. When Jesus came, people were obligated to now accept him as the Prophet of God and not doing so would remove them from being defined as Believers – even though they may have accepted Moses as a prophet. These Christians were now the Believers till the time the Prophet Muhammad was sent. After which any person claiming to submit to the will of God would have to accept the prophethood of Muhammad and not doing so would excommunicate them from being a true Believer in God.

**Q: If everything is pre-ordained and decided, where is the free will?**

A: The question of 'fate and freewill' has baffled people for many centuries; but Islām has given a clear answer. The first point to be noted in this respect is that the Islāmic concept of Qadar and Qadha' is quite different from fatalism, determinism and predestination, as understood by most people. In Arabic, the words Qadar and Qadha are often used for fate and destiny. The word, Qadha means to decide; to settle; to judge. A Qadhi is a judge who decides a matter between disputants. From the Islāmic view, the events of the world take place within God's Knowledge and Will.

Read the following verses:

1. "And not an atom's weight in the earth or in the sky escapes your Lord, nor what is less than that or greater than that, but it is (written) in a clear Book." (Yunus 10:61)

2. "No disaster strikes upon the earth or among yourselves except that it is in a register before We bring in into being – indeed that, for God, is easy – In order that you not despair over what has eluded you and not exalt [in pride] over what He has given you. And God does not like everyone self-deluded and boastful." (al-Hadid 57:22-23).

The above verses speak of God Almighty's power and control over His creation, as well as of His will and plan. This is one aspect of His Qadar. There is also another aspect of Qadar, which is concerned with human freewill.

B: On human freedom and responsibility read the following verses:

1. "Corruption has appeared throughout the land and sea by [reason of] what the hands of people have earned so He [i.e., God] may let them taste part of [the consequence of] what they have done that perhaps they will return [to righteousness]." (ar-Rum 30:41)

2. "...The truth is from your Lord, so whoever wills - let him believe; and whoever wills - let him disbelieve." (al-Kahf 18:29)

The above verses speak of the special status of humans as beings with a role and mission. God's power over His creation and His fore-knowledge of all our actions and their results do not preclude that status. God's Qadar and Qadha – which could be loosely rendered as 'Divine decree and human destiny' – include a certain amount of freedom for humans. We may say that God Almighty has willed that we must have the freedom to choose between good and bad, and take the course of action we decide, i.e to the extent we are permitted. It is God Who created us with all our talents and gifts, and if we do not have the freedom to use them, what would be the meaning of those blessings? And remember that God gave us, not merely our intellectual faculties but also the power of moral judgment. And what is more, He sent us His Guidance through His chosen Prophets and Books, to help us make the right choices. So in Islām, there is no contradiction between belief in Divine Preordainment on the one hand, and the freedom of man on the other.

**Q: Why do bad things happen?**

A: First of all, God has not made this a permanent world. This is a temporary world and everything here has a time limit. Neither the good things of this world are forever, nor the bad things eternal. We are here for a short time and we are being tested – those who pass the test will find an eternal world that is perfect and permanent. "And when We let the people taste mercy, they rejoice therein, but if evil afflicts them for what their hands have put forth, immediately they despair." [ar-Rum 30:36]

Things we consider bad may happen for a number of reasons:

1. As a punishment where the laws of God have been violated as in the case of the people of Noah and Lot: "Has there not reached them the news of those before them - the people of Noah and [the tribes of] 'Aad and Thamūd and the people of Abraham and the companions [i.e., dwellers] of Madyan and the towns overturned? Their messengers came to them with clear proofs. And God would never have wronged them, but they were wronging themselves." (Surah at-Tawbah 9:70)

2. Sometimes God allows people to be afflicted by the consequences of their actions as a sign and reminder in order that they have the opportunity to repent and reform themselves. "Corruption has appeared throughout the land and sea by [reason of] what the hands of people have earned so He [i.e., God] may let them taste part of [the consequence of] what they have done that perhaps they will return [to righteousness]." (ar-Rum 30:41)

   "And whatever strikes you of disaster - it is for what your hands have earned; but He pardons much." [ash-Shura 42:30]

3. Suffering can also be a test and trial for some people. God allows some people to suffer in order to test their patience and steadfastness. Even God's Prophets and Messengers were made to suffer. Prophet Job is mentioned in the Qur'ān as a Prophet who was very patient. Through these trials and tribulations, one has the opportunity to draw closer to God.

4. God sometimes allows some people to suffer to test others, how they react to them. When you see a person who is sick, poor and needy, then you are tested by God to test your charity and faith. God says in a [hadith qudsi], 'Verily, Allah will say to his slave when He will be taking account of him on the Day of Judgement, 'O son of Adam, I was hungry and you did not feed me.' He will answer: 'How could I feed you? You are the Lord of the worlds!' He will say: 'Did you not know that my slave so and so who is the son of so and so felt hunger, and you did not feed him. Alas, had you fed him you would have found that (i.e. reward) with Me.' 'O son of Adam, I was thirsty and you gave Me nothing to drink.' He will reply: 'How could I give You drink? You are the Lord of the worlds!' He will say: 'Did you not know that my slave so and so, the son of so and so felt thirsty and you did not give him drink. Alas, if you had given him, you would have found that (i.e. reward) with me.' 'O son of Adam, I became sick and you did not visit Me.' He will answer: 'How can I visit You? You are the Lord of the worlds!' He will say: 'Did you not know that my slave so and so, the son of so and so became sick and you did not visit him. Alas, had you visited him, you would have found Me with him."

## Frequently Asked Questions about Islām

**Q: How many Muslims are there?**

A: There are currently 1.6 Billion Muslims in the world, with about 2-3 million living in the United Kingdom. Contrary to popular perception, only 20% of Muslims are Arabs and live in the Middle East. The countries with the largest Muslim populations are India and Indonesia with about 175 million Muslims each.

**Q: Is it true that all Arabs are Muslims, and that all Muslims are Arabs?**

A: No! Any person who reads, writes and speaks the Arabic language is called an Arab. There are about 1.6 billion Muslims in the world. 20% are considered Arabs while the rest are non-Arabs. Among the Arab people there are about 8% who are non-Muslims, such as Christians, Jews, Assyrians, Atheists, Agnostics, etc. However, every Muslim has to study and learn the Arabic language so that he/she will be able to pray daily and to read Qur'ān and the Arabic language.

**Q: Are the Arabs superior to others?**

A: The Prophet said in his farewell pilgrimage, 'All mankind is from Adam and Eve, an Arab has no superiority over a non-Arab nor a non-Arab has any superiority over an Arab; also a white has no superiority over a black nor a black has any superiority over white except by piety and good action. Learn that every Muslim is a brother to every Muslim and that the Muslims constitute one brotherhood.'

**Q: What are the legal sources of Islām?**

A: The sources of Islām are the Qur'ān, the Hadith (sayings of the Prophet) and the Unanimous decisions of the early Muslim scholars.

**Q: What is the difference between Hadith and Sunnah?**

A: Hadith is the exact sayings of the Prophet with quote and unquote. The Sunnah of the Prophet are his deeds, actions and his tacid approval, i.e. actions done by others in his presence which he didn't comment.

**Q: What does Jihād mean – linguistically and practically?**

A: Jihād linguistically means the process of 'exerting the best efforts,' involving some form of 'struggle' and 'resistance' to achieve a particular goal. In the Qur'ān this word has been used in different connotations – entailing to struggle in the way of God, verbally, monetarily and physically. In the context of war, the Qur'ān legislates the performance of Jihād in order to make His word the highest in the land, defend or establish the religion, remove oppression from weak men, women and children and to remove turmoil and corruption. A point to note – there are strict laws governing the engagement of the enemy and the treatment of prisoners of war – all of which was laid down by God and demonstrated by His Prophet.

**Q: What is a Fatwa?**

A: A Fatwa is a religious ruling to a question based on Islāmic law and issued by Islāmic scholars.

**Q: In secular countries, the Pledge of Allegiance is to the flag of the country. How do Muslims look at such a pledge?**

A: Any person who makes his Pledge of Allegiance to the flag of his country, he is legally responsible to defend that country according to what the political leaders decide. The leaders may decide to invade other countries and commit all types of injustices, atrocities, and crime. A Muslim's loyalty is to God. He will never obey political leaders unless they themselves obey God. Invading other countries and killing other people are among the biggest crimes. Therefore, the masses as well as the leaders should make a Pledge of Allegiance to God, the Creator of the whole universe.

**Q: Since the Pledge of Allegiance of Muslims is only to God, what is that Pledge, and what does it mean?**

A:Yes, the Pledge of Allegiance of Muslims is only to God, the Creator of the Universe. Muslims have to say daily the Pledge in the language of the Qur'ān, i.e., Arabic. They have to recite it vocally individually and collectively. They may pronounce it verbally, privately, and silently too.

The Pledge goes as follows:

"Ashhadu Anla ilaha Illa Allah...Wa Ashhadu Anna Muhammadan RasooluAllah."

"I bear witness that there is no one worthy of worship except God (Allah)... And I bear witness that Prophet Muhammad is the Messenger of God."

**Q: Can you explain the Shariah and secularism in Islām?**

A: Islām teaches that the Believer cannot make any agreement with any person or government to displease God; they cannot make any deal with any group to decide any matter against what God has already decided. In Islām, State and Religion are to abide their total life according to the teachings of God. No one has the right to separate the state from religion - otherwise, we are creating two gods: One god for our daily life and one god for the spiritual life. This type of approach is totally rejected and unacceptable. In Islām, God created the whole universe. He is the Real Legislator of all systems of life for us and He knows exactly what we need. He legislated the Shariah (Islāmic Law) - that we should abide by. Then and only then we will live in peace and harmony in this life and the hereafter.

**Q: I heard that there is something called Seerah. Would you kindly tell me what it is?**

A: Generally speaking, Seerah means the life history of someone. Any time Muslims talk about the Sirah, they mean the biography of Prophet Muhammad. Muslims are to study the Sirah of the Prophet so that they will be able to imitate him, emulate him, and benefit from his wisdom and his teachings. The early followers of Islām have written a series of books about the Sirah of the Prophet Muhammad to act as a guide to all the new generations to come.

**Q: How does Islām view women?**

Refer to article in the appendices, 'Women in Islām'

**Q: Why do Muslim women cover themselves?**

A: They do so in submission to God. He has asked them to hide their beauty except to those whom He permits and any woman who does so fulfills the command that God has placed on her. God has legislated for all members of society and each individual will be judged according to commands that were ordained for him or her. The rights a wife has on her husband, or a son on his mother or a brother to his sister all vary – and although they are different, quintessentially our submission to God is judged according to how we observe them. In addition, however, their Hijab (covering) protects them and demands respect from men who otherwise would have judged them by their looks as opposed to what they say or do. The concept of keeping a womans beauty hidden is not unique to Islām but exists in many other faiths including Christian Nuns who wear similar attire to some Muslim women.

**Q: How does Islām view human rights?**

A: Freedom of conscience is laid down by the Qur'ān itself: "There shall be no compulsion in [acceptance of] the religion.." (2:256) The life, honour and property of all citizens in an Islāmic state are considered sacred whether the person is Muslim or not.

> **"O mankind, indeed We have created you from male and female and made you peoples and tribes that you may know one another. Indeed, the most noble of you in the sight of God is the most righteous of you. Indeed, God is Knowing and Acquainted."**
>
> Qur'ān 49:13

**Q: Where can I learn more about Islām?**

A: Online at www.quranproject.org - you will find relevant audio, video, books and articles which will expand on all the above questions.

# Brief Index of the Qur'ān

## A

## B

## C

## D

## E



## F

## G

## I

# J

## K

## L



## M

## N



## O



## P

## S

## Z

# Free Online Library

www.quranproject.org

Below are some of the titles we recommend you to read -
All these and many more are available to download for free

Discover Islām

A Brief Illustrated Guide to Islām

33 Lessons For Every Muslim

Al-Qur'ān Miracle of Miracles

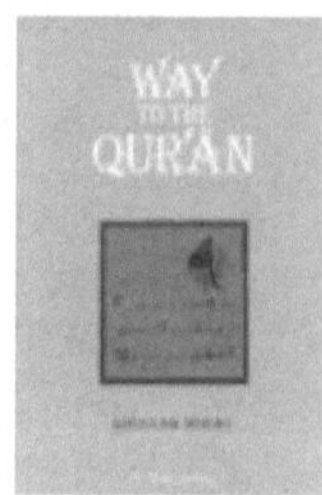


Way to the Qur'ān

Conditions of Testimony of Faith

Islām is your Birthright

Towards Understanding Islām

Christianity: Original and Present Reality

Concept of God in Major Religions

Is the Bible God's Word?

The Qur'ān and Modern Science

Stories of the Qur'ān

Stories of New Muslims

Milestones

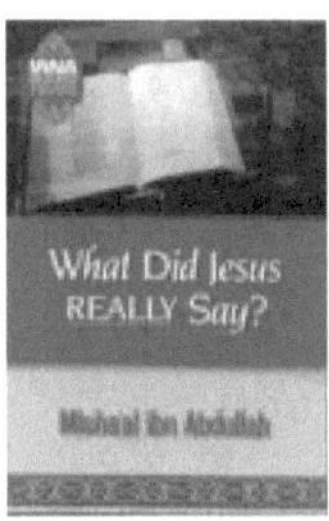

Sincere Advice to Every Christian

What Did Jesus Really Say?

The Choice – Islām and Christianity

Promised Prophet of the Bible

Jihād in the Qur'ān and Sunnah

Obligations Muslim owe to the Qur'ān

Program of Studies for New Muslims

Fortress of the Muslim (prayer book)

Major Sins

In Pursuit of Allah's Pleasure

Tafsir Ibn Kathir (complete explanation of the Qur'ān)

Language of the Qur'ān

Help yourself in Reading the Qur'ān

Fundamentals in Classical Arabic

Descriptions of Paradise and Hellfire

Developing Humility in Prayer

In the Early Hours – Reflections on Spirituality

Fiqh us Sunnah Rulings on Worship

Why do We Pray?

The Nature of Fasting

Zakah and Fasting

Hajj and Umrah AtoZ

Polygamy in Islām

Patience and Gratitude

The Hijab - Why?

The World of the Jinn and Devils

Belief in Angels

I want to Repent, But…..

Music and Singing in Islām

The Ideal Muslim

Collection of Biographies of the Companions

Stories of the Prophets

Men around the Messenger

Why God decrees Wars and Catastrophe's

Etiquettes of Marriage

This is our Belief

Autobiography of Malcolm X

Dealing with Worries and Stress

Religion of Ibrahim

Signs before the Day of Judgement

Ideal Muslim Woman

40 Recommendations for the Muslim Home

The Fiqh of Love Marriage in Islām

Islām and Love

Islām the Misunderstood Religion

# DONATION PAGE

## I want to Support The Qur'ān Project's Efforts

Our Aim - To produce a free and simple translation of the Qur'ān which includes additional chapters beneficial for the seekers of truth in as many countries as possible.

You can donate and help with the cost of printing further copies - Logon to make a donation

www.quranproject.org

## How can I obtain a free copy?

- Order your free copy at www.quranproject.org
- Read or download it in full online at the Qur'ān Project website
- A full listing of Islāmic Bookstores where you can obtain a free copy are available online

## How can I donate?

- Logon to www.quranproject.org/donate
- Pay direct in to the bank account

  Bank: Islamic Bank of Britain
  Acc name: The Quran Project
  Sort code: 30-00-83
  Acc number: 01200001

Made in United States
Troutdale, OR
02/10/2024